D1126952

THE OXFORD HANDBOOK OF

RELIGION, CONFLICT, AND PEACEBUILDING

THE OXFORD HANDBOOK OF

RELIGION, CONFLICT, AND PEACEBUILDING

Edited by

ATALIA OMER, R. SCOTT APPLEBY,

and

DAVID LITTLE

OXFORD
UNIVERSITY PRESS

OXFORD
UNIVERSITY PRESS

Oxford University Press is a department of the University of
Oxford. It furthers the University's objective of excellence in research,
scholarship, and education by publishing worldwide.

Oxford   New York
Auckland   Cape Town   Dar es Salaam   Hong Kong   Karachi
Kuala Lumpur   Madrid   Melbourne   Mexico City   Nairobi
New Delhi   Shanghai   Taipei   Toronto

With offices in
Argentina   Austria   Brazil   Chile   Czech Republic   France   Greece
Guatemala   Hungary   Italy   Japan   Poland   Portugal   Singapore
South Korea   Switzerland   Thailand   Turkey   Ukraine   Vietnam

Oxford is a registered trademark of Oxford University Press
in the UK and certain other countries.

Published in the United States of America by
Oxford University Press
198 Madison Avenue, New York, NY 10016

Library of Congress Cataloging-in-Publication Data
The Oxford handbook of religion, conflict, and peacebuilding / edited by Atalia Omer, R. Scott Appleby,
and David Little.
pages cm. — (Oxford handbooks) Includes index.
ISBN 978–0–19–973164–0 (hardcover : alk. paper) — ISBN 978–0–19–021794–5 (ebook)
1. Peace—Religious aspects—Handbooks, manuals, etc.   2. Peace-building—Handbooks, manuals, etc.
3. Religion and politics—Handbooks, manuals, etc.   4. Conflict management—Handbooks, manuals, etc.
5. War—Religious aspects—Handbooks, manuals, etc.   6. Violence—Religious aspects—Handbooks,
manuals, etc.   I. Omer, Atalia, editor.   II. Appleby, R. Scott, 1956– editor.   III. Little, David,
1933– editor.   IV. Title: Handbook of religion, conflict, and peacebuilding.
BL65.P4O94 2015
201′.7273—dc23
2014017167

1 3 5 7 9 8 6 4 2
Printed in the United States of America
on acid-free paper

Contents

PART FOUR PEACEBUILDING IN PRACTICE: STRATEGIES, RESOURCES, CRITIQUE

PART FIVE THE GROWING EDGE
OF THE CONVERSATION

PREFACE

IT is now common knowledge that the events of the Iranian Revolution of 1979 began the slow process, culminating with the tragic Tuesday morning of September 11, 2001, of dissipating the "secular myopia" of political analysts, policymakers, and academics in the "West." Notwithstanding this halting progress, the discourses of secularism and orientalism and the modernist assumptions they convey concerning religion and its relevance to conflict in the contemporary world remain analytically dominant. More often than not, religion continues to be dismissed as illusionary or pathological, a form of "false consciousness" and thus a resource for manipulation by political elites. A related reductive strategy is to portray religion or "civilizational identity" as a reified, ahistorical, essentialized set of characteristics.

Regardless of one's chosen form of reductionism (religion is either epiphenomenal or at the very root of conflict), it is clear that "religion" remains a critical variable to contend with, whether in attempting to explain various forms of violence or in recognizing the empirical realities on the ground. Humans are embedded within and inhabit historical, religious, social, political, and cultural imaginations and contexts that inform their motivations and commitments to various forms of violence and, potentially, to various modes of peacebuilding and resistance. These overlapping contexts, however, are internally pluralistic, multifaceted, and always open to scrutiny and reframing. This Oxford Handbook takes this non-reductionist insight as its point of departure. What results from this effort, or so we intend, reflects the inevitably multidisciplinary nature of the interrelations between religion, conflict, and the very practical orientations and pragmatic concerns of peacebuilding efforts. One nexus of our inquiry, therefore, is highly attentive to the connections and possible synergies between theory and practice.

An early and still growing aspect of the study of religion, conflict, and peacebuilding is the effort to discover what discourses, warrants, and resources each of the world religious traditions have for both legitimating violent conflict and calling for its cessation. Could religions contribute to a transformed social, political, and economic order in which violence would give way to more peaceful relations among peoples? The field around this valuable inquiry has grown increasingly sophisticated, with new questions arising about the modes of religious interaction with such modern realities as the nation-state and its supposed legitimate monopoly on violence; global migration and diasporic communities shaped in part by communications technologies; contemporary forms of social life (including urbanization and the breakdown of traditional family and religious authorities); the modern human rights regime; shifting realities and awareness of gender; and new forms and dynamics of secularism, to name a few.

Accordingly, this volume extends the inquiry of religion, conflict, and peacebuilding beyond its previously prescribed parameters. Our objective is to provide a handbook that orients readers to the state of the field—to its central concepts, thinkers, and debates. In doing so, however, we aspire to advance an interdisciplinary conversation, and its attendant arguments, over what the central concepts, exemplars, and debates of the field actually are, as well as how the terrains of religion, conflict, and peacebuilding can and ought to be configured. In this effort we have in mind a reading audience of fellow scholars, students, practitioners, and inquirers who may have yet to realize that their interests, aims, and purposes overlap with those of the broad complex of peace studies.

Hence, among the impressive group of authors we recruited for this volume, we included many who have made their marks in parallel or cognate fields but who traditionally have not considered themselves part of, or have not been included in, conversations inquiring into the role of religion in conflict and peacebuilding. In February 2012 we convened all the authors at the Kroc Institute for International Peace Studies at the University of Notre Dame to discuss both the content of this volume and possibilities for further collaboration. The discussions that took place in the workshop, which now unfold across the pages of this volume, encouraged the contributors to articulate normative orientations (what is the scholar's implicit or explicit theory of justice?), to engage in critique (what are the contested histories and meanings of the categories we use in the analysis of religion?), to scrutinize the relevance of religion to an expansive account of violence as encompassing cultural, systemic, structural, as well as deadly manifestations, and to imagine various connections between theory and practice. It is our hope as well that this volume will encourage a robust flowering of future scholarship in this area, particularly in non-Western contexts.

While these orienting threads are interlaced in many junctures, the volume is divided into four parts. The first offers a mapping of the literatures on religion and violence as well as religion and peace. The second part engages the historical legacies of religion, peace, and nationalism as well as the historicist and deconstructive accounts of these legacies. Prominent in this discussion are the post-structuralist challenges to the very categories under scrutiny: religion, nationalism, peace, justice, and violence. These historical and historicist accounts prepare the transition to the third part of the volume, which engages contested issues at the heart of the emerging subfield of religion, conflict, and peacebuilding. The analysis in this part encompasses cognate disciplinary and practice-oriented conversations as well. Here authors address the issues of religion and development, violent and nonviolent religious militancy, religion and state violence, the legal discourse of religious freedoms and its implications for peacebuilding globally, and the complex conceptual and practical issues surrounding the synergy of gender theory, religion, and women's roles in peacebuilding.

The scrutiny devoted to contested conceptual issues with significant ramifications for policy and practice leads directly to the fourth part of the volume, titled "Peacebuilding in Practice: Strategies, Resources, Critique." Herein authors engage the internal dynamics of religious peacebuilding—for example, the role of religious actors as they operate in various contexts and within the internal hermeneutics of various traditions; the possibilities and limits of interreligious dialogue and scriptural reasoning as peacebuilding practices; the constructive potential of youth who are transforming conflict through interfaith engagements on American university campuses and within the framework of multicultural discourse; the role of religious and nonreligious rituals in conflict transformation; the convergent horizons of theology and peacebuilding practice; and the cultivation of the spiritual imagination and virtues of peacebuilding under fire. Part Four also considers the enduring relevance of comparative religious ethics to questions and virtues of peacebuilding and devotes equal attention to religious issues beyond the religious community itself (e.g., religion and political reconciliation; the role of religious actors in social change; secular militancy as an obstacle for peacebuilding processes; the colonial and missionary legacies of peacebuilding; and the meanings of religion as they intersect with the formation of solidarity activism with distant causes of national and other forms of liberation).

In the conclusion, Atalia Omer, one of the editors, offers a synthetic reflection on the volume and how its various chapters relate to one another and to the broader framing questions.

Atalia Omer
R. Scott Appleby
David Little

CONTRIBUTORS

R. Scott Appleby is Professor of History and the Marilyn Keough Dean of the Keough School of Global Affairs at the University of Notre Dame. His research examines the roots of religious violence and the potential of religious peacebuilding. Appleby co-chaired the Chicago Council on Global Affairs' Task Force on Religion and the Making of U.S. Foreign Policy, which released the influential report "Engaging Religious Communities Abroad: A New Imperative for U.S. Foreign Policy." He also directs Contending Modernities, a major multi-year project to examine the interaction among religious and secular forces in the modern world. Appleby is the author of *The Ambivalence of the Sacred: Religion, Violence and Reconciliation* (2000), and editor of *Spokesmen for the Despised: Fundamentalist Leaders of the Middle East* (1997). With Martin E. Marty, he co-edited the five-volume Fundamentalism Project.

Elizabeth A. Clark is Associate Director of the International Center for Law and Religion Studies at Brigham Young University. She has taken part in drafting commentaries and legal analyses of pending legislation and developments affecting religious freedom and has written amicus briefs on international religious freedom issues for the US Supreme Court. She has published numerous articles and book chapters on church-state issues and has been an associate editor of the books *Facilitating Freedom of Religion and Belief: A Deskbook* and *Law and Religion in Post-Communist Europe*. Professor Clark has also testified before Congress on religious freedom issues. Prior to joining the J. Reuben Clark Law School at Brigham Young University, she was an associate in the Washington, DC, office of Mayer, Brown & Platt, where she was a member of the Appellate and Supreme Court Litigation Group. She also clerked for Judge J. Clifford Wallace on the US Court of Appeals for the Ninth Circuit.

Heather M. DuBois is a doctoral student in peace studies and theology at the University of Notre Dame. She holds master's degrees in systematic theology (Fordham University) and conflict resolution (University of Bradford). Her research interests include Christian interpretations of suffering, experiences of divine presence/absence, and practices of accompaniment amidst violence.

W. Cole Durham, Jr. is the director of the International Center for Law and Religion Studies and Susa Young Gates University Professor of Law at J. Reuben Clark Law School, Brigham Young University. He has received multiple honors, including appointment as co-chair of the OSCE Advisory Panel of Experts on Freedom of Religion or Belief, and service as vice president of the International Academy for Freedom of Religion and Belief. A graduate of Harvard College and Harvard Law School, he has been heavily involved in comparative constitutional law and church-state relations throughout his career. He has published widely on comparative law, has served in the past as the chair of both the Comparative Law Section and the Law and Religion Section of the American Association of Law Schools, and is a member of several U.S. and international advisory boards dealing with religious freedom and church-state relations.

Marc Gopin is the Director of the Center for World Religions, Diplomacy, and Conflict Resolution (CRDC) and the James H. Laue Professor at the School for Conflict Analysis and Resolution at George Mason University. His research covers a wide range of topics from globalization, development, and social justice to the relationship between global trends in nonviolence and new approaches to global conflict resolution. Dr. Gopin has trained thousands of people worldwide in peacebuilding strategies for complex conflicts. He is the author of five books, including, most recently, *Bridges Across an Impossible Divide: The Inner Lives of Arab and Jewish Peacemakers* (2012).

Susan Hayward works in the Religion and Peacebuilding program at the US Institute of Peace (USIP) and is completing her doctorate in Buddhist and Christian studies at Georgetown University. In her work as a practitioner and researcher, she focuses on pluralism, the impact of the religious sector on peace, gender relations and religion, and identity formation in conflict. Hayward has worked extensively in Sri Lanka, Myanmar, Iraq, and Colombia. She co-led a three-year initiative analyzing the intersection of women, religion, conflict, and peacebuilding as a collaboration between USIP and Georgetown. An edited volume that is the fruit of this initiative is forthcoming.

Scott Hibbard is an Associate Professor in the Department of Political Science at DePaul University, where he teaches courses on American foreign policy, Middle East politics, and international relations. Hibbard has a PhD from Johns Hopkins University and advanced degrees from the London School of Economics and Political Science and Georgetown University. He is the author of *Religious Politics and Secular States: Egypt, India, and the United States* (2010) and coauthor (with David Little) of *Islamic Activism and U.S. Foreign Policy* (1997).

Janna Hunter-Bowman is earning her PhD in peace studies and theology through the Kroc Institute for International Peace Studies and theology department at the University of Notre Dame. In her dissertation studies, she plans to draw on theologies of witness and accounts of witness from an anthropological perspective to analyze forms of agency in highly constrained environments of protracted armed conflict. She will be Assistant Professor of Peace Studies and Social Ethics at Associated Mennonite Biblical Seminary beginning in 2015. During her eight years in Colombia as a practitioner, she developed and directed a national program monitoring political violence and peacebuilding, led fact-finding missions, and authored in-depth investigative reports, book chapters, and popular journal articles.

Slavica Jakelić is an Assistant Professor of Humanities and Social Thought at Valparaiso University's Honors College and an Associate Fellow of the Institute for Advanced Studies in Culture at the University of Virginia. Her scholarly interests and publications center on religion and identity, theories of religion and secularism, the relationship between religious and secular humanisms, and conflict resolution. Professor Jakelić has worked at or been a fellow of several interdisciplinary institutes: the Erasmus Institute for the Culture of Democracy in Croatia, the Institute for the Study of Economic Culture at Boston University, the Institut für die Wissenschaften vom Menschen in Vienna, Austria, the Erasmus Institute at the University of Notre Dame, the Martin Marty Center at the

University of Chicago, and the Notre Dame Institute for Advanced Study. Professor Jakelić is a co-editor of two volumes, *The Future of the Study of Religion* and *Crossing Boundaries: From Syria to Slovakia*, a co-editor of *The Hedgehog Review*'s issue "After Secularization," and, most recently, the author of *Collectivistic Religions: Religion, Choice, and Identity in Late Modernity*. She is working on a book entitled *The Practice of Religious and Secular Humanisms*.

S. Ayse Kadayifci-Orellana is Visiting Assistant Professor in Georgetown University's MA Program in Conflict Resolution and directs the Conflict Resolution Field Program. Dr. Kadayifci-Orellana has authored *Standing On an Isthmus: Islamic Narratives of War and Peace in the Palestinian Territories* and co-edited the volume *Anthology on Islam and Peace and Conflict Resolution in Islam: Precept and Practice*.

John Kelsay is Distinguished Research Professor and Chair of the Department of Religion at Florida State University. He is the author of *Islam and War: A Study in Comparative Ethics* (1993) and *Arguing the Just War in Islam* (2007), as well as other works dealing with the role of religion in the cultural regulation of armed force.

John Paul Lederach is Professor of International Peacebuilding at the Kroc Institute for International Peace Studies at the University of Notre Dame. His books include *The Moral Imagination: The Art and Soul of Building Peace, Building Peace: Sustainable Reconciliation in Divided Societies,* and (with Angela Jill Lederach) *When Blood and Bones Cry Out: Journeys through the Soundscape of Healing and Reconciliation.*

David Little retired in 2009 as Professor of the Practice in Religion, Ethnicity, and International Conflict at Harvard Divinity School, and as an associate at the Weatherhead Center for International Affairs at Harvard University. He is now a fellow at the Berkley Center for Religion, Peace, and World Affairs at Georgetown University. Until the summer of 1999, he was Senior Scholar in Religion, Ethics and Human Rights at the United States Institute of Peace in Washington, DC. Before that, he taught at the University of Virginia and Yale Divinity School. From 1996 to1998, he was member of the Advisory Committee to the State Department on Religious Freedom Abroad. Little is coauthor with Scott W. Hibbard of the USIP publication *Islamic Activism and U.S. Foreign Policy* (1997) and author of two volumes in the USIP series on religion, nationalism, and intolerance (RNI), *Ukraine: Legacy of Intolerance* (1991) and *Sri Lanka: The Invention of Enmity* (1994). The RNI conference report on Tibet, *Sino-Tibetan Coexistence: Creating Space for Tibetan Self-Direction*, written by Little and Hibbard, also appeared in 1994. In 2007 he published two volumes, *Religion and Nationalism in Iraq: A Comparative Perspective* (with Donald K. Swearer) and *Peacemakers in Action: Profiles of Religion in Conflict Resolution.* In the past several years, Little has authored a number of articles on religion and human rights, the history of rights and constitutionalism, and religion and peace, and he will soon publish a collection of essays entitled *Essays on Religion and Human Rights: Ground to Stand On.*

Cecelia Lynch is Professor of Political Science and Director of International Studies at the University of California, Irvine. Her books include *Beyond Appeasement: Interpreting Interwar Peace Movements in World Politics* (1999, winner of the 1999 Furniss Award for best book in international security studies and the 1998-99 Myrna Bernath Book Award of the Society for Historians of American Foreign Relations), *Law and Moral Action in World*

Politics (co-edited with Michael Loriaux, 2000), *Strategies for Research in Constructivist International Relations* (with Audie Klotz, 2007), and the co-edited *On Rules, Knowledge, and Politics: Friedrich Kratochwil and the Study of International Relations* (2010). She has been awarded fellowships from the Social Science Research Council, MacArthur Foundation, Andrew W. Mellon Foundation, and the Henry Luce Foundation, and her articles on religion have appeared in *Millenium, Ethics and International Relations, International Theory*, and other journals and edited volumes. She is completing one book on tensions in Western (Christian) religious ethics on violence and researching another on Islamic, Christian, and interfaith religious ethics in world crises. She edits the blog "Critical Investigations into Humanitarianism in Africa," or The CIHA Blog, at www.cihablog.com.

Patrick Q. Mason is Associate Professor of Religion and Howard W. Hunter Chair of Mormon Studies at Claremont Graduate University. He is the author of *The Mormon Menace: Violence and Anti-Mormonism in the Postbellum South*, and co-editor of *War and Peace in Our Time: Mormon Perspectives*.

Cassie Meyer is Director of Academic and Curricular Initiatives at Interfaith Youth Core (IFYC), where she oversees IFYC's faculty programming and the development of online educational resources. She has an MA from the University of Chicago Divinity School, where she focused on American religious history. She has taught courses on interfaith engagement at numerous institutions including the University of Chicago Divinity School, Princeton Theological Seminary, and Northwestern University and has written extensively about interfaith topics. Her current interest focuses on pedagogies for engaging interfaith issues in the classroom.

Tam Ngo is a Research Fellow at the Max Planck Institute for the Study of Religious and Ethnic Diversity in Göttingen. She studies the relation between media and various forms of religiosity in contemporary Vietnam. She is the author of *The New Way: Protestantism and the Hmong in Contemporary Vietnam* (forthcoming).

Peter Ochs is Edgar Bronfman Professor of Modern Judaic Studies at the University of Virginia, where he also directs religious studies graduate programs in "Scripture, Interpretation, and Practice," an interdisciplinary approach to the Abrahamic traditions. He is cofounder of the (Abrahamic) Society for Scriptural Reasoning. He writes on Jewish philosophy, rabbinics and semiotics, Judaism and Christian theology, and the logic of inter-traditional, scriptural dialogue.

A. Rashied Omar is Research Scholar of Islamic Studies and Peacebuilding at the Kroc Institute for International Peace Studies at the University of Notre Dame. His research and teaching focus on the roots of religious violence and the potential of religion for constructive social engagement and inter-religious peacebuilding. He is a coauthor of *Religion in Public Education: Options for a New South Africa* (1994).

Atalia Omer is an Assistant Professor of Religion, Conflict, and Peace Studies at the Kroc Institute for International Peace Studies at the University of Notre Dame. She earned her PhD from the Committee on the Study of Religion at Harvard University. Her research interests include the theoretical study of the interrelation between religion and nationalism; religion, nationalism, and peacebuilding; the role of national/religious/ethnic diasporas in the dynamics of conflict transformation and peace; multiculturalism as a framework for conflict transformation and as a theory of justice; the role of subaltern narratives in reimagining questions of peace and justice; intra-group dialogue and the contestation of citizenship in ethno-religious national contexts; innovation and reframing of religious traditions in response to empathy with others' sufferings; and the symbolic appropriation of the Palestinian-Israeli conflict in other zones of conflict. Her first book, *When Peace Is Not Enough: How the Israeli Peace Camp Thinks about Religion, Nationalism, and Justice* (2013), examines the way the Israeli peace camp addresses interrelationships between religion, ethnicity, and nationality and how it interprets justice vis-à-vis the Palestinian conflict. The book highlights how hybrid identities may provide creative resources for peacebuilding, especially in ethno-religious national conflicts where political agendas are informed by particularistic and often purist conceptions of identity.

Eboo Patel is the Founder and President of Interfaith Youth Core (IFYC), a Chicago-based organization building the interfaith movement on college campuses. He is the author of the books *Acts of Faith* (2007), which won the Louisville Grawemeyer Award in Religion, and *Sacred Ground* (2012). He served on President Obama's inaugural Advisory Council of the White House Office of Faith-based and Neighborhood Partnerships and holds a doctorate in the sociology of religion from Oxford University, where he studied on a Rhodes Scholarship. He has taught courses on interfaith cooperation at many institutions including the University of Chicago, Princeton Theological Seminary, Northwestern University, and Dominican University (IL) where he was the Lund-Gill Chair.

Daniel Philpott is Professor of Political Science and Peace Studies and Director of the Center for Civil and Human Rights at the University of Notre Dame. He is the author most recently of *Just and Unjust Peace: An Ethic of Political Reconciliation* (2012).

Lisa Schirch is Director of Human Security at the Alliance for Peacebuilding and Research Professor at Eastern Mennonite University's Center for Justice & Peacebuilding. A former Fulbright Fellow in East and West Africa, Schirch has worked in more than twenty countries and has authored five books in the field of conflict prevention and peacebuilding. Schirch holds a BA in international relations from the University of Waterloo, Canada, and an MS and PhD in conflict analysis and resolution from George Mason University.

Timothy Samuel Shah is Associate Director and Scholar-in-Residence with the Religious Freedom Project of the Berkley Center for Religion, Peace, and World Affairs at Georgetown University and Visiting Assistant Professor in the Department of Government, also at Georgetown University.

Dan Smyer Yu, a Research Group Leader at the Max Planck Institute for the Study of Religious and Ethnic Diversity, is an anthropologist of religion and an ethnographic filmmaker. He is the author of *The Spread of Tibetan Buddhism in China: Charisma, Money, Enlightenment* (2012) and *Mindscaping the Landscape of Tibet: Place, Memorability, Eco-aesthetics* (2014).

Jason A. Springs is Assistant Professor of Religion, Ethics, and Peace Studies at the Kroc Institute for International Peace Studies at the University of Notre Dame, where he also holds an appointment as faculty fellow in the Center for the Study of Religion and Society in the Department of Sociology. His research and teaching focus on ethical perspectives on restorative justice; conceptions of religious toleration and the challenges posed by oppositional forms of moral and religious pluralism for transforming conflict in European and North American contexts; religious nationalism; and lenses of structural and cultural violence for peacebuilding. His articles addressing the role of religion and conflict in modern public life appear in *Journal of Religion, Journal of Religious Ethics, Modern Theology, Journal of the American Academy of Religion, Contemporary Pragmatism*, and *Soundings: An Interdisciplinary Journal*. His broader interests include the ethical and political dimensions of American pragmatist thought and postliberal theology. He is the author of *Toward a Generous Orthodoxy: Prospects for Hans Frei's Postliberal Theology* (2010) and coauthor (with Atalia Omer) of *Religious Nationalism* (2013).

Peter van der Veer is Director of the Max Planck Institute for the Study of Religious and Ethnic Diversity in Göttingen and Distinguished University Professor at Utrecht University. He studies religion and nationalism in Asia and Europe with a focus on India and China. Among his many books are *Religious Nationalism* (1994), *Imperial Encounters* (2001), and *The Modern Spirit of Asia* (2014).

PART ONE

MAPPING THE FIELD

CHAPTER 1

··

RELIGIOUS PEACEBUILDING
The Exotic, the Good, and the Theatrical

··

ATALIA OMER

INTRODUCTION

NUMEROUS works and commentaries in the post-9/11 era begin with an urgent articulation of the need to theorize about religion and violence. A preoccupation with the relationship between religion and violence also has given rise to a concomitant booming of religious peacebuilding. Most of what takes place in the field of religious peacebuilding has been grounded, implicitly or explicitly, in Scott Appleby's *The Ambivalence of the Sacred: Religion, Violence, and Reconciliation* and his phenomenological approach to religion.[1] Drawing on theologian Rudolf Otto's view of religion in *The Idea of the Holy* as the *mysterium tremendum et fascinans*, Appleby argues that religion, or rather the experience of the sacred (the *mysterium tremendum* or *numen*), can generate ambivalent phenomena or responses, ranging from violent to nonviolent militancy.[2] This point of departure further is linked to a non-reductive view of religious traditions as internally plural and multifaceted. Illuminating the special proclivity of religious actors to engage in nonviolent militancy in the pursuit of change and justice underscores the potential constructive and instrumental roles of religion, religious leaders, and institutions, in particular, in processes of peacebuilding. The sociological assumptions undergirding this approach are that religious leaders may have certain credibility within the society and/or religious institutions could provide ready networks to propagate attitudinal shifts (in the same manner that they supposedly are available for the recruitment of radical violent warriors).

Because of its focus on the potentially constructive role of religion in transforming conflicts, the "ambivalence of the sacred" thesis also confronts reductionist accounts such as Bernard Lewis's and Samuel Huntington's "the Clash of Civilizations" argument. While the "clash" thesis does take religion seriously on its own terms as a causal factor in international relations and global politics, it renders religion as an ahistorical, monolithic, and unchanging *essence*.[3] This lens produces an overly simplistic, belligerent, skewed, and deterministic picture of religion and conflict in the post–Cold War era. This picture is an appealing one precisely because of its simplicity; it consequently functions as a self-fulfilling prophecy with both Islamists and xenophobic Western commentators rendering their objectives in terms of ineradicable and irreconcilable differences between civilizations.[4] The "ambivalence of the sacred" thesis, on the other hand, is grounded in recognition of the internal pluralities of religious traditions, consequently articulating a non-essentialist and non-reductionist constructive and contextually sensitive framework. It is this insight that sparked the industry of religious peacebuilding and carved out space for a theological and hermeneutical focus on peace-promoting motifs and resources within religious traditions.

However, this insight is misapplied if the preoccupation with theological retrieval and appropriation precludes a consideration of how historical contexts and interpretations of events from multiple perspectives might, and perhaps even should, challenge and transform religious traditions and political ideologies.[5] Religious peacebuilding amounts to more than the inverse image of the Huntingtonian frame, and so does the "ambivalence of the sacred," with its often overlooked emphasis on fallibility and context—an emphasis conceptually grounded in the aforementioned critical distinction between *numen* and phenomena. Rethinking religious peacebuilding, therefore, will necessitate moving beyond a simplistic and unreflective application of the idea that a supposedly "authentic" religion (one that is not perverted by violent "alien" motifs) is and can do good. Such a simplistic formulation gives rise to the same kind of essentialism and ahistoricity that characterize the "clash of civilizations." Likewise, with its inattentiveness to the task of discursive critique, religious peacebuilding is not always in tune with the broader objectives of peacebuilding.

This article provides an overview of the various trends and trajectories of religious peacebuilding. The trends include theological excavations of "good" religion (to combat "bad" or "perverted" religion and to imagine reconciliatory ethics), the role of religion in the theatrics and processes of peacebuilding, the spirituality and inspiration of peace practitioners, the instrumentality of religious leaders and networks in diplomacy and in shifting societal attitudes, and the exoticization of religious peacebuilders by the "industry" component of the field. To be academically rigorous, religious peacebuilding needs to move beyond the exotic, the theatric, and the good and the kinds of limitations they impose on the analysis of religion, conflict, and peacebuilding. I begin with a brief mapping of the field of religious peacebuilding and continue by challenging its presuppositions and agendas primarily with respect to questions arising from structural and cultural violence and broad discursive formations. I refer to this challenge as the "justice dilemma."

MAPPING THE FIELD

The dominant themes in religious peacebuilding include the ethnographic study of interfaith dialogues (IFD), the retrieval of peace-promoting motifs from within the resources of individual religious traditions, the instrumental role of "religious networks" in the dynamics of conflict and peacebuilding, and, more broadly, the role of "faith diplomacy."

I refer to this area of research and activism as the *conflict transformation* approach. This thread of scholarship provides an inductive theory about praxis as well as a focus on the retrieval of theological resources for peacebuilding. The conflict transformation approach, generally, explores the relevance of culture and religion in processes of conflict transformation as they pertain to those who are both directly and indirectly connected to the specific landscapes of the conflict. There are currents within this thread that are thoroughly instrumentalist, asking how it is possible to capitalize on religious networks to further peace and development agendas.[6] Other currents are more theological in that they represent the intimate interlinking between peacebuilding and religious vocations. In what follows, I divide my discussion of this approach into "the theatrical," "the inspirational," and "the theological."

The Theatrical

On the level of praxis, one way in which religion is relevant to questions of peacebuilding is in providing a specific model or technique for conflict transformation. The works of Marc Gopin and Lisa Schirch represent two notable examples of this approach. Gopin has been instrumental in integrating religion into the field of conflict resolution. He focuses on the role of religion in emotional training, interpersonal relations and encounters, respect and appreciation of mourning processes, forgiveness, and honor—all constitutive of meaningful peacebuilding.[7] Schirch captures the ritualistic elements of religious practice as a framework for designing and analyzing the possibility of constructive change. She explicitly deploys the lens of ritual theory in order to outline the "best approaches" for and effectiveness of the actual practice of peacebuilding. Her work on rituals in peacebuilding signals a focus on the theatrics of peacebuilding. The theatrical thread illuminates the practice of peacebuilding as a highly ritualistic engagement, one that optimally might produce liminal spaces and transformative moments when adversaries or enemies move beyond reified interpretations of their respective identities. Reaching a certain degree of receptivity to liminal spaces often resonates with and draws upon religious motifs and symbols. Hence, the theatrical mode that instrumentalizes religion is never too far removed from an intricate sensitivity to religious and cultural memories and narratives as well as to interfaith theological and cultural exchanges and hermeneutics.[8]

The Spiritual/Inspirational

The focus on the particular qualities and cultural sensitivity, creativity, and moral imagination of the peace practitioner has occupied significant space in the literature that connects religion to peacebuilding practitioners. Religion interrelates with conflict transformation through three primary models, which are referred to by Appleby as "crisis mobilization," "saturation," and "interventionist."[9] Triggered by exigencies, crisis mobilization emerges spontaneously but fails to routinize (to use the Weberian term) the charisma of leaders such as Martin Luther King Jr. or Gandhi and thus falls short of substantially transforming social and religious institutions in the post-crisis era. The saturation model denotes precisely that—saturation with some degree of permanence of inter- and intra-religious mechanisms for conflict transformation. While this model does focus on the long haul, its success deeply depends on a strong civil society, democratic traditions, and institutional frameworks and thus is unlikely to materialize on its own in contexts devastated by destruction. Therefore, the "interventionist" model, with its emphasis on the instrumental role of external actors in facilitating the indigenous emergence of a saturation model, is deemed the most successful in offering long-term processes of reform and in cultivating, through educational and other initiative-empowering mechanisms, what scholar-practitioner John Paul Lederach calls "constituencies of peace."[10] This focus on the interventionist model unsurprisingly brings to the fore an introspection of the motivations and guiding principles of interventions.

The interrelation between the saturation and the interventionist models sparked a preoccupation with indigenous leaders as well as with the morality and religiosity of "interventionist" peacebuilders. Some works look at the role of spiritual and religious formation as motivating and inspirational background. To this extent, these works are anecdotal and their proliferation and systematization could and do offer insights concerning spirituality and peacebuilding across different cultural and religious contexts. They often emphasize the prophetic function of religion, the resources that enable courageous individuals to speak truth to power while in the midst of fire, and the significance of self-scrutiny and, at times, uncritical celebration of the interventionist/practitioner's own religious and cultural trappings.[11]

Two key authors and practitioners who highlight the (obvious) relevance of culture and religion to peacebuilding processes are Kevin Avruch and John Paul Lederach.[12] Peacebuilding must be a contextually sensitive enterprise, one that is self-conscious about the cultural biases and baggage that the peace practitioner carries on her back as well as the cultural specificity of the contexts of conflict. "Getting to yes," without a complex comprehension of on-the-ground perspectives, memories, and dreams, has no traction beyond the thin accomplishment of getting some people (male elites, mainly) to agree to terminate direct forms of violence. A move from the "episodes" to the "epicenters" of conflict, the guiding principle of Lederach's approach to conflict transformation, requires thick familiarity with and immersion in the languages, memories, and meanings embedded on the ground.[13] Other works, as indicated above, engage in an explicitly theological hermeneutics in order to locate peace-promoting motifs; sometimes these motifs resonate in the background as part of the spiritual formation and sense of vocation of the peace practitioner and activist. Here the well-known case of the Catholic Community of Sant'Egidio in Mozambique usually is cited. Sometimes those motifs come to the surface through capitalizing on religious networks, and this is when religious peacebuilding connects with the subfield of religion and development. This subfield further explores the implications and often even the inevitability of capitalizing on and collaborating with religious institutional networks and leaderships in the process of providing aid and supporting local efforts for developing infrastructures to cultivate programs to promote better quality of life. In the development business, to ignore the role of religious networks in advancing and implementing objectives amounts to blindness about the realities on the ground.

Theologies of Peacebuilding and the Instrumentalization of Religious Networks

As in the pursuit of sustainable development, religious peacebuilding that focuses on cultivating saturation through intervention and empowerment operates on various fronts. Sant'Egidio was indeed instrumental in mediating peace agreements. Religious leaders, however, also could become influential in national reconciliation (Cambodian Buddhists[14]) and in transnational religious reform (the Gülen movement). It is the synergy among these various fronts that is deemed most conducive for sustainable peacebuilding.[15] The focus on

religion and techniques of peacebuilding, therefore, probes into ho[ ]
moral and spiritual formation of the peacemaker. An example o[ ]
the work of Lederach, who reflected on how his Mennonite back[ ]
tudes in the field (in conflict zones) and his sense of vocation. Le[ ]
with Cynthia Sampson,[16] *From the Ground Up: Mennonite Con[ ]*
Peacebuilding, attempts to reflect not only the connections be[ ]
ground and the commitment to peacebuilding, but also the v[ ]
stances propelled internal processes of change, whereby pacifi[ ]
into isolationism, but rather into active and meaningful peaceful activism tow[ ]
ing direct forms of violence and transforming conflicts. Interlaced with this peace activism
are Christian theological concepts such as love, justice, forgiveness, mercy, and hope.

The above overview shows there is a body of literature that documents and analyzes religious peacebuilding as a practice and a vocation. Beyond an exploration of individual peacebuilders, this line of research also is compounded by an explosion of organizations, research centers, and single-tradition and ecumenical peacebuilding networks. Various Mennonite networks and numerous committed Mennonite peacemakers have been pivotal in processes of peacebuilding, including trauma healing and development initiatives around the world. Likewise, the global institutional network of Catholics lends itself to religious peacebuilding around the globe.[17] Other transnational single-tradition networks include the Gülen movement,[18] Baptist Peace Fellowship,[19] Buddhist Peace Fellowship,[20] and Christian Peacemaker Team,[21] among numerous other organizations. Representatives of ecumenical "interventionists" include International Committee for Peace Council[22] and World Conference on Religion and Peace.[23] The business of religious peacebuilding is expanded further to research institutions such as the Berkley Center for Religion, Peace, and World Affairs at Georgetown University in Washington, DC,[24] and the Program on Religion, Conflict, and Peacebuilding at the Kroc Institute for International Peace Studies at the University of Notre Dame.[25]

The study of individual prophetic voices and institutional faith networks, featured in great volume in the literature, interrelates and oscillates between an instrumentalization of religion for peacebuilding and development and for fulfilling religious vocations. This is where distinctions need to be drawn between praxis and theory. The importance of this task will become clear in my exposition of the theological thread and its complex relation to questions of justice and change.

The Theological

As indicated, Appleby's "ambivalence of the sacred" undergirds practice and theory in religious peacebuilding.[26] Theologically, the insight about the constructive and causal qualities of religion translated into sustained efforts to retrieve and cultivate nonviolent and peaceful motifs within diverse religious traditions. The act of retrieval presupposes internal plurality.

Gopin's *Between Eden and Armageddon: The Future of World Religions, Violence, and Peacemaking* echoes the insight concerning the internal diversity and plurality of a community and the subsequent need to analyze why certain violent, exclusive, or otherwise peace-inhibiting interpretations of religious symbols, texts, and other narratives gained dominance. Such exploration, Gopin suggests, might be pivotal for conflict analysis as well as conflict transformation. At the heart of these processes, therefore, is recognition of

tive hermeneutics as a key peacebuilding method. The analyst may engage in an
ation of the tradition, seeking possible marginalized motifs that would promote peace-
lding ideals and concerns with justice. Applying a psychodynamic approach to conflict,
Gopin traces the patterns of change within religious traditions, that is, what circumstances
led to the adaptation of violent motifs and by which subgroups.[27] This approach typifies a
presumption that violent motifs constitute inauthentic or perverted interpretations of religion. In other words, the task of religious peacebuilding amounts to a recovery of good
religion.

This archeological approach later reverberates in the work of scholar-practitioner
Mohammed Abu-Nimer.[28] Abu-Nimer underscores the dynamic character of Islamic
sources and Islam itself as a continuous, lived revelation. His work consequently exemplifies the premise, despite proclamations of various literalists to the contrary, that religions
are internally plural and thus that sacred sources are subject to continuous interpretations.
Abu-Nimer labors to develop a nonviolent paradigm for peacebuilding from within the
sources of Islam (underscoring core Islamic values such as justice, benevolence, patience,
and forgiveness). This theological genre resonates with works on forgiveness, nonviolence,
and reconciliation that likewise seek to identify an ethics and practice of reconciliation and
peace from within the resources of a given tradition.[29] The growing preoccupation with the
retrieval of theological resources that are consistent with principles of nonviolence represents an expansion of the traditional theological focus on the ethics of the use of force.
Traditionally, this paradigm has been the most dominant scholarly thread, engaging the
questions of religion and conflict, along with an interrelated focus on how religion informs
pacifism and "holy wars."[30] The focus on how religion relates to the legitimate and/or illegitimate use of force intersects with the field of ethics, although ethics is not yet an intentional
interlocutor with religious peacebuilding, specifically, and peace studies, more broadly.
On the part of comparative ethics, an underdeveloped interface with peace studies may be
attributed to the enduring persistence of the dichotomous focus on only war and pacifism.

On the part of religious peacebuilding, the lack of interface with comparative ethics and
comparative religious studies is costly because it does not account for the decades of methodological critiques and conversations concerning the delicate act of comparison. Comparison
without self-reflexivity and discursive analysis risks an essentializing naiveté.[31] As a result of
this disciplinary gap, a recent effort within the religious peacebuilding subfield to develop an
ethics of political reconciliation may be subject to some of the same critiques conventionally
aimed at comparative ethics (as well as comparative religion, more generally).[32]

Political theorist and peace studies scholar Daniel Philpott articulates such an ethics of
political reconciliation in the aftermath of atrocities. Philpott's model highlights restoration of right relations within the political realm. He grounds this ethics in an encyclopedic
retrieval and cataloguing of motifs from within Judaism, Islam, and Christianity that are
consistent with a view of political reconciliation as entailing building just institutions and
relations between and among states, acknowledgement of wrongdoing, reparation, punishment, apology, and forgiveness. This project is in conversation with liberal political theory
and ideas concerning a pragmatic endurance of the principle of overlapping consensus and
of the tradition of human rights as an instrument designed to identify injustice.[33]

Philpott's approach, however, diverges significantly from a view of liberal peace (the corollary of an unrevised liberal political theory) with its distinct presuppositions about religion
and how it relates to conflict, peace, and public discourse. These premises involve analyzing

religious violence as a matter of epistemological dispute, the solution of which necessitated the rise of the modern liberal state and conceptions of toleration.[34] The field of religious peacebuilding, as I show below in further detail, has not challenged these premises, but rather has operated within them. Philpott offers a correction that resonates with a rich body of literature and, by now, a perhaps increasingly resolved conversation in religious ethics that challenges and revises presumptions concerning the non-publicity of religion.[35] Tapping into the religion and public life debates, however, proves a valuable maneuver, indicating the need to theoretically enrich religious peacebuilding. Yet unawareness of theoretical and methodological debates that take place in the study of religion can diminish the effectiveness of theorizing about religion in the religious peacebuilding subfield. This may be the case with the model of political reconciliation cited above.

Similar to other exercises in comparative ethics, the pitfall of the attempt to develop an ethics of peacebuilding across different religious terrains is to elide, however inadvertently, meaningful and often problematic differences, making them all conform to categories of justice that are indebted to a particular religious and cultural context. From the perspective of the analyst, this model of political reconciliation selectively extracts and essentializes interpretations of contextually specific particularities, practices, and on-the-ground innovative applications and subversions of norms. The model of political reconciliation, like the conventional project of the comparative ethicist, therefore, can become inattentive, blind, and even complicit with underlying structural and cultural injustice.

Distilling an ethics of reconciliation from within Judaism, for instance, does not provide the constructive tools needed to deconstruct and reframe the meta-injustices undergirding the discussion of peace and justice in Israel/Palestine. Israeli liberalism, despite its secularity and even anti-religious stance, embodies a distinct political theology. Religious peace activism in Israel also operates within the parameters set out by this political theology. This is where I identify the limitations of religious peacebuilding in the Israeli case and other cases more broadly.[36] Without explicating and interrogating this theology (a particular reading of Jewish history and identity) from within the religious, historical, and lived sources of Judaism, a radical transforming of the Palestinian-Israeli conflict will not materialize. This kind of contestation of symbolic boundaries (axiomatic conceptions of identity) I term the *hermeneutics of citizenship*. It emerges as a response to challenges from the victims of Zionist practices (internal and external) who appeal to broad (human rights norms) rather than particularistic frames of justice, which, by themselves, are not sufficient as a framework for rethinking the symbolic boundaries authorizing unjust practice. (They primarily serve a diagnostic and empowering function.)

The limitations of religious peacebuilding, therefore, revolve around the secularist framing of religion as a belief and as a distinct variable, empirically manifest but thoroughly ahistorical and transcultural. Another related conceptual limitation is the inclination to articulate religious peacebuilding as a unidirectional process in which religion as an ahistorical and transcultural essence can function positively to influence peacebuilding processes. This conceptualization of religious peacebuilding as a unidirectional process precludes thinking about how historical developments, intercultural exchanges, and multiperspectival demands of justice might work in the other direction as an occasion to transform religion, religious institutions, and the interfaces between religion and ideological formations.[37] But a model of political reconciliation that essentializes and selectively extracts from the sources of religious traditions can afford only a unidirectional view of change. It deploys the "ambivalence of the sacred" thesis in the comparative imagining of an ethics of political reconciliation. However, in the process, it merely inverses the essentializing of religion (as bad) that Appleby sets out to challenge.

The arena of comparative ethics, as indicated, has fallen on occasion into similar pitfalls. Even when expanded beyond a preoccupation concerning the use of force and principles of peace to a related discussion of religion and human rights, it tends to distill selectively what works in accordance with a predetermined theory of justice.[38] Avoiding the complexities, divergences, and subversive spaces on the ground limits this approach's effectiveness as a framework for peacebuilding. However, comparative ethicist David Little, whose earlier work largely framed the subfield of comparative religious ethics, illustrates in his later preoccupation with the comparative study of ethno-religious national conflicts where fruitful connections between ethics and religious peacebuilding can unfold.[39] A critical divergence from Philpott's model of political reconciliation is Little's view of the tradition of human rights, not as ontologically distinct from the ethics found in the three Abrahamic traditions, but as already representing a multiperspectival, dynamic, and interpretive tradition, with an inbuilt mechanism for self-correction.[40] This view of human rights is indispensible for Little's engagement with questions of peace and justice. While operating with an a priori theory of justice, Little's focus on theological retrieval as an instrument of peacebuilding is thoroughly contextual and anchored within the framework of the nation-state and its mythologies. He asks what kind of interpretations of religion will promote more or less exclusionary conceptions of identity, with the presumption that greater exclusivity relates to violent practices. Yet Little's view, as apparent from his work with Appleby, is non-reductive, taking into account how institutional and structural conditions also influence and play into cultural and national formations.[41] It is not about religions in abstraction as systems of meanings informing behavior but as interpreted and embodied in the complex interplay between social practices and institutional formations.

To reiterate, critical to Little's view of religious peacebuilding is an approach that is at once historical and localized yet also ahistorical and universal in its commitment to human rights.[42] This commitment gestures to a central conceptual divergence from Philpott's articulation of the tradition of human rights as potentially in conflict with the religious traditions. The tension that arises from discussions concerning the relation between religion and human rights brings to the fore the urgency of analyzing the theory of justice underlying the field of religious peacebuilding.

Religious Peacebuilding and the Justice Dilemma

In Search of Silent Violence

Peacebuilding is intricately associated with questions of justice or "positive" peace and the transformation not only of direct and obvious violence, but also of structural and cultural forms of violence. As I indicate in my discussion of an ethics of political reconciliation, the concept of "positive" peace challenges "negative" or "liberal" interpretations of peace that understand peace *negatively* as the absence of direct violence, a view that not only has informed various conventions of international relations, conflict resolution, and diplomacy, but that also is indebted to certain political-philosophical conceptions of toleration that could, at once, gloss over meta-forms of injustice and function to reify those structural problems.

A subgenre in political theory that focuses on democracy in ethno-religious majoritarian national contexts (ethnocracies) usually does not make it onto reading lists in religious peacebuilding.[43] But it should because a careful analysis might expose how religion relates to meta-injustices (in Israel, for instance, "multiculturalism" is encouraged within strict ethno-religious boundaries), or it can trace the patterns of increased or decreased inclusivity.[44] The blinders imposed by a theological approach would amount to overlooking an analysis of power and discourse. To return to the case of Israel, the question that is not asked is why a particular hegemonic interpretation of Jewish-Israeli identity emerged as an axiomatic frame. Within the theological thread, the belief that Jewish religious destiny entails political hegemony is framed as a "right" that needs to be respected. This framing already hints at a potential dissonance between the discourse of religious freedom, which attained currency in the early twenty-first century as the main idiom for discussing the plight of minorities abroad and identity politics at home (in the context of the United States), and justice concerns guided by a human rights framework. I return to this point shortly. For now, it suffices to underscore that the language of "rights" and "liberties," if unreflective of its own categories, assumptions, and locations, can become complicit with injustice. The tool of critique is pertinent for religious peacebuilding. Without discursive critique, creative hermeneutics (a hallmark of religious peacebuilding) risks becoming overly backward-looking and reactionary, diminishing its transformative potential.

Substantially engaging in a discursive critique could expand not only the theoretical scope of religious peacebuilding but also its practical implications. By discursive critique, I mean an analysis that is self-aware of the genealogy and historicity of its categories. Political theorist Elizabeth Shakman Hurd has effectively highlighted how the discourses of secularism have produced preconceptions that have dominated how the so-called "phenomenon of religious resurgence" has been analyzed and how it determined what kind of questions were deemed pertinent to the analysis of religion and politics. That "religious resurgence" is interpreted as subversive and threatening and that religious violence is especially associated with Islam, Hurd argues, illuminates the Euro- and Judeo-Christo-centricity of the discussion as well as its undergirding orientalism. What conventional analyses of public and/or "resurgent" religion overlook is an exposition of historical contexts of displacement, marginalization, and colonization and how and why the "resurgence" of religion signals attempts to renegotiate the meanings of the secular in various contexts.[45]

While the raison d'être of the religious and peacebuilding industry is to combat overly deterministic renderings of religion as divisive, belligerent, and irrational, it remains rather unreflective about how this outlook is born out of particular modalities or discourses that dominate how "religious" and "secular" are analyzed. Because religious peacebuilding operates within the secularist discourse, it focuses overwhelmingly on direct and obvious violence, overlooking how religion relates to structural and cultural violence. A conceptual shift beyond the secularist frame gave rise to the aforementioned attempt to construct an ethics of political reconciliation that nonetheless reproduced a secularist rendering of "religion" as an ahistorical body of dogmas, rituals, and texts. Exploring discursive formations therefore is intricately relevant to questions of peace and justice. As in the analogous preoccupation in political theory with a discussion of "religion and democracy," what is considered generically "religious" privileges Christo-centric and Western assumptions about the "religious" and the "political."

When religious peacebuilding in Israel glosses over the *hermeneutics of citizenship*, it appears as a good force for peace and justice, despite operating within meta-injustice. Cultural anthropologist Saba Mahmood's deconstructive reading of the discourse of religious freedoms and liberties as an umbrella for a host of non-governmental and governmental advocacy and activism likewise illustrates why, despite its apparent positive connotations, deploying this lens may be delimiting because it reflects the universalization of particularistic conceptions of conscience and freedom not easily translated across cultural terrains. Moreover, through the articulation of religious freedom as a universal and ahistorical good, one glosses over historical engagements with the experiences of colonialism and post-colonialism, hegemonic secularist frames of international relations with their Orientalist undertones, and ongoing geopolitical agendas.[46]

To allude to what a geopolitical agenda entails in this respect is to look at how supposed attacks on religious freedoms, primarily of Christians in the Middle East, figure into broader discourses about Islam and Muslims and how those discourses function to authorize belligerence in the region. A curious exception is the case of Christian Palestinians; their silencing in the mainstream corporate media, for example, is, at best, problematic. In the words of a courageous Palestinian Quaker woman Jean Zaru: "Although we are really the modern heirs of the disciples of Jesus in Jerusalem, we have become unknown, unacknowledged, and forgotten. Despite all of this, we are a community that has maintained a strong witness to the gospel in the land of the incarnation and resurrection. . . unfortunately, a community that is diminishing every day as a result of the political, economic, and religious pressures of the Israeli occupation."[47] What is at stake here for Zaru is to combat—among other forms of violence—religious, cultural, and structural violence; by this she refers to the stereotyping of Palestinians and Arabs in the media, the imposition of other cultures and value systems, the destruction and shelling of cultural heritage sites, the language of chosenness (deployed both by Jewish and Christian Zionists), and the demonization of Islam, among other issues. In the brief excerpt I just cited, Zaru locates her silencing most immediately with the Israeli occupation but also more globally in discursive formations that enable the kind of marginalization she is combating. Her inability to flourish in Palestine is not classified as a matter of religious freedom. If it is, it is in reference to Muslim-Christian relations within Palestine and not in reference to the Israeli occupation. This enables the perpetuation of a broader paradigm about Christian peril in Muslim contexts, divorcing this discussion from the historical realities of Israeli occupation. This disconnect substantiates the point about the importance of unpacking the political and cultural underpinnings of framing something as a matter of "religious freedom." What goes into this decision politically?

In describing the inherent biases of the International Religious Freedom Act of 1998 Mah-mood claims that one needs to engage in a critical exploration of what precisely gets to be classified as a violation of religious freedoms and liberties, along with the ramifications that such classification may have on the formulation of American foreign policy. This exploration involves historicizing why a philosophically, religiously, and culturally embedded articulation of religion as a matter of individual conscience and belief has been universalized and construed as an ahistorical moral good.[48] However, differentiating religion as a belief from religion as a national and historical consciousness, as in cases such as Sri Lanka and Israel, overlooks the complex ways in which religion interrelates with other indices of identity. If the establishment of a political hegemony is considered the fulfillment of a religious destiny, should not ensuring this project be classified as the exercise of a religious freedom? Are the boundaries of those freedoms confined to private spaces and to individual consciences? Do they become collectivized only insofar as they translate into the language of minority rights and cultural and religious autonomy? This language, while designed to accommodate collective rights, is still philosophically grounded in culturally specific conceptions of personhood, religion, and freedom. The politics enabled by the idiom of religious freedoms could—under the banner of providing a normative good—naturalize and normalize meta-injustices, as when the case of the Palestinian-Israelis is framed as merely involving questions about minority rights. There are always enduring questions, not only with regard to broad geopolitical frames, but also with regard to the implicit normalcy of who constitutes the majority within those contexts where the plights of religious minorities are debated and how religious narratives, symbols, and institutions may be interlaced into the construction and deconstruction of national ethos.

The testimony of Zaru is especially illustrative of the need to engage in wide-ranging discursive analyses that move beyond the rhetoric of local conflicts. Her analysis not only moves beyond obvious dichotomies between Muslims and Jews or West and East. It also highlights how broader discourses of orientalism, militarism, imperialism, chosenness, and patriarchy are relevant. The stereotyping of Arabs and Muslims (often through the mere conflation of these identity indices) in the American media, for example, is part of the problem. It betrays a long history of orientalism that informs the making of American foreign policy while also being constitutive of imagining American Judeo-Christian identity. Zaru is confronting the "silent" structural violence that enables the perpetuation of the Israeli occupation of Palestine on so many levels.[49] It follows that if media representation and stereotyping are part of the problem, part of the solution will involve engaging in discursive critiques that deconstruct received narratives. This kind of critique and engagement goes beyond the geopolitical boundaries of this particular conflict zone and points to global interconnections. Zaru also looks internally at questions of gender and patriarchy. She recognizes intuitively and through her own marginality as a Christian Palestinian woman that domestic gender injustice is not unrelated to the pervasive direct, structural, and cultural forms of violence she so aptly illuminates. I mention this because one fallacy of the field of religious peacebuilding is to privilege occasionally the "local" by myopically obscuring the pertinence of how religion relates to broader questions of "silent" violence.

Discourse Analysis as Peacebuilding

A conceptual turn that challenges the privileging of the "international" focus of religious peacebuilding would also move beyond the premises informing the extensive involvement of the United States Institute of Peace (USIP) with religious peacebuilding initiatives. Consistent with the broader mandate of the USIP, the study of issues related to religion and peacebuilding excludes a focus on the United States. This mandate imposes critical conceptual blinders on peace studies, generally, and religious peacebuilding, more specifically. What it excludes from the analysis are questions about the relevance of the legacies of colonialism, post-colonialism, US imperialism, and the global discourse of neoliberalism to local concerns with conflict and peace.[50]

To move in these new directions, it is important to reflect on the enduring (and somewhat ironic) hold of secularist discourses. It is ironic because religious peacebuilding emerged as a supposed antidote to the reductive dismissal of or essentializing alarmism about religion plaguing the social sciences and the popular media. From its inception, religious peacebuilding presented itself as a "supplement" rather than a radical challenge to the logic of international relations. Douglas Johnston and Cynthia Sampson's pioneering work *Religion: The Missing Dimension of Statecraft*[51] highlights the potential but untapped role of religion in international relations and in peacebuilding. It generated a series of subsequent works on the role of religion in diplomacy and peacebuilding.[52] These works typify the "instrumental approach" to religious peacebuilding. The usual motif of this instrumental approach is that dogmatic realism in international relations blocks the possibility of recognizing how one's actions are informed by values and religious orientations and how one's processes of healing and religious resources, narratives, and leadership might be instrumental in overcoming trauma and transforming conflicts. The role of religion in diplomacy, subsequently, is referred to as "Track II diplomacy" or "faith-based diplomacy."

Indeed, this subgenre makes significant strides in highlighting the need to take religion seriously in international relations. However, the framing of religion's involvement in international relations and specifically in peacebuilding as "faith-based" is a problematic proposition. It is problematic because it presupposes "faith," a contextually specific category, to be universally applicable and interchangeable with religion. The critical study of religion and the secularism and post-secularism debates alluded to above shed light on why religion-qua-faith is not only a delimiting classification but also one deeply entrenched in the discourses of colonialism and orientalism.

While the now extensive documentation of various faith-based initiatives and success stories proves to be a wealth of resources for analyzing religion as it relates to questions of peacebuilding, the rendering of faith-based diplomacy as a supplementary but necessary venue for realpolitik is insufficient and problematic. In fact, such a construal overlooks the need to substantially engage in a discursive analysis that brings to bear how unrevised secularist and modernist ontologies and epistemologies inform how we think about the role of religion in international relations. Hence, while on the surface the faith diplomacy thread challenged political realism, it did not depart in any significant way from the undergirding secularist discourses that informed conventional modes of thinking about international relations. This includes the international relations (IR) paradigm of constructivism that presupposes "beliefs" in international relations as merely a function of cognition. Hence, despite the relevant and important correction that the faith diplomacy and the related IFD foci offer to international relations theory and practice, their general acceptance of religion as having to do with belief, morality, and altogether "soft"[53] power shows the theoretical thinness of the field and suggests possibilities for further research and scholarship.[54]

In fact, engaging in the theoretical questions that deconstruct how secularist and orientalist discourses have informed the modalities of thinking about religion in international relations can transform the field of religious peacebuilding. The field would shift from its primary preoccupation with constructive religious leadership or faith-based initiatives and interventions in the dynamics of conflict and peacebuilding to a deeper engagement with the rather messy role of religion-qua-politics as well as the intricate philosophical relations between religion and morality. A constructive retrieval of theological and other religious resources is insufficient as a method of peacebuilding, if there is no accompanying engagement with the kind of historicism and discursive critique that might expose undergirding injustice. Therefore, in a different essay, I highlight religious peacebuilding as entailing a process of "critical caretaking," a synthesis of the constructive, non-reductive insights of religious peacebuilding as encapsulated in Appleby's thesis of the "ambivalence of the sacred" and the deconstructive analytic tools of discursive critique.[55] The various functions of the language of "religious freedoms" typify this observation concerning the need for "critical caretaking" and hint at the conceptual blinders and potential pitfalls of the theological thread as an instrument for the pursuit of a multiperspectival (as distinct from parochial) justice.

Where the field of religious peacebuilding is entirely lacking, therefore, is in recognizing the full spectrum of its potential contribution. This is not merely a problem of scope; it also reflects deep theoretical blinders born out of the misapplication of the insights and potentialities of the "ambivalence of the sacred." While construing the militancy of the nonviolent religious warrior as the inverse of the religiously motivated suicide bomber frees religion from material or ideal reductionism, it also generates conceptual and practical blind-spots that need to be deconstructed for scholarship in the field of religious peacebuilding to grow in a meaningful way. Importantly, the constructive hermeneutics inherent in the "ambivalence of the sacred" could, if expanded to integrate the tool of critique, avoid the power reductionism that constitutes the pitfall of discursive analysis.

Justpeace and the Conversion Trap

It may be obvious how religion relates to "direct" forms of violence in the Crusades, the messianic theology of Jewish settlers in the West Bank, and the events of September 11, 2001. It is not, however, so obvious how religion relates to the authorization of state violence and a sense of national entitlement, superiority, and destiny. It is not only that even in the cases of the Crusades, the European Wars of Religion, and the settlement movement in Israel/Palestine, a simple rendering of religion as a cause of violence and conflict is highly decontextualized and ahistorical. It is also the case that this rendering enables both analysts and practitioners to overlook internal pluralities and contestations as well as nuanced analyses of the interrelationship between conceptions of religion, ethnicity, nationality, and culture. Bracketing religion as a "belief" and an essence outside of history (despite its empirical manifestations in historical space and time) enables the analyst (and by extension the peace practitioner) to gloss over critical junctures between religion and nationalism where religion (often silently) reifies and vindicates exclusive political and social practice. This, as mentioned, is also the limitation of the theological constructivism entailed in the model of political reconciliation. This is also where Little's attention to the contexts of nationalism and the legacy of colonialism in each instance of ethno-religious national conflict offers important corrections to the essentialism endemic to a methodologically naive comparison.

I, therefore, frame the topic as one about religious peacebuilding rather than religion and peace to capture the dynamic, multidisciplinary, multidirectional, and deeply contextual frameworks that need to guide one's exploration of theory and praxis about religion, conflict, and peacebuilding. The concept of peacebuilding entails an active engagement with particular conflicts. It is not a general and decontextualized reflection on religion and peace. The peace sought is this-worldly (social, political, economic), although the this-worldliness should not be viewed as necessarily dichotomous with inner-spirituality or with other-worldly and transcendent conceptions of peace. There is a presumption here that religious peacebuilding as an academic pursuit (and certainly as a practice) focuses on justice as distinct from peace. However, because the field is not sufficiently critical of its own discursive formations, it enables a disconnection between peace and justice, which translates into a lack of reflexivity about how religion relates to structural and cultural violence. This lack of scrutiny, on occasion, also gives rise to curtailing the possibility of reform within religious traditions. The central philosophical issue is whether we historicize and submit religious traditions to a broader conception of morality. Philosophical conversations on religion and human rights and political-theoretical debates (including feminist critiques) on the "justness" of multicultural frameworks and identity politics need to become front and center in thinking about religious peacebuilding.[56] Without such a multidisciplinary interrogation, religious peacebuilding, I argue below, becomes missionary and mono-perspectival in its pursuit of justice.

The recently articulated concept of strategic peacebuilding provides an especially effective lens to think through the role of religion in conflict transformation. Strategic peacebuilding as defined in a co-authored essay by Appleby and Lederach entails a comprehensive, multidimensional, multifocal, and multidisciplinary process, normatively guided by a pursuit of justice or *justpeace*.[57] The normative and comprehensive compass that strategic peacebuilding affords, with its focus on the continuous striving toward this neologism of *justpeace*, viewing it as a contested and continuously debated framework rather than a fixed telos, is especially helpful in exploring how religion might relate to "peace" as the cessation of direct violence. It might also be helpful in exploring how it interrelates with cultural, structural, and even "secular" forms of violence. The prism of strategic peacebuilding, therefore, recognizes the instrumental relevance of religious networks and leadership as well as substantive theological and hermeneutical contestations and critique of the endurance of unrevised secularist assumptions in IR.[58] It is potentially consistent with the task of "critical caretaking." On the other hand, "uncritical caretaking" is endemic within religious peacebuilding because it can contribute not only to a reified interpretation of religion, but also could enable the perpetuation of injustice. Conversely, the merely deconstructive turn is power reductionistic (reducing the analysis to power as a monocausal variable), unable to extricate critically refined theological and religious content from its negation of colonial discursive formations; in short, throwing out the baby with the bath water. While this power reductionism is further susceptible to the charge of relativism, the religion and reconciliation subfield (in addition to its essentializing and ahistoricity) falls into the colonial fallacy that privileges and universalizes culture- and tradition-specific categories such as "forgiveness" and "love." This thread already occupies a fine line between religious peacebuilding and proselytizing, not only through decontextualizing "Judaism" or "Islam," but also through forcing non-Christian worlds of associations to conform to Christian-specific categories.

I refer to this as the conversion trap. This trap also is present on the level of practice. Is it acceptable that the work of religiously motivated "aid" organizations also involves teaching the gospel? This question goes back to a deeper debate about the meanings of humanitarian assistance and whether neutrality should be an unsullied principle. It also highlights the need to reflect on the ethics of peacebuilding intervention. When missionaries claim to engage in peacebuilding efforts and demonstrate a lack of self-reflexivity about the historical colonial undertones of this enterprise, as well as the profound disrespect toward other religions and alternative orientations, they contribute to the delegitimization of the subfield of religious peacebuilding as an important and serious scholarly enterprise with immense practical ramifications for real situations. The conversion trap, however, has permeated both scholarship and practice.

Therefore, for religious peacebuilding to develop beyond the enduring dominance of secularist categories, it will have to assume a thoroughly interdisciplinary approach. This will also require an exploration not only of where religious peacebuilding is limited by its own conceptual and theoretical assumptions, but also how these presuppositions could potentially derail the field altogether.

Derailment

The task of theological excavation is highly necessary for the field of religious peacebuilding. If one takes religion seriously on its own terms, it is indeed of substantive relevance to engage religious traditions comprehensively and to develop the same kind of fluency in "religion and peace" that was devoted to the study of religion and violence and/or the use of force. However, as I argue elsewhere, this needs to avoid the charge of ahistoricity and essentialism by deploying the tools of critique. This is where operationalizing the "ambivalence of the sacred" thesis is lacking and delimiting. At times, it is even misguided.

It is misguided when religious peacemakers are "exoticized" and when their narratives are presented as a form of theater, as if they perform some peculiar native dance, usually elsewhere and in a different language. Countless times, I have witnessed such exoticization during academic conferences on religion and peacebuilding. This exoticization is, in part, the upshot of the "local" bias of the field. Related to this exoticization of "religion and peacebuilding" is the work of organizations that foster and feature, on different levels, faith-based peacebuilders. Some of these organizations indeed represent the "industry" aspects of religious peacebuilding (the Tanenbaum Center for Interreligious Understanding, for example); others include representatives of religious groups whose peacebuilding work is missionary. The fact that faith motivates missionary work and that this work is perceived as "peacebuilding," "development," or "humanitarianism" is relevant to the academic study of religious peacebuilding. But to overlook the need for a second-order reflection on systemic and moral issues, such as aggressive proselytism in a post-colonial context, is not only deficient; it also relinquishes the kind of critical rigor necessary for scholarship.[59] The main paradigms of religious peacebuilding as a field of study, however, are conducive to this kind of deficiency. The issue at stake is not that focusing on particular religious leaders and their activism with respect to processes of conflict transformation or on various missionary forms of peacebuilding is irrelevant to the study of religious peacebuilding. Rather, the focus of this scrutiny is that the field of religious peacebuilding needs to move beyond the secularist, the exotic, the apologetic (and the missionary), and the mere reportage mode that has come to dominate the field.

Back to the Ambivalence and the Quest
for Critical Caretaking

Regardless of how admirable the actions of various religious actors may seem, one cannot relinquish the critical-analytic lens. This will spell the difference between scholarship and mere showcasing or even crude and unreflective evangelizing. Certainly, showcasing various religious actors in academic conferences may be enriching and humbling. But if this showcasing is not followed by a systematic analysis that probes into the patterns of religious peacebuilding (e.g., what does it mean in various contexts, and what might be the limitations of this undertaking?), this showcasing remains just that—a theater. As such, it not only confirms the suspicion of various critics who either render religious peacebuilding as "soft," "kumbaya" extra-curricular activities in the otherwise brutal realities of international and local *real* politics, but it also risks exoticizing religious peacebuilding and religious actors. Therefore, religious peacebuilding easily can shift from the task of a careful analysis of religion and conflict transformation to an "uncritical caretaking," masquerading as scholarship. The missionary trap is the greatest obstacle for the maturation of the field of religious peacebuilding as a scholarly enterprise with a real potential to think creatively and multidirectionally about *justpeace* in different contexts.

But a rereading of Appleby's thesis shows that the task of religious peacebuilding is not a simple search for the most authentic interpretation of religion, presuming that this interpretation is also "good" and "just." Appleby's thesis is more complex than the mere framing of the "religious peacebuilder" as the mirror image of the "religious terrorist": the one perfects religion, the other perverts it. Both constructs are problematic and deserve a sustained interrogation of the question of causality: Does religion cause violence? Can religion cause peace? Appleby never wants to ask those questions in a decontextualized manner. Neither does he forgo a view of the fallible and historical characteristics of religious phenomena or of a deeply pluralistic society. The theoretical poverty of religious peacebuilding can be attributed to missing these points about fallibility and contextual yet non-reductive interpretations of religion and their relevance to sociopolitical and economic institutional frameworks. Missing those points also facilitates the creeping in of an uncritical treatment of religion, conflict, and peacebuilding, one that overlooks internal and external power constraints so that the missionary woman cannot view the structural and cultural violence within which she self-righteously and faithfully operates.

While many volumes have been written documenting how religious people do good around the world and about locating resources within religious traditions that resemble normative motifs such as forgiveness and reconciliation, there has been very little theoretical reflection and engagement with the premises undergirding these interrelated enterprises. Hence, the limits of religious peacebuilding revolve around a simplistic appropriation of the thesis of the "ambivalence of the sacred." This has included illuminating internal plurality within a tradition solely as an act of retrieval in order to access resources to combat explicit belligerence authorized by other religious claims. A deeper understanding of plurality also will involve submitting religious practices and ideas to critique and possibly reform, in light of questions of justice.

This inquiry would include a global analysis of the endurance of orientalist frames in international relations and how it might transpire in distinct conflict zones. The inquiry also would encompass debating on a case-by-case basis how religion, ethnicity, and culture interface with the construction and reproduction of secular national identities and why, especially within explicitly ethnocentric national frames, distinguishing between religion-qua-belief and religion-qua-national identity may function myopically to conceal and reproduce injustice. The tools of critique likewise will be employed in the analysis of the idiom of "religious freedoms" and how it operates within a multiperspectival tradition of human rights norms. The question of whether an American man can circumcise his daughter or kill his wife on the basis of a "religious conviction" is not beyond the scope of religious peacebuilding (although it has been debated primarily within political theory). In fact, this topic is conceptually connected to the need to deconstruct and interrogate the main discursive formations within which those questions arise locally and globally.

Another related trajectory would involve developing a conceptual framework that would enable a multiperspectival prism for the analysis of questions of peace and justice, one that would enable one's particularistic narration of justice to be confronted by others' contextual counter-narratives (including "domestic" underdogs and those who experience gender injustice). This multiperspectival lens confronts the unidirectionality inherent in the phenomenological framing of much of the discussion of religious peacebuilding. Moving religious peacebuilding from the level of spectacle to rigorous academic scrutiny would necessitate asking not only how religion works in conflict and peacebuilding, but also whether a multiperspectival approach to justice can change traditions themselves when they appear to be inconsistent with justice concerns. Here the academic study of religion and peacebuilding cannot merely report, feature, and inductively theorize about praxis; it must also reflect critically by historicizing religious knowledge and practice. Feminist theories have engaged in such critique in order not only to gain agency and equal standing, but also to reimagine the meanings of the religious tradition itself. Feminist theorist Judith Plaskow's *Standing Again at Sinai* is about highlighting the need to view women coreligionists as equal to men, as well as deeply challenging male normativity and reimagining the covenantal moment in Sinai through a gendered lens.[60] Such a transformative process would have substantial structural ramifications for questions of religious leadership and household management, among various other loci.

This discussion of feminist critique exemplifies that change depends upon acts of critique, introspection, and reframing. There is limited scholarship that connects gender analysis with religion, conflict, and peacebuilding, however. The inclination is to illuminate the idiom of folk rather than official religiosity (thus private, female religiosity) as potentially subversive and instrumental in its critique, coping with devastation and trauma and anti-militarist organizing (while there is also a thread in the literature stressing that women are as prone to violence as men).[61] At the same time that a gender critique challenges the undergirding categories of political formations (see especially works on gender and nationalism), the interlinking between gender and religion falls back into the same discursive formations that relegated the feminine to the home, the supposed "private sphere." On a different scholarly front, Mahmood's study of the pious Egyptian women—who in inhabiting the norms of submissiveness and humility, became agents in transforming Egyptian secularism—correctly highlights that (female) agency is more complex than mere overt resistance to patriarchy, as conventional feminist theory has it.[62] Yet this theoretical framework does not permit a constructive space to reimagine the normative presuppositions that the pious women inhabit, ipso facto suggesting a kind of relativism inconsistent with the normative orientation of peace studies. What is lacking is a kind of critical caretaking that would rethink the norma-tive presuppositions of religious and political identities in light of critique and through the prism of *justpeace*.

To conclude, the study of religion and peace is a precarious enterprise, one fraught with conceptual traps. While aspiring to move beyond negative "peace" to an engagement with questions of justice or positive peace, religious peacebuilding as a scholarly focus has stud-ied "religion" merely as an addendum to conventional modes of analyzing and mitigating violent conflicts, thereby leaving the conceptual limitation of such approaches intact. In order to avoid the charges of irrelevance and/or mere "soft" background relevance, religious peacebuilding conceptually needs to shift away from the secularist presuppositions under-lying the field. Differentiating religion as a distinct variable reinforces secularist presump-tions in that it subscribes to a neat compartmentalization of the "religious" and the "secular." Certainly, this differentiation enabled the flourishing of the field of religious peacebuilding because it carved out relevance for religion by articulating its distinctiveness as a resource of peace, both on the level of theologies and ideas as well as on the practical level of religious institutional networks and individual leadership. This is where the paradoxical turn to cri-tique comes into play. In order to combat the conversion trap, religious peacebuilding needs to avoid the "uncritical caretaking" that amounts to an overly simplistic application of the logic of the "ambivalence of the sacred."

Cultivating the field of religious peacebuilding as a rigorous academic reflection therefore would entail self-reflexivity concerning the field's reliance on secularist presumptions about religion, which facilitate complicity with religion's relevance to cultural and systemic injus-tices; the presumption of the unidirectionality of religion and historical change; and the dis-connect from broader conversations about religion in public life. Future trajectories would need to focus on the method of the *hermeneutics of citizenship* and its reliance on a multiper-spectival approach to justice for critique and reframing. Here the philosophical problem is whether we submit traditions as well as political theologies to a broader concept of morality that is already, as Little understands it, multiperspectival (reflecting cross-cultural and inter-religious negotiations) rather than disembodied and ontologically distinct.

Another fruitful trajectory would challenge the Westphalian assumptions undergird-ing the field of peacebuilding. While an emphasis on the institutional aspects of trans-national religious networks is well evident in the religious peacebuilding literature, the privileging of the "local" as the site of conflict still is evident and delimiting of the discus-sion of global discursive formations that are intricately related to local manifestations of cultural, structural, and direct forms of violence. The "local" bias also imposes con-straints on where peacebuilding work might take place. The locus of peacebuilding can be as much with expatriate and diaspora communities in the urban centers of Western cities like New York, London, and Paris than in the "exotic" and far-off villages of Colombia, Palestine, and Sri Lanka. This is not to dismiss the heroism of peacebuilders and the need to identify and rethink axiomatic claims through the counter-hegemonic embodied experiences of indigenous and subaltern victims, but rather to gesture toward the pos-sibility of pluralizing the fronts of peacebuilding. To move beyond the exotic, the good (as in the conversion trap), and the theatrical, as I suggest above, calls for a thoroughly interdisciplinary enterprise, centrally synthesizing the insights of critique with the non-reductive, creative hermeneutics that already dominates religious peacebuilding.

NOTES

1. R. Scott Appleby, *The Ambivalence of the Sacred: Religion, Violence, and Reconciliation* (Lanham, MD: Rowman and Littlefield, 2000).
2. Appleby, *Ambivalence*, especially 28.
3. Samuel Huntington, *The Clash of Civilizations and the Remaking of World Order* (New York: Simon and Schuster, 1996). For critiques of Huntington's argument, see Emran Qureshi and Michael Anthony Sells, eds., *The New Crusades: Constructing the Muslim Enemy* (New York: Columbia University Press, 2003).
4. See José Casanova, "Immigration and the New Religious Pluralism: A European Union/United States Comparison," 59–83; Sam Cherribi, "Politicians' Perceptions of the 'Muslim Problem': The Dutch Example in European Context," 113–132; and Danièle Hervieu-Léger, "Islam and the Republic: The French Case," 203–222 in *Democracy and the New Religious Pluralism*, ed. Thomas Banchoff (Oxford: Oxford University Press, 2007).
5. In suggesting that the theoretical insights of the "ambivalence of the sacred" are mis-applied, contributing to a diminishing relevance of religious peacebuilding and reaffirming secularist presuppositions and even parochial agendas (intentionally or inadvertently), I depart from Katrien Hertog's assessment of how this thesis has informed religious peacebuilding; see Hertog, *The Complex Reality of Religious Peacebuilding: Conceptual Contributions and Critical Analysis* (Lanham, MD: Lexington Books, 2010), especially 19.
6. For works on development and religion that take an instrumentalist approach, see Katherine Marshall, "Religion and Global Development: Intersecting Paths," in *Religious Pluralism: Globalization and World Politics*, ed. Thomas Banchoff (Oxford: Oxford University Press, 2008), 195–228; Marshall and Richard March, *Millennium Goals for Development and Faith Institutions: Common Leadership Challenges* (Washington, DC: World Bank, 2003); Marshall and Marisa Bronwyn, *Development and Faith: Where Mind, Heart, and Soul Work Together* (Washington, DC: World Bank, 2007); and Jeffrey Haynes, *Religion and Development: Conflict or Cooperation?* (New York: Palgrave Macmillan, 2007).
7. Marc Gopin, *Between Eden and Armageddon: The Future of World Religions, Violence, and Peacemaking* (New York: Oxford University Press, 2000). See also Gopin, "Religion, Violence and Conflict Resolution," *Peace and Change* 22, no. 1 (1997): 1–31; Gopin, "Forgiveness as an Element of Conflict Resolution in Religious Cultures: Walking the Tightrope of Reconciliation and Justice," in *Reconciliation, Justice and Coexistence: Theory and Practice*, ed. Mohammed Abu-Nimer (Lanham, MD: Lexington Books, 2001), 87–100; and Gopin, *Holy War, Holy Peace: How Religion Can Bring Peace to the Middle East* (New York: Oxford University Press, 2002).
8. Lisa Schirch, *Ritual and Symbol in Peacebuilding* (Bloomfield, CT: Kumarian Press, 2005). Numerous other works reflect on the ritualistic aspects of peacebuilding and on how religion explicitly fits into such processes. Some of these works fall under the broad preoccupation with the instrument of interfaith dialogue. See, for example, Mohammed Abu-Nimer, *Reconciliation, Justice, and Coexistence: Theory and Practice* (Lanham, MD: Lexington Books, 2001) and Abu-Nimer, Amal Khoury, and Emily Welty, *Unity in Diversity: Interfaith Dialogue in the Middle East* (Washington, DC: US Institute of Peace Press, 2007).
9. Appleby, *Ambivalence*, 230–238.

10. See John Paul Lederach, *Building Peace: Sustainable Reconciliation in Divided Societies* (Washington, DC: US Institute of Peace Press, 1997).

11. For examples of interventionists' framing of their faith-motivation and training, see Tricia Gates Brown, *Getting in the Way: Stories from Christian Peacemaker Teams* (Scottdale, PA: Herald Press, 2005); Mary Ann Cejka and Thomas Bamat, eds., *Artisans of Peace: Grassroots Peacemaking among Christian Communities* (New York: Orbis Books, 2003); David W. Chappel, ed., *Buddhist Peacework: Creating Cultures of Peace* (Somerville, MA: Wisdom Publications, 1999); Adam Curle, *True Justice: Quaker Peace Makers and Peace Making* (London: Quaker Home Service, 1981); Eknath Easwaran, *A Man to Match His Mountains: Badshah Khan, Nonviolent Soldier of Islam* (Petaluma, CA: Nilgiri Press, 1984); John McConnell, *Mindful Mediation: A Handbook for Buddhist Peacemakers* (Thailand: Buddhist Research Institute and Mahachula Buddhist University, 1995); Mennonite Conciliation Service, *Mediation Training Manual: Skills for Constructive Conflict Transformation* (Philadelphia: Mennonite Conciliation Service, 1992); Swami Agnivesh, *Religion, Spirituality and Social Action* (Haryana: Hope India Publications, 2003); Thich Nhat Hanh, *Being Peace* (Berkeley, CA: Parallax Press, 1987); Hanh, *Touching Peace* (Berkeley, CA: Parallax Press, 1992); Hanh, *Love in Action: Writings on Nonviolent Social Change* (Berkeley, CA: Parallax Press, 1993); Marc Ellis, *Unholy Alliance: Religion and Atrocity in Our Time* (Minneapolis: Fortress Press, 1997); and Yehezkel Landau, *Healing the Holy Land: Interreligious Peacebuilding in Israel/Palestine* (Washington, DC: US Institute of Peace Press, 2003). For an example of external reportage of indigenous religious peacebuilders, see Tanenbaum Center for Interreligious Understanding, *Peacemakers in Action: Profiles of Religion in Conflict Resolution*, ed. David Little (Cambridge: Cambridge University Press, 2007).

12. See Kevin Avruch, *Culture and Conflict Resolution* (Washington, DC: US Institute of Peace Press, 1998); John Paul Lederach, *Preparing for Peace: Conflict Transformation across Cultures* (New York: Syracuse University Press, 1996); Lederach, *Building Peace; and* Lederach, *The Moral Imagination: The Art and Soul of Building Peace* (New York: Oxford University Press, 2005).

13. See John Paul Lederach, *The Little Book of Conflict Transformation* (Intercourse, PA: Good Books, 2003).

14. In connection to the question of religion and national reconciliation, much has been written in reference to the Truth and Reconciliation Commission in South Africa; see, for instance, Audrey R. Chapman and Bernard Spong, *Religion and Reconciliation in South Africa: Voices of Religious Leaders* (Philadelphia: Templeton Foundation Press, 2003); James R. Cochrane, John de Gruchy, and Stephen Martin, *Facing the Truth: South African Faith Communities and the Truth and Reconciliation Commission* (Cape Town: Ohio University Press, 1999); and Charles Villa-Vicencio, *Looking Back, Reaching Forward: Reflections on the Truth and Reconciliation Commission of South Africa* (Cape Town: University of Cape Town Press, 2000).

15. See R. Scott Appleby, "Building Sustainable Peace: The Roles of Local and Transnational Religious Actors," in *Religious Pluralism: Globalization and World Politics*, ed. Thomas Banchoff (New York: Oxford University Press, 2008),.

16. John Paul Lederach and Cynthia Sampson, *From the Ground Up: Mennonite Contributions to International Peacebuilding* (New York: Oxford University Press, 2000).

17. For an insightful reflection on Catholicism and peacebuilding, see Robert J. Schreiter, R. Scott Appleby, and Gerard F. Powers, eds., *Peacebuilding: Catholic Theology, Ethics, and Praxis* (Maryknoll, NY: Orbis Books, 2010).

18. For an overview, see John L. Esposito and Ihsan Yilmaz, eds., *Islam and Peacebuilding: Gülen Movement Initiatives* (New York: Blue Dome Press, 2010).

19. Baptist Peace Fellowship of North America, http://www.bpfna.org/home.

20. Buddhist Peace Fellowship, http://www.bpf.org/.

21. Christian Peacemaker Team, http://www.cpt.org/.

22. International Committee for Peace Council, http://www.peacecouncil.org/index.html.

23. World Conference on Religion and Peace, http://www.wcrp.org.

24. Berkley Center for Religion, Peace, and World Affairs, http://berkleycenter.georgetown.edu.

25. Kroc Institute for International Peace Studies, http://kroc.nd.edu.

26. The conceptual framework for religious peacebuilding is also explicated in David Little and Scott Appleby, "A Moment of Opportunity?," in *Religion and Peacebuilding*, eds. Harold Coward and Gordon S. Smith (Albany: State University of New York Press, 2004).

27. See Gopin, *Between Eden and Armageddon*, especially 9, 59, and 168.

28. See Mohammed Abu-Nimer, *Nonviolence and Peace Building in Islam: Theory and Practice* (Gainesville: University Press of Florida, 2003). For a similar work (in the same subgenre), refer to Abdul Aziz, Nathan Funk, and Ayse S. Kadayifci, eds., *Peace and Conflict Resolution in Islam: Precept and Practice* (Lanham, MD: University Press of America, 2001).

29. Examples of such works include: Jerald D. Gort, Henry Jansen, and Hendrik M. Vroom, eds., *Religion, Conflict and Reconciliation: Multifaith Ideals and Realities* (Amsterdam: Rodopi, 2002); Thomas Scheffler, *Religion Between Violence and Reconciliation* (Beirut: Orient-Institu, 2002); John Ferguson, *War and Peace in the World's Religions* (London: Sheldon Press, 1977); James Heft, ed., *Beyond Violence: Religious Sources of Social Transformation in Judaism, Christianity and Islam* (New York: Fordham University Press, 2004); Raymond G. Helmick, SJ, and Rodney L. Petersen, eds., *Forgiveness and Reconciliation: Religion, Public Policy, and Conflict Transformation* (Philadelphia: Templeton Foundation Press, 2001); James Turner Johnson, *The Quest for Peace: Three Moral Traditions in Western Cultural History* (Princeton, NJ: Princeton University Press, 1987); Ronald Kraybill, "From Head to Heart: The Cycle of Reconciliation," *Conciliation Quarterly* 7, no. 4 (1998): 2–38; Donald Shriver, *An Ethic for Enemies: Forgiveness in Politics* (New York: Oxford University Press, 1995); Daniel Smith-Christopher, ed., *Subverting Hatred: The Challenge of Nonviolence in Religious Traditions* (Cambridge, MA: Boston Research Center for the 21st Century, 1998); David Smock, *Perspectives on Pacifism: Christian, Jewish, and Muslim Views on Nonviolence and International Conflict* (Washington, DC: US Institute of Peace Press, 1995); and Gerrie ter Haar and James J. Busuttil, eds., *Bridge or Barrier: Religion, Violence and Visions of Peace* (Leiden-Boston: Brill, 2005).

30. In an attempt to articulate a systematic approach to religious peacebuilding, Hertog explains that increased "interreligious encounters" in a time of an evident association of religion with violence prompted some intra-religious theological reflections and assessments of violent motifs. This historical moment, therefore, opens up the possibility for introspection and possible reform. A second development posed by the apparent "urgency of certain global problems," such as poverty, global warming, nuclear proliferation and so forth, also sheds new light and enables novel paths for interreligious cooperation and exchange (see *The Complex Reality of Religious Peacebuilding*, 17). But the dominant thread of ethical engagement remains within the dual focus on just war and pacifism. See, for examples, James Johnson Turner and John Kelsay, eds., *Cross, Crescent, and Sword: The Justification and Limitation of War in Western Islamic Tradition* (Westport: Greenwood

Press, 1990); Turner and Kelsay, eds., *Just War and Jihad: Historical and Theoretical Perspectives on War and Peace in Western and Islamic Traditions* (Westport: Greenwood Press, 1991); Kelsay, *Arguing the Just War in Islam* (Cambridge, MA: Harvard University Press, 2007); and Lisa Cahill, *Love Your Enemies: Discipleship, Pacifism and Just War Theory* (Minneapolis: Fortress Press, 1994).

31. For a condensed account of the issues and risks involved in the comparative enterprise, see Kimberley C. Patton and Benjamin C. Ray, eds., *A Magic Still Dwells: Comparative Religion in the Postmodern Age* (Berkeley: University of California Press, 2000).

32. Instructive of the conceptual problems inherent in such comparativist attempts would be the methodological debates that unfolded among comparative religious ethicists in response to the field's shaping work of David Little and Barney Twiss's *Comparative Religious Ethics* (San Francisco: Harper and Row, 1978). Those responses include, for example, Jeffrey Stout, "Weber's Progeny Once Removed," *Religious Studies Review* 6 (October 1980): 289–295; Little, "The Present State of the Comparative Study of Religious Ethics," *Journal of Religious Ethics* 9, no. 2 (1981): 210–227; and Stout, "Holism and Comparative Ethics: A Response to Little," *Journal of Religious Ethics* 11, no. 2 (1983): 301–316. Stout revisits the general lesson from this exchange more recently in his *Democracy and Tradition* (Princeton, NJ: Princeton University Press, 2004), 283–286.

33. Daniel Philpott, *Just and Unjust Peace* (New York: Oxford University Press, 2012). See also Philpott, ed., *The Politics of Past Evil: Religion, Reconciliation, and the Dilemmas of Transitional Justice* (Notre Dame, IN: University of Notre Dame Press, 2006).

34. For a deconstructive analysis of the liberal discourse and its relation to the "myth of religious violence" as the defining narrative of modernity, see William Cavanaugh, *The Myth of Religious Violence: Secular Ideology and the Roots of Modern Conflict* (New York: Oxford University Press, 2009); chapter 3 is especially devoted to this historicist exercise.

35. These conversations have unfolded now among religious ethicists over decades; for a succinct overview, see Jason Springs, "On Giving Religious Intolerance its Due: Prospects for Transforming Conflict in a Post-Secular Society," *The Journal of Religion* 92, no. 1 (2012): 1–30, especially 2–7.

36. This point is perhaps grotesquely evident in the profiling of Rabbi Menachem Froman as one of the select "peacemakers" of the Tanenbaum Center. Froman is a settler whose ideological and religious formations are both selective (as a discursive analysis will show) and enabling of the very root causes of the Palestinian-Israeli conflict. Froman can talk about peace and reconciliation, but as long as this talk is stricken by the kind of amnesia I articulate, it is problematic to categorize him as a "peacebuilder." See Tanenbaum Center, *Peacemakers in Action*.

37. For extensive discussions of the method of the *hermeneutics of citizenship* and for my analysis of Israeli peace activism, specifically, see Atalia Omer, *When Peace Is Not Enough: How the Israeli Peace Camp Thinks about Religion, Nationalism, and Justice* (Chicago: University of Chicago Press, 2013) and Omer, "The Hermeneutics of Citizenship as a Peacebuilding Process: A Multiperspectival Approach to Justice," *Journal of Political Theology* 11, no. 5 (2010): 650–673.

38. See, for example, Abdulaziz Abdulhussein Sachedina, *Islam and Human Rights* (New York: Oxford University Press, 2010); Sachedina, *The Islamic Roots of Democratic Pluralism* (New York: Oxford University Press, 2001); Ann Elizabeth Mayer, *Islam and Human Rights: Tradition and Politics* (Boulder, CO: Westview Press, 2007); Abdullahi An-Na'im, *Islam and Human Rights: Selected Essays of Abdullahi An-Na'im*

(Farnham: Ashgate, 2010); An-Na'im, *Toward an Islamic Reformation: Civil Liberties, Human Rights, and International Law* (Syracuse, NY: Syracuse University Press, 1990); Irene Oh, *The Rights of God: Islam, Human Rights, and Comparative Ethics* (Washington, DC: Georgetown University Press, 2007); David Novak, *Conventional Rights: A Study in Jewish Political Theory* (Princeton, NJ: Princeton University Press, 2000); and Novak, *Natural Law in Judaism* (Cambridge: Cambridge University Press, 1998).

39. See Little, "Belief, Ethnicity, and Nationalism," in *Nationalism and Ethnic Politics* 1, no. 2 (1995): 284–301; Little, "Ground to Stand On: A Philosophical Reappraisal of Human Rights Language," in *Essays by David Little* (Cambridge: Cambridge University Press, forthcoming); and Little, "Peace, Justice, and Religion," in *What Is a Just Peace?*, ed. Pierre Allan and Alexis Keller (New York: Oxford University Press, 2006), 149–175.

40. Little often cites the work of Johannes Morsink in documenting the kind of cross-cultural debating that went into the drafting of the Universal Declaration of Human Rights; see Morsink, *The Universal Declaration of Human Rights: Origins, Drafting, and Intent* (Philadelphia: University of Pennsylvania Press, 1999).

41. See Little and Appleby, "A Moment of Opportunity?"

42. This approach informs Timothy Sisk, ed., *Between Terror and Tolerance: Religious Leaders, Conflict, and Peacemaking* (Washington, DC: Georgetown University Press, 2011). This work studies the potential constructive and destructive roles of religious leaders within the nexus of religion, nationalism, and state formation as well as in relation to supra-national doctrinal disputes, as in the Sunni-Shi'a divide.

43. See, for instance, Oren Yiftachel, *Ethnocracy: Land and Identity Politics in Israel/Palestine* (Philadelphia: University of Pennsylvania Press, 2006).

44. See Scott Hibbard, *Religious Politics and Secular States: Egypt, India, and the United States* (Baltimore, MD: The Johns Hopkins University Press, 2010).

45. Elizabeth Shakman Hurd, *The Politics of Secularism in International Relations* (Princeton, NJ: Princeton University Press, 2008).

46. See, for example, Saba Mahmood, "The Politics of Freedom: Geopolitics, Minority Rights, and Gender," the annual Helen Pond McIntyre '48 Lecture, Barnard College, New York, New York, November 5, 2009, http://mrzine.monthlyreview.org/2009/mahmood231109.html.

47. Jean Zaru, *Occupied with Nonviolence: A Palestinian Woman Speaks* (Minneapolis: Fortress Press, 2008), 42.

48. Mahmood (in collaboration with Shakman Hurd) explains that the principle of religious freedom is intricately related to the story of the emergence of the secular-liberal democratic state. A genealogy of this development shows the carving of religion out of the political and the framing of religion as a belief and/or faith and as a phenomenon also characterized by doctrines, creeds, institutions, and rituals. While this framing seems to make sense in a particular context, its universalization, through a process of colonial classification and domination, was precisely that of an imposition of alien categories, even if those categories may have been eventually internalized and appropriated by colonial subjects.

49. Zaru, 62.

50. In June of 2011, I attended a conference entitled "Local Peacebuilding and Religion: Conflict, Practice, and Models" at Emory University. A small number of the presentations moved beyond the paradigm that privileges the far and the exotic over discursive self-examination. In a paper titled "Sacrifice, Civil Religion, and Obstacles to Peacebuilding in the U.S.," Kelly

Denton-Borhaug probed into the relevance of deconstructing an ethos of exceptionalism and sacrifice as key for moving constructively from the belligerent and imperialistic paradigms of American foreign policy. This process of introspection involves an analysis of the selective deployment of religious imaginaries in the construal and reproduction of an American civil religion. Denton-Borhaug's project, therefore, suggests that "religion" can be involved in peacebuilding through a process of critique and rethinking "empire" and "national destiny." Another presentation by William O'Neil challenged the premises and categories of restorative justice as pivotal for rethinking peacebuilding in the United States. Likewise moving beyond the *far* as the focus of peacebuilding (and religion as it relates to conflict), Jason Springs discussed "Peacebuilding in Contexts of Structural and Cultural Violence: The Case of the Headscarf Controversy in France." Here the focus is western Europe and rising Islamophobia. The analysis of this trend requires one to deploy the tools of cultural theory as well as peace studies. Structural and cultural forms of violence as embodied in the ethos of laïcité in France, for example, necessitate a deconstructive critique of secularism, colonialism, orientalism, and multiculturalism. For an illustrative example of what this kind of critique might look like, see Joan Wallach Scott, *The Politics of the Veil* (Princeton, NJ: Princeton University Press, 2007).

51. Douglas Johnston and Cynthia Sampson, *Religion: The Missing Dimension of Statecraft* (Washington, DC: Center for Strategic and International Studies, 1994).

52. Douglas Johnston, ed., *Faith-Based Diplomacy: Trumping Realpolitik* (New York: Oxford University Press, 2003); Thomas Scott, *The Global Resurgence of Religion and the Transformation of International Relations: The Struggle for the Soul of the Twenty-First Century* (New York: Palgrave Macmillan, 2005); David Smock, ed., *Religious Contributions to Peacemaking: When Religion Brings Peace, Not War* (Washignton D.C.: United States Institute of Peace, 2006), http://www.usip.org/sites/default/files/resources/PWJan2006. pdf and "Faith-based NGOs and International Peacebuilding," www.usip.org/pubs/specialreports (2001); Marc Gopin, *To Make the Earth Whole: The Art of Citizen Diplomacy in an Age of Religious Militancy* (Lanham, MD: Rowman and Littlefield, 2009); and Coward and Smith, *Religion and Peacebuilding*.

53. Here I allude to the concept of "soft power" developed by Joseph S. Nye in *Soft Power: The Means to Success in World Politics* (New York: Public Affairs, 2004).

54. The designation "faith-based" suggests that religious peacebuilding did not pose a radical challenge to the operative theoretical frameworks in international relations (realism, liberalism, and constructivism). Therefore, it is not surprising that Emily Cochran Bech and Jack Snyder, in their conclusion to an edited volume *Religion and International Relations Theory* (New York: Columbia University Press, 2011), argue that challenges from discursive critiques, as in Shakman-Hurd, only illuminate some correctable limitations in each of these conventions.

55. See Atalia Omer, "Can a Critic Be a Caretaker Too? Religion, Conflict, and Conflict Transformation," *Journal of the American Academy of Religion* 79, no. 2 (2011): 459–496.

56. See, for instance, Susan Okin, *Is Multiculturalism Bad for Women?* (Princeton, NJ: Princeton University Press, 1999).

57. Lederach and Appleby, "Strategic Peacebuilding: An Overview," in *Strategies of Peace: Transforming Conflict in a Violent World*, eds. Daniel Philpott and Gerard F. Powers (New York: Oxford University Press, 2010). See also Lederach, "Justpeace," in *People Building Peace: 35 Inspiring Stories from Around the World*, ed. Paul Van Tongeren (Utrecht: European Centre for Conflict Prevention, 1999), 27–36.

58. A notable stride in this direction was the convening by the Chicago Council on Global Affairs of a task force to explore the role of global religions in international politics and diplomacy. It is no surprise that co-chairing this task force was R. Scott Appleby, whose earlier work set the parameters for the study of religious peacebuilding.

59. One way to open up the discussion to critique would be through integrating the philosophical explorations of religion and human rights, especially the issue of proselytizing. See, for instance, Jean Bethke Elshtain, "Toleration, Proselytizing, and the Politics of Recognition," and John Witte Jr., "The Rights and Limits of Proselytism in the New Religious World Order," in *Religious Pluralism, Globalization, and World Politics*, ed. Thomas Banchoff (New York: Oxford University Press, 2008), 89–104 and 105–124.

60. Judith Plaskow, *Standing Again at Sinai: Judaism from a Feminist Perspective* (San Francisco: Harper and Row, 1990).

61. See Marshall, "Women, Religion, and Peacebuilding Interview Series," US Institute of Peace, the Berkley Center for Religion, Peace, and World Affairs, and the World Faiths Development Dialogue (WFDD), http://berkleycenter.georgetown.edu/projects/women-religion-and-peace-experience-perspectives-and-policy-implications. For an analysis that centrally incorporates gender theory (not only an account of women, religion, and conflict/peace), see Monique Skidmore and Patricia Lawrence, eds., *Women and the Contested State: Religion, Violence, and Agency in South and Southeast Asia* (Notre Dame, IN: University of Notre Dame Press, 2007).

62. Mahmood, *Politics of Piety: The Islamic Revival and the Feminist Subject* (Princeton, NJ: Princeton University Press, 2005).

BIBLIOGRAPHY

Abu-Nimer, Mohammed, ed. *Reconciliation, Justice, and Coexistence: Theory and Practice.* Lanham, MD: Lexington Books, 2001.

Abu-Nimer, Mohammed. *Nonviolence and Peace Building in Islam: Theory and Practice.* Gainesville: University Press of Florida, 2003.

Abu-Nimer, Mohammed, Amal Khoury, and Emily Welty. *Unity in Diversity: Interfaith Dialogue in the Middle East.* Washington, DC: US Institute of Peace Press, 2007.

Agnivesh, Swami. *Religion, Spirituality and Social Action.* Haryana: Hope India Publications, 2003.

An-Na'im, Abdullahi. *Toward an Islamic Reformation: Civil Liberties, Human Rights, and International Law.* Syracuse, NY: Syracuse University Press, 1990.

An-Na'im, Abdullahi. *Islam and Human Rights: Selected Essays of Abdullahi An-Na'im.* Farnham: Ashgate, 2010.

Appleby, R. Scott. *The Ambivalence of the Sacred: Religion, Violence, and Reconciliation.* Lanham, MD: Rowman and Littlefield, 2000.

Appleby, R. Scott. "Building Sustainable Peace: The Roles of Local and Transnational Religious Actors." In *Religious Pluralism: Globalization and World Politics*, edited by Thomas Banchoff, 125–154. New York: Oxford University Press, 2007.

Avruch, Kevin. *Culture and Conflict Resolution.* Washington, DC: US Institute of Peace Press, 1998.

Baptist Peace Fellowship of North America. http://www.bpfna.org/home.

Bech, Emily Cochran, and Jack Snyder. "Religion's Contribution to International Relations Theory." In *Religion and International Relations Theory*, edited by Jack Snyder, 200–209. New York: Columbia University Press, 2011.

Berkley Center for Religion, Peace, and World Affairs. http://berkleycenter.georgetown.edu.

Buddhist Peace Fellowship. http://www.bpf.org.

Cahill, Lisa. *Love Your Enemies: Discipleship, Pacifism and Just War Theory*. Minneapolis: Fortress Press, 1994.

Casanova, José. "Immigration and the New Religious Pluralism: A European Union/United States Comparison." Paper presented at the conference on "The New Religious Pluralism and Democracy," Georgetown University, Washington, DC, April 21–22, 2005.

Cavanaugh, William. *The Myth of Religious Violence: Secular Ideology and the Roots of Modern Conflict*. New York: Oxford University Press, 2009.

Cejka, Mary Ann, and Thomas Bamat, eds. *Artisans of Peace: Grassroots Peacemaking among Christian Communities*. New York: Orbis Books, 2003.

Chapman, Audrey R., and Bernard Spong. *Religion and Reconciliation in South Africa: Voices of Religious Leaders*. Philadelphia: Templeton Foundation Press, 2003.

Chappel, David W., ed. *Buddhist Peacework: Creating Cultures of Peace*. Somerville, MA: Wisdom Publications, 1999.

Cherribi, Sam. "Politicians' Perceptions of the 'Muslim Problem': The Dutch Example in European Context." In *Democracy and the New Religious Pluralism*, edited by Thomas Banchoff, 113–132. New York: Oxford University Press, 2007.

Christian Peacemaker Teams. http://www.cpt.org.

Cochrane, James R., John de Gruchy, and Stephen Martin. *Facing the Truth: South African Faith Communities and the Truth and Reconciliation Commission*. Cape Town: Ohio University Press, 1999.

Coward, Harold, and Gordon S. Smith, eds. *Religion and Peacebuilding*. Albany: State University of New York Press, 2004.

Curle, Adam. *True Justice: Quaker Peace Makers and Peace Making*. London: Quaker Home Service, 1981.

Denton-Borhaug, Kelly. "Sacrifice, Civil Religion, and Obstacles to Peacebuilding in the U.S." Paper presented at "Local Peacebuilding and Religion: Conflict, Practice, and Models" conference, Emory University, Atlanta, GA, June 2011.

Easwaran, Eknath. *A Man to Match His Mountains: Badshah Khan, Nonviolent Soldier of Islam*. Petaluma, CA: Nilgiri Press, 1984.

Ellis, Marc. *Unholy Alliance: Religion and Atrocity in Our Time*. Minneapolis: Fortress Press, 1997.

Elshtain, Jean Bethke. "Toleration, Proselytizing, and the Politics of Recognition." In *Religious Pluralism, Globalization, and World Politics*, edited by Thomas Banchoff, 89–104. New York: Oxford University Press, 2008.

Esposito, John L., and Ihsan Yilmaz, eds. *Islam and Peacebuilding: Gülen Movement Initiatives*. New York: Blue Dome Press, 2010.

Ferguson, John. *War and Peace in the World's Religions*. London: Sheldon Press, 1977.

Gates Brown, Tricia. *Getting in the Way: Stories from Christian Peacemaker Teams*. Scottdale, PA: Herald Press, 2005.

Gopin, Marc. "Religion, Violence and Conflict Resolution." *Peace and Change* 22, no. 1 (1997): 1–31.

Gopin, Marc. *Between Eden and Armageddon: The Future of World Religions, Violence, and Peacemaking*. New York: Oxford University Press, 2000.

Gopin, Marc. "Forgiveness as an Element of Conflict Resolution in Religious Cultures: Walking the Tightrope of Reconciliation and Justice." In *Reconciliation, Justice and Coexistence: Theory and Practice*, edited by Mohammed Abu-Nimer, 87–100. Lanham, MD: Lexington Books, 2001.

Gopin, Marc. *Holy War, Holy Peace: How Religion Can Bring Peace to the Middle East*. New York: Oxford University Press, 2002.

Gopin, Marc. *To Make the Earth Whole: The Art of Citizen Diplomacy in an Age of Religious Militancy*. Lanham, MD: Rowman and Littlefield, 2009.

Gort, Jerald D., Henry Jansen, and Hendrik M. Vroom, eds. *Religion, Conflict and Reconciliation: Multifaith Ideals and Realities*. Amsterdam: Rodopi, 2002.

Haynes, Jeffrey. *Religion and Development: Conflict or Cooperation?* New York: Palgrave Macmillan, 2007.

Heft, James, ed. *Beyond Violence: Religious Sources of Social Transformation in Judaism, Christianity and Islam*. New York: Fordham University Press, 2004.

Helmick, Raymond G., SJ, and Rodney L. Petersen, eds. *Forgiveness and Reconciliation: Religion, Public Policy, and Conflict Transformation*. Philadelphia: Templeton Foundation Press, 2001.

Hertog, Katrien. *The Complex Reality of Religious Peacebuilding: Conceptual Contributions and Critical Analysis*. Lanham, MD: Lexington Books, 2010.

Hervieu-Léger, Danièle. "Islam and the Republic: The French Case." In *Democracy and the New Religious Pluralism*, edited by Thomas Banchoff, 203–222. New York: Oxford University Press, 2007.

Hibbard, Scott. *Religious Politics and Secular States: Egypt, India, and the United States*. Baltimore, MD: The Johns Hopkins University Press, 2010.

Huntington, Samuel. *The Clash of Civilizations and the Remaking of World Order*. New York: Simon and Schuster, 1996.

International Committee for the Peace Council. http://www.peacecouncil.org.

Johnson, James Turner. *The Quest for Peace: Three Moral Traditions in Western Cultural History*. Princeton, NJ: Princeton University Press, 1987.

Johnson, James Turner, and John Kelsay, eds. *Cross, Crescent, and Sword: The Justification and Limitation of War in Western Islamic Tradition*. Westport: Greenwood Press, 1990.

Johnson, James Turner, and John Kelsay, eds. *Just War and Jihad: Historical and Theoretical Perspectives on War and Peace in Western and Islamic Traditions*. Westport: Greenwood Press, 1991.

Johnston, Douglas, ed. *Faith-Based Diplomacy: Trumping Realpolitik*. New York: Oxford University Press, 2003.

Johnston, Douglas, and Cynthia Sampson, eds. *Religion: The Missing Dimensions of Statecraft*. Washington, DC: Center for Strategic and International Studies, 1994.

Kelsay, John. *Arguing the Just War in Islam*. Cambridge, MA: Harvard University Press, 2007.

Kraybill, Ronald. "From Head to Heart: The Cycle of Reconciliation." *Conciliation Quarterly* 7, no. 4 (1998): 2–38.

Kroc Institute for International Peace Studies. http://kroc.nd.edu.

Landau, Yehezkel. *Healing the Holy Land: Interreligious Peacebuilding in Israel/Palestine*. Washington, DC: USIP Press, 2003.

Lederach, John Paul. *Preparing for Peace: Conflict Transformation across Cultures*. New York: Syracuse University Press, 1996.

Lederach, John Paul. *Building Peace: Sustainable Reconciliation in Divided Societies*. Washington, DC: US Institute of Peace Press, 1997.

Lederach, John Paul. "Justpeace: The Challenge of the 21st Century." In *People Building Peace: 35 Inspiring Stories from Around the World*, edited by Paul Van Tongeren, 27–36. Utrecht: European Centre for Conflict Prevention, 1999.

Lederach, John Paul. *The Little Book of Conflict Transformation*. Intercourse, PA: Good Books, 2003.

Lederach, John Paul. *The Moral Imagination: The Art and Soul of Building Peace*. New York: Oxford University Press, 2005.

Lederach, John Paul, and R. Scott Appleby. "Strategic Peacebuilding: An Overview." In *Strategies of Peace: Transforming Conflict in a Violent World*, edited by Daniel Philpott and Gerard F. Powers, 19–44. New York: Oxford University Press, 2010.

Lederach, John Paul, and Cynthia Sampson. *From the Ground Up: Mennonite Contributions to International Peacebuilding*. New York: Oxford University Press, 2000.

Little, David. "The Present State of the Comparative Study of Religious Ethics." *Journal of Religious Ethics* 9, no. 2 (1981): 210–227.

Little, David. "Belief, Ethnicity, and Nationalism." *Nationalism and Ethnic Politics* 1, no. 2 (1995): 284–301.

Little, David. "Peace, Justice, and Religion." In *What Is a Just Peace?*, edited by Pierre Allan and Alexis Keller, 149–175. New York: Oxford University Press, 2006.

Little, David. "Ground to Stand On: A Philosophical Reappraisal of Human Rights Language." In *Essays by David Little*. Cambridge: Cambridge University Press, forthcoming.

Little, David, and R. Scott Appleby. "A Moment of Opportunity? The Promise of Religious Peacebuilding in an Era of Religious and Ethnic Conflict." In *Religion and Peacebuilding*, edited by Harold Coward and Gordon S. Smith, 1–23. Albany: State University of New York Press, 2004.

Little, David, ed., with the Tanenbaum Center for Interreligious Understanding. *Peacemakers in Action: Profiles of Religion in Conflict Resolution*. New York: Cambridge University Press, 2007.

Little, David, and Barney Twiss. *Comparative Religious Ethics: A New Method*. San Francisco: Harper and Row, 1978.

Mahmood, Saba. *Politics of Piety: The Islamic Revival and the Feminist Subject*. Princeton, NJ: Princeton University Press, 2005.

Mahmood, Saba. "The Politics of Freedom: Geopolitics, Minority Rights, and Gender." Lecture, The Sixth Annual Helen Pond McIntyre '48 Lecture from Barnard College, New York, NY, November 5, 2009.

Marshall, Katherine. "Religion and Global Development: Intersecting Paths." In *Religious Pluralism: Globalization and World Politics*, edited by Thomas Banchoff, 195–228. New York: Oxford University Press, 2008.

Marshall, Katherine. "Women, Religion, and Peacebuilding." Interview Series, US Institute of Peace, the Berkley Center for Religion, Peace, and World Affairs, and the World Faiths Development.

Marshall, Katherine, and Marisa Bronwyn. *Development and Faith: Where Mind, Heart, and Soul Work Together*. Washington, DC: World Bank, 2007.

Marshall, Katherine, and Richard March. *Millennium Goals for Development and Faith Institutions: Common Leadership Challenges*. Washington, DC: World Bank, 2003.

Mayer, Ann Elizabeth. *Islam and Human Rights: Tradition and Politics*. Boulder, CO: Westview Press, 2007.

McConnell, John. *Mindful Mediation: A Handbook for Buddhist Peacemakers*. Thailand: Buddhist Research Institute and Mahachula Buddhist University, 1995.

Mennonite Conciliation Service. *Mediation Training Manual: Skills for Constructive Conflict Transformation*. Philadelphia: Mennonite Conciliation Service, 1992.

Morsink, Johannes. *The Universal Declaration of Human Rights: Origins, Drafting, and Intent.* Philadelphia: University of Pennsylvania Press, 1999.

Nhat Hanh, Thich. *Being Peace.* Berkeley, CA: Parallax Press, 1987.

Nhat Hanh, Thich. *Touching Peace.* Berkeley, CA: Parallax Press, 1992.

Nhat Hanh, Thich. *Love in Action: Writings on Nonviolent Social Change.* Berkeley, CA: Parallax Press, 1993.

Novak, David. *Natural Law in Judaism.* Cambridge: Cambridge University Press, 1998.

Novak, David. *Conventional Rights: A Study in Jewish Political Theory.* Princeton, NJ: Princeton University Press, 2000.

Nye, Joseph S. *Soft Power: The Means to Success in World Politics.* New York: Public Affairs, 2004.

Oh, Irene. *The Rights of God: Islam, Human Rights, and Comparative Ethics.* Washington, DC: Georgetown University Press, 2007.

Okin, Susan Moller. *Is Multiculturalism Bad for Women?* Princeton, NJ: Princeton University Press, 1999.

Omer, Atalia. "The Hermeneutics of Citizenship as a Peacebuilding Process: A Multiperspectival Approach to Justice." *Journal of Political Theology* 11, no. 5 (2010): 650–673.

Omer, Atalia. "Can a Critic Be a Caretaker Too? Religion, Conflict, and Conflict Transformation." *Journal of the American Academy of Religion* 79, no. 2 (2011): 459–496.

Omer, Atalia. *When Peace Is Not Enough: How the Israeli Peace Camp Thinks about Religion, Nationalism, and Justice.* Chicago: University of Chicago Press, 2013.

Patton, Kimberley C., and Benjamin C. Ray, eds. *A Magic Still Dwells: Comparative Religion in the Postmodern Age.* Berkeley: University of California Press, 2000.

Philpott, Daniel, ed. *The Politics of Past Evil: Religion, Reconciliation, and the Dilemmas of Transitional Justice.* Notre Dame, IN: University of Notre Dame Press, 2006.

Philpott, Daniel. *Just and Unjust Peace.* New York: Oxford University Press, 2012.

Plaskow, Judith. *Standing Again at Sinai: Judaism from a Feminist Perspective.* San Francisco: Harper and Row, 1990.

Qureshi, Emran and Michael Anthony Sells, eds. *The New Crusades: Constructing the Muslim Enemy.* New York: Columbia University Press, 2003.

Sachedina, Abdulaziz Abdulhussein. *The Islamic Roots of Democratic Pluralism.* New York: Oxford University Press, 2001.

Sachedina, Abdulaziz Abdulhussein. *Islam and Human Rights.* New York: Oxford University Press, 2010.

Said, Abdul Aziz, Nathan Funk, and Ayse S. Kadayifci, eds. *Peace and Conflict Resolution in Islam: Precept and Practice.* Lanham, MD: University Press of America, 2001.

Scheffler, Thomas. *Religion Between Violence and Reconciliation.* Beirut: Orient-Institute, 2002.

Schirch, Lisa. *Ritual and Symbol in Peacebuilding.* Bloomfield, CT: Kumarian Press, 2005.

Schreiter, Robert J., R. Scott Appleby, and Gerard F. Powers, eds. *Peacebuilding: Catholic Theology, Ethics, and Praxis.* Maryknoll, NY: Orbis Books, 2010.

Scott, Joan Wallach. *The Politics of the Veil.* Princeton, NJ: Princeton University Press, 2007.

Scott, Thomas. *The Global Resurgence of Religion and the Transformation of International Relations: The Struggle for the Soul of the Twenty-First Century.* New York: Palgrave Macmillan, 2005.

Shakman Hurd, Elizabeth. *The Politics of Secularism in International Relations.* Princeton, NJ: Princeton University Press, 2008.

Shriver, Donald. *An Ethic for Enemies: Forgiveness in Politics*. New York: Oxford University Press, 1995.

Skidmore, Monique, and Patricia Lawrence, eds. *Women and the Contested State: Religion, Violence, and Agency in South and Southeast Asia*. Notre Dame, IN: University of Notre Dame Press, 2007.

Smith-Christopher, Daniel, ed. *Subverting Hatred: The Challenge of Nonviolence in Religious Traditions*. Cambridge, MA: Boston Research Center for the 21st Century, 1998.

Smock, David. *Perspectives on Pacifism: Christian, Jewish, and Muslim Views on Nonviolence and International Conflict*. Washington, DC: US Institute of Peace Press, 1995.

Smock, David. "Faith-based NGOs and International Peacebuilding." Report presented at a United States Institute of Peace workshop, Washington, DC, June 20, 2001.

Smock, David, ed. *Religious Contributions to Peacemaking: When Religion Brings Peace, Not War*. Washignton D.C.: United States Institute of Peace, 2006. http://www.usip.org/sites/default/files/resources/PWJan2006.pdf.

Springs, Jason. "Peacebuilding in Contexts of Structural and Cultural Violence: The Case of the Headscarf Controversy in France." Presentation at "Local Peacebuilding and Religion: Conflict, Practice, and Models" conference, Emory University, Atlanta, GA, June 2011.

Springs, Jason. "On Giving Religious Intolerance its Due: Prospects for Transforming Conflict in a Post-Secular Society." *The Journal of Religion* 92, no. 1 (2012): 1–30.

Stout, Jeffrey. "Weber's Progeny Once Removed." *Religious Studies Review* 6, no.4 (1980): 289–295.

Stout, Jeffrey. "Holism and Comparative Ethics: A Response to Little." *Journal of Religious Ethics* 11, no. 2 (1983): 301–316.

Stout, Jeffrey. *Democracy and Tradition*. Princeton, NJ: Princeton University Press, 2004.

ter Haar, Gerrie, and James J. Busuttil, eds. *Bridge or Barrier: Religion, Violence and Visions of Peace*. Leiden-Boston: Brill, 2005.

Sisk, Timothy D., ed. *Between Terror and Tolerance: Religious Leaders, Conflict, and Peacemaking*. Washington, DC: Georgetown University Press, 2011.

Villa-Vicencio, Charles. *Looking Back, Reaching Forward: Reflections on the Truth and Reconciliation Commission of South Africa*. Cape Town: University of Cape Town Press, 2000.

Witte, John, Jr. "The Rights and Limits of Proselytism in the New Religious World Order." In *Religious Pluralism, Globalization, and World Politics*, edited by Thomas Banchoff, 105–124. New York: Oxford University Press, 2008.

Yiftachel, Oren. *Ethnocracy: Land and Identity Politics in Israel/Palestine*. Philadelphia: University of Pennsylvania Press, 2006.

Zaru, Jean. *Occupied with Nonviolence: A Palestinian Woman Speaks*. Minneapolis: Fortress Press, 2008.

CHAPTER 2

....

RELIGIOUS VIOLENCE
The Strong, the Weak, and the Pathological

....

R. SCOTT APPLEBY

How do we begin to account for the human act of violating another person? What are we to make of the brutalities of rape, torture, and the slaughter of innocents? How do the advocates and perpetrators of violence justify unspeakable deeds? What of violence that falls short of "atrocity" but nonetheless seeks to harm, debase, and possibly kill?

And then we come to the question of agency. Are those who enact deadly violence to be considered pathological and beyond the pale, or can violence be considered legitimate, just, indeed valorous under certain circumstances? And who is to decide? Does the modern nation-state have the legitimate monopoly on violence, as Weber famously asserted? Or may protest movements, rebellions, and revolutions displace the state and do so with compelling ethical and legal justification?

Such fundamental and enduring questions, typically the province of lawyers, constitutionalists, political philosophers, and ethicists, become ever more complicated when religion and religious actors are implicated in deadly violence. And lately they have been. Indeed, the last three decades have witnessed a thematically and methodologically incoherent outpouring of books, articles, and multimedia documentaries on "religious violence." Triggered by the rise of virulent religious movements in the 1970s, this avalanche of reportage, analysis, and commentary ranges in subject matter from lone assassins, apocalyptic cults, and religiously ambiguous terrorists to networks of Hindu militants crisscrossing India, Jewish irredentist movements in Israel, and the Sikh extremists of Punjab.[1] Everyone, it seems, has a pet theory as to the who and why of religious violence, including those who see it as a reified construct distracting attention from the structural and supposedly "legitimate" physical violence of the modern nation-state.[2] Meanwhile, the westernized global media has helped to open a profitable market for books with titles featuring the words "sacred terror" and "holy war."[3] The relative lack of sophistication regarding religion, not least in policy circles, combined with the advent of a skeptical secularism as the default mode of public discourse in North America and Europe, has abetted both the exoticizing of religion and the conflation of public religion with fundamentalism and fundamentalism with terrorism.[4] That "religion and violence" has "arrived" as an academic sub-field is evident in the recent or imminent appearance of "readers," "companions," and "handbooks" for use by teachers, students, and researchers.[5] In short, it has been a seller's market for scholars, public intellectuals, and pundits trafficking in expertise in religious extremism.

The plethora of scholarly publications alone suggests the need to identify broad interpretive categories and review a few representative titles for each. Accordingly, in this survey of "the state of the field" I use the term *strong religion* to cluster works which see religion itself as the source of, or justification for, deadly violence, or which emphasize distinctive religious practices, beliefs, and ideologies as the decisive ingredients in violent movements that may also draw on nationalist, ethnic, or other motivations.[6] My second category, *weak religion*, refers to works that present religion as a dependent variable in deadly violence, the primary source of which is secular in origin (e.g., enacted by the state, or by nationalist or ethnic extremists). Finally, a network of scholars explores what might be termed *pathological religion*, namely, religious actors whose embrace of fundamentalist or extremist religious modes of behavior reflect symptoms of psycho-social deviance. The meaning and content of "religion" itself fluctuates within and across these interpretive modes, as I indicate below.

Strong Religion

Authors writing in the "strong religion" camp focus on the phenomenology and history of religion itself as sufficient to inspire and authorize deadly violence, which may be enacted by the self-styled "true believers" themselves or by their religiously less literate or committed surrogates.

The most influential author in this category is the sociologist of religion Mark Juergensmeyer, who spices his selections of scriptures and traditions of divine warfare with observations and insights derived from field interviews, gleanings from websites, and evocative quotations from extremist treatises and apocalyptic "novels" such as *The Turner Diaries*.[7] In his role as a synthesist, Juergensmeyer has been criticized for skimming the surface and conflating different types of religious (and nonreligious) actors, but his conceptual contributions to the field are undeniable. His best-known work, *Terror in the Mind of God: The Global Rise of Religious Violence*, tapped into the intense anxiety provoked by the events of 9/11. Written in accessible prose, its cover adorned with menacing close-ups of three then-prominent—and strikingly disparate, not to say incomparable—"religious terrorists" (Timothy McVeigh, Osama bin Laden, and Shoko Asahara of Aum Shinrikyo), the book reinforced the impression that religious violence is a ubiquitous and particularly lethal threat to world order and security. It also provided a showcase for key concepts that Juergensmeyer had been developing as his signal contribution to the field.

The most cited of these is the notion of cosmic war. Religious extremists—reveling in myths of a martial past, believing themselves to be enacting God's will, and viewing the current military campaign as but a chapter in a glorious and protracted battle between good and evil—adopt a calculus of warfare that is radically different, and less strictly rational, than that governing the tactics of secular combatants. The true believers, Juergensmeyer argues, see themselves engaged in a metaphysical struggle, the ultimate stakes of which dwarf mere territorial or political ambitions and justify endless, self-renewing, ultra-violent enactments of divine wrath. "What makes religious violence particularly savage and relentless is that its perpetrators have placed such religious images of divine struggle—cosmic war—in the service of worldly political battles," he writes.[8]

Religious narratives of martyrdom, sacrifice, and conquest inform the notion of cosmic war, which in turn provides the script that is played out in the performative as well as the tactical violence of al-Qaeda, Aum Shinryko, the Christian Identity militias, and many more. Performative violence—extremist acts which are primarily symbolic in nature—gestures toward an infinite horizon of meaning beyond the immediate strategic or practical considerations of the present battle. (Such acts may also carry "demonstration effect," which can deliver quite practical propaganda and recruiting results, as in: See what a few true believers/suicide plane hijackers, empowered by faith and equipped only with courage, zeal, and a few box-cutters, can do—bring the mighty, pagan America to its knees in terror!) Cosmic war, Juergensmeyer contends, is central to a religious worldview and it thereby valorizes religious commitment as a path of honor and virtue, endows individuals as well as societies with nobility and meaning, justifies otherwise despicable acts, and provides political legitimization to its warriors.[9]

But is "cosmic war" *central* to a religious worldview or is it derived mainly from the extremist wing of contemporary religious movements? And is it accurate to apply this notion broadly, to religious movements in general? Juergensmeyer's published work oscillates between holding religion itself accountable for violence authorized or enacted by religious actors ("strong religion"), and laying the blame on nationalist or ethnic actors who manipulate religious sensibilities, symbols, and actors toward decidedly nonreligious ends ("weak religion"). But he nonetheless applies cosmic war as a theoretical canopy overarching secular as well as religious actors. "The Palestinian conflict," he writes in a typical passage, "is conceived as something larger than a contest between Arabs and Jews: it is a cosmic struggle of Manichaean proportions."[10]

An elastic definition of religion and who counts as religious creates certain analytical challenges for the theorist and comparativist of religious violence. So, too, do the substantive and organizational differences between the religious groups engaged in deadly violence. These include fundamentalist movements that emerge within multigenerational global religions such as Islam and Christianity and draw on their ideological and organizational resources; less organizationally robust and pervasive sects and "new religious movements," including cults such as the Branch Davidians and Aum Shinryko, which depend heavily on a charismatic leader; and loosely affiliated networks such as the Christian Identity militias.[11] In addition, there are significant variations within these clusters, and one must consider how the variations might affect the use or frequency of various forms of violence. "Structurally, the radical right is a confusing, seemingly anarchic world," writes Michael Barkun, an expert on Christian extremism and apocalyptic violence.[12]

Other scholars of religious violence writing in the "strong religion" mode have also struggled with the challenges of differentiating religious from other motivations, isolating distinctively religious dynamics, and accounting for the ways religion is embedded in specific historical and cultural contexts. They are aware that some of their colleagues in the study of religion argue that what we call religion, in addition to being a category of analysis developed in the modern period and complicit in Western colonial and imperial efforts to conquer and control non-Western populations, is so fluid, contingent, and adaptive that it cannot responsibly be posited as a stable source of identity and behavior. The most radical expression of this view holds that the concept of "religion" is "manufactured, constructed, invented or imagined, but does not correspond to an objective reality 'out there' in the world." The term should therefore be dropped altogether.[13]

In her chapter on religious peacebuilding in this volume, Atalia Omer offers a generous and sympathetic rendering of my own work in the "strong religion" mode, *The Ambivalence of the Sacred: Religion, Violence, and Reconciliation*. Without repeating her lucid summary of that book's main themes and argument, I can say simply that I am certainly not in the "there is no such thing as religion" camp. Rather, I accept the "reality" of the human experience of the numinous, which cannot be reduced to the totality of its psychological, social, economic, cultural, and other dimensions. That this cross-cultural and cross-generational experience, or set of experiences, finds expression in historically contingent practices, beliefs, and institutions, and is already always "reduced" semiotically as well as linguistically—that is, contained and truncated within connotative and allusive as well as denotative (and thus "naive") discursive modes—is undeniable. The challenge, however, is to determine, as far as possible, how these different cultural, social, and psychological "placements" of religious experiences condition the concrete working-out of a behavioral response within the range of violent and nonviolent options available to the devout. To acknowledge that religion is a modern construct, differentiated from the state in order to be constrained by secular power, does not absolve the interpreter from the task of scrutinizing its present configurations.

One thread of historical continuity is precisely the ongoing construction of the sacred. Deadly violence against the impure, the heretic, and the infidel, I have argued, is an authentic, if not necessarily legitimate, response to the encounter with the sacred, the power of which is rendered, variously, as awesome, imposing, creative, destructive, fascinating, liberating, and commanding. When people believe themselves to be acting in response to the sacred, the timing, nature, duration, targets, audience(s), and understood purpose of their acts draw heavily on the sensibilities, symbols, rituals, precepts, and doctrines available within the discursive community. Such action is always "militant," according to the terminology I employ; that is, driven by "a passion for the infinite" and a corresponding spirit of self-denial, sacrifice, and zeal for doing "God's will." It is "extremist" (in my usage) when the dynamics of "othering" and demonizing kick in, to a degree that the annihilation of the enemy is considered a religious obligation.

In underscoring the distinctively religious character of some expressions of religious violence, my approach accords with the "strong religion" explanatory framework. As Omer notes, however, I find in "the ambivalence of the sacred"—that is, in the pre-moral, pre-interpreted, "raw" (if always mediated) experience of the radical mystery of the numinous—a powerful source of nonviolent peacebuilding, compassion, and love of enemy. In accounting for religious violence as well as religious peacebuilding, hermeneutics is everything, contestation is inevitable, and struggle within and outside the enclave is the norm.[14]

The corollaries of both the cosmic war thesis and the ambivalence thesis hold explanatory power. Martial themes and symbols abound in the religious imagination, as one would expect from peoples convinced that human existence is a never-ending face-off between the elect and the reprobate, the pure and impure.[15] Religious "militance"—absolute and unconditional devotion to the sacred cause—makes compromise unlikely; this helps to explain why religious actors are among the major rejectionists of peace processes and agents of spoiler violence.[16] Related motifs of divine wrath and judgment, rituals of purification, and contestations over sacred space also inhabit the religious imaginary and provide evidence for the "strong religion" interpretation of religious violence. Indeed, an array of scholars, spanning the disciplines of ritual studies, history, semiotics, cultural anthropology, theology, ethics, and peace and conflict studies, has explored the potential for inciting violence in behaviors and practices typically seen as constitutive of religion.

DESIRE, MIMESIS, RITUAL

"In many rituals the sacrificial act assumes two opposing aspects, appearing at times as a sacred obligation to be neglected at grave peril, at other times as a sort of criminal activity entailing perils of equal gravity." Thus begins *Violence and the Sacred*, the influential text of the French literary critic René Girard, who sets forth his theory of mimetic desire, ritual sacrifice, and the dual function of religion to authorize and contain violence. By "mimetic desire" Girard refers to the tendency of a tribe to emulate the desirable traits of an other who is perceived as strong, noble, "ideal," but whose perceived superior status and power ultimately become the source of envy, jealousy, resentment, and often bitter competition and loathing. Such visceral impulses must be channeled and managed, lest they destroy the host community. Through the sacrifice of a scapegoat, the collective anger and aggression that build up in a community and can threaten to turn its members against against one another are transferred to a "safe" victim. In Girard's view, "the function of ritual is to 'purify' violence; that is, to 'trick' violence into spending itself on victims whose death will provoke no reprisals."[17] In this sense, Girard comments, "ritual is nothing more than the regular exercise of 'good violence.'"[18] When sacrificial rituals break down, religious symbols and myths can be turned to justify aggression against outsiders, often in the form of a "holy war." In short, as Charles Selengut comments, "religion, by sacralizing and legitimating violence against enemies or promoting ritual enactments of mythic violence, rids a society of its own intragroup violence."[19]

Girard's influence is far-ranging. The Christian writer Gil Bailie sees Girard's focus on the "redemptive victim" as a "breakthrough" that relieves society of the need for religious or ethnic war. The logic of sacred violence, Bailie argues, "is nowhere expressed more succinctly nor repudiated more completely than in the New Testament, where the high priest solemnly announces its benefits and the crucifixion straightaway reveals its arbitrariness and horror."[20] Scholars find Girardian theory a useful analytical lens. While acknowledging that mimetic desire and the crisis of ritual sacrifice do not comprehend the entire range of motivations for religious violence, Selengut points out that Girard's theory "is particularly helpful because it incorporates myth, ritual and the unconscious and refuses to explain violence as [merely] the result of logical goals or political strategy." While religious violence may not make military or political sense, in other words, it may make religious and psychological sense by "resolving" certain internal problems for a society. Intriguingly, Selengut uses scapegoating and mimetic desire as a lens for analyzing intragroup Israeli dynamics in the context of the struggle against the religious and ethnic Palestinian other.[21]

Taking a page from Girard (while drawing explicitly on other theorists of religion such as Wayne Proudfoot), Hugh Nicholson argues that religious and theological discourse, driven by rivalry, is inherently polemical—and thereby all the more creative and adaptive. The need to distinguish oneself from one's intra- and/or inter-religious adversaries, he suggests, inspires "a process of abstraction and sublimation" even as it compels religious communities into oppositional political modes.[22]

Along similar lines, Regina Schwartz's elegant analysis of "the violent legacy of monotheism," *The Curse of Cain*, traces the origin of violence to identity formation, specifically to "imagining identity as an act of distinguishing and separating from others, of boundary marking and line drawing." The Bible, she argues, narrates and instantiates the "sibling rivalry" born of competition for scarce resources. Along the way Schwartz engages the notion of substitutive sacrifice, noting that "Girard. . . stresses that for identification in sacrificial ritual to work, the original object of violence must not be lost sight of in the substitution." Yet too often in Biblical narratives, she observes, the symbolic enactment is eschewed and violence is "literalized."[23]

A related subject of inquiry is the role of ritual and symbol in sacralizing mass violence. Natalie Zemon Davis, a historian of the early modern period, studied religious riots in sixteenth-century France. The goal of the rioters was "ridding the community of dreaded pollution. . . [which] would surely provoke the wrath of God." While Catholics and Protestants timed and framed their acts of violence differently, they shared a goal "reminiscent of the insistence of revolutionary millenarian movements that the wicked be exterminated that the godly may rule." "Is there any way we can order the terrible, concrete details of filth, shame, and torture reported from both Protestant and Catholic riots?" Davis ponders. "I would suggest that they can be reduced to a repertory of actions from the Bible, from the liturgy, from the action of political authority, or from the traditions of popular folk justice, intended to purify the religious community and humiliate the enemy and thus make him less harmful."[24]

Similar patterns of religious violence recur in more contemporary clashes between religious activists. What Davis argues for sixteenth-century France—namely, that "the occasion for most religious violence was during the time of religious worship or ritual and in the space which one or both groups were using for sacred purposes"[25]— applies equally to the bloody confrontations between Jews and Muslims worshipping at Temple Mount/Haram al-Sharif in Jerusalem; Muslim and Hindu riots in India triggered by Hindu nationalists who destroyed the Babri Mosque of Ayodhya to build the temple of the Lord Ram on that site in 1992; the storming of the Golden Temple of Amritsar, where Sikh extremists had taken refuge, and the retaliatory violence, including the assassination of Indira Gandhi by her Sikh bodyguards; and the "rites of violence" among religious and ethnic groups of South Asia examined by anthropologist Stanley Tambiah.[26]

FUNDAMENTALISMS AND VIOLENCE

A formidable subset of modern movements, groups, and organizations vying for cultural influence, social capital, and political power display a pronounced religious dimension. The vast and "incoherent" literature on religious violence fails to cohere, inter alia, on the question of whether religious movements of this power-seeking sort are more prone to violence than their secular counterparts. Much of the analysis of political Islam moves in this direction, for example.[27] A related question, dealt with effectively in Atalia Omer's opening chapter, is whether so-called "civilizational blocs," á la Huntington, replicate the contestation over sacred space and resources.

Another sprawling body of scholarship, dissecting "the radical right," includes authors who place at least part of the phenomenon—especially its millenarian wing—in the category of politicized religious violence. The Christian Identity movement is the most prominent and analyzed exemplar of what Michael Barkun calls the "racist right." These anti-government movements do not fall neatly into the categories of ecclesial polity; they tend to be less structured and less explicitly religious than cults or sects, for example, though some branches feature one or more of the following religious elements: a charismatic leader claiming direct divine authority or access to special revelation; religious or quasi-religious rituals and practices; a polemical claim to be the sacred remnant or true inheritor of the religious tradition; biblical proof-texts; and a social imaginary drenched in apocalyptic discourse.[28] The scholars of violence David Rapoport and Jeffrey Kaplan have toiled, with considerable success, to map the shadowy world of international terrorism, including its recent stage of inward-turning localism, what Kaplan calls "the new tribalism." Religious actors and themes inhabit corners of this world but do not define it.[29]

Less ambiguously, religious dynamics are at the core of the "power-seeking" movements and organizations labeled "fundamentalist." Do fundamentalisms "tend toward" violence? Are they *inherently* violent? Or, on the contrary, is it erroneous to posit a necessary connection between fundamentalism and violence? If the ambivalence thesis is correct, then to acknowledge fundamentalist movements as religious at their core does not necessarily imply that they are automatically violent as well. Yet fundamentalisms are viewed in some quarters as interpretations of religion that amplify its destructive power to such a degree as to mute its counterbalancing trajectory toward empathy and embrace. Thus the question becomes: if *religions* have the capacity to sublimate or spiritualize militancy, and even to channel energies toward nonviolent peacebuilding, do *fundamentalisms* have that capacity as well?

Scholars, as one might expect, disagree on this pivotal matter. One's response to the question depends on how one defines and assesses fundamentalism. (As one Baptist from Chicago complained: "How dare they compare us to the Ayatollah Khomeini? We do *not* store guns in the basement of Moody Bible School!") In 1988 the American Academy of Arts and Sciences launched a multi-year, interdisciplinary project on "global fundamentalisms," which ultimately involved more than seventy scholars and produced essays on dozens of movements around the world, published in five encyclopedia-sized volumes, followed by a co-authored capstone volume.[30] Even this massive project accounts only for a fraction of the books and articles on fundamentalisms, both tradition-specific and comparative, published since the term crept into the international lexicon in the late 1970s.[31] Among the more stimulating works are those that deconstruct the term, mount a critique of the naive or politically charged use of it, or offer theoretically interesting "explanations" of the phenomena to which it points, however inadequately.[32]

With respect to the responsible use of the term as a comparative construct, a degree of definitional consensus emerged among the fifteen or so core contributors to the Fundamentalism Project; they see "fundamentalism" as a modern religious logic and a mode of politicized religion available to conservative, orthodox, and traditional as well as "disembedded" practitioners (e.g., cyberspace jihadists, religiously illiterate youth). In this modest consensus view, "fundamentalism" functions in roughly the same way that "modernism," "liberalism," and other modern interpretive/behavioral schools represent their own distinctive reactions to the complex set of material and structural conditions and accompanying philosophies and worldviews which together constitute modernity/modernities.[33]

Ideologically, fundamentalist movements are both reactive and selective. They react primarily to the marginalization of religion—that is, to the displacement of "true religion" by nationalist political leaders, rival religious or ethnic groups, and scientific and cultural elites (feminists being a particular bête noir). And they select elements of both the religious tradition and techno-scientific modernity; once "updated" and instrumentalized, these retrieved practices, precepts, and doctrines constitute the foundation for an alternative worldview and set of institutions capable of challenging the hegemony of secularism. To this end fundamentalists also embrace *absolutism* and *dualism* as tactics of resistance. In an attempt to protect the holy book or hallowed tradition from the depredations of historical, literary, and scientific criticism—that is, from criteria of validity and ways of knowing that deny the transcendence of the sacred—fundamentalist leaders claim inerrancy and infallibility for their religious knowledge. The truth revealed in scriptures and traditions is neither contingent nor variable, but absolute. Each movement selects from its host religion certain scandalous doctrines (i.e., beliefs not easily reconcilable to scientific rationality, such as the imminent return of the Hidden Imam, the virgin birth of Christ, the divinity of the Lord Ram, the coming of the Messiah to restore and rule "the Whole Land of Israel"). These "supernatural dicta" they embellish, reify, and politicize. The confession of literal belief in these hard-to-swallow "fundamentals" sets the self-described true believers apart from the "Westoxicated" masses. Moreover, it marks them as members of a sacred remnant, an elect tribe commissioned to defend the sacred against an array of "reprobate," "fallen," and "polluted" coreligionists—and against the forces of evil that have corrupted the religious community.[34]

Already one recognizes the religious core of fundamentalisms, and evidence mounts of a propensity toward aggression, at the very least, as one considers which elements of the historic religious repertoire are chosen and how they are adapted. That is, the vulnerability of some religious actors to the seductions of an absolute truth and unambiguous moral clarity shapes *identity formation* over against a demonized other (Schwartz). Desire to manipulate the *awesome power of the numinous* (Rudolf Otto[35]) seems to serve an (often awkward) emulation of the idealized (secular) other—reflecting a grudging admiration which quickly curdles into resentment and will to power (Girard).

That the dominative power perceived within the sacred holds a perhaps irresistible appeal to the fundamentalist becomes ever more evident in the final ideological trait, namely, the retrieval and embellishment of the *millennial* or *apocalyptic* dimension of the religious imagination. By these two terms I mean to include the array of combustible eschatological doctrines, myths, and precepts embedded in the history and religious imagination of the major religious traditions of the world. Islam, Christianity, and Judaism all anticipate a dramatic moment in time, or beyond time, in which God will bring history to a just (and often bloody) culmination. In certain religious communities, such as Shi'ite Islam or evangelical Protestant Christianity, this expectation is highly pronounced and developed. (Indeed, the term "millennialism" refers to the prophesied thousand-year reign of the Christ, following his return in glory to defeat the Anti-Christ.) What is striking, however, is the recent retrieval of apocalyptic themes, images, and myths by fundamentalists from religious communities with a muted or underdeveloped strain of "end times" thought.[36]

How does this retrieval and embellishment of apocalyptic or millennial themes function within fundamentalist movements that seek recruits from among their orthodox coreligionists? Leaders seeking to form cadres for jihad, crusade, or anti-Muslim (or anti-Jewish, etc.) riots must convince the believer that violence is justified in religious terms. Luckily for them, most scriptures and traditions contain ambiguities and exceptions—including what might be called "emergency clauses." Thus the Granth Sahib, the holy book and living guru of the Sikhs, repeatedly enjoins forgiveness, compassion, and love toward enemies. It does, however, also contain an injunction calling believers to arms, if necessary, if the Sikh religion itself is threatened with extinction—a passage put to use by Jarnail Singh Bhindranwale, the Sikh militant who cut a swath of terror through the Punjab in the early 1980s.[37] Such "emergency clauses" can be found in the Qur'an, the Hebrew Bible, and the New Testament as well. And what better "emergency" than the advent of the predicted "dark age" or reign of evil that precedes the coming of the Messiah, the return of the Mahdi, the vindication of the righteous at God's hands? The fundamentalist invocation of "millennialism," in short, strives to convince believers that they are engaged not merely in a mundane struggle for territory or political power or financial gain, but in a cosmic war (Juergensmeyer), a battle for the soul and for the future of humanity. In such a context, violence is not only permissible; it is obligatory.

Case studies illustrating these dynamics proliferated after the Islamic revolution in Iran and, again, after 9/11.[38] While fundamentalists are not portrayed uniformly as irrational, much less pathological, most authors of the scholarly literature are not themselves fundamentalists (and many are not religious in any sense), and they leave little doubt that movements with a strong religious or "fundamentalist" element are indeed prone to pursue power through the barrel of a gun. Bruce Lawrence, an American scholar of Islam who authored a seminal analysis of comparative fundamentalisms that helped launch that sub-field of study, provides a more nuanced treatment.[39] *Shattering the Myth: Islam Beyond Violence* successfully steers a middle course between apologetics and polemics by demonstrating how the variability of Islam—the book considers and compares Islamist leaders and movements in Tunisia, Egypt and Syria, Indonesia and Malaysia—fosters a spectrum of Muslim attitudes toward violence, including strategies for averting the cyclical violence that feeds on patterns of revenge and retaliation.[40]

WEAK RELIGION

"Strong religion" as an interpretive approach, as we have seen, encompasses works that underscore the capacity of religions themselves to enjoin or legitimate deadly violence, as well as studies of movements, groups, networks, and organizations driven primarily by religious goals and dynamics. Yet few movements that foment violence are wholly or "purely" religious—including "strong religious" networks such as al-Qaeda, Hezbollah, or Gush Emunim. Most collectives are "mixed" in membership—composed, that is, of "true believers" as well as bureaucratic functionaries, armed militias, ideological fellow travelers, displaced youth, and bandwagon-jumpers.

Even more to the point is the fact that contemporary and recent reformist, revolutionary, fundamentalist, and other politicized social movements have emerged in the context of "hyper-modernity," an era characterized by unprecedented globalizing trends, ideologies of nationalism, and the omnipresent "totalizing" nation-state.[41] In this milieu, religion is seldom the sole player, and religious actors themselves are susceptible to worldviews and habits of mind embedded in structures and processes derived not from religious but from "worldly" (secular) trajectories. Accordingly, innumerable books and articles published over the last few decades modify the category "religious violence" by embedding religious agency within encompassing nationalist and ethnic narratives. I call these works examples of a "weak religion" interpretive approach, because many of these accounts subordinate the religious motivations and dynamics of violence-prone actors (inaccurately, in some cases) and also because a recurrent explanation for the "dependent" role of religious actors within a "mixed" movement, or for the mixed motives of religious actors themselves, is the vulnerability of religious leaders and institutions to the manipulations of state, nationalist, and ethnic forces in their societies. The religious element, that is, is relatively "weak."

Two clarifications are in order. First, rather than construe "strong" and "weak" religious presences as two wholly separate, isolated realities, as if some movements are always or essentially "purely" religious, and others always or essentially diluted, it is more accurate to use these terms as indicators of points on a continuum of configurations across which religious actors move over time (in different directions). The interesting question is not (only): Which movements are strong or weak at a given time? Rather, it is: Under what conditions are religious actors (leaders, individuals, movements, institutions) more and less vulnerable to nonreligious forces?

Second, the field of religious violence studies is evolving (perhaps an optimistic choice of words) on this interpretive issue. Accordingly, several key authors have written both in the "strong religion" *and* the "weak religion" mode. Juergensmeyer's *Terror in the Mind of God* falls more squarely in the former, for example, while his other major work on religious violence, *The New Cold War?: Religious Nationalism Confronts the Secular State* (1993)—updated and reissued in 2008 under the title *Global Rebellion: Religious Challenges to the Secular State, from Christian Militias to Al Qaeda*—is premised on the claim that militant religious actors of the twentieth century have adopted the modern ideology of nationalism from their secular counterparts as their political vehicle of choice. While Juergensmeyer does not call these religious actors "weak," exactly, three factors suggest their continuing vulnerability to being defined by their putative adversaries: their reliance on a historically secular (i.e., alien) model of political and social order; their serial failures to transform it into an effective religious model (with the debatable case of Iran being the major possible exception); and the "mixed" (religious and vaguely religious or even irreligious) character of these political movements.

Juergensmeyer's approach, while persuasive in some respects, attempts to squeeze all major violent religious actors into one procrustean category, "religious nationalism," thereby eliminating from view the important and numerous militant religious actors who decry "the idolatry of the state" into which their coreligionists have fallen, and/or who offer a different political model (e.g., the restored caliphate) around which to rally the troops.[42] The term "fundamentalism" has its own deficiencies, but it does encompass a broader range of "militantly antisecularist and antimodernist" political options. In *Shattering the Myth*, Lawrence attempts to settle this debate by presenting "religious nationalism" as a subset or species of the genus "fundamentalisms."[43]

RELIGION, NATIONALISM, AND VIOLENCE

One of the themes of the vast theoretical literature on nationalism is the exclusionary nature of the process of national formation, which is linked to the sacralization of the nation itself.[44] Befitting an interpretive approach to religious violence that emphasizes the susceptibility of religious militants to manipulation by nationalists, several recent studies focus on the pattern whereby, as the political scientist Scott Hibbard puts it, "ostensibly secular state actors sought to coopt the ideas and activists associated with religious fundamentalisms."[45] A small mountain of literature, much of it by social scientists, explores how politicians recruited religious actors in Sudan, Sri Lanka, Iran, Israel, and elsewhere to do their "dirty work," including the violent persecution of religious and ethnic minorities.[46] Hibbard's own recent book, *Religious Politics and Secular States: Egypt, India, and the United States*, adds a new wrinkle to this interpretive camp by focusing on state actors and on the partly unintended consequences of their machinations. "The invocation of illiberal renderings of religious tradition provided state actors with a cultural basis for their claims to rule and an effective means of mobilizing popular sentiment behind traditional patterns of social and political hierarchy," he writes. As a result, "secular norms were displaced by exclusive forms of religious politics."[47] "Weak" religion gains a boost of power, welcome or not, in this transition.

A subtle and provocative variation on the "religious versus secular" theme places aggressive religious and secular actors in the same interpretive frame. For example, Joyce Dalsheim's analysis of right-wing religious settlers in Gaza and their leftist and secular antagonists situates these opposing camps within a broader account of the social and cultural work they inadvertently collude to accomplish. Their antagonism "reinscribes existing categories, setting the boundaries of ways of being, and the limits of public debate," she writes. "The appearance of incommensurable discourses in conflict conceals continuities and commonalities among these Israelis who are all part of the settler project in Palestine and who are all subject to the disciplining processes of state rationality."[48]

Further down the road to crediting religious agency in nationalist campaigns are studies in which the term "religious nationalism" appears prominently. The subcontinent of India is the locus of many such organizations and movements.[49] The anthropologist and professor of comparative religion Peter van der Veer calls attention to the nationalist appropriation of widespread religious practices such as the ritual performance of pilgrimage, as well as traditional discourse on the body and the family, for the purpose of nation building in India and Sri Lanka. While van der Veer acknowledges the complicity of religious actors in this appropriation, he emphasizes the priority granted by them to nationalist discourse:

> Nationalism reinterprets religious discourse on gender, on the dialectics of masculinity and femininity, to convey a sense of belonging to the nation. It appropriates the disciplinary practices, connected to the theme of the management of desire, in the service of its own political project. Nationalism also grafts its notion of territory onto religious notions of sacred space. It develops a ritual repertoire, based on early rituals of pilgrimage, to sanctify the continuity of the territory.[50]

Indeed, a major theme in the literature argues that the manipulation of South Asian communities of practice by colonial and imperial powers left them in a "weakened" religious condition—weakened, in no small part, by their reduction to the status of a "religion" differentiated from the political authority and from other local or regional communities of practice. Harjot Oberoi traces this disintegrative process in Sikhism, which ultimately led to the rupture of the Sikh community, the construction of religious boundaries, the (re)valorization of a warrior caste, and vicious intra- as well as inter-religious conflict.[51]

ETHNO-RELIGIOUS VIOLENCE

The relationship between ethnicity and religion can become a vicious circle. On the one hand, religions yield their independence and autonomy when they sacralize ethnic identity. On the other, as David Little observes, "religiously shaded 'ethnic tension' appears to be latent in the very process of ethnic classification."[52] Whenever supposedly "primordial" ties of blood, land, and birth assume a transcendent dimension, whenever religious authorities invoke the idea of a 'chosen people,' they thereby sanctify the quest for ethnic hegemony and appear to provide justification for engaging in deadly violence against rival ethnic groups. Folk religion—"the religion of the people"—therefore claims a special relationship to, or authority over, national consciousness.

The reverse is also true: ethnonationalist leaders can and do exploit a religion's identification with "the people," especially at times when a heightened perception of threat destabilizes society. According to Michael Sells, the Bosnian War of 1992 to 1995 featured the perpetration of religiously justified violence elicited by ethnonationalist extremism. In his riveting account, *The Bridge Betrayed*, Sells demonstrates how the Serbian politician Slobodan Milosevic manipulated the folk and nationalist elements of the Serbian Orthodox Church, turning potential critics into allies, or silent bystanders, as he launched a campaign of ethnic cleansing. Milosevic orchestrated the events of June 28, 1989, for example, when the Serb Orthodox patriarch led a procession of priests in scarlet robes marking the death of Prince Lazar, the hero of Serb nationalist mythology, at the battle of Kosovo. Nearby, on the plain of Gazimestan, where the battle had taken place, a vast crowd gathered. Milosevic mounted a stage with a backdrop depicting peonies, the flower that symbolized the blood of Lazar, and an Orthodox cross at each of its four corners. (The symbol stands for the slogan "Only Unity Saves the Serb.") The crowd chanted "Kosovo is Serb" and "We love you, Slobodan, because you hate the Muslims." The former communist "had adroitly transformed himself into an ethnoreligious nationalist," Sells comments, and within three years, those who had directed the "festivities" at Gazimestan were organizing unspeakable depravities against Bosnian civilians.[53]

Analysts who downplay the presence of religious elements in the Bosnian War point to the secular orientation of the generals or to the manipulation of naive or weak religious officials. One misreads the religious sensibilities of a people, however, by judging from the behavior of their military or government leaders. "The genocide in Bosnia . . . was religiously motivated and religiously justified," Sells argues. "Religious symbols . . . myths of origin (pure Serb race), symbols of passion (Lazar's death), and eschatological longings (the resurrection of Lazar) were used by religious nationalists to create a reduplicating Milos Obilic [the assassin of Sultan Murat], avenging himself on the Christ killer, the race traitor, the alien, and, ironically, the falsely accused 'fundamentalist' next door." When the Serb and Croat armies systematically targeted libraries, museums, mosques, and churches, they were destroying the evidence of five hundred years of inter-religious life in Bosnia. To evaluate such acts as being religious in motivation and character is not to deny the explanatory power of political and economic analyses. Neither is it to equate "genuine" religious behavior with moral atrocities. Still less is it to valorize the acts in question as "holy" by calling them religious. Unfortunately, the numinous power of the sacred—accessible to human beings through multivalent symbols, elastic myths, and ambiguous rituals and conveyed through the imperfect channels of intellect, will, and emotion—does not come accompanied by a moral compass. The seeds of Serbian, Croatian, and Bosnian religiosity were not stamped out under communist rule, even among the so-called secularized masses; but neither were they nurtured. Scattered and left untended, they were eventually planted in the crude soil of ethno-nationalism. "The human capacity for acknowledging religiously based evil," Sells concludes, "is particularly tenuous."[54]

In some prominent accounts of deadly conflict, religion is *rendered* "weak" by methods and analyses that artificially subordinate religious motivations to economic, political, and other factors. Such reductionist accounts distort the role of religion by failing to perceive or "measure" religious agency and give an accurate account of its subtle power. Religious dimensions of violence, in short, should not be evaluated as "weak" simply because they escape certain kinds of social scientific methods of inquiry.[55]

Pathological Religion

Prior to 9/11 Charles B. Strozier, a practicing psychoanalyst and currently a professor of history and the director of the Center on Terrorism at the John Jay College, CUNY, was not exactly a voice crying in the wilderness; from the publication of Freud's *The Future of an Illusion* (1927), religion has been pathologized by a long and distinguished line of psychoanalysts, social psychologists and social scientists more generally. Freud himself saw "clinging to religion" as a neurotic regression to satisfy infantile desires and needs. Developing insights of Freud and his successors, social philosophers and critical theorists such as Michel Foucault and Judith Butler have presented ideas associated with the religious imagination as formative of a subject who emerges through "passionate attachment" to his or her own subordination.[56] But Strozier, working at times with the psychiatrist Robert Jay Lifton, went a step further. While working with fundamentalist Christians imprisoned at Riker's Island and preparing his 1994 book, *Apocalypse: On the Psychology of Fundamentalism in America*, Strozier read the growing literatures on fundamentalism and modern apocalyptic movements though the lens of psychoanalytic theory.[57]

Around that time, a group of social psychologists, clinical psychologists, psychoanalysts, and cultural historians began to explore what they call *The Fundamentalist Mindset*.[58] While the editors of the volume claim they do not intend to present fundamentalism within a deviant frame, they nonetheless draw a straight line between the mindset and a psychological disposition toward violence—and terrorism. In fact, the book details the profile not of a religious logic, but a patho-logic. The true believers, in short, suffer from the symptoms of a mental disorder, an identifiable disease. Strozier and coauthor Katharine Boyd contend that "the fundamentalist mindset, wherever it occurs, is composed of distinct characteristics, including dualistic thinking; paranoia and rage in a group context; an apocalyptic orientation that incorporates distinct perspectives on time, death, and violence; a relationship to charismatic leadership; and a totalized conversion experience."[59] In her essay "The Unsettling of the Fundamentalist Mindset," Lee Quinby develops the notion of an "apocalyptic subjectivity" to which fundamentalists are prone—"a psychology subjected to the teachings and the values found in the Book of Revelation." Foundational to that psychology, Quinby asserts, are "gender dualism, messianic rescue, and obedience to authority."[60]

This interpretive approach turns both the strong and weak religion camps on their heads, in that it sees militant religion (many varieties of which are included in their analyses) as the distilled essence of a mindset discoverable in secular as well as strictly religious actors. Thus the authors committed to the "pathological religion" thesis attempt to make a case for the recurrent manifestation of a paranoid habit of mind, shaped by the alienating experience of humiliation (or close identification with the humiliated), that can be perceived not only in individuals but in bloodthirsty movements, groups, and parties ranging from the Jacobins of 1789 to the genocidaires of twentieth-century Nazi Germany, Rwanda, and Cambodia. They cite theorists and theories of violence such as Jerrold Post's typology of terrorist movements, Vamik Volkan's conceptualization of ethnic violence around concepts of a "chosen trauma" and a "chosen glory," and the work of Melanie Klein, Otto Kernberg, and Wilfrid Bion on what might be called the pathology of ideology. In Strozier and company's rendering, fundamentalism is not only religious, but secular, not only modern but primordial, ancient, and medieval—and it is exceedingly violent in its trajectory and telos. This conceptual slipperiness is justified by reference to the supposed "benefits of ambiguity, which makes for a larger conceptual umbrella . . ."[61]

Yet such ambiguity invites chaos as well as creativity. Not least, it erodes the theoretical foundations supporting an empirically accurate portrait of fundamentalists as unmistakably modern, selective retrievers of the elements of religious traditions, including apocalyptic and dualist habits of mind, for the purpose of constructing religiously nuanced alternatives to an overweening, hostile, secular political and cultural milieu. *One* of the alternatives is the creation of a theocratic state or transnational community by means of extremist violence, including terrorism. But there are literally hundreds of millions of "true believers" within global religious communities who have adopted the fundamentalist mode of religiosity while rejecting any form of terrorism or violent apocalypticism. Confident in their use of synecdoche, however, the "pathological religion" camp chooses the extreme point on the spectrum as the representative of the whole. They fail to explain why the vast majority of the world's fundamentalists *do not* take up the sword. In sum, the phenomenon under scrutiny in *The Fundamentalist Mindset* might more coherently be called *The Extremist Mindset*, toward which a subset of religious fundamentalists arguably are drawn.

An interpretive approach informed by a psychological perspective need not be reductive or unhelpfully destabilizing of even elastic definitions of religion, as the psychoanalyst Sudhir Kakar demonstrates in his nuanced study of communal conflict in India, *The Colors of Violence*.[62] An extended case study of the Hindu-Muslim riots in Hyderabad in 1990, triggered by the Babri Masjid conflict, the argument unfolds through consideration of information collected from interpretive interviews with both Hindu and Muslim leaders of violent mobs as well as with the victims of violence. The psychological mechanism that Kakar most often uncovers is Freudian "projection," whereby one ethno-religious group, employing a kind of reverse mimetic desire, projects its own insecurities and self-doubt upon the reified other (e.g., Hindus characterize Muslims as "sexual animals," "polluted," "dirty," etc.). The displacement and feelings of alienation that invariably accompany rapid but haphazard modernization and urbanization, Kakar suggests, increase the appeal of membership in groups with absolute value systems and with little tolerance for deviation from their norms. Yet Kakar, observing with a critical empathy, refrains from equating membership in such communities with a psychological disorder.

Conclusion: The Promise of Coherence

My abbreviated and inevitably selective review of the field raises the question of what the field should be called. I have used the term "religious violence" to underscore my conviction that religion is indeed "something apart" from other modes of belief, behavior, practice, and social organization, and that it can generate violence through (always internally contested) self-understandings excavated from the depths of an identifiably religious logic and religious dynamics. Yet I also resist—and the evidence does not support—the automatic identification of a fundamentalist or militant religious orientation, much less any intense religious sensibility whatsoever, with an inclination toward deadly violence, or with a deviant or pathological mindset (apart from the argument that *any* act of violation of another person might justifiably be considered "deviant"). The paired words "religious violence," however, might create the unfortunate (to my mind) impression of a natural connection between the two.

And so we study "religion and violence," and therefore ponder the question: When does religion become violent? The "strong religion" line of analysis reviewed above, granting decisive agency to the religious actors themselves, points to the calculations of religious leaders and their reading of the external environment. Is the struggle perceived as a defense of basic identity and dignity? Is the religious community threatened with extinction if it does not take up arms? Are there certain religious values that take priority over life itself (e.g., witness to the truth, the protection of innocents, etc.) and are these values at risk in the conflict? Is this, then, the time to retrieve elements of the religious imagination, scriptures, traditions that might transform worshippers into warriors?[63]

The "weak religion" line of analysis points, instead, to exogenous triggers, especially the encroachments of secular actors, the compelling identification of blood, land, birth with "sacred priorities." Yet it does not ignore the contributions of structural or psychological aspects of the religious community itself. An ecclesiology that holds church and nation to be ontologically united, divinely twinned and thus inseparable; a lack of moral formation and religious instruction (catechetical training, preaching, practices, etc.) that cultivates a prophetic voice and fosters a measure of independence from external influences; a failure of religious leadership—such conditions, owing to internal dynamics, increase the vulnerability of the religious group or community to intervention by unsympathetic outsiders.

Insights from the still-evolving "pathology" camp, if not yet developed into a coherent and satisfying master narrative of religion and violence, lend depth and nuance to our understanding of the strong-to-weak spectrum.

In the opening of this chapter I described the "avalanche" of publications that have issued forth over the last three or four decades as "incoherent." Yet there is much to be admired in the sheer volume of data collected and concepts developed to order it. In addition, one can perceive distinct lines of analysis and interpretive "schools" taking shape. This amounts, one might become convinced, to a mighty groaning toward coherence. Can a first sustained attempt at a comprehensive general theory of religious violence be far off?[64]

Notes

1. *Israeli Assassins: Yigal Amir* (General Books LLC, 2010); Jayne Seminare Docherty, *Learning Lessons from Waco: When the Parties Bring Their Gods to the Negotiation Table* (Syracuse, NY: Syracuse University Press, 2001); Lou Michel and Dan Herbeck, *American Terrorist Timothy McVeigh and the Tragedy at Oklahoma City* (New York: HarperCollins, 2002); Christophe Jaffrelot, *The Hindu Nationalist Movement in India* (New York: Columbia University Press, 1993); Ian S. Lustick, *For the Land and the Lord: Jewish Fundamentalism in Israel* (New York: Council on Foreign Relations Press, 1988); Cynthia Keppley Mahmood, *Fighting for Faith and Nation: Dialogues with Sikh Militants* (Philadelphia: University of Pennsylvania Press, 1996).

2. See, for example, William T. Cavanaugh, *The Myth of Religious Violence: Secular Ideology and the Roots of Modern Conflict* (New York: Oxford University Press, 2009). Substantive definitions of religion, Cavanaugh claims, posit a transhistorical and transcultural essence of religion and foster the notion that a special kind of violence exists in the world, one that is exceptionally deadly, dangerous, and immune in its virulence from the limits imposed by ordinary strategic, economic, and political considerations. This notion is false, however, Cavanaugh argues, and the distinction it underwrites between secular and religious violence is "unhelpful, misleading and mystifying" and "should be avoided altogether." Public-private, religion-politics, and church-state dichotomies, rather than describing reality as it is, justify a certain configuration of power. In the early modern period, for example, they provided the rationale for the state's colonial expansion and claim to a monopoly over internal violence. "To construe Christianity as a religion, therefore, helps to separate loyalty to God from one's public loyalty to the nation-state," Cavanaugh writes. "The idea that religion has a tendency to cause violence—and is therefore to be removed from public power—is one type of this essentialist construction of religion" (9).

3. To take merely a handful of the dozens of examples: Daniel Benjamin and Steven Simon, *The Age of Sacred Terror: Radical Islam's War Against America* (New York: Random House, 2003); John K. Cooley, *Unholy Wars: Afghanistan, America and International Terrorism* (London: Pluto Press, 2000); Ron E. Hassner, *War on Sacred Grounds* (Ithaca, NY: Cornell University Press, 2009); Karen Armstrong, *The Battle for God* (New York: Alfred A. Knopf, 2000); John L. Esposito, *Unholy War: Terror in the Name of Islam* (Oxford University Press, 2002); Lloyd Steffen, *The Demonic Turn: The Power of Religion to Inspire or Restrain Violence* (Cleveland: The Pilgrim Press, 2003).

4. Elizabeth Shakman Hurd, *The Politics of Secularism in International Relations* (Princeton: Princeton University Press, 2008); R. Scott Appleby, "What's in a Name? 'Fundamentalism' and the Discourse about Religion," in *How Should We Talk about Religion?: Perspectives, Contexts, Particularities*, ed. James Boyd White (Notre Dame, IN: University of Notre Dame Press, 2006), 87–103.

5. See, for example, Andrew R. Murphy, ed., *The Blackwell Companion to Religion and Violence*, Blackwell Companions to Religion (West Sussex: Wiley-Blackwell, 2011); and, Mark Juergensmeyer and Margo Kitts, eds., *Princeton Readings in Religion and Violence* (Princeton: Princeton University Press, 2011).

6. In the current chapter I use the term "strong religion" more broadly than my co-authors and I did in a book of the same name, where it referred only to the form of "strong religion" known as "fundamentalism": Gabriel A. Almond, R. Scott Appleby, and Emmanuel Sivan, *Strong Religion: The Rise of Fundamentalisms Around the World* (Chicago: University of Chicago Press, 2003).

7. Andrew McDonald [William Pierce], *The Turner Diaries* (New York: Barricade Books, 1996, first published 1978 by National Alliance Vanguard Books). *The Turner Diaries* is written in the form of an ideological tract posing as a novel. Through its story of a heroic band of freedom fighters enduring an against-all-odds war against a dictatorial government, Pierce incited the apocalyptic and excessively violent imaginations of a cadre of activists who established clandestine networks and militias dedicated to opposing a hegemonic secularism imposed on America by a conspiracy of Jews and liberals bent on undermining the nation's Christian foundation. Sound familiar?

8. Mark Juergensmeyer, *Terror in the Mind of God: The Global Rise of Religious Violence* (Berkeley: University of California Press, 2000), 146.

9. "To live in a state of war is to live in a world in which individuals know who they are, why they have suffered, by whose hand they have been humiliated, and at what expense they have persevered. The concept of war provides cosmology, history, and eschatology and offers the reins of political control. Perhaps most important, it holds out the hope of victory and the means to achieve it. In the images of cosmic war this victorious triumph is a grand moment of social and personal transformation, transcending all worldly limitations. One does not easily abandon such expectations" (Juergensmeyer, *Terror*, 155).

10. Juergensmeyer, *Terror*, 150. Doubts about the religious motivations of some of his central subjects do not deter Juergensmeyer from including them in the pantheon of "religious extremists." Oklahoma City bomber McVeigh, one of the exemplars of *Terror in the Mind of God*, acknowledged that he was an agnostic, for example: "In his letter, McVeigh said he was an agnostic but that he would 'improvise, adapt and overcome,' if it turned out there was an afterlife. 'If I'm going to hell,' he wrote, 'I'm gonna have a lot of company.' His body is to be cremated and his ashes scattered in a secret location," Julian Borger, "McVeigh faces day of reckoning," *Guardian*, June 11, 2001; "McVeigh is agnostic. He doesn't believe in God, but he won't rule out the possibility," noted McVeigh biographer Lou Michel. "I asked him, 'What if there is a heaven and hell?' He said that once he crosses over the line from life to death, if there is something on the other side, he will—and this is using his military jargon—'adapt, improvise, and overcome.' Death to him is all part of the adventure," "Authors Lou Michel and Dan Herbeck on their book about Timothy McVeigh," interview, *CNN.com*, April 4, 2001, http://www.cnn.com/COMMUNITY/transcripts/2001/04/04/michelherbeck/.

11. See David G. Bromley and J. Gordon Melton, eds., *Cults, Religion and Violence* (Cambridge: Cambridge University Press, 2002).

12. Michael Barkun, "Militias, Christian Identity and the Radical Right," *The Christian Century* 112, no. 23 (1995): 739. "Survivalists, militias, Klans, neo-Nazis, Christian Identity churches, skinheads and Christian constitutionalists do not inhabit neatly defined segments. Their styles of rhetoric, dress and symbolism are not mutually exclusive, and often interpenetrate and overlap. A person may be a survivalist Christian Identity believer who likes skinhead music, has a fondness for Nazi symbols, and is sympathetic to Christian constitutional arguments. Another participant in the movement might accept some parts of this world but not others. The memberships of right-wing organizations often overlap, and the groups themselves (like those on the far left) are often riven by factionalism and

internal conflicts," Barkun explains (739). "It is not surprising, therefore, that months after the Oklahoma City bombing journalists still have difficulty describing suspect Timothy McVeigh's relationship to the Michigan Militia and to Christian Identity groups. Within the subculture, individuals migrate easily from group to group, sometimes appropriating one set of ideas and symbols, sometimes another, sometimes several simultaneously. It is not clear whether Timothy McVeigh had Christian Identity associations. . ."

13. Kevin Schilbrack, "Religions: Are There Any?" *Journal of the American Academy of Religion* 78, no. 4 (2010): 1113.

14. R. Scott Appleby, *The Ambivalence of the Sacred: Religion, Violence, and Reconciliation* (Lanham, MD: Rowman and Littlefield, 2000).

15. For examples, see Appleby, *Ambivalence*, 11–12; Michael K. Jerryson and Mark Juergensmeyer, eds., *Buddhist Warfare* (New York: Oxford University Press, 2010); Oliver McTernan, *Violence in God's Name: Religion in an Age of Conflict* (London: Darton, Longman and Todd, 2003), 45–76; J. Harold Ellens, ed., *The Destructive Power of Religion: Violence in Judaism, Christianity and Islam*, vol. 1, *Sacred Scriptures, Ideology and Violence* (Westport, CT: Prager, 2004).

16. John Darby, *The Effects of Violence on Peace Processes* (Washington, DC: US Institute of Peace Press, 2001), 54–57; Steven J. Stedman, "Spoiler Problems in Peace Processes," *International Security* 22, no. 2 (1997): 5–53.

17. René Girard, *Violence and the Sacred*, trans. Patrick Gregory (Baltimore: Johns Hopkins University Press, 1977), 36.

18. Girard, *Violence*, 37.

19. Charles Selengut, *Sacred Fury: Understanding Religious Violence* (Walnut Creek, CA: AltaMira Press, 2003), 54. On Girard and religion as a "stupendous collective deception," see also David Rapoport, "Some General Observations on Religion and Violence," in *Violence and the Sacred in the Modern World*, ed. Mark Juergensmeyer (London: Frank Cass, 1991), 118–140.

20. Gil Bailie, *Violence Unveiled: Humanity at the Crossroads* (New York: Crossroad, 1995), 7.

21. Selengut, *Sacred Fury*, 54; for his discussion of Meir Kahane's exploitation of Israeli Jewish secular and religious extremism, see *Sacred Fury*, 55–69.

22. Hugh Nicholson, *Comparative Theology and the Problem of Religious Rivalry* (New York: Oxford University Press, 2011).

23. Regina M. Schwartz, *The Curse of Cain: The Violent Legacy of Monotheism* (Chicago: University of Chicago Press, 1997), 23.

24. Natalie Zemon Davis, "The Rites of Violence," *Past and Present* 59 (1973): 53.

25. Davis, "The Rites of Violence," 72.

26. Stanley J. Tambiah, *Leveling Crowds: Ethnonationalist Conflicts and Collective Violence in South Asia* (Berkeley, CA: University of California Press, 1997).

27. Michael Mazarr, *Unmodern Men in the Modern World: Radical Islam, Terrorism, and the War on Terror* (New York: Cambridge University Press, 2007); Gilles Kepel, *Muslim Extremism in Egypt: The Prophet and the Pharoah* (Berkeley, CA: University of California Press, 1993); Emmanuel Sivan, *Radical Islam: Medieval Theology and Modern Politics* (New Haven, CT: Yale University Press, 1990); Daniel Pipes, *In the Path of God: Islam and Political Power* (New York: Basic Books, 1983); Bassam Tibi, *The Crisis of Modern Islam* (Salt Lake City: University of Utah Press, 1988).

28. Michael Barkun, *Religion and the Racist Right: The Origins of the Christian Identity Movement*, rev. ed. (1994; repr., Chapel Hill, NC: University of North Carolina Press, 1997);

see also Jeffrey Kaplan, *Radical Religion in America: Millenarian Movements from the Far Right to the Children of Noah* (Syracuse, NY: Syracuse University Press, 1997).

29. Jeffrey Kaplan, *Terrorist Groups and the New Tribalism: Terrorism's Fifth Wave* (2010; repr., London: Routledge, 2012); David C. Rapoport, "Four Waves of Modern Terrorism," in *Attacking Terrorism: Elements of a Grand Strategy*, ed. Audrey Kurth Cronin and James M. Ludes (Washington, DC: Georgetown University Press, 2004), 46–73; Rapoport, "The Four Waves of Rebel Terror and September 11," *Anthropoetics* 8, no. 1 (2002).

30. Martin E. Marty and R. Scott Appleby, eds., *Fundamentalisms Observed* (Chicago: University of Chicago Press, 1991); *Fundamentalisms and the State: Remaking Polities, Economies, and Militance* (Chicago: University of Chicago Press, 1993); *Fundamentalisms and Society: Remaking the Sciences, the Family and Education* (Chicago: University of Chicago Press, 1993); *Accounting for Fundamentalisms: The Dynamic Character of Movements* (Chicago: University of Chicago Press, 1994) and *Fundamentalisms Comprehended* (Chicago: University of Chicago Press, 1995); Almond, Appleby, and Sivan, *Strong Religion*.

31. Representative titles include: R. Hrair Dekmejian, *Islam in Revolution: Fundamentalism in the Arab World* (Syracuse, NY: Syracuse University Press, 1985); George M. Marsden, *Fundamentalism and American Culture: The Shaping of Twentieth Century Evangelicalism, 1870–1925* (New York: Oxford University Press, 1980); Niels C. Nielsen Jr., *Fundamentalism, Mythos, and World Religions* (Albany, NY: State University of New York Press, 1993); Martin Riesebrodt, *Pious Passion: The Emergence of Modern Fundamentalism in the United States and Iran*, trans. Don Reneau (Berkeley, CA: University of California Press, 1993); Ernest R. Sandeen, *The Roots of Fundamentalism: British and American Millenarianism 1800–1930* (Chicago: University of Chicago Press, 1970); Ali Tariq, *The Clash of Fundamentalisms: Crusades, Jihads, and Modernity* (London: Verso, 2002).

32. See, for example, Mahmood Mamdani, *Good Muslim, Bad Muslim: America, the Cold War, and the Roots of Terrorism* (New York: Doubleday, 2004); Olivier Roy, *Holy Ignorance: When Religion and Culture Part Ways* (New York: Columbia University Press, 2010); Bruce Lincoln, *Holy Terrors: Thinking About Religion after September 11* (Chicago: University of Chicago Press, 2002).

33. R. Scott Appleby, "Rethinking Fundamentalism in a Secular Age," in *Rethinking Secularism*, ed. Craig Calhoun, Mark Juergensmeyer, and Jonathan VanAntwerpen (New York: Oxford University Press, 2011), 225–247.

34. Appleby, "Rethinking Fundamentalism," 230–233.

35. Rudolf Otto, *The Idea of the Holy*, trans. John W. Harvey (1914; repr., New York: Oxford University Press, 1958).

36. Barbara Freyer Stowasser, "A Time to Reap," *Middle East Studies Association Bulletin* 34, no. 1 (2000): 1–13.

37. T. N. Madan, "The Double-Edged Sword: Fundamentalism and the Sikh Religious Tradition," in *Fundamentalisms Observed*, ed. Marty and Appleby, 598.

38. For examples, see Emmanuel Sivan and Menachem Friedman, eds., *Religious Radicalism and Politics in the Middle East* (New York: State University of New York Press, 1990); Laurence J. Silberstein, ed., *Jewish Fundamentalism in Comparative Perspective: Religion, Ideology, and the Crisis of Modernity* (New York: New York University Press, 1993); Samuel Heilman, *Defenders of the Faith: Inside Ultra-Orthodox Jewry* (New York: Schocken Books, 1992); Olivier Roy, *Islam and Resistance in Afghanistan* (Cambridge: Cambridge University Press, 1985). Ahmed Rashid, *Taliban: Militant Islam, Oil, and Fundamentalism*

in Central Asia (New Haven, CT: Yale University Press, 2000); Mansoor Moaddel and Kamran Talattof, eds., *Modernist and Fundamentalist Debates in Islam: A Reader* (New York: Palgrave MacMillan, 2002); Lawrence Wright, *The Looming Tower: Al-Qaeda and the Road to 9/11* (New York: Vintage Books, 2006).

39. Bruce B. Lawrence, *Defenders of God: The Fundamentalist Revolt against the Modern Age* (San Francisco: Harper and Row, 1989).

40. Bruce B. Lawrence, *Shattering the Myth: Islam Beyond Violence* (Princeton, NJ: Princeton University Press, 1998).

41. On "late modernity," see Anthony Giddens, *The Nation-State and Violence* (Cambridge: Polity, 1985); Giddens, *Modernity and Self-Identity: Self and Society in the Late Modern Age* (Stanford, CA: Stanford University Press, 1991); and Giddens, *The Consequences of Modernity* (Cambridge: Polity, 1990.)

42. A. Rashied Omar, "Religion, Violence and the State: A dialogical encounter between activists and scholars" (PhD diss., University of Cape Town, 2006).

43. Lawrence, *Shattering the Myth*, 51–106.

44. See, for example, Anthony Smith, "The Sacred Dimension of Nationalism," *Millennium Journal of International Studies* 29, no. 3 (2000); Anthony Marx, *Faith in Nation: Exclusionary Origins of Nationalism* (New York: Oxford University Press, 2003), 197.

45. Scott W. Hibbard, *Religious Politics and Secular States: Egypt, India, and the United States* (Baltimore: Johns Hopkins University Press, 2010), 4.

46. Seyyed Vali Reza Nasr, *Islamic Leviathan: Islam and the Making of State Power* (New York: Oxford University Press, 2001); Francis Deng, *War of Visions: Conflict Identities in Sudan* (Washington, DC: Brookings Institution Press, 1995); David Little, *Sri Lanka: The Invention of Enmity* (Washington, DC: US Institute of Peace, 1994); Mark Tessler, "The Origins of Popular Support for Islamist Movements," in *Islam, Democracy, and the State in North Africa,* ed. John Entelis (Bloomington, IN: Indiana University Press, 1997), 93–126.

47. Hibbard, *Religious Politics and Secular States*, xii.

48. Joyce Dalsheim, *Unsettling Gaza: Secular Liberalism, Radical Religion, and the Israeli Settlement Project* (New York: Oxford University Press, 2011), 5.

49. For an influential analysis of communal violence in India that locates religious vulnerability and volatility to the lack of inter-religious civic and associational life, see Ashutosh Varshney, *Ethnic Conflict and Civic Life: Hindus and Muslims in India* (New Haven, CT: Yale University Press, 2002).

50. Peter van der Veer, *Religious Nationalism: Hindus and Muslims in India* (Berkeley, CA: University of California Press, 1994), 201–202.

51. Harjot Oberoi, *The Construction of Religious Boundaries: Culture, Identity, and Diversity in the Sikh Tradition* (Chicago: University of Chicago Press, 1994). See other influential post-colonial critical studies of religion and nationalisms in India and Asia, such as Gayatri Chakrabarty Spivak, *Nationalism and the Imagination* (London: Seagull Books, 2010) and Peter van der Veer, *Imperial Encounters: Religion and Modernity in India and Britain* (Princeton, NJ: Princeton University Press, 2001).

52. David Little, "Introduction," in *Religion and Nationalism in Iraq: A Comparative Perspective*, ed. David Little and Donald K. Swearer (Cambridge, MA: Harvard University Press, 2007), 9.

53. Michael Sells, *The Bridge Betrayed: Religion and Genocide in Bosnia* (Berkeley, CA: University of California Press, 1996), 123.

54. Sells, *The Bridge Betrayed*, 123. See also Appleby, *Ambivalence of the Sacred*, 69–72.
55. See, for example: James D. Fearon and David D. Laitin, "Ethnicity, Insurgency, and Civil War," *American Political Science Review* 97, no. 1 (2003): 75–90; Paul Collier, "Economic Causes of Civil Conflict and Their Implications for Policy," in *Turbulent Peace: The Challenges of Managing International Conflict*, ed. Chester A. Crocker, Fen Osler Hampson, and Pamela Aall (Washington, DC: US Institute of Peace Press, 2001), 143–162; Ted Robert Gurr (with contributors), *Minorities at Risk: A Global View of Ethnopolitical Conflict* (Washington, DC: US Institute of Peace Press, 1993).
56. Judith Butler, *The Psychic Life of Power* (Stanford, CA: Stanford University Press, 1997), 6–7; Michel Foucault, "Sexuality and Power" (1978) in *Religion and Culture: Michel Foucault*, ed. Jeremy R. Carette (New York: Routledge, 1999).
57. Charles B. Strozier, *Apocalypse: On the Psychology of Fundamentalism in America* (Boston: Beacon Press, 1994).
58. Charles B. Strozier, David M. Terman, and James W. Jones, eds. (with Katharine A. Boyd), *The Fundamentalist Mindset: Psychological Perspectives on Religion, Violence, and History* (New York: Oxford University Press, 2010).
59. Strozier et al., *The Fundamentalist Mindset*, 11.
60. Quinby, "The Unsettling of the Fundamentalist Mindset," in *The Fundamentalist Mindset*, ed. Strozier et al., 125.
61. Strozier et al., *The Fundamentalist Mindset*, 11.
62. Sudhir Kakar, *The Colors of Violence: Cultural Identities, Religion, and Conflict* (Chicago: University of Chicago Press, 1996).
63. See Juergensmeyer, *Terror in the Mind of God*, 161–162.
64. For an interesting exercise in typologizing varieties of Islamist politics, see Said Amir Arjomand, "Unity and Diversity in Islamic Fundamentalism," in *Fundamentalisms Comprehended*, ed. Marty and Appleby, 179–199.

Bibliography

Ali, Tariq. *The Clash of Fundamentalisms: Crusades, Jihads, and Modernity.* London: Verso, 2002.
Almond, Gabriel A., R. Scott Appleby, and Emmanuel Sivan. *Strong Religion: The Rise of Fundamentalisms Around the World.* Chicago: University of Chicago Press, 2003.
Appleby, R. Scott. *The Ambivalence of the Sacred: Religion, Violence and Reconciliation.* Lanham, MD: Rowman and Littlefield, 2000.
Appleby, R. Scott. "What's in a Name? 'Fundamentalism' and the Discourse about Religion." In *How Should We Talk about Religion?: Perspectives, Contexts, Particularities*, edited by James Boyd White, 87–103. Notre Dame, IN: University of Notre Dame Press, 2006.
Appleby, R. Scott. "Rethinking Fundamentalism in a Secular Age." In *Rethinking Secularism*, edited by Craig Calhoun, Mark Juergensmeyer, and Jonathan VanAntwerpen, 225–247. New York: Oxford University Press, 2011.
Arjomand, Said Amir. "Unity and Diversity in Islamic Fundamentalism." In *Fundamentalisms Comprehended*, edited by Martin E. Marty and R. Scott Appleby, 179–199. Chicago: University of Chicago Press, 2004.
Armstrong, Karen. *The Battle for God.* New York: Alfred A. Knopf, 2000.
Bailie, Gil. *Violence Unveiled: Humanity at the Crossroads.* New York: Crossroad, 1995.

Barkun, Michael. "Militias, Christian Identity and the Radical Right." *The Christian Century* 112, no. 23 (1995): 738–740.

Barkun, Michael. *Religion and the Racist Right: The Origins of the Christian Identity Movement.* 1994. Reprint, Chapel Hill, NC: University of North Carolina Press, 1997.

Benjamin, Daniel, and Steven Simon. *The Age of Sacred Terror: Radical Islam's War Against America.* New York: Random House, 2003.

Bromley, David G., and J. Gordon Melton, eds. *Cults, Religion and Violence.* Cambridge: Cambridge University Press, 2002.

Butler, Judith. *The Psychic Life of Power.* Stanford, CA: Stanford University Press, 1997.

Cavanaugh, William T. *The Myth of Religious Violence: Secular Ideology and the Roots of Modern Conflict.* New York: Oxford University Press, 2009.

Collier, Paul. "Economic Causes of Civil Conflict and Their Implications for Policy." In *Turbulent Peace: The Challenges of Managing International Conflict,* edited by Chester A. Crocker, Fen Osler Hampson, and Pamela Aall, 143–162. Washington, DC: US Institute of Peace Press, 2001.

Cooley, John K. *Unholy Wars: Afghanistan, America and International Terrorism.* London: Pluto Press, 2000.

Dalsheim, Joyce. *Unsettling Gaza: Secular Liberalism, Radical Religion, and the Israeli Settlement Project.* New York: Oxford University Press, 2011.

Darby, John. *The Effects of Violence on Peace Processes.* Washington, DC: US Institute of Peace Press, 2001.

Davis, Natalie Zemon. "The Rites of Violence." *Past and Present* 59, no. 1 (1973): 51–91.

Dekmejian, R. Hrair. *Islam in Revolution: Fundamentalism in the Arab World.* Syracuse, NY: Syracuse University Press, 1985.

Deng, Francis. *War of Visions: Conflict Identities in Sudan.* Washington, DC: Brookings Institution Press, 1995.

Docherty, Jayne Seminare. *Learning Lessons from Waco: When the Parties Bring Their Gods to the Negotiation Table.* Syracuse, NY: Syracuse University Press, 2001.

Ellens, J. Harold, ed. *The Destructive Power of Religion: Violence in Judaism, Christianity and Islam.* Vol. 1, *Sacred Scriptures, Ideology and Violence.* Westport, CT: Prager, 2004.

Esposito, John L. *Unholy War: Terror in the Name of Islam.* New York: Oxford University Press, 2002.

Fearon, James D., and David D. Laitin. "Ethnicity, Insurgency, and Civil War." *American Political Science Review* 97, no. 1 (2003): 75–90.

Foucault, Michel. "Sexuality and Power (1978)." In *Religion and Culture: Michel Foucault,* edited by Jeremy R. Carette, 115–130. New York: Routledge, 1999.

Giddens, Anthony. *The Nation-State and Violence.* Cambridge: Polity, 1985.

Giddens, Anthony. *The Consequences of Modernity.* Cambridge: Polity, 1990.

Giddens, Anthony. *Modernity and Self-Identity: Self and Society in the Late Modern Age.* Stanford, CA: Stanford University Press, 1991.

Gurr, Ted Robert (with contributors). *Minorities at Risk: A Global View of Ethnopolitical Conflict.* Washington, DC: US Institute of Peace Press, 1993.

Hassner, Ron E. *War on Sacred Grounds.* Ithaca, NY: Cornell University Press, 2009.

Heilman, Samuel. *Defenders of the Faith: Inside Ultra-Orthodox Jewry.* New York: Schocken Books, 1992.

Hibbard, Scott W. *Religious Politics and Secular States: Egypt, India, and the United States.* Baltimore: The Johns Hopkins University Press, 2010.

Israeli Assassins: Yigal Amir. General Books LLC, 2010.

Jaffrelot, Christophe. *The Hindu Nationalist Movement in India.* New York: Columbia University Press, 1993.

Jerryson, Michael K., and Mark Juergensmeyer, eds. *Buddhist Warfare.* New York: Oxford University Press, 2010.

Juergensmeyer, Mark. *Terror in the Mind of God: The Global Rise of Religious Violence.* Berkeley, CA: University of California Press, 2000.

Kakar, Sudhir. *The Colors of Violence: Cultural Identities, Religion, and Conflict.* Chicago: University of Chicago Press, 1996.

Kaplan, Jeffrey. *Radical Religion in America: Millenarian Movements from the Far Right to the Children of Noah.* Syracuse, NY: Syracuse University Press, 1997.

Kaplan, Jeffrey. *Terrorist Groups and the New Tribalism: Terrorism's Fifth Wave.* 2010. Reprint, London: Routledge, 2012.

Kepel, Gilles. *Muslim Extremism in Egypt: The Prophet and the Pharoah.* Berkeley, CA: University of California Press, 1993.

Lawrence, Bruce B. *Defenders of God: The Fundamentalist Revolt against the Modern Age.* San Francisco: Harper and Row, 1989.

Lawrence, Bruce B. *Shattering the Myth: Islam Beyond Violence.* Princeton, NJ: Princeton University Press, 1998.

Lincoln, Bruce. *Holy Terrors: Thinking About Religion after September 11.* Chicago: University of Chicago Press, 2002.

Little, David. *Sri Lanka: The Invention of Enmity.* Washington, DC: US Institute of Peace Press, 1994.

Little, David. "Introduction." In *Religion and Nationalism in Iraq: A Comparative Perspective,* edited by David Little and Donald K. Swearer. 1–42 Cambridge, MA: Harvard University Press, 2007.

Lustick, Ian S. *For the Land and the Lord: Jewish Fundamentalism in Israel.* New York: Council on Foreign Relations Press, 1988.

Nielsen, Niels C., Jr. *Fundamentalism, Mythos, and World Religions.* Albany, NY: State University of New York Press, 1993.

Madan, T. N. "The Double-Edged Sword: Fundamentalism and the Sikh Religious Tradition." In *Fundamentalisms Observed,* edited by Martin E. Marty and R. Scott Appleby, 594–627. Chicago: University of Chicago Press, 2010.

Mahmood, Cynthia Keppley. *Fighting for Faith and Nation: Dialogues with Sikh Militants.* Philadelphia: University of Pennsylvania Press, 1996.

Mamdani, Mahmood. *Good Muslim, Bad Muslim: America, the Cold War, and the Roots of Terror.* New York: Doubleday, 2004.

Marsden, George M. *Fundamentalism and American Culture: The Shaping of Twentieth Century Evangelicalism, 1870–1925.* New York: Oxford University Press, 1980.

Marty, Martin E., and R. Scott Appleby, eds. *Fundamentalisms Observed.* Chicago: University of Chicago Press, 1991.

Marty, Martin E., and R. Scott Appleby, eds. *Fundamentalisms and Society: Remaking the Sciences, the Family and Education.* Chicago: University of Chicago Press, 1993.

Marty, Martin E., and R. Scott Appleby, eds. *Fundamentalisms and the State: Remaking Polities, Economies, and Militance.* Chicago: University of Chicago Press, 1993.

Marty, Martin E., and R. Scott Appleby, eds. *Accounting for Fundamentalisms: The Dynamic Character of Movements.* Chicago: University of Chicago Press, 1994.

Marty, Martin E., and R. Scott Appleby, eds. *Fundamentalisms Comprehended*. Chicago: University of Chicago Press, 1995.

Marx, Anthony. *Faith in Nation: Exclusionary Origins of Nationalism*. New York: Oxford University Press, 2003.

Mazarr, Michael. *Unmodern Men in the Modern World: Radical Islam, Terrorism, and the War on Terror*. New York: Cambridge University Press, 2007.

McDonald, Andrew [William Pierce]. *The Turner Diaries*. New York: Barricade Books, 1996. First published 1978 by National Alliance Vanguard Books.

McTernan, Oliver. *Violence in God's Name: Religion in an Age of Conflict*. London: Darton, Longman and Todd, 2003.

Michel, Lou, and Dan Herbeck. *American Terrorist Timothy McVeigh and the Tragedy at Oklahoma City*. New York: HarperCollins, 2002.

Moaddel, Mansoor, and Kamran Talattof, eds. *Modernist and Fundamentalist Debates in Islam: A Reader*. New York: Palgrave MacMillan, 2002.

Nasr, Seyyed Vali Reza. *Islamic Leviathan: Islam and the Making of State Power*. New York: Oxford University Press, 2001.

Nicholson, Hugh. *Comparative Theology and the Problem of Religious Rivalry*. New York: Oxford University Press, 2011.

Oberoi, Harjot. *The Construction of Religious Boundaries: Culture, Identity, and Diversity in the Sikh Tradition*. Chicago: University of Chicago Press, 1994.

Omar, A. Rashied. "Religion, Violence and the State: A dialogical encounter between activists and scholars." PhD diss., University of Cape Town, 2006.

Otto, Rudolf. *The Idea of the Holy*. Translated by John W. Harvey. New York: Oxford University Press, 1958.

Pipes, Daniel. *In the Path of God: Islam and Political Power*. New York: Basic Books, 1983.

Rapoport, David C. "Some General Observations on Religion and Violence." In *Violence and the Sacred in the Modern World*, edited by Mark Juergensmeyer, 118–140. London: Frank Cass, 1991.

Rapoport, David C. "The Four Waves of Rebel Terror and September 11." *Anthropoetics* 8, no. 1 (2002). http://www.anthropoetics.ucla.edu/apo801/terror.htm.

Rapoport, David C. "Four Waves of Modern Terrorism." In *Attacking Terrorism: Elements of a Grand Strategy*, edited by Audrey Kurth Cronin and James M. Ludes, 46–73. Washington, DC: Georgetown University Press, 2004.

Rashid, Ahmed. *Taliban: Militant Islam, Oil and Fundamentalism in Central Asia*. New Haven, CT: Yale University Press, 2000.

Riesebrodt, Martin. *Pious Passion: The Emergence of Modern Fundamentalism in the United States and Iran*. Translated by Don Reneau. Berkeley, CA: University of California Press, 1993.

Roy, Olivier. *Islam and Resistance in Afghanistan*. Cambridge: Cambridge University Press, 1985.

Roy, Olivier. *Holy Ignorance: When Religion and Culture Part Ways*. New York: Columbia University Press, 2010.

Sandeen, Ernest R. *The Roots of Fundamentalism: British and American Millenarianism 1800–1930*. Chicago: University of Chicago Press, 1970.

Schilbrack, Kevin. "Religions: Are There Any?" *Journal of the American Academy of Religion* 78, no. 4 (2010): 1112–1138.

Schwartz, Regina M. *The Curse of Cain: The Violent Legacy of Monotheism*. Chicago: University of Chicago Press, 1997.

Selengut, Charles. *Sacred Fury: Understanding Religious Violence.* Walnut Creek, CA: AltaMira Press, 2003.

Sells, Michael. *The Bridge Betrayed: Religion and Genocide in Bosnia.* Berkeley, CA: University of California Press, 1996.

Shakman Hurd, Elizabeth. *The Politics of Secularism in International Relations.* Princeton: Princeton University Press, 2008.

Silberstein, Laurence J., ed. *Jewish Fundamentalism in Comparative Perspective: Religion, Ideology, and the Crisis of Modernity.* New York: New York University Press, 1993.

Sivan, Emmanuel. *Radical Islam: Medieval Theology and Modern Politics.* New Haven, CT: Yale University Press, 1990.

Sivan, Emmanuel, and Menachem Friedman, eds. *Religious Radicalism and Politics in the Middle East.* New York: State University of New York Press, 1990.

Smith, Anthony. "The Sacred Dimension of Nationalism." *Millennium Journal of International Studies* 29, no. 3 (2000): 791–814.

Spivak, Gayatri Chakrabarty. *Nationalism and the Imagination.* London: Seagull Books, 2010.

Stedman, Steven J. "Spoiler Problems in Peace Processes." *International Security* 22, no. 2 (1997): 5–53.

Steffen, Lloyd. *The Demonic Turn: The Power of Religion to Inspire or Restrain Violence.* Cleveland, OH: The Pilgrim Press, 2003.

Stowasser, Barbara Freyer. "A Time to Reap." *Middle East Studies Association Bulletin* 34, no. 1 (2000): 1–13.

Strozier, Charles B. *Apocalypse: On the Psychology of Fundamentalism in America.* Boston: Beacon Press, 1994.

Strozier, Charles B., David M. Terman, and James W. Jones, eds. (with Katharine A. Boyd). *The Fundamentalist Mindset: Psychological Perspectives on Religion, Violence, and History.* Oxford University Press, 2010.

Tambiah, Stanley J. *Leveling Crowds: Ethnonationalist Conflicts and Collective Violence in South Asia.* Berkeley, CA: University of California Press, 1997.

Tessler, Mark. "The Origins of Popular Support for Islamist Movements." In *Islam, Democracy, and the State in North Africa,* edited by John Entelis, 93–126. Bloomington, IN: Indiana University Press, 1997.

Tibi, Bassam. *The Crisis of Modern Islam.* Salt Lake City, UT: University of Utah Press, 1988.

van der Veer, Peter. *Religious Nationalism: Hindus and Muslims in India.* Berkeley, CA: University of California Press, 1994.

van der Veer, Peter. *Imperial Encounters: Religion and Modernity in India and Britain.* Princeton, NJ: Princeton University Press, 2001.

Varshney, Ashutosh. *Ethnic Conflict and Civic Life: Hindus and Muslims in India.* New Haven, CT: Yale University Press, 2002.

Wright, Lawrence. *The Looming Tower: Al-Qaeda and the Road to 9/11.* New York: Vintage Books, 2006.

PART TWO

THE HISTORICAL AND THE HISTORICIST

CHAPTER 3

....

RELIGION, PEACE, AND THE ORIGINS OF NATIONALISM[*]

....

DAVID LITTLE

INTRODUCTION

....

Nationalism and the Liberal Peace

NATIONALISM is a matter of increasing interest to scholars of religion, conflict, and peace. An important reason is that in recent times, many lethal conflicts appear to involve religiously-colored disputes over the boundaries and character of nation-states, as in the cases of Northern Ireland, the former Yugoslavia, Sri Lanka, Kashmir, Sudan, Nigeria, Iraq, and Israel-Palestine. Other countries, like India and Egypt, were subject in the 1970s and 1980s to sectarian strife and executive assassination, with a potential for greater violence generated by appeals to one or another version of "religious nationalism."[1] At issue in all such cases is the makeup of the "nation" or "people" who control the state of a given territory. Religion plays a role by helping to define national identity or "peoplehood," thereby influencing the ideals and values according to which the state is organized and legitimated. The process by which nation and state coalesce and interact is fraught with political, economic, cultural, and territorial competition, and as a result, too frequently, with violent conflict.

Some students of the subject distinguish between two types of nationalism, "liberal" or "civic" and "illiberal" or "ethnic," as a way of tracking the connection between nationalism and peace.[2] They are advocates of what is known as "the liberal peace." They maintain that the orderly and properly sequenced development of robust liberal political and economic institutions is a critical condition of national and international peace,[3] while illiberal or ethnically exclusivist institutions increase the probability of violence.

According to Jack Snyder, violence is restrained by means of "thick versions of liberal or constitutional democracy," consisting "of an ample set of preconditions for "a stable, productive, peaceful society." There is "a certain degree of wealth, the development of a knowledgeable citizenry, the support of powerful elites, and the establishment of a whole panoply of institutions to insure the rule of law and [equal] civic rights."[4] Similarly, Michael Doyle and Nicholas Sambanis, on the basis of their detailed study of conditions for successfully resolving civil war, conclude that "the rule of law and constitutional consent," including "a basic framework of rights and duties of citizens," are crucial foundations for durable peace.[5] By contrast, the presence of illiberal or ethnic nationalism, which "bases its legitimacy on common culture, language, religion, shared historical experience, and/or the myth of shared [ethnicity], and. . . use[s] these criteria" as the exclusive basis for citizenship, engenders a high risk of violence of either an institutionalized sort, as in authoritarian systems, or outside institutional control, as in insurgencies and civil wars.[6]

A particularly important recent study highlights the urgency of protecting "a basic framework of rights and duties of citizens," and especially freedom of conscience, for the sake of peace. The study is by Brian J. Grim and Roger Finke and called *The Price of Freedom Denied: Religious Persecution and Conflict in the Twenty-First Century*.[7] On the basis of a broad and rigorous empirical survey, the authors express strong support for the liberal peace. They conclude: "to the extent that governments and societies restrict religious freedoms, physical persecution and conflict increase."[8]

To be sure, this typology of "liberal/civic" versus "illiberal/ethnic" nationalism has been challenged. Skeptics point out that national identity, even in the allegedly most "liberal" or "civic" of countries, like the United States or France, "comes loaded with inherited cultural baggage that is contingent upon their peculiar histories," including a privileged language or religion, or a domineering ethnic group or economic class. In fact, the skeptics continue, "claims about. . . authentic or original identity most often represent ways of silencing debate about the interpretation of. . . complex and often contradictory cultural legacies."[9] In short, a national image advertised as liberal and civic typically conceals illiberal or ethnically preferential and economically unjust components.

A second criticism is that if liberal or civic nationalism means a commitment to universal equal freedom, it is questionable how liberal a system of segmented, diversely populated, nation-states can be when each state has as its primary obligation favoring the interests of its own citizens.[10] The problem is both internal and external. Domestically, granting completely equal status to all of a nation's diverse cultural and social ideals is not feasible. Some degree of preference and ranking is unavoidable. As to the international aspect, even the most liberal nation-state thwarts the universal spread of equal freedom, politically and economically, to the extent it is called upon, as it frequently is, to protect the security and welfare of its own citizens at the expense of others.

A third criticism challenges the coherence of the notion of religious freedom as a purported ingredient of the liberal peace by calling it "impossible" to define and apply without bias,[11] and by arguing that legal and other attempts to do so inevitably produce perverse results.[12] The claim is that modern law bearing on religious freedom has typically favored privatized, individualistic, and voluntary, or "protestant," forms of religion, while disfavoring public, communal, and ascribed forms, conditions that are now supposed to be changing to some extent. In the United States, for example, it is asserted that the law increasingly privileges religious groups over nonreligious ones, creating a new kind of discrimination.[13] Beyond such claims, this line of attack goes further and calls into question the worth of a liberal order as such, including the rule of law and human rights standards in general.[14]

It needs to be stressed that however arresting these criticisms are, they do not altogether refute the claims of the advocates of liberal peace. That is because those claims rest on extensive evidence showing that *relative* differences in the incidence of liberal or illiberal attributes in given nation-states in fact match important variations in the probability of peace or violence, duly defined and measured. Any successful refutation would have to expose flaws in the procedures and conclusions of such studies.

Still, even if the data generally hold up as claimed (a not unimportant conclusion), there is merit to some of the criticisms. To establish that, as with any ideal typology, boundaries distinguishing one type from another are usually more porous, more subject to cross-boundary "slippage" in the real world, than is often admitted, could be significant for the study of peace. Acknowledging that nationalism by nature incorporates illiberal or ethnically exclusive and economically unjust elements serves at once to dispel complacency and draw attention to the lurking sources of antagonism and grievance that provoke violence.

The same is true of efforts to resolve political, economic, cultural, and territorial contests within the nation-state, as well as conflicts between national and international obligations outside it. Acute awareness of the difficulty of finding equitable compromises to the daunting "dilemmas of nationalism" would appear to be the beginning of wisdom. It could inspire new, imaginative ways of negotiating and accommodating as peacefully and as justly as possible the congeries of interests and obligations characteristic of modern nation-states. Even the general charges against liberalism, including the rule of law and the right to religious freedom and other human rights, might generate sensitivity to legal and political blind spots and to inadvertent forms of discrimination. Whether the benefits extend beyond that remains to be seen.

Justpeace: An Alternative?

It is such considerations as these that underlie a broader critique of the liberal peace associated with the concept *justpeace*, something of central concern to the editors and authors of this volume. The concept involves a notion of "strategic peacebuilding" that is "comprehensive," "architectonic," and "sustainable," where all relevant factors are considered in relation to each other in an "interdependent" and "integrative" way.[15] Viewed from that perspective, some proponents regard the liberal peace as "far too narrow,"[16] and something to "move beyond."[17] At issue are not only the shortcomings of overlooking the persistent, subtle, and complex interaction of liberal and illiberal forces constitutive of nationalism, or of disregarding the domestic and international "dilemmas of nationalism" alluded to above. Also in question, say some justpeace proponents, is the limited range of concerns identified with the liberal peace, namely, "to end armed violence and to establish human rights, democracy, and market economies [premised on] the liberal tradition that arose from the Western Enlightenment."[18]

According to one proponent, peacebuilding "is far wider, deeper, more encompassing and involves a far greater array of actors, activities, levels of society, links between societies, and time horizons than the dominant [liberal peace] thinking realizes."[19] That would mean, for one thing, giving more attention to the role of religion in peacebuilding than secularly-oriented descendants of the Enlightenment are inclined to do.[20] As one example, religious resources favoring forgiveness, reconciliation, and restorative justice might be consulted as a way of supplementing, if not replacing, exclusive reliance on retributive justice characteristic of the liberal peace.[21] For another thing, it would imply seriously reevaluating the close association between neoliberal economic policies and the liberal peace. "Marketization strategies that ignore social welfare" and perpetuate inequality and poverty in postconflict settings are exacerbated by a global economic order indifferent to "local culture, customs, institutions and processes."[22] Similarly, it is argued that the liberal peace is too closely tied to the traditional structure of the nation-state. What the justpeace approach calls for is a substantial expansion of horizons to include peace efforts at the international and transnational level and, simultaneously, at the "subnational" or local and grassroots level.[23]

In sum, without intending to refute the essential conclusions of liberal peace advocates—that liberal or civic nationalism promotes peace of a certain kind, while illiberal or ethnic nationalism promotes the opposite—justpeace proponents seek to expand the discussion to include a more comprehensive range of considerations relevant to achieving a truly durable and just peace. What remains unclear among justpeace proponents is whether the liberal peace framework "can be salvaged and improved" or whether "more radical thought is required to go beyond this paradigm of peacebuilding."[24]

One important step toward clarifying that issue is to examine afresh the historical origins of nationalism as background to the idea of liberal peace. The objective is to sharpen understanding of what exactly the idea means, the better to decide what to make of it. That involves determining how pertinent the "liberal/civic" versus "illiberal/ethnic" typology is to the beginnings of nationalism, and assessing, from a historical point of view, how accurate the charges are against the typology and related aspects of the notion of liberal peace. In particular, we shall have to sort out the role and significance of religion, as well as characterize the attitudes of early nationalists toward corrective and economic justice, and toward negotiating and accommodating both transnational and subnational interests and obligations. We shall also need to begin, at least, to come to terms with the more general assault on liberalism we mentioned, including the rule of law, the idea of freedom of religion, and other human rights.

THE ORIGINS OF NATIONALISM

The Scholarly Setting

Undertaking the task we have set ourselves is especially demanding since we must work against considerable historical neglect and misunderstanding. Claiming as we shall that the Protestant Reformation marks a decisive point of origin, we have to make up for the fact that students of nationalism have either neglected the Reformation altogether,[25] or commented on it only in passing.[26] Others have mischaracterized its influence by overlooking or misconstruing the contribution of the Calvinist wing of Reformed Christianity.[27] Historians who have commented on the Reformation and its aftermath have either made the same mistake,[28] or written inconsistently on the subject.[29]

Besides three notable exceptions to this general picture,[30] a sophisticated and sustained account of the role of the Reformation in the rise of nationalism is contained in Anthony Marx's *Faith in Nation: Exclusionary Origins of Nationalism*.[31] For Marx, the Reformation decisively affected the ideas of nationhood in sixteenth- and seventeenth-century Protestant England and France under the influence of the Catholic Counter-Reformation, as the result of sometimes violent interactions between the state and the respective religious communities. However, his argument that the idea of national identity was in each case simply the product of a state-manipulated policy of religious uniformity ignores the independent role of religion, as well as the competing conceptions of nation advocated by different segments of the Reformation, and the diverse effects those conceptions had on subsequent forms of nationalism.[32]

The Reformation and New Notions of "Peoplehood"

The Protestant Reformation, appearing just as the medieval Catholic establishment in Europe was dissolving into a collection of separate self-governing territorial states, involved reimagining the meaning of "nation" or "people" to go along with these new states. Through publications in the vernacular and related means of mobilizing the public, the Reformation elevated in various ways, often in an innovative theological idiom, a politically oriented popular consciousness, implying a new sense of popular awareness, political empowerment, and national identity or "peoplehood."

Behind this new thinking lay two sources, Renaissance humanism and Catholic conciliarism. Both undoubtedly had an impact on the early nationalist attitudes of the Reformers, though the role of humanism was less direct and less salient, except, perhaps, in the case of England. To be sure, recent scholarship has demonstrated a decided preoccupation with national identity on the part of the humanist movement. "Towards the end of the fifteenth century, German, French, Spanish and English scholars fashioned themselves simultaneously as humanists of [classical] Italian greatness and as champions of a free and authentic nation. In both roles they claimed to contribute to the honor of their nation."[33] Still, the nationalist spirit associated with the humanist movement was not, in general, connected to the new populism that would become so important.[34] There is some debate about the Florentine humanists,[35] but the northern humanists appear to have supported consistently "a traditionally hierarchical picture of political life"[36] and "a durable oligarchic rule" in relation to which they performed "a mainly celebratory function."[37]

By contrast, conciliarism radically challenged existing authority, ecclesiastical and political. Reaching its peak of influence at the Council of Constance in 1414–1415, the movement favored rule by church council rather than papal monarchy. In various ways and degrees, its advocates introduced constitutionalism as a way to ecclesiastical and political peace, proposing to limit the power of both church and state by distinguishing and carefully defining their respective jurisdictions and functions by means of "definite laws and statutes," as Jean Gerson, one of the leaders, put it.[38] Gerson held that the two societies, "ecclesiastical" and "secular," are each "perfect," or self-sufficient, in their own right. Ecclesiastical authorities have no right or aptitude for interfering in worldly matters, especially in regard to the administration of physical force.[39]

Conciliarists interpreted their key principle, "the people's welfare is the ultimate law," in accord with a doctrine of natural rights that added to the sense of popular empowerment, and they based membership in the councils on representation from what they called "the four *nationes*—the *Gallicana, Italiana, Anglicana,* and *Germanica*."[40] "Each nation could elect its own president, ... hold its meetings in a proper assembly room, dispatch delegates to the committees, and most importantly, pass a single vote for all its members."[41]

Nicholas of Cusa (1401–1464), one of the more progressive leaders, sought to expand the significance of the 'contractual' or 'covenantal' relationship between the rulers and the "people" in both church and state. "Since all men are by nature free," he wrote, "it follows that every government, whether it rests its authority on written law or on the voice of the prince, derives solely from the common consent and agreement of the subjects." Officials of the Christian church likewise depend on the voluntary assent of the faithful, and, according to Nicholas, "it would be well that this ultimate popular derivation of Church authority should be emphasized in his own day by the revival of the primitive practice of congregational election of bishops and priests."[42]

It should be emphasized that despite its (variable) emphasis on the freedom of the people and their right to participation, conciliarism nowhere favored anything close to a modern view of freedom of conscience where the doctrines of the church were concerned. The Council of Constance regarded itself as a duly constituted legal institution, and, going back on its renunciation of the right of the church to use force, "claimed coercive powers over the entire Christendom."[43]

However, as to the political order, conciliarists made "deeply influential contributions to the evolution of a radical and constitutionalist view of the sovereign State."[44] For Gerson, wherever a ruler is above the law, there can be no authentic political community. That is because political order is fundamentally grounded in the necessity to restrain arbitrary power, something that can be achieved only by adopting common constitutional standards. In a "strongly anti-Thomist and anti-Aristotelian style," Gerson, like other conciliarists, believed that, because of the fall, human beings were otherwise unable to control bias, partiality, passion, and revenge in pursing their interests.[45] Rulership, unregulated by constitutional standards, simply reverts to the chaotic conditions of what later would be called the state of nature.

Though conciliarism lost out to papalism within the Roman Catholic Church, its central tenets had an important impact on some of the Reformation ideas about peoplehood and citizenship, albeit in different ways and degrees. Three quite divergent movements stemming from the Reformation may be singled out: *accommodationism*, *renovationism*, and *reformism*. *Accommodationism* is an example of "illiberal" or "ethnic" nationalism, whereby religion accommodates or acquiesces, among other things, to a centralized, territorial state[46]; *renovationism*, in reaction, represents a radical, utopian version of "liberal" or "transethnic" nationalism; and *reformism* tries, erratically and with considerable ambivalence, to work out a middle way between the two options. In short, reformism exhibits oscillation between liberal and illiberal nationalism, as well as between national and transnational responsibilities. Much of the instability associated with modern nationalism, including struggles over the two dilemmas—the tension between liberal and illiberal forms, and between national and international obligations—is eloquently foreshadowed in reformist experience.

Accommodationism

The key feature of accommodationism is the mobilization of popular support for a consolidated, unitary[47] territorial state closely allied with an exclusive national religion and a hereditary, hierarchical system of authority and status. Despite some fits and starts, the German reformer Martin Luther (1483–1546) eventually encouraged such an arrangement, and two influential leaders of the English Reformation, Archbishop John Whitgift (1530–1604) and Richard Hooker (1554–1600), advocated it consistently and without reservation.

Luther is a complicated case. While he sometimes adopted the nationalist idiom of the humanists, as when he characterized the French as duplicitous, the Scots as haughty, the Spanish as cruel, and the Italians as insidious, treacherous, and untrustworthy,[48] he refused to follow the humanist custom of singularly elevating his own people.[49] But his influence, if circuitous, was no less important. Unlike the humanists, he helped inspire the "new populism" that eventually transformed the elitist and politically marginal activities of the humanists into a mass movement.[50] The new populism was to a certain extent a function of the rejection of Latin and the astonishing spread of vernacular literature, made possible by the invention of printing in the late fifteenth century,[51] and successfully exploited by Luther in making his writings popularly accessible. It was also the result of his anticlericalism, illustrated by his famous slogan "the priesthood of all believers," and of his conciliarist sympathies, which led him to prefer representative councils over the papacy, and occasionally, if inconsistently, to condone political resistance to oppressive rule.

But, preponderantly, Luther's legacy is associated with his conviction that the people are best served by supporting a strong, religiously uniform, unitary government. That conviction rested on his growing fear of anarchy, and a certain indifference and passivity regarding the institutional reform of both church and state. At first, Luther wanted to remove icons and images from the churches because of their association with Catholicism. But he changed his mind when he saw people taking things into their own hands. Such practices would create "pretty preliminaries to riot and rebellion," and a loss of respect for order and authority.[52] Hadn't St. Paul counseled a duty of passive obedience to temporal rulers? Luther thought so and said as much in responding to the Peasants' Revolt in Germany of 1524–25. He reminded the rebels that the wickedness and injustice of rulers do not excuse rebellion, and that in defying their obligations to temporal authority, the peasants "forfeited body and soul," and thereby "abundantly merited death."[53] He displayed no compunctions whatsoever about the methods used by the princes in subduing the peasants, or about the appalling costs of such action.[54] In one place, Luther even goes so far as to say that tyrants exist not because they are scoundrels, but "because of the people's sin."[55]

Luther came to favor an established national church in close alliance with a unitary territorial government as the only secure bulwark against chaos. Despite occasional utterances limiting the authority of state to "life, property, and other external things on earth," and precluding it from regulating religious belief and practice,[56] Luther gravitated not only "to attacking the jurisdictional powers of the Church [of the medieval period], but also to filling the power-vacuum this created by mounting a corresponding defense of the secular authorities," including the right of the prince "to appoint and dismiss the officers, as well as to control and dispose of Church property."[57]

This is the key to "Luther's nationalist influence."[58] According to the principle *cuius regio eius religio*—"a territory's religion is that of its ruler," a principle Luther stalwartly supported—the people of a state must take on the faith of the ruler, which, in turn, becomes the primary index of national identity. Uniform religion is the essential link between "nation" and "state." This principle was first officially implemented by the Peace of Augsburg in 1555 as the basis for political sovereignty and order among the Lutheran and Catholic territories that made up Germany at the time. Having embraced the ruler's religion, any believers found out of place were at liberty either to emigrate to the territory where their religion was practiced, or to stay put and acquiesce. Proselytism across or within political borders was strictly prohibited. A century later, the agreement was expanded to include other religious groups and other parts of Europe in the Peace of Westphalia of 1648, something that laid down important legal and political foundations for the modern nation-state system.

When it came to working out the institutional structures of church and state, Luther was more devoted to tearing down than building up. As to the church, he sought to liberate Germany from the domination of the papacy and canon law, and as to the state, he was happy to accept whatever powers that were, so long as they, too, were liberated from Catholic control. His indifference to the organization of the state never really changed; there is no evidence he ever reflected on the comparative merits of monarchy, aristocracy, or democracy, or sought to integrate his disparate comments on the restraint of political power into any kind of general theory of government.

On the subject of church order, Luther's policies were the result of inadvertence. Without much reflection, he at first recommended replacing the discredited Catholic tradition with simple New Testament norms. When that failed, as the result of a series of severe social, political, and economic crises in the 1520s and '30s, he acquiesced to a kind of accidental reappropriation of Catholic canon law, so long as it was shorn of all traces of papal authority. He went along, as Quentin Skinner puts it, so as to fill the power vacuum that had been created by the removal of the Catholic system. Authority over spiritual and temporal matters, invested in the church in medieval times, now became the responsibility of the unitary state.[59] "By the mid-1550s, the medieval canon law had returned to . . . German society, but now largely under the control of civil authorities and under the color of civil law."[60]

It should be emphasized that by encouraging the substantial extension of state authority over church affairs, Luther weakened significantly one tenet of conciliarist thought, the independence of the church. While conciliarists never succeeded in putting into practice their commitment to the separation of the spiritual and temporal communities, the idea was very much there in theory. By definition, accommodationism minimizes the separation of church and state.

J. N. Figgis's claim that Luther, along with the sixteenth-century Anglican leaders Whitgift and Hooker, transferred "to the State most of the prerogatives that had belonged in the Middle Ages to the Church,"[61] applies more directly and with less qualification to the Anglicans than to Luther. Whitgift and Hooker were accommodationists par excellence because they developed elaborate theological and other warrants for defending a unitary territorial government against the threats of both Catholic recusants and a growing number of Reformed Protestant agitators. For them, national identity consisted in the exclusive alliance of the state with the national—"English"—church, causing them to set aside even the limited space for popular independence and resistance admitted by Luther. Except for the conciliarist emphasis on the national character of the church, they were less indebted to conciliarism than Luther and closer to some aspects of humanist teaching on nationalism, especially its traditionally hierarchical picture of political life.

Archbishop John Whitgift and Richard Hooker were children of and leading apologists for the Henrician and Elizabethan settlements in England. Taken together, these two arrangements—the one occurring in 1532 when Henry VIII (1509–1547) broke with Rome and "nationalized" the English church, and the other in 1559, when Elizabeth I (1558–1603), shortly after ascending the throne, secured passage of the Supremacy and Uniformity Acts—consolidated the English Reformation. According to the Supremacy Act, the English monarch, a layperson, became "Supreme Governor" of the church, and anyone not acknowledging the queen's ultimate religious authority would be ineligible for public office or for a university degree. Later, authorizing still severer punishments, the Uniformity Act established Anglicanism as the only lawful religion of England.

While Elizabeth, partly by temperament, partly by political instinct, was at first ill-disposed to enforce Anglicanism too rigidly, she was, nevertheless, prompted by circumstance to unify state and nation by means of an increasingly exclusionary religious policy.[62] She created thereby a remarkable early example of "religious nationalism," according to which one religion, uniformly imposed by the state upon the inhabitants of a given territory, is a key determinant of national identity, and thus of popular political consciousness and loyalty.

The strong current of anti-Catholicism Elizabeth inherited, inspired by widespread revulsion toward the fervent pro-Catholic policies of her half-sister, Mary Tudor (1553–1559), formed an important part of the strategy by which she would solidify support for her government. It was helped along by a series of consequential events: a pattern of intimidating efforts undertaken in the early years of her reign by the pope; the challenge to the English crown of the Catholic claimant, Mary Queen of Scots; the ominous designs of Catholic Spain, which were finally terminated in the dramatic defeat of the Armada in 1588; and the continuing military conflicts with Catholic Ireland.

The other part of the strategy, namely, the efforts from the 1550s onward to domesticate the growing body of Reformed Protestant opposition to the Elizabethan settlement, the so-called "Puritan movement," was less successful, at least in the long run. Thanks to the efforts of Whitgift, Elizabeth weakened the movement temporarily, but it would prove harder over time to contain this group and gain control of its considerable energies. Though the movement was complex and various, many Puritans had religious, national, and political goals deeply at odds with the prevailing system. In a profound sense, the contest between Elizabeth—together with her Stuart successors, James I (1603–1625) and Charles I (1625–1649)—and much of the Puritan movement was over the kind of nationalism that would eventually prevail in England, the Tudor-Stuart version, or something quite different.

Though Elizabeth tried to suppress "Catholic sedition" with increasing ardor during the 1580s, and though Whitgift and Hooker supported her efforts, it was especially the Puritan threat that they had in mind in mounting their spirited defense of the Elizabethan order. Whitgift was appointed archbishop in 1583, and immediately declared war on the Puritans, whom Hooker disparagingly referred to as "patrons of liberty." It is they who "shaketh universally the fabric of government, . . . overthroweth kingdomes, churches, and whatsoever now is through the providence of God by authority and power upheld."[63] By means of new authority and newly perfected inquisitorial techniques, Whitgift went about stringently enforcing subscription by the clergy to the Acts of Supremacy and Uniformity. Hooker's *Laws of Ecclesiastical Polity*, dedicated to Whitgift, provided the theory for Whitgift's practices.[64]

At the heart of their position is the idea, familiar to accommodationists, that the temporal commonwealth is best entrusted with the coercive supervision of all "outward action." Hooker rejected the claims of Catholics and Puritans that the church has the right to supervise its own affairs, and like Luther, though more consistently, Whitgift and Hooker believed the effects of the Gospel are but inward or "ghostly." Accordingly, the English crown does not overstep its authority in regulating outward action, including the faith and life of the church, so long as it respects the traditions of the English Reformation, understood "as a return to the past, a vindication of the rights of the Crown against usurped [papal] jurisdiction."[65]

Recovering and exercising legitimate political and ecclesiastical jurisdiction is the very soul of peace and tranquility. First, monarchy is incomparably better than polyarchy. "Where many rule, there is no order," declares Whitgift, taking issue with a Puritan preference for electoral government.[66] Second, proper order depends on conforming to what is established and traditional. "There are few things known to be good," writes Hooker, "till such time as they grow to be ancient."[67] What was decided in the dim past binds the present since "corporations are immortal," and "we were alive in our predecessors and they in their successors do still live."[68] That is the proper meaning of the adage "the voice of the people is the voice of God." The age-old "general and perpetual voice of the people" has from time immemorial reaffirmed the inseparable unity of church and state under the guidance of the earthly monarch. "There is not any man of the Church of England but the same man is also a member of the commonwealth, nor any man a member of the commonwealth which is not also of the Church of England," wrote Hooker.[69]

Thirdly, national peace and security also depend on maintaining the existing political, social, and religious status system established from ancient times. In the allocation of political power and authority, "hereditary birth giveth right unto sovereign dominion," as Hooker put it, and the same is true of social rank. "The Church of God esteemeth [the nobility to be of] more worth than thousands,"[70] and any proposal "which bringeth equally high and low unto parish churches," or in any way challenges "the majesty and greatness of English nobility" is utterly intolerable.[71]

Even more than Luther, Hooker played down the independence of the church advocated by the conciliarists. While admitting that church councils have some significance in determining the church's life and thought, and that its rulings may have advisory value, he believed that the "just authority" of the established civil government in overseeing the church "is not therefore to be abolished."[72]

Renovationism

The various individuals and groups who made up the "Radical Reformation" represented, in one way or other, a fundamental and widespread repudiation of accommodationism. Most offensive was the close identification of Christianity with the new, post-medieval territorial state, and particularly with the emerging patterns of authoritarian control over the church, including the enforcement of religious uniformity and the willingness to accept as the basis for church order the dominant hierarchical, unitary, and territorial forms of political and social organization. Impatient with what they regarded as dishonorable compromises with the world, these people "espoused, rather, a radical rupture with the immediate past and all its institutions, and [were] bent upon either the restoration of the primitive Church or the assembling of a new Church, all in an eschatological mood far more intense than anything to be found in normative Protestantism or Catholicism."[73]

> A new kind of Christian had emerged, . . . not a reformer but a converter, not a parishioner but . . . a sojourner . . . whose true citizenship was in Heaven, ... no longer primarily . . . German or . . . Gentile, . . . husband or . . . wife, . . . nobleman or . . . peasant, but a saint . . ., a fellow of the covenant . . ., a bride of Christ . . . . The Radical Reformation [transformed] the Lutheran doctrine of the priesthood of all believers [into] a universal lay apostolate[, mainly] the common man and woman, [but also] former friars, monks, and nuns, . . . as well as patricians and noblemen.[74]

The term "renovationism" is designed to convey how profound and extensive were the social revolutionary implications of the Radical Reformation. That the radicals themselves declined to advocate social programs, but instead generally withdrew from and were indifferent to worldly institutions, does not obscure the fact that their message bespoke a total and final renovation of the world and everything in it. Nor should the implications of their preaching be overlooked because most of their attention was devoted not to the temporal kingdom, but to the heavenly one yet to come. It is hardly surprising that what these renovators said and did struck the authorities as seditious in the extreme.

Some of the radicals, like Thomas Muentzer (1488?–1525), were standard revolutionaries, inciting armed rebellion, as he did as a leader of the Peasants' Revolt of 1525. Most Anabaptists rejected Muentzer's violent apocalypticism, but they shared his antipathy to the political and religious establishment, as well as his high regard for the common lay people and for those victimized by the existing system.

These predilections seriously challenged the prevailing ideas of "nation" and "state." What it means to be a "people," and, by implication, what form of government might best accommodate such an understanding, were profoundly reconceived. Most of the radicals were Anabaptists, and their central belief in adult baptism epitomized the point. For Anabaptists, the conventional practice of infant baptism subverted an indispensable feature of the Christian life, *mature individual conscientious consent*. In particular, the practice exemplified four objectionable features of accommodationism. It was authoritarian for being forced upon the under-aged by authorities not consensually appointed. It determined membership on the basis of birth, elevating as key marks of Christian identity accidental, ascribed factors, such as ethnic identity and inherited status. It discouraged a spirit of intentional, responsible participation in favor of passivity and subservience, and, given the close connection between church and state, it was, above all, coercive. The prescribed practice was under the supervision of the state, and any defection from the obligations of baptism would be civilly punished.

Though differences existed among the Anabaptists, there were also salient continuities. Basic was the impulse to form a consensual or "free church," as Conrad Grebel, founder of the Swiss Brethren, emphasized. Christians must "go forward with the Word and establish a Christian church" on the basis of "common prayer and decision according to faith and love, without command or compulsion."[75] The true church is a "voluntary association of the faithful" that "on principle administers its own affairs without the aid or the interference of the temporal government," and where "the free will of the individual and liberty from the constraints of the authorities were . . . the distinct marks."[76] In a word, the "individual congregation had no superior; it was independent and democratically organized."[77]

The Anabaptist idea of "participatory lay religion" was combined with the belief that a Christian's primary obligation was to a "universal Church not linked to race or nation," but to "a People . . . transcending any earthly state and never to be subsumed under one."[78] Most Anabaptists acknowledged that the earthly government is divinely ordained to restrain transgressions in "outward affairs," but there its jurisdiction ended. As an early Mennonite leader put it, "the ruler has received his sword not to sit in judgment . . . over spiritual matters, but to keep his subjects in good order and peace, and to protect the good and to punish the wicked."[79] Their notion of true people- or nationhood implied a state with drastically limited authority. Only those states that respected and tolerated freedom of conscience were truly legitimate.

Though limited government of that kind is to be respected, Anabaptists generally refused to serve as civil authorities because it would mean complicity in the use of force. In their early statement of faith, the Schleitheim Confession of 1527, they declared that "it is not appropriate for a Christian to serve as a magistrate because . . . the . . . magistracy is according to the flesh, but [the discipline of Christians] is according to the spirit: their citizenship is in this world, but the Christians' citizenship is in heaven; the weapons of their conflict and war are carnal and against the flesh only, but the Christians' weapons are spiritual, against the fortification of the devil."[80]

The suggestion that such "apolitical" beliefs were socially irrelevant is misleading. However much Anabaptists may have isolated themselves, the political impact of their views was critical. They contributed to revolutionizing conceptions of nation and state by offering a vision of limited government and an expanded role for "civil society" that encouraged increased voluntary political and civil participation and new opportunities for the free exercise of conscience, or, beyond that, by implying that state interests are circumscribed by compelling transnational conditions and obligations. Specifically, their views implied the principle of conscientious objection to military service, something that would assume enormous significance in the development of liberalism. In keeping with their fundamental beliefs, Anabaptists invoked a "higher right," based on conscience, to exemption from participation in a primary function of the state, the use of force. Although commonplace now, the idea that ordinary citizens, in addition to clergy and monastics, had a right to exemption was earthshaking at the time. By their statements and actions—typically viewed in the sixteenth century as desperate and futile—Anabaptists were laying down precedents for transforming life in the West.[81]

Anabaptists introduced other radical ideas, which, to be sure, were not always consistently put into practice. While the "cultural gap between educated leadership and uneducated clergy and laity characteristic of the Roman church and the Protestant established churches was narrowed drastically among Anabaptists," their ability to overcome "the patriarchal principle of men over women" in regard to marriage and social relations was by no means uniformly successful.[82] There is considerable evidence that what was affirmed in principle was not widely realized in fact.[83] That is also true of the tendency over time of Anabaptist communities to take on the characteristics of ethnic enclaves, altogether out of keeping with their original inspiration. Nevertheless, the revolutionary potential of their early message was always there.

That potential was important in two other respects. Except in a few extreme groups, Anabaptists regarded private property as a God-given trust that entailed a stringent obligation to share possessions with those in need, both inside and outside the community. "Extravagance was forbidden, while everything beyond the actual need of the individual member was placed at the disposal of the whole group."[84]

It is also reasonable to attribute to Anabaptists the early practice of what has come to be called "restorative justice." Forsaking retributive, usually coercive, punishment associated with the earthly magistrate, Anabaptists emphasized consensual acts of forgiveness and mercy aimed at overcoming estrangement and restoring right relations among offender, victim, and community. Expelling a resolutely unrepentant offender from the group was the closest they came to practicing retributive justice, and even that was non-violent in character.

Reformism

Reformism represents a middle way between accommodationism and renovationism. Its representatives try to mediate and negotiate between the radical differences of the two types. That leads to enormous disruption, innovation, and dynamism in regard to national and international institutions, and to considerable tension and difference of opinion among the individuals and groups who make up this unstable type.

The tensions and disagreements may be evaluated as to whether they tend more toward accommodationism or renovationism. While reformists are distinguished from either extreme by their efforts to hold features of both sides together, there are still significant variations in emphasis. Some incline, with certain reservations, toward a religiously uniformist understanding of the state, thereby endorsing a more expansive role for state authority in religious and other matters than Anabaptists could ever accept. Others incline in the opposite direction, though with a difference. They favor certain renovationist ideas about limiting government, reconceiving citizenship, and protesting social, legal, and economic injustice. At the same time, their commitment to institutional reform, and thus to active involvement in the political and legal order, sets them apart from the renovationists. Anabaptists, adopting a more utopian or eschatological outlook, had little confidence in human efforts to reconstruct society. They did attempt, locally, to put into practice some of their radical views concerning church order and social life, but those efforts were intended more as testimony to the coming kingdom than as a scheme for social reform.

The leading example of reformism is the Calvinist branch of the Reformation, starting with the Genevan reformer John Calvin (1509–1564).[85] There is clear evidence of the ambiguous effects of the movement's influence on the development of nationalism in premodern Switzerland, France, Holland, England, and colonial New England. With the accommodationists, Calvin essentially took a "people" or nation where he found it—situated, that is, within the territorially administered boundaries of post-medieval Europe. He came to favor a close alliance between the state and an exclusive national religion, and up to a point tolerated inherited patterns of status and authority. At the same time, he sought to reform those "new nations" in accord with key renovationist values, such as the independence of church from state, freedom of conscience, new ideas of citizenship, participatory government, special protection for the deprived and vulnerable, and transnational obligations. His far-flung spiritual offspring reflected much of the same ambivalence.

Calvin interacted extensively with Anabaptist refugees in Geneva, even marrying the widow of one of them. While he sometimes harshly opposed their views, "his assertions that discipline and suffering were characteristic of the true Church were also Anabaptist themes . . . [and] many of Calvin's followers proved over the next century that they could be as . . . politically revolutionary as any Anabaptist."[86] Though modified and reformulated, radical Anabaptist conceptions of peoplehood and citizenship played an important role in reformist thinking.

Calvin encountered both humanism and conciliarism as a student, and he was undoubtedly exposed to the early forms of nationalist discourse expressed by both movements. However, the influence of conciliarism was particularly evident in Calvin's commitment to constitutionalism, as applied to both state and church. Consistent with conciliarist theory, constitutional government became for him the vehicle for expressing the voice of "the people" by means of national representation, the separation of ecclesial and civil powers, plural authority, and a provision for the fundamental rights of communities and individuals. All this contributed considerable impetus and shape to the "new populism" associated with the Protestant Reformation.

Drawing on the conciliar tradition, Calvin elaborated a position approximating in various ways the characteristics of modern constitutionalism. As to the state, Calvin held the following:

- "Every commonwealth rests upon laws and agreements," preferably written,[87] that are regarded as fundamental to the protection of the "freedom of the people,"[88] a term he frequently invoked. Written law is "nothing but an attestation of the [natural law], whereby God brings back to memory what has already been imprinted in our hearts."[89]
- The structure of government should be polyarchic rather than monarchic, "a system compounded of aristocracy and democracy."[90] For "it is very rare for kings so to control themselves that their will never disagrees with what is just and right, or for them to have been endowed with such great keenness and prudence, that each knows how much is enough. Therefore, mens' fault or failing causes it to be safer and more bearable for a number to exercise government."[91]
- "The best condition of the people [is] when they can choose, by common consent, their own shepherds: for when any one by force usurps the supreme power, it is tyranny."[92]
- "Certain remedies against tyranny are allowable, for example when magistrates and estates have been constituted, to whom has been committed the care of the commonwealth; they shall have power to keep the prince to his duty and even to coerce him if he attempt anything unlawful."[93] Especially toward the end of his life, and facing the Huguenot revolt in France, Calvin welcomed duly authorized redress on the part of "constitutional magistrates," as he called them, countenancing armed rebellion under their authority in extreme cases.[94] Shortly before he died, Calvin even went so far as to condone acts of individual resistance against tyrannical rulers.[95]
- A set of basic rights and freedoms are taken to undergird the founding agreement, and to comprise an imprescriptible limit on governmental power. They are a collection of what are best described as the "original natural rights of freedom," "associated with the second table of the Decalogue," and stressing especially the protection of "personal liberty and property," as well as the rights of conscience.[96]

A few comments on the rights of liberty and property, as well as conscience, are in order. Underlying Calvin's commitment to constitutional government, as with the conciliarists, was an abhorrence of arbitrary power. Gradually, he came to support constitutionally authorized armed rebellion aimed at resisting "the fierce licentiousness of kings" "who violently fall upon and assault the lowly common folk,"[97] or as he puts it elsewhere, exercise "sheer robbery, plundering houses, raping virgins and matrons, and slaughtering the innocent."[98] To tolerate such atrocities is both to violate the natural "inborn feeling" "to hate and curse tyrants," and to "betray the freedom of the people."

It is, then, the fundamental purpose of constitutions, and the basic rights they protect, to restrain arbitrary power, defined as taking life, inflicting severe pain and suffering, expropriating property, and inhibiting thought and action basically for self-serving purposes. Such behavior is taken to be both wrong in itself and likely to provoke violent resistance.

Accordingly, restraining the impulse to act that way—an impulse believed to be endemic to human experience—is the primary justification for constitutional government.[99]

While particular constitutions may vary in certain ways, they all have as their ultimate purpose to limit power by "equally press[ing] toward the same goal," namely what Calvin calls "equity." It is "equity alone," he says, that "must be the goal and rule of all laws."[100] As the essence of the moral law "God has engraved upon the [human mind]," the idea consists of two rules: firstly, "that everyone's rights should be safely preserved,"[101] and, secondly, that everyone "be beneficent to neighbors," and "helpful to the necessities of others," relieving indigence with abundance.[102] Particularly the second rule of equity recalls the stringent obligation, assumed by the Anabaptists, to share wealth with those in need.

But the idea of equity had another significance for Calvin, related, again, to Anabaptist ideals, namely their commitment to "restorative justice." Understood as "voluntary moderation" and "abatement of severity" directly associated with Christian love, equity tempers the strong human impulse "to demand our right with unflinching rigor."[103]

> Almost all are so blinded by a wicked love of themselves, that . . . they flatter themselves that they are in the right . . . Christ reproves that obstinacy . . . and enjoins his people to cultivate moderation and equity, and to make some abatement of the highest rigor, that, by such an act of justice, they may purchase for themselves peace and friendship.[104]

Perfect justice, Calvin seems to be saying, is justice informed by love. Although never ignored, claims for the meticulous protection of everyone's rights by means of a rigorous application of retributive justice must always be assessed in the light of the higher, overriding claims of "peace and friendship." While (to my knowledge) Calvin nowhere attempts to institutionalize restorative justice in anything like the forms being proposed these days, he clearly and persistently supported such ideals.

Civilly and politically, Calvin did labor during his career in Geneva to expand the rules of due process[105] and enlarge substantially the civil franchise,[106] and eventually, as we have mentioned, he supported armed rebellion abroad aimed at restraining tyrannical power. As to economic justice, he embraced a theory of property rights going back to monastic theologians and developed by the conciliarists.[107] It involved drawing a distinction between "inclusive rights," which naturally entitle all human beings to adequate sustenance and health, and "exclusive rights," which protect private property, but only so long as the inclusive rights are provided for. While Calvin nowhere spelled out specific state obligations, he defined "a just and well-regulated government" as one that upholds "the rights of the poor and afflicted" "who are exposed as easy prey to the cruelty and wrongs of the rich,"[108] and he favored and supported welfare efforts in Geneva, both public and private.[109]

Calvin's ideas on the rights of conscience are tied to his theory of the church, and, it turns out, to a deep and pervasive ambivalence concerning constitutional government. On the one hand, he defends a very high doctrine of the sovereignty of conscience, which depends on a critical distinction between the "internal" and "external" forum. The first concerns personal, inward deliberation regarding fundamental belief and practice regulated by "spiritual power," meaning reliance on reasons and argument. The second concerns "external" or public deliberation regarding "outward behavior"—the needs of "the present life," such as food, clothing, and the laws of social cooperation—that are regulated by the "power of the sword," something that limits the sovereignty of conscience.

Expositing the thirteenth chapter of the Epistle to the Romans early in his career, Calvin declared that the proper jurisdiction of a well-ordered government is exclusively that "part of the law that refers to human society," or the second table of the Decalogue, whose basic principle is that "all individuals should preserve their rights." "There is no allusion at all," he asserts, "to the first table of the law, which deals with the worship of God." Since "the whole of [Paul's] discussion [only] concerns civil government," "those who bear rule over consciences attempt to establish their blasphemous tyranny . . . in vain."[110] In short, the subject matter of the first table is the province of conscience, which, except when it threatens to subvert the civil and economic rights of others, ought to be entirely free from state regulation.

In keeping with this line of thought, the church, for Calvin, is the locus of what he calls "liberated consciences." Its members comprehend more fully than non-Christians the "goal and rule of all laws"—the principle of equity (respect for the rights of all supplemented by special concern for the deprived and vulnerable)—and they are endowed with a new capacity to embrace and act upon its requirements by means of the "law of the spirit," *not* the "law of the sword." For this reason, Calvin is particularly emphatic about constitutionalizing the church, about carefully defining and separating the powers of church government so as to maximize the opportunity for voluntary participation by "the people," thereby protecting their fundamental rights, including, above all, their right to conduct their affairs free of state interference. It was, of course, regarding just such issues that Calvin was expelled from Geneva in 1538 by town fathers jealous of their authority over church life. That he was invited back in 1541 marked a certain concession on their part to his belief in an independent church.[111]

It should be stressed that this more liberal side of Calvin's thought presupposed the existence of a natural moral law that is universally both accessible and obligatory. Otherwise, it would not be possible to hold non-Christians accountable, and therefore legitimately subject to coercion, for violations of the restrictions on arbitrary power. It is clear Calvin held such a view; but he held it only some of the time.[112]

That brings us to the "other side" of Calvin's thought regarding the proper shape of constitutional government. While, in my view, he was always ambivalent about the natural moral capability of human beings, he became increasingly skeptical toward the end of his life, somewhere, perhaps, around 1553 with the trial and execution of Michael Servetus, as John Witte Jr. suggests.[113] It is after that event that he specifically reversed himself with regards to limiting the jurisdiction of the state to the second table of the Decalogue, now calling upon civil magistrates to enforce "the outward worship of God" as well as "sound doctrine of piety and the position of the Church."[114] Obviously, such prescriptions radically restricted the right to freedom of conscience, and, by implication, the exercise and enjoyment of other rights, as well. To establish religion, to bring both tables of the Decalogue more directly under the control of the state, is to limit the opportunities of citizens not only religiously, but also politically, civilly, and economically. While Geneva during Calvin's career was never free of such regulation, it appears to have intensified after 1555 when Calvin reached his full powers of influence.

Calvin's growing skepticism about natural moral capabilities appears also to have colored his constitutional preferences in both church and state. While at pains to expand democratic participation in both places, he was undoubtedly biased, in the final analysis, toward the "aristocratic" side of his constitutional proposals. What he said about the administration of the church could also go for the civil order: special deference to officials is required in elections, as in the general conduct of affairs, "in order that the multitude may not go wrong either through fickleness, through evil intentions, or through disorder."[115] Moreover, his deepening suspicion of natural moral capabilities also strengthened in his mind the indispensability of the Reformed Church as the locus of true righteousness, and therefore as the exclusive foundation of state authority and practice.

While Calvin made considerable room theoretically for a "liberal" interpretation of constitutional government, based on an expansive understanding of the right to freedom of conscience, both inside and outside the church, he very much qualified that interpretation in practice—increasingly, in the latter years of his tenure in Geneva.

This ambivalence on Calvin's part toward liberal nationalism, expressed in irresolution and vacillation with regard to the scope of the constitutional protection of freedom of conscience, was central to his legacy as it spread throughout northern Europe, and especially England and colonial New England, after his death. Calvinism was directly associated with severe political convulsions in Europe and the British Isles from the 1550s throughout much of the seventeenth century. They occurred in Holland beginning with the Dutch Protestant insurgency against the Catholic Hapsburgs in 1581, in France with the long-running civil war between the Huguenots and Catholics, in Scotland beginning with the Scottish Reformation of 1560, in England with the Puritan challenges to the Anglican establishment starting in the 1560s and leading up to the Civil War and Interregnum, and in New England with the Puritan community's struggles over religious freedom beginning in the 1630s. All of these contests concerned national constitutional reform, and especially the relations of state to religion. In all of them, Calvinist participants exhibited, in different ways and degrees, ambivalence over the meaning of the "rights of the people," particularly as they applied to religious freedom, but with significant consequences for the broader enjoyment of civil, political, and economic rights as well.[116]

The most striking example of the tension between liberal and illiberal nationalism implicit in the Calvinist tradition is the case of colonial New England. While they by no means agreed on everything, American Puritans, "in their covenanted towns and congregations," as David Hall puts it, *were* of one mind that the "crucial feature of all covenants" is "a people's willing consent," that "covenant [is an] instrument and expression of popular decision-making."[117] That common conviction underlay their commitment to constitutional government, and, in fact, explains their pioneering role in the rise of modern constitutionalism.

According to a leading authority, the Charter of Massachusetts Bay of 1629 "was not strictly a popular constitution, because it was in form and legal effect a royal grant, but in its practical operation after the transfer, it approximated a popular constitution more closely than any other instrument of government in actual use up to that time in America or elsewhere in modern times."[118] Moreover, Massachusetts Bay authorities went well beyond the original wording, claiming that their charter permitted an astounding degree of political independence. As early as 1641, they refused help from the English Parliament because the colony might "then be subject to all such laws as [the Parliament] should make or at least such as [it] might impose upon us."[119] When in 1646 the authorities were criticized for considering themselves "rather a free state than a colony or corporation of England," they agreed! Parliament might have authority in England, but "the highest authority here is in [our legislature], *both by our charter and by our own positive laws . . . [O]ur allegiance binds us not to the laws of England any longer than we live in England*."[120] This same interpretation applied to the charters of the other colonies, as well. Though American Puritans were slow to admit it, it was not a large step to the eventual replacement of the authority of the English crown, as well as of Parliament, with the will of "the people" who inhabited the colonies.[121]

Of greatest importance was the impulse in Massachusetts Bay and other colonies to adopt declarations of rights as an important feature of their early constitutions. The Body of Liberties was adopted by the Massachusetts Bay legislature in 1641, and amounted to an exceptionally lengthy list of fundamental rights.[122] Though it incorporated provisions from English statutes and precedents, it went well beyond them. It redefined and restructured the traditional rights of English subjects in the light of Puritan Christianity, adding modified portions of biblical law, and some "daring rights proposals"[123] from left-wing English Puritan pamphleteers.

The document opens, significantly, by referring to "such liberties, immunities, and privileges" that "humanity, civility, and Christianity call for as due to every man in his place and proportion without impeachment or infringement," highlighting the several grounds, religious *and* natural, that rights were believed to rest on.[124] In the first article, the document goes on to enumerate certain fundamental protections against taking life or property, or imposing penalties and burdens, "unless it be by some virtue or equity of some express law . . . established by the [legislature] and sufficiently published. . . ."[125] Hall makes much of the idea of equity in Puritan New England, echoing what it meant for Calvin (respect for the rights of all supplemented by a special concern for the deprived and vulnerable). Equity "may best be understood," he says, "as expressing strong hopes for even-handedness in a world where 'unrighteousness and iniquity were visibly present in the workings of English politics, civil society, ecclesiastical governance, and the law, each of which was aligned with structures of privilege and power.'"[126] He mentions several kinds of legal reform present in the Body of Liberties aimed at creating a more "equitable society."

One was "a cluster of rights and privileges for plaintiffs and defendants with virtually no equivalent in English law," including a "more impartial method of selecting juries than was the norm in England."[127] Another was significantly limiting capital punishment, and abolishing what the code calls "revolting barbarities of the English law." Still another was the abolition of monopolies, which in England had been arbitrarily dispensed to favorites of the Crown, and abolishing as well the practice of primogeniture. In its place was established (though not always observed) a more equitable system of inheritance, including provisions for female children. In that way and others, according to Hall, "the colonists eliminated all but a few traces of the social privileges that pervaded the English system and remade justice into a matter of equal treatment before the law."[128] Incidentally, in respect to the distribution of wealth, Hall stresses that Puritan rhetoric was fervently and repeatedly addressed to the obligations of the affluent for the indigent, accompanied by efforts to make tax policy more equitable than was the case in England,[129] and in places to guarantee "each adult male" "some land, free and clear."[130]

There was, however, one part of the Body of Liberties that generated a particularly strong division of opinion: the rights pertaining to religious belief and practice, namely, section 95, articles 1 through 11, identified as "A Declaration of the Liberties the Lord Jesus hath given to the Churches." According to these articles, all members of the colony have "full liberty" to practice religion according to conscience, though only so long as they "be orthodox in judgment," and "every church has full liberty to elect church officers," "provided they be able, pious and orthodox."

This was of course the basis of what John Cotton, a prominent clergyman in the colony, referred to as the "theocratic" character of Massachusetts Bay, namely, a state governed by officials regarded as divinely guided.[131] Cotton and other leaders did believe that church and state should not be "confounded," so that magistrates were precluded from holding church office, and church officials from holding civil office. At the same time, he and his associates affirmed with equal resolution that only church members might vote in civil elections, that churches and clergymen should receive direct public support through taxes and other donations, and that religious beliefs and practices should be extensively and severely regulated by laws covering blasphemy, irreverence, profanity, idolatry, and "schismatic" activity.

Although the position was widely shared, by no means all Puritans agreed with the official Massachusetts Bay policy concerning the meaning of "full liberty" of religious belief and practice, or with the commitment to established religion. Roger Williams, a controversial figure from the time he set foot in the New World in 1631, and himself evicted from the colony for unorthodox beliefs five years later, strongly opposed the Massachusetts Bay establishment, and, from his newfound perch in Rhode Island, took up the case against it in a lengthy and heated dispute in print with none other than John Cotton himself.

In essence, the conflict between Cotton and Williams personified dramatically the two sides of the Calvinist background. Both figures were staunch constitutionalists, favoring limited government, and most of the protections enunciated in the Body of Liberties—though they differed, of course, on the *degree* of limits and the *range* of protections. Both were committed to Reformed doctrine and use of scripture in guiding faith and morals, though Williams was increasingly skeptical, as Cotton was not, of Reformed ecclesiology. He seemed to take to extremes the motto, "the church reformed, always reforming."[132]

What divided them most fundamentally was the right to the freedom of conscience and the implications of that difference for the organization of church-state relations and the enjoyment of civil and political rights. Williams put the issue between them as sharply as possible quoting passages that pitted Calvin against himself. When Calvin declared that Romans 13 restricts the jurisdiction of the state exclusively to the second table, he was an "excellent servant of God," as Williams writes in *The Bloody Tenent of Persecution*, published in 1644.[133] But when Calvin assigned "Christ's ordinances and administrations of worship . . . to a civil state, town or city, as [in] the instance of Geneva," Williams rejected that practice unconditionally as a contradiction of Calvinist principles.[134]

Williams proceeded to develop his case against Massachusetts Bay very much within the framework of Calvin's "liberal" side. There is the same reliance on the distinction between the "inward" and the "outward" forum, and the accompanying distinction between "spirit" and "sword," and between the two tables of the Decalogue, that Calvin presupposed. There is the same belief that human beings are, within limits, naturally capable of recognizing violations of "second table crimes" prior to and independent of special religious enlightenment, and insofar as they do not violate those prohibitions, they may—and should—be left free to determine their religious convictions as their consciences dictate. It is important to emphasize that in constructing his position, Williams (like Calvin) invoked several separate arguments: some based explicitly on reason and experience, others derived from scripture and doctrine. To his mind, these arguments all worked together, suggesting a constructive relation between the two tables of the Decalogue, properly implemented.[135] In particular, he repeatedly emphasized that the persecution of conscience "fills the streams and rivers with blood," in keeping with the findings of Brian J. Grim and Roger Finke, mentioned above.[136]

It is, of course, on these grounds, taken together, that Williams opposed so fervently all forms of established, or what he called "National," religion so prevalent at his time. He was very clear: Given forms of political "power, might or authority [are] not religious, Christian, etc., but natural, humane, and civil."[137] The "wall of separation" between church and state Williams favored was not for protecting the church from an invariably corrupt state, as is so frequently asserted, but for protecting church and state equally from what he called the "wilderness of National religion," a condition that utterly confuses the proper roles of *both* institutions.[138] Along with religious warrants, his commitment to the principle of non-establishment is based on a belief in an independent natural moral law accessible to and obligatory upon all people, and it led to a remarkable expansion not only of the rights of con-science but of civil, political, and economic rights as well, as expressed in the Rhode Island Civil Code of 1647 and the Rhode Island Charter of 1663.

Martha Nussbaum has demonstrated convincingly in her book *Liberty of Conscience*[139] that it is Roger Williams, not John Locke, Thomas Jefferson, or James Madison, who pro-vided the intellectual foundations for the expansive constitutional protection of conscience that, she believes, Jefferson and Madison also intended. The only shortcoming in Nussbaum's otherwise excellent book is the failure to appreciate the Calvinist background, or at least one side of it. She mistakenly invokes the Stoics as the basis for Williams's approach, and thereby neglects the tradition of constitutionalism and natural rights that Calvin and many of his fol-lowers so clearly, if sometimes so ambivalently, represented.

Of course, the contribution of the Williams-Jefferson-Madison lineage to the ideals of lib-eral nationalism has constituted only one part of the American experience. That lineage has had to contend persistently with strong tendencies in the opposite direction, tendencies that have promoted one or another form of religious establishment at both state and national levels, or, more recently, the preservation of "Anglo-Protestant Culture," something Samuel P. Huntington has considered an indispensable expression of American national identity that to him is at present under severe threat.[140] These tendencies reflect the illiberal side of the Calvinist back-ground, and they are reflected in other ways as well. Despite the fact that Rhode Island adopted one of the first American anti-slavery laws in 1652, and that Roger Williams had an impressive record of deep respect and equal regard for native Americans, he assisted in rounding up native Americans and selling them into slavery after King Philip's War of 1675–1676, probably as the result of an uncharacteristic flash of vengefulness over the destruction done. Williams's ambiva-lence toward slavery set the tone for similar ambivalence on the part of Jefferson and Madison, though, in their case, with even more baleful consequences for the ideals of liberal nationalism.

A concluding and very significant example of reformist attitudes toward early nationalism is the work of Alberico Gentili (1552–1608), an Italian-born Calvinist[141] who taught interna-tional law at Oxford around the turn of the seventeenth century. "As the precursor of [Hugo] Grotius, and the one who substantially and effectively prepared the way for him, Gentili is [arguably] the real 'father' of the modern law of nations."[142] In sum, "the pioneer work of Gentili was in harmony with the larger movement of the sixteenth century which witnessed a transformation of society, the establishment of a new spirit and wider outlook, the decline of theocracy, and the rise of the modern State."[143] Central to the idea of the modern law of nations, already incipient in the earlier thinking of the conciliarists and Catholic theorists like Victoria and Suarez, is the extension of the norms of constitutionalism, including, espe-cially, the universal protection of rights, to a new international order made up of a multiplic-ity of independent national states. That meant establishing general laws and practices able to restrain arbitrary power, not only *within* the new nations, but *among* them, as well, and particularly in regard to the use of force.

Calvin did not comment at length on the law of nations, but he did support the idea over against those who wanted to make universal "the political system of Moses."[144] Whatever the variations in detail and degrees of punishment among the law codes of the world, all nations, he said, enforce second-table rights and may be called to account in respect to them. These rights are expressions of natural law and equity, which, in turn, underlie the law of nations.[145] In that connection, he also devoted some attention to the "right of the government to wage war"[146] and its duty to observe "restraint and humanity in war,"[147] briefly invoking some of the standards of the just war tradition, albeit ambivalently.[148]

Gentili elaborated on the law of nations and the law of war at much greater length and with more serious study and expertise than Calvin. However, he shared Calvin's general perspective, as well as some of the deep ambivalence of his thought, now developing certain liberal themes, now veering toward more illiberal ones.

An important part of Gentili's theory of force accords with Calvin's views, and, up to a point, particularly his "early" thinking. Like Calvin, Gentili distinguished sharply between the two tables of the Decalogue: the laws of religion "are divine, that is between God and man; they are not human, namely between man and man."[149] "Religion is a matter of the mind and . . . will, which is always accompanied by freedom."[150] "Therefore, no man's rights are violated by a difference in religion, nor is it lawful to make war because of religion."[151] "Force in connexion with religion is unjust."[152] Gentili registered strong support for religious freedom and pluralism, both among and, more surprisingly, *within* states, thereby challenging the principle of religiously uniform states authorized by the Peace of Augsburg and Westphalia.[153]

Accordingly, human laws alone—second-table rights—are the proper domain of earthly government, in both domestic and international relations. "Now this is a just cause [for the use of force, if] our own rights have been interfered with. . . . Everyone is justified in maintaining his rights."[154] The only truly just cause for using force, inside or outside national borders, is the protection of the legitimate temporal and material rights of nation-states and their citizens. Excluding religion as a cause for war, whether civil or international, and expanding the society of states to include infidel and even barbarian nations that are independent and politically organized,[155] is an indispensable condition of peace. By developing his approach to international law in this way, Gentili advanced the secularization and liberalization of international law.[156]

Like other sixteenth-century Calvinist authors, Gentili supported constitutional restrictions on political power and authority, including a right of rebellion in extreme cases. However, he occasionally equivocated on the subject, exemplifying ambivalence about these matters characteristic of reformist thinking. On the one hand, rulers who betray their subjects by failing to defend them or by breaking agreements with them, may be replaced, and, in fact, rebellions may be assisted licitly by outside powers, as in the case of the support given to the Dutch Revolt of 1581 by Queen Elizabeth of England.[157] On the other hand, Gentili temporized at times. He worried that things might go too far, and concluded that since anarchy is worse than tyranny,[158] considerable indulgence is owed earthly rulers. Now and again, he suggested that they have overriding authority that must be submitted to, appearing at times to disregard the authority of "constituted lesser magistrates" to stand up to a deviant ruler that was countenanced even by Calvin himself.[159] For example, Gentili stated that rulers may not be put on trial by their people, and that while they are not entitled to deprive their people of property without just cause, a ruler has the final say as to whether a just cause exists![160]

Gentili's thoughts on international obligations during wartime also reveal some further ambivalence. Along with respect for religious diversity, he strongly emphasized protection of noncombatants, restraints against cruelty to prisoners, moderation of vengeance against a conquered enemy, and conservation of religious buildings and other architectural and artistic treasures. Nevertheless, he countenanced the enslavement of conquered peoples, the right of booty, the sacking of cities, and the use of reprisals.[161]

Conclusion

Following the advocates of "the liberal peace," we have assumed that "liberal nationalism," consisting of the orderly and properly sequenced development of constitutional democracy, including provisions for economic prosperity, is a critical condition of national and international peace, while the presence of illiberal institutions, namely those that are seriously fractured religiously, ethnically, economically, and in other ways, promise a high probability of violence. At the same time, we have paid attention to some of the challenges to those assumptions represented by adherents of the new idea of "justpeace," such as the neglect of religion, questionable neoliberal convictions about economic justice, an exclusive devotion to the merits of retributive justice, and the benefits of state-centered solutions to violent conflict. In addition, we have acknowledged the inescapable dilemmas of nationalism, such as the intermixture of liberal and illiberal elements, and the abiding tension between national and international obligations, as well as the complications of attempting to administer a system of equal rights fairly and equitably.

Accordingly, we have reexamined the historical origins of nationalism and offered a fresh account that does two things: First, it reveals the saliency of religion by establishing the centrality of the Protestant Reformation and the complexity of its influence on the rise of nationalism. The three types of attitude toward a new understanding of nation- or people-hood—accommodationism, renovationism, and reformism—give clear evidence of the conflicting tendencies between liberalism and illiberalism that have become central to the study of nationalism, and they help explain why the conflicts are so deep-seated and so persistent. Second, it reveals some significant intellectual resources for reevaluating and correcting our understanding of the liberal peace, which will bring it more closely into line with the ideals of the advocates of justpeace.

By demonstrating that religion was "present at creation," our account shows why religion and nationalism have up until now been so closely associated, as well as why the dilemmas of nationalism, both domestic and international, are not likely to go away. It also reveals, especially where reformists—mainly liberal Calvinists—give prominence to renovationist ideas, how the concept of the liberal peace can be improved. In particular, the Calvinist notion of equity, drawing as it does upon Anabaptist impulses to modify both economic inequality and the severity of retributive law, contributes to adjustments in approaches to peacemaking that seem abundantly confirmed by experience. That is also true of the liberal Calvinist emphasis, again adapted from central Anabaptist convictions, on limiting the state and expanding the sphere of conscientious belief and action, religious and otherwise. That development makes way for supplementing state-centered peacemaking policies with a broad array of nongovernmental innovation.

For all these reasons, it is imperative to take a new look at the origins of nationalism.

NOTES

* The author expresses special appreciation to Atalia Omer for urging fuller attention to some of the criticisms of modern nationalism that exist in the literature, and to David Y. Kim for assistance in assembling invaluable source materials, particularly in regard to the discussion of Luther and the Anabaptists.

1. See Scott W. Hibbard, *Religious Politics and Secular States: Egypt, India, and the United States* (Baltimore: Johns Hopkins University Press, 2010).

2. Jack Snyder, *From Voting to Violence: Democratization and Nationalist Conflict* (New York: W.W. Norton and Co., 2000), 316–317. See also Edward D. Mansfield and Jack Snyder, *Electing to Fight: Why Emerging Democracies Go to War* (Cambridge, MA: MIT Press, 2005); Edward D. Mansfield and Jack Snyder, "Democratic Transitions and War: From Napoleon to the Millennium's End," in *Turbulent Peace: The Challenges of Managing International Conflict*, ed. Chester A. Crocker, Fen Osler Hampson, and Pamela Aall (Washington, DC: United States Institute of Peace Press, 2001), 113–126; David Little, "Religion, Nationalism, and Intolerance," and some of the other essays in *Between Terror and Tolerance: Religious Leaders, Conflict, and Peacemaking*, ed. Timothy L. Sisk (Washington, DC: Georgetown University Press, 2011); David Little and Donald K. Swearer, eds., *Religion and Nationalism in Iraq: A Comparative Perspective* (Cambridge, MA: Harvard University Press, 2006) for a comparison of the dynamics of ethnoreligious nationalism in four postcolonial cases (Bosnia-Herzegovina, Sudan, Sri Lanka, and Iraq); Hibbard, *Religious Politics and Secular States*. Jürgen Habermas, in "The European Nation-State: Its Achievements and Its Limits," in *Mapping the Nation*, ed. Gopal Balakrishnan (London: Verso, 1996), comes to similar conclusions using slightly different terminology.

   In addition to studies drawing explicit connections between constitutional democracy, nationalism, and peace, there is a broad literature relating constitutional democracy and peace that is relevant to the literature on nationalism. Of special importance is a new collection of essays on the subject by Michael W. Doyle, *Liberal Peace: Selected Essays* (New York: Routledge, 2012). Doyle emphasizes that "democratic institutions" "promote peace and mutual respect among democratic peoples," "enhance human rights, produce higher levels of political participation, and decrease state repression," "serve to protect the mass of the population from state indifference during a natural disaster," and stimulate economic growth and inclusiveness, and that weak democratic institutions foster violence (202–203). Cf. 214–216, supporting the conclusion that "empirical confirmation of the liberal peace is exceptionally strong" (216), though also admitting both that further theoretical testing continues to be required (216), and that while liberal states are generally peaceful toward one another, they are also guilty of bellicosity toward nonliberal states, as in the imperialist and colonialist wars of the nineteenth century (67). See also R.J. Rummel, *Power Kills: Democracy as a Model of Nonviolence* (New Brunswick, NJ: Transaction, 2004); Morton H. Halperin, Joseph T. Siegle, and Michael M. Weinstein, *Democracy Advantage: How Democracies Promote Prosperity and Peace* (New York: Routledge, 2005). Examples of special relevance to nationalism are Ted Robert Gurr, *Peoples versus States: Minorities at Risk in the New Century* (Washington, DC: United States Institute of Peace Press, 2000); Gurr and Barbara Harff, *Ethnic Conflict in Global Politics* (Boulder,

CO: Westview Press, 2004); Michael W. Doyle and Nicholas Sambanis, *Making War and Building Peace: United Nations Peace Operations* (Princeton, NJ: Princeton University Press, 2006); Larry Diamond, *The Spirit of Democracy: The Struggle to Build Free Societies throughout the World* (New York: Times Books, 2008); Roland Paris, *At War's End: Building Peace after Civil Conflict* (New York: Cambridge University Press, 2004).

3. Scholars like Snyder, Mansfield, Gurr, and Paris, among others, emphasize the importance of "orderly development," or proper sequencing in the creation of liberal institutions. A disorderly transition from authoritarianism to democracy, where, for example, elections precede the creation of stable political, civil, and economic institutions, can greatly increase the likelihood of violence. "The rule seems to be: Go fully democratic, or don't go at all" (Edward D. Mansfield and Jack Snyder, "Democratic Transitions and War," in Crocker, Hampson, and Aall, eds., *Turbulent Peace*, 124). Cf. Gurr, *Peoples versus States*, and Paris, *At War's End*.

4. Snyder, *From Voting to Violence*, 316–317.

5. Michael W. Doyle and Nicholas Sambanis, *Making War and Building Peace: United Nations Peace Operations* (Princeton, NJ: Princeton University Press, 2006), 340.

6. Snyder, *From Voting to Violence*, 24 and 352–353. There is controversy among scholars over how important political, economic, and social grievances are in causing civil wars. One dissenter is Paul Collier, "Economic Causes of Civil Conflict and Their Implications for Policy," in Crocker, Hampson, and Aall, eds., *Turbulent Peace*, where he defends his now-famous aphorism "greed not grievance" (see 144ff.). For a critique of Collier's views and the similar views of other social scientists, see comments in the Introduction in David Little and Donald K. Swearer, eds., *Religion and Nationalism in Iraq: A Comparative Perspective* (Cambridge: Harvard University Press, 2006), 5–6.

7. Brian J. Grim and Roger Finke, *The Price of Freedom Denied: Religious Persecution and Conflict in the Twenty-First Century* (New York: Cambridge University Press, 2011).

8. Grim and Finke, *The Price of Freedom Denied*, 222.

9. Bernard Yack, "Myth of the Civic Nation," in *Theorizing Nationalism*, ed. Ronald Beiner (Albany, NY: State University of New York Press, 1999), 106. Cf. Samuel P. Huntington, *Who Are We? The Challenges to America's National Identity* (New York: Simon and Schuster, 2004), 30ff.

10. Judith Licthenberg, "How Liberal Can Nationalism Be?" in Beiner, *Theorizing Nationalism*, 167–188.

11. Winnifred Fallers Sullivan, *The Impossibility of Religious Freedom* (Princeton, NJ: Princeton University Press, 2005).

12. Winnifred Fallers Sullivan, "Religious Freedom and the Rule of Law: Exporting Modernity in a Postmodern World?" *Mississippi College Law Review* 22 (2002–2003): 181ff, accessed via HeinOnline.

13. Winnifred Fallers Sullivan, "'The Conscience of Contemporary Man': Reflections on *U.S. v. Seeger* and *Dignitatis Humanae*," *U.S. Catholic Historian* 24 (2006): 119–123.

14. Sullivan, *The Impossibility of Religious Freedom*, 154–157. Along with Peter Danchin, Elizabeth Shakman Hurd, and Saba Mahmood, Sullivan is part of a group of lawyers, anthropologists, and international relations scholars who regularly contribute to a blog, "The Immanent Frame" (http://blogs.ssrc.org/tif/about/), that is dedicated to criticizing various aspects of the "liberal hegemony," in a phrase of Sullivan's. They all exhibit, sometimes explicitly, the influence of Talal Asad, who has made a career of "problematizing" the liberal order as such, including the language of human rights. See, for example, Talal Asad,

Formations of the Secular: Christianity, Islam, and Modernity (Stanford, CA: Stanford University Press, 2003).

15. John Paul Lederach and R. Scott Appleby, "Strategic Peacebuilding: An Overview," in *Strategies of Peace: Transforming Conflict in a Violent World*, ed. Daniel Philpott and Gerard F. Powers (New York: Oxford University Press, 2010), 40–41.

16. Daniel Philpott, "Introduction: Searching for Strategy in an Age of Peacebuilding," in Philpott and Powers, eds., *Strategies of Peace*, 4. Cf. Daniel Philpott, *Just and Unjust Peace: An Ethic of Reconciliation* (New York: Oxford University Press, 2012), 2, 9, 70–73, 176–177, 207, 209.

17. Oliver P. Richmond, "Conclusion: Strategic Peacebuilding beyond the Liberal Peace," in Philpott and Powers, eds., *Strategies of Peace*, 361.

18. Philpott, "Introduction," 4.

19. Philpott, "Introduction," 4.

20. Philpott, "Introduction," 4, and Gerard F. Powers, "Religion and Peacebuilding," in Philpott and Powers, eds., *Strategies of Peace*, 319–322. Such a complaint applies to Grim and Finke, *The Price of Freedom Denied*. Their "religious economies" approach, holding that deregulated religion is beneficial in the same way as a deregulated market, relies on three Enlightenment figures, Voltaire, David Hume, and Adam Smith. Grim and Finke take them to believe that every religion characteristically seeks to dominate by repressing competitors, and the best way to prevent that is to increase the number of competitors, making it hard for any one religion to gain a monopoly. On their account, to believe in the superiority of one's religion is necessarily to regard competitors as "dangerous and wrong" (46) and to warrant repression, as exemplified, they think, by the New England Puritans. Such a claim, of course, disregards radical English and American Puritans, not to mention Anabaptists, who helped constitute the "free church" tradition in Western Christianity. Members of that tradition regularly believed in the superiority of their religion, and simultaneously favored, often at great cost, the universal protection of the freedom of conscience.

21. Philpott, "Reconciliation: An Ethic for Peacebuilding," in Philpott and Powers, eds., *Strategies of Peace*, 91–118.

22. Richmond, "Conclusion," 360.

23. Lederach and Appleby, "Strategic Peacebuilding," 26–27.

24. Richmond, "Conclusion," 361.

25. E.g., E. J. Hobsbawm, *Nations and Nationalism: Programme, Myth, Reality* (Cambridge: Cambridge University Press, 1991); Walker Conner, *Ethnonationalism: The Quest for Understanding* (Princeton, NJ: Princeton University Press, 1994); Mark Jurgensmeyer, *The New Cold War? Religious Nationalism Confronts the Secular State* (Berkeley, CA: University of California Press, 1993).

26. For example, Ernest Gellner, *Nations and Nationalism* (Ithaca, NY: Cornell University Press, 1983); Benedict Anderson, *Imagined Communities* (London: Verson, 1991); Anthony D. Smith, *Chosen Peoples: Sacred Sources of National Identity* (Oxford: Oxford University Press, 2003); William R. Hutchison and Hartmut Lehmann, eds., *Many Are Chosen: Divine Election and Western Nationalism* (Minneapolis, MN: Fortress Press, 1994); and Caspar Hirschi, *Origins of Nationalism: An Alternative History from Ancient Rome to Early Modern Germany* (Cambridge: Cambridge University Press, 2012).

27. For example, Liah Greenfeld, *Nationalism: Five Roads to Modernity* (Cambridge, MA: Harvard University Press, 1993); Monica Duffy Toft, Daniel Philpott, and Timothy

Samuel Shah, *God's Century: Resurgent Religion and Global Politics* (New York: W.W. Norton and Co., 2011).

28. For example, Brad S. Gregory, *The Unintended Reformation: How a Religious Revolution Secularized Society* (Cambridge, MA: Harvard University Press, 2012). Gregory does not say much about nationalism, but he believes the "entire tradition of modern liberal thought" is represented by Thomas Hobbes, who is supposed to have opposed any mixing of religion and politics (162). Gregory's claim is mistaken in two ways. 1) As a consummate Erastian, Hobbes did not exclude religion but subordinated it to his ideal of an all-powerful "unitary executive." 2) Most Calvinists vigorously rejected Hobbes's ideal, holding out, to one degree or another, for a church independent of the state. Even the most separationist-minded of them, like Roger Williams, did not favor completely divorcing religious belief from political life (see note 135).

    A second example is Philip Hamburger's book, *Separation of Church and State* (Cambridge, MA: Harvard University Press, 2002), contending that the "separation of church and state" in American legal history is a radical nineteenth-century doctrine, invented by nativist Protestants in reaction to Catholic immigrants, that is sharply distinct from the earlier idea of the disestablishment of religion, and that has only the most oblique connection to the Calvinist wing of the Reformation (22ff.). For one thing, Hamburger has seriously overstated the differences between the ideas of disestablishment and separation of church and state in the American legal tradition, as Kent Greenawalt has shown in his telling review (*California Law Review* 93 (2005): 367). For another, Hamburger vastly oversimplifies the nineteenth-century data, as Jeremy Gunn amply demonstrates in "The Separation of Church and State versus Religion in the Public Square: The Contested History of the Establishment Clause," in *No Establishment of Religion: America's Contribution to Religious Liberty*, ed. T. Jeremy Gunn and John Witte Jr. (New York: Oxford University Press, 2012), esp. 26–38. Lastly, and most important for our purposes, Hamburger's tendentious reading of Roger Williams overlooks extensive supplementary appeals to "reason and experience" Williams makes that warrant at once a sharp separation between churches and civil authority and a basis for constructive relations between them. These are themes that lie deep in the Calvinist tradition and that conflict with or significantly modify Hamburger's account. (See our analysis of the Calvinist tradition and of Williams's place in it in the section "Reformism" later in this chapter, especially notes 134 and 135. See also Little, "Roger Williams and the Puritan Background of the Establishment Clause," in Gunn and Witte, eds., *No Establishment of Religion*, 100–124.) Winifred Sullivan expresses strong support for Hamburger's book in "Religious Freedom and the Rule of Law," 181, and her book, *Impossibility of Religious Freedom*, is generously endorsed by Hamburger on the book jacket.

29. Diarmaid McCullough, *The Reformation: A History* (New York: Viking, 2004). Early in the book, McCullough dismisses the relevance of the idea of nationalism until the eighteenth century (42). But later he reverses himself and announces that the Reformation promoted "a common cultural and religious identity" as the basis for state power, thereby encouraging the evolution of a "state-nation" into a "nation-state" (649).

30. J. N. Figgis, *From Gerson to Grotius: 1414-1625* (Cambridge: Cambridge University Press, 1956); Philip S. Gorski, *The Disciplinary Revolution: Calvinism and the Rise of the State in Early Modern Europe* (Chicago: University of Chicago Press, 2003); and Ernest Barker, "Book I: State and Society," esp. "The Sixteenth Century and the National State," in *Principles of Social and Political Theory* (Oxford: Clarendon Press, 1956), 13–29. Speaking of the relation of the Protestant Reformation to the "rise of national feeling," Barker says

that in the Lutheran and Anglican cases "a return was made to the classical unity of the Greek city-state," "but not, or not to the same extent, in the area of Calvinism" (14–15). Later he says that in some places Calvinism "stood for the cause of the minorities and the rights of the 'gathered' Free Church based upon voluntary compact," leading to "an argument against . . . absolutism, and a plea for the contracted rights of the people" as the basis for the national state (17). See also "Christianity and Nationality" in Barker, *Church, State, and Education* (Ann Arbor, MI: University of Michigan Press, 1957), 131–150, for a related line of argument concerning the contribution of "Nonconformity" in England to the rise of liberal nationalism.

31. Anthony Marx, *Faith in Nation: Exclusionary Origins of Nationalism* (New York: Oxford University Press, 2003). Marx defines "nationalism" as "a collective [or mass] sentiment or identity, bounding and binding together those individuals who share a sense of large-scale political solidarity aimed at creating, legitimating, or challenging states." "Nationalism is the potential basis of popular legitimacy or expression of support for state power, and as such the two are tied by definition" (6). Marx's definition of nationalism, and his analysis of its development, place him somewhere in between two different, and competing, schools of thought on the subject, the "modernists" and the "primordialists." Modernists (e.g., Ernest Gellner and E. J. Hobsbawm) hold that nationalism does not exist until the appearance of modern states like France and the United States in the eighteenth century. (The term was coined by Johann Gottfried Herder in the late 1770s.) Critical to this understanding is the capacity of the modern state to consolidate a "people" into a "mass society" by means of new, inclusive techniques of communication, commerce, education, law enforcement, and bureaucratic control. In contrast, primordialists (e.g., Anthony Smith) emphasize the importance of popular or "national" consciousness or identity without reference to the state, a characteristic that may be accentuated and intensified by the modern state, but that, in many cases, antedates the modern state by centuries. I follow Marx's "middle way." The heart of nationalism is the link between "nation" and "state," but the origins of the link, and the process of its development, significantly precede the eighteenth century. In fact, that process of development is very important in the shaping of the modern state.

32. The same defects can be found in McCullough's second comment (on 649 in *Reformation: A History*) mentioned in note 29.

33. Hirshi, *Origins of Nationalism*, 152.

34. Hirshi, *Origins of Nationalism*, 215.

35. At *Origins of Nationalism*, 137, Hirshi takes issue with Quentin Skinner's characterization of "civic humanists" like Bruni as taking an active part in running the commonwealth (Skinner, *Foundations of Modern Political Thought*, vol. 1, *The Renaissance* (New York: Cambridge University Press, 1979), 77).

36. Skinner, *Foundations*, vol. 1, 238–239.

37. Hirshi, *Origins of Nationalism*, 135.

38. Cited by Matthew Spinka, *John Hus and the Council of Constance* (New York: Columbia University Press, 1965), 19.

39. See Skinner, *Foundations of Modern Political Thought*, vol. 2, *The Reformation*, 114–123.

40. Hirshi, *Origins of Nationalism*, 82.

41. Hirshi, *Origins of Nationalism*, 44.

42. John B. Morrall, *Political Thought in Medieval Times* (New York: Harper and Bros., 1962), 129.

43. Spinka, *Jan Hus and the Council of Constance*, 69.

44. Skinner, *Foundations*, vol. 2, 115.

45. Skinner, *Foundations*, vol. 2, 116.

46. "Accommodationism" as used in this chapter means something opposite to what it means in the hands of legal scholars like Martha Nussbaum. For her, it defines a policy whereby the state allows for exemptions on grounds of religion to neutral and generally applicable laws. See Nussbaum, "The Struggle Over Accommodation," in *Liberty of Conscience: In Defense of America's Tradition of Religious Equality* (New York: Basic Books, 2008), 115–174, and *The New Religious Intolerance: Overcoming the Politics of Fear in an Anxious Age* (Cambridge, MA: Harvard University Press, 2012), 68ff.

47. "Unitary" here means a system of government in which the powers of the constitutent parts of government are vested in a strong central executive authority, sometimes referred to as "absolutist."

48. Hirshi, *Origins of Nationalism*, 202.

49. Hirshi, *Origins of Nationalism*, 203.

50. Hirshi, *Origins of Nationalism*, 215. The phrases "new populism" and "mass movement" are Hirshi's. He makes the important point that despite Luther's skepticism about the humanist brand of nationalist language, he eventually accelerated the rise of nationalism by means of effective "religious propaganda" (206). But Hirshi also makes some dubious points, such as labeling Luther a "religious fundamentalist" (205) responsible for the rise of "confessionalization" that temporarily retarded the rise of nationalism. These terms and claims are neither well defended nor consistent with what he says elsewhere.

51. Anderson, *Imagined Community*, 39.

52. Quoted in Carlos Eire, *War against the Idols: The Reformation of Worship from Erasmus to Calvin* (Cambridge: Cambridge University Press, 1986), 72.

53. Skinner, *Foundations*, vol. 2, 18.

54. Philip Schaff, *History of the Christian Church*, vol. 6, *Modern Christianity: The German Reformation* (New York: Charles Scribner's Sons, 1888), 447–448; cited in James Turner Johnson, *Just War Tradition and the Restraint of War: A Moral and Historical Inquiry* (Princeton, NJ: Princeton University Press, 1981), 52–53.

55. Cited by Skinner, *Foundations*, vol. 2, 19.

56. John Witte Jr., *Reformation of Rights: Law, Religion, and Human Rights in Early Modern Calvinism* (Cambridge: Cambridge University Press, 2007), 131.

57. Skinner, *Foundations*, vol. 2, 14–15.

58. Figgis, *From Gerson to Grotius*, 60.

59. Figgis, *From Gerson to Grotius*, 76.

60. John Witte, Jr., *Law and Protestantism: Legal Teachings of the Lutheran Reformation* (Cambridge: Cambridge University Press, 2002), 83–84.

61. Figgis, *From Gerson to Grotius*, 55.

62. The thesis that "exclusionary religion" inspires early nationalism in sixteenth-century England and elsewhere in Western Europe is the central claim of Marx in his *Faith in Nation*. There are, as we shall see, strengths and weaknesses to this thesis. While Marx is rather good on what we call "accommodationist" Protestantism, he is considerably weaker on the character and role of the Puritan reformists, to whom we shall turn in a later section.

63. Richard Hooker, *Laws of Ecclesiastical Polity* (1593; repr., London: J.M. Dent and Sons, 1958), vol. 1, 362–363.

64. In *Separation of Church and State*, 32–38, Philip Hamburger makes much of the fact that Hooker mischaracterized the Puritan dissenters as seeking a strong version of separation, rather than a more benign form of disestablishment. But if the distinction between separation and disestablishment is not as sharp as Hamburger claims (see note 28), then it is

likely that Hooker's description matched the views of some segments of a complex movement, views that would become more prominent in the seventeenth century, as in the case of Roger Williams.

65. Maurice Powicke, *The Reformation in England* (New York: Oxford University Press, 1961), 51.

66. Cited in David Little, *Religion, Order, and Law* (Chicago: University of Chicago Press, 1984), 143.

67. Hooker, *Laws of Ecclesiastical Polity*, vol. 2, 29.

68. Hooker, *Laws of Ecclesiastical Polity*, vol. 1, 195.

69. Works of Richard Hooker, John Keble, ed. 3 vols. (Oxford: Clarendon Press, 1888), vol. 3, 330.

70. Hooker, *Laws of Ecclesiastical Polity*, vol. 2, 475.

71. Hooker, *Laws of Ecclesiastical Polity*, vol. 2, 475.

72. Skinner, *Foundations*, vol. 2, 105.

73. George Hunston WIlliams, *The Radical Reformation* (Kirkville, MO: Sixteenth Century Journal Publications, Inc., 1992), 1303.

74. Williams, *Radical Reformation*, 1277.

75. Conrad Grebel and friends, "Letters to Thomas Müntzer," in *Spiritual and Anabaptist Writers*, ed. George Hunston Williams, (Philadelphia: Westminster Press, 1958), 79.

76. Hans-Jurgen Goertz, *The Anabaptists* (London: Routledge, 1996), 86.

77. Claus Peter Clasen, *Anabaptists: A Social History* (Ithaca, NY: Cornell University Press, 1972), 426.

78. Williams, *Radical Reformation*, 1286–1287.

79. Cited by James M. Strayer, *Anabaptists and the Sword* (Lawrence, KS: Coronado Press, 1976), 320.

80. Cited at Strayer, *Anabaptists and the Sword*, 121. There were related reservations about paying taxes, particularly in support of the use of force, though on that matter some Anabaptists were willing to compromise.

81. See MacCulloch, *The Reformation: A History*, 682: "Radical thinkers and preachers in the early stages of the Reformation [were at the time] marginalized and rejected by Catholics and Protestants alike . . . [M]ainstream Christianity is only now reexamining [their] alternative views of the future and recognizing how much value there is in them. A modern Anglican . . . is likely to be more like a sixteenth-century Anabaptist in belief than . . . a sixteenth-century member of the Church of England."

82. Clasen, *Anabaptists: A Social History*, 426.

83. Williams, *Radical Reformation*, note 15, 763, 762.

84. Peter James Klassen, *Economics of Anabaptism, 1525–1560* (London: Mouton and Co., 1964), 42.

85. Parts of what follows are borrowed from a forthcoming essay by the author, "Calvinism, Constitutionalism, and the Ingredients of Peace," in John Bowlin, ed., Kuyper Center Review. Calvinism and Democracy (Grand Rapids: Eardmans, 2014).

86. MacCulloch, *The Reformation: A History*, 190.

87. Calvin, *Homilies on I Samuel*, 10, cited in Herbert D. Foster, "Political Theories of Calvinists," in *Collected Papers of Herbert D. Foster* (privately printed, 1929), 82.

88. John Calvin, *Institutes of the Christian Religion*, ed. John T. McNeill, trans. Ford Lewis Battles (Philadelphia: Westminster Press 1960), bk. 4, ch. XX, para. 31, 1519.

89. Calvin, *Commentary on the Psalms* ch. 119, cited in Foster, *Collected Papers*, 82.

90. Calvin, *Institutes*, bk. 4, ch. XX, para. 8, 1493.

91. Calvin, *Homilies on I Samuel*, 8, cited in Foster, *Collected Papers*, 82.

92. Calvin, *Commentary on Micah*, 5:5.

93. Calvin, *Homilies on I Samuel*, cited in Foster, "Political Theories of the Calvinists," 82.

94. Calvin, *Institutes*, bk. 4, ch XX, para. 31, 1518–1519, and note 54.

95. See Willem Nijenhuis, "The Limits of Civil Disobedience in Calvin's Last-Known Sermons," in *Ecclesia Reformata: Studies on the Reformation*, vol. 2 (New York, Leiden and Köln: E.J. Brill, 1994), 73–94, discussing Calvin's *Homilies on 1 and II Samuel*.

96. Josef Bohatec, *Calvins Lehre von Staat und Kirche mit besonderer Berucksichtigung des Organismusgedankens* (Aalen: Scientia, 1961), 94–95. (Translations are mine.)

97. Calvin, *Institutes*, bk. 4, ch. XX, para. 31, 1519.

98. Calvin, *Institutes*, bk. 4, ch. XX, para. 24, 1512.

99. This conviction, central to Calvin's thought, is an important point of connection to what Judith Shklar has called the "liberalism of fear" in her classic essay by that name (in *Liberalism and the Moral Life*, ed. Nancy L. Rosenblum (Cambridge, MA: Harvard University Press, 1989), 21–38). Because of the deep-seated and widespread human disposition toward the exercise of arbitrary power—to inflict, that is, severely aversive consequences for self-serving purposes—plural government and the legal protection of individual rights (against arbitrary killing, torture, enslavement, persecution of "conscience, religion or belief," etc.) are urgently required on a universal basis. This general point is either not addressed, or addressed confusingly (see note 134, below), by critics of liberalism, the rule of law, and existing human rights norms, such as Danchin, Hurd, Mahmood, Sullivan, and their mentor, Asad, mentioned in note 14. (See David Little, "Religion, Human Rights, and Secularism: Preliminary Clarifications and Some Islamic, Jewish, and Christian Responses" in *Humanity Before God: Contemporary Faces of Jewish, Christian, and Islamic Ethics*, ed. William Schweiker, Michael A. Johnson, and Kevin Jung (Minneapolis: Fortress Press, 2006), 262–273, for a critique of Asad's attack on human rights language.) While particular governments, including constitutional democracies, must of course be called to account according to constitutional, rule of law, and human rights standards, it is those very standards that are taken by "liberals of fear" best to protect against the violations resulting from the exercise of arbitrary power, and to reduce the related occurrence of violence. Any successful refutation must begin by addressing the extensive evidence that by now supports that position (see note 2, above).

100. Calvin, *Institutes*, bk. 4, ch. XX, para. 16, 1504.

101. Calvin, Four Last Books of the Pentateuch, Exodus, http://www.studylight.org/commentaries/cal/view.cgi?bk=ex&ch=20:15, vol. 3.

102. Calvin, *Epistles of Paul the Apostle to the Romans and to the Thessalonians*, trans. Ross Mackenzie (Grand Rapids, MI: Eerdmans, 1976), II Thessalonians 3:12, 420.

103. Calvin, *Commentary on Matthew* 5:25, cited in David Yoon-Jung Kim, "Law, Equity, and Calvin's Moral Critique of Protestant Faith," ThD diss., Harvard Divinity School, 2012, 164, 171. I am indebted to Kim's dissertation for illuminating the central importance of the idea of equity in Calvin's thought, as well as the connection of the idea to a "natural law conception of rights."

104. Calvin, *Commentary on Matthew* 5:25.

105. Witte, *Reformation of Rights*, 52.

106. Foster, "Calvin's Programme for a Puritan State," in *Collected Papers*, 65.

107. Brian Tierney, *Idea of Natural Rights: Studies on Natural Rights, Natural Law and Church Law* (Atlanta, GA: Scholars Press, 1997), chs. IX, X.

108. Calvin, *Commentary on the Psalms*, http://www.ccel.org/ccel/calvin/calcom08.html, 82:3.

109. Robert M. Kingdon, "Social Welfare in Calvin's Geneva," in *Church and Society in Reformation Europe* (London: Variorum Reprints, 1985), 50–69; and Jennine E. Olson, *Calvin and Social Welfare: Deacons and the Bourse Francaise* (London: Associated University Presses, 1989).

110. Calvin, *Epistles of Paul the Apostle*, 283–286.

111. Philip Benedict, *Christ's Churches Purely Reformed: A Social History of Calvinism* (New Haven, CT: Yale University Press, 2002), 7, 120.

112. See David Little, "Calvin and Natural Rights," *Political Theology* 10 (2009): 3.

113. Witte, *Reformation of Rights*, 67–70.

114. Calvin, *Institutes*, bk. 4, ch. XX, para. 2, 1487.

115. Calvin, *Institutes*, bk. 4, ch. III, para. 15, 1066.

116. See Chapters 2, 3, and 4 of Witte, *Reformation of Rights*, on Theodore Beza, Johannes Althusius, and John Milton, respectively. These chapters discuss the evolving thoughts on constitutionalism, the protection of rights, and church-state relations of the three figures toward violent struggles over national reform in France (Beza), the Netherlands (Althusius), and England (Milton) in the sixteenth and seventeenth centuries.

117. David D. Hall, *A Reforming People: Puritanism and the Transformation of Public Life* (New York: Alfred A. Knopf, 2011), 157.

118. C. H. McIlwain, *Constitutionalism and Its Changing World* (Cambridge: Cambridge University Press, 1939), 241.

119. From *Winthrop's Journal*, cited in McIlwain, *Constitutionalism and Its Changing World*, 234.

120. From *Winthrop's Journal*, cited in McIlwain, *Constitutionalism and Its Changing World*, 235, emphasis added.

121. Donald S. Lutz, *Origins of American Constitutionalism* (Baton Rouge, LA: Louisiana State University Press, 1988), 37.

122. Edmund S. Morgan, *Puritan Political Ideas, 1558–1794* (Indianapolis, IN: Bobbs-Merrill Co., 1965), 171–197.

123. Witte, *Reformation of Rights*, 280.

124. Morgan, *Puritan Political Ideas*, 172–173. I have modernized and here and there "translated" some of the archaic words and forms of speech in the Body of Liberties, and in some of the subsequent citations from Puritan writings.

125. Morgan, *Puritan Political Ideas*, 173.

126. Hall, *A Reforming People*, 147.

127. Hall, *A Reforming People*, 150

128. Hall, *A Reforming People*, 152.

129. Hall, *A Reforming People*, 67–70.

130. Hall, *A Reforming People*, 64–65.

131. Cotton actually uses the term to describe what in his mind is "the best form of government in the commonwealth, as well as the church," in Morgan, *Puritan Political Ideas*, 163.

132. It is this aspect of Williams's views that Hamburger devotes exclusive attention to in expositing Williams's thinking on church-state relations (*Separation of Church and State*, 38–53). Hamburger refers to Williams's insistence on purifying the church of all worldly influence, including his radical anticlericalism, as favoring "a sort of separation" (484), though a position Hamburger regards as idiosyncratic, if not just plain weird. On Hamburger's construction, this obsession with church purification, leading Williams eventually to abandon membership in any congregation, and to oppose all existing forms of church organization, caused him to turn his back on the state and all "worldly

activities" (42), and thereby to embrace, if circuitously, his highly peculiar view of church-state separation. Clearly, Hamburger's objective is to marginalize Williams's contribution. However, this is a seriously distorted interpretation of Williams's position. For one thing, it ignores several other prominent lines of argument employed by Williams in favor of separating church and state (alluded to in the text) that are quite consistent both with (liberal) Calvinist thinking and with subsequent eighteenth-century approaches to the subject. For another, Williams's convictions concerning the purification of the church have little bearing on his broader theory of church-state relations, which explicitly leaves the matter of religious belief and practice, including religious organization, entirely up to the consciences of others. Williams nowhere demands adherence on the part of others to his anticlerical or anti-ecclesiastical views.

It is distressing that Hamburger's characterization of Williams continues to be highly influential on reputable historians and legal scholars alike. See, for example, Gordon S. Wood's comments on a recent book on Williams in a review entitled "Radical, Pure, Roger Williams," *New York Review of Books* (May 10, 2012). "Williams's beliefs were too extreme, too eccentric, too individualistic to have much relevance today." As with Hamburger, Wood's argument for Williams's alleged irrelevance is that he was gradually disillusioned with all forms of organized Christianity and isolated himself from any corporate religious experience. Hamburger's misrepresentations of Williams's views replicate in many ways the similarly mistaken but widely echoed claims of Mark DeWolfe Howe, *The Garden and the Wilderness* (Chicago: University of Chicago Press, 1965). One particularly distressing example of Howe's distorting influence on the understanding of Williams is in the otherwise compelling and insightful writings on law and religious liberty by Douglas Laycock, *Religious Liberty: Overviews and History* (Grand Rapids, MI: Eerdmans, 2011), 68. Citing Howe, Laycock says that for Williams "religion is sacred and the state corrupt, so that separation of church and state is necessary to protect religion from corruption by the state." See notes 136 and 138 for the discussion of Williams's idea of the "wall of separation."

133. Roger Williams, *A Bloody Tenent of Persecution*, in *Complete Writings of Roger Williams*, vol. 3 (New York: Russell and Russell, 1963), 153.

134. Williams, *A Bloody Tenent of Persecution*, 225. A key implication of Williams's critique of Calvin here is that legal protection of the rights of conscience is an indispensable means of preventing the state from exercising arbitrary power, an insight Calvin himself appreciated and asserted early in his career, even if he went back on it later. Ironically, Williams's central conviction is well-expressed by Winifred Sullivan, a putative critic of freedom of religion, rule of law, and human rights. Surprisingly, freedom of religion stands, after all, for something of which she strongly approves: "*the right of the individual, every individual, to life outside the state*—the right to live as a self on which many given, as well as chosen, demands are made" (*Impossibility of Religious Freedom*, 158–159; italics added). Her central conclusion in *Impossibility of Religious Freedom* that this right to a "life outside the state" "may not best be realized through laws guaranteeing religious freedom but by laws guaranteeing equality" (159) is undercut by an earlier claim of hers that "religion is . . . arguably different from speech, movement, association and the like"—the legal protection of which presumably guarantees equality! "To be religious is, in some sense, to be obedient to a rule outside of oneself and one's government, whether that rule is established by God, or otherwise. It is to do what must be done. . . and doing so at some personal cost" (156). This is the standard idea of the "sovereignty of conscience"

and its *special* right to protection over against the authority of the state. Her additional claim that "to be religious is not to be free, but to be faithful" (156) is true in regard to conscience, but *not* in regard to the state. That's the whole point: Being subject to the one means being free, at least in part, from the other.

The problem is Sullivan's concessions here deeply compromise her recurring attacks, and those of her colleagues, against what they consider to be the perverse influence of "protestant" "hyper-privatization" on questions of religious freedom. On the one hand, Sullivan's formulation—completely consistent with Williams's ideas—presupposes an irreducible individualism (what I have called elsewhere "conscientious individualism"). Despite the indispensable influence of social experience, it is, finally, *individuals who have consciences*, which, according to the implication of Sullivan's formulation, are to be protected *as such* by a well-ordered state against undue coercion or restraint. On the other hand, there is no reason to assume, as Sullivan and associates seem to do, that protection of conscience is hopelessly wedded to a preoccupation with "private belief" understood as unrelated to behavior, group membership, or public life in general. Williams respected "free exercise" or practice as well as belief, and he also respected the "non-protestant" groups many people at the time identified with, such as Jews, "Mohammedans," and native Americans, so long as they complied, as many of them did on his account, with "second table standards," and allowed, in one way or another, for the "right of the individual" "to life outside the state," a principle Sullivan herself endorses. As to the public aspect of freedom of conscience, Williams never tired of arguing that protecting individual rights of conscience enabled the state to do its true job, namely to ensure to all citizens *impartially and equally* the *public goods* of peace, safety, and civic welfare. Continuing to consider, in accord with due process, "challenges of conscience" to the state's jurisdiction performs a critically public function of calling the state to account in this regard.

Sullivan also seems sympathetic to an idea Williams favored, namely extending freedom of conscience to those, in Williams's words, "who turn atheistical and irreligious" (*Complete Writings of Roger Williams*, vol. 7, 181), although she disregards the fact that human rights standards follow Williams by enshrining that very idea (see *Impossibility of Religious Freedom*, 157). In "The Conscience of Contemporary Man," Sullivan affirms the Supreme Court's extension of the right of conscience to nonreligious people (as in *U.S. v. Seeger*), but then, inexplicably, goes on to portray such a development as "outdated" by invoking a number of recent anthropological studies without making clear what bearing they have on the issue of conscience and state. A similar criticism might be leveled against her interpretation of the ruling in *Warner v. Boca Raton*, the central focus of her argument throughout *Impossibility of Religious Freedom*. It is hard to follow why, *on Sullivan's own assumptions,* she would not favor a ruling that, on grounds of conscience inclusively understood, extended the right to erect upright gravestones in an area otherwise legally limited to flat gravestones. She here and there toys with such a conclusion, but nowhere forthrightly embraces it (see, e.g., 136–137). Cf. Kent Greenawalt, *Religion and the Constitution*, vol. 2, *Establishment and Fairness* (Princeton, NJ: Princeton University Press, 2008), 330–331, for a related criticism.

135. Williams writes: "I affirm that state policy and state necessity, which (for the peace of the state and the preventing of rivers of civil blood) [safeguards] the consciences of men, will be found to agree most punctually with the rules of the best politician that ever the world saw, the King of kings and Lord of lords." He speaks of the civil protection of conscience as an "absolute rule of this great politician for the peace of the field, which is

the world, and for the good and peace of the saints, who must have a civil being in the world" (*Complete Writings of Roger Williams*, vol. 3, 178–179). The point is that the teachings and life of Jesus, based on appeals to conscience, not coercion, match and flourish in a civil order that protects conscience, and make a critical contribution to civil or "worldly" peace for which Jesus's true followers, "the saints," have a singular responsibility. At the same time, there is nothing compulsory about the convergence; Williams's view of Christianity, though compelling for him, is by no means an "official requirement" for a constitutional system to work, as he makes clear more than once. In fact, he believed most Christians of his time and place, by turns predatory and overbearing, had much to learn about the authentic Christian message by respecting the equal rights of native Americans and interacting with them sympathetically. (See Nussbaum's moving discussion of Williams's contribution to the ideals of "respect and sympathetic imagination" as exemplified by his attitudes toward the Narragansett Indians whom he befriended (*The New Religious Intolerance*, 149–158).)

136. See note 8.

137. *Complete Writings of Roger Williams*, vol. 3, 398.

138. See Little, "Roger Williams and the Puritan Background of the Establishment Clause," in *No Establishment of Religion*, ed. Gunn and Witte, 111–112, for an elaboration of this critical point.

139. Martha C. Nussbaum, *Liberty of Conscience: In Defense of America's Tradition of Religious Equality* (New York: Basic Books, 2008).

140. Huntington, "Anglo-Protestant Culture," in *Who Are We?*, 59–80. See David Little, "Culture, Religion, and National Identity in a Postmodern World," *Anuario del Derecho Eclesiastico del Estado* XXII (2006), for a critique of Huntington's argument.

141. In her definitive study of Gentili, *Alberico Gentili and the Development of International Law* (Amsterdam: H. J. Paris, 1937), Gezina H.J. van der Molen makes a strong case for Gentili's Calvinism, both theologically (249–256) and politically (201–221).

142. Coleman Phillipson, "Introduction," in Alberico Gentili, *De Iure Belli Libri Tres*, trans. John C. Rolfe (1612; repr., Oxford: Clarendon Press, 1933), 18a.

143. Phillipson, "Introduction," 25a.

144. Calvin, *Institutes*, bk. 4, ch. XX, sect. 14, 1502.

145. Calvin, *Institutes*, bk. 4, ch. XX, sect. 16, 1502.

146. Calvin, *Institutes*, bk. 4, ch. XX, sect. 11, 1499.

147. Calvin, *Institutes*, bk. 4, ch. XX, sect. 12, 1500.

148. Calvin, *Institutes*, bk. 4, ch. XX, sect 16, 1505: "There are countries which unless they deal cruelly with murderers by way of horrible examples, must immediately perish from slaughters and robberies. There are ages that demand increasingly harsh penalties."

149. Gentili, *De Iure Belli*, bk. 1, ch. IX, 41.

150. Gentili, *De Iure Belli*, bk. 1, ch. IX, 39.

151. Gentili, *De Iure Belli*, bk. 1, ch. IX, 41.

152. Gentili, *De Iure Belli*, bk. 1, ch. IX, 38.

153. Gentili, *De Iure Belli*, bk. 1, ch X, 43–46: "Violence should not be employed against subjects who have embraced another religion than that of the ruler. . . with the reservation, 'unless the state suffer some harm in consequence' [such as disturbance of the peace— a fully modern limitation].. . . I for my part hear of battles and wars where no place is given to religion. I do not hear of them where there is room for different religions." In this regard, Gentili was considerably more liberal than Grotius, who favored religious pluralism and freedom internationally but *not* domestically.

154. Gentili, *On the Laws of War*, bk. 1, ch. XVIII, 83.

155. Phillipson, "Introduction," in Gentili, *De Iure Belli*, 25a.
156. Van der Molen, *Alberico Gentili*, 214ff.
157. Van der Molen, *Alberico Gentili*, 237.
158. Van der Molen, *Alberico Gentili*, 236.
159. Van der Molen, *Alberico Gentili*, 239.
160. Van der Molen, *Alberico Gentili*, 133, 136.
161. Van der Molen, *Alberico Gentili*, 244.

Bibliography

Anderson, Benedict. *Imagined Communities*. London: Verso, 1991.

Asad, Talal. *Formations of the Secular: Christianity, Islam, and Modernity*. Stanford, CA: Stanford University Press, 2003.

Barker, Ernest. *Principles of Social and Political Theory*. Oxford: Clarendon Press, 1956.

Barker, Ernest. *Church, State, and Education*. Ann Arbor, MI: University of Michigan Press, 1957.

Benedict, Philip. *Christ's Churches Purely Reformed: A Social History of Calvinism*. New Haven, CT: Yale University Press, 2002.

Bohatec, Josef. *Calvins Lehre von Staat und Kirche mit besonderer Berucksichtigung des Organismusgedankens*. Aalen: Scientia, 1961.

Calvin, John. *Institutes of the Christian Religion*. Edited by John T. McNeill. Translated by Ford Lewis Battles. 2 vols. Philadelphia: Westminster Press, 1960.

Calvin, John. *Epistles of Paul the Apostle to the Romans and to the Thessalonians*. Translated by Ross Mackenzie. Grand Rapids, MI: Eerdmans,1976).

Calvin, John. *Commentary on Micah*. Translated by John King. www.sacred-texts.com/chr/calvin/cc28/index.htm.

Calvin, John. *Commentary on the Psalms*. http://www.ccel.org/ccel/calvin/calcom08.html.

Calvin, John. *Four Last Books of the Pentateuch*. http://www.ccel.org/ccel/calvin/comment3/comm_vol03/comm_vol03.rtf.

Clasen, Claus Peter. *Anabaptists: A Social History*. Ithaca, NY: Cornell University Press, 1972.

Collier, Paul. "Economic Causes of Civil Conflict and their Implications for Policy." In *Turbulent Peace: The Challenges of Managing International Conflict*, edited by Chester A. Crocker, Fen Osler Hampson, and Pamela Aall, 143–162. Washington, DC: US Institute of Peace Press, 2001.

Conner, Walker. *Ethnonationalism: The Quest for Understanding*. Princeton, NJ: Princeton University Press, 1994.

Diamond, Larry. *The Spirit of Democracy: The Struggle to Build Free Societies throughout the World*. New York: Times Books, 2008.

Doyle, Michael W. *Liberal Peace: Selected Essays*. New York: Routledge, 2012.

Doyle, Michael W., and Nicholas Sambanis. *Making War and Building Peace: United Nations Peace Operations*. Princeton, NJ: Princeton University Press, 2006.

Eire, Carlos. *War against the Idols: The Reformation of Worship from Erasmus to Calvin*. Cambridge: Cambridge University Press, 1986.

Figgis, J.N. *From Gerson to Grotius: 1414–1625*. Cambridge: Cambridge University Press, 1956.

Foster, Herbert D. "Political Theories of Calvinists." In *Collected Papers of Herbert D. Foster*. Privately printed, 1929.

Gellner, Ernest. *Nations and Nationalism*. Ithaca, NY: Cornell University Press, 1983.

Gentili, Alberico. *De Iure Belli Libri Tres*. 1612. Reprint translated by John C. Rolfe. Oxford: Clarendon Press, 1933.

Goertz, Hans-Jurgen. *The Anabaptists*. London: Routledge, 1996.

Gorski, Philip S. *The Disciplinary Revolution: Calvinism and the Rise of the State in Early Modern Europe*. Chicago: University of Chicago Press, 2003.

Greenawalt, Kent. "History as Ideology: Philip Hamburger's Separation of Church and State." Review of *Separation of Church and State*, by Philip Hamburger. *California Law Review* 93, no. 1 (2005): 367–396.

Greenawalt, Kent. *Religion and the Constitution*. 2 vols. Princeton, NY: Princeton University Press, 2006, 2008.

Greenfeld, Liah. *Nationalism: Five Roads to Modernity*. Cambridge, MA: Harvard University Press, 1993.

Gregory, Brad S. *The Unintended Reformation: How a Religious Revolution Secularized Society*. Cambridge, MA: Harvard University Press, 2012.

Grim, Brian J., and Roger Finke. *The Price of Freedom Denied: Religious Persecution and Conflict in the Twenty-First Century*. New York: Cambridge University Press, 2011.

Gunn, T. Jeremy. "The Separation of Church and State versus Religion in the Public Square: The Contested History of the Establishment Clause." In Gunn and Witte, eds., *No Establishment of Religion*, 15–44.

Gunn, T. Jeremy, and John Witte Jr., eds. *No Establishment of Religion: America's Contribution to Religious Liberty*. New York: Oxford University Press, 2012.

Gurr, Ted Robert. *Peoples versus States: Minorities at Risk in the New Century*. Washington, DC: US Institute of Peace Press, 2000.

Gurr, Ted Robert, and Barbara Harff. *Ethnic Conflict in Global Politics*. Boulder, CO: Westview Press, 2004.

Habermas, Jürgen. "The European Nation-State: Its Achievements and Its Limits." In *Mapping the Nation*, edited by Gopal Balakrishnan, 281–294. London: Verso, 1996.

Hall, David D. *A Reforming People: Puritanism and the Transformation of Public Life*. New York: Alfred A. Knopf, 2011.

Halperin, Morton H., Joseph T. Siegle, and Michael M. Weinstein. *Democracy Advantage: How Democracies Promote Prosperity and Peace*. New York: Routledge, 2005.

Hamburger, Philip. *Separation of Church and State*. Cambridge: Harvard University Press, 2002.

Hibbard, Scott W. *Religious Politics and Secular States: Egypt, India, and the United States*. Baltimore: Johns Hopkins University Press, 2010.

Hirschi, Caspar. *Origins of Nationalism: An Alternative History from Ancient Rome to Early Modern Germany*. Cambridge: Cambridge University Press, 2012.

Hobsbawm, E.J. *Nations and Nationalism: Programme, Myth, Reality*. Cambridge: Cambridge University Press, 1991.

Hooker, Richard. *Laws of Ecclesiastical Polity*. 2 vols. 1593. Reprint, London: J.M. Dent and Sons, 1958.

Hooker, Richard. *Works of Richard Hooker*. Edited by John Keble. 3 vols. Oxford: Clarendon Press, 1888.

Howe, Mark DeWolfe. *The Garden and the Wilderness*. Chicago: University of Chicago Press, 1965.

Hutchison, William R., and Hartmut Lehmann, eds. *Many Are Chosen: Divine Election and Western Nationalism*. Minneapolis, MN: Fortress Press, 1994.

Huntington, Samuel P. *Who Are We? The Challenges to America's National Identity.* New York: Simon and Schuster, 2004.

Johnson, James Turner. *Just War Tradition and the Restraint of War: A Moral and Historical Inquiry.* Princeton, NJ: Princeton University Press, 1981.

Jurgensmeyer, Mark. *The New Cold War? Religious Nationalism Confronts the Secular State.* Berkeley, CA: University of California Press, 1993.

Kim, David Yoon-Jung. "Law, Equity, and Calvin's Moral Critique of Protestant Faith." ThD diss., Harvard Divinity School, 2012.

Kingdon, Robert M. "Social Welfare in Calvin's Geneva." In *Church and Society in Reformation Europe*, 50–69. London: Variorum Reprints, 1985.

Klassen, Peter James. *Economics of Anabaptism, 1525–1560.* London: Mouton and Co., 1964.

Laycock, Douglas. *Religious Liberty: Overviews and History.* 2 vols. Grand Rapids, MI: Eerdmans, 2011.

Lederach, John Paul, and R. Scott Appleby. "Strategic Peacebuilding: An Overview." In *Strategies of Peace: Transforming Conflict in a Violent World*, edited by Daniel Philpott and Gerard F. Powers, 19–44. New York: Oxford University Press, 2010.

Lichtenberg, Judith. "How Liberal Can Nationalism Be?" In *Theorizing Nationalism*, edited by Ronald Beiner, 167–188. Albany, NY: State University of New York Press, 1999.

Little, David. *Religion, Order, and Law: A Study in Pre-Revolutionary England.* Chicago: University of Chicago Press, 1984.

Little, David. "Culture, Religion, and National Identity in a Postmodern World." *Anuario del Derecho Eclesiastico del Estado* XXII (2006): 19–35.

Little, David. "Religion, Human Rights, and Secularism: Preliminary Clarifications and Some Islamic, Jewish, and Christian Responses." In *Humanity Before God: Contemporary Faces of Jewish, Christian, and Islamic Ethics*, edited by William Schweiker, Michael A. Johnson, and Kevin Jung, 256–283. Minneapolis, MN: Augsburg Fortress, 2006.

Little, David. "Calvin and Natural Rights." *Political Theology* 10, no. 3 (2009): 411–430.

Little, David. "Religion, Nationalism, and Intolerance." In *Between Terror and Tolerance: Religious Leaders, Conflict, and Peacemaking*, edited by Timothy L. Sisk, 9–28. Washington, DC: Georgetown University Press, 2011.

Little, David. "Roger Williams and the Puritan Background of the Establishment Clause." In Gunn and Witte, eds., *No Establishment of Religion*, 100–124.

Little, David, and Donald K. Swearer, eds. *Religion and Nationalism in Iraq: A Comparative Perspective.* Cambridge, MA: Harvard University Press, 2006.

Lutz, Donald S. *Origins of American Constitutionalism.* Baton Rouge, LA: Louisiana State University Press, 1988.

Mansfield, Edward D., and Jack Snyder. "Democratic Transitions and War: From Napoleon to the Millennium's End." In *Turbulent Peace: The Challenges of Managing International Conflict*, edited by Chester A. Crocker, Fen Osler Hampson, and Pamela Aall, 113–126. Washington, DC: US Institute of Peace Press, 2001.

Mansfield, Edward D., and Jack Snyder. *Electing to Fight: Why Emerging Democracies Go to War.* Cambridge, MA: MIT Press, 2005.

Marx, Anthony. *Faith in Nation: Exclusionary Origins of Nationalism.* New York: Oxford University Press, 2003.

McCullough, Diarmaid. *The Reformation: A History.* New York: Viking, 2004.

McIlwain, C.H. *Constitutionalism and Its Changing World.* Cambridge: Cambridge University Press, 1939.

Morgan, Edmund S. *Puritan Political Ideas, 1558–1794*. Indianapolis, IN: Bobbs-Merrill Co., 1965.

Morrall, John B. *Political Thought in Medieval Times*. New York: Harper and Bros., 1962.

Nijenhuis, Willem. "The Limits of Civil Disobedience in Calvin's Last-Known Sermons." In *Ecclesia Reformata: Studies on the Reformation*, vol. II,. New York, Leiden and Köln: E.J. Brill, pp. 78–97, 1994.

Nussbaum, Martha C. *Liberty of Conscience: In Defense of America's Tradition of Religious Equality*. New York: Basic Books, 2008.

Nussbaum, Martha C. *The New Religious Intolerance: Overcoming the Politics of Fear in an Anxious Age*. Cambridge, MA: Harvard University Press, 2012.

Olson, Jennine E. *Calvin and Social Welfare: Deacons and the Bourse Francaise*. London: Associated University Presses, 1989.

Paris, Roland. *At War's End: Building Peace after Civil Conflict*. New York: Cambridge University Press, 2004.

Phillipson, Coleman. Introduction to *De Iure Belli Libri Tres*, by Alberico Gentili, translation of the 1612 edition by John C. Rolfe. Oxford: Clarendon Press, 1933.

Philpott, Daniel. "Introduction: Searching for Strategy in an Age of Peacebuilding." In Philpott and Powers, eds., *Strategies of Peace*, 3–18.

Philpott, Daniel. "Reconciliation: An Ethic for Peacebuilding." In Philpott and Powers, eds., *Strategies of Peace*, 91–118.

Philpott, Daniel. *Just and Unjust Peace: An Ethic of Reconciliation*. New York: Oxford University Press, 2012.

Philpott, Daniel, and Gerard F. Powers, eds. *Strategies of Peace: Transforming Conflict in a Violent World*. New York: Oxford University Press, 2010.

Powicke, Maurice. *The Reformation in England*. New York: Oxford University Press, 1961.

Oliver P. Richmond. "Conclusion: Strategic Peacebuilding beyond the Liberal Peace." In Philpott and Powers, eds., *Strategies of Peace*, 353–368.

Rummel, R.J. *Power Kills: Democracy as a Model of Nonviolence*. New Brunswick, NJ: Transaction, 2004.

Schaff, Philip. *History of the Christian Church*. Vol. 4, *Modern Christianity: The German Reformation*. New York: Charles Scribner's Sons, 1888.

Shklar, Judith N. "Liberalism of Fear." In *Liberalism and the Moral Life*, edited by Nancy L. Rosenblum, 21–38. Cambridge, MA: Harvard University Press, 1989.

Skinner, Quentin. *Foundations of Modern Political Thought*. 2 vols. New York: Cambridge University Press, 1979.

Smith, Anthony D. *Chosen Peoples: Sacred Sources of National Identity*. Oxford: Oxford University Press, 2003.

Snyder, Jack. *From Voting to Violence: Democratization and Nationalist Conflict*. New York: W.W. Norton and Co., 2000.

Spinka, Matthew. *John Hus and the Council of Constance*. New York: Columbia University Press, 1965.

Strayer, James M. *Anabaptists and the Sword*. Lawrence, KS: Coronado Press, 1976.

Sullivan, Winifred Fallers. "Religious Freedom and the Rule of Law: Exporting Modernity in a Postmodern World?" *Mississippi College Law Review* 22, no. 2 (2002–2003): 173–183. HeinOnline. http://heinonline.org/HOL/LandingPage?collection=journals&handle=hein.journals/miscollr22&div=15&id=&page=.

Sullivan, Winifred Fallers. *The Impossibility of Religious Freedom*. Princeton, NJ: Princeton University Press, 2005.

Sullivan, Winifred Fallers. "'The Conscience of Contemporary Man': Reflections on *U.S. v. Seeger* and *Dignitatis Humanae.*" *U.S. Catholic Historian* 24 (2006): 107–123.

Tierney, Brian. *Idea of Natural Rights: Studies on Natural Rights, Natural Law and Church Law.* Atlanta, GA: Scholars Press, 1997.

Toft, Monica Duffy, Daniel Philpott, and Timothy Samuel Shah., *God's Century: Resurgent Religion and Global Politics.* New York: W.W. Norton and Co., 2011.

van der Molen, Gezina H.J. *Alberico Gentili and the Development of International Law.* Amsterdam: H. J. Paris, 1937.

Williams, George Hunsten, ed. *Spiritual and Anabaptist Writers.* Philadelphia: Westminster Press, 1958.

Williams, George Hunsten. *The Radical Reformation.* Kirksville, MO: Sixteenth Century Journal Publishers, Inc., 1992.

Williams, Roger. *Complete Writings of Roger Williams.* 7 vols. New York: Russell and Russell, 1963.

Witte, John, Jr. *The Reformation of Rights: Law, Religion, and Human Rights in Early Modern Calvinism.* New York: Cambridge University Press, 2007.

Witte, John, Jr., *Law and Protestantism: The Legal Teachings of the Lutheran Reformnation,* Cambridge: Cambridge University Press, 2002.

Wood, Gordon S. "Radical, Pure, Roger Williams." *New York Review of Books,* May 10, 2012.

Yack, Bernard. "Myth of the Civic Nation." In *Theorizing Nationalism,* edited by Ronald Beiner, 103–118. Albany, NY: State University of New York Press, 1999.

CHAPTER 4

RELIGION, NATIONALISM, AND THE POLITICS OF SECULARISM

SCOTT HIBBARD

INTRODUCTION

THE relationship between religion and the modern nation-state has been the source of much discord, debate, and conflict. At one level, the contention involves ongoing debates over the proper role of religion in public life. Should the religion of a dominant community inform the institutions of nation and state, or ought the political structures of a given society (and government policy) be neutral in regard to matters of religion and belief? In other words, should the state (and/or nation) be religious or secular? At a deeper level, the central concern involves questions about the nature of society, and whether membership in the national community ought to be inclusive or exclusive. These disputes pit religious activists against their secular counterparts, minority populations against majorities, and coreligionists against one another. These debates also raise questions about the very idea of secularism. Is secularism a matter of neutrality in matters of religion—and largely consistent with liberal or modernist understandings of religion—or is secularism, by definition, hostile toward religious belief of all kinds?

This chapter will examine these questions in turn. Its point of departure is the recognition that neither modernity nor states are invariably secular, nor is secularism necessarily hostile to religion. On the contrary, there are multiple interpretations of secularism, some of which are consistent with expressions of religion in public life, while others are not. Similarly, both religion and nationalism are defined by high degrees of variation, ranging from the liberal and tolerant to the chauvinistic and intolerant. In this context, religion refers to "a complex of socially prescribed beliefs and practices relating to a realm of reality conceived as sacred."[1] It is this connection between the immanent and transcendent—more specifically, a transcendent moral order—that gives religion its continuing utility in modern politics. Religion provides a normative language for political action, informs nationalist mythologies, and helps to define collective identities. More to the point, religion and religious ideologies remain important mechanisms for reifying particular patterns of social and political power, and, thus, for shaping the contours of social life. Hence, the important question is not whether states are religious or secular per se, but rather, how do different interpretations of religion (and secularism) inform competing visions of the nation?

The first part of the chapter will focus on the larger issue of religion and public life, and the failure of the secularization thesis to account for the continuing relevance of religion to modern politics. In doing so, this opening section will elaborate on the relationship between religion, nationalism, and the modern state. Particular emphasis will be devoted to the competition between those who argue for state neutrality and those who believe religion (or, more accurately, a particular interpretation of religion) ought to be given preference within the institutions of nation and state. This first section will also examine the variability of religion, and the manner in which different interpretations of religious tradition inform competing visions of the nation. Both of these latter two issues raise important questions about the persistence of religious sectarianism, and the compatibility of certain forms of religious belief with the requirements of an open, tolerant, and inclusive society.

The second section will then turn to the secular tradition and review the different interpretations of secularism as well as the debates over its relative merits. One of the challenges here is that secularism has come to mean different things to different people. For many, secularism is seen as the antithesis of religion—akin to atheism—or, more simply, as an overt hostility toward religion. This type of "irreligious secularism" embodies a "competing intellectual and moral vision"[2] that seeks to remove all traces of religion from the public sphere. However, there is an alternative variant, "ecumenical secularism," that is defined by neutrality, not hostility, in matters of religion and belief. Given the absence of societal agreement on religious issues, it is argued that state policy must be premised upon "a civil politics of primordial compromise"[3] whereby each faith community relinquishes its claim for preference in exchange for all other communities doing likewise. This is central to the construction of a social order consistent with the requirements of a "justpeace," though one that has remained elusive in practice.

The last two sections of the chapter will explore the critiques of secularism and a re-conceptualized vision of secularism. At the heart of the "politics of secularism" is a claim—some would argue a recognition—that, whatever the theory, secularism in practice has failed to accommodate religion of any sort. From this view, there is within the very idea of secularism an inherent hostility toward religion, and secularism can only allow certain types of religion into the public square. Secularism, from this perspective, systematically excludes certain ideas and peoples from public life, and is deeply implicated in the power structures of states and markets. More to the point, it is said to foster the kind of extremism it is meant to eschew. A key challenge, then, for achieving a truly just society—one free of the institutional violence that the justpeace paradigm is committed to addressing—lies in resolving this tension between secularism in theory and secularism in practice. What this might look like—and whether a genuinely inclusive vision of social life means abandoning secularism altogether—is the final topic of the chapter.

RELIGION, NATIONALISM, AND THE STATE

A review of modernization theory and its corollary, the secularization thesis, provides a useful starting point for this inquiry. At the heart of modernization theory was the premise that religion would diminish in importance—both for the individual and in public life—as economic and political development progressed. As the ideas and institutions of modernity became more pronounced, it was argued, religion would become less important and, ultimately, disappear. A key feature of this argument was its recognition of the growing influence of modern states and market capitalism over social organization. As these core institutions of the "modern" world became more influential, it was assumed that they would displace the church (or other formal religious organizations) as the dominant institutions of public life. It was also assumed that personal belief would decline as religious myths lost their hold on the popular imagination. Just as markets and states marginalized the church, science and reason would displace religious belief. Insofar as religion endured, it would be a personal affair and limited to individual matters of conscience. Modernity subsequently came to be defined by a differentiation of social life into a variety of spheres: secular vs. religious, on the one hand, and public vs. private on the other.

Although this theory was largely descriptive in nature, it also had a prescriptive component. The programs of social engineering that defined Turkish government policy in the early twentieth century—as well as related efforts to control religion in Iran and Egypt—were informed by a worldview that equated religion with a backward tradition and secularism with a progressive modernity. Similarly, in the post–World War II period, economic and political development was thought to require a diminution of religious belief. It was this latter perspective that informed government policy for many countries—and the field of development economics—well into the latter part of the twentieth century.

The proliferation of religious politics in the post–Cold War era forced a re-evaluation of these ideas. To be fair, some elements of modernization theory have held true. The first, and perhaps most important, is that the authority of organized religion has been greatly diminished vis-à-vis the state and the market. Churches as centers of social life do not have the same degree of influence they once did. Moreover, as the World Values Survey has demonstrated, there is a correlation between levels of affluence and religiosity, even if this is not uniform. On the other hand, it is clear that science and rationalism have not displaced religious belief on a personal level, even in affluent societies such as the United States. As Peter Berger has rightfully noted, the world is "as furiously religious" as ever.[4] Similarly, economic change has not undermined religion in the manner predicted by these earlier theories. Rather, the dislocation associated with economic modernization (and globalization) has ironically had the opposite effect.[5] The destruction of traditional societies by global capitalism—and with that the web of relationships that bound historical communities together—has spurred a return to religion on a large scale as individuals have sought to find a home in their transformed world. Far from diminishing religion, economic change in this context has reinforced it.[6]

If modernization theory cannot account for the continued relevance of religious politics, what can? Does the contemporary "resurgence" embody a genuine return to religion—a "de-secularization of the world," as Berger and others would argue—or does it merely reflect the utility of religion for articulating political purpose? A comprehensive answer to these questions is beyond the scope of this chapter, but a brief overview of the dominant approaches is useful. One of the more commonly held views is that the religious politics of recent years embodies a popular rejection of secularism and secular norms. This "deprivatization of religion," some argue, springs from the deep desire of religious populations to "re-normativize" the public sphere, and otherwise assert themselves in an overtly secular (or atheistic) society.[7] From this perspective, religious mobilization in the post–Cold War era represents a rebellion of religious populations against secular elites, and pits those who seek to infuse public life with the "traditional values" of religion against a state that embodies the irreligious values of secular modernity.[8]

An alternative perspective views the issue less in terms of religion—and religious revival— than of politics. This latter approach perceives the failure of the modern state to address basic human needs as the source of a popular discontent that has found expression in religious terms. While such political movements may articulate their grievances in a religious and cultural idiom, the underlying impetus is economic and political.[9] It is a mistake to interpret contemporary activism as "religious" since the source of grievance is material. Religious fundamentalisms, then, ought to be seen as a byproduct of a rapidly changing economic, social, and political environment, and not as a return to religion per se.

A third approach sees the larger trend as *both* thoroughly religious and political. It is this last view that shapes this chapter. While the driving impetus for much religious activism may, indeed, be socioeconomic or political in nature, it is nonetheless significant that it is religion to which political actors appeal, and not some other ideological resource. This is indicative of the continued salience—and power—of religion in modern life. To begin with, religion speaks to fundamental questions of human existence: life, death, and moral purpose. While science and reason help to explain the mechanical operations of the world, they are less able to address the normative questions faced by both individuals and society. Moreover, religion provides a language to articulate moral purpose, sanction the exercise of power, and otherwise situate contemporary issues in a wider, normative framework. Religion also remains central to the construction of identity, and particularly collective identities. Hence, even if there is a formal separation of church and state—that is, a separation of religious authority from political authority—religious ideas and beliefs continue to provide a basis for social cohesion and a language for contemporary politics.

It is for these reasons that even ostensibly secular states have invoked religious narratives to legitimate their authority. This last point warrants elaboration. A key failing of modernization theory was the assumption that modern states were invariably hostile to religious belief of all sorts. This assumption was incorrect. While some states tried to eradicate religion—or greatly restrict it—this was by no means universal. More commonly, states sought to control, regulate, or otherwise use religion to their own ends. As other chapters in this volume illustrate, religion was (and remains) a central feature of the nationalist project, and nationalist narratives provided a new means by which religion could enter the public sphere. As Anthony Marx has argued:

> [Within the European context,] religious fanaticism was the basis for popular engagement with—for or against—centralizing state authority. . . . Nationalism emerged when the masses were invited onto the political stage or invited themselves in. But that invitation did not come inclusively from books, enrichment, or schooling, but rather from sectarian conflicts, enraging sermons and callings. The passions of faith were the stuff of which the passions for the state were built.[10]

The point is that nationalism emerged from the cauldron of religious sentiment, and the latter continues to provide an emotive—and moral—foundation to modern political structures. This influence is evident in the religious symbols and narratives that inform modern nationalisms, including such recurring themes as "chosen peoples," divine favoritism, and providential mission.[11] The religious dimension of nationalism also offers a narrative within which individual sacrifice is given transcendent meaning, associating it with both a mythic past and an ostensibly better future. These features of modern nationalism derive in part from the covenant tradition of biblical religion, and provide a moral and spiritual foundation to secular societies and institutions. These forms of "civil religion" are an important mechanism for binding nationalist communities together, justifying political authority, and lending a universal and sacred quality to a particular set of political arrangements.[12]

Part of the explanation for the contemporary resurgence of religion, then, is that religion never went away. It was always a part of modern political discourse, even if its particular manifestations varied across time and place. What is most interesting about the post–Cold War resurgence, however, involves the type of religion with which it is associated. What defined this era was not a resurgence of religion per se, but rather a resurgence of *illiberal* visions of religion at the expense of *liberal* ones. In the mid-twentieth century, the type of religion that was dominant in public life was liberal and modernist—that is, the dominant interpretations of religion eschewed a literalist reading of scripture for metaphorical, and emphasized tolerance and ecumenical coexistence. These liberal interpretations of religion were consistent with secular norms of neutrality and informed a vision of society that was (theoretically) inclusive. Modernist religion was also associated with the political left, the promotion of social justice, and the eradication of poverty. On the other hand, illiberal religion—interpretations that claimed a monopoly on truth, placed an emphasis upon scriptural literalism, and tended to be intolerant of alternative beliefs—were commonly associated with the political right and traditional patterns of social and political hierarchy.

In the mid-twentieth century, illiberal and dogmatic forms of religion (and the organizations that espoused them) were politically marginalized and commonly repressed. This marginalization was perceived as a harbinger of religion's future writ large, and the trend informed the secularization thesis. However, the relative influence of these competing interpretations of religion began to change in the 1970s and early 1980s. During this period, mainstream political actors came to see religious fundamentalisms as a bulwark against socialism and a useful carrier of a patriotic majoritarianism (vis-à-vis a more explicit religious nationalism). In this Cold War context, religious activists gained support on a variety of continents from state actors who had come to see illiberal religious movements as a constituency to be courted, not a threat to be marginalized.[13] The resurgence of religious politics that transpired in the 1990s, then, was characterized by the rise of illiberal religion at the expense of its liberal counterpart. Significantly, this trend was associated with a larger ideological shift defined by the embrace of neoliberal economic policies, and the abandonment by state actors of earlier commitments to social justice, equality, and diversity.

These last points highlight an important part of the broader narrative: different interpretations of religion inform competing visions of social life.[14] Liberal or modernist interpretations are commonly associated with inclusive political structures and have provided the basis for a civic nationalism and "inclusive universal and transcending [identities]." Illiberal renderings of religious belief, on the other hand, tend to inform the "exclusive particularist and primordial [identities]" associated with ethnic nationalisms.[15] When we speak of the "struggle to define the nation," we refer to this competition over both religious interpretation and social order.

The assumption, then, that modernity is secular (and liberal) and "tradition" is religious (and illiberal) is highly misleading. Rather, secularism, religion, and nationalism all have their liberal and illiberal variants, and neither religion nor secularism is necessarily hostile to the demands of an inclusive and open society. Similarly, the assumption that secular forms of nationalism are invariably hostile to religion is a misreading of history. As the early to mid-twentieth century illustrates, modernist or liberal interpretations of religion were a common feature of the secular public square (at least in those societies that were tolerant of religious and ideological pluralism) and were entirely consistent with the "ecumenical secularism" that will be discussed below. Conversely, exclusive interpretations of secularism (i.e. those that are intolerant of all religious expression) were less accommodating to ideological pluralism, and tended to be associated with closed conceptions of society.[16] This was the case in the former Soviet states (as well as in modern China), where religion was perceived as a competing source of individual loyalty, and, hence, a threat to the state.

A more nuanced depiction of the religious-secular divide, then, would distinguish between four interpretations of social order, each reflecting a different way in which religion and secularism inform competing visions of the nation. These include inclusive conceptions of both religion and secularism ("civil religion" and ecumenical secular nationalism, respectively) as well as exclusive conceptions of religion and secularism (religious nationalism and irreligious secular nationalism). A simple typology would link inclusive interpretations of both religion and secularism with cosmopolitan norms of national identity. Conversely, exclusive (illiberal or sectarian) interpretations of religion and secularism tend to correlate more closely with closed conceptions of community.[17] (See Table 4.1 below.) Hence, the liberal interpretation of religion is more inclined toward a cosmopolitan interpretation of national identity, while those who claim a unique understanding of the sacred are more likely to institutionalize a privileged position for their religious or communal identity. The main point here is that there is nothing antithetical between religion and the demands of an inclusive society; rather, the issue is how a given religious tradition (or official secularism) is interpreted, and whether or not this interpretation tolerates diversity.

Table 4.1

	Conceptions of Social Order	
	Inclusive/Open	Exclusive/Closed
Religious	Liberal or Civic Nationalism (Informed by a 'Civil Religion')	Religious or Ethnic Nationalism
Secular	Ecumenical Secular Nationalism	Irreligious Secular Nationalism

THE POLITICS OF SECULARISM

Like debates over religion, debates over the relative merits—or failings—of secularism are complicated by the absence of a common understanding of the term. The root word, "secular," typically refers to worldly or temporal affairs. That is, not ecclesiastical or clerical, nor involving a separate "realm of reality conceived as sacred." In this regard, the "secular" and the "religious" make up a binary phenomenon that is "mutually constitut[ing],"[18] though made up of distinct parts. The former pertains to things of "this world"—the immanent or natural—and the latter to things associated with an eternal, transcendent, or spiritual realm. Secularism as a doctrine reflects this distinction, and is alternately interpreted as either a separation of spheres—with an emphasis upon the temporal as opposed to the spiritual—or as a set of beliefs or habits that "makes no reference to supernatural beliefs."[19] While one understanding acknowledges the existence of two separate realms, the other denies the existence of the transcendent altogether. In either case, secularism as a worldview typically understands the functioning of both social and natural order without reference to God or some form of spiritual power. It is this worldly perspective that Taylor has referred to as the "immanent frame," and which defines our era as a "secular age."[20]

Secularization similarly reflects the dichotomous essence of "secular" but refers not to a philosophy or doctrine, but to the process by which religion is diminished or marginalized. In this sense, secularization refers to the evolution of a worldview that is self-contained and devoid of spiritual reference. It can also refer to the historical process whereby areas of social life that were once regulated by religious rules and institutions come to be governed by secular norms and institutions (e.g., states). The process of secularization need not require the eradication of religion, but it certainly demands a differentiation of spheres. It also gives priority to the immanent over the transcendent. In this regard, secularization is not without normative judgments. The marginalization of religion has been commonly perceived as a matter of "emancipating" humanity from the grip of superstition, and thus as essential to human progress. This is perhaps the most controversial aspect of the secularization thesis: the assumption that secularization is a universal process whereby human freedom and development are invariably (or necessarily) tied to religion's demise. From this view, the natural evolution of social life is "from the primitive sacred to the modern secular."[21]

This last point reveals a latent bias within the secular tradition. While secularism does not necessarily entail the rejection of religion, it has come to be seen as the antithesis of religion. This understanding derives in part from the classic formulation of secularism as an ideology (and movement) that developed in nineteenth-century England.[22] In this context, secularism was understood as a moral and political doctrine that was rationalist in orientation and concerned solely with worldly affairs. Morality was derived not from scriptural commandments (or the divine), but rather from the requirements of humanism. The tendency toward atheism that was associated with the movement reflected the historical tensions between reason and faith, and between church and state. While this understanding of secularism is just one interpretation, it has come to shape popular perceptions. The assumption that secularism is the antithesis of religion is especially pronounced among religious populations in the Muslim world, where secularism is commonly equated with unbelief, atheism, and Western domination.

From this discussion, we can distinguish between two very distinct but related interpretations of secularism.[23] The first, *irreligious secularism*, is best understood as hostility to religion, and may be summarized as "a doctrine oriented toward human earthly well-being that excludes all consideration of religious belief and practice."[24] It emphasizes the exclusion of religion from public life. This understanding is rooted in the emancipatory project discussed above, and operates under the premise that governments ought to remove religion from the public sphere and diminish religious belief among its subject population. Irreligious secularism sees religion as inherently illiberal, intolerant, and supportive of oppressive social institutions. Consequently, religion is assumed to be inimical to human flourishing and in need of regulation and control. Moreover, the tendency in the early to mid-twentieth century to equate secularism with modernity—and to link economic and social progress with the diminution of religious beliefs and institutions—meant that the process of secularization was not just descriptive, but often prescriptive as well. This accounts for the efforts by many states to eradicate religion—or otherwise diminish its influence—as a means of facilitating economic and social development.

The alternative version of secularism is one defined by neutrality, not hostility, in matters of religion. Secularism, from this view, is sympathetic but impartial toward religion and fundamental beliefs, neither privileging nor excluding particular religions or denominations. This alternative, *ecumenical secularism*, can be defined as "a doctrine oriented toward human earthly well-being in a narrow or restricted sense that otherwise supports protection of religious belief and practice."[25] This alternative is concerned with two related sets of issues. The first is protecting religion and conscience from political intrusion. Secularism, in this sense, circumscribes the authority of the state to regulate religious belief, and provides the basis for the institutional separation of church and state. This separation is premised upon a distinction between two realms: the inner realm of conscience and the outer realm of worldly affairs. Matters of religion and belief fall within the inner realm of conscience, where persuasion, not the coercive power of the state, is legitimately exercised. This realm differs from the outer one, which involves matters of public order, and where the coercive power of the state is legitimately employed. As Locke argued in his *Letter Concerning Toleration*, government's rightful business is with the latter and not the former. Hence, the jurisdiction of the state is limited to the concerns of this world—security, health, and well-being—"in which all members of a political community, regardless of religious differences, are assumed to share a common interest."[26] In matters of religion and belief, however, it is the church—and conscience—that are to be the final arbiters of truth.

A second concern of ecumenical secularism is protecting religious minorities from discrimination and persecution. This issue reflects the pragmatic considerations from which many secular states emerged. It also embodies the basic compromise of multiethnic, multi-religious societies not to privilege one interpretation of religion (and, hence, one community) at the expense of all others. Recognizing that most societies are defined by a high degree of religious diversity, the separation of religious and political authority, and the development of inclusive governmental institutions, are intended to provide a basis of social solidarity that is not rooted in a religious or sectarian identity. By separating religion from political authority—and de-linking civil status from religious identity—secularism as non-discrimination is meant to protect minority populations from persecution and marginalization. To do otherwise—to give a preferential status to one religion or denomination—necessarily relegates minority sects and populations to a second-class status. It also provides the basis for ongoing conflict and division.

The heart of ecumenical secularism, from this latter view, is the creation of both a national identity *and* a political order that are not premised upon the exclusion of certain communities or the privileging of others. The secular project of the mid-twentieth century reflected this view and was driven by the desire to create "over-arching [political] loyalties that transcend the more primordial ones of ethnic affiliation, religious affiliation and linguistic identity."[27] Without some common basis for social life—including a minimal notion of shared identity—it was feared that inter-communal rivalries would tear weak political communities apart.[28] Similarly, the common interest—or common good—that provided a foundation for society had to be defined by a shared commitment to constitutional rule, the protection of rights, and the equal treatment of its diverse citizens.

These various understandings of secularism and secularization are evident in the different cases in which secular norms have provided a guiding ideology. The strong version of secularism as hostility to religion, or irreligious secularism, is evident in the Turkish understanding of Kemalism developed under Mustafa Kemal Ataturk, the father of modern Turkey. In this instance, state policy was informed by a conscious effort to remove religion from the public sphere. The motivation behind this policy was to reorient Turkish society away from the Muslim Middle East and toward a European and Western vision of modernity. The secular project in Turkey was, thus, informed by an assumption that religion had hindered the development of Ottoman society, and tied the population to a backwards, Muslim East. To be modern, from this view, was to be secular, and to be religious was to be backwards. Consequently, the eradication of religion was considered a necessary prerequisite for the development and modernization of the new Turkish republic. Given the historical context— which included the demise and dismemberment of the Ottoman Empire—the founders of modern Turkey saw a complete transformation of society as necessary to compete with their European rivals. This transformation would be economic, political, and, above all, cultural.

Similarly, the French secular tradition, *laïcité*, emerged from a desire to minimize the continuing influence of the Catholic Church on both French state and society. *Laïcité* therefore differentiated between the public and private spheres, and restricted religion to the latter. Since *laïcité* was born of the French Revolution—and had distinct anticlerical overtones— this differentiation was seen as protecting "citizens from religion, not, as in the American case, to also protect religion from the state."[29] Political freedom in this context was not coextensive with religious freedom. Olivier Roy (as well as others), however, has argued that *laïcité* does not necessarily entail a rejection of religious values, or a broader notion of the sacred. Rather, the political doctrine of *laïcité* "aims to free political, but also public, space from religious control. [It] does not aim to replace religious discourse by a new ethics."[30] This ambiguity is not surprising. The anticlerical strains of French history vie with the continuing influence of Catholicism on national identity. In more recent years, *laïcité* has been interpreted in a more aggressively exclusionary manner, at least in regard to headscarves and other outward symbols of personal religious faith. The 2004 law banning headscarves is perceived by many as discriminatory and as an infringement upon the individual religious freedom it is said to protect. The headscarf ban in public schools, of course, involves much more than religion, but ties into larger issues regarding the ability—and desirability—of integrating a dispossessed Muslim minority into contemporary French life.

The understanding of secularism as neutrality in matters of belief is evident in the cases of both India and the United States. In each instance, the religious pluralism of society prompted the government to develop official policies of tolerance and non-discrimination in matters of religion. These governments also sought to create a political identity that would transcend religious and sectarian division.

In the American experience, the proliferation of religious denominations within the early colonies precluded the establishment of any one church. Fearful that the dominance of one tradition or sect would entail the persecution of all others, representatives of the various faith groups accepted state neutrality as a founding compromise. They agreed, in short, to recognize others' religious freedom in exchange for their own. This compromise was manifest in the First Amendment to the Constitution, which precludes the establishment of any one particular religion, while also preserving the free exercise of religion. Very much influenced by both John Locke and Roger Williams, many of the founding fathers believed the state ought *not* to involve itself in the business of promoting particular interpretations of religion. They also believed that government ought *not* to ally with religious authorities "in the joint names of Caesar and God to impose their will on the people."[31] More to the point, the framers agreed that the Constitution should not privilege one group above all others, but rather "put contending sectarians on an equal footing by giving special status to none."[32] This vision of an ecumenical secularism has been the basis of America's inclusive civic nationalism, a vision that has been challenged variously by those who seek a more overt expression of Christianity in public life as well as by those who seek to eradicate religion altogether. Indeed, it is this competition between strict separationists, liberal accommodationists, and Christian nationalists that informs a broad spectrum of thought on matters of faith in American public life.

Similarly, in India, an ecumenical secularism was seen by Jawaharlal Nehru, Mohandas Gandhi, and other early leaders as the only viable basis for domestic harmony. Fearful of the sectarian divisions that marked the Partition of India, state elites committed themselves to creating a public square defined by official neutrality. This notion of official tolerance is exemplified by the Indian understanding of secularism as "equal distance" to religion, and embodies a genuinely pluralist conception of fundamental belief. This type of "primordial compromise" was seen as a necessary prerequisite for social harmony, and is embodied in Nehru's description of India's secular state:

> We call our State a secular one. The word "secular" perhaps is not a very happy one and yet for want of a better, we have used it. What exactly does it mean? It does not obviously mean a society where religion itself is discouraged. It means freedom of religion and conscience, including freedom for those who may have no religion. It means free play for all religions, subject only to their not interfering with each other or with the basic conceptions of our state.[33]

Secularism's Critics and Challenges

Finding the proper balance between religion and state—and institutionalizing a nondiscriminatory vision of secularism—has remained a challenge. Some critics of the secular tradition emphasize its failure to achieve this goal, while others reject the goal altogether. Among the latter group are many religious activists who see secular norms as a betrayal of faith and nation. For such activists, the self-actualization of a given community requires a close association between religion and state. Official preference ought to be given to the religious and ethnic motifs of the dominant community, and civil status be tied to religious identity. Such ethnic or religious nationalisms are based on the belief that "social unity and concord requires agreement on a general and comprehensive religious, philosophical or moral doctrine."[34] In other words, social cohesion is seen as requiring a shared religious (or national) identity, and political unity as best achieved through a high degree of cultural uniformity. Tolerance of religious diversity—and, hence, an ecumenical compromise on matters of religion and belief—is perceived as either a threat to social order, or as the "acquiescence in heresy."[35] It follows, then, that state authority has both the right and the obligation to regulate religious thought and practice.

There are numerous examples of such assertive religious nationalisms. This trend is evident among those who argue that the United States is a Christian nation, and that conservative Christian ideas ought to be promoted through government institutions (particularly education). Similar arguments are made in favor of an Islamic state in Egypt, the defining feature of which is government implementation of Islamic law. In such debates, it has been argued that "the unity of the nation can only be cemented by ensuring unity of thought."[36] The struggle to define Indian nationalism similarly pits Hindu nationalists against their civic opponents. In this case, religious activists offer an exclusive vision of Indian society—one that privileges upper-caste Hindus—against their secular counterparts. In these (as well as other) cases, debates over the role of religion in state institutions reflect long-standing disputes between those who want to construct an inclusive social order and those who believe that the state ought to give priority to the religion of the majority population. The religious nationalisms of the former Yugoslavia, culminating in the wars of the 1990s, represent the extreme version of this trend, and embodied both intense chauvinism and a corresponding proclivity toward violence.

These extreme expressions of religious nationalism are the most significant challenge to secularism of either variant. Such debates involve basic questions of social life, and whether society (and, hence, the nation) ought to be defined along cosmopolitan lines—and inclusive of diversity—or whether such inclusiveness is itself discriminatory. These debates pit majority demands for self-assertion against minority concerns of equal treatment, and highlight the difficulty of accommodating exclusive visions of religion and nation. In each of the cases mentioned in the previous paragraph, the call for a preferential role for conservative or illiberal religion was tied to a majoritarian impulse that saw secular nationalism not as neutrality, but as privileging minority populations at the expense of the majority. Whatever the philosophical intention, secular norms, from this view, were seen as banishing religion from the public sphere, not accommodating it.

This last point ties into a second set of critiques. For many, secularism as a worldview is simply incapable of accommodating religion in any manner aside from a subordinate one. There are several aspects to this view. The first is that secularism has, in practice, abandoned any sense of neutrality. Critics like Ashis Nandy and T. N. Madan, for example, have argued that states (or at least the Indian state) have fallen into the trap of "illiberal secularism" and refuse to recognize the manner in which religion legitimately informs human life and society.[37] In doing so, they argue, secularists have made things worse, not better. By attempting to remove religion altogether—and by transforming secularism into a totalizing worldview—state policies have inadvertently contributed to the kind of religious assertiveness and fanaticism that secularism was meant to combat. While Nandy and Madan focus on the Indian experience, this argument can be applied to any number of other cases, including the United States. From this view, secularism is the "dream of a minority that wishes to shape the majority in its own image."[38]

A similar critique is offered by William Connolly and Elizabeth Shakman Hurd, both of whom argue that secularism—and the secular state—has set itself up as the authoritative (and intolerant) arbiter of truth in the modern world.[39] From this view, secularism is not just a set of state policies but an authoritative discourse that structures human relations. It is, in this sense, both an ingrained worldview—filled with assumptions about what is natural, right, and just—as well as "an exercise of power" whose strength derives from its perceived objectivity and "taken for granted" status. The ideas that constitute the secular imaginary, in other words, exercise their influence indirectly through the social and political structures that they inform. This is evident in the perceived neutrality of ecumenical secularism (what Shakman Hurd refers to as Judeo-Christian secularism), which is embedded in the cultural and political institutions of the West. Although secularism is inclusive at one level—tolerating, as it does, different Christian denominations—it nonetheless "[retains] the civilizational hegemony of Christianity in a larger sense."[40] This prejudice reflects a lack of self-awareness, an assumed 'naturalness,' and a pernicious quality given the close association of secularism to both Western power structures and global capitalism.

Talal Asad takes this argument a step further and asserts that secularism (like, ostensibly, the liberal tradition from which it derives) is necessarily premised on the exclusion of certain ideas and peoples. Political speech may, in theory, be free, but in practice only certain types of speech are tolerated, let alone allowed into the public square. From this view, secularism is premised upon the exclusion of ideas and individuals that do not conform to particular norms, and, as a result, various forms of dissent are simply not given serious consideration. Asad goes on to argue that this is not an unintended consequence but a constitutive feature of the inequitable power relations (and inherent coercion) that constitute the secular public sphere. Secularism as a worldview, in other words, "presupposes new concepts of religion, ethics and politics." Traditional religious ideas and practices must conform to certain (modernist and liberal) criteria in order to be tolerated. Just as the freedoms of the liberal tradition are not absolute, secularism entails proscribed limits of acceptability that constitute the institutions of social order. As a consequence, such freedoms "are not open equally to everyone"[41] and never will be.

The question remains whether the ecumenical version of secularism has failed to live up to its promise, or whether the secular idea is itself inherently flawed. In short, can secularism be redeemed or must it be abandoned? This question goes to the heart of the critique: whether an inclusive secularism is possible, or whether the secular order is invariably based on the exclusion of certain beliefs (and peoples) and, thus, is incapable of tolerating genuine diversity. The converse of this last question also needs to be asked. Can secularism stand up to the assault of illiberal religious actors? The resurgence of illiberal religious ideologies represents a significant challenge to the liberal vision of an open society, and highlights the weak appeal of secular norms and identities. On the one hand, the attraction of religious fundamentalisms reflects the inherent limitations of a public sphere shorn of religious imagery, and the inability of liberal norms to provide certitude in a world defined by constant change. On the other hand, the appeal of fundamentalisms reflects the political utility of religion and its ability to provide a sense of belonging in a fragmented world. The failings of secularism, in short, are inherent in the challenge of providing a normative basis to political life without reference to the divine, and raise questions about whether an inclusive social order is even viable within the multiethnic, multi-religious societies that define our age.

A Justpeace Approach

Secularism is, indeed, in a state of crisis. So where lies its future? Is secularism—as noted above—so flawed as to warrant its complete abandonment, or can it be redeemed? If it is to be abandoned, what would be the alternative? What kind of institutions and values would be offered in the place of a secular order? It is in regard to this last query—and the absence of a viable alternative to a liberal vision of secularism as neutrality—that many have concluded that secularism must be rehabilitated, not forsaken.[42] The following section will expand upon this idea, and offer a re-conceptualized notion of secularism that takes the issue of neutrality and equal distance seriously, and rejects the exclusive tendencies that have proven so problematic. In formulating such an alternative, one can look to the emerging lens of just-peace as a guide for re-conceptualizing secular ideas and institutions, and to provide a normative benchmark by which to judge the efficacy of a reconceived secular order.

One of the key challenges for any society is the unrestrained exercise of power, and the coercion and violence associated with it. A second challenge is providing a shared ethic or moral basis to diverse societies. Political liberalism (which informs ecumenical secularism) arose in response to precisely these issues. In regard to the first, liberalism as a political tradition sought to restrain the arbitrary exercise of power through constitutional limits and the rule of law. This includes the protection of individual rights, freedom of conscience, and a commitment to equal treatment. In regard to the second issue, religious diversity, opposing political views and differences over conceptions of justice are just a few of the obstacles to developing a vision of social life that "goes beyond a mere *modus vivendi*."[43] Rawlsian political liberalism—which is reflected in secularism as non-discrimination—sought to address this challenge by differentiating political conceptions of justice from the overarching worldviews that inform them. The assumption was that members of society *can* agree on political values and policies, even if they cannot agree on comprehensive moral doctrines. This is the basis of a compromise that ensures equal treatment of individuals and groups.

Here, the central critique of ecumenical secularism needs to be addressed directly. As Asad notes, "it is not enough for liberals to [argue] that although the public sphere is less than perfect as an actual forum for rational debate, it is still an ideal worth striving for. The point here is that the public sphere is a space necessarily (not just contingently) articulated by power [and] everyone who enters it must address power's disposition of people and things."[44] While Asad's last point is self-evidently true, does it mean that the elimination of constitutional restraint would be preferable? The construction of a social order without power relations would appear utopian, so the alternative must be to mitigate—as far as possible—the abuses and exploitation associated with any concentration of power, be it economic, political, or religious. In regard to questions of religious and ethnic pluralism, there is a legitimate debate over whether traditional notions of liberal tolerance are sufficient, or whether they need to be expanded to embrace a "multicultural" (or deeply pluralist) model of coexistence. This would, among other things, require tolerating those who are outside the bounds of traditional acceptability and who "may have to disrupt existing assumptions in order to be heard."[45]

The evolving field of justpeace, with its emphasis upon strategic peacebuilding, offers a guide to address these challenges. As Scott Appleby and John Paul Lederach argue, the goal of strategic peacebuilding is to "[nurture] constructive human relations. . . [and focus] on transforming inhumane social patterns, flawed structural conditions and open violent conflict that weaken the conditions necessary for a flourishing human community."[46] A key component of this vision is the reduction of violence—both overt and institutional—and a respect for individual human rights, transparent government, and other elements of constitutional liberalism. Lederach and Appleby also identify a commitment to economic and social justice as a central feature of a just social order. The strength of this justpeace alternative—and its difference from the liberal tradition—is that it seeks to address directly the exclusionary tendencies of secularism in practice, the privileging of certain economic and political classes, and the tendency to associate neoliberal economic policies with the "liberal peace" thesis. Finally, a true justpeace would include interdependence among communities and a genuine collaboration in the articulation and pursuit of "the common good"[47] (about which more will be said below). This would, it appears, entail the engagement of a broad spectrum of religious actors and groups, and require a re-conceptualization of the nation in a manner that is genuinely inclusive and cosmopolitan.

Ecumenical secularism—rightly conceived and implemented—can facilitate the goals of a justpeace as envisioned above. Each emphasizes mitigating the systemic sources of conflict, marginalization, and oppression that have historically been associated with the liberal tradition. Moreover, a genuinely ecumenical vision of secularism can pursue justpeace without degenerating into the kind of relativism that is latent within the critique mentioned above. While an ecumenical secularism would not presume a particular "telos" for human society—particularly not one that requires a diminution of religious belief or the removal of religion from the public square—it would require a basic commitment to freedom of conscience and to the norms of non-discrimination and equal treatment. More to the point, an inclusive secularism would require a re-conceptualization of the nation that rejects the exclusive tendencies of both the religious nationalist and the irreligious secular nationalist. State and nation would, in short, need to tolerate social, religious, and political difference, though such tolerance could be based on either religious or secular reasons.

What might an ecumenical secularism entail in practice? A necessary first step would be to take a more accommodating approach to religion. This would require, above all else, abandoning the anti-religious sentiments latent within the secular worldview, and instead recognizing the constructive role that religion can play in human affairs. The "de-privatization" of religion should be seen as offering a source of meaning and moral authority, and not necessarily be perceived as a source of contention and conflict.[48] A re-conceptualized secularism would, moreover, see religion *not* as a separate (and autonomous) sphere, but rather as part of the social fabric that binds communities together, and that informs the norms and identities of both individuals and groups. In this context, an ecumenical secularism must take the commitment to equal treatment and non-discrimination seriously, and reflect that commitment in the institutions of nation and state. To this end, the state cannot support one version of religion above all others—sanctioning intra-religious or inter-religious domination—nor should it treat religious perspectives differently from nonreligious ("secular" or atheistic) views. Just as one tradition should not be favored over another, a neutral state cannot favor "religion over against nonbelief in religion or *vica versa*."[49]

This last point is important. As Charles Taylor notes, one of our key mistakes is in thinking that secularism has to do with religion, when "in fact it has to do with the (correct) response of the democratic state to diversity."[50] A social order that embodies the values of a justpeace, and a re-conceptualized vision of secularism, will be defined by non-discrimination and equal treatment of *all* citizens. In Taylor's view, this would require the pursuit of three goals. The first would be to ensure freedom of religion and conscience (i.e. the right to believe or not), as embodied in the notion of religious liberty. Second, this liberty must be available to all, equally. In other words, there must be equal treatment of all faith communities and worldviews, and none should "enjoy a privileged status, let alone be adopted as the official view of the state."[51] The third goal would move beyond non-discrimination and ensure a positive role in society for "all spiritual families," along with a concerted commitment to harmonious relations between groups.

What is interesting about Taylor's alternative is that it identifies goals, not particular institutional arrangements. This is intentional. Taylor recognizes that all societies have different cultural and historical contexts, and that one size does not fit all. Rajeev Bhargava agrees on this point, noting that a particular configuration of secularism will have to be "context-sensitive."[52] Nonetheless, there are certain overarching themes that need to be respected regarding both conscience and the free exercise of religion. First, even if one can legitimately criticize particular religious practices or doctrines, religious belief needs to be protected and free from persecution. Second, there needs to be an element of reciprocity in matters of tolerance. This is similar to (though distinct from) Alfred Stepan's "twin tolerations," which argues that democratic institutions require a degree of freedom from religion, in the same manner that "citizens need to be given sufficient space by democratic institutions to exercise their religious freedom."[53] Finally, this re-conceptualized secularism "cleaves very strongly to certain political principles: human rights, equality, the rule of law and democracy."[54] That such recommendations draw from the liberal canon should not be surprising given the priority liberalism places upon the restraint of power, and they should not be rejected on this basis.

There are, of course, a variety of challenges to achieving such a re-conceptualized vision of secularism. One involves the tension between the various goals. As Taylor rightly notes, to ensure that "every voice is heard" does not mean that each will be heard equally. Hence, there will always be some tension between the competing goals of liberty and equality, particularly in matters of belief. Second, there will remain differences of opinion on fundamental issues of social and political life that are not easily reconciled. This is particularly relevant to questions of fundamental purpose, and the absence of a shared conception of the good towards which society (and human existence) is ostensibly directed. What, in short, does it mean to commit oneself to human flourishing when there are competing visions of what that entails? Finally, the very notion of consensus is premised on the existence of a *common* interest, when, in fact, democratic societies are defined by competing—and often mutually exclusive—interests.

How, then, can diverse societies find a common ethic or shared moral vision for their collective life? More to the point, can this be resolved without coercion, marginalization, or the exclusion of at least some voices? These questions have been the subject of much debate, and only a very brief summation is possible here. Many, including John Rawls and Jürgen Habermas, believe that consensus on matters of political purpose and justice is possible, though it must be sought through persuasion and negotiation. In terms of content, this would entail, at minimum, a shared commitment to the equal protection of rights, and such public goods as health, safety, order, and the rule of law.[55] How such a vision would be justified is another matter. Rawls, in particular, has argued that support for such public goods is facilitated by the use of a universal language that is subject to "reasoned" debate. In other words, to develop a genuine consensus on the ethical underpinnings of public life, the arguments over law and government must appeal to "secular reasons," and not to religion. This claim assumes that religious arguments are unpersuasive (if based upon scriptural commandment), irrational (i.e., not rooted in secular reason), or parochial (if not grounded in natural law or some shared human experience). Needless to say, this claim has been the source of much contention. To marginalize religion from such debates, it is argued, will create a moral void and pave the way for "the intolerant, the trivial, and other misguided moralisms."[56]

How, then, to address this challenge? Do citizens need to check their religion at the door, or can overt expressions of religion be tolerated in a secular public square? The answer, at least in an inclusive secular order, is that religion and religious expression must be a part of this discourse. The teachings of a given religion can be appealed to in the public realm—and this should be welcomed—though not to justify the exclusion of other religious communities or ideas. The acceptance of religious reasoning is evident in a growing consensus (at least in American political circles) that recognizes the positive contributions that religion can make to the secular public sphere. Although appeals to church dogma or biblical literalism will have limited effectiveness when those views run counter to prevailing opinion, it is nonetheless important that such voices be heard. An argument similar to this was made by then-Senator Barack Obama in a speech he gave in 2006, when he argued that secularists (of the strict separationist sort) ought to shed their bias against religion in public discourse. Religion, he noted, is part of the fabric of American culture and politics, and should neither be excluded nor feared. By embracing—and not avoiding—religion, all parties "might recognize some overlapping values that both religious and secular people share when it comes to the moral and material direction of our country."[57]

The challenge remains, though, how to deal with those who espouse *intolerant* ideologies (whether religious or secular) or who otherwise promote violence and injustice. In other words, how ought society treat those who reject the fundamental principles of equal treatment and mutual tolerance? This poses a conundrum for the advocates both of justpeace and of a re-conceived secularism. In any society, there will be members (and groups) who believe themselves to be uniquely informed, and all others to be errant, on matters of religion and politics. Such certitude provides modern zealots with the belief that they ought rightly "direct and control the behavior of people *outside* the faith as well as inside it."[58] It also precludes such activists from accepting any political arrangement that does not give priority to their beliefs. The question, then, is: ought the rights and privileges of membership in a political community be granted to those who refuse to extend similar rights to others? If not, are illiberal beliefs and activists necessarily—and legitimately—excluded from the democratic process?[59]

There are no easy answers to these questions. A re-conceptualized secularism would begin by recognizing that intolerance is not something unique to religion. Hence, the problem is not religion per se, but the exclusive qualities of any belief system. Moreover, as long as those espousing intolerant views abide by the minimal requirements of peaceful coexistence, then there is an obligation to respect their right to hold contrarian views. In other words, dogmatic (and intolerant) ideas will need to be tolerated, though not "in the way adherents would want to have their beliefs accepted."[60] This claim is based upon several assumptions. First, tolerance necessarily entails a willingness to accept (though not necessarily embrace) objectionable and uncomfortable opinions. Second, to do otherwise—to exclude illiberal opinions from public life—has historically proven to be counterproductive (as noted in the section "Secularism's Critics and Challenges"). Of course, those who engage in violence, infringe upon others' civil liberties, or otherwise engage in violations of the standards set by the justpeace alternative are legitimately excluded or restrained. However, the reason for exclusion would not be their beliefs, but their actions. Finally, one can assume that ideas put forward in a public manner will be subject to dialogue and debate, and that the inclusion of all views in the public square is the best means of restraining chauvinism. As Pope Benedict XVI argued, the only solution to the pathologies of religion is to allow "the divine light of reason" to serve as a controlling organ. Similarly, the "pathologies of reason" ought to be checked by the spiritual lessons offered by the "great religious traditions of mankind."[61] Religion, in short, can—and ought—to play a positive role in the re-conceptualization of the secular public square.

CONCLUSION

In seeking accommodation on matters of religion in public life, a few points are evident. First, it is necessary to recognize that neither states nor modernity are necessarily secular (let alone liberal), nor is secularism invariably hostile to religion and religious pluralism. Similarly, religion is not, by definition, either irrational or inimical to human progress. While religious violence and extremism may capture headlines, those present only a part of the influence of religion in human experience. Religion can, and should, be a part of public discourse, and can provide a basis for peaceful coexistence. Similarly, secularism as a tradition or worldview is *not* a unitary phenomenon, but rather is itself defined by variation and diversity. Some interpretations are consistent with inclusive visions of social life and the nation, while others are not. What is ultimately at stake in these debates, then, is not religion or secularism, but diversity, and the tension between those who are willing to peacefully coexist with other communities and those who are not.

Moving beyond such preconceptions is a necessary first step for imagining a more constructive relationship between religion, nation, and state. It also creates an opportunity to re-conceptualize a vision of secularism that eschews its intolerant strains and affirms those elements consistent with the goals of justpeace. Such a re-conceptualized secularism would require (1) an ecumenical tolerance, in which particular expressions of various religions are neither excluded nor privileged; (2) that all faith traditions and communities enjoy equal treatment under law, and (3) that social order (i.e., the nation) be characterized by an inclusivity that does not link civil status to religious identity. Admittedly, this vision of ecumenical secularism is distinctly liberal insofar as its emphasis is on constitutional governance and the protection of the "inner forum" of conscience.[62] However, this emphasis—along with the commitment to non-discrimination—remains consistent with the basic requirements of justpeace regarding the marginalization of populations and the institutionalized violence associated with unregulated market capitalism and unfettered state power.

Such a re-conceptualized secularism is, necessarily, an ideal type, and one that may remain insufficiently "reformed" or inclusive for many. Nonetheless, it does consciously seek to break with secularism's troubled past, particularly in regard to secularity's materialist worldview and the tradition's historical intolerance. Of course, some will argue that any form of secular nationalism—or even religious tolerance—will invariably contain cultural and religious bias. Be that as it may, what this alternative hopes to offer is the requirements of a genuine and viable political compromise on matters of faith and conscience. Such a compromise would need to recognize that religion cannot—and should not—be excluded from public life, nor should state power be used to coerce belief of any sort. The legitimate exercise of state power is, consequently, limited to questions of public order, and not to the regulation of religious ideas and practices (except insofar as they encroach upon legitimate concerns of public order and safety). Finding the proper balance between religious freedom and equality will necessarily vary depending on particular circumstances. Moreover, these issues and debates will never be easily nor permanently resolved, but will always remain a matter of negotiation, debate, and contestation. "But such is the nature of the enterprise that is the modern secular state. And what better alternative is there for diverse democracies?"[63]

Notes

1. Gianfranco Poggi, *Forms of Power* (Malden, MA: Polity Press, 2001), 63.
2. Linell Cady and Elizabeth Shakman Hurd, *Comparative Secularisms in a Global Age* (New York: Palgrave MacMillan, 2010), 4.
3. Clifford Geertz, "The Integrative Revolution," in *Old Societies and New States: The Quest for Modernity in Asia and Africa*, ed. Clifford Geertz (New York: The Free Press of Glencoe, 1963), 157.
4. Peter Berger, "The Desecularization of the World: A Global Overview," in *The Desecularization of the World: Resurgent Religion and World Politics*, ed. Peter Berger (Washington, DC: Ethics and Public Policy Center, 1999), 2.
5. See for example Saad Eddin Ibrahim, "The Changing Face of Islamic Activism," in *Egypt, Islam, and Democracy: Twelve Critical Essays* (Cairo: American University in Cairo Press, 1996), 69–80.
6. Norris and Inglehart consequently argue that there is a strong correlation between the lack of human security and the continuing strength of religious belief. They also argue that high levels of existential security drive the secularization process. Pippa Norris and Ronald Inglehart, *Sacred and Secular: Religion and Politics Worldwide* (New York: Cambridge University Press, 2006).
7. José Casanova, *Public Religions in the Modern World* (Chicago: University of Chicago Press, 2004), 5.
8. Mark Juergensmeyer, *Global Rebellion: Religious Challenges to the Secular State, from Christian Militias to al-Qaeda* (Berkeley, CA: University of California Press, 2008).
9. See Mark Tessler, "The Origins of Popular Support for Islamist Movements," in *Islam, Democracy, and the State in North Africa*, ed. John Entelis (Bloomington: Indiana University Press, 1997), 93–126.
10. Anthony Marx, *Faith in Nation: Exclusionary Origins of Nationalism* (New York: Oxford University Press, 2003), 197.
11. See for example Anthony Smith, "The Sacred Dimension of Nationalism," *Millennium: Journal of International Studies* 29, no. 3 (2000): 791–814. See also David Little, "Belief, Ethnicity and Nationalism," in *Nationalism and Ethnic Politics* 1, no. 2 (1995): 284–301.
12. Robert Bellah, "Civil Religion in America," in *Beyond Belief: Essays on Religion in a Post-Traditionalist World* (Berkeley, CA: University of California Press, 1991), 168–189.
13. For more on this topic, see Scott W. Hibbard, *Religious Politics and Secular States: Egypt, India, and the United States* (Baltimore: Johns Hopkins University Press, 2010).
14. R. Scott Appleby, *The Ambivalence of the Sacred: Religion, Violence, and Reconciliation* (New York: Rowman and Littlefield, 2000), 27.
15. Casanova, *Public Religions*, 4.
16. For more on the distinction between secularism as hostility to religion and secularism as neutrality, see Charles Taylor, "Modes of Secularism," in *Secularism and its Critics*, ed. Rajeev Bhargava (Delhi: Oxford University Press, 1998), 31–53.

17. An alternate typology would add a third variable, and distinguish between genuinely "pluralist" as opposed to simply inclusive notions of religion, the distinction being whether alternative viewpoints are genuinely embraced as opposed to merely tolerated. This threefold typology of inclusive, exclusive, and pluralist is offered by Diana Eck, and referenced in Appleby, *Ambivalence of the Sacred*, 15.

18. José Casanova, "The Secular, Secularizations, Secularisms," in *Rethinking Secularism*, ed. Craig Calhoun, Mark Juergensmeyer, and Jonathan VanAntwerpen (New York: Oxford University Press, 2011), 54.

19. Graeme Smith, *A Short History of Secularism* (New York: I. B. Taurus, 2008), 22.

20. Charles Taylor, *The Secular Age* (Cambridge: Harvard University Press, 2007).

21. Casanova, "The Secular, Secularizations, and Secularisms," 54.

22. See for example George Jacob Holyoake, *The Principles of Secularism Briefly Explained* (Bristol Selected Pamphlets, 1859).

23. There are, of course, numerous variations on the relationship of state and religion, ranging from complete separation to various forms of accommodation. For more on these, see Ahmet Kuru, *Secularism and State Policies Toward Religion: The United States, France, and Turkey* (New York: Cambridge University Press, 2009) and Jonathan Fox, ed., *Religion, Politics, Society, and the State* (Boulder, CO: Paradigm Publishers, 2012).

24. David Little, "The Global Challenge of Secularism to Religious Freedom," in *Trends of Secularism in a Pluralistic World*, ed. Jaime Contreras and Rosa Maria Martinez de Codes (Madrid: Iberoamericana–Vervuert, 2013), 3.

25. Little, "Global Challenge," 4.

26. Little, "Global Challenge," 4.

27. David Apter, "Political Religion in the New Nations," in Geertz, *Old Societies and New States*, 80.

28. Clifford Geertz, "The Integrative Revolution." pp. 105–157.

29. Cady and Shakman Hurd, *Comparative Secularisms*, 13.

30. Olivier Roy, *Secularism Confronts Islam* (New York: Columbia University Press, 2007), 22.

31. Frank Lambert, *The Founding Fathers and the Place of Religion in America* (Princeton, NJ: Princeton University Press, 2003), 161.

32. Lambert, *Founding Fathers*, 238. It should noted that these clauses did not apply to states, which had various forms of establishment and bans on clergy in politics until the early 1800s.

33. Jawaharlal Nehru, cited in *India After Independence*, by Bipan Chandra, Mridula Mukherjee, and Aditya Mukherjee (New Delhi: Penguin Books, 1999), 48.

34. John Rawls, *Political Liberalism* (New York: Columbia University Press, 1996), xxvii.

35. Rawls, *Political Liberalism*, xxvi.

36. Samir Amin, "Pluralism Spurs Innovation," *Al-Ahram Weekly*, April 1994.

37. See T. N. Madan, "Secularism in Its Place," 297–320 and Ashis Nandy, "The Politics of Secularism and the Recovery of Religious Toleration," 321–344, in Bhargava, *Secularism and Its Critics*.

38. Madan, "Secularism in Its Place." p. 298.

39. See William E. Connolly, *Why I Am Not a Secularist* (Minneapolis, MN: University of Minnesota Press, 1999), and Elizabeth Shakman Hurd, *The Politics of Secularism in International Relations* (Princeton, NJ: Princeton University Press, 2008).

40. Shakman-Hurd, *Politics of Secularism*, 6. A similar critique of secularism's Christian roots is offered by Saba Mahmood in "Can Secularism Be Otherwise?" in *Varieties of Secularism*

in a Secular Age, ed. Michael Warner, Jonathan VanAntwerpen, and Craig Calhoun (Cambridge: Harvard University Press, 2010), 282–299.

41. Talal Asad, "Religion, Nation-State, Secularism," in *Nation and Religion: Perspectives on Europe and Asia*, ed. Peter van der Veer and Hartmut Lehmann (Princeton, NJ: Princeton University Press, 1999), 180.

42. See for example Rajeev Bhargava, "Rehabilitating Secularism," in Calhoun et al., *Rethinking Secularism*, 92–113.

43. Jürgen Habermas, in *The Dialectics of Secularization: On Reason and Religion*, by Jürgen Habermas and Joseph Ratzinger (San Francisco: Ignatious Press, 2005), 22.

44. Asad, "Religion, Nation-State, Secularism," in van der Veer and Lehmann, *Nation and Religion*, 180.

45. Asad, "Religion, Nation-State, Secularism," 181.

46. John Paul Lederach and R. Scott Appleby, "Strategic Peacebuilding: An Overview," in *Strategies of Peace: Transforming Conflict in a Violent World*, ed. Daniel Philpott and Gerard F. Powers (New York: Oxford University Press, 2010), 22.

47. Lederach and Appleby, "Strategic Peacebuilding," 23.

48. Gerard F. Powers, "Religion and Peacebuilding," in Philpott and Powers, *Strategies of Peace*, 322.

49. Charles Taylor, "Why We Need a Radical Redefinition of Secularism," in *The Power of Religion in the Public Sphere*, ed. Eduardo Mendieta and Jonathan VanAntwerpen (New York: Columbia University Press, 2011), 37.

50. Taylor, "Radical Redefinition," 37.

51. Taylor, "Radical Redefinition," 35.

52. Bhargava, "Rehabilitating Secularism," 108.

53. Alfred Stepan, "The Multiple Secularisms of Modern Democratic and Non-Democratic Regimes," in Calhoun et. al., *Rethinking Secularism*, 114.

54. Taylor, "Radical Redefinition," 37.

55. David Little expands upon this idea by noting that a constitutive (but not inclusive) piece of the common good would include a "broad common commitment to the protection of rights (ideally, both nationally and internationally defined) in accord with the Constitution and the rule of law." Other elements would include such basic public goods as "health, order and safety, which are the appropriate concerns of government." Beyond this, he notes, a shared vision of the common good will need to be a matter of negotiation and debate, and "left to whatever is commonly agreed to on the basis of the proper functioning of constitutional procedures." David Little in correspondence.

56. Michael Sandel, *Liberalism and the Limits of Justice* (New York: Cambridge University Press, 1998) 216–217.

57. Barack Obama, "Call to Renewal" keynote address, Washington DC, June 28, 2006.

58. David Little, "Tolerating Intolerance: Some Reflections on the Freedom of Religion as a Human Right," *Reflections* (Summer/Fall 1995): 18–25. Emphasis added.

59. Bargava, "Rehabilitating Secularism," 101.

60. Little, "Tolerating Intolerance," 25.

61. Joseph Cardinal Ratzinger, "That Which Holds the World Together," in Habermas and Ratzinger, *Dialectics of Secularization*, 77.

62. The liberal roots of this argument reflect the philosophical commitment to inclusivity, restraint on power, and equal treatment inherent in the broader tradition. That liberalism has often manifest in illiberal ways does not detract from the philosophical commitments

upon which it is founded, and it is for this reason that the argument in this chapter returns to the liberal tradition. The author owes a debt of gratitude to Joseph Margulies for his thoughts on this topic.

63. Taylor, "Radical Redefinition," 51.

Bibliography

Works Cited

Appleby, R. Scott. *The Ambivalence of the Sacred: Religion, Violence and Reconciliation.* New York: Rowman and Littlefield, 2000.

Apter, David. "Political Religion in the New Nations." In Geertz, *Old Societies and New States,*.

Asad, Talal. "Religion, Nation-State, Secularism." In *Nation and Religion: Perspectives on Europe and Asia,* edited by Peter van der Veer and Hartmut Lehmann, 178–196. Princeton, NJ: Princeton University Press, 1999.

Bellah, Robert. "Civil Religion in America." In *Beyond Belief: Essays on Religion in a Post-Traditionalist World,* 168–189. Berkeley, CA: University of California Press, 1991.

Berger, Peter L. "The Desecularization of the World: A Global Overview." In *The Desecularization of the World: Resurgent Religion and World Politics,* edited by Peter L. Berger, 1–18. Washington, DC: Ethics and Public Policy Center, 1999.

Bhargava, Rajeev, ed. *Secularism and Its Critics.* Delhi: Oxford University Press, 1998.

Bhargava, Rajeev. "Rehabilitating Secularism." In Calhoun, Juergensmeyer, and VanAntwerpen, *Rethinking Secularism,* 92–113.

Cady, Linell, and Elizabeth Shakman Hurd. *Comparative Secularisms in a Global Age.* New York: Palgrave MacMillan, 2010.

Calhoun, Mark, Mark Juergensmeyer, and Jonathan VanAntwerpen, eds. *Rethinking Secularism.* New York: Oxford University Press, 2011.Casanova, José. *Public Religions in the Modern World.* Chicago: University of Chicago Press, 2004.

Casanova, José. "The Secular, Secularizations, Secularisms." In Calhoun, Juergensmeyer, and VanAntwerpen, *Rethinking Secularism,* 54–74.

Chandra, Bipan, Mridula Mukherjee, and Aditya Mukherjee. *India After Independence.* New Delhi: Penguin Books, 1999.

Connolly, William E. *Why I Am Not a Secularist.* Minneapolis, MN: University of Minnesota Press, 1999.

Fox, Jonathan, ed. *Religion, Politics, Society and the State.* New York: Oxford University Press, 2012.

Geertz, Clifford, ed. *Old Societies and New States: The Quest for Modernity in Asia and Africa.* New York: The Free Press of Glencoe, 1963.

Geertz, Clifford. "The Integrative Revolution." In Geertz, *Old Societies and New States,* 105–157.

Habermas, Jürgen. "Pre-Political Foundations of the Democratic Constitutional State." In *The Dialectics of Secularization: On Reason and Religion,* by Jürgen Habermas and Joseph Ratzinger, 19–52. San Francisco: Ignatious Press, 2005.

Hibbard, Scott W. *Religious Politics and Secular States: Egypt, India, and the United States.* Baltimore: Johns Hopkins University Press, 2010.

Holyoake, George Jacob. *The Principles of Secularism Briefly Explained.* Bristol Selected Pamphlets, 1859.

Hurd, Elizabeth Shakman. *The Politics of Secularism in International Relations*. Princeton, NJ: Princeton University Press, 2008.

Ibrahim, Saad Eddin. *Egypt, Islam, and Democracy: Twelve Critical Essays*. Cairo: American University in Cairo Press, 1996.

Juergensmeyer, Mark. *Global Rebellion: Religious Challenges to the Secular State, from Christian Militias to al-Qaeda*. Berkeley, CA: University of California Press, 2008.

Kuru, Ahmet. *Secularism and State Policies Toward Religion: The United States, France, and Turkey*. New York: Cambridge University Press, 2009.

Lambert, Frank. *The Founding Fathers and the Place of Religion in America*. Princeton, NJ: Princeton University Press, 2003.

Little, David. "Tolerating Intolerance: Some Reflections on the Freedom of Religion as a Human Right." *Reflections* (Summer/Fall 1995): 18–25.

Little David. "Belief, Ethnicity and Nationalism." *Nationalism and Ethnic Politics* 1, no. 2 (1995): 284–301.

Little, David. "The Global Challenge of Secularism to Religious Freedom." In *Trends of Secularism in a Pluralistic World*, edited by Jaime Contreras and Rosa Maria Martinez de Codes, 31–58. Madrid: Iberoamericana–Vervuert, 2013.

Lederach, John Paul, and R. Scott Appleby. "Strategic Peacebuilding: An Overview." In Philpott and Powers, *Strategies of Peace*, 19–44.

Madan, T. N. "Secularism in Its Place." In Bhargava, *Secularism and Its Critics*, 297–320.

Mahmood, Saba. "Can Secularism Be Otherwise?" In Warner, VanAntwerpen, and Calhoun, *Varieties of Secularism*, 282–299.

Marx, Anthony. *Faith in Nation: Exclusionary Origins of Nationalism*. New York: Oxford University Press, 2003.

Mendieta, Eduardo, and Jonathan VanAntwerpen, eds. *The Power of Religion in the Public Sphere*. New York: Columbia University Press, 2011.

Nandy, Ashis. "The Politics of Secularism and the Recovery of Religious Toleration." In Bhargava, *Secularism and Its Critics*, 321–344.

Norris, Pippa, and Ronald Inglehart. *Sacred and Secular: Religion and Politics Worldwide*. New York: Cambridge University Press, 2006.

Obama, Barack. "Call to Renewal" keynote address. Washington, DC, June 28, 2006.

Philpott, Daniel, and Gerard F. Powers, eds. *Strategies of Peace: Transforming Conflict in a Violent World*. New York: Oxford University Press, 2010.

Poggi, Gianfranco. *Forms of Power*. Malden, MA: Polity Press, 2001.

Powers, Gerard F. "Religion and Peacebuilding." In Philpott and Powers, *Strategies of Peace*, 317–352.

Ratzinger, Joseph Cardinal. "That Which Holds the World Together." In *The Dialectics of Secularization*, by Jürgen Habermas and Joseph Ratzinger, 53–80. San Francisco: Ignatius Press, 2005..

Rawls, John. *Political Liberalism*. New York: Columbia University Press, 1996.

Roy, Olivier. *Secularism Confronts Islam*. New York: Columbia University Press, 2007.

Sandel, Michael. *Liberalism and the Limits of Justice*. New York: Cambridge University Press, 1998.

Smith, Anthony. "The Sacred Dimension of Nationalism." *Millennium: Journal of International Studies* 29, no. 3 (2000): 791–814.

Smith, Graeme. *A Short History of Secularism*. New York: I. B. Taurus, 2008.

Stepan, Alfred. "The Multiple Secularisms of Modern Democratic and Non-Democratic Regimes." In Calhoun, Juergensmeyer, and VanAntwerpen, *Rethinking Secularism*, 114–144.

Taylor, Charles. "Modes of Secularism." In Bhargava, *Secularism and its Critics,*.

Taylor, Charles. *A Secular Age*. Cambridge: Harvard University Press, 2007.

Taylor, Charles. "Why We Need a Radical Redefinition of Secularism." In Mendieta and VanAntwerpen, *The Power of Religion in the Public Sphere*, 34–59.

Tessler, Mark. "The Origins of Popular Support for Islamist Movements." In *Islam, Democracy, and the State in North Africa*, edited by John Entelis, 93–126. Bloomington, IN: Indiana University Press, 1997.

Warner, Michael, Jonathan VanAntwerpen, and Craig Calhoun, eds. *Varieties of Secularism in a Secular Age*. Cambridge, MA: Harvard University Press, 2010.

Further Reading

An-Naim, Abdullahi. *Islam and the Secular State: Negotiating the Future of Shari'a*. Cambridge, MA: Harvard University Press, 2010.

Asad, Talal. *Formations of the Secular: Christianity, Islam, Modernity*. Stanford, CA: Stanford University Press, 2003.

Bellin, Eva. "Faith in Politics: New Trends in the Study of Religion and Politics." *World Politics*, Volume 60, no. 2 (2008): 315–346.

Bruce, Steve, ed. *Religion and Modernization: Sociologists and Historians Debate the Secularization Thesis*. New York: Oxford University Press, 1992.

Brown, L. Carl. *Religion and State: The Muslim Approach to Politics*. New York: Columbia University Press, 2000.

Chandhoke, Neera. *Beyond Secularism: The Rights of Religious Minorities*. New Delhi: Oxford University Press, 2002.

Contreras, Jaime, and Rosa Maria Martinez de Codes, eds. *Trends of Secularism in a Pluralistic World*. Madrid: Iberoamericana—Vervuert, 2013.

Esposito, John, and Assam Tamimi, eds. *Islam and Secularism in the Middle East*. New York: New York University Press, 2000.

Fatton, Robert, and R. K. Ramazani, eds. *Religion, State and Society: Jefferson's Wall of Separation in Comparative Perspective*. New York: Palgrave Macmillan, 2008.

Hargreaves, Alec G., John Kelsay, and Sumner B. Twiss, eds. *Politics and Religion in France and the United States*. Lanham, MD: Lexington Books, 2007.

Hashemi, Nader. *Islam, Secularism, and Liberal Democracy: Toward a Democratic Theory for Muslim Societies*. New York: Oxford University Press, 2009.

Hirschkind, Charles, and David Scott, eds. *Powers of the Secular Modern: Talal Assad and His Interlocutors*. Stanford, CA: Stanford University Press, 2006.

Keddie, Nicki. "Secularism and its Discontents." *Daedalus*, Vol. 132, no. 3 (2003): 14–30.

Kuru, Ahmet T. "Passive and Assertive Secularism: Historical Conditions, Ideological Struggles and State Policies Toward Religion." *World Politics*, Vol. 59, no. 4 (2007): 568–594.

Lilla, Mark. *The Stillborn God: Religion, Politics and the Modern West*. New York: Alfred A. Knopf, 2007.

Little, David. "Religion, Human Rights and Secularism: Preliminary Clarifications and Some Islamic, Jewish and Christian Responses." In *Humanity Before God: Contemporary Faces of Jewish, Christian and Islamic Ethics*, edited by William Schweiker, Michael Johnson, and Kevin Jung, 256–283. Minneapolis, MN: Augsburg Fortress, 2006.

Little, David, and Donald Swearer, eds. *Religion and Nationalism in Iraq: A Comparative Perspective*. Cambridge, MA: Harvard University Press, 2006.

John Locke. *A Letter Concerning Toleration*. Edited by James Tully. Cambridge, MA: Hackett, 1983.

Monsma, Stephen, and Christophen Soper. *The Challenge of Pluralism: Church and State in Five Democracies*. New York: Rowan and Littlefield, 2008.

Srinivasan, T. N., ed. *The Future of Secularism*. New Delhi: Oxford University Press, 2007.

Tamadonfar, Mehran, and Ted G. Jelen. *Religion and Regimes: Support, Separation, and Opposition*. Lanham, MD: Lexington Books, 2013.

Tepe, Sultan. *Beyond Sacred and Secular: Politics of Religion in Israel and Turkey*. Stanford, CA: Stanford University Press, 2008.

CHAPTER 5

....

SECULAR-RELIGIOUS ENCOUNTERS AS PEACEBUILDING*

....

SLAVICA JAKELIĆ

MANY scholars in international affairs today are rediscovering the importance of religion, but the past and the present status they ascribe to it often reveal the same modernist bias. If religions used to be dismissed because of a belief in their unavoidable decline, they are now frequently perceived as a significant albeit irrational and divisive social force.[1] The latter perspective is not without reason: religious elites and religious institutions have often provided justifications or served as an impetus for social conflicts.[2] But as a number of scholars has recently argued, the root of distrust and neglect of religions in international affairs and, more generally, the social sciences, is not simply in the lessons of history but in secularism as a normative disposition. It is the "secularist paradigm" or "the politics of secularism,"[3] scholars maintain, that direct social analysis toward the a priori evaluation of religions as either irrelevant or as a problem, for social life in general and conflict resolution in particular. Awareness of the dominance of secularist bias in the social sciences has at least two important repercussions for peace studies. Firstly, secularism emerges as a problem for the very practice of peacebuilding: it overemphasizes the role of secular nation-states and economics and neglects the positive role of religious symbols, elites, and institutions in the context of peacebuilding.[4] The politics of secularism, in other words, does not allow us to acknowledge and explore what Scott Appleby aptly calls the "ambivalence of the sacred": the simple but important fact that the fervor of religious commitments can be a foundation of conflict and exclusion but also the source of reconciliation and justice.[5]

Secondly, the identification of the secularist paradigm in the consideration of religion means that one important task for scholars and practitioners of peace studies is to distinguish between those religious elites and institutions that legitimize conflicts and those that play the role of peacemakers.[6] We thus see the possibility for two directions in the theory and practice of peace studies—one that recognizes the proper place of religion and the other that critiques the normative assumptions and negative implications of secularism. Both of these directions present us with the temptation to dismiss secularism as unhelpful or even unnecessary for our thinking about peacebuilding.

At first sight, this chapter seems to follow that trajectory. It begins with a critique of secularism: it acknowledges the crisis in religious-secular encounters as well as the urgency of moving away from secularist parochialism. In pursuing that line of discussion, however, the chapter also recognizes a great danger of falling into another extreme—that of marginalizing and neglecting the positive role of secularism for establishing and sustaining peace. The marginalization of the constructive, positive role of secularism presents peace studies with a practical problem: as Gerard Powers reminds us, religious actors do not act alone when it comes to building and sustaining peace.[7] Even more importantly, disregarding secularism or focusing solely on its critique stand as a moral problem for peace studies when the end of peacebuilding is envisioned as justpeace. The latter can emerge only from the participation of both religious and secular members of society[8]—only if believers and nonbelievers participate in the development of "local and national communities that respect the dignity of each individual" and want to "promote authentic human flourishing" of all, religious and secular people alike.[9]

Put differently, if the critique of secularism is an unavoidable prerequisite to exploring the proper place of religions in peacebuilding, moving beyond the critique of secularism is indispensable in order to grasp both the institutional and ethical potential of secular-religious encounters for building and sustaining justpeace. This chapter's call for religious-secular collaboration, then, is not instrumental but deeply normative in character. Its departing point is the view of religious-secular pluralism as a value that constitutes social life, and which needs to be explored and sustained if we are to promote the conditions of human flourishing in all contemporary societies, especially those undergoing conflict transformation.

The chapter is divided into two parts. In the first, theoretical part, I elaborate on two critiques that dominate the current scholarship on secularism—the critique of the secular state and the critique of secular agency. The discussion affirms the legitimacy of such critical views of secularism, but its goal is also to indicate these views' limitations and the need to move beyond the discourse of critique. One of the purposes of my discussion is to develop a thicker understanding of secular agency and of secularisms. This theoretical move shapes the constructive thrust of the chapter: it attempts to posit religions and secularisms as two equal and mutually enriching agents of peacebuilding, rather than as obstacles for each other.

The constraints of a critical approach to secular agency become particularly evident in the second part of the chapter, which considers the meanings and actions of secular agency in the context of Solidarity, the 1980s social movement in Communist Poland. The richness of historical detail in the Solidarity movement allows us to appreciate the complex phenomenology of secular agency as it is practiced in specific social contexts and in relation to religion—religious ideas but also concrete religious institutions and actors. Secularism here ceases to be just a matter of power, politics, and ideology; it stands as a moral orientation toward the world, reflected in people's ideas and their lives, and As constitutive of social movements. Secularism, in other words, reveals itself as a worldview *and* practice that serves to disclose rather than to legitimize state power.[10]

In a trajectory I propose below—a trajectory that links critical theoretical considerations of secularism with the affirmation of secularism as articulated and practiced by individual actors—I hope to broaden the horizons of peace studies in two ways: first, by affirming a "multilayered view" of secularism that will recognize religious-secular differences and practical difficulties in their encounters without drawing unbridgeable distinctions between them,[11] and second, by opening the space for a greater appreciation of religious-secular encounters as these happen among the range of local actors, in the context of civil society, and not solely on the level of secular states or established religious institutions.

Secularism as a Problem

As the growing body of literature on "secularism" demonstrates, defining this notion is a complicated endeavor. Most scholars (from social scientists such as Ahmet Kuru, Jocelyne Cesari, Tariq Modood, José Casanova, or Elizabeth Shakman Hurd to legal scholars such as Silvio Ferrari and Winnifred Fallers Sullivan), focus on secularism as an organizational principle of a political community—the principle of separation between politics and religion and, in national contexts, between the state and religious institutions.[12] These discussions are important because they reveal the porous boundaries between the religious and the secular, and the wide range of political models of secularism. But the discussions in question also point out that, while secularism is given different symbolic and institutional expressions, the Western Christian roots of secularism often continue to live even in different institutionalizations of secularist principles. For T. N. Madan and Adam Seligman, the Western Christian origins of secularism make it inherently problematic for either political practice or social analysis in non-Western contexts.[13] For moral philosopher Charles Taylor, however, the particular theological roots of secularism do not imply that one current of its normative history could not be retrieved and developed as a principle for all democratic (liberal) societies, Western or non-Western.[14]

Even though much of the current scholarship focuses on the political aspects and politics of secularism, this notion does not indicate just a form of political governance. Secularism, it is important to underline, may also refer to a worldview, an ideology, a political doctrine, a type of moral philosophy, or a belief that the scientific method is sufficient to understanding the world in which we live (as is the case with some advocates of the "New Atheism").[15] The definition of secularism is also complicated because of its proximity to the notion of "secularization," which has long been used to refer to the processes that accompany modernization. These processes, however, cannot be understood as a natural or neutral progression toward less religious societies. David Martin and Jeffrey Hadden argued decades ago that secularization processes are inseparable from the philosophical, political, and ideological aspects of secularisms,[16] while the American sociologist Christian Smith and his collaborators meticulously documented that the secularization of American public life did not happen on its own but was introduced by concrete historical agents whose goals included the institutionalization of various secularist principles.[17] In the words of Christian theologian John Milbank, secularization did not just happen, it was established; the world did not become secular, it was made such.[18]

Secularism, then, is a conceptual problem: it has developed and acquired a range of meanings, historical applications, and institutional arrangements that depend on specific histories and circumstances. As a result, secularism cannot be thought of in the singular, only in the plural.[19] Secularism is also a political and a normative problem. Scholars today agree that secularism is an urgent political question due to the crises of secular states all over the world—crises that are shaped by the challenges of public religions, religious fundamentalisms, and the changing nature of cultural pluralism.[20] The crisis of secularism also has an internal or normative dimension. Its claims to universality, neutrality, and rationality are unsustainable, we are told, once we recognize its Western Christian roots, its parochial views of agency and authority, which form secular sensibilities and secular politics that justify the power of the secular state.[21]

For the discussion of secularism in the context of peace studies, the normative critics of secularism are of particular concern. Although different in their disciplinary approaches—they include theologians, political philosophers, anthropologists, and social scientists—the normative critics of secularism generally represent the larger critique of Western modernity, and all of them reject secularism's claims to universality, rationality, and neutrality.[22] I focus here on critiques of the secular state and secular agency. The former is pertinent to the theory and practice of peace studies because it highlights the need to move beyond the scope of nation-state in thinking about the peacebuilding processes; the latter is relevant because it tackles the prejudice against religions in the context of peacebuilding.

The Critique of the Secular State

According to common interpretations of the liberal-democratic doctrine, Partha Chatterjee writes, the secular state is based on three principles: liberty, equality, and neutrality.[23] This means that the secular state is to permit the practice of any religion, and that it does not give preference to any religious or non-religious beliefs. In affirming these principles, scholars explain, the secular state, "does not just promise the progress brought about by emancipation. It also promises peace, or at least a more peaceful resolution to conflicts." [24]

The reality of the secular state, critics suggest, is quite different. In the case of the United States, Michael Sandel argues, the secular state is far from being neutral: it moved from religious choice as a possibility to religious choice as a norm and, ultimately, as a legal principle.[25] In doing so, according to Sandel, the state affirmed a voluntarist, liberal conception of the human person, a notion that gives priority of the right over the good and that posits the individual's self-mastery and self-government at the center. In the name of neutrality, the secular state legislated a particular, liberal idea of personhood and established that idea at the foundation of democratic polity.

The failed promise of neutrality is also the subject of critique among those who write about the Indian secular state. The advocates of the Indian model of secularism—Amartya Sen, Raymond Panikkar, Rajeev Bhargava, Zoya Hasan—think that its normative ideals need to be emphasized if the state is to ensure equality of all religious groups and individuals in the multi-religious society burdened by the legacies of the caste system.[26] For T. N. Madan, however, it is precisely the normative foundations of Indian secularism that present a problem: they lead into a narrow definition of religion due to which the state does not take religious differences seriously but marginalizes and privatizes religion. Secularism, Madan argues, is impossible as a foundation of the Indian democratic state: it cannot be sustained as a shared credo of life because most Indians are religious, and it cannot serve as the foundation of equality because the state privileges some religious traditions over others (in the Indian case, it privileges religious minorities). Partha Chatterjee elaborates that the interventions of the Indian secular state in the religious traditions and life of some communities, while done in the name of social reforms, represent an example of how the state "flagrantly violated the principle of separation of state and religion."[27] The outcome, according to some critics, is that the state is not only "incapable of countering religious fundamentalism[,] fanaticism,"[28] and conflict but is actually conducive to them.

The French *laïcité* model also calls for critiques of the interventionist character of political secularism. *Laïcité* was not some unencumbered development: it emerged from within very specific French philosophical, political, and legal traditions, and in relation to French religious history and the most powerful of religious institutions—the Catholic Church. Due to this embedded nature of *laïcité*, its meanings and institutions have always been porous. And, while in the beginning it was Catholicism and *laïcité* that have been constitutive of each other's boundaries and sensibilities, it is Islam that now challenges the normative contents and institutional boundaries of *laïcité*. In the words of Talal Asad, *laïcité* as the constitutional principle of the French state and the cultural foundation of the French national identity is "not blind to religiously-defined groups in public" but, to the contrary, "is suspicious of some (Muslims) because of what it imagines they may do... [and] is ashamed in relation to others (Jews) because of what they have suffered at the hands of Frenchmen."[29]

For the critics, in other words, secularism at the foundation of the modern state claims to solve the problem of conflict while it actually only replaces one type of violence (religious) with another—that of the nation-state. Secularism promises progress and peace; it claims to mitigate the challenges of religious pluralism. Instead, embodied in the institutions of powerful nation-states, secularism causes more injustice by virtue of marginalizing religious identities—by focusing on individual freedoms as opposed to collective religious identities—and thus often strengthens religious fundamentalisms.

The Critique of Secular Agency

One of the most influential critics of secularism, anthropologist Talal Asad, argues that secularism is grounded in distinctive politics, knowledges, and sensibilities, which are reflected in its parochial view of agency and authority. Asad writes that secular agency is constituted by the "romance of resistance."[30] The purpose of the secular agent is self-empowerment—opposition to the external power that oppresses her. The framework of the action of the secular agent is history-making, with the objective to remove suffering from human life. Contrary to what conceptions of secular agency assume, Asad maintains, there is not one but many different grammars and different forms of action that define what agency is.[31] Thus, while secular agency is defined by opposition to suffering, many if not most religions understand suffering as constitutive of the human condition.[32] The positive orientation toward human suffering in early Christian communities, as Asad explains, countered the dominant approach to suffering in their surroundings.[33] This Christian self-subjection to suffering and pain,[34] in Asad's view, is not the absence of agency but a particular form of agency—the act of suffering that is meaningful with regard to those who suffer and with regard to the world in which they suffer.[35]

Drawing on Asad's ideas, anthropologist Saba Mahmood critiques the manner in which the secular view of agency structures the feminist approach to freedom and empowerment. Mahmood studies the women's piety grassroots in Cairo mosques. She points out that the usual interpretations of these women's actions happen within the trope of resistance, and within the framework of suppression/subversion.[36] As a result, the mosque women's movements are seen as either working "against Western politico-cultural domination" or as a protest "against the failed modernization project of postcolonial Muslim regimes."[37] The leading question in these analyses is not what the Islamic women's reform movements stand for; the leading question is what they stand against.[38]

Such interpretations, Mahmood writes, stem from the progressive feminist view of agency. According to this view, agency means one's "capacity to realize one's own interest against. . . custom, tradition, transcendental will, or other obstacles."[39] However, Mahmood proposes, our capacity for agency "is entailed not only in those acts that resist the norms but also in the multiple ways in which one inhabits norms,"[40] not only in how we oppose traditions, but also in how we embody them.

The core of Asad's and Mahmood's normative critique of secularism is a rejection of the notion of agency that secularism assumes and employs. Asad and Mahmood see two main problems with this notion. First, it is now thought of as a natural and universal concept while it is in fact particular and parochial. Secondly, secular agency has come to be defined as the use of reason against the passions ascribed to the realm of religious subjectivity. When someone passionately supports secular beliefs, that is regarded as the public expression of "objective principle."[41] At the same time, secular agency does make strong assumptions about human nature, it treats these assumptions as norms, and it does so in ways that are fraught with emotions.[42]

Moving Beyond the Critiques of Secularism

The normative critiques of secularism propose that secularism is not a political problem because of the challenges of immigration or religious pluralization; secularism is a political problem because of its normative assumptions.[43] It is easy to agree with the main objectives of these critiques—with the rejection of secularism's claims to universal justice and rationality or with the suggestions about the normative problems in, and the problematic political implications of, secularism's approach to moral pluralism. The relevance of these arguments becomes especially evident when one considers them in relation to the power of contemporary secular states. The genealogies of modern secular states show that each secular state is embedded in its own history and embodies the institutional, cultural, and especially religious legacies of the place and time in which it emerged. As a result, secular states are never neutral actors but always privilege some worldviews over others: secularism or atheism over religious traditions, one religious community over the other. In the vocabulary of peace studies, secular states may be the key players in processes of conflict resolution, but they also often cause and sustain social conflicts.

Notwithstanding the significant insights of the normative critiques of secular states and secular agency, however, there are several important reasons why these critiques ought to be problematized. Among the first tasks is the need to unpack the relationship among nationalism, secular states, *and* religion. For the critics of secularism, it is a commonplace to identify nations and states[44] and to do so by positing the secular nation-states against religions. In many cases, however, the establishment of modern nation-states did not imply the marginalization of religious institutions and elites but quite the opposite: it was precisely the religious elites who had a vital role in placing religious ideas at the center of nationalist platforms and who employed the institutional infrastructure of religions in the process of nation-building.[45]

The secular critics' identification of nation with the (secular) state, in other words, is problematic when it becomes an obstacle for recognizing the powerful agency of religion in the very construction of both the ideologies of nationalism and the institutions of the nation-state. As a result, the focus is on secularists' attempts to use or control religion, without attending to religious actors who established or authorized the place of religion in collective identities—often intending to link, and not reduce, religion to national identity. This last point is important theoretically: it enables us to appreciate continuities in the collectivistic meanings of religions, that is, to see them as phenomena that are not necessarily associated with the rise of modern states and are not just the epiphenomena of secularization.[46]

Historicizing the link among religion, nationalism, secularism, and modern state also has repercussions for the practice of strategic peacebuilding: the focus on the agency of religious actors makes it possible to distinguish between those interested in national homogenization at the expense of pluralism and those who, even when embedded in specific communities, remain concerned with the conditions of justpeace for all members of society.

The framework that pits secular nation-states against religions points to the second larger question that needs to be raised with regard to the critics of secularism, and that is the notion of modernity with which they implicitly or explicitly operate. The critics generally envision modernity as a uniform, hegemonic project that has a unified philosophical, political, and economic platform. The outcome is somewhat paradoxical: while developing a forceful rejection of Western modernity and of secularism as its constitutive element, the critics in effect reinforce the vision in which the only relation between the secular and the religious is one of conflict. Yet, as we know, even inside the Western world, modernity is not one but many. Modernization (industrialization, urbanization, technological development) changes all societies, structurally and culturally. However, this does not happen in a vacuum and has neither the same beginning nor the same end. It is for these reasons that the notion of "multiple modernities," introduced by a number of social scientists, is especially important.[47] First, it does not assume the opposition of secularity and religiosity; rather, it sustains the tension between tradition and change, between generalizable and particular trends. Second, the notion of multiple modernities is analytically open: it affirms the idea that different cultural and political programs of modernity are possible without limiting what their interactions might be. The concept of multiple modernities, finally, allows space for a critique of the view of Western European modernity as a secular ideal that ought to be implemented everywhere. It reflects a normative stance that the plurality of cultural and political programs of modernity in which secular and religious exist together, is not a problem to solve, but a value to uphold. This normative point, which constitutes the multiple modernities framework in important ways, shapes the analytic angle of this discussion of religions and secularisms, and it is indispensable for every theoretical or practical approach to justpeace that can be, it was suggested earlier, sustained only if it involves all members of some society.

The third question that ought to be raised in response to the normative critiques of secularism regard the claims made about the nature—values and actions—of secular agency. Asad is correct to argue that we can have only an impoverished view of agency if its grammar—being and action—is determined exclusively by what he identifies as a secular sensibility and if only that secular view of agency is taken as natural. However, what happens with our view of *secular* agency if we read it the way Asad and other critics do—only in relation to the power of secular states and solely in terms of self-empowerment? Is it possible to explore the complex phenomenology of secular agency if we posit it exclusively within the framework of power and in the context of the state-politics, or does such an approach flatten our analytic perspective?

In order to fully appreciate the ways in which secular agency is embodied and embedded, it is vital that we fully embrace Asad's own proposal—the idea that we can only understand what *any* agency, secular agency included, is, if we ask "how, by whom, and in what context the concept of agency is defined and used."[48] As will become clear in a moment, precisely this approach to agency makes possible the analysis of the norms and actions of secular agents in the Solidarity movement in Poland, and shows a possible trajectory for exploring the positive synergy in secular-religious encounters in the context of building justpeace.

Finally, the normative critiques of secularism are also problematic because of how they point to the future of secularism as a concept, as an idea, and as an ideal. Some critics of secularism suggest that we ought to reject the notion altogether; others hope to undo the religious-secular binary in order to open the space for new configurations; still others propose that we replace this binary with that of tradition of practices vs. practice of tradition.[49]

The question of what we are to do with secularism is central for contemporary peace studies. There is an emerging consensus among scholars and practitioners in the field, according to which the secularist paradigm marginalized and excluded religious institutions and actors from peacebuilding in many contexts. With the awareness that secularism has had such a negative role both in the processes of peacebuilding and in the study of these processes, it is important to ask: Should peace studies focus primarily on critiques of secularism? Should peace studies, moreover, adopt the trajectory currently suggested in several academic disciplines, according to which secularism should be understood first and foremost as a political ideology and a model of governance embodied in the power of nation-states?

To answer these questions, it is useful to reiterate two arguments made thus far. First, it was suggested that the normative critiques of secularism and the recognition of the ways in which secularism is embodied in the power of nation-states offer very important insights for peace studies—for their understanding of what secularisms are and how they came to be defined and positioned with regard to religions, analytically and practically. Second, it was proposed that, while vital for any discussion of religious-secular relations in peace studies, the critical and reflexive views of secularism also have serious limitations. They offer a narrow conceptualization of modernity (due to which religions, paradoxically, emerge without much agency in relation to nationalism and modern states) and result in an impoverished notion of secular agency and a thin understanding of secularism. If the critical and reflexive approaches to secularism are to be meaningful for peace studies; if they are, furthermore, to be useful for both the theory and practice of peacebuilding, these approaches cannot stand alone but ought to be complemented by an additional, more constructive trajectory. Instead of criticizing or rejecting secularism, a more constructive approach requires that we reappraise it.

The Indian political theorist Rajeev Bhargava writes that the problem for contemporary secularism is not that it is normative, but rather that it forgot its normative origins.[50] I draw on Bhargava's ideas when I propose that we define secularism not only as a political model of governance or as an ideology that can be reduced to anti-religiousness. Secularism, I suggest, is also a moral orientation and practice toward and in the world, often guided by a drive to enable the human flourishing of all.

This definition of secularism is relevant for the vision of peacebuilding that is founded on, and has as its moral end, the development of productive human relationships among all members of society, religious and secular alike. Secularism as a moral orientation, rather than as an ideology, also emerges from the analysis of the encounter between secular and religious worldviews in the Polish Solidarity movement.[51] In the section that follows, I consider the meanings of secularisms and of secular agency by examining the secular-religious alliance that shaped Solidarity and by looking at the ideas, actions, and influence of

Adam Michnik. The outcome is a thicker view of secular agency and a richer account of religious-secular relations—relations defined through confrontation *and* an active dialogue between religious and secular worldviews, thus relations that affirm the religious-secular differences but also highlight the sites of encounter.

Secularism Embodied and Embedded: Secularism in the Context of the Polish Solidarity Movement[52]

Solidarity emerged in the summer of 1980 as the first independent trade union in the Soviet bloc. Within one year, it grew into a social movement of ten million Poles of all ranks—workers, engineers, intelligentsia, clergy. These Poles did not only demand better wages, shorter working hours, and better working conditions; they also protested food shortages, deteriorating health care, the privileged status of the regime supporters, and violations of freedom of religion and freedom of speech.[53]

Solidarity was not the first protest of Polish citizens against the Communist government's broken promises of equality and freedom. But compared to public dissents in 1956, 1968, or 1970, Solidarity was different. Its leaders remembered the lost battles of the past and, alert of the possibility of Soviet intervention, they did not call for a change of social order but for negotiations with the regime. They used the strategy of peaceful civil opposition, which they learned from the Workers' Defense Committee (KOR).[54] The KOR, created in mid-1970s, was respected in Poland because it provided practical assistance to people[55] but also because it did something that no one else had done before: in countering the regime's workings in secrecy, KOR spelled out the name of each of its members giving an identity to its own actions, and pronouncing the possibility of agency in a society filled with fear. Thus, while the sixteen months of the Solidarity movement did bring social conflict to its peak, this revolution was different from all other revolutions because it "killed nobody."[56] Challenging the very foundations of an oppressive Communist regime, Solidarity insisted on peaceful and dignified resistance and became associated with non-violence, hunger strikes, and with the ban on alcohol among its members (this in a country in which, by 1980, "one million Poles were classified as alcoholics").[57]

While Solidarity's peaceful methods and negotiating tactics resulted from the political realism of some of its leaders, the movement was both a political and a moral revolution—a civil protest against economic and political injustices of the radical secular state, as well as a call for a moral transformation of the Polish nation. The moral nature of Solidarity was inspired by religious faith. The Solidarity leaders spoke of the dignity of every human person and the inherent value of work, the language they could hear in the homilies of the Polish Cardinal Wyszyński,[58] and in the speeches of the charismatic Polish Pope John Paul II. Solidarity was also deeply embedded in Catholic practices and symbolism. Pictures of the pope were on the walls of the Solidarity halls, while the Gdańsk workers waited on their knees during lunch breaks to have their confessions heard and to receive Holy Communion.[59]

As deeply immersed as Solidarity was in Catholic traditions, its moral character, especially its emphasis on limits and restraint—hence the term "self-limiting revolution"[60]—cannot be understood without appreciating the revolutionary character of the secular-religious coalition it created. This "confluence of the secular and the religious,"[61] this "tacit alliance"[62] of believing and nonbelieving Poles, was important but also surprising: the history of the relations between secular and Catholic Poles was characterized by a lack of trust, especially after the victory of Communism. The Communist regime and the secular elites of the Left had important ideological differences and conflicts, but both believed that the Polish Catholic Church was nationalistic and anti-Semitic. For the Catholic Church, the differences between the Communist state and secular leftist intellectuals did not matter too much: trust was impossible whenever the other side had any sympathy for Marxist ideology.

Yet the religious-secular alliance that emerged and gave Solidarity its moral force and sense of restraint did not come out of nowhere. After Stalin's death, Poland not only grew into a leading place of reflection on Marxist theory; its secular Left also presented serious challenges to Marxist dogmas and practices of the Communist regime.[63] Philosopher Leszek Kołakowski, for example, moved from militant atheism toward a critique of the Communist regime, to ultimately offer a powerful affirmation of Marxist humanism.[64] In 1964, Jacek Kuron and Karol Modzelewski authored the "Open Letter to the Party," in which they attacked the Communist regime and due to which they were sent to prison.[65]

The examples of the Polish secular Left, intellectuals and activists, who critiqued and opposed the regime and ended up in its prisons, carry an important insight for the problem of secularism, conflict, and peacebuilding. These cases tell us that, even in the context of an oppressive Communist system, there is no one meaning of secularity and secularism. Kołakowski, Kuron, Modzelewski—they all point out that secularism is not just a political platform but can also be a moral and humanistic stance, used to critique and reject the official secular (Marxist) worldview, its politics, and its institutions. Put another way, secularism as lived and practiced by some members of the Polish secular Left had a role of disclosing rather than legitimizing the power of the secular state.

On the Catholic side, where many members of the church hierarchy and lower clergy remained suspicious of the secular Left, there were Catholic thinkers, especially in the liberal Catholic circles gathered around the Catholic magazine *Tygodnik Powszechny*, who were interested in a more nuanced understanding of Marxism. Some of the most insightful points were offered by Father Józef Tischner. For this philosopher and theologian, also a good friend of John Paul II, there was a common ground between Christianity and Marxism, especially in the questions of human dignity and alienation.[66] With the election of the Polish pope, whose thinking was immersed in personalist theology but also carried an awareness of the historicity of all religious experience, the Polish Catholic Church as a whole became more open to nonreligious others. Church representatives increasingly spoke in humanistic terms about the need to protect the "human rights of all Poles, believers and non-believers" alike,[67] offering a vision of a society that would be just for all and not just those who identified with the narrow meaning of the term *Polak-katolik*.[68]

Yet when it comes to dialogue and collaboration between the secular Left and Polish Catholics, nobody offered reasons more specific and made a greater impact on religious-secular encounters in the context of Solidarity than Adam Michnik—the son of Marxist parents, a secular liberal activist, a student of both Kołakowski and Kuron, and a political prisoner of the Communist regime.

Michnik's book *The Church and the Left*, published in Paris in 1977, brought the claim that the concepts and strategies used to explore the relations between the Left and the church in Poland had to be revised.[69] His was a call for dialogue,[70] and to some extent a call that came out of pragmatic considerations. Michnik was convinced that only together, only through dialogue and collaboration, could the Left and the Catholic Church in Poland win against the Communist state. Michnik also argued that the church had to be made an ally, because as such it would not be isolated and, in its isolation, opposed to modernity.

His pragmatism notwithstanding, however, the most striking features of Michnik's invitation to dialogue—his critique of the Left and his praise of the Polish Catholic Church and Christianity—went beyond the matters of politics. Michnik condemned the anti-clericalism of the Left, especially its understanding that religious beliefs and the Catholic Church are "synonymous for reaction and dim-witted obscurantism."[71] In Michnik's view, such anticlericalism was ahistorical. We fear and reject, Michnik wrote, the conservative, nationalistic, all-powerful institution that the Polish Catholic Church once was. But this is now a different church, he maintained, the church "stubbornly on the side of the persecuted and the oppressed,"[72] the only public institution in Poland to speak bravely on behalf of freedom and the rights of every human being. And, not only does the Polish secular Left need to enter a dialogue with the Catholic Church; not only does it need to reject the obtuse, primitive, and harsh atheism of Communist states, Michnik writes,

> "our search must go deeper. It must touch the very roots of that oh-so-haughty conviction that it is we. . . who really do know the true path of progress and reason. The truth, of course, is that we do not know this path. Neither we nor anyone else in this world knows the road along which history will travel. . . . [So] let us respect those who believe that a supernatural world has been revealed to them. Let us judge them by their deeds, not by words that are twisted and distorted by others.[73]

Michnik demands two things from the secular Left and, thus, from himself: a self-critique and a respect toward the religious others, the latter because of the ability for historical transformation but also because of what he identifies as an inherent dignity of religious worldviews. To be sure, Michnik's view of Catholicism in Poland is multilayered: he is partial toward the liberal Catholic faction in Poland[74] and warns against Catholicism as a state religion, while also being a self-confessed Polish nationalist who understands all too well the cultural role the Catholic Church has had and would continue to have in Polish history.[75]

Michnik's call that the Polish secular Left start respecting the dignity of religious Poles, and his recognition of the Catholic Church's emphasis on human rights, at least partly stem from the same political platform—liberalism concerned with the rights of individuals. But his ideas about the role of the Catholic Church and the nature of rights also transcend one particular tradition of liberalism. He does not speak of religion as a private matter; he emphasizes the centrality of Catholicism and of the Catholic Church in the history of the Polish nation. And, even as he grew more critical of the church, Michnik continued to think that it "is impossible to imagine a Poland of the future without the Roman Catholic Church and its enormous influence on society."[76] His approach to religion within the context of Polish national history, in other words, contains a call for a "different interfacing between the 'religious' and the 'secular.'"[77]

Perhaps most importantly for our discussion, Michnik makes two larger points about religion that fully uncover the content of his philosophical stance. First, he admires the moral force of religion, especially Christianity's notion of limits,[78] which he sees as "serving a noble political purpose"[79] and which he adopts while speaking about the limits of human knowledge. Michnik's ideas therefore are not a simple reflection of a liberal secular agenda. His is a view of a chastened secular humanism, or secularism aware of the limits of human power and willing to learn about those limits from its religious other. Michnik's discourse of rights also moves beyond his liberal worldview—or, rather, broadens and enriches it. "The point is," he writes, "that our affection for civil liberties would be rather suspect were we to desire them only for ourselves."[80] He believes that it is his role, as a representative of the secular Left, to fight for the freedom of the Catholic Church and the freedom of religion. To paraphrase philosopher Nicholas Wolterstorff: Michnik does not use the language of rights to affirm his own but to affirm the rights of the other.

The reception of Michnik's ideas and his call for collaboration between the Polish Left and the Catholic Church was complex. Some Catholic thinkers especially accused him of condescension, and did not welcome his point about good and bad church.[81] Father Tischner, while never losing sight of the differences between Catholic and secular leftist ontological perspectives, remarked: "What is left for me if I do not support the ideals of the Left? Nothing but 'chauvinism, national oppression, obscurantism, lawlessness' and similar atrocities."[82] The secular Left also had its fears, and it was suspicious of whether the Catholic Church would truly held to democratic ideals. The reactions to Michnik's public call for dialogue between believers and nonbelievers, between the Catholic Church and the secular Left, show that it is not easy to build trust and bridges between those who have long been opposed and who affirm different worldviews. The responses to Michnik's invitation to dialogue also suggest that only those prepared for self-critique can have a chance at resolving their differences to recognize that they also have ideals in common.

However, Michnik's impact on the secular Left and its openness to rapprochement with the Catholic Church cannot be overstated. After 1976, the Left "did make its leap of faith and embraced the Church. . . . Its excited pride in the Polish pope, its unswerving support for workers marching behind religious symbols in 1980, its praise for the episcopate and willingness, even eagerness, to see the Church regain a prominent public presence all testify to the intelligentsia's readiness to disown its anti-clerical past."[83] Even though Michnik was initially skeptical of what Solidarity could achieve, it was beyond doubt that he made a mark on it. It is difficult, if not impossible, to imagine Solidarity—its dignified spirit, its openness to both religious and secular voices, its affirmation of pluralism—without Michnik's platform for a dialogue between the Left and the Catholic Church. His *mea culpa* on behalf of the Polish secular Left, his rejection of anticlericalism, his affirmation of the dignity of religious beliefs, his recognition of the Catholic Church's courage in Communist Poland—all helped to shape "the attitude of a generation of intellectuals that contributed so much to the Solidarity movement as a whole."[84]

SECULAR-RELIGIOUS COLLABORATIONS
AND JUSTPEACE

If secular agency is defined by self-empowerment, as Talal Asad asserts and many scholars seem to accept, how are we to understand Michnik's call for the self-examination of the

Polish secular Left—his call for the rejection of secularists' ideas about, and their practices toward, Catholicism? How to account for the fact that Michnik and other secular activists used the language of rights not only for self-empowerment but to empower the others—religious believers?

Using Asad's notion of secular agency, how should Michnik's and Kuron's years of imprisonment be interpreted—are they a result of the secular "romance of resistance" or are they more akin to the suffering of early Christians, where the act of suffering is meaningful with regard to those who suffer and with regard to the world in which they suffer? Finally, how should we classify secularisms in the works of Polish secular intellectuals? Can they be reduced to ideology or anti-religiousness if they recognized the moral force of Catholicism and created an alliance with Catholic intellectuals and workers? Or are these secularisms, developed in a very particular historical moment, moral orientations toward and in the world driven by a desire to affirm the human flourishing of all?

These questions are historical, sociological, and normative in character, and as such they are directly pertinent to conversations about peacebuilding and justpeace. They ought be raised not only because they point out the limitations of a narrow focus on political secularism and the role of secular states. These questions need to be asked in order to highlight the problems of the uncritical approach to secular agency as necessarily opposed to, and different from, religious agency. While the ontological differences between most secular and religious orientations need to be recognized—something that Michnik and Tischner, for example, understand deeply and do very clearly—it is equally important to appreciate the internal heterogeneity of the religious and the secular as well as the productive sites of their encounter. For example, drawing a sharp distinction between secular and religious agency— the resistance mode of the former and the acceptance of suffering by the latter—is difficult once we acknowledge that both religious and non-religious forms of sacrifice ("sacrifice to" and "sacrifice for," to use the distinctions of Moshe Halberta) are ultimately, despite all their important differences, acts of self-transcendence.[85] Similarly, the very notion of "religious agency" against which Asad and others posit "secular agency" becomes problematic once we recognize that even the martyrdom of early Christians—and their religious agency—did not have one but multiple meanings.[86]

The case of the Polish secular Left can help scholars and practitioners in peace studies by complicating the normative critiques of secularism and secular agency. On the most general level, the Polish case underscores that the meanings and boundaries of every agency have to be historicized and explored empirically if they are to be understood in all their complexity and potentiality. To use Asad's words, we can appreciate the capacities that certain actors have for peacebuilding only if we ask how, by whom, and in what context some agency is defined. Furthermore, the case of the Polish secular Left indicates that secular agency, just like religious agency, has many grammars and forms of action. Here, it was the secular agents who critiqued the secular state, affirmed religion and religious perspectives, and helped create a powerful social movement that weakened (and ultimately ended) an oppressive Communist regime.

The practice of secularism in the context of Solidarity, it is important to note, is not just an isolated case that contradicts some dominant forms of secularism in the modern world.

If the Polish case were compared with other cases—for example, the early twentieth-century labor movement and civil rights movement in the United States, or the anti-apartheid movement in South Africa—the conclusion would be similar: we cannot, and should not, reduce the grammar and actions of secular agency only to questions of self-empowerment or the drive to create a secular nation-state.

The historical outcomes of all the mentioned movements show the accuracy of Adam Michnik's conviction that "only through dialogue between secular and religious forces can a good and desirable democratic order be constructed."[87] The religious-secular alliances in these cases also confirm Gerard Powers's insight that, in working to build just and sustainable peace, religious actors rarely act alone. We should therefore not take the Polish episode of Solidarity as a historical exception. Rather, we should think of it as a rich referent for addressing what is, in my view, an urgent question for peace studies today: how can religions and secularisms, while keeping their differences, become two equal and mutually enriching agents of peacebuilding, rather than obstacles to one another? Social activists in today's Poland—from those dedicated to gender equality to those who correctly recognize that the right to work is a vital component of human rights—could also learn from revisiting the discourses and practices that shaped the Solidarity movement's secular-religious encounters. The Solidarity experience would remind them that in the pursuit of a more just society, the internal heterogeneity of religious-secular categories can contribute to the success of various humanistic alliances. In the post-Communist context, in which there are many disagreements about the moral and cultural direction that Polish society should take, retrieving the narratives of Solidarity could help Poles, religious and secular alike, rediscover the ideal of a national community in which authentic human flourishing can be built and sustained only if it is constituted by a plurality of voices.

Notes

* This chapter was written with the generous support of the Notre Dame Institute for Advanced Study. While thinking about the problem of religion, secularism, and peace studies, I greatly benefited from conversations with Jason Varsoke, Atalia Omer, Jason Springs, and Joseph Wawrykow. I remain especially indebted to the editors of this volume for their critical and constructive comments and questions.

1. For a similar point, see Gerard Powers, "Religion and Peacebuilding," in *Strategies of Peace: Transforming Conflict in a Violent World*, ed. Daniel Philpott and Gerard F. Powers (New York: Oxford University Press, 2010), 318. On the neglect of the positive role of religion in peacemaking, see *Forgiveness and Reconciliation: Religion, Public Policy, and Conflict Transformation*, ed. Raymond G. Helmick, SJ, and Rodney L. Petersen (Philadelphia: Templeton Foundation Press, 2001); also Marc Gopin, *Between Eden and Armageddon: The Future of World Religions, Violence, and Peacemaking* (Oxford: Oxford University Press, 2000); John Brewer, Gareth I. Higgins, and Francis Teeney, *Religion, Civil Society, and Peace in Northern Ireland* (Oxford: Oxford University Press, 2011); Slavica Jakelić, "Religion, Collective Identity, and Violence in Bosnia and Herzegovina," *The Hedgehog Review* 6, no. 1 (2004): 51–70.

2. Scholars are correct to argue that religions can be the source of conflict but they can also be the tools of tolerance and peace. Among the most significant contributions to the discussions of the dual role that religions play in societies was R. Scott Appleby's *The Ambivalence of the Sacred: Religion, Violence, and Reconciliation* (Lanham, MD: Rowman and Littlefield, 2000). In this book, Appleby points out an inherent ambivalence of religious symbols, ideas, and traditions. As he argues, the same ideas of the sacred can be the

source of conflict and exclusion, as well as the foundation of peace and tolerance. Next to the religious radicals who subscribe to the ideas and practices of crusades or jihad as the war against the infidels, we find religious radicals standing on the side of peace. For a comparative examination of the peacemaking and war-legitimizing roles of the representatives of the same religious organization, see the historical and sociological study of the Roman Catholic Church in Bosnia and Herzegovina and Croatia in Slavica Jakelić, *Collectivistic Religions: Religion, Choice, and Identity* (Burlington, VT: Ashgate, 2010).

3. See Powers, "Religion and Peacebuilding," 318; Elizabeth Shakman Hurd, *The Politics of Secularism in International Relations* (Princeton, NJ: Princeton University Press, 2008); William Cavanaugh, *The Myth of Religious Violence: Secular Ideology and the Roots of Modern Conflict* (New York: Oxford University Press, 2009).

4. Powers, "Religion and Peacebuilding," 317–318.

5. Appleby, *Ambivalence of the Sacred.*

6. Jakelić, *Collectivistic Religions.*

7. Powers, "Religion and Peacebuilding."

8. John Paul Lederach and R. Scott Appleby, "Strategic Peacebuilding: An Overview," in *Strategies of Peace: Transforming Conflict in a Violent World,* ed. Daniel Philpott and Gerard F. Powers (New York: Oxford University Press, 2010), 23–24.

9. Lederach and Appleby, "Strategic Peacebuilding," 41.

10. I draw here on the argument that humanism can play the role of disclosing rather than legitimizing power. See Frits de Lange as quoted in John W. de Gruchy, "Christian Humanism: Reclaiming a Tradition; Affirming an Identity," *CTI Reflections* 8, no. 19 (2009).

11. Lederach and Appleby, "Strategic Peacebuilding"; also Powers, "Religion and Peacebuilding."

12. See Shakman Hurd, *Politics of Secularism*; Ahmet T. Kuru, *Secularism and State Policies toward Religion: The United States, France, and Turkey* (Cambridge: Cambridge University Press, 2009); Silvio Ferrari and W. Cole Durham Jr., eds., *Law and Religion in Post-Communist Europe* (Leuven: Peeters, 2003); Winnifred Fallers Sullivan, *The Impossibility of Religious Freedom* (Princeton, NJ: Princeton University Press, 2005).

13. One of the first to point out the problems of the Western Christian roots of political secularisms was T. N. Madan; see, for example, his "Secularism in Its Place," in *Secularism and Its Critics,* ed. Rajeev Bhargava (New York: Oxford University Press, 1998), 297–320 (piece originally written in 1986). For the arguments that the particularity of the origins of secularism means that it cannot be used as a tool of social inquiry in non-Western, non-Christian contexts, see Adam Seligman, "Secularism: A Necessary Condition for Social Inquiry?" (conference paper, Forli, Italy, May 18–19, 2007).

14. Charles Taylor, "Modes of Secularism," in Bhargava, *Secularism and Its Critics,* 31–53; Shakman Hurd, *Politics of Secularism.*

15. See Slavica Jakelić, "Secularism: A Bibliographic Essay," *The Hedgehog Review* 12, no. 3 (2010): 49–55. The idea that secularism is founded in the sciences has particularly been popularized by the so-called "New Atheists"; for versions of that view, see Richard Dawkins, *The God Delusion* (New York: Bantam, 2006); Daniel Dennett, *Breaking the Spell: Religion as a Natural Phenomenon* (New York: Penguin, 2006); Christopher Hitchens, *God Is Not Great: How Religion Poisons Everything* (New York: Twelve, 2007). For powerful critiques of such views, see Terry Eagleton, *Reason, Faith, and Revolution: Reflections on the God Debate* (New Haven, CT: Yale University Press, 2009); Harold W. Attridge, ed., *The Religion and Science Debate: Why Does It Continue?* (New Haven, CT: Yale University

Press, 2009); Barbara Herrnstein Smith, *Natural Reflections: Human Cognition at the Nexus of Science and Religion* (New Haven, CT: Yale University Press, 2010).

16. For reflection on his older critique of the theories of secularization, see David Martin, *On Secularization: Towards a Revised General Theory* (Burlington, VT: Ashgate, 2005). See also Jeffrey K. Hadden, "Toward Desacralizing Secularization Theory," *Social Forces* 65, no. 3 (1987): 587–611.

17. Secularization is always a result of the intertwined relations among diverse variables and agents—from the unintended consequences of the medieval religious reforms and the Protestant Reformation, to the Enlightenment philosophies, the birth of the modern nation-state, and actors whose explicit objective was to secularize law, education, politics, and economics. For an important account of variables and agents involved in the secularization of American society, see Christian Smith, ed., *The Secular Revolution: Power, Interests, and Conflict in the Secularization of American Public Life* (Berkeley, CA: University of California Press, 2003).

18. John Milbank, *Theology and Social Theory: Beyond Secular Reason* (Cambridge, MA: Basil Blackwell, 1990).

19. See Janet Jakobsen and Ann Pellegrini, *Secularisms* (Durham, NC: Duke University, 2008); also see Jakelić, "Secularism: A Bibliographic Essay."

20. On the global political crisis of secularism, see, for example, T. N. Srinivasan, "Introduction" to *The Future of Secularism*, ed. T. N. Srinivasan (New Delhi: Oxford University Press, 2007), 4. On cultural and religious pluralization, or as Bhargava calls it, the increase of "religious diversity," see Rajeev Bhargava, "The Distinctiveness of Indian Secularism," in *The Future of Secularism*, ed. T. N. Srinivasan (New Delhi: Oxford University Press, 2007), 23–24. Tariq Modood is among the few scholars who question the nature and the depth of the current crisis of secularism; see Modood, "Is There a Crisis of Secularism in Western Europe?," *Sociology of Religion* 73, no. 2 (2012): 130–149.

21. While Madan, for example, recognizes the extent to which the secular ideology of the modern Indian state emerges from the Hindu tradition and its approach to tolerance, he sees the Christian provenance of modern political secularism that affirms the secular-religious binary as incompatible with the Indian cultural ethos and its experience of religion as a public and collective phenomenon. See Madan "Indian secularism: A Religio-Secular Ideal," in Cady and Shakman Hurd, Comparative Secularisms, *Comparative Secularisms in a Global Age*, ed. Linell E. Cady and Elizabeth Shakman Hurd (New York: Palgrave Macmillan, 2010), 181-196.

22. Ashis Nandy argues that "to accept the ideology of secularism is to accept the ideologies of progress and of modernity," and thus places his critique of secularism in India within the larger critiques of instrumental rationality and Western modernity; see Nandy, "Politics of Secularism and the Recovery of Religious Tolerance," in Bhargava, *Secularism and Its Critics*, 321–344. See also Nandy, "The Politics of Secularism and the Recovery of Religious Tolerance," as quoted in Amartya Sen, "Secularism and Its Discontents," in Bhargava, *Secularism and Its Critics*, 460. Secularism, Chakrabarty tells us, can be all these different things to different people because it is profoundly intertwined with modernity: it is its "foundational [political] category" (Chakrabarty in Shakman Hurd, *Politics of Secularism*, 15). For a similar argument, see also Jakobsen and Pellegrini, *Secularisms*, 7.

23. See Chaterjee, "Secularism and Tolerance," 358.

24. Jakobsen and Pellegrini, *Secularisms*, 9.

25. See Michael Sandel, "Religious Liberty: Freedom of Choice or Freedom of Conscience," in Bhargava, *Secularism and Its Critics*, 86, 87.

26. According to Panikkar, for example, the fact that Indian cultural traditions differ from Western secularism do not call for the dismissal of secularism as a whole but for the reform of Indian cultural traditions. See Panikkar described in Rajeev Bhargava, "The 'Secular Ideal' before Secularism: A Preliminary Sketch," in *Comparative Secularisms in a Global Age*, ed. Linell E. Cady and Elizabeth Shakman Hurd (New York: Palgrave Macmillan, 2010), 159. See also Zoya Hasan, "Not Quite Secular Political Practice," in *Comparative Secularisms in a Global Age*, ed. Linell E. Cady and Elizabeth Shakman Hurd (New York: Palgrave Macmillan, 2010) 195–214.

27. Chatterjee refers here primarily to the enactment of the 1955 Hindu Code Bill that introduced changes to personal law: it legalized intercaste marriage, legalized divorce, and prohibited polygamy. See Chaterjee, "Secularism and Tolerance," in Bhargava, *Secularism and Its Critics*, 356–357.

28. Madan, "Secularism in Its Place," 298.

29. Talal Asad, "French Secularism and the 'Islamic Veil Affair,' " *The Hedgehog Review* 8, no 1–2 (2006): 93–106, 102.

30. Talal Asad, *Formations of the Secular: Christianity, Islam, Modernity*, (Stanford, CA: Stanford University Press, 2003), 71.

31. Asad, *Formations of the Secular*, 73.

32. Asad, *Formations of the Secular*, 67.

33. Asad, *Formations of the Secular*, 86.

34. Asad, *Formations of the Secular*, 67.

35. Asad, *Formations of the Secular*, 87.

36. This is the case even in the work of Judith Butler, says Saba Mahmood in her *Politics of Piety: The Islamic Revival and the Feminist Subject* (Princeton, NJ: Princeton University Press, 2005), 22.

37. Mahmood, *Politics of Piety*, 24.

38. Mahmood, *Politics of Piety*, 25.

39. Mahmood, *Politics of Piety*, 8.

40. Mahmood, *Politics of Piety*, 15.

41. Asad, "French Secularism."

42. Mahmood, *Politics of Piety*, 5.

43. Some of these critics focus on secularism as the epistemological foundation of the social sciences; others highlight the way in which secularism is problematic because it is experienced as a way of life. Saba Mahmood writes that "secular liberalism cannot be addressed simply as a doctrine of the state, or a set of juridicial conventions: in its vast implications, it defines. . . something like a way of life," and something "natural and given" (*Politics of Piety*, 191).

44. My point about the complex nature of the religion-nationalism-secularism-state link emerged as a response to Atalia Omer's important insight about the ways in which the secular critics identify state and nation.

45. See the discussion of the Bosnian, Croatian, Greek, Irish, and Polish cases in Jakelić, *Collectivistic Religions*.

46. Jakelić, *Collectivistic Religions*, especially the introduction and first chapter.

47. See Shmuel N. Eisenstadt, "Multiple Modernities," *Daedalus* 129, no. 1 (2000): 1–29.

48. Asad, *Formations of the Secular*, 99.

49. See Madan, "Secularism in Its Place," for the rejection of secularism; see Jakobsen and Pelegrini, *Secularisms*, for the view that we should undo the binary religious-secular;

and see Adam Seligman "Secularism: A Necessary Condition for Social Inquiry?," for the introduction of the new binary, Tradition of Practices vs. Practice of Tradition which he sees as "more structural, less particularistic, historicist and Whiggish a way of conceptualizing what is usually understood as the dichotomy between religious and secular individuals, cultures and communities" (conference paper, Forli, Italy, May 18–19, 2007).

50. See Rajeev Bhargava, "Introduction," in Bhargava, *Secularism and Its Critics*, 1–28.

51. Jakobsen and Pellegrini, *Secularisms*.

52. The discussion of secularisms in the context of Polish Solidarity draws on my essay about the practice of religious and secular humanisms in 1980s Poland; see Slavica Jakelić, "Engaging Religious and Secular Humanisms," in *At the Limits of the Secular: Reflections on Faith and Public Life*, Grand Rapids, Michigan/Cambridge, UK: William B. Eerdmans Publishing Company, 2014.

53. Timothy Garton Ash, *The Polish Revolution: Solidarity*, 3rd ed. (London: Jonathan Cape, 1983; New Haven, CT: Yale University Press, 2002), 30, 37. Citations refer to the Yale University Press edition.

54. Aleksander Smolar, "Towards 'Self-limiting Revolution': Poland 1970--1989," in *Civil Resistance and Power Politics: The Experience of Non-violent Action from Gandhi to the Present*, eds. Adam Roberts and Timothy Garton Ash, (Oxford: Oxford University Press, 2009),; 127–143, 127.

55. KOR helped people who lost their jobs and those, whose family members were arrested, imprisoned, or killed by the Ccommunist regime.

56. Garton Ash, *The Polish Revolution*.

57. Garton Ash, *The Polish Revolution*, 124, 30.

58. On the importance of this aspect of Polish Catholicism for its vitality during the Communist period, see Barbara Strassberg, "Changes in Religious Culture in Post War II Poland," *Sociological Analysis* 48, no. 4 (1988): 342–354.

59. Garton Ash, *The Polish Revolution*.

60. The term "self-limiting revolution" was coined by sociologist Jadwiga Staniszkis in her book *Poland's Self-Limiting Revolution* (Princeton, NJ: Princeton University Press, 1984). For this, see also Garton Ash, *The Polish Revolution*.

61. David Ost, Introduction to *The Church and the Left*, by Adam Michnik (Chicago: University of Chicago Press, 1993), 1.

62. Garton Ash, *The Polish Revolution*, 27.

63. Helena Czosnyka, *The Polish Challenge: Foundations for Dialogue in the Works of Adam Scaff and Józef Tischner* (Atlanta, GA: Scholars Press, 1995), x.

64. Garton Ash, *The Polish Revolution*, 23.

65. Kuron was one of the founders of KOR; both Kuron and Modzelewski served as advisers to Solidarity.

66. For an elaborate discussion of Marxism, see Tischner's essays on alienation, superstructure, and historical determinism in his *Marxism and Christianity: The Quarrel and the Dialogue in Poland* (Washington, DC: Georgetown University Press, 1987). For discussion of Tischner's view of the shared ground between Marxism and Christianity, see Czosnyka, *The Polish Challenge*. It is important to note that Tischner's views became more critical of every type of Marxism in the post-Communist context. This period was also significant for Adam Michnik's analysis of the Catholic Church and its role in Polish society, which became much less generous than it had been in the late 1970s and 1980s. For Michnik's recent critique of the Polish Catholic Church, see "The Democrat-Skeptic Reads Cardinal

Ratzinger: Democracy between Relativism and the Absolute," *The Hedgehog Review* 9, no. 1 (2007): 32–46.

67. Garton Ash, *The Polish Revolution*, 23.

68. For the problematization of the Polak-katolik identity, its exclusive and inclusive meanings, see Slavica Jakelić, "Beyond Religious Nationalism," *The Immanent Frame*, March 2014, http://blogs.ssrc.org/tif/2014/03/04/beyond-religious-nationalism/.

69. Ost, "Introduction," 4.

70. Father Tischner's and Michnik's approaches to dialogue were similar. For Tischner, dialogue was "not. . . a question of compassion but of. . . the recognition that someone else, from his point of view, is always to some extent right," *The Spirit of Solidarity* (San Francisco: Harper and Row, 1984), 11. Michnik follows Tadeusz Mazowiecki's idea of dialogue as "a readiness to understand the validity of someone else's position" and "a method by which an ideologically diverse society can learn to live together" (Ost, "Introduction," 4–5).

71. Michnik, *The Church and the Left* (Paris: Seuil, 1977; repr., Chicago: University of Chicago Press, 1993), 181. See also Ost, "Introduction," 4.

72. Michnik, *The Church and the Left*, 182.

73. Michnik, *The Church and the Left*, 128.

74. "He champions the 'social Catholic' tendency represented by Jerzy Turowicz and the weekly *Tygodnik Powszechny* in Kraków, and by Tadeusz Mazowiecki and the monthly *Więź* in Warsaw. Increasingly prominent in intellectual circles even while scarce among the hierarchy, strongly influenced by the "personalism" of French theologians like Jacques Maritain and Immanuel Mounier, this tendency claimed for Catholicism the liberal values of openness, tolerance, and diversity" (Ost, "Introduction," 9–10.)

75. Michnik *The Church and the Left*, 134.

76. Michnik, *The Church and the Left*, 134.

77. I am grateful to Atalia Omer for this point. One similar example is Chris Hanni, one of the Marxist leaders of the anti-apartheid movement in South Africa, who simultaneously advocated socialism and the role of the Christian churches as a foundation for South African civil society—as institutions that can help "combat illiteracy [and] enable people to rediscover moral and social values without which no nation can survive." See Hanni in Charles Villa-Vicencio, *The Spirit of Freedom: South Africa Leaders on Religion and Politics* (Berkeley, CA: University of California Press, 1996), 117.

78. Ost, "Introduction," 25.

79. Ost, "Introduction," 14.

80. Michnik, *The Church and the Left*, 131.

81. Ost, "Introduction," 10.

82. Tischner, *Marxism and Christianity*, 153.

83. Ost, "Introduction," 18.

84. Ost, "Introduction," 1.

85. For the distinction between "sacrifice to" and "sacrifice for" see Moshe Halberta, *On Sacrifice* (Princeton, NJ: Princeton University Press, 2012). Halberta suggests that the common feature of both types of sacrifice is violence, and offers a critique of "sacrifice for" when this is linked to "an unworthy and misguided cause," especially the power of the modern state, 116.

86. Candida Moss, *Ancient Christian Martyrdom: Diverse Practices, Theologies, and Traditions* (New Haven, CT: Yale University Press, 2012).

87. Ost, "Introduction," 10.

BIBLIOGRAPHY

Works Cited

Appleby, R. Scott. *The Ambivalence of the Sacred: Religion, Violence, and Reconciliation.* Lanham, MD: Rowman and Littlefield, 2000.

Asad, Talal. *Formations of the Secular: Christianity, Islam, Modernity.* Stanford, CA: Stanford University Press, 2003.

Asad, Talal. "French Secularism and the 'Islamic Veil Affair.'" *The Hedgehog Review* 8, no 1–2 (2006): 93–106.

Ash, Timothy Garton. *The Polish Revolution: Solidarity.* Third edition. New Haven, CT: Yale University Press, 2002. First published 1983 by Jonathan Cape.

Bhargava, Rajeev, ed. *Secularism and Its Critics.* Oxford: Oxford University Press, 1998.

Bhargava, Rajeev. "The 'Secular Ideal' before Secularism: A Preliminary Sketch." In *Comparative Secularisms in a Global Age,* edited by Linell E. Cady and Elizabeth Shakman Hurd, 159–180. New York: Palgrave Macmillan, 2010.

Brewer, John, Gareth I. Higgins, and Francis Teeney, eds. *Religion, Civil Society, and Peace in Northern Ireland.* Oxford: Oxford University Press, 2011.

Cavanaugh, William. *The Myth of Religious Violence: Secular Ideology and the Roots of Modern Conflict.* New York: Oxford University Press, 2009.

Chaterjee, Partha. "Secularism and Tolerance," in Bhargava, *Secularism and Its Critics,*345–381.

Czosnyka, Helena. *The Polish Challenge: Foundations for Dialogue in the Works of Adam Scaff and Józef Tischner.* Atlanta, GA: Scholars Press, 1995.

Eisenstadt, Shmuel N. "Multiple Modernities." *Daedalus*129, no. 1 (2000): 1–29.

Ferrari, Silvio, and W. Cole Durham Jr., eds. *Law and Religion in Post-Communist Europe.* Leuven: Peeters, 2003.

Gopin, Marc. *Between Eden and Armageddon: The Future of World Religions, Violence, and Peacemaking.* New York: Oxford University Press, 2000.

Hadden, Jeffrey K. "Toward Desacralizing Secularization Theory." *Social Forces* 65, no. 3 (1987): 587–611.

Halberta, Moshe. *On Sacrifice.* Princeton, NJ: Princeton University Press, 2012.

Hasan, Zoya. "Not Quite Secular Political Practice." In *Comparative Secularisms in a Global Age,* edited by Linell E. Cady and Elizabeth Shakman Hurd, 195–214. New York: Palgrave Macmillan, 2010.

Helmick, Raymond G., SJ, and Rodney L. Petersen, eds. *Forgiveness and Reconciliation: Religion, Public Policy and Conflict Transformation.* Philadelphia: Templeton Foundation Press, 2001.

Jakelić, Slavica. "Religion, Collective Identity, and Violence in Bosnia and Herzegovina." *The Hedgehog Review* 6, no. 1 (2004): 51–70.

Jakelić, Slavica. *Collectivistic Religions: Religion, Choice, and Identity.* Burlington, VT: Ashgate, 2010.

Jakelić, Slavica. "Secularism: A Bibliographic Essay." *The Hedgehog Review* 12, no. 3 (010): 49–56.

Jakelić, Slavica. "Engaging Religious and Secular Humanisms," in *At the Limits of the Secular: Reflections on Faith and Public Life,* edited by William A. Barbieri Jr., Grand Rapids, Michigan/Cambridge, UK: William B. Eerdmans Publishing Company, 2014, 305-330.

Jakelić, Slavica. "Beyond Religious Nationalism," *The Immanent Frame,* March 2014, http://blogs.ssrc.org/tif/2014/03/04/beyond-religious-nationalism/.

Jakobsen, Janet, and Ann Pellegrini. *Secularisms.* Durham, NC: Duke University Press, 2008.

Kuru, Ahmet T. *Secularism and State Policies toward Religion: The United States, France, and Turkey.* Cambridge: Cambridge University Press, 2009.

Lederach, John Paul, and R. Scott Appleby. "Strategic Peacebuilding: An Overview," in *Strategies of Peace: Transforming Conflict in a Violent World*, edited by Daniel Philpott and Gerard F. Powers, 19–44. New York: Oxford University Press, 2010.

Madan, T. N. "Secularism in Its Place." In Bhargava, *Secularism and Its Critics*, 297–320.

Mahmood, Saba. *Politics of Piety: The Islamic Revival and the Feminist Subject.* Princeton, NJ: Princeton University Press, 2005.

Martin, David. *On Secularization: Towards A Revised General Theory.* Burlington, VT: Ashgate, 2005.

Nandy, Ashis. "Politics of Secularism and the Recovery of Religious Tolerance." In Bhargava, *Secularism and Its Critics*, 321–344.

Michnik, Adam. *The Church and the Left.* Edited and translated by David Ost. Chicago: University of Chicago Press, 1993. First published 1977 by Seuil.

Michnik, Adam. "The Democrat-Skeptic Reads Cardinal Ratzinger: Democracy between Relativism and the Absolute." *The Hedgehog Review* 9, no. 1 (2007): 32–46.

Milbank, John. *Theology and Social Theory: Beyond Secular Reason.* Cambridge, MA: Basil Blackwell, 1990.

Modood, Tariq. "Is There a Crisis of Secularism in Western Europe?" *Sociology of Religion* 73, no. 2 (2012): 1–20.

Moss, Candida. *Ancient Christian Martyrdom: Diverse Practices, Theologies, and Traditions.* New Haven, CT: Yale University Press, 2012.

Ost, David. Introduction to *The Church and the Left*, by Adam Michnik, 1–28.Chicago: University of Chicago Press, 1993.

Powers, Gerard. "Religion and Peacebuilding." In *Strategies of Peace: Transforming Conflict in a Violent World*, edited by Daniel Philpott and Gerard F. Powers, 317–352. New York: Oxford University Press, 2010.

Sandel, Michael. "Religious Liberty: Freedom of Choice or Freedom of Conscience." In Bhargava, *Secularism and Its Critics*, 73–93.

Seligman, Adam. "Secularism: A Necessary Condition for Social Inquiry?" Conference paper, Forli, Italy, May 18–19, 2007.

Sen, Amartya. "Secularism and Its Discontents." In Bhargava, *Secularism and Its Critics*, 454–485.

Shakman Hurd, Elizabeth. *The Politics of Secularism in International Relations.* Princeton, NJ: Princeton University Press, 2008.

Smith, Christian, ed. *The Secular Revolution: Power, Interests, and Conflict in the Secularization of American Public Life.* Berkeley, CA: University of California Press, 2003.

Smolar, Aleksander. "Towards 'Self-limiting Revolution': Poland 1970–1989," in *Civil Resistance and Power Politics: The Experience of Non-violent Action from Gandhi to the Present*, edited by Adam Roberts and Timothy Garton Ash, 127–143. Oxford: Oxford University Press, 2009.

Srinivasan, T. N. Introduction to *The Future of Secularism*, edited by T. N. Srinivasan, 1–7. New Delhi: Oxford University Press, 2007.

Sullivan, Winnifred Fallers. *The Impossibility of Religious Freedom.* Princeton, NJ: Princeton University Press, 2005.

Staniszkis, Jadwiga. *Poland's Self-Limiting Revolution.* Princeton, NJ: Princeton University Press, 1984.

Strassberg, Barbara. "Changes in Religious Culture in Post War II Poland." *Sociological Analysis* 48, no. 4 (1988): 342–354.

Taylor, Charles. "The Meaning of Secularism." In Bhargava, *Secularism and Its Critics*, 31–53.

Tischner, Józef. *Marxism and Christianity: The Quarrel and the Dialogue in Poland.* Washington, DC: Georgetown University Press, 1987.

Tischner, Józef. *The Spirit of Solidarity.* San Francisco: Harper and Row, 1984.

Villa-Vicencio, Charles. *The Spirit of Freedom: South Africa Leaders on Religion and Politics.* Berkeley, CA: University of California Press, 1996.

Further Reading

Secularism, Sciences, and Religion

Attridge, Harold W., ed. *The Religion and Science Debate: Why Does It Continue?* New Haven, CT: Yale University Press, 2009.

Dawkins, Richard. *The God Delusion.* New York: Bantam, 2006.

Dennett, Daniel. *Breaking the Spell: Religion as a Natural Phenomenon.* New York: Penguin, 2006.

Eagleton, Terry. *Reason, Faith, and Revolution: Reflections on the God Debate.* New Haven, CT: Yale University Press, 2009.

Herrnstein Smith, Barbara. *Natural Reflections: Human Cognition at the Nexus of Science and Religion.* New Haven, CT: Yale University Press, 2010.

Hitchens, Christopher. *God Is Not Great: How Religion Poisons Everything.* New York: Twelve, 2007.

Secularism, the State, and Democracies

An-Na'im, Abdullahi. *Islam and Human Rights, Collected Essays in Law.* Edited by Mashood A. Baderin.. Aldershot: Ashgate, 2010.

Bowen, John R. *Why the French Don't Like Headscarves: Islam, the State, and Public Space.* Princeton, NJ: Princeton University Press, 2008.

Cesari, Jocelyne, and Sean McLoughlin, eds. *European Muslims and the Secular State.* Aldershot: Ashgate, 2005.

Janis, Mark W., and Carolyn Evans, eds. *Religion and International Law.* The Hague: Martinus Nijhoff, 1999.

Marty, Martin E., and R. Scott Appleby, eds. *Fundamentalisms and the State: Remaking Polities, Economies, and Militance.* Chicago: University of Chicago Press, 1996.

Roy, Olivier. *Secularism Confronts Islam.* New York: Columbia University Press, 2007.

CHAPTER 6

··

STRUCTURAL AND CULTURAL VIOLENCE IN RELIGION AND PEACEBUILDING

··

JASON A. SPRINGS

RECENT work in religion, conflict, and peacebuilding demonstrates the vast resources that scholars and practitioners working with and/or within religious traditions and institutions can contribute (and have contributed) to transforming conflict, conceptualizing and cultivating justice, and building sustainable peace.[1] What happens when this important engagement between religious peacebuilding and peace studies more generally becomes intentionally bidirectional? What insights, lenses, and approaches emerge from peace studies that uniquely fit the purposes and practices of religious peacebuilding?

This chapter explores ways that the analytical lenses of structural and cultural violence that have emerged in peace studies debates since the 1960s aid in illuminating and addressing religious and cultural dimensions of conflict, violence, and peacebuilding that are of specific interest to religious peacebuilders. These analytical lenses have been powerfully applied across cases pertaining to poverty, development, gender, and race. Yet their application to concerns about religion and peacebuilding are comparatively underdeveloped.[2] I argue that they are equally incisive when applied to religious identity–based forms of violence and injustice, and the social, spiritual, emotional, and psychological effects of those forms. Critical attention to the processes and debates by which these analytical lenses emerged in peace studies will illuminate an array of theoretical points of contact, overlap, and possibilities for mutual enrichment between peace studies as a still emerging field, and the flourishing literature on religion and peacebuilding.

In what follows I demonstrate two ways that developing analytical lenses of structural and cultural violence, and incorporating them into religion, conflict, and peacebuilding, importantly expands and deepens that field. First, I argue that integrating these lenses into the conceptual framework of religion and peacebuilding requires critically revising that subfield's temptation toward an overly narrow focus upon "deadly violence." This correction makes possible multifocal forms of critical analysis in religion and peacebuilding, thereby rendering more sensitive and fine-grained the identification and assessment of the manifold forms that violence may take, and the compound and multi-layered effects those forms may produce. Such multidimensionality eludes the prevailing conceptions of violence in religion and peacebuilding insofar as those are conceived primarily (or perhaps exclusively) as physical and/or deadly. At one level, then, the resulting analytical framework becomes more encompassing in the simple sense that it now aims to assess multiple types of violence. It is deepened in the sense that this expansion results in greater nuance and precision both in detecting frequently acute distinctions between forms of violence, and diagnosing the sometimes tacit or non-explicit modes by which those different forms of violence mutually reinforce one another or relate symbiotically.

Second, I demonstrate that achieving analytical command of the lenses of structural and cultural violence is particularly imperative for those who are critically conversant with, or who draw upon and utilize the resources of, religious traditions, practices, and institutions for the purposes of peacebuilding. This is the case for three reasons. First, these lenses illuminate manifestations and effects of violence to which scholars and practitioners laboring in religion and peacebuilding are likely to be particularly attuned and motivated or potentially well-equipped to understand and constructively respond. These forms of violence surface in the account below as deprivation of "identity needs" and "well-being needs." To this end, the second portion of this chapter examines some thinkers and activists who demonstrate in their work the ways that religious peacebuilding has been (can be) uniquely attuned to structural and cultural violence. I make the case that, in the instances I examine, this attunement derives from the incisiveness, sensitivity, and self-reflexivity afforded by the religious knowledge, religious orientation, and/or religious character of the peacebuilding effort.

At the same time, by no means are "identity" and "well-being" needs exhaustive of the forms of violence with which religious peacebuilders will be concerned, and may find themselves especially well-appointed to address. Neither are these forms of needs-deprivation exclusively the jurisdiction of those who work within or evince a critically reflective grasp of the resources provided by religious traditions. Nor, for that matter, are participants within religious traditions adept at such modes of reflection *by default*. As these provisos indicate, I deploy the conception of "religious peacebuilder" in a sense that is broader than what one may find in other chapters of this volume. While the figures I examine in this chapter are motivated and informed by their own religious commitments and identification with religious traditions, as I use the term, one need not be motivated by personal religious commitments nor identify or affiliate with a religious tradition to be a "religious peacebuilder." I include in this category activists, practitioners, and thinkers who acquire proficiency in a religious tradition in order to work with the resources available there—for both critical and constructive purposes—in the interests of reducing violence in its various forms, and cultivating conditions for a just and sustainable peace. Such figures need not be participants in (i.e., self-identifying "insiders" to) the tradition(s) in question in order to be what Max Weber called "religiously musical" in their scholarship and activism. Rather, they may acquire an intimate grasp of a religious tradition, and develop the skills necessary to engage and deploy its features and elements, for ad hoc purposes, and in the interests of developing a conception, or pursuing conditions, of justpeace (which may be consistent or overlap with that of the tradition in question).[3]

These provisos lead to the second reason that analytical lenses of structural and cultural violence are imperative for so-called religious peacebuilders. Inclusion of structural and cultural violence lenses in religion and peacebuilding is indispensable because structures and cultures interweave to shape many of the most broadly occurring features of historical religious traditions, for example, symbolic and linguistic practices, rituals, exercises of identity- and self-formation, textual interpretive practices, and institutional arrangements. Lenses that draw light to the ways that violence may embed and exert itself (whether visibly or tacitly) in these forms—even as they strive to contribute to peacebuilding processes— are crucial for those who work in peacebuilding with particular attention to the challenges raised by, and resources especially available to, religious traditions, institutions, practices, and identities. Thus, lenses of structural and cultural violence afford indispensable forms of critical self-reflexivity that are frequently absent from conceptions of inter-religious peace-building engagement and dialogue.[4]

A correlate of this second reason forms the third basis on which I claim that analytical lenses of structural and cultural violence are of particular value for religion and peacebuild-ing. These forms of critical self-reflexivity aim to facilitate constructive and practical work at the same time that they persist in diagnostic self-inventory and, ideally, self-correction. They emerged out of concerns surrounding peace*building*. They were fashioned in order ultimately to contribute to the positive processes of cultivating and fostering the condi-tions of just and sustainable peace. I make the case that these lenses facilitate an equilibrium between self-reflexive critical analysis, on one hand, and constructive objectives of cultivat-ing conditions of justice and peace, on the other, that are uniquely tailored to the purposes of peacebuilding. This sidesteps temptations to subvert such constructive reflection and prac-tice through interminable systemic analysis of power and domination (a temptation, I dem-onstrate, to which analyses of power and domination in critical theory are prone). Insofar as peacebuilding initiatives born of, or drawing upon, religious traditions and institutions aim to build constructive alternatives to violence and injustice, lenses of structural and cultural violence serve to critically chasten their efforts at the same time that they facilitate those efforts in indispensable ways.

THE STRUCTURE AND CLAIMS OF THIS CHAPTER

In Part I of this chapter, I set forth a genealogical account of the emergence of analysis of structural and cultural forms of violence in peace studies. Here I account for the central concepts in and around structural and cultural violence, and provide a critical narrative of their emergence. I examine their theoretical roots and objectives in order to illuminate both their strengths and liabilities in comparison with analytical options with which they share influences and family resemblances (e.g., critical theory, reflexive sociology). I identify the concerns and purposes in response to which these lenses were derived, and reexamine the arguments by which they were contested and refined over ensuing decades. This genealogy culminates in demonstrating how these lenses illuminate the indefensibility—and, in fact, debilitating deficiency—of materialist-reductionist conceptions of peace research, and the security studies orientation that ensued therefrom.

As we will see, the emergence of these lenses challenges peace researchers with the need to recognize and attend to forms of violence and injustice "that work on the soul." Moreover, they illuminate the necessity of studying and addressing the ways that organized religious traditions, and the array of institutional orders, language and symbol systems, ritual and tex-tual practices, and modes of identity formation that constitute them, may be lived out in ways that enforce, conceal, and perpetuate such violence. Yet they raise a converse possibility that these same complex practices, systems, institutions, and traditions might also be conceptualized, embodied, and deployed in ways that foster peace and combat injustice. As we will see, religiously conversant and religiously motivated scholars and practitioners can be especially well-positioned to identify and address certain forms and effects of violence that the lenses of structural and cultural violence disclose, and the possibilities for peace they intimate.

To substantiate these characterizations, in the second portion of this chapter I examine the work of two figures whom I position within the ambit of religion and peacebuilding: Martin Luther King Jr. and Cornel West. I demonstrate how each of these thinkers and activists has formulated and deployed modes of criticism that anticipate or parallel those lenses that peace studies scholars theoretically articulated. In each case, the respective thinker critically identifies and constructively responds to what are, in effect, structural and cultural forms of violence. Moreover, the respective interventions are compelled, and rendered especially discerning and incisive, in virtue of the religious commitments and traditions from which their analyses derive. Their analyses anticipate, largely parallel—and in important ways, surpass— the accounts of structural and cultural violence as articulated by peace studies scholars. Each figure accomplishes this separately from the genealogical emergence of those concepts as formal lenses within peace studies proper. And yet the instructive family resemblances are there to be explored and developed. In fact, identifying and developing these resemblances enriches both sets of resources, and contributes to a more integrative vision of the relation between religion and peacebuilding, on one hand, and peace studies more broadly.

I. Violence: The Missing Dimensions of Religion and Peacebuilding

In a pivotal essay in the religion and peacebuilding scholarship, subtitled "The Promise of Religious Peacebuilding in an Era of Religious and Ethnic Conflict," David Little and Scott Appleby make the case that religious peacebuilding contains unique resources capable of transforming conflict and restructuring societies in the wake of deadly violence. Religious peacebuilding consists of "the range of activities performed by religious actors and institutions for the purpose of resolving and transforming deadly conflict, with the goal of building social relations and political institutions characterized by an ethos of tolerance and nonviolence."[5] The authors position religious peacebuilding as a multidimensional and multi-phase process in which practices of conflict transformation unfold across moments of *conflict management* ("the replacement of violent with nonviolent means of settling disputes") and *conflict resolution* ("removing, to the extent possible, the inequalities between the disputants, by means of mediation, negotiation, and/or advocacy"), which merge into processes of *structural reform* ("efforts to build institutions and foster civic leadership that will address the root causes of the conflict and develop long-term practices and institutions conducive to peaceful, nonviolent relations in the society").[6] Attending to—and, ideally, reforming—the social and political structures that mark out the context of conflict is what Little and Appleby refer to as a "post–deadly conflict phase of the process."[7]

Clearly, these seminal passages advance a multidimensional conception of peacebuilding, with particular attention to how religiously identified or motivated actors and religious traditions have contributed, and might contribute, to intervening in circumstances of explicit (or direct) violence, resolving the violence in question, and cultivating sustainable conditions of peace. Little and Appleby are not content to conceive of peacebuilding in terms of what peace researchers and practitioners have come to call "negative peace"—peace understood as the absence of war or visible, deadly conflict. They focus on the sustainability and quality of the peace that is built, the cultivation of institutions and sociopolitical structures necessary to maintain and promote such peace, and simultaneously, to address the root causes of the conflict that had to be contained in the first place.

At the same time, however, forms of conflict that are *deadly* provide the orienting concern for Little and Appleby—the focal point around which the other parts of their account orbit. So, for instance, attention to the structures and root causes of the conflict in question occurs during—indeed, largely constitutes—the "post–deadly conflict phase" of the process of peacebuilding. Concern for the impact of structural conditions and causes of violence prior to the eruption of deadly conflict is not prohibited on this approach. In fact, it is to be encouraged. And yet, in their approach, attention to such causes and conditions would, nonetheless, be motivated by the liability of those to give rise to conflict that is deadly. In this pivotal sense (and perhaps others), deadly conflict presents a conceptual center of gravity— an orientational spin—for the analytical attention and practical interventions of religious peacebuilding.

On the one hand, there is an important reason for their emphasis on deadly conflict. If deadly violence erupts, analyses and interventions that aim to assuage or contain it may be, at that particular point in time, the most pressing item on the peacebuilding agenda. And yet, on the other hand, an orientation to physically deadly conflict, while crucial, risks limiting the scope of religious peacebuilding, which Appleby and Little actually aim to develop and expand. It is at this point that efforts to integrate religion and peacebuilding set the stage for a mutually instructive engagement with peace studies more broadly, as well as with resources afforded by critical theory and discourse analysis.

A Genealogy of Violence in Peace Studies Since the Sixties

Questions over the extent to which deadly conflict ought to provide the impetus and orientation for peace theory, analysis, and practice have fueled wide-ranging debates among peace scholars since the 1960s. This question has, at once, sustained disagreement about, and inspired innovation and development of, some of the most pivotal analytical tools that peace studies has to offer to the related concerns of religion, conflict, and peacebuilding.

In his 1964 essay on the subject, sociologist and peace researcher Johan Galtung identified "negative peace" as "the absence of violence, the absence of war," and positive peace as "the integration of human society."[8] He later sharpened the concept of "negative peace," defining it as "the absence of organized violence between such major human groups as nations, but also between racial and ethnic groups because of the magnitude that can be reached by internal wars." Positive peace he further positioned as "a pattern of cooperation and integration between major human groups."[9]

Negative peace (peace understood as the absence of explicitly violent conflict) is, on its own, an inadequate conceptualization of the aims and objectives of peacebuilding. At the same time, however, it remains indispensable as a concern. In other words, to conceptualize and pursue peace in its "negative dimension" (i.e., containment, reduction, cessation of direct and physical forms of violent conflict) is still necessary and, in many cases, urgently so. And yet, however compelling the pursuit of such objectives, at no point could it be sufficient by itself. Rather, negative peace must be embedded within, and pursued in tandem with, positive peace. "How narrow it is to see peace as the opposite of war, and limit peace studies to war-avoidance studies, and more particularly avoidance of big wars or super-wars (defined as wars between big powers or superpowers), and even more particularly to the limitation, abolition, or control of super-weapons," Galtung wrote. "Important interconnections among types of violence are left out, particularly the way in which one type of violence may be reduced or controlled at the expense of controlling another."[10]

Such claims aim not simply to expand the scope of peace studies and practice beyond the debilitatingly narrow boundaries of security studies and international relations. The more fundamental conceptual point is that addressing immediate conflict situations and presenting forms of direct and personal violence must be combined with the simultaneous pursuit of social justice. "Peace" conceived or pursued in the absence of an intentional and sustained, simultaneous pursuit of justice (understood relationally, in terms of mutual recognition, reciprocal accountability, protection against the violation of basic rights, even integration between persons and groups) limits itself to the cessation or suppression of direct violence or overt conflict. Holding explicit and direct forms of violence in abeyance—keeping order or "keeping the peace"—is entirely compatible with and often accompanies conditions of injustice, repression, disenfranchisement, exploitation, and myriad other forms of dehumanization. The latter constitute what Mohandas Gandhi described as akin to "the seeds of war"—often precursors to explicitly violent conflict but also, simultaneously, warfare of its own kind.[11] Moreover, insofar as such conditions become normal and are institutionalized, attending only to direct and explicit forms of violence in pursuit of negative peace is most assuredly to leave the roots of the violent conflict extensively in place.

There are further lessons to derive from this formulation. Even to mis-order the relation of positive to negative peace—to give an orientational emphasis to "negative peace"—risks making peace studies "crisis-driven." It risks raising concern for justice and attention to the deeper causes and conditions of peace only after the fact; after attention-demanding direct violence has erupted in some particular circumstance. The analytical lenses emerging in peace studies challenged this imbalance. "There is no temporal, logical, or evaluative preference given to one or the other," Galtung argued. "Social justice is not seen as an adornment to peace as absence of personal violence, nor is absence of personal violence seen as an adornment to peace as social justice."[12] Peace researchers and practitioners would need to combine and promote both dimensions of peace—("the absence of personal violence with the fight against social unjustice" [sic][13]). This gestured toward the symmetry—indeed, the conceptual interdependence—and orientational normativity that peace scholars and practitioners would strive to convey with the neologism justpeace several decades on.[14]

This bidimensional account of negative and positive peace necessitated a multifocal lens for re-conceptualizing and identifying violence. The term structural violence came to refer to indirect, unintentional, or nonphysical forms of violence. At its most general level, the term denoted the causes and conditions of the gap in human functioning and flourishing between the potential and the realized or actual—"those factors that cause people's actual physical and mental realizations to be below their potential realizations." Calling such forms "structural" identified a form of violence that is perpetrated apart from the purposeful or goal-directed action of a particular actor or group, but rather, occurs through the normal functioning of the social system. Usually, traces of such violence show up as vast differentials of power, agency, need-fulfillment, or well-being (among other indicators). The causes of these differentials are inscribed in social structures that result in drastic deficits in "life chances." "Individuals may do enormous amounts of harm to other human beings without ever intending to do so, just performing their regular duties as a job defined in the structure," Galtung argued, ". . . [or] as a process, working slowly in the way misery in general, and hunger in particular, erode and finally kill human beings."[15] He elsewhere explained:

> Thus, when one person beats his wife there is a clear case of personal violence, but when one million husbands keep one million wives in ignorance there is structural violence. Correspondingly, in a society where life expectancy is twice as high in the upper class as in the lower classes, violence is exercised even if there are not concrete actors one can point to directly attacking others, as when one person kills another.[16]

So formulated, structural violence lenses aim to detect and analyze violence that does not manifest itself physically or visibly ("to the naked eye"). In part, it aims at violence "that works on the soul"—"lies, brainwashing, indoctrination of various kinds, etc. that serve to decrease mental potentialities."[17] Its conceptualization of such processes is indebted to appropriations from critical theory. And while this debt is not frequently recognized, it is actually important to understand. For precisely what is appropriated from critical theory, and what is refused, sheds light upon the crucial difference between structural violence and analyses of power and domination that often fall under the heading of "critique."

The Virtue of "Under-Theorizing" Peace Studies?: Critical Theory and the Roots of Structural Violence

Critical theory appeared as a mode of social and political analysis in the inter-war years in Germany. It emerged from the complex integration of Karl Marx's analysis of capitalist political economy, Freudian psychoanalytic theory, Max Weber's account of the ascendancy and predominance of the "legal rational" (*Zweckrationalitat*) administration of society and "dis-enchantment" of the modern world (e.g., the extirpation of religious understanding as a necessary ingredient in the working of the natural and social world, and its relegation to the sphere of private and personal life), among other analytical resources. Though different, these resources overlapped in their capacity to lay bare the fact that the emergence of the modern world presented itself as—and was widely presumed to embody—the triumph of reason over archaic superstition, science's mastery of the natural world through experimental methods of prediction and control, modern industry's manifestation of that scientific mastery, and the liberation of the sovereign, self-determining individual from the shackling duties imposed in previous epochs by roles dictated within religious and cultural traditions and communities.

Yet these (purportedly) fulfilled promises of the Enlightenment actually concealed insidious forms of un-freedom, self-alienation, and repression. Thinkers such as Max Horkheimer, Theodor Adorno, Erich Fromm, Walter Benjamin, and Herbert Marcuse distinguished "critical theory" from "traditional theory" in virtue of its basic objective of "human emancipation"—seeking to unfetter people from their captivity to the illusion that Enlightenment forms of knowledge (e.g., the predominance of scientific positivism and instrumental means-ends and cost-benefit forms of rationality) and modern modes of life had made them rational and set them free within an increasingly rational and free society. In overcoming archaic vestiges of history, the Enlightenment had actually internalized and insidiously re-instantiated much of what it believed it had eliminated.

Critical theory sought to expose people's alienation from their true interests. What people (mis)recognized as forms of freedom actually manifest forms of social repression and domination to which those people were subject, but were less and less equipped to recognize. One aspect of critical theory's emancipatory impulse was relentless "ideology critique." Such critique deploys modes of criticism (sociological, economic, psychotherapeutic, political, and so forth) that seek to expose the ways that seemingly given and stable attitudes, ideas, practices, and institutions actually mystify and conceal the relations of power that constitute them, and normalize the forms of social domination in which they result. Critical theory, thus, aimed to expose modern and allegedly enlightened forms of social organization and individual identity as, in fact, forms of false consciousness or "ideological illusion" (processes in which "the real motive forces impelling [a thinker] remain unknown to him"[18]). The critique of ideology aimed to unmask concealed modes of domination and repression in the present in hopes of redeeming the seeds of utopia that the Enlightenment had actually contained.[19]

The subtle influence of critical theory on early developments in peace studies has significant implications. First, these resources enabled recognition that forms of structural violence may manifest as negative constraints that are not readily visible (e.g., psychological, spiritual, and emotional conditioning that delimits and prohibits whole ranges of potentialities). At the same time, and more importantly, insights from critical theory enabled recognition that structural violence may also exert itself in the social processes in and through which individual consciousness is positively shaped and formed (where, for example, persons are seemingly rewarded for participation and cooperation, thereby cultivating the kinds of habits, desires, dispositions, personalities, and consciousness valued by the influencers or influencing structures). This illuminated the need for powerful and systemic critiques of, for instance, consumer societies' capacities to form and cultivate desires, and to generate perceived needs and ideals that only that form of society purports to be able to fulfill.[20]

Of course, the impulses of critical theory that fuel criticism of these forms are prone to characterize structural repression and systemic domination as so pervasive as to produce a form of practical paralysis in the critic herself. Typically, this results from either a critical-analytical refusal to speak constructively and practically at all (for fear of implicating oneself—however inevitably—in some version of the very thing one is subjecting to relentless analysis), or finding violence and domination so pervasive that it becomes, in effect, impossible to identify (or perhaps even conceive of) circumstances that are not saturated by it in multiple varieties. To make the move from "the relentless criticism of all existing conditions"[21] to constructive—and ostensibly practicable—prescription would be to open oneself to the relentless interrogation of critical theory itself.[22] Thus, on one hand, incorporating elements of critical theory into structural violence ensures rigorous analysis that cuts deeply beneath surface-level appearances, and into the social and historical processes by which apparently fixed realities are constituted. At the same time, concern for practical results and constructive applicability required newly enriched—even newly imagined—conceptions of peace and justice that could steer clear of the Pandora's box of analytical temptations to which critical theory and its heirs are prone (namely, fetishizing critique, and ultimately, forms of practical impotence that quickly ensue therefrom).

Is Structural Violence Really "Violent" If It Is Not Deadly?

From their inception, the lens of structural violence faced criticisms of being too vast, too encompassing, and allegedly, too normative. Is there some particular benefit in identifying a particular form of injustice as a type of *violence*? Or is this simply a case of the peace researcher and peacebuilder projecting her preconceptions onto the world around her? "From many points of view," wrote one critic, "an explicit recognition of the notion of 'violence' as a normative concept, with a meaning varying according to the value structure of the user, would have its advantages. It would at least reduce the possibilities for semantic manipulation, resulting in quasi-scientific propositions about what violence 'really is'. It would be clear that 'violence' is simply the cause of what the user of the term does not like."[23]

Kenneth Boulding—economist, peace researcher, and Galtung's key critical interlocutor—complained of the attenuation of analytical precision and the practical clumsiness that typically follow when one's critical lenses become overly holistic, as he claimed that Galtung's multi-variant account of violence had.[24] Boulding wrote:

> The metaphor [of structural violence] is that poverty, deprivation, ill health, low expectation of life, a condition in which more than half the human race lives, is 'like' a thug beating up the victim and taking his money away from him in the street, or it is 'like' a conqueror stealing the land of the people and reducing them to slavery. The implication is that poverty and its associated ills are the fault of the thug or the conqueror and the solution is to do away with thugs and conquerors. While there is some truth to the metaphor, in the modern world at least there is not very much. Violence, whether of the streets and the home, or of the guerilla, of the police, or of the armed forces, is a very different phenomenon from poverty.... There is a very real problem of the structures which lead to violence.... Violence in the behavioral sense, that is, somebody actually doing something to somebody else and trying to make them worse off, is a 'threshold' phenomenon, rather like the boiling over of a pot.... The [structural violence] concept has been expanded to include all the problems of poverty, destitution, deprivation, and misery. These are enormously real and are a very high priority for research and action, but they belong to systems which are only peripherally related to the structures which produce violence.[25]

Boulding argued that attending to processes of dehumanization, poverty, and sociopolitical exclusion should not be the objectives of peace research unless they are deployed so as to lead directly to explicit violence that is intentionally perpetrated by some actor or group against another. Without such identifiable parameters, the analytical purposes of structural violence—while certainly noble—were far too vast and, at best, only tangentially related to "actual" violence (i.e. agent-originating, intentional, objective-directed, and deadly). The result was researchers' asking important questions, but questions conceived and articulated in a way that obscured the possibility of answering them.

One response to such charges is to answer them on their own terms, delineating precisely whose interests and purposes structural violence serves, and how its manifestations contribute to the "threshold conditions" for direct violence of which Boulding spoke. So, for instance, the sociologist Peter Uvin rearticulated the category of structural violence to entail "the joint occurrence of high inequality, social exclusion, and the humiliation characteristic of symbolic violence."[26] This account avoids the unwieldy diffusion of violence as (allegedly) anywhere and everywhere, for instance, by acknowledging the unavoidability of some inequalities in a world characterized by finite resources. Only when material inequality becomes viciously disproportionate, and is concurrent with forms of exclusion and humiliation, do those conditions amount to structural violence.

Exclusion may take more visible forms in discrimination based on racial, sexual, ethnic, and other characteristics. These may occur through processes, structures, and actions that "actively deny rights and entitlements to certain categories of marginalized people," either officially or informally.[27] At the same time, exclusion may exert itself in seemingly more justified or inevitable forms (e.g., legal forms of exclusion[28]). This latter frequently occurs as a predicate of unavoidable inequalities. High inequality (e.g., some living in abundance and super-abundance while many others go hungry) raises difficulties on its own. However, if some having more *is predicated upon* others having less—if it is a condition achieved and maintained in virtue of others having less—then that inequality is induced owing to the structure of the relationship, and simultaneously imposes a form of exclusion.[29] High inequality and exclusion—distinguishable for analytical purposes—are likely to emerge interdependently and to reinforce one another. Economic inequality that manifests itself in political and socioeconomic structures (either officially or in effect) quickly devolves into exploitation.

To take but one possible example, insofar as vast economic disparity translates into vastly greater social and political access, influence, and public voice for those who possess resources, and that disparity in resources is used to protect and augment the power of those in power (thereby further perpetuating disparities), such conditions of inequality amount to de facto exclusion of those who have less. These high inequality–exclusion dynamics result in political influence and governance being dominated by a highly enfranchised, wealthy few. In such cases, what is, in fact, oligarchy and plutocracy may be justified or disguised by the fact that the political context in question remains "democratic" in name (and in certain of its surface-level operations). Though impoverished, marginalized, and incapacitated, people recognized as citizens in such circumstances have, in principle, rights of free expression, political participation, and a vote. While these rights may be invoked as indicators of the justness of the political context, they actually camouflage—and aid in perpetuating—massive structural violence (extreme inequality that is structurally interlocked with exclusion) masquerading as substantive justice and democracy.

Uvin's third ingredient of structural violence reaches beyond the explicit violation of rights. It encompasses the myriad of processes through which denials of dignity and attrition of self-worth and self-respect, sometimes subtly or tacitly, occur (i.e., psychological, spiritual, or emotional effects that can be categorized as "humiliation"). This treats the effects of poverty (for example) in the form of identifiable effects and experiences of social inferiority, isolation, physical weakness, vulnerability, powerlessness, and the psychological effects of poverty. "Poor people are acutely aware of their lack of voice, power, and independence, which subject them to exploitation. Their poverty also leaves them vulnerable to rudeness, humiliation, and inhuman treatment by both private and public agents."[30] Such an example makes evident how this lens illuminates dynamics and forces that may exert themselves in contexts in which human and civil rights are legally in place, and in some cases, even where a seemingly theoretically robust and much-discussed account of "justice" is in force.[31]

Answering Boulding's criticisms on their own terms (in effect), Peter Uvin parsed the ways that structural violence promotes, and is liable to lead to, direct or "acute" violence. The constitutive features of structural violence contribute directly to the "threshold conditions" of direct violence along four primary vectors.[32] First, those who are structurally subjugated are liable to use explicit forms of violence, such as rioting, violent protest, or revolutionary or insurgent activity, in attempts to challenge and change the structures that oppress them. Second, those who benefit from the structures are liable to use violence to preserve them (police or military enforcement of unjust laws involving the use or threat of violent force to preserve "law and order," "keep the peace," and hold the status quo in place). Third, where certain resources are scarce or unavailable due to conditions held in place by structural violence, competition for those resources is liable to lead to direct violence between marginalized groups. Fourth, rather than generate solidarity among subjugated groups by, for instance, fueling efforts to challenge and alter oppressive structures, structural violence tends to highlight and balkanize the identity boundaries of structurally subordinated groups, harden those boundaries, and turn the groups against one another. Structural violence is prone to produce scapegoating of purportedly inferior groups, a process which often results in explicit violence.

These are indices of how structural violence relates directly to forms of acute and deadly violence. In each case, the diagnostic lens of structural violence aims to identify and lay bare the complex, subterranean root systems from which direct violence is likely to spring. The objective and unique contribution of this analysis is to identify, assess, and thereby aid in addressing acute violence at the levels of its causes, conditions, complex background, and histories.

But what if structural violence does *not* lead to direct or deadly violence? Is it no longer a primary concern of the peacebuilder? In such cases, one responds to Boulding's behaviorist (agent-specific and objective-directed) constraints upon violence not by striving to meet the challenge on its own terms, but rather, by further expanding and enriching the multifocal conceptualization of violence, and its role in articulating peace interwoven with justice. Positive peace—the reduction of direct violence and simultaneous pursuit of justice—cannot be limited to treating physical violence and deadly conflict at its roots (addressing its causes and conditions). It requires more.

Thus, Galtung expanded his earlier appeal to the somatic basis for conceptualizing violence (the differential between the potential and actual in physical functioning) to include a "spiritual/mental" focus as well. In fact, it was necessary to overcome the deficiencies of the "materialist bias"—or tendency toward material reductionism—to which both peace studies and development studies gravitated.[33] This required recalibrating the definition of violence to refer to the deprivation of basic needs—"Avoidable insults to basic human needs, and more generally to life, lowering the real level of needs satisfaction below what is potentially possible"—in four basic categories: survival, well-being, freedom, and identity.[34]

"How difficult I find it to see what is right in front of me": The Emergence of Cultural Violence[35]

Recasting the definition of violence illuminates the arguably more insidious layers of structural violence, namely, its normalizing functions. In many cases, the power of structural violence consists precisely in its capacity to hold exploitative, repressive, and dehumanizing conditions in place *without producing direct or deadly violence*. In fact, frequently, it is in virtue of not leading to direct violence or deadly conflict that structural violence avoids drawing attention to itself in ways that direct forms of violence typically do, thereby attracting the recognition and intervention of those concerned to understand and combat direct violence (or structural violence identifiably related to direct violence). Direct violence may be resolved, successfully managed, or held at bay in ways that actually contribute to maintaining, perpetuating, or even increasing structural violence.

For instance, direct violence is only one reaction to being deprived of basic needs. Other reactions to structural violence, not involving direct violence, are all the more insidious and destructive because the possibilities of active resistance and explicit violence are pre-empted or seemingly resolved. Such reactions may include quiet acquiescence to conditions of poverty, exclusion, and humiliation. They may entail the subjugated groups' complicity in and even active perpetuation of the very structural processes, practices, and institutions by which they are exploited, incapacitated, and enmeshed in misery.[36] "[Direct violence] is not the only reaction [to needs deprivation]," Galtung came to explain:

> There could also be a feeling of hopelessness, a deprivation/frustration syndrome that shows up on the inside as self-directed aggression and on the outside as apathy and withdrawal. Given a choice between a boiling, violent and a freezing, apathetic society as reaction to massive needs-deprivation, topdogs tend to prefer the latter. They prefer 'governability' to 'trouble, anarchy.' They love 'stability.'[37]

Galtung came to be persuaded of the analytical insufficiency of the *structural violence* lens for these purposes. Detecting the violence diffused in impersonal, sometimes unintended, even anonymous operations of social, political, and economic structures was important, but insufficient. In fact, a greater danger—the *cunning* of structural violence, as it were—is not that the conditions, causes, and effects of such forms of violence are normalized, but that they contribute to processes of normalization. They come to appear, to present themselves, as "natural," even "necessary" or "inevitable." They become accepted within—interwoven with—average, workaday, normal perceptions; in effect, they colonize the common sense of both the people benefitting from them and those harmed by them.

Structural violence is sometimes rendered invisible—camouflaged and difficult to recognize—precisely by its apparently uncontroversial, inconspicuous diffusion throughout the routinized functioning of society. Moreover, to illuminate and lay bare the structures in question—and the fact that well-meaning people are complicit in, indeed, often beneficiaries of, those structures—is liable to inspire denial, refusal, rejection of structural analyses by those many well-intentioned and concerned people. Efforts to lay bare structural violence risk hitting too close to home.

The realities of structural violence are not merely neglected because of their everydayness, or denied because they are seemingly uncontroversial or necessary. They are also positively justified and legitimized by conceptions of "the way the world is." Thus, the great challenge presented by thinking in terms of structural violence is not merely tracking it in the operations of social, political, economic structures, but figuring out how to *denaturalize* its operations—to render it visible and expose its effects. One analytical challenge particularly important for peacebuilding, then, is to re-conceptualize or counter-conceptualize such dynamics and processes as forms of violence needing to be addressed as such. This re-conceptualization struggles against the grain of what presents itself as the natural, necessary—and, perhaps most significantly, seemingly innocuous—ways it has been conceptualized or unrecognized heretofore. For these purposes, Galtung derived a further analytical lens—that of *cultural violence*.

Cultural violence Galtung defined as "those aspects of culture, the symbolic sphere of our existence—exemplified by religion and ideology, language and art, empirical science and formal science, that can be used to justify or legitimize direct or structural violence."[38] He continued, "Cultural violence makes direct and structural violence look, even feel, right, or at least not wrong.. . . The study of cultural violence highlights the way in which the act of direct violence and the fact of structural violence are legitimized and thus rendered acceptable in society."[39] This development expanded and linked the earlier critical-theoretical dimensions of the account—particularly those addressing consciousness formation—to the "spiritual effects" of structural violence. He wrote:

> A violent structure leaves marks not only on the human body but also on the mind and the spirit. [These] can be seen as parts of exploitation or as reinforcing components in the structure. They. . . [impede] consciousness formation and mobilization, two conditions for effective struggle against exploitation. Penetration, implanting the topdog inside the underdog so to speak, combined with segmentation, giving the underdog only a very partial view of what goes on, will do the first job. And marginalization, keeping the underdogs on the outside, combined with fragmentation, keeping the underdogs away from each other, will do the second.[40]

This account retrieves and further develops the much earlier incorporation of consciousness formation and enculturation, but aims to further expand these in terms of psychological, emotional, and spiritual impact. These correlate with two importantly different forms of exploitation.

"Exploitation A," as Galtung termed it, occurs when those subjected to structural violence are so disadvantaged that the effects of the exploitative relationship result in premature or unnecessary mortality, that is, "the underdogs die" (starve, waste away from disease). This form of exploitation is justified or rendered uncontroversial by forms of cultural violence that construe it as (however sadly) "unavoidable," "tragic," or perhaps "self-inflicted," or that let it go unrecognized.[41]

Exploitation B occurs when some person or group is left in a permanent, unwanted state of misery. This may include malnutrition and illness, but may not, in these instances, lead identifiably to premature or unnecessary mortality or deadly conflict.[42] Moreover, the invisibility or perceived legitimacy of this form of exploitation may be augmented by that very fact (that such conditions are not "deadly"). One example would be gender-identified violence, in which, statistically, women may have lower morbidity and mortality rates than men (provided that they evade gender-specific perils manifest across many cultures and societies such as gender-specific abortion and infanticide, gender-preferential prenatal care and treatment in the first years of childhood, and so forth), but live subject to arbitrary treatment, lack of voice in decisions directly affecting their life chances, strictly delimited social status, and cultural conditions that promote and perpetuate attenuated self-respect, destructive forms of self-abnegation, and reduced emotional well-being.[43]

One vector along which Exploitation B manifests itself is a form of "spiritual death." In this condition life is experienced as having little or no meaning, engendering apathy and passivity, disengagement, and an abiding sense of hopelessness. This is related to—but importantly distinct from—what Galtung termed a "silent holocaust" (in contrast to a holocaust that aims explicitly to exterminate) by which violent structures gradually exploit, causing hunger and illness that "erode and finally kill human beings."[44] The miseries born of physical (somatic) incapacitation are horrific. Yet conditions of spiritual misery—apathy, passivity, self-hatred, abiding hopelessness, the fatigue of despair, and Sisyphean struggle for bare survival—would tend not to show up in statistics concerned with deadly conflict or direct violence, as they would not be explicitly linked to premature mortality. This form of spiritual deprivation he called "alienation."

From Analysis to Engagement: Summary of Part I

So far I have traced the historical emergence and conceptual development of structural and cultural violence in peace studies. At the same time, I have described how these lenses empower multidimensional forms of critical analysis. Such multidimensional analysis, I argued, renders the identification and assessment of violence more sensitive and fine-grained; it enables detecting the manifold forms of violence as well as their modes of interrelation and the different levels at which the effects of violence take hold. I have also demonstrated how these lenses facilitate critical analysis and self-reflexivity that serve constructive objectives, sidestepping temptations to subvert such reflection and practice through interminable systemic analysis of power and domination (the paralysis of analysis).

The upshot is that nonphysical and non-deadly structural forms of violence must become (where they are not already) central concerns of the peacebuilder. These are forms of violence categorized as deprivation of "identity needs" and "well-being needs." As we have seen, they take forms of alienation and exploitation that "work on the soul." Under this heading we find categorized forms and effects such as:

- processes of consciousness- and self-formation in which "the topdog is implanted inside the underdog" (i.e. "penetration"), and ensuing experiences of inferiority, self-devaluation, self-abnegation, shame, humiliation, and stigmatization;
- internalized and self-directed aggression, rage, and despair;
- invisibility or negligibility through social and legal marginalization and voicelessness (civic or social death);
- diminished agency, disempowerment, and isolation through exclusion, segregation and partition ("segmentation");
- the denuding of nurturing communal bonds and nourishing relationships ("fragmentation");
- stereotyping and/or scapegoating, and the ensuing experiences of being terrorized, hunted, or endangered; existential angst resulting from pariah status;

- Sisyphean conditions void of care and compassion, and interlaced experiences of abiding hopelessness, purposelessness, and lovelessness; misery-induced apathy and passivity;
- the effects of efforts to anesthetize spiritual, emotional, mental suffering (substance abuse, alcoholism, dependency and addiction, and so forth).

These are examples of forms and effects of violence that the lenses of structural and cultural violence bring to light. All of them deprive people of basic needs. None of them need be deadly. In fact, some of these forms of violence are more widespread and persistent precisely because they are not deadly. The cultural violence lens illuminates cultural practices, perceptions, and convictions that camouflage, justify, or normalize these forms and effects, making them seem natural, necessary, or right—or "at least not wrong," if not altogether invisible.

In what ways are these analytical lenses especially fit for the interests and purposes of religiously informed or religiously motivated peacebuilders? How is it that they are acutely effective in illuminating manifestations and effects of violence to which those working in religion and peacebuilding are likely to be particularly attuned to and motivated or well-equipped to understand and constructively address? I answer these questions by turning to specific examples in which religious peacebuilders have demonstrated acute awareness of, critically diagnosed, and provided constructive prescriptions for structural and cultural forms of violence.

II. Structural and Cultural Violence in Religious Peacebuilding: Parallels and Precursors

As is often the case, the analytical lenses and insights developed by theorists follow on the heels of the insights and experiences of practitioners on the ground. In many ways the most seminal studies of structural and cultural violence are but analytically articulated footnotes to the work that activists and practitioners already firmly grasped and powerfully articulated. In this second section I examine two examples of such activists: Martin Luther King Jr. and Cornel West. My examination will seek to answer two questions in each case: 1) How are his efforts to combat injustice and to cultivate justpeace consistent with and describable in terms of the above accounts of structural and cultural violence? 2) How does his work as a "*religious* peacebuilder" (his knowledge of, engagement with, and motivation born of religious traditions) equip him to be acutely attuned to the forms and impact of such violence?

Martin King: From Racial Inequality to Cultural Homicide

Central threads of my genealogy of the emergence and development of structural and cultural violence in peace studies find robust antecedents in the life and work of Martin Luther King Jr. In fact, some years before Galtung first invoked the field-demarcating distinction between negative and positive peace (1964), King had deployed such a distinction to explain and justify to Southern moderates and liberals the tactics of civil disobedience used by the Student Nonviolent Coordinating Committee (e.g., boycotts, sit-ins, freedom rides, and so forth) in 1961. The white moderates and liberals he addressed were sympathetic to the movement's aims, but were decidedly gradualist in their ideas about how racial segregation should be altered. Many such Southerners claimed that race relations had been peaceful for many years and that explicit forms of Jim Crow segregation needed measured reform, but ultimately that "only time can solve this problem."

King acknowledged the surface-level appearance of tranquil race relations, but explained that the student movement was intentionally in revolt against the "negative peace" that had suffused the Southern United States for many decades.[45] The movement aimed not at desegregation, but at the full-fledged integration of black people in American life. Anything less would be cosmetic integration, and as a result, superficial democracy. In revolting against negative peace, the movement aimed to dramatize repressed tension and deploy that tension—nonviolently, but disruptively— in order to bring latent conflict out into plain view, to illuminate the full depths of injustices and confront them directly so as to transform them constructively. King describes the absence of explicit tensions, conditions under which black people quietly accepted their plight, using the term "negative peace." The movement aimed to struggle for "positive peace." Peace of this sort was not merely the absence of hostility and conflict. It would be "the presence of justice and brotherhood."[46]

Though Galtung never cites King's use of the "positive/negative" distinction and the "presence of justice and integration of groups" as a source, the similarity of their terms is startling. Galtung is credited by many peace researchers as the originator of these ideas, but clearly he is not.[47] From where does King derive these concepts? Working as a Christian theologian and Baptist preacher, King derives them from his interpretation of Jesus's claim that he has "come not to bring peace but a sword" (Matthew 10:34–39). King reads this as Jesus's rejection of negative peace, with its characteristic complacency and impassiveness that typically gets portrayed as tranquility. As King has it, whenever Jesus comes, "conflict is precipitated between the old and new... [and] struggle takes place between justice and injustice, between the forces of light and the forces of darkness." In this, Jesus's coming precipitates the struggle for positive peace: the pursuit of justice, brotherhood and sisterhood, and the kingdom of God.[48] In short, King derives his integrated account of positive and negative peace from Christian Scriptures. This exemplifies what King's fellow civil rights activist Andrew Young refers to as his use of "biblical critique."

The implications of King's articulation of the student campaign as a "revolt against negative peace" and "struggle for positive peace"—its explicit confrontation of latent tension, suppressed conflict, and repressed injustices—meant that, eventually, he would have to take up what peace researchers would come to identify as violence perpetrated structurally and culturally. Here again, King derived a conception of structural change from Christian Scripture, specifically, the story of Jesus and Nicodemus (John 3:1–21). King interprets Jesus's instruction to the lawyer Nicodemus that in order to be saved he must be born again to indicate that his "whole structure must be changed." The structural implication for King's context meant that the "thing-ification" of black people under 244 years of slavery continues to exert itself through the economic exploitation of people of color, and of poor people more generally. Moreover, economic exploitation at home relates to international investments and interests that must be preserved and protected militarily. King's point is that these strands of oppression are tightly interwoven (related structurally) and must be addressed in tandem.

As a result, he declared—echoing Jesus's instruction to Nicodemus—"America, you must be born again!"[49] On these bases, King came to expand and deepen his interests and purposes beyond the pursuit of equality in the face of racist and discriminatory laws—beyond what he called as late as 1966 the "racial revolution to 'get in,'" and receive a fair share economically, educationally, and in social opportunities.[50]

By August of 1967, King realized that positive peace required training his attention on the structures and cultural conceptions that held discriminatory dispositions, habits, manners, and mores in place long after discriminatory laws had been wiped from the books. He spoke of the pursuit of justice that is available only by coming to the full recognition of—and struggling to transform—the systemic injustices that hold discriminatory and prejudicial structural relationships and patterns in place. To transpose this into terms of my genealogical account in Part I, "Violence: The Missing Dimensions of Religion and Peacebuilding," King recognized the depths that were obscured by the meagerness of what the words "discrimination" and "prejudice" had come to signify. He recognized the necessity of addressing the cultural processes, dispositions, and symbolic practices that prop up and perpetuate the forms of exclusion, humiliation, and subtler (but no less radical) inequalities that persisted even after the revolution of equal rights and legal recognition effected by the civil rights movement.

Several years after receiving the Nobel Prize for Peace, and standing alongside President Johnson as witness to the signing of the Civil Rights Act (1964) and the passage of the Voting Rights Act one year later, King called for mobilizing against the persistence of what he identified as the "cultural homicide" of black people. With this phrase, he illuminated the forms of violence that exert themselves through language, embodiment, and consciousness formation. He pointed to the fact that average, workaday ways of speaking—as well as the meanings of words held firmly in place by Webster's Dictionary and Roget's Thesaurus—were laced with, and perpetuated, abiding forms of inferiority and self-abnegation layered into the consciousness and inscribed across the bodies of people of color in the United States after several hundred years of slavery and Jim Crow.

Dynamics of humiliation could not be isolated only in the socioeconomic marginalization or in the legalized inequality and exclusion of groups of people. Rather, the psychological and spiritual dimensions of such types of humiliation provide a kind of cultural mortar holding the elements of structural and direct violence firmly in place. This point of analysis does not simply address the adverse impact of white supremacy that shaped the everyday operations of culture and society. It also lays bare the various examples of what peace studies categories described as processes of "penetration" by which "top dogs" become "implanted" inside the "underdogs" (exemplifying what Galtung would only much later came to call cultural violence). They make forms of structural and direct violence appear natural or necessary—to look, to even feel, right; or at least not wrong. They are manifest in the forms of psychological and spiritual self-abnegation that King described as the results of "cultural homicide."

In effect, such cultural forms of violence are as debilitating as direct forms of violence. Exposing and challenging them is even more fundamental to pursuing freedom from domination and to developing the capacities by which to cultivate positive conditions of a just and sustainable peace. And yet, cultivating self-respect and self-love was a task that could not be measured by the standards firmly entrenched in a society that had suffered from the cultural effects of white supremacy for so long. Certain forms of subjugation were already inscribed in established standards and ideals. Such work required challenging and transforming the less visible and often internalized metrics of value and beauty by which prevailing structures both legitimized and asserted themselves. These metrics had come to be written, as it were, upon the bodies and shot through the personalities, the unreflective self-conceptions, of people of color subject to cultural violence. They had come to be acculturated and habituated, and inscribed through dynamics of consciousness-formation.

To describe these culturally articulated, seldom reflected-upon metrics of value as internalized is not to suggest that they are impervious to being recognized and illuminated through social-analytical lenses and other tools of redescription, and then critically interrogated and revised. In fact, this is precisely the kind of analysis that lenses of structural and cultural violence facilitate. King brought such analysis to bear by way of his training in and the resources of the Christian theological tradition.

As we saw in the genealogical account above, structural/cultural violence lenses' sensitivity to the inscription of person-diminishing violence in and through consciousness formation has roots in the tradition of critical social theory (Herbert Marcuse and his Frankfurt School forebears). From where did King derive his equally incisive analysis of violence in and through consciousness formation? Again, in this case, we must look to the analytical resources he drew from the Christian theological tradition and Jewish philosophy.

King's conception of human personhood, the ultimate origins of human dignity in the personhood of God, and what these conceptions necessitated of justice were based upon his commitment to theological and philosophical personalism. Thus he invoked St. Augustine and St. Thomas Aquinas in appealing to the moral law to which all human laws are accountable for their justness ("An unjust law is no law at all"). At the same time, to give concrete content to the implications of this principle, he employed the terms of personalism.[51] Laws that degrade human personality are unjust, and those that protect and honor its dignity are just. On this basis, all segregationist laws are unjust because they "distort the soul and damage the personality" of all the people affected by them. Those who benefit from segregation are endowed with the false perception that they are superior. Those who are subjugated by segregationist laws absorb a false sense of subordination and inadequacy. King borrowed the terms of the Jewish philosopher Martin Buber to make the point that such personality-degrading laws "substituted an 'I-it' relationship for an 'I-thou' relationship."[52] This consigns persons to the status of things, or at least to the status of "less than fully human." As King had it, the degradation of human personality "distorts the soul." This is consistent with what peace researchers later came to refer to as "violence that works on the soul."

From King's Christian theological perspective, such violence obscures or attempts to deny the reality that the human person bears the image of God, and that, in virtue of this image, his or her dignity and inestimable value inheres in his or her personhood by default. Such violence "distorts the soul" by projecting as real the unreality, or promoting internalization of the lie, that the person is *not* born out of God's extravagant agapic love (and thus is not created with intrinsic dignity), when in fact, he or she is. This nature and basis of personhood mean that persons have been created for the purposes of giving and receiving forms of love through mutual recognition and mutual respect, reciprocal accountability, and humanizing and constructive relationships that derive therefrom. Laws, social and political structures, and cultural processes consistent with this reality will protect and promote human dignity and value, and protect against all forms of arbitrary and dehumanizing treatment. Moreover,

King's understanding of agapic love meant that, in the fight for justice, even one's enemy was to be recognized as a bearer of dignity, to be respected, and whose well-being was to be pursued. To pursue his opponent's well-being through nonviolence meant that the struggle for justice should promote the liberation of King's opponents from the blinding, spiritual sickness of white supremacy, in the hope of opening possibilities for reconciliation. Most importantly, agapic love impelled King to call for loving the person who participates in evil (i.e., loving one's enemy), while simultaneously hating and struggling against the evil in which that person participates.[53]

In virtue of these insights, King recognized dehumanizing cultural formations as violence that must be combatted and positively countered in order to build positive peace interwoven with justice and the integration of human groups ("brotherhood and sisterhood"). As King addressed these motifs, structural and cultural forms of violence pertain to the condition of the human soul, inseparable as it was (as he understood it) from the psychological, emotional, and physical. Such a position refuses the possibility of construing "the spiritual" in abstraction from (as somehow wholly separable and discrete, or secreted away within or transcending) the mundane.

In re-describing these elements of King's work in terms of religious peacebuilding, we find further support for my central claim that modes of consciousness formation are central to the concerns of peacebuilding not simply insofar as they might relate to direct violence or deadly conflict. Rather, the forms and effects of cultural violence are, in themselves, just that: forms of violence. They hold injustice and humiliation in place at the same time that they hold forms of deadly or direct forms of violence in abeyance. They render populations docile, and by generating psychological and spiritual apathy, those people accept their own marginalization—their having been rendered invisible, negligible—as normal.

Cornel West: Nihilism as a Spiritual Condition

We are now in a position to see how the lenses of structural and cultural violence, as they make visible dimensions of consciousness formation, relational needs, and identity needs, may illuminate the spiritual impact of cultural violence. Just such analytical motifs inform the criticism of the structural impact of poverty and culture of consumption deployed by the philosopher, social critic, and activist Cornel West. Once the parameters of religious peacebuilding are expanded to include structural and cultural (in conjunction with direct) forms of violence, West's work can be seen to fall squarely within the category of religious peacebuilding.

Among contemporary thinkers and activists, it is West who perhaps most clearly carries forward the legacy of Martin Luther King Jr. He takes prophetic streams of the Christian tradition as indispensable for analyzing and responding to the catastrophic conditions that compel activists and practitioners to strive for justice and decrease violence in all its forms. His reasons for drawing upon religion are both political and grounded in his existential commitments. "The culture of the wretched of the earth is deeply religious," he explains. "To be in solidarity with them requires not only an acknowledgment of what they are up against but also an appreciation of how they cope with their situation. This appreciation does not require that one be religious; but if one is religious, one has wider access into their life-world." At the existential level he explains that Christianity is, for him, an enabling tradition. It provides the ground for hope in the face of the tragic realities against which he struggles. And yet, he does not advocate an uncritical and undiscriminating reliance upon Christian tradition. It must be persistently subjected to self-reflexive analysis and critique.[54]

It is the prophetic dimensions of the Christian tradition that compel West to seek solidarity with the wretched of the earth. The prophetic also provides resources by which he assesses the causes and conditions of the wretchedness in question. This entails a struggle for justice and the reduction of violence. In his critical and self-reflexive retrieval of resources from the Christian tradition—motivated and normatively oriented by Jesus's instruction for any who would follow him to live and work in solidarity with the oppressed (e.g., Jesus's words, "Just as you have done it to the least of these, you have done it unto me," Matthew 25:31–46)—West models a form of "religious peacebuilding."

What do West's "religiously musical" solidarity and profound personal conviction enable him to identify that reflects the distinctive fit between the aims of a religiously informed or motivated critic and activist, and the uses of structural and cultural violence lenses? Religious resources inform West's diagnosis, his prescription for change, and the grounds of his hope in the midst of catastrophic conditions that are dismissed as self-inflicted or tragically unavoidable, or else are casually ignored.

In the wake of the 2008 economic collapse and ensuing "great recession," West points out, "The catastrophic conditions and circumstances right now, in light of corporate elites and financial oligarchs, with greed running amok, looting billions and billions of dollars, when 21 percent of America's children live in poverty—that's a crime against humanity."[55] And yet, to identify as forms of violence the savagely and disproportionately high rates of incarceration, infant mortality, unemployment, and crime among people hovering around and beneath the poverty line, and people of color more generally, is to diagnose only one part of the relevant violence. As West has it, these conditions must be addressed in terms of their spiritual dimensions—insight afforded him uniquely in virtue of his recognition of the role of religion and the existential nature of his own religious commitments. It is in virtue of his religious commitments, as well as his use of the prophetic streams of the Christian and Jewish traditions, that West sees that these conditions cannot be accounted for solely in terms of poverty, racial inequality, and material destitution. Rather, adequate diagnoses require recognition that these conditions are interwoven with and interdependent upon a form of the spiritual condition of nihilism. West explains:

> I am not just talking about the one out of five children who live in poverty. I am not just talking about the one out of two black and two out of five brown children who live in poverty. I am talking about the state of their souls. The deracinated state of their souls. By deracinated I mean rootless. The denuded state of their souls. By denuded, I mean culturally naked. Not to have what is requisite in order to make it through life. Missing what's needed to navigate through the terrors and traumas of death and disease and despair and dread and disappointment. And thereby falling prey to a culture of consumption. A culture that promotes addiction to stimulation. A culture obsessed with bodily stimulation. A culture obsessed with consuming as the only way of preserving some vitality of a self. You are feeling down, go to the mall. Feeling down, turn on the TV. The TV with its spectator passivity. You are receiving as a spectator, with no sense of agency, no sense of making a difference. You are observing the collapse of an empire and feeling unable to do anything about it.. . . A market culture that promotes a market morality. A market morality has much to do with the unprecedented violence of our social fabric.. . . You need market forces as necessary conditions for the preservation of liberties in the economy. But when the market begins to hold sway in every sphere of a person's life,

market conceptions of the self, market conceptions of time, you put a premium on distraction over attention, stimulation over concentration, then disintegrate [sic] sets in.. . . We are talking about larger cultural tendencies that affect each and every one of us. It takes the form of self-destructive nihilism in poor communities, in very poor communities. The lived experience of meaninglessness and hopelessness and lovelessness. Of self-paralyzing pessimism among stable working-class and lower working-class people.[56]

These lines offer a glimpse of what it looks like to identify and assess the impact of poverty in terms of spiritual deprivation. As West illuminates these effects, they can neither be reduced to terms of social psychology, nor socioeconomic class. Rather, "nihilism" gets repositioned as something more fundamental than a philosophical doctrine. In light of my genealogy in Part I, we can describe it in terms of the spiritual effects of structural and cultural violence. As West has it, nihilism is "the lived experience of coping with a life of horrifying meaninglessness, hopelessness, and (most importantly) lovelessness. . . . Nihilism is a disease of the soul."[57]

How does this vision inform West's prescription? "Nihilism is not overcome by arguments or analyses; it is tamed by love and care," he responds. "Any disease of the soul must be conquered by a turning of one's soul. This turning is done through one's own affirmation of one's worth—and affirmation fueled by the concern of others. A love ethic must be at the center of a politics of conversion."[58] Like King, West is quick to point out that the love ethic he prescribes has nothing to do with sentimental emotion, or being kind and gentle. An adequate conception of Christian love—and its implication that Christians must take responsibility for the justness of the structures and conditions in which they live here and now—recognizes the indispensability of seeing the complex interrelation of love with justice and power. "Power without love is reckless and abusive, and love without power is sentimental and anemic," King wrote. "Power at its best is love implementing the demands of justice, and justice at its best is power correcting everything that stands against love."[59] Such an analysis opens horizons for the peacebuilder whose conceptualization of violence needs to be deepened and broadened. It opens necessary horizons for the work of peacebuilders addressing not only physical violence, but violence in all its forms.

What Does "Religious Peacebuilding" Accomplish that Social Psychology Does Not?

To those for whom religious traditions are unfamiliar, so much of what these lenses detect may sound like merely social psychology: cultural and structural forms of violence affect the psyche, mental functioning, and emotional health. These interweave with, and are dimensions of, the spiritual, ethical, and emotional concerns of the religious peacebuilder. At one level, this is accurate. These forms of violence admit of varying descriptions, and different descriptions may help illuminate different features and the multiple levels at which response is needed. And yet, they cannot be reduced to social psychology without a loss of their content, without becoming something other than what they are.

The effects of nihilism, meaninglessness, and hopelessness might be anesthetized with Prozac and Wellbutrin, much like some people self-medicate their effects with illegal drugs, alcohol, and other forms of dependency and addiction. And yet, as West and King make the case, ultimately, nihilism is a disease of the soul. It can only be countered by lived practices of love, care, compassion, personal integrity, and self- and other-respect. Can these only be provided by the Christian tradition or exclusively by religious traditions more broadly?

As I argued previously, a peacebuilder need not be personally religious to intervene in and respond to violence and despair. However, as the examples of King and West indicate, religious peacebuilders can be especially well-equipped to perceive, diagnose, and respond to these facets of human existence and the forms and effects of violence that "work on the soul." In the cases I examined, acute awareness of structural and cultural forms of violence comes to light by looking at the inescapability of power through the lens of agapic love. Must one be Christian to agree? In my judgment, the answer must be "no." While clearly grounded in Christian theological particularity (i.e. irreducibility), King also deployed the concept of love at the level of what may be described as an "intermediate norm"—a normative orientation for practice and analysis that might accommodate (or find analogical agreement with, or overlap for ad hoc purposes with) a number of normative conceptions articulated within other religious, ethical, or cultural traditions. Of course, it is important to note that this conception of analogy (or intermediate normativity) seeks agreement redescriptively and provisionally—at an intermediate level, and for ad hoc purposes—rather than reductively. In other words, it is not asserting that particular claims and traditions are "reducible" to a more basic unified conception of, say, "the sacred," that all of these different traditions are, at their core, "really about the same thing" or are "paths up different sides of the same mountain," or even that different traditions' central concepts and claims translate easily into each other without remainder. For example, the conception of agapic love that King and West share is not identical to, yet is in many ways consistent with, Gandhi's commitment to "ahimsa"— meaning literally "non-injury," but which Gandhi came to construe as a positive state of non-violence toward the world.[60] At an intermediate level, the relational implications of agapic love, arguably, similarly accommodate the human rights–oriented conception of love as mutual respect and the inviolable implications of human dignity.[61]

At the same time, a strong caution is in order for any who would engage in peacebuilding from religious and theological quarters. These activists and critics must be especially aware of the temptation toward esoteric insider-speak and similar postures and languages directed at a religious or theological "ghetto" to which some intra-traditional or intra-communal religious discourse is prone regarding matters of justice and peace. King and West speak forthrightly—at moments, quite explicitly—from, and in the terms of, their primary tradition-specific, theological motivations. Each is simultaneously eclectic and improvisational, pragmatic, strategic, and multilingual—even while normatively oriented by their commitment to be faithful—in how they articulate their claims, and how they enrich and compound their analyses. These capacities enable them to avoid the great temptation (and, for many, the great pitfall) of religious voices in conflict, war, and peacebuilding: the temptation of preaching to themselves. These powerful exemplars demonstrate that anyone who would approach peacebuilding from within religion-specific traditions, and (in these cases) Christian theological commitments, must hold their theological commitments, understandings, and practices flexibly and conversantly at the same time that they engage and enrich their own accounts with the conceptual tools of non-theological resources and conversation partners. Moreover, on this point, there is a lesson to be taken from Johan Galtung.

Galtung was not a religious peacebuilder. And yet, he stood within the predominantly social-scientific, quasi-positivist, security studies–oriented enterprise of peace research that was emerging in the middle of the twentieth century, at the same time that he cut deeply against it. He challenged and pressed beyond the deficiencies of the conception of conflict, violence, and peace that prevailed at that time. As my genealogical account above makes clear, this required moving beyond the safety of rigid academic disciplinary boundaries and becoming multilingual and conceptually innovative. Galtung rejected materialist reductionism and opened peace studies to the spiritual, emotional, and psychological dimensions of peacebuilding. In doing so, he opened vistas within peace studies that had long been unfolding and that are ideally suited for the dynamics of religious peacebuilding today.

Conclusion

The purpose of this chapter has been to identify, genealogically explicate, and juxtapose several analytical tools and research currents within peace studies that are uniquely compatible with the interests and purposes, contents and resources of religiously conversant peacebuilding. I have sought, further, to examine what the idea of "violence" entails when one holds justice and peace together as a normative orientation ("positive peace" or "justpeace"). Those convinced of the necessity of holding justice and peace in tandem (who recognize that each is essential to the other) cannot afford to limit their analytical vision to an exclusive or even orientational focus upon conflict that is deadly. Nor, I have argued, can we risk an easy compartmentalization of these analytical lenses. The assumption that if social structures and cultural understandings and practices have not identifiably contributed to deadly conflict, then they need not be tracked and addressed, ultimately truncates the full scope and interests of positive peace.

Read charitably and with attention to their concern for altering the "roots of the conflict" as those persist in social, institutional, and procedural forms, Little and Appleby set forth an analytical framework that is consistent with the full breadth of concerns that I have brought to light in this chapter. But their pull toward deadly conflict seems orientational—it serves as a conceptual center of gravity—and therefore overly constricts the focus and potential impact of religious peacebuilding. Something weighty is at stake in this point of difference, namely that to the degree that deadly conflict is orientational for peacebuilding practice and theory, the range of concerns that the peacebuilder must take up is delimited. A primary focus on deadly conflict causes peacebuilders to neglect those points at which the forms of violence and its effects take on psychological, emotional, and spiritual dimensions.[62]

The implication is that structural and cultural forms of violence ought be the objects of peace research and religion and peacebuilding not simply as they are understood to be causes and conditions of direct, deadly violence, but also as equally orientational objects of analysis in themselves. Such analytical tools and practical interventions offer a multi-focal, and expansive analytical conceptions of non-deadly conflict and violence. In this way the lenses and concepts of structural and cultural violence facilitate probing for, attending to, and strategizing about how best to intervene in conditions of structural and cultural forms of conflict which are not explicitly deadly, but are, as such, not only violent, but all the more insidiously so.

Once structural forms of violence are given equally orientational weight to direct and deadly violence, we arrive at a further enriched understanding of the concept of *justpeace*—now understood to entail *the reduction of violence in all its forms (i.e., direct, structural, cultural, deadly/non-deadly), and the simultaneous pursuit and cultivation of justice in the full range of its varieties (e.g., social, distributive, restorative, reparative, and so on).* A risk attendant to overlooking or downplaying the effects of structural and cultural forms of violence is that efforts at peacebuilding will be out of synch with the logic of "justpeace." In short, there is actually much at stake in the seemingly minor semantic difference between focusing upon "deadly violence" as opposed to "violence in all its forms." Not only does the multidimensional lenses for identifying and assessing violence dramatically expand the scope and validity of peacebuilding, but it also draws upon developments in the peace studies literature which are, arguably, most directly relevant to religious peacebuilding.

Notes

1. In addition to Gordon Smith and Harold Coward, eds., *Religion and Peacebuilding* (New York: SUNY, 2004), see also Robert J. Schreiter, R. Scott Appleby, and Gerard F. Powers, eds., *Peacebuilding: Catholic Theology, Ethics, and Praxis* (Maryknoll, NY: Orbis Books, 2010), David Little, ed., *Peacemakers in Action* (Cambridge: Cambridge University Press, 2006) and Daniel Smith-Christopher, ed., *Subverting Hatred: The Challenge of Nonviolence in Religious Traditions* (Maryknoll, NY: Orbis Books, 2007); Douglas Johnston, ed., *Faith Based Diplomacy: Trumping Realpolitik* (Oxford: Oxford University Press, 2003); Douglas Johnston and Cynthia Sampson, eds., *Religion: The Missing Dimension of Statecraft* (Oxford: Oxford University Press, 1995), among numerous others.

2. A secondary task of this chapter is to locate and map exemplary studies and texts that deploy analyses of structural and cultural violence toward the ends of peacebuilding (broadly construed). I identify and map the literature on structural and cultural violence primarily in the endnotes throughout this chapter. The relevant entries intend to provide the reader with an overview of works assessing structural and cultural violence across several subfields of peace and justice studies, with specific attention to such studies in the subfield of religion and peacebuilding.

3. While I do not engage any such figures in the present chapter, in my judgment, Jeffrey Stout, Romand Coles, and John Kelsay fall into this category of peacebuilders who are "religiously musical" though not participants in the religious tradition(s) with which each works. To consider a helpfully instructive example, Stout demonstrates command of the features of Christian ethical and theological reflection in order to both criticize and constructively correct deficient currents internal to that tradition insofar as they relate to his work for justice and democratic practice in US contexts. He has demonstrated at length that, on certain readings of the tradition, its institutions and practices are indispensable for pursuing forms of just and sustainable peace that committed Christian citizens in the United States, and citizens of other religious traditions, or no tradition, can, and should, share interests in pursuing by substantive democratic means. Read in the way I propose, his texts *Democracy and Tradition* and *Blessed are the Organized* operate in tandem to exemplify the broadly construed conception of "religious peacebuilding" I am articulating here. In *Democracy and Tradition*, Stout deployed immanent criticism—a form of criticism in which a critic either takes up and uses the reasoning and resources of his or her interlocutor to demonstrate that the interlocutor's position is self-subverting on its own terms, or conversely, works more constructively by presuming

the premises, reasoning, and resources of his or her interlocutor in order to demonstrate how those move in the direction of the immanent critic's conclusions. Whether deployed critically or constructively, this form of engagement requires a charitable—even intimate—grasp of the tradition, and high proficiency in engaging and deploying its resources and modes of reasoning. This is one sense in which one may be a "religious peacebuilder" without holding personal religious commitments or identifying as a practitioner of a religious tradition. In Stout's case, it has led some Christian theologians to identify him as "the church's best secular ally in America." For examples of Stout's "religiously musical" immanent criticism (in its critical mode) see "The New Traditionalism" and "Virtue and the Way of the World," *Democracy and Tradition* (Princeton: Princeton University Press, 2004), chaps. 5–6, and in a more constructive mode see, among others, "A Prophetic Church in a Post-Constantinian Age: The Implicit Theology of Cornel West," *Contemporary Pragmatism* 4, no. 1 (2007): 39–45, and Stout's contribution in Jason Springs (ed), Cornel West, Richard Rorty, Stanley Hauerwas, Jeffrey Stout, "Pragmatism and Democracy: Assessing Jeffrey Stout's *Democracy and Tradition*," *Journal of the American Academy of Religion* 78, no. 2 (2010): 413–448. For Stout's exposition and argument for the indispensability of Christian, Jewish, and Muslim religious communities, in addition to nonreligious civic groups, in the United States for cultivating justice and reducing violence through grassroots democratic, broad-based community organizing—an account largely inspired by the work of Saul Alinsky and consistent with the aims and approach of strategic peacebuilding—see Stout's *Blessed Are the Organized: Grassroots Democracy in America* (Princeton, NJ: Princeton University Press, 2010), esp. chap. 18.

4. For an overview that maps the variety of ways that the field of religion and peacebuilding has suffered from a dearth of critical reflexivity, see Atalia Omer's "Religion and Peacebuilding" in the present volume.

5. David Little and Scott Appleby, "A Moment of Opportunity? The Promise of Religious Peacebuilding in an Era of Religious and Ethnic Conflict," in *Religion and Peacebuilding*, ed. Harold Coward and Gordon S. Smith (Albany, NY: State University of New York Press, 2004), 5.

6. Little and Appleby, "A Moment of Opportunity?," 5–6.

7. Little and Appleby, "A Moment of Opportunity?," 6.

8. Johan Galtung, "An Editorial," *Journal of Peace Research* 1, no. 1 (1964): 2.

9. Johan Galtung, "Peace," in *International Encyclopedia of the Social Sciences, Vol. 11*, ed. David Sills (New York: The Macmillan Company and The Free Press, 1968), 487.

10. Galtung, "Cultural Violence," *Journal of Peace Research* 27, no. 3 (1990): 293.

11. It was the integrative and holistic conception of nonviolence that Gandhi drew from multiple religious and ethical traditions that led him to see the draconian excesses of commercialization and commodification—in as far as they find their impetus in human greed—as forms of violence. "An armed conflict between nations horrifies us," he wrote, "But the economic war is no better than an armed conflict. This is like a surgical operation. An economic war is prolonged torture. And its ravages are no less terrible than those depicted in the literature on war properly so called. We think nothing of the other because we are used to its deadly effects. Many of us in India shudder to see blood spilled.... but we think nothing of the slow torture through which by our greed we put our people.... But because we are used to this lingering death, we think no more about it." Gandhi, "Nonviolence—The Greatest Force," *The World Tomorrow*, Oct. 1926.

12. Johan Galtung, "Violence, Peace, and Peace Research," *Journal of Peace Research* 6, no. 3 (1969): 185.

13. Galtung, "Violence, Peace, and Peace Research," 186.
14. John Paul Lederach, "Justpeace: The Challenge of the 21st Century," in *People Building Peace: 35 Inspiring Stories from Around the World*, ed. Paul Van Tongeren (Utrecht: European Centre for Conflict Prevention, 1999), 27–36. See also Lederach and R. Scott Appleby, "Strategic Peacebuilding: An Overview," in *Strategies of Peace: Transforming Conflict in a Violent World*, ed. Daniel Philpott and Gerard F. Powers (Oxford: Oxford University Press, 2009), 19–44 (esp. 23–35, and 42 n. 3).
15. Galtung, "Twenty-Five Years of Peace Research: Ten Challenges and Some Responses," *Journal of Peace Research* 22, no. 2 (1985): 145.
16. Galtung, "Violence, Peace, and Peace Research," 171.
17. Galtung, "Violence, Peace, and Peace Research," 170 (here quoting 169).
18. Frederick Engels, "Letter from Engels to Franz Mehring in Berlin, London, July 14, 1893," in *The Marx-Engels Reader*, ed. Robert C. Tucker (New York: W.W. Norton & Company, 1978), 766.
19. For an important intellectual history and socio-philosophical exposition of the Frankfurt School, see Martin Jay's *The Dialectical Imagination: A History of the Frankfurt School and the Institute of Social Research, 1923–1950* (Berkeley, CA: University of California Press, 1996). Seyla Benhabib offers powerful critical exposition in *Critique, Norm, and Utopia* (New York: Columbia University Press, 1986).
20. See, for instance, Galtung, "Violence, Peace, and Peace Research," 170. Galtung invoked Herbert Marcuse's 1964 text, *One Dimensional Man: Studies in the Ideology of Advanced Industrial Society* (Boston: Beacon Press, 1991), which, itself, drew upon prior analyses of "mass culture" of which Max Horkheimer and Theodor Adorno's 1944 *Dialectic of Enlightenment* (New York: The Continuum Publishing Company, 2000) (esp. chap. 4) and Erich Fromm's *Escape from Freedom* (New York: Avon, 1941) stand as but two pronounced exemplars.
21. Karl Marx, "An Exchange of Letters," in *Writings of the Young Marx on Philosophy and Society*, edited and translated by Loyd D. Easton and Kurt H. Guddat (Indianapolis, IN: Hacket, 1997), 212.
22. This is exemplified in how the concept of "utopia" (the ideal of "society made rational") functions in critical theory of Adorno and Horkheimer. In order for critique to remain un-assimilated to the domination that saturates the present, it must remain in a negative mode. One maintains this negative posture only by virtue of one's perpetual engagement in criticism. The utopian ideal can never be stated discursively, that is, articulated in positive and definite terms. While affording indispensable critical resources, arguably, such conceptions of critique and utopia provide far too slender a groundwork upon which to base the constructive objectives entailed in cultivating peace that is just and sustainable. See Max Horkheimer, "Reason Against Itself," in *What Is Enlightenment?*, ed. James Schmidt (Berkeley, CA: University of California Press, 1996), 359–367; Jay, *The Dialectical Imagination*, 54–56; Benhabib, *Critique, Norm, Utopia*, 167–171.
23. Kjell Eide, "Note on Galtung's Concept of 'Violence,'" *Journal of Peace Research* 8, no. 1 (1971): 71.
24. Kenneth Boulding, "Twelve Friendly Quarrels with Johan Galtung," *Journal of Peace Research* 14, no. 1 (1977): 75–86 (here 85).
25. Boulding, "Twelve Friendly Quarrels," 83, 84.
26. Peter Uvin, "Global Dreams and Local Anger: From Structural to Acute Violence in a Globalizing World," in *Rethinking Global Political Economy: Emerging Essays, Unfolding Odysseys*, ed. Mary Ann Tetreault, Robert A. Denemark, Kenneth P. Thomas, and Kurt Burch (New York: Routledge, 2003), 149.

27. Uvin, "Global Dreams and Local Anger," 150.
28. To give a textbook example: being convicted of a felony in the US criminal justice system results in "legal discrimination"—exclusion from access to public housing and public assistance benefits (e.g., welfare support, supplemental nutrition assistance), prohibition from voting, exclusion from employment and education opportunities, and more insidious forms of "civic death." See Michelle Alexander's *The New Jim Crow: Mass Incarceration in the Age of Colorblindness* (New York: The New Press, 2010), esp. chaps. 4–5.
29. See, for example, Galtung, "Only One Quarrel with Kenneth Boulding," *Journal of Peace Research* 24, no. 2 (1987): 200–201.
30. Uvin, "Global Dreams and Local Anger," 150–151.
31. In the final chapter of *The Decent Society*, Avishai Margalit makes the case that John Rawls's principles of justice could be fulfilled, and the society still be characterized by forms of institutional humiliation. See *The Decent Society* (Cambridge, MA: Harvard University Press, 1996), esp. chap. 1 and the conclusion. Along these lines, the restorative justice movement is largely predicated on the claim that many retributive models of criminal justice, and the criminal justice system in the United States in particular, inflict wide-reaching forms of humiliation in seeing that "justice is served." For exposition of these themes amid the vulnerabilities of the low-wage working poor in the U.S., see Barbara Ehrenreich's *Nickel and Dimed: On (Not) Getting By in America* (New York: Henry Holt and Company, 2001).
32. Uvin positions these vectors extensively within the literature and documents them at length. "Global Dreams and Local Anger," 155–156. See also Uvin's *Aiding Violence: The Development Enterprise in Rwanda* (Hartford, CT: Kumarian Press, 1998), esp. chap. 6.
33. Galtung, "Twenty-Five Years of Peace Research," 145–147.
34. Galtung, "Cultural Violence," 292; see also "The Basic Needs Approach," in *Human Needs: A Contribution to the Current Debate*, ed. Katrin Lederer, David Antal, and Johan Galtung (Cambridge, MA: Oelgeschlager, Gunn and Hain, 1980), 55–125.
35. Ludwig Wittgenstein, *Culture and Value*, trans. Peter Winch (Chicago: University of Chicago Press, 1977), 39e.
36. To take a severe example, this was one of the pivotal—and most controversial—insights brought to light in Hannah Arendt's *Eichmann in Jerusalem: A Report on the Banality of Evil* (New York: Penguin, 2006). The "banality of evil" exerted itself most insidiously in the Nazis' efforts to make the Jews accomplices to the extermination of their people through various bureaucratic, procedurial, and work-a-day ministrations of the Jewish Councils through European communities.
37. Galtung, "Cultural Violence," 295.
38. Galtung, "Cultural Violence," 291.
39. Galtung, "Cultural Violence," 296.
40. Galtung, "Cultural Violence," 299. At this point, the complex interrelation of structural and cultural violence in Galtung's account overlaps with several basic insights in sociologist Pierre Bourdieu's account of "symbolic violence," understood as the complex interaction between the structurally embodied modes of domination that are internalized by both the dominant and the dominated, such that the latter do not recognize the economy in which domination is embodied as domination, turning whatever resultant aggression may emerge among the dominated inward or toward one another in ways that perpetuate the system of domination. For a particularly powerful assessment of structural violence in US inner-city illegal drug economies and cultures conducted explicitly through the

lens of Bourdieu's account of "symbolic violence," see Phillipe Bourgois, "U.S. Inner-city Apartheid: The Contours of Structural and Interpersonal Violence," in *Violence in War and Peace*, ed. Nancy Scheper-Hughes and Phillip Bourgois (Oxford: Blackwell, 2004), 301–307.

The challenge presented by Bourdieu's account is that he so emphasizes the anonymity and structural diffusion of domination that the personal or direct (agent-oriented) dimension gets minimized, if not altogether washed out. As a result, power, domination, and violence become conceived as forces that no one subject to them can really recognize, render explicit, critique, resist, or alter. This difficulty manifests the temptations of critical theory that I mentioned earlier in this chapter. When viewed in terms of the multifocal lens of violence developed here (direct/structural/cultural), Bourdieu's account risks removing altogether the direct vector of the tri-part relationship (i.e., the personal, agent-originating, and directed), thus portraying any slender possibility of resistance as a by-product of reflexive sociological analysis itself. By contrast, as I am construing it here, the tri-focal lens accounts for anonymous and structurally and culturally diffused forms of violence while retaining their interconnectedness with direct and personal (i.e., agential) forms of violence and domination. Representative statements of Bourdieu's category occur in Pierre Bourdieu and Loic Wacquant, "Language, Gender, and Symbolic Violence," in *An Invitation to Reflexive Sociology* (Chicago: University of Chicago Press, 1992), esp. 167–173, and Bourdieu, *Masculine Domination* (Stanford: Stanford University Press, 2001), esp. 34–42.

For a treatment of these features of Bourdieu and Michel Foucault and an effort to bring individual agency as a means of critique, resistance, and innovation back to the center of the analysis (in tandem with structural and cultural dimensions), see Michel de Certeau, *The Practice of Everyday Life*, xiv, and especially chap. 4 ("Foucault and Bourdieu"). See also Jason A. Springs, "'Dismantling the Master's House': Freedom as Ethical Practice in Robert Brandom and Michel Foucault," *Journal of Religious Ethics* 37, no. 3 (2009): 419–448. For a clear and sympathetic exposition of the deep tensions in Bourdieu's account regarding the possibilities of constructive change in light of domination illuminated by reflexive sociology (e.g., through the plasticity of the habitus), see David Couzens Hoy, *Critical Resistance: From Poststructuralism to Post-Critique* (Cambridge: MIT Press, 2005), 114–139.

41. Here an exemplary study is Nancy Scheper-Hughes's study of structural causes and conditions for—as well as the cultural bases for widespread acceptance of, inattention to, or mis-recognition of—the exorbitantly high infant mortality rates in Brazilian slums. Scheper-Hughes treats what she calls "invisible genocides and small holocausts" in her text *Death Without Weeping: The Violence of Everyday Life in Brazil* (Berkeley, CA: University of California Press, 1992). For a more wide-ranging study that takes Galtung's account of structural violence as an analytical touchstone, see the work by medical anthropologist Paul Farmer, *Pathologies of Power: Health, Human Rights, and the New War on the Poor* (Berkeley, CA: University of California Press, 2003).

42. Galtung, "Cultural Violence," 198.

43. Joshua Price provides a powerful examination of the multiple and mutually interpenetrating layers of various forms of gender-identified violence that mobilizes and applies Galtung's account of structural violence. This text deploys the lens of structural violence both to illuminate the multiple forms of violence ("Exploitation A" and "Exploitation B") that are rendered invisible by the institutionalized category "domestic violence." See

Price's *Structural Violence: Hidden Brutality in the Lives of Women* (Albany, NY: SUNY, 2012). Price's study suggests that an integrated analysis of personal and structural violence, and their legitimation and perpetuation through cultural modes of violence, is most liable to adequately lay bare the complexities of the (often silent and internalized) brutalities suffered by women in contemporary US contexts (see, in particular, chap. 2). For additional work on gender-identified structural violence oriented by Galtung's accounts, see Lubna Nazir Chaudhry, "Reconstituting Selves in the Karachi Conflict: Mohjir Women Survivors and Structural Violence, *Cultural Dynamics* 16, no. 2–3 (2004): 259–289; and Mary Anglin, "Feminist Perspectives on Structural Violence," *Identities: Global Studies in Culture and Power* 5, no. 2 (1998): 145–152.

44. Galtung, "Twenty-Five Years of Peace Research," 146–147.

45. King, "Love, Law, and Civil Disobedience," in *A Testament of Hope: The Essential Writings and Speeches of Martin Luther King, Jr.*, ed. James M. Washington (New York: Harper Collins, 1991), 43–53 (here 50).

46. King, "Love, Law, and Civil Disobedience," 50–51.

47. Kathleen Maas-Weigert rightly traces Galtung's use of these terms with their earlier formulation in Quincy Wright's *A Study of War* (Chicago: University of Chicago Press, 1942), 1089–1093, 1305–1307. In fact, prior to King's invocation of the terms, Jane Addams had written of the deficiencies of "negative peace" (as the absence of war) and the necessity of "positive ideals of peace" in her book of 1902, *Newer Ideals of Peace*. See Berenice Carroll and Clinton Fink, "Introduction to the Illinois Edition," in *Newer Ideals of Peace*, ed. Jane Addams (Urbana, IL: University of Illinois Press, 2007), xvii–xviii. For a helpfully condensed examination of structural violence see Maas-Weigert, "Structural Violence," in *Encyclopedia of Violence, Peace, and Conflict*, ed. Lester Kurtz (San Diego, CA: Academic Press, 1999), 2004–2011.

48. King, "Love, Law, and Civil Disobedience," 51.

49. King, "Where Do We Go from Here?," in *I Have a Dream: Speeches and Writings that Changed the World*, ed. James M. Washington (New York: Harper, 1992), 177.

50. King, "Nonviolence: the Only Road to Freedom," in Washington, *I Have a Dream*, 130–131.

51. See King, "An Encounter with Niebuhr (1 Sept. 1958)," in *The Papers of Martin Luther King, Jr.*, vol. 4, *Symbol of the Movement, January 1957–September 1958*, ed. Clayborn Carson et al. (Berkeley, CA: University of California Press, 2000), 480.

52. King, "Letter from Birmingham City Jail" (April 1963), in Washington, *A Testament of Hope*, 289–302. For the crucial philosophical and theological background for King's understanding of personalism, see Martin Buber's *I and Thou* (New York: Touchstone, 1970).

53. King, "Letter from Birmingham City Jail."

54. West, *The American Evasion of Philosophy: A Genealogy of Pragmatism* (Madison, WI: University of Wisconsin Press, 1989), 233–234. See also West, "Prophetic Religion and the Future of Capitalist Civilization," in *The Power of Religion in the Public Sphere*, ed. Eduardo Mendieta and Jonathan VanAntwerpen (New York: Columbia University Press, 2011), 92–100.

55. West, *American Evasion of Philosophy*, 97–98.

56. West, "Beyond Eurocentrism and Multiculturalism," in *Prophetic Thought in Postmodern Times* (Monroe, ME: Common Courage, 1993), 16–19. For a more recent example of West engaging these issues of poverty; cultures of consumption and free market fundamentalism; hopelessness and meaninglessness as conditions in which spiritual and material deprivation are wholly interwoven, see West and Tavis Smiley, *The Rich and the Rest of Us* (New York: Smiley Books, 2012).

57. West, Race Matters (Boston: Beacon Press, 2001), pp. 14, 18.

58. A piece particularly pronounced in West's corpus along these lines is "Nihilism in Black America," in Race Matters (New York: Vintage, 2001), esp. 22 and 29.

59. King, "Where Do We Go from Here?," 172.

60. It was in his articulation of ahimsa that Gandhi reinterpreted the classic passages in the Bhagavad Gita typically invoked to justify the obligations of the caste system, and the necessity of engaging in violent struggle and warfare. This stands out as a powerful example of a thinker working within a tradition to read its more orienting values correctively against prevailing readings of passages taken to justify both direct violence and the violent social structures held in place by the Hindu caste system as a whole. "Krishna's Counsel in a Time of War" of the Gita has long been taken to justify some of the most repellent duties of direct violence (what may become the warrior's duty to kill even those who nurtured and cared for him). It is also taken to justify and reinforce the Hindu caste system more broadly, and as such, structural violence. Moreover, when deployed for such justifying purposes, the Gita serves as an example of cultural violence. Thus, Gandhi's efforts to reread and interpret the Gita against the grain of those traditional uses stands as an example of combatting cultural violence from within the particular tradition itself, and with resources (perhaps uniquely) available there. See Gandhi, "Anasaktiyoga: The Message of the Gita," in The Gospel of Selfless Action or The Gita According to Gandhi, ed. Mahadev Desai (Ahmedabad: Navajivan Publishing House, 1929), 125–134.

61. For an effective example, see the articulation of human rights and other regard by Barbara Deming in "Violence and Equilibrium," in Revolution and Equilibrium (New York: Grossman, 1971), esp. 207 and 221. On the complexities of Gandhi's position, see Thomas Kilgore, "The Influence of Gandhi on Martin Luther King, Jr." in Gandhi's Significance for Today, ed. John Hick and Lamont Hempel (New York: St. Martin's Press, 1989), 236–243. For a helpful entry-level account of a non-reductionist approach to conceptualizing what are taken to be the major religious traditions, see Stephen Prothero's God is Not One: The Eight Rival Traditions that Run the World—and Why their Differences Matter (New York: Harper, 2010). For a more technical treatment of inter-religious cooperation that sidesteps the violence done to religious traditions when their differences are construed as surface-level trappings that reduce to shared grounding in "the sacred," see Mark Heim, Salvations: Truth and Difference in Religion (New York: Orbis, 1995). For a fuller theological tradition-specific account of non-reductionist inter-religious engagement and dialogue, see William Placher, Unapologetic Theology: A Christian Voice in a Pluralistic Conversation (Louisville, KY: Westminster/John Knox, 1989), esp. Chapters 7–9.

62. As is clear in the sample of literature I have referenced throughout (though far from exhaustively), engagement in peacebuilding through lenses of structural and cultural violence requires expanding the attention and efforts of peacebuilders to encompass matters of poverty and development (Scheper-Hughes, Uvin, Farmer, Ehrenreich); gender (Price, Chaudhry, Anglin); race, ethnicity, religious identities and institutions (King, West, see also Jean Zaru's Occupied with Nonviolence: A Palestinian Woman Speaks (Minneapolis, MN: Fortress, 2008); the interface of religion, ethnicity, and nationalism (Atalia Omer's When Peace Is Not Enough: How the Israeli Peace Camp Thinks About Religion, Nationalism, and Justice (Chicago: University of Chicago Press, 2013) and Michael Sells's The Bridge Betrayed: Religion and Genocide in Bosnia (Berkeley, CA: University of California Press, 1998); and law, criminal justice, and prison systems (Bourgois, Alexander). It trains attention and efforts of peacebuilders equally upon dimensions of environmental peace and justice, though these have not been addressed above. On this topic, see, for example, Rob

Nixon, *Slow Violence and the Environmentalism of the Poor* (Cambridge, MA: Cambridge University Press, 2013). Other pivotal resources include James Gilligan, *Violence: Our Deadly Epidemic and Its Causes* (New York: Putnam and Sons, 1996) and Veena Das, Arthur Kleinman, Mamphela Ramphele, and Pamela Reynolds, *Violence and Subjectivity* (Berkeley, CA: University of California Press, 2000).

BIBLIOGRAPHY

Addams, Jane. *Newer Ideals of Peace.* Urbana, IL: University of Illinois Press, 2007.

Alexander, Michelle. *The New Jim Crow: Mass Incarceration in the Age of Colorblindness.* New York: The New Press, 2010.

Anglin, Mary. "Feminist Perspectives on Structural Violence." *Identities: Global Studies in Culture and Power* 5, no. 2 (1998): 145–152.

Arendt, Hannah. *Eichmann in Jerusalem: A Report on the Banality of Evil.* New York: Penguin, 2006.

Benhabib, Seyla. *Critique, Norm, and Utopia.* New York: Columbia University Press, 1986.

Boulding, Kenneth. "Twelve Friendly Quarrels with Johan Galtung." *Journal of Peace Research* 14, no. 1 (1977): 75–86.

Bourdieu, Pierre. *Masculine Domination.* Stanford, CA: Stanford University Press, 2001.

Bourdieu, Pierre, and Loic Wacquant. "Language, Gender, and Symbolic Violence." In *An Invitation to Reflexive Sociology*, 140–173. Chicago: University of Chicago Press, 1992.

Bourgois, Phillipe. *In Search of Respect: Selling Crack in El Barrio.* Cambridge: Cambridge University Press, 2003.

de Certeau, Michel. *The Practice of Everyday Life.* Berkeley, CA: University of California Press, 1988.

Buber, Martin. *I and Thou*, translated by Walter Kaufman. New York: Touchstone, 1970.

Chatterjee, Margaret. *Gandhi's Religious Thought.* Notre Dame, IN: University of Notre Dame Press, 1983.

Chaudhry, Lubna Nazir. "Reconstituting Selves in the Karachi Conflict: Mohjir Women Survivors and Structural Violence." *Cultural Dynamics* 16, no. 2–3 (2004): 259–289.

Das, Veena, Arthur Kleinman, Mamphela Ramphele, and Pamela Reynolds. *Violence and Subjectivity.* Berkeley, CA: University of California Press, 2000.

Demming, Barbara. "Violence and Equilibrium." In *Revolution and Equilibrium*, 194–221. New York: Grossman, 1971.

Eide, Kjell. "Note on Galtung's Concept of 'Violence.'" *Journal of Peace Research* 8, no. 1 (1971): 71.

Ehrenreich, Barbara. *Nickel and Dimed: On (Not) Getting By in America.* New York: Henry Holt and Company, 2001.

Engels, Frederick. "Letter from Engels to Franz Mehring in Berlin, London, July 14, 1893." In *The Marx-Engels Reader*, edited by Robert C. Tucker, 765–767. New York: W.W. Norton & Company, 1978.

Farmer, Paul. *Pathologies of Power: Health, Human Rights, and the New War on the Poor.* Berkeley, CA: University of California Press, 2003.

Fromm, Erich. *Escape from Freedom.* New York: Avon, 1941.

Galtung, Johan. "An Editorial." *Journal of Peace Research* 1, no. 1 (1964): 1–4.

Galtung, Johan. "Peace." In *International Encyclopedia of the Social Sciences, Vol. 11*, edited by David Sills, 487–496. New York: The Macmillan Company and The Free Press, 1968.

Galtung, Johan. "Violence, Peace, and Peace Research." *Journal of Peace Research* 6, no. 3 (1969): 167–191.

Galtung, Johan. "A Structural Theory of Imperialism." *Journal of Peace Research* 8, no. 2 (1971): 81–117.

Galtung, Johan. "The Basic Needs Approach." In *Human Needs: A Contribution to the Current Debate*, edited by Katrin Lederer, David Antal, and Johan Galtung, 55–125. Cambridge, MA: Oelgeschlager, Gunn and Hain, 1980.

Galtung, Johan. "Twenty-Five Years of Peace Research: Ten Challenges and Some Responses." *Journal of Peace Research* 22, no. 2 (1985): 141–158.

Galtung, Johan. "Only One Quarrel with Kenneth Boulding." *Journal of Peace Research* 24, no. 2 (1987): 199–203.

Galtung, Johan. "Cultural Violence." *Journal of Peace Research* 27, no. 3 (1990): 291–305.

Gandhi, Mohandas. "Anasaktiyoga: The Message of the Gita." In *The Gospel of Selfless Action or The Gita According to Gandhi*, edited by Mahadev Desai, 125–134. Ahmedabad: Navajivan Publishing House, 1929.

Gilligan, James. *Violence: Our Deadly Epidemic and Its Causes*. New York: Putnam and Sons, 1996.

Heim, Mark. *Salvations: Truth and Difference in Religion*. New York: Orbis, 1995.

Horkheimer, Max. "Reason Against Itself." In *What Is Enlightenment?*, edited by James Schmidt, 359–367. Berkeley, CA: University of California Press, 1996.

Horkheimer, Max, and Theodor Adorno. *Dialectic of Enlightenment*. New York: The Continuum Publishing Company, 2000.

Hoy, David Couzens. *Critical Resistance: From Poststructuralism to Post-Critique*. Cambridge, MA: MIT Press, 2005.

Jay, Martin. *The Dialectical Imagination: A History of the Frankfurt School and the Institute of Social Research, 1923–1950*. Berkeley, CA: University of California Press, 1996.

Kilgore, Thomas. "The Influence of Gandhi on Martin Luther King, Jr." In *Gandhi's Significance for Today*, edited by John Hick and Lamont Hempel, 236–243. New York: St. Martin's Press, 1989.

King, Martin Luther, Jr. *A Testament of Hope: The Essential Writings and Speeches of Martin Luther King, Jr.* Edited by James M. Washington. New York: Harper Collins, 1991.

King, Martin Luther, Jr. *I Have a Dream: Speeches and Writings that Changed the World*. Edited by James M. Washington. New York: Harper, 1992.

King, Martin Luther, Jr. *The Papers of Martin Luther King, Jr.*, vol. 4, *Symbol of the Movement, January 1957–September 1958*, edited by Clayborn Carson et al. Berkeley, CA: University of California Press, 2000.

Lederach, John Paul. "Justpeace: The Challenge of the 21st Century." In *People Building Peace: 35 Inspiring Stories from Around the World*. Edited by Paul Van Tongeren, 27–36. Utrecht: European Centre for Conflict Prevention, 1999.

Lederach, John Paul, and R. Scott Appleby. "Strategic Peacebuilding: An Overview." In *Strategies of Peace: Transforming Conflict in a Violent World*, edited by Daniel Philpott and Gerard F. Powers, 19–44. Oxford: Oxford University Press, 2009.

Little, David, and Scott Appleby, "A Moment of Opportunity? The Promise of Religious Peacebuilding in an Era of Religious and Ethnic Conflict." In *Religion and Peacebuilding*, edited by Harold Coward and Gordon S. Smith, 1–26. Albany, NY: State University of New York Press, 2004.

Maas-Weigert, Kathleen. "Structural Violence." In *Encyclopedia of Violence, Peace, and Conflict,* edited by Lester Kurtz, 2004–2011. San Diego, CA: Academic Press, 1999.

Marcuse, Herbert. *One Dimensional Man: Studies in the Ideology of Advanced Industrial Society.* Boston: Beacon Press, 1991.

Margalit, Avishai. *The Decent Society.* Cambridge, MA: Harvard University Press, 1996.

Marx, Karl. "An Exchange of Letters." In *Writings of the Young Marx on Philosophy and Society,* edited and translated by Loyd D. Easton and Kurt H. Guddat, 203–215. Indianapolis, IN: Hacket, 1997.

Mendieta, Eduardo, and Jonathan VanAntwerpen, eds. *The Power of Religion in the Public Sphere.* New York: Columbia University Press, 2011.

Nixon, Rob. *Slow Violence and the Environmentalism of the Poor.* Cambridge, MA: Cambridge University Press, 2013.

Omer, Atalia. *When Peace Is Not Enough: How the Israeli Peace Camp Thinks About Religion, Nationalism, and Justice.* Chicago: University of Chicago Press, 2013.

Placher, William. *Unapologetic Theology: A Christian Voice in a Pluralistic Conversation.* Louisville, KY: Westminster/John Knox, 1989.

Price, Joshua. *Structural Violence: Hidden Brutality in the Lives of Women.* Albany, NY: SUNY, 2012.

Prothero, Stephen. *God Is Not One: The Eight Rival Traditions that Run the World—and Why Their Differences Matter.* New York: Harper, 2010.

Scheper-Hughes, Nancy. *Death Without Weeping: The Violence of Everyday Life in Brazil.* Berkeley, CA: University of California Press, 1992.

Scheper-Hughes, Nancy, and Phillip Bourgois, eds. *Violence in War and Peace.* Oxford: Blackwell, 2004.

Schreiter, Robert J., R. Scott Appleby, and Gerard F. Powers, eds. *Peacebuilding: Catholic Theology, Ethics, and Praxis.* Maryknoll, NY: Orbis Books, 2010.

Sells, Michael. *The Bridge Betrayed: Religion and Genocide in Bosnia.* Berkeley, CA: University of California, 1998.

Smiley, Tavis, and Cornel West. *The Rich and the Rest of Us: A Poverty Manifesto.* New York: Smiley Books, 2012.

Springs, Jason A. " 'Dismantling the Master's House': Freedom as Ethical Practice in Robert Brandom and Michel Foucault." *Journal of Religious Ethics* 37, no. 3 (2009): 419–448.

Springs, Jason A., Cornel West, Richard Rorty, Stanley Hauerwas, and Jeffrey Stout. "Pragmatism and Democracy: Assessing Jeffrey Stout's *Democracy and Tradition*." *Journal of the American Academy of Religion* 78, no. 2 (2010): 413–448.

Springs, Jason A. "Following at a Distance (Again): Freedom, Equality, and Gender in Karl Barth's Theological Anthropology." *Modern Theology* 28, no. 3 (2012): 446–477.

Stout, Jeffrey. *Democracy and Tradition.* Princeton, NJ: Princeton University Press, 2004.

Stout, Jeffrey. "A Prophetic Church in a Post-Constantinian Age: The Implicit Theology of Cornel West." *Contemporary Pragmatism* 4, no. 1 (2007): 39–45.

Stout, Jeffrey. *Blessed Are the Organized: Grassroots Democracy in America.* Princeton, NJ: Princeton University Press, 2010.

Uvin, Peter. *Aiding Violence: The Development Enterprise in Rwanda.* Hartford, CT: Kumarian Press, 1998.

Uvin, Peter. "Global Dreams and Local Anger: From Structural to Acute Violence in a Globalizing World." In *Rethinking Global Political Economy: Emerging Essays, Unfolding*

Odysseys, edited by Mary Ann Tetreault, Robert A. Denemark, Kenneth P. Thomas, and Kurt Burch, 147–163. New York: Routledge, 2003.

West, Cornel. *The American Evasion of Philosophy: A Genealogy of Pragmatism.* Madison, WI: University of Wisconsin Press, 1989.

West, Cornel. *Prophetic Thought in Postmodern Times.* Monroe, ME: Common Courage, 1993.

West, Cornel. *Race Matters.* New York: Vintage, 2001.

West, Cornel. "Prophetic Religion and the Future of Capitalist Civilization." In *The Power of Religion in the Public Sphere,* edited by Eduardo Mendieta and Jonathan VanAntwerpen, 92–100. New York: Columbia University Press, 2011.

Wright, Quincy. *A Study of War.* Chicago: University of Chicago Press, 1942.

Zaru, Jean. *Occupied with Nonviolence: A Palestinian Woman Speaks.* Minneapolis, MN: Fortress, 2008.

PART THREE

CONTESTED ISSUES

CHAPTER 7

THE NEW NAME FOR PEACE? RELIGION AND DEVELOPMENT AS PARTNERS IN STRATEGIC PEACEBUILDING

R. SCOTT APPLEBY

"DEVELOPMENT is the new name for peace," declared Pope Paul VI in the encyclical *Populorum Progressio* (1967). Today, forty-seven years after that papal proclamation, the promising partnership between development practitioners, peacebuilders, and religious communities is still in its infancy. As I demonstrate in this chapter, however, there is growing awareness among the three sets of actors regarding the affinities and opportunities for collaboration among them.[1] In what follows I argue that their previously separate and self-contained understandings and practices are converging in three areas, creating a nexus for collaboration, a common ground that should be cultivated by religious leaders, development experts, and peacebuilders alike. These areas of convergence are: 1) a focus on the local community, engaged in its full creative potential by external actors, through an elicitive method of discernment and practice; 2) an emerging consensus regarding the "rules of engagement" with local communities; and 3) a growing recognition, rooted in reflective practice, that the criteria for "authentic" human development must be articulated and addressed on a case-by-case basis.

THE EVOLUTION OF DEVELOPMENT

Each of the players in this drama of convergence contains multitudes. "Religion," "development," and "peacebuilding" are contested terms that admit of multiple meanings. Peacebuilding and development are decades rather than centuries old, but religion, adaptive to its late modern globalizing environment, is no less fluid in meaning and expression. All three are "professions" in the classical sense and all three, under the pressure of secular modernity, have been undergoing a kind of rationalization and bureaucratization—a forced-march "professionalization" that has disaggregated and sometimes confused ritual, service, and social ethic. The designation "religious actors," for example, serves as a billowy canopy overarching disparate lay, clerical, religious, and monastic ranks; local and regional communities of practice; transnational networks and institutions; and "faith-based organizations" (FBOs). "Peacebuilding," itself a neologism, attempts to convey the potentially awkward marriage of the technical, the political, and the spiritual. In a volume filled with definitions and interpretations of both religion and peacebuilding, however, the changing conception of "development" deserves special attention here.

A recently published survey of the field defines development as "the process by which the people and states outside the industrial world attempt to improve their conditions of life, through material and social means."[2] The reference to "the industrial world" is quaint, for development is no longer portrayed as synonymous with modernization—that is, with industrialization accompanied by economic and organizational efficiency, bureaucratization, rational decision-making, and the fundamental alteration of premodern social and cultural patterns. The postindustrial shift to service economies; the shadow of doubt cast on mechanistic, techno-scientific rationalism by its failure to eradicate or even significantly diminish poverty; the reduced levels of aid triggered by the economic crisis of 2008 and beyond—these and other dilemmas of secular, top-down developmentalism have turned previous assumptions on their head. Echoing other critics of Western-led development, Damien Kingsbury laments "the commodity producing and subsistence economics of most of the world's states, in which wages are low, employment conditions usually bad and unregulated." Such countries, he notes, also often lack technical and organizational capacity and have limited access to resources. "There has been a trickle down of technology to developing countries, [where] health conditions remain poor, medical support is limited or unaffordable, literacy is at marginal levels, and opportunities for personal growth are virtually non-existent."[3]

Decades of encounter between developed and underdeveloped societies have had a leveling effect. Previously resisted by state, intergovernmental, and nongovernmental agencies alike, the idea that the recipients of humanitarian aid might possess wisdom of their own regarding the meaning and means of human flourishing is now increasingly plausible. No longer openly countenanced is the tendency to read "local culture" as a code for "uneducated," "benighted," and "anti-modern." Writing in July 2010, James D. Wolfensohn, president of the World Bank from 1995 to 2005, acknowledged that "[the major development institutions] need to be guided by a more comprehensive and more complex view of societies" and become more keenly aware that "economic policy and management of public institutions are always embedded in an environment that is shaped by the societies themselves, and especially their history and culture." He pointed to "non-economic factors that affect the quality of life in developing countries," such as governance, the regulation of markets, management of the natural environment, and attention "to both inherited and living culture."[4] In this respect Wolfensohn was echoing what has become the conventional wisdom in secular circles, namely, that development "is a multidimensional and, by definition, interdisciplinary field in which economic, political, technological, social and cultural factors interact."[5]

Indeed, the category "development" has expanded to include a host of practices that overlap, replicate, and coincide with some of the practices of peacebuilders as well as religious actors. (Whether development experts are aware of, much less acknowledge, the path blazed by these potential collaborators is another matter altogether.) Development in practice is constituted today by a broad range of priorities, notes John A. Rees, "from crisis relief to long-term reconstruction, from environmental sustainability to gender empowerment, from good governance at the international level to community consultation at the local level, and many others."[6] Influential secular thinkers who disagree on the details have nonetheless recognized the fundamental need to embed the discourse of development within a richer anthropological and philosophical vision of human flourishing, whether development's proper goal is cast as "enhancing human freedom," or as "creating human capabilities."[7] Even more recently, "integral development" has come into use—a term with strong resonances to the Roman Catholic concept of "integral human development."[8]

Paying Attention to Religion

While this constitutes progress of a sort, spiritual and religious dimensions of human flourishing remain neglected in secular versions of "integral development." Attitudes toward religion (uncloaked by the anodyne term "culture") are still evolving. Wolfensohn himself recognized the need to bring religion, per se, to the attention of development experts:

> In exploring these broader dimensions of the development environment, it struck me forcibly that religion was a pervasive force in many of the World Bank's client countries. . . Religion has an effect on many peoples' attitudes to everything, including such matters as savings, investment and a host of economic decisions. It influences areas we had come to see as vital for successful development, like schooling, gender equality, and approaches to health care. In short, religion could be an important driver of change, even as it could be a brake to progress. . . . I came to realize how far religious ideas and attitudes that are linked to them underpin vital facets of societies like social trust and cohesion. If development is to succeed, development policies must truly be integral in scope. Religion, therefore, cannot be excluded from the debate.[9]

Despite such exhortations, quite a few development theorists continue to think of religion as an obstacle to progress, "inasmuch as they suppose religion to stand in the way of a rational view of the world and thus to hamper material progress, or they see religion as a medium sustaining embedded cultural attributes inimical to development," writes Gerrie ter Haar.[10] Expertise in local or regional religious histories, practices, and institutions has not been integrated into development planning. When development actors do engage religion, ter Haar notes, they focus primarily on the organizational aspect of religion—religious institutions—that development workers often regard as particularly useful for service delivery. Yet the religious ideas inspiring these institutions and the religious practices shaping communal life tend to be overlooked.

The nexus between religion and development is best understood, perhaps, as a manifestation of the co-constitutive nature of the religious and the secular. Among a handful of theoretically informed development experts, there is an appreciation of the ways in which what we refer to as religion encompasses and orders both the sacred and the secular (the profane) within it.[11] This awareness, in turn, has given rise to attempts to map the convergences between religion and development, as well as the centrifugal patterns pushing them apart.

Deploying a "dynamics of religion model," for example, John Rees charts the relationships between the respective *orthodox* (i.e., mainstream, secular) and *critical* approaches to development, on the one hand, and three modes of religion—secular religion, integrated religion, and sacral religion—on the other. The *secular* elements of religion, according to this typology, display the subordination of religious actors and interests to other structures, such as the state, and to other priorities, such as the imperatives of markets and political ideologies. By contrast the *sacral* elements of religion display the primacy of spiritual and "otherworldly" actors and interests; this dimension of religion poses formidable if not always insuperable obstacles to collaboration with secular development actors.

The mean is what Rees terms *integrated religion*, which displays a balance of secular and sacral interests and dynamics. From an orthodox development perspective, he writes, integrated religion is generally welcomed as an agent in the turn to "authenticity," with religions collaborating in capitalist development; whereas from a critical perspective on development, integrated religion is celebrated when it produces religiously inspired or inflected social movements of resistance to the pernicious aspects of the capitalist development agenda, and when it generates theologies of liberation that share basic assumptions held by critics of development. Among the virtues of Rees's analytical model is the play it gives to the internal diversity and plurality of actors and interests within a local religious community, not to mention within the host religious tradition in its historical and transnational presences and modes.[12]

In *Sacred Aid*, their seminal study of faith and humanitarian relief agencies, editors Michael Barnett and Janice Gross Stein, as well as most of the other contributors, rely on a more conventional separation of the religious, which they identify more consistently with the otherworldly or sacred, and the secular, which they identify more consistently with the profane or mundane.[13] Nonetheless they call attention repeatedly to the co-imbrication and mutual constitution of the religious and the secular, from the time of the establishment of organized humanitarian assistance in the early nineteenth century to the present.[14] The formula "no religion, no humanitarianism" sums up the origins and early development of their subject. The close relationship between religious agency and humanitarian aid reached its peak during the era of the world wars; the interwar period, in particular, saw religious missionaries becoming heavily involved in the campaign to establish international human rights conventions and otherwise promote a national and international commitment to vulnerable foreign populations. A shift to state and other funders and agents of secular relief (e.g., nongovernmental organizations like CARE) occurred after the Second World War; faith-based organizations such as Catholic Relief Services (CRS) and World Vision adapted to the new climate by downplaying their religious identity. Up through the 1980s, secular agencies proliferated and budgets grew. In the 1990s, however, Christian relief agencies, especially those run by evangelical Christians, began a sustained expansion, as did the American Jewish World Service and some Islamic aid organizations. (Islamic Relief, one of the most prominent, was founded in England in 1984.)[15]

In narrating these developments, Barnett and Stein speak of the simultaneous secularization *and* sanctification of humanitarianism, with secularism evident in the growing role of states and commercial enterprises, and in the fundraising, bureaucratization, and empirical metrics associated with professionalism. By contrast, sanctification is manifest in an insistence on a "space apart," a zone of activism informed by an ethos of altruism unsullied by political and financial calculations—a world in which values and ethics trump interests and instruments. "Secularization and sanctification are enduring aspects of humanitarianism, evolving in historically dynamic ways, shaping its trends, practices, and tensions," Barnett and Stein conclude.[16]

To his credit Rees avoids this sharp dichotomy between the sacred and the secular, creating a model that captures something of the complexity of the ongoing negotiations within and between so-called faith-based and secular organizations. When it adapted to the new professional standards imposed by the state and by privately funded aid agencies in the postwar era, was Catholic Relief Services becoming a "secular" relief and development organization? While some of their critics, enamored of a dualistic approach to "religion and the world," hurled this accusation at CRS, it is more accurate to invoke Rees's "integrated religion" mode in analyzing the evolution of CRS as a government-funded agency, but one which resisted certain government mandates, accommodated others, and continued to apply the principles of Roman Catholic social teaching in their choice of sites and clients, and in their methods of envisioning and delivering aid. Similar adaptations have characterized the evolution of World Vision, MercyCorps, and other Christian relief and development organizations.[17]

Islamic agencies are not immune from these internal negotiations and adaptations. As it has grown and gained recognition, Islamic Relief has adopted secular development discourse and demonstrated its conformity to norms of the international aid system such as neutrality, impartiality, and nondiscrimination. For example, Islamic Relief has declared its commitment to meeting the Millennium Development Goals. It shares platforms with Christian and secular NGOs, and touts its policy of working with local communities "regardless of race, color, political affiliations, gender or belief." Ajaz Ahmed Khan notes that Islamic Relief finds it necessary to be "bilingual." In order to stay true to its founding vision and mission, and to appeal to its conservative Muslim donors, the organization must underscore the unique qualities and contributions of Islam to human development. At the same time, it has to project a secularized mode of Islam, one that conforms in significant respects to "mainstream" Western practices, procedures, and values—some of which may be regarded as inimical to Islam. Khan reports that some of the organization's members question whether it is even possible to develop an "Islamic approach to development."[18]

Notwithstanding the ideological motivations of some of their internal critics, these religiously inspired relief and development organizations are shaping worldwide development practices and policies as well as being shaped by them. The comparative advantages they bring to the field of development include closer proximity and greater access to religious actors on the ground, who are already, as part of their ordinary ongoing mission, providing essential "relief and development"–type services to local and hard-to-reach populations. The secular development organizations are "catching up," however. In 2013 the scholarly literature, as well as policy guidelines adopted by both secular and faith-based development organizations, reflected a broad consensus regarding the inevitability and indeed the desirability of interacting regularly with religious agents of development.[19]

Barnett and Stein themselves soften the dichotomy between the sacred and the secular by speaking of "processes" of sanctification and of secularization—processes which are "messy" in that they entail constant trespassing and policing, encounters through which both sacred and secular forms change as they engage the other. The acknowledgment that these sacred and secular forms can be contained within any given faith-based or secular governmental or nongovernmental agency does not in itself obscure the fact that secularism and sacralism are not merely processes but also strategies used by religious and secular elites to advance their agendas and restrain the authority of their counterparts.[20] In this respect we observe yet again the fluidity of religious as well as secular boundaries, and the adulterated character of religious and secular motivations.

Paying Attention to Peacebuilding

If development practitioners must not overlook religion, the new thinking continues, neither must they ignore the dynamics of twenty-first century war and peace. On this score the evolution of development is comparable to its incorporation of religious and spiritual dimensions and partners. That is to say: the experts are increasingly aware of the various unintended consequences of development programs, both in terms of igniting or deepening conflict and in terms of hindering (and sometimes advancing) peacebuilding efforts. But they are still discovering the ways peacebuilding and development projects could be constructively integrated. Many remain cautious of carrying the collaboration too far: we are not trained to resolve conflicts, they reasonably respond. For their part, peacebuilders are grateful when development projects do not *trigger* violent conflicts.

The peoples and governments of most developed countries, in addition to acknowledging their postcolonial responsibilities to the "liberated" and poorer countries, have long recognized that building local economies and creating international markets is in their own economic self-interest. But in an era of non-state combatants and resource wars, they are now more keenly attuned to the relationship between development and conflict. The seeds of awareness of this relationship were sown during the Cold War, when the two major ideological blocs used aid as a guarantor of loyalty and tool of control. As the Cold War ended and the arena of violent conflict shifted to local communities and regions, international humanitarian relief and development agencies began to consider the dynamics of violent conflict as they were affected, for good and ill, by major development programs. Peacebuilders concerned with sustaining "a negative peace"—the minimal material, social, and political conditions necessary for the cessation or reduction of organized armed violence—pleaded with development actors to "do no harm."[21]

Gradually there emerged among development practitioners a sensitivity to the myriad ways in which an epistemologically and culturally narrow development project might exacerbate existing tensions between ethnic, religious, and local economic sectors of society. Which subgroup benefits from the external intervention, and which subgroups are left out, resentful of the implicit or explicit favoritism? How might development planning and implementation reflect a more sophisticated understanding and appreciation of local and regional political and cultural dynamics? Careful consideration of these questions seemed essential amid the escalation of intra-state, territorial, ethnic, and religious tensions, as well as the rise of the virulent anti-Western, anti-secular, global jihadist ideology.[22]

The need to address the correlation between poverty, underdevelopment, and conflict also took on a new urgency. Gradually development theorists made the turn to studying the conditions for "positive peace"—a state of affairs characterized by the presence of the economic, cultural, political, and social requirements for sustained human flourishing and the nonviolent resolution of conflict. In 2001 Marc Lindenberg and Coralie Bryant, in their study of the globalization of NGOs dedicated to relief and development, penned a pioneering chapter entitled "Building Positive Peace: Reducing Poverty and Social Exclusion." Acknowledging that poverty reduction remained the stated goal of most such NGOs, and citing the World Bank's *World Development Report 2000: Attacking Poverty*, the authors argued that the persistence of poverty can be understood only within the context of growing global inequalities and "social exclusion," protracted conflict and civil wars, the resulting creation of refugees and internally displaced persons (IDPs), failed states, epidemics, and environmental crises.[23] Drawing on seminal works by Mary Anderson (*Do No Harm*), Amartya Sen (*Development as Freedom*), Peter Uvin (*Aiding Violence*), and peace scholar Johan Galtung, Lindenberg and Bryant argued that the development community, by its refusal to recognize the relationship between political violence, structural violence, and global poverty, and adjust its policies accordingly, was complicit in the suffering of hundreds of millions of people.[24] They quoted Anderson approvingly:

> When international aid agencies arrive in conflict zones to provide assistance to people affected by war, their programs often miss the local capacities for peacebuilding. They design programs, make decisions, distribute goods, employ and deploy staff in ways that ignore, and negate other realities—those on which past peace rested and future peace could be built. What additional good could be done by assistance that is provided in conflict areas if, while emergency needs were being met, local capacities for peace were also recognized, supported, encouraged and enlarged.[25]

In dozens of conflict settings around the world, religious actors constitute Anderson's "local capacities for peace." Dedicated to working with poor, ill, and marginalized groups and individuals, religious actors often serve (and belong to) populations remote from the cities and larger towns and villages. They excel in grassroots initiatives addressing peace-related issues ranging from disaster relief and health care delivery to education and conflict mediation. Religious leaders also enjoy a "vertical reach" to higher levels of politics and society by virtue of the networks and hierarchies to which they belong. And, as Ashutosh Varshney demonstrated in his study of Hindus and Muslims in India, religiously and ethnically integrated organizations, including business, trade, and other associations, are effective means for building ties across ethnically and religiously divided groups, even leading to "an institutionalized peace system."[26]

CONVERGENCES

Perhaps it should not be surprising, then, that after decades of self-imposed secular myopia, the fields of humanitarian aid and development are finally adjusting to a putatively inconvenient truth: religious actors, despite stubborn predictions to the contrary, continue to play pervasive instrumental roles among the populations served by the aid agencies and development organizations. The rapid rise and continued growth of FBOs is one marker of the new professional landscape, as is the hiring and promotion of religiously and culturally literate development staff. Lagging behind is the integration of insights from the literature on religion and grassroots peacebuilding into development texts, manuals, and protocols. The competitiveness of FBOs nonetheless constitutes a trend toward what Rees calls "an integrated religious presence" in the field of development.[27]

The acceptance of religion as an enduring force in underdeveloped societies is also reshaping the field of peacebuilding itself. Other chapters in this volume amplify the critique of the constraining secularist assumptions of the model for development predicated on "the liberal peace" and explore the tension between what has been called "liberal peacebuilding" and an alternative method and conceptualization known as "strategic peacebuilding."[28] The former, as mentioned, has tended to be almost exclusively secular, Western, bureaucratic, ends-driven, materialist, and top-down; powered by wealthy nation-states and the international community; and driven by humanitarian concerns, certainly, but also by enlightened state self-interest regarding security, markets, and the preservation of order. According to the advocates of the so-called liberal peace, the measure of peace is the regulation of armed conflict or its reduction ("negative peace") and the securing of trade and other economic relations among states. The "development" of societies is conceived in largely material and economic terms.

It is important to recognize that the most sophisticated advocates of the liberal peace do not deny the importance and desirability of moving beyond these basic economic interests and security issues in order to address concerns of justice, human rights, and integral human development. But they continue to imagine the realization of these goods as sequential rather than concurrent. Achieving a sustainable peace in most longstanding "hot conflict" settings is particularly implausible, for such a state of affairs is dependent upon the prior restoration of order and law, the application of which defends and perpetuates familiar structures of power and resource allocation.

This volume offers a corrective to the model of liberal peace by challenging the assumption that a negative peace must precede efforts to create a more just social order. The correction is derived from a model of peacebuilding that insists on the priority of peace with justice (a "justpeace") and which offers concrete strategies for building the kind of robust multiethnic, multi-religious, cross-generational relationships and partnerships capable of transforming conflict, over the long term, toward a condition of justpeace. Peacebuilding that is relational, comprehensive, and strategic in this way cannot and does not wait upon the cessation of violent conflict, the restoration of order, or a return to "normalcy"; rather, it challenges the very desirability of a return to the pre-violence status quo or some facsimile thereof, and it sees the just (and therefore more effective) provision of "law and order" as possible only alongside and concurrent with the striving toward "positive peace."

In making room for religion qua religion, strategic peacebuilding expands the horizon of possibilities for constructive partnership beyond the secular confines of the liberal peace. If not entirely liberated from the weight of secular, liberal frames and expectations in every case, religious actors have nonetheless begun to make a mark in peacebuilding. Several chapters in this volume explore the dynamics of religious or faith-based peacebuilding.[29] And now development experts have also come to realize that religious actors are often the key that unlocks the dynamics and meanings of local culture.

The rules of engagement governing interaction between "experts" and "locals" have evolved accordingly. Indeed, development experts and peacebuilding practitioners have much to learn from one another regarding effective methods of collaboration with local actors, including religious actors. For example, religious insiders—actors native to the country or region under development—were systematically excluded from consultation in the not too distant past. Now, however, nongovernmental development organizations (NDGOs) and humanitarian international nongovernmental organizations (INGOs) interact with the religious insiders, whom they invite to become partners in the field.[30]

As we look to the future, I perceive three emerging points of convergence between the liberal and strategic peacebuilding models at the nexus between religion and development.

The Priority of the Local, and the Elicitive Method

Basic human needs are universal, but the means of meeting them and the way in which they are understood to contribute to human flourishing are particular to a specific time and place. This seemingly unobjectionable observation stands in considerable tension with a purely prescriptive approach to development (or to peacebuilding), that is, an approach that depends heavily on the knowledge and skill sets of experts and minimally on the knowledge and practices of the recipients of aid and development projects. Informing the prescriptive approach is the assumption that the transfer of knowledge, techniques, skills, and models of development moves in one direction, from expert to participant. In its most naive form, the prescriptive approach embraces an uncritical view of the universality of technology and deems it a "neutral" tool, thereby ignoring the ways in which every model bears its own cultural and ideological presuppositions. Based on the premises of transferability and universality, the prescriptive approach offers concrete "solutions" and, under ideal conditions, promotes new ways of thinking in local settings and thus empowers local actors to participate in the development of their own society—to learn to fish in their own ponds.[31]

Associated with modernization theory, the prescriptive approach did not rule out participation by receiving populations; indeed, "participation," of a sort, became the new orthodoxy during the height of the influence of modernization theory after World War II. The early institutionalized forms of participation were community development programs, wherein villagers in India and other developing countries were mobilized to increase agricultural output and improve rural infrastructure through self-help efforts, and cooperatives, in which the collective management and ownership of small businesses was intended to socialize rural populations into the economic and civic patterns seen as constitutive of liberal democracy. While these forms of participatory development achieved some success, too often they were undermined by mismanagement and political manipulation by local and regional elites.[32] Reflection on the nature, purpose, and limits of these forms of participation led to innovative responses from Brazilian educator and philosopher Paulo Freire, whose influential book *Pedagogy of the Oppressed* (1968) presented a method of "conscientization" by which landless and powerless peasants might take political action to confront the economic and political structures that exploited them; and from the founders of *comunidades eclesiales de bases* (basic Christian communities), which mushroomed in number in Latin America during the 1970s and 1980s. Such efforts to radicalize the meaning and practice of "participation" prefigured the appeal and potential of religious actors on the democratization and development horizon. The BCCs, for example, were small groups of poor people who came together to "combine consciousness-raising, bible-study, worship, mutual help and political action in defense of their rights."[33] Other alternatives to a "pure" prescriptive approach emerged in the late 1970s, including a technique known as PRA (participatory rural appraisal). PRA developed from a method of participatory enquiry involving semi-structured interviews and decision-making processes designed to allow poor people to define what sort of development they wanted, and to become empowered through its methods.[34]

During the 1980s, such experiments won the endorsement of international financial institutions and the United Nations, as development experts grew increasingly frustrated with the corrupt practices of aid-receiving governments and the inefficient or politically manipulated distribution of resources to the intended target populations. This endorsement coincided with a renewed emphasis on the building of social capital and civil society as essential ingredients of democratization and economic development. All of this helped to stimulate the explosion of a new wave of NGOs, which were seen as organizationally nimble, relatively transparent and honest, responsive, skilled, and participatory: from 1970 to 2000, the amount of development funding spent by international NGOs nearly quadrupled, from $3.64 billion to $12.4 billion.[35]

Not long after participatory processes had been absorbed into the mainstream of development practice, however, it attracted a cohort of critics alert to the strong link between the distribution of power and the establishment and maintenance of structures of inequality and poverty. Drawing on postmodernist suspicions of grand narratives of linear progress, and feminist and environmentalist critiques of the exclusionary tendencies of neoliberal policies and policymakers, this array of academics and former practitioners noted that "participation" in practice often meant consultation for the purpose of providing and receiving information, rather than the support of community initiatives for collective discernment and action. By this account, development workers' grasp of local and indigenous cultures was shallow and their images and understandings of the people's values, desires, and needs simplistic. From practitioners of the PRA came a declaration of the importance of a "self-critical epistemological awareness" on the part of development practitioners. Concluding that the development enterprise itself was hopelessly dependent upon discredited aspects and assumptions of modernization theory, the most radical critics began in the late 1980s to construct an analysis from the perspective of subaltern peoples, leading to what Uma Kothari has called a "methodological revisionism that enables a wholesale critique of Western structures of knowledge and power." The advocates of this "postdevelopment" approach call for an end to neoliberal designs on the so-called underdeveloped world.[36]

An equally radical but more constructive approach, based in part on the critical pedagogical method of Freire, emerged around the same time in the writing of the Mennonite peacebuilder John Paul Lederach (see Chapter 21 in this volume).[37] Unlike the prescriptive approach, with its heavy dependence on external actors and expertise, the "elicitive model" places emphasis "not only on empowerment as participating in creating models, but also in seeking resource and root in the cultural context itself."[38] Originally formulated as a method for training practitioners of conflict resolution, the elicitive model is easily adapted to development practice. Its constitutive activities include the move from implicit to explicit knowledge through *discovery* and *naming* (what do we value as central to human security and human flourishing? how do we hope to realize these values?); the process of critical self-reflection or *evaluation and adaptation* (what do we do that helps us achieve our values? what gets in the way? what do we lack? what needs to be changed, and how do we change?); and the testing of the emergent model through *practical application* (do the new behaviors and practices move us closer to the goal of realizing our values?). The elicitive approach does not overlook the need of local actors to master new techniques, including those offered by outsiders; Lederach and Freire recognize that cross-cultural exchanges are invaluable means by which a people learn and move beyond their current practices. But the elicitive method sets their ambitions higher. By building on and critically assessing "local knowledge," and by disembedding and articulating previously unexamined communal values, it aims to deepen and transform the participation of local actors in the development (or peacebuilding) process.[39] "Participants' natural knowledge, their way of being and doing, their immediate situation, their past heritage, and their language are seen as the seedbed" in which the new development techniques will be planted and take root.[40]

The elicitive method has expanded over the past two decades, becoming a staple of what Wolfgang Dietrich calls "the transrational shift in peace politics."[41] In the field of development, it is available to theorists and practitioners alike, alongside another closely related and not yet fully integrated tradition closer to home, namely, development ethics. Together, the elicitive method of conflict transformation and the ethics of global development establish the priorities for development, which in turn dictate the rules of engagement at the nexus of religion, development, and peacebuilding.

Deriving Markers of Authentic Development

Who is to say what constitutes "authentic human development"? Could such a formulation ever be non-reductive? Denis Goulet, a pioneer in development ethics, responded to this implied accusation of neo-imperialism with an attempt to balance the local and the universal, the contingent and the irreducibly human. Any external intervention would fail and produce unintended consequences, he argued, if it was not preceded by careful study of the demography of the setting, the patterns of corruption, the potential for disarmament, the dynamics of an economy of needs, the optimal levels of national sovereignty, and—not least—the local aesthetic and spiritual resources for conflict transformation.[42] In this way savvy development and peacebuilding professionals would become the agents of "integration"—the *orchestrated* "convergences" of internal and external actors, resources, and expertise.

Goulet proposed the integrative method as a means of crafting a value-laden, ethically precise, locally resonant development discourse. Thus, he set developmental ethicists the task of serving as the mediator between the worlds of religion, spirituality, and culture; the technical expertise of the engineer, demographer, and agronomist; and the social scientific acumen of the economist, political scientist, and psychologist. In order to bridge these various professional practices and discourses, each of which must contribute to what Goulet called "culturally authentic" human development, the developmental ethicist must be a polymath of sorts.[43] In that respect the "integrative" development ethicist plays a role analogous to that of the peacebuilder who acts and thinks strategically.

Goulet's approach to development emerged from his reading of secular as well as religious philosophy and his discernment of what Roman Catholic activists of his generation, citing the Second Vatican Council, were calling "the signs of the times." In 1976, nine years after Pope Paul VI had issued the clarion call of religion, peace, and development, *Populorum Progressio*, but well before the rhetoric of globalization penetrated popular consciousness, he insisted that global human solidarity had become a moral necessity. To be human in our globalized economy, he wrote, is to observe the distinction between "having" and "being." If people are beholden solely to macroeconomic forces beyond their control, they are reduced to mere buyers, defined by their "needs" as construed according to the metrics of the market. This reduction of the human to a narrow category of needs and desires, specified in an ever-expanding, morally colonizing content, stifles any kind of aspiration beyond the strictly material. Such distortion of the capacity and meaning of human life grips the populations of developed as well underdeveloped nations, Goulet contended. The less materially affluent nations are defined by the standards of the richer ones; their value is measured solely in terms of the production and consumption that generate material wealth—or what passes for material wealth—in the system. Exacerbating the distortion of the meaning of the human person is the Western exaltation of the individual, conceptualized as an autonomous moral agent operating in an atomized society. From Roman Catholic social doctrine, Goulet understood the community, not the individual, to be the basic unit of society: from birth to death, the person is enmeshed in a network of relationships—conceived "in community," nurtured in another's womb, born into a family, and fundamentally dependent or interdependent throughout life. "Solidarity" is the fundamental existential and ontological condition[44]:

> All countries have the duty to work with prudence and realism, but also with imagination, discipline, and sacrifice, to tend in the direction of laws, structures, and networks of relationships which come ever closer to the requirements of global solidarity, of the active respect of persons, and of the establishment of political and economic regimes suited to meeting all human needs—needs of the body and spirit [which include] all human registers: spiritual, intellectual, artistic, social, familial, personal, psychological, and biological. [45]

Although these words were written in 1960, they were echoed and amplified almost verbatim by Pope Francis in 2013.[46]

A corollary of Goulet's view of authentic development is the re-conceptualization of agency. Who are the appropriate agents of authentic human development? What is the nature of their agency? According to Goulet's synthesis of religious and secular ethical traditions, human beings, valued as subjects, are called actively to participate in the formation and direction of their lives. "Called to" indicates that they are oriented by their nature to the task of self-expression and self-fulfillment through the exercise of free will and moral agency. Accordingly, the development expert must consider first and foremost people's needs, desires, and aspirations in the full sense described above. If people are subjects and masters of their own destiny, if they are the agents of change in the first instance, then they are the ones who must decide what changes are needed, and they are the ones who must design the methods and means to achieve the goals they establish.[47] Goulet's imperative challenged the cult of technical expertise of his day, which, many have argued, has led time and again to serious errors in development policy and methods, sometimes producing ecologically and culturally devastating consequences.[48]

Conventional markers of development based exclusively on the cult of technical expertise are therefore ethically deficient. The growth paradigm of development, Goulet notes, assigns the highest priority to increasing aggregate gross national product, with little regard for the equity in the distribution of its fruits. That same paradigm also emphasizes planning from the top down, and stimulates resource transfers from foreign sources in ways that weaken local and national self-reliance and perpetuate relationships of dependency. This approach also leads to undue destruction of cultural values, because it is uncritically biased in favor of techno-scientific modernity, which it treats in every important respect as superior to tradition. Moreover, "by concentrating on aggregate gains in industrial output, export trade and financial earnings, growth oriented strategies prove both wasteful of resources and environmentally destructive."[49]

Authentic sustainable development, by contrast, depends on a new definition of human wealth. Goulet found it "more accurate" to assign only instrumental value to economic riches. True human wealth consists in other, qualitative kinds of goods—public goods that are available to all, and whose production creates "right livelihoods" for all. He considered this shift indispensable for new thinking about what constitutes culturally resonant, ethically correct development. No less than "a new mode of living" based in "genuine human solidarity" is required. If finite resources are to be distributed in a way consistent with justice, society must embrace a life of "austerity," limitation, and discipline.[50]

Implied in this idealistic and humanistic proposal was a radical reorientation of values and priorities. The creation of wealth should lead to improved material conditions for all sectors of society, measured as well-being in health, education, housing, and employment. The political corollary to this form of economic distributism, Goulet wrote, would valorize and uphold "human rights, political freedom, legal enfranchisement of persons, and some form of democracy." The dynamic of development along these lines, furthermore, must be sustainable (based on strategies to replenish consumed resources), ecologically sound, and culturally resonant. To instantiate the culture's deepest values, development must strive for the social realization of a "full-life paradigm," that is, for a society whose goods and practices reflect what the people hold to be "the ultimate meaning of life and history."[51]

In this section I have focused on the work of one thinker, Denis Goulet, in part because while he addressed largely a secular audience of ethicists and development theorists, he drew heavily on a specific religious tradition. Nonetheless, like-minded non-Catholic and nonreligious economists and philosophers of development influenced Goulet and were influenced by him; many elements of his thought are found in their writings. Specifically, the broad themes and arguments sketched above can be found, mutatis mutandis, in the writings of, inter alia, Amartya Sen,[52] Herman Daly,[53] Paul Ekins,[54] and the aforementioned Martha Nussbaum. Goulet's basic analysis has also been applied rigorously in various faith-based and religious critiques of globalization.[55]

Rules of Engagement

From the writings of these economists, philosophers, and ethicists, one can derive rules of engagement with local communities and local actors; strikingly, similar "rules" are also found in the handbook of the strategic peacebuilder.[56]

The consensus revolves around four deceptively simple rules:

1. *The people most directly affected by proposed development programs or peace processes must participate extensively in planning them and carrying them out.* Sen, Kothari, Nussbaum, and other scholars consider elitism in its various manifestations the most daunting obstacle to effective development and sustainable peace. Too often, development practitioners and local elites (religious as well as secular) exclude the people to be affected from decisions regarding the goals of development, tolerable costs, who should bear the burden, and who should enjoy the benefits. Failing to incorporate the perspective of the people will almost certainly lead to bad decisions and unjust programs.[57]

Yet *how* are "the people" to participate "extensively" in the processes and planning? To be avoided is "passive participation," cases in which an elite tells a non-elite what it has done or plans to do, and the people listen or ask questions, but have little impact on the process. Only slightly less ineffective is "participation [merely] through information-giving," by which non-elites provide elites with information or opinions, but the elites themselves do not interact with the people. Slightly higher on the scale is "participation by consultation," by which non-elites give their proposals and perhaps deliberate the issues with the elites—but the decision is still fully in the hands of the elites. Similarly, "participatory implementation" is a process that enables elites to determine the goals and means, while non-elites implement the goals, and make decisions only about tactics. The optimal mode of collaboration, of course, is deliberative participation, by which non-elites and sometimes elites deliberate together and make decisions.[58]

A second and closely related rule of engagement:

2. *Be as inclusive as possible in eliciting values, concerns, insights, and interests, paying special attention to marginalized and aggrieved groups.* On too many occasions, development professionals in particular have been known to violate the coherence of the local worldview by ignoring certain central elements of it, especially the elements that do not conform to, or that openly challenge, Western values and priorities. Here the fields of development and conflict prevention overlap significantly. The perception that outsiders are setting aside or supplanting traditional and cultural values can lead to counterproductive and sometimes literally deadly results. Backlash can occur in several disparate psychological and social settings: when clumsy or imperious development projects ignite long-standing popular grievances against local elites; when a development project (or peace negotiation) privileges one tribe or sect over others; when development workers, peacebuilders, health care providers, and other external actors compete with one another, inadvertently or directly, for local support and affiliation.[59]

While the first two rules of engagement lean heavily in the direction of local priorities and values, the external actors must not remain passive or fail to contribute alternative views where possible and desirable for the overall goal of elicitive development or peacebuilding. Thus:

3. *Provide space for conflict among divergent values and support for accommodations, by insiders and outsiders alike.* Peacebuilding professionals have had some success in eliciting new practices that do not destroy traditional sites, customs, and practices, but preserve their meaning while advancing technical development goals. To support traditional values in this way demonstrates a basic trust in the people to "improve their lives, to understand the social forces that affect them, and eventually to harness these forces to processes of genuine human and societal development."[60]

Finally, development experts and peacebuilders alike must balance the interests of the state and local governments, on the one hand, and private citizens and local actors, on the other. The latter "constituency" often feels, with justification, that the state holds all the cards and seeks nothing but top-down control of the process from start to finish. Local elites may fear that supporting traditional values will produce negative reactions by governments that seek "development" at any cost. Accordingly:

4. *Practice transparency in engaging local elites, religious actors, and state officials at every stage of the planning and implementation process.* Practicing transparency and open communication across various sectors and levels of society will not in itself resolve the inevitable

conflicts, but it has been proven to be a strong measure for reducing mistrust and preventing the exacerbation of differences.[61]

INTEGRATING RELIGIOUS ACTORS:
THE EVIDENCE THUS FAR

While multilevel political conflict is a realistic possibility in many settings, local religious and cultural leaders might play a role in neutralizing it. Indeed, religious actors are potential allies in regularizing the rules of engagement discussed above. Judith Mayotte, surveying the intersection of religion and development, notes that religious groups have important qualities that "lead the development community in new directions." Not least, their core values "often transcend the social, political and economic issues of a community," making religious actors invaluable mediators between state and local interests. Owing to the fact that "religion is transformational, not simply transitional," she continues, "[w]hen religion informs social change, the effects of development transcend the physical and material by reaching what is important to people. The community is encouraged to base development choices on its deeper, broader values." [62] Indeed, religious values are sometimes the only thread connecting elite and lower-class people of a society. Mayotte's argument is underscored by the fact that development projects unfold not only in war-torn societies but also in communities attempting to transition from violence to negative peace. In such settings, religious actors have been critical (even if secondary) players in reconciliation and transitional justice efforts.[63]

The potential *negative* impact of religious activism in development contexts is also considerable, however. Religious groups bent on conversion—and on using development as leverage for proselytism—can complicate efforts to provide comprehensive development, to say the least.

Moreover, religious visions of "authentic human development" often clash with one another and with secular human rights standards. Powerful elements within Islam and Christianity, for example, diverge from the liberal consensus on women's rights, reproductive practices, scientific research, and other matters touching the hierarchy of human values. A system of transcendent meaning, such as Islam or Christianity, Goulet himself warned, can be "a powerful developmental force... but also suspicious and subversive of global order, and not necessarily in a constructive or creative way."[64]

The theologian Gregory Baum notes that religious groups, including indigenous ones, are equally suspicious of secular, liberal actors.[65] They recognize in the offer of "partnership" threats to religion itself: how, for example, will activism in public affairs change the nature of worshipping communities? Development experts will find important lessons in the documented cases of religious peacebuilding, which demonstrate not only the many benefits to the religious community of active participation in peace processes, but also the risks for religious communities when activism in public affairs divides the observant, or when religiously motivated activists who receive adequate professional training in complex socioeconomic and political issues become divorced from their religious base in the process.

Notwithstanding these genuine concerns, the record of religious involvement in peacebuilding is promising, if complicated. That is, when we narrow the field of religious actors to those religiously motivated or "faith-based" individuals, groups, and organizations who have joined or led efforts in conflict prevention, mediation, peace negotiations, trauma healing, political or social reconciliation, and other constitutive dimensions of peacebuilding, we find numerous well-documented cases of "positive" impact—religious agency that contributes to the nonviolent resolution of conflict, to the common good, and to the pursuit of a justpeace. On the other hand, religious and secular or liberal worldviews, values, and behaviors are not fully commensurate even in the best cases, and they diverge significantly in other circumstances. The manner in which high-profile religious leaders in Cambodia and South Africa responded to atrocities committed by the Khmer Rouge and the apartheid regime, respectively, is a case in point. The religious leaders' apparent willingness to prioritize forgiveness and reconciliation over imprisonment and other forms of retributive justice mandated by state law was a source of scandal in some secular—and religious—quarters.[66] In short, religious agency for peace is complex in motivation and impact, as critics as well as supporters of Desmond Tutu, Maha Ghosananda, or Menachem Froman, Sant'Egidio or the Islamic Society of North America would testify.

This volume is possible only because scholars and practitioners have been studying and writing about the complexities of "religious peacebuilding" systematically for two decades, dating back to the appearance of a seminal volume entitled *Religion: The Missing Dimension of Statecraft.*[67] By contrast the examination of the contours of religious agency in "development" is less than a decade old. Thanks to the work of a few pioneering scholars such as Gerrie ter Haar and Michael Barnett, and to the recent efforts of a team of researchers into global FBO operations, however, we are learning more about the dynamics of religious engagement in development. As with peacebuilding, which is often closely tied to development in the minds and actions of religious leaders, the motivations and impact of religious actors is sui generis. One of the catalysts of the global study of religion and development is Katherine Marshall, currently a senior fellow at Georgetown University's Berkley Center for Religion, Peace, and World Affairs and previously a senior advisor for the World Bank on issues of faith and development.[68] In her capacity as executive director of the World Faiths Development Dialogue (WFDD), Marshall led a team of researchers who, from 2006 to 2011, collected data about religious engagement in development and interviewed relevant religious (and secular) actors in several countries around the world. The research covered six different broadly defined world regions and eight development issues, produced twenty-eight background reviews, fourteen consultation events and corresponding meeting reports, and some two hundred formal interviews with development practitioners, religious leaders, and scholars.[69]

The researchers' findings confirmed the general themes of the extant literature on the strength of religious communities and faith-inspired organizations at the grassroots and country levels. Faith-inspired actors remain a visible core of local communities almost everywhere in Latin America, Africa, and Asia. Religious leaders are widely respected for their ability to influence and mobilize their "congregations" and to provide a stable social infrastructure for community development projects: "we were here long before the government or NGOs and will remain long after you are gone." The WFDD survey responses underscored the trust that communities have for faith leaders and their communities, which provide services in places where state and private-sector services are inadequate or absent. Yet Marshall and her colleagues remain uncertain how to build on these two related strengths of presence and trust, given the fact that the priorities and mandate of many faith

communities are sometimes in tension with or exclude important dimensions of development (from a secular perspective). Excluding the religious voices is folly, however, they conclude. The platform religious leaders enjoy for exhorting the community is the envy of those
working for behavioral change. Engaging the communication skills and genius of faith leaders has led to important successes in programs to combat HIV/AIDS and malaria, for example. On the other hand, religious leaders have been known to accentuate social practices that
undermine development progress, as, for example, when they reinforce stigmas against people living with HIV/AIDS or tuberculosis. On other occasions they have condoned or even
encouraged the marriage of young girls. The USAID "Leaders of Influence" program in Asia
is one attempt to educate and engage with religious leaders in deliberate efforts to change this
kind of social behavior.[70]

The WFDD reports also provide nuanced accounts of how and why religious and secular development actors differ in their understandings of what constitutes proselytization
and evangelization. Who has the authority to establish and monitor the proper boundaries between provision of services and resources, sharing of one's faith commitments, and
active prosyletism? While the question is hotly contested within and among faith communities themselves, secular development workers draw the line strictly at provision of services. Some of the religious actors interviewed by WFDD researchers argued that sharing
one's faith is "a right"—an exercise of religious freedom. Others, religious as well as secular, complain that any type of unsolicited faith-sharing can generate hostility toward all
faith-based organizations. Obviously, the situation of religious actors deteriorated rapidly
in the numerous reported cases of aggressive proselytizing, which were seen to threaten the
social standing or core beliefs of local individuals or groups. Any such insensitive behavior on the part of religious individuals or FBOs is seen as disrespectful of the culture and
social norms of local communities. In order to combat the stereotypes of the "imperious
Westerners," the larger and more visible FBOs have adopted international standards of best
practice (including Sphere standards and Geneva Convention norms), and they include
strong anti-proselytizing language in their organizational policy. At the same time, most
organizations distinguish between proselytizing, which is forbidden, and speaking about
personal and organizational motivations, which is permitted under certain circumstances.[71]

Finally, the WFDD reports underscore three areas in which religious actors have demonstrated special expertise and commitment. First, religions tend to invest in and provide
high-quality education at all levels (especially for males) by creating and sustaining schools,
colleges, seminaries, and universities whose faculty, programs, and facilities outshine their
local and regional competitors. In addition, many prestigious faith-based education institutions have specific mandates to reach the poor and underserved. Second, what the WFDD
calls "faith-inspired health services" leads the field of preventive and recuperative health
care. Religious actors staff many of these facilities; they tend to see the delivery of affordable
and reliable medical care as an integral dimension of their spiritual commitment.

Third, and relatedly, religious actors excel in the care of orphans and vulnerable children.
In the knowledge that the Prophet Muhammad was an orphan, Islam brings an especially
strong commitment to this work. Roman Catholics have long specialized in institution-based
care (orphanages and boarding schools). Other Christian and Jewish organizations specialize in community-based care systems (e.g., the granny care system in Swaziland), and
provide support for adoption and sponsorship programs. Indeed, all the major religious traditions express a clear calling to care for orphans. And yet, as in other areas where religions

have been traditionally active, their work is also a source of controversy. For example, some religious norms clash with liberal standards and international norms for the care of orphans, which have changed since the times when orphanages were generally the optimal or only available solution. And recent highly publicized cases of sexual abuse of minors by a tiny minority of Roman Catholic clergy and religious, although perpetrated at a percentage paralleling that of other religious and secular agencies, has done immeasurable damage to the reputation of that institution.[72]

The opportunities and pitfalls introduced into the development equation by religious actors are on display in the WFDD pilot project on Cambodia, where the vast majority of the population is Buddhist and where the sangha (community of monks) played a central role in the history of nation-building and governance. Buddhist leaders were intricately linked to the evolution of the monarchy and to the functioning of the economy, and the ethos and values of Buddhism are inseparable from what is seen as the Cambodian or Khmer identity. Buddhist teachings and rituals were and remain central features of daily life. Accordingly, Buddhism plays a major role in the direction and character of Cambodia's post-genocide development path and in forging the practical connections between development strategies and Buddhist values and organizations.[73] Several interviewees insisted that restoring Buddhism to its former strength, prior to the Khmer Rouge massacres of the 1970s that drastically depleted its ranks, is an essential element in developing Cambodia and building a peaceful society—not least because Buddhism remains the primary source of services and compassion for Cambodia's poorest citizens.

Despite the genocide and the targeted destruction of Buddhist structures by the Khmer Rouge, the Buddhist pagodas, or *wats* (numbering approximately four thousand), and the sangha (numbering between sixty and seventy thousand monks) remain ubiquitous presences in Cambodia. Pagodas have long served as community centers, especially in rural areas, and they continue to provide education and basic health care for orphans, widows, and the disabled. The pagoda committee, typically made up of five to ten elected older individuals from surrounding villages, is the bridge between the monastic and lay communities. Its members must be literate, for they manage the pagoda funds, which are provided by donations from the lay community and used to feed and clothe the monks, novices, and nuns, maintain the pagoda grounds and buildings, and support the building of new structures. The pagoda committee, active in organizing and funding cash associations, rice associations, and communal projects, is the natural partner for development workers.[74] Accordingly, NGOs make use of the community space provided by pagodas. The "bottom line," according to Marshall and colleagues, is that the pagoda "is both a center and a resource, and the pagodas and monks offer many opportunities for partnership." Through existing Buddhist structures, "development actors have opportunities to reach more communities more effectively, and to find and support truly sustainable development projects, especially in rural areas." By working in partnership with the pagoda and its structures, development organizations would be able to tap into grassroots networks that already exist, "bypassing the need to create inorganic committees that so often fail."[75]

As in other cases of inchoate partnerships between religious actors and external development experts, however, a combination of cultural, political, and locally specific contingencies presents obstacles to grounding development in local structures and groups. In the case of Cambodian Buddhism, these include the after-effects of the near demolition of Buddhist organizations during the civil war, which left the sangha with few experienced and respected

Buddhist teachers and a weak understanding of traditional roles and Buddhist teachings. The loss of senior leadership inevitably weakened connections between the lay community and the sangha, leaving younger Cambodians untutored in Buddhist values and precepts.

In addition, Cambodian Buddhism is not immune from the internal divisions and rivalries afflicting most religious communities. Tensions between and within the Mahanikay and Thommayut schools have created a divide, exacerbated by the *boran* movement and its special links to wealth and power, between "socially engaged" Cambodian Buddhists and their politically conformist coreligionists. With the periodic blessings of the King and despite some unease of the Cambodian government, some leaders, notably the late Maha Ghosananda and Yos Hut, acted to engage Buddhist organizations directly in policy matters, while proclaiming what they saw as the right path for Cambodia's development. The tensions played out in debates about the role of the sangha in politics: how the monks should behave in elections, or as part of political parties, and whether they should engage in advocacy on land tenure, treatment of HIV/AIDS, and the monitoring of deforestation.

And, as in other settings, as noted above, the religious leadership must be aware of, and often wary of, the prerogatives of the state. In recent Cambodian history, Buddhist national leadership has generally allied itself with state power, but a few Buddhist leaders have taken on broader roles that are not directly linked to the official hierarchy, whether through Buddhist organizations or the media (especially radio). At the local level the picture is far more fragmented, with monks, nuns, and lay people alike engaged in the slow effort to rebuild the Buddhist ethos after the years of destruction. The sharp discontinuity in Buddhist practice as a result of Cambodia's wars is a central concern of these local workers. They worry over the "missing generation" of monks and laypeople. Some young men are said to enter the monkhood less from firm religious beliefs or convictions, than because they view it as an opportunity to have access to education, and to obtain a scholarship to study at the university level. Indeed, many monks attend university and benefit from the community support that they receive as they live in pagodas. Yet Buddhist sages such as the venerable Yos Hut remind Cambodians that Buddhism is a way of life that will enrich their business, economic, and political pursuits. In the same spirit, another Buddhist patriarch, Venerable Vandong, encourages young Buddhists to participate in development projects and take leadership in reinforcing Buddhist values: "Donors give us money because they say they trust us . . . I want to connect modern society and Buddhist culture to make them closer than before. If people make Buddhist culture part of their lives, then the modern society will be free of violence, free of killing, free of stealing, free of sexual misconduct, and free of lying. That's my goal and my vision for the future." Heng Monychenda, a former monk, founded Buddhism for Development, a faith-based NGO committed to "healing the nation" after the conflict and war. Through the pagoda system, another interviewee commented, development actors can support Khmer communities in rebuilding Buddhist structures and trust, while also working toward development goals.[76]

The authors of the WFDD report see the Cambodian situation as a "glass half full." Despite the formidable obstacles, they conclude, the international development community would be served well by learning more about the history and practices of Cambodian Buddhism and by practicing what this chapter calls the elicitive method of development practice and policy. Strengthening strategic alliances with "Buddhist peacebuilders," so to speak, is a first step in this next stage of "the evolution of development." Indeed, drawing on data collected in several world regions, the WFDD team offered similar findings and recommendations to development practitioners in Africa, Asia, and Latin America.[77]

CONCLUSION: FROM CONVERGENCES TO PARTNERSHIPS?

In this chapter we have identified three sectors of society devoted to alleviating suffering, reducing violent conflict, and improving the situation of the poor and displaced peoples of the world: development, peacebuilding, and religion. Each of these sectors is complicated, riven by internal differentiation and contestation, and each struggles toward a unity forged by the common purpose of "repairing the world." And there remain between these sectors significant philosophical and methodological gaps, which need to be negotiated if their potential synergies are fully to be realized. In addition, proponents of the liberal peace, including hundreds of workers for nongovernmental organizations operating under its secular canopy, are only now beginning to recognize the potential for good that would become available if these sectors were to work in closer collaboration. Insights from the literature on strategic peacebuilding, which offers a corrective to the (previously?) religiously tone-deaf liberal peace model, point in this direction.

One such insight is the priority of the local community and the need to practice an "elicitive method" of tapping into the local community's moral imagination and spiritual resources for development and peacebuilding. Through this method, the actual members of the conflicted and underdeveloped societies in question are called to partnership with professional peacebuilders and development experts to play a decisive role in the direction and shape of their future.

Agents of the liberal peace have reason to be wary of the processes of repairing the world "from the ground up"—for the ground is more complex, unruly, formally undereducated, religiously vital, and unpredictable than many imagined. It can make a humanitarian aid worker dizzy with anxiety and filled with frustration; hence the widely reported tendency of foreign NGO workers to adopt a hands-on, can-do, follow-us approach to the populations they seek to serve. To call such workers aloof is surely unfair; they are often risking their health if not their very lives to provide humanitarian service to people in need. But they tend not to become integrated into the societies they serve, perhaps not least because they know there is a definite temporal limit to their service, which is often governed by funding cycles and metrics of success derived from a corporate mentality quite alien to the rhythms of life on the ground, and to the local populations' own criteria regarding what counts for "peace" and "development."

Religions complicate this mix, adding to the headaches of the liberal do-gooders. Asked to provide a checklist of what constitutes "development," for example, a Buddhist monk or Catholic nun or Muslim imam might tick off some familiar items: reliable health care, paved streets, electricity, clean running water, a stable bridge over which to transport harvested crops. But the imam might prioritize the building of a mosque for worship and the monk demand merit-earning support for his fellow members of the sangha. And the nun might argue that a Catholic school, where spiritual and doctrinal precepts are inculcated into students, is far more important to the "integral human development" of the villagers than almost anything else. And she might be required, or require herself, to object to the outside provision of "reliable health care" if it includes certain kinds of reproductive services.

How to respond to, much less integrate or even manage, this kind of diversity of actors and values pervasive in settings of violent conflict, systemic poverty, and gross underdevelopment? Should we not expect the NGO workers and religious actors and development experts to fly apart from one another in a fury? Perhaps. But there is also an almost irresistible invitation to converge, to meet at the sites of disaster and violence, illness and poverty—the epicenters of development, conflict, and faith. This chapter has argued that these three sectors can and must come together to share the insights, resources, and best practices they have culled from their respective experiences. More ambitiously, they must learn to collaborate actively for the common good.

NOTES

1. "Religious voices are likely to be heard more frequently in future development debates, with repercussions for development thinking and practice." Katherine Marshall, "Ancient and Contemporary Wisdom and Practice on Governance as Religious Leaders Engage in International Development," *Journal of Global Ethics* 4, no. 3 (2008): 217–229.
2. Damien Kingsbury, introduction to *International Development: Issues and Challenges*, ed. Damien Kingsbury, John McKay, Janet Hunt, Mark McGillivrary, and Matthew Clarke, 2nd ed. (Basingstoke, UK: Palgrave MacMillan, 2012), 13.
3. Kingsbury, "Introduction," 3. Based on the overall fall in official development assistance from developed countries as a proportion of their GDP, Kingsbury writes, "it is clear that 'fatigue' has set in, and the global contest driving much work has ended. Certainly, the gap between developed countries and many, perhaps most developing countries continues to widen, meaning that the world is increasingly a less equal, rather than more equal, place." To underscore the relatively rapid change in perceptions, note the persistence of earlier secular, materialist, and narrow economic focus and assumptions in Gerald M. Meier and James E. Rauch, *Leading Issues in Economic Development*, 8th ed. (New York: Oxford University Press, 2005).
4. James D. Wolfensohn, foreword to *Religion and Development: Ways of Transforming the World*, ed. Gerrie ter Haar (New York: Columbia University Press, 2011), xviii.
5. Kingsbury, "Introduction," 3.
6. John A. Rees, *Religion and International Politics and Development: The World Bank and Faith Institutions* (Cheltenham, UK: Edward Elgar, 2011), 46–47.
7. Martha Nussbaum, *Creating Capabilities: The Human Development Approach* (Cambridge, MA: Harvard University Press, 2011); Amartya Sen, *Development as Freedom* (New York: Knopf, 1999).
8. The term "integral human development" is found and defined in the encyclical *Populorum Progressio* (1967) by Paul VI and in the encyclical *Caritas in Veritate* (2007) by Pope Benedict XVI.
9. Wolfensohn, "Foreword," xvii.
10. Gerrie ter Haar, "Religion and Development: Introducing a New Debate," in ter Haar, *Religion and Development*, 5.

11. An insight explored originally by the great historian of religion Mircea Eliade (*The Sacred and the Profane* (New York, NY: Harcourt, Brace 1957)) and his disciples, and recently revived and elaborated by Charles Taylor (*A Secular Age* (Cambridge, MA: Harvard University Press, 2007)), Talal Asad (*Formations of the Secular* (Stanford, CA: Stanford University Press, 2003)), and others.

12. Rees, *Religion and International Politics and Development*, 46–67.

13. "By sanctification of humanitarianism, we mean creation of the sacred, establishment and protection of a space that is viewed as pure and separate from the profane." Michael Barnett and Janice Gross Stein, "Introduction: The Secularization and Sanctification of Humanitarianism," in *Sacred Aid: Faith and Humanitarianism*, ed. Michael Barnett and Janice Gross Stein (New York: Oxford University Press, 2012), 8.

14. See Peter Stamatov, "Activist Religion, Empire, and the Emergence of Modern Long-Distance Advocacy Networks," *American Sociological Review* 75, no. 4 (2010): 607–628.

15. Faith-based and evangelical Christian agencies accounted for 80 percent of the new aid organizations after 1990. In the first decade of the twenty-first century, Barnett and Stein report, Americans increased their giving to overseas missions by 50 percent, to $3.7 billion. Barnett and Stein, *Sacred Aid*, 5.

16. Barnett and Stein, *Sacred Aid*, 8.

17. See Loramy C. Conradi Gerstbauer, "Having Faith in NGOs? A Comparative Study of Faith-Based and Secular NGOs Engaged in International Peacebuilding" (PhD dissertation, University of Notre Dame, 2001).

18. Ajaz Ahmed Khan, "Religious Obligation or Altruistic Giving? Muslims and Charitable Donations," in Barnett and Stein, *Sacred Aid*, 91–92.

19. "The closer development actors come to communities the more keenly aware they become of the central role and extraordinary work of many faith actors." This statement is included in Michael Bodakowski et al., "Faith-Inspired Development: Lessons Learned and Next Steps: Appraising the Luce/SFS Program on Religion and Global Development" (Washington, DC: Berkley Center for Religion, Peace, and World Affairs, 2012, http://berkleycenter.georgetown.edu/publications/faith-inspired-development-work-appraising-the-luce-sfs-program-on-religion-and-development) (hereafter "Faith-Inspired Development"), a draft summary report that was prepared for the "capstone" conference at Georgetown University on November 7, 2011. It summarizes the findings of a multi-year exploration of the religion-development nexus, sponsored by the Henry R. Luce Foundation as part of its initiative on Religion and International Affairs, and supported by the Georgetown University Walsh School of Foreign Service (SFS) and Berkley Center for Religion, Peace, and World Affairs (working with the World Faiths Development Dialogue). The report summarizes and draws on the project's whole series of documents and interviews, which are all available on the Berkley Center website at http://berkleycenter.georgetown.edu/programs/religion-and-global-development.

  The project also took a collaborative approach, engaging with some parallel efforts, notably involving the World Bank, the United Nations Population Fund (UNFPA), the University of Birmingham Religions and Development Program, the Center for Interfaith Action on Global Poverty, and the Tony Blair Faith Foundation.

20. Barnett and Stein, "Introduction," 8–10.

21. Mary Anderson, *Do No Harm: Supporting Local Capacities for Peace Through Aid* (Cambridge, MA: Local Capacities for Peace Project, 1996).

22. See Katherine Marshall and Marisa Van Saanen, *Development and Faith: Where Mind, Heart, and Soul Work Together* (Washington, DC: The World Bank, 2007), 83–85.

23. For a firsthand account of the relationship between such convergences and terrorism, see Kennedy Odede, "Terrorism's Fertile Ground," *New York Times*, January 8, 2014, http://www.nytimes.com/2014/01/09/opinion/terrorisms-fertile-ground.html?smid=fb-share&_r=0.

24. Marc Lindenberg and Coralie Bryant, *Going Global: Transforming Relief and Development NGOs* (West Hartford, CT: Kumarian Press, 2001), 118.

25. Anderson, *Do No Harm*, quoted in Lindenberg and Bryant, *Going Global*, 118.

26. Ashutosh Varshney, *Ethnic Conflict and Civic Life: Hindus and Muslims in India* (New Haven, CT: Yale University Press, 2002), 46.

27. Rees, *Religion and International Politics and Development*, 48.

28. See the introduction to this volume and Daniel Philpott, "Introduction: Searching for Strategy in an Age of Peacebuilding," in *Strategies of Peace: Transforming Conflict in a Violent World*, ed. Daniel Philpott and Gerard F. Powers (Oxford: Oxford University Press, 2010), 3–18.

29. See the chapters in this volume by Marc Gopin (Chapter 14), S. Ayse Kadayifci-Orellana (Chapter 17), Susan Hayward (Chapter 12), Patrick Q. Mason (Chapter 8), and John Paul Lederach (Chapter 21).

30. Religions for Peace is perhaps the largest and best-known organization dedicated to building partnerships between governments, NGOs, and NGDOs: http://www.rfp.org/node/89. FBOs such as World Vision and Catholic Relief Services pioneered partnerships with local religious actors, beginning with inter-religious dialogue efforts and extending to community development alliances: http://crs.org/peacebuilding/dialogue.cfm. The partnerships between development organizations and religious actors began on the international level; the most notable early intervention of religious organizations was their leadership of a coalition urging debt relief for developing nations. The coalition, which had its origins in Latin America and Africa during the 1970s, burgeoned into a global network in the 1980s, proclaiming the year 2000 a "Year of Jubilee"—a term invoking the biblical promise of a year of debt forgiveness in recognition of and thanks for God's forgiveness of sin. The Jubilee 2000 Coalition came eventually to include more than sixty-five countries and hundreds of organizations. The debt relief campaign was truly an inter-religious effort. The Catholic Church in Latin America and Africa had a major influence in clarifying and raising the human effects of injustice caused by unpayable debt burdens, while the Vatican's Pontifical Council for Justice and Peace and the United States Conference of Catholic Bishops (USCCB) played particularly influential roles in lobbying for debtor countries in creditor countries and at international financial lending institutions. As early as the 1980s, Catholic and Protestant religious organizations were working together to create a unified message with a broad base. The Catholic Church leadership, in its national bodies and in conjunction with the World Council of Churches, issued draft statements evaluating the ethics of the debt crisis. Christian Aid UK, Oxfam, and the European Network on Debt and Development, a Washington-based coalition of church and anti-poverty groups, were among the organizations that called attention to the harmful consequences of debt and structural adjustment policy. In April 1996 British groups, led by the overseas relief agencies of the Anglican and Catholic Churches, launched the United Kingdom's own Jubilee 2000 campaign. For more details, see http://www.usccb.org/issues-and-action/human-life-and-dignity/debt-relief/jubilee-debt-forgiveness.cfm.

31. John Paul Lederach, *Preparing for Peace: Conflict Transformation Across Cultures* (Syracuse, NY: Syracuse University Press, 1995), 47–53.

32. Alastair Greig, David Hulme, and Mark Turner, *Challenging Global Inequality: Development Theory and Practice in the 21st Century* (New York: Palgrave Macmillan, 2007), 233–235.

33. Philip Berryman, "Basic Christian Communities and the Future of Latin America," *Monthly Review* 36, no. 3 (1984): 27.

34. Greig et al., *Challenging Global Inequality*, 235.

35. Greig et al., *Challenging Global Inequality*, 236.

36. Uma Kothari, "Feminist and Postcolonial Challenges to Development," in *Development Theory and Practice: Critical Perspectives*, ed. Uma Kothari and Martin Minogue (Basingstoke, UK: Palgrave, 2002), 39.

37. Lederach acknowledges his debt to Freire, and also to Quaker peace theorist Adam Curle, who was among the first to criticize exclusively prescriptive conflict resolution methods as ineffective, and insisted that "it is essential to consider the peacemaking potential within the conflicting communities themselves," in Adam Curle, *Making Peace* (London: Tavistock Publications, 1971), 34.

38. Lederach, *Preparing for Peace*, 55.

39. Lederach, *Preparing for Peace*, 59–61.

40. Lederach, *Preparing for Peace*, 67.

41. "The idea, once considered heretical, has meanwhile gained stature in the debates on conflict transformation." Wolfgang Dietrich, *Elicitive Conflict Transformation and the Transrational Shift in Peace Politics* (New York: Palgrave Macmillan, 2013), 11.

42. Denis Goulet, *Development Ethics at Work: Explorations—1960–2002* (New York: Routledge, 2006), 9–10.

43. See William R. Walters, review of *The Cruel Choice*, by Denis Goulet, *Journal of Economic Literature* 10, no. 4 (1972): 1228.

44. Denis Goulet, "Being and Having: The Use of Ethics in Development Planning," in *Development Ethics at Work*, 26–29. Goulet adds: "In an era of globalization, during which 'relationship' becomes an indisputable fact of life on a worldwide scale as a result of economic, environmental and cultural interdependence, one can add, with the force of conviction: As long as these needs are not met in any part of the world, and the world is focused on consumerism with a narrowly economic rather than a fully human understanding of values, all of humanity is demeaned. In this sense development is a truly universal project, both in terms of geography and anthropology: even the apparently physically isolated project will have consequences in other regions of the global economy and eco-system, and it will have implications for the human person in her communal, psychological, spiritual and cultural—as well as merely 'material'—reality."

45. Goulet, "Development Ethics for our Time," in *Development Ethics at Work*, 7.

46. Of many possible examples, see Pope Francis, *The Joy of the Gospel*, apostolic exhortation (Vatican: The Holy See, 2013), 53–62. A sample: "*No to an economy of exclusion* Just as the commandment 'Thou shalt not kill' sets a clear limit in order to safeguard the value of human life, today we also have to say 'thou shalt not' to an economy of exclusion and inequality. Such an economy kills. How can it be that it is not a news item when an elderly homeless person dies of exposure, but it is news when the stock market loses two points? This is a case of exclusion. Can we continue to stand by when food is thrown away while people are starving? This is a case of inequality. Today everything comes under the laws of competition and the survival of the fittest, where the powerful feed upon the

powerless. As a consequence, masses of people find themselves excluded and marginalized: without work, without possibilities, without any means of escape. Human beings are themselves considered consumer goods to be used and then discarded. We have created a 'throw away' culture which is now spreading. It is no longer simply about exploitation and oppression, but something new. Exclusion ultimately has to do with what it means to be a part of the society in which we live; those excluded are no longer society's underside or its fringes or its disenfranchised—they are no longer even a part of it. The excluded are not the 'exploited' but the outcast, the 'leftovers'. In this context, some people continue to defend trickle-down theories which assume that economic growth, encouraged by a free market, will inevitably succeed in bringing about greater justice and inclusiveness in the world. This opinion, which has never been confirmed by the facts, expresses a crude and naïve trust in the goodness of those wielding economic power and in the sacralized workings of the prevailing economic system. Meanwhile, the excluded are still waiting. To sustain a lifestyle which excludes others, or to sustain enthusiasm for that selfish ideal, a globalization of indifference has developed. Almost without being aware of it, we end up being incapable of feeling compassion at the outcry of the poor, weeping for other people's pain, and feeling a need to help them, as though all this were someone else's responsibility and not our own. The culture of prosperity deadens us; we are thrilled if the market offers us something new to purchase. In the meantime all those lives stunted for lack of opportunity seem a mere spectacle; they fail to move us."

47. See R. Scott Appleby and Carl J. Bindenagel, "The Economy of the Spirit: Religion, Ethics, and Development in the Thought of Denis Goulet and in Contemporary Practice" in *New Directions in Development Ethics: Essays in Honor of Denis Goulet*, ed. Charles K. Wilber and Amitava Dutt (Notre Dame, IN: University of Notre Dame Press, 2010), 281–307.

48. See, for example, David Keen, *Complex Emergencies* (Cambridge: Polity Press, 2008), 116–148.

49. Goulet, "Culture and Traditional Values in Development," in *Development Ethics at Work*, 139.

50. Goulet, "Culture and Traditional Values," 143.

51. Goulet, "Culture and Traditional Values," 150.

52. Sen, *Development as Freedom*; see also Amartya Sen, "Equality of What?" (Tanner Lecture on Human Values, Stanford University, Stanford, CA, May 22, 1979).

53. Herman Daly, *Beyond Growth: The Economics of Sustainable Development* (Boston: Beacon Press, 1966).

54. Paul Ekins, *Economic Growth and Environmental Sustainability: The Prospects for Green Growth* (New York: Routledge, 2000).

55. For example, three Christian economists suggest that various modern kinds of idolatries are preventing the emergence of global solidarity. Echoing Goulet's denunciations of waste and excessive materialism, they lay the blame at the feet of the idols of "progress," technology, and modernity. A psychological condition afflicts humanity, they suggest, marked by "heightening anxiety about the future" mingled with "elements of loss of perspective, helplessness, and even despair." Their diagnosis is also Goulet's: many people in today's society "feel they no longer have a significant impact on the events that most influence their lives." Bob Goudzwaard, Mark Vander Vennen, and David Van Heemst, *Hope in Troubled Times: A New Vision for Confronting Global Crises* (Grand Rapids, MI: Baker Academic, 2007), 19. For a second example of a Goulet-inflected approach, this one explicitly theological, see D. Stephen Long, *The Divine Economy* (New York: Routledge, 2000). For a

Catholic liberationist perspective, see Daniel G. Groody, *Globalization, Spirituality, and Justice: Navigating a Path to Peace* (Maryknoll, NY: Orbis, 2007).

56. See John Paul Lederach and R. Scott Appleby, "Strategic Peacebuilding: An Overview," in Philpott and Powers, eds., *Strategies of Peace*, 19–44.

57. See for example, Amartya Sen, *The Idea of Justice* (Cambridge, MA: Harvard University Press, 2009), 87–113.

58. Lederach, *Preparing for Peace*, 144.

59. For a summary of "the debates that never happened" over these issues, see William Easterly, *The Tyranny of Experts: Economists, Dictators and the Forgotten Rights of the Poor* (New York: Basic Books, 2014), 17–42.

60. Goulet, "Culture and Traditional Values," 155.

61. Lederach and Appleby, "Strategic Peacebuilding," 22.

62. Judith A. Mayotte, "Religion and Global Affairs: The Role of Religion in Development," *SAIS Review* 18, no. 2 (1998): 66.

63. The most comprehensive summary of the literature on religious actors and transitional justice is found in Daniel Philpott, *Just and Unjust Peace: An Ethic of Political Reconciliation* (Oxford: Oxford University Press, 2013).

64. Goulet, *Development Ethics at Work*, 62.

65. Gregory Baum writes: "First Nation peoples, whether they are Christian or practice their traditional cosmic religion, regard with great suspicion the secular approach to life taken for granted in business, government, economics and other social sciences. As all these endeavors systematically exclude the spiritual dimension of life, native peoples often regard them as a form of brainwashing designed to undermine their cultural identity.... [T]he Western economic empire makes people in Africa and Asia suffer 'anthropological oppression,' that is, the people find themselves caught in institutions and overwhelmed by a set of symbols that rob them of their cultural identity and produce religious anguish." Baum, "Solidarity with the Poor," in *The Lab, the Temple, and the Market: Reflections at the Intersection of Science, Religion, and Development*, ed. Sharon M. P. Harper (West Hartford, CT: Kumarian Press, 2000), 63.

66. See the accounts of the backlash in R. Scott Appleby, *The Ambivalence of the Sacred: Religion, Violence and Reconciliation* (Lanham, MD: Rowman and Littlefield, 2000) 34–40, 197–204.

67. Douglas Johnston and Cynthia Sampson, eds., *Religion: The Missing Dimension of Statecraft* (New York: Oxford University Press, 1994).

68. Marshall's long career with the World Bank (1971–2006) involved leadership on a wide range of issues relevant to development in Africa, Asia, and Latin America, including conflict resolution, the role of women, and, toward the end of her term, the integration of local values and ethics into World Bank deliberations. After departing the World Bank, in 1998 she helped to establish and became executive director of the World Faiths Development Dialogue, a not-for-profit organization working at the intersections of faith and development (http://berkleycenter.georgetown.edu/wfdd/about).

69. Bodakowski et al., "Faith-Inspired Development Work."

70. Bodakowski et al., "Faith-Inspired Development Work."

71. Bodakowski et al., "Faith-Inspired Development Work." The meaning, practice, and purpose of "mission" is not static over time. As with other practices and beliefs, religious communities adapt to changing circumstances and may even move to a significantly altered expression, as both the Mennonite and Catholic communities did over the course of the twentieth century. For details, see Appleby, *Ambivalence of the Sacred*, 40–47, 143–151.

72. "Orphanages are seen today as open to abuse, separating children from their community and roots and alternative approaches are preferred. This is a telling example both of varying approaches, of the depth of the impetus to compassion, and how these approaches and theologies can have practical manifestations." Bodakowski et al., "Faith-Inspired Development Work." On the prevalence of sexual abuse, see Philip Jenkins, *Pedophiles and Priests: Anatomy of a Contemporary Crisis* (New York: Oxford University Press, 1996).

73. Ian Harris, *Cambodian Buddhism: History and Practice* (Honolulu, HI: University of Hawaii Press, 2008).

74. Community members are able to borrow rice or money from these associations in times of need and avoid the high interest rates associated with loans from other sources. In 1997, the German development organization GTZ, in an effort to increase food security and reduce poverty, began working in partnership with pagoda associations in Kampong Thom province. GTZ provided half the start-up capital of rice or cash and provided training in basic management skills. See Bodakowski et al., "Faith-Inspired Development Work."

75. Bodakowski et al., "Faith-Inspired Development Work."

76. Bodakowski et al., "Faith-Inspired Development Work."

77. "If there are two clear themes that emerge, they are the depth and pervasive nature of faith engagement and its extraordinary diversity," write the authors of the WFDD report. "We can affirm that for every development goal, every challenge, there is a faith dimension. The challenge is to see these dimensions more clearly and to explore what we can learn, why they matter, and their implications for development policy and practice." Bodakowski et al., "Faith-Inspired Development Work."

Bibliography

Anderson, Mary. *Do No Harm: Supporting Local Capacities for Peace Through Aid*. Cambridge, MA: Local Capacities for Peace Project, 1996.

Appleby, R. Scott. *The Ambivalence of the Sacred: Religion, Violence, and Reconciliation*. Lanham, MD: Rowman and Littlefield, 2000.

Appleby, R. Scott, and Carl J. Bindenagel. "The Economy of the Spirit: Religion, Ethics, and Development in the Thought of Denis Goulet and in Contemporary Practice." In *New Directions in Development Ethics: Essays in Honor of Denis Goulet*, edited by Charles K. Wilber and Amitava Dutt. Notre Dame, IN: University of Notre Dame Press, 2010.

Asad, Talal. *Formations of the Secular: Christianity, Islam, Modernity*. Stanford, CA: Stanford University Press, 2003.

Barnett, Michael, and Janice Gross Stein, eds. : *Faith and Humanitarianism*. New York: Oxford University Press, 2012.

Pope Benedict XVI. *Caritas in Veritate*. Encyclical letter. Vatican: The Holy See, 2007.

Berryman, Philip. "Basic Christian Communities and the Future of Latin America." *Monthly Review* 36, no. 3 (1984): 27.

Binder, Leonard. *Islamic Liberalism: A Critique of Development Ideologies*. Chicago: University of Chicago Press, 1988.

Bodakowski, Michael, et al. "Faith-Inspired Development Work: Lessons Learned and Next Steps." Washington, DC: Berkley Center for Religion, Peace, and World Affairs, 2012. http://berkleycenter.georgetown.edu/publications/faith-inspired-development-work-appraising-the-luce-sfs-program-on-religion-and-development.

Curle, Adam. *Making Peace*. London: Tavistock Publications, 1971.

Daly, Herman E. *Beyond Growth: The Economics of Sustainable Development*. Boston: Beacon Press, 1966.

Dietrich, Wolfgang. *Elicitive Conflict Transformation and the Transrational Shift in Peace Politics*. New York: Palgrave Macmillan, 2013.

Easterly, William. *The Tyranny of Experts: Economists, Dictators and the Forgotten Rights of the Poor*. New York: Basic Books, 2014.

Ekins, Paul. *Economic Growth and Environmental Sustainability: The Prospects for Green Growth*. New York: Routledge, 2000.

Eliade, Mircea. *The Sacred and the Profane: The Nature of Religion*. Translated by Willard R. Trask. New York: Harcourt and Brace, 1959. First published 1957 by Rowohlt Taschenbuch Verlag GmbH.

Fowler, Alan. *Striking a Balance: A Guide to Enhancing the Effectiveness of Non-Governmental Organisations in International Development*. London: Earthscan Pubications, 1997.

Pope Francis. *The Joy of the Gospel*. Apostolic exhortation. Vatican: The Holy See, 2013. http://www.vatican.va/evangelii-gaudium/en/.

Gerstbauer, Loramy C. Conradi. "Having Faith in NGOs? A Comparative Study of Faith-Based and Secular NGOs Engaged in International Peacebuilding." PhD diss., University of Notre Dame, 2001.

Goudzwaard, Bob, Mark Vander Vennen, and David Van Heemst. *Hope in Troubled Times: A New Vision for Confronting Global Crises*. Grand Rapids, MI: Baker Academic, 2007.

Goulet, Denis. *Development Ethics at Work: Explorations—1960–2002*. New York: Routledge, 2006.

Greig, Alastair, David Hulme, and Mark Turner. *Challenging Global Inequality: Development Theory and Practice in the 21st Century*. New York: Palgrave Macmillan, 2007.

Groody, Daniel G. *Globalization, Spirituality, and Justice: Navigating a Path to Peace*. Maryknoll, NY: Orbis, 2007.

Harper, Sharon M. P., ed. *The Lab, the Temple, and the Market: Reflections at the Intersection of Science, Religion, and Development*. West Hartford, CT: Kumarian Press, 2000.

Harris, Ian Charles. *Cambodian Buddhism: History and Practice*. Honolulu, HI: University of Hawaii Press, 2005.

Ikenberry, G. John. *Liberal Leviathan: The Origins, Crisis, and Transformation of the American World Order*. Princeton, NJ: Princeton University Press, 2011.

Jenkins, Philip. *Pedophiles and Priests: Anatomy of a Contemporary Crisis*. New York: Oxford University Press, 1996.

Johnston, Douglas, and Cynthia Sampson, eds. *Religion: The Missing Dimension of Statecraft*. New York: Oxford University Press, 1994.

Keen, David. *Complex Emergencies*. Cambridge: Polity Press, 2008.

Kingsbury, Damien, John McKay, Janet Hunt, Mark McGillivrary and Matthew Clarke, eds. *International Development: Issues and Challenges*. 2nd ed. Basingstoke, UK: Palgrave MacMillan, 2012.

Kothari, Uma. "Feminist and Postcolonial Challenges to Development." In *Development Theory and Practice: Critical Perspectives*, edited by Uma Kothari and Martin Minogue. Basingstoke: Palgrave, 2002.

Lederach, John Paul. *Preparing for Peace: Conflict Transformation Across Cultures*. Syracuse, NY: Syracuse University Press, 1995.

Lindenberg, Marc, and Coralie Bryant. *Going Global: Transforming Relief and Development NGOs*. West Hartford, CT: Kumarian Press, 2001.

Long, D. Stephen. *The Divine Economy: Theology and the Market*. New York: Routledge, 2000.

Marshall, Katherine. "Ancient and Contemporary Wisdom and Practice on Governance as Religious Leaders Engage in International Development." *Journal of Global Ethics* 4, no.3 (2008): 217–229.

Marshall, Katherine, and Marisa Van Saanen. *Development and Faith: Where Mind, Heart, and Soul Work Together*. Washington, DC: The World Bank, 2007.

Mayotte, Judith A. "Religion and Global Affairs: The Role of Religion in Development." *SAIS Review* 18, no. 2 (1998): 65–69.

Meier, Gerald M. and James E. Rauch. *Leading Issues in Economic Development*, 8th ed. New York: Oxford University Press, 2005.

Nussbaum, Martha. *Creating Capabilities: The Human Development Approach*. Cambridge, MA: Harvard University Press, 2011.

Pope Paul VI. *Populorum Progressio*. Encyclical letter. Vatican: The Holy See, 1967.

Philpott, Daniel, and Gerard F. Powers, eds. *Strategies of Peace: Transforming Conflict in a Violent World*. Oxford: Oxford University Press, 2010.

Philpott, Daniel. *Just and Unjust Peace: An Ethic of Political Reconciliation*. Oxford: Oxford University Press, 2013.

Rees, John A. *Religion and International Politics and Development: The World Bank and Faith Institutions*. Cheltenham, UK: Edward Elgar Publishing, 2011.

Schreiter, Robert J., R. Scott Appleby, and Gerard F. Powers, eds. *Peacebuilding: Catholic Theology, Ethics, and Praxis*. Maryknoll, NY: Orbis Books, 2013.

Sen, Amartya. *Development as Freedom*. New York: Alfred A. Knopf, 1999.

Sen, Amartya. "Equality of What?" (Tanner Lecture on Human Values, Stanford University, Stanford, CA, May 22, 1979).

Sen, Amartya. *The Idea of Justice*. Cambridge, MA: Harvard University Press, 2009.

Stamatov, Peter. "Activist Religion, Empire, and the Emergence of Modern Long-Distance Advocacy Networks." *American Sociological Review* 75, no. 4 (2010): 607–628.

Taylor, Charles. *A Secular Age*. Cambridge, MA: Harvard University Press, 2007.

ter Haar, Gerrie, ed. *Religion and Development: Ways of Transforming the World*. New York: Columbia University Press, 2011.

Uvin, Peter. *Aiding Violence: The Development Enterprise in Rwanda*. West Hartford, CT: Kumarian Press, 1998.

Varshney, Ashutosh. *Ethnic Conflict and Civic Life: Hindus and Muslims in India*. New Haven, CT: Yale University Press, 2002.

Walters, William R. "Review of Denis Goulet, *The Cruel Choice*." *Journal of Economic Literature* 10, no. 4 (1972): 1227–1228.

CHAPTER 8

VIOLENT AND NONVIOLENT RELIGIOUS MILITANCY

PATRICK Q. MASON

ONE of the central questions that bedevils scholars, in peace studies and beyond, is why some people are violent and others are not, even when they share similar cultural, economic, political, and educational backgrounds. The question also has clear policy implications as we think about such issues as criminal justice, rehabilitation and reintegration, conflict resolution, and educational planning and pedagogy, to name a few. Even where studies have been able to describe, ex post facto, the conditions (from the psychological to the macro-structural) that led to a particular expression of violence, our current tools of analysis remain inadequate in their predictive capacity, particularly when it comes to the individual actor. By the same token, no definitive answer exists for why some people are militantly peaceful to the point of choosing to lay down their lives rather than commit aggression or even act in self-defense. Rather than advancing a grand theory, this chapter employs a descriptive and analytical approach to understanding the phenomenon of religious militancy in both its violent and nonviolent forms.

"Religious militancy" is equated in the minds of many observers with "religious violence." The long-standing relationship of religion and violence has provided critics with a powerful argument that, in the words of the late Christopher Hitchens, "God is not great," and "religion poisons everything." Hitchens opened a chapter on religious violence—subtly titled "Religion Kills"—with an epigraph from John Stuart Mill speaking about his father's "aversion to religion," which he decried as a "great moral evil" that required obedience to a being "on whom it lavishes indeed all the phrases of adulation, but whom in sober truth it depicts as eminently hateful." According to Hitchens, the problem with religion—or at least one problem of many—is its absolutism. Because believers claim to possess the grand interpretive scheme that allows them to decipher all of life and the cosmos, they translate that sacred knowledge into divinely ordained authoritarianism: "The true believer cannot rest until the whole world bows the knee. Is it not obvious to all, say the pious, that religious authority is paramount, and that those who decline to recognize it have forfeited their right to exist?" The enactment of deadly violence is the most dramatic expression of this denial of the right of others to exist. Hitchens sees a clear connection between piety and the inclination and capacity for violence, claiming that the al-Qaeda operatives who hijacked the planes on September 11, 2001, "were beyond any doubt the most sincere believers on those planes." Their jihadism in turn resurrected a strand of Christian crusaderism that found expression in the public sermons and statements of ministers, pundits, and politicians across the United States (including, briefly, the president) and helped contribute to the Iraq War. From the former Yugoslavia to the Middle East to Sri Lanka, the evidence is in, Hitchens reckoned, and religion is found guilty of widespread and wanton murder. "As well as a menace to civilization," he concluded, "[religion] has become a threat to human survival."[1]

Even setting aside Hitchens' characteristic bombast and hyperbole, the claim that religion has been the prime mover behind the world's violence is commonly made not only by atheist critics but also by many believers. For instance, Charles Kimball, a religion scholar and Baptist minister, opened his best-selling book *When Religion Becomes Evil* with the assertion: "It is somewhat trite, but nevertheless sadly true, to say that more wars have been waged, more people killed, and these days more evil perpetrated in the name of religion than by any other institutional force in human history."[2] Though powerful, and commonly held, this particular claim is empirically false. The fact is that, especially in the modern world, the secular nation-state is far and away the greatest purveyor of violence. The human toll of Nazi death camps, Stalinist and Maoist purges, the Khmer Rouge's killing fields, and the Rwandan genocide—all secular and state-sponsored affairs—vastly outranks anything to be laid at the feet of religion. To be fair, the relatively lower body count of religious violence may simply be a matter of capacity, as religious actors typically do not command the organizational wherewithal, let alone firepower, that allowed agents of the state to murder as many as 262 million people worldwide in the twentieth century.[3]

This is not to let religion off the hook. The scope and severity of the violence perpetrated in the name of religion need not be inflated to be seriously analyzed and critiqued. But beyond interrogating some of the more overblown claims about religion and violence, especially relative to the destructiveness of state-sponsored violence, one of the most productive developments in this area in recent years has been the increasing recognition that religion is not only violent, but that it also contributes powerfully to peace and justice movements around the world, not to mention inspiring countless individual and organizational acts of charity and compassion. To argue that religion is either inherently violent or peaceful is to peddle in crass reductionism, ignoring tremendous diversity within and between religious traditions as well as the complexity and, indeed, messiness naturally attendant to human relations and institutions (of which religion is among the most historically significant).

One of the most important articulations of this more nuanced thesis—and a foundational text for the field of religion, conflict, and peacebuilding—is R. Scott Appleby's book *The Ambivalence of the Sacred*. Appleby contends that religion, precisely because it deals with matters of the divine, calls on its adherents to make (or at least be prepared to make) the ultimate commitment and sacrifice on behalf of what is perceived to be the godly cause. In its unmoderated form, religion naturally produces what he terms "militants"—those who are consumed with "sacred rage." Contra Hitchens's unidirectional relationship between religion and violence, however, Appleby's key insight is that religious militancy takes different forms, including "rage"-filled protesters who fight against the very forms of physical, structural, and cultural violence that their coreligionists wreak. Religious militants of different stripes can simultaneously be found systematically violating human rights and organizing campaigns to protect and enforce those rights. As Appleby observes, "Militant religion, in short, produces a broad spectrum of religious actors with differing attitudes toward the pursuit of political power and the use of violence." Applying a taxonomy in which "militant" is the generic term and "extremist" describes those who use violence to accomplish their ends, he continues:

> Both the extremist and the peacemaker are militants. Both types "go to extremes" of self-sacrifice in devotion to the sacred; both claim to be "radical," or rooted in and renewing the fundamental truths of their religious traditions. In these ways they distinguish themselves from people not motivated by religious commitments—and from the vast middle ground of believers. Yet the peacemaker renounces violence as an acceptable extreme and restricts the war against oppressors and injustice to noncoercive means. The extremist, by contrast, exalts violence as a religious prerogative or even as a spiritual imperative in the quest for justice.

The ultimate difference between religious peacemakers and extremists, Appleby asserts, lies not in their commitment but rather in their orientation. The religious peacemaker is motivated by and seeks "reconciliation or peaceful coexistence with the enemy [as] the ultimate goal," whereas the violent extremist "is committed primarily to victory over the enemy," and thus may sanction the use of violence as a godly means of achieving her sacred ends.[4]

This chapter builds upon the fundamentally sound premises of Appleby's arguments by further examining the concept and nature of religious militancy, first in general terms by considering selected key concepts, and then through a historical illustration of the competing dynamics of religious militancy present in the struggle over black civil rights in the American South in the 1950s and 1960s. Operating within the normative framework associated with peace studies, I will conclude by offering tentative reflections on how religious militancy might be deployed in the service of "justpeace" rather than further contributing to cycles of structural, cultural, and physical violence.

This chapter commonly refers to "religion" as a generic umbrella term of convenience. I do so recognizing that a considerable body of literature has emerged in recent years both historicizing and deconstructing the analytical and political usages of the term "religion" and even questioning whether it can still be considered a meaningful category. As demonstrated by these scholars, what is called religion in the modern West is in fact an intellectual, cultural, and even political product of the modern West, rather than a transhistorical and transcultural reality. Religion became useful as a category of analysis in Euro-American colonial and imperial projects on every continent, reifying the superiority and normativity of a particular historical phenomenon (often Anglo-American Protestantism) over competing ways of knowing and being. The definition and application of the concept religion, then, historically has been an inherently political act, drawing boundaries around certain beliefs and behaviors that are considered "enlightened" and "civilized"—meaning friendly to a certain set of liberal Western cultural norms and political structures—while marginalizing and often repressing beliefs and behaviors (and the people embodying them) as regressive and even dangerous to a modern (meaning secular and liberal) sociopolitical order. This constitutes an even deeper challenge than the readily acknowledged problem that Western notions of religion and religiosity typically privilege a certain constellation of traits characteristic of the Abrahamic traditions of Judaism, Christianity, and Islam.[5] Some scholars have noted an imperialistic tendency within the contemporary academic study of religion (as practiced primarily in the Christian or post-Christian West), and there have been recent calls to drop the term altogether.[6]

I acknowledge the general outlines of this critique. On the one hand, it is now somewhat unremarkable to note that the category of religion, like all human ideas and institutions, is contingent, always operating within and in turn shaping its particular historical, social, cultural, political, intellectual, and economic settings. Nevertheless, the careful historicist and deconstructive work performed by scholars of religion in the past generation becomes a helpful tool in approaching the subject of religious militancy in all its complexity. Indeed, a recognition that religion is constantly being reconstructed, reimagined, and reinvented should help prevent an uncritical argument that religion is inherently anything, including violent. An important recent example of how critical approaches to the study of religion can illuminate the subject of religious militancy is William Cavanaugh's book *The Myth of Religious Violence.* Tracing the historical construction of the term religion and associating it with the rise of the Westphalian political order, Cavanaugh argues that "a transhistorical and transcultural concept of religion that is essentially prone to violence is one of the foundational legitimating myths of the liberal nation-state. . . . This myth can be and is used in domestic politics to legitimate the marginalization of certain types of practices and groups labeled religious, while underwriting the nation-state's monopoly on its citizens' willingness to sacrifice and kill."[7]

The most effective studies of religion are those that carefully delineate the specific formations of "religion" in a certain time and place. This chapter will at least gesture in the direction of that desirable particularity through a historical treatment of the ways that specific expressions of Protestant Christianity led to different forms of religious militancy in the mid-twentieth-century American South. At other places in the chapter, however, I will for the sake of convenience speak of religion in more generic terms when referring to broad trends that can be traced across various times and places. As Scott Appleby observes in Chapter 2 of this volume, "To acknowledge that religion is a modern construct, differentiated from the state in order to be constrained by secular power, does not absolve the interpreter from the task of scrutinizing its present configurations." I adopt a similarly pragmatic approach that retains religion as a meaningful category of scholarly analysis precisely because it is a meaningful category of lived reality for wide swaths of humanity, both historically and contemporarily—conditioned and contingent, politicized and the product of a long intellectual genealogy, to be sure, but no less real in the present. This is particularly true for agentive subjects whose self-understanding of themselves, and particularly their militancy, is explicitly religious.

WHENCE RELIGIOUS MILITANCY?

How do we explain religious militancy? For that matter, what exactly is "religious" about religious militancy? In asking these and similar questions, it is essential to remember that religious militancy cannot be reduced to its violent manifestations. If that were so, we could simply refer to the substantial body of literature on religion and violence.[8] Instead, we can outline, in necessarily selective fashion, a handful of concepts that illuminate the internal logic of what spurs religious actors toward militant attitudes and behavior. My goal is not to provide an exhaustive survey of the extant literature or a thorough analysis—let alone unqualified endorsement—of the thinkers cited here. I have selected them for their relative utility and accessibility, drawing on particular insights that they originated or concisely expressed rather than evaluating the respective merits of their work as a whole.

In his widely read 1957 book *Dynamics of Faith*, the influential mid-twentieth-century Protestant theologian Paul Tillich defined faith as "the state of being ultimately concerned." Though grounded in Tillich's own Christian tradition, his notion of faith as concern with "the ultimate, the unconditional, the absolute, the infinite" provides an instructive foundation for considering the broader phenomenon of religious militancy. The dynamics of this ultimate concern include not only the "unconditional demand" required of believers but also "the promise of ultimate fulfillment" that entices them as the reward for a faithful life. Tillich noted that "Faith as ultimate concern is an act of the total personality. It happens in the center of the personal life and includes all its elements." Faith is not simply the sum total of one's commitments, beliefs, and actions, but rather transcends and exercises a "decisive impact on each of them." Tillich differentiated between "true faith," in which "the ultimate concern is a concern about the truly ultimate," and "idolatrous faith," in which "preliminary, finite realities are elevated to the rank of ultimacy." Phenomenologically, Tillich recognized that there may not be a meaningful distinction between the two brands of faith; after all, "idolatrous faith is still faith. The holy which is demonic is still holy." The seeds of Appleby's ambivalence thesis are present here: "This is the point where the ambiguous character of religion is most visible and the dangers of faith are most obvious: the danger of faith is idolatry and the ambiguity of the holy is its demonic possibility. Our ultimate concern can destroy us as it can heal us."[9]

Tillich recognized the political implications of ultimate concern, and that its application is by no means limited to what we might commonly refer to as the "religious." In illustrating his concept, he initially pointed not to scripture or sacred history but rather to the modern secular nation-state. He incisively observed:

> If a national group makes the life and growth of the nation its ultimate concern, it demands that all other concerns, economic well-being, health and life, family, aesthetic and cognitive truth, justice and humanity, be sacrificed. The extreme nationalisms of [the twentieth] century are laboratories for the study of what ultimate concern means in all aspects of human existence, including the smallest concern of one's daily life. Everything is centered in the only god, the nation—a god who certainly proves to be a demon, but who shows clearly the unconditional character of an ultimate concern.[10]

While faith as ultimate concern may not encompass the totality of human experience, the value of Tillich's analysis is its elasticity. One can readily perceive the dynamics of ultimate concern operationalized by all kinds of masters who would claim absolute authority, from Jehovah of the Hebrew Bible to any number of modern totalitarian political leaders. Tillich viewed the latter as definitionally and operationally idolatrous, trading in the wares of the "preliminary" and "finite" rather than truly ultimate, but from a distance we can see that the devoted Maoist would turn the same critique back on Tillich's Christian faith. The danger of using "idolatry" as a category is that it seriously questions the legitimacy of any concern that is not, in the observer's eyes, ultimate. This raises the question of the subjectivity inherent in the perception and experience of truth, particularly as refracted through the lenses of deep pluralism. Short of a complementary ethic of pluralism, Tillich's notion of faith can produce prejudice toward and even the extermination of rival sources of ultimate concern.

Its possible dangers notwithstanding, Tillich's concept has resonated far beyond his immediate circle of Euro-American Protestant theology. For instance, in considering the rise of "extremist" religious groups in modern Israel, political scientist Charles Liebman began from the Tillichian premise that "religion claims absolute truth about ultimate reality," then concluded that "extremism is an understandable and, other things being equal, the most obvious consequence of religious commitment"; in short, "extremism is the religious norm." As a logical corollary, then, "it is not religious extremism but religious moderation that requires explanation." Liebman elaborated his basic thesis:

> A propensity to religious extremism does not require explanation since it is entirely consistent with basic religious tenets and authentic religious orientations. It is religious moderation or religious liberalism, the willingness of religious adherents to accommodate themselves to their environment, to adapt their behavioral and belief patterns to prevailing cultural norms, to make peace with the world, that requires explanation.... Extremism is a tendency to which every religiously oriented person is attracted.[11]

Given the totalizing demands made by the sacred, extremism—or in this chapter's parlance, "religious militancy"—is the default position. To find scriptural support for this position one can easily invoke the Hebrew Bible ("You shall love the Lord your God with all your heart, and with all your soul, and with all your might"[12]), or the Qur'an ("there is no god but I; therefore worship and serve Me"[13]), or the Bhagavad Gita ("Fix your mind on Me, be devoted to Me, offer service to Me, bow down to Me, and you shall certainly reach Me"[14]), or even the *I Ching* ("The Superior Man, taking his stance as righteousness requires, adheres firmly to heaven's decrees"[15]).

Liebman was less interested in the scriptural and theological than the sociological and political dimensions of religious extremism. And it must be said that he seems blind to the secular analogues of what he calls here *religious* extremism; many forms of nationalist "absolutism" would qualify by his definition of "extremism." Nevertheless, he argued that "the religious impulse," whoever exhibits it, lends itself to extreme expression such as lethal violence against the Other. Liebman identified multiple, and even conflicting, tendencies among religious extremists. These range from seeking to impose their agenda on society to isolating themselves and withdrawing from engagement, perhaps as a realistic assessment of their own weakness as they await some sort of divine intervention that will enable them to enact their (or rather, God's) agenda.[16] In its purest sense, Liebman admitted, extremism exists only as "an ideal typical impulse rather than as objectified in individuals or institutions." Precisely when it becomes embodied, extremism begins to be moderated. This often occurs as a result or in the process of achieving its own success, as various goals—whether it be pursuing converts, seeking to protect the community from the outside, or endeavoring to transform the political or economic system—necessitate the approval of others. Contact and especially robust engagement with outsiders introduce an element of compromise, adaptation, or accommodation that serves to moderate, on at least some level, the original extremist impulse. This may lead to purges or schisms and the resultant creation of a new, "purified" community, but that group, if it seeks anything beyond survival in radical isolation (which is not possible in most parts of the modern world) will then be subject to the same dynamics that created it.[17]

Liebman noted that an advanced stage of secularization—characterized by religion being differentiated or set apart from the formal structures of the public sphere, most notably in politics, economics, and public policy—ironically serves as an incubator for religious extremists. In seeking to explain this counterintuitive finding, he argued that religion's general decline in prestige and influence in society means that ambitious, worldly, accommodative individuals who might have sought leadership in religious institutions find less incentive to do so. Concomitantly, the ranks of religious leadership are filled more by those who are less given to accommodation with general societal mores. Furthermore, extremists earn a certain cultural cachet by mobilizing discourses of stability based on eternity and inerrancy that become attractive to people affected by the destabilizing and disorienting changes attendant to modern political and economic processes. Thus, "the rejectionists are not only unaffected but perhaps even strengthened by the contrast between their own seemingly uninterrupted unchanging culture and that which surrounds them. The affirmationists, on the other hand, face the dilemma of reconciling their religious conceptions with this self-consciously changing culture." The relative authority and perceived devotion of extremists therefore increase while those of the moderates decrease. The decline of moderating influences within the broader religious community, as well as increased critiques of secular society's ability to deliver on its promises of prosperity and full human flourishing, only reinforces the trends that strengthen the extremists' position and appeal.[18]

Though helpful at multiple points, Liebman's argument that extremism is the religious norm is open to serious critique. One problem is that he selects one manifestation of religious behavior and belief—which he labels extremism—and then declares it as normative for all religion. Beginning with extremism as the religious norm contributes to a particular liberal secular discourse that identifies practitioners of "strong religion" as marginal, aberrant, and perhaps even dangerous; indeed, it becomes difficult to determine where "religion" ends and "the lunatic fringe begins." Finally, the claim that extremism requires no analytical explanation fails to pay adequate attention to the dynamics in which practitioners exercise agency in choosing or legitimating a particular religious leader, movement, or worldview.[19] Militancy as an ideal type that embodies the absolutist claims and tendencies within religious discourse must be differentiated from a descriptive project that characterizes the belief and practice of the vast majority of religious adherents. Speaking descriptively, moderation or accommodationism is far more the norm than is militancy. It is more accurate to say that extremism (or militancy) is *a* religious norm rather than *the* religious norm. Such a distinction avoids an overly deterministic focus on religious militancy that characterizes some if not much of the literature on the dynamics of religious belief and behavior.

For much of the twentieth century, secularization theorists posited (and most intellectual, cultural, and political elites believed) that religion was in the final stages of succumbing to the steady march of progress and secular enlightenment; any brief flare-up of religion in the public sphere was simply a manifestation of the desperate last gasps of a dying God. Yet the question of whether God was dead—as *Time* magazine famously mused on the cover of its April 8, 1966, issue—was answered by believers around the world with a decisive "No!" French scholar Gilles Kepel memorably dubbed this global trend "the revenge of God," which he described as "a new religious approach. . . aimed no longer at adapting to secular values but at recovering a sacred foundation for the organization of society—by changing society if necessary."[20] Sociologist José Casanova argued that the world was witnessing a "deprivatization" of religion, meaning "that religious traditions throughout the world are refusing to accept the marginal and privatized role which theories of modernity as well as theories of secularization had reserved for them."[21] In short, any secularization narrative that predicted the complete demise of religion, or even its effective relegation to the privacy of homes and churches, is at best incomplete.

The most striking, and troubling, aspect of this resurgence of religion in the public sphere has been the highly visible and globalized outbreak of religiously inspired violence, of which the September 11, 2001, terrorist attacks in the United States are only the most famous. In his widely popular examination of the global rise of religious violence, *Terror in the Mind of God*, political sociologist Mark Juergensmeyer argued that "The era of globalization and postmodernity creates a context in which authority is undercut and local forces have been unleashed." Chief among these "local forces" is religion, which, because of the comprehensive worldview it offers believers, is "capable of providing the ideological resources for an alternative view of public order," particularly in areas where the modern ideologies and processes of liberal democracy, capitalism, and especially secularism have been perceived to fail to deliver on their promises of advancing humanity to a new stage of peace and prosperity.[22]

Juergensmeyer profiled a number of cases of religiously motivated violence across several of the world's major traditions, including Christian abortion clinic bombers and paramilitary groups in the United States, Jewish and Sikh assassins of political leaders, Muslim suicide bombers, and the Japanese Buddhist Aum Shinrikyo poison gas attack in Toyko. In each of these cases, the perpetrators did not believe that theirs was a first-strike attack; rather, they held "a widely shared perception that the world was already violent: it was enmeshed in great struggles that gave their own violent actions moral meaning." Although recognizing the explicitly political motivations of these acts of violence, Juergensmeyer insisted that they were, at heart, acts of religious militancy: "Religion is crucial for these acts, since it gives moral justification for killing and provides images of cosmic war that allow activists to believe that they are waging spiritual scenarios." This notion of "cosmic war," in which the participants are part of a much broader struggle between the forces of good and evil in which they are called to play a decisive role, is central to Juergensmeyer's analysis; indeed, it is the key element of his argument that there is "a strain of violence that may be found at the deepest levels of religious imagination." Acknowledging that his cases represent a minority strand in the broad spectrum of religious experience and behavior, he nevertheless located the central logic of religious violence in the essential core of "the religious imagination, which always has had the propensity to absolutize and to project images of cosmic war."[23]

The very popularity of Juergensmeyer's book, especially in the undergraduate classroom, testifies to the problem of normalizing and essentializing what is in fact a relatively fringe phenomenon of highly destructive religiously motivated violence. This is further problematized by the fact that some of the subjects in Juergensmeyer's case studies, such as Timothy McVeigh, did not consider themselves to be particularly religious. This speaks to a more substantive critique that Juergensmeyer—like numerous other authors who write on religious violence—is unable to draw a clear distinction between religious violence on the one hand and secular political violence on the other.[24] Isolating the religious variable in acts of violence actually inspired by multiple crosscurrents reinforces the notion that religion is inherently dangerous.

The point is not to dismiss or excuse violence committed by religious militants. It is simply that many of the dynamics ascribed to religion that are claimed to produce violence are generally not, as presented by many scholars, unique to religion. Many if not most of those same traits and processes are present in secular movements as well; thus, an obsession with *religious* violence not only essentializes the phenomenon but potentially distracts attention from more common (and decidedly unreligious) forms of violence. Even acts of violence that clearly have a religious quality can never be fully comprehended by isolating only one variable labeled "religion" while ignoring political, economic, psychological, and other factors. Anything approaching a complete understanding of religiously motivated violence thus requires a multidimensional and multifactorial analysis. It may be helpful to isolate religion for heuristic purposes—as I am largely doing in this chapter—but an examination of the part should never be confused for comprehension of the whole.[25]

A recent attempt to consider the corresponding dynamics of certain types of religious and secular violence comes from a group of psychologists examining what they call "the fundamentalist mindset." These scholars delink the term fundamentalism from its typical association with religion. They identify a series of traits that characterize "fundamentalist" actors, both religious and secular: dualistic thinking; group paranoia or rage; apocalypticism; charismatic leadership; and a totalized conversion experience.[26] This allows them to analyze the Terror of the French Revolution alongside contemporary apocalyptic Christianity in the United States, and Nazism alongside Hindu-Muslim violence in post-partition India. Recognizing that extremism is not the exclusive preserve of religion is a useful step analytically and comparatively. However, the cumulative result of their study is to draw a straight line from the "fundamentalist mindset" to a pathological psychology disposed toward violence and terrorism.[27] Unlike the Fundamentalism Project, which identified fundamentalism as a distinctly and authentically religious response to modernity, here fundamentalism is equated with pathology. Embedded in the "fundamentalist mindset" literature is a meta-narrative about modernity that presupposes its liberal, secular, hyper-rational characteristics. A psychological approach to religious (and all other forms of) militancy is a welcome addition, and no doubt much violence is connected to real individual or social psychological pathologies. However, future researchers should take care not to essentialize one particular modern worldview at the normative expense of competing alternatives. Furthermore, considerably more work needs to be done mapping the psychological profile of "the peacemaker mindset," thus exploring more constructive dimensions of religious militancy.[28]

This is not only an academic debate, in the narrow sense of the term. By continuing to equate religious militancy with violence, scholars—not to mention the mass media and general public—will continue to subtly, if often unintentionally, reify certain secularist assumptions that religion is a problem that needs to be solved if not altogether outgrown. Furthermore, the common association of religion and violence serves to marginalize religion's potential as a constructive social actor. Such an assumption renders the task of religiously militant peacemakers that much more difficult, as they must argue for their own legitimacy within both peacemaking and religious circles even before making their argument with violence. The human fascination with violence is well established, but there is a moral as well as analytical duty for scholars to expand their circle of inquiry to give due attention to all forms of religious militancy—from the violent to the nonviolent. We legitimize what we name, and thus the field will do well to move beyond privileging studies of "religion and violence" to a more encompassing consideration of "religion, conflict, and peacebuilding." The next section illustrates how this broader view helps bring into focus the dynamics of religious militancy as we locate them in operation in a particular historical context, namely the struggle for black civil rights in post–World War II America.

Religious Militancy in Action: A Historical Illustration

The mid-twentieth-century African American civil rights movement has been embraced as one of the core narratives of modern American history, politics, and culture; its most prominent spokesman, Martin Luther King Jr., has now been memorialized on the National Mall in Washington, DC. Historians and schoolchildren alike often interpret the civil rights movement as a logical and in many ways culminating step in the inevitable march of human progress and freedom, a teleological framing of history that lies at the heart of modern liberalism. Generally lost, however, is the fact that, at its core, the movement was a profoundly religious contest, and that its primary battlegrounds were "theaters of complex theological drama."[29] As recent scholars including Charles Marsh and David Chappell have pointed out, many if not most of the principal combatants in the struggle viewed the arenas of battle in Montgomery, Little Rock, Nashville, Birmingham, Oxford, and the Supreme Court as proximate sites in a cosmic struggle between good and evil, including but ultimately transcending competing ideas of racial identity or constitutional democracy. To be sure, the movement featured its share of protagonists who operated within a dominantly secular paradigm, but for the foot soldiers of the struggle on both sides—from nonviolent civil rights activists to violent Ku Klux Klansmen—theirs was God's work, and it demanded their ultimate concern and sacrifice.

We can rightly frame the civil rights movement as a battle of competing religious militancies, ranging from the radically nonviolent to the heinously violent, because that is how the combatants themselves framed it. Textbooks and popular hagiographies have typically painted Martin Luther King as a moderate figure, thus forgetting that in his most famous missive he critiqued moderates and self-identified as a militant. In his 1963 "Letter from a Birmingham Jail," one of the classics in American letters, he responded to some of his critics who had accused him of extremism:

> But though I was initially disappointed at being categorized as an extremist, as I continued to think about the matter I gradually gained a measure of satisfaction from the label. Was not Jesus an extremist for love. . . . Was not Amos an extremist for justice. . . . Was not Paul an extremist for the Christian gospel. . . . Was not Martin Luther an extremist. . . . And Abraham Lincoln. . . . And Thomas Jefferson. . . . So the question is not whether we will be extremists, but what kind of extremists we will be. Will we be extremists for hate or for love? Will we be extremists for the preservation of injustice or for the extension of justice?. . . Perhaps the South, the nation and the world are in dire need of creative extremists.[30]

We see in this passage not only the multiple trajectories of religious militancy, including King's preferred militancy for love and justice, but also the profoundly religious roots of King's worldview. This was not isolated to King, an ordained minister—who in this particular letter was writing to other ministers and thus would naturally invoke biblical language and precedent. Indeed, this deeply biblical worldview suffused the movement, particularly on the level of the grassroots black activists in the South.

Historian David Chappell has contrasted the worldview of these black activists with the confidence held by mid-twentieth-century liberals in the force of human reason and progress to gradually overcome racial prejudice and other vestiges of an unenlightened past. Because they had faith that the process was natural and inevitable, liberals had no burning motivation to undertake drastic action to accomplish their desired ends. Black activists, on the other hand, were "driven not by modern liberal faith in human reason, but by older, seemingly more durable prejudices and superstitions that were rooted in Christian and Jewish myth." They drank from the wells of the Judeo-Christian prophetic tradition, stretching from the Hebrew prophets of ancient Israel to Reinhold Niebuhr in the twentieth century. Accordingly, they inherited a darker, more pessimistic view of human history in which the world and its institutions could not, when left to their own devices, be expected to improve with time. This understanding of history led them away from a comfortable view of human progress toward a more afflicted conviction of human sinfulness, and toward a prophetic activism in which "they had to stand apart from society and insult it with skepticism about its pretensions to justice and truth."[31]

Accompanying this view of history and human corruption was a powerful faith that they were on God's side and that God was on theirs. This was not a shallow invocation of divine favor but a testimony born of "ritualistic expressions of religious ecstasy" experienced in the mass meetings that sustained the movement's rank and file. Although the black church had largely been politically quiescent for the first half of the twentieth century, it revived what Chappell calls "a militant tradition" in the 1950s that hearkened back to its nineteenth-century roots and inspired, legitimated, and sacralized a new generation of militant activists for peaceful social change.[32]

The movement was successful, according to Chappell, precisely because "black southern activists got strength from old-time religion," whereas white liberals and conservatives alike failed "to inspire solidarity and self-sacrificial devotion to their cause." Martin Luther King's self-professed extremism has already been noted. Religious militancy also suffused the lesser-known ranks of the movement. Modjeska Simkins, a radical activist in South Carolina from the 1940s onward, framed the struggle in biblical terms, citing the Apostle Paul's letter to the Ephesians: "For we wrestle not against flesh and blood, but against principalities and powers, against the rulers of darkness of this world, against spiritual wickedness in high places." James Lawson, in his address at the founding conference of the Student Nonviolent Coordinating Committee in 1960, spoke of a battle against sin and evil that demanded complete renunciation, opposition, and self-sacrifice, not a temperate liberal faith in "progress." He asserted that "the nonviolent effort has convicted us of sin," and that the sit-in movement constituted "a judgment upon middle-class, conventional, half-way efforts to deal with radical social evil." Both Reverend Fred Shuttlesworth and student leader John Lewis, both of whom were frequent victims of white supremacist intimidation and violence, referred to the movement as a "crusade." Shuttlesworth in particular invoked militant discourse: "This is a religious crusade, a fight between light and darkness, right and wrong, good and evil, fair play and tyranny. We are assured of victory because we are using weapons of spiritual warfare."[33]

One of the most powerful voices of the movement was Mississippi sharecropper-turned-activist Fannie Lou Hamer. She is commonly remembered for her political mobilizing of poor blacks in rural Mississippi and her powerful testimony at the Democratic National Convention in Atlantic City in 1964, where she described the physical and sexual torture she had undergone at the hands of the state as punishment for her activism. What compelled Hamer to persist through beatings and threats and molestation to establish a new society based on freedom, justice, and most of all love, was not a faith in American constitutionalism or Enlightenment notions of human progress. Rather, her motivation was a radical Christian faith that "was not separable from her practical conception of action in the day-to-day world." In fact, she critiqued those who saw the struggle in purely secular terms. Hamer told the mostly white, liberal students coming to Mississippi to register blacks to vote during Freedom Summer in 1964 that they would need to engage the "extreme" religious devotion among the black masses they came to organize. She was as critical of the black church as of America's hypocrisy, calling out the churches' leaders for their bourgeois moderation. The real Christians—the religious militants—were the activists who were willing to sacrifice everything, including their own lives, for the cause.[34] For Hamer, if religion was not radical—militant—then it was not real religion. "Christ was a revolutionary person," she asserted, "out there where it was happening." Similarly, she pronounced, "If Christ were here today, He would be just like these young people who the Southerners called radicals." The purpose of the movement, for Hamer, was not to fulfill Jefferson's creed but rather to hasten "the beginning of a New Kingdom [of God] right here on earth." Hamer's theology held together "the miraculous and the militant Christ," a creative synthesis that gave her, in Charles Marsh's estimation, "one of America's most innovative religious imaginations."[35]

Black civil rights activists were not the only Southerners compelled by militant religious convictions. Will Campbell, a chaplain at the University of Mississippi before joining the civil rights movement, publicly condemned Southern white churches for their support of racism, accusing them of being extensions of the Ku Klux Klan. He charged that the Klan's appeal was "essentially religious in character," and that the issue of race was fundamentally spiritual for Southerners: "No subject has more religious relevance and arouses more religious support than the subject of race in the South today. . . . The stamp of racism has become a part of [our] religious heritage and it is almost impossible to break through."[36] Most white churches and ministers in the South were "moderate" on the issue of race, meaning (in the parlance of the day) that they believed that relations between whites and blacks were basically harmonious and that greater equality would be achieved over time, without the need for agitation or activism. This moderation frustrated more radical churchgoers, both white and black; Martin Luther King confessed to being "gravely disappointed with the white moderate. . . who is more devoted to 'order' than to justice; who prefers a negative peace which is the absence of tension to a positive peace which is the presence of justice."[37] Yet that same churchly moderation is the very reason David Chappell offers for the ultimate failure of the segregationists, in terms of their inability to rally the masses to give active support to the cause. It was, in his estimation, "the franker racists of the white South [who came] up with more exciting, more inspiring battle cries."[38]

Among the most militant of these "franker racists" was Sam Bowers, Imperial Wizard of the White Knights of the Ku Klux Klan. Bowers led a four-year campaign of terror in Mississippi in which he orchestrated multiple murders, dozens of bombings of black churches, and hundreds of assaults, beatings, and other bombings. Charles Marsh characterizes him as "the animating force behind white Mississippi's journey into the heart of militant rage, the Kurtz at the heart of darkness of the anti-civil rights movement." Bowers was motivated not simply by racial hatred, but also by what he believed was a divine calling and destiny to eliminate the "heretics." In a recruiting poster he referred to civil rights workers as "dedicated agents of Satan" who were "absolutely determined to destroy Christian Civilization and all Christians." By contrast, he and his followers were the true followers of

Jesus who were "MILITANTLY DETERMINED" to preserve their nation, their liberty, and their religion. Bowers's hate was not limited to non-Anglo-Saxon racial groups; he also furiously denounced Jews and "Papists" (Roman Catholics). Bowers's life had for the most part been without distinction until he heard God speak to him in a powerful epiphany that left him convinced that he had a special role to play in a larger cosmic drama in which the forces of good and evil were arrayed against one another. He acknowledged that he had gone beyond the point of moderate, socially acceptable religion, claiming, "To be saved one must go to the point of insanity." Bowers decided to devote his life to doing anything that God called him to do in preserving the purity and soul of his native Mississippi.[39]

What God called Bowers to do was to lead an armed vigilante movement against the "outside agitators" who were invading his home state and threatening to undermine its white Christian character. A voracious reader of religious texts, Bowers knew that the teachings of Jesus were not readily put to use in justifying terrorist violence. His answer reveals the elasticity of scripture and theology to support a desired agenda:

> As Christians we are disposed to kindness, generosity, affection and humility in our dealings with others. As militants we are disposed to use physical force against our enemies. How can we reconcile these two apparently contradictory philosophies? The answer, of course, is to purge malice, bitterness and vengeance from our heart. . . . If it is necessary to eliminate someone, it should be done with no malice, in complete silence and in the manner of a Christian act.

Sam Bowers was the archetypal Christian militant, an ardent believer in the radical sovereignty of God. Since God's majesty filled all time and space, he demanded complete and unequivocal loyalty and obedience. The greatest sinner is the heretic, who must be responded to decisively and eliminated so that the heresy does not spread. Just as John Lewis and Fred Shuttlesworth saw their struggle for black equality as a crusade, Bowers understood his role as a high priest or prophet-warrior leading a holy war in which the enemy, as the enemy of God, could be given no quarter. Attacks against selected targets "should, of course, be as severe as circumstances and conditions will permit." Human laws and due process could be suspended precisely because it was a time of crisis and the enemies would try to "twist" the law "away from its original Divine design" and toward their own nefarious purposes. As Bowers framed it, Southern Christians faced one of two choices: "SEGREGATION, TRANQUILITY AND JUSTICE, or BI-RACISM, CHAOS AND DEATH." Or, even more starkly, "It is simply what it has always been for centuries: Christ versus Satan." Those who willfully opted for biracialism, chaos, death, and Satan were "devoid of grace" and, by divine decree, "*must be eliminated*."[40] With the murders of civil rights activists Vernon Dahmer, Andrew Goodman, James Chaney, and Michael Schwerner, as well as the hundreds of other acts of violence and intimidation against blacks and whites fighting for interracialism and equality, Bowers proved the depth of his militant commitments. It would be incorrect to say that religion was the exclusive source or inspiration for Bowers's militancy, but his theological convictions did play a substantial role in his self-understanding and public framing of the violent battle he waged.

The lives and worldviews of activists on all sides of the battle over black civil rights were powerfully shaped by their respective individual and communal images of God and readings of scripture and tradition. All were convinced that theirs was a righteous cause and that God was on their side, yet their religious militancy, though drawing from the same Christian scriptures and invoking the same Christian God, led them down radically different paths.

For all of these militants, from the nonviolent Fannie Lou Hamer to the violent Sam Bowers, God demanded everything of them—their total commitment, ultimate concern, and complete willingness to sacrifice their own lives if necessary in a righteous cause.

No doubt secular causes muster similar devotion—one need look no further than the millions who have killed and died for their country since the advent of nationalism. But at least in this particular context, it was those activists motivated by deep-seated religious commitments born of radical encounters with the divine who were most willing to give up their lives and bodies (or, in the case of Bowers, other people's lives and bodies) for their apprehension of the coming kingdom of God. Chappell proposes that no other explanation suffices for the ultimate commitment demonstrated by the powerful nonviolent witness of the core civil rights activists:

> It is hard to imagine masses of people lining up for years of excruciating risk against southern sheriffs, fire hoses, and attack dogs without some transcendent or millennial faith to sustain them. It is hard to imagine such faith being sustained without emotional mass rituals—without something extreme and extraordinary to link the masses' spirits. It is impossible to ignore how often the participants carried their movement out in prophetic, ecstatic biblical tones.[41]

Similarly illustrative scenarios could easily be drawn from virtually any other country and religious tradition. Together they provide an empirical base of case studies upon which scholars can continue to theorize and problematize the roots, nature, and dynamics of religious militancy, in both its violent and nonviolent manifestations. In the end, our theories and analyses will only be as valuable as the concrete realities they purport to explain.

HARNESSING RELIGIOUS MILITANCY FOR PEACE

In many ways a retrospective account of a bipolar struggle over black civil rights offers a deceptively simple scenario in which hatred, injustice, and violence are arrayed against love, justice, and peace; few people would look back and identify with Sam Bowers's brand of religious militancy over Fannie Lou Hamer's. That judgment only makes sense, however, when acknowledged as being normatively informed. From a strictly utilitarian standpoint, Hamer's self-sacrificial commitment to justice and compassion makes no more sense than Bowers's devotion to rooting out what he saw as the gravest threats to societal integrity, morality, and stability. Particularly in cases that feature competing value systems, each operating under their own respective logics of ultimate concern, peacebuilding must adopt an ethical perspective in order to make value-based judgments and strategic determinations that privilege certain ideas and behaviors over others—put simply, elevating peace over violence, justice over injustice.

This includes a willingness to critique all actors in a conflict—as they may all have blood on their hands—and then to transcend judgment in a move toward reconciliation. It was a politician, Abraham Lincoln, who made perhaps the profoundest American theological statement along these lines. In his Second Inaugural Address, given only a month before the end of the devastating American Civil War and six weeks before his assassination, Lincoln reflected that citizens and leaders of both the Union and Confederacy "read the same Bible and pray to the same God, and each invokes His aid against the other." Given these competing religious militancies, "The prayers of both could not be answered. That of neither has been answered fully. The Almighty has His own purposes." Lincoln thus drew as the only possible conclusion an ethic of peacebuilding striking in its foundations in humility and compassion: "With malice toward none, with charity for all, with firmness in the right as God gives us to see the right, let us strive on to finish the work we are in, to bind up the nation's wounds. . . to do all which may achieve and cherish a just and lasting peace among ourselves and with all nations."[42]

An ethical commitment to peacebuilding in the face of "the ambivalence of the sacred" also requires a certain boldness in asserting, as Gerard Powers says, "that an interpretation of a religious tradition or certain religious practices that promote violence and injustice are 'inauthentic,' whereas those that are a force for peace and justice are 'authentic.'"[43] In one sense Powers's argument is tautological: peacebuilders' version of religion is authentic simply because they say so. But no doubt those who invoke religious arguments in the service of violence, such as Sam Bowers or Osama bin Laden—and for that matter, George W. Bush— would claim the same for themselves; indeed, no religious militant would admit that their invocation of religion is *prima facie* inauthentic. Given the internal pluralism characteristic of all the world's great religious traditions and texts, the peacebuilding religious militant's claim to authenticity—and the scholar's recognition of such—can only operate when grounded upon a normative commitment to something akin to John Paul Lederach's and Scott Appleby's concept of "justpeace," which they define as "a dynamic state of affairs in which the reduction and management of violence and the achievement of social and economic justice are undertaken as mutual, reinforcing dimensions of constructive change."[44]

Given the normative commitments of the peacebuilder, then, we can proceed—cautiously—in making value-laden assessments about the types of activities that will harness the self-emptying power of religious militancy into an ethic of nonviolence rather than holy war. As Powers notes, religious peacebuilders are operative at every point along the multiple stages of conflict, immersing themselves in a range of activities including observation and witness, education and formation, advocacy and empowerment, and conciliation and mediation.[45] Without wanting to minimize in the least the crucial importance of religious peacebuilders' work at other points within the conflict cycle, here I want to emphasize the essential work to be done by peace-oriented religious militants on the front edge of the cycle, before underlying patterns of cultural and structural violence escalate into full-blown killing and other horrors. I operate under the same assumptions as the contemporary medical profession: namely, that preventive medicine is by no means the only legitimate type of medicine to be practiced, but its success greatly reduces the likelihood that other forms of interventionist medicine will come into play, as well as mitigating the severity of the presenting symptoms and underlying system failures that will require future treatment if left unaddressed.

In the arena of conflict prevention, religious peacebuilders must engage on at least three fronts: seriously confronting, and then besting, the arguments of violent militants; finding ways to capture the great mass of people who are not militants at all, but rather follow the broad path of casual moderation; and directly naming and challenging the underlying violence of the modern nation-state. Peacebuilding is best served usually not by completely defusing the fervor of religious militancy but rather by harnessing its potency in the direction of nonviolence and justice. The precise dynamics of how this plays out in a given situation will vary. In some cases a challenge from peacebuilders who are religious but not members of the religious community in question could be well received as insider-outsider impartials. In other cases, members of the religious community serving as insider-impartials may be more effective. Finally, insiders who represent one party (presumably the nonviolent one) may be successful as insider-partials.[46]

The primary battle for believers' hearts and minds is fought within each individual tradition, often at the local level of the church, the synagogue, the mosque, or the temple. It is not enough to casually dismiss violence as an "inauthentic" expression of faith; it is a temptation for peacebuilders to be glib about their own righteousness while dismissing their violent opponents as hopelessly misguided and malicious—thus mimicking the very processes of demonization and othering that help give rise to violence. Rather, recognizing that religious traditions operate according to their own distinctive logics and that every tradition is internally plural, peacebuilding militants must be able to mount a convincing, even overwhelming, argument, based squarely on the theology, ritual, and ethics of their particular tradition, that will resonate with the faithful majority of religious leaders and laity who have not had the training or occasion to think deeply about these issues and who can otherwise be swayed by the seductive logic of violence in a moment of crisis. In doing so, they must seriously engage the rhetoric, symbols, and narratives that are invoked by violent militants in convincing fellow believers that theirs is God's cause.

There are any number of examples of scholars and religious leaders who have identified the powerful resources within their scriptures and tradition that exhort the faithful to a life dedicated to peace and justice. But many of these otherwise admirable endeavors adopt the tactic of reading selectively, excising the problematic texts and stories that would undermine their purposes. By so doing they are not only engaged in the same method of selective retrieval that is employed by violent militants in picking out the elements of the tradition that will inspire people to violence, but they are setting up the faithful for a sense of betrayal if and when they encounter the contrary passages and narratives on their own. One model that may address this problem is to acknowledge with brutal honesty the blood and violence within one's own tradition, rather than avoiding it or shamefully shoving it into the closet.

A recent example of this method is Philip Jenkins's book *Laying Down the Sword*, in which he argues against the selective editing of the Bible that Christians have done for centuries in their formal, liturgical readings of scripture. While Jenkins acknowledges a certain utility in institutional and individual forgetting, the trouble is that the nettlesome, violent texts have not been purged from the scripture but remain there dormant, waiting for a Sam Bowers or some other engineer of violence to discover and apply them. Jenkins's strategy is for religious traditions—he deals primarily with Christianity and Islam—to admit their bloody origins, "come to terms with them, and understand where they fit into the broader scheme of the faith." Rather than ignoring the difficult passages, he demonstrates how they can be "absorbed, comprehended, and freely discussed." What emerges from Jenkins's proposed reading of the scripture in its totality is a "deeper-rooted faith" that requires a profound level of humility and a chastening—if not rejection—of triumphalist notions that *ours* is a peaceful faith while *theirs* encourages violence. In short, what Jenkins calls for is "a process of truth and reconciliation" in which even the hardest sayings of the Bible are encountered "without compromise or apology."[47] The intention behind this approach is not to dilute the potency of religious commitment but to shine light into the corners of the tradition and thus dispel their dark, fearful power. This form of pedagogical peacebuilding encourages a strong formation in the faith that would resist facile manipulations by religious militants—though it must be reiterated that the textual cherry-picking performed by many aspiring peacemakers is a casualty of this approach just as much as that of the violent extremists.

An endorsement of any peacebuilding tactic that relies largely on ideas and texts must come with the stoutest of caveats: no matter how essential theories, theologies, and histories are in constructing an intellectual and religious rationale for the pursuit of peace and justice, peacebuilding cannot be merely an intellectual project. This is particularly true of "strategic peacebuilding," which emphasizes the blending of theory and praxis. There is no shortage of intellectuals and religious adepts (this author included) who have offered eloquent apologias for peace. The challenge is disseminating those ideas among the masses so as to transform the entire discursive paradigm in which the faithful operate. This has been accomplished on both micro- and macro-levels in every tradition, so precedent is available for recovery and appropriate application. It will typically be accomplished within the bounds of the tradition, with religious leaders who have acquired spiritual capital among the faithful leading adults, youth, and children in new paths of religious formation that steer the militancy of ultimate concern toward peace. The work of leaders such as Martin Luther King and James Lawson in marshaling the distinctive spiritual resources of the African American community not just for a nonviolent protest campaign but also for the personal transformation of participants is emblematic of this approach.[48] Such a transformation can also be accomplished in ecumenical settings, as is done by the Chicago-based Interfaith Youth Core, which encourages its student participants to explore the depths of their own tradition to find resources for pluralism, tolerance, and cooperation and then coming together to enact those values in concrete projects working alongside members from other traditions.[49]

In short, it is not enough to have two parallel discourses that can be exploited by religious militants inclined either toward nonviolence or violence. Peacebuilders must try to win the argument. This is not a foolproof strategy, as textual and historical warrants for violence will persist in every tradition. The challenge, therefore, is to make the aspirations and practice of justpeace normative within the tradition, working within the assumptions, discourses, symbols, rituals, worldview, and political and cultural structures of the religious community. Doing so will help crowd out arguments in favor of violent extremism, as well as empowering ordinary believers and practitioners—not just the religious leadership—to identify with and intentionally enact the peaceable elements of their tradition. It is for this reason that Appleby compellingly argues for giving greater attention to religious education and formation. "Deep formation in the peaceable heart of a religious tradition," he argues, "is fundamental to the religious militancy that can serve conflict transformation, whether through participation in humanitarian intervention, peacekeeping, rights advocacy, community organizing, election monitoring, conflict mediation, or dialogue with aggrieved members of rival ethnic or religious communities."[50] Paying sufficient and strategic attention to religious militancy on the front end of the conflict cycle can yield long-term dividends by minimizing religiously legitimated violence and enhancing the proclivities and capacities of religious actors to work for peace.

Religious militants for peace will not only denounce religiously motivated extremism but also level a poignant critique of the structures, practices, and widespread acceptability of the violence of the secular state. Religious militants need not be critical of secularism per se. Indeed, a liberal secular pluralism that grants the public recognition and influence of religion and religious actors may be the best pragmatic, political option in many if not most places, and it can be congenial to the aims of religiously militant peacebuilders. The excesses and idolatries of religious nationalism are easily spotted targets here, as are religious actors who use the state machinery—in both democratic and totalitarian systems—to advance their own often exclusionary and even violent purposes.[51] But a deep religious commitment to peace and justice will also seek to historicize and deconstruct the monopoly on violence that has been at the foundation of the modern statebuilding project from Westphalia to the present. Religious peacebuilders will not seek to reclaim the right to violence from the state, but rather to call out all the forms of physical, structural, and cultural violence wrought by the ultimate concern of secular nationalism.[52] Religiously militant peacebuilders must therefore go beyond (without neglecting) individualist ethics and think systemically, accounting for the structures of power, inequality, and violence that are endemic in a world dominated by sovereign nation-states and transnational corporations. Again, this does not necessarily entail an assault on the accommodating processes of a pluralistic, and presumably secular, public sphere, though questions can and should be asked about who is privileged in particular arrangements. But militants for peace cannot settle for countering the violent extremism within their own religious tradition or others. They must adopt a comprehensive approach that considers state violence, gender-based violence, economic violence, and other impediments to a fuller realization of a social order characterized by justpeace.

NOTES

1. Christopher Hitchens, *God Is Not Great: How Religion Poisons Everything* (New York: Twelve Books, 2007), 15, 25, 31–32.

2. Charles Kimball, *When Religion Becomes Evil* (San Francisco: HarperSanFrancisco, 2002), 1.

3. See R. J. Rummel, "20th Century Democide," http://www.hawaii.edu/powerkills/20TH. HTM; and "What? Only 35,000,000 Killed in 20th Century War?," http://democratic-peace.wordpress.com/2008/11/30/what-only-35000000-killed-in-20th-century-war/. Rummel notes that most of these deaths resulted from authoritarian regimes. Lower estimates—between 180 and 231 million killed by the state—are provided by Matthew White, "Wars, Massacres and Atrocities of the Twentieth Century," http://users.erols. com/mwhite28/war-1900.htm; and Milton Leitenberg, "Deaths in Wars and Conflicts in the 20th Century" (occasional paper, Cornell University Peace Studies Program, 2006), http://www.cissm.umd.edu/papers/files/deathswarsconflictsjune52006.pdf.

4. R. Scott Appleby, *The Ambivalence of the Sacred: Religion, Violence, and Reconciliation* (Lanham, MD: Rowman and Littlefield, 2000), 7, 11, 13.

5. The relevant literature is vast, but important theoretical works include Talal Asad, *Formations of the Secular: Christianity, Islam, Modernity* (Stanford, CA: Stanford University Press, 2003); and William T. Cavanaugh, *The Myth of Religious Violence: Secular Ideology and the Roots of Modern Conflict* (New York: Oxford University Press, 2009). For specific examples, see Philip Almond, *The British Discovery of Buddhism* (Cambridge: Cambridge University Press, 1998); Richard King, *Orientalism and Religion: Postcolonial Theory, India and "the Mythic East"* (London: Routledge, 1999); Ann Taves, *Fits, Trances, and Visions: Experiencing Religion and Explaining Experience from Wesley to James* (Princeton, NJ: Princeton University Press, 1999); Tomoko Masuzawa, *The Invention of World Religions; or, How European Universalism Was Preserved in the Language of Pluralism* (Chicago: University of Chicago Press, 2005); Tisa Wenger, *We*

Have a Religion: The 1920s Pueblo Indian Dance Controversy and American Religious Freedom (Chapel Hill: University of North Carolina Press, 2009); and J. Spencer Fluhman, *"A Peculiar People": Anti-Mormonism and the Making of Religion in Nineteenth-Century America* (Chapel Hill: University of North Carolina Press, 2012).

6. See Russell T. McCutcheon, "The Imperial Dynamic in the Study of Religion: Neocolonial Practices in an American Discipline," in *Post-Colonial America*, ed. C. Richard King (Urbana: University of Illinois Press, 2000), 275–302; and Kevin Schilbrack, "Religions: Are There Any?" *Journal of the American Academy of Religion 78*, no. 4 (2010): 1112–1138.

7. Cavanaugh, *Myth of Religious Violence*, 4.

8. See Mark Juergensmeyer, Margo Kitts, and Michael Jerryson, eds., *The Oxford Handbook of Religion and Violence* (New York: Oxford University Press, 2012). For a brief literature review, see Chapter 2 of this volume.

9. Paul Tillich, *Dynamics of Faith* (New York: Harper and Brothers, 1957), 1–2, 4, 9, 12, 16.

10. Tillich, *Dynamics of Faith*, 1–2.

11. Charles S. Liebman, "Extremism as a Religious Norm," *Journal for the Scientific Study of Religion 22*, no. 1 (1983): 75, 79, 84–85. It should be noted that Liebman's usage of "extremism" does not necessarily equate the term with violence the way that Appleby's taxonomy does.

12. Deut. 6:5; recapitulated by Jesus in the Christian New Testament at Matt. 22:37, Mark 12:30, and Luke 10:27.

13. Qur'an 21:25.

14. Bhagavad Gita 18:65.

15. John Blofeld, trans., *I Ching: The Book of Change* (New York: Penguin, 1991), 183 (Hexagram 50: *Ting*—A Sacrificial Vessel).

16. This insight resonates with the fourfold pattern of fundamentalists' interaction with the world—world conqueror, world transformer, world creator, and world renouncer—outlined in Gabriel A. Almond, Emmanuel Sivan, and R. Scott Appleby, "Explaining Fundamentalisms," in *Fundamentalisms Comprehended*, ed. Martin E. Marty and Appleby (Chicago: University of Chicago Press, 1995), 426–429.

17. Liebman, "Extremism as a Religious Norm," quote from 79.

18. Liebman, "Extremism as a Religious Norm," quote from 82–83.

19. John Cumpsty, "Glutton, Gourmet or Bon Vivant: A Response to Charles S. Liebman," *Journal for the Scientific Study of Religion 24*, no. 2 (1985): 217–221. William Cavanaugh makes a similar critique of Enlightenment formulations that construct religion "as an irrational and dangerous impulse that must give way in public to rational, secular forms of power" (Cavanaugh, *Myth of Religious Violence*, 4). Scott W. Hibbard, in *Religious Politics and Secular States: Egypt, India, and the United States* (Baltimore: Johns Hopkins University Press, 2010), theorizes diverse patterns of interaction between the secular and the religious in various political contexts.

20. Gilles Kepel, *The Revenge of God: The Resurgence of Islam, Christianity and Judaism in the Modern World*, trans. Alan Braley (University Park: Pennsylvania State University Press, 1994), 2.

21. José Casanova, *Public Religions in the Modern World* (Chicago: University of Chicago Press, 1994), 5.

22. Mark Juergensmeyer, *Terror in the Mind of God: The Global Rise of Religious Violence*, 3rd ed., rev. and updated (Berkeley: University of California Press, 2003), xii.

23. Juergensmeyer, *Terror in the Mind of God*, xi, 6, 12, 248.

24. See Cavanaugh, *Myth of Religious Violence*, 30–31.

25. See James W. Jones, *Blood that Cries Out From the Earth: The Psychology of Religious Terrorism* (New York: Oxford University Press, 2008), 21–22.

26. Charles B. Strozier and Katharine Boyd, "Definitions and Dualisms," in *The Fundamentalist Mindset: Psychological Perspectives on Religion, Violence, and History*, ed. Charles B. Strozier, David M. Terman, and James W. Jones, with Katharine A. Boyd (New York: Oxford University Press, 2010), 11.

27. A popular example building on similar assumptions is Jon Krakauer, *Under the Banner of Heaven: A Story of Violent Faith* (New York: Anchor Books, 2004).

28. Charles B. Strozier and David Terman, "Introduction," in Strozier et al., *The Fundamentalist Mindset*, 3, 7. One parallel approach has been to profile the lives, work, and philosophies of a number of religious peacemakers. See David Little, ed., with the Tanenbaum Center for Interreligious Understanding, *Peacemakers in Action: Profiles of Religion in Conflict Resolution* (New York: Cambridge University Press, 2007).

29. Charles Marsh, *God's Long Summer: Stories of Faith and Civil Rights* (Princeton, NJ: Princeton University Press, 1997), 3.

30. Martin Luther King Jr., *Why We Can't Wait* (1964; repr., New York: Signet Classic, 2000), 76–77.

31. David L. Chappell, *Stone of Hope: Prophetic Religion and the Death of Jim Crow* (Chapel Hill: University of North Carolina Press, 2004), 3.

32. Chappell, *Stone of Hope*, 5, 94. On the historical and theological trajectory of African American Christianity in the twentieth century from deradicalization to re-radicalization, see Gayraud S. Wilmore, *Black Religion and Black Radicalism: An Interpretation of the Religious History of African Americans*, 3rd ed. (Maryknoll, NY: Orbis Books, 1998), chapters 7–9.

33. Chappell, *Stone of Hope*, 8, 66, 71, 75, 88; biblical quote from Eph. 6:12.

34. Chappell, *Stone of Hope*, 71–73.

35. Marsh, *God's Long Summer*, 5, 33, 39, 46.

36. Jason Sokol, *There Goes My Everything: White Southerners in the Age of Civil Rights, 1945–1975* (New York: Vintage Books, 2006), 101–102.

37. King, *Why We Can't Wait*, 72–73.

38. Chappell, *Stone of Hope*, 7.

39. Marsh, *God's Long Summer*, 49–50, 54; emphasis in original.

40. Marsh, *God's Long Summer*, 61, 66, 70, 73, 80; emphasis in original.

41. Chappell, *Stone of Hope*, 102.

42. Second Inaugural Address of Abraham Lincoln (Washington, DC, March 4, 1865), available online at http://avalon.law.yale.edu/19th_century/lincoln2.asp.

43. Gerard F. Powers, "Religion and Peacebuilding," in *Strategies of Peace: Transforming Conflict in a Violent World*, ed. Daniel Philpott and Gerard F. Powers (New York: Oxford University Press, 2010), 322.

44. John Paul Lederach and R. Scott Appleby, "Strategic Peacebuilding: An Overview," in Philpott and Powers, *Strategies of Peace*, 23.

45. Powers, "Religion and Peacebuilding," 323.

46. See Paul Wehr and John Paul Lederach, "Mediating Conflict in Central America," in *Resolving International Conflicts: The Theory and Practice of Mediation*, ed. Jacob Bercovitch (Boulder, CO: Lynne Rienner Publishers, 1996), 55–74. For further discussion of the relevant issues, see Richard K. Betts, "The Delusion of Impartial Intervention";

Saadia Touval and I. William Zartman, "International Mediation in the Post–Cold War Era"; and R. Scott Appleby, "Religion as an Agent of Conflict Transformation and Peacebuilding," all in *Turbulent Peace: The Challenges of Managing International Conflict*, ed. Chester A. Crocker, Fen Osler Hampson, and Pamela Aall (Washington, DC: US Institute of Peace Press, 2001).

47. Philip Jenkins, *Laying Down the Sword: Why We Can't Ignore the Bible's Violent Verses* (New York: HarperOne, 2011), 23–26.

48. See Taylor Branch, *Parting the Waters: America in the King Years, 1954–63* (New York: Touchstone, 1988). For evidence that nonviolent leaders such as King and Lawson were not universally heeded, even in the black community, see Christopher B. Strain, *Pure Fire: Self-Defense as Activism in the Civil Rights Era* (Athens: University of Georgia Press, 2005).

49. More information on the Interfaith Youth Core can be found at its website, http://www. ifyc.org/. See also Eboo Patel, *Acts of Faith: The Story of an American Muslim, the Struggle for the Soul of a Generation* (Boston: Beacon Press, 2007), especially 151–182, as well as Chapter 18 in this volume, co-authored by Patel and Cassie Meyer.

50. Appleby, *Ambivalence of the Sacred*, 286.

51. See Atalia Omer and Jason Springs, *Religious Nationalism: A Reference Handbook* (Santa Barbara, CA: ABC-CLIO, 2013). For individual illustrations, see Michael A. Sells, *The Bridge Betrayed: Religion and Genocide in Bosnia* (Berkeley: University of California Press, 1996); Stanley J. Tambiah, *Leveling Crowds: Ethnonationalist Conflicts and Collective Violence in South Asia* (Berkeley: University of California Press, 1997); Mark A. Noll, *The Civil War as a Theological Crisis* (Chapel Hill: University of North Carolina Press, 2006).

52. See A. Rashied Omar, "Religion, Violence and the State: A Dialogical Encounter between Activists and Scholars" (PhD diss., University of Cape Town, 2006).

BIBLIOGRAPHY

Almond, Gabriel A., Emmanuel Sivan, and R. Scott Appleby. "Explaining Fundamentalisms." In *Fundamentalisms Comprehended*, edited by Martin E. Marty and R. Scott Appleby, 425–444 Chicago: University of Chicago Press, 1995.

Almond, Philip. *The British Discovery of Buddhism*. Cambridge: Cambridge University Press, 1998.

Appleby, R. Scott. *The Ambivalence of the Sacred: Religion, Violence, and Reconciliation*. Lanham, MD: Rowman and Littlefield, 2000.

Appleby, R. Scott. "Religion as an Agent of Conflict Transformation and Peacebuilding." In Crocker et al., *Turbulent Peace*, 821–840.

Asad, Talal. *Formations of the Secular: Christianity, Islam, Modernity*. Stanford, CA: Stanford University Press, 2003.

Betts, Richard K. "The Delusion of Impartial Intervention." In Crocker et al., *Turbulent Peace*, 285–294.

Blofeld, John, trans. *I Ching: The Book of Change*. New York: Penguin, 1991.

Branch, Taylor. *Parting the Waters: America in the King Years, 1954–63*. New York: Touchstone, 1988.

Berger, Peter L. "The Desecularization of the World: A Global Overview." In *The Desecularization of the World: Resurgent Religion and World Politics*, edited by Peter L. Berger, 1–18. Washington, DC: Ethics and Public Policy Center, 1999.

Casanova, José. *Public Religions in the Modern World*. Chicago: University of Chicago Press, 1994.

Cavanaugh, William T. *The Myth of Religious Violence: Secular Ideology and the Roots of Modern Conflict*. New York: Oxford University Press, 2009.

Chappell, David L. *Stone of Hope: Prophetic Religion and the Death of Jim Crow*. Chapel Hill: University of North Carolina Press, 2004.

Crocker, Chester A., Fen Osler Hampson, and Pamela Aall, eds. *Turbulent Peace: The Challenges of Managing International Conflict*. Washington, DC: US Institute of Peace Press, 2001.

Cumpsty, John. "Glutton, Gourmet or Bon Vivant: A Response to Charles S. Liebman." *Journal for the Scientific Study of Religion* 24, no. 2 (1985): 217–221.

Fluhman, J. Spencer. *"A Peculiar People": Anti-Mormonism and the Making of Religion in Nineteenth-Century America*. Chapel Hill: University of North Carolina Press, 2012.

Hibbard, Scott W. *Religious Politics and Secular States: Egypt, India, and the United States*. Baltimore: Johns Hopkins University Press, 2010.

Hitchens, Christopher. *God Is Not Great: How Religion Poisons Everything*. New York: Twelve Books, 2007.

Jenkins, Philip. *Laying Down the Sword: Why We Can't Ignore the Bible's Violent Verses*. New York: HarperOne, 2011.

Jones, James W. *Blood that Cries Out From the Earth: The Psychology of Religious Terrorism*. New York: Oxford University Press, 2008.

Jergensmeyer, Mark. *Terror in the Mind of God: The Global Rise of Religious Violence*, 3rd ed. Berkeley: University of California Press, 2003.

Juergensmeyer, Mark, Margo Kitts, and Michael Jerryson, eds. *The Oxford Handbook of Religion and Violence*. New York: Oxford University Press, 2012.

Kepel, Gilles. *The Revenge of God: The Resurgence of Islam, Christianity, and Judaism in the Modern World*. Translated by Alan Braley. University Park: Pennsylvania State University Press, 1994.

Kimball, Charles. *When Religion Becomes Evil*. San Francisco: HarperSanFrancisco, 2002.

King Martin Luther, Jr. *Why We Can't Wait*. New York: Signet Classic, 2000. First published 1964 by Harper and Row.

King, Richard. *Orientalism and Religion: Postcolonial Theory, India and "the Mythic East."* London: Routledge, 1999.

Krakauer, Jon. *Under the Banner of Heaven: A Story of Violent Faith*. New York: Anchor Books, 2004.

Lederach, John Paul, and R. Scott Appleby. "Strategic Peacebuilding: An Overview." In *Strategies of Peace: Transforming Conflict in a Violent World*, edited by Daniel Philpott and Gerard F. Powers, 19–44. New York: Oxford University Press, 2010.

Leitenberg, Milton. "Deaths in Wars and Conflicts in the 20th Century." Occasional Paper #29, 3rd ed., Cornell University Peace Studies Program, Ithaca, NY, 2006. http://www.cissm.umd.edu/papers/files/deathswarsconflictsjune52006.pdf.

Liebman, Charles S. "Extremism as a Religious Norm." *Journal for the Scientific Study of Religion* 22, no. 1 (1983): 75–86.

Lincoln, Abraham. Second Inaugural Address. Washington, DC, March 4, 1865. Available online at http://avalon.law.yale.edu/19th_century/lincoln2.asp.

Little, David, ed., with the Tanenbaum Center for Interreligious Understanding. *Peacemakers in Action: Profiles of Religion in Conflict Resolution*. New York: Cambridge University Press, 2007.

McCutcheon, Russell T. "The Imperial Dynamic in the Study of Religion: Neocolonial Practices in an American Discipline." In *Post-Colonial America*, edited by C. Richard King, 275–302. Urbana: University of Illinois Press, 2000.

Marsh, Charles. *God's Long Summer: Stories of Faith and Civil Rights*. Princeton, NJ: Princeton University Press, 1997.

Masuzawa, Tomoko. *The Invention of World Religions; or, How European Universalism Was Preserved in the Language of Pluralism*. Chicago: University of Chicago Press, 2005.

Noll, Mark A. *The Civil War as a Theological Crisis*. Chapel Hill: University of North Carolina Press, 2006.

Omar, A. Rashied. "Religion, Violence and the State: A Dialogical Encounter between Activists and Scholars." PhD diss., University of Cape Town, 2006.

Omer, Atalia, and Jason Springs. *Religious Nationalism: A Reference Handbook*. Santa Barbara, CA: ABC-CLIO, 2013.

Patel, Eboo. *Acts of Faith: The Story of an American Muslim, the Struggle for the Soul of a Generation*. Boston: Beacon Press, 2007.

Powers, Gerard F. "Religion and Peacebuilding." In *Strategies of Peace: Transforming Conflict in a Violent World*, edited by Daniel Philpott and Gerard F. Powers, 317–352. New York: Oxford University Press, 2010.

Rummel, R. J. "20th Century Democide." http://www.hawaii.edu/powerkills/20TH.HTM.

Rummel, R. J. "What? Only 35,000,000 Killed in 20th Century War?" http://demo-craticpeace.wordpress.com.   http://democraticpeace.wordpress.com/2008/11/30/what-only-35000000-killed-in-20th-century-war/.

Schilbrack, Kevin. "Religions: Are There Any?" *Journal of the American Academy of Religion* 78, no. 4 (2010): 1112–1138.

Sells, Michael A. *The Bridge Betrayed: Religion and Genocide in Bosnia*. Berkeley: University of California Press, 1996.

Smith, Jonathan Z. "Tillich['s] Remains. . ." *Journal of the American Academy of Religion* 78, no. 4 (2010): 1139–1170.

Smith, Wilfred Cantwell. *The Meaning and End of Religion*. Minneapolis, MN: Fortress, 1962.

Sokol, Jason. *There Goes My Everything: White Southerners in the Age of Civil Rights, 1945–1975*. New York: Vintage Books, 2006.

Soloveitchik, Haym. "Migration, Acculturation, and the New Role of Texts in the Haredi World." In *Accounting for Fundamentalisms: The Dynamic Character of Movements*, edited by Martin E. Marty and R. Scott Appleby, 197–235 Chicago: University of Chicago Press, 1994.

Strozier, Charles B., and Katharine Boyd. "Definitions and Dualisms." In *The Fundamentalist Mindset: Psychological Perspectives on Religion, Violence, and History*, edited by Charles B. Strozier, David M. Terman, and James W. Jones, with Katharine A. Boyd, 11–15. New York: Oxford University Press, 2010.

Strozier, Charles B., and David Terman. Introduction to *The Fundamentalist Mindset: Psychological Perspectives on Religion, Violence, and History*, edited by Charles B. Strozier, David M. Terman, and James W. Jones, with Katharine A. Boyd, 3–7. New York: Oxford University Press, 2010.

Strain, Christopher B. *Pure Fire: Self-Defense as Activism in the Civil Rights Era*. Athens: University of Georgia Press, 2005.

Tambiah, Stanley J. *Leveling Crowds: Ethnonationalist Conflicts and Collective Violence in South Asia*. Berkeley: University of California Press, 1997.

Taves, Ann. *Fits, Trances, and Visions: Experiencing Religion and Explaining Experience from Wesley to James*. Princeton, NJ: Princeton University Press, 1999.

Tillich, Paul. *Dynamics of Faith*. New York: Harper and Brothers, 1957.

Touval, Saadia, and I. William Zartman. "International Mediation in the Post-Cold War Era." In Crocker et al., *Turbulent Peace*, 427–444.

Wehr, Paul, and John Paul Lederach. "Mediating Conflict in Central America." In *Resolving International Conflicts: The Theory and Practice of Mediation*, edited by Jacob Bercovitch, 55–74. Boulder, CO: Lynne Rienner Publishers, 1996.

Wenger, Tisa. *We Have a Religion: The 1920s Pueblo Indian Dance Controversy and American Religious Freedom*. Chapel Hill: University of North Carolina Press, 2009.

White, Matthew. "Wars, Massacres and Atrocities of the Twentieth Century." http://users.erols.com/mwhite28/war-1900.htm.

Wilmore, Gayraud S. *Black Religion and Black Radicalism: An Interpretation of the Religious History of African Americans*. 3rd ed. Maryknoll, NY: Orbis Books, 1998.

CHAPTER 9

··

RELIGIOUS VIOLENCE
AND STATE VIOLENCE

··

A. RASHIED OMAR

Notwithstanding Max Weber's definition of the modern state as "the association that claims the monopoly of the legitimate use of violence," religious leaders have often refused to yield authority on the question: the state's legal monopoly of violence does not render moral its every use of violence.[1]

THIS chapter seeks to address a palpable neglect of systemic violence and state-sponsored terror in the literature on religion and violence.[2] This glaring omission of the role of the state tends to reinforce the biased assumption that religious violence and terrorism are the preserve of non-state actors. As I will demonstrate in what follows, the tendency to attribute deadly violence almost exclusively to non-state religious actors obscures the larger view of the interaction between religious and state actors and seriously distorts analysis of the phenomenon of religious involvement in deadly conflict.

There are a few rare exceptions to this myopia with respect to state violence, such as the context-specific studies of David Chidester (*Shots in the Streets: Violence and Religion in South Africa*[3]), Michael A. Sells (*The Bridge Betrayed: Religion and Genocide in Bosnia*[4]), and Paul Brass (*The Production of Hindu-Muslim Violence in Contemporary India*[5]). More recently, William T. Cavanaugh (2009) has produced a seminal study, *The Myth of Religious Violence: Secular Ideology and the Roots of Modern Conflict*,[6] in which he turns on its head the "founding myth" of the dominant secularist paradigm of the twentieth century—that religion is inherently sectarian and thus has a distinctive proclivity for violence—and makes a compelling argument that the modern nation-state provoked the violence that has been credited to religion. These atypical and revisionary analyses illustrate the state's complicity in fomenting violence.[7] The lessons from them however, have been largely ignored in comparative and theoretical studies on religion and violence. I am curious to discover why.

This fault line is nowhere better illustrated than in the work of the American sociologist Mark Juergensmeyer, one of the leading figures in current scholarship on religion and violence.[8] Juergensmeyer is emblematic of a larger trend in the literature in which this analytical slippage occurs. In his influential work *Terror in the Mind of God: The Global Rise of Religious Violence* (2000), while acknowledging that of "all of the worst incidences of genocidal killings this century have been perpetrated by public officials invoking a sort of state terrorism," Juergensmeyer nevertheless proceeds to deal exclusively with the violence of non-state actors.[9] As a result, the chief focus of his study is to describe the psychological mindset of these non-state actors, which renders them vulnerable to appropriate the violent elements of their religious texts.[10] What he omits in his hermeneutical reading is that social text or context contributes equally to the violent appropriation of the sacred. Looming large in the social context is the state and its coercive ideological apparatuses.

Juergensmeyer's widely read study ignores the dialogical nature of violence. Thus he concentrates solely on one side of the equation and denudes the state of any agency and responsibility in the production of violence. Unwittingly his monocausal analysis buttresses state authority and obscures the role of the state in complex conjunctions of violence.

The inattention to the role of the state in fomenting violence is striking, and it seems all the more anomalous given the fact that the hegemonic paradigm of most contemporary scholars is that of "modernity," and political modernity, as the influential German sociologist Max Weber (d. 1920) recognized, depended upon the centralized state monopolizing the legitimate use of violence.[11] Since Weber, every scholar of modernity acknowledges that not only political discourses but also ethical and sociological discourses are informed by and configured within the dominance and prerogatives of the state; it shapes every discourse, vision, and theory. S. Parvez Manzoor usefully captures this aspect of modernity. "The modern perception of reality," Manzoor argues, "not only of the political world but also of the moral, aesthetic and intellectual dimensions of our existence, is largely through the prism of the state."[12] Why, then, is the state largely absent in current academic analyses of the role of religion in violence?

This chapter contends that there is an urgent need, in the words of some political theorists, to "bring the state back in[to]" theoretical discourses on religion and violence.[13] My central argument is that an understanding of the state's role in conflict, and in particular a critical appraisal of how it obtains its legitimacy and exercises its "monopoly of violence," is crucial to a more nuanced grasp of the relationship between religion and violence. Such a balanced understanding of religious violence, in addition to increasing the accuracy of analysis, would contribute to the development of more effective methodologies in the subfield of religion, conflict transformation, and strategic peacebuilding.

In pursuit of my goal, I raise three interrelated research questions: First, how does the post–Cold War literature deal with the issue of systemic institutional violence and state-sponsored terror? Second, under what conditions and through which mechanisms are religious discourses and actors enlisted in legitimating the state's use of violence? And, last but not least, how do current theories on religion and violence challenge and/or serve state interests in coercive practices?

In what follows, I argue that Western scholarly perspectives on religion and violence (which have become a growth industry since September 11, 2001) are artificially slanted toward state interests, to the detriment of those resisting state excesses in various contexts. In this regard, scholars and experts radically misunderstand the big picture of religions' intersection with violence in the post–Cold War era. Are there examples of alternative scholarship that provide a corrective to this error?

My key hypothesis is that rethinking the nexus between religion and violence to include the role of the state will inevitably lead us to a different appreciation of the relationship between religion and violence. The "religion and violence" school of thought must be firmly and radically expanded to constitute a triad of religion, violence, and the state. It is my hope that this expanded analysis will augment the intellectual efforts of Cavanaugh and others to develop what I call a polycentric (as opposed to Eurocentric and Weberian)[14] theory of religion, violence, and the state that expands and deepens our understanding of religious violence and provides new resources for conflict transformation and strategic peacebuilding.

By exploring the intricate connections between religion, violence, and the state in three diverse contexts—the anti-apartheid struggle in South Africa (1948–1994), the war in Bosnia-Herzegovina (1992–1995), and the "communal" conflict in the Gujarat state of India (2002)—this chapter seeks to amplify the rare existing studies that highlight the critical role of the modern state in the production of violence.[15] The three case studies developed in this chapter identify different aspects of the nexus between religion and violence. But all three point to the critical role of the state and illuminate the ways in which religion can sanctify state-sponsored violence.

RELIGION AND VIOLENCE UNDER APARTHEID SOUTH AFRICA

From 1948 to 1994, South Africa was governed by a system of structural violence known as "apartheid." This vicious system institutionalized the oppression and dehumanization of people of color. It legalized racial discrimination, sociopolitical oppression, and economic exploitation. Non-whites were forced to live in separate areas and were not allowed to vote. According to David Chidester, under the apartheid system, "violence was everywhere. It was an integral part of the discourses, practices and social formations through which human beings struggled to be human."[16] This was the grim reality that South Africans had to contend with for close to half a century until the historic nonracial elections held on April 27, 1994, that brought Nelson Mandela to power.

What is significant for our purpose here is that the white supremacist policy of apartheid was created in the name of Calvinist Christianity. Many of the key leaders of the oppressive apartheid regime were also devout adherents of the Dutch Reformed Church (DRC). The discriminatory apartheid education policy was labeled "Christian National Education." These facts spurred the composition of an important theological document, *The Kairos Document* (1985), produced by black South Africans, which lamented this Christian legitimation of the structural violence of apartheid.[17]

I have found a conspicuous neglect of the South African case in the deluge of literature on religion and violence that has flooded the market since the end of the Cold War. For example, the bibliography of religion and violence compiled by Christopher Candland lists just over a dozen entries.[18] Furthermore, Candland's choice of bibliographical subheadings is intriguing. He lists case studies such as "Religious Violence in Nigeria and the Sudan," "Religion in the Conflict in Northern Ireland," and "Violence and Religious Nationalism in South Asia." To categorize the South African situation, he chooses the curious title of "Afrikaner Violence and Liberation Theology in Southern Africa."[19] The general impression is that religion was not implicated in the violence of apartheid, and that its roots lay elsewhere, in Afrikaner nationalism, and if indeed religion was involved in legitimating violence at all, it was doing so in support of the liberation movement. This one-sided perspective appears to be pervasive in the scholarship and thinking about religion and violence under apartheid.

The most prominent title in the scant catalogue on religion and violence in South Africa is an edited volume, *Violence and Theology*, by one of the most prolific scholars in the field, Charles Villa-Vicencio.[20] He collected nineteen articles in which some of the most influential anti-apartheid theologians in South Africa, including Desmond Tutu, debated the theological roots of mainstream Christianity's legitimation of state violence and its consequent disinclination to legitimate revolutionary violence in the struggle against apartheid.[21] Most of the authors argue that the time for debating whether the church should support the revolutionary violence in South Africa is over, for by the mid-1980s, the conditions in apartheid South Africa were ripe for the application of the just war criteria set forth by classical theologians such as Augustine of Hippo, Thomas Aquinas, Martin Luther, and John Calvin. This theological position is usefully depicted by Albert Nolan and Mary Armour: "The criteria of the just-war being present [in the South African situation] is not really at issue, in that ample evidence exists as regards the existence of a manifest longstanding tyranny."[22]

Theology and Violence powerfully captures the critique of anti-apartheid theologians regarding mainstream Christianity's duplicitous position on the question of religion and violence. Along the way, the authors note the dominant tradition of the church blessing the state's use of violence, while condemning violent revolution against the ruling authorities. "Suffice it to say that held captive to the dominant forces of what has come to be known as 'Western Christian civilization,' the Christian religion has come to be an important part of the ideological framework that has supported the existence of successive regimes in different parts of the world who affirm the dominant values of the West," writes Villa-Vicencio. "And the inclination of the church to legitimate the use of violence by these regimes, while opposing revolutionary violence to overthrow such regimes, is a natural consequence of this ideological captivity."[23]

The rich essays contained in Villa-Vicencio's edited volume are by far the most widely cited materials on religion and violence in South Africa.[24] However, due to an explicit theological position, more general literature on religion and violence does not afford it a central location. Perhaps the reason for its neglect in the academy is its theological bias. For while this anthology includes some compelling arguments in support of revolutionary violence, and does raise some interesting theoretical questions, especially about the historical predisposition of the powerful elites for the religious legitimation of state violence, it is essentially a theological inquiry. The only two works that place the South African case within the context of the theoretical debate on religion and violence are *Shots in the Streets*, by David Chidester, and *The Ambivalence of the Sacred*, by Scott Appleby.

Chidester's contribution is the only volume that deals exclusively with religion and violence in South Africa. More importantly, he is the only scholar who has applied the theoretical insights gained from the international debate to explicate the diverse ways in which religion was implicated in the violence of apartheid. Unlike most historians of religion, Chidester does not avoid the difficult challenge of defining violence. He confronts it head-on and not surprisingly chooses to start his analysis not with a single definition of violence but with four: direct physical harm, the violation of humanity, illegitimate force, or legitimate liberation.[25] He identifies three types of religious violence in South Africa as the focus of his study: ritual killing, dehumanization through torture, and the spiritual politics of the armed struggle against apartheid.[26] Utilizing insights gleaned from the theory of René Girard on sacrifice and scapegoating, Chidester successfully demonstrates that two notorious cases of public violence—the execution of eight black pedestrians in the capital city of Pretoria by a white supremacist, Barend Strydom, and the public killing of a black community counselor by a gang of black township residents—followed a religious logic of sacrificial killing and ritual elimination.[27]

Chidester's pioneering attempt to theorize violence and religion in South Africa has, however, made little impact on the broader debate within the Western academy.[28] For example, in *The Ambivalence of the Sacred,* one of the only instances I have found of a significant treatment of the South African case in the theoretical literature on religion and violence, Chidester's volume is not cited. Nevertheless, Appleby's work deals with the South African case both within the broader theological as well as the theoretical debates on the religious legitimation of violence. He argues tangentially that during the apartheid era, the Dutch Reformed Church, as well as some charismatic and evangelical churches, deliberately chose not to challenge the oppressive apartheid system and that under "conditions of systemic, state-supported violence this was an unacceptable option" and essentially meant "support for the status quo by default." Appleby employs the *Kairos Document* in making the case that both state theology and church theology were implicated in legitimating apartheid. In church theology, synthesizing the Kairos position, Appleby avers that "violence becomes part of the state propaganda. It refers to the actions of those who seek to overthrow unjust structures, but not to the violence of the structures, nor to the violence of the State in maintaining such structures."[29]

Demonstrating religious complicity with apartheid violence is, however, not Appleby's major thesis. On the contrary, he invokes the South African case as a plausible Christian argument for legitimating revolutionary violence in resisting and even overturning the apartheid state. Appleby carefully analyzes the theological positions on religion and violence in the context of apartheid of some of the most prominent South African anti-apartheid clerics, including Alan Boesak, Frank Chikane, and Buti Tlhagale. The following quotation from Desmond Tutu usefully captures the duplicity black Christians saw in the "mainstream tradition" on violence: "Dietrich Bonhoeffer, who plotted to murder Hitler, came to be regarded as a modern-day martyr and saint. But when it comes to the matter of black liberation, the West and most of the Church suddenly begins to show pacifist tendencies."[30]

Curiously, Appleby does not invoke the South African case as a model of any of his three typological patterns of religious violence, which he enumerates as fundamentalism, ethno-religious nationalism, and liberationism.[31] However, one anthropologist who studies comparative religions, Richard T. Antoun, has made the case for one or other strand within the Afrikaner Reformed Church to be considered as typically fundamentalist.[32] Antoun uses the Afrikaner reading of the Bible as a concrete example of what he calls "traditioning," one of the key features of a fundamentalist movement. In my view, the DRC's justification of apartheid would have made a useful example of ethno-religious nationalism. More pertinent, however, is Appleby's cogent synthesis of the moral arguments marshaled by the anti-apartheid churches in making a credible case to legitimate counter-violence against the apartheid state. This, in my perspective, may be an appropriate example of the liberationist prototype and could be used to strengthen this unexplored dimension of Appleby's typology.[33]

Regrettably, Appleby's important reference to the South African case has not been recognized in any of the plethora of reviews of his book. Neither has this been taken up by any of the unprecedented number of books on religion and violence that have been written since its publication in 2000. Perhaps this is due in part to the fact that his analysis of the South African case is tucked away in the middle of chapter 1, in which he is elaborating elements of a theory of religion and violence rather than analyzing the case substantively on its own merits. Appleby's treatment of apartheid South Africa is not unique but in the lack of attention it received, it shares the same plight as Chidester's study; the scant impact of both show the striking neglect of the apartheid case in the proliferating literature on religion and violence.

The question of why this is so gets to the heart of my critique. I suggest three possible reasons for this neglect. The first might be that many scholars are not convinced that religion was implicated in apartheid violence. The second centers on the hypothesis of South African exceptionalism: the notion that the apartheid case is so unique that it does not correspond to other contexts in which religion has been implicated in violence.

But the third, and to my mind, most compelling explanation of this oversight is powerfully brought to the fore by the anti-apartheid Kairos theologians, who wrote that that "the Christian religion has come to be an important part of the ideological framework that has supported successive regimes in different parts of the world who affirm the dominant values of the West. And the inclination of the Church to legitimate the use of violence by these regimes is a natural consequence of this ideological captivity."[34] Transposing this critique to the Western academy, one may make a comparable proposal: *Is the scholarly neglect of the South African case a reflection of the pro-state bias in the dominant literature on religion and violence?*

In the next section of this essay, I explore how the lessons that might have been learned from the South African experience have eluded theorists in their attempts to account for the religious dimensions of the violence that engulfed the Balkans in the mid-1990s, ironically at the same time that South Africa was being liberated from apartheid.

The Role of Religion in the Bosnian War: An Assessment of the Literature

> A resurgence of religious violence has caught the post–cold war world off guard. From the subways of Tokyo to the ruins of the mosque in India, from the World Trade Center and the federal building in Oklahoma City to a Jerusalem rally for the Israeli prime minister, religious militants have transgressed the boundaries of civil society in pursuit of their aims. Bosnians have faced the most brutal religious violence unleashed in the aftermath of the cold war.[35]

The quotation is taken from *The Bridge Betrayed: Religion and Genocide in Bosnia*, by Michael Sells. In the book, Sells makes a compelling case that the war in Bosnia and Herzegovina, which lasted from March 1, 1992, until December 14, 1995, should be considered a "religious genocide" in that "it was religiously motivated and religiously justified." Sells argues that Serb aggression "was religious genocide in several senses: the people destroyed were chosen on the basis of their religious identity; those carrying out the killings acted with the blessings and support of Christian church leaders; the violence was grounded in a religious mythology that characterized the targeted people as race traitors, and their extermination as a sacred act; and the perpetrators of the violence were protected by the policy makers of a Western world that is culturally dominated by Christianity."[36] Sells was fully aware that his "religious genocide thesis" was provocative and challenged conventional wisdom. In fact, this seems to have been one of the key purposes of the book.

Miroslav Volf takes issue with Sells' interpretation of the role of religion in the Bosnian genocide. He argues that the "primary motivation for the war was not religious but rather political, economic and cultural." When they claimed to be "fighting for our faith, the Serbian Orthodox Church," Volf writes, were not "offering either the primary motivation or primary justification for their actions." Rather, "religious rhetoric," he goes on to argue, "is only one of the many rhetorics employed, and a subordinate one at that."[37] Another Croatian historian of religion, Paul Mojzes, who has written extensively on the role of religion in the Balkans conflict, acknowledges the liberal use that was made of religious symbols and myths, as well as the complicity of high-profile religious leaders in supporting the atrocities. Nonetheless Mojzes also concludes that the war was primarily "ethnonationalist" not religious.[38]

Notwithstanding this robust debate among scholars concerning the precise role of religion in the Bosnian War, no attention is given to the Bosnian conflict in the global survey of contemporary religious terror in Juergensmeyer's *Terror in the Mind of God*—a disconcerting fact. Among the eighty-five interviewees and correspondents he lists at the back of his book, there is not a single individual from the Balkans.[39] Moreover, Juergensmeyer mentions Bosnia only twice. Interestingly, the first time he refers to it is in the context of "state terrorism" and the second time he simply notes that "During the height of the conflict in Bosnia in the mid-1990's . . . mosques stayed open and the symphony orchestra of Sarajevo kept to its concert schedule, performing to mixed audiences [*sic*]."[40]

Highlighting this inconsistency in scholarship on the role of religion in the Bosnian conflict, Appleby argues that "some Western analysts, following the lead of the apologists for religion on the scene, downplayed the religious dimension of the war and argued that political, economic, and cultural factors were far more prominent in causing and sustaining it—as if 'culture' were a category somehow independent of religion."[41] Appleby goes on to argue that by "exculpating the religious leaders on the grounds that they were protecting their respective religious and cultural communities," the "'religion did not do it' camp" inadvertently undermined their own claims.[42]

In attempting to correct this apparent contradiction in Western scholarship on the role of religion in legitimating the violence in Bosnia, Appleby proceeds to develop a sophisticated analysis of what he calls "ethnoreligious" violence "because it is virtually impossible to disaggregate the precise roles of religion and ethnicity."[43] He furthermore argues that "for many people, *religion is intrinsically a part of the sense of ethnicity*" and that religion more often than not does not break down ethnic barriers; on the contrary, it frequently fortifies them.[44] Drawing on the twin themes of mimesis and the scapegoat advanced by René Girard, Appleby's analysis of the Bosnian conflict lends credence to the claim that it is sameness rather than difference that leads to mimetic rivalry and lies at the heart of the conflict. In support of his thesis he argues that the Serbs and Croats, "twinned tribes mutually scornful and yet imitative of each other, each desiring its own sacred nation with expanded 'purified' borders, found a handy scapegoat in the Muslims of Bosnia. Latecomers to the ways of eth-noreligious nationalism, the Bosnian Muslims fell prey to the genocide-legitimating propa-ganda by which Christian extremists deemed them 'race traitors' and 'apostates.'"[45]

Appleby's account of the role of religion in the Bosnian War, however helpful and nuanced, falls short, ironically, of giving ethno-religious violence a subordinate position within his broader typology of post–Cold War religious violence. He gives it less weight than what he defines as "fundamentalist violence." For Appleby, in the case of the for-mer, religion is an *accomplice* to violence. But in "fundamentalist violence," religion plays a preeminent role unencumbered by "ethnic" and "nationalist" considerations. While to his credit Appleby does argue that not all fundamentalists are violent, he still leaves the question open as to why it is that when Christians are complicit in legitimating violence, as was the case in the Balkans, the role of religion is inferior or dependent—unlike when Muslims are implicated, as for example in the cases of Lebanon and the Sudan, both of which Appleby depicts as fundamentalist types of violence. Recent events in both of these countries have adequately demonstrated that the conflicts cannot be reduced to religion. The March 2005 assassination of the former Lebanese prime minister Rafiq al-Hariri sparked widespread protests in that country, supported equally by Muslims and Christians. Moreover, the brutal campaigns by the Arab-dominated northern Sudanese regime to put down a rebellion by black tribes in the Darfur region of Western Sudan has shown that the conflict in that country has, in addition to the religious dimension, strong racial and eth-nic overtones. How else is one to explain the fact that the Arab North as well as its Darfur adversaries are both predominantly Muslim?[46]

Almost two decades after the war in Bosnia there are still vigorous debates concerning the causes and nature of the conflict. Sells has argued that the Belgrade regime under the leader-ship of Slobodan Milosevic and the newly established Croatian state under the leadership of Franco Tudjman were directly implicated in generating the atrocities perpetrated against Bosnian Muslims. His view resonates with the conclusions of some of the most influential scholars who have written on the Bosnian War, such as Roy Gutman and Norman Cigar.[47] All these scholars agree that the war can be classified as ethnic cleansing and genocide and that it would not have been possible without the active involvement of the state. More signifi-cantly, this perspective has been buttressed by a judgment handed down at the International Criminal Tribunal for the former Yugoslavia (in The Hague).[48]

Of course, other scholars have denied the plausibility of genocide.[49] How does one make sense of such diverse scholarly assessments of the Bosnian War? I contend that this diver-gence of scholarly opinion, while in itself reflecting an essential part of the nature of the academy, is not immune to political conditioning. This vulnerability is not unique to the academy, however, but is even more apparent in international institutions. For example, all the major international institutions, including the UN and the European Union, failed to fully appreciate the role of state authorities in the Bosnian conflict. Underscoring such a cri-tique, de Graaff maintains that "the centrality of the state was often overlooked in the West, because state actors in Former Yugoslavia tried to hide that they were behind the violence, as well as how they aimed at creating new states."[50] I would add that hegemonic intellectual paradigms, which privilege the state, have also contributed to obscuring the insidious role of the state.

We turn now to India, complicating the picture further by looking at a discourse yet more alien to the Western academy—that of Hinduism.

GUJARAT: A HARVEST OF HATE?[51]

> Indian government officials have acknowledged that since February 27, 2002, more than 850 people have been killed in communal violence in the state of Gujarat, most of them Muslims.. . . The attacks on Muslims are part of a concerted campaign of Hindu national- ist organizations to promote and exploit communal tensions to further the [Bharatiya Janata Party's] political rule—a movement that is supported at the local level by militant groups that operate with impunity and under the patronage of the state.

The above quotation comes from a Human Rights Watch report on the communal vio- lence that engulfed the Western Indian state of Gujarat in February and March of 2002.[52] Its conclusion states: "State officials of Gujarat, India, were directly involved in the killings of hundreds of Muslims since February 27 and are now engineering a massive cover-up of the state's role in the violence." This statement confirms an earlier, independent report by India's National Human Rights Commission.[53] Not surprisingly however, the charge of state com- plicity in the violence was highly controversial and contested.[54]

It is to be expected that opinions about a sensitive topic such as the causes of an outbreak of violence between members of two different religious groups will invariably differ radi- cally. One of the most striking aspects of the case of the Gujarat violence of 2002, however, is the near unanimity of the judgment. More than sixty national and international agencies who investigated the 2002 Gujarat violence all concluded that officials of the Gujarat state were complicit.[55] Scholarly opinions have been no less unanimous. Paul Brass,[56] Ashutosh Varshney,[57] Peter van der Veer,[58] Upendra Bax,[59] and Ashgar Ali Engineer[60] all agree that the violence was not a spontaneous reaction but was in fact orchestrated by groups closely aligned to the *Sangh Parivar* and the Bharatiya Janata Party (BJP) government. Two of these scholars who hold opposing theoretical perspectives—Brass and Varshney—have both felt confident enough to declare the 2002 communal violence of Gujarat a "pogrom." In the case of Varshney, this is particularly revealing: he has never applied this strong label to any other incident of violence in post-independence India, including the anti-Sikh violence that broke out in Delhi after the assassination of Indira Gandhi in 1984. In fact, he has been at the fore- front of arguing against scholars such as Brass that the anti-Sikh violence of 1984 was *not* a pogrom.[61] This time, albeit cautiously, Varshney says, "Unless later research disconfirms the proposition, the existing press reports give us every reason to conclude that the riots in Gujarat were the first full-blooded pogrom in independent India."[62]

Varshney has been careful to nuance his bold position by arguing that the existing evi- dence suggested that at least in March if not in April 2003 the culpability of the state lay in condoning the killings.[63] He suggested that the contention that the government officially encouraged anti-Muslim violence cannot be conclusively proved on the basis of existing evi- dence. He did, however, leave the door open for such a proposition to be proven by later research.

In contradistinction, Brass has taken a much bolder position and has invoked the Gujarat 2002 case as clear evidence in support of his major thesis that most, if not all, of the commu- nal violence in contemporary India does not arise spontaneously but rather is consciously orchestrated, or in his words, "produced by institutionalized riot systems."[64] One is tempted to ask: Could this be the case with the Gujarat riots of 2002?

More than a decade after the tragedy, the condemnation and calls for justice for the victims have not dissipated but become even stronger. In January 2005, Amnesty International released their investigative report on the 2002 communal violence in Gujarat:

> [I]n relation to the violence in Gujarat in 2002, India has not fulfilled its obligations to protect fundamental rights guaranteed in its constitution and in international treaties to which it is a party. Reports received from human rights groups in India indicate that the Government of Gujarat may have been complicit in at least part of the abuses perpetrated in Gujarat in 2002. There is evidence of connivance of authorities in the preparation and execution of some of the attacks and also in the way the right to legal redress of women victims of sexual violence has been frustrated at every level. Furthermore, the Gujarat state has failed to meet their international obligations to bring to justice perpetrators of crimes against humanity.[65]

Like all the investigative reports, the Amnesty International report makes for shocking reading. It concludes that the violence in Gujarat was not merely a failure of law and order, but was deliberately planned with the active knowledge and involvement of key government and police officials.

In March 2005, a campaign was launched in the United States by the Coalition Against Genocide to prevent the Gujarat Chief Minister, Narendra Modi, from entering the country to speak at the Annual Convention and Trade Show convened by the Asian American Hotel Owners Association in Florida on March 24–26, 2005.[66] On the same visit, Modi was also scheduled to speak at Madison Square Garden in New York on March 20. In their memorandum calling on the US State Department to withdraw Modi's visa, the coalition claimed that Modi was in violation of the International Religious Freedom Act of 1998 and other international laws and that the Modi government in Gujarat was responsible for the deaths of thousands of its citizens, organized violence, large-scale displacement of minority populations, and continuing denial of justice. The coalition also noted that two civil suits had been filed against Modi for crimes against humanity and genocide. Not least, "a climate of terror permeates civil society in Gujarat even today."[67]

To the astonishment of many observers, the coalition's demand was heeded and Modi's US visa was revoked. In a statement justifying the visa withdrawal, the US embassy in India said that the visa had been revoked under "Section 604 of the International Religious Freedom Act which makes any foreign official who has engaged in particularly severe violations of religious freedom inadmissible to the US."[68] Modi claimed that it was the Gujarat government's stand against religious conversions in the state that was the main reason for the withdrawal of his visa. "They [Americans] think that by providing monetary benefits, they can conduct [religious] conversions in the state. But that person (Modi) did not allow it to happen and so was denied a visa," he said in a press statement afterwards.[69] Through this statement, Modi was of course cynically trying to exploit one of the major sources of religious conflict in contemporary India, namely, that of the Hindu opposition to Christian proselytism. This is a useful example of the manner in which a highly placed politician may appeal to religious grievances in order to advance his political agenda and interests.

After a comprehensive survey of the welter of investigative reports, proliferating scholarly opinions, and active human rights campaigns, one may safely conclude that the BJP government of the state of Gujarat and its supporting Hindu religious network, the *Sangh Parivar*, were complicit in the violence directed against Muslims in 2002. What implications does this clear-cut case of state-sponsored violence targeting a community defined by ethno-religious boundaries hold for theories of religion and violence?

It is instructive to note that a decade later, there are very few scholarly treatises within the Western academy focusing on the Gujarat case.[70] In fact, most of them are edited volumes that have been published in India. There appears to be a palpable neglect of scholarly works that clearly implicate the state. I propose that one reason why instances such as that of Gujarat are unconsciously ignored is that they do not fit into what I would describe as the pro-statist Weberian paradigm within which much of the current research on religion and violence operates. The unfortunate result is that religious violence is reduced to the activities of non-state actors. The state is often absent from, or occupies a very small role in contemporary accounts of religious violence. Applying this to the case of India, the dominant discourse defines the Kashmir and Sikh activists seeking self-determination as terrorists par excellence, while the role of the Indian state in spawning religious violence is ignored, and would only become visible in an extreme case such as that of the former Taliban regime of Afghanistan.

It is here that there appears to be a major problem in the perspectives of scholars who are more attuned to recognizing the awesome power of the state in fomenting violence. Swami Agnivesh argues that the modern nation-state has been wrapped in "a certain aura of legitimacy."[71] This, he claims, is why people initially found it hard to believe that the Gujarat state was implicated in the brutal killings of Muslims in 2002. Agnivesh contends that the chief lesson from the Gujarat tragedy is the following: "What is far more dangerous and reprehensible in the contemporary age [than the religiously motivated violence of non-state actors] is the potential of the state itself becoming an instrument of genocide or carnage." The reasons for this, he claims, are twofold: "First, the real actor [in state violence] is faceless, and second, state-sponsored genocide is legitimized and camouflaged by the fact that government has come to power through democratic means and has the support of the constitution."[72] He provides Hitler and the Nazi regime as a clear example of this: "Hitler came to power through democratic means and used his position to exterminate the Jews." He further argues:

> One of the chief reasons why Hitler was able to get away with his policy of genocide against the Jews was that it took a long time for people to realize what was happening. When it was happening many people did not realize it, because they were deluded by the fact that it was a democratically elected government. The case of the BJP-led government of Narendra Modi and his Gujarat pogrom is very similar. I have been warning people about it for a long time, but no one cared to listen.[73]

Agnivesh believes that religious activists as well as other civil society activists, should be vigilant, constantly monitoring the state so as to counterbalance the tendency not to question the exercise of its awesome coercive powers. This is precisely how he conceives of his own role in relationship to politics and the state. His constructive example of the role of religion in the public sphere is, however, not unique. There are numerous other examples that need to be lifted up so that the reality of religion in public life is evaluated in a more positive and comprehensive manner in the academic literature. But what about the key theoretical question of the ever-present potential of the state to become an instrument of carnage and genocide? When will this be taken seriously by scholars of religion and violence?

It is encouraging to note that recently a few scholars have, in fact, tried to incorporate the destructive potential of the state into their theorizing of the question of violence. These scholars have been drawing on the theories of the biopolitical state first formulated by the French philosopher Michel Foucault (1926–1984) and later taken up slightly differently by the Italian scholar Giorgio Agamben. [74] Both critics attempted to uncover and denaturalize the logic of state sovereignty and power.

One of the Indian scholars associated with the Subaltern Studies project, Angana P. Chatterji, has already begun to apply some of these novel insights into her analysis of Hindu nationalism and communal violence in India.[75] Anthropologist Veena Das has raised the vexing question of how the biopolitical state, which is invested with the responsibility of preserving and managing bare life, can also allow and even cause the death of significant parts of the population.[76] "We are living in an era in which the state is more in the business of producing killable bodies than that of managing life," she contends.[77] In support of her contention, she cites the mass killings and plundering of Muslims in Gujarat in February and March 2002 as an instructive example.

These new theoretical perspectives provide us with some hope for the emergence of a polycentric perspective of religion and violence that fully integrates the important role of the state into its analysis. It is disconcerting to note, however, that these scholarly endeavors, especially those of the Subaltern school, are not considered part of mainstream scholarship in the Western academy. Their novel and challenging theoretical insights are currently marginalized in the mainstream disciplines of the social sciences. They are conspicuously absent from the growing sub-discipline of religion and violence.

The case of the communal violence in Gujarat in 2002 once again illustrates the critical importance of holding onto a broader definition of violence that does not exclude systemic and structural violence. The tragic lesson from Gujarat is that the aura surrounding the awesome power of the modern nation-state has further buttressed the inherent tendency of the state to commit excesses in the execution of its legitimate coercive force. This, I propose, needs to be challenged. Unfortunately, theorists of religion and violence in the Western academy have not yet taken this perspective on the state seriously enough. Such a polycentric theoretical focus is, however, evident in the research work of the Subaltern Studies project and especially in the work of Veena Das.

The analysis of Gujarat in this essay concludes my three case studies and represents a third instance of how the modern nation-state is deeply implicated in the production of violence, and how organized religion, instead of countering it, only too often serves to further legitimize it.

Towards a Theory of Religion, Violence, and the State

A survey of the scholarly writing on religion and violence over the past two decades has led me to conclude that it is *inadequate* in accounting for systemic violence, in that it tends to ignore state-sponsored terror. The paradigm stands: the state is a neutral or an unmarked category, while non-state activists are the religiously motivated purveyors of violence.

Inattention to the lessons of the South African case exposes the deficiencies of theories on religion and violence and reminds us of the conditioning effect of power on scholarly analysis of the causes of violence.[78] I offer at least two possible explanations for this bias in the prevailing theoretical perspectives on religion and violence. First, I attribute it to the widely held assumption derived from the state-centric Weberian paradigm that state violence is "legitimate." From this vantage point, state violence by definition is viewed as force gone wrong. By implication, therefore, the force employed by the state, even if it results in direct physical harm, cannot be regarded as violence, since it is employed in order to enforce the law. Such definitions that privilege the state's use of violence inevitably have the double effect of delegitimizing the use of violence by non-state actors under any and all circumstances and obscuring the excesses of the state in the exercise of its power.

Second, I point to the conditioning influence of political location in the framing of academic discourse. In this matter, anthropologist Jeffrey Sluka observes that "academics, media and governments neglect state terror in their diagnosis of violence due to their own political and ideological biases rather than empirical evidence."[79] Sluka's contention has been confirmed by the findings of an international comparative study conducted at the University of Hawaii. The study found that state-sponsored violence, measured by the number of killings, far outweighs that of the violence perpetrated by non-state actors.[80] Yet despite this compelling empirical evidence, one hears more about the terror and violence perpetrated by non-state actors than those of the state.

Demonstrating the complicity of the scholarly community in such distorted analysis, Chidester reinforces Sluka's claim by stating that "academic institutions, disciplines, teaching and research are necessarily implicated in the ceremonies of power in the network of social relations within which they operate."[81] Illustrating that problem, Mahmood Mamdani calls to our attention the fact that two of the leading proponents of the "Clash of Civilizations" thesis, Bernard Lewis and Samuel Huntington, have both served as political advisors to the United States policy establishment dating back to the end of the Vietnam War.[82]

The three case studies to which I have drawn attention—South Africa, Bosnia-Herzegovina, and Gujurat, India—accentuate different aspects of the nexus of religion and violence. However, they have one key thing in common: they point to the critical role of the state. In particular, all three illuminate the manner in which religion can buttress and sanctify state-sponsored violence.

The case of apartheid South Africa provides a particularly compelling critique of the existing theories on religion and violence. It exposes their paucity and underscores the importance of broadening the existing academic definition of violence to include that of systemic state violence. The fact that David Chidester's endeavor to apply the theoretical insights gained from the apartheid case to the international discourse on religious violence has been completely disregarded in the broader debate within the Western academy is instructive in this regard.

The case of the state of Gujarat in India provides further empirical support for the view that state-sponsored violence is one of *the* most important sources of contemporary violence. The aura that surrounds the awesome power of the modern nation-state has further reinforced the state's natural tendency toward excess in the execution of its "legitimate" coercive force. Although a few scholars such as the anthropologist Veena Das have studied the issue, this perspective on the state has unfortunately not yet been taken seriously enough by most theorists of religion and violence in the Western academy.

The Bosnian case illustrates the difficulty of disentangling the religious from the ethnic, and these in turn, from the socio-economic and political factors in situations of deadly conflicts. It also provides a strong example of the denial of the complicity of religion in state-sponsored violence. Is this perhaps one reason why Michael Sells's seminal study on religious genocide and the critical role of the Serbian state in Bosnia has been largely ignored in the comparative and theoretical studies on religion and violence?

CONCLUSION

The conclusion that these three cases lead us to is inescapable: the modern nation-state has to be brought centrally into our theorizing of religion and violence.

At the outset of my essay, I hypothesized that incorporating the role of the state into the existing theory of religion and violence would make it possible to construct a more nuanced and polycentric (as opposed to Eurocentric) theory of religion, violence, and the state. Instead of aiming for a single overarching and all-comprehensive *theory* to add to the religion and violence literature, I propose a new *framework* for the analysis of situations of religious violence. I choose a framework rather than a typology in order to accommodate the range of empirical circumstances with which we are confronted when we observe religion and violence. Through reviewing the religion and violence literature, I note the primarily *dyadic* quality of most scholars' analyses. The frame of discourse moves from the pole of religion to the pole of violence, remaining mute regarding the role of the governing state. I propose, therefore, that a frame of analysis that is *triadic* rather than dyadic be foundational to the field of religion and violence—and the state. This framework is illustrated in Figure 9.1.

Of course, not every case in which religion and violence are implicated involves the state. Nor does every case in which the state confronts a violent insurgency contain a religious element. The religious and nonreligious variables in deadly conflict are configured differently in disparate contexts. In the frame of analysis I propose, one of the elements may well be null in any given case. The point is, however, that in today's world it has become clear—as illustrated in the three cases examined in this essay—that one must *start* with the assumption of a threefold rather than twofold framework. That is the essential contribution of this essay.

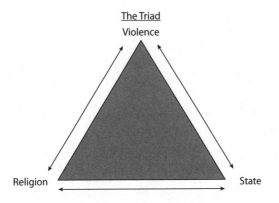

FIGURE 9.1

A Eurocentric and Weberian view, as I have demonstrated, privileges the state and treats state violence as sui generis, not comparable to all other forms of violence. By contrast, a polycentric theory of religion, violence, and the state will end this privileging and introduce a dialogical relationship in what I call a triad of elements.

Perhaps we have celebrated the death of the state too soon. Certainly those who have suffered the state's excesses, such as those survivors of crimes against humanity fighting for justice in The Hague, or those who continue to suffer arbitrary detention in many parts of the world, or those increasing victims of targeted assassinations by drones, do not doubt that the state continues to live, flourish, and kill.

Notes

1. R. Scott Appleby, *The Ambivalence of the Sacred: Religion, Violence, and Reconciliation* (New York: Rowman and Littlefield, 2000), 34–35.

2. For an overview of the proliferation of books on religion and violence since September 11, 2001, see Charles K. Bellinger, "Religion and Violence: A Bibliography," *The Hedgehog Review* 6, no. 1 (2004): 111–119. For an expanded online version of that article, see http://www.wabashcenter.wabash.edu/resources/article2.aspx?id=10516. See also *Spotlight on Teaching* 18, no. 4 (2003), published by the American Academy of Religion, on "Teaching about Religion and Violence." It contains a useful list of references and research projects. For a recent bibliography, see Jeffrey Ian Ross, *Religion and Violence: An Encyclopedia of Faith and Conflict from Antiquity to the Present* (Armonk, NY: M.E. Sharpe, 2010).

3. David Chidester, *Shots in the Streets: Violence and Religion in South Africa* (Boston: Beacon Press, 1991).

4. Michael A. Sells, *The Bridge Betrayed: Religion and Genocide in Bosnia* (Berkeley: University of Californian Press, 1996).

5. Paul Brass, *The Production of Hindu-Muslim Violence in Contemporary India* (Seattle: Washington University Press, 2003).

6. William T. Cavanaugh, *The Myth of Religious Violence: Secular Ideology and the Roots of Modern Conflict* (Oxford: Oxford University Press, 2009).

7. There are, of course, a few others, but these are few and far between, and their insights have not been taken up seriously in the dominant emerging theories on religion and violence in the post–Cold War era.

8. Mark Juergensmeyer is Director of the Orfalea Center for Global and International Studies and Professor of Global and International Studies at the University of California, Santa Barbara. He is the 2004 recipient of the Silver Medal Award of the Queen Sofia Center for the Study of Conflict in Valencia, Spain. He is currently recognized as one of the world's foremost experts on "religious violence." For a full biography, see http://www.global.ucsb.edu/faculty/juergensmeyer.html.

9. Mark Juergensmeyer, *Terror in the Mind of God: The Global Rise of Religious Violence* (Berkeley: University of California Press, 2000), 5.

10. Another study that focuses on the psychological dimensions of religious militants is Jessica Stern, *Terror in the Name of God: Why Religious Militants Kill* (New York: Ecco, 2003).

11. Max Weber, *Sociological Writings*, ed. Wolf Heydebrand (London: Continuum International Publishing Group, 1994).

12. S. Parvez Manzoor, review of *The Rise and Decline of the State*, by Martin van Creveld, *Islam* 21 (October 2000): 15–16.

13. Peter B. Evans, Dietrich Rueschemeyer, and Theda Skocpol, eds., *Bringing the State Back In* (Cambridge: Cambridge University Press, 1985). For the argument for granting the state agency in our analysis of resurgent religion, see Seyyed Vali Reza Nasr, *Islamic Leviathan: Islam and the Making of State Power* (Oxford: Oxford University Press, 2001).

14. The Egyptian scholar Samir Amin first proposed the concept of polycentricity as an alternative to Eurocentrism. Polycentrism critiques the presumptions, methodologies, and goals that underpin the study of social sciences in the Western academy. See Amin, *Eurocentrism*, trans. Russell Moore (London: Zed Books, 1989) and Amin, *Delinking: Towards a Polycentric World* (London: Zed Books, 1990).

15. Here I will be drawing extensively from my doctoral thesis, "Religion, Violence, and the State: A Dialogical Encounter Between Activists and Scholars" (University of Cape Town, 2005).

16. Chidester, *Shots in the Streets*, 7.

17. Kairos Theologians, *The Kairos Document: Challenge to the Church; A Theological Comment on the Political Crisis in South Africa*, 2nd ed. (Grand Rapids, MI: Eerdmans, 1986).

18. See Christopher Candland, *The Spirit of Violence: An Interdisciplinary Bibliography of Religion and Violence*, Occasional Papers of the Harry Frank Guggenheim Foundation, no. 6 (1992): 71–73.

19. For this categorization, see "Contents" in Candland, *The Spirit of Violence* 71–72.

20. Charles Villa-Vicencio has been one of the most productive scholars in analyzing the debate about the role of Christianity in relation to apartheid. For some of his work, see Villa-Vicencio, *Trapped in Apartheid: Socio-Theological History of the English-Speaking Churches* (Maryknoll, NY: Orbis Books, 1988).

21. Charles Villa-Vicencio, ed., *Theology and Violence: The South African Debate* (Grand Rapids, MI: Eerdmans, 1988).

22. Albert Nolan and Mary Armour, "Armed Struggle as a Last Resport: The Roman Catholic Position," in *Theology and Violence: The South African Debate*, ed. Charles Villa-Vicencio (Grand Rapids, MI: Institute for Contextual Theology, 1987), 209.

23. Villa-Vicencio, *Theology and Violence*, 2.

24. See, for example, Appleby, *Ambivalence of the Sacred*, p. 318 nn. 41, 45, and 48.

25. Chidester, *Shots in the Streets*, x–xii and p. 173 n. 3. For a later elaboration of his views on the contested definitions of violence, see Chidester, "Comprehending Political Violence," in *Dealing with Diversity: Keywords for a New South Africa*, ed. Emile Boonzaier and John Sharp (Cape Town: David Phillip, forthcoming).

26. Chidester, *Shots in the Streets*, 33–37

27. Chidester, *Shots in the Streets*, 1–21.

28. One reviewer has suggested that the reason Chidester's contribution has not made a wider impact is its "de- and reconstructionist" style. See Pierre L. van den Berghe, review of *Shots in the Streets: Violence and Religion in South Africa*, by David Chidester, *Contemporary Sociology* 21, no. 3 (1992): 324–325.

29. Appleby, *Ambivalence of the Sacred*, 37–39.

30. Appleby, *Ambivalence of the Sacred*, 28.

31. Appleby, *Ambivalence of the Sacred*, 57–120.

32. Richard T. Antoun, *Understanding Fundamentalism: Christian, Islamic, and Jewish Movements* (Lanham, MD: Rowman and Littlefield, 2001).

33. Appleby allocates two full chapters to considering fundamentalism and ethno-religious nationalism. In contradistinction, he discusses liberationism in three pages. See Appleby, *Ambivalence of the Sacred*, 34–40.

34. Kairos Theologians, *The Kairos Document*, http://kairossouthernafrica.wordpress.com/2011/05/08/the-south-africa-kairos-document-1985/.

35. Michael A. Sells, *The Bridge Betrayed: Religion and Genocide in Bosnia* (Berkeley: University of California Press, 1996), xiii.

36. Sells, *Bridge Betrayed*, 89.

37. Miroslav Volf, review of *The Bridge Betrayed: Religion and Genocide in Bosnia*, by Michael A. Sells, *Journal of the American Academy of Religion* 67, no. 1 (1999): 250.

38. Paul Mojzes, *Yugoslavian Inferno: Ethnoreligious Warfare in the Balkans* (New York: Continuum, 1994), 147.

39. Juergensmeyer, *Terror in the Mind of God*, 281–284.

40. Juergensmeyer, *Terror in the Mind of God*, 241.

41. Appleby, *Ambivalence of the Sacred*, 67.

42. Appleby, *Ambivalence of the Sacred*, 68.

43. Appleby, *Ambivalence of the Sacred*, 61.

44. Appleby, *Ambivalence of the Sacred*, 62. Appleby provides the examples of Bosnia, which included "Bosnian Serbs," "Bosnian Croats," and "Bosnian Muslims," as well as Sri Lanka, where the Sinhala majority "invoked Buddhism as a basis for legitimating Sinhala cultural and political preeminence in Sri Lanka." In each case, it was religion wed to ethnicity that distinguished each "ethnic" group from the other.

45. Appleby, *Ambivalence of the Sacred*, 79.

46. For such a view, see Mahmood Mamdani, *Saviors and Survivors: Darfur, Politics, and the War on Terror* (New York: Doubleday, 2004).

47. See, for example, Roy Gutman, *A Witness to Genocide: The 1993 Pullitzer Prize-winning Dispatches on the 'Ethnic Cleansing" of Bosnia* (New York: Macmillan Pub. Co, 1993); Norman Cigar, *Genocide in Bosnia: The Policy of 'Ethnic Cleansing'* (College Station, TX: Texas A&M University Press, 1995).

48. For example, see International Criminal Tribunal for the former Yugoslavia, "The Vice-President of Herceg-Bosna and Five Other Prominent Bosnian Croats Indicted for the 'Ethnic Cleansing' of the Lasva Valley Area," *The Hague*, November 13, 1995, http://www.icty.org/sid/7222.

49. See, for example, Edward Herman, "The Politics of the Srebrenica Massacre," *Znet*, July 7, 2005, http://zcomm.org/znetarticle/the-politics-of-the-srebrenica-massacre-by-edward-herman/.

50. de Graaff, "The Wars in the Former Yugoslavia in the 1990s: Bringing the State Back In," in *Rethinking the Nature of War*, ed. Isabelle Duyvesteyn and Jan Angstrom (New York: Frank Cass, 2005), 162.

51. The term "harvest of hate" comes from the title of Swami Agnivesh's book and is very suggestive of his overall thesis that the Gujarat massacres were not spontaneous but the outcome of a well-orchestrated plan that had been in the making for some time. Swami Agnivesh and Valson Thampu, eds., *Harvest of Hate: Gujarat Under Siege* (Delhi: Rupa and Co., 2002).

52. Human Rights Watch, "'We Have No Orders To Save You': State Participation and Complicity in Communal Violence in Gujarat," *Human Rights Watch Report* 14, no. 3(C) (2002): 4, http://www.hrw.org/reports/2002/India/.

53. The complicity of the state in the Gujarat violence was first claimed on April 3, 2002, in a preliminary report released by India's National Human Rights Commission (NHRC), "Case No. 1150/6 2001-2002," http://nhrc.nic.in/gujratorders.htm.

54. For an example of critiques of the Human Rights Report, see Arvin Bahl, "Politics by Other Means: An Analysis of Human Rights Watch Report on Gujarat," in *Gujarat After Godhra: Real Violence, Selective Outrage*, ed. Ramesh N. Rao and Koenraad Elst (New Delhi: Har-Anand Publications, 2003), 172–200. A slightly revised version of this critique was published by the South Asia Analysis Group, Paper no. 891, 12.01.2004, http://www.saag.org/papers9/paper891.

55. For some of these, see Syeeda Hameeda, Ruth Manorama, Malini Ghose, Sheba George, Farah Naqvi, and Mari Thekaekara, "The Survivors Speak: How has the Gujarat massacre affected minority women?;. Fact-finding by a Women's Panel," Citizen's Initiative, April 16, 2002, http://cac.ektaonline.org/resources/reports/womensreport.htm; Kamal Mitri Shenoy, S. P. Shukla, K. S. Subramanian and Achin Vanaik, Kamal Mitra Chenoy, S.P Shukla, K.S. Subramanian, and Achin Vanaik, "Gujarat Carnage, 2002: A Report to the Nation," April 10, 2002, http://www.sacw.net/Gujarat2002/GujCarnage.html; "Maaro! Kaapo! Baalo!: State, Society, and Communalism in Gujarat," *People's Union for Democratic Rights*, May 2002, http://www.onlinevolunteers.org/Gujarat/reports/pudr/.

56. Brass, *The Production of Hindu-Muslim Violence.*

57. Varshney, "Understanding Gujarat Violence," *Contemporary Conflicts*, March 26, 2004, http://conconflicts.ssrc.org/gujarat/varshney/.

58. van der Veer, "Tradition and Violence in South Asia" (keynote address, conference of the Kroc Institute's Program in Religion, Conflict, and Peacebuilding, University of Notre Dame, Notre Dame, IN, April 11–12, 2003). For a report on the conference, see *Peace Colloquy*, no. 4 (Fall 2003): 18–19.

59. Upendra Bax, "The Second Gujarat Catastrophe," in *Fascism in India: Faces, Fangs and Facts*, ed. Chaitanya Krishna (Delhi: Manak Publications, 2003), 58–96.

60. Ashgar Ali Engineer, *The Gujarat Carnage* (New Delhi: Orient Longman, 2003).

61. "It is sometimes suggested that the anti-Sikh violence in Delhi, after the assassination of Indira Gandhi on October 30, 1984, was the first pogrom of independent India. This argument is not plausible." Varshney, "Understanding Gujarat Violence."

62. Varshney, "Understanding Gujarat Violence." I have not seen any subsequent writings by Varshney that would contradict his initial judgment that it was a pogrom.

63. Varshney, "Understanding Gujarat Violence."

64. Brass, *The Production of Hindu-Muslim Violence*, 32.

65. Amnesty International, "India: Justice, the victim—Gujarat state fails to protect women from violence," January 27, 2005, http://web.amnesty.org/library/index/engasa200012005.

66. This coalition represents a spectrum of organizations and individuals in the United States and Canada that have come together in response to the Gujarat genocide to demand accountability and justice.

67. Coalition Against Genocide, "Genocide in Gujarat: The Sang Parivar, Narendra Modi, and the Government of Gujarat," March 2, 2005, http://www.coalitionagainstgenocide.org/reports/2005/cag.02mar2005.modi.pdf.

68. "Statement by David C. Mulford, US Ambassador to India," Embassy of the United States: New Delhi, March 21, 2005, http://newdelhi.usembassy.gov/wwwhipr032105.html.

69. "Anti-Conversion Stand Led to US Visa Denial: Modi," *The Times of India*, April 13, 2005, http://timesofindia.indiatimes.com/articleshow/1081402.cms.

70. I have not found a single volume written exclusively on the communal violence of Gujarat 2002. Paul Brass has contributed a few pages to it in the conclusion of his latest book (*Production of Hindu-Muslim Violence*, 386–392).

71. Swami Agnivesh, interview with author, February 25, 2005.

72. Agnivesh, interview.

73. Agnivesh, interview.

74. Giorgio Agamben, *Homo Sacer: Spvereogn Power and Bare Life* (Stanford, CA: Stanford University Press, 1998) and for Michel Foucalut's relevant work, see *Discipline and Punish: The Birth of the Prison* (New York: Vintage, Reprint Edition, 1995).

75. Chatterji, "The Biopolitics of Hindu Nationalism," *Cultural Dynamics* 16, no. 2–3 (2004): 319–372.

76. Veena Das, Deborah Poole, and Richard M. Leverthall, eds., *Anthropology in the Margins of the State* (Santa Fe, NM: School of American Research Press, 2004).

77. Veena Das, "Women and the Contested State: Religion, Violence and Agency in South Asia" (keynote address, conference of the Kroc Institute's Program in Religion, Conflict, and Peacebuilding, University of Notre Dame, Notre Dame, IN, April 11–12, 2003). For a report on the conference, see *Peace Colloquy*, no. 4 (Fall 2003): 18–19.

78. Juergensmeyer has written widely on religion and violence, but I have not found any references to the South African case in any of his work.

79. Jeffrey Sluka, "Introduction: State Terror and Anthropology," in *Death Squad: The Anthropology of State Terror*, ed. Jeffrey Sluka (Philadelphia: University of Pennsylvania Press), 2000, 1.

80. R. J. Rummel, *Death by Government* (New Brunswick, NJ: Transaction Books, 1994), 25.

81. David Chidester, *Savage Systems: Colonialism and Comparative Religion in Southern Africa* (Charlottesville: University of Virginia Press, 1996), xi.

82. Mamdani, *Good Muslim, Bad Muslim: America, the Cold War, and the Roots of Terror* (New York: Three Leaves Press, 2009), 20–21.

BIBLIOGRAPHY

Works Cited

Agamben, Giorgio. *Homo Sacer: Sovereign Power and Bare Life.* Trans. Daniel Heller-Roazen. Stanford: Stanford University Press, 1998.

Agnivesh, Swami and Valson Thampu, eds. *Harvest of Hate: Gujarat Under Siege.* Delhi: Rupa and Co., 2002.

Amin, Samir. *Eurocentrism.* Trans. Russell Moore. London: Zed Books, 1989.

Amin, Samir. *Delinking: Towards a Polycentric World.* Trans. Michael Wolfers. London: Zed Books, 1990.

Appleby, R. Scott. *The Ambivalence of the Sacred: Religion, Violence, and Reconciliation.* New York: Rowman and Littlefield, 2000.

Antoun, Richard T. *Understanding Fundamentalism: Christian, Islamic, and Jewish Movements.* Lanham, MD: Rowman and Littelfield, 2001.

Bax, Upendra. "The Second Gujarat Catastrophe." In *Fascism in India: Fangs and Facts*, edited by Chaitnya Krishna, 58–96. Delhi: Manak Publications, 2003.

Brass, Paul. *The Production of Hindu-Muslim Violence in Contemporary India.* Seattle: Washington University Press, 2003.

Candland, Christopher, comp. *The Spirit of Violence: An Annotated Bibliography on Religious Violence.* New York: Harry Frank Guggenheim Foundation, 1992.

Carnegie Commission on Preventing Deadly Conflict. *Preventing Deadly Conflict.* Washington, DC: Carnegie Commission on Preventing Deadly Conflict, 1997.

Cavanaugh, William T. *The Myth of Religious Violence: Secular Ideology and the Roots of Modern Conflict*. Oxford: Oxford University Press, 2009.

Chidester, David. *Shots in the Streets: Violence and Religion in South Africa*. Boston: Beacon Press, 1991.

Chidester, David. *Savage Systems: Colonialism and Comparative Religion in Southern Africa*. Charlottesville: University of Virginia Press, 1996.

Chidester, David. "Comprehending Political Violence." In *Dealing with Diversity: Keywords for a New South Africa*, edited by Emile Boonzaier and John Sharp. Cape Town: David Phillip, forthcoming.

Coalition Against Genocide. "Genocide in Gujarat: The Sang Parivar, Narendra Modi, and the Government of Gujarat." March 2, 2005. http://www.coalitionagainstgenocide.org/reports/2005/cag.02mar2005.modi.pdf.

Das, Veena, Deborah Poole, and Richard M. Leverthall, eds. *Anthropology in the Margins of the State*. Santa Fe, NM: School of American Research Press, 2004.

de Graaff, Bob. "The Wars in the Former Yugoslavia in the 1990s: Bringing the State Back in." In *Rethinking the Nature of War*, edited by Isabelle Duyvesteyn and Jan Angstrom, 159–176. New York: Frank Cass, 2005.

Engineer, Ashgar Ali. *The Gujarat Carnage*. New Delhi: Orient Longman, 2003.

Evans, Peter B., Dietrich Rueschemeyer, and Theda Skocpol, eds. *Bringing the State Back In*. Cambridge: Cambridge University Press, 1985.

Herman, Edward. "The Politics of the Srebrenica Massacre." *Znet*, July 7, 2005. http://zcomm.org/znetarticle/the-politics-of-the-srebrenica-massacre-by-edward-herman/.

Human Rights Watch. "'We Have No Orders To Save You': State Participation and Complicity in Communal Violence in Gujarat." *Human Rights Watch Report* 14, no. 3(C) (2002): 1–68. http://www.hrw.org/reports/2002/india/.

Juergensmeyer, Mark. *Terror in the Mind of God: The Global Rise of Religious Violence*. Berkeley: University of California Press, 2000.

Lincoln, Bruce. *Holy Terrors: Thinking About Religion after September 11*. Chicago: University of Chicago Press, 2003.

Mamdani, Mahmood. *Saviors and Survivors: Darfur, Politics, and the War on Terror*. New York: Doubleday, 2004.

Mamdani, Mahmood. *Good Muslim, Bad Muslim: America, the Cold War, and the Roots of Terror*. New York: Three Leaves Press, 2009.

Manzoor, S. Parvez. 2000. Review of *The Rise and Decline of the State*, by Martin van Creveld. *Islam* 21 (October 2000).

Mojzes, Paul. *Yugoslavian Inferno: Ethnoreligious Warfare in the Balkans*. New York: Continuum, 1994.

Omar, A. Rashied. "Religion, Violence, and the State: A Dialogical Encounter Between Activists and Scholars." PhD diss., University of Cape Town, 2005.

Nasr, Seyyid Vali Reza. *Islamic Leviathan: Islam and the Making of State Power*. Oxford: Oxford University Press, 2001.

Rao, Ramesh N., ed. *Gujarat After Godhra: Real Violence, Selective Outrage*. New Delhi: Har-Anand Publications, 2007.

Ross, Jeffrey Ian, ed. *Religion and Violence: An Encyclopedia of Faith and Conflict from Antiquity to the Present*. Armonk, NY: M.E. Sharpe, 2010.

Rummel, R. J. *Death by Government*. New Brunswick, NJ: Transaction Books, 1994.

Sells, Michael A. *The Bridge Betrayed: Religion and Genocide in Bosnia*. Berkeley: University of California Press, 1996.

Sluka, Jeffrey, ed. *Death Squad: The Anthropology of State Terror.* Philadelphia: University of Pennsylvania Press, 2000.

Stern, Jessica. *Terror in the Name of God: Why Religious Militants Kill.* New York: Ecco/HarperCollins, 2003.

The Kairos Theologians. *The Kairos Document: Challenge to the Church; A Theological Comment on the Political Crisis in South Africa.* 2nd ed. Johannesburg: Skotaville Press, 1986.

Varshney, Ashutosh. *Ethnic Conflict and Civic Life: Hindus and Muslims in India.* New Haven, CT: Yale University Press, 2002.

Varshney, Ashutosh. "Understanding Gujarat Violence." *Contemporary Conflicts*, March 26, 2004. http://conconflicts.ssrc.org/archives/gujarat/varshney/.

Villa-Vicencio, Charles, ed. *Theology and Violence: The South African Debate.* Grand Rapids, MI: Eerdmans, 1987.

Villa-Vicencio, Charles. *Trapped in Apartheid: Socio-Theological History of the English Speaking Churches.* Maryknoll, NY: Orbis Books, 1988.

Volf, Miroslav. Review of *The Bridge Betrayed*, by Michael A. Sells. *Journal of the American Academy of Religion* 67, no. 1 (1999).

Weber, Max. *Sociological Writings.* Edited by Wolf Heydebrand. London: Continuum International Publishing Group, 1994.

Further Reading

Apter, David E., ed. *The Legitimation of Violence.* New York: New York University Press, 1997.

Arendt, Hannah. *On Violence.* London: Allen Lane, 1970.

Asad, Talal. *Formations of the Secular: Christianity, Islam, Modernity.* Stanford, CA: Stanford University Press, 2003.

Ateek, Naim. *Justice and Only Justice: A Palestinian Theology of Liberation.* Maryknoll, NY: Orbis Books, 1989.

Bailie, Gil. *Violence Unveiled: Humanity at the Crossroads.* New York: Crossroads, 1995.

Barkun, Michael, ed. *Millenialism and Violence.* London: Frank Cass, 1996.

Bellinger, Charles K. "Religion and Violence: A Bibliography." *The Hedgehog Review* 6, no. 1 (2004)

Beuken, Wim, and Karl-Josef Kuschel, eds. "Religion as a Source of Violence?" Special issue, *Concilium*, no. 4 (1997).

Brown, Robert McAfee. *Religion and Violence.* 2nd ed. Philadelphia: Westminster Press, 1987.

Casanova, José. *Public Religions in the Modern World.* Chicago: University of Chicago Press, 1994.

Chatterji, Angana P. "The Biopolitics of Hindu Nationalism." *Cultural Dynamics* 16, no. 2–3 (2004): 319–372.

Chidester, David. *Patterns of Power: Religion and Politics in American Culture.* Englewood Cliffs, NJ: Prentice Hall, 1988.

Chomsky, Noam, and Edward Herman. *The Washington Connection and Third World Fascism.* Vol. 1 of *The Political Economy of Human Rights.* Nottingham: Spokesman, 1979.

Cigar, Norman. *Genocide in Bosnia: The Policy of 'Ethnic Cleansing'.* College Station, TX: Texas A&M University Press, 1995.

Das, Veena. "Women and the Contested State: Religion, Violence and Agency in South Asia" (keynote address, conference of the Kroc Institute's Program in Religion, Conflict, and Peacebuilding, University of Notre Dame, Notre Dame, IN, April 11–12, 2003).

de Vries, Hent. 2002. *Religion and Violence: Philosophical Perspectives from Kant to Derrida*. Baltimore: John Hopkins University Press, 2002.

Ellis, Marc H. *Unholy Alliance: Religion and Atrocity in Our Time*. Minneapolis, MN: Fortress Press, 1997.

Esposito, John L. *Unholy War: Terror in the Name of Islam*. Oxford: Oxford University Press, 2002.

Falla, Ricardo. 1994. *Massacres in the Jungle: Ixcan, Guatemala, 1975–1982*. Translated by Julia Howland. Boulder, CO:Westview Press, 1994.

Fanon, Frantz. *The Wretched of the Earth*. Hamondsworth: Penguin Books, 1967.

Foucalut, Michel. *Discipline and Punish: The Birth of the Prison*. New York: Vintage, Reprint Edition, 1995.

Foucault, Michel. *Power/Knowledge: Selected Interviews and Other Writings 1972–1977*. New York: Pantheon Books, 1980.

Girard, René. *The Scapegoat*. Baltimore: Johns Hopkins University Press, 1986.

Gutman, Roy. *A Witness to Genocide: The 1993 Pullitzer Prize-winning Dispatches on the 'Ethnic Cleansing" of Bosnia*. New York: Macmillan Pub. Co, 1993.

Haynes, Jeff. *Religion in Third World Politics*. Boulder, CO: Lynne Rienner, 1994.

Hecht, Richard, and Roger Friedland. "The Bodies of Nations: A Comparative Study of Religious Violence in Jerusalem and Ayodhya." *History of Religions* 38, no. 2 (1998): 101–149.

Heft, James L, ed. *Beyond Violence: Religious Sources of Social Transformation in Judaism, Christianity, and Islam*. New York: Fordham University Press, 2004.

Hoffman, Bruce. *"Holy Terror": The Implications of Terrorism Motivated by a Religious Imperative*. Santa Monica, CA: RAND Corporation, 1993.

Kakar, Sudhir. *The Color of Violence*. Chicago: University of Chicago Press, 1996.

Kimball, Charles. *When Religion Becomes Evil*. New York: HarperCollins, 2002.

Larson, J. P. *Understanding Religious Violence: Thinking Outside the Box of Terrorism*. Aldershot, UK: Ashgate, 2004.

Lawrence, Bruce. *Shattering the Myth: Islam Beyond Violence*. Princeton, NJ: Princeton University Press, 1998.

Lewy, Guenter. *Religion and Revolution*. New York: Oxford University Press, 1991.

Mahmood-Keppley, Cynthia. 1996. *Fighting for Faith and Nation: Dialogues with Sikh Militants* ..Philadelphia: University of Pennsylvania Press.

Majid, Anour. *Unveiling Traditions: Postcolonial Islam in a Polycentric World*. Durham, NC: Duke University Press, 2000.

Marty, Martin E., and R. Scott Appleby, eds. *Fundamentalisms Comprehended*. Chicago: University of Chicago Press, 1995.

McTernan, Oliver. *Violence in God's Name: Religion in an Age of Conflict*. Maryknoll, NY: Orbis Books, 2003.

Nandy, Ashis. *The Savage Freud and Other Essays on Possible Retrievable Selves*. Princeton, NJ: Princeton University Press, 1995.

Nasr, Seyyid Vali Reza. *Islamic Leviathan: Islam and the Making of State Power*. Oxford: Oxford University Press, 2001.

Nolan, Albert and Mary Armour. "Armed Struggle as a Last Resort: The Roman Catholic Position." In *Theology and Violence: The South African Debate*, edited by Charles Villa-Vicencio, 209–214 (Grand Rapids, MI: Institute for Contextual Theology, 1987).

Noor, Farish A, ed. *Terrorising the Truth: The Shaping of Contemporary Images of Islam and Muslims in Media, Politics, and Culture; A Report on the International Workshop Organised by Just World Trust (JUST) from 7–9 October, 1995.* Penang: Just World Trust, 1997.Rudolph, Susanne Hoeber, and James Piscatori, eds. *Transnational Religion and Fading States.* Boulder, CO: Westview Press, 1997.

Said, Edward. *Orientalism.* New York: Vintage Books, 1979.

Said, Edward. *Covering Islam.* New York: Pantheon Books, 1981.

Stohl, Michael, and George A. Lopez, eds. *The State as Terrorist.* Westport, CT: Greenwood Press, 1984.

Tambiah, Stanley J. *Buddhism Betrayed? Religion, Politics, and Violence in Sri Lanka.* Chicago: University of Chicago Press, 1992.

Tambiah, Stanley J. *Leveling Crowds: Ethnonationalist Conflicts and Collective Violence in South Asia.* Berkeley: University of California Press, 1996.

Van den Berghe, Pierre L. Review of *Shots in the Streets: Violence and Religion in South Africa,* by David Chidester. *Contemporary Sociology* 21, no. 3 (1992): 324–325.

Westerlund, David, ed. *Questioning the Secular State: The Worldwide Resurgence of Religion in Politics.* London: Hurst, 1996.

CHAPTER 10

....

THE COMPARATIVE STUDY
OF ETHICS AND THE PROJECT
OF THE JUSTPEACE

....

JOHN KELSAY

EARLY on in his study of the "conditions" that make for peace, E. H. Carr writes:

> It cannot be too often repeated—for it is still not widely understood—that neither security
> nor peace can properly be made the object of policy.. . . A generation which makes peace and
> security its aim is doomed to frustration. The only stability attainable in human affairs is the
> stability of the spinning top or the bicycle. . . the condition of security is continuous advance.
> The political, social, and economic problems of the post-war world must be approached with
> the desire not to stabilize, but to revolutionize.[1]

As a consummate realist in matters of political life, Carr may seem out of place in an essay on
peacebuilding. And yet, his point is one that John Paul Lederach, R. Scott Appleby, and others make with respect to the project of the justpeace. Peace is not a static condition, achieved
once and for all. Nor ought it be identified as the absence of conflict. Given the dynamics of
group life, conflict is a more or less constant factor. The goal is to build relationships that can
bear conflict and to forge institutions that sustain those relationships. To endure, the condition we describe as peace must be dynamic. One might say that building and sustaining
peace requires constant attention and adjustment to developments in social life.

Many of the chapters in this volume focus on the positive contributions religious people
and practices make, or at least *can* make, to the project of building peace. Particularly with
respect to the contemporary tendency to focus on religion as a cause of violence, this is an
important point. As one engaged in the comparative study of ethics, and in particular of the
normative vocabularies developed in the service of the cultural regulation of armed force,
however, it seems to me that there is a significant lacuna in these accounts. For the Muslim
tradition of "judgments pertaining to jihad," as for the Christian analogue of *jus ad bellum*
and *jus in bello*, the goal was and remains to direct military force in ways that serve legitimate
political purposes, and in so doing to delimit more anarchic forms of violence.[2] Identifying
and describing vocabularies like these is thus an important aspect of the discussion of religion and peacebuilding.

Not that these vocabularies always work well. As Carr's dictum reminds us, we have always to account for changing conditions. In order to play the role I suggest, discourse about jihad or just war requires a reasonably stable political order. In that connection, these traditions play what might be called an order-preserving role. When political institutions break down, so that there is a crisis of legitimacy, the vocabulary of jihad or just war takes on a different cast, as groups of people claim the mantle of tradition in the service of order transformation.

In the service of thinking about religion and peacebuilding, then, it seems necessary to take account of the ways historic frameworks intended to regulate armed force are chang-ing in the here and now. We want an answer to the question at which comparative studies of ethics always aim: what is going on? In this chapter, I shall focus in particular on dis-course regarding jihad.[3] As I shall indicate, historic Muslim thinking took the Qur'an and the example of the Prophet to indicate that armed force could be a legitimate means of pursuing peace and justice in connection with the command or guidance of God. In the context of the Abbasid Caliphate, this judgment and the sources upon which it was based helped to foster a war convention, in the sense of a set of institutions designed to channel armed force in ways that served legitimate political purposes. Despite disagreement regarding some hard cases, the order-preserving purpose of such discourse seems clear.

As the tradition developed, however, it also developed a vocabulary for emergencies—that is, for times when the ordinary structures of command and control might break down. As we turn to the very different political situation of the last two centuries, we find that this vocabu-lary, by which fighting becomes a duty incumbent on every individual believer, moves to a place of prominence. Thus contemporary Muslim discourse about war points to a crisis of legitimacy, in which there is little if any consensus about the shape of a just political order. Taking account of this, I suggest, is one way of heeding Carr's advice. And the difficulty this presents—say, in a case like the Syrian civil war—serves to remind us that the project of just-peace requires substantial investments of time and other resources. It also requires people with certain characteristics, or even virtues. I close with a gesture in this direction, by way of reflecting on some themes in the speeches of Dag Hammarskjold, whose emphasis on the role of patience in building peace seems particularly apt.

Historic Islam and the Notion of Peace

We may begin with a story from the biography of the Prophet. When he began to proclaim the message and to call the citizens of Mecca to Islam, only a few responded favorably. Indeed, Muhammad's reception was overwhelmingly negative. Leading figures in the city perceived his message as a challenge to long-standing practices. In this they were correct. The proclamation "there is no god but God" set the Prophet and his companions in opposi-tion to the Arab way, in which people thought of a pantheon of deities, some functioning as patrons of particular tribes and others as exercising power with respect to children, illness, or the time of one's death. As revelation, the Qur'an claimed priority over the "beaten path" of the ancestors. As for the promise of postmortem resurrection with an accompanying final judgment, most of those listening to Muhammad simply found it bewildering.

The Qur'an reflects some of the give and take between the Muslims and the citizens of Mecca. The opposition of the latter was not only verbal, however. Standard biographies present tales of economic boycott, death threats, even torture. In this connection, we understand when we read that some of the believers approached the Prophet and requested he authorize a response in kind. Their idea was that a show of force might serve as a deterrent. Once the opposition understood the determination and power of the Muslims, the physical threat would cease.

Muhammad responded that he had received no order to fight. At this point, God only authorized him to preach. Thus he could not grant his companions' request. Unless and until God gave a command to the contrary, the proper response of Muslims—as those who submit to or obey the commandments of God and thus display *taqwa*, or godly fear—would involve endurance, along the lines indicated in Qur'an 2:153 and similar passages:

> O believers! Seek help with patient perseverance [*bi-l-sabri*] and prayer, for God is with those
> who patiently persevere.[4]

As the narrative proceeds, the order to fight does come, in connection with the migration to Medina in 622. When it does, the first instantiation presents fighting as something "permitted."

> Those who have been attacked are permitted to take up arms because they have been
> wronged—God has the power to help them—those who have been driven unjustly from
> their homes only for saying, "Our Lord is God." If God did not repel some people by means
> of others, many monasteries, churches, synagogues, and mosques, where God's name is much
> invoked, would have been destroyed. (22:39–41)

In the order presented by standard biographies, the language of the Qur'an changes as the conflict between the Muslims and their enemies intensifies. Thus at 2:216, we read that "fighting is written for you, though you do not like it"; at 2:190–94, the order is to "fight them as they are fighting you, but do not violate the limits." At 4:75, believers are challenged by the question "Why should you not fight in God's cause and for those oppressed men, women, and children who cry out, 'Lord, rescue us from this town whose people are oppressors! By your grace, give us a protector and helper.'" At 8:39, the imperative mood is operative as God says, "Believers, fight them [the unbelievers] until there is no more persecution. . ." Finally, at 9:5, in connection with the charge that the Meccans violated a treaty with the Muslims, the text reads:

> When the forbidden months are over, wherever you find the polytheists, kill them, seize them,
> besiege them, ambush them. . .

That is, unless and until they repent. Even in this, perhaps the most vigorous of the Qur'anic verses on fighting, we find the notion of limits.

The point, for our purposes, is this: fighting or not fighting is not the central thing. Rather, the pattern of the discourse in the Qur'an and the example of the Prophet stress obedience to the commands of God. Muslims developed this notion into a full-blown convention intended to regulate armed force, to make it serve a particular conception of social and political life. As those who contributed to the tradition would have said, the "judgments pertaining to armed struggle" were developed in order to foster peace.

We begin to get a sense of the particular conception of peace operative in historic Islam by attending to the report of the Prophet's orders to those leading Muslim armies.

> Whenever the Apostle of God sent forth an army. . . he charged its commander personally to fear God. . . and he enjoined the Muslims who were with him to do good. . . [he said]: : Fight in the name of God and in the path of God. Combat [only] those who disbelieve in God. Do not cheat or commit treachery, nor should you mutilate anyone or kill children. Whenever you meet your polytheist enemies, invite them [first] to adopt Islam. If they do so, accept it, and let them alone.. . . If they refuse [to accept Islam], then call upon them to pay the jizya (poll tax); if they do, accept it and leave them alone..⁵

Only upon refusal of these options does fighting commence.

There is much of interest in this text, but for our purposes, the important point has to do with the attempt to bring a potential enemy into a proper relation with the Muslim community. The order envisioned in the text involves some sort of established regime by which Islam and the values associated with it "reign supreme." The most efficient and best way of attaining this goal is through the enemy's acceptance of the call to faith. A community that responds positively is no longer an enemy, but an ally.

Failing such acceptance, however, there is another option by which fighting may be avoided. In this case, the enemy chooses to pay tribute. The reference to *al-jizya* suggests an arrangement of "protection." As outlined in judgments pertaining to the "people of the Book" (Jews, Christians, and others), the members of a non-Muslim community promise not to take up arms against the Islamic state, or to cooperate with its enemies. As well, those living under the protection of Islam promise to abide by a set of proprieties designed to protect the priority of Muslim revelation. They will not attempt to convert Muslims, for example; nor will they revile or insult the Qur'an, the Prophet, or other important symbols. In exchange, they enjoy certain rights, within boundaries deemed necessary to good public order.

Finally, refusal of the options of conversion or protection brings the test of war. Again, the goal is the establishment of a particular kind of order, in which the primacy of Islam is established, and the leadership pledges to implement the commands of God. As developed in the territories that came under the control of Muslims in a series of campaigns following the death of Muhammad in 632, the characteristics of the new order of Islam may be summarized as follows. First, the ruler is a Muslim, to whom the believers pledge allegiance. In turn, the ruler pledges to rule according to the Qur'an and the example of the Prophet. He thus takes the title *khalifa*, in the sense of one who "follows" the Prophet.

Second: in order to ensure such a rule of law, the ruler establishes a practice of consultation (*al-shura*) with recognized members of the religious class or *ulama*. The term suggests those who are learned in the sources by which divine guidance may be ascertained. Those are primarily the Qur'an and reports of the Prophet's example, of course, though through the centuries, the *fatawa* or opinions of members of the learned class with respect to the rights and wrongs of particular courses of action came to constitute important precedents in themselves. And in cases where something new occurs, members of the *ulama* attempted to reason from approved texts and established precedents in order to render sound judgments. The practice of Shari`a reasoning thus involved a kind of transgenerational conversation regarding Muslim practice, not least in matters of war and peace.

Third: a legitimate government—the kind indicated by the term *khilafat*, and thus entitled to rule over the territory or "house" of Islam—ensures that Muslims are citizens of the first rank, with non-Muslims living under the protection of Islam. As described previously, this involves recognition of some degree of autonomy for the latter. At the same time, the rights and duties of protected peoples are circumscribed, especially as compared with those of Muslims, who are free to call others to faith, to exhort others to do what is right and avoid what is wrong, to aspire to positions of power and prestige, and in the case of males, to marry members of the protected peoples. In general, the order envisioned in historical Islam establishes a set of hierarchical relationships in which citizens are under the protection of rulers, non-Muslims under the protection of Muslims, women under the protection of men, children under the protection of parents, and slaves under the protection of their owners.

Fourth: the territory of Islam stands in a relation of contrast to the territory or "house" of war. The orders attributed to the Prophet already suggest something along these lines, as the commanders of Muslim forces are directed to engage with non-Muslims in an attempt to extend the territory under Muslim control. Assuming the report is genuine, the particular context is the Arabian Peninsula between 622 and 632. As the tradition developed, however, the territorial dimension of these orders took on a different cast, so that the "opening" of new regions of the world by means of military force became an important aspect of Islamic tradition. Historians suggest a variety of explanations for this, not the least being economic. But from the Muslim point of view, the answer to the question "why territorial expansion?" involves two interrelated responses. The first is connected to the notion that the community of believers has a mission, as in Qur'an 3:110:

> You are the best community singled out for people: you order what is right, forbid what is wrong, and you believe in God.

Here, the idea is that in the history of God's quest for a community that will actually carry out the "trust" given to human beings who agree to serve as God's viceregent or *khalifa* on earth, Muslims represent the last and final act. Their calling is to remind humanity of its destiny. In political terms, this came to be associated with the spread of Islamic government, which would provide human beings with their best chance to live in peace and attain a modicum of justice.

The second answer rests on the notion that, once established, an Islamic order must find ways to guarantee its security. In this regard, most accounts point to the campaigns of Muhammad against the Meccans and their allies, suggesting that believers can never rest easily, so long as unbelief has its strongholds. The expansion of Islamic government thus involves a kind of extension of the normal meaning of defense. The territory of Islam is a zone of security, safeguarding the ability of the believers to practice their faith.

In either case, the terminology for non-Muslim territory is apt. It is the territory of war. If one is thinking in terms of the mission of Islam, the sense of such a characterization has to do with notions that apart from divine guidance, human beings are prone to fight with one another. Thus non-Muslim territory is conceived as a zone of *fitna* or civil strife. To bring it under the protection of Islam is a blessed act, by which a more stable order becomes possible. By contrast, if one is thinking of the need for Muslim security, the characterization "territory of war" suggests that non-Muslim polities are ruthlessly expansionist, their unbelief serving as a motive by which their rulers and citizens will strive to put out the light shed abroad by Islam. Fighting, particularly of the type envisioned in the orders of the Prophet, becomes a means by which believers attempt to achieve the goals of establishing, maintaining, and defending an order characterized by peace and justice.

THE MUSLIM WAR CONVENTION

The earliest collections of texts related to these matters come from the late eighth and early ninth centuries—that is, the early years of the Abbasid caliphate. And since the Abbasids established Baghdad as their capital, it is not surprising that some of the more thorough texts are attributed to scholars in the tradition of Abu Hanifa (d. 767), which in this early period of development had its home in Iraq. In particular, Abu Yusuf and Muhammad ibn Idris (known as al-Shaybani), both disciples of Abu Hanifa, produced collections of judgments pertaining to politics and war. As well, each served at one point or another as the chief *qadi* or judge for the Abbasid caliphs, providing advice related to matters of policy.

A story from the caliphate of Harun al-Rashid, who held power from 786 to 809, provides insight into the workings of the war convention at this point. In the history of al-Tabari, we read of al-Rashid's attempts to quell a rebellion led by Yahya ibn ʾAbdullah ibn Hasan.[6] Scion of the family of Ali, Yahya led a force based in Daylam. The region, located in what we would think of as Iran, was not at that point under the control of the Abbasids, so al-Rashid could not deal with Yahya's forces directly. Instead, he sent an emissary, who offered a sizeable sum of money to the local ruler in exchange for Yahya. Once Yahya understood the situation, we are told that he agreed to turn himself in on the condition that he receive a written *aman*, or guarantee of protection, signed by the caliph. Al-Rashid and his advisors agreed to this, and Yahya was soon in custody at court.

As al-Tabari has it, Yahya and the caliph engaged in several blunt conversations. Yahya complained of ill treatment on the part of al-Rashid. Noting that the family of Ali and the Abbasid clan had been partners against the Umayyads, he suggested that al-Rashid was neglecting the relationship. In response to such policies, Yahya argued, a use of armed force seemed justified as a means of obtaining Alid rights.[7]

In response, al-Rashid suggested that Yahya's resort to force constituted a formal act of rebellion, along the lines of Qur'an 49:9:

> If two groups of the believers fight, you should try to reconcile them; if one of them is oppressing the other, fight the oppressors until they submit to God's command, then make a just and even-handed reconciliation between the two of them: God loves those who are even-handed. The believers are brothers, so make peace between your two brothers and be mindful of God, so that you may be given mercy.

Yahya and his forces are thus in the position of oppressing other Muslims. The caliph is thereby justified in sending forces to quell the rebellion, unless and until the schismatic warriors lay down their arms.

With such a beginning, it is perhaps unsurprising that the story takes a negative turn. The next time we encounter Yahya, he is in chains, summoned to appear before the caliph. This time, however, al-Rashid is joined by several members of the learned class, including al-Shaybani. Al-Rashid explains the situation, noting that he granted Yahya an *aman*, and thus that the prisoner possesses a guarantee of protection. Addressing the assembled scholars, the caliph asks for a ruling: Is he bound by the guarantee? Al-Shaybani answers in the affirmative. Al-Rashid has given his word. Yahya cannot be kept in chains, and upon release, even were Yahya to return to fighting and then be captured, the guarantee of security would remain in effect.

Al-Rashid's displeasure was apparent. He would receive another opinion, however, from one of the other scholars present. Abu al-Bakhtari argued that Yahya's behavior placed him in the category of a rebel or worse. Given this, no writ of protection could hold, and the caliph could deal with his prisoner as with a common criminal. Proclaiming to al-Bakhtari "You are the supreme judge!," al-Rashid tore the paper in pieces, then threw it to the floor. Al-Bakhtari then spat on it. In the end, Yahya died in prison.

Whatever we think of this outcome, the story of Yahya and al-Rashid provides a nice example of the way political structures in historic Islam functioned. Yahya's audience with the caliph takes place in a way that accords with the requirement of a consultation between rulers and recognized members of the learned class. While this does not guarantee a just outcome, it suggests a process by which state policy may be evaluated in accordance with God's law. The disagreement between scholars present and offering opinions does not in itself weigh against such a characterization. While some Muslim commentators suggest that "the fix was in" regarding Yahya, we need not read the story in that way. Shari`a reasoning aims at discerning the guidance of God by way of members of the learned class articulating a "fit" between textual precedent and the facts of a case. In this instance, ascertaining the status of Yahya (and by implication, those who fought with him) is the goal, and opinions differed. As with any adult male believer, al-Rashid has the right to take the opinion he thinks best, when scholars disagree. In the absence of more information, perhaps we will do best to regard this as a case in which procedures are followed, even if the outcome seems questionable.

And in any case, the story helps us in understanding how the opinions collected in a text like al-Shaybani's *Siyar* or "Movements" between the territory of Islam and the territory of war were developed. Here, we see a scholar at work, responding to a wide range of questions regarding the justification and conduct of armed force. The opinions take shape in connection with the political order outlined in the section "Historic Islam and the Notion of Peace." Since this order is understood to be legitimate, and thus to offer human beings their best chance for peace, al-Shaybani's rulings may be understood as an attempt to regulate or channel armed force in order to extend, maintain, and defend this goal.

In connection with this, it is interesting that al-Shaybani's rulings deal with several different types of fighting. In the first, Muslim forces are deployed in an attempt to extend the territory of Islam. In this case, we are to understand that an invitation to Islam or to terms of peace has been proffered and refused. Fighting ensues; in al-Shaybani's opinion, it would be commendable for the Muslim forces to re-issue the invitation, though it is not required. There follows a quick summary of the tactics permitted to the Muslim forces in the territory of war.

> The army may launch the attack by night or by day and it is permissible to burn fortifications with fire or to inundate them with water. If [the army] captures any spoil of war, it should not be divided up in enemy territory until [the Muslims] have brought it to a place of security and removed it to the territory of Islam.[8]

The permission to use fire or flooding against the enemy seems to establish wide latitude for the Muslim armies. And indeed, al-Shaybani generally favors allowing Muslim forces to employ any means necessary to a victorious outcome. Thus we read his answer to the query "Do you think it is objectionable for the believers to destroy whatever towns of the territory of war that they may encounter?":

No. Rather do I hold that this would be commendable. For do you not think that it is in accordance with God's saying, in His Book: "Whatever palm trees you have cut down or left standing upon their roots, has been by God's permission, in order that the ungodly ones might be humiliated." So, I am in favor of whatever they did to deceive and anger the enemy.[9]

Or again, when asked about the permissibility of flooding, burning, or using hurling machines against an enemy city in which one may presume the presence of slaves, women, old men, and children, al-Shaybani replies that he would approve any of these tactics. He says:

If the Muslims stopped attacking the inhabitants of the territory of war for any of the reasons that you have stated, they would be unable to go to war at all, for there is no city in the territory of war in which there is no one of all these you have mentioned.[10]

Even in cases where there are Muslim inhabitants or merchants present in an enemy city, al-Shaybani takes a hard line.[11]

That is not to say there are no limits on the Muslim forces, however. As we have seen, the orders attributed to the Prophet expressly forbid direct and intentional attacks on children. In other reports, the prohibition of direct targeting is extended to include women, the old, the insane, religious specialists, and others who are presumed to be noncombatants.[12] Indeed, this is the background of the question posed to al-Shaybani with respect to attacks on enemy cities—how can Muslim armies employ the tactics mentioned, when the Prophet forbade the direct and intentional killing of the categories of persons mentioned?

Al-Shaybani's reply will be familiar to anyone acquainted with the just war tradition. An action may have more than one effect. The first, which is both foreseen and intended, makes the act legitimate—as in bringing the blessings of Islamic governance to portions of the territory of war. The second, which is foreseen but not intended, involves the deaths of some noncombatants, in the pursuit of a legitimate military target. Thus:

If the Muslims besieged a city, and its people from behind the walls shielded themselves with Muslim children, would it be permissible for the Muslim [warriors] to attack them with arrows and hurling machines? He replied: Yes, but the warriors should aim at the inhabitants of the territory of war and not the Muslim children.

I asked: Would it be permissible for the Muslims to attack them with swords and lances if the children were not intentionally aimed at? He replied: Yes.[13]

So sure is al-Shaybani on this point that he responds in the negative to a query regarding the need for Muslim fighters who engage in such activities to pay blood money to relatives of innocent victims or to perform acts of expiation.[14] Again an analogy to the just war tradition is helpful, as al-Shaybani is trying to walk the fine line between respect for the protected status of noncombatants and military necessity. Muslim armies should never deliberately violate the former. In the service of the latter, however, they may indirectly and thus unintentionally do harm to noncombatants.

What of the other provision in al-Shaybani's opening judgment, namely, that any spoil captured should not be divided until the Muslim forces return to a place of security? This I think we must read as a way of ensuring that fighters do not separate themselves from their comrades. To put it another way, this judgment reminds us that al-Shaybani is providing rules of engagement intended to discipline an army. Further judgments make the point that all soldiers follow the orders of a unit commander, who in turn follows the orders of the leader of the general army. That person in turns responds to directives from authorities, who ultimately carry out policies set by the caliph and his advisers according to the practice of consultation. In the Muslim war convention, fighting is not a private matter. It is a public affair, in which authority belongs to established leaders according to a chain of command. It is also tied to a notion of just cause, in this instance the expansion of legitimate (that is, Islamic) order and the retraction of the territory of war. The queries about noncombatants and proportionality in turn reflect the importance of right intention. It is important to note with respect to this last that al-Shaybani's opinions do not stand unchallenged. A scholar like al-Mawardi judged cases like those involving children as hostages differently, so that Muslim armies unable to carry out attacks without inflicting significant numbers of unintended though foreseen deaths to noncombatants should withdraw and return to fight at another time.[15] The point, for our purposes, is the existence of a set of rules intended to regulate armed force in the service of a particular set of political arrangements—a Muslim instantiation of a balance between peace, order, and justice.

The order-preserving character of these judgments pertaining to armed struggle is further demonstrated by two other kinds of fighting discussed by al-Shaybani. In the first, a set of opinions crafted in response to questions about groups of people classified as *al-bughat* or "rebels" suggests a way of dealing with those who would take up arms against the state. Recalling the example of Yahya ibn `Abdallah ibn Hasan, we already know that Qur'an 49:9 set a precedent in this connection.

> If two groups of the believers fight, you should try to reconcile them; if one of them is oppressing the other, fight the oppressors until they submit to God's command, then make a just and even-handed reconciliation between the two of them: God loves those who are even-handed. The believers are brothers, so make peace between your two brothers and be mindful of God, so that you may be given mercy.

Al-Shaybani adds to this, citing several reports of the practice of `Ali ibn `abi Talib, the nephew and son-in-law of the Prophet, who during his brief career as leader of the Muslims (656–661) dealt with a variety of rebellious groups. If Harun al-Rashid's treatment of Yahya suggests the way that the Qur'anic text authorizes fighting such groups of "oppressors," `Ali ibn `abi Talib's practice picks up on the idea that the ultimate goal should be reconciliation, in the service of the unity praised at Qur'an 3:103–106:

> Hold fast to God's rope all together; do not split into factions. Remember God's favor to you: you were enemies and then He brought your hearts together and you became brothers by His grace; you were about to fall into a pit of fire and He saved you from it—in this way God makes His revelations clear to you so that you may be rightly guided. Be a community that calls for what is good, urges what is right, and forbids what is wrong: those who do this are the successful ones. Do not be like those who, after they have been given clear revelation, split into factions and fall into disputes: a terrible punishment awaits such people.

As the reports cited by al-Shaybani have it, `Ali's public reply to a challenge from dissenters was to acknowledge their sincerity, while disputing their reasons. As well, he established firm limits on the establishment response, saying

> We shall not prohibit you from entering our mosques to mention His name; we shall not deny you a share in the war prizes, so long as you join hands with us; nor shall we fight you until you attack us.[16]

Or on another occasion, `Ali reportedly laid down the following rules of engagement for forces encountering Muslim rebels:

> Whoever flees shall not be chased, no prisoner of war shall be killed, no wounded in battle shall be dispatched, no enslavement [of women and children] shall be allowed, and no property shall be confiscated.[17]

From these precedents, al-Shaybani crafts a set of responses to questions that clearly indicate the priority of preserving an order reflective of the unity of Muslims, while dealing realistically with internal challenges. The rules of engagement are more restrictive than in the case of fighting in the territory of war, even as the ultimate aims of fighting are more in the nature of policing than of war-making. Again, right authority belongs to the caliph and his associates; just cause is a matter of maintaining legitimate order; and right intention is demonstrated by adherence to the standards of just conduct.

A second example of fighting intended to preserve legitimate order is found in the judgments pertaining to apostates (*al-murtadd*) and the people of protection (*ahl al-dhimma*). The former includes Muslims who in some way "turn back" from the faith, while the latter are groups of Jews, Christians, and others who pay special taxes in return for the protection against war provided by the Muslim state. In either case, the issue is dealt with as a matter of contract. A Muslim who turns from Islam in a public way violates a contract with God and with the Muslim state. In a classic precedent in this regard, Abu Bakr (first caliph after the Prophet, ruling from 632 to 634) authorized the use of force against Arab tribes who refused to send the required *zakat*, or payment of alms, to Medina for the caliph's use. Since their refusal was joined with a declaration of the *shahada*, there is a sense in which they seemed to remain Muslims. As Abu Bakr had it, however, a refusal to perform such a basic duty violated the terms of these tribes' agreement with the Prophet, and should not be tolerated. As al-Shaybani's judgments suggest, by his time, apostasy typically involved individuals whose public pronouncement of a turn from Islam entailed some breach of propriety—say, insulting the Prophet or desecrating the Qur'an. In such cases, he accepted the standard procedure by which the miscreant should be given the opportunity to repent and, if he or she failed to do so, should be punished by death.[18]

A small number of rulings suggest a different kind of case, however. Here we understand that a group of Muslims turns. In one scenario, they establish "their ascendancy in the territory in which" they live, and acquire "property belonging to Muslims and Dhimmis." So long as they remain apostate, they should be fought, and the goal should be to offer them the opportunity to repent, or else suffer the prescribed penalty. If the apostates seek terms of peace—for example, asking to be put in the status of *dhimmis*—their request should be refused. The Muslim forces are in the position of enforcing an established contract, not negotiating a new one. And if the group does return to Islam, the members are allowed to keep the property they acquired—again, the goal is to get them to return.[19]

Similarly with protected peoples. If they violate their agreement with the Muslims, for example, by refusing to pay the required tribute or by taking up arms in an attempt to establish independence, they are to be fought until the prior agreement is restored. The right of war belongs to the Muslim state. Its goal is the preservation of legitimate poitical order. And its forces act in a manner consistent with that aim.

What happens, though, when that order is seriously threatened? The response of the learned to this question has to do with the notion of fighting as an "individual" duty (*fard `ayn*). The concept needs some explanation. In one sense, Muslim scholars looking to the Qur'an and the prophetic example understood the order to fight as a duty incumbent on all adult Muslim men. In particular, a text like Qur'an 4:75, with its query "And why should you not fight?," suggests that those who "hang back" are failing in their duty.

At the same time, the stories of campaigns against the opposition indicate that some were always left behind, not only because of age, gender, or physical capacity, but in order to carry out other duties. Given this, the consensus of the learned was that fighting should be construed as *fard kifaya*. Usually translated as "collective" or "communal" duty, the phrase indicates that if the caliph has sufficient forces for the task at hand, others may stay behind and carry out their normal tasks.

In some circumstances, jihad remains an individual duty, however: as more than one scholar wrote, fighting can be a duty comparable to prayer and fasting, so that no one can perform it for another. Standard examples include soldiers "in the line"—that is, someone in the army who is engaged in battle has an obligation not to leave his post; indviduals who make a vow to participate in a campaign; people "called up" by the caliph or his representative, perhaps because they possess particular skills; and finally, in a situation of emergency, as when the territory of Islam comes under attack.

As the last example suggests, fighting becomes an individual duty in connection with the defense of important values. In a sense, we have a continuation of the order-preserving function of discourse about jihad. And yet, the language of scholars suggests something a bit more extreme. Given that part of the caliph's duty had to do with protecting the borders of Muslim territory, we are to envision an instance in which forces from the territory of war have overwhelmed Muslim soldiers assigned to protect one or more outposts. According to some accounts, fighting then becomes obligatory for each individual. In a standard trope, we read that an underage male may fight without having permission from his parents, and a woman may fight without having permission from her male guardian. In the immediate task of defense, no one needs to wait for orders. Of course, these beleaguered Muslims should send messages to the authorities requesting help. But they are not to wait. And should the authorities prove unwilling or unable to respond, believers located at some distance should rally in the task of defense.

In this case, scholars envisioned a kind of emergency, in which ordinary lines of command and control break down. An important example is provided by the Crusades, for which we have the texts of al-Sulami, a publicist who simultaneously admonishes the authorities in Damascus for failures with respect to the duty of jihad and appeals to other authorities to bring forces to assist locals in resisting the advance of *al-faranj*, the Franks in Syro-Palestine.[20] Another is provided by the various rulings of Ibn Taymiyya (d. 1328), in connection with the Mongol victories that deposed the Abbasid caliph in Baghdad in 1258.[21] No doubt Ibn Taymiyya hoped the Mamluk sultan would provide sufficient forces to repel the invaders, but his rhetoric appeals to fighting as an individual duty. So long as the Mongols remained "outside Islam"—a condition which in some of Ibn Taymiyya's rulings held even after their leaders made a public profession of faith—fighting in the service of repelling the invaders remained obligatory for every believer.

Fighting as an individual duty thus suggests a different angle on jihad, in which the discourse of scholars hearkens back to the time of the Prophet's original campaigns. Here the position of the Muslims is uncertain, and the security or even the survival of the community and its faith is in question. One is fighting to change that situation, so that a legitimate order may be established and fulfill the mission of commanding right and forbidding wrong from a position of strength. The political purpose of force is clear. But the command-and-control functions that regulate fighting and thus delimit more anarchic forms of violence are less certain. Even in cases where defense becomes an individual obligation, it makes sense for groups of believers to organize their efforts, of course. If the fight goes on in different locations, however, and communication becomes difficult, or if sectarian differences make cooperation among defenders troublesome, then we have an effective deregulation of armed force. In the service of order transformation, we may expect conflict that is both more extensive and, since we are dealing with fighters who may lack the formal training and discipline of a regular army, more characterized by violations of the conduct of war provisions laid out in the orders of the Prophet.

Modern Jihad

This account of the historical Muslim war convention provides important background for understanding contemporary Muslim discourse about fighting. That this discourse develops in a political context very different from that of al-Shaybani and Harun al-Rashid is often noted. The expansion of European influence in the territory of Islam began in the middle of the eighteenth century. By 1820, British power in India became so pervasive that an influential member of the learned class like Shah `Abd al-Aziz could issue a formal judgment that India could not longer be considered *dar al-Islam*. By the early twentieth century, the French and the British controlled large segments of North Africa and the Middle East. And when a cadre of Turkish military officers led by Mustafa Kemal declared that, following the defeat of Ottoman forces in the First World War, they would no longer support the sultan and other institutions of imperial rule, the last vestiges of the old order of Islam faded from view.

In this connection, the intensive debate over legitimacy that drives modern Islamic thought makes sense. As Hamid Enayat notes, the number of books, essays, and tracts responding to the question "What constitutes an Islamic state?" published in the twentieth century far exceeded any other topic.[22] Certainly there were Muslim reformers who saw the passing of the old forms as an opportunity to fulfill some neglected aspects of Islamic tradition. Advocates of democracy argued that the old understandings of consultation, for example, effectively restricted the practice in ways that ignored the basic equality of believers. All deserved a place at the table of power, and institutions should be arranged to ensure this, including elections; parliamentary procedures; separation of executive, legislative, and judicial powers; and constitutional guarantees of rights.

Others saw such proposals as reflective of the continuing influence of non-Muslims, however. Hasan al-Banna and Abul A`la Mawdudi argued that God required Muslims to develop institutions in accord with the Shari`a, the point of which should be to ensure that the believers continue their mission of commanding right and forbidding wrong. Wherever advocates of democracy suggested a form of social order that would grant equal rights to non-Muslims, women, or groups of Muslims considered irregular or heretical, more "traditionalist" authors and movements saw a drift away from historic Muslim values. To be sure, *khilafat* could be interpreted along lines different from those prominent in an earlier period. *Shura* could in principle involve the development of parliamentary procedures and elections. But an Islamic state should have God's law as its guiding light. And thus, any legitimate state should involve an establishment of Islam, with a consultation between religious and political leaders dedicated to crafting policies consistent with divine standards, and ensuring the kind of order in which Muslims exercise leadership with respect to non-Muslims, men with respect to women, and the young receive strong guidance from their elders.

Al-Banna and Mawdudi wrote widely read treatises on jihad, among other issues.[23] Their work provided others with forceful restatements of historic tradition. To move from these early twentieth-century figures to contemporary jihadists, however, another step is required. Given the continuing lack of consensus about the form of an Islamic state, as well as the continued dominance of Europe and, following World War II, of the United States in the international arena, it was perhaps inevitable that groups would emerge and claim the mantle of jihad as a mode of resistance. When they did, one of the most consistent arguments presented involved appeals to fighting as an individual duty, particularly in connection with the judgment that the influence and in some cases, the presence of military outposts, of non-Muslim powers constituted an invasion or occupation of the territory of Islam. In such texts as *The Neglected Duty*, the Hamas Charter, or the World Islamic Front's "Declaration on Armed Struggle against Jews and Crusaders," groups of Muslims claimed the mantle of historical discourse on jihad, appealing among others to Ibn Taymiyya and his responses to questions occasioned by the Mongol invasion.[24]

The World Islamic Front's "Declaration" can stand as our example.[25] Here, Usama bin Ladin, Ayman al-Zawahiri, and several other militant leaders present the "facts" of contemporary international politics, as of February 1998. The power of the United States and its allies is paramount, with deleterious effects in the historically Muslim lands. In Iraq, a regime of sanctions imposed following the Gulf War has brought great suffering, with thousands of deaths from malnutrition and lack of basic medical supplies. In the Arabian Peninsula, a compliant government has allowed the United States to establish a continuing military presence, contrary to the directive of the Prophet regarding non-Muslim residence in the vicinity of Mecca and Medina. And in Palestine, US support allows Zionists to maintain their "petty state" in an area God entrusted to the Muslims. The situation constitutes an emergency, in which the unanimous precedent of the learned class indicates that fighting should be considered an individual duty, to be carried out by anyone able to do so, in any country where that is possible, against "Americans and their allies, civilians and soldiers" alike. Attacks on US embassies in Kenya and Tanzania the following August; the 9/11 attacks on the World Trade Center, the Pentagon, and the US Capitol; the 7/7/2004 bombings in London and those in 2005 in Madrid; various "lone wolf" attacks such as those attempted by Richard Reid and Umar Farouk Abdulmutallab; all these and many other operations may be understood to come under the umbrella of the "Declaration." As Ayman al-Zawahiri promised following the London bombings, these attacks will not cease until the Americans, the British, and others "depart from the lands of Muhammad, leaving the Muslims free to develop" a Shari`a state, with institutions that ensure the freedom of believers to carry out their mission of commanding right and forbidding wrong.[26]

The claims articulated in the "Declaration" occasioned a great deal of debate.[27] Considering the historical conventions associated with jihad, one can understand why. We may begin with right authority, and thus with Muslims who argue that, notwithstanding the Declaration's claims about the hegemony of the United States and its allies, Muslims remain in control of much of the historical territory of Islam. Established regimes in Egypt, Jordan, Turkey, Saudi Arabia and other Gulf States, Pakistan, and elsewhere institutionalize Muslim values. Whatever their faults, they maintain an order in which Muslims are secure and able to carry out their religious duties. As well, the growing Muslim populations in the United States, the United Kingdom, and the European Union suggest a future in which Islamic influence in those regions will increase. Given these facts, those who act on the basis of the "Declaration" may be deemed naive, at best; at worst, they sow dissension and are thus enemies of God. The authors of the "Declaration" and like-minded Muslims reply that the so-called Muslim governments mentioned are in various ways in violation of God's directives. Their adherence to Shari`a is half-hearted. They lack vigilance with respect to the security of Muslim lands. As to the hopes expressed for Muslim influence in the West, the evidence indicates that many of the believers are being seduced by non-Muslim ideas. In the absence of real leadership from established Muslim states, authority for war falls to a vanguard of believers who will carry out the "neglected duty" incumbent on individuals when the security of Islam is under threat.

What of just cause? As the "Declaration" has it, the influence of enemy forces in the territory of Islam constitutes an occasion for defense. In passing, the authors note that prior to 1998, some disputed this. They think the various facts cited suggest the issue is no longer susceptible of such argument. And it must be said that following the NATO action in Afghanistan, the US-led operation in Iraq that began in 2002, and the continuing war on terror, the drift of Muslim discourse indicates some degree of acceptance of this judgment. Where there is dispute, the focus is on (1) the goals of resistance, namely, the Shari`a state and (2) on the means employed. I shall comment briefly on the first focus, and more extensively on the second.

If defense constitutes a just cause for fighting, what sort of order are those involved defending? To put it another way, what do the authors of the "Declaration on Armed Struggle" and similar texts propose as a replacement for regimes they consider unsatisfactory? To say that they will implement the Shari`a is insufficient. For many Muslims, the examples most closely associated with the World Islamic Front are not encouraging—the rule of the Taliban in Afghanistan, for example, or more recently the imposition of Shari`a in areas coming under the control of the group styling itself the Islamic State in Iraq and Syria. Such examples suggest a harsh and particularly rigorist enforcement of traditional norms, which does not accord with the sentiment of many Muslims. Acknowledgment of the priority of God's law, institutions that show the importance of Muslim leadership, protection of Islamic family values—these are important. They should not be pursued in ways that inhibit an exchange of views, or that ignore changing conditions, however. And so in many circles, such evidence as we have suggests that sympathy with the notion that some portions of the territory of Islam are under attack does not translate into support for the alternative represented in militant statements.

As to means: Here we have an extended debate, beginning with the World Islamic Front's claims that fighting is required of Muslims "in any country where it is possible," and that the targets include "Americans and their allies, civilians and soldiers alike." In a variety of pronouncements, successive holders of the title Shaykh al-Azhar have judged that operations in countries outside the historic territory of Islam are prohibited.[28] Defense of the type associated with fighting as an individual duty applies only to regions where there was or is an order identified with Islam. The goal is to repel invading forces. Operations outside the specified territory follow a different model, analogous to the kind of fighting al-Shaybani and others understood as just in connection with bringing the blessings of Islamic governance to peoples riven by civil strife. For that sort of fighting, the order of a caliph or an equivalent authority is required.

In specifically Muslim terms, the argument of these traditionally respected authorities involves a distinction between the "near" enemy and the "far" enemy. As suggested already, individual Muslims may fight the former. Indeed, they are bound to do so. The latter presents a different case. For this type of fighting, order is needed. Otherwise, one might imagine individuals or small groups conducting a private campaign to extend the boundaries of Islam, without due consideration to the possibilities for success, proportionality of costs and benefits to Muslims, arrangements for supplies, and the like. The responses of bin Ladin, Zawahiri, and others take on this distinction, arguing that the world at present is more complex than the simple division between near and far admits. In effect, the extended hegemony of the United States and its allies constitutes a campaign aimed at undermining the ability of Muslims to carry out their mission. One cannot effectively resist by fighting only on the "near" front. One must take the war to the enemy, raising the cost to its people so that they will bring pressure to bear on policy-makers, hopefully leading to withdrawal.

This leads organically to other tactical issues, for example, the eliding of distinctions between civilian and military targets. The historic requirement of a good-faith effort to avoid direct targeting of the former seems clear enough. While realists like al-Shaybani allowed for a significant amount of collateral damage in the interests of pursuing victory, it does not seem that they envisioned a situation in which the distinction would be moot. For bin Ladin and others, however, the idea that citizens in democratic states enjoy opportunities to change the course of policy, and thus the judgment that they bear responsibility for unjust initiatives, particularly if such remain in place under successive administrations, is deemed convincing. In addition, the notion that the United States and its allies are responsible for the deaths of Muslim civilians justifies retaliation, even if those deaths were not directly intended. In response, more establishment figures argue that the direct and intentional targeting of civilians is never permitted in Islam. Anyone carrying out an attack that does not respect this prohibition does not deserve the honor due to a legitimately Islamic fighter, even if that person sacrifices his or her own life in the attempt.

We can bring this discussion of the modern relevance of fighting as an individual duty to a close with a brief consideration of the Syrian conflict. When fighting began in 2010, government forces were responding to a series of demonstrations expressing a desire for change. The immediate inspiration for these was the success of similar tactics in Egypt, Tunisia, and other countries in which the Arab Spring took hold. A longer-term explanation would point to the importance of policy decisions in which the Assad regime provided support for some domestic allies to develop large-scale farming operations along the lines of American agribusiness. The use of massive irrigation equipment (by regional standards) began to draw down the water table, leading to expressions of alarm from international groups interested in the phenomenon. When this trend was joined with a long drought beginning in 2004, the impact on small, family-oriented farming enterprises was immediate. In some cases, entire clans moved to cities like Aleppo, Damascus, and Homs, which increased demands for basic services. The government would not, or could not, comply.

The demands of the demonstrators thus had a longer-term economic and environmental basis, as well as a political one. Bashar al-Assad inherited a coalition built by his father, in which the Alawite minority joined with Christians and some others to forge a government in which perhaps 25 to 30 percent of the population governed the rest. While the original parties in the demonstrations did not employ religious language, it was perhaps predictable that, once the regime responded with force and fighting began, the historical distinctions between the Shia (the Alawites being a kind of heterodox variation of that side of the Muslim divide, and with strong associations with the Lebanese Hezbollah and its Iranian sponsor) and the majority Sunni Syrian population would come to the fore.

As the Sunni identity became more prominent for groups opposing the Assad regime, important religious figures began to speak about the fighting as a kind of defense, in which a government both tyrannical and heretical, and with international support, sought to impose its will on orthodox, Sunni Muslims. A figure like Yusuf al-Qaradawi, noteworthy for his al-Azhar training and his activism in association with the Muslim Brotherhood, did not quite invoke the language of individual duty—after all, he (like the Shaykh al-Azhar) understood that notion in very specific terms, in which foreign forces invaded Islamic lands.[29] Qaradawi came close, however, as he argued that all Muslims able to do so should come to the aid of those engaged in resistance, and criticized the governments of Egypt and other historically Sunni states for their unwillingness to provide support. Ideally, Qaradawi declared, these governments would sponsor armed support for the resistance. If they could not or would not do that, they should at least not put up obstacles (travel regulations and the like) to those Muslims willing to go. The conflict in Syria is a great test, Qaradhawi argued. The Assad regime and its Shiite supporters must be fought, even as the Qur'an indicates in 49:9.

What shall we make of this? The notion of fighting as an individual duty is a legitimate aspect of historic Muslim discourse about war. As such, it is a piece of a war convention, intended to regulate resort to and conduct of force, and is in the service of delimiting more anarchic forms of violence. At the same time, the notion is invoked in connection with judgments that legitimate order is under attack, or even in such disarray as to be non-operational. In that sense, the widespread invocation of the notion, and the ensuing disputes over it, are symptomatic of a deep crisis of legitimacy in the historically Muslim lands. Those who would consider the relationship of religion and peacebuilding in this case must count this an important datum, even as they seek ways for religion to function as a constructive aspect of the project of a justpeace.[30]

How to Proceed

Given the foregoing discussion of Islam's crisis of legitimacy, the stalemate among policy-makers is hardly surprising. What to do, to stop the killing in Syria? To bring peace to Afghanistan, or to Pakistan's northwest frontier? To address Iran's nuclear ambitions, or the anxiety of Saudi Arabia and other historically Sunni states over the ways Iran's foreign policy suggests an aspiration to become the region's hegemon? And these are only a few of the conflicts one might mention in thinking about historically Muslim areas.

I shall not address any of these directly. I do not think that the comparative study of ethics, in and of itself, suggests particular answers. Rather, in the sense I have suggested, comparative ethics stands as a descriptive or hermeneutical enterprise, in which the goal is to contribute to an answer to the question "what is going on?"[31] In the case at hand, Muslim argument concerning the historical judgments pertaining to armed struggle indicates a deep social crisis, which is only compounded when one considers factors like climate change, economic development, and interventions by a variety of international actors.

In addition to description of a problem, however, I think that there is another angle by which the comparative study of ethics may be relevant to the project of pursuing justpeace. And that is by way of an account of the qualities or virtues necessary to building peace Consider, for example, a few lines from one of the speeches of Dag Hammarskjold:

> Politics and diplomacy are no play of will and skill, where results are independent of the character of those engaging in the game. Results are determined not by superficial ability but by the consistency of the actors in their efforts and by the validity of their ideals. Contrary to what seems to be popular belief, there is no intellectual activity which more ruthlessly tests the solidity of a man than politics. Apparently easy successes with the public are possible for a juggler, but lasting results are achieved only by the patient builder.[32]

As a recent biography of Hammarskjold suggests, these speeches present a rich vein of materials regarding the virtues of peacebuilders. In the passage quoted above, patience is cited. As the metaphor of building suggests, however, patience is not simply a matter of waiting things out. It is joined with activity that has an aim. The attributes of those who would build peace thus include justice, and patience itself is paired with perseverance. Thus

> The United Nations is faith and works—faith in the possibility of a world without fear and works to bring that faith closer to realization in the life of men.[33]

As Hammarskjold's biographer has it, the late secretary-general considered fear "the root of all evil."[34] The United Nations served as a moral force for taming this vice, he believed, whenever its decisions and actions conform to the values of the Charter and the Universal "Declaration" of Human Rights. The holder of the secretary-general's post is uniquely placed with a mandate to exercise some part of that moral force. And

> the first thing required is patience, the patience inspired by a firm faith in our ability to reach the goal. But we need more than patience in the passive sense. We need perseverance, of the kind that equips us not to take defeats to heart, in the knowledge that defeats are unavoidable, and that if our efforts do not seem to get results, it may be because we have not yet applied the necessary degree of perseverance.[35]

A certain kind of confidence is required of a peacebuilder, in that he or she must maintain faith in the possibility of a good result; at the same time, the task requires practical wisdom, both in the sense of recognizing obstacles and in the willingness to craft "provisional solutions" that build on "small zones of common ground." Comparing peacebuilding to mountain climbing, Hammarskjold speaks of the importance of

> perseverance and patience, a firm grip on realities, careful but imaginative planning, a clear awareness of the dangers but also of the fact that fate is what we make it and that the safest climber is he who never questions his ability to overcome all difficulties.[36]

In medical terms, peacebuilding shares more with the activities of nurses or midwives than of surgeons. That is because of the attention to detail and the willingness to provide long-term care; peacebuilders should not expect to make news in the way surgeons or, one supposes, those who create new techniques or medical devices might.[37]

In other settings, Hammarskjold often spoke of the importance of faith, in the sense of an "awareness of something greater than oneself, realistic acknowledgement of others' mastery, willingness to play one's role to the extreme limit of one's ability. . ."[38] And as his personal journal indicates, he drew on an eclectic set of sources for inspiration and wisdom.

In terms of the comparative study of ethics, Hammarskjold's speeches bear a striking resemblance to a number of accounts of the virtues—that is, of those excellences of character that entail the power to combine a sense of justice with practical wisdom, and also to discipline oneself so as to overcome personal obstacles to doing the right. In the account of Thomas Aquinas, for example, prudence travels with justice, so that one understands how to act in a given set of circumstances. Without prudence, justice is blind or lacks direction; without justice, prudence devolves into a kind of cunning. Courage deals with aspects of a situation that are repulsive, like high levels of danger. Temperance addresses other temptations, by which one's actions may be overly colored by desires for praise or other things most would count as pleasant. Interestingly, Thomas's discussion of patience puts this character trait in the service of courage. As Josef Pieper writes, patience is "a necessary component of fortitude," not least because of Thomas's description of endurance as the primary component of courage. And yet, patience does not stand alone. It is not the "indiscriminate acceptance of any and every evil. . . [but] means to preserve cheerfulness and serenity of mind in spite of injuries that result from the realization of the good. [Patience] keeps [a human being] from the danger that [his or her] spirit may be broken by grief and lose its greatness." But "patience by itself does not constitute the whole of fortitude, no more, nay, less than does endurance, to which patience is subordinated. The brave [person] not only knows how to bear inevitable evil with equanimity; he [or she] will also not hesitate to 'pounce upon' evil and to bar its way, if this can reasonably be done." In this regard, Thomas assigns to anger a "positive relation to the virtue of fortitude."[39]

From another context, the great Nasir al-Din Tusi (1201–1274) develops a Muslim account of virtues. Like Thomas, Tusi builds from Aristotle a notion that wisdom, justice, courage, and temperance express the most general aspects of an excellent character, and courage in particular "signifies that the irascible should submit to the rational." That is, courage addresses "passions" that tempt one away from the performance of duty, particularly by taming the tendency to "become agitated in perilous affairs." In dangerous or challenging circumstances, one may err in the direction of fear, which leads to withdrawal or flight. One may also err in the direction of foolhardiness, by rushing into danger before due consideration of what actions are the most apt, the most wise and just. And since courage requires "long-suffering," "perseverance," "calmness," and "vigor," among other things, we have in Tusi an account that is not only consistent with Aquinas, but which bears comparison with the speeches of Hammarskjold.[40]

The power of Tusi as an example may be amplified if we note that the term translated as long-suffering ultimately derives from the Arabic root *s-b-r*, which denotes steadfastness, endurance, stick-to-it-iveness, and related terms. In various forms, this notion constitutes one of the most characteristic themes of the Qur'an, so that the call to submit by struggling in the way of God might even be said to require it. Interestingly, it is often joined with the practice of prayer.

> Seek God's help with patient perseverance [bi-l-sabri] and prayer. This is indeed hard, except for those who are humble. (2:45)
>   O believers! Seek help with patient perseverance [bi-l-sabri] and prayer, for God is with those who patiently persevere. (2:153)

In other verses, s-b-r is a command, as at 40:55, in which it is joined with asking for forgiveness of sin, as well as with worship.

> Patiently, then, persevere [asbir], for the promise of God is true. And ask forgiveness for your fault, and celebrate the praises of your Lord in the evening and in the morning.

And in the context of dealing with enemies, we read,

> Have patience [asbir] with what they say, and separate from them with a noble separation. (73:10)

Or:

> If you punish, let your punishment be proportionate to the wrong that has been done to you. But if you show patience [sabartum] that is indeed best.. . . Be patient [asbir] because your patience [sabruka] exists by the help of God. Do not grieve over them, and do not distress yourself because of their plots. (16:126–127)

As noted, Hammarskjold's various statements on the qualities necessary for peacebuilders resonate with the points made by John Paul Lederach in this volume. And I think one could argue that the comparisons with Thomas Aquinas and Nasir al-Din Tusi suggest religious resources for peacebuilders, along the lines of other contributions to this handbook.

There is, however, something else to say, by way of bringing the conversation back to religious traditions and the cultural regulation of armed force. As Hammarskjold worked to quell tensions and build peace during the Suez Canal crisis, with respect to Arab-Israeli tensions, and finally in the deeply conflicted Congo, he drew more and more on the wisdom of military experts. Peacekeeping missions became his "specialty."[41] These were the early days of such missions, and questions about the rules of engagement for such forces, when and how they would be authorized to intervene, and other matters were much under debate. Importantly, though, as a "provisional solution" to specific cases, Hammarskjold thought these military moves important.

Earlier in this chapter I suggested that tracking the development of discourse about jihad contributes to an answer to the question "what is going on?" In cases like Syria, or in the discourse of the World Islamic Front, we learn that the historic references to fighting as an individual duty reveal that the Muslim community feels beleaguered. Now we need to say something more. These appeals point as well to a judgment that the current order of things is illegitimate. Indeed, despite the prevalence of calls for governance by the Shari`a, there is very little consensus even among Muslims as to what this would mean. We are dealing here with a deep political crisis, in which those who aim at peace must commit to the long term; in which patience and perseverance are joined to a capacious vision, while prudence proceeds through the identification of small zones of common ground and begins with provisional solutions. And this last must not, if we follow Hammarskjold's example, rule out the use or threat of armed force. How to make use of this tool—for example, in connection with the development of conceptions of the responsibility of the United Nations to protect the peoples of the world from genocide and other abuses of human rights—is a question that deserves wide discussion. We cannot in any simple way draw on the historic frameworks of jihad, just war, or other long-standing cultural traditions for guidance. Our political condition is distinctive, and building peace in the historically Muslim regions, as elsewhere, requires building consensus in ways that are more egalitarian, more inclusive than jurists like al-Shaybani or Ibn Taymiyya could imagine.

Nevertheless, I do not think we will get far without attending to the question such frameworks were designed to address. Which brings us back to the role of religions in the cultural regulation of armed force. They provided and still provide vocabularies by which human beings may discern the difference between better and worse uses of military force. For peacebuilders like Hammarskjold (or one might say like Thomas Aquinas and Nasir al-Din Tusi), these frameworks also play a role in connection with the life of virtue: they assist in the attempt to develop policies that are both wise (fitting for a particular situation) and just. One should admit the difficulties of calling on such traditions in the service of peacebuilding. They do not guarantee "correct" answers to our questions; they may be misused; and even when employed with the purest of motives, they may in the end prove unsuccessful. And yet, can peacebuilding afford to ignore them?

Notes

1. Edward Hallett Carr, *Conditions of Peace* (New York: Macmillan, 1942), xxiii–xxiv.
2. John Kelsay, "Just War and Legal Restraints," in *The Oxford Handbook of Religion and Violence*, ed. Mark Juergensmeyer et al. (New York: Oxford University Press, 2013), 306–314.
3. A reasonable person might well ask about this focus on Islam. As will become clear, I think tracking Muslim arguments about jihad provides a unique window through which to analyze conditions in one of the more troubled regions of the contemporary world. As well, this discourse, while framed as a set of judgments about the rights and wrongs of military force, helps to illumine the interrelations of conceptions of peace, order, and justice in the task of building peace.
4. Throughout this essay, I draw on the translation of M. A. S. Abdel Haleem, *The Qur'an* (New York: Oxford University Press, 2008), with alterations when I judge this necessary to convey the sense of the Arabic text.
5. Majid Khadduri, *The Islamic Law of Nations: Shaybani's Siyar* (Baltimore: Johns Hopkins University Press, 1966), 75–76.
6. Abu Ja'far Muhammad b. Jarir al-Tabari, *The 'Abbasid Caliphate in Equilibrium*, vol. 30 of *The History of al-Tabari,* trans. C. E. Bosworth (Albany: State University of New York Press, 1989), 115ff.
7. al-Tabari, *The 'Abbasid Caliphate in Equilibrium.*
8. Khadduri, *Islamic Law of Nations*, 95–96.
9. Khadduri, *Islamic Law of Nations*, 99.
10. Khadduri, *Islamic Law of Nations*, 102.
11. Khadduri, *Islamic Law of Nations*, 102.

12. Khadduri, *Islamic Law of Nations*, 87.
13. Khadduri, *Islamic Law of Nations*, 102.
14. Khadduri, *Islamic Law of Nations*, 102.
15. Abu al-Hasan al-Mawardi, *The Ordinances of Government*, trans. Wafaa H. Wahba (Reading, UK: Garnet Publishing, 1996), 45.
16. Khadduri, *Islamic Law of Nations*, 231.
17. Khadduri, *Islamic Law of Nations*, 231.
18. Khadduri, *Islamic Law of Nations*, 195–229.
19. Khadduri, *Islamic Law of Nations*, 222–223.
20. Emmanuel Sivan, "La genese de la Contre-Croisade: Un traite damasquin du debut du XII siècle," *Journal Asiatique* 254 (1966): 197–224.
21. Omar A. Farrukh, *Ibn Taymiyya on Public and Private Law in Islam* (Beirut: Khayats, 1966).
22. Hamid Enayat, *Modern Islamic Political Thought* (Austin: University of Texas, 1982), p. 1
23. Charles Wendell, trans., *Five Tracts of Hasan al-Banna (1906–1949)* (Berkeley: University of California Press, 1978), 133–162; Sayyid Abul A`la Mawdudi, *Jihad in Islam* (Lahore: Islamic Publications, 1976).
24. John Kelsay, *Arguing the Just War in Islam* (Cambridge, MA: Harvard University Press, 2007), 244–245.
25. For a convenient translation, see Intelligence Resource Program of the Federation of Scientists, "Jihad Against Jews and Crusaders: World Islamic Front Statement," http://www.fas.org/irp/world/para/docs/980223-fatwa.htm.
26. IntelCenter, "Ayman al-Zawahiri Audio/Video Release Analysis," August 5, 2005, http://www.intelcenter.com/AZAVRA-PUB-v1-1.pdf, especially 12–13.
27. Kelsay, *Arguing the Just War in Islam*.
28. Kelsay, *Arguing the Just War in Islam*, 142–143.
29. BBC, "Syria conflict: Cleric Qaradawi urges Sunnis to join rebels," June 1, 2013, http://www.bbc.com/news/world-middle-east-22741588.
30. As I read over the copyedited version of this chapter, the advance of Islamic State in Iraq and Greater Syria (the leadership of which now wishes to be known as the State of the Islamic Caliphate) renders the situation even more complex. A report from the Rand Corporation provides evidence of a growing number of groups appealing to the notion of fighting as an individual duty. See Seth Jones, *A Persistent Threat: The Evolution of al-Qa`ida and Other Salafi Jihadists* (Washington, D.C.: Rand Corporation, 2014).
31. This is perhaps the place to note a difference between my own conception of the comparative study of ethics and that of some others. For example, Daniel Philpott's argument that an ethic of reconciliation provides a theme that links Christianity, Judaism, and other traditions to the project of building peace proceeds with an explicitly normative agenda. Here as elsewhere, I proceed with a rough distinction between the analytic and interpretive work of understanding what is going on in a particular case, and any normative agenda one wishes to pursue. The task of comparative studies of ethics is thus usually not directly connected to a purpose like building democracy or the project of justpeace, although the findings of scholars engaged in comparative study may well assist in identifying resources for, as well as obstacles to, the attainment of such goals. For Philpott, see not only the chapter in this volume, but also his *Just and Unjust Peace: An Ethic of Political Reconciliation* (New York: Oxford University Press, 2012).
32. Roger Lipsey, *Hammarskjöld: A Life* (Ann Arbor: University of Michigan Press, 2013), 6.
33. Lipsey, *Hammarskjöld*, 175.

34. Lipsey, *Hammarskjöld*, 190.
35. Lipsey, *Hammarskjöld*, 191.
36. Lipsey, *Hammarskjöld*, 122.
37. Lipsey, *Hammarskjöld*, 290–291, 104.
38. Lipsey, *Hammarskjöld*, 130.
39. Josef Pieper, *The Four Cardinal Virtues*, trans. Richard and Clara Winston, et al. (New York: Harcourt Brace World, 1965), 129.
40. Nasir ad-Din Tusi, *The Nasirean Ethics*, trans. G. M. Wickens (London: George Allen and Unwin, 1964), 79–83.
41. Lipsey, *Hammarskjöld*, 258.

Bibliography

IntelCenter. "Ayman al-Zawahiri Audio/Video Release Analysis." August 5, 2005. http://www.intelcenter.com/AZAVRA-PUB-v1-1.pdf.

Carr, Edward Hallett. *Conditions of Peace*. New York: Macmillan, 1942.

Enayat, Hamid. *Modern Islamic Political Thought*. Austin: University of Texas, 1982.

Farrukh, Omar A. *Ibn Taymiyya on Public and Private Law in Islam*. Beirut: Khayats, 1966.

Haleem, M. A. S. Abdel. *The Qur'an*. New York: Oxford University Press, 2008.

Intelligence Resource Program of the Federation of Scientists. "Jihad Against Jews and Crusaders: World Islamic Front Statement." February 23, 1998. http://www.fas.org/irp/world/para/docs/980223-fatwa.htm.

Jones, Seth. *A Persistent Threat: The Evolution of al-Qa'ida and Other Salafi Jihadists*. Washington, D.C.: Rand Corporation, 2014.

Kelsay, John. *Arguing the Just War in Islam*. Cambridge, MA: Harvard University Press, 2007.

Kelsay, John. "Just War and Legal Restraints." In *The Oxford Handbook of Religion and Violence*, edited by Mark Juergensmeyer et al. New York: Oxford University Press, 2013: 306–314.

Khadduri, Majid. *The Islamic Law of Nations: Shaybani's Siyar*. Baltimore: Johns Hopkins University Press, 1966.

Lipsey, Roger. *Hammarskjöld: A Life*. Ann Arbor: University of Michigan Press, 2013.

al-Mawardi, Abu al-Hasan. *The Ordinances of Government*. Translated by Wafaa H. Wahba. Reading, UK: Garnet Publishing, 1996.

Mawdudi, Sayyid Abul A`la. *Jihad in Islam*. Lahore: Islamic Publications, 1976.

Philpott, Daniel. *Just and Unjust Peace: An Ethic of Political Reconciliation*. New York: Oxford University Press, 2012.

Pieper, Josef. *The Four Cardinal Virtues*. Translated by Richard and Clara Winston, et al. New York: Harcourt Brace World, 1965.

Sivan, Emmanuel. "La genese de la Contre-Croisade: Un traite damasquin du debut du XII siècle." *Journal Asiatique* 254 (1966): 197–224.

al-Tabari, Abu Ja`far Muhammad b. Jarir. *The `Abbasid Caliphate in Equilibrium*. Vol. 30 of *The History of al-Tabari*. Translated by C. E. Bosworth. Albany: State University of New York Press, 1989.

Tusi, Nasir ad-Din. *The Nasirean Ethics*. Translated by G. M. Wickens. London: George Allen and Unwin, 1964.

Wendell, Charles, trans. *Five Tracts of Hasan al-Banna (1906–1949)*. Berkeley: University of California Press, 1978.

CHAPTER 11

....

THE PLACE OF RELIGIOUS FREEDOM IN THE STRUCTURE OF PEACEBUILDING

....

W. COLE DURHAM JR. AND ELIZABETH A. CLARK

FREEDOM of religion or belief is fundamental to the structure of peacebuilding. Without it, no society can be fully just, and processes aimed at achieving stable and lasting peace are necessarily incomplete. This fundamental human right has long been considered a critical tool for ending and averting religious warfare, but it also provides necessary footings needed to begin crystallizing peace out of conflict.

Yet focus on this fundamental constitutional and human right may appear to be at once too broad and too narrow to have relevance to the resolution of hot conflicts. The focus seems too broad because it relates to a range of conflicts arising in "normal" situations that don't typically mobilize experts in conflict resolution. Recurrent issues such as public display of religious symbols, the wearing of religious garb, the place of religion in education, religious discrimination in employment, and countless other similar issues reflect social tensions, but not necessarily tensions of an intensity that typically calls for professional peacebuilders. On the other hand, the focus may seem too narrow, since religious freedom is only one of many human rights: one of many tools that can help build "justpeace," one of many elements constituting a just and stable society, one of many relational and cultural factors vital to peacebuilding in a modern world.

These considerations serve to highlight aspects of the place of religious freedom in the overall structure of peacebuilding. While many religious tensions scarcely register on the scale of matters requiring governmental or other external intervention, we neglect such tensions at our peril. Problems related to religious freedom often lack the urgency of disappearances, imprisonment, torture, and other egregious violations of human rights, but if simmering religious tensions are neglected, forces build up that can explode. Protecting freedom of religion can help avert such escalation, and if explosions do occur, it is vital to unwinding such conflict afterwards. It is clearly not the only tool of peacebuilding, but it is a vital one. Freedom of religion and belief straddles the gap between "liberal peace," revolving around human rights and the law, and more holistic peacebuilding efforts that focus on building a just peace through the involvement of many actors, including religious ones.[1] While freedom of religion and belief is merely one part of an overall just peace, it can be a significant force in strategic peacebuilding and can facilitate the contributions of religious groups and individuals.

In what follows, we examine the place of freedom of religion or belief in the structure of peacebuilding at the level of theory, at the level of relevant legal structures, and at the level of contributing to other social goods that are important constituents of just and lasting peace. But first, we need to address the relationship of religion to conflict itself.

I. Religion, Pluralism, and Conflict

Hobbes famously described peace as a residue left after subtracting out all times of war: "The nature of War consisteth not in actual fighting; but in the known disposition thereto, during all the time there is no assurance to the contrary. All other time is PEACE."[2] Religion, unfortunately, has all too often been a detractor from rather than a contributor to that slender residue. Like romantic love, religion is deeply implicated in much that is highest, but also in much that is lowest, in the human condition.[3] Religion provides significant resources for building peace, but part of the "ambivalence of the sacred"[4] arises from its all-too-frequent contributions to conflict and violence. Any discussion of the role of religion (and freedom of religion) in peacebuilding necessarily grapples with this ambivalence.[5]

It has become a commonplace to say that religion is a major cause of social tensions. The essential picture is both simple and plausible. We live in an increasingly pluralistic world. A significant part of this sociological pluralism is rooted in divergent religious views. Religion involves transcendent values that people may treasure more than life itself, and it generates loyalties that run deeper than ties to any earthly sovereign. Because religious differences are deep and nonnegotiable, they lead to intractable conflicts that have littered the pages of history. Building on this picture, a standard account portrays religious freedom as a tool that emerged from the cauldron of post-Reformation religious wars to quell the violence of nascent religious pluralism. In this picture, religious freedom is a secularist tool designed to contain the otherwise destructive force of religion.

While there is considerable truth to this account, recent scholarship suggests that this picture overstates the dark side of religion. In a significant recent book, William Cavanaugh argues persuasively that liberal political theory exaggerates the hazard that religious difference poses for social stability and peace. The title of his book, *The Myth of Religious Violence*, no doubt overstates his thesis.[6] He is not claiming that religion is never implicated in violence. But the assumption that religion is the key causal factor in violence skews analysis. In Cavanaugh's view, the myth of religious violence is part of an entrenched Enlightenment narrative, according to which religion has essential transhistorical and transcultural features distinct from secular features of society. Part of this essence, rooted in the irrationality of religion, is a peculiarly dangerous inclination to promote violence. Religion must thus be tamed by submitting it to, and restricting its access to, public power. Religion as an irrational and dangerous impulse must give way in public to rational, secular forms of power.

According to Cavanaugh, there are a number of significant difficulties with this picture. In fact, religions are no more inclined to violence than secular institutions and ideologies such as nationalism, Marxism, capitalism, and liberalism. Religions are not more absolutist, divisive, or irrational than their secular counterparts. In fact, there is really no convincing way to distinguish between religious and secular violence. One is not inherently more suspect than the other, and it cannot simply be assumed that religion is in fact the predominant causal factor in narratives in which religion is painted as the villain. As an example, Cavanaugh focuses on what he calls the "founding myth of the secular state": the idea that the modern state was born as a peacemaker, resolving religious conflicts rooted in the intransigence of Catholics and Protestants. The difficulty with this picture is that while the "religious" wars certainly occurred, closer historical examination shows that most of the warfare occurred long before the secular state emerged, and leaving that aside, the battle lines often did not track religious divides. The much more typical pattern was that conflicts emerged to resist the state-building efforts of centralizing monarchs. State restrictions on religion flowing from state-building initiatives were often the real cause of conflict. It turns out that more careful historiography shows that it was not so much religious difference, but state-imposed restrictions on religion that explain the violence.[7]

That the role of religion as a causal factor in conflict should not be overemphasized is confirmed by research coming from two other directions. Recent studies analyzing causal influences in conflict situations recognize the significance of religion as a factor, but also emphasize that its role can easily be exaggerated. Gerard Powers has taken a careful look at data on violent conflicts and argues that only 22 percent of conflicts between 1989 and 2003 involved religious claims and that religious terrorists only make up 36 percent of terrorist groups in the world.[8] These are not, of course, insignificant amounts, but the percentages are much lower than one might have expected. Along these lines, Monica Duffy Toft acknowledges that religious terrorism has increased in recent years and that it tends to be more lethal than nonreligious terrorism.[9] She also notes that religious civil wars made up more than a third of all civil wars fought between 1940 and 2010.[10] Powers, relying on data from the Uppsala Conflict Data Program, suggests that while conflicts over religious questions are more intractable than other conflicts, conflicts between groups of differing religious identities are not.[11] In analyzing the extent to which religion is involved in conflict, it is important to remember that data sets, arguments, and even the individuals involved do not always clearly distinguish between conflicts caused by religious motivations and ones where religious identity merely serves as a marker in a conflict over other issues.

Another line of study suggesting caution in blaming religion for violent conflict emerges from the sociological work of Brian Grim and Roger Finke. In their seminal work, *The Price of Freedom Denied*,[12] Grim and Finke summarize extensive empirical research based on data compiled from a variety of major international studies of restrictions on freedom of religion. A key finding was that restrictions on religious freedom are highly correlated with and appear to be a significant factor in causing religious violence. Religious freedom, in contrast, correlates more strongly with peace and stability. This work has profound policy implications. It suggests that those wielding state power need to be particularly cautious about imposing governmental restrictions aimed at religious difference, because they are more likely to cause religious violence than to cure it. The data reinforce Cavanaugh's historical argument that religious violence in the era of religious wars was more likely a result of centralizing governmental restrictions than of religious difference itself. Religious violence is more likely to be a defensive or retaliatory reaction to interference with religious values than a spontaneous irrational eruption of violence.

The foregoing analysis of the relationship of religion to violence does not deny the ambivalence of the sacred, or the reality of harm caused by religion. What it emphasizes is the need for great caution in assuming that religion is a problem that should be dealt with by repression rather than with respect. Respect need not be naive and can remain cautious, but reconciliation and stable peace ultimately need to find ways for people with deeply differing worldviews to live together with mutual respect for each other and each others' rights. Shedding the perception that religion is inherently prone to violence may make it easier for peacebuilders to open channels of tolerance, trust, reconciliation, and ultimately respect. It may also lessen temptations to think of religion as an issue that should be avoided or downplayed or suppressed in the process of seeking peaceful solutions, precisely because such approaches send messages of exclusion or disrespect that are likely to undermine peacebuilding initiatives.

II. Religious Freedom Theory
and the Structure of Peacebuilding

The foregoing reflections on the relationship of religion and conflict provide a natural transition to a discussion of the place of religious freedom theory and its connection to peacebuilding. Ultimately, conflict situations pose the critical test for the broader theory of religious freedom. The difficulty is that this means that religious freedom theory in its entirety is germane to thought about conflict prevention and resolution situations, at least insofar as they involve religion in some way. All that can be done here is to reflect briefly on a few focal areas in this vast domain. In what follows, a series of key theoretical issues are addressed, each treated here as footnotes on or corrections to John Locke's theory of religious liberty.[13] The aim with each of the "footnotes" is to draw attention to starting points at the foundation of liberal theory, and to point out how historical experience has shown the need to further liberalize liberalism.

A. The Pluralist Insight

Perhaps most fundamental is a Lockean insight into the possibilities of social pluralism that paved the way for modernity. For much of human history, it was assumed that religious homogeneity was a necessary ingredient of social peace. Religion provided a kind of social glue holding society together, providing legitimacy for social institutions and vital incentives (in the form of eternal rewards or punishments) for voluntary compliance with social norms. Dissenters constituted the ultimate threat to social order, breaching vital standards of loyalty and raising the risk of civil war. Against this background, Locke's thought was revolutionary, constituting a "Copernican revolution" in political theory. It shifted the focus from securing homogeneity to respecting difference, recognizing paradoxically that the latter could provide a stronger basis for stability than coerced uniformity.

The key passage is found toward the end of his famous *Letter Concerning Toleration*:

> Now if that church which agrees in religion with the prince be esteemed the chief support of any civil government, and that for no other reason. . . than because the prince is kind and the laws are favorable to it; *how much greater will be the security of government, where all good subjects, of whatsoever church they be, without any distinction upon account of religion, enjoying the same favor of the prince and the same benefit of the laws, shall become the common support and guard of it,* and where none will have any occasion to fear the severity of the laws but those that do injuries to their neighbors and offend against the civil peace?[14]

Locke recognized that the real source of religious violence is not religious difference itself, but defensive conduct when conscientious convictions are threatened by efforts to coerce social monism. This insight provides the theoretical explanation for contemporary empirical findings that government restrictions on religion are a predominant factor accounting for religious violence. Building a just peace necessarily takes this pluralist insight as a starting point. This is the deep reason that freedom of religion needs to be treated as a non-derogable right, even in times of national emergency, as recognized by the International Covenant on Civil and Political Rights (ICCPR).[15] Religious pluralism is both a potential threat to social harmony and an inherent aspect of social life that must be taken into account if peace is to be achieved. The question is how to domesticate this ultimate source of social tension and how to achieve just reconciliation. Not surprisingly, it was often religious dissenters—figures such as Roger Williams and William Penn—who helped to articulate the reasons for thinking that religious freedom is critical to the answer.[16]

B. Limitations Theory

1. Limitations on Accommodations of Religious Freedom

Of course, religious freedom is not boundless. Locke understood this, but miscalculated the scope of the needed limitations. In the first place, he had an insufficiently flexible notion of the way law interacts with conscience. He thought that so long as laws related to matters within the magistrate's civil authority (and not to purely spiritual issues), there was no need to exempt conscience from the reach of civil law. The public good aimed at by law would seldom clash with private conscience, but if it did, the private conscientious objector should bear the legal consequences of following conscience, because the private judgment of a person "does not take away the obligation of that law, nor deserve a dispensation."[17]

Whether and under what conditions religious freedom justifies differential (even deferential) treatment under general and neutral laws remains a controversial question. This has been the central debate in free exercise jurisprudence of the United States for the past quarter-century,[18] and also calls for sensitive balancing in international and European law.[19] The debate can be understood as one between early thinkers, who thought that the rule of law would be sufficient to resolve the underlying social tensions generated by religious difference, and later thinkers who had actually experienced rather than merely forecast the validity of the Lockean insight. The later thinkers were more acutely conscious that legal rules are not always "faithfully administered and. . . directed to the public good."[20] Rules that are formally "general and neutral" on their face can be manipulated to persecute particular

religious groups, or perhaps more typically, may have the unintended effect of creating conflicts of conscience for some believers. Legal regimes sensitive to the problem have recognized that both the intrinsic justice and the stability-strengthening potential of religious
freedom are enhanced if the law is construed to avoid conscientious conflict, except where
there is a compelling need to override conscience that cannot be achieved in some less
restrictive way.[21]

a. Accommodations and Equality

Egalitarians worry that deferring to conscience in this way creates discriminatory exceptions that are themselves a source of social tension and injustice. But this overlooks the fact
that respect for religious difference constitutes a legitimate ground for making distinctions
in a substantive rather than formal theory of equality. Moreover, in an integralist theory of
law,[22] statutes need to be understood not only in isolation, as disconnected commands of
the sovereign, but in harmony with broader constitutional norms. Understood in this way,
accommodating conscience is not an anomaly or an exception to legal ordering, but a con-
touring of individual rules to conform to the overall constitutional order.

b. Rule of Law Constraints

This richer understanding of the rule of law opens space for the legal order to incorporate
Locke's pluralist insight. In contrast, insisting on formal equality where this is not necessary
to furthering a compelling or proportionate public good is the prototypical contemporary
version of violating Locke's pluralist insight. Excessive insistence on formal equality creates
pressures for homogeneity that undermine freedom and true protection of human dignity.
The Lockean insight and its genuine respect for difference are as important as a counter-
weight to excessive egalitarian homogeneity as they are to excessive religious homogeneity.
Peacebuilding depends on finding ways to respect the dignity of difference and to integrate
even deep difference in a common social life. The right to equality remains a pseudo-right if
it confuses a right to sameness with an equal right to be different.

2. General Limitations Theory

A second area in which Lockean theory was insufficiently supple was in setting the outer
limits of religious freedom protections. Briefly stated, the Lockean view was that there are
four groups with no right to be tolerated: "(1) those whose opinions undermine the interests
of civil society; (2) the intolerant; (3) those who serve a foreign power; and (4) atheists."[23]

a. Necessity Constraints

The principle behind selection of the first of these groups is problematic only in that it is so
abstract that it is difficult to be certain of concrete applications. As Locke states the principle,
"no opinions contrary to human society, or to those moral rules which are necessary to the
preservation of civil society, are to be tolerated by the magistrate."[24] This included in particular teachings that "manifestly undermine the foundations of society."[25] This principle can be
read as Locke's version of a "compelling state interest" test, or perhaps even more clearly, his
elucidation of the principle in international and European law that only those limitations on
religious freedom that are strictly "necessary" can withstand scrutiny.[26] Exactly what meets

this test needs to be evaluated in light of the particular considerations relevant in particular contexts, but it is clear that only a fairly restricted set of public policies or interests will qualify.

b. Tolerance and the Intolerant

In many ways the second excluded group is most fundamental: the other groupings simply reflect particularly significant types of intolerance that need not be tolerated. There is something almost Kantian about the principle that religious freedom does not require toleration of the intolerant. Intolerant maxims of action cannot be universalized, and therefore cannot support a categorical imperative.[27] The difficulty is that Locke applied the general principle that "the intolerant need not be tolerated" far too broadly. In his view, Catholics and Muslims need not be tolerated to the extent that they are subservient to foreign powers. A magistrate granting such toleration would "give way to settling of a foreign jurisdiction in his own country."[28] Atheists are a hazard because "promises, covenants, and oaths, which are the bonds of human society, can have no hold upon an atheist. The taking away of God, though but even in thought, dissolves all."[29] Locke thus appears to limit toleration in England essentially to different brands of Protestantism, and perhaps to Jews.[30] Even they will be suspect to the extent they "arrogate to themselves and to those of their own sect some peculiar prerogative. . . opposite to the civil right of the community."[31] Not surprisingly, subsequent historical experience has confirmed that the basic Lockean insight can function successfully in societies with a far broader range of pluralization. Accordingly, under international law, all human beings (not just citizens) have the right to freedom of religion, and this is now understood to be a right to freedom of religion *or belief*, out of respect for the convictions of those not holding religious beliefs.

While imperfectly applied, however, Locke's basic understanding of the structure (if not the reach) of the limitations on religious freedom remains sound. At least since Hitler used the instruments of democracy to destroy a democratic regime, theorists have understood the need for principles of "militant democracy" capable of withstanding those who would undermine the foundations of constitutional order. Fears of fifth columnists among individuals with ties to foreign organizations are obviously not totally unreasonable, especially in a world alert to the risks of foreign terrorism. Broad latitude should be given to rights of dissent, religious or otherwise, but this does not extend to tolerating views that pose imminent threats to existing constitutional institutions. Drawing the necessary lines in this area is profoundly difficult. Decisions in cases such as *Refah Partisi v. Turkey*,[32] which sustained dissolution of a religious party because of the threat it allegedly posed to secular democratic order, or the secular takeover in Egypt ousting a democratically elected Muslim Brotherhood regime, may have gone too far. But the core insight remains valid, and stands in fact not only as a fundamental constraint on theories of religious freedom, but more generally as a limit on liberal theory as a whole. Peacebuilders face the particularly challenging task of discerning when radical dissent threatens the very institutions that make pluralism possible, and when, on the other hand, new forms of accommodation can make a common life possible for all. What we have learned since Locke is that pluralistic societies can accommodate wide diversity of strongly held and even exclusivist beliefs, so long as there is genuine commitment within those value systems to respect for the dignity of others.

C. The Temporal/Spiritual Divide

The final feature of Locke's picture of religious freedom to be mentioned here is in many ways most fundamental to his thought on religion and the state. As he states the issue, "I esteem it above all things necessary to distinguish exactly the business of civil government from that of religion, and to settle the just bounds that lie between the one and the other."[33] In his view, the jurisdiction of the civil magistrate extends only to "life, liberty, health, and indolency of body; and the possession of outward things, such as money, lands, houses, furniture and the like,"[34] and does not reach matters regarding "the salvation of souls."[35] Civil jurisdiction does not extend to the religious sphere in Locke's view for several reasons: first, because God has never conferred such jurisdiction; second, because individuals cannot leave the care of their salvation to others, including through "consent of the people"; third, meaningful religious conduct must reflect sincere inner belief; and fourth, the power of the magistrate "consists only in outward force," whereas "true and saving religion consists in the inward persuasion of the mind." The magistrate may at most attempt to persuade, but cannot compel.[36] Locke envisions religious organizations essentially as private associations, which individuals can voluntarily join or leave.[37] He acknowledges that some religious communities may have more hierarchical structures, and they have freedom to so organize themselves so long as they are not using the tools of coercive power that belong to civil government.[38] In short, he draws a sharp distinction between temporal and spiritual authority, and carefully limits the reach of civil authority to the temporal domain. This line has deep roots in legal history, particularly in countries with long Christian heritage, and underlies structural features of many national constitutions that insist on separation of religion and state.[39]

1. Contrasting the Public/Private Divide

There has been a tendency to equate the temporal/spiritual divide with the more general public/private divide in many legal systems, but this can be misleading if it is construed to mean that religion must be excluded from the public sphere. It is one thing to say that religious individuals and religious communities may not exercise the power of the state, and quite another to say that they must be barred altogether from the public sphere. Religious practice virtually always has communal dimensions, and to that extent necessarily lives in social and thus public space. Religious thought can make significant contributions to public debate,[40] and despite prominent arguments to the contrary,[41] the principles of the freedom of expression do not and should not impose unique limits on the right to express religious convictions in the marketplace of ideas.[42]

Recognizing that religious freedom rights extend into the public sphere is important to peacebuilding in a variety of ways. It is particularly vital in avoiding the mistaken inference that separation of religion and state necessarily requires sanitizing all forms of religious presence from the public sector. The facts that religious communities may not use public coercive power and that public authority may not intervene in internal religious affairs do not mean that religious resources may not be tapped in resolving conflicts or that the religious and public sectors may not work together in appropriate and synergistic ways. Particularly in peacebuilding situations, efforts to suppress religious involvement may be read as signals of exclusion that reduce trust and exacerbate rather than heal conflicts.

2. Remembering the Significance of Religious Organizations as Mediating Institutions

Part of the peril of assuming that religion belongs exclusively to the private sector is that this may undermine religion's vital role in buffering individuals from state power and in providing contexts in which individuals can find meaning and form close social bonds. Of course, one could simply define the private sector to include both the intimate sphere of private life and the larger sphere of mediating institutions between the individual and the state, and to restrict the conception of the public sector narrowly to governmental institutions commanding obedience through the use of coercive sanctions. But the point is that religious life is experienced and lived as something more than purely private. Moreover, religious communities, however structured, also have an identity-forming value: particularly for religious believers, they provide a context vital for the development of individual personality. They also have an envisioning value. In the context of a neutral state, religious groups are part of a larger collection of necessary social institutions that help create, advocate, and maintain moral values. Locke's temporal/spiritual divide is significant, but needs to be understood in ways that protect rather than disrupt the role of religious communities as mediating institutions within pluralistic societies. Peacebuilders must understand the significance of these intermediate institutions and protect their ability to function, while assuring that those within such organizations can leave them voluntarily.

3. Secularity vs. Secularism

Equating the temporal/spiritual divide with the public/private divide and relegating spiritual aspects of life to a narrowly defined private sphere can lead to a problematic distortion of the secular ordering of society: to the replacement of secularity with secularism. Briefly, the contrast is between secularism as an ideological position and secularity as a framework within which different comprehensive views—both religious and secular—can be held. Both ideas are linked to the general historical process of secularization, but as used here, the terms have significantly different meanings and practical implications. "Secularism" connotes an ideological position that is committed to promoting a secular order as an end in itself. "Secularity," in contrast, means an approach to religion-state relations that avoids identification of the state with any particular religion or ideology (including secularism itself) and that provides a neutral framework capable of accommodating or cooperating with a broad range of religions and beliefs.[43] In most legal systems, there are advocates of both of these types of secular ordering, with the result that key debates turn on differences between the two approaches. Historically, French *laïcité* is closer to secularism; American separationism is closer to secularity. But there are debates in both societies about how strictly secular the state (and the public realm) should be.

This tension between two conceptions of the secular runs through much of religion-state theory in contemporary settings.[44] Secularism, as the more rigid approach,

> would accord more importance to the principle of neutrality than to freedom of conscience and religion, attempting to relegate the practice of religion to the private and communal sphere, leaving the public sphere free of any expression of religion. Also termed

"a-religiousness," this concept of secularism is obviously less compatible with religious accommodation, as well as antithetical to the recognition of the place of pluralism in the modern state.[45]

In contrast, secularity constitutes a more "flexible" or "open" approach, which

is based on the protection of freedom of religion, even if this requires a relaxation of the principle of neutrality. In this model, state neutrality towards religion and the separation of Church and State are not seen as ends in themselves, but rather as the means to achieving the fundamental objectives of respect for religious and moral equality and freedom of conscience and religion. In open secularism, any tension or contradiction between the various constituent facets of secularism should be resolved in favour of religious freedom and equality. [46]

The "flexible" and "open" (secularity) approach is the one recommended in Canada by the highly publicized Bouchard-Taylor Commission constituted in Quebec in 2007, and it appears to be the approach followed by Canadian Courts.[47] As stated in a landmark Canadian case, "a truly free society is one which can accommodate a wide variety of beliefs, diversity of tastes and pursuits, customs and codes of conduct."[48]

Secularity favors substantive over formal conceptions of equality and neutrality, taking claims of conscience seriously as grounds for accommodating religiously motivated difference. Secularity is likely to give more favorable treatment to a wide range of conscientious objection claims. Because of the conceptual and rhetorical similarity of secularism and secularity claims, it is all too easy to slip from the optimal and open practices of secularity to the more hostile and restrictive approach of secularism. The cost is measured in increased restrictions on religious life, a greater tendency to rule religion off-limits in the public square, and an expanded range of potential conflicts between the state and religious believers and organizations.

Secularism fails to understand that Locke's pluralist insight applies to integrating both secular and religious worldviews in a common social world. The Lockean notion that temporal and spiritual realms are separate does not revoke the insight that greater stability is achieved by respecting differences of worldview, whether religious or secular, than by coercing homogeneity—even secular homogeneity. As the European Court of Human Rights has repeatedly recognized, tensions inevitably arise when communities are divided on religious or ideological lines, but "this is one of the unavoidable consequences of pluralism," and the "role of the authorities [including peacebuilding authorities] in such circumstances is not to remove the cause of tension by eliminating pluralism, but to ensure that the competing groups tolerate each other." [49]

4. Religious Freedom and Theories of Justice

The idea of religious freedom and religious tolerance figures prominently not only in liberal theory,[50] as suggested by the foregoing "footnotes on Locke," but in other philosophical and religious traditions as well. It can easily be squared with a philosophy of reconciliation.[51] It is one of the touchstones that persuasive theories of justice must take into account in reaching what John Rawls referred to as "reflective equilibrium."[52] Rawls himself has argued that except on the basis of "equal liberty of conscience and freedom of thought," "firmly founded and publicly recognized, no reasonable political conception of justice is possible."[53] Freedom of religion is in fact a fundamental criterion of justice, of ethics, and very simply, of how we treat "the other."

III. Peacebuilding and the Legal Structures of Religious Freedom

A. The Normative Core of Legal Protections

The legal structures protecting religious freedom are the distillation of over three centuries of theoretical debate since Locke, coupled with expanding historical experience confirming that the core theoretical insights work in practice. Because religion and other belief systems are central to life and culture, actual legal institutions are subject to constant reinterpretation and adjustment, but the normative core of legal protections is reasonably clear. It includes an absolute right to internal freedom of belief; a strong right to manifest that freedom, subject to carefully constrained limitation; freedom from coercion in religious matters; non-discrimination on the basis of religion; sensitivity to claims of parents, children, and the state in family contexts where religion is involved; the rights of religious communities themselves to autonomy in their own affairs and to protection of their institutional rights; limitations strictly limited by rule of law constraints and the need to demonstrate that any limitations are "necessary to protect public safety, order, health, or morals or the fundamental rights of others";[54] and finally, non-derogability.[55]

This normative core is now embodied, with considerable variation in detail, in the constitutions of the overwhelming majority of nations on earth,[56] as well as in major documents of international and regional human rights law.[57] There is also significant support for the notion that the core requirements of religious freedom have acquired the status of international customary law.[58] The aim of this section is not to describe this extensive body of legal materials in any detail, but to reflect on ways that peacebuilding needs to use these legal footings in its work.

B. Peacebuilding in Constitutional Contexts

The most dramatic situation for peacebuilding arises when a hot conflict has toppled a prior regime and the path forward calls for a fresh constitutional start. There is a tendency to think of the exercise of constituent power at such constitutional moments as writing on a tabula rasa, but this is not really the case. In the first place, constitutional discussions do not go on in a theoretical vacuum. The rich heritage of religious freedom theory and debate hinted at above shapes the constitutional debates. Linguistic and other factors may affect the range of theoretical discourse that is easily accessible. Historical background in the particular country, including particular historical problems, will inevitably focus concerns and affect the constitutional framework that emerges. Fear of relapse into civil war, and the residual strength of various groupings following conflict, will inevitably create pressures. Retention of weapons by Maoist forces in Nepal has stalled constitutional progress for years.

Moreover, the constitutional drafters do not live behind a Rawlsian veil of ignorance. Various political parties and other interest groups negotiate constitutional provisions with an eye to their future institutional and political needs. Moreover, they need to forecast what types of institutions hold the best promise for achieving just results for the future. How can institutions key to the rule of law, such as a competent and independent judiciary, be structured? How can risks of corruption be contained? Beyond the national scene, there are inevitable foreign policy pressures. In our highly interconnected world, failed regimes are an international problem. Foreign pressures typically include strong contingents monitoring the quality of human rights protections built into new constitutional provisions.

A consideration often overlooked is that, at pre-constitutional moments, society does not consist simply of an array of individuals. It consists of countless cross-cutting groups, among which religious communities play a prominent role. Peacebuilding needs to take this reality into account. In part, this is an aspect of respecting the importance of intermediate institutions between the individual and the state, as we have mentioned.[59] But the issue goes deeper with religious communities. To draw on images from classic social contract theory, religious individuals and the communities to which they belong have little incentive to accede to the social contract if that risks destroying the pre-existing religious community or violating its conscientious commitments. As James Madison recognized in his "Memorial and Remonstrance," religious freedom protections constitute a reservation clause on the social contract: if a citizen "who enters into any subordinate Association, must always do it with a reservation of his duty to the general authority; much more must every man who becomes a member of any particular Civil Society, do it with a saving of his allegiance to the Universal Sovereign."[60] That is, groups and individuals are likely to resist a new peace structure, unless respect is assured for certain key conscientious convictions that they believe take precedence over other social obligations. It is precisely by sustaining the legitimacy of this constitutional "reservation clause" that constitutional protection of religious freedom makes room for Locke's plurality insight. Peacebuilding needs to be sensitive to addressing such pre-constitutional commitments, and to allow them to be embodied in constitutional law, legislative and judicial accommodations of conscientious convictions, and in day-to-day administrative practice.

C. International Legal Frameworks

Another factor often forgotten is the relevance of international law itself to constitutional change. Once adopted and ratified, international human rights treaties constitute binding legal norms against which new constitutional provisions must be assessed. This is true whether new provisions are considered at the time of wholesale revamping of a constitution, or merely in the process of amending particular provisions. The general rule with regard to international treaty obligations following a change of regime is the principle of continuity. Specifically, this rule holds that "notwithstanding internal alterations in the organization of government, or in the constitutional structure of a particular state, the state itself continues to be bound by its rights and obligations under international law, including treaty rights and obligations."[61] The rationale behind the continuity rule is straightforward. Other parties to a treaty are entitled to rely on existing treaty provisions regardless of internal power shifts occurring within other sovereign states. Unilateral revision of treaty obligations is not permissible. Once a country is bound by a treaty, the obligations it imposes can be revised only by mutual consent of the parties.[62] Multilateral treaties such as the ICCPR are even less subject to revision, particularly where the change reflects an intention to authorize human rights violations. In general, "a party may not invoke the provisions of its internal law as justification for its failure to perform a treaty."[63] Constraints on unilateral modification of treaty obligations include prohibitions on unilateral narrowing of those obligations. In the context of international religious freedom norms, laws or judicial decisions that unduly broaden permissible limitations on religion, thereby narrowing religious freedom protections, may run afoul of this principle.[64]

International law today thus constitutes an important starting point for peacebuilding at the level of constitution formation. For the 167 countries that are parties to the ICCPR as of the beginning of 2014, Article 18 of that Covenant constitutes a legal requirement that should govern future constitutional revisions. For the rest, there are arguable customary law obligations. These obligations are reinforced to the extent that these same parties are also bound by various regional human rights treaties. Of course, countries may breach their treaty obligations, and the exact consequences of doing so are not always clear. What has become increasingly evident, however, is that civil society organizations, the media, and the general citizenry are conscious of these human rights obligations, and substantial deviations from widely accepted norms trigger strong responses, both at home and abroad. At a minimum, failure to comply erodes a state's long-term legitimacy. What this means is that national and international norms provide powerful persuasive tools to help forge new constitutional and legal frameworks that can help assure all sides to a conflict that fundamental religious and worldview differences can be protected, at least within the limits that have been developed under limitations clauses, such as Article 18(3) of the ICCPR and Article 9(2) of the European Convention for the Protection of Human Rights and Fundamental Freedoms (ECHR).

D. Legal Arrangements and Time

Of course, much conflict is less dramatic and more mundane. The circumstances range from conditions of transitional justice, involving radical transformation of political institutions, to conflicts involving typical bureaucracies. It is not always easy to tell the situations apart. Precisely because religious communities often have substantially longer histories than particular constitutional arrangements, longer-term solutions may be necessary. For example, one sensitive area following the collapse of communism in Central and Eastern Europe in the 1990s was the need to deal with claims for the restoration of religious property. This created complex issues of transitional justice, many of which have proven intractable and remain unresolved twenty-five years later. But to put this in perspective, a substantial percentage of the current budgets of the major churches in Germany comes from payments they receive as part of a church property settlement with Napoleon, dating back to 1803.[65] What was no doubt in some ways a transitional arrangement has become a standard feature of the religious landscape in Germany. There are a variety of ways in which adjusting timelines may give both state and religious actors greater time to achieve accommodations or other solutions.

E. Filtering the Ambivalence of the Sacred

One of the most significant contributions that the legal institutions protecting religious free-dom make to peacebuilding is their capacity to play a filtering role that helps optimize the social goods generated by religion, while allowing appropriate constraints to be imposed on its evils. That is, religious liberty constitutes more than a one-sided guarantee of benefits for religion. It is in fact a finely honed tool that restrains the dark side of religion, while protect-ing core values of pluralism, freedom, and dignity. The structure of this filtering mechanism has evolved over the centuries since Locke's time, and not surprisingly, has taken different forms in differing national and international settings. The primary adjustments to this filter-ing mechanism take the form of adjusting limitation clauses in international, constitutional, and other legal documents, and of refining the tests governing judicial review of religious freedom claims.

Broadly, the legal filtering structures have the following elements. Protections under international and constitutional law create strong presumptions in favor of religious free-dom, and aim to deter the temptation for government officials to impose excessive (and potentially counterproductive) constraints on religious freedom. Absolute protection is afforded to the "internal forum" of thoughts and beliefs, including the right to change one's beliefs. In effect, the filtering mechanism does not become relevant until religious beliefs begin to have concrete impacts in the external world. Once that threshold is reached, the typical limitation clauses (e.g., ICCPR, art. 18(3) and ECHR, art. 9(2)) focus on three key issues to determine whether limitations are permissible. First, they insist that any limitation be "prescribed by law," which has come to be understood as a requirement that limitations conform more generally to the rule of law. This requires both that the limitation be formally grounded in a rule adopted by proper legal authority and that the rule meet standard quali-tative standards associated with the rule of law—for example, that the rule is general, clear, and not retroactive. There tend also to be expectations that the rule can be reviewed by an independent judiciary. Second, the limitation must further one of a relatively small number of social interests—public health, safety, order, morals, and the fundamental rights of oth-ers (not just any right or social interest). Third, the limitation must be genuinely necessary in that it furthers a pressing social need or compelling state interest, in that the limitation is proportionate in the sense of the state interest being sufficiently important to outweigh the countervailing religious freedom claim, and in that this interest cannot be furthered in some less intrusive way. In practice, the third part of the "filter" has tended to be the most significant. Religious freedom rules also screen out religious discrimination, and this applies among other things to limitations that have discriminatory purposes or effects. Finally, the typical filtering mechanisms provide strong deference to the autonomy of religious institu-tions, provided that adequate rights to exit the institutions are in place.

The impact of this filtering system is profound, and the efforts of peacebuilders will be strengthened if they respect such filtering where appropriate mechanisms are in place, or if they find ways to institute functionally equivalent mechanisms where formal legal institu-tions with these filtering features are not yet in place. Credible filtering measures of this type give individual believers confidence that their dignity will be protected and respected. They also assure other members of society that religious freedom protections are rational and appropriately limited. The filter assures that the government is in fact limited—that there are domains beyond the authority of the state, and that state power is limited and not absolute. In short, the state is more Lockean than Hobbesian. Significantly, the religious liberty filter creates an ongoing process of negotiation that takes citizens' conscientious claims seriously and facilitates peacebuilding (and the generation of other social goods) by religious groups.

IV. RELIGIOUS FREEDOM, SOCIAL GOODS, AND STRATEGIC PEACEBUILDING[66]

The religious freedom filtering mechanisms just described help to explain the numerous and complex ways that religious freedom can contribute to strategic peacebuilding. Current empirical research demonstrates strong correlations between protections of religious freedom and countless other social goods—including other civil rights, gender empowerment, longevity of democracy, lower poverty levels, economic freedom, higher percentage of GDP spent on health, lower inflation, lower income inequality, more foreign direct investment, and higher earned income for women.[67] But these are correlations, and it is not always clear in which direction causation runs. It may be helpful to reflect on various pathways through which religious freedom protections (and filtering) may contribute positively to advancement of other social goods, and in the process, to strategic peacebuilding and ultimately to the achievement of just and lasting peace. While not conclusive, this helps to make the case that religious freedom forms part of the basis of a just peace, with an impact that goes far beyond the mere elements of a liberal peace. The latter assumes that "stable peace, human rights, democracy, and market economies are the primary ends; intergovernmental institutions, state governments, and warring parties are the primary actors." Religious freedom goes further, and contributes to "the holism of strategic peacebuilding."[68] As Lederach and Appleby have explained, strategic peacebuilding is "the capacity to develop strategies to maximize the impact of initiatives for constructive change" within the complexity of multiple societal levels and "potentially polarizing lines of ethnicity, class, religion, and race."[69] It is not possible in this brief essay to identify all the ways that religious freedom can contribute both directly and indirectly to strategic peacebuilding, but identifying a number of these can help confirm the important role that religious freedom plays in this regard.

A. Direct Contributions

The filtering aspect of religious freedom promotes peacemaking directly in a variety of ways. Among other things, by protecting religious freedom, it promotes the proliferation of religious peacemakers, both in number and in diversity. As a practical matter, religious freedom secures the ability of religious leaders to assume peacebuilding roles as trusted conflict mediators, and to encourage peacebuilding by their followers. Properly understood, religious freedom protects not only worship and ritual practices, but the right of religious institutions to provide needed social services, either directly or through religiously affiliated legal entities. As a more general matter, "religious communities are most likely to support democracy, peace, and freedom for other faiths, and least likely to take up the gun or form dictatorships, when governments allow them freedom to worship, practice, and express their faith freely and when religious communities in turn renounce their claims to permanent offices or positions of policy-making authority."[70] Religious freedom also helps cultivate an array of socially productive virtues: tolerance, reflective thinking, generosity, altruism, law-abidingness, honesty, helpfulness to others, and social trust.

B. Opening Channels of Dialogue and Negotiation

Religious freedom can also open a variety of processes involving dialogue and human interaction that can facilitate strategic peacebuilding. In this sense, religious freedom can be better conceptualized not as a static end, but as a process of negotiating societal tensions involving religion. Religious freedom enables discourse in a society that engages individual believers, religious communities, and the state in a holistic process that cuts across ethnic, cultural, and religious lines. It engages each of what Lederach and Appleby have called the "three distinct transformative processes at the heart of peacebuilding—striving for social justice, ending violent conflict, and building healthy cooperative relationships in conflict-ridden societies."[71] Protecting religious belief and expression allows religion to flourish,[72] bringing positive benefits and social goods that address issues of social justice, ending conflict, and building cooperative relationships.

C. Providing Peacebuilding Personnel

Religious freedom also produces a number of significant social goods that assist in strategic peacebuilding. One of the more obvious contributions is making key mediating personnel available to peace processes. Religious freedom recognizes and values the contributions of religious actors and ideas, which can empower both religious leaders and members to become helpful resources for peace processes. Religious communities may contribute personnel and other organizational resources to peace processes. Note that religious freedom may help maintain the independence of important peace actors, making it possible for them to maintain some distance from state actors and to avoid being suppressed altogether.[73]

D. Contributing to the Material Foundations for Just Peace

Religious freedom can contribute in a variety of ways to strengthening the material foundations for justpeace. As discussed earlier in connection with Locke's plurality insight, religious freedom has proven itself over time to be a massive contributor to social stability and citizen loyalty. But it makes profound contributions in other ways. Of course, it often does so indirectly, by facilitating the positive contributions that religion makes to society. To the extent religious freedom frees religious communities from focusing major portions of their energy on self-preservation and avoiding persecution, it frees their resources to make more productive contributions. This can easily lead to increased service to society in many ways.

It has long been known that in the United States, religious attendance is associated with higher rates of volunteering and monetary donations. Significantly, global data suggest that this relationship exists in almost all countries[74] and across all the major world religions, including Christianity, Islam, Judaism, Hinduism, and Buddhism.[75] In part this is a reflection of the fact that religions teach altruism, and believers implement this altruism in charitable activity. Ram Cnaan and colleagues have documented, however, that involvement in a congregation enhances the altruism effect. There are countless ways that interaction with other congregation members firms up altruistic resolutions. It may simply be that concrete requests for help are made in the congregational setting; it may be that links to concrete initiatives are facilitated; working with other friends in the congregation may be more meaningful; and so on.[76] All of these processes enhancing altruistic resolve are naturally enhanced if freedom of worship protects the right to gather in congregations.

Increasing the vitality of religion in society may be a potent antidote to problems of corruption. Particularly in countries with extremely limited financial resources, corruption is often endemic, and it is very difficult to know how to combat it. A state's limited financial tools are typically of limited utility, because they can be outbid by forces of corruption. Religious inculcation of values such as honesty and integrity is one of the few forces that can effectively counter the temptations of corruption (and of course, it is not a perfect remedy, either).

Faith-based facilities acount for 30 to 50 percent of global health care providers. Religious institutions are often the most likely to reach out to rural and otherwise marginalized populations, especially outside Europe. Also, religious organizations can facilitate reception, understanding, and distribution of health care, as in the cases of malaria and AIDS. Religious organizations often play critical roles in other social service areas, such as addressing the orphan crisis in Africa. They are also known for making significant contributions in other areas such as disaster relief, environmental projects, housing initiatives, anti-corruption efforts, and last but not least, in peacebuilding initiatives. Here again, religious freedom broadly construed to grant a high degree of autonomy to religious organizations in carrying out what they perceive as their own affairs could facilitate the charitable activities of religious organizations.

Religion and religious freedom can help instill values that contribute to hard work, stewardship of resources, honesty, and general productivity. It can in many ways be a "force multiplier" providing peace dividends and oher benefits.[77]

In short, religious organizations and charities contribute to social harmony and development and in general to the material foundations of justpeace in countless ways. These contributions are organized in diverse ways that reflect religious differences, practical realities, and human ingenuity. Given the importance of religious charities and related features of religious life, legal structures that protect and facilitate the religious factor in social development are vital, as international experience has demonstrated. This points to the need both for general religious freedom protections for charitable work and for ease of access to legal entity status for religiously affiliated organizations.

V. Conclusion

Everything we know about human beings suggests that religion or belief is an ineradicable aspect of human anthropology and culture. Part of the story is that worldviews are central to dignity and finding meaning in life. Another part is that differences in fundamental orientations toward religion can produce tension and conflict. The result is that it is vital that states provide strong protection for the freedom of religion or belief, and at the same time, that they put certain narrow limitations in place to protect against abuse of the right, and to ensure that the benefits flowing from religion (including from diversity of religions) be optimized while keeping serious problems in check.

Discussing freedom of religion or belief from the vantage point of its relevance to peacebuilding yields insights into both the inherent importance of this fundamental freedom and the structuring of peace processes. The peacebuilding context underscores the fact that freedom of religion or belief is a key foundation for the building of stable and lasting peace. It provides the footings or starting points for bringing wary enemies to a point where peace processes can begin. As the footings solidify into firmer foundations on which peace can be built, it can serve as a framework for peacebuilding across a range of social situations, from dramatic historical moments when new constitutions are being drafted to much more mundane encounters between state officials and individual believers. Experience with religious freedom in the peacebuilding context, in turn, highlights a number of techniques drawn from the resolution of religious freedom cases that can be put to productive use in peacebuilding initiatives.

Our analysis has emphasized that religious freedom is a more powerful stabilizing force than is often realized. This is in part because some of the problems often blamed on religion may actually be more a result of state action or other social forces threatening religious groups. That is, the framework of religious freedom may be more effective than expected because its problems are not as acute as typically assumed, and in any event, the framework targets a primary source of problems: excessive intervention in religious affairs by the state. But there are also powerful positive reasons why religious freedom enhances stability. By guaranteeing respect for differences in religion or belief, it yields dividends in enhanced loyalty to the state flowing from gratitude felt by those whose core rights are secured. Moreover, protecting religious freedom frees up other social forces that help produce other social goods. That is, protecting religious freedom yields a peace dividend. Religious actors freed from the need to spend energy defending their beliefs can turn their altruism to more productive social causes, with positive results in many areas. Of course, there are times when limitation on manifestations of religion is justified, but only under narrowly circumscribed circumstances. In the long run, better protection of religious rights, rather than greater use of state force, will provide the best solutions to social tensions.

NOTES

1. See Daniel Philpott, "Introduction: Searching for Strategy in an Age of Peacebuilding," in *Strategies of Peace: Transforming Conflict in a Violent World*, ed. Daniel Philpott and Gerard F. Powers (Oxford: Oxford University Press, 2010), 1–15 (discussing the distinctions between "liberal peace" and strategic building of a just peace).
2. Thomas Hobbes, *Of Man, Being the First Part of Leviathan* XIII para. 8 (vol. 34 of *Harvard Classics*, New York: P. F. Collier and Son, 1909–1914), http://www.bartleby.com/34/5/13. html.
3. We are indebted to Gerhard Robbers for this comparison.

4. R. Scott Appleby, *The Ambivalence of the Sacred* (Lanham, MD: Rowman and Littlefield, 2000).

5. See, e.g., Mark Gopin, *Between Eden and Armageddon* (Oxford: Oxford University Press, 2000); David Little and R. Scott Appleby, "A Moment of Opportunity? The Promise of Religious Peacebuilding in an Era of Religious and Ethnic Conflict," in *Religion and Peacebuilding*, ed. Harold Coward and Gordon S. Smith (Albany: State University of New York Press, 2004), 1–23; Gerrie ter Haar, "Religion: Source of Conflict or Resource for Peace?," in *Bridge or Barrier: Religion, Violence, and Visions for Peace*, ed. Gerrie ter Haar and James J. Busuttil, 3–34 (Leiden: Brill, 2005); Mark Juergensmeyer, *Terror in the Mind of God: The Global Rise of Religious Violence*, 3rd ed. (Berkeley: University of California Press, 2003); Gerard F. Powers, "Religion and Peacebuilding," in Philpott and Powers, *Strategies of Peace*, 317–352; Monica Duffy Toft, "Religion, Terrorism, and Civil Wars," in *Rethinking Religion and World Affairs*, ed. Timothy Samuel Shah, Alfred Stepan, and Monica Duffy Toft (Oxford: Oxford University Press, 2012), 127–148.

6. Cavanaugh, *The Myth of Religious Violence: Secular Ideology and the Roots of Modern Conflict* (Oxford: Oxford University Press, 2009).

7. Cavanaugh, *The Myth of Religious Violence*, 123–180.

8. Powers, "Religion and Peacebuilding," 319–320.

9. Toft, "Religion, Terrorism, and Civil Wars," 141–142.

10. Toft, "Religion, Terrorism, and Civil Wars," 138.

11. Powers, "Religion and Peacebuilding," 320.

12. Brian J. Grim and Roger Finke, *The Price of Freedom Denied: Religious Persecution and Conflict in the 21st Century* (Cambridge: Cambridge University Press, 2011).

13. If, as Alfred North Whitehead suggested [*Process and Reality* (New York: Free Press, 1979), 63], "the safest general characterization of the European philosophical tradition is that it consists of a series of footnotes to Plato," it is perhaps no exaggeration to think of religious liberty theory as footnotes on Locke.

14. John Locke, *A Letter Concerning Toleration* (1689, cited edition: Indianapolis: Bobbs-Merrill, 1955), 55 (emphasis added). Locke further maintained (52) that accusations that religious dissenters are "nurseries of factions and seditions. . . would soon cease if the law of toleration were once so settled that all churches were obliged to lay down toleration as the foundation of their own liberty, and teach that liberty of conscience is every man's natural right, equally belonging to dissenters as to themselves; and that nobody ought to be compelled in matters of religion either by law or force. The establishment of this one thing would take away all ground of complaints and tumults upon account of conscience."

15. ICCPR, art. 4(2). See Koji Teraya, "Emerging Hierarchy in International Human Rights and Beyond: From the Perspective of Non-derogable Rights," *European Journal of International Law* 12, no. 5 (2001): 917, 922–923 (suggesting that non-derogability reflects not only a hierarchy of value, but also the functional nature of the rights—that non-derogable rights perform functions needed in dealing with states of emergency).

16. Nicholas P. Miller, *The Religious Roots of the First Amendment: Dissenting Protestants and the Separation of Church and State* (Oxford: Oxford University Press, 2012).

17. Locke, *A Letter Concerning Toleration*, 50.

18. For an overview of developments, see W. Cole Durham Jr. and Robert T. Smith, "Religion and the State in the United States at the Turn of the Twenty-first Century," in *Law and Religion in the 21st Century*, ed. Silvio Ferrari and Rinaldo Cristofori (Farnham, UK: Ashgate, 2010), 79, 82–96; William Bassett, W. Cole Durham Jr., and Robert T. Smith,

Religious Organizations and the Law (New York: Thomson Reuters/West, updated annually, latest edition 2013), §§ 2:55–2:71.

19. For a study of European-style proportionality analysis as used in religion cases in the European Court of Human Rights and most European jurisdictions, see W. Cole Durham Jr. and Brett G. Scharffs, *Law and Religion: National, International and Comparative Perspectives* (New York: Wolters Kluwer Law and Business, 2010), 231–234, 243, 383–389, 429–434.

20. Locke, *A Letter Concerning Toleration*, 48.

21. The compelling state interest test was rejected by the United States Supreme Court in *Employment Division v. Smith*, 494 U.S. 872 (1990); reinstituted by the federal Religious Freedom Restoration Act, Pub. L. No. 103–141; codified at 42 U.S.C.A. §§ 2000bb et seq.; struck down as applied to the states, *City of Boerne v. Flores*, 521 U.S. 507 (1997); and partially reasserted in various pieces of federal legislation that apply in limited domains. At the state level, as of December 2013, eighteen states have passed their own Religious Freedom Restoration Acts, and an additional eleven states have invoked heightened scrutiny in construing state constitutional provisions protecting freedom of religion (see Eugene Volokh, "What Is the Religious Freedom Restoration Act?" The Volokh Conspiracy, December 2, 2013, http://www.volokh.com/2013/12/02/1a-religious-freedom-restoration-act/). Canada has adopted a particularly sensitive test for analyzing religious freedom claims. To pass constitutional scrutiny, state action infringing a religious freedom right "must be sufficiently important to warrant limiting a constitutional right" and "the means chosen by the state authority must be proportional to the objective in question." To this end, there must be a rational connection between the means chosen and the state objective, and the limitation "must minimally impair the right or freedom that has been infringed." *Multani v. Commission Scolaire Marguerite-Bourgeoys*, Supreme Court of Canada, [2006] 1 S.C.R. 256, 2006 SCC 6.

22. On the relevance of the contrast between legalist or positivist and integralist theories of law, see W. Cole Durham Jr., "Religion and the World's Constitutions," in *Law, Religion, Constitution: Freedom of Religion, Equal Treatment, and the Law*, ed. W. Cole Durham Jr. et al. (Farnham, UK: Ashgate, 2013), 1, 20–24.

23. Patrick Romanell, "Editor's Introduction," in Locke, *A Letter Concerning Toleration*, 10.

24. Locke, *A Letter Concerning Toleration*, 50.

25. Locke, *A Letter Concerning Toleration*, 50.

26. ICCPR, art. 18(3); ECHR, art. 9(2); UN Human Rights Committee, General Comment 22 (48), para. 8, adopted July 20, 1993, UN Doc. CCPR/C/21/Rev.1/Add.4 (1993), reprinted in UN Doc. HRI/GEN/1/Rev.1 at 35 (1994).

27. Immanuel Kant, *Fundamental Principles of the Metaphysic of Morals* (1797), trans. Thomas Abbott Kingsmill (New York: Liberal Arts Press, 1949).

28. Locke, *A Letter Concerning Toleration*, 51.

29. Locke, *A Letter Concerning Toleration*, 52.

30. See Locke, *A Letter Concerning Toleration*, 36–37, 45, 56.

31. Locke, *A Letter Concerning Toleration*, 50.

32. *Refah Partisi (The Welfare Party) v. Turkey* (ECtHR Grand Chamber, App. Nos. 41340/98, 41342/93, 41343/98, and 41344/98, 13 February 2003).

33. Locke, *A Letter Concerning Toleration*, 17.

34. Locke, *A Letter Concerning Toleration*, 17.

35. Locke, *A Letter Concerning Toleration*, 17.

36. Locke, *A Letter Concerning Toleration*, 18.

37. Locke, *A Letter Concerning Toleration*, 20.

38. See Locke, *A Letter Concerning Toleration*, 20–27.

39. For general comparative analysis of such constitutions, see W. Cole Durham, Jr. and Javier Martínez-Torrón, "General Report," in *Religion and the Secular State: National Reports/ La Religion et l'État laïque: Rapports nationaux*, ed. Javier Martinez-Torron and W. Cole Durham, Jr. (interim edition 2010), 19–24.

40. See generally Jeffrey Stout, "Religious Reasons in Political Argument," in *Democracy and Tradition* (Princeton, NJ: Princeton University Press, 2004), 63–92 ("The free expression of religious premises is morally underwritten not only by the value we assign to the freedom of religion, but also by the value we assign to free expression, generally"); Richard John Neuhaus, *The Naked Public Square* (Grand Rapids, MI: Eerdmans, 1984); Douglas G. Smith, "The Illiberalism of Liberalism: Religious Discourse in the Public Square," *San Diego Law Review* 34, no. 4 (1997): 1571; Robert P. George, "Public Reason and Political Conflict: Abortion and Homosexuality," *Yale Law Journal* 106, no. 8 (1997): 2475; Michael J. Perry, "Why Political Reliance on Religiously Grounded Morality Does Not Violate the Establishment Clause," *William and Mary Law Review* 42, no. 3 (2001): 663, 679, 682.

41. See, e.g., Bruce Ackerman, "Why Dialogue?," *Journal of Philosophy* 86, no. 1 (1989): 20; Stephen Macedo, "The Politics of Justification," *Political Theory* 18, no. 2 (1990): 295; John Rawls, "The Idea of Public Reason Revisited," *University of Chicago Law Review* 64, no. 3 (1997): 766.

42. See generally Christopher J. Eberle, *Religious Conviction in Liberal Politics* (Cambridge: Cambridge University Press, 2002); Kent Greenawalt, *Private Consciences and Public Reasons* (Oxford: Oxford University Press, 1995); and Michael J. Perry, *Religion in Politics: Constitutional and Moral Perspectives* (Oxford: Oxford University Press, 1997).

43. One finds advocates of secularity in both religious and secular thought. Pope Pius XII spoke already in 1958 of the "healthy secularity of the state" ("*sana laïcité dello stato*"). "Alla vostra filiale," *Acta Apostolicae Sedis* 50 (March 1958): 220. See also Paul VI, *Evangelii Nuntiandi*, apostolic exhortation (1975), para. 55. Former French President Nicolas Sarkozy also noted the distinction: "Allocution de M. le Président de la République dans la sallede la signature du Palais de Latran" (December 20, 2007), http://tempsreel.nouvelobs.com/file/456435.pdf.

44. See Javier Martínez-Torrón and W. Cole Durham Jr., "General Report," in *Religion and the Secular State/La Religion et l'État laïque*, Interim National Reports Issued for the Occasion of the XVIIIth International Congress of Comparative Law, ed. Javier Martínez-Torrón and W. Cole Durham Jr. (Provo, UT: International Center for Law and Religion Studies, 2010), 3–5, http://www.iclrs.org/content/blurb/files/General%20Report.pdf.

45. José Woehrling and Rosalie Jukier, "Religion and the Secular State in Canada," in Martínez-Torrón and Durham, *Religion and the Secular State*, 185.

46. Woehrling and Jukier, "Religion and the Secular State in Canada," 185.

47. Woehrling and Jukier, "Religion and the Secular State in Canada," 185–186.

48. *R. v. Big M. Drug Mart* [1985] 1 S.C.R. 295 at para. 94, 18 D.L.R. (4th) 321 (Dickson, C.J.).

49. *Serif v. Greece* (ECtHR, App. No. 38178/97, 14 December 1999), § 53.

50. Noel Reynolds and W. Cole Durham Jr., *Religious Liberty in Western Philosophical Thought* (Atlanta: Emory University, 1996).

51. See, e.g., Daniel Philpott, *Just and Unjust Peace: An Ethic of Political Reconciliation* (Oxford: Oxford University Press, 2012).

52. John Rawls, *A Theory of Justice* (Cambridge, MA: Harvard University Press, 1971), 18–22, 46–53.

53. John Rawls, *Political Liberalism* (New York: Columbia University Press, 1993), xxvi; see also Daniel A. Dombrowski, *Rawls and Religion* (Albany: State University of New York Press, 2001).

54. ICCPR, art. 18(3); ECHR, art. 9(2).

55. For a more extensive discussion of the normative core, see Tore Lindholm, W. Cole Durham Jr., and Bahia Tahzib-Lie, eds., *Facilitating Freedom of Religion or Belief: A Deskbook* (Leiden: Martinus Nijhoff, 2004), xxxvi–xli.

56. For an overview of constitutional provisions, see Martínez-Torrón and Durham, "General Report," 6–17.

57. Universal Declaration of Human Rights (UDHR), art. 18; ICCPR, art. 18; 1981 UN Declaration on the Elimination of All Forms of Intolerance and of Discrimination Based on Religion or Belief (1981 Declaration); ECHR, art. 9, 213 UNTS 222 (entered into force September 3, 1953); American Convention of Human Rights, art. 12, OAS Treaty Series No. 36, at 1, OEAS/serL/V/II.23, Doc. Rev. 2 (entered into force July 18, 1978). All relevant documents can be found in Tad Stahnke and J. Paul Martin, *Religion and Human Rights: Basic Documents* (New York: Columbia University Press, 1993), http://www.religlaw.org/international/.

58. W. Cole Durham Jr., Matthew K. Richards, and Donlu D. Thayer, "The Status of and Threats to International Law and Freedom of Religion or Belief," in *The Future of Religious Freedom: Global Challenges*, ed. Allen Hertzke (Oxford: Oxford University Press, 2012), nn. 24–29 (collecting sources).

59. See the section "Remembering the Significance of Religious Organizations as Mediating Institutions" in this chapter.

60. James Madison, "Memorial and Remonstrance Against Religious Assessments," in *The Writings of James Madison*, ed. G. Hunt (New York: G. P. Putnam's Sons, 1901), 2, § 1.

61. I. A. Shearer, *Starke's International Law*, 11th ed. (London: Butterworths, 1994), 305.

62. Vienna Convention on Treaties, § 39.

63. Vienna Convention on Treaties, §§ 27, 46.

64. Portions of this paragraph derive from Durham, Richards, and Thayer, "The Status of and Threats to International Law and Freedom of Religion or Belief," 36–37.

65. See, for example, Herbert A. L. Fisher, *Studies in Napoleonic Statesmanship: Germany* (New York: Haskell House Publishers, 1903).

66. Portions of this section draw on presentations prepared in cooperation with Brett G. Scharffs and Donlu D. Thayer.

67. Grim and Finke, *The Price of Freedom Denied*.

68. Philpott, "Introduction: Searching for Strategy in an Age of Peacebuilding," 8.

69. John Paul Lederach and R. Scott Appleby, "Strategic Peacebuilding: An Overview" in Philpott and Powers, *Strategies of Peace*, 22.

70. Shah, Stepan, and Toft, eds., *Rethinking Religion and World Affairs*, 18, 216.

71. John Paul Lederach and R. Scott Appleby, "Strategic Peacebuilding: An Overview," in *Strategies of Peace*, ed. Daniel Philpott and Gerard F. Powers (Oxford: Oxford University Press, 2010), 27.

72. See, e.g., Robert D. Putnam and David E. Campbell, *American Grace: How Religion Divides and Unites Us* (New York: Simon and Schuster, 2010), 550 ("The U.S. Constitution's

prohibitions both on an established religion. . . and religious tests for public office helped to create a flourishing religious ecosphere.").

73. Shah et al., *Rethinking Religion and World Affairs*, 18, 205–206.

74. Buster G. Smith and Rodney Stark, "Religious Attendance Relates to Generosity Worldwide: Religious and the secular more charitable if they attend services," Gallup, September 4, 2009, http://www.gallup.com/poll/122807/religious-attendance-relates-generosity-worldwide.aspx.

75. Smith and Stark, "Religious Attendance."

76. See generally Ram Cnaan et al., *The Invisible Caring Hand: American Congregations and the Provision of Welfare* (New York: New York University Press, 2002); Stephanie Boddie and Ram Cnaan, *Faith-Based Social Services: Measures, Assessments, and Effectiveness* (Abingdon, UK: Routledge, 2012); Ram Cnaan, *The Other Philadelphia Story: How Local Congregations Support Quality of Life in Urban America* (Philadelphia: University of Pennsylvania Press, 2006).

77. Shah et al., *Rethinking Religion and World Affairs*, 217.

BIBLIOGRAPHY

Ackerman, Bruce. "Why Dialogue?" *Journal of Philosophy* 86, no. 1 (1989): 5–22.

Bassett, William, W. Cole Durham Jr., and Robert T. Smith. *Religious Organizations and the Law*. New York: Thomson Reuters/West, updated annually, cited edition 2013.

Boddie, Stephanie, and Ram Cnaan. *Faith-Based Social Services: Measures, Assessments, and Effectiveness*. Abingdon, UK: Routledge, 2012.

Cavanaugh, William T. *The Myth of Religious Violence: Secular Ideology and the Roots of Modern Conflict*. Oxford: Oxford University Press, 2009.

City of Boerne v. Flores. 521 U.S. 507 (1997).

Cnaan, Ram. *The Invisible Caring Hand: American Congregations and the Provision of Welfare*. New York: New York University Press, 2002.

Cnaan, Ram. *The Other Philadelphia Story: How Local Congregations Support Quality of Life in Urban America*. Philadelphia: University of Pennsylvania Press, 2006.

Council of Europe. *Convention for the Protection of Human Rights and Fundamental Freedoms as amended by Protocols No. 11 and No. 14* (European Convention on Human Rights). CETS No.: 005. Entered into force September 3, 1953. http://conventions.coe.int/Treaty/en/Treaties/Html/005.htm.

Dombrowski, Daniel A. *Rawls and Religion*. Albany: State University of New York Press, 2001.

Durham, W. Cole, Jr. "Religion and the World's Constitutions." In *Law, Religion, Constitution: Freedom of Religion, Equal Treatment, and the Law*, edited by W. Cole Durham Jr., Silvio Ferrari, Cristiana Cianitto, and Donlu Thayer, 3–36. Farnham, UK: Ashgate, 2013.

Durham, W. Cole, Jr., and Robert T. Smith. "Religion and the State in the United States at the Turn of the Twenty-first Century." In *Law and Religion in the 21st Century: Cultural Diversity and the Law*, edited by Silvio Ferrari and Rinaldo Cristofori, 79–110. Farnham, UK: Ashgate, 2010.

Durham, W. Cole, Jr., Matthew K. Richards, and Donlu D. Thayer. "The Status of and Threats to International Law and Freedom of Religion or Belief." In *The Future of Religious Freedom: Global Challenges*, edited by Allen Hertzke, 31–66. Oxford: Oxford University Press, 2012.

Eberle, Christopher J. *Religious Conviction in Liberal Politics*. Cambridge: Cambridge University Press, 2002.

Employment Division, Department of Human Resources of Oregon v. Smith. 494 U.S. 872 (1990).

Fisher, Herbert A. L. *Studies in Napoleonic Statesmanship: Germany*. New York: Haskell House Publishers, 1903.

George, Robert P. "Public Reason and Political Conflict: Abortion and Homosexuality." *Yale Law Journal* 106, no. 8 (1997): 2475–2504.

Gopin, Mark. *Between Eden and Armageddon*. Oxford: Oxford University Press, 2000.

Greenawalt, Kent. *Private Consciences and Public Reasons*. Oxford: Oxford University Press, 1995.

Grim, Brian J., and Roger Finke. *The Price of Freedom Denied: Religious Persecution and Conflict in the 21st Century*. Cambridge: Cambridge University Press, 2011.

Hobbes, Thomas. *Of Man, Being the First Part of Leviathan*. Vol. 34 *of Harvard Classics*. New York: P. F. Collier and Son, 1909–1914. http://www.bartleby.com/34/5/13.html.

Juergensmeyer, Mark. *Terror in the Mind of God: The Global Rise of Religious Violence*. 3rd ed. Berkeley: University of California Press, 2003.

Jukier, Rosalie, and José Woehrling. "Religion and the Secular State in Canada." In Martínez-Torrón and Durham, *Religion and the Secular State*, 185–212.

Kant, Immanuel. *Fundamental Principles of the Metaphysic of Morals*. Translated by Thomas Abbott Kingsmill. New York: Liberal Arts Press, 1949. First published 1797.

Lederach, John Paul, and R. Scott Appleby. "Strategic Peacebuilding: An Overview." In Philpott and Powers, *Strategies of Peace*, 19–44.

Lindholm, Tore, W. Cole Durham Jr., and Bahia Tahzib-Lie, eds. *Facilitating Freedom of Religion or Belief: A Deskbook*. Leiden: Martinus Nijhoff, 2004.

Little, David, and R. Scott Appleby. "A Moment of Opportunity? The Promise of Religious Peacebuilding in an Era of Religious and Ethnic Conflict." In *Religion and Peacebuilding*, edited by Harold Coward and Gordon S. Smith, 1–23. Albany: State University of New York Press, 2004.

Locke, John. *A Letter Concerning Toleration*. Translated by William Popple, with an introduction by Patrick Romanell. Indianapolis: Bobbs-Merrill, 1955.

Macedo, Stephen. "The Politics of Justification." *Political Theory* 18, no. 2 (1990): 280–304.

Madison, James. "Memorial and Remonstrance Against Religious Assessments." In *The Writings of James Madison*, edited by G. Hunt, vol. 2. New York: G. P. Putnam's Sons, 1901.

Martínez-Torrón, Javier, and W. Cole Durham Jr., eds. *Religion and the Secular State/La Religion et l'État laïque*. Interim National Reports Issued for the Occasion of the XVIIIth International Congress of Comparative Law. Provo, UT: International Center for Law and Religion Studies, 200.

Martínez-Torrón, Javier, and W. Cole Durham Jr. "General Report." In Martínez-Torrón and Durham, *Religion and the Secular State*, 1–56.

Miller, Nicholas P. *The Religious Roots of the First Amendment: Dissenting Protestants and the Separation of Church and State*. Oxford: Oxford University Press, 2012.

Multani v. Commission Scolaire Marguerite-Bourgeoys. Supreme Court of Canada, [2006] 1 S.C.R. 256, 2006 SCC 6.

Neuhaus, Richard John. *The Naked Public Square*. Grand Rapids, MI: Eerdmans, 1984.

Organization of American States. *American Convention of Human Rights*. OAS Treaty Series No. 36, OEAS/serL/V/II.23, Doc. Rev. 2. Entered into force July 18, 1978.

Pope Paul VI. *Evangelii Nuntiandi*. Apostolic exhortation. Vatican: The Holy See, 1975.

Perry, Michael J. *Religion in Politics: Constitutional and Moral Perspectives*. Oxford: Oxford University Press, 1997.

Perry, Michael J. "Why Political Reliance on Religiously Grounded Morality Does Not Violate the Establishment Clause." *William and Mary Law Review* 42, no. 3 (2001): 663–683.

Philpott, Daniel. "Introduction: Searching for Strategy in an Age of Peacebuilding." In Philpott and Powers, *Strategies of Peace*, 3–18.

Philpott, Daniel. *Just and Unjust Peace: An Ethic of Political Reconciliation*. Oxford: Oxford University Press, 2012.

Philpott, Daniel, and Gerard F. Powers, eds. *Strategies of Peace: Transforming Conflict in a Violent World*. Oxford: Oxford University Press, 2010.

Pope Pius XII. "Alla vostra filiale." *Acta Apostolicae Sedis* 50 (March 1958): 216–220.

Powers, Gerard F. "Religion and Peacebuilding." In Philpott and Powers, *Strategies of Peace*, 317–352.

Putnam, Robert D., and David E. Campbell. *American Grace: How Religion Divides and Unites Us*. New York: Simon and Schuster, 2010.

Rawls, John. *A Theory of Justice*. Cambridge, MA: Harvard University Press, 1971.

Rawls, John. *Political Liberalism*. New York: Columbia University Press, 1993.

Rawls, John. "The Idea of Public Reason Revisited." *University of Chicago Law Review* 64, no. 3 (1997): 766–807.

Refah Partisi (The Welfare Party) v. Turkey. European Court of Human Rights, Grand Chamber. Application Numbers 41340/98, 41342/93, 41343/98, and 41344/98. 13 February 2003.

Religious Freedom Restoration Act of 1993. Pub. L. No. 103–141. Codified at 42 U.S.C.A. §§ 2000bb et seq.

Reynolds, Noel, and W. Cole Durham Jr. *Religious Liberty in Western Philosophical Thought*. Atlanta: Emory University, 1996.

Romanell, Patrick. "Editor's Introduction." In John Locke, *A Letter Concerning Toleration*, translated by William Popple. Indianapolis: Bobbs-Merrill, 1955.

Sarkozy, Nicolas. "Allocution de M. le Président de la République dans la sallede la signature du Palais de Latran." December 20, 2007. http://tempsreel.nouvelobs.com/file/456435.pdf.

Shah, Timothy Samuel, Alfred Stepan, and Monica Duffy Toft, eds. *Rethinking Religion and World Affairs*. Oxford: Oxford University Press, 2012.

Smith, Buster G., and Rodney Stark. "Religious Attendance Relates to Generosity Worldwide: Religious and the secular more charitable if they attend services." Gallup. September 4, 2009. http://www.gallup.com/poll/122807/religious-attendance-relates-generosity-worldwide.aspx.

Smith, Douglas G. "The Illiberalism of Liberalism: Religious Discourse in the Public Square." *San Diego Law Review* 34, no. 4 (1997): 1571–1641.

Stahnke, Tad, and J. Paul Martin. *Religion and Human Rights: Basic Documents*. New York: Columbia University Press, 1993.

Stout, Jeffrey. *Democracy and Tradition*. Princeton, NJ: Princeton University Press, 2004.

ter Haar, Gerrie. "Religion: Source of Conflict or Resource for Peace?" In *Bridge or Barrier: Religion, Violence, and Visions for Peace*, edited by Gerrie ter Haar and James J. Busuttil, 3–34. Leiden: Brill, 2005.

Teraya, Koji. "Emerging Hierarchy in International Human Rights and Beyond: From the Perspective of Non-derogable Rights." *European Journal of International Law* 12, no. 5 (2001): 917–941.

Toft, Monica Duffy. "Religion, Terrorism, and Civil Wars." In *Rethinking Religion and World Affairs*, edited by Timothy Samuel Shah, Alfred Stepan, and Monica Duffy Toft, 127–148. Oxford: Oxford University Press, 2012.

United Nations General Assembly. Declaration on the Elimination of All Forms of Intolerance and of Discrimination Based on Religion or Belief. A/RES/36/55. November 25, 1981.

United Nations General Assembly. International Covenant of Civil and Political Rights. Resolution 2200A (XXI) of December 16, 1966. Entered into force March 23, 1976.

United Nations General Assembly. Universal Declaration of Human Rights. Resolution 217 A (III). December 10, 1948.

Volokh, Eugene. "What Is the Religious Freedom Restoration Act?" The Volokh Conspiracy. December 2, 2013. http://www.volokh.com/2013/12/02/1a-religious-freedom-restoration-act/.

Warner, Carolyn M., Ramazan Kilnic, Christopher W. Hale, Adam B. Cohen, and Kathryn A. Johnson. "Religion and Public Goods Provision: Experimental and Interview Evidence from Catholicism and Islam." Paper presented at the AALIMS-Princeton workshop, Princeton, NJ, October 18–19, 2013. Revised version of paper presented at the 2013 American Political Science Association conference. http://www.princeton.edu/bobst/events/aalims/Warner-Religion_and_Public_Goods_ExperimentsInterviews-10_2013.pdf.

Whitehead, Alfred North. *Process and Reality*. New York: Free Press, 1979.

CHAPTER 12

WOMEN, RELIGION, AND PEACEBUILDING

SUSAN HAYWARD

As the field of conflict resolution theory and practice developed over the second half of the twentieth century, it grew more sophisticated, nuanced, and complex. This is due not only to the emergence and growth of a theoretical and practical field of conflict resolution, but also to the changing nature and definition of war. War, as Mary Kaldor has described in her work, generally was understood from post-Westphalia Europe into the mid-twentieth century as a regulated exercise between two (or more) state military forces concluded either through military victory or formal political negotiations between elite government representatives.[1] Today, our understanding of war, and war itself, have become more complex. Contemporary wars are fought and sustained by multiple social actors and factors, including non-state organizations; are often asymmetric in nature; use unconventional tactics; and are driven and shaped by local and global forces. Given this changed nature and understanding of war, contemporary peacebuilding sees formal negotiations as one small piece of a larger agenda of social, political, and economic transformations necessary for sustainable peace. The consequence has been greater recognition of the important roles civil society plays in the building of peaceful societies and institutions. Of course, civil society itself is a complex animal, composed of various sectors with unique influence, and so conflict resolution theory and practice have expanded to include a wider array of sectors such as media, education, and youth, seeking to understand their niche roles in creating and sustaining peace with justice. The very existence of this volume attests to a significant increase in scholarship at the intersection of religion and peacebuilding over the past several decades, particularly, in the United States, following the events of September 11, 2001.[2] Moreover, a practical field of religious peacebuilding—defined as peacebuilding practices that target religious ideas, actors, and institutions—has emerged over the last two decades.[3] These emerging scholarly and practical fields have argued that religious dynamics in conflict must be grappled with seriously, and that the religious sector—as a key element of civil society that has historically been marginalized from peacebuilding—should be engaged effectively in comprehensive and strategic peace programming.

In a similar vein, as long as the work of peace was defined by hardball negotiations between armed actors and political elites, the work of peace was almost exclusively a male enterprise. However, even as peacebuilding work began to encompass a wider array of actors and constituencies, women, like religious actors, were absent from these efforts. This is reflective of the larger, historically male-dominated field of international relations, in which women have been noticeably marginalized and to which they have been less visible.[4] In recent years, however, scholarly and practical fields exploring women's experiences in conflict and peacebuilding have grown considerably.[5] This growth is illustrated and motivated by the passage of United Nations Security Resolution 1325, which calls for the equal participation of women in peacebuilding.

Despite the advances in understanding and engagement of religious actors and women in peacebuilding, the scholarship at the intersection of women, religion, and peacebuilding remains thin.[6] A good deal of existing religious peacebuilding scholarship has focused on exemplary male religious figures or failed to address with depth gender dynamics in (and implications of) religious peacebuilding. Meanwhile, the scholarship on gender, conflict, and peace has focused little on religious dynamics hampering or facilitating women's full participation in peacebuilding (particularly religious dynamics *propelling* women into peace work).

This is not a reflection of the state of the field *in* the field, however. Spend a few days in conflict contexts, and one will find many women participating in religious peacebuilding work, particularly in the implementation of projects at the grassroots. Spend time with women peacebuilders who operate in the "secular" peacebuilding world (that is, peacebuilding advanced through organizations or institutions not defined as religiously motivated or rooted, or peacebuilding practices that do not explicitly draw on religious resources), and one discovers that their work is connected to their faith in various ways. Consider, for example, two of the winners of the 2011 Nobel Peace Prize, Leymah Gbowee and Tawakkol Karman, both of whom credit their faith as an important aspect of their identity and a source inspiring and shaping their work.[7] Several studies and international conferences in recent years have devoted increased attention to the unique experiences, including the opportunities and challenges, of women of faith seeking to advance peacebuilding.[8] This chapter will outline some of this recent scholarship and its findings, after first reviewing the field of women and peacebuilding by way of laying a foundation to which the religious lens can be introduced. As we will find, women of faith have historically "fallen through the cracks" of the scholarship and practice of religious peacebuilding and women's peacebuilding, marginalized from both fields. Religious women peacebuilders often find themselves caught between, on the one hand, deeply patriarchal religious institutions that prevent them from serving in key positions of authority and influence for peacebuilding, and on the other hand, a women's peacebuilding sector shaped by Western feminism that tends to operate at a distance from a religious sector perceived to be a barrier to women's empowerment. Despite these barriers, and indeed at times seeking to leverage their position at the margins, women of faith across many traditions and throughout the world have practiced creative, dynamic forms of peacebuilding.

DEFINITIONS AND CONSIDERATIONS

It behooves us to pause first to define what we mean by a woman-of-faith peacebuilder. Essentially, I consider women who have important and formative links to their religion as a source of inspiration and formation or, more practically, who use religious resources as a central component of their peace work, to be religious women peacebuilders. More particularly, I include traditional women religious leaders. Women hold clerical authority in various traditions, exemplified by Buddhist or Catholic nuns. Other women preach and lead religious rituals throughout the world, particularly in Protestant Christian, Muslim, and indigenous traditions. Increasingly, Islamic *madrassas*, Christian seminaries, and Jewish rabbinical schools produce women clergy, scholars, and even Islamic shariah judges in countries such as Morocco, Egypt, and Palestine.[9] In Syria, Huda al-Habash runs religious schools for girls that educate them on Qur'anic interpretation and Islamic law while at the same time encouraging them to think critically, to pursue secular education, and to empower themselves as leaders. In Egypt, Dr. Su'ad Saleh has a weekly television show through which people solicit her judgments (fatwas) based on Islamic law.[10] Women offer religious education to children through formal and informal institutions throughout the world. Often women religious leaders are on the margins of religious institutions and their authority is limited in crucial ways. Nonetheless, many play important roles as peacebuilders. Also included in this paper's conception of women-of-faith peacebuilders are those women working through faith-based organizations, social service or other arms of religious bodies, or university scholarship to advance justice and peace. And finally, I include as well those women operating in "secular" arenas who cite important links to their faith, often as a force inspiring and shaping their work.

In discussing warfare, a similar pause for definition is required. As has been noted, gone are the days when violent conflict was defined primarily as exercises between state militaries or as large-scale civil wars. Increasingly, violent conflict is driven by local militias, armed criminal gangs, local resource–related conflict, trafficking (particularly narco-trafficking), or local conflicts with transnational ideological connections (for example, those movements across Africa, Asia, and the Middle East that are associated with al-Qaeda). Oftentimes, conflicts contain several of these elements, interlinked and mutually driving one another.[11] Modern violent conflict is defined as having three characteristics: 1) Non-cooperative, destructive, widespread, and persistent actions; 2) violation of property rights concerning assets, persons, or institutions; and 3) instigation by some degree of group activity.[12] The examples used in this chapter are among these complex contemporary scenarios.

Finally, a preliminary note of caution is required. There is always a risk in talking about women's work for peace that we essentialize them—describing them as nurturers, connectors, or integrationalists who are somehow more suited for relationship-building, healing, and peacebuilding than men.[13] While focusing on the peacebuilding work of women of faith, I do not make the generalization that all women, and particularly women of faith, are natural peacebuilders. The work of scholar Mia Bloom, among others, sheds light on the roles women have played in propelling both secular and religious violent movements, including participating as suicide bombers, shaping cults of martyrdom, cajoling men into fighting, and nurturing religiously biased attitudes or exclusivist forms of nationalism.[14] Moreover, an unintended consequence of essentializing women in these ways is that we trap them in "soft" forms of peacebuilding at the community level, as though they are less suited for the "hard" work of negotiations, political decisionmaking, and civil resistance that also constitute peacebuilding. This can, in turn, perpetuate gender power imbalances that drive the emergence or re-emergence of violent conflict. That said, women's social and political positions, and their gendered experiences, certainly afford them particular capacities, insights, and priorities they bring to their work to build peace, as we will explore further below.

WOMEN, WAR, AND PEACE

The changing nature of war from a violent, controlled exercise of interstate relations to intra-state and informal conflicts that involve and impact a larger variety of actors and factors has shifted calculations about how to bring peace. Ending modern conflict requires more than a negotiated agreement between heads of state who may have little control over the irregular violent forces that mark contemporary warfare, including organized criminal activity, illegal trafficking, and interethnic violence. As evidenced in Iraq and Afghanistan in the beginning of the twenty-first century, economic insecurity, weak democratic structures, retaliatory justice, high levels of inter-group distrust, lack of social services, and unresolved trauma can feed continued violence. Importantly, this shift in peacemaking strategy from a state security–dominated lens to one that takes into account human security and inter-group relations (peacebuilding) has led to greater awareness of the role of gender in international relations and the experience of women in war, historically realms dominated by and understood through the perspective of men.[15]

The reality of modern warfare means utter social disruption that has serious consequences for women. Increasingly, violence occurs in populated centers rather than on battlegrounds at a distance from civilians. Medical and educational infrastructure is often decimated. As the distinctions between soldier, rebel, insurgent, revolutionary, and narco-trafficker are blurred, civilian populations become targets of violence and forced displacement.[16] While it is notoriously difficult to gather data on conflict casualties with reliability,[17] overall trends show that more civilians die as a consequence of violent conflict than ever before. While in the First World War 5 percent of deaths were civilians, in the 1990s it was estimated that up to 90 percent of casualties were civilians.[18] This means that relatively more women and children are dying as a consequence of modern war.[19] Civilian populations also suffer from the breakdown in economic security and social order; increased levels of lawlessness and human rights abuses; and the lack of medical care, reliable economic opportunities, and access to humanitarian relief. Finally, civilians are deliberately targeted in modern warfare, particularly in acts of genocide, ethnic cleansing, terrorism, disappearances, rape campaigns, and forced displacement. In short, civilians living in conflict zones are rendered extremely vulnerable by modern warfare.

Sexual violence against women is a common element of violent conflict (though I hasten to add that sexual violence afflicts men and children in wartime as well). In many wars of the last century, including those in the Balkans, Mozambique, and Northern Uganda, women were systematically raped in private and public, particularly in the presence of family members, as a tactic of warfare or were taken as sex slaves by combatants.[20] These are acts not only perpetrated against individuals, but against whole communities, meant to tear them apart and undermine social stability. In response to this epidemic, the United Nations Security Council passed Resolutions 1820 and 1888, which recognize sexual violence as a security issue demanding a security response.[21] Notably, these rapes have not only been perpetrated by armed combatants, but also by humanitarian aid workers and UN peacekeepers sent to provide security to local populations.[22]

In the midst of this disruption, women struggle to provide for their families, protect their communities, and survive. Women are not merely passive victims of violence, however. The literature on women and war has sought to recognize women's agency in the midst of war.[23] The disruption caused by war often thrusts women into untraditional roles in their communities. While combatants in warfare are primarily male, they are not exclusively so. Not only are women increasingly integrated into state militaries, but in Sri Lanka, Colombia, Nepal, Zimbabwe, Eritrea, and other countries, women have actively participated in insurgent armed movements as combatants, spies, or logistical support. Indeed, some women may seek out these opportunities as a means to gain training or authority not granted them in their home communities, though more often they are compelled to participate as a result of force or economic necessity.[24] More commonly, however, women remain home while adult male members of their household engage in war.

While in pre-war times women's authority and responsibilities may have been limited to the domestic sphere, during wartime women are compelled to take on responsibilities in the public sphere, including roles normally held by men, such as family breadwinner. Although overall unemployment rates tend to increase in countries at war, the unemployment rate of women, on average, shows a slight decrease.[25] In some situations, with men vulnerable to being picked up and targeted by armed groups, women increasingly leave the home to enter public spaces, including detention centers, refugee camps, and police offices, looking for loved ones. Women increasingly are thrust into roles as community leaders, ensuring that community needs are met in the midst of disruption. Finally, women take on many and varied roles in peacebuilding in their communities, including advocacy, social reconciliation, engaging and reintegrating armed actors, and providing rehabilitation to survivors. In this way, at the same time that war brings obvious suffering for women, it creates a shift in traditional gender norms and opens opportunities for women's empowerment.[26]

The end of war does not necessarily mean greater security for women. In fact, the return of (primarily male) combatants to local communities can translate into an increase in violence against women, particularly as men seek to reassert their control and authority to pre-war levels. Meredeth Turshen has argued that men seek to reassert their authority through social violence (such as private acts of sexual and domestic violence); political violence (for example, co-opting women's organizations to serve their political parties or discounting their political voice); and economic violence (reparation and rehabilitation programs, for instance, often target men at the expense of women).[27] Meanwhile, the gains women make during wartime with respect to employment and leadership are often turned back. As Meintjes, Turshen, and Pillay argue, the little attention women are given in post-conflict settings frequently comes too late to transform patriarchal norms, structures, and relations, and leads to a failure to consolidate women's wartime gains.[28] There is often a reassertion of traditional gender norms and roles in order to "correct" the transformations that occurred during wartime.[29]

The unique challenges women face during and after wartime, and their resulting needs, have historically not been adequately addressed by peace processes that have been shaped and constituted by men. Focusing specifically on formal peace negotiations, a sample of twenty-one major peace processes in the years from 1992 to 2009 revealed that only 2.4 percent of signatories to peace agreements were women, and that women represented only

5.9 percent of the participants in the ten delegations for which this information was available.[30] Those involved in negotiations at peace tables, after all, are typically those who led armed efforts, generally men. The consequences of this marginalization are catastrophic for women. Peace negotiations are not just about the conditions for ending war, but about creating the conditions for peace, including decisions about what state assistance will be offered for reconstruction and rehabilitation, how political and legal structures will be reformed, and economic recovery. When women are not included in these discussions, their post-war needs are less likely to be addressed. Women's grassroots peacebuilding initiatives have also suffered from lack of support from the state and international communities. Some theorists argue that the lack of attention to women's agency in wartime is a result of the militarization of conflict zones, which has meant a certain "masculinization" in which the space and recognition for women's agency becomes reduced.[31]

In 2000, the United Nations Security Council passed Resolution 1325 on women, peace, and security. The resolution recognizes that women face unique challenges requiring particular forms of protection during wartime, and called for the equal participation of women in conflict prevention, conflict resolution, and post-conflict reconciliation efforts.[32] Its passage came as a result of a movement catalyzed in 1995 at the United Nations' Fourth World Conference on Women held in Beijing, which, in the aftermath of the events in Rwanda and the Balkans, put the atrocities women face in wartime on the international agenda, as well as highlighted the active roles women took to resist violence in these and other conflict zones. UNSCR 1325 has itself catalyzed the practical field of women's peacebuilding, granting greater attention, funding, and impetus to women's participation across a spectrum of peacebuilding activities. A number of organizations seek to advance the objectives of UNSCR 1325 through advocacy, peacebuilding training and capacity building for women, and public awareness raising, particularly about women's rights and experiences in war and peace.

Much (though certainly not all) of the major literature on women, war, and peacebuilding has been blind to religion, if not antagonistic toward it, reflecting a secular bias. Rarely is religion given systematic treatment as a form of support or empowerment for women in conflict situations, nor is there significant attention to religious women leaders and their positions and experiences in violent conflict. When mentioned, religion is often referred to as a primary source for the creation and sustenance of deeply patriarchal norms that shape policy and institutions, and so described as a barrier to women's advancement and protection. In short, women are described as victims of religion.[33] This despite the fact that in places like "South and Southwest Asia, grassroots activism and the creation and maintenance of women's networks often emerges from a particular religious framework."[34] In interviews, women peacebuilders cite "spirituality" as one of their primary motivations.[35] Major organizations (particularly those in the West) involved in women's peacebuilding have, like the theoretical field, tended to be highly secular, historically not engaging religion or faith-based institutions in their work.

WOMEN OF FAITH BUILDING PEACE

While women have been marginalized from peacebuilding generally, the emerging field of religious peacebuilding has been particularly challenging for women. With formal religious authority primarily vested in men in most major religious traditions throughout the world, those women seeking to work through religious institutions or to shape pro-peace religious attitudes often struggle to find spaces to lead efforts or exert influence. Despite these challenges, many women of faith pursue peace actively both within and outside of religious institutions. These efforts are exemplified by women such as the late Dekha Ibrahim of Kenya, Venerable Mae Chee Sansanee of Thailand, and Sister Marie-Bernard Alima of the Democratic Republic of Congo.

Dekha Ibrahim lived and worked as a peacebuilder in Kenya until her death in 2011, serving as trustee of the Coalition for Peace in Africa and of NOMADIC, a pastoralist organization based in Wajir, Kenya. She was also one of the founders of the Wajir Peace and Development Committee and Action for Conflict Transformation. She received several international awards for her peacebuilding contributions, including the 2007 Right Livelihood Award presented at the Swedish parliament "for showing in diverse ethnic and cultural situations how religious and other differences can be reconciled, even after violent conflict, and knitted together through a cooperative process that leads to peace and development."[36] A devout Muslim, Dekha often referred to the foundation her faith provided for her work, and the way specific Qur'anic teachings influenced her peacebuilding approach.[37] She was dedicated to deepening inter-religious relationships.

Buddhist nun Mae Chee Sansanee founded and directs the Sathira-Dhammasathan Center outside Bangkok, a retreat center that runs numerous programs providing support to victims of domestic violence, prisoners, and unwed mothers. When conflict broke out between Buddhists and Muslims in southern Thailand, Mae Chee led a peace walk in the south and reached out to Muslim women, bringing them to her retreat center to build relationships with Buddhist women. As Co-Chair of the Global Peace Initiative of Women, Mae Chee participates in and leads interfaith dialogue in conflict zones around the world. She describes all her work as about breaking cycles of violence.[38]

Catholic Sister Marie-Bernard Alima has worked for more than two decades to advance peace and to strengthen the capacity of women peacebuilders. In 2001, she created a civil society network called the Coordination of Women for Democracy and Peace to train and support women peace leaders. This network now includes thousands of women across the Democratic Republic of Congo (DRC) who provide leadership in human rights, transitional justice, widening women's participation in the political sphere, and combating sexual and gender-based violence, a pernicious problem in the DRC. Sister Alima is the first woman to serve as the General Secretary of the DRC Episcopal (Bishops') Commission for Justice and Peace, where she guides the Catholic Church's Justice and Peace Program in a country where half the population is Catholic. Under her leadership, the commission has become more heavily engaged in advocacy to prevent sexual and gender-based violence and to offer rehabilitative support to its victims.[39]

Despite the existence of countless women religious peacebuilders such as these in conflict zones around the world, rarely are their experiences highlighted in the major literature on religious peacebuilding, which tends instead to focus on exemplary male figures, or on initiatives led by men. Tellingly, Katrien Hertog's 2010 review of religious peacebuilding, which comprehensively summarizes the major literature shaping the field, makes little reference to women religious peacebuilders aside from reference to "lay religious" or "religious actors."[40] Moreover, historically it is male religious clerics who have been targeted by the international community in the practice of religious peacebuilding, particularly in highly visible and well-funded initiatives. "A Common Word Between Us and You," for instance, is a movement sparked by a letter sent from Muslim scholars to the Christian world in 2007 calling for greater dialogue and engagement for the purpose of mutual understanding and peace. The letter was signed by 137 men and one woman.[41] The Council of Religious Institutions of the Holy Land and its antecedent, the Alexandria Process in Israel/Palestine, have not included any female members.[42] The Tanenbaum Center for Interreligious Understanding based in New York City has struggled to receive nominations of women peacemakers for its annual religious peacemakers award.[43] It is no wonder that in 2011 Heiner Bielefeldt, the United Nations Special Rapporteur on Freedom of Religion or Belief, remarked on "a current imbalance in the composition of high-level interreligious dialogue events where women tend to be marginalized."[44]

Even when women are included in these initiatives, they frequently have a difficult time shaping the agenda and claiming an equal seat in the process. Power differentials between ordained male clerics and lay women prove difficult to manage in current processes of religious peacebuilding. In Sri Lanka, for example, Muslim activist Jezima Ismael speaks of her challenges serving as one of very few women in the Sri Lankan Council of Religions for Peace, saying cultural traditions shaping gender relations, coupled with social deference to religious clergy, pose significant challenges to sharing an equal voice with male religious clerics on the council.[45]

In recognition of the challenge of including women in religious peacebuilding, and their historic marginalization, a number of organizations involved in religious peacebuilding have created separate women's initiatives. Religions for Peace, formally created in 1970 (and formerly known as the World Conference of Religions for Peace), created a Women's Mobilization Network in 1998 in an effort to integrate women into all of its programming.[46] The Global Peace Initiative for Women, an organization based in New York City, was created in response to the marginalization of women at the 2000 Millennium Summit of Religious Leaders.[47] However, these attempts to create women's initiatives give rise to new challenges. They create greater competition for funds within the religious peacebuilding sector, face a difficult time receiving funding, and can lead to further fragmentation of the field of religious peacebuilding and peacebuilding more generally, which already struggles with collaboration and coordination.[48] They often end up ghettoizing women's religious peace initiatives, rather than mainstreaming them.

Given the lack of documentation of the work on the ground of women of faith to build peace, it is challenging to offer a comprehensive picture of their work. That said, from analysis of what studies are available, anecdotes, and direct field observation, some trends emerge about the sort of work they are drawn to and the values that shape these activities. Scholar Cynthia Sampson has categorized the various roles faith-based actors play in peacebuilding as observer, educator, advocate, and intermediary.[49] Likewise, scholar Judy El-Bushra has categorized women's peacebuilding work as focused on survival and basic needs, peacebuilding and mediation at different levels, advocacy, women's rights and participation, and community outreach and building.[50] Note that the categories below, which emerge from a focus on women religious peacebuilders, bridge these two scholars' categories.

Cross-Boundary Work

Time and again women generally, and particularly women of faith, reach across religious, political, ethnic, and other divides in conflict zones to build bridges between communities through deepening interpersonal relationships, and to create broad-based movements and constituencies for peace. Scholar Cynthia Cockburn has documented these efforts in several settings marked by identity-based conflict, including Israel/Palestine, Northern Ireland, and the Balkans. In these contexts, Cockburn asserts, women have been "caught up in coercive and narrowing identity processes... marked by highly mobilized ethnicities." Women peace-builders' cross-boundary work brings them together to create spaces "in which such differences would be respected, not collapsed into a spurious unity. At the same time... allowing closeness, even intimacy, in which differences are not so reified as to determine expectations and limit the range of responses."[51] The relationships built allow women to understand and deconstruct national, ethnic, religious, or political identity narratives that are fueling division and conflict without ignoring (and indeed, by engaging) legitimate underlying concerns of particular communities. Often motivated by their own experiences of gender-based marginalization and oppression, women in these initiatives struggle over what it means to be a "good" Christian, Muslim, Tamil, Marxist, and so on. They grapple with coercive identity formation processes that often mark conflict environments and rethink their own sense of self in relation to various group identities.[52]

For some women, the desire to reach out across divides comes as a result of their experience as victims of the conflict, "fed up with" the suffering imposed on their families and communities by continued violence.[53] In Sri Lanka, for example, Visaka Dharmadasa founded the Association of War Affected Women (AWAW) in 2002, which brings together women from both sides of the conflict who lost sons and husbands during the civil war for dialogue and to work together to end violence. Beginning in 2009, AWAW began a program called Team 1325 to train women to run for political office. In Liberia in the 1990s, Nobel Peace Prize winner Leymah Gbowee brought together Christian and Muslim women who were fed up with the violence that had saturated their communities, destroying families. One survey had shown that nearly half of Monrovia's women and girls had been abused by a soldier or fighter, and another showed that 61 percent of Monrovian high school students had seen someone killed, raped, or tortured.[54] "We are tired!" Leymah Gbowee cried out, speaking for the Christian Women's Peace Initiative she had recently founded, to a church full of visiting bishops. "We are *tired*. We feel it's now time to rise up and speak." To which a Muslim woman rose up and pledged to join the effort, creating a coalition of Liberia's Christian and Muslim women that asserted "We are tired of our children being killed! Tired of being raped! Women, wake up—you have a voice in the peace process."[55] It was through coming together in solidarity that the women began to feel "a new source of power and strength [in] each other" through shared prayer and advocacy.[56]

For many of the women involved in this work, the relationships they build are crucial and transformative. Indeed, many note that women's work for peace is often very relational,[57] that is, focused on building and deepening interpersonal relationships that can be both individually and socially transformative. Diane D'Souza notes that "women's groups have tended to devote more time to dialogue and to building relationships than mixed gender groups have done.. . . An inclination toward engagement, toward listening and struggling to establish positive relationships seems characteristic of such initiatives."[58] But oftentimes their goal in bridging these divides is as much strategic as it is about relationship-building for its own sake: as a group with little political influence, particularly in an environment in which those carrying guns are those with political or other forms of agency, women need larger coalitions in order to exert influence and to be heard. Like the women in Liberia, women from different sides of the conflict in Bougainville came together through the vehicle of church groups to advocate for peace.[59] Moreover, where as individuals the women might be more vulnerable to violent retaliation, particularly in rural areas, through working corporately they benefit from greater security.

To some degree, women's marginalization from the top tier of institutional religious and political leadership situates them for this sort of cross-boundary work. Less visible and less constrained by institutional commitments, they are freer to make moves that would otherwise be considered politically or socially risky.

Advocacy

In a similar vein, women of faith seek to influence political decision-making in the midst of conflict in order to advance peace. Because they are frequently excluded from direct participation in political decision-making, citizen advocacy becomes their means to do so. Women often advocate on behalf of the community, youth, and women—those suffering the brunt of war. Sometimes this advocacy keeps women's rights central, but not always. Consider Nobel Peace Prize winner Tawakkol Karman, who led resistance movements—marches, sit-ins, other forms of civil disobedience—to end war or dictatorship. In Colombia, many religious women, especially Catholic nuns, advocate against corporate powers that profit from operating in the chaos of war. Similarly, nuns in the Philippines, exposed to the suffering inflicted by martial law in the 1970s and '80s, often became activists able to use their "moral power" and their perceived lack of political opportunism to serve as a successful pressure group.[60] As observed by Nadine Naber, urban women from Cairo and those from villages joined factory workers in Egypt in 2008 to create the movement that led its 2011 revolution and the overthrow of Hosni Mubarak in efforts to address poverty and advance human rights.[61] Women played a similarly important role in the overthrow of the shah in Iran in 1979, many compelled by concerns about corruption, poverty, and the failures of secular nationalist rule.[62] In Honduras, religious women, including Catholic nuns from the Sisters of Mercy order, have been at the forefront of advocacy movements following the 2009 coup and subsequent violence, using religious ritual, song, and prayer as central components of their public protests. Their activist stance has often put them in opposition to the official Catholic Church's position.[63] Women, and women of faith in particular, often seek to draw together various groups—particularly disempowered or minority groups—in order to mount an effective resistance to powers propelling violence.

Psycho-Social and Spiritual Support to Survivors

"Peacebuilding to me isn't about ending a fight by standing between two opposing forces," writes Lehmah Gbowee in her autobiography. "It's healing those victimized by war, making them strong again, and bringing them back to the people they once were. It's helping victimizers rediscover their humanity so they can once again become productive members of their communities."[64] In the midst of conflict, women of faith seem particularly drawn to providing psychosocial care to victims in conflict zones. In northern Uganda, Catholic Sister Pauline Acayo, a member of the Acholi Religious Leaders Peace Initiative, has coordinated

Catholic Relief Services' projects offering psychosocial trauma counseling and reintegration to former child combatants from the Lord's Resistance Army (in addition to her work organizing women peacebuilders).[65] Soraya Jamjuree, a Muslim woman living in southern Thailand, invokes Islamic ideals of compassion in her work to provide emotional, psychological, and practical support to families touched by violence.[66]

Women religious appear to be well positioned to offer support to women and men survivors of sexual-based violence, who may not feel comfortable going to male religious leaders for support. While religious communities are sometimes accused of not doing enough to combat violence against women—including rape and sex slavery in warfare, human trafficking, and domestic violence that spikes when soldiers come home—certainly, women of faith have sought to push this issue more to the center of religious peace- and justice-building priorities. This is evidenced by Sister Alima's efforts to mainstream responses to sexual and gender-based violence within the Catholic Church in the DRC, as noted in the section "Women of Faith Building Peace." Similarly, the Centre Olame, a Catholic social assistance agency in South Kivu, under director Mathilde Muhindo Mwamini provides psychological and practical assistance to victims of sexual violence.[67] Andrea Blanch, president of the Center for Religious Tolerance and trained social psychologist, comments that "religion and faith tap into people's deepest beliefs and can provide one tool to begin addressing the trauma and the conflict at a personal and societal level."[68]

Mediation/Intermediaries

Though less common, there are examples of women of faith serving as direct intermediaries between parties in conflict or between local communities and armed actors. They are able to approach these actors in part because as religious women, they are less likely to be seen as a threat by armed actors. This is particularly true with respect to local mediation with armed actors to create zones of security and protection, such as takes place in Colombia. Ayse Kadayifci-Orellana documents the story of a Somali woman, Asha Hagi Elmi, who was able to secure a place in political negotiations in part by advocating for her participation within an Islamic framework.[69] Betty Bigombe, a Christian Ugandan woman and recipient of the Tanenbaum Religious Peacemakers Award, twice served as a principle mediator for the Ugandan government's direct negotiations with the Lord's Resistance Army.

Community Development

Women of faith are also heavily involved in activities that might traditionally be ascribed to the development sector, but which play a role in strategic peacebuilding: education, public health, and humanitarian relief, for instance. These women recognize that peace is about more than a ceasefire or negotiated agreement to end immediate forms of violence; it is also about expanding peace to wider constituencies, addressing the economic drivers of conflict. In 2010, the Niwano Peace Prize was awarded to Ela Bhatt, founder of the Self-Employed Women's Network. This underscored that addressing structural poverty is an essential aspect of peacebuilding.

Taking into account this focus on sustainable development, as well as those other activities named above, one notes that religious women's peacebuilding practices align with the goal of creating a "justpeace," described by Lederach and Appleby as an understanding of peace that takes into account both "the reduction and management of [overt] violence and the achievement of social and economic justice" that necessitates the "building of constructive personal, group, and political relationships."[70] The work described above sees individual and social transformation and healing, the development of personal and communal relationships and identities that are mutually constructive, and the work of advocacy and mediation as interrelated aspects of building peace.

Moreover, the peacebuilding work shaped and implemented by women of faith often reflects several values, namely inclusive processes, an eye toward justice as a central component of peace, and affirmation of the inherent dignity of all people, including victims and combatants. Perhaps as a result of women's own marginalization in patriarchal societies, they tend to see cross-cutting forms of oppression and structural violence that travel "from the bedroom to the battlefield," all driving the larger conflict.[71] Therefore, these women tend to be very conscious of structural injustice and entrenched institutional and social inequalities, and they seek a peace solution that takes into account justice concerns that are directly and indirectly related to the conflict. They also prize participatory and democratic processes, aware of how external power dynamics, including between urban elite and rural poor, between majority and minority communities, and between identity groups, can seep into peacebuilding programs and processes in which certain social groups have greater access to funding or more power to shape decisions over agendas, priority issues, and goals. In Sri Lanka, Buddhist peace practitioner Dishani Jayaweera strives to ensure that her interfaith peace programming is shaped and implemented through inclusive decision-making processes. This, she states, is in order to ensure that the process of her work itself reflects her larger goal: the transformation of a highly centralized state apparatus overwhelmingly influenced by the majority ethno-religious community, one of the root drivers of Sri Lanka's conflict.[72]

Something more fundamental is also at play. For many women facing persistent violence and suffering, their faith becomes a rock on which to stand when political, social, and economic systems seem untrustworthy or unstable. It is a source that shapes and inspires their work, while also providing spiritual sustenance for the hard slog of peacebuilding.

PROCESSES, CHALLENGES, OPPORTUNITIES

Many of the women involved in peace work through religious institutions acknowledge the patriarchal roadblocks they inevitably run up against in their traditions—religious laws, authorities, or teachings that would constrain their work. In response, religious women peacebuilders frequently draw from the theological and textual sources of their religious traditions to defend their agency to others and to empower themselves. That is to say, in addition to pulling from the religious sources theorists regularly identify as shaping religious work for *justpeace* in each tradition— particular teachings, practices, stories, exemplary figures—women simultaneously mine traditions for material that affirms their experiences in wartime and empowers them, specifically as women, to assume active social and political roles. For example, women participants in a 2010 workshop in Colombia in which I participated repeatedly referred to biblical women who either served as leaders in their communities (Esther and Vashti standing up to men's violence, early Christian women leaders like Priscilla) or who were victims of men's violence and war. Women highlight religious support for their active participation to inspire themselves as individuals, to challenge gender-oppressive religious claims that would limit their work (put forward by clerical authorities as well as husbands, relatives, and others), and to undergird theologically an effort to transform structural gender inequalities—both within and outside religious institutions. These resources are used not just to challenge gender-oppressive voices within religious traditions, but also secular forces, or outside actors, that define their religion as inherently and irrevocably opposed to women's progress. These activities reveal how just as religious traditions are inherently plural when it comes to violence and peace, so too are they plural in offering both sources for oppression and sources for empowerment for women.[73]

In nearly every global religious tradition, formal interpretive authority (not to mention the writing of foundational texts in the first instance) has traditionally been vested in men. Feminist critique of hermeneutics has revealed the ways in which scriptures and other primary religious texts have been written and interpreted so as to maintain gender norms that privilege male authority and power.[74] While historically women have been involved in religious interpretation, their work has tended to be informal and less documented. Contemporary feminist movements within different religious traditions have sought to place feminist interpretation within the mainstream, to lift up those textual currents that are friendly to women, and to deconstruct and challenge those considered harmful to women.[75] In Morocco, for example, women clergy and religious scholars have sought to "take Islam back," criticizing scholars from the Wahhabi school of Islam for being obsessed with women's bodies and outdated interpretations. They point to examples of women's leadership in early Islam and their protection and empowerment within the bounds of Islamic law.[76] In other traditions as well, particularly when women religious peacebuilders stand in opposition to mainstream or institutional positions or understandings, women religious peacebuilders often engage in these gender-aware hermeneutics in order to negotiate their peacebuilding agency and authority from within their religious traditions.

Interestingly, as women come to understand how their religious traditions have been interpreted in ways that have disempowered them, sometimes in manners contradicting earlier interpretations, they begin to question many of their long-held assumptions. Monica Maher and Andrea Blanch have written about how these exercises often awaken women's political critique of those with power in Latin America and Israel/Palestine, respectively.[77] Monica Maher explains how women begin to "question the unquestionable," further writing that "by challenging what they had been taught as final and absolute truth about female nature and the historical religious tradition, women often begin to question authorities, finding their voices in political activism toward justice for women."[78] These practices also seem to contribute to helping them find their voice in working for peace—particularly when it comes to challenging religious interpretations that have legitimated and propelled violence.

However, not all feminist theologies that arise through women's hermeneutical engagement with their traditions result in similar forms of agency in resistance to traditional or conservative interpretations of women's roles. Saba Mahmood's work reveals the manner in which the Egyptian women's piety movement led to stricter adoption of female behavior codes and practices that would be considered anti-progressive by Western feminist standards. Yet their study of scripture and tradition led these women to embrace standards, even against growing trends in wider society, as a form of agency and protest, seeking to protect their dignity and autonomy as women.[79]

Religion, of course, plays a significant role in shaping norms of acceptable gendered behavior. And religion has played an undeniable role in providing ideological infrastructure for social norms and political and economic systems in which women are disadvantaged. In the midst of war, however, women are often forced to assume roles outside these norms.[80] In so doing, they shake off traditional cultural and religious restrictions. In other words, the violent conflict itself breaks open space for new hermeneutics, as women begin to play a more active role in shaping religious attitudes and behaviors in their communities, and even to take on leadership roles in faith-based institutions. Pentecostal women in Colombia, for example, in the midst of disruption and displacement, have become church and community leaders, particularly in displaced communities.[81] Of course women are seldom the traditional or formal interpretive authorities in their traditions, and are not always educated in hermeneutics. But that is not to say they lack interpretive authority. Across traditions and geographies, women shape religious interpretations of their context and shape "proper" religious response to injustice and violence—in ways that both propel and hamper peace. In the midst of war as they assume more leadership roles in the community, their influence as religious authorities can also be amplified. However, in the aftermath of war, peacebuilding work to restore communities often means turning back advances women have made, to reinstate a status quo that existed before the violence broke out.[82] Certainly in several contexts we see religious institutions and leaders spearheading conservative backlashes against women's public roles in conflict and post-war scenarios.[83]

Making Lemonade: Operating from the Margins

The fact that much of the prominent, well-funded, religious peacebuilding work is designed and dominated by men has many downsides for women of faith. It means that issues affecting women, issues of priority to women, and crucial understandings of conflict that women have as a result of their experiences, as well as their interpretation of community needs, are not as likely to be addressed in religious peacebuilding in practice. Also problematic for women of faith is that the emerging field of women's peacebuilding has not tended to engage religious actors and organizations. Given that in much of the world, constraints on women's public roles are justified on religious grounds, these groups should feel compelled to partner with religious forces who can challenge and transform those roadblocks. And, of course, women of faith who are involved in peace work have a lot to contribute to the wider world of women's peacebuilding. More practically, however, the invisibility and marginalization of women of faith have very real implications for their own practice of peacebuilding: these women often lack funding, training, and support. It also means their work is less documented, and so not as well understood, posing a challenge for those outside organizations that would like to offer them strategic support. International nongovernmental organizations, international organizations, and governments are increasingly engaging religious actors, but these tend to be male clerics. These same bodies are engaging women, but these tend to be elite, secular-oriented women. So one has to ask, whose peace are these outside actors supporting? And are they reinforcing systems that privilege men at the expense of women, or secular women rather than religious women?

However, religious women peacebuilders have also insisted that their very invisibility can be useful in pushing forward radical changes. This "strategic invisibility" allows them to operate under the radar of armed actors and religious gatekeepers who would otherwise create barriers to their work, or who would make them, and those with whom they work, vulnerable to retribution.

Moreover, women's marginalization from traditional power structures has afforded them a certain flexibility and wisdom. "The fact that they are often not at the top levels of institutions may mean that they are more open to institutional change," notes Virginia Bouvier.[84] Some argue that women, as victims of power systems, are more attuned to violent dynamics of power in a manner that can serve the development of sophisticated tools for advocacy and structural transformation. It also creates flexibility, and develops skills at erecting and mobilizing effective decentralized networks outside of traditional power structures. But ending our analysis with this glorification of the results of women's oppression does little to transform structures that privilege men. In fact, it risks sanctifying women's disempowered status and keeping their perspectives and contributions out of more formal aspects of peacemaking, including political negotiations and decision-making. Given that strategic and sustainable peacebuilding seeks the creation of more just systems and structures, recognizing inequalities as a root driver of violence,[85] one must be sensitive to this risk. Moreover, as noted above, the marginalization of women from peacebuilding processes has led to the failure to fully eradicate violence from post-war societies, in which violence has tragically moved into the private sphere, impacting women and children in particular. As such, the strategic invisibility or marginality of religious women's work for peace, and religious women's operation within religiously derived gender norms that may appear contradictory to human rights or Western feminist norms, must be considered alongside strategic peacebuilding practices that seek to transform structures, relationships, and norms that drive overt and covert forms of violence against women and others.

Conclusion: Between Religious Patriarchy and Secular Feminism

The lack of attention to the implications of the development of religious peacebuilding for women is worrisome. Only recently have activists and theorists begun to question *whose* peace religious peacebuilders are advocating, whether that peace addresses the needs and priorities of women, or if it simply reifies attitudes and systems that are harmful to women and sets back the goals expressed in Resolution 1325 of the UN Security Council.[86] Because religion plays such an important role in shaping gender norms and attitudes, and because women have been historically marginalized from mainstream peacemaking efforts and so seldom had their needs addressed in post-conflict restructuring and building of societies, this question is pressing. Conflict can provide opportunities for women to take on new forms of leadership, and ideally, peacebuilding practices should seek to capitalize on and reinforce those gains to create more gender-inclusive social, economic, and political power relations in post-conflict societies.[87] As has been argued, societies in which structural injustices, whether based on gender, race, class, or other differences, have been transformed through peace processes are more likely to achieve sustainable peace.[88] Thus, eradication of gender discrimination should be regarded as an essential component of strategic peacebuilding processes, reflecting the gender-inclusive society they seek to build. Gender-inclusive religious peacebuilding would ensure women have an equal part in design and implementation of processes, as well as ensure they benefit equally from it.[89] Religious peacebuilding would then come to play a role in creating permanent transformations of social norms around violence, gender, and power; a crucial role to play given religion's role in shaping these norms historically.

The barriers to religious women's participation in the growing field of women's peacebuilding create similar challenges. Many factors feed the mutual suspicion between religious and women peacebuilding movements, but it often comes down to rather extreme views, on the one side, of religious authority as irrevocably oppressive or insensitive toward women and on the other, of Western feminist agendas as irrevocably anti-religion.[90] This alienates many women of faith who fall in the middle of this divide, and feel forced to choose between their religion and women's rights—a false choice, as demonstrated by the women highlighted in this chapter. Fortunately, a growing number of initiatives seek to bridge these divides, recognizing that attempts to reform gender relations that do not take into account religion are likely to fail, particularly in postcolonial environments in which initiatives that do not show any deference or sensitivity to local religious and cultural practices are likely to be resisted as neocolonial tools of the West.[91] Despite the rise in projects that bring together women's rights, development, and religious organizations, the relationship remains tense. This is a vital issue that has real impacts on the peacebuilding practice of women-of-faith, particularly in their ability to form coalitions that can shape the local and global context.

Nonetheless, as religious women advance peace, typically with little support, they are beginning to redefine their societies—shaping new religious narratives in support of women's agency and peace with justice, often in distinction to predominant patriarchal religious narratives that legitimate violence. While often operating from the margins, in isolation, these women are able to leverage their positions to advance their goals for holistic peace.

NOTES

1. Mary Kaldor, *New and Old Wars: Organized Violence in a Global Era* (Cambridge: Polity Press, 1999), 14–15.

2. David Smock, ed., *Interfaith Dialogue and Peacemaking* (Washington, DC: US Institute of Peace Press, 2002) and special issue, *Peaceworks*, no. 55 (January 2006). "Religious Contributions to Peacemaking: When Religion Brings Peace Not War," special issue, *Peaceworks*, no. 55 (January 2006); Douglas Johnston, ed., *Faith-Based Diplomacy: Trumping Realpolitik* (New York: Oxford University Press, 2003); Mohammed Abu-Nimer, *Nonviolence and Peace Building in Islam* (Gainesville: University Press of Florida, 2003); Harold Coward and Gordon S. Smiths, eds., *Religion and Peacebuilding* (Albany: State University of New York Press, 2004); Mark Rogers, Tom Bamat, and Julie Ideh, eds., *Pursuing Just Peace: An Overview and Case Studies for Faith-Based Peacebuilders* (Baltimore: Catholic Relief Services, 2008); Sampson, Cynthia, "Religion

and Peace Building," in *Peacemaking in International Conflict: Methods and Techniques*, ed. William Zartman and L. Rasmussen (Washington, DC: US Institute of Peace Press, 1997); Tsjeard S. Bouta, Ayse Kadayifci-Orellana, and Mohammed Abu-Nimer, *"Faith-Based Peace-Building: Mapping and Analysis of Christian, Muslim and Multi-Faith Actors"* (The Hague: Netherlands Institute for International Relations 'Clingendael,' 2005); Sheherazade Jafari, "Local Religious Peacemakers: An Untapped Resource in U.S. Foreign Policy," *Journal of International Affairs* 61, no. 1 (2007): 111–130.

3. Katrien Hertog, *The Complex Reality of Religious Peacebuilding* (Lanham, MD: Lexington Books, 2010); Susan Hayward, *"Religion and Peacebuilding: Reflections on Current Challenges and Future Prospects,"* Special Report 313 (Washington, DC: US Institute of Peace, 2012).

4. Spike Peterson, "The Gender of Rhetoric, Reason and Realism," in *Refiguring Realism: International Relations and Rhetorical Practices*, ed. Francis A Beer. and Robert Hariman (East Lansing, MI: Michigan State University Press, 1996).

5. Kathleen Kuehnast, C. de Jonge Oudraat, and H. Hernes, eds., *Women and War: Power and Protection in the 21st Century* (Washington, DC: US Institute of Peace Press, 2011); Rita Manchanda, ed., *Women, War, and Peace in South Asia: Beyond Victimhood to Agency* (New Delhi: Sage Publications, 2001); Krishna Kumar, ed., *Women and Civil War: Impact, Organizations, and Action* (Boulder, CO: Lynne Rienner Publishers, 2001); Susie Jacobs, Ruth Jacobson, and Jennifer Marchbank, *States of Conflict: Gender, Violence, and Resistance* (New York: Zed Books, 2000); Cynthia Cockburn, *The Space Between Us: Negotiating Gender and National Identities in Conflict* (New York: Zed Books, 1998); Sanam Anderlini, *Women Building Peace: What They Do, Why it Matters* (Boulder, CO: Lynne Rienner Publishers, 2007); Sheila Meintjes, Anu Pillay, and Meredeth Turshen, eds., *The Aftermath: Women in Post-Conflict Transformation* (New York: Zed Books, 2001); Elisabeth Rehn and Ellen Johnson Sirleaf, *Women, War and Peace: The Independent Experts' Assessment on the Impact of Armed Conflict on Women and Women's Role in Peacebuilding* (New York: United Nations Development Fund for Women, 2002).

6. A number of recent initiatives have sought to fill this gap, including Luce Foundation–funded research programs at Yale University and Arizona State University. Patricia Lawrence and Monique Skidmore produced a book from an exploration at the inter-section conducted at Notre Dame University: *Women and the Contested State: Religion, Violence, and Agency in South and Southeast Asia* (Notre Dame, IN: University of Notre Dame Press, 2007).

7. See an interview with Tawakkol Karman: Nadia Al-Sakkaf, "'There Is No Turning Back,'" *The Daily Beast*, October 9, 2011, http://www.thedailybeast.com/articles/2011/10/09/tawakul-karman-interview-nobel-peace-prize-could-help-arab-spring.html.   Karman states, "About Islam in particular, I am so glad that this prize was given to me being the person who I am because it will help the world break the stereotypes about Islam and Muslim women." Leymah Gbowee's book *Mighty Be Our Powers: How Sisterhood, Prayer, and Sex Changed a Nation at War* (New York: Beast Books, 2011) is rife with references to her faith and the role of prayer, religious institutions, and inspirational historical religious women who served as inspiration for her movement.

8. For example, see Isabelle Gueskens, Merle Gosewinkel, and Jose de Vries, eds., *"(Inter)faith-Based Peacebuilding: The Need for a Gender Perspective"* (The Hague: International Fellowship on Reconciliation Women Peacemakers Program, 2010). In 2009, Yale University organized a conference on women, religion, and globalization that included

a panel on women, religion, and peacebuilding. The Center for Religious Tolerance organized a women's interfaith leadership development workshop in Jordan in 2007. In June 2011, the Joan B. Kroc School of Peace Studies at the University of San Diego, in partnership with a number of other organizations and schools, held an international symposium in the Dominican Republic entitled "Peacebuilding in Society and Religion: Feminist Practices of Intercultural Transformation." Georgetown University's Berkley Center for Religion, Peace, and World Affairs and the US Institute of Peace's Religion and Peacemaking Program launched a multi-year project on women, religion, conflict, and peace in 2010. See Katherine Marshall and Susan Hayward, with Claudia Zambra, Esther Breger, and Sarah Jackson, "Women in Religious Peacebuilding," special issue, *PeaceWorks*, no. 71 (May 2011).

9. In Morocco in 2000, the Ministry of Islamic Affairs appointed approximately two hundred women to serve as preachers in mosques. In 2004, the king appointed thirty women to the Ulama Council. For more, see Zakia Salime, *Between Feminism and Islam: Human Rights and Sharia Law in Morocco* (Minneapolis: University of Minnesota Press, 2011).

10. See, for example, the documentary *Veiled Voices* by Brigid Maher, which profiles Ghina Hammoud in Lebanon, Dr. Su'ad Saleh in Egypt, and Huda al-Habash in Syria. Brigid Maher, *Veiled Voices* (Seattle: Typecast Films, 2009).

11. World Bank, "World Development Report 2011: Conflict, Security, and Development" (Washington, DC: The World Bank, 2011), http://wdr2011.worldbank.org/sites/default/files/pdfs/WDR2011_Full_Text.pdf, 53–54.

12. Mats Berdal and David M. Malone, *Greed and Grievance: Economic Agendas and Civil War* (Boulder, CO: Lynne Rienner Publishers, 2000).

13. In 1998, Francis Fukuyama published a paper entitled "Women and the Evolution of World Politics" that argued for a biological basis for sex differences in international affairs and critiqued feminist international relations scholars whom he thought focused too narrowly on culture (*Foreign Affairs* 77, no. 5 (1998): 24–40). For a critique of his argument, see Hilary Charlesworth, "Are Women Peaceful?: Reflections on the Role of Women in Peacebuilding," *Feminist Legal Studies* 16, no. 3 (2008): 347–361. See also Louise Vincent, "Engendering Peace in Africa: A Critical Inquiry into Some Current Thinking on the Role of African Women in Peacebuilding," *African Journal in Conflict Resolution* 2, no. 1 (2001): 9–20.

14. Mia Bloom, *Bombshell: The Many Faces of Women Terrorists* (Toronto: Penguin, 2011). See also Jean Elshtain, *Women and War* (Chicago: University of Chicago Press, 1995).

15. Kuehnast et al., *Women and War*, 1.

16. Kuehnast et al., *Women and War*, 19.

17. Military data tend to focus on military casualties rather than civilian deaths. Meanwhile, NGOs and relief agencies, which are more likely to include civilians, do not use consistent definitions of wartime-related deaths.

18. See para. 24 of Graça Machel, "Impact of Armed Conflict on Children: Report of the Expert of the Secretary General," UN document A/51/306 (New York: United Nations and UNICEF, 1996).

19. Human Security Report Project, *Human Security Report 2009/2010: The Causes of Peace and the Shrinking Costs of War* (New York: Oxford University Press, 2011).

20. UNIFEM, United Nations Department of Peacekeeping Operations, and UN Action against Sexual Violence in Conflict, "Addressing Conflict-Related Sexual Violence: An Analytical Inventory of Peacekeeping Practice" (New York: UN Development Fund for

Women, 2010), http://www.unifem.org/attachments/products/Analytical_Inventory_of_
Peacekeeping_Practice_online.pdf.

21. As described by Resolution 1820, sexual violence amounts to a tactic of war when it is
    used to "humiliate, dominate, instill fear in, disperse and/or forcibly relocate civilian
    members of a community or ethnic group" and it "can constitute a war crime, a crime
    against humanity, or a constitutive act with respect to genocide" (preamble and opera-
    tive paragraph 4). UN Security Council, Resolution 1820, June 19, 2008, http://www.secu-
    ritycouncilreport.org/atf/cf/%7B65BFCF9B-6D27-4E9C-8CD3-CF6E4FF96FF9%7D/
    CAC%20S%20RES%201820.pdf and Resolution 1888, September 30, 2009, http://www.
    securitycouncilreport.org/atf/cf/%7B65BFCF9B-6D27-4E9C-8CD3-CF6E4FF96FF9
    %7D/WPS%20SRES%201888.pdf.

22. See United Nations Office of Internal Oversight, "Investigation into Sexual Exploitation
    of Refugees by Aid Workers in West Africa," UN document A/57/465, October 11,
    2002. In response to these allegations, the UN has taken measures to track, respond
    to, and prevent further sexual violence by UN workers. See, for example, UN General
    Assembly, Resolution 57/306, May 22, 2003, http://www.un.org/en/ga/search/view_doc.
    asp?symbol=A/RES/57/306&Lang=E; Secretary-General's Bulletin, "Special Measures for
    Protection from Sexual Exploitation and Sexual Abuse," UN document ST/SGB/2003/13,
    October   9,   2003,   http://www.pseataskforce.org/uploads/tools/1327932869.pdf.   In
    response, Secretary-General Kofi Annan reported annually on the number of allegations
    of sexual violence by UN humanitarian workers and peacekeepers and the status of the
    investigations. See, as an example, the report of 2005 in which 340 new allegations of sex-
    ual abuse by peacekeepers were reported: UN Report of the Secretary-General, "Special
    Measures for Protection from Sexual Exploitation and Sexual Abuse," UN document
    A/60/861, May 24, 2006, http://daccess-dds-ny.un.org/doc/UNDOC/GEN/N06/360/40/
    PDF/N0636040.pdf?OpenElement.

23. Christine Moser and Fiona Clark, eds., *Victims, Perpetrators, or Actors?: Gender, Armed
    Conflict, and Political Violence* (London: Zed Books, 2001); Manchanda, *Women, War and
    Peace in South Asia*; Rehn and Sirleaf, *Women, War, and Peace*.

24. Kuehnast et al., *Women and War*, 95–96. See also Patricia Lawrence, "The Watch of Tamil
    Women: Women's Acts in a Transitional Warscape," in *Women and the Contested State*,
    ed. Monique Skidmore and Patricia Lawrence (South Bend, IN: Notre Dame University
    Press, 2007), 89–116; and Sheila Meintjes, "War and Post-War Shifts in Gender Relations,"
    in Meintjes et al., *The Aftermath*, 63–77.

25. The World Bank, World Development Indicators 2008, http://data.worldbank.org/
    data-catalog/world-development-indicators/wdi-2008.

26. Sanam Anderlini, *Women Building Peace: What They Do, Why It Matters* (Boulder,
    CO: Lynne Rienner Publishers, 2007).

27. Meredeth Turshen, "Engendering Relations of State to Society in the Aftermath," in
    Meintjes et al., *The Aftermath*, 84.

28. Meintjes et al., "There Is No Aftermath for Women," in *The Aftermath*, 8–15; Krishna,
    Women and Civil Wars, 23.

29. For example, during World War II, the typical symbol of women in the United States was
    the strong and independent Rosie the Riveter, who stepped up to keep the country func-
    tioning while men fought overseas, taking on jobs in the public sphere. Following the end
    of the war, 1950s America's iconic woman was Joan Cleaver, the housewife who personi-
    fied women's traditional domestic roles.

30. UNIFEM, "Women's Participation in Peace Negotiations: Connections between Presence and Influence," August 2010, http://peacemaker.un.org/sites/peacemaker.un.org/files/WomensParticipationInPeaceNegotiations_UNIFEM2010.pdf.

31. Manchanda, *Women, War, and Peace in South Asia*.

32. UN Security Council, Resolution 1325, October 31, 2000, http://daccess-dds-ny.un.org/doc/UNDOC/GEN/N00/720/18/PDF/N0072018.pdf?OpenElement.

33. For example, Meintjes, Pillay, and Turshen ask, "What is the role of religious institutions in the process of reconstruction?" and answer their question by offering examples of how (male) religious leaders have curtailed women's rights. They go on to describe how clergy are "agents of socialization. . . who legitimize the oppression of women." "There Is No Aftermath for Women,", 15, 40. Meanwhile, Rita Manchanda points out that in the Kashmiri conflict men who felt "emasculated by a powerful armed enemy" responded to the shift in gender roles brought about by the emergence of women-headed households by reasserting their control over women through a campaign to veil Muslim women. Manchanda also points out that many women activists joined this campaign, which often put them at odds with urban, elite, and more secular-oriented women activists. "Women in the Kashmiri Conflict," in *Women, War and Peace in South Asia*, 45.

34. Lawrence and Skidmore, *Women and the Contested State*, 4.

35. Ann Jordan, "Women and Conflict Transformation: Influences, Roles, and Experiences," in *Development, Women, and War: Feminist Perspectives*, ed. Haleh Afshar and Deborah Eade (Oxford: Oxfam GB, 2004), 133–151.

36. Right Livelihood Award Foundation, "2007 Laureates: Dekha Ibrahim Abdi (Kenya)," http://rightlivelihood.org/abdi.html.

37. Ayse Kadayifci-Orellana and Meena Sharify-Funk, "Muslim Women Peacemakers as Agents of Change," in *Crescent and Dove: Peace and Conflict Resolution in Islam*, ed. Qamar-ul Huda (Washington, DC: US Institute of Peace Press, 2010), 179–204; "A Discussion with Dekha Ibrahim," Berkley Center for Religion, Peace, and World Affairs, http://berkleycenter.georgetown.edu/interviews/a-discussion-with-dekha-ibrahim-founder-wajir-peace-and-development-committee-kenya.

38. Dena Merriam, "Creating Peaceful and Sustainable Communities through the Spiritual Empowerment of Women" (paper submitted for the Women, Religion, Conflict, and Peace Initiative, US Institute of Peace and the Berkley Center for Religion, Peace, and World Affairs, Georgetown University, Washington, DC, January 2012). For more, visit Sathira Dhammasathan's website: http://www.sathira-dhammasathan.org/. Mae Chee's biography on the Global Peace Initiative of Women website can be found at http://www.gpiw.org/MaeCheeSansanee.html.

39. Maryann Cusimano Love, "Catholic Women Building Peace: Invisibility, Ideas, and Institutions Expand Participation" (paper submitted for the Women, Religion, Conflict, and Peace Initiative, US Institute of Peace and the Berkley Center for Religion, Peace, and World Affairs, Georgetown University, Washington, DC, January 2012).

40. Hertog, *The Complex Reality of Religious Peacebuilding*.

41. "A Common Word," http://www.acommonword.com.

42. Susan Hayward and Lucy Kurtzer-Ellenbogen, "Religion: Inter- and Intrafaith Dialogue," in *Facilitating Dialogue*, ed. David Smock and Dan Serwer (Washington, DC: US Institute of Peace Press, 2012), 67–89.

43. Marshall et al., *Women in Religious Peacebuilding*.

44. Bielefeldt, statement before the 66th Session of the UN General Assembly, New York, October 20, 2011.

45. Interview with author. Colombo, Sri Lanka. October 2011.

46. Religions for Peace website, http://www.religionsforpeace.org/initiatives/women/.

47. "A Discussion with Dena Merriam," Berkley Center for Religion, Peace, and World Affairs, April 7, 2010, http://berkleycenter.georgetown.edu/interviews/a-discussion-with-dena-m erriam-global-peace-initiative-of-women.

48. "A Discussion with Mohammed Abu-Nimer," Berkley Center for Religion, Peace, and World Affairs, June 13, 2010, http://berkleycenter.georgetown.edu/intervi ews/a-discussion-with-mohammed-abu-nimer-professor-school-of-internati onal-service-american-university.

49. Cynthia Sampson, "Religion and Peacebuilding," in *Peacemaking in International Conflict: Methods and Techniques*, ed. William Zartman and L. Rasmussen (Washington, DC: US Institute of Peace Press, 1997), 273–326.

50. El-Bushra, "Feminism, Gender, and Women's Peace Activism," *Development and Change* 38, no. 1 (2007): 139.

51. Cockburn, *The Space Between Us*, 15.

52. Cockburn, *The Space Between Us,* 216.

53. Manchanda, *Women, War, and Peace in South Asia.* Many of these organizations and movements, perhaps epitomized by the Mothers of the Disappeared in Argentina, seek to assert their authority by leveraging their gender roles, particularly as mothers, taking their private grieving into the public sphere and attempting to shame mostly male leadership. These efforts have been criticized by some Western feminists as reinforcing gender roles. As described by Judy El-Bushra: "The problem is that women's role as mothers provides them with a platform on which to approach and appeal to powerful men, but it simultaneously undermines their desire to be taken seriously as political players," "Feminism, Gender and Women's Peace Activism,",140. See also Louise Vincent, "Engendering Peace in Africa: A Critical Inquiry into Some Current Thinking on the Role of African Women in Peacebuilding," *African Journal in Conflict Resolution* 2, no. 1 (2001) 9–20.

54. Gboweh, *Mighty Be Our Powers*, 69.

55. Gboweh, *Mighty Be Our Powers*, 124–126.

56. Gboweh, *Mighty Be Our Powers*, 137.

57. Marshall et al., "Women in Religious Peacebuilding," 8; Jordan, "Women and Conflict Transformation," 139.

58. Diane D'Souza, "Creating Spaces: Interreligious Initiatives for Peace," in Coward and Smith, *Religion and Peacebuilding*, 172.

59. Charlesworth, "Are Women Peaceful?" 352–353.

60. Mina Roces, "The Militant Nun as Political Activist and Feminist in Martial Law Philippines," in *Women, Activism, and Social Change*, ed. Maja Mikula (London: United Kingdom: Routledge, 2008), 136–156.

61. Nadine Naber, "Women and the Arab Spring: Human Rights from the Ground Up," *II Journal* (Fall 2011), 11.

62. Note that this discontent with the shah's secular nationalist regime did not necessarily translate into support for the particular brand of Islamic theocracy that became the basis for rule in Iran.

63. Monica Maher, "Women Peacebuilders in Post-Coup Honduras: Their Spiritual Struggle to Transform Multiple Forms of Violence" (paper prepared for Women, Religion, Conflict and Peace Initiative, US Institute of Peace and the Berkley Center for Religion, Peace, and World Affairs, Georgetown University, Washington, DC, January 2012).

64. Gbowee, *Mighty Be Our Powers*, 81.

65. Emiko Noma, *Born in the Borderlands, Living for Unity: The Story of a Peacebuilder in Northern Uganda* (San Diego: Joan B. Kroc Institute for Peace and Justice, 2005).

66. Kadayifci-Orellana and Sharify-Funk, "Muslim Women Peacemakers," 196.

67. Marshall et al., "Women in Religious Peacebuilding," 17.

68. "A Discussion with Andrea Blanch," Berkley Center for Religion, Peace, and World Affairs, June 13, 2010, http://berkleycenter.georgetown.edu/interviews/a-discussion-with-andre a-blanch-president-center-for-religious-tolerance.

69. Ayse Kadayfici-Orellana, "Muslim Women's Peace Building Initiatives" (paper prepared for Women, Religion, Conflict and Peace Initiative, U.S. Institute of Peace and the Berkley Center for Religion, Peace, and World Affairs, Georgetown University, Washington, DC, January 2012).

70. John Paul Lederach and R. Scott Appleby, "Strategic Peacebuilding: An Overview," in *Strategies of Peace*, ed. Daniel Philpott and Gerard F. Powers (New York: Oxford University Press, 2010), 23–24. This comprehensive definition of peace as being more than the absence of violent conflict corresponds as well to an earlier description by Johan Galtung of positive peace, constituting an environment conducive to human flourishing in which people have collaborative and supportive relationships, and in which there is a lack of what he called structural and cultural violence: the suffering caused by economic and political structures of exploitation and repression, and the aspects of culture, including religion and ideology, used to legitimize violence. See Galtung, "Peace by Peaceful Means: Peace and Conflict, Development and Civilisation" (Oslo: Peace Research Institute of Oslo, 1996).

71. Cockburn, *The Space Between Us*, 8.

72. As shared with the author in interviews and conversations.

73. Emma Tomalin, ed., *Gender, Faith, and Development* (Warwickshire, UK: Practical Action Publishing, 2011), 5.

74. For examples from Buddhism, Christianity, and Islam, see R. M. Gross, *Buddhism After Patriarchy: A Feminist History, Analysis, and Reconstruction of Buddhism* (Albany: State University of New York Press, 1993); Elisabeth Schussler Fiorenza, *In Memory of Her: A Feminist Theological Reconstruction of Christian Origins* (New York: Crossroad, 1994) and *Rhetoric and Ethic: The Politics of Biblical Studies* (Minneapolis: Fortress Press, 1999); Amina Waded, *Qur'an and Women: Rereading the Sacred Text from a Woman's Perspective* (New York: Oxford University Press, 1999).

75. Tomalin, *Gender, Faith, and Development*, 4–6.

76. Salime, *Between Feminism and Islam*, 124. In the 2011 documentary *The Light in Her Eyes* (http://thelightinhereyesmovie.com/), Syrian Houda al-Habash asks her young female students: "Does the shariah say you cannot be president? No, it doesn't."

77. Andrea Blanch, "Women Reborn: A Case Study of the Intersection of Women, Religion and Peace Building in a Palestinian Village in Israel" (paper prepared for Women, Religion, Conflict and Peace Initiative, US Institute of Peace and Berkley Center for Religion, Peace, and World Affairs, Washington, DC, January 2012).

78. Monica Maher, "The Truth Will Set Us Free: Religion, Violence, and Women's Empowerment in Latin America," in *Global Empowerment of Women: Responses to Globalization and Politicized Religion*, ed. C. M. Elliott (London: Routledge, 2007), 265–284.

79. Saba Mahmood, *The Politics of Piety: The Islamic Revival and the Feminist Subject* (Princeton, NJ: Princeton University Press, 2005).

80. Krishna Kumar, ed., *Women and Civil War: Impact, Organization, and Action* (Boulder, CO: Lynne Rienner Publishers, 2001).
81. Sara Miller Llana, "In Colombia, Women Use New Faith to Gain Equality," *Christian Science Monitor*, December 19, 2007.
82. Meintjes, Turshen, and Pillay, *The Aftermath*.
83. Gueskens et al., "(Inter)faith-Based Peacebuilding," 3.
84. Marshall et al., "Women in Religious Peacebuilding."
85. Lederach and Appleby, "Strategic Peacebuilding."
86. Marshall et al., "Women in Religious Peacebuilding."
87. Kuehnast et al., *Women and War*, 4.
88. R. Baksh-Sodeen, ed., *Gender Mainstreaming in Conflict Transformation* (London: Commonwealth Secretariat, 2005).
89. This reflects recommendations made by Elaine Zuckerman and Marcia Greenburg for a rights-based approach to post-conflict reconstruction work. See E. Zuckerman and M. Greenburg, "The Gender Dimensions of Post-Conflict Reconstruction: An Analytical Framework for Policymakers," *Gender and Development* 12, no. 3 (2004): 70–82.
90. See Fatima Adamu, "A Double-Edged Sword: Challenging Women's Oppression within Muslim Society in Northern Nigeria," in Tomalin, *Gender, Faith, and Development*, 97–104.
91. Tomalin, *Gender, Faith, and Development*.

BIBLIOGRAPHY

Abu-Nimer, Mohammed. *Nonviolence and Peace Building in Islam*. Gainesville: University Press of Florida, 2003.
Afshar, Haleh, and Deborah Eade, eds. *Development, Women, and War: Feminist Perspectives*. Oxford: Oxfam GB, 2004.
Albright, Madeleine. *The Mighty and the Almighty: Reflections on America, God, and World Affairs*. New York: HarperCollins, 2006.
Amor, Abdelfattah. Special Rappatouer. "Civil and Political Rights, Including the Question of Religious Intolerance." United Nations Economic and Social Council. Commission on Human Rights. April 24, 2009.
Anderlini, Sanam. *Women Building Peace: What They Do, Why It Matters*. Boulder, CO: Lynne Rienner Publishers, 2007.
Baksh-Sodeen, R., ed. *Gender Mainstreaming in Conflict Transformation*. London: Commonwealth Secretariat, 2005.
Bielefeldt, Heiner. Special Rapporteur on Freedom of Religion or Belief. Statement before the 66th Session of the UN General Assembly. New York. October 20, 2011.
Blanch, Andrea. "Women Reborn: A Case Study of the Intersection of Women, Religion and Peace Building in a Palestinian Village in Israel." Paper prepared for Women, Religion, Conflict and Peace Initiative, US Institute of Peace and the Berkley Center for Religion, Peace, and World Affairs, Georgetown University, Washington, DC, January 2012.
Berdal, Mats and David M. Malone. *Greed and Grievance: Economic Agendas and Civil War*. Boulder, CO: Lynne Rienner Publishers, 2000.
Bloom, Mia. *Bombshell: The Many Faces of Women Terrorists*. Toronto: Penguin, 2011.

Bouta, Tsjeard S., Ayse Kadayifci-Orellana, and Mohammed Abu-Nimer. "Faith-Based Peace-Building. Mapping and Analysis of Christian, Muslim and Multi-Faith Actors." The Hague: Netherlands Institute for International Relations 'Clingendael,' 2005.

Braybrooke, Marcus. *Pilgrimage of Hope: One Hundred Years of Global Interfaith Dialogue.* New York: Crossroad, 1992.

Caiazza, Amy. *The Ties That Bind: Women's Public Vision for Politics, Religion, and Civil Society.* Washington, DC: Institute for Women's Policy Research, 2005.

Charlesworth, Hilary. "Are Women Peaceful?: Reflections on the Role of Women in Peacebuilding." *Feminist Legal Studies* 16, no. 3 (2008): 347–361.

Cockburn, Cynthia. *The Space Between Us: Negotiating Gender and National Identities in Conflict.* New York: Zed Books, 1998.

Coward, Harold and Gordon S. Smith, eds. *Religion and Peacebuilding.* New York: State University of New York Press, 2002.

Cusimano Love, Maryann. "Catholic Women Building Peace: Invisibility, Ideas, and Institutions Expand Participation." Paper submitted for the Women, Religion, Conflict, and Peace Initiative, US Institute of Peace and the Berkley Center for Religion, Peace, and World Affairs, Georgetown University, Washington, DC, January 2012.

El-Bushra, Judy. "Feminism, Gender and Women's Peace Activism." *Development and Change* 38, no. 1 (2007): 131–147.

Elliott, C. M., ed. *Global Empowerment of Women: Responses to Globalization and Politicized Religion.* London: Routledge, 2007.

Elshtain, Jean. *Women and War.* Chicago: University of Chicago Press, 1995.

Ferris, Elizabeth. *Women, War and Peace. Research Report 14.* Uppsala: Life and Peace Institute, 1993.

Fukuyama, Francis. "Women and the Evolution of World Politics." *Foreign Affairs* 77, no. 5 (1998): 24–40.

Galtung, Johan. *"Peace by Peaceful Means: Peace and Conflict, Development and Civilisation."* Oslo: Peace Research Institute of Oslo, 1996.

Gbowee, Leymah. *Mighty Be Our Powers: How Sisterhood, Prayer, and Sex Changed a Nation at War.* New York: Beast Books, 2011.

Gross, R. M. *Buddhism After Patriarchy: A Feminist History, Analysis, and Reconstruction of Buddhism.* Albany: State University of New York Press, 1993.

Gross, R. M. *Feminism and Religion: An Introduction.* Boston: Beacon Press, 1996.

Gueskens, Isabelle, Merle Gosewinkel, and Jose de Vries, eds. *"(Inter)faith-Based Peacebuilding: The Need for a Gender Perspective."* The Hague: International Fellowship on Reconciliation Women's Peacemakers Program, 2010.

Hertog, Katrien. *The Complex Reality of Religious Peacebuilding.* Lanham, MD: Lexington Books, 2010.

Hayward, Susan. *"Religion and Peacebuilding: Reflections on Current Challenges and Future Prospects."* Special Report. Washington, DC: US Institute of Peace Press, 2012.

Hayward, Susan, and Lucy Kurtzer-Ellenbogen. "Religion: Inter- and Intrafaith Dialogue." In *Facilitating Dialogue*, edited by David Smock and Dan Serwer, 67–89. Washington, DC: US Institute of Peace Press, 2012.

Jacobs, Susie, Ruth Jacobson, and Jennifer Marchbank. *States of Conflict: Gender, Violence, and Resistance.* New York: Zed Books, 2000.

Jafari, Sheherazade. "Local Religious Peacemakers: An Untapped Resource in U.S. Foreign Policy." *Journal of International Affairs* 61, no. 1 (2007): 111–130.

Johnston, Douglas, ed. *Faith-Based Diplomacy: Trumping Realpolitik*. New York: Oxford University Press, 2003.

Kadafiyci, Ayse. "Muslim Women Peacemakers." In *Crescent and Dove: Islam and Conflict Resolution*, edited by Qamar-ul Huda, 179–204. Washington, DC: US Institute of Peace Press, 2010.

Kadafiyci, Ayse. "Muslim Women's Peace Building Initiatives." Paper prepared for Women, Religion, Conflict and Peace Initiative, US Institute of Peace and the Berkley Center for Religion, Peace, and World Affairs, Georgetown University, Washington, DC, January 2012.

Kaldor, Mary. *New and Old Wars: Organized Violence in a Global Era*. Cambridge: Polity Press, 1999.

Karam, Azza. "Women in War and Peacebuilding: The Roads Traversed, the Challenges Ahead." *International Feminist Journal of Politics* 3, no. 1 (2001): 2–25.

Kuehnast, Kathleen, C. de Jonge Oudraat, and H. Hernes, eds. *Women and War: Power and Protection in the 21st Century*. Washington, DC: US Institute of Peace Press, 2011.

Kumar, Krishna, ed. *Women and Civil War: Impact, Organization, and Action*. Boulder, CO: Lynne Rienner Publishers, 2001.

Lawrence, Patricia, and Monique Skidmore, eds. *Women and the Contested State: Religion, Violence, and Agency in South and Southeast Asia*. Notre Dame, IN: University of Notre Dame Press, 2007.

Little, David, ed., with the Tanenbaum Center for Interreligious Understanding. *Peacemakers in Action: Profiles of Religion in Conflict Resolution*. New York: Cambridge University Press, 2007.

Llana, Sara Miller. "In Colombia, Women Use New Faith to Gain Equality." *Christian Science Monitor*, December 19, 2007.

Maher, Monica. "The Truth Will Set Us Free: Religion, Violence, and Women's Empowerment in Latin America." In *Global Empowerment of Women: Responses to Globalization and Politicized Religion*, edited by C. M. Elliott, 265–284. London: Routledge, 2007.

Maher, Monica. "Women Peacebuilders in Post-Coup Honduras: Their Spiritual Struggle to Transform Multiple Forms of Violence." Paper prepared for Women, Religion, Conflict and Peace Initiative, US Institute of Peace and the Berkley Center for Religion, Peace, and World Affairs, Georgetown University, Washington, DC, January 2012.

Mahmood, Saba. *The Politics of Piety: The Islamic Revival and the Feminist Subject*. Princeton, NJ: Princeton University Press, 2005.

Manchanda, Rita, ed. *Women, War, and Peace in South Asia: Beyond Victimhood to Agency*. New Delhi: Sage Publications, 2001.

Machel, Graça. "Impact of Armed Conflict on Children: Report of the Expert of the Secretary-General." UN document A/51/306. New York: United Nations and UNICEF, 1996.

Marshall, Katherine, and Susan Hayward, with Claudia Zambra, Esther Breger, and Sarah Jackson. "Women in Religious Peacebuilding." Special issue, *PeaceWorks*, no. 71 (May 2011).

Meintjes, Sheila, Anu Pillay, and Meredeth Turshen. *The Aftermath: Women in Post-Conflict Transformation*. New York: Zed Books, 2001.

Merriam, Dena. "Creating Peaceful and Sustainable Communities through the Spiritual Empowerment of Women." Paper submitted for the Women, Religion, Conflict, and Peace Initiative, US Institute of Peace and the Berkley Center for Religion, Peace, and World Affairs, Georgetown University, Washington, DC, January 2012.

Mikula, Maja, ed. *Women, Activism and Social Change*. London: Routledge, 2008.

Moser, Christine, and Fiona Clark, eds. *Victims, Perpetrators, or Actors?: Gender, Armed Conflict, and Political Violence*. London: Zed Books, 2001.

Naber, Nadine. "Women and the Arab Spring: Human Rights from the Ground Up." *II Journal* (Fall 2011): 11–13.

Noma, Emiko. *Born in the Borderlands, Living for Unity: The Story of a Peacebuilder in Northern Uganda*. San Diego: Joan B. Kroc Institute for Peace and Justice, 2005.

Peterson, V. Spike. "The Gender of Rhetoric, Reason and Realism." In *Post Realism: The Rhetorical Turn in International Relations*, edited by Francis A. Beer and Robert Hariman, 257–276. East Lansing, MI: Michigan State University Press, 1996.

Razavi, Shahra and Anne Jenichen. "The Unhappy Marriage of Religion and Politics: Problems and Pitfalls for Gender Equality." *Third World Quarterly* 31, no. 6 (2010): 833–850.

Rehn, Elisabeth and Ellen Johnson Sirleaf. *Women, War and Peace: The Independent Experts' Assessment on the Impact of Armed Conflict on Women and Women's Role in Peacebuilding*. New York: United Nations Development Fund for Women, 2002.

Rogers, Mark, Tom Bamat, and Julie Ideh, eds. *Pursuing Just Peace: An Overview and Case Studies for Faith-Based Peacebuilders*. Baltimore: Catholic Relief Services, 2008.

Salime, Zakia. *Between Feminism and Islam: Human Rights and Sharia Law in Morocco*. Minneapolis: University of Minnesota Press, 2011.

Sampson, Cynthia. "Religion and Peace Building." In *Peacemaking in International Conflict: Methods and Techniques*, edited by William Zartman and L. Rasmussen, 273–326. Washington, DC: US Institute of Peace Press, 1997.

Schussler Fiorenza, Elisabeth. *In Memory of Her: A Feminist Theological Reconstruction of Christian Origins*. New York: Crossroad, 1994.

Schussler Fiorenza, Elisabeth. *Rhetoric and Ethic: The Politics of Biblical Studies*. Minneapolis, MN: Fortress Press, 1999.

Smock, David, ed. *Interfaith Dialogue and Peacemaking*. Washington, DC: US Institute of Peace Press, 2002.

Smock, David, ed. "Religious Contributions to Peacemaking: When Religion Brings Peace Not War." Special issue, *Peaceworks*, no. 55 (January 2006).

Tomalin, Emma, ed. *Gender, Faith, and Development*. Warwickshire, UK: Practical Action Publishing, 2011.

Vincent, Louise. "Engendering Peace in Africa: A Critical Inquiry into Some Current Thinking on the Role of African Women in Peacebuilding." *African Journal in Conflict Resolution* 2, no. 1 (2001): 9–20.

Wadud, Amina. *Qur'an and Woman: Rereading the Sacred Text from a Woman's Perspective*. New York: Oxford University Press, 1999.

World Bank. "*World Development Report 2011: Conflict, Security, and Development*." Washington, DC: The World Bank, 2011. http://wdr2011.worldbank.org/sites/default/files/pdfs/WDR2011_Full_Text.pdf.

Zuckerman, E., and M. Greenburg. "The Gender Dimensions of Post-Conflict Reconstruction: An Analytical Framework for Policymakers." *Gender and Development* 12, no. 3 (2004): 70–82.

PART FOUR

PEACEBUILDING IN PRACTICE: STRATEGIES, RESOURCES, CRITIQUE

CHAPTER 13

....

RECONCILIATION, POLITICS, AND TRANSITIONAL JUSTICE

....

DANIEL PHILPOTT

ONE novel trend in global politics over the past generation is the wave of efforts to address the political injustices of past war, genocide, dictatorship, and other large-scale evils, such as abuses of native peoples. Numerous institutions and practices have arisen that previously had little place in global politics. More than forty truth commissions have taken place. Reviving the precedent of the Nuremberg trials, two major international tribunals arose during the 1990s, one for Yugoslavia and one for Rwanda, and were then succeeded by a permanent International Criminal Court. Several countries have held national-level trials. Countries like Rwanda and Timor-Leste have transmuted traditional tribal practices into judicial forums. Apologies by political leaders have become a common practice. In several countries, forgiveness is reported to have taken place widely among populations. Monuments, memorials, commemorations, and civil society initiatives have all multiplied. To describe these doings, the term "transitional justice" has arisen.

During the same period, a separate trend in global politics has developed: the resurgence of religion in global politics.[1] Reversing several centuries of the decline of religion's influence relative to the state's, from the 1960s onward, religious actors have reasserted their influence in the political realm. They played a major role in the global wave of democratization that began in 1974 and continues even today in the Arab Spring. Religious forms of terrorism have emerged. Religion fuels civil wars far more commonly than before. Religious leaders mediate peace agreements. Religion shapes economic development, education, gender relations, and numerous other areas of social and political life around the world in a way that it did not half a century ago.

Having arisen simultaneously and globally, it is only natural that these two trends—resurgent religion and transitional justice—have intersected. Transitional justice is another area of politics that religious actors have shaped. Religious leaders and communities have campaigned for and conducted truth commissions, demanded trials and reparations, called for and practiced forgiveness, promoted reconciliation among enemies, remembered deceased victims, supported living victims, and reflected theologically on addressing past sin in the political sphere.

In responding to past injustices, though, religious leaders and communities have accomplished something wider and more momentous. They have articulated what is arguably a paradigm of peacebuilding and even of justice itself: reconciliation. Reconciliation stands as a globally prominent alternative paradigm, I will argue, to the view of transitional justice and of peacebuilding that dominates the thinking of the international community—the liberal peace.

In this chapter, I seek to articulate reconciliation as an ethic of peacebuilding and demonstrate how it is rooted in religious traditions.[2] I show how the texts and practices of Judaism, Christianity, and Islam support this ethic, though it might well be grounded in other traditions as well. I then apply the ethic to the political sphere and situate it in the context of transitional justice. I will show how it both overlaps and contrasts with the liberal peace. Finally, I will suggest that forgiveness, the practice that most stands in tension with the liberal peace and is most emblematic of religious reconciliation, is a promising avenue for future research in this area.

The Setting of Transitional Justice

Transitional justice became a common term for describing political efforts to deal with the past in the 1990s. Most broadly, the term denotes the subject of how to address past injustices justly. Transitional justice can also refer, however, to a particular approach to justice that is shared by a network of international lawyers, human rights activists, officials in international organizations like the United Nations, and like-minded scholars and journalists—a network that much overlaps with the liberal peace. The standard ingredients of this approach include the rule of law, judicial punishment, vetting, truth and transparency, and restitution for victims, all of these conceived through the language of rights and law.[3]

I gladly use the term transitional justice here but with two clarifications. First, I use the term in the broad, open-ended sense, not as the particular answer to justice shared by the transitional justice network. As I shall argue, reconciliation differs significantly from what the transitional justice network has in mind. Second, I use the word "transitional" with caution. It was adopted because so many of the trials and truth commissions of the 1990s took place just after transitions from dictatorship to democracy. The same practices, though— along with reparations, apologies, memorialization, and so on—sometimes take place years after injustices have occurred and entirely apart from any transition in regime or from war to peace. Consider, for instance, Germany's intense public debate about the Holocaust in the 1980s, accompanied by apology, reparations, and the construction of museums and monuments; or Spain's contested examination of the deeds of the Franco dictatorship in the 2000s; or recent debates about addressing slavery and the maltreatment of native peoples decades earlier in Canada, the United States, Australia, and New Zealand. To exclude these activities from the dimension of peacebuilding that addresses past injustices is arbitrary, even if they are not strictly transitional justice. But if the term transitional justice can be used loosely, expansively, and not always literally, then I am happy to employ it to refer to the setting for the central question at hand: What is the meaning of justice in the wake of massive injustice?

THE LIBERAL PEACE

The globally dominant answer to this question is the liberal peace. It is globally dominant because it pervades the thinking of what is often called the international community—the United Nations, Western governments, and international lawyers and human rights activists. The liberal peace means three things. First, it is a concept of justice. Springing from the Enlightenment, its unifying ideas are individual rights and liberties, equality, and the rule of law.

Second, the liberal peace is a set of contemporary actors and institutions that have adopted this conception of justice and promoted it in peacebuilding—essentially, the international community. The "magisterium" of the UN—the secretary-general and other leading officials in the permanent bureaucracy—is the most important promoter. Western governments have also been guided by the liberal peace in their own peacebuilding operations, as the United States has been in Bosnia, Iraq, and Afghanistan. The liberal peace can be found in the reports of Amnesty International and Human Rights Watch and is prominent in the International Center for Transitional Justice, the most prominent NGO dedicated to transitional justice.

Third, the liberal peace is the set of activities that these actors carry out: establishing the rule of law, human rights, and free markets; carrying out elections; and implementing the range of measures that promote relief and settlement at the end of armed conflict. Pride of place, though, belongs to international judicial punishment, which advocates of the liberal peace tout as the alternative to a culture of impunity. *Nunca más!* they cry. The International Criminal Court is their signature accomplishment.

Because of the prestige of the liberal peace, sociologist Jonathan VanAntwerpen calls it the global "orthodoxy" of peacebuilding.[4]

THE HETERODOXY OF RECONCILIATION

By contrast, VanAntwerpen calls reconciliation the global "heterodoxy" of peacebuilding, meaning that it is espoused widely and prominently enough to constitute an alternative paradigm—though it is still a challenger—to the liberal peace. It is predominantly the religious who have introduced the heterodoxy of reconciliation to the world. Not exclusively: there are secular proponents of reconciliation, just as there are religious proponents of alternative approaches to the past. There exists, though, a strong "elective affinity," to use Max Weber's term, between the religious and reconciliation.

Although no definitive story has been told about how the religious brought reconciliation into global politics, some scholars have pointed to strands of a genealogy. In Christian theology, reconciliation is axial: It is what God did and does for humanity. But it was not until the late nineteenth and early twentieth centuries, as theologian John de Gruchy describes, that Christian theologians applied reconciliation to modern political orders—theologians as different as liberal Protestant Albrecht Ritschl and more orthodox Protestants like Karl Barth and Dietrich Bonhoeffer.[5] Bringing reconciliation more directly into politics, argues scholar Erik Doxtader, were theologians and religious leaders in the struggle against the apartheid government of South Africa from the 1960s onward.[6] It was they who laid the groundwork for Archbishop Desmond Tutu to bestow global prominence on reconciliation through his famous performance in South Africa's Truth and Reconciliation Commission in the mid-1990s. A Catholic genealogy can be traced as well. During the era of Barth, Pope Benedict XV urged reconciliation and forgiveness upon European nations after World War One.[7] During the era of Tutu, Pope John Paul II advocated reconciliation and forgiveness in politics (as well as in the Church's own history) and, like Tutu, lent global fame to these ideas.[8]

Meanwhile, theologians, clerics, and religiously motivated politicians who are foot soldiers by comparison have promoted reconciliation in more local contexts. Theologians and religious scholars like Miroslav Volf, Donald Shriver, Rabbi Marc Gopin, Emmanuel Katongole, and Mohammed Abu-Nimer have theorized reconciliation as a theologically grounded and politically relevant concept.[9] Religious leaders and activists have brought reconciliation into politics on the ground over the past generation in Chile, Brazil, Guatemala, El Salvador, Timor-Leste, Germany, Iraq, Afghanistan, Morocco, Sierra Leone, Poland, Northern Ireland, Bosnia, the Czech Republic, South Africa, and other countries.[10] They have promoted and helped to conduct truth commissions, for instance, as they did in South Africa, of whose commission Tutu was the chair. In most of these cases, they framed their support of truth commissions in the language of reconciliation. The very strongest case of this was the Guatemalan Catholic Church's formation and conduct of the Recovery of Historical Memory Project (REMHI) under the leadership of Bishop Juan Gerardi. Notable for its "personalism," REMHI trained and sent out eight hundred "animadores," or agents of reconciliation, to rural villages where they took the testimony of victims and provided them with emotional, spiritual, and psychological support. Two days after Gerardi presented REMHI's report in Guatemala City's Metropolitan Cathedral in April 1998, thugs under the command of Guatemala's military bludgeoned him to death in his garage.[11]

In other ways, too, religious leaders and groups have promoted reconciliation. Muslim and Christian clerics in Nigeria have sought to increase peace among their followers through public forums in which they quote from the other faith's scriptures.[12] In 2002 in Israel and Palestine, Muslim, Christian, and Jewish leaders forged a common document, the Alexandria Declaration, that called for the cessation of violence and of demonization among faiths.[13] In the aftermath of the Khmer Rouge genocide in Cambodia, Buddhist leader Samdech Preah Maha Ghosananda created a popular movement for compassion and forgiveness rooted in the traditional teaching and practice of Buddhism.[14] Perhaps the most accomplished faith-based peacemaker is the Community of Sant'Egidio, a Catholic lay association that, in 1992, mediated an end to a civil war in Mozambique and consequently has been called upon to mediate conflicts in Kosovo, Algeria, Guatemala, Uganda, Burundi, and Liberia.[15]

Along with the caveat that it is not only the religious who promote reconciliation belongs the caveat that the religious do not always promote reconciliation. Many religious leaders and groups have had little influence on the politics of past injustices or even have collaborated with dictators or armed factions. In Argentina, for instance, the bishops of the Catholic Church mostly (but not unanimously) supported that country's military dictatorship during the Dirty Wars of 1976 to 1983. As a result, the Catholic Church had little role in shaping the truth commission that looked back on the crimes of this conflict. In 1995 the bishops issued an apology, but a muted one. Similarly, in Rwanda, major Christian churches, including the Catholic and Anglican Churches, were so closely linked with the Hutu government that they could offer little resistance to the genocide of 1994. In the aftermath these churches had little influence on national decisions about how to address the crimes of the genocide, though they did play a constructive role at the village level. Stories of churches that were weakened in their influence on the politics of the past, whether on behalf of reconciliation or any other ideal, can also be told in the Czech Republic, Hungary, Estonia, Latvia, Cameroon, Uganda, Uruguay, Bulgaria, Romania, Greece, Ukraine, and Russia. That not all of the religious promote reconciliation, though, does not detract from the role that those who do promote reconciliation have played in giving it the status of heterodoxy in the global politics of peacebuilding.

RECONCILIATION AS A CONCEPT OF JUSTICE

If reconciliation has spread widely in global politics and if religious people have done much to spread it, just what does it mean as a concept of peacebuilding? And how does it differ from the liberal peace? In its numerous deployments across the globe, in scholarship and practice alike, reconciliation has taken on multiple meanings, many of them differing with respect to how they treat reconciliation in relationship to justice. Here, I wish to develop one of these meanings that I find particularly distinctive and promising. It is found in Judaism, Christianity, and Islam and resonates with secular articulations of restorative justice, many tribal traditions around the world, as well as "relational theories" of justice, espoused especially by Western feminists.[16]

In this version, reconciliation is itself a concept of justice. This will grate on Western listeners, for whom justice is a matter of rights, entitlements, and deserved punishment, not reconciliation. But in the three religious traditions at hand, justice means the comprehensive set of obligations that define right relationship in all spheres of life. Like all notions of justice, justice in these traditions has two valences: right conduct and right response to wrong conduct. Justice is both holistic right relationship and the restoration of right relationship after an injustice has ruptured it. Crucial for the present argument, reconciliation is also defined in terms of right relationship. Reconciliation is the restoration of relationship that wrongs have ruptured; when it is achieved, what results is a state of being reconciled, where right relationship is observed. In these traditions, then, reconciliation and justice carry virtually the same meaning, allowing us to say that reconciliation is a concept of justice.

The texts of each of these three faith traditions bear out this claim. In the Hebrew scriptures, the word "justice" is translated from the same words that translate to "righteousness"—*sedeq* (or, in its feminine form, *sedeqah*) and *mishpat*. Especially in the case of *sedeq*, righteousness is comprehensive, connoting the duties and obligations that pertain to all spheres of life as set forth by God's covenants. The concept of righteousness is not only a set of norms governing how Israel ought to live but also describes God's restoration of the world after evil has broken it apart. Since comprehensive righteousness (as a state and as restoration) is none other than the right relationship that is reconciliation (again as state and as restoration), the Hebrew scriptures support the notion that reconciliation is a concept of justice.

The same notion resurfaces in the New Testament. Here, reconciliation is central and explicit. In most translations of the New Testament, the word "reconciling" or "reconcile" appears some fifteen times, twelve of them in the letters of the Apostle Paul. Reconciliation describes God's exchanging places with humanity, taking sin upon himself, and restoring humanity to right relationship with God and with one another. In the New Testament can also be found the close relationship of justice and righteousness. Here, several Greek words beginning with the *dik-* stem (perhaps most prominently *dikaiosunē*) are the same words that translate *sedeq* and *mishpat* in the Greek version of the Old Testament and thus carry forth the close relationship of justice and righteousness found in these words. In Paul's concept of justification, justice describes the atoning work of Christ, through which Christ restores the world to right relationship, that is, reconciles it.[17]

In the Arabic of the Qur'an, the words that translate into justice do not translate so readily into righteousness as do Hebrew and Greek words in the Bible. Still, justice in the Qur'an, translated most commonly from the words *'adl* and *qist*, arguably approximates comprehensive righteousness, understood both as a state and as a restoration, and is presented as set forth by God.[18] If justice is comprehensive righteousness, then once again, justice is equivalent to reconciliation.

From the scriptures of these three traditions, then, can be derived the proposition that reconciliation is a concept of justice that means comprehensive right relationship. Is this comprehensive justice—right relationship in all spheres of life, including family, business, civil society, and religious life—the business of the modern political order? In my view, no. Here, an adaptation must take place. The state, I argue, properly concerns itself with political reconciliation, a subset of comprehensive reconciliation that is confined to those dimensions of relationship that concern the duties and virtues of citizens within states and of states in their relations with other states in the international system. For the state, justice as right conduct involves respect for human rights, including features of democracy like elections and the rule of law, and core features of international justice like the laws of war. With respect to this valence, there is little difference between reconciliation and the liberal peace. It is in redressing past injustices—the other valence of justice—that reconciliation proves far more distinctive. As I shall describe below, reconciliation seeks to heal the many wounds that political injustices inflict through a wide range of practices that restore persons and relationships.

Reconciliation is not only a concept of justice but also one of peace. Peace corresponds to a state of right relationship or of being reconciled once the wounds of injustice have been redressed. In the Hebrew scriptures, the word for peace is shalom, which connotes right relationship in all spheres of life. *Eirene* is the word that translates shalom into Greek and appears in the New Testament with all of the connotations that shalom carries. The Arabic *salam*, which represents peace in the Qur'an, similarly means a holistic condition of harmony within a community.[19] As with justice, the peace of political reconciliation is narrower than the comprehensive peace of the religious scriptures. Still, though, it is wider and more substantive than the "negative peace" of a mere settlement or even the "positive peace" of liberalism, involving rights, democracy, and the like, for it also entails a condition in which the many wounds of political injustice have been redressed.[20]

Beyond justice and peace, reconciliation also includes the concept of mercy—indeed, that is its animating virtue. Mercy in the ethic of reconciliation is, as Pope John Paul II defined it, "manifested in its true and proper aspect when it restores to value, promotes and draws good from all the forms of evil existing in the world and in man."[21] In the Hebrew scriptures, mercy is denoted by *hesed*, God's willingness to restore his people, and by *rahamim*, connoting the strong love of a mother for her children. In Christianity, mercy is the action through which God restored humanity through Jesus Christ. The Qur'an's *rahma* closely resembles the Hebrew word *rahamim* and carries its connotation of feminine compassion and a constant willingness to restore. If peace is the condition that corresponds to the state of relationship that results from reconciliation, mercy is the virtue that attends the restorative processes through which reconciliation takes place—that is, the aspect of justice that addresses past misconduct. This notion of mercy differs markedly from the modern notion of mercy, which means letting someone "off the hook" from deserved punishment and thus stands in tension with justice. By contrast, the wider, more restorative notion of mercy is compatible with justice, the justice of reconciliation.

It is not only in the concepts of justice, peace, and mercy found in the scriptures of Judaism, Christianity, and Islam that an ethic of reconciliation is supported, but in other aspects of these traditions as well. Each tradition also contains a notion of God's response to evil that involves restoration of right relationship. This is especially pronounced in Christianity, where God's redemptive action is explicitly portrayed as one of reconciliation, but it is echoed in Judaism and Islam as well. On the other hand, Judaism and Islam contain especially strong resources for reconciliation in holistic rituals for repairing wrongs within communities that developed in their post-biblical or post-Qur'anic period. Arabic Islamic tribal cultures, for instance, developed *musalaha*, or reconciliation, rituals that combine truth-telling, reparations, apology, forgiveness, and a ceremony that reintegrates offenders back into the community.[22]

A justice that restores relationship, a peace of being reconciled, a mercy that wills to restore all that is broken—at this point the ethic will strike many as utopian, even if it is understood that political reconciliation is less ambitious than comprehensive reconciliation. That political reconciliation is stated in terms of its full realization, however, makes it no more utopian than are concepts like human rights or economic equality, whose realization in the world falls far short of the achievement of these principles. Reconciliation, even political reconciliation, will always be partially achieved, occurring in pieces and parts, obstructed by the powerful, hindered by damaged institutions and the chaotic aftermath of dictatorship and war, and challenged by the sheer complexity of the practices that it involves. But it is also the case that each of the practices that bring reconciliation into politics that I describe below has taken place in tens of countries around the world, has often achieved partial success, and sometimes has attained even more. Neither full achievement nor complete absence or failure is the fate of the ethic; rather it exists in the broad middle between these extremes.

Reconciliation in Modern Political Orders

The vision of reconciliation—expressed through distinctive concepts of justice, peace, and mercy, that is found in Judaism, Christianity, Islam, and restorative justice as well as in other schools of thought—contrasts with the dominant orthodoxy, the liberal peace. While the core concepts of the liberal peace are rights and the rule of law, at the heart of reconciliation is the more encompassing notion of restoration of right relationship. These core concepts, though, do not specify how they are to be enacted in modern political orders—like Rwanda after the genocide, Germany after the fall of the Berlin Wall, or perhaps the United States or Canada addressing a history of slavery or maltreatment of native peoples. Nevertheless, as I have mentioned, contemporary representatives of the faith traditions as well as the restorative justice school of thought have sought, each in their own way, to apply their notions of reconciliation to modern politic. Here I offer my own effort to theorize this application.

Two further concepts prove pivotal for realizing reconciliation in modern politics: the wounds of injustice, and practices of reconciliation. The sort of justice that entails restoration of relationship addresses the wide range of ways in which political injustices inflict wounds. Political injustice means a violation of human rights or the laws of war. A wound is any diminishment to persons and right relationship that political injustices inflict. There are at least six wounds of political injustice:

1) *The violation of the victim's basic human rights.* This wound, of course, matches the very definition of political injustice. It is identified as a wound because rights involve a respect that is violated when acts of injustice are committed, a form of harm that extends over and beyond other, more palpable harms to the person.

2) *Harm to the person of the victim.* These include death of the victim, death of his or her family and friends, permanent injury, psychological and emotional damage, loss of property and livelihood, grief, humiliation, sexual violation, or the defilement of the victim's race, ethnicity, religion, nationality, or gender.

3) *Ignorance of the source and circumstances of the political injustices.* Evidence from truth commissions and other transitional justice proceedings from around the world reveals that lack of knowledge compounds the harm from the injustice itself. This wound was depicted by the mother of a missing South African political activist when she demanded, "If they can just show us the bones of my child, where did they leave the bones of my child?"[23]

4) *A lack of acknowledgment of the suffering of victims on the part of the surrounding political community (or a separate political community in the case of war between states).* This lack may stem either from ignorance or indifference and deepens the harm to the victims. In failing to acknowldge suffering, the government and surrounding community withhold a recognition of the dignity of persons.

5) *The "standing victory" of the political injustice that the perpetrator committed.* In committing a political injustice, a perpetrator severs right relationship not only with his victim but also with the community whose role it is to recognize and uphold the victim's rights. His injustice continues to "stand over" the victim and against the community. The idea of the standing victory of injustice helps to explain what human rights activists wanted to address when they insisted on the prosecution of General Augusto Pinochet long after he had left office and was infirm and disempowered.

6) *Harm to the person of the wrongdoer.* This wound is rarely stressed by the liberal peace, which focuses on victims, but it is easily recognizable to the three faith traditions and restorative justice and was expressed by thinkers like Plato in the *Gorgias*. Committing evil injures the perpetrator's soul, leaves lasting psychological damage, and often leads to further injustices.

These six wounds are ones that political injustices inflict directly and thus may be called "primary wounds." They also lead to derivative injustices that may be called "secondary wounds."

Secondary wounds result from prior primary wounds through a chain of memories, emotions, and judgments that the primary wounds spark. These judgments may be a decision for revenge or simply a withholding of approval for a new peace settlement or democracy. Collectively experienced secondary wounds can sustain cycles of conflict, as they have in Bosnia, Northern Ireland, the Basque Country, Iraq, South Africa, China, Korea, and Japan.

Following the restorative logic of reconciliation, six practices redress these wounds— though not corresponding with them one-to-one—with the aim of restoring persons and relationships in or between political orders. That the ethic of reconciliation at hand revolves around practices rather than rules reflects the religious traditions' sense of God's response to evil as one of action. Each of the six practices entails a unique sort of restorative action, usually involving a communication, between victims, perpetrators, members of the community at large, and the state. They include: 1) building socially just institutions; 2) acknowledgment; 3) reparations; 4) punishment; 5) apology; and 6) forgiveness. Insofar as each practice increases human flourishing directly, through its very performance, it effects what may be called a primary restoration. Then, parallel to the concept of secondary wounds, primary restorations may then bring about "secondary restorations," which might include an increase in positive evaluations of government institutions or of a peace settlement, in trust in fellow citizens, in commitment to a common national identity, or in willingness to engage in democratic deliberation.

Let us consider each of the six practices in greater depth.

Building Socially Just Institutions

Building socially just institutions is the practice that most converges with the liberal peace. It involves replacing war and dictatorship with institutions based on human rights and the rule of law. Human rights include not only political and civil rights but also social and economic ones, as well as the obligations between states set forth by international human rights agreements and humanitarian law. Since 1974, in what political scientist Samuel P. Huntington called the "third wave of democratization," some ninety societies across the world have striven to replace dictatorships with democracies.[24] Human rights and democratic institutions are also standard elements of civil war settlements.

Building socially just institutions is also a practice of political reconciliation. Human rights, the duties and claims that they involve and the dignity of the person that they honor when they are enshrined by law, are themselves a form of right relationship. Reconciliation is cheap when it proposes a compromise that fails to uphold human rights, a critical dimension of justice. Rights, of course, have been prominent in the liberal tradition and are found in the thought of John Locke, Immanuel Kant, John Stuart Mill, and John Rawls. But they also predate modern liberalism in religious traditions. Rights are found in the Hebrew scriptures and are advocated by contemporary Jewish intellectuals.[25] Christianity, of course, shares Judaism's scriptures and has given rights an important place in its own tradition. Historian Brian Tierney argues that rights can be found in medieval canon law.[26] Later, the Spanish scholastics gave rights explicit expression in their defense of native peoples in the New World. Today, the Catholic Church and virtually every major Protestant church have embraced human rights. In Judaism and Christianity, rights are grounded in the dignity of the person as created in the image of God and in obligations that are grounded in the law of

God and are fulfilling of the person—a far thicker, more relational account of rights than liberal versions, which are rooted in self-preservation. Islam, by contrast, has had a more ambivalent relationship to rights, which are prominent neither in the Qur'an nor in the tradition. Today, rights are widely endorsed by both Muslim scholars and Muslim states, though certain ones remain disputed, especially the rights of women, the right of religious freedom, and claims surrounding certain harsh forms of punishment.

Which rights are truly universal human rights is one of the several controversies that attend the practice of building socially just institutions—and cannot be settled here. Another controversy involves structural economic and gender inequalities. It is not enough, the criticism runs, to restore rights and the rule of law. Justice also requires transforming structures of inequality, which are not only unjust in themselves but potentially spark further conflict if not addressed. Reconciliation that involves a holistic restoration of right relationship hardly can ignore this dimension of relationship, so indeed it would be wrong to omit this dimension of justice. The question of how economic inequality is to be rectified, however, involves much greater complexity and is none other than the central issue in development economics—and another question that cannot be settled here.

Acknowledgment

The wounds that political injustices inflict on victims are compounded when the surrounding community fails to recognize the victim's suffering. The lack of recognition is itself a primary wound but also a source of victims' hostility toward fledgling political orders and thus a secondary wound. Acknowledgment is the action by which a political official or body of officials, speaking on behalf of the political order, recognizes victims as having suffered a political injustice, as having been wounded by this injustice, and as being full citizens again. When other citizens affirm this recognition, acknowledgment is enhanced.

In the past generation's proliferation of peacebuilding activity, acknowledgment has been practiced primarily by truth commissions, more than forty of which have taken place worldwide. Other forms of acknowledgment have appeared as well. A unique one is the German government's decision to make available to victims the files that the Stasi, or East German police, kept on them over decades of Communist rule. Other forms of acknowledgment include memorials, museums, monuments, days of commemoration, and public rituals. In some countries, public school textbooks acknowledge past injustices by teaching children about them and thus attempting to lodge them in public memory.

Unearthing the truth about past injustices has become a standard component of the liberal peace. International lawyers now speak regularly of a "right to truth." In an ethic of reconciliation, though, acknowledgment performs restorations that extend beyond what a right to truth describes. Acknowledgment is a form of solidarity with the suffering that alleviates their condition of isolation. The best forms of acknowledgment are characterized by personalism—direct, empathetic attention to individual victims. The more that public officials and onlookers exercise recognition of the victim, support the victim through any trauma that the exercise of acknowledgment may elicit, assist in the long-term healing of the victim, and encourage the integration of the victim into the community, the more restorative the acknowledgment becomes. One of the best examples of personalism is the REMHI project in Guatemala, mentioned above, in which victims received personal attention and were encouraged to participate in the work of discovering truth. The ability of acknowledgment to heal the wound of social indifference finds expression in Judaism, Christianity, and Islam, which portray a God who hears the cry of the poor and marginalized, comforts them by communicating awareness and love, calls members of the religious community and their leaders to join in this recognition, and connects this acknowledgment to justice. The Book of Job (34: 24–28), for instance, takes to task "mighty men" who cause "the cries of the poor to reach [God]" and describes God as one who has "heard the plea of the afflicted." In the Christian tradition, the justice of acknowledgment is found most strongly in interpretations of Christ's death on the cross as an act of solidarity with forgotten victims.[27] The Catholic Church understands acknowledgment through the concept of solidarity found in its social thought. Pope John Paul II taught that solidarity is exercised when members of a society "recognize one another as persons" and demonstrate awareness of the poor.[28] One can find acknowledgment expressed in Islam through Allah's commands not to forget the poor and the oppressed. In these religions, then, can be found acknowledgment in the wide, restorative sense.

Reparations

Reparations are a material payment to victims of political injustices. Usually it is the government that pays them, though sometimes perpetrators do, too. They may take the form of money, mental and physical health services, and the like. Reparations, too, have become more common in recent years. In the early 1980s, Argentina agreed to a comparatively generous payment to victims of the Dirty Wars. Other countries have followed suit—Chile, for instance, which agreed to make a sizable reparations payment to Pinochet's victims. Far overshadowing any other reparations payments, though, are those that Germany has paid to survivors of the Holocaust over several decades, beginning with the 1952 Luxembourg Agreement, in which the German government pledged three billion Deutschmarks to Israel.[29] Meanwhile, reparations have come to enjoy an important place in international law, finding inclusion in several international conventions. The United Nations' Basic Principles and Guidelines of 2005 stands as a major legal commitment to reparations.

Several rationales for reparations are on offer. They have been justified both on punitive and distributive justice grounds. The liberal tradition offers another rationale for reparations: *restitutio in integrum*. Insofar as it is possible, reparations restore the victim to his condition prior to the injustice. Clearly, "insofar as it is possible" is an important phrase. Both the nature of victims' wounds—not least the loss of life and limb—and a lack of resources will limit the degree to which persons and relationships can be restored. Still, *restitutio in integrum* remains a major rationale for restoration.

Of course, the concept has its dilemmas. How to adjudicate the reparations claims of descendants of victims who are no are no longer alive?[30] How to settle the property claims of those whose possessions were seized by a dictatorial regime or through war, sometimes decades earlier, as in Communist Eastern European states or in states like Burundi and Uganda? How are reparations justly distributed when resources are lacking? All of these dilemmas require making more complex the rationale of *restitutio in integrum*; none of them eviscerates the rationale.[31]

In part, the reconciliation ethic advanced here can incorporate the liberal rationale into its own thinking. It involves an effort to address harms to the person of the victims, one of the six wounds of political injustice. The reconciliation ethic, though, broadens the liberal rationale for reparations. A major justification for reparations resembles the major justification for acknowledgment: They confer recognition on victims, thus addressing the wound of social ignorance. Reparations are acknowledgment fortified materially. Through reparations, the state communicates a message to victims and to the community at large that recognizes the victim's suffering at the hands of the political order, affirms her restored citizenship, and delegitimates the standing victory of the injustice. Often, this communication will require more than merely a financial payment. In the 1990s, a deal for a $5 billion payment from the German government to victims of forced labor and slavery in the Holocaust went through only when the government agreed to offer an accompanying apology and to tell the story of forced labor in school textbooks. Reparations alone, victims would have considered "blood money."[32]

Reparations have a strong place in the religious traditions and in restorative justice. In the Jewish tradition, the Torah prescribed reparations for restoring shalom between injured parties; the Mishnah prescribed compensation for five kinds of harm; while reparations were also essential in rituals of *teshuva*, or repentance.[33] Reparations, performed as an act of penance, also exist in the Christian tradition, though their role has waxed and waned over the centuries. Even today, the *Catechism of the Catholic Church* states, "one must do what is possible in order to repair the harm [of wrongs] (e.g., return stolen goods, restore the reputation of someone slandered, pay compensation for injuries)."[34] The Islamic tradition strikingly allows murderers to pay reparations to their victims' family members as an alternative to the punishment of death, while in *musalaha* rituals, compensation is a crucial step toward reconciliation. Likewise, in restorative justice, reparations, along with apologies, truth-telling, and forgiveness, are a crucial practice in restoring right relationship. In these traditions, reparations are incorporated into a wide, holistic restoration of human flourishing.

Apology

With apology, the fourth practice of reconciliation, the primary responsibility belongs to the perpetrator. In apologizing, he confesses that he committed the wrongful act, recognizes its wrongfulness, voices regret for having done it, expresses this regret to the victim, takes responsibility for his action, and vows not to perform the wrong again. Apologies in the political context, too, have grown more common in the past generation. Aaron Lazare, a psychiatrist who studied political apologies, found that they emerged in the 1990s and sharply increased over the course of this decade.[35] Still, we do well to remember that apologies remain dwarfed by the scale of political injustices.

Who makes apologies in the political realm? Most commonly, heads of state voice them for injustices committed by leaders of past governments. As with reparations, Germany is the global leader in apologies. From Konrad Adenauer on forward, German presidents and chancellors have apologized for Germany's past, perhaps most famously in the case of Chancellor Willy Brandt, who fell to his knees before a memorial to victims of the Nazis in Warsaw in 1971. Many other examples of apologies by heads of state can be found, too—for instance, US President George H. W. Bush's apology to Japanese-Americans, whom the US government interned during World War II.

It is far rarer for leaders who committed political injustices or ordered them to be committed to apologize. But it does sometimes happen. South Africa in its transition away from apartheid is a site where apologies were relatively common (though still rare among officials) and were voiced by the last president of the apartheid government, F. W. de Klerk, by President Nelson Mandela (for crimes committed by the African National Congress), and by other top officials. Even these instances contained complexities, as when de Klerk went on to deny knowledge of crimes committed by members of his government and to renounce responsibility for them.[36] Nor are apologies always successful in their reception. When Japanese leaders apologized in the 1990s for crimes committed during World War II, they were met with a strong nationalist backlash.[37]

Apologies in the political context play little role in the liberal peace. Though a few international law documents mention apology briefly, it is not among the practices for dealing with the past that the international community regularly advocates. By contrast, in the religious traditions that undergird the reconciliation ethic, apology is prominent and understood restoratively. Among the wounds of injustice that political apologies redress, the most important is the standing victory of injustice, which the perpetrator delegitimizes by renouncing his own act. Apology is prominent in the Jewish tradition both in the Bible and in restorative rituals of *teshuva*. Repentance is crucial in Christianity as well, essential in the sinner's reception of God's forgiveness and in the sacrament of reconciliation. In Islam, the Qur'an commends repentance, repeating the term for it eighty-seven times, and repentance is crucial to *musalaha* rituals. Finally, repentance is integral to the theory and practice of restorative justice.

Punishment

Debates about transitional justice all over the world pit punishment against reconciliation. Reconciliation is equated with mercy and forgiveness and is said to promote impunity for human rights violators. But punishment need not be at odds with reconciliation and indeed can be part of practicing it. This requires, though, justifying punishment through a different rationale from liberalism, which, since the Enlightenment, has oscillated between retributivism, which stresses payment, and consequentialism, which stresses the effects of punishment, particularly in terms rehabilitating criminals and deterring crime.

In an ethic of reconciliation, on the other hand, punishment is entirely justified by its restorative function. Restorative punishment does not deny that perpetrators of crimes deserve proportionate punishment; however, its rationale is not balancing payments but restoring persons, relationships, and societies. Punishment restores by redressing the wounds that sever right relationship. Most of all, the wound that punishment addresses is the standing victory of the injustice and the disorder in the soul of the perpetrator. Like the other practices, punishment entails communication performed by the state. Here, it is a message of censure, directed first to the perpetrator for violating the community's just moral standards and then to invite his restoration, and second to the community, whose standards of justice are reinforced.

Restorative punishment converges closely with restorative justice, which has been applied most directly to the criminal justice systems of Western countries. Punishment, restorative justice holds, should take a form that restores the perpetrator's relationship with, and involves the participation of, victims and related members of the community. From the scriptures and traditions of Judaism, Christianity, and Islam, a strong case for restorative punishment can be made, though it has not been shared unanimously within these traditions. Although, in the Hebrew scriptures, there is no consistent and explicit rationale common to all the episodes where God delivers punishment, still, a purpose of restoring the people of Israel can be discerned. Within the community of the Israelites, restorative punishment is evident in the practice of restitution in response to crime and in an interpretation of the "eye for an eye" passages as limiting punishment rather than as a prescription for revenge. Today, both the Catholic Church and many Protestant churches call for restorative justice in judicial systems. In Islam, restorative punishment is prescribed for *qisas* crimes, including murder, as well as for crimes of *ta'zir*, which are smaller in scale, though not admittedly for *hudud* crimes, for which the Qur'an prescribes specific punishments in advance.

What does restorative punishment imply for judicial punishment in contexts of transitional justice? Institutions for judicial punishment have expanded greatly in the last couple of decades, with the founding of two international criminal tribunals, a permanent international criminal court, and numerous national tribunals. For those who violate human rights most gravely, only long-term imprisonment imposed by courts like these can adequately communicate the gravity of their offense. Expressing restorative punishment far more fully are community-level forums that bring together perpetrators, victims, members of the community, and village elders to discuss the crime and its effects and to prescribe a form of punishment that reintegrates the perpetrator and restores the community. These can be employed for lower-level perpetrators and in situations in which the judicial punishment of more serious criminals is not possible. Rwanda's *gacaca* courts and Timor-Leste's Community Reconciliation Panels are examples of such forums that achieved significant success, although not without drawbacks and controversies.

Forgiveness

Of the six practices of reconciliation, forgiveness is the one that most stands in tension with the liberal peace. The liberal peace centers on rights, but forgiveness is something to which nobody has a right; rather, it is a gift conferred by a victim. Liberals also criticize forgiveness for forgoing just retribution, disempowering victims, disrespecting the autonomy of victims, especially when it is pressured, and wrongly importing religion into politics. By contrast, forgiveness is the practice most emblematic of religiously informed reconciliation.

Forgiveness, like the discourse of reconciliation, is a relatively recent entrant into global politics. It is practiced mostly by ordinary victims and is present in the political discourse of South Africa, Rwanda, Uganda, Sierra Leone, Chile, El Salvador, Timor-Leste, Guatemala, Bosnia, Northern Ireland, Poland, and Germany. Rarely is it voiced by heads of state, in contrast to its counterpart, apologies. An exception is Nelson Mandela, who forgave apartheid officials after the apartheid government had fallen, though importantly, he spoke for himself and not for any group. Often it is encouraged by civil society leaders, especially church leaders.

Forgiveness is an act through which victims renounce justified anger, resentment, and claims against a perpetrator, but also, importantly, one through which a victim wills to construct right relationship by looking at a perpetrator as a person "in good standing." Forgiveness is difficult. But if it is genuine, then it neither condones nor forgets injustice. It does not involve neglecting laws, structures, or conditions of injustice, or ceasing to oppose them. In my view, a victim's forgiveness of a perpetrator does not contradict the justice of judicial punishment for the perpetrator; the two are made compatible by the restorative justification behind both forgiveness and punishment. Though forgiveness always involves some restoration of right relationship, it need not involve full restoration—for instance, an abused wife returning to live with her husband or a swindled merchant again doing business with the swindler. Forgiveness defeats the standing victory of injustice, invites the restoration of the perpetrator's soul, and, importantly, restores and strengthens the victim by enabling him, who was once utterly objectified by the political injustice, to exercise agency and construct justice.

Forgiveness is most pronounced in the Christian tradition. There, forgiveness is a command of Jesus, but even more so, a participation in the life of the Trinity and in God's restoration of the world through Jesus. Judaism and Islam both strongly commend forgiveness, though both tend to stress the importance of a prior apology more than Christianity does. Forgiveness is also strongly favored as a component of restorative justice. Though the question is disputed, in my view, a moral case for forgiveness can also be made in secular terms—as an act of constructive benevolence. To be sure, secular versions lack the divine justification and enablement offered by religious rationales. But the potential of secular justification makes the possibility all the stronger that forgiveness can come to play a constructive role in global politics.

DIRECTIONS FOR FUTURE RESEARCH

Not only has forgiveness been sidelined by the international community, but it has also been under-studied by the academic community, which has devoted far less attention to forgiveness than to truth commissions and the courts that try war criminals. Forgiveness is therefore one of the most untilled plots of ground for research in the area of transitional justice. It is fertile ground, too, due to the possibility that forgiveness has played a far larger role in countries' efforts to face the past than either scholars or practitioners of transitional justice have realized. This lack of regard is due in part to the tension between forgiveness and the liberal peace, but is probably also due to forgiveness taking place out of sight of the high politics of presidents and parliaments and instead in villages and megacities and in churches, mosques, and synagogues, thus eluding Western sensors. Research might investigate how often and under what conditions forgiveness takes place, what it means to its practitioners, what sorts of actions and words it consists of, and how it affects victims, perpetrators, and societies. If it turns out that forgiveness is a robust factor in restoring peace and justice, these findings will only strengthen the conclusion that reconciliation, advanced largely by the religious, is a globally prominent and widely practiced paradigm of peacebuilding.

NOTES

1. This trend is documented in Monica Duffy Toft, Daniel Philpott, and Timothy Samuel Shah, *God's Century: Resurgent Religion and Global Politics* (New York: W. W. Norton, 2011).

2. The chapter draws from Daniel Philpott, *Just and Unjust Peace: An Ethic of Political Reconciliation* (New York: Oxford University Press, 2012).

3. In her excellent "conceptual history of transitional justice," Paige Arthur describes the field of transitional justice as "an international web of individuals and institutions whose internal coherence is held together by common concepts, practical aims, and distinctive claims for legitimacy" that formed in common response to practical dilemmas. "The field of transitional justice, so defined, came directly out of a set of interactions among human rights activists, lawyers and legal scholars, policymakers, journalists, donors, and comparative politics experts concerned with human rights and the dynamics of 'transitions to democracy,' beginning in the late 1980s." Arthur also discusses debates that occurred within this web despite their broad agreement on certain values—over the desirable extent of and justification for judicial punishment, for instance. See Paige Arthur, "How 'Transitions' Reshaped Human Rights: A Conceptual History of Transitional Justice," *Human Rights Quarterly* 31, no. 2 (2009): 324, 353, 354, 358. For other helpful surveys and assessments of transitional justice, see Bronwyn Leebaw, "The Irreconcilable Goals of Transitional Justice," *Human Rights Quarterly* 30, no. 1 (2008): 95–118; and Ruti G. Teitel, "Transitional Justice Genealogy," *Harvard Human Rights Journal* 16 (2003): 69–94.

4. Jonathan VanAntwerpen, "Reconciliation as Heterodoxy" (unpublished manuscript, 2011).

5. John W. de Gruchy, *Reconciliation: Restoring Justice* (Minneapolis: Fortress Press, 2002), 67–76.

6. Erik Doxtader, *With Faith in the Work of Words: The Beginnings of Reconciliation in South Africa,1985–1995* (East Lansing: Michigan State University Press, 2008).

7. Pope Benedict XV, *Pacem, Dei Munus Pulcherrimum*, encyclical letter, 1920.

8. Pope John Paul II, *Dives in Misericordia*, encyclical letter, 1980; "Offer Forgiveness and Receive Peace," Message for the Celebration of the World Day of Peace, January 1, 1997; "No Peace Without Justice, No Justice Without Forgiveness," Message for the Celebration of the World Day of Peace, January 1, 2002.

9. Mohammed Abu-Nimer, Nonviolence and Peace Building in Islam (Gainesville: University Press of Florida, 2003); Miroslav Volf, Exclusion and Embrace: A Theological Exploration of Identity, Otherness and Reconciliation (Nashville, TN: Abingdon Press, 1996); Emmanuel Katongole, The Sacrifice of Africa: A Political Theology for Africa (Grand Rapids, MI: Eerdmans, 2010); Donald W. Shriver, An Ethic for Enemies: Forgiveness in Politics (New York: Oxford University Press, 1995); Marc Gopin, Between Eden and Armageddon: The Future of World Religions, Violence, and Peacemaking (New York: Oxford University Press, 2000).

10. For a broad survey of religion's impact on transitional justice and an effort to explain variation in this impact, see Daniel Philpott, "When Faith Meets History: The Influence of Religion on Transitional Justice," in *The Religious in Response to Mass Atrocity: Interdisciplinary Perspectives*, ed. Thomas Brudholm and Thomas Cushman (New York: Cambridge University Press, 2009), 174–212.

11. Paul Jeffrey, *Recovering Memory: Guatemalan Churches and the Challenge of Peacemaking* (Uppsala, Sweden: Life & Peace Institute, 1998), 28–63.

12. David Little, ed., with the Tanenbaum Center for Interreligious Understanding, *Peacemakers in Action: Profiles of Religion in Conflict Resolution* (New York: Cambridge University Press, 2007), 247–277.

13. Canon Andrew White, "Bringing Religious Leaders Together in Israel/Palestine," *Peaceworks* 55 (January 2006): 9–11.

14. R. Scott Appleby, *The Ambivalence of the Sacred: Religion, Violence, and Reconciliation* (Lanham, MD: Rowman and Littlefield, 2000), 123–140.

15. Andrea Bartoli, "Forgiveness and Reconciliation in the Mozambique Peace Process," in *Forgiveness and Reconciliation: Religion, Public Policy, and Conflict Transformation*, ed. Raymond G. Helmick, SJ, and Rodney L. Petersen (Philadelphia: Templeton Foundation Press, 2001), 351–372.

16. The ethic of political reconciliation described herein is drawn from Philpott, *Just and Unjust Peace*. On relational theories, see, for instance, Joan C. Tronto, *Moral Boundaries: A Political Argument for An Ethic of Care* (London: Routledge, 1993).

17. Here I rely on de Gruchy, *Reconciliation: Restoring Justice*, 68–112; and Christopher D. Marshall, *Beyond Retribution: A New Testament Vision for Justice, Crime, and Punishment* (Grand Rapids, MI: Eerdmans, 2001).

18. Here, I have relied on Majid Khadduri, *The Islamic Conception of Justice* (New York: Johns Hopkins University Press, 1984).

19. Abu-Nimer, *Nonviolence and Peace Building in Islam*, 60.

20. For the earliest statements of the distinction, see Martin Luther King Jr., "Nonviolence and Racial Justice," in *A Testament of Hope: The Essential Writings and Speeches of Martin Luther King, Jr.*, ed. James M. Washington (New York: HarperCollins, 1986), 5–9; Johan Galtung, "An Editorial," *Journal of Peace Research* 1, no. 1 (1964): 1–4; Kenneth Boulding, "Toward a Theory of Peace," in *International Conflict and Behavioral Science*, ed. Roger Fisher (New York: Basic Books, 1964), 70–87.

21. John Paul II, *Dives in Misericordia*, para. 6.

22. On these rituals, see George E. Irani and Nathan C. Funk, "Rituals of Reconciliation: Arab-Islamic Perspectives," *Arab Studies Quarterly* 20, no. 4 (1998): 53–73; and Abu-Nimer, *Nonviolence and Peace Building in Islam*, 91–127.

23. Quoted in Brandon Hamber and Richard A. Wilson, "Symbolic Closure through Memory, Reparation and Revenge in Post-Conflict Societies," *Journal of Human Rights* 1, no. 1 (2002): 40.

24. See Samuel P. Huntington, *The Third Wave: Democratization in the Late Twentieth Century* (Norman: University of Oklahoma Press, 1991); and Larry Diamond, "The Democratic Rollback: The Resurgence of the Predatory State," *Foreign Affairs* 87, no. 2 (2008): 36–48.

25. For a modern Jewish account of rights, see David Novak, *Covenantal Rights: A Study in Jewish Political Theory* (Princeton, NJ: Princeton University Press, 2000).

26. See Brian Tierney, *The Idea of Natural Rights: Studies on Natural Rights, Natural Law, and Church Law, 1150–1625* (Atlanta: Scholars Press, 1997).

27. See, for instance, Jürgen Moltmann, *The Crucified God: The Cross of Christ as the Foundation and Criticism of Christian Theology* (Minneapolis: Fortress Press, 1993), 46, 53.

28. John Paul II, *Solicitudo Rei Socialis*, encyclical letter, 1987, paras. 39 and 40.

29. Pablo de Greiff, "Introduction. Repairing the Past: Compensation for Victims of Human Rights Violations," in *The Handbook of Reparations*, ed. Pablo de Greiff (Oxford, UK: Oxford University Press, 2006), 1–18.

30. See, for instance, the arguments of Jeremy Waldron in "Superseding Historical Injustice," *Ethics* 103, no. 1 (1992): 4–28; and "Settlement, Return, and the Supersession Thesis,"

Theoretical Inquiries in Law 5, no. 2 (2004): 237–268. See my discussion in *Just and Unjust Peace*, 194–195.

31. I make a more extended case for this claim in *Just and Unjust Peace*, 191–198.

32. J.D. Bindenagel, "Justice, Apology, Reconciliation and the German Foundation: Remembrance, Responsibility, and the Future," in *Taking Wrongs Seriously: Apologies and Reconciliation*, eds. Elazar Barkan and Alexander Karn (Palo Alto, CA: Stanford University Press, 2006), 306.

33. John Hayes, "Atonement in the Book of Leviticus," *Interpretation* 52, no. 1 (1998): 11; "Tractate *Baba Qamma*," in *The Mishnah: Translated From the Hebrew with Introduction and Brief Explanatory Notes*, trans. H. Danby (Oxford: Oxford University Press, 1993), 8:1; Gopin, *Between Eden and Armageddon*, 187–188.

34. para. 1459.

35. Aaron Lazare, *On Apology* (New York: Oxford University Press, 2004), 6–7.

36. Trudy Govier and Wilhelm Verwoerd, "The Promise and Pitfalls of Apology," *Journal of Social Philosophy* 33, no. 1 (2002): 77–79.

37. Jennifer Lind, *Sorry States: Apologies in International Politics* (Ithaca, NY: Cornell University Press, 2008), 26–78; and Yinan He, *The Search for Reconciliation: Sino-Japanese and German-Polish Relations Since World War II* (New York: Cambridge University Press, 2009), 115–288.

Bibliography

"Tractate Baba *Qamma*." In *The Mishnah: Translated From the Hebrew with Introduction and Brief Explanatory Notes*. Translated by H. Danby. Oxford: Oxford University Press, 1993.

Abu-Nimer, Mohammed. *Nonviolence and Peace Building in Islam*. Gainesville: University Press of Florida, 2003.

Appleby, R. Scott. *The Ambivalence of the Sacred: Religion, Violence, and Reconciliation*. Lanham, MD: Rowman and Littlefield, 2000.

Arthur, Paige. "How 'Transitions' Reshaped Human Rights: A Conceptual History of Transitional Justice." *Human Rights Quarterly* 31, no. 2 (2009): 321–367.

Bartoli, Andrea. "Forgiveness and Reconciliation in the Mozambique Peace Process." In *Forgiveness and Reconciliation: Religion, Public Policy, and Conflict Transformation*, edited by Raymond G. Helmick, SJ, and Rodney L. Petersen, 351–372. Philadelphia: Templeton Foundation Press, 2001.

Bindenagel, J.D. "Justice, Apology, Reconciliation and the German Foundation: Remembrance, Responsibility, and the Future." In *Taking Wrongs Seriously: Apologies and Reconciliation*, edited by Elazar Barkan and Alexander Karn, 286–310. Palo Alto, CA: Stanford University Press, 2006.

Pope Benedict XV. *Pacem, Dei Munus Pulcherrimum*. Encyclical letter. Vatican: The Holy See, 1920.

Boulding, Kenneth. "Toward a Theory of Peace." In *International Conflict and Behavioral Science*, edited by Roger Fisher, 70–87. New York: Basic Books, 1964.

de Gruchy, John W. *Reconciliation: Restoring Justice*. Minneapolis: Fortress Press, 2002.

Diamond, Larry. "The Democratic Rollback: The Resurgence of the Predatory State." *Foreign Affairs* 87, no. 2 (2008): 36–48.

Doxtader, Erik. *With Faith in the Work of Words: The Beginnings of Reconciliation in South Africa, 1985–1995*. East Lansing: Michigan State University Press, 2008.

Galtung, Johan. "An Editorial." *Journal of Peace Research* 1, no. 1 (1964): 1–4.

Gopin, Marc. *Between Eden and Armageddon: The Future of World Religions, Violence, and Peacemaking.* New York: Oxford University Press, 2000.

Govier, Trudy, and Wilhelm Verwoerd. "The Promise and Pitfalls of Apology." *Journal of Social Philosophy* 33, no. 1 (2002): 67–82.

De Greiff, Pablo. "Introduction. Repairing the Past: Compensation for Victims of Human Rights Violations." *The Handbook of Reparations*, edited by Pablo de Greiff, 1–18. Oxford, UK: Oxford University Press, 2006.

Hadley, Michael L., ed. *The Spiritual Roots of Restorative Justice.* Albany: State University of New York Press, 2001.

Hamber, Brandon, and Richard A. Wilson. "Symbolic Closure through Memory, Reparation and Revenge in Post-Conflict Societies." *Journal of Human Rights* 1, no. 1 (2002): 35–53.

Hayes, John. "Atonement in the Book of Leviticus." *Interpretation* 52, no. 1 (1998): 5–15.

He, Yinan. *The Search for Reconciliation: Sino-Japanese and German-Polish Relations Since World War II.* New York: Cambridge University Press, 2009.

Huntington, Samuel P. *The Clash of Civilizations and the Remaking of World Order.* New York: Simon and Schuster, 1996.

Irani, George E., and Nathan C. Funk. "Rituals of Reconciliation: Arab-Islamic Perspectives." *Arab Studies Quarterly* 20, no. 4 (1998): 53–73.

Jeffrey, Paul. *Recovering Memory: Guatemalan Churches and the Challenge of Peacemaking.* Uppsala, Sweden: Life & Peace Institute, 1998.

Pope John Paul II. *Dives in Misericordia.* Encyclical letter. Vatican: The Holy See, 1980.

Pope John Paul II. *Solicitudo Rei Socialis.* Encyclical letter. Vatican: The Holy See, 1987.

Pope John Paul II. "Offer Forgiveness and Receive Peace." Message for the Celebration of the World Day of Peace, January 1, 1997.

Pope John Paul II. "No Peace Without Justice, No Justice Without Forgiveness." Message for the Celebration of the World Day of Peace, January 1, 2002.

Katongole, Emmanuel. *The Sacrifice of Africa: A Political Theology for Africa.* Grand Rapids, MI: Eerdmans, 2010.

Khadduri, Majid. *The Islamic Conception of Justice.* New York: Johns Hopkins University Press, 1984.

King, Martin Luther, Jr. "Nonviolence and Racial Justice." In *A Testament of Hope: The Essential Writings and Speeches of Martin Luther King, Jr.*, edited by James M. Washington, 5–9. New York: HarperCollins, 1986.

Lazare, Aaron. *On Apology.* New York: Oxford University Press, 2004.

Lederach, John Paul. *Building Peace: Sustainable Reconciliation in Divided Societies.* Washington, DC: US Institute of Peace Press, 1997.

Leebaw, Bronwyn. "The Irreconcilable Goals of Transitional Justice." *Human Rights Quarterly* 30, no. 1 (2008): 95–118.

Lind, Jennifer. *Sorry States: Apologies in International Politics.* Ithaca, NY: Cornell University Press, 2008.

Little, David, ed., with the Tanenbaum Center for Interreligious Understanding. *Peacemakers in Action: Profiles of Religion in Conflict Resolution.* New York: Cambridge University Press, 2007.

Marshall, Christopher D. *Beyond Retribution: A New Testament Vision for Justice, Crime, and Punishment.* Grand Rapids, MI: Eerdmans, 2001.

Moltmann, Jürgen. *The Crucified God: The Cross of Christ as the Foundation and Criticism of Christian Theology.* Minneapolis: Fortress Press, 1993.

Novak, David. *Covenantal Rights: A Study in Jewish Political Theory*. Princeton, NJ: Princeton University Press, 2000.

Philpott, Daniel. "When Faith Meets History: The Influence of Religion on Transitional Justice." In *The Religious in Response to Mass Atrocity: Interdisciplinary Perspectives*, edited by Thomas Brudholm and Thomas Cushman, 174–212. New York: Cambridge University Press, 2009.

Philpott, Daniel. *Just and Unjust Peace: An Ethic of Political Reconciliation*. New York: Oxford University Press, 2012.

Philpott, Daniel, and Gerard F. Powers, eds. *Strategies of Peace: Transforming Conflict in a Violent World*. New York: Oxford University Press, 2010.

Shriver, Donald W. *An Ethic for Enemies: Forgiveness in Politics*. New York: Oxford University Press, 1995.

Teitel, Ruti G. "Transitional Justice Genealogy." *Harvard Human Rights Journal* 16 (2003): 69–94.

Tierney, Brian. *The Idea of Natural Rights: Studies on Natural Rights, Natural Law, and Church Law, 1150–1625*. Atlanta: Scholars Press, 1997.

Toft, Monica Duffy, Daniel Philpott, and Timothy Samuel Shah. *God's Century: Resurgent Religion in Global Politics*. New York: W. W. Norton, 2011.

Tronto, Joan. *Moral Boundaries: A Political Argument for an Ethic of Care*. London: Routledge, 1993.

VanAntwerpen, Jonathan. "Reconciliation as Heterodoxy." Unpublished manuscript, 2011.

Volf, Miroslav. *Exclusion and Embrace: A Theological Exploration of Identity, Otherness and Reconciliation*. Nashville, TN: Abingdon Press, 1996.

Waldron, Jeremy. "Superseding Historical Injustice." *Ethics* 103, no. 1 (1992): 4–28.

Waldron, Jeremy. "Settlement, Return, and the Supersession Thesis." *Theoretical Inquiries in Law* 5, no. 2 (2004): 237–268.

White, Canon Andrew. "Bringing Religious Leaders Together in Israel/Palestine." *Peaceworks* 55 (January 2006): 9–11.

CHAPTER 14

....

NEGOTIATING SECULAR AND RELIGIOUS CONTRIBUTIONS TO SOCIAL CHANGE AND PEACEBUILDING

....

MARC GOPIN

INTO discussions of religious peacebuilding, including many in this volume, there can creep signs of an implicit binary, separating religious and secular approaches to social change and peacebuilding into two unbridgeable camps, with the promoters of religious agency claiming that religion has a unique contribution to make and therefore deserves a seat at the table. Meanwhile, secular actors resent being subordinated in this discourse to a secondary role, when religious people can hardly claim for organized religion a history of choosing peace over war, tolerance over exclusion.

This chapter joins a growing intellectual and popular questioning of this binary, on the grounds that it is based on some misleading assumptions on both presumed sides. Constructively, and drawing on my thirty years of experience with religion and peacebuilding, I attempt to demonstrate the effectiveness of the justpeace lens threaded through the chapters in this volume. In other words, there could be one comprehensive approach to peacebuilding that builds on the virtues of both approaches to peace, what I will refer to as "the liberal peace" or "secular peace" and what I will refer to as "the elicitive, religious-cultural peace" models. I will argue that a comprehensive, integrative approach is truly "strategic" for the purposes of effecting sustained positive change, as well as peace with justice.

For the purposes of this essay, I will define the liberal or secular peace as peace that is pursued and achieved through commitment to the idea of a social contract for all citizens of a state (and by extension, today, to all citizens of the world), regardless of religious affiliation, belief, or commitments. This approach to peace is especially rooted in Enlightenment thinking; it draws in particular on John Locke's vision of the social contract, and on Immanuel Kant's idea of the universal moral commitments that the individual adheres to in his or her treatment of others. But many others are associated with this tradition, right up to contemporaries such as John Rawls. Classifying this stream of thought as secular is not to say that these figures are nonreligious or anti-religious by any means, but that in it, the foundations of actions and behaviors are not religious or sectarian texts, tenets, or laws, but rather universal commitments to fellow citizens with no *necessary* basis in religious commitment. The human rights agenda emerges strongly from this line of thinking in recent centuries.

The model of elicitive, cultural-religious peace, on the other hand, is rooted more in specific texts, traditions, faith positions, dogmas, and laws that appeal to people adhering to specific religious or spiritual traditions. Their motivation to act and work toward peace comes from those specific beliefs and practices.

The point of this chapter is that this dichotomy can be overdrawn, producing ambivalence and complications, sometimes right inside the conscience of the thinkers and actors committed to lasting peace. The struggle between these two poles of motivation and styles of action needs to be addressed, in order to create a stronger bridge between the two and a more effective and integrated approach to promoting global social change.

The Source of the Animosity

Let me give an illustration of this dichotomy and its potentially harmful effects by analyzing my own professional field. The field of conflict analysis (CA) and resolution (CR) is fairly new, perhaps thirty years old. The field of religion, conflict analysis, and conflict resolution is even newer, perhaps no more than twenty years old. Religious people have been both war-makers and peacemakers since the beginning of time, and they have been supported in both by their religious traditions. But the academic and professional interaction between the secular constructs of CA and CR theoreticians and practitioners, on the one side, and religious actors on the other has been fraught with complexity from the beginning of these professional disciplines. Mutual suspicion (and at times, outright disdain for religious thinking) has created a divide that only recently has begun to be bridged.

For many professionals, academics, and peace activists, religion is *the* problem from which they are trying to help people escape. This is understandable given the quantity and quality of human rights abuses, torture, and even mass murder committed in the name of religion in human history. At the same time, this bias against including religion and religious people as part of conflict analysis and resolution has made life for religious practitioners of peacebuilding quite difficult. Furthermore, many professionals coming out of the Judeo-Christian Western legacy desire and intend to keep church and state separated. This intention can complicate addressing problems in other religious contexts, especially Middle Eastern ones, where ignoring or sidelining religious people can be quite unhelpful. At the same time, it has been the author's experience in many parts of the globe that the separation of religion and state does over time reduce the amount of violence, and certainly the amount of corrupting uses to which states can put religion.

Some analysts have concluded, based on years of frustration in Washington, that bias against religion and the separation between church and state in the United States (porous though it sometimes may seem) have enabled many policy-makers to indulge their personal biases while ignoring religion.[1] The neglect has rendered some members of the Washington establishment less than dexterous at understanding and dealing with the ways in which religion and culture intertwine, and it allows the destructive elements of religious communities or traditions to come to caricature entire religions (i.e., Islam is a warlike religion). Some seem to hold to the "clash of civilizations" thesis made popular by Samuel P. Huntington's 1993 article.[2] An insistence that religion is a private matter persists in many Western analysts' and officials' view of religion and international relations, which in turn has led to many mistakes in international relations, conflict analysis, and conflict management.[3]

More importantly for peacebuilding, the constructive potential of religion is left unseen and untapped. In their rather negative approach to religion, especially in its public expression, many Western policy-makers do not acknowledge sufficiently the creative, peacebuilding resources in religious traditions and people. This is not conducive to analyzing the complex interactions between the many factors of history, geopolitics, and economics that influence the course and direction of religion's presence in public and international affairs.

An attempt to refine—correct—the approach of policy-makers began in the 1990s. It was led by Douglas Johnston and Cynthia Sampson, whose volume *Religion, the Missing Dimension of Statecraft* (1994) marks the beginning of the post–Cold War literature in the field of conflict, religion, and peacebuilding.[4] Of course, the Iranian Revolution of 1979 shocked Western policy-makers. But it was not until the events of September 11, 2001, that the political and foreign affairs establishment truly awoke to the role of religion in shaping politics, culture, and international relationships.

In light of the large presence religion continues to have on the world stage, numerous authors have critiqued the neglect of religion. Recently three scholars of international relations, for example, have argued in a co-authored work that religious leaders and institutions are an untapped resource in interstate relations and can provide strategic value to governments. I would argue that to the degree to which governments want to play a constructive role in peacebuilding, they should recognize this asset. In the last chapter of their volume, *God's Century: Resurgent Religion and Global Politics*, Monica Duffy Toft, Daniel Philpott, and Timothy Samuel Shah give ten rules for "surviving God's century," one of which is, "Learn to live with the fact that it is not whether, but when and how, religious actors will enter public life and shape political outcomes."[5] They explore what they describe as enduring relationships between religion and democratization, politics, human rights, humanitarian aid, peace, and conflict.[6] Elsewhere, and in line with many of the critiques of unreconstructed secularism one finds in various disciplines, Dennis Hoover and Douglas Johnston draw a distinction between "secularization theory" and "anti-religious secularism." The latter is a *normative position*, according to them, which holds that "secularity is the *correct* direction of history."[7] This position, which they claim is commonly found amongst Western policymakers and intelligentsia, functions to exclude religious perspectives despite their importance to understanding, preventing, and resolving conflict. Yet not only is modernization not driving out religion, it actually may be contributing to the rise of religious revivalism—for example, by enabling religious groups to mobilize and organize members with ever greater efficiency and impact amid a crisis of unrealized expectations of nationalism, which some scholars claim is secular.[8] Nationalism, I would argue, has deep religious roots as well, but whatever the roots, chauvinistic forms of nationalism are and always have been a dangerous phenomenon, and responding to such phenomena nonviolently requires a deeper alliance of religious and secular institutions committed to peacebuilding. This is plainly evident from all of our experience as peacebuilders operating in many global arenas, with explicit religiosity and through processes that may be defined as "religious peacebuilding."

SECULAR AND RELIGIOUS PEACEBUILDING: A CLEAR DISTINCTION?

Even among those academics and professionals who now acknowledge the enduring importance of religion in public and international affairs, there is an unspoken assumption that religion is "the other"—a player who cannot necessarily be trusted, who must remain contained, on the margins of "real" diplomacy and conflict resolution. This is understandable given the fact that in the minds of many people, the secular state is a fortress standing against religious coercion. Nevertheless, the latent distrust creates some problems, reflective of the internalizing of secularism that reads this phenomenon through a modernist binary prism.

Many of my colleagues in religion and peacebuilding experience a wide range of identity challenges resulting from these concerns and dichotomies. On the one hand, there are many practitioners, whether they self-identify as secular or as spiritual, who are fundamentally ambivalent about organized religion. But they work in religion and peacebuilding with practitioners of organized religion. They do so because they have arrived at a fundamental "realist" and empirical truth that most of the world's violent conflicts involve deeply religious people who are either willing participants in religious violence or who are being cleverly manipulated to religious violence by powerful state and nonstate entities.[9] Therefore, it is irrational, these scholars have concluded, *not* to engage religion and peacebuilding as an essential strategy of global social change.

For other practitioners, peacebuilding is a part of their own *religious* identity. They have been influenced by what are known generally as secular commitments to peace and human rights or democracy, but their own religious motivations for peacebuilding come from the way those "secular" values resonate with religious reality and religious interpretation. Sometimes they believe that peace, human rights, and democracy are in fact fundamentally religious practices and goals, with a long history of precedents that gave rise to the secular constructs of international peacebuilding, conflict resolution, human rights advocacy, democratization, and so on. The rootedness of modern Enlightenment civilization in religious thinkers such as Grotius and Kant lend credence to their intuitive sense that the boundaries between secular and religious are better understood as the differences between the political realms of organized religion and the political realm of power constructs of many modern states and civilizations.

The differences in worldview, discourse, and practices between secular Enlightenment constructs and the world of religious life and communities can cause quite a bit of identity confusion, though for some people these are in perfect harmony. There is sometimes a gnawing question of whether and how religions contribute something *unique* to peacebuilding and social change. This is where one hears questions about the difference between "liberal peace" and peacebuilding that incorporates and at times even privileges religion and culture. *There is, in short, an alleged distinction between the "liberal peace" and religious conceptions of just peace and peacebuilding. I wish to explore and challenge that distinction.*

First, the terms "liberal peace" and traditional religious notions of "justpeace" and peacebuilding, need clearer definition in order to support the distinction. Let me quote from a conversation that followed the workshop held in preparation for this volume:

> We devoted important conversation during the workshop to the tension between the complex concept of justpeace and the more familiar tradition of "liberal peace.". . . The justpeace concept, we believe, complements and also supplements the liberal peace by, among other virtues, giving greater attention to how religion interfaces not only with direct but also structural and cultural forms of violence as well as how religion and culture provide resources in the building of peace; conceptualizing the peacebuilding horizon in decades, not months or years; and emphasizing the role of local actors and the need to elicit from them "cues" for effective relationship-building. This, in short[,] is a normative orientation we ask you to wrestle with in your essay, and one that aspires to encompass that which is indispensable within the so-called "liberal peace."[10]

Grounding their discussions in R. Scott Appleby and John Paul Lederach's overview of the comprehensive, interdisciplinary, and multidimensional concept of "strategic peacebuilding,"[11] the participants did not set up a dichotomy between liberal peace and religious notions of justpeace and peacebuilding. Rather, they suggested the possibility of complementarity or a deepening of liberal peace through an exposition of the cultural, religious, orientalist, and colonial legacies of this orientation. They then imagined how the expansive lens of justpeace could open up potential spaces for the participation of religious people and traditions in processes of conflict transformation.

I would like to respond to this binary of secular and religious peace drawing upon my experience as a practitioner. "Religion" does not contribute in one uniform way to war and peace; as Appleby described it so succinctly,[12] the contribution of religion is fundamentally "ambivalent" and often dichotomous. Sometimes, in my experience, religious institutions and religious people make conflicts much worse than they would be otherwise, but sometimes they make them better.

For example, some claim that religion is adept at analyzing and addressing structures of injustice. Is that really true? Organized religion has been one of the most important handmaidens and apologists for the worst empires and states of history, not only failing to analyze structural injustice but actively constructing the most long-standing forms of structural injustice against nonbelievers, against women, against homosexuals, even against children sometimes, and it has always been available to bless the destruction of enemies beyond the borders of the empire or state. On the other hand, one must distinguish between the great prophets of religious traditions and the religious, political, and military institutions built in their names. There is no question that the prophetic figures of many major religions have, across many cultures and throughout history, exposed the deepest structures of injustice and cruelty, while envisioning the most enlightened and saintly forms of human interaction. What I refer to here is, of course, the familiar and persistently useful categories of priestly vs. prophetic religion, which do in fact correspond to actual and paradoxical realities in the history of many religions.

In addition, it is problematic to place a critique of structures squarely in the hands of religious voices. Is it true that only prophetic religious voices challenge the structures of society? In the past few centuries, humanistic and even anti-religious philosophies of socialism gave rise to the strongest critiques of structures of injustice. In what way, then, is the critique of unjust structures a unique asset of religion for the purposes of conflict resolution and peacebuilding? More broadly, what is unique about religious contributions to peacebuilding? There is always counter-evidence to the claim of uniqueness, and, as far as I have been able to discern, there are always secular parallels to the positive claims made about religion.

The theoretical questions about whether religion brings a unique perspective to the subject of conflict analysis, or about its capacity to critique the structures of society, have practical parallels. For example, is there a place for religious actors in official settings of conflict resolution and peacebuilding, and if so, what is their role? Is it through engagement with nongovernmental organizations (NGOs), faith-based diplomacy through unofficial or official channels, or citizen diplomacy and work with grassroots initiatives in religious understanding? Is it in an advisory capacity, where scholars and practitioners quietly advise governments on how to engage and how not to engage religious populations? Can they help diplomats and others make sense of religious texts that appear to both endorse and prohibit violence? How do we make progress against movements that utilize only the violent aspects of a tradition, and are religious practitioners and advisors in a unique position to help in this endeavor?

As authors attempt to answer these questions, they uncover a multitude of potential roles for religious actors. For example, in his edited volume on *Faith-Based Diplomacy*,[13] Johnston argues with Brian Cox for the presence of faith-based diplomats engaged in Track Two diplomacy who, by virtue of their religious affiliation or spiritual charisma, have credibility with other religious leaders and believers. They have a deep understanding of the intricacies of other religions and their potential for conflict and for practices of peacebuilding, reconciliation, and tolerance (even love) of the other. He and Cox also advocate for the establishment of a religion attaché position within the US Foreign Service whose role would be to establish relationships with local religious leaders and groups with the aim of developing trust, understanding religious imperatives, and integrating these insights into larger US activities abroad.

In discussions with foreign policy teams in government over the course of the decade following the events of September 11, 2001, many experts and a series of task force reports on religion and US foreign policy[14] expressed concern about pigeonholing religion into one bureaucrat's portfolio or one department. Sequestering religion in this way ignores the broad range of governmental and nongovernmental political, social, and economic programs that should pay attention to religious actors and religious sensibilities. For example, programs on the needs of women, programs on entrepreneurship, programs on reconstruction—all of these should incorporate analysts and program officers addressing the inclusion of religious communities in or their exclusion from these activities. Conflict analysis and resolution at their most basic level would predict the onset of destructive conflict when the human needs of religious actors are excluded from *any* of these activities. Johnston and I, among several others, have conveyed these concerns and strategies in several venues over many years to government officials who are interested in helping the system work more effectively with religious actors globally.

I have alluded to the creative peacebuilding potential of religious actors. Many scholars have detailed the myriad of ways in which religious texts and communities engage in peacemaking around the world. Religious peacemakers (in official and unofficial capacities, including laypeople) often have contributed at every point in conflict, from raising awareness of a conflict, to intervention, to eventual peacebuilding and reconciliation.[15]

Harnessing the positive potential of religion depends, however, on a powerful nonviolent religious narrative bolstered by hermeneutics. Here the literature in the field gets richer by the day. I argue for a creative hermeneutic that allows religious people to access values such as tolerance (even love) of the other, the importance of resolving conflict nonviolently, and the sanctity of all human life.[16] Religious texts can take on a multiplicity of meanings depending on historical context, the current political and social climate, and the philosophical position of the reader. The goal is to employ a hermeneutic that elicits the positive messages and themes of religious stories. For example, Mohammed Abu-Nimer, in his work *Nonviolence and Peacebuilding in Islam*, provides deep and insightful analysis of the peaceful messages in the Qur'an and Hadith texts, and the culture of Islam.[17] The many people around the world already engaged in such education and peacemaking work need support for their efforts.[18]

This will be especially necessary in the future, because states are here to stay, and secular states can often become infected by forms of ultranationalism that are very prone to religious manipulation. It is a commonplace of so-called secular nationalism that it is often blessed by official religion, and the harm or violence it seeks to do, either to a minority or to an enemy over the border, becomes sacralized through official sermons and texts or through sanctification of the ethnic "purity" of a particular group, where ethnicity easily converges with religious and cultural connotations of identity. Thus, it becomes all the more important to develop a solid set of peacebuilding hermeneutics that are available for every major religion in all its different denominations.

Religious ideas can also support efforts of reconciliation, despite their dangers as a handmaiden to nationalism. Daniel Philpott[19] shows that reconciliation is largely missing from Western political discourse and law, which tends to focus on retributive rather than restorative models of justice, with little or no room for narrative, forgiveness, and grace.

While Philpott's point is well-taken, religion as a social and moral force in this sphere remains ambivalent. Although forgiveness and grace are present in religious approaches to law, crime, and punishment, it is also the case that religious institutions have a checkered reputation at best when it comes to applying said values to all people without regard to their status inside or outside the religious community. In religious systems there is nothing comparable on a global scale to, for example, universal human rights that guarantee equal treatment under the law; there is nothing to guarantee that forgiveness or grace, for example, could even be a reliable mode of response in legal systems controlled by religious authority. On the other hand, it is unquestionably true that such religious ideas and values as forgiveness, borrowed from religious traditions, can enhance and further humanize secular international and national legal systems already in place, which do have guarantees of equal treatment under the law.

There are additional problems with religious categories in ethics, such as forgiveness, apology, grace, compassion, and mercy. For various reasons, historically these can be associated more with one religion than another, and thus may be interpreted, when integrated into peacebuilding, as a form of cultural imperialism.[20] This critique is important, as I have demonstrated in my own writings. Nevertheless, it is unfair to dismiss their contribution to peacebuilding. After all, human rights themselves have been dismissed also as a Western cultural imposition. There is no escaping accusations of cultural bias when it comes to interventions in and between cultures. But it is possible, whether with religious values or Western constructs of law, to engage conflictual situations with respect. Both secular constructs, such as human rights, and religious constructs, such as forgiveness, can be useful in deepening processes of conflict resolution and peacebuilding, if and when they are integrated in a collaborative way by all parties.

Philpott argues, for example, that there are good reasons to include religious leaders and language in processes of reconciliation, and that reconciliation is an idea that can take diplomacy much further in preventing war and mitigating conflict. Jewish, Islamic, and Christian traditions offer great reservoirs of wisdom that can contribute to a political ethic of reconciliation. Particularly in conflicts where religion has played a large role, it is quite helpful to use religion in the making of peace, encouraging people to discover any peacemaking potential that lies within their sacred texts and traditions. Philpott is not arguing for a strictly religious approach, but rather a "grafting in which religious justifications are offered fully and publicly but are accompanied by secular justifications and in which concepts from ancient scripture merge with ideas drawn from the modern liberal tradition."[21] In this way it is possible for religion to make a major contribution to negotiation, mediation, and peacebuilding.[22] As I have argued in all my books, hermeneutics is essential to the establishment of religious practices that contribute to the improvement of the human condition, and Philpott is basically arguing that these hermeneutic engagements with religious traditions and laws can be quite helpful, even sometimes indispensable, in secular diplomatic processes that are usually based on modern liberal traditions.

I want to suggest a different way of looking at the secular-religious divide in conflict analysis and resolution. I would like to ask, is the divide today between secular and religious approaches to conflict and peacebuilding truly confined to the modern era? Is it possible that we are witnessing no more than a more self-examined and self-conscious divide that has always existed in human consciousness? I return to the fact that the terms "secular" and "religious" to describe official and unofficial actors and institutions may in fact not be significantly different from ancient and biblical divides between the monarchy, the priesthood, and social critics known as the biblical prophets. Is it possible that what we sometimes call a religious-secular divide in the execution of foreign policy, for example, is actually quite the same as ancient prophetic critiques of kings who failed to sufficiently attend to the needs of the weak and disenfranchised? The kings were putatively religious, but the prophets railed against them as impious for their theft and violence. Religious peacebuilders find often in their entry into the halls of power that there is a resonance with age-old struggles between spiritual or humanitarian values and state or empire interests.

More importantly, the ancient role of the religious priestly class is re-created in these contexts: many states have religious hierarchies that dutifully endorse all state activities, including the most savage wars, just like the ancient biblical priesthood did for corrupt kings. But the great Jewish social prophets, such as Isaiah, Ezekiel, and Amos, stood apart from those priests and said, "Wait a second. What about the waste of human life? What about the fairness of this war, or this plan of action, or this pattern of commerce—or theft? This is anti-religious, this is against God's wishes." Thus today there may be not so much a divide between religion and secularism when it comes to conflict analysis and resolution, as a divide between idealistic religious values and the levers of power that do not want those values to interfere with imperialistic, state, or aristocratic goals. In other words, religious institutions or modes of religious expansionism, from American Christian to Sunni to Shiite, are often functioning in the field as mere fronts for state and aristocratic power or imperialistic designs. Many conflicts today are being spearheaded by states that pour billions of dollars into very aggressive forms of evangelism over against a competitor, Sunni, Shiite, or Christian. Now conflict analysts may interpret this to mean that religion is essentially an obstacle to peace, and I can sympathize with that analysis. But this mistakenly conflates the contribution of *religion as such* with organized religious constructs that may be functioning as entities of power or power-grabbing that are essentially violent. Our field of conflict analysis and resolution must learn to see these fine differences within the world of what is called religion.

THE IDENTITY ISSUES OF RELIGION, PEACEBUILDING, AND SECULAR/SCIENTIFIC CIVILIZATION

Let us now delve more deeply into the question of the present and future relationship between what we currently refer to as secular and religious modes of peacebuilding and social change. Reflection on the experience of engaging religion strategically in peacebuilding suggests the need for a flexible and evolving exploration of the boundaries of religion and peacebuilding practices as they are influenced by and in turn influence so-called secular models of social change. I frame this reflection by asking: Why are we looking for something unique that religion has to contribute? What is the motivation to want to suggest that religious peacebuilding has something that is *additional to* or *deeper than* "liberal peace"? Why are we framing the issues this way? I pose these questions for the religious peacebuilding community—the intellectuals and practitioners who are contributing to this volume and to the broader field. I do so to invite an exercise in self-reflection and self-examination, for this topic of religious and secular "modes" of conflict resolution has been very important to my research and practice in recent years.[23]

There are two possible motivations for claiming that religious peacebuilding offers something extra: 1) the conviction that it is possible to demonstrate the superiority of the religious model of ethical intervention in global problems over against liberal or secular forms of intervention, and 2) the conviction that religious actors should be awarded a respected place at the table in national and global policy-making.

I want to argue, first of all, that demonstrations of religion's supposed superiority in peacebuilding are problematic at an intellectual level, and better left as a faith position by those who espouse it. The second motivation—the desire to create a place for the religious at the policy table—is a legitimate concern, and I have been making that case in policy circles for a long time. I would add a caveat, however, that such claims can be treacherous because it is so easy to end up aligning oneself with those religious actors who want to supplant liberal peace—and liberals—rather than just be included at the same table. The United States is enmeshed in an intra-Christian culture war over this very issue, and it is perilous to be involved in this conflict, especially in the halls of power. It has complicated my professional contribution to peacebuilding in Washington for decades. It would be unethical to become an unwitting partner in an exercise to usurp the public space for religion, so one has to be very cautious in lobbying for such positions in the public domain. I have nevertheless lobbied for religious involvement in policy-making, but it is a treacherous undertaking. Whatever one does in the halls of power, for those of us committed to religious peacebuilding, creating a place for religious actors at the table is not always a helpful motivation, for it is an intellectually weak position. Approaches to peacebuilding that emphasize long-term commitment, for example, are not unique to religion or religious people, nor is a critique of structures of justice and injustice, which (as I have suggested) may have deep and ancient prophetic roots—but also anti-religious Marxist roots. I have seen many of my agnostic compatriots from development work come to the same conclusions based on a set of values and ideologies very different from religion. In fact, it weakens the argument for religion to say that "religion is uniquely x or y." When others adopt those same approaches without recourse to religion, when they arrive at the same destination by another way, then the religious contribution seems unnecessary or redundant. In other words, it sets up religious people for planned obsolescence.

The argument that religion makes some unique contribution to peacebuilding is also unnecessary: the simple truth is that religious people should be at the table of the social contract and global social peace because they constitute much of the planet's population. Religious voices must be there and deserve to be there, not because there is some secret formula they possess that will be superior to other formulas, but because they have a right to be there.

Another great benefit of the contemporary approach to peace has been the emphasis on a shared public space in which no one group or religion has a monopoly. Space that is thoroughly shared and that honors all equally is rare in history, and we owe it to the Enlightenment's creation of a collective public space that is shared by a plurality of groups and individuals. This is a necessity in democracies. Of course, many of the architects of the Enlightenment began that process from a religious cultural orientation. But it has grown more and more radically inclusive and secular as its logic has been pursued.

That new public space need not be bereft of all religious symbols or character, however, and it need not be radically secular in order to achieve the aims of tolerance and peace. But neither can any one group, religious or secular, now have a monopoly on that space and still claim to favor democracy. This plural reality and the state democratic constructs that gave rise to it have become a vital contribution to the future, for they have stimulated new and creative religious ethics and philosophy as well—a new progressive religious hermeneutic in support of this plural public space.

The point is that this secularizing trend of the Enlightenment has brought benefits, a positive evolution of moral thinking, and enrichment to the religious world itself, for having to share the public space with others often brings traditions back to their best ethical moorings. The secular human rights agenda has, for example, spurred far greater attention to the religious obligations owed to needy and vulnerable others, not to mention benefitted religious minorities across the world in securing their right to practice their religion freely. The secular human rights agenda is one of the greatest guarantors of the increasing nonviolence of the planet, including nonviolence to religious people. At the same time, the secular champions of this trend need not deny room in that public space to religious people, and in fact they would undermine the very concept of that shared, democratic space in doing so.

We can acknowledge that the secularizing trends of the Enlightenment have been at least partly responsible for the massive growth in state and international commitments to human rights. But now we encounter a major point in favor of religion's contribution to peacebuilding. Once organized religion is drawn into ethical reflection on human rights, as it has been in numerous traditions that have a very clear "left wing" or progressive wing, it undeniably can reach into the hearts of millions of people. Witness, for example, the documents of Vatican II on issues vital for human rights, or the positions of the Organization of Islamic Countries, the largest organization of states in the world after the United Nations, and one can be astonished by just how much success human rights has achieved, at least in theory. As of 2012, the most conservative religious government on the planet was Saudi Arabia, but that year the King of Saudi Arabia established an unprecedented interfaith center for peace and coexistence, whose board included representatives from all the major faiths and denominations, and whose charter specifically committed itself to international agreements on human rights.[24] This would have been unthinkable just *ten* years before. To judge by the course and direction of the last fifty years, religious cultures are changing rapidly in favor of human rights.

In practice there are points of severe disagreement about religion and human rights as to the extension and application of those rights, such as regarding women or homosexuals, for example, by these conservative institutions. But we must not forget the astounding success of the new confluence of secular and religious commitments to human rights that we have witnessed in recent decades, on an interfaith basis as well as in individual traditions. This seemed to have grown at quite an accelerated pace even since the beginning of the twenty-first century. That means that there are now thousands of clerics around the world teaching these human rights values as *religious* values. Voltaire and Spinoza might be shocked, Marx might be horrified, Kant and Grotius might be pleased, and Jefferson might be pleasantly surprised.

Here is the most important point about the value added of religion. There would be far less violence in the name of religion if millions of clerics were teaching these values every week. Religious bodies, when seriously engaged, have the power to socialize millions if not billions of people into human rights thought, which would contribute massively to the increasing global consensus on these matters. They could draw on a substantial literature among modern religious thinkers and legal decision-makers as to the efficacy of human rights as expressions of valid and important religious values and laws.[25]

In addition, organized religions have interesting ways of integrating and balancing values. They do this somewhat more successfully than do government bureaucrats. Balancing rights and responsibility, individualism and communitarianism, is necessary for the global future. If organized religions help set the tone for societies trying to hold these two poles in balance, there would be a strengthening of personal, social, and political ethics. As I argue below, interfaith efforts at building a just peace are a prime example of the wisdom of such ethical integration. Indeed, the integration of values is religion's greatest strength. But here I refer to religion as conceived and framed since the Enlightenment, in which organized religion is tempered and controlled by the free society of the social contract. Here we see the best side of religion emerge, along withwisdom at practicing the integration of ethical values, of rights and responsibilities. The less power that organized religions have over the lives of citizens, the better they have been at modeling this balance. We need the society of the Enlightenment, its social contract with all variety of citizens, as the foundation upon which religions build the integration of practices such as compassion, justice, peace-seeking, reconciliation, and forgiveness.

Accordingly, we cannot escape the liberal peace model and its guarantee of rights for all. In his treatise on perpetual peace, Kant showed he knew that, as did other religious thinkers of the Enlightenment.[26] At the same time, the liberal model needs constant critique and direction. For example, we should not proceed with secular and democratic experiments based on free-market capitalism alone. Also necessary are the tempering effects of the values expressed by religiously inspired just peacemaking. This is what is directly implied in

Adam Smith's embrace of the free market. For Smith, the market by itself would not lead to the good society; only if it were accompanied by a serious commitment to the moral senses, especially values such as compassion, would it do so. [27] This suggests the way in which moral values, whether inspired by secular constructs of ethics or religious ones, would be critical to the proper functioning of the free society. I want to explore this now with some concrete examples.

In the last twenty years, religious individuals committed to peacebuilding have made a significant impact on a very wide range of conflicts globally. Both clerics and lay people have been involved, and sometimes they motivate the organized structures of their religions to participate in peacebuilding or in using nonviolent methods to inspire social change. The pioneering work of individual clerics or lay people on behalf of the poor, for example, or environmental justice often leads over time to official clerical and theological shifts on an official level. Some of the analysis of religion and peacebuilding focuses more on organizations dedicated to religion and social change. Some of these organizations operate at a more elite level of interfaith dialogue among religious leaders, whereas other organizations, such as United Religions Initiative, are highly oriented to grassroots and democratic processes of inter-religious engagement for peace.

A number of practitioners are based in academia and function as scholar-practitioners. These divide their time between theory-building and practice, research and practice, or teaching and training and practice, and sometimes teaching and training *as practice*, especially in the field. Some are firmly rooted in conflict analysis and peacebuilding programs, such as Gopin, Lederach, Appleby, and Abu Nimer, whereas others are more firmly rooted in graduate religion programs. Some are more clearly in the field as practitioners or scholar-practitioners, whereas others have primarily contributed to the field through scholarship and the construction of academic programs, while still others operate through governmental or semi-governmental agencies of research and training, such as the United States Institute of Peace.

Some scholar-practitioners' research has focused particularly on methodologies of peacebuilding in their unique cultural settings that would resonate with some religious actors in particular, such as interpretations of ancient laws involving the pursuit of peace, mediation, the practice of humility, or compassion, that are then extended into their implications for conflict resolution theory and practice. This has been the case in several faith traditions, including Judaism, Islam, Christianity, and Buddhism. [28] Other forms of analysis focus on the ways religious approaches to peacebuilding may reach a level of psychosocial depth that more secular approaches may not achieve, such as we saw before in the work of Philpott. Some have engaged in advocacy and increased literacy on this subject through the construction of dedicated websites, such as Joseph Montville's Family of Abraham. [29] All of the literature acknowledges that organized religions can contribute to both peace and violence based on competing interpretations and attest to the hermeneutical potential of religious peacebuilding.

There are also organizations in this field, active in advocacy and practice, that take a distinct faith trajectory advocating a particular religion, such as World Vision. Nevertheless they have dedicated themselves unmistakably to peacebuilding activities that cut across religious lines. Then there is a distinct literature of a more purely theological kind that focuses on the legal and religious theological foundations for peacebuilding. [30]

Finally, and not least, a persistent strain of this field is focused on and builds upon inter-faith dialogue. Interfaith dialogue has a long and distinguished history, and it is often seen as a form of peacebuilding by activists, scholars, and public officials. I have distinguished that work from my own interventions in the field, and yet dialogue is a consistent label for all of our work. I have made it clear in my writings and also in my practice that dialogue is an insufficient depiction of the kind of transformative relationship-building that I consider optimal for interfaith conflict resolution. But I will still get enthusiastic support for my work, sometimes from high officials like former President Bill Clinton, in praise of my work in interfaith dialogue![31] Clearly, whether interfaith dialogue is or is not sufficient as a phrase or experience to capture the full range of this field's work, it has captured the imagination and support of a broad range of political and religious leaders. Without a doubt, there is a great diversity of practices and actors in this field of religious peacebuilding.

INTERFAITH JUST PEACEBUILDING: AN INTEGRATIVE MOMENT FOR LIBERAL AND RELIGIOUS VALUES

Among these various contributions there is an unprecedented opportunity to bring together the great power of personal conscience, which gave birth to a radical human rights agenda such as the world had never seen, with the tremendous organizing capacity, popular educa-tional capacity, and family-friendly power of organized religions. Let me explain this with an analytical synopsis of just peacemaking, a term which refers to a particular instantiation of what the editors and contributors to this volume typically refer to as the task of building a justpeace.

Interfaith just peacemaking and its predecessor of Christian just peacemaking are good examples of how the integration of secular and religious values can demonstrate its greatest power. A synopsis of Christian just peacemaking has been articulated by Glen Stassen,[32] but the implications for interfaith just peacemaking are clear. Stassen's description corresponds to my own analysis of the creative integration of the religious and secular paradigms of human rights and social justice. We both agree that there are some interesting and seamless integrations emerging in terms of global peace and justice culture, and these integrations are aiding the global community to reach unprecedented levels of human nonviolence, at least statistically.[33]

Hermeneutics itself is a vital form of religious growth and creative change that goes back thousands of years. The just peacemaking priorities outlined by Stassen are a good example of the unfolding of new religious paradigms that marry the best of modern secular thinking and religious spiritual categories to explore the questions of justice and peace. For example, Stassen explains that while pacifism and just war theory both intend to prevent some wars or all wars, they focus on discerning whether war is justified or not. "Recognizing a practi-cal stalemate between the arguments for pacifism and just war," he says, "the theory of just peacemaking seeks to define and implement practices that *prevent* violent conflict and *create* peace. Notice, however, that pacifism and just war theory, while they certainly have roots in religious traditions, are secular constructs as well, having old roots in many wisdom and legal traditions. Notice also that, moving beyond the binaries of just war and pacifism, just peacemaking emphasizes the power of human agency, every individual's agency, as opposed to the just war tradition, which arrogates to religious leaders the moral decision about whether secular wars are justified or not. Thus, just peacemaking goes back to biblical roots that emphasize personal, not clerical, responsibility, but also seems strongly influenced by modern commitment to the individual's agency in the world as a basic right, or a foundation of human rights.

Similarly, Stassen's just peacemaking approach calls for support of nonviolent direct action by governments, social movements, and individuals. Of course there is a strong biblical basis for nonviolence in Jesus's own example and way of transforming conflict (cf. Mt 5:38ff.). But the movements of recent nonviolent change cited by Stassen (in the Philippines, Eastern Europe, and elsewhere) clearly involved both secular and religious actors with religious and nonreligious liberal motivations. Stassen adds an important textual religious hermeneutic that lends depth to seeing the religious expression of nonviolent direct action in its ancient roots.

A second practice of just peacemaking, according to Stassen, is to take independent initiatives to reduce threat. These include steps, independent of the slow process of negotiation, that decrease threat perception and distrust but do not leave the initiator weak. These initiatives are verifiable actions carried out at the announced time regardless of the other side's bluster; they have their purpose clearly announced—to shift toward de-escalation and to invite reciprocation. Although they have a biblical basis, these measures might also be seen as secular confidence-building measures and the kind of gestures that promote trust between negotiators. In short, they have their origins in both secular and religious wisdom traditions.

A third just peacemaking practice is to use cooperative conflict resolution. It has a biblical basis (Mt 5:21ff.: "Go, make peace with your adversary while there is time"). But it is also derived from and expresses itself in clear secular constructs of conflict resolution practice. Crucially, conflict resolution is not separated from justice. It is hard to know in the development of conflict resolution theory and practice in recent years who influenced whom more on the centrality of justice as integral to authentic conflict resolution—religious or secular practitioners? Having played a role in building this field, I believe that, oddly enough, both the religious peacebuilders and the more socialist or Marxist theoreticians have been the ones to champion the indispensability of justice in conflict resolution. The classic secular liberal exponents, however, in various elite institutions, have often "settled" for conflict resolution practices that are closer to negotiations and liberal models that more easily cooperate with governmental, corporate, and international institutions of a rather conservative nature. The question of how justice became more central to conflict resolution requires more study, but the point here is that the reader should see how hard it is to separate secular and religious contributions to the combination of peace and justice as indispensable to conflict resolution.

This becomes clear yet again in Stassen's advice to acknowledge responsibility for conflict and injustice and seek repentance and forgiveness. He invokes the examples of Germany since World War II, the South African Truth and Reconciliation Commission, and other actions designed to heal long-standing bitterness. The religious foundations of repentance and forgiveness are self-evident, yet Stassen combines them seamlessly with secular state models of apology that have played constructive roles in moving beyond cycles of violence in recent history.

Just peacemaking theory also exposes the secular and religious roots of democracy, human rights, and religious freedom. It may seem odd to some to hear of religious liberty as a cardinal principle of religious ethics, considering the often violent history of biblical monotheism. But the argument for religious pluralism is a very real element in monotheistic philosophical and mystical history from the beginning. It should come as no surprise, therefore, that here too is a great potential for common cause between secular and religious ethics in terms of the right to freedom of religion, and the best practices of conflict resolution that will realize that outcome.

Stassen and others also note the secular-religious consensus on the need to foster sustainable economic development; the importance of forming and sustaining voluntary associations for peace, international exchanges, communications, transactions, and networks; and the centrality of the United Nations and international efforts for cooperation and human rights.

Stassen rightly perceives that the United Nations is a hard-headed but highly imperfect instantiation of the biblical command to love one's enemies. In other words, it is a place to deal and negotiate with many enemies; that is its purpose. That it disappoints often on humanitarian and human rights issues should come as no surprise because that is exactly where enemy perceptions of the other will come to those very conclusions. It is effectively a place of nonviolent battle, as it should be. For example, many at the UN see the developed countries, especially the United States, as the principal supporters of human rights violations, whereas many in the United States might see less democratic developing countries as using the UN to deflect blame onto the West and distract their own people. Despite these problems, there is a confluence of a religious ideal of loving your enemies (or, in Judaism, helping your enemies) with the practical effects of the United Nations system. Despite our focus on some sensational failures, United Nations missions all over the world quietly succeed in preventing bloodshed and maximizing a humanitarian approach to problem-solving. Those saved lives are attributable to the uncomfortable way in which the great and small powers are forced to sit with each other and stomach each other's prevarications. As Stassen indicates, even if biblical traditions are foreign to the actual motivations and rationales of international actors, this is classical nonviolent diplomacy and weapons reduction.

Just peacemaking is hard; it is about dealing with enemies rather than killing them, which requires a strong inner motivation. Stassen provides that motivation in this case through a controversial religious virtue, loving your enemies. I can imagine other ethicists reaching the same mindset of dealing with enemies through meditation and yoga, for example, or compassion, or through utilitarian ethical calculations. The point is that we must see the multiple intellectual and emotional paths by which secular and religious thinking can reach the same destination.

The confluence of religious organizations and secular organizations struggling for common goals has had obvious benefits for any number of global struggles for peace and justice. This has been true in the United States, for example, almost since the birth of the country. But, as Stassen is implying with the practice for building justpeace, bringing the religious and secular together in a common effort should become a more self-conscious activity, more deliberately embraced by both communities, rather than the product of stumbling into an uncomfortable alliance and sometimes hostile relationship. The alliance has been very productive on matters ranging from the abolition of slavery centuries ago, to the withdrawal from Vietnam and the birth of an environmental movement that has produced many significant gains for the earth. But the relationship could be far more productive if there were a kind of religious-secular social contract of common interests and values, with an agreement to disagree where it is unavoidable. This can enhance justice and peace in the United States and become a better model for other highly divided societies where the hatred between secular Left and religious Right is so intense that there is no productive synergy at all for common interests and values.

Two recent innovations and experiments within my own conflict resolution practice show how interfaith just peacemaking practices provide a useful integration of secular and religious principles and practices, an integration that exists both in reality and in my own combinations as a practitioner. I am indebted to an Enlightenment narrative of tolerance and civility, along with my inheritance of religious values, and both play into specific instances of collaboration in conflict zones.

INTERVENTION IN SYRIA

The Arab Spring has pushed to the forefront of human civilization the question of nonviolent resistance, popular demonstration, and the question of what power, if any, the masses of people have to change history and the political structure of their countries. An astonishing variety of cultures and states across the Arab world have felt the power of people to shake and move history in a different direction. Just as powerfully, however, the Arab Spring has problematized the question of violent versus nonviolent resistance, and therefore taken us back to the origins of the field of conflict resolution, namely the search for forms of conflict prevention, management, mitigation, and resolution that offer a way of accomplishing social change other than simple resistance, violent or nonviolent.

In my attempts to continue years of work on citizen diplomacy and conflict resolution training in Syria together with my Syrian peace partners, it became obvious that we could no longer support an evolutionary approach of reform to the country's problems. For seven years we had worked quietly on public forms of citizen diplomacy inside Syria, focusing mostly on interfaith relations because that is all that the government would allow; we were watched and challenged in every detail of what we did. Nevertheless, we made great strides in sharing our interfaith public debates with millions of people through the media and modeling nonviolent debate on vital political issues that was coupled with common ethical commitments.[34]

Eventually we added conflict resolution training to our work in Syria as something we could "get away with" underneath the nose of the government, due to the mutual trust and nonthreatening character of our relations with everyone. We had students in conflict resolution from every walk of life, every religion and ethnic group, and we even had a number of government workers taking our classes. The psychology of conflict resolution training, the emphasis on empathic skills in role-plays and the art of compromise, were good—and subversive—skills for opening up Syrian society even in a dictatorship. We were opening up the possibility of "a culture of debate," Hind Kabawat's words for the rudimentary elements of democratic deliberation.[35]

It became more and more obvious, however, as the reaction of the Syrian government to the demonstrations of 2011 became more and more barbaric, that we could no longer believe in or support an evolutionary approach to Syria. We needed to express solidarity with the innocent and courageous nonviolent citizens who were dying in the streets at the hands of the corrupt and brutal security services. This realization came to me at the same time that I was becoming fascinated with the benefits of nonviolent resistance activities in Palestine as well as Iran.

I was introduced in the last few years to Michael Nagler's work[36] and reacquainted with the work of Mubarak Awad[37] and many others whose work has been the application of non-violence theory to the concrete challenges facing suffering people across the world. This had a profound effect on me, because I had been troubled by a weakness in ways nonviolent resistance came to be employed over the decades. That weakness involves the dynamic of demonization that has afflicted violent and nonviolent forms of resistance alike. One of the most important schools of conflict analysis, the psychodynamic school, has rightly empha-sized the destructive nature of demonization as a generator of radical violence and conflict acceleration.

Nonviolent resistance training in the West, as far as I have observed, has tended to accept and even encourage demonization of the authoritarian regime in question, especially as advocated by Gene Sharp.[38] This development in nonviolent resistance was the opposite of the intentions of Gandhi, King, Nagler, and others, in my opinion. Gandhi and King's ultimate aims seemed to be nicely aligned with conflict resolution theory and practice, but I worried that nonviolent resistance as framed by Sharp and others would produce more destructive violence, not less, and only elicit a greater spiral of violence. In fact, the very purpose of demonizing the dictator is to provoke violence from oppressive regimes, create martyrs, and bring out the masses even more. I understand the rationale behind this strat-egy and its focus on generating sympathy among third-party observers. My concern with such an approach emerges from an ethical point of view. Gandhi constantly had his hand reached out to the British, at every stage. He hated demonization and knew that it was the enemy of his whole philosophy and purpose. Notably, nonviolence as a method of resis-tance has, since Gandhi and King's movements of mass resistance, differentiated itself from explicitly religious ground in order to be more broadly applied as a tool to crumble down, as the renowned scholar of nonviolent resistance Gene Sharp illuminated, the pillars of power upon which the legitimacy of dictatorships and other authoritarian regimes rests.

The sense of dissonance I experienced between my understanding of the ethical grounds of nonviolent resistance and the patterns of demonization I observed in later deployments of nonviolent resistance presented me with a dilemma regarding my own interventions in Syria. Years of work in citizen diplomacy had proven to me that there was no category of people to demonize, not in governments, not in militaries, not in intelligence, not in terror-ist groups. Despite some serious criminality, for which they should be brought to justice, people from such groups often feel themselves to be making supreme sacrifices for what they believe is right and good and best for people, often for their own people.

I myself would never participate in any of their violent subcultures. (I have never touched a gun.) But I realized that extending a hand to all of them in engagement, dialogue, resis-tance to violence—but resistance with invitation even to violent groups and governments— was the only way out of the hell of endless cycles of violence. The only evil is the cycle of violence itself that consumes innocent children like a hungry monster. That was my only chosen enemy. I therefore faced a dilemma between the world of hardcore nonviolent resistance and the world of citizen diplomacy, conflict resolution, diplomatic engagement with all parties—an approach that fundamentally resists demonization. I knew that I could not embrace as an ideal a form of political engagement, nonviolent resistance, that *by definition* demonized leaders or governments,[39] just as surely as I could not embrace warriors who would consider the art of killing as optimal. But the atrocities and astonishing war crimes that the Syrian government officials perpetrated and outsourced to the *shabiha* in these years of revolution from 2010 through 2013 have been a difficult test for all of us committed to nonviolence.

I also faced a dilemma in terms of secular, academic, NGO, and governmental bureaucratic tendencies to separate ethical engagements with the world that should not be separated or separable. For example, resisting oppressive governments and utilizing conflict resolution skills, citizen diplomacy, and interfaith peacebuilding to reach out to all parties should not be mutually exclusive activities. But they often are divided as either/or options. The same goes for providing humanitarian aid to victims and doing conflict resolution work with divided ethnic and religious minorities. They were both necessary with the same Syrian refugees, for example.

My sense was that the very interesting and effective world of nonviolent resistance training was doing important work, but that they were in danger of getting people killed by their unnecessary levels of demonization and disengagement from those in power, especially Alawites and Christians who needed to be encouraged to join the opposition to form a new democratic Syria. Conversely, I felt that conflict resolution practices devolved sometimes into engagements that under-serve the cause of justice, especially of those most oppressed. I was sure the two fields, nonviolent resistance and conflict resolution, both academically and in NGO communities, could learn more from each other and cooperate more, but facilitating this cooperation was hard, due to over-specialization, over-classification, and resulting tribal competitions.

This is where I realized that the blending of values encouraged by interfaith just peacemaking practices makes available the contributions of integrated systems of religious ethics. In turn, these religiously integrated values could inform professional and bureaucratic practices of global interventions, such as bridging the imperatives of nonviolent resistance professionals and conflict resolution professionals. While religious actors in history tend to restrict the scope of ethical concern to one saved or favored group, the best aspect of religious ethics is the effective prophetic integration of peace and social justice practices that *together* create a compassionate, more integrated, and holistic approach to a very complicated and difficult world.

This realization led us in the Syrian crisis to a cautious embrace of nonviolent resistance work and training combined with vital conflict resolution training and skill-building. The goal is to maximize the chance of building a new, peaceful Syria among the survivors who hail from such different and mutually wounding backgrounds. This is the kind of training that our CRDC team from Syria has undertaken. It resists the tribalization of intervention efforts into either the armed resistance camp or the nonviolent resistance camp. Instead, it weaved together a Gandhian-style commitment to resistance that is highly "invitational," constantly reaching out to enemy others in order to cast a wide net for a future of Syria that is tolerant, diverse, and just.

SOCIALLY RESPONSIBLE TOURISM

I have discovered the same need for integration of values, championed so well in religious values, through our experiments in social business as peacebuilding. A crisis in my peace work in Israel/Palestine began after 2000, with the suicide bomb phenomenon from Hamas, which was triggered in part by the aggressive settlement movement and the Goldstein massacre in Hebron in 1994 (there were no suicide bombs before this unprecedented massacre of Muslim worshippers). The continual wars, the rockets, the so-called "Security Wall," all created the ingredients of a deteriorating relationship between Palestinians and Israelis that all of our nonprofit work seemed incapable of reversing. NGOs in Israel were out-maneuvered and out-financed by the forces of conflict and war; this was a depressing, demoralizing predicament indeed.

My colleagues and I wanted to do something utterly different and new that would integrate several ethical and social aims that were not usually integrated in an effort to challenge "the status quo," meaning complete stalemate between the sides. The status quo was one of almost constant militarization and war, enormous imbalance of power, and failure to make progress in the project of equality and coexistence between Israel and Palestine. The just peacemaking categories integrate a range of values and goals that captured our thinking. We discovered that instead of focusing exclusively on political approaches to social change, such as dialogue and conflict resolution strategies, which had lost all credibility with both sides, we would use a cultural institution that had been deeply indigenous to the Palestinian and Jewish psyche for thousands of years: business. But we would add to business a set of qualities in relationship between enemies that would make it a powerful and irresistible model of social change.

We found a commodity that everyone loved to contribute to and benefit from—tourist dollars. We discovered that if the lure of tourist dollars were wedded deeply to Palestinian/Jewish partnership at every level, if that partnership embraced both narratives equally, if the economic benefits were equally shared, and in particular if fair wage methods guaranteed that the profits filtered down to the poor, and to poor peacebuilders, then and only then could we push the trends of war in a direction of conflict transformation. We could push toward more equality between classes on both sides, more equality between Jews and Palestinians, more honor of two narratives, more evidence that peace pays off despite the obvious misery caused by militants and unscrupulous leaders and institutions. The traditional liberal constructs of negotiations at elite levels had totally failed to transform the cultures, or to include religious people committed to new relations. We discovered that enacting the values of peace, fairness, equality, and justice in a very practical way could engage religious and secular alike, rich and poor alike. Thus, although we were committed to liberal and secular efforts to achieve peace, we felt that the model of social change needed to go much deeper. The secular liberal model of the Oslo peace process did contain commitments to business, but it was business among mostly neoliberal elites, which left most Israelis economically unaffected and most Palestinians even more disadvantaged. This was incompatible with prophetic religious values that focus on the bottom of society and their needs. Thus, our model was an artful combination of religious and secular values and one utterly consistent with the lens of justpeace informing this volume.

In a short time of operation, just three years, we managed to inject approximately $500,000 into the Palestinian and Israeli economy that filtered down to middle-class and poor families—and to peacebuilders on both sides who have been trained as our tour guides for the dual narrative tours.

The Enlightenment philosopher Immanuel Kant, one of the truly great visionaries of the mechanics of nonviolent human interaction, predicted in *Perpetual Peace*, previously referred to, that "gentle commerce," when done well and justly, could become a key vehicle of conflict prevention and conflict resolution. That is exactly what we have discovered, although many orders of magnitude more commerce is necessary to spur a true paradigm shift of thinking and behavior in the Israeli/Palestinian conflict, which would in turn generate new political leadership or push the present leadership in a better direction, as President Obama urged in a recent lecture to Israelis.[40] Of course, Kant is frequently retrieved as pivotal for conceptions of a liberal peace. An emphasis on commerce, therefore, needs to be held in a creative tension with the prophetic framing of just peacemaking, its focus on the margins of society, and its emphasis on positive rather than negative peace.

The essential point for the purposes of this discussion is the following. Professional secular categories of conflict resolution, dialogue, development, or even nonviolent resistance were not sufficiently integrative of the ethical values necessary to build our new paradigm. We were searching for a combination of love of peace, justice, honor, equality, care for families, humble engagement with poor shopkeepers, respect for business, that could generate a new experiment. Thus we combined the recommendations of the German Pietist Kant for equal treatment with the analytic value of the conflict resolution "contact" hypothesis.[41] This brought to bear the essence of Kant's categorical imperative—the embrace of the rule of law, of gentle commerce, of the centrality of deeds, not just words, and of investment in people, not just roads (in Kant's language, a kingdom of ends). We combined all of that with tours that generate compassion, listening, and humility. The combination of secular professional approaches to development and conflict resolution with classical Abrahamic ethics of engagement created a unique venture. This kind of synergy between ethics rooted in traditional values of piety, together with secular constructs of business and conflict resolution engagement, suggests religious and secular approaches to peacebuilding should be embraced around the globe. There is a clear line between the emerging impact of global tourism done well, on the one side, and, on the other, Kant's pioneering approach to global governance and gentle commerce centuries ago. He pioneered rather secular institutions of global governance, and yet he constructed his universal categories inspired by his hermeneutic of German Christian piety.

The integrated values of just peacemaking, like many religious ethical disciplines around the world, capture the kind of personal and collective ethical commitments that give rise to new experiments and approaches in seemingly intractable conflicts. Nothing about these combinations requires faith in God or some set of dogma. It is simply that religious approaches to ethics and social transformation make for a rich and productive environment in which to innovate for peace and justice at a deep level.

NOTES

1. Jonathan Fox, "Religion as an Overlooked Element of International Relations," *International Studies Review* 3, no. 3 (2001): 53–73; Eric Patterson, *Politics in a Religious*

World: Building a Religiously Literate U.S. Foreign Policy (New York: Continuum Books, 2011).

2. See http://www.foreignaffairs.com/articles/48950/samuel-p-huntington/the-clash-of-civilizations. For an excellent critique of the Huntington thesis from a conflict resolution perspective, see Kevin Avruch, *Context and Pretext in Conflict Resolution: Culture, Identity, Power, and Practice* (Boulder, CO: Paradigm Publishers, 2012), 81–95.

3. See Elizabeth Shakman Hurd, *The Politics of Secularism in International Relations* (Princeton, NJ: Princeton University Press, 2008).

4. Douglas Johnston and Cynthia Sampson, eds., *Religion, the Missing Dimension of Statecraft* (New York: Oxford University Press, 1994).

5. Monica Duffy Toft, Daniel Philpott, and Timothy Samuel Shah, *God's Century: Resurgent Religion and Global Politics* (New York: W. W. Norton, 2011), 221.

6. Additionally, see Timothy Samuel Shah, Alfred Stepan, and Monica Duffy Toft, eds., *Rethinking Religion and World Affairs* (New York: Oxford University Press, 2012).

7. See generally Dennis Hoover and Douglas Johnston, eds., *Religion and Foreign Affairs: Essential Readings* (Waco, TX: Baylor University Press, 2012).

8. Emile Sahliyeh, ed., *Religious Resurgence and Politics in the Contemporary World* (New York: State University of New York Press, 1990), 6.

9. Pakistan, Afghanistan, Gaza, Syria, Burma, Egypt, and Israel, to name just a few.

10. R. Scott Appleby and Atalia Omer, email communication with author and others, March 2012.

11. John Paul Lederach and R. Scott Appleby, "Strategic Peacebuliding: An Overview," in *Strategies of Peace: Transforming Conflict in a Violent World*, ed. Daniel Philpott and Gerard F. Powers (New York: Oxford University Press, 2010), 19–44.

12. R. Scott Appleby, *The Ambivalence of the Sacred: Religion, Violence, and Reconciliation* (Lanham, MD: Rowman and Littlefield, 2000).

13. Douglas Johnston and Brian Cox, "Faith-Based Diplomacy and Preventive Engagement," in *Faith-Based Diplomacy: Trumping Realpolitik*, ed. Douglas Johnston (New York: Oxford University Press, 2003), 11–29.

14. See, for example, R. Scott Appleby, Richard Cizik, and Thomas Wright, "Engaging Religious Communities Abroad: A New Imperative for U.S. Foreign Policy," Report of the Task Force on Religion and the Making of U.S. Foreign Policy, sponsored by the Chicago Council on Global Affairs, 2010, http://www.thechicagocouncil.org/Files/Studies_Publications/TaskForcesandStudies/Religion_2010.aspx; and Maria Otero, "Remarks to the Religion and Foreign Policy Working Group," US Department of State, October 18, 2011, http://www.state.gov/j/176344.htm.

15. Appleby, *The Ambivalence of the Sacred*; George W. Wolfe, *The Spiritual Power of Nonviolence: Interfaith Understanding for a Future Without War* (Austin, TX: Jomar Press, 2011); Katrien Hertog, *The Complex Reality of Religious Peacebuilding: Conceptual Contributions and Analysis* (Lanham, MD: Lexington Books, 2010); Johnston and Cox, "Faith-Based Diplomacy and Preventive Engagement"; Timothy D. Sisk, ed., *Between Terror and Tolerance: Religious Leaders, Conflict, and Peacemaking* (Washington, DC: Georgetown University Press, 2011).

16. On this methodology, see generally Marc Gopin, *Between Eden and Armageddon: The Future of World Religions, Violence, and Peacemaking* (New York: Oxford University Press, 2000).

17. As do Abdul Aziz Said, Nathan C. Funk, and Ayse S. Kadayifci, eds., *Peace and Conflict Resolution in Islam: Precept and Practice* (Lanham, MD: University Press of America,

2001); and Qamar-ul Huda, ed., *Crescent and Dove: Peace and Conflict Resolution in Islam* (Washington, DC: US Institute of Peace Press, 2010).

18. Marc Gopin, *To Make the Earth Whole: The Art of Citizen Diplomacy in an Age of Religious Militancy* (Lanham, MD: Rowman and Littlefield, 2009), 66–73.

19. Daniel Philpott, *Just and Unjust Peace: An Ethic of Political Reconciliation* (New York: Oxford University Press, 2012).

20. See Marc Gopin, *Holy War, Holy Peace* (New York: Oxford University Press, 2002), 108–143.

21. Philpott, *Just and Unjust Peace*, 9.

22. Daniel Philpott and Gerard F. Powers, eds., *Strategies of Peace: Transforming Conflict in a Violent World* (New York: Oxford University Press, 2010).

23. Marc Gopin, *Bridges Across an Impossible Divide: The Inner Lives of Arab and Jewish Peacemakers* (New York: Oxford University Press, 2012).

24. See http://www.kaiciid.org/en/the-centre/the-centre.html.

25. An interesting bibliography in this area was compiled by the International Center for Law and Religion Studies. Notice how much research has evolved on the important interaction of religion and human rights. The roots of this evolution go back many centuries, to authors such as Grotius. See "Religion and the Secular State: Selected Bibliography," International Center for Law and Religion Studies, http://www.iclrs.org/content/blurb/files/Selected%20Bibliography.1.pdf.

26. Immanuel Kant, *Toward Perpetual Peace and Other Writings on Politics, Peace, and History*, edited and with an Introduction by Pauline Kleingeld, translated by David L. Colclasure (New Haven, CT: Yale University Press, 2006).

27. Adam Smith, *The Wealth of Nations*, ed. Edwin Cannan (London: Methuen, 1904), Book III, Chapter IV, 448.

28. The appreciation of sacred text and text study, for example, has become an important bridge between Jews, Christians, and Muslims, for finding common values and narratives, as well as deepening mutual respect and tolerance. See, for example, http://www.scripturalreasoning.org, a website run by the Cambridge Inter-faith Programme, on the phenomenon of engaging scriptural reasoning across many traditions. But this is preceded by decades of deep interfaith interaction between Jews, Christians, and Muslims on text study, a practice with ancient roots that was unfortunately suppressed and only engaged covertly for many generations. Conflict resolution methodologies indigenous to the Arab world, such as *Sulha*, have become an important traditional precursor to and advance of conflict resolution methodology. See, for example, Zoughbi Zoughbi, ed., *Sulha: Community Based Mediation in Palestine* (Alexandria, VA: Holistic Solutions, Inc., 2013) and http://www.sulha.com. Recently, new Jewish rituals are appearing in very traditional settings, such as the institution of a ritual day of constructive conflict. See "9 Adar: Jewish Day of Constructive Conflict," Pardes Center for Judaism and Conflict Resolution, http://pcjcr.pardes.org/courses/study-materials-for-global-machloket-leshem-shamayim-day/, a project that is the brainchild of Rabbi Dr. Daniel Roth.

29. Abrahamic Family Reunion, http://abrahamicfamilyreunion.org/uniting-the-children-of-abraham/.

30. I am thinking here of the works of Sheikh Qadri, Arthur Green, Arthur Waskow, Chief Rabbi Jonathan Sacks, Abdulaziz Sachedina, and Abdolkorim Soroush, among many others. See Dr. Muhammad Tahrir-ul-Qadri, *Fatwa on Terrorism and Suicide Bombings* (London: Minhaj-ul-Quran International, 2010), http://www.quranandwar.com/

FATWA%20on%20Terrorism%20and%20Suicide%20Bombings.pdf, and http://www.fatwaonterrorism.com/; Arthur Green, *Radical Judaism: Rethinking God and Tradition* (New Haven, CT: Yale University Press, 2010); Joan Chittister, Murshid Saadi Shakur Chishti, and Arthur Waskow, *The Tent of Abraham: Stories of Hope and Peace for Jews, Christians, and Muslims* (Boston: Beacon Press, 2006); Jonathan Sacks, *The Dignity of Difference: How to Avoid the Clash of Civilizations*, 2nd ed. (London: Bloomsbury Academic, 2003); Jonathan Sacks, *To Heal a Fractured World: The Ethics of Responsibility* (New York: Schocken Books, 2005); Abdulaziz Sachedina, *The Islamic Roots of Democratic Pluralism* (New York: Oxford University Press, 2001); Abdolkarim Soroush, *Reason, Freedom, and Democracy in Islam: Essential Writings of Adbolkarim Soroush*, translated, edited, and with a critical introduction by Mahmoud Sadri and Ahmad Sadri (New York: Oxford University Press, 2000); and Glen Stassen, ed., *Just Peacemaking: The New Paradigm for the Ethics of Peace and War* (Cleveland, OH: Pilgrim Press, 2008).

31. Marc Gopin, *Holy War, Holy Peace*, 49–52.

32. Glen Stassen, "Holistic Hermeneutical Method for Just Peacemaking Practices," Just Peacemaking Initiative, http://justpeacemaking.org/the-holistic-hermeneutical-method/.

33. Steven Pinker, *The Better Angels of Our Nature* (New York: Penguin Books, 2011).

34. See Joshua Landis, "Hind Kabawat and Marc Gopin Work for Peace," SyriaComment.com, May 7, 2005, http://faculty-staff.ou.edu/L/Joshua.M.Landis-1/syriablog/2005/05/hind-kabawat-and-marc-gopin-work-for.htm; and Gilah Langer, "The Evolution of an American Rabbi: A Conversation with Marc Gopin," *Kerem* 12 (2010): 45–72, http://kerem.org/wp-content/uploads/2010/09/A-Conversation-with-Marc-Gopin.pdf. A full story of the events is also reported in Gopin, *Bridges Across an Impossible Divide*.

35. See Gopin, *To Make the Earth Whole*, 93–160, for an overview of this work.

36. Michael Nagler, *The Search for a Nonviolent Future* (Novato, CA: New World Library, 2004).

37. Mubarak Awad is the founder of Nonviolence International, http://nonviolenceinternational.net/.

38. See, for example, Gene Sharp, *The Role of Power in Nonviolent Struggle* (Cambridge, MA: Albert Einstein Institution, 1990).

39. See, for example, this revealing interview of the nonviolent resistance movement leaders in Serbia: Bryan Farrell and Eric Stoner, "Bringing Down Serbia's Dictator, 10 Years Later: A Conversation with Srdja Popovic," Waging Nonviolence, October 5, 2010, http://wagingnonviolence.org/feature/bringing-down-serbias-dictator-10-years-later-a-conversation-with-nonviolent-movement-leader-srdja-popovic/. I admire the leaders on many levels, and in their case the movement led to great success. But in many cases, such forms of ridicule can lead to backlash and needless casualties that I cannot in good conscience support, neither ethically nor analytically.

40. "In Full: President Obama's Speech to Israeli Students in Jerusalem," *The Jewish Chronicle Online*, March 25, 2013, http://www.thejc.com/news/israel-news/103857/in-full-president-obama's-speech-israeli-students-jerusalem.

41. Gordon Allport is generally credited with pioneering the view that the right kind of intergroup contact ultimately reduces prejudice and violent conflict. See Gordon Allport, *The Nature of Prejudice* (Cambridge, MA: Perseus Books, 1954).

BIBLIOGRAPHY

Allport, Gordon. *The Nature of Prejudice.* Cambridge, MA: Perseus Books, 1954.

Appleby, R. Scott. *The Ambivalence of the Sacred: Religion, Violence, and Reconciliation.* Lanham, MD: Rowman and Littlefield, 2000.

Avruch, Kevin. *Context and Pretext in Conflict Resolution: Culture, Identity, Power, and Practice.* Boulder, CO: Paradigm Publishers, 2012.

Chittister, Joan, Murshid Saadi Shakur Chishti, and Arthur Waskow. *The Tent of Abraham: Stories of Hope and Peace for Jews, Christians, and Muslims.* Boston: Beacon Press, 2006.

Duffy Toft, Monica, Daniel Philpott, and Timothy Samuel Shah. *God's Century: Resurgent Religion and Global Politics.* New York: W. W. Norton, 2011.

Fox, Jonathan. "Religion as an Overlooked Element of International Relations." *International Studies Review* 3, no. 3 (2001): 53–73.

Gopin, Marc. *Between Eden and Armageddon: The Future of World Religions, Violence, and Peacemaking.* New York: Oxford University Press, 2000.

Gopin, Marc. *Holy War, Holy Peace.* New York: Oxford University Press, 2002.

Gopin, Marc. *To Make the Earth Whole: The Art of Citizen Diplomacy in an Age of Religious Militancy.* Lanham, MD: Rowman and Littlefield, 2009.

Gopin, Marc. *Bridges Across an Impossible Divide: The Inner Lives of Arab and Jewish Peacemakers.* New York: Oxford University Press, 2012.

Green, Arthur. *Radical Judaism: Rethinking God and Tradition.* New Haven, CT: Yale University Press, 2010.

Hertog, Katrien. *The Complex Reality of Religious Peacebuilding: Conceptual Contributions and Analysis.* Lanham, MD: Lexington Books, 2010.

Hoover, Dennis, and Douglas Johnston, eds. *Religion and Foreign Affairs: Essential Readings.* Waco, TX: Baylor University Press, 2012.

Huda, Qamar-ul, ed. *Crescent and Dove: Peace and Conflict Resolution in Islam.* Washington, DC: US Institute of Peace Press, 2010.

Johnston, Douglas, ed. *Faith-Based Diplomacy: Trumping Realpolitik.* New York: Oxford University Press, 2003.

Johnston, Douglas, and Brian Cox. "Faith-Based Diplomacy and Preventive Engagement." In *Faith-Based Diplomacy: Trumping Realpolitik*, edited by Douglas Johnston, 11–29. New York: Oxford University Press, 2003.

Johnston, Douglas, and Cynthia Sampson, eds. *Religion, the Missing Dimension of Statecraft.* New York: Oxford University Press, 1994.

Lederach, John Paul, and R. Scott Appleby. "Strategic Peacebuilding: An Overview." In *Strategies of Peace: Transforming Conflict in a Violent World*, edited by Daniel Philpott and Gerard F. Powers, 19–44. New York: Oxford University Press, 2010.

Nagler, Michael. *The Search for a Nonviolent Future.* Novato, CA: New World Library, 2004.

Patterson, Eric. *Politics in a Religious World: Building a Religiously Literate U.S. Foreign Policy.* New York: Continuum Books, 2011.

Philpott, Daniel. *Just and Unjust Peace: An Ethic of Political Reconciliation.* New York: Oxford University Press, 2012.

Philpott, Daniel, and Gerard F. Powers, eds. *Strategies of Peace: Transforming Conflict in a Violent World.* New York: Oxford University Press, 2010.

Pinker, Steven. *The Better Angels of Our Nature.* New York: Penguin Books, 2011.

Sachedina, Abdulaziz. *The Islamic Roots of Democratic Pluralism*. New York: Oxford University Press, 2001.

Sacks, Jonathan. *The Dignity of Difference: How to Avoid the Clash of Civilizations*. 2nd ed. London: Bloomsbury Academic, 2003.

Sacks, Jonathan. *To Heal a Fractured World: The Ethics of Responsibility*. New York: Schocken Books, 2005.

Sahliyeh, Emile, ed. *Religious Resurgence and Politics in the Contemporary World*. New York: State University of New York Press, 1990.

Said, Abdul Aziz, Nathan C. Funk, and Ayse S. Kadayifci, eds. *Peace and Conflict Resolution in Islam: Precept and Practice*. Lanham, MD: University Press of America, 2001.

Shah, Timothy Samuel, Alfred Stepan, and Monica Duffy Toft, eds. *Rethinking Religion and World Affairs*. New York: Oxford University Press, 2012.

Shakman Hurd, Elizabeth. *The Politics of Secularism in International Relations* Princeton, NJ: Princeton University Press, 2008.

Sharp, Gene. *The Role of Power in Nonviolent Struggle*. Cambridge, MA: Albert Einstein Institution, 1990.

Sisk, Timothy D., ed. *Between Terror and Tolerance: Religious Leaders, Conflict, and Peacemaking*. Washington, DC: Georgetown University Press, 2011.

Soroush, Abdolkarim. *Reason, Freedom, and Democracy in Islam: Essential Writings of Abdolkarim Soroush*. Translated, edited, and with a critical introduction by Mahmoud Sadri and Ahmad Sadri. New York: Oxford University Press, 2000.

Stassen, Glen. "Holistic Hermeneutical Method for Just Peacemaking Practices." Just Peacemaking Initiative. http://justpeacemaking.org/the-holistic-hermeneutical-method/.

Stassen, Glen, ed. *Just Peacemaking: The New Paradigm for the Ethics of Peace and War*. Cleveland, OH: Pilgrim Press, 2008.

Tahir-ul-Qadri, Muhammad. *Fatwa on Terrorism and Suicide Bombings*. London: Minhaj-ul-Quran International, 2010. http://www.quranandwar.com/FATWA%20on%20Terrorism%20and%20Suicide%20Bombings.pdf.

Wolfe, George W. *The Spiritual Power of Nonviolence: Interfaith Understanding for a Future Without War*. Austin, TX: Jomar Press, 2011.

CHAPTER 15

SECULAR MILITANCY AS AN OBSTACLE TO PEACEBUILDING

TIMOTHY SAMUEL SHAH

INTRODUCTION

WHAT features of the current global context constitute essential background for understanding the dynamics of religion, conflict, and peacebuilding today? If the geopolitical competition between European great powers implied one kind of agenda for scholars and practitioners concerned about religion and peace in the nineteenth century, and the worldwide clash between largely secular political and economic ideologies implied another very different agenda for such scholars and practitioners for much of the twentieth century, what are the most important and relevant global dynamics today?

That is, what do we need to know about the trajectory of world affairs in order to understand the interrelationship of religion, conflict, and peacebuilding in the twenty-first century? In particular, what, if anything, is new and distinctive about the place and trajectory of religion in world affairs in the current context? What is new and distinctive in the religious field itself, one might say, in terms of religion's configurations and practices? And what dominant patterns and trajectories, if any, characterize the relationship between the religious field and political dynamics in ways that bear on patterns of religious conflict and religious peacebuilding?

In trying to answer these questions, caution is immediately in order. As Robert Nisbet bracingly articulated nearly two generations ago, elegant generalization about the trajectory of "the world" or of "history" is, strictly speaking, impossible. How indeed "does one make an entity out of [world history's] far-flung and diversified conglomerate of peoples and acts?"[1] This question arises whether we are talking about the distant past of ancient civilizations or what one might call the contemporary past of current history. And it is as relevant to attempts to generalize about global religious dynamics as to efforts to generalize about "secular" or nonreligious trends, patterns, and developments. The extraordinarily wide range of the world's religious actors and ideas and dynamics intersects with the extraordinarily wide range of the world's social and political contexts in an extraordinarily wide range of ways, giving us an array of religious permutations so numerous and disparate that the slightest temptation on the part of any student of history to squeeze all this diversity into a single grand narrative deserves the application of a large bucket of icy water.

Even on Nisbet's terms, however, it is not systematic thinking as such that should be resisted, but systematic thinking that reduces global complexity to a single "entity" or trajectory. Precisely inquiry that aims at science or Wissenschaft cannot do without systematic thought that runs the risk of simplistic and even reductionist generalization. Since Thomas Kuhn, we know that scientific inquiry cannot do without "paradigms." We want and need to understand the world. Yet it is by now a truism that we cannot understand and illuminate the world—or any part of it—without simplifying it. And we cannot simplify it usefully without Kuhnian paradigms. For "something like a paradigm is prerequisite to perception itself."[2]

So we are caught between two epistemic imperatives as we seek to illuminate the world and its complex dynamics of religion, conflict, and peacebuilding. On one hand, we must make every effort to avoid "grand narratives" that are grossly simplistic, univocal, and reductionist. On the other hand, we have no choice but to employ paradigms that are radically simplifying. Indeed, the paradigms that we must employ—"must" in both a strong sense of inevitability and normativity—necessarily focus our attention on some phenomena relevant to our inquiry while systematically screening out other phenomena that may also be relevant to our inquiry. But it is not only that our paradigms predetermine what data we see. The data appear to us only through the lens of our paradigms and therefore laden with a quality and significance they would lack save for our paradigms.

In this paper I suggest a paradigm for understanding the place of religion in this current historical moment vis-à-vis both the ongoing horrors of violence in our world and struggles to build peace. This paradigm, I think, lays stress on some features of religion that have characteristically been neglected by other paradigms that have dominated much thinking about religion in the modern world—above all, secularization theory. The paradigm seeks to respect both of the epistemic imperatives noted above. That is, it aspires to at least some epistemic modesty, recognizing the danger and futility of grandiose narratives that look for a single arc or trajectory or causal driver of global dynamics. But it also unapologetically embraces a paradigm that is simple and simplifying. This paradigm represents a particular outlook conditioned by particular assumptions, experiences, convictions, and, frankly, normative commitments. Only armed with such an outlook can we register what we know about the world and hope to expand somewhat our stock of knowledge and understanding.

To navigate between the shoals of overconfident dogmatism and the "bloomin' buzzin' confusion" of skepticism, I propose that a useful way to illuminate the realities and dynamics of religion, conflict, and peacebuilding today is through a paradigm of "persistent unsecularity." As befits the imperative of epistemic modesty, this paradigm does not replace the dogmatism of overconfident modernization and secularization theories with the dogmatism of an overconfident paradigm of "sacralization" or "desecularization." Instead, its claims are more humble. If I may, the significance of the little prefix "un" in "unsecularity" parallels the insight of the apophatic approach in theology. According to this approach, one builds one's knowledge of God not through the dogmatic proclamation of what or who God is but through the cumulative knowledge of what God is *not* and *cannot* be.

By analogy to apophatic theology, the paradigm I propose holds that we know too little about the world to be confident that its political and social dynamics—including its wars and its efforts to build peace—will always and everywhere be thoroughly religious or sacral in the sense of being directly and self-consciously oriented to some more-than-human source and framework of reality. We know too little to be able to say that the whole world is moving along a single trajectory toward greater "religiosity," however defined. However, I believe we know enough to be able to say something about what the world and its political dynamics are *not* and will *not* be: in the main, the world's peoples and their conflicts will *not* be systematically or thoroughly shut off from, closed to, or indifferent to religious questions, longings, concerns, ideas, practices, and communities.

"We know too little to be dogmatists," to quote Pascal, "but we know too much to be skeptics."[3] We know very little relative to what we would like to know, but we know enough to have some confidence about what the world is not. And we can be confident that neither our world nor our age taken as a whole is secular or secularizing. Indeed, as I explore below, the very zeal and dogmatism of secular ideas and projects and movements themselves betray a messianic and in some cases paradoxically religious or quasi-religious character. Such religious zeal and dogmatism and the power of "unsecularity" are evident, in fact, in the historical and conceptual roots of the very "scientific" paradigm that claims that modernity inevitably spells the demise of religious zeal and dogmatism and the triumph of secularity—secularization theory—which, as I explore in the course of this essay, is itself best understood not as a value-free theory but as a Kuhnian paradigm that emerged from within a particular matrix of normative and indeed religious commitments. In fact, the secularization paradigm, at least in some of its forms, is best interpreted as a religious ideology. And it is a religious ideology with enormous, demonstrated potential to generate global misunderstanding, division, and destructive conflict.

Secularization as Paradigm

It is necessary to begin with a brief exploration of what has been and remains the dominant paradigm for understanding the place and trajectory of religion in the modern world—dominant, at any rate, among the sociologically peculiar tribe responsible for authoritative knowledge production in Western societies, what Andrew Greeley calls the "intellectual ethnic group." This of course is the paradigm of secularization, which remains the default framework—indeed, the default grand narrative—for understanding the place and trajectory of religion in the modern world. Analytical exploration of its distinctive features is a prerequisite to clear articulation of the paradigm of persistent unsecularity, not least because the secularization paradigm itself is an instance of the persistence of unsecularity.

Paradigms are "universally recognized scientific achievements that for a time provide model problems and solutions to a community of practitioners."[4] That is, paradigms share "two essential characteristics." First, "their achievement was sufficiently unprecedented to attract an enduring group of adherents away from competing modes of scientific activity." Second, "it was sufficiently open-ended to leave all sorts of problems for the redefined group of practitioners to resolve." For Kuhn, the significance of the concept lay in the fact "that some accepted examples of actual scientific practice—examples which include law, theory, application, and instrumentation together—provide models from which spring particular coherent traditions of scientific research."[5]

A paradigm is thus always retrospective and prospective. It always begins in some past "achievement"—some widely accepted breakthrough, some unprecedented step in favor of human progress. And this past breakthrough then becomes the basis for developing a model or pattern for all future inquiry and activity in the relevant domain. An exemplar is so significant that it frames all subsequent inquiry and activity, yet it also leaves a wide range of questions unanswered. The convincing success of the exemplar in the past makes inquiry possible, while its intrinsic inability to settle all relevant questions in advance makes continuing inquiry necessary.

Precisely as a paradigm in this sense, the theory of secularization originally emerged from the confluence of the French Enlightenment and French Revolution. The enormously influential thinkers of the French Enlightenment and their progeny, such as Condorcet and Comte, interpreted the virtually coterminous French Revolution as a demonstration—an exemplar—of a universal law. In Kuhnian terms, the French Enlightenment and French Revolution were "sufficiently unprecedented to attract an enduring group of adherents" from competing modes of intellectual activity. These new adherents were converted, as it were, to an exemplar that they considered the unprecedented and indispensable basis of revolutionary human progress. But this exemplar, though it was believed to provide a necessary pattern for all human progress, was not sufficient. It did not in itself answer all questions about how progress would be achieved and institutionalized, or how it would be sustained and spread.

That is, the conjoined intellectual and political upheavals of the Enlightenment and revolution drew a sociologically significant portion of the French elite to abandon the traditional mode of intellectual reflection on religion and society in favor of a completely new intellectual pattern—a new paradigm. In particular, it compelled them to reverse the traditional view that adherence to orthodox Christianity was the necessary and only possible basis for social and political progress. Instead, those thinkers of the French Enlightenment who exercised a preponderant influence on authoritative knowledge production just before and after the French Revolution concluded that the "unprecedented" intellectual awakening and political progress achieved in France in the final years of the eighteenth century were supremely significant "achievements" that (a) depended on the marginalization of traditional religious authorities and ideas and (b) would and should, in time, generate the complete collapse of traditional religious authorities and ideas. Rousseau's *Social Contract* (1762) is an excellent example of this pattern of Enlightenment thought, with its frontal assault on traditional Christianity in general and Catholicism in particular as barriers to progress toward true republican liberty. Of course, prospectively, this pattern of thought exercised an enormous influence on the architects of the French Revolution. And retrospectively, after 1789, the revolution itself (with its real albeit partially reversed success in overthrowing the Ancien Régime) seemed to Condorcet and others of his ilk a harbinger of unstoppable global progress.[6]

In other words, the French Revolution as interpreted (and to some degree caused) by the intellectual revolutionaries of the French Enlightenment became an extraordinary exemplar—a paradigm case—of a radically new intellectual and social tradition. This new tradition was one part normative social theory and one part descriptive sociology. The normative social theory was this: to make real social and political progress, a moral or normative imperative must be respected—namely, religious tradition should give way to reason, or at least be radically reinterpreted in the light of reason. The upshot of this normative social theory is *the recommendation of secularization as a moral imperative and program of action.*[7]

The descriptive sociology was this: the achievement of intellectual and political progress through the gradual achievement of the rule of reason will in time generate the decline of traditional religious ideas, authorities, and communities. As Condorcet put it in 1795, the "enlightened" "principles of the French constitution. . . are too widely disseminated, and too openly professed, for the efforts of tyrants and priests to prevent them from penetrating by degrees into the miserable cottages of their slaves."[8] The upshot of this descriptive sociology was the *formulation of secularization as a theory of linear social progress or development.*

In Tocqueville's lapidary summary, the philosophers of the eighteenth century held the "theory" that "religious zeal . . . will be extinguished as freedom and enlightenment increase."[9] For the first time in history, an influential corps of elites in an influential society self-consciously formulated *the idea of secularization* (if not necessarily the term) as both a normative ideal and a descriptive theory.

To confirm the extent to which the roots of the secularization paradigm lie in the ways in which the French Enlightenment inferred universal moral imperatives and sociological laws from the achievement of the French Revolution, consider the semi-official genealogy of secularization theory drawn up by perhaps the purest and most influential secularization theorist of the late twentieth century, Bryan Wilson. In the very first lines of the very first paragraph of perhaps his most elegant statement on the origins and chief characteristics of the secularization "model," Wilson writes:

> Auguste Comte is not now much remembered, even by sociologists, whose discipline he both shaped and named. Sociologists of religion, however, have special reason to remember him, and with him his immediate precursor, Saint-Simon, since *they defined the new science of society with specific reference to, and in direct contrast with, the previously existing body of social knowledge.* Man, society, and the world were, hitherto, explained—in the Western tradition, but perhaps in all traditions—by reference to transcendent laws, states, or beings. *As a methodology for interpreting society, sociology was, from its first enunciation, directly set over against theology.* Quite explicitly, Comte indicated the contrast between theological and (social) scientific ways of knowing. Although he did not use the term, and his interests were certainly broader, *Comte provided a comprehensive account—its many factual errors notwithstanding—of a process of secularization.*[10]

According to Wilson's quasi-canonical Genesis narrative of the conjoined origins of sociology and secularization, in the beginning Saint-Simon and Comte said, in effect, "Let there be light!" In an approach that "was directly set over against theology," the two Frenchmen invented a new and unprecedented science of sociology, which, in turn, generated an account of secularization as a general process. If secularization was their creation, however, it was not created *ex nihilo*. Writing less than two generations after the French Revolution, Comte developed his "scientific" account of secularization as a universal process—in which humanity as a whole evolves from a theological to a metaphysical and finally to a scientific stage—explicitly and directly from the material of French history.

Comte's pioneering understanding of secularization is thus readily classifiable as a "paradigm" in the strict Kuhnian sense. It draws a permanent, prospective intellectual pattern from a past concrete exemplar that is considered an unprecedented achievement. In other words, secularization is based on the historical reconstruction of a specific exemplar—one that is a historically particular and putatively unprecedented achievement—that becomes a paradigm in the fullest sense in that it is believed to provide an intellectual model. And, in turn, this intellectual model forms the core of a coherent (though still somewhat varied and open-ended) tradition of inquiry. Wilson confirms all this as his Genesis narrative assumes the form of a biblical genealogy, in which the secularization theory of Comte begets the increasingly mature secularization theories of Marx, Weber, and Veblen.[11]

In other words, if Comte begat sociology and the secularization paradigm, descendants as numerous as the starry host soon appeared in the firmament, with the result that the tradition of regarding secularization as a paradigm that provides the basis of a continuing scientific tradition is still with us. So when Oliver Tschannen offers a systematic summary of secularization theory, he recognizes that it is best understood as "the secularization paradigm."[12] And when sociologist of religion Steve Bruce, perhaps the leading defender of secularization theory writing today, provides a one-page schematic of the theory in his 2002 book, *God Is Dead: Secularization in the West*, he refers to the theory as, simply, "the secularization paradigm."[13]

To a remarkable degree, then, the secularization paradigm—in its broad outlines and basic assumptions—has remained remarkably coherent and consistent since its origins in the late eighteenth century. For example, the concept of modernity at the heart of the secularization paradigm is, at bottom, more or less identical to the desideratum of the French Enlightenment: the unfettered rule of scientific reason over every sphere of society, or what later came to be called rationalization. "Modernity is characterized, if not defined, by a widely held commitment to the proposition that ordinary people should govern their affairs in accord with the canons of rationality."[14] And it was the thinkers of the French Enlightenment, particularly Condorcet, who perhaps did more than anyone to make the dichotomy of "religious" tradition and "rational" modernity canonical in the Western imagination. With modernity understood as the sovereignty of reason, the secularization paradigm conceives of modernity as the dominant, creative, and agenda-setting force in world history, intrinsically able and intrinsically worthy to sweep away all "superstition" and "tyranny" as it advances. The clarity and confidence of Condorcet's *Outlines of an Historical View of the Progress of the Human Mind* (1795) in making this claim are probably unmatchable.[15] For Condorcet, modernity first dawned during the Renaissance, for it was then that "the sciences and philosophy threw off the yoke of authority"—by which he meant, of course, theological and ecclesiastical authority.[16] And reason's complete global triumph is only a matter of time. Priests, with their superstitions, "will no longer exist but in history and upon the stage." And what guarantees this eventual victory is nothing other than the sheer "force of reason."

An important corollary of the secularization paradigm is that religion can survive only to the extent that it conforms to modernity and the rule of reason. And the primary way religion conforms to modernity is by withdrawing from any authoritative role in shaping the public, rationally organized system of modern society. For under conditions of modernity,

> It is the *system* that becomes secularized. . . . The system no longer functions, even notionally, to fulfill the will of God. Neither institutions nor individuals operate primarily to attain supernatural ends. As Comte predicted, and in ways that Max Weber indicated, rational planning and the deployment of new technology invoke as their justification the goal of human well-being, not the greater glory of God. Human consciousness is itself depicted as changing in response to the increasingly rational patterns of social organization and the imposition on man of increasingly abstract patterns of role playing. Men learn to regulate their behavior to the rational premises built into the social order; action must be calculated, systematic, regulated, and routinized.[17]

Note that in Wilson's view the entire social system of modernity is understood to be under the governance—"sovereign sway" would not be too strong a phrase—of "rational planning," "rational patterns," and "rational premises." On his construction, in fact, it is as if late-twentieth-century modernity perfectly fulfills Condorcet's late-eighteenth-century predictions of a world in which the nations "acknowledg[e] no other master than their reason."

The place left for religion—which, importantly, Wilson's value-free sociology characterizes as based on "arbitrary unexplained authority"[18]—in an increasingly rational and rationalized world is vanishingly small and insignificant. If religion survives at all, it must confine itself to a sphere that is not only private but also irrational and verging on the unreal. In his own striking words, religion under conditions of modernity is reduced to enabling "individuals privately to take up the vestiges of ancient myths and arcane lore and ceremonies, in the search for authentic fantasy, power, possibilities of manipulation, and alternative sources of private gratification. In this sense, *religion remains an alternative culture, observed as unthreatening to the modern social system, in much the same way that entertainment is seen as unthreatening.*"[19] Or as he puts it starkly elsewhere, "The secularization thesis implies the privatization of religion."[20]

THE BACKBONE OF THE SECULARIZATION PARADIGM: SIX PROPOSITIONS

What do we learn from this review of the origins and contours of the secularization paradigm? We learn that the secularization paradigm in some of its classical and most influential forms consists in a small set of simple propositions. Indeed, its very elegance is one more respect in which it has the quality of a Kuhnian paradigm. And these propositions, furthermore, have remained remarkably consistent since the age of Condorcet and Comte. I believe the following *six propositions* are among the most salient and significant components of the secularization paradigm.

First, a core proposition of the secularization paradigm is that the most important and decisive forces and factors driving change *inside* the religious field lie *outside* the religious field. The political, social, and economic dynamics of modernity—which are assumed to proceed entirely independently of religion, even if it is allowed that religious factors (such as the Protestant Reformation) may have helped to set them in motion in the very distant past—either swallow up religion more or less completely or constitute the dominant action to which religion is merely the (equal and opposite) reaction. In all of the versions of the secularization paradigm, including the variations that take "fundamentalism" seriously, religion does not enjoy sufficient agency or power to reverse or significantly modify what Bryan Wilson calls the "modern social system." It either lacks effective agency altogether, reduced to the equivalent of "unthreatening" private entertainment in the midst of cultures and systems pervasively indifferent to its claims, as in the treatments of Bryan Wilson or Steve Bruce. Or its agency and agenda are derivative, defined in diametric opposition ("You say 'X,' we say 'not X' ") to the creative and prior action and initiative of modernity and secularity, as in the "fundamentalism" studies of Scott Appleby et al.[21] That is, concerning the relationship between modernity and religion, they share a basic premise of *presumptive exogeneity*—in the sense that everything important that is happening *to* and *in* religion comes from *outside* religion, a premise borrowed from both Marxian/structural social theory and from Weberian sociology (in the latter case particularly evident in the fatalistic and melancholic closing pages of *The Protestant Ethic and the Spirit of Capitalism*).[22]

At least part of the explanation of the secularization paradigm's tendency to invest the central driver(s) of secularization with a high degree of agency may lie in grammar. The word "secularization" is a nominalization—that is, a noun formed from other parts of speech. It is of course formed from an adjective, "secular," and a verb, "secularize." The characteristic problem with nominalization is that it "fails to tell us *who* is doing *what*." In fact, as Helen Sword memorably puts it, "nominalizations are 'zombie nouns' because they cannibalize active verbs, suck the lifeblood from adjectives and substitute abstract entities for human beings."[23] That last point is a perfect description of the characteristic tendency of the secularization paradigm—namely, to invest abstract entities with the powers of personal agency. The particular abstract entity that is invested with agency differs across versions of the secularization paradigm. In some cases, as with sociologist Anthony Wallace, the driver of secularization is the "increasing adequacy and diffusion of scientific knowledge."[24] In other cases, the driving force behind the abstract nominalization of secularization is another abstract nominalization, as in Ronald Inglehart's view that "secularization is *inherently* linked to Modernization."[25] The point is that, by an extraordinary kind of transfusion, the secularization paradigm sucks the lifeblood of vital personal agency (including powers of intentionality, coordination, and efficacy) from actual human actors, especially religious ones, and pumps it into abstract, impersonal entities and concepts.

Second, the secularization paradigm conceives of the force or forces responsible for secularization as unstoppable and the secularization process itself as irreversible. In other words, the secularization paradigm not only invests the impersonal force (or forces) responsible for secularization with personal or quasi-personal agency, but invests it (or them) with an extraordinary and essentially irresistible power. The single *locus classicus* of this view is probably Weber's conclusion in *The Protestant Ethic and the Spirit of Capitalism* that "material goods have gained an increasing and finally an inexorable power" such that "modern man is in general even with the best will unable to give religious ideas a significance for culture and national character which they deserve."[26] Whether through the rationalization and materialism engendered by modern capitalism or the unstoppable force and agency of "science," "belief in supernatural powers is doomed to die out, all over the world," as Anthony Wallace not-so-subtly puts it.[27] Regardless of how the driver of secularization is conceived, the result is always the same. In Bryan Wilson's brutal, laconic summary, "religions are always dying" in the modern world.[28]

To put it another way, the secularization paradigm invests an agentless, trans-historical force or entity—"modernity," "reason," "rationalization"—with the qualities of an all-powerful, god-like, causative agent. One may call this reification. Or one may think of this as investing modernity or rationality with an ultimate, ontic status. But one may also see this tendency of the secularization paradigm as a form of personification or deification—as investing an impersonal force with a specific purposiveness and directiveness and capacity to achieve specific and coordinated outcomes that are normally reserved for *descriptions of divine agents*. For the remarkable implication of the secularization paradigm is that whatever the driver of secularizing change is taken to be somehow stands above and outside religious dynamics—almost above history—yet at the same time acts decisively on religious dynamics in a way that profoundly weakens, reshapes, or eliminates them altogether. In short, according to Warren Nord, "the secularization of the modern world is not the work of secularists."[29] Secularization is rather a great happening that results either from some exceptionally powerful single force or entity or from a variety of powerful forces that somehow align and reinforce each other so perfectly as to generate a single linear process and a single coherent outcome. In this connection, it is irresistible to wonder whether the secularization paradigm in its classical forms does not bear the imprint of a panentheist, Hegelian philosophy of history. For the putative drivers of secularization are invested with more than ordinary agency. They are invested with a kind of omnipotence and "cunning" that guarantee a single final outcome.[30]

Third, the secularization paradigm in its classical forms conceives of secularization as universal and unlimited in scope. In its original form as articulated by the French *philosophes* (such as Condorcet) and in the classic claims of modern sociology from the nineteenth century onward, secularization is understood to be a truly global process that respects no geographic, cultural, or religious boundaries. It is certainly not restricted to the West or to North Atlantic societies. For example, in Daniel Lerner's influential formulation in 1958, modernization was fast becoming just as operative and powerful in the Middle East as anywhere else, making an eventual secular outcome as inevitable and complete as it was expected to be in Western countries. His modern classic, *The Passing of Traditional Society: Modernizing the Middle East*, cites a consensus of scholars in concluding that Islam was "absolutely defenseless" in the face of the rationalist and positivist spirit of modernity and that secularization would inevitably follow the rapid urbanization of Egypt and other Arab countries.[31] Not only Islam, according to the great English historian Arnold Toynbee, but "*all* current religions. . . have been losing their hold on the hearts and consciences and minds of their former adherents." He underscored that he did not have only the West in mind by adding, "*all* the non-Western religions. . . are now experiencing the same crisis of faith and allegiance that the Western Christian churches had begun to experience before the close of the 17th century."[32] As Peter Berger argued in 1968, the scope of the "secular culture" that was rapidly and inexorably displacing religious authority was literally "world-wide."[33]

Fourth, embedded in the secularization paradigm is a radical notion of an "Other" that is the inevitable opponent of reason, progress, and modernity. Conjoined with this radical notion of alterity is a radical notion of incommensurability. One of the core propositions of the secularization paradigm is that modernity and religion represent radically different epistemic, moral, and indeed ultimate orientations to the world. That is, the secularization paradigm is committed to the proposition that there is a *presumptive and ineliminable incommensurability* between modernity and religion. According to Wilson, the secularization paradigm holds that modern science and traditional religion represent "diametrically opposite approaches." On one hand, modern science, including sociology, is "empirical, man-centered, this-worldly, [and] matter-of-fact," not to mention "value-free," "positivistic," "objective," and "neutral." On the other hand, religion is oriented to "supernatural entities (beings, laws, events, places, and actions) which [it] project[s] as of real, determining importance in man's affairs."[34] The animating spirit of modernity is the rational understanding and organization of a human-centered world. The animating spirit of religion is the non-rational projection or construction of a theocentric and supernaturalistic universe or "sacred canopy."

The upshot of this view is that there is bound to be a zero-sum conflict between the spirit of modernity and the spirit of religion whenever the two come into direct contact. Where one rises, the other falls. As Vilho Harle notes in *The Enemy with a Thousand Faces: The Tradition of the Other in Western Political Thought*, "The modernization hypothesis had claimed that the modern, rational, and secular society had no space for... primitive passions. According to Talcott Parsons, modernization was to produce an emotionally restrained, self-interested individual to whom racism, superstition, and ethnicity are unknown."[35] If "a dualistic or Manichaean worldview is one in which reality is considered to be uncompromisingly divided into light... and darkness" and one in which "ultimately, light will triumph over darkness,"[36] there is little question that a literally Manichaean worldview constitutes a core component of the secularization paradigm.

Fifth, characteristic of the secularization paradigm is what Christian Smith has described as an under-specification of the causal mechanisms or pathways of the secularization process. Secularization is conceived as relentless and universal, but it is somehow opaque at the same time. As we have noted, the secularization paradigm advances extraordinarily ambitious claims concerning the inexorable displacement of "religious" and "traditional" values by "modern" and "rational" ones. "The moral intimations of Christianity do not belong to a world ordered by conveyor belts, time-and-motion studies, and bureaucratic organizations," insists Bryan Wilson. "The very thought processes which these devices demand of men leave little place for the operation of the divine."[37] But as Christian Smith asks, "why should we automatically believe that God and conveyor belts are incompatible?" The simple fact is that "we are not told."[38] An impersonal force or agency—typically described in terms of an abstract nominalization such as "modernization" or "industrialization"—is believed to generate secular outcomes in an ineluctable fashion. But this "causal" story typically lacks not only a concrete *who* (as explored above) but also a concrete *how*.

One might add, furthermore, that it lacks a concrete *when*. When, precisely, was the great "age of faith" of the historical past when "all our ancestors" were "literally" religious believers "all of the time," as Peter Laslett claimed in his modern classic, *The World We Have Lost*?[39] And when, precisely, were "we" supposed to have "lost" this comprehensively religious "world"? The historical assumption that once upon a time an omnipotent and pervasive "sacred canopy" hung over the whole creation is an essential and foundational assumption of the secularization paradigm in almost of all of its forms, from the French Enlightenment onward. The difficulty is that this essential historical baseline—the linchpin of the whole trajectory and narrative arc of the secularization story—is almost never specified with any chronological precision or substantiated with serious and systematic evidence. The "golden age of faith" is, as it were, an article of faith. And it helps to make the causal claims at the heart of the secularization paradigm impenetrably opaque if not actually mythological.

Sixth, many secularization theorists have embraced the secularization paradigm in such a way that it is effectively unfalsifiable. At one point, Bryan Wilson claims, "Certainly it is an open question whether secularization is reversible." But in the very next sentence he insists, "It would be difficult to demonstrate that any such reversals have ever occurred."[40] In other words, it may be an "open question" in theory whether secularization is reversible, but it turns out to be an absolutely closed question in practice. Thus, the position of the secularization paradigm as classically articulated and widely held is not that 75, 80, or 95 percent of all apparent reversals of secularization can be explained away. The position is that "it would be difficult to demonstrate that *any* such reversals have *ever* occurred." Indeed, Wilson's position is that 100 percent of all apparent reversals of secularization or resacralization can be explained not merely as insignificant but as advancing the march of secularization (thus reminding one of Hegel again). "Closer examination of . . . sudden upsurges in religious activity . . . are interpreted according to the secularization thesis as revealing the long-term effect of revitalization movements—not so much a restoration of the past as an accommodation of the pressing claims of the present." Eventually, in all such movements, "the magical and emotional elements receded, and what was left—for as long as it lasted—was an ethical deposit" that was "effectively secularized." But if any and every apparent instance of religious revitalization that has "ever" occurred is just further proof of secularization, then it is hard to avoid the conclusion that the secularization paradigm is effectively unfalsifiable and a species of untestable dogma.

But what about all the well-known outbursts of passionate, vital, and socio-politically consequential religiosity, from Tehran to Topeka, that appeared with accelerating frequency from the 1970s onward? Were not these outbursts a set of increasingly powerful "anomalies" (to use a Kuhnian term) that falsified the secularization paradigm or at least rendered it implausible in its classical form? After all, it suddenly appeared that a non-trivial number of religious groups—certainly more than the secularization paradigm led one to expect, and in more regions of the world—developed the will and the capacity under some conditions to put up a fight in the face of modernity and secularity and at least make a bid to influence the social and political systems of numerous societies. In other words, they seemed to defy one of the core predictions of the secularization paradigm: namely, that the inevitable (and desirable) outcome of secularization would be the "privatization of religion."

In fact, many if not most of those secularization theorists who tried to reckon with such trends did so in a way that suggested that they continued to believe that the secularization paradigm was not falsified—and perhaps could not be falsified—by any apparent "resurgence" of religion in global politics. Since the secularization paradigm continued to frame what Thomas Kuhn calls "normal science" concerning the place of religion in the modern world, many of those who theorized about the apparent anomaly of religion's global resurgence did not see it as a reason to question the fundamental assumptions of secularization—just as Kuhn's own account of the stubborn persistence of paradigms would have predicted. For those who remain convinced adherents of the secularization paradigm, that there are bursts of religious revival or reaction may simply mean, for example, that modernity had not been introduced in a sufficiently complete form in the given context(s)—in other words, that the creation of modern states, modern economies, and a modern system of science-based education had not sufficiently progressed (as Steve Bruce has claimed).[41] Or, as Bryan Wilson has often argued, activism on the part of religious groups may actually reveal an internal secularization whereby they achieve new relevance at the price of assuming secular or worldly functions that have no reference to the transcendent.[42] Or religion's apparent revitalization may mean that modernity had been introduced in a complete form but a cultural lag was at work; the full secularizing consequences of modernity would take time to work their way down and across all the various sectors, segments, and classes of society (as Bryan Wilson, Ronald Inglehart, and Pippa Norris have argued).[43] Or it may mean that the very power and effectiveness of secularization in most of the world—and in most parts of most societies—drove a few individuals and communities into an increasingly panicked sense of embattlement and isolation. On this last view, by an analogy to Newtonian physics, the very power of the *action* of secularization was generating in some quarters an equal and opposite religious *reaction*—or, if not a reaction fully equal to the vast political and cultural power of secularization, at least a reaction that was forceful and determined.[44]

It is of course debatable whether falsifiability is a remotely adequate criterion of truth or epistemic progress. One might argue that if the secularization paradigm runs afoul of the positivist criterion of falsifiability, then so much the worse for the positivist criterion of falsifiability. But that option is not open to many of the most influential proponents of the secularization paradigm in its classical form. In Bryan Wilson's rendering, the classic form of the secularization paradigm explicitly affirms that part of the advance of rational modernity over religious tradition consists in its replacement of irrational dogmas with "falsifiable propositions." It would be singularly awkward, then, if the secularization paradigm itself turned out to be an ensemble of unfalsifiable propositions and thus patently inconsistent with its own test of epistemic progress.

In sum, the secularization paradigm in some of its classical and most influential forms casts secularization as:

(1) the product of a quasi-personal, transcendent, and virtually omnipotent agency ("modernity" or "rationality"), which generates

(2) a process that is unstoppable and irreversible as well as

(3) global and universal, with the result that there is everywhere

(4) a Manichaean conflict and zero-sum interaction between the secularizing forces of modernity and rationality and the traditional forces of religion and custom, which are conceived as incommensurable and diametrically opposed, yet

(5) these secularizing forces generate the decline of religion and the construction of an increasingly secular world through a causal logic that is under-specified and ultimately mysterious, and

(6) in accordance with a theory that is unfalsifiable and seemingly untestable.

To round out our analysis of the secularization paradigm, it takes no leap of the imagination to identify a clear implication of all that has been said so far.

The secularization paradigm is a religious worldview. It is not merely functionally religious. It does not merely occupy a place in the hearts and minds of its adherents that is the equivalent of a religion. In many key respects, it is *literally religious.* If religion is "concerned with the Ultimate on which reality rests," the secularization paradigm is thoroughly religious in that it believes that there is now an Ultimate Driver of world history—"modernity" and its basic principle of scientific reason—that is the key to grasping the meaning and trajectory of reality.[45] Moreover, the secularization paradigm has the quality of a religion in the further sense that it "is not simply a set of theoretical beliefs about reality."[46] Rather, like all genuine religions, it tells people "how [they] must live in order that [they] might be at harmony with ultimate reality."[47] One might say that the secularization paradigm is not just the truth; it is also the way and the life. To be on the right side of history and achieve harmony with ultimate reality, one must shed all superstition and inherited tradition and simply obey "the force of reason." Precisely as a paradigm in the Kuhnian sense, in fact, the secularization paradigm was an "achievement" inspired by a moral imperative and program of action before it was a scientific theory of linear social progress.

But the religious character of the secularization paradigm runs deeper. At its heart is a genuine *theology* whereby it posits (worships?) a quasi-transcendent, quasi-personal agency as the driving force of history and the key to humankind's progress and development. Moreover, this agency enjoys a virtually omnipotent capacity to initiate transformative change and overcome resistance, and a power to mold the whole of humanity. Another constitutive element of the secularization paradigm is a kind of *eschatology*, by virtue of its belief in the irreversible and universal movement of history toward the conjoined outcomes of rationalization, modernization, and secularization. It also features a *demonology*, insofar as it embraces a Manichaean dichotomy between modern rationality and traditional religion. Epistemologically, the secularization paradigm includes a high degree of *faith* and *mystery*, since it offers little clarity or evidence concerning the specific mechanisms, processes, or timeline whereby modernity is supposed to generate secularity. In fact, it continues to be embraced with such extraordinary equanimity and fervor even in the face of countervailing trends that it appears to be an effectively unfalsifiable *dogma*.

At least in broad outline if not in every detail, Robert Bellah fully grasped the religious nature of secularization theory nearly two generations ago. Secularization "is a myth," he wrote in *Beyond Belief* in 1970, "because it functions to create an emotionally coherent picture of reality. It is in this sense religious, not scientific at all. This theory or myth is that of the Enlightenment, which views science as the bringer of light relative to which religion and other dark things will vanish away."[48] Who knows how many of the world's people—particularly the world's disproportionately Western-educated elites whom Samuel Huntington once deliciously called "Davos people"[49]—have abandoned the traditional religions of their fathers and mothers for an emotionally satisfying faith in the mytho-poetic grand narrative of secularization? One thing we do know is that the optimal way to describe such conversions is not under the rubric of "secularization." For at the heart of these transformations is not the adoption of a genuinely worldly, scientific, immanent, or positivist viewpoint but the substitution of one religious faith for another. For an indeterminate though probably disproportionately influential segment of the world's people, secular modernity is the "sacred canopy" under which they live.

Religious Conflict and Religious Peacebuilding: Five Commandments

So what does all this mean for understanding the interaction of religion, violence, and peace in the contemporary world? I believe the account I have developed yields several unabashedly normative commandments—indeed, "five commandments"—that should frame the way we understand religion, conflict, and peacebuilding today.

First Commandment: Recognize the profound religiosity of secularization and secularism in many of their leading forms. Of course, not every version of secularization theory or belief in secularism is religious in the way I have described. But I believe what Bellah called the religious "myth" of secularization underpins some of the most important social, intellectual, and political projects of the modern world. Some of these projects—such as international communism—are now largely exhausted, though in China, Vietnam, Cuba, and a few other countries it remains an important force. Others flourish and derive no small amount of energy and purpose from a sense of historical destiny that is inexplicable, I think, apart from the secularization paradigm. Indeed, both the American and French republics—and republicanism itself—were inspired from the beginning by a sense that some quasi-divine force not readily identifiable with the biblical God endowed them with "the power to begin the world all over again," in the words of Thomas Paine in 1776. This was not "secularism" so much as a new kind of religion, as Tocqueville understood so well when he observed that the French Revolution, in all its "striving for the regeneration of the human race even more than for the reform of France," was actually "a new kind of religion" that "like Islam, flooded the earth with its soldiers, apostles and martyrs."[50]

The religion of secularization continues to frame and inspire numerous social and political projects in the contemporary world. The myth of secularization underpins what Michael Latham has called "modernization as ideology," that is, the use of modernization theory by American policy-makers from the 1950s onward to catapult numerous "traditional" societies into the "modern world," often by violence.[51] Since September 11, it is a major factor in framing the response of the American foreign policy establishment to "religious militancy." In 2006, when longtime *Washington Post* foreign policy columnist James Hoagland paused to observe a litany of militant religious movements exercising growing influence around the world, he consoled himself by reciting the creed of secularization: "[Religious militants] and their devout followers fight back in their own ways against the spreading vulgarization and secularization of societies that seem tempted to dispense with religion altogether. *These are by and large counterrevolutionary movements, out of step with a secularizing march by history* that many of them would destroy rather than accept."[52] Whatever short-term challenges religious militants might pose for the United States and other modern societies, Hoagland says, in effect, it should give no small comfort to the makers of Western foreign policy that the direction and destination of the "march" of "history" remain foreordained. ("Damn the torpedoes," those steering the ship of the secular state can say, "full speed ahead!")

Second Commandment: Acknowledge the enormous potential of the religious ideology of secularization for militancy and violence. The French Revolution, Russian Revolution, Mexican Revolution, Spanish Republicanism, some forms of fascism, Stalinism, Ba'athism in Syria and Iraq, the Cultural Revolution in China, and the Cambodian Revolution undertaken by the Khmer Rouge were all forms of messianic secular militancy underpinned by at least some of the key propositional components of the secularization paradigm. The most striking contemporary example of the militancy of secularization is perhaps the remorseless bloodbath now being perpetrated by the acolytes of the secular political religion of Ba'athism against Sunnis and other religious communities in Syria. After Ba'athist forces crushed protests in Hama in August 2011, they scrawled on the city's walls, "No God but al-Assad" and "God falls down and Assad lives."

If it is thought that it is unfair to focus on such an extreme example as indicative of the militant tendency of secularization, one might reply that it is no more unfair than focusing on al-Qaeda or Hezbollah or the Lord's Resistance Army as indicative of the militant or violent potential of religious "fundamentalism." As it happens, based on the most sophisticated analysis we have of fundamentalism, the secularization paradigm possesses four of the five "ideological characteristics" of militant religious fundamentalism, including a high degree of reactivity; moral Manichaeanism; epistemological absolutism; and millennialism and messianism.[53] It is at least arguable, then, that the mythology of secularization is itself classifiable as a species in the broad genus of fundamentalism, one that bears a strong "family resemblance" to many other forms of fundamentalist militancy.[54]

In fact, it would appear undeniable that the religious militancy of the secularization paradigm makes this religious ideology and some of its proponents a major source of violence
and conflict and a significant threat to world peace and stability. Today, militant groups such
as al-Qaeda are considered the quintessential source of "violent religion" and "militant fundamentalism" in the modern world. But it is at least arguable that paradigms and programs of
secularization—not only Leninism, Maoism, and Stalinism but also the Mexican Revolution
as well as American "pacification" campaigns in the Vietnam War and American support for
"modernizing," secular regimes such as in pre-1979 Iran and elsewhere—have generated far
greater and more systematic violence than any other species of religion the world has seen
since the eighteenth century (if not in the entirety of world history). Ideologies of modernization and secularization have been, and remain, fierce partisans in the world's conflicts,
and they have been, and remain, powerful engines of militant proselytization, repression,
and violence.

This is not just a historical point. Even today, it may well be that the modern religion
of relentless secular progress and its gods of nationalism, rationalism, and economic
development—particularly through the onslaught unleashed on the environment in every
part of the globe—remain at least as great a threat to world peace and the rights of the weak
and vulnerable as the commitments or practices of any of the so-called "traditional" religious communities. Of course, not all of this onslaught and violence can be directly attributed to the secularization paradigm, any more than all apparently "religious violence" in the
conventional sense can be directly attributed to specifically "religious" motives or factors.[55]
But I believe it is clear enough that the propositional components of the secularization paradigm help to frame and motivate at least some of the destructive political, developmental,
and "modernization" schemes undertaken by a wide array of governments, multinational
corporations, and multilateral development organizations.[56] (It should go without saying
that I am far from thinking that all development schemes and political projects underpinned
in whole or in part by the secularization paradigm are destructive; in this sense, secularization, like other "sacred" frameworks and projects, is morally ambivalent.)

Third Commandment: Admit that the secularization paradigm bears witness against
itself. If there is any truth at all in any part of my suggestion that the secularization paradigm
is religious and in some sense a religious worldview, then the secularization paradigm itself
is good reason to doubt the adequacy of the secularization paradigm. One way to characterize the religious nature of the secularization paradigm is simply to say that it provides
ultimate answers to ultimate questions based on an implicit or explicit faith in an ultimate
reality. Michael Perry eloquently describes the character of such ultimate questions:

> One's most fundamental convictions and commitments. . . are the yield of one's response to
> what are sometimes called "ultimate" questions, such as: Who are we? Where did we come
> from; what is our origin, our beginning? Where are we going; what is our destiny, our end?
> What is the meaning of suffering? Of evil? Of death? And there is the cardinal question, the
> question that comprises many of the others: Is human life ultimately meaningful or, instead,
> ultimately bereft of meaning, meaning-less, absurd? If any questions are fundamental,
> these questions—what Catholic theologian David Tracy has memorably called "religious or
> limit questions"—are fundamental. Such questions—"naive" questions, "questions with no
> answers," "barriers that cannot be breached"—are "the most serious and difficult. . . that any
> human being or society must face. . ." And one's answers to such questions obviously bear
> strongly on this fundamental question: What sort of life is constitutive of, or conducive to,

one's religious (or, if you prefer, "spiritual") and/or moral well-being?.... Historically extended communities—"traditions"—are principal matrices of answers to all such "religious or limit questions."[57]

Is human life ultimately meaningful? What sort of life is most conducive to one's well-being? Beginning in the late eighteenth century, as I have shown, a "historically extended communit[y]" of thinkers and practitioners has produced a coherent tradition of reflection—the secularization paradigm—that in fact addresses many of these "religious or limit questions." One characteristic of this community is that it seeks to provide answers to these ultimate questions in a way that suits the conditions and demands of the modern world. Furthermore, not only are the questions addressed by the secularization paradigm of a religious or "liminal" character, but its answers presuppose a number of robust religious commitments.

The implication of this fact is clear. The widespread intellectual and political projects of secularization in the modern world—the global ascendancy and influence of which I have explored elsewhere[58]—suggest that "secularization" is not actually occurring in any strict sense. The more ardently the secularization paradigm is believed and promoted, the more it betrays its dependence on unfalsifiable articles of faith and religious commitments—theologies, eschatologies, demonologies—that violate its own professed canons of "modern," scientific rationality and its own normative and descriptive images of modernity. This probably makes the vast majority of us religious "believers" of one sort or another, with some being "secular" religious believers and others being "religious" religious believers.[59] But if the religious features of the secularization paradigm are genuine, they have the awkward feature of rendering the paradigm in its classic form self-referentially incoherent if not self-refuting.

Fourth Commandment: Realize that the self-refutation of the secularization paradigm does not represent a dead end but points to an alternative paradigm of "persistent secularity." The claim that the secularization paradigm is self-refuting is not a mere debating point or feat of deconstruction. The point of emphasizing the religious features of the secularization paradigm is a positive one. Its purpose is to underscore that the construction of religious meaning is a widespread and persistent feature of human experience.

It is necessary and important to absorb the negative lesson: the secularization paradigm does not reflect the reality of the modern world. But we do not need to invoke the self-refuting religiosity of the secularization paradigm to doubt its adequacy. The secularization paradigm's core claim that the world's social and political systems would (and should) be evacuated of "traditional" religious actors and symbols and that religion would retreat to an "unthreatening" position in the private realm has been subjected to devastating empirical, theoretical, and normative criticism. To take one recent example, Jonathan Fox analyzed the latest data in his massive Religion and State data set to determine whether religion became a greater or lesser factor in world politics over the nearly twenty-year period between 1990 and 2008. Specifically, he examined official patterns of legislation and discrimination concerning religion in *the political and legal systems* of 177 countries—the very systems that Bryan Wilson long claimed would become increasingly closed to religion. After examining the trends in these countries, which represent more than 99 percent of the world's population, Fox concludes that both religious discrimination and legislation have increased significantly between 1990 and 2008. This increase is robust. It remains consistent across world regions and major religious traditions. States where levels of religious discrimination and legislation increased greatly outnumber states where it dropped.... *The multivariate analysis also shows that economic development, which secularization theory predicts will result in less government support for religion, is significantly correlated with the opposite. This strongly confirms [the hypothesis of religious resurgence] that the extent of religious legislation and discrimination will be uniformly significant and increase over time.... This has significant implications for our understanding of the relationship between religion and politics.... Secularism is not an inevitable process. It is an ideology which seeks to play a role in guiding society and politics that was formerly exclusive to religion....* Given this, it is impossible to avoid the conclusion that religion is, for the foreseeable future, inextricably intertwined with politics across the globe.[60]

Entirely apart from the self-contradictions of the secularization paradigm, therefore, we have ample reasons for thinking that its core propositions and predictions are unpersuasive.

The religious character of the secularization paradigm shows something more interesting than that its core propositions are off the mark. It suggests the deep-seated quality of humankind's hunger for an all-encompassing framework of meaning, purpose, and direction. As many have observed, the innate biological capacities and genetic coding of human beings do not suffice to provide the sense of meaning, purpose, and orientation to reality that human beings need in order to live with a minimum of stability and functionality. "Man is therefore a symbolizing, conceptualizing, meaning-seeking animal, not by choice, but by absolute biological necessity. His culture, and the meaning that the culture provides, is not an option for him. Quite the contrary, man creates and operates according to his 'meaning templates' whether he wants to or not. Man is *driven* to the search for meaning."[61] Why are human beings driven to seek meaning? The reason, according to Clifford Geertz, is that "the events through which we live are forever outrunning the power of our ordinary, everyday, moral, emotional, and intellectual concepts to construe them, leaving us, as a Javanese image has it, like a water buffalo listening to an orchestra."[62] Among the most important of these "meaning templates" are those religious symbolic systems and conceptual frameworks that purport to bring human beings into an informed harmony with whatever ultimate frame and source of reality there might be. If I am correct, the secularization paradigm appears to be one such religious symbolic system.

By investing history with overarching meaning and an inevitable direction that derive from a transcendent or quasi-transcendent, superempirical agency, the secularization paradigm itself demonstrates the stubborn persistence of "unsecularity" in the modern world. The point is not that every quest for meaning inevitably leads to a religious conclusion. But the "unsecular" tendencies of the secularization paradigm, along with the evidence of cognitive psychology, suggest that human beings develop beliefs about unseen, transcendent agents with remarkable ease and naturalness. In this context, it is of enormous significance that at the very point where modern people are aspiring to be maximally secular, immanent, and worldly—by constructing the intellectual and political paradigm of secularization—they are in fact telling a religious or sacred story about what they take to be the meaning and destiny of the modern world. Indeed, the very architects and adherents of the secularization paradigm are throwing a canopy of sacred meaning over what they are doing and where they are going.

Fifth Commandment: Acknowledge that both large-scale human conflict and large-scale peacebuilding are fields of human activity that lend themselves to "unsecular" interpretation, activity, and engagement.

This is true first of all because all human striving in relation to violence—whether to inflict it, promote it, or stop it—revolves around life and death. It involves the life and death of individuals. And it sometimes involves the life and death of whole communities, societies, nations, and civilizations. In the nature of the case, to inflict or promote violence is to push individuals or even large groups of individuals "over the brink," as it were, from life to death. Of its very nature, then, violence is liminal: it touches that point where our seen world drops below (or above) the visible horizon of our experience into an unseen world. It intrinsically involves pushing human life and experience over or beyond the limit of "our world"—our own here-and-now world of the living—to what we often significantly call "the beyond."

To confront the prospect of death is thus ipso facto to confront questions about the nature of ultimate reality or "the beyond." As Michael Perry notes in the passage quoted above, among the ultimate questions or "religion and limit questions" are: "Who are we? Where did we come from; what is our origin, our beginning? Where are we going; what is our destiny, our end? What is the meaning of suffering? Of evil? Of death?" In the most peaceful of contexts, "the possibilities of death or disaster for persons and societies can be reduced but never obviated totally."[63] In situations of violent conflict, the possibilities of death or disaster cannot help but be vivid realities, confronting perpetrators and victims alike with unavoidable immediacy. In this sense, large-scale human conflict and violence of their nature tilt toward "unsecularity."

There is another sense in which large-scale modern violence tilts the human beings involved in it toward unsecularity. It is not merely that it makes death and therefore ultimate issues unavoidable. It forces those involved to ask themselves how it is at least possible and tolerable, if not rational and justifiable, to push other human beings—many other human beings—"over the brink" of life into death.

I take it for granted that large-scale violence as it has evolved in the modern world always outrageously violates the norms of ordinary morality to one degree or another. This is so much the case that the societies and individuals that engage in it normally must justify it by an appeal to some extraordinarily powerful and compelling source or logic, often if not usually rooted in some transcendent concept or discourse. Either the enemy must be identified with a transcendent evil and thus "demonized," or one's own camp and cause must be sacralized, or one must develop a special account of why there is a special, transcendent justification for the massive violence one's community is inflicting on another. None of this guarantees that individuals and communities will turn to religious discourses or symbols to frame and justify large-scale violence. But such factors lead one to expect that they will often and persistently do so. In other words, there is a logic whereby violence intrinsically tilts toward unsecularity—not, I might add, that religion intrinsically or necessarily tilts toward violence. Thus what has been called the "religionization of conflict" has roots not only in the logic of ideological and organizational mobilization but in anthropology and the nature of modern violence.

In a different vein, there is what Peter Berger calls "the argument from damnation," which "refers to experiences in which our sense of what is humanly permissible is so fundamentally outraged that the only adequate response to the offense as well as to the offender seems to be a curse of supernatural dimensions.... [This] negative form of the argument makes the intrinsic intention of the human sense of justice stand out much more sharply as a signal of transcendence over and beyond socio-historical relativities."[64] In other words, the horrific evils and injustices of global conflict themselves drive many people to a profound sense that there must be a transcendent moral order that grounds and ratifies our sense of outrage at these evils and injustices—and perhaps one that even grounds or promises a final "rectification" of all wrongs. There is, then, a dual sense in which the nature of evil and injustice prompts a turn to transcendence. The very transcendence of the evil of violence and injustice invests efforts to stop such violence and evil with a corresponding transcendence and a correspondingly sacred character. Tellingly, when Kofi Annan announced his resignation on August 2, 2012, as the special peace envoy of the United Nations and the Arab League to Syria, he said, "I accepted this task, which some called 'Mission: Impossible,' for I believed it was a *sacred duty* to do whatever was in my power to help the Syrian people find a peaceful solution to this bloody conflict."[65] It is a sign of the persistence of unsecularity in the modern world that many even relatively secular figures throughout modern history have seen their missions to bring peace and reconciliation in religious or quasi-religious terms. Indeed, the Nobel Peace Prize can be seen as a kind of quasi-religious, quasi-secular conferral of modern sainthood.

The implication of the foregoing analysis is clear. It is not that "religion" must be "brought" to the issues of conflict, violence, injustice, and peacebuilding, or harnessed so as to be "made relevant" to these problems. It is not fundamentally a matter of devising and applying "religious" techniques and frameworks to real-world problems—an approach that presupposes that the techniques and frameworks are purely extrinsic to the conflicts and contexts of violence in question. Rather, it is that one should expect that religious structures, frameworks, symbols, and actors of some sort—though perhaps of a very unconventional sort—are already radically and pervasively present in the realities and dynamics of conflict, violence, and peacemaking. The assumption that human experience and human societies are naturally and pervasively unsecular means that we should assume that many of the conflicts and peacebuilding efforts we find in the real world—whether the world of history or the world of the present day—will already be thoroughly and systematically invested with a sense of sacral meaning, purpose, and direction.

In other words, the field of human activity that concerns scholars of violence and peace—war, organized violence, conflict, as well as efforts to stop such violence and conflict and build peace—is itself soil that naturally lends itself to the growth and presence of religion in its various forms. Contrary to fashionable thinking, this is not so much because religion is naturally violent. Instead, it is because violence is naturally religious. That is, violence and conflict cry out for religious construction, interpretation, and legitimation, not least because death itself cries out for religious interpretation and intervention. And the very unacceptability of violence naturally and consistently invests efforts to stop it—efforts to build peace—with a transcendent moral and religious significance. The paradigm of persistent unsecularity is nowhere more clearly vindicated than in the unsecular character of human conflict and human peacemaking.

Conclusion

The upshot of this view of the world as persistently unsecular is (as befits an "apophatic" approach) negative: the world is not shifting decisively in either a religious or secular direction. The movement of world history—usually understood in terms of the ugly nominalizations of "globalization" or "modernization"—is not putting religious individuals, communities, or structures on the back foot. But nor is it putting "secular" or nonreligious individuals, communities, modes of life, or structures on the back foot. As it probably always has been, the world is and will forever remain a highly complex interaction—sometimes collaborative, sometimes conflictual—between more religious and more worldly individuals, institutions, personalities, concerns, and orientations, often jostling for dominance, moreover, in the very same communities, cultures, and even individual psyches.

A further implication is that the secularization paradigm and its accompanying intellectual and political projects cannot be considered neutral frameworks or mechanisms for fostering inter-religious peace and understanding. Any effort to make theoretical or practical progress in global peacebuilding must begin with an appreciation of this fact, and recognize the reality of persistent and widespread unsecularity. For, among other reasons, global peacebuilding must include profound and respectful dialogue and reconciliation between self-identified religious individuals and communities, on one hand, and self-identified secular individuals and communities, on the other. The secularization paradigm, however, is founded on premises that clearly make it unsuitable as common ground or as a foundation of mutual respect, understanding, or reconciliation. On the contrary, the secularization paradigm has been, and remains, a major engine of militancy, violence, and conflict in the modern world.

By design, this picture has none of the elegance or arc or satisfying storyline of a grand narrative. That is the point. The world is not being determined by a handful of actors or systems or causes we can count on one hand. The world is a meeting place—or rather a set of innumerable and sometimes interlocking meeting places—in which various individuals and communities on a continuum between religious and secular interact, collaborate, and conflict in ways that yield radically indeterminate and unpredictable outcomes. Or to put it another way, the world is a teeming and untidy crossroads—an unregulated intersection of the sort one meets every hundred yards or so in the metropolises of the Global South such as Bangalore, India, where I am writing this essay—of more or less religious actors and ideas and more or less secular actors and ideas. Sometimes these actors are moving in the same direction, even assisting each other—giving each other "a lift"—as they make their way on a common journey. Sometimes they are moving in orthogonal directions, heading to different destinations but not moving at direct cross-purposes. Sometimes they are moving in opposite directions, set on a collision course, usually swerving to avoid each other but not infrequently meeting head-on to violent effect.

If the world is a meeting place of the religious and secular, why should it be called "unsecular"? Why couldn't it just as well be called "unreligious" or "unsacred"? Shouldn't it be called something more neutral?

I believe the world occupies a space somewhere between outright secularity and outright sacrality, between immanence and transcendence, but this space is a few notches closer to the transcendent pole of the continuum than the immanent. Why do I think so? I freely confess to be so inspired by the admirably iconoclastic and prescient work by the late Andrew Greeley published more than forty years ago, *Unsecular Man: The Persistence of Religion*, that I feel that numerous features of human experience—including the dynamics of war and peace themselves—tilt human beings away from pure secularity or a strictly "immanent frame" or orientation towards something like "unsecularity," as I have tried to show. I hope

I honor Greeley with my humble attempt to revise his insight that this tilt towards unsecularity does not necessarily "make" all or even most human beings deeply or "authentically" religious (whatever "authentic" religion would be precisely). But it renders all human beings and all human societies permanently fertile soil for the growth of religious longings, strivings, ideas, practices, modes of life, and communities. The same goes for all human activities, including those involved in violent human conflict and peacebuilding. The presence of such fertile soil does not guarantee religious growth, but it explains why the growth is so predictable, consistent, and persistent.

Notes

1. "One must view skeptically. . . reconstructions of the past in the forms of cycles or trajectories. By arbitrarily accepting some data and excluding much other data, some kind of cycle can no doubt be discerned in the history of, for example, the Roman people. Or, if one insists upon conceiving civilization as a single great whole, one can deal with it in terms of some assumed direction in time. Civilization, we say, has moved from the homogeneous to the heterogeneous, or from the communal to the individualistic, or from handicraft to computer technology, or from the original goodness of the Golden Age to present corruption and misery. We can say any of these things, and we do. The question is, do we mean anything when we say them? I repeat, in any concrete, empirical, substantive sense, 'civilization' or 'mankind' can only be taken to mean the vast, nearly incommensurable totality of ways of living of all the peoples who have ever existed on earth. How does one make an entity out of this far-flung and diversified conglomerate of peoples and acts? The answer is, we cannot." Robert Nisbet, *The Social Bond: An Introduction to the Study of Society* (New York: Knopf, 1970), 360–361.
2. "Something like a paradigm is prerequisite to perception itself. What a man sees depends both upon what he looks at and also upon what his previous visual-conceptual experience has taught him to see. In the absence of such training there can only be, in William James's phrase, 'a bloomin' buzzin' confusion.'" Thomas Kuhn, *The Structure of Scientific Revolutions* (Chicago: University of Chicago Press, 1970), 113.
3. Quoted in Paul Eidelberg, *On the Silence of the Declaration of Independence* (Amherst: University of Massachusetts Press, 1976), 50. But I admit that this oft-cited line of Pascal is less a direct quotation than a paraphrase—a broadly accurate one—of his penetrating discussion of dogmatism and skepticism in the *Pensées*; see Blaise Pascal, *Pensées*, edited and translated by Roger Ariew (Indianapolis, IN: Hackett Pub. Co, 2005), 34–38.
4. Kuhn, *Structure of Scientific Revolutions*, viii.
5. Kuhn, *Structure of Scientific Revolutions*, 10.
6. "If we take a survey of the existing state of the globe, we shall perceive, in the first place, that in Europe the principles of the French constitution are those of every enlightened mind. We shall perceive that they are too widely disseminated, and too openly professed, for the efforts of tyrants and priests to prevent them from penetrating by degrees into the miserable cottages of their slaves, where they will soon revive those embers of good sense, and rouse that silent indignation which the habit of suffering and terror have failed totally to extinguish in the minds of the oppressed." Marquis de Condorcet, Marie-Jean-Antoine-Nicolas de Caritat, *Outlines of an Historical View of the Progress of the Human Mind* (Philadelphia: Lang and Ultick, 1795), 253.

7. To a large extent, this normative social theory based on the disfavoring of religious tradition in favor of reason was based on a radicalization and extension of the thought of John
Locke, who was almost universally venerated by the thinkers of the French Enlightenment
as "*le sage* Locke."

8. Condorcet, *Outlines*, 253.

9. Alexis de Tocqueville, *Democracy in America*, translated by Harvey Claflin Mansfield and
Delba Winthrop (Chicago: University of Chicago Press, 2000), 282.

10. Bryan Wilson, "Secularization: The Inherited Model," in *The Sacred in a Secular Age*, ed.
Phillip E. Hammond (Berkeley: University of California Press, 1985), 9. Emphasis mine.

11. "Sociology's charter as a discipline [as formulated by Comte] implied from the outset
that it was to be an empirical, man-centered, this-worldly, matter-of-fact explanation of
human organization and development. The work of Comte's major successors, beginning
from different starting points, using different terms, and within different frameworks of
argument, reinforced this general orientation: Marx's emphasis on materialism; Weber's
Entzauberung; Durkheim's pursuit of a rational ethic; Veblen's 'matter-of-fact' thinking.
Sociology documented a secularizing process" (Wilson, "Secularization," 9).

12. Oliver Tschannen, "The Secularization Paradigm: A Systematization," *Journal for the
Scientific Study of Religion* 30, no. 4 (1991): 395–415.

13. Steve Bruce, *God Is Dead: Secularization in the West* (Malden, MA: Wiley-Blackwell,
2002), 4.

14. Christopher J. Eberle, *Religious Conviction in Liberal Politics* (Cambridge: Cambridge
University Press, 2002), 15.

15. "Every thing seems to be preparing the speedy downfall of the religions of the East, which,
partaking of the abjectness of their ministers, left almost exclusively to the people, and,
in the majority of countries, considered by powerful men as political institutions only,
no longer threaten to retain human reason in a state of hopeless bondage, and in the eternal shackles of infancy.. . . Then will arrive the moment in which the sun will observe in
its course free nations only, acknowledging no other master than their reason; in which
tyrants and slaves, priests and their stupid or hypocritical instruments, will no longer exist
but in history and upon the stage; in which our only concern will be to lament their past
victims and dupes, and, by the recollection of their horrid enormities, to exercise a vigilant
circumspection, that we may be able instantly to recognise and effectually to stifle by the
force of reason, the seeds of superstition and tyranny, should they ever presume again to
make their appearance upon the earth" (Condorcet, *Outlines*, 257–259).

16. Condorcet, *Outlines*, 145.

17. Wilson, "Secularization," 19. Emphasis is Wilson's.

18. Wilson, "Secularization," 13.

19. Wilson, "Secularization," 20. Emphasis mine.

20. Wilson, "Secularization," 19.

21. See the five edited volumes of the Fundamentalism Project directed by R. Scott Appleby
and Martin Marty published by the University of Chicago Press between 1991 and 1995.
A fine synthetic monograph summarizing the key findings of the Fundamentalism Project
later appeared, as "one born out of due time": Gabriel A. Almond, R. Scott Appleby, and
Emmanuel Sivan, *Strong Religion: The Rise of Fundamentalisms Around the World*
(Chicago: University of Chicago Press, 2003).

22. Max Weber, *The Protestant Ethic and the Spirit of Capitalism* (New York: Charles Scribner,
1958).

23. Helen Sword, "Zombie Nouns," *NYtimes.com*, July 23, 2012, http://opinionator.blogs. nytimes.com/2012/07/23/zombie-nouns/?_php=true&_type=blogs&_r=0.

24. Anthony Wallace, *Religion: An Anthropological View* (New York: Random House, 1966), 265.

25. Ronald Inglehart, *Modernization and Postmodernization: Cultural, Economic, and Political Change in 43 Societies* (Princeton: Princeton University Press, 1997), 72.

26. Weber, The Protestant Ethic and the Spirit of Capitalism, 181–183.

27. Wallace, *Religion*, 265.

28. Bryan Wilson, *Contemporary Transformations of Religion* (Oxford: Oxford University Press, 1976), 116.

29. Warren Nord, *Religion and American Education* (Chapel Hill: University of North Carolina Press, 1995), 39.

30. The reference here of course is to Hegel's notion of the "cunning of Reason," whereby the great driving agent of history achieves its purpose by harnessing a variety of sub-rational forces, means, and agents, including human passions.

31. Daniel Lerner, *The Passing of Traditional Society: Modernizing the Middle East* (New York: The Free Press, 1958), 45–48, 230.

32. Arnold Toynbee, preface to *Religion in a Secular Age*, by John Cogley (New York: Frederick Praeger, 1968), xvi. Emphasis mine.

33. Peter L. Berger, "A Bleak Outlook Is Seen for Religion," *New York Times*, February 25, 1968, 3.

34. Wilson, "Secularization," 10–11.

35. Vilho Harle, *The Enemy with a Thousand Faces* (Westport, CT: Praeger, 2000), 2.

36. Almond et al., *Strong Religion*, 95.

37. Wilson, Contemporary Transformations of Religion, 6.

38. Christian Smith, "Introduction: Rethinking the Secularization of American Public Life," in *The Secular Revolution: Power, Interests, and Conflict in the Secularization of American Public Life*, ed. Christian Smith (Berkeley: University of California Press, 2003), p. 21.

39. Peter Laslett, *The World We Have Lost: Further Explored*, 4th ed. (London: Routledge, 2004), 71.

40. Wilson, "Secularization," 17.

41. Bruce, God Is Dead.

42. Wilson, "Secularization," 18.

43. See Bryan Wilson's various writings, including *Contemporary Transformations of Religion* and see Pippa Norris and Ronald Inglehart, *Sacred and Secular: Religion and Politics Worldwide* (Cambridge: Cambridge University Press, 2011).

44. For example, many of the compelling empirical and theoretical studies carried out under the multi-volume Fundamentalism Project led by Martin E. Marty and R. Scott Appleby proceed, I think, under some combination of these assumptions. In other words, these studies of fundamentalism not only do not depart from the secularization paradigm but in fact presuppose the fundamental truth and power of secularization as an overwhelming and essentially irreversible global process. Consider the concise one-volume summary of the Fundamentalism Project, (Alomond et al., *Strong Religion*). The book summarizes fundamentalist groups as "militant and highly focused antagonists of secularization" that "call a halt to the centuries-long retreat of the religious establishment before the secular power" (2). In other words, it is the very reality and power of secularization that inspires the formation and mobilization of fundamentalist militancy. But the authors do not for a moment believe that secularization is realistically reversible. Fundamentalism may

amount to a kind of "rebuff" to modernization and secularization. Yet the important question is whether fundamentalism could realistically alter the system and direction of the modern world. And on that question, the authors of *Strong Religion* conclude that "fundamentalism qua fundamentalism (i.e., as an aggressive, enclave-based movement with absolutist, reactive, and inerrantist tendencies)... is quintessentially a local phenomenon, a struggle for cultural and political influence over the 'tribe,' whether conceived along narrow or expansive geographical lines.. . . International developments and affiliations will continue to influence fundamentalisms, but they will remain confined ideologically within the boundaries set by fundamentalists' selectively traditional and selectively modern, inerrantist, and Manichean worldviews.... Chances are, [fundamentalism] will thrive mostly in opposition as a dissenting minority, although in some settings it may assume power directly or by infiltration.. . . Nonetheless, the move from disrupting the social/political order to taking actual power remains a quantum leap" (242).

45. Andrew Greeley, *Unsecular Man: The Persistence of Religion* (Indiana University: Schocken Books, 1972), 60.

46. Joseph Boyle, "The Place of Religion in the Practical Reasoning of Individuals and Groups," *The American Journal of Jurisprudence* 43(1998): 3.

47. Greeley, *Unsecular Man*, 63.

48. Robert Bellah, *Beyond Belief: Essays on Religion in a Post-Traditional World* (New York: Harper and Row, 1970), 237.

49. Samuel P. Huntington, *The Clash of Civilizations and the Remaking of World Order* (New York: Simon and Schuster, 1997), 57.

50. Alexis de Tocqueville, *The Old Regime and the Revolution*, edited by François Furet and Françoise Mélonio, translated by Alan S. Kahan (Chicago: University of Chicago Press, 1998), 101.

51. Michael Latham, *Modernization as Ideology* (Chapel Hill: University of North Carolina Press, 2000).

52. James Hoagland, "Facing Faith as Politics," *Washington Post*, January 15, 2006, http://www.washingtonpost.com/wp-dyn/content/article/2006/01/13/AR2006011301699.html.

53. Almond et al., *Strong Religion*, 93–97.

54. One could also argue that the religious ideology of secularization is more literally "militant" and dangerous than some (other) forms of religious fundamentalism, because it makes human beings co-creators (with "reason" or "history" or "modernity") of an "immanentized eschaton," to paraphrase Eric Voegelin. In other words, human beings must and can do some of the important work of "mak[ing] the world all over again," to quote Paine, including work that may well be militant and violent. This contrasts with many religious and even fundamentalist visions, in which human beings depend entirely on a god—conceived as outside time and history—to take the initiative and exercise his sovereign power to bring history to its final consummation in the eschaton, new age, or final judgment.

55. William T. Cavanaugh, *The Myth of Religious Violence: Secular Ideology and the Roots of Modern Conflict* (New York: Oxford University Press, 2009).

56. For a suggestive analysis of the ways in which belief in inevitable secular progress is both pervasive in the modern world and has some of the features of a religion, see Christopher Lasch, *The True and Only Heaven: Progress and Its Critics* (New York: W. W. Norton, 1991).

57. Michael J. Perry, "The Right to Religious Freedom: An Elaboration and Defense (with Particular Reference to Same-Sex Marriage)," unpublished paper presented to an

International Conference on Religious Law and State Affairs, Bar Ilan University, Faculty of Law, Tel Aviv, Israel, May 29–31, 2011, 6–8.

58. Monica Toft, Daniel Philpott, and Timothy Shah, *God's Century: Resurgent Religion and Global Politics* (New York: W. W. Norton, 2011), Chapter 3.

59. Christian Smith, *Moral, Believing Animals: Human Personhood and Culture* (Oxford: Oxford University Press, 2003).

60. Jonathan Fox, "Is It Really God's Century? An Evaluation of Religious Legislation and Discrimination from 1990 to 2008," paper presented at the University of Maryland, February 2012. Emphasis mine.

61. Greeley, *Unsecular Man*, 58. Emphasis mine.

62. Clifford Geertz, *Islam Observed* (New Haven, CT: Yale University Press, 1969), 101. Quoted in Greeley, *Unsecular Man*, 64.

63. Nisbet, *The Social Bond*, 239–240.

64. Peter Berger, *The Sacred Canopy: Elements of a Sociological Theory of Religion* (New York: Knopf, 1968), 73–77.

65. Kofi Annan, "Press conference by Kofi Annan, Joint Special Envoy for Syria," Geneva, Switzerland, August 2, 2012.

BIBLIOGRAPHY

Almond, Gabriel A., R. Scott Appleby, and Emmanuel Sivan. *Strong Religion: The Rise of Fundamentalisms Around the World*. Chicago: University of Chicago Press, 2003.

Annan, Kofi. "Press Conference by Kofi Annan, Joint Special Envoy for Syria." Geneva, Switzerland, August 2, 2012.

Bellah, Robert. *Beyond Belief: Essays on Religion in a Post-Traditional World*. New York: Harper and Row, 1970.

Berger, Peter. *The Sacred Canopy: Elements of a Sociological Theory of Religion*. New York: Knopf, 1968.

Berger, Peter L. "A Bleak Outlook Is Seen for Religion." *New York Times*, February 25, 1968, 3.

Boyle, Joseph. "The Place of Religion in the Practical Reasoning of Individuals and Groups." *The American Journal of Jurisprudence* 43, no. 1 (1998): 1–24.

Bruce, Steve. *God Is Dead: Secularization in the West*. Malden, MA: Wiley-Blackwell, 2002.

Cavanaugh, William T. *The Myth of Religious Violence: Secular Ideology and the Roots of Modern Conflict*. New York: Oxford University Press, 2009.

de Caritat, Marie-Jean-Antoine-Nicolas, Marquis de Condorcet. *Outlines of an Historical View of the Progress of the Human Mind*. Philadelphia: Lang and Ultick, 1795.

Eberle, Christopher J. *Religious Conviction in Liberal Politics*. Cambridge: Cambridge University Press, 2002.

Eidelberg, Paul. *On the Silence of the Declaration of Independence*. Amherst: University of Massachusetts Press, 1976.

Fox, Jonathan. "Is It Really God's Century? An Evaluation of Religious Legislation and Discrimination from 1990 to 2008." Paper presented at the University of Maryland, February 2012.

Geertz, Clifford. *Islam Observed*. New Haven, CT: Yale University Press, 1969.

Greeley, Andrew. *Unsecular Man: The Persistence of Religion*. New York: Schocken Books, 1972.

Harle, Vilho. *The Enemy with a Thousand Faces*. Westport, CT: Praeger, 2000.

Hoagland, James. "Facing Faith as Politics." *Washington Post*, January 15, 2006. http://www.washingtonpost.com/wp-dyn/content/article/2006/01/13/AR2006011301699.html.

Huntington, Samuel P. *The Clash of Civilizations and the Remaking of World Order*. New York: Simon and Schuster, 1997.

Inglehart, Ronald. *Modernization and Postmodernization: Cultural, Economic, and Political Change in 43 Societies*. Princeton: Princeton University Press, 1997.

Kuhn, Thomas. *The Structure of Scientific Revolutions*. Chicago: University of Chicago Press, 1970.

Lasch, Christopher. *The True and Only Heaven: Progress and Its Critics*. New York: W. W. Norton, 1991.

Laslett, Peter. *The World We Have Lost: Further Explored*, 4th ed. London: Routledge, 2004. First published in 1965 by Methuen & Co.

Latham, Michael. *Modernization as Ideology*. Chapel Hill: University of North Carolina Press, 2000.

Lerner, Daniel. *The Passing of Traditional Society: Modernizing the Middle East*. New York: The Free Press, 1958.

Nisbet, Robert. *The Social Bond: An Introduction to the Study of Society*. New York: Knopf, 1970.

Nord, Warren. *Religion and American Education*. Chapel Hill: University of North Carolina Press, 1995.

Paine, Thomas. *Rights of Man, Common Sense, and Other Political Writings*. Oxford: Oxford University Press, 1995.

Perry, Michael. "The Right to Religious Freedom: An Elaboration and Defense (with Particular Reference to Same-Sex Marriage)." Unpublished paper presented to an International Conference on Religious Law and State Affairs, Bar Ilan University, Faculty of Law, Tel Aviv, Israel, May 29–31, 2011.

Pascal, Blaise. *Pensées*, edited and translated by Roger Ariew. Indianapolis, IN: Hackett Pub. Co, 2005.

Norris, Pippa and Ronald Inglehart. *Sacred and Secular: Religion and Politics Worldwide*. Cambridge: Cambridge University Press, 2011.

Rousseau, Jean-Jacques. *Discourse on Political Economy and the Social Contract*. Oxford: Oxford University Press, 1999.

Smith, Christian. *Moral, Believing Animals: Human Personhood and Culture*. Oxford: Oxford University Press, 2003.

Smith, Christian. "Introduction: Rethinking the Secularization of American Public Life." In *The Secular Revolution: Power, Interests, and Conflict in the Secularization of American Public Life*. Berkeley: University of California Press, 2003.

Sword, Helen. "Zombie Nouns." *NYtimes.com*, July 23, 2012. http://opinionator.blogs.nytimes.com/2012/07/23/zombie-nouns/?_php=true&_type=blogs&_r=0.

de Tocqueville, Alexis. *The Old Regime and the Revolution*, edited by François Furet and Françoise Mélonio, translated by Alan S. Kahan. Chicago: University of Chicago Press, 1998.

de Tocqueville, Alexis. *Democracy in America*, translated by Harvey Claflin Mansfield and Delba Winthrop. Chicago: University of Chicago Press, 2000.

Toft, Monica, Daniel Philpott, and Timothy Shah. *God's Century: Resurgent Religion and Global Politics*. New York: W. W. Norton, 2011.

Toynbee, Arnold. Preface to *Religion in a Secular Age* by John Cogley, v–xxiv. New York: Frederick Praeger, 1968.

Tschannen, Oliver. "The Secularization Paradigm: A Systematization." *Journal for the Scientific Study of Religion* 30, no. 4 (1991): 395–415.

Voegelin, Eric. *The New Science of Politics*. Chicago: University of Chicago Press, 1952.

Wallace, Anthony. *Religion: An Anthropological View*. New York: Random House, 1966.

Weber, Max. *The Protestant Ethic and the Spirit of Capitalism*. New York: Charles Scribner, 1958.

Wilson, Bryan. *Contemporary Transformations of Religion*. Oxford: Oxford University Press, 1976.

Wilson, Bryan. "Secularization: The Inherited Model." In *The Sacred in a Secular Age*, edited by Phillip E. Hammond, 9–20. Berkeley: University of California Press, 1985.

CHAPTER 16

···

RELIGION AND PEACE
IN ASIA

···

TAM NGO, DAN SMYER YU, AND
PETER VAN DER VEER

WITH four billion people, Asia is the home to more than half of the world's population. The nineteenth century saw the colonial conquest and imperial domination of much of Asia, while the twentieth century was marked by Japanese aggression, civil war, and wars of independence. Large parts of the population were pitted against each other in the Cold War by communists and anti-communists, as in North and South Vietnam, North and South Korea, Taiwan and China, or in communalist separatism by Hindu and Muslim nationalists as in India and Pakistan.

Religious communities were and still are deeply involved in these conflicts. Their traditions can be regarded as either among the sources of conflict or among the solutions to them. The legacies of these wars and conflicts are crucial to understanding the contemporary predicament of these societies, as are processes of peacebuilding and reconciliation. In this chapter we examine peacebuilding and reconciliation as these practices resonate within Asian religious contexts. Christianity and Islam are minority religions in Asia. While they belong to the complex religious tapestry of Asia, they do not dominate it. Of crucial importance are other religious traditions, such as Hinduism and Buddhism. This implies that we have to deal with other legacies, other vocabularies and genealogies, than in Western traditions that are deeply imbued with Abrahamic understandings of peace and conflict. This difference from the West is further complicated by the specific histories of imperialism and anti-imperialism (nationalism, communism) in Asia, which explain why religious conversion is so fraught with conflict and impedes peacebuilding. This is not to say that we can understand peacebuilding within the Asian religious context solely from the perspective of *difference*. On the contrary, the specificity of Asian modernity has been developed in interaction with Western power and values.[1] This specificity, however, requires attention to the historical context in which peacebuilding takes place. A major argument in this contribution will be that personalistic, charismatic models for peacebuilding play a central role in Asia, while the ideas conveyed by these personalities are coming out of interactions between Asian and Western traditions. Peacebuilding, like reconciliation, refers to a specific set of practices, informed by theory, designed to alleviate human suffering and create the conditions for human flourishing. However, much of the theoretical apparatus of peacebuilding and reconciliation seems to come out of the West and build on elements of the Christian tradition. In the two extended vignettes on Mozambique and Colombia that John Paul Lederach and R. Scott Appleby offer in their overview of strategic peacebuilding, the Catholic Church is the protagonist of peacebuilding. In Asia the Church cannot easily play such a role of negotiator and arbiter, since nationalists see Christianity as a colonial legacy and the Church itself is targeted by state violence in China, Vietnam, and North Korea, and by communal violence in India and Pakistan. Christianity is not only relatively marginal in Asia, but also a bone of contention, so that we have to look at the majority traditions for sustainable peacebuilding. One of the great theoretical and practical problems that peacebuilders face is the relation between violence and social justice. How can one obtain justice without violence? In developing their argument about *justpeace* as "a dynamic state of affairs in which the reduction and management of violence and the achievement of social and economic justice are undertaken as mutual, reinforcing dimensions of constructive change," Lederach and Appleby seem to downplay the inherent tension (and sometimes opposition) between the reduction of violence and the achievement of economic justice.[2] One can sustain peace for a long time by not allowing challenges to an unjust social system. At the same time, one can obtain social and economic justice by violent revolution. Much violence in Asia has been directed at dominant groups that were considered to be obstacles to economic justice. Religions were seen, at least by communists, as a legitimating structure for class oppression. At the same time, the suppression of rebellion can sustain an unjust social structure.

We argue in this chapter that non-Christian Asian traditions contribute perspectives on peacebuilding that are different from those offered by major Western traditions. That is not to say that, for example, Christian ideas of peacebuilding and reconciliation are not applied in Asian contexts. An important example is forgiveness, which is a particularly Christian idea that is generally seen as crucial to reconciliation.[3] Forgiving is an alternative to seeking revenge and retribution and thus enhances peace. According to Hannah Arendt, "The discoverer of the role of forgiveness in the realm of human affairs was Jesus of Nazareth. The fact that he made this discovery in a religious context and articulated it in religious language is no reason to take it any less seriously in a strictly secular sense."[4]

The question before us, however, is less whether a Christian idea can be carried over to a Christian-secular context than whether it is translatable to non-Christian contexts. The root of the concept of forgiveness is "gift," implying a giver, a recipient, and an object that is given. As Marcel Mauss has observed, the gift demands something in return, forces reciprocity. Forgiveness requires a relationship that is initiated by apology. To be able to forgive, then, one needs to be given an apology.[5]

Japan after World War II offers a rich example of the complexity of apology in Asian cultural contexts.[6] Japan's neighbors, Korea and China, have repeatedly asked Japan to apologize for its misdeeds in the war, but the repeated apologies by Japanese leaders have failed to satisfy Japan's victims. The apologies are not felt to be "sincere" since they are contradicted by visits of politicians to the Yasukuni shrine in Tokyo (where war criminals are included among the memorialized dead) and by controversies about the depiction of the war in Japanese history textbooks. The difficulty with "sincere" apologies in the Japanese case is that the Japanese have not been willing to see themselves as straightforward perpetrators of unjust war, but continue to see themselves, at least in part, as the victims of the war. By contrast, postwar Germany has addressed the process of *Vergangenheitsbewältigung* (dealing with the past) much more thoroughly and even vigorously.

It is clear from the Japanese example that the transactional model of apology and forgiveness, amplified by the Protestant demand for "sincerity," is crucial to the processes of peacebuilding and reconciliation in large swaths of Asia. However, the language of forgiveness is only one element of religious tradition that is relevant in Asia—and it derives from Christianity, which after all is only a minority religion there. The major religious traditions of Asia—Hinduism, Buddhism, Islam, Daoism, and Confucianism—all carry important ideas that are relevant to peacebuilding and conflict resolution.

Essential to translating these ideas into "useful" concepts to stimulate and inform actual peacebuilding among and within Asian nations and within local communities is a deep awareness of and reckoning with the bitter legacies of colonialism, imperialism, and intra-religious wars (often promoted by foreign powers or resulting in part from imperial policies). Before we can turn to some positive examples of religious contributions to just-peace, *we have to consider some of the historical complexities within which peacebuilding in Asia takes place.*

A religious conviction held by more than one of all religious traditions in general is a variant on the claim that universal conversion to "the one true faith" would result in world peace. A deadly corollary to this notion holds that so-called holy wars may indeed be instrumental to the spread of the religious Truth—a necessary evil or "inconvenience" in light of the ultimate goal of uniting people in that Truth and transcending the antagonisms that cause warfare in the first place. This corollary has its secular counterpart, of course, not least in post-Christian societies: not only holy warfare, but also secular wars or conflict in general can lead to a future of peace.

While these convictions have underwritten the spread of various "imperial" versions of Christianity and Islam over huge areas, they have not been shared universally. Indeed, we recognize with our colleagues in this volume that there is no such thing as "Islam" or "Christianity" in some encompassing monolithic sense, but only many Islams and Christianities, and so on. And yet the idea of universal truth and the corollary commitment to spreading the truth by force lent a violent, deadly cast to the history of expansion in Asia. That memory is still very much alive in the present day. This is, for example, a crucial element in the popular understanding of Muslim conversion in South Asia. Whatever the correct historical interpretation may be, the image of Sultan Mahmud of Ghazni, hailing from what is today Afghanistan, destroying the Hindu temple in Somnath in 1025 CE pervades Indian popular memory and textbook education.[7] It provides the legitimizing narrative for anti-conversion campaigns, in which Hindu leaders accuse Muslims of using Gulf oil wealth to entice poor Hindus to convert, as in the important incident of the conversion of an untouchable community in Meenakshipuram in 1980.[8] Such memories, too easily constructed and manipulated by exploitative politicians and extremist movements, also provided the legitimation for the campaign to destroy a mosque that was allegedly built in the sixteenth century by the Mughal emperor Babar on the birthplace of the Hindu god Rama in the North Indian pilgrimage center Ayodhya. The campaign to "liberate Rama's birthplace" succeeded in 1992 and dominated Indian politics for at least two decades.

One finds such popular "memories" of violent Islamic expansion everywhere in Asia. They stand in the way of peaceful coexistence and reconciliation between Muslims and others (Muslims and Hindus in India, Muslims and Buddhists in Thailand, Muslims and

Christians in Indonesia and Malaysia). Secular scholars in the more recent past have conducted meticulous research and published more accurate and less inflammatory accounts of the historical interaction between Muslims, Hindus, and others. But this professional history has not really "trickled down" to the population at large.[9]

COUNTERING RELIGIOUS EXTREMISM THROUGH SYNCRETISM

Religious responses to the manipulation of memory and exploitation of religious differences are both more complex and more promising. At the popular level, there is considerable interpenetration of religious traditions, especially in tomb worship in Sufi Islam. The sacred power of the saint and his tomb bring people of different communities to forms of syncretism that promote peace and reconciliation. *Indeed, syncretism is the most important channel of dealing with religious diversity, because it crosses boundaries and allows hybridity.* The phenomenon of mixing and matching and blending religious and cultural ideas and practices is too complex to be reduced to a simple story of multicultural tolerance, but it shows religious creativity in diffusing conflict and promoting coexistence.[10] Hindus and Muslims both visit Sufi shrines and believe in the power of the saints worshipped there.[11] The history of Islamic expansion is not forgotten, but creatively reworked in ballads and folklore that celebrates magical power (*baraka*) that transcends communal politics and helps devotees to overcome suffering. Particularly striking is the worship of Muslim warrior-saints (ghazi) by Hindus in India.[12] The story of these warriors is at one level that of conquest, but at a deeper level one of virginal martyrdom that is reminiscent of the death of Jesus Christ on the cross and inspires similar devotion. It is in these devotional practices that large parts of mostly rural populations come together to celebrate victory over death. The sites where these saints are worshipped are still of crucial importance in India and in places where Muslims are part of plural societies, such as Yugoslavia. What happens here is what one could call antagonistic tolerance.[13]

CONVERSION A STUMBLING BLOCK

Conversion to Christianity in Asia is at least as fraught with tension as conversion to Islam. Popular memory focuses particularly on the modern period of Western imperialism. Christianity is often seen in Asia as foreign and a handmaiden of imperial expansion. An especially important memory for the Chinese is the Opium Wars of the nineteenth century, which opened China not only to trade (especially of opium), but also to Christian missions. The Treaty of Tianjin in 1858 allowed Western powers not only to enter China for trading, but also allowed Christian missionaries to proselytize there. This had been forbidden since an edict of Pope Clement XI forbidding Christian participation in Confucian rites had let to a ban on Christian activities by Emperor Kangxi in 1721.

Feelings of humiliation by Western imperialism remain widespread in Asia today, and Christian conversion is seen in India, Vietnam, and China as a threat to post-imperial sovereignty. In India there are anti-conversion laws in place,[14] and the atheistic communist governments of Vietnam and China have severely restrain Christian activities. In India, Christian missionaries have been violently attacked by Hindu nationalists, while in Vietnam and China Christians are subject to strict surveillance and considerable repression by the state.[15] Their connections with churches and organizations outside of Asia are especially suspicious in the eyes of nationalists and state authorities. Since Christian proselytism has been successful among hill people in border areas (such as the Nagas in India and the Hmong in Laos and Vietnam), these suspicions are couched in the language of national security. This situation is aggravated by US agencies, such as the State Department's Office of Religious Freedom, who pressure the governments of Asian states with Christian minorities to legalize religious freedom, including the right to proselytize. In communist states, vivid memories of Christian anti-communism during the Cold War (framed as a global conflict between the God-fearing and the godless) exacerbate the situation and pit the state against Christian minorities.[16]

Notwithstanding these burdens, Asian Christianity has been in many ways a core contributor to indigenous nationalism. Sun Yat-sen as well as Chiang Kai-shek were Christians and leaders of Chinese nationalism. In East Asia, Christianity can perhaps be seen as an alternative to communism, which may limit Christians' ability to play a role in reconciling North and South Vietnam after the American War. Catholics were too much a party in the conflict and on the losing side, while Protestants are seen as agents of American imperialism.[17] In contrast, Christians can and do play a significant role in Korea. In the aftermath of the Korean War, they have helped North Korean refugees to China come to South Korea and assimilate into society by way of converting to Christianity. Since the mid-1990s, when North Korea began suffering from severe famine, many North Koreans began crossing the border into China in search of food. It is the Korean Protestant Church that not only established an "underground railroad" through which many of the border crossers travel via China to South Korea, but that also provides religious and nonreligious services for North Koreans when they settle in South Korea. Eighty to 90 percent of the North Koreans who reach South Korea identify themselves as Protestant. Protestants see the reunification of the two Koreas as a "spiritual war." There can be little doubt that in any reunion of the two Koreas, Christians will play a central role in the process of reconciliation.[18]

However, in general, promoting peace and reconciliation in Asian religious traditions may require a campaign, against the Abrahamic grain, to deemphasize or even abandon the notion and practice of individual conversion: one should not convert, or attempt to make converts, but leave people in the collective faith into which they were born. Inculcating respect for each religious tradition and community would have the added benefit of strengthening the culture of tolerance that is an integral dimension of building peace.

Such an orientation resonates with Hinduism's natural affinity for pluralism, expressed through a hierarchical inclusivism that stresses that there are many paths that lead to spiritual liberation. Such a thought is intimately related to the doctrine of transmigration of the soul, in which deeds done in past lives determine one's birth and thus one's caste. By emphasizing difference and separation, Hindu traditions legitimize a social order of extreme inequality but relatively little violence. Buddhism and Jainism add to this an abhorrence of animal sacrifice, which is extended to vegetarianism and nonviolence in general. It also leads to a relativizing of suffering, since suffering is seen as the human condition. While Buddhism has expanded over a large part of Asia (and has disappeared almost entirely from India), the social memory of that expansion carries an altogether different salience than the conquests of peoples by Islam and Christianity. Of course, Buddhism has aligned itself with political power in different periods of history as it clearly does today in Tibet, Thailand, Burma, and Sri Lanka. But it has been more relativistic and tolerant of popular syncretism by focusing on monastic rather than lay practice for a long part of its history. Lay practice is, more or less, seen as a lesser practice and thus not in need of reform, while monastic practice is the "true" practice of renunciation.

The absence of a strong sense of conversion in the Indic traditions sets them apart from Abrahamic traditions. Antipathy toward conversion is strongly felt in India, as we will see below in our discussion of Gandhi. This has led to quite strict legislation in independent India against proselytism. Ironically these laws are believed to safeguard religious freedom, since they proscribe "forced conversions" induced by charity. They are considered to protect tribal people and untouchables, considering them (fallaciously) to be "naturally" Hindu. As expressions of Indian secularism, these laws in fact attempt to produce a homogeneous Hindu nation.[19]

In the context of legislation that is intended to prevent untouchbles and tribals from defecting from the Hindu majority, the conversion to Buddhism of the untouchable Bhimrao Ambedkar in the 1950s is important. Ambedkar, one of the great untouchable leaders of Congress and architect of India's secular constitution, came to the conclusion that the secular, liberal state (liberal peace and justice) could not solve the problems of untouchability that were deeply embedded in codes of honor and respect. While early in his career he demonstrated his stance against Hinduism by burning Hindu Law Books in public, at the end of his life he decided to convert to Buddhism in order to escape from the Hindu caste system.[20] In a very original manner he came to grips with the dualism of redistribution (class) and recognition (caste). His conversion shows that religious conversion can address these issues sometimes better than conversion to secular ideologies like socialism or liberalism. It is an attempt at justpeace that can be sustained over time that motivated Ambedkar and millions of his followers to convert to Buddhism, in principle a much more egalitarian worldview than Hinduism. Ambedkar argued that only a radical rejection of the Hindu values underlying the caste system would undermine the cultural basis of systematic discrimination. By pointing out Hinduism's legitimation of exploitation and slavery, Ambedkar refuted the claim that it was a creed of tolerance and peace.

RENUNCIATION AS A PATH TO PEACE?

Asian religious traditions, it can be argued, converge around the idea that a person seeking a superior moral life and liberation from suffering should focus on renunciation and self-cultivation. Such a person is a moral exemplar, one whose path, if widely imitated, would enhance the prospects for world peace, tolerance, and reconciliation. The Shakyamuni Buddha is such a person, and the stories of his life (Jatakas) are moral instructions on how to lead one's life. In Buddhist meditation, metta (kindness and compassion) is cultivated in order to expel every form of hostility and envy. The potentially individualistic practice and aim of renunciation is tempered by the ideal of loving kindness of all sentient beings that is also at the root of the doctrine of the bodhisattva, a being who does not disappear into nirvana but watches the universe to protect and assist those who suffer. Avalokitesvara (the Lord who looks down) is one of the most revered bodhisattvas in Mahayana Buddhism and is worshipped in China as Guanyin, while in Tibet he is thought to be incarnated in the Dalai Lama. He (or she in China) has postponed Buddhahood to support humanity in its suffering and is characterized by loving kindness.

This tradition of the moral exemplar is still alive in Asian religious traditions. Properly understood, it may be the most significant resource for processes of peacebuilding and reconciliation.[21] It is important to see this not as a phenomenological interpretation of religious traditions, but as practical religion and practical peacebuilding. Within Asia there are many examples of the role of moral exemplars in building peace, but by far the most inspiring and important figures who exemplify this tradition are Mahatma Gandhi in India, the Dalai Lama in Tibet, and Thich Nhat Hanh in Vietnam. They have practically confronted some of the world's most complex situations of conflict and shown leadership in justpeace and reconciliation: Hindu-Muslim antagonism and violence in India; Chinese oppression of the Tibetan people; and the American War and the unification of North and South Vietnam.

Mahatma Gandhi

The most significant conflict in the Indian subcontinent is that between Hindus and Muslims. Political competition between the two in British India led to widespread violence, culminating in disastrous ethnic cleansing during the Partition of independent India and Pakistan in 1947. The emergence of two independent nation-states after bloody conflict caused further armed conflict about Kashmir in 1947 and 1965 as well as another war in 1971 around the separation of Bangladesh from Pakistan. One can speak of a continuous state of tension between India and Pakistan as exemplified in the Kargil border conflict of 1999 and the terrorist attack on Mumbai in 2008. At the same time, Hindu-Muslim conflict within India has remained a prominent feature of political life, especially after the demolition of the Babar mosque in Ayodhya in 1992 and the Gujarat pogrom against Muslims in 2002. Considering the importance of the Indian subcontinent (India, Pakistan, Bangladesh), Hindu-Muslim antagonism and periodic violence are one of the most contentious issues for today's peacebuilding.

This makes the contribution to justpeace by the most important protagonist of nonviolence in the twentieth century, Mahatma Gandhi, so important.

In 1910, when he began writing on India's struggle for independence in his book *Hind Swaraj*, Mohandas Gandhi (1869–1948) was aware of the deep connection between spirituality and anti-imperialism in British intellectual circles. Gandhi himself saw that struggle as primarily a spiritual one. The sources for that spiritual perspective were multiple: Hindu tradition, Tolstoy's interpretation of Christian spirituality, Ruskin's thoughts about industry, Nordau's views on civilization.[22] We would argue that Gandhi's "experiments with truth," as he called his political and spiritual struggle, were a product of the imperial encounter of Britain and India. The man whom Churchill dismissed as a "half-naked faqir" was as much a product of that encounter as Churchill himself.[23]

Gandhi formulated his ideas in universalistic terms, but the idiom of universalism always emerges from a particular place and history. In Gandhi's case it came from the Hindu tradition into which he had been socialized. His vegetarianism derived from well-established traditions of the Hindu and Jain trading castes, but could be universalized as a general moral practice, connecting to theories of the connections between body and spirit that had become popular in Britain in the second half of the nineteenth century. His nonviolence was again a particular interaction between Hindu and Jain traditions and European repertoires of radical protest (like the boycott). More than simply perceiving a connection between Eastern and Western traditions, Gandhi contributed to the transformation of them in the context of a history of interaction. This history continued in a new direction when American blacks adopted some of Gandhi's ideas and tactics in their own struggle for civil rights.[24]

Gandhi's "experiments with truth" were attempts to attain moral truth through disciplines of the body, like fasting and celibacy. At the same time such disciplines, like fasting unto death, could be used as political instruments in the struggle for India's independence. A strong element in this was the notion of "inner-worldly" asceticism, a spiritual rejection of the materialism of Western (colonial) civilization. Gandhi called himself a *karmayogi*, a man who practices the yoga of activity, in this way combining revolutionary spirit and the ancient spiritual tradition of inner tranquility. He modernized and nationalized yoga. He was also quite obsessed with public hygiene and public health as signs of national morality. In this he was as much influenced by Hindu bio-moral thought about food (hot and cold) and its effect on one's nature and actions as by Western bio-moral thought on the benefits of vegetarianism as well as the effects of bathing. With Gandhi we truly have body politics in the sense that he was using his body as a field of experimentation and as an exemplar for society to follow.[25]

His spirituality was not conceived as a traditional quest for religious insight or redemption, but as the opposite of the Western materialism that he saw as the basis of imperialism. Gandhi wanted economic progress for India, but saw the materialism of imperial power as one of the causes of India's decline. He had a universalistic view of the various religious traditions in the sense that he thought they had a spiritual core in common. That was one of the reasons why he felt that one should not proselytize, as Christian missionaries were doing in India, but let people discover the unifying moral and spiritual essence in their own and other traditions while sticking to the one in which they had been socialized. In Gandhi's view, one obtained truth through one's experiments with truth (satyagraha), but it was a moral truth that had to be experienced and indeed shown to others through one's example. One should not criticize those who had not realized such truth and while criticism is already a kind of violence, one should in general avoid violently imposing truth upon others who are not convinced by one's example. Truth, then, is moral, while cognitive truth is only important in helping us to realize our moral goals rather than destroy us through materialism.[26] It was this emphasis on the authenticity of one's upbringing in a tradition and the rootedness of these traditions in India that led Gandhi to a spiritual nationalism. Unlike Tagore, he was never very excited by Pan-Asian cosmopolitanism, despite his acknowledgment that the spirituality of the West had been corrupted and that it was the task of Asia to bring the spiritual message to the world. At the political level it was Nehru who was interested in Pan-Asianism and in India's spiritual leadership of the non-aligned world during the Cold War. Nehru's efforts culminated in the Bandung Conference of 1955, but ended miserably in the Indian defeat by China in the Sino-Indian War of 1962.[27] What Gandhi offers is a spiritual contribution to justpeace. He emphasized what he saw as specifically Indian civilizational ideas about nonviolence and tolerance as well as selfless devotion to others. Important is that he saw these ideas as not so much belonging to Hinduism as a religion, but to world spirituality. That is why he did not see a need for conversion, since these spiritual notions can be found in all religious traditions, Islam and Christianity included. The great enemy is not the "other religion," but selfish materialism and destructive capitalist imperialism. In a romantic move, Gandhi celebrated simple, rural life as an alternative to exploitative industrial life. There is a sense that this anti-materialist, spiritual life can create both peace between religious communities and justice of economic distribution.

For justpeace as a practice, Gandhi is an excellent model, since he was simultaneously a spiritual leader and a shrewd political and diplomatic negotiator. Though he was only once elected for a year as president of the Indian Congress Party in 1924 and refused to have an official position in the party, he was the great mover and shaker behind the scenes. There was nothing "otherwordly" about Gandhi; he set his goals very clearly and used methods like non-cooperation and hunger strikes to attain them. On the other hand, he showed through his own example that his actions were grounded in a deep moral understanding of himself and of the world. His view of independence (swaraj) was immediately connected with his views of self-control (swaraj).

How successful was Gandhi in attaining independence through nonviolence? This is a question that is answered in diametrically opposed ways by historians. The end result of the Indian independence struggle was, as we have seen, the Partition, and this was clearly the complete opposite of what Gandhi wanted. We may say that Gandhi showed an extraordinary commitment to justpeace and that he gave the world a model to follow. That model may or may not be ultimately successful in the obtaining of justpeace, but it at least takes some significant steps toward this goal.

The Dalai Lama

Since the Dalai Lama went into exile in 1959, the so-called Tibet Question has been not merely a bilateral dispute between Tibet and China but has been internationalized. Over the last half-century, the Tibet Question has evolved as a multidimensional question involving territorial disputes, geopolitical contentions, humanitarian issues, and tensions between traditional values and modern practices. From a deeply contested historical perspective, China claims to have been ruling over Tibet since the Yuan dynasty.[28] Many scholars outside China argue that the Yuan dynasty saw an integrative phase of Mongolia, Tibet, and China; however, they see the Sino-Tibet or rather Tibet-Mongol relation as a "teacher-patron relation,"[29] referring to Tibet's position as the religious counsel to Mongol's Yuan dynasty, while the Yuan court provided Tibet with protection and material offerings. This relation continued well into the Qing dynasty or the Manchu Empire (1644–1911).

After the ending of the Qing dynasty in 1911, Sino-Tibet relations entered their modern phase of territorial dispute. The new Republic of China was too weak to exercise its rule over Tibet. The territorial status of Tibet between 1911 and 1951 is often seen as a "de facto independence" by scholars.[30] The Tibetan government then also took the initiative to establish a de jure independence by seeking support from Western countries;[31] however, the idea of the modern, progressive nation-state did not take root in Tibet as the majority members of Tibet's government then preferred its traditional governing system known as *chösinyitrel*

(ཆོས་སྲིད་ཟུང་འབྲེལ), meaning the conjoinment of religion and the state in the modern sense. *Chösinyitrel* is often presented as "theocracy" among Tibet scholars. From the Tibetan native perspective, it is best understood as a polity governed with a Buddhist orientation or simply as a Buddhist nation. This traditional Tibetan governing system was intact until 1959 when the People's Republic of China suppressed an uprising of Tibetans in Lhasa; thereafter the young Fourteenth Dalai Lama went into exile in India. Since then, the Tibet Question in essence has become what we see as a "Dalai Lama Question," a complex international issue.

Since the 1970s, when China's rule over Tibet was officially acknowledged by the UN, the United States, and other countries, China has fully exerted its. The territorial dispute over Tibet in the current dialogue between the Chinese state and the Tibetan government in exile becomes less pressing, but issues of human rights, religious freedom, and environmental degradation in Tibet are ever becoming a global humanitarian concern. On the side of Tibet's exile government, the Fourteenth Dalai Lama since the late 1980s has been advocating a higher autonomy for Tibet, equivalent to China's renewed rule over Hong Kong and Macau, known as "one country with two systems" (一国两制 *yiguo liangzhi*). The Dalai Lama accepts Tibet as a part of China but prefers an autonomy that protects Tibet's traditional religious practices, cultural customs, and environmental integrity.[32]

However, China rejects the Dalai Lama's proposition. It continues to look upon him as a separatist and puts out a range of international diatribes against his representation of Tibetan people. To Chinese statesmen, the Dalai Lama's proposition is *fubi* (复辟) or "turning the clock back"[33] to an alleged feudal serfdom replete with cruelty and superstition. The Chinese state's atheistic, anti-religious position particularly hinders its statesmen from seeing the relevance of the Buddhist-oriented peace proposal by the Dalai Lama. Since 2008, the Chinese state has reaffirmed this position by producing and re-airing documentaries and fiction films such as *Dalai Lama* (2009),[34] *50 Years of Democratic Reform in Tibet* (2009),[35] *The Story of Tibet's Serfs* (2009),[36] and *The Serf* (1963).[37] All these productions attribute the agonies of Tibetan common people then to their religious customs. This is the center of the current Sino-Tibetan tension and conflict, which reflect the current popular Tibetan civil disobedience against the Chinese state, in the forms of demonstration, self-immolation, and public discourses online.

The Dalai Lama proposed that Tibet be a zone of peace in his five-point plan in 1987.[38] According to him, that would mean "the conversion of the entire Tibetan plateau into a Zone of Ahimsa, a sanctuary of peace and nonviolence where human beings and nature can live in peace and harmony."[39] We are aware that the timing of his plan coincided with the cultural phenomenon that Donald Lopez calls "New Age Orientalism,"[40] a critique leveled at both Tibetans and non-Tibetans who emphasize Buddhist spirituality as the core of Tibetan culture or who treat Tibet as an object of fantasy. Herein we do not wish to dwell on this polemic, but do acknowledge the relevancy of the Dalai Lama's proposition in peacebuilding. We see his proposition as being rooted not only in his practice of Mahayana Buddhism but also in the history of Tibetan civilization with the historical fact that the successive Dalai Lamas have been regarded by their people as *chosgyal* (ཆོས་རྒྱལ), or kings of Dharma. The Dalai Lamas, as the kings of Tibet, were instrumental in solidifying Tibet's Buddhist identity since the sixteenth century. In this respect, Buddhism in traditional Tibet was simultaneously a spiritual tradition, a source of political and moral principles, and a symbol of Tibetan national pride. Every Dalai Lama in history, including Tenzin Gyatso, the current

Dalai Lama, is an incarnation of Chenrezig (སྤྱན་རས་གཟིགས།) or Bodhisattva Avalokiteshvara—the ultimate representation of the Great Compassion in Mahayana Buddhism.

Prior to the advent of its modern era in the late 1950s, Western travelers and spiritual seekers, imperial officers, Chinese Buddhist pilgrims, and officers and soldiers of the People's Liberation Army (PLA) witnessed the overwhelming Buddhist presence in Tibetan society. Alexandra David-Neel (1868–1969),[41] Lama Anagarika Govinda (1898–1985, born Ernst Lothar Hoffman),[42] Francis Younghusband (1863–1942),[43] and Lin Tian[44] (former PLA journalist) all noted the importance of Buddhism in traditional Tibet. Undoubtedly Tibet was a land of Buddha Dharma, which was built into its governing system and social ethos.

From this historical perspective and considering the current state of affairs of the world, the Dalai Lama's proposition of Tibet as a zone of peace has three objectives. First, Tibet would be a place of his global experiment for peace and human flourishing; second, Tibet's Buddhist civilization and cultural heritage would be restored; and third, Tibet would also pragmatically acknowledge China's territorial sovereignty and neighboring nations' regional strategic interests.[45] When the idea of a zone of peace is placed in the context of contemporary Sino-Tibetan relations, it would enable Tibetans to have a higher autonomy and, in the meantime, would put China in a position of safeguarding Tibet as a world heritage and a zone of peace with a Buddhist orientation.[46] The Dalai Lama's peace proposition shows his maximum compassion toward the Chinese state in relation to its national interests and geopolitical strategic needs. The zone of peace puts into practice his ideas of universal consciousness and interdependence.[47]

The spiritual terms of the Dalai Lama's proposition have been ill-received by the Chinese state. Especially since the Tibetan uprisings in March 2008, the Chinese state has consistently alleged that he is "a separatist in monk's robe."[48] As a matter of fact, the Chinese state is aware of how deeply Buddhism is embodied in Tibetan cultural practices but in a negative fashion. Chinese policy-makers and state-sanctioned scholars often interpret the Dalai Lama's Buddhist-oriented peace proposal from the perspective of their national security interests. They see the growth of one monastery as the growth of separatism.[49] Unlike its former communist counterparts in Eastern Europe, China's territory has become more unified than ever as control of Hong Kong and Macau were returned to Mainland China. The Chinese state retains tight administrative and military control over Tibet. In this regard, separatism, allegedly supported by the Dalai Lama, is not a viable threat.

However, the overwhelming return of Tibetan Buddhism in contemporary Tibet[50] again shows that is is the ballast of Tibetan culture. In reference to the seminal position of Buddhism in Tibetan history, Tsering Dongrub, a contemporary Tibetan archivist and historian based in Sichuan, extensively emphasizes in his *A General History of Tibetan People*[51] that most Tibetans in traditional Tibet referred themselves as *chosde* (ཆོས་སྡེ།) or "subjects of Dharma."[52] The late Dawa Norbu, studying the impact of China's socialist revolution in Tibet, found that the Chinese implementation of class struggle in Tibetan regions encountered stiff popular resistance that was spontaneous rather than organized and mostly involved common Tibetans. In his comment on Tibetan uprisings in Kham in the 1950s, Norbu pointed out "The Chinese liberators were called *brtan dgra* (བསྟན་དགྲ)—enemies of the faith; the Khampa guerrillas who led the Tibetan nationalist movement were popularly called *brtan srung* (བསྟན་སྲུང་)—defenders of the faith; and the main aim of the movement was the defense of Tibetan Buddhism as personified by the Dalai Lama."[53]

Since the late 1980s, incidents of Tibetan civil disobedience in Lhasa have also shown a clear pattern of Buddhist participation, particularly among the monks from the Drepung, Gandan, and Sera Monasteries. In his study of contemporary Sino-Tibetan relations, Ronald Schwartz says, "By combining *bskor-ba* [khorra སྐོར་ར། or circumambulation] with symbols of Tibetan nationhood—the Dalai Lama, the flag—the Drepung monks forged a link between the powerful motivation that underlies religious ritual and the national consciousness that divides Tibetans from Chinese."[54]

The Tibet Question, as the Dalai Lama Question, is not as simplistic and black and white as the Chinese state perceives. It is a question of a living belief in "a conscious reincarnation of Avalokiteshvara, the bodhisattva of universal compassion"[55] in all Tibetan regions. "Dalai Lama" is not the name of a person, but is a religious and cultural institution of Tibet. It is an integral part of the Tibetan Buddhist cultural system called *tulkus* (སྤྲུལ་སྐུ།), which means reincarnation. It also refers to incarnate lamas. The current Dalai Lama is the most well-known incarnate lama among Tibetans. In the history of Tibetan Buddhism, the retroactive recognition of *tulkus* also took place with the institution as well as the individual incarnations of the Dalai Lama. In 1578, after Altan Khan, the de facto Mongol King then, bestowed the title of the Dalai Lama on Sonam Gyatso, then head of Gelukpa, Sonam Gyatso's two predecessors, Gendun Drup and Gendun Gyatso, were retroactively recognized as the first and the second Dalai Lamas, respectively.[56] The Mongol's conferring of the title is often understood as the result of the strategic alliance of Gelukpa with Altan Khan; however, the retroactive inclusion of Gendun Drup and Gendun Gyatso in the lineage of the Dalai Lama was based on Sonam Gyatso's spiritual achievement, which was considered identical to theirs.[57] In both historical and Buddhist senses, a *tulku* lineage is an institution, but a *tulku* himself possesses demonstrated spiritual merits that either connect him with his previous incarnations or qualify him as the origin of a lineage. Similar practices for the retroactive recognition of *tulkus* are also seen among other *tulku* lineages in Tibet.

In the early 1980s, when China began its nationwide economic reform, it allowed the Dalai Lama's fact-finding delegations to visit Tibetan regions. The Chinese statesmen were expecting common Tibetans' outright denouncement of the delegations as the representatives of the old, oppressive Tibetan ruling class. Arjia Rinpoche, the abbot of Kunbum Monastery who is currently in exile in the U.S., was one of the Chinese state's representatives escorting the members of the four delegations sent by the Dalai Lama. In an interview with Dan Smyer Yu's, Arjia Rinpoche recalled:

> Because they [the Chinese statesmen] were afraid that the "liberated serfs" in Lhasa would get revenge on the "feudal lords," they made sure to have the delegates protected. However, when one of the delegations led by the Dalai Lama's sister arrived in Lhasa, what happened there surprised the Chinese government. Thousands of "liberated serfs" surrounded the delegates like an unstoppable tide. They did not take revenge on them, but were tearfully asking for blessings from the delegates.

Obviously, an incarnate lama is not merely a conventional person. He possesses a dual descent, meaning that in addition to descending from his biological parents, he is an embodiment of a spiritual lineage; therefore, he is a public figure with a sacred character. Its institutionality precedes the individuality of the person who bears the title. Dalai Lama, as Tibet's foremost institution, has been sustained by successively chosen individuals based on prophecies and oracle readings. Melvyn Goldstein and Paljor Tsarong emphatically recognize the

Tibetan monastic system as "one of human history's most ambitious and radical and social psychological experiments" and suggest it as "a cultural template,"[58] in which the ideals of Buddhism are rigorously cultivated beyond the monastic establishment of Tibet.

The strong religiosity of Tibetan culture has been denounced by the Chinese state as a part of premodern Tibet's serfdom. To the Chinese state, reversing the course of history from the present socialist modern Tibet to the past serfdom is not an option. Thus the contemporary revival of Tibetan Buddhism is permitted but subject to being performed as a "socialist Buddhism" or a Buddhism "compatible" with China's socialist system.[59] The Chinese state is not engaging what the Dalai Lama actually wishes to discuss regarding Tibet: that is, making it an experimental site for world peace with new ideas pertaining to the well-being of both Tibetans and the Chinese.

Global Peacebuilding Through the Preservation of Tibet's Heritage

Returning to the proposition of Tibet as a zone of peace, the Dalai Lama is most innovative on both moral and spiritual ground. His peace proposition to China is not meant to turn the clock back to the traditional governing system of Tibet; instead, he is advocating a global, collective experiment for peacebuilding. As a philosophical idea, the zone of peace accords with the Dalai Lama's global vision of peace, but it would be implemented in specific regions of the world. Unlike the Cold War era, during which Tibetans' national cause was fought over in armed struggles supported by Western countries,[60] as the Dalai Lama points out in his speech "The Global Community," which emphasizes building the oneness of humankind based on "positive human qualities such as tolerance, generosity and love."[61] The pattern of the Dalai Lama's global peacebuilding act clearly lays itself out in a sequence of inner and outer transformations from the individual to the institutional, the national, and the international. Zones of peace, according to him, will serve as experimental sites of world peace:

> Zones of peace within regional communities would serve as oases of stability. While paying their fair share of the costs of any collective force created by the community as a whole, these zones of peace would be the forerunners and beacons of an entirely peaceful world and would be exempt from engaging in any conflict. If regional communities do develop in Asia, South America[,] and Africa[,] and disarmament progresses so that an international force from all regions is created, these zones of peace will be able to expand, spreading tranquility as they grow.[62]

Thus, Tibet as a zone of peace would serve the ultimate goal of the Dalai Lama to build a new international order of peace based on his recognition of the universal needs of humankind. The Dalai Lama's global peace work in the case of Tibet is calling for the "mundane awakening" of the nation-states for the purpose of building and sustaining peace as a work of inter-communities and inter-nations.[63] Tibetan Buddhism in this context is not only spiritually, socially, and globally engaged, but has fully merged with the planetary discourse of peace and sentient flourishing. As a zone of peace, Tibet would be one of many global sites of compassion in practice as what the Dalai Lama calls "the pillar of world peace."[64]

To resolve the tensions and conflicts between the Tibetan government in exile and the Chinese state, it is clear that we must see the current Dalai Lama in a new light as a global peacebuilder and the Tibetan Buddhism he practices as globally engaged, not the same as its traditional counterpart prior to the arrival of China's socialism. The Dalai Lama's peacebuilding is grounded in his practice of Mahayana Buddhism, which is a manifestation of his lived awareness that all sentient beings desire peace and happiness. He has spoken of this fundamental aspect of our sentience on numerous occasions: "The desire or inclination to be happy and to avoid suffering knows no boundaries. It is in our nature."[65] Many of us perceived this multifaceted man as a Tibetan, a monk, and a political leader, in that order. However, from a careful reading of his global itineraries and the contents of his public speaking and publications over the last half-century, it is evident that he is a global peacebuilder. In both Buddhist and non-Buddhist contexts, the Dalai Lama emphasizes that his being a human being precedes all his other identities: "I am human before I am Tibetan," as he states again in his *Ethics for the New Millennium*,[66] his global proclamation of peace and sentient flourishing at the turn of the new century. He has never given in when he advocates his Tibet cause; however, his vision of global peace and happiness entails a fair, just, and peaceful Sino-Tibetan relationship in the future. In this respect, we see his peacebuilding as global in nature when he proposes ways to alleviate human suffering and create conditions for human flourishing throughout the world. "Our basic sameness as humans"[67] is consistently professed and emphasized in his peacebuilding.

Thich Nhat Hanh

In war, according to Graham Greene, "one must take sides, if one is to remain human".[68] This observation is especially true for a war like the Vietnam War. In the Vietnam War, for all Vietnamese, North or South, pitted against each other, to remain neutral seemed impossible. To pronounce the word "peace" was equally unthinkable, for it could have led one to be branded a communist or a defeatist, or both. To utter the word was to risk a life in exile. And yet, that was exactly what Thich Nhat Hanh did in 1964 when he composed a painful antiwar poem entitled "Peace."[69]

The most influential living Buddhist Zen master in the world today, who is respectably called Thay (the Master) by his followers, Thich Nhat Hanh has dedicated his whole life to fight for peace, not just in the world but also in each human being's mind and heart. At the time he composed the poem, the Vietnam War had begun to pit North and South Vietnamese against one another in horrendous bloodbaths. The war also confronted the monasteries with the question of whether to adhere to contemplative life and remain meditating in the monasteries, or to help the villagers suffering under bombings and other forms of devastation. Not only did the Master choose "engaged Buddhism" as the answer but also, born and ordained into monkhood in a war-torn world, he chose peacebuilding as the principal object and ultimate aim in his life, dedicating himself to the work of inner transformation for the benefit of individuals and society.

Unlike the Dalai Lama, his Tibetan contemporary, for whom peace is an external object, locatable in time and place (Tibet as a zone of peace) and globally transportable via the vehicle of love and compassion, Thich Nhat Hanh sees peace as much more an internal object coming from and vanishing in each human being's mind. The responsibility of war lies with all individuals of a society, not just the army or the politicians, because war is the eruption of our prejudices, fears, and ignorancefrom within our own minds. Creating peace means uprooting war "from ourselves and from the hearts of men and women."[70] Instead, he recommends "interbeing" (*Tiep Hien*) as the method of coexistence. In his teaching, the Master has consistently focused on how our interdependence with others makes partisan conflict unintelligible. Our interbeing with others implies that whether we are called "oppressors" or "the oppressed," we all contribute to injustice and violence in the world. This is because we are not just interconnected and interdependent as human to human, but also as human beings to the physical and spiritual world around us. Our consumption has immediate effects on nature, whose response could be quickly felt by us and other beings. The cause of peace and justice thus could be imperiled by the mere act of segregating people and things into violent and nonviolent categories and denying violent tendencies within ourselves. Taking a side in a violent world does not make sense, even when the side one chooses is that of nonviolence, because every side is "our side" and violence is at the heart of both sides. In the Master's view, if we do not change our lifestyles, our economic consumption, and our spiritual and emotional responses, new generations of violence will emerge. We are all part of the problem.[71]

Thich Nhat Hanh's action for peace started in the mid-1950s with the establishment of the School of Youth for Social Services (SYSS) in Saigon.[72] This grassroots relief organization worked to rebuild villages, set up schools, establish medical centers, and resettle families left homeless because of the war. In 1963, after studying comparative religion for three years at Princeton University, he returned to Vietnam to aid his fellow monks in their nonviolent peace efforts. Their nonviolent approach for peace, however, was not shared by many other forces in Saigon at the time. Beside the attacks from the pro-war Catholic politicians, quite a few prominent Buddhist monks also kept their distance from Thich Nhat Hanh's engaged Buddhist philosophy and preferred to stay "disengaged." This is perhaps the reason why after Thich Nhat Hanh left again for the United States in 1965. After that some of the chancellors of Van Hanh University wanted to sever ties with Thich Nhat Hanh and his SYSS and accused Sister Chan Khong, who was left in charge of the SYSS, of being a communist. Meanwhile, in the United States, seeing his trip to the country that was the root of the Vietnam War as a peace mission, Thich Nhat Hanh gave numerous lectures and talks at universities and rallies to call for an end to the war. In 1966 he met Martin Luther King Jr., who was deeply moved by his peace efforts. The following year, King nominated Thich Nhat Hanh for the Nobel Peace Prize. It has been said that Thich Nhat Hanh was not given the prize because King had made his nomination public and thus violated the prize's protocol and procedure. But one cannot help but be astonished by the irony that six years later, when the Vietnam War's violent destruction reached its fullest scale, the Nobel Peace Prize was awarded to Henry Kissinger, one of the key architects of this war.

Although the verses of "Peace" express a burning desire to speak up against war and violence, what the poet wants us to see is the danger of division between "us" and "them," "violence" and "nonviolence." "We do not need to take sides," he declares. Taking sides, according to the Master, implies a dualistic response motivated by anger that ultimately leads us toward polarization. In contrast, an appropriate response aims at reconciliation and peace rather than conflict. At the heart of reconciliation is love that embraces the whole of reality. This involves listening to each side and describing to each one the suffering of the other. Thus, in addition to social justice, the Master appeals to the importance of reconciliation and peace between all the involved parties. This approach differs significantly from a pursuit of justice via demands for apologies and subsequent forgiveness.

Like Gandhi, Thich Nhat Hanh turns the human body into a site of peace and salvation. Access to a peaceful state of being can be achieved at every moment via the simple bodily acts of breathing, listening, and walking: "Each step we make should be peace.. . . We don't need future.. . . Everything we want is right here in the present moment."[73] Thich Nhat Hanh brought "engaged Buddhism" to another level when he introduced the method of mindfulness. A form of meditation that seeks awareness of the states of one's mind, mindfulness is the essence of ways of achieving peace. This practice aspires to instill compassion for other beings, very much along the lines of the Christian love ethic. Thich Nhat Hanh deeply believes that true success in "doing peace" depends on our "being peace." "The only way out of violence and conflict is for us to embrace the practice of peace, to think and act with compassion, love, and understanding."[74] Mindfulness is thus a practice of daily transformation, of cultivating peace within so that one can obtain peaceful relations with others and do one's best in social action.

Thich Nhat Hanh argues that more than the correction of systemic injustice is in order. Moving beyond the concern for justice and truth, he anchors social justice in a peaceful dialogue that stems from compassion for all involved parties. Recognizing the limited scope of all our visions and our co-responsibility for the suffering of others, we should not aim at getting others to recognize the rightness of our conclusions.[75] Compassionate consideration for others facilitates a dialogue that avoids dogmatism, prevarication, and unnecessary polarization. This is the spirit of the Master's teaching, which he has managed to maintain regardless of the constant obstacles of political realities that he has faced in life.

It was his refusal to take sides and his belief in peace and reconciliation that caused the anti-communist South Vietnam government to forced the Master into exile in 1973. His situation did not improve much after the unification of the country in 1975 as the Communist government continued to ban his return to Vietnam.[76] His engaged Buddhism and Order of Interbeing have been strongly suspected by the Vietnamese authorities as being of "potential reactionary nature." Connection between Buddhist monks and lay practitioners inside Vietnam and members of the Plum Village, a Buddhist monastery in southern France founded by Thich Nhat Hanh in 1982, was discouraged by Vietnamese authorities until recently. In 2005, after thirty-nine years of exile, the Master, at the age of eighty, was at last able to return to Vietnam at the invitation and with the blessing of the Vietnamese government, after a lengthy negotiation. His visit was enthusiastically welcomed by thousands and inspired many young people to become monastics and devote their lives to meditation. During his second visit to Vietnam in 2007, the Master's primary objective was to organize three large Requiem Masses, aiming at bringing healing to the sufferings and internecine conflicts of the war. The support of Buddhist churches in Vietnam and local authorities for these events was enthusiastic in Ho Chi Minh city (the South), but unreliable in Hue (the Central) and fragile in Hanoi. During his third visit to Vietnam in 2008, the Master openly expressed his advocacy of democratic reform and the abolishment of Communist rule in the country. At the same time, conflicts were growing between the local Buddhist authority and members of the Ban Nha, a monastery in the style of Plum Village established in 2005 through the support of the Master and his followers. The combination of these two factors led Thich Nhat Hanh to be again banned from returning to Vietnam. In spite of his unfailing efforts, the walk to peace and reconciliation in his native country seems again to be a lengthy one.

CONCLUSION

Building justpeace in Asia requires tapping religious and spiritual sources precisely because religion and spirituality are major elements of conflict. In some cases, like in Korea, Christianity can play a positive role in reconciling and reintegrating part of the population as well as in taking the peace process forward. In other cases it has been too closely identified, incorrectly but understandably, with foreign imperialism and thus it is perceived as a threat to national sovereignty. In India Christianity is targeted by Hindu nationalists, while in China, Tibet, and Vietnam it is targeted by communists. Asia's majority religions, like Hinduism and Buddhism, have to provide the resources for justpeace in the complex contexts of postcolonial India, Vietnam, and China-Tibet.

In Asian traditions, the moral exemplar is of great significance. It is the saint, the guru, the spiritual master who can show a way out of the suffering caused by war and conflict. Their success, however, depends on the extent to which traditional renunciation of secular life can be harnessed to the daily existence of common people. Engaged Buddhism develops from an older tradition of the bodhisattva who takes pity on the world and does not claim Buddhahood, but remains engaged with the world. The Dalai Lama is the incarnation of the Bodhisattva Avalokiteshvara. In India, Mahatma Gandhi was deeply inspired by the selfless devotion to duty that can be found in the Bhagavad Gita. However, it is important to understand that all these traditions are constantly reinterpreted in changing contexts. From the nineteenth century onwards, they have been reinterpreted in relation to Western ideas, partly derived from Christianity, about peace and justice, social welfare, and being spiritually active in society. The most creative interpreter of this interaction of Asian and Western ideas has been Mahatma Gandhi, who was deeply influenced by both Hindu and Western ideas about nonviolence, simple living, and vegetarianism. Gandhi's personal form of building justpeace was a model for Martin Luther King, the Dalai Lama, and Thich Nhat Hanh. This shows that it is transportable as a model of charismatic leadership. When the moral exemplar dies, it is hard to sustain the enthusiasm created by his personal example. Nvertheless, as the Gandhian movement in India and the US civil rights movement show, some of the methods developed by these leaders survive to be practiced by later generations.[77]

NOTES

1. Peter van der Veer, *Imperial Encounters: Religion and Modernity in India and Britain* (Princeton, NJ: Princeton University Press, 2001); Peter van der Veer, *The Spirit of Asia: The Spiritual and the Secular in China and India* (Princeton, NJ: Princeton University Press, 2013).

2. John Paul Lederach and R. Scott Appleby, "Strategic Peacebuidling: An Overview," in *Strategies of Peace: Transforming Conflict in a Violent World*, ed. Daniel Philpott and Gerard F. Powers (New York: Oxford University Press, 2010), 23.

3. Daniel Philpott, "Reconciliation: An Ethic for Peacebuilding," in *Strategies of Peace: Transforming Conflict in a Violent World*, ed. Daniel Philpott and Gerard F. Powers (New York: Oxford University Press, 2010), 92.

4. Hannah Arendt, *The Human Condition* (Chicago: University of Chicago Press, 1958), 258.

5. J. Angelo Corlett, "Forgiveness, Apology, and Retributive Punishment," *American Philosophical Quarterly* 43, no. 1 (2006): 25–42.

6. Jane W. Yamazaki, *Japanese Apologies for World War II: A Rhetorical Study* (New York: Routledge, 2006).

7. For a recent historical evaluation by the eminent Indian historian Romilla Thapar, see *Somanatha, The Many Voices of History* (London: Verso, 2005).

8. For an extensive and detailed discussion, see Peter van der Veer, *Religious Nationalism: Hindus and Muslims in India* (Berkeley: University of California Press, 1994).

9. See Veronique Benei, *Schooling Passions: Nation, History, and Language in Contemporary Western India* (Palo Alto, CA: Stanford University Press, 2008).

10. Peter van der Veer, "Syncretism, Multiculturalism and the Discourse of Tolerance," in *Syncretism/Anti-Syncretism: The Politics of Religious Synthesis*, ed. Charles Stewart and Rosalind Shaw (London: Routledge, 1994), 196–212.

11. Peter van der Veer, "Playing or Praying: A Sufi Saint's Day in Surat," *Journal of Asian Studies* 51, no. 3 (1992): 545–564.

12. For an extensive historical analysis of one of the most important saints of North India, Ghazi Miyan, see Shahid Amin, "Un Saint Guerer: Sur le Conquete de l'Inde du Nord par les Turcs aux XI siecle," *Annales: Histoire, Sciences Sociale* 60, no. 2 (2005): 265–292.

13. Robert M. Hayden, "Antagonistic Tolerance: Competitive Sharing of Religious Sites in South Asia and the Balkans," *Current Anthropology* 43, no. 2 (2002): 205–231.

14. "'Religious Freedom Acts': Anti-Conversion Laws in India," American Center for Law and Justice, June 26, 2009, http://media.aclj.org/pdf/freedom_of_religion_acts.pdf.

15. The missionary Graham Staines was killed with his two sons in Orissa (India) in 1999. For Vietnam, see Tam Ngo, "Missionary Encounters at the China-Vietnam Border: The Case of the Hmong," in *"Religious Networks in Asia and Beyond,"* ed. Peter van der Veer, special issue, *Encounters*, no. 4 (2011): 113–131.

16. Dianne Kirby, ed., *Religion and the Cold War* (Basingstoke, UK: Palgrave, 2002).

17. For more detail on the role of Catholicism in the Vietnam War era, see Lan T. Chu, "Catholicism vs. Communism, Continued: The Catholic Church in Vietnam," *Journal of Vietnamese Studies* 3, no. 1 (2008): 151–192.

18. Jin-heon Jung, "Underground Railroads of Christian Conversion: North Korean Migrants and Evangelical Missionary Networks in Northeast Asia," in *"Religious Networks in Asia and Beyond,"* ed. Peter van der Veer, special issue, *Encounters*, no. 4 (2011): 163–191.

19. "'Religious Freedom Acts': Anti-Conversion Laws In India"; Laura Dudley Jenkins, "Legal Limits on Religious Conversion in India," *Law and Contemporary Problems* 71, no. 2 (2008): 109–127.

20. For Ambedkar's ideas, see Christophe Jaffrelot, *Ambedkar and Untouchability: Fighting the Indian Caste System* (New York: Columbia University Press, 2005).

21. John A. Coleman, S.J., argues that Christianity today has more or less lost this tradition. See Coleman, "After Sainthood," in *Saints and Virtues*, ed. J. S. Hawley (Berkeley: University of California Press, 1987), 205–225.

22. Richard G. Fox, *Gandhian Utopia: Experiments with Culture* (Boston: Beacon Press, 1989).

23. Peter van der Veer, *Imperial Encounters* (Princeton, NJ: Princeton University Press, 2001).

24. Sean Chabot, *Transnational Roots of the Civil Rights Movement: African American Explorations of the Gandhian Repertoire* (Plymouth, MA: Lexington Books, 2011).

25. Joseph S. Alter, *Gandhi's Body: Sex, Diet, and the Politics of Nationalism* (Philadelphia: University of Pennsylvania Press, 2000).

26. Akeel Bilgrami, "Gandhi's Integrity: The Politics Behind the Philosophy," *Postcolonial Studies* 5, no. 1 (2002): 79–93.

27. Carolien Stolte and Harald Fischer-Tiné, "Imagining Asia in India: Nationalism and Internationalism (ca. 1905–1940)," *Comparative Studies in Society and History* 54, no. 1 (2012): 65–92.

28. Zhu Xiaoming, "Regarding the History and the Current State of the Research on Tibet as a Part of China Since the Ancient Time," *Red Flag Journal*, no. 4 (2012): 16–20.

29. Melvyn Goldstein, *A History of Modern Tibet, 1913–1951: The Demise of the Lamaist State* (Berkeley: University of California Press, 1997), 28.

30. Goldstein, *History of Modern Tibet*, 30; Gray Tuttle, *Tibetan Buddhists in the Making of Modern China* (New York: Columbia University Press, 2005), 35.

31. On de facto independence, see Goldstein, *History of Modern Tibet*, 391.

32. Dalai Lama, "Five-Point Peace Plan for Tibet" (address to the US Congressional Human Rights Caucus, Washington, DC, September 21, 1987).

33. Xu Chang'an, "Scholars Admonishing the Dalai Lama: Turning the Clock Back Will Meet a Dead End," *Chinese News*, March 27, 2010, www.ln.chinanews.com.

34. Li Xiaoshan, director, *Dalai Lama*, documentary film, 1997, China Central Television.

35. Li Xingyan, director, *50 Years of Democratic Reform in Tibet*, documentary film, 2009, China Central Television.

36. Dai Wei, director, *The Story of Tibet's Serfs*, documentary film, 2009, China Central Television.

37. Li Jun, *The Serf*, fiction film, 1963, PLA August 1st Film Studio.

38. Dalai Lama, "Five-Point Peace Plan."

39. Dalai Lama, "The 14th Dalai Lama—Acceptance Speech" (speech delivered to accept the Nobel Peace Prize at the University of Oslo, Oslo, Norway, December 10, 1989), http://www.nobelprize.org/nobel_prizes/peace/laureates/1989/lama-acceptance.html.

40. Donald S. Lopez Jr., "New Age Orientalism: The Case of Tibet," *Tricycle* 3, no. 3 (1994): 36–43.

41. Alexandra David-Neel, *My Journey to Lhasa* (New York: Harper Perennial, 2005).

42. Lama Anagarika Govinda, *The Way of the White Clouds*, (New York: Overlook, 2005).

43. David Matless, "Nature, the Modern and the Mystic: Tales from Early Twentieth Century Geography," *Transactions of the Institute of British Geographers* 16 (1991): 272–286.

44. Lin Tian, *The Diaries of My Tibet Journey* (Beijing: Chinese Tibetology Press, 1997).

45. Dalai Lama, "Strasbourg Proposal 1988" (address to the Members of the European Parliament, Strasbourg, France, June 15, 1988), http://www.dalailama.com/messages/tibet/strasbourg-proposal-1988.

46. Dalai Lama, "A Human Approach to World Peace," 1987, http://www.dalailama.com/messages/world-peace/a-human-approach-to-peace.

47. Sallie B. King, "An Engaged Buddhist Response to John Rawls's 'The Law of Peoples,'" *Journal of Religious Ethics* 34, no. 4 (2006): 637–661.

48. Wang Zuoan, "The Religious Circle Should Play Its Positive Role in Cultural Building," the United Front Work Department of CPC Central Committee, 2011, http://www.zytzb.org.cn/publicfiles/business/htmlfiles/tzb2010/S1821/201112/719164.html.

49. He Zhenhua, "Political Conspiracy in the Disguise of Religion," *The People's Daily*.

50. Melvyn Goldstein and Matthew T. Kapstein, eds., *Buddhism in Contemporary Tibet: Religious Revival and Cultural Identity* (Berkeley: University of California Press, 1998).

51. Tsering Dongrub, *A General History of Tibetan People: A Vase of Treasures* (Lhasa, China: Tibetan People's Publishing House, 2001).

52. Tsering Dongrub, interview with Dan Smyer Yu, 2003.

53. Dawa Norbu, *China's Tibet Policy* (Richmond, UK: Curzon Press, 2001), 226.

54. Ronald D. Schwartz, *Circle of Protest: Political Ritual in the Tibetan Uprising* (London: Hurst and Company, 1994), 236.

55. Robert Thurman, *Why the Dalai Lama Matters: His Act of Truth as the Solution for China, Tibet, and the World* (New York: Atria Books, 2008), 3.

56. Qingying Chen, *The Biographies of the Successive Dalai Lamas* (Beijing: China Tibetology Publishing House, 2006), 81.

57. Chen, *Biographies*, 81.

58. Melvyn Goldstein and Paljor Tsarong, "Tibetan Buddhist Monasticism: Social, Psychological and Cultural Implications," *Tibet Journal* 10, no. 1 (1985): 17.

59. Dan Smyer Yu, *The Spread of Tibetan Buddhism in China: Charisma, Money, Enlightenment* (London: Routledge, 2011), 176–177.

60. See John Kenneth Knaus, *Orphans of the Cold War: America and the Tibetan Struggle for Survival* (New York: Public Affairs, 1999); Mikel Dunham, *Buddha's Warriors: The Story of the CIA-Backed Tibetan Freedom Fighters, the Chinese Invasion, and the Ultimate Fall of Tibet* (New York: Jeremy P. Tarcher/Penguin, 2004); and Kenneth Conboy and James Morrison, *The CIA's Secret War in Tibet* (Lawrence: University Press of Kansas, 2002).

61. Dalai Lama, "The Global Community," 1999, http://www.dalailama.com/messages/world-peace/the-global-community.

62. Dalai Lama, "The Global Community."

63. Kathryn Poethig, "Movable Peace: Engaging the Transnational in Cambodia's Dhammayietra," *Journal for the Scientific Study of Religion* 41, no. 1 (2002): 19–28.

64. Dalai Lama, "A Human Approach."

65. Dalai Lama and Howard C. Cutler, *Ethics for the New Millennium* (New York: Putnam Books, 1999), 5.

66. Dalai Lama and Cutler, *Ethics for the New Millennium*, 19.

67. Dalai Lama and Cutler, *Ethics for the New Millennium*, 3.

68. Graham Greene, *The Quiet American* (New York: Viking Press, 1955).

69. Thich Nhat Hanh, "Peace," in *The Cry of Vietnam* (Santa Barbara, CA: Unicorn Press, 1969).

70. Thich Nhat Hanh, foreword to *Hell, Healing, and Resistance: Veterans Speak*, by Daniel William Hallock (Farmington, PA: Plough Publishing House, 1998), xii.

71. Wioleta Polinska, "Christian-Buddhist Dialogue on Loving the Enemy." *Buddhist-Christian Studies* 27, no. 1 (2007): 94.

72. http://www.architectsofpeace.org/architects-of-peace/thich-nhat-hanh.

73. Thich Nhat Hanh, *Peace Is Every Step: The Path of Mindfulness in Everyday Life* (New York: Bantam Books, 1991), 42.

74. Thich Nhat Hanh, *Creating True Peace: Ending Violence in Yourself, Your Family, Your Community and the World* (New York: Free Press, 2003), 6.

75. Polinska, "Christian-Buddhist Dialogue on Loving the Enemy," 103.

76. John Chapman, "The 2005 Pilgrimage and Return to Vietnam of Exiled Zen Master Thich Nhat Hanh," in *Modernity and Re-enchantment: Religion in Post-revolutionary Vietnam*, ed. Philip Taylor (Singapore: Institute of Southeast Asian Studies, 2007).

77. T. K. Oommen, *Charisma, Stability, and Change: An Analysis of Bhoodan-Gramdan Movement in India* (Delhi: Thomson Press, 1972).

BIBLIOGRAPHY

Alter, Joseph S. *Gandhi's Body: Sex, Diet, and the Politics of Nationalism*. Philadelphia: University of Pennsylvania Press, 2000.

Amin, Shahid. "Un Saint Guerer: Sur le Conquete de l'Inde du Nord par les Turcs aux XI siecle." *Annales: Histoire, Sciences Sociale* 60, no. 2 (2005): 265–292.

Arendt, Hannah. *The Human Condition*. Chicago: University of Chicago Press, 1958.

Benei, Veronique. *Schooling Passions: Nation, History, and Language in Contemporary Western India*. Palo Alto, CA: Stanford University Press, 2008.

Bilgrami, Akeel. "Gandhi's Integrity: The Politics Behind the Philosophy." *Postcolonial Studies* 5, no. 1 (2002): 79–93.

Chabot, Sean. *Transnational Roots of the Civil Rights Movement: African American Explorations of the Gandhian Repertoire*. Plymouth, MA: Lexington Books, 2011.

Chapman, John. "The 2005 Pilgrimage and Return to Vietnam of Exiled Zen Master Thich Nhat Hanh." In *Modernity and Re-enchantment: Religion in Post-revolutionary Vietnam*, edited by Philip Taylor (Singapore: Institute of Southeast Asian Studies, 2007).

Chen, Qingying. *The Biographies of the Successive Dalai Lamas*. Beijing: China Tibetology Publishing House, 2006.

Chu, Lan T. "Catholicism vs. Communism, Continued: The Catholic Church in Vietnam." *Journal of Vietnamese Studies* 3, no. 1 (2008): 151–192.

Coleman, John A. "After Sainthood." In *Saints and Virtues*, edited by J. S. Hawley, 205–225. Berkeley: University of California Press, 1987.

Conboy, Kenneth, and James Morrison. *The CIA's Secret War in Tibet*. Lawrence: University Press of Kansas, 2002.

Corlett, J. Angelo. "Forgiveness, Apology, and Retributive Punishment." *American Philosophical Quarterly* 43, no. 1 (2006): 25–42.

Dalai Lama. "Five-Point Peace Plan for Tibet. Address to the US Congressional Human Rights Caucus, Washington, DC, September 21, 1987.

Dalai Lama. "A Human Approach to World Peace." 1987. http://www.dalailama.com/messages/world-peace/a-human-approach-to-peace.

Dalai Lama. "Strasbourg Proposal 1988." Address to the Members of the European Parliament, Strasbourg, France, June 15, 1988. http://www.dalailama.com/messages/tibet/strasbourg-proposal-1988.

Dalai Lama. "The 14th Dalai Lama—Acceptance Speech." Speech delivered to accept the Nobel Peace Prize at the University of Oslo, Oslo, Norway, December 10, 1989. http://www.nobel-prize.org/nobel_prizes/peace/laureates/1989/lama-acceptance.html.

Dalai Lama. "The Global Community." 1999. http://www.dalailama.com/messages/world-peace/the-global-community.

Dalai Lama and Howard C. Cutler. *Ethics for the New Millennium*. New York: Putnam Books, 1999.

David-Neel, Alexandra. *My Journey to Lhasa*. New York: Harper Perennial, 2005.

Dongrub, Tsering. *A General History of Tibetan People: A Vase of Treasures*. Lhasa, China: Tibetan People's Publishing House, 2001.

Dunham, Mikel. *Buddha's Warriors: The Story of the CIA-Backed Tibetan Freedom Fighters, the Chinese Invasion, and the Ultimate Fall of Tibet*. New York: Jeremy P. Tarcher/Penguin, 2004.

Fox, Richard G. *Gandhian Utopia: Experiments with Culture*. Boston: Beacon Press, 1989.

Greene, Graham. *The Quiet American*. New York: Vikig Press, 1955.

Goldstein, Melvyn. *A History of Modern Tibet, 1913–1951: The Demise of the Lamaist State*. Berkeley: University of California Press, 1997.

Goldstein, Melvyn, and Paljor Tsarong. "Tibetan Buddhist Monasticism: Social, Psychological and Cultural Implications." *Tibet Journal* 10, no. 1 (1985): 14–31.

Goldstein, Melvyn, and Matthew T. Kapstein, eds. *Buddhism in Contemporary Tibet: Religious Revival and Cultural Identity*. Berkeley: University of California Press, 1998.

Hayden, Robert M. "Antagonistic Tolerance: Competitive Sharing of Religious Sites in South Asia and the Balkans." *Current Anthropology* 43, no. 2 (2002): 205–231.

Govinda, Lama Anagarika. *The Way of the White Clouds*. New York: Overlook, 2005.

He Zhenhua. "Political Conspiracy in the Disguise of Religion." *The People's Daily*, 2009.

Jaffrelot, Christophe. *Ambedkar and Untouchability: Fighting the Indian Caste System*. New York: Columbia University Press, 2005.

Jin-heon Jung. "Underground Railroads of Christian Conversion: North Korean Migrants and Evangelical Missionary Networks in Northeast Asia." In *"Religious Networks in Asia and Beyond,"* edited by Peter van der Veer, special issue, *Encounters*, no. 4 (2011): 163–191.

King, Sallie B. "An Engaged Buddhist Response to John Rawls's 'The Law of Peoples.'" *Journal of Religious Ethics* 34, no. 4 (2006): 637–661.

Kirby, Dianne, ed. *Religion and the Cold War*. Basingstoke, UK: Palgrave, 2002.

Knaus, John Kenneth. *Orphans of the Cold War: America and the Tibetan Struggle for Survival*. New York: Public Affairs, 1999.

Lederach, John Paul, and R. Scott Appleby. "Strategic Peacebuilding: An Overview." In *Strategies of Peace: Transforming Conflict in a Violent World*, edited by Daniel Philpott and Gerard F. Powers, 19–44. New York: Oxford University Press, 2010.

Lopez, Donald S., Jr. "New Age Orientalism: The Case of Tibet." *Tricycle* 3, no. 3 (1994): 36–43.

Matless, David. "Nature, the Modern and the Mystic: Tales from Early Twentieth Century Geography." *Transactions of the Institute of British Geographers* 16(1991): 272–286.

Ngo, Tam. 2011 "Missionary Encounters at the China-Vietnam Border: The Case of the Hmong." In *"Religious Networks in Asia and Beyond,"* edited by Peter van der Veer, special issue, *Encounters*, no. 4 (2011): 113–131.

Nhat Hanh, Thich. "Peace." In *The Cry of Vietnam*. Santa Barbara, CA: Unicorn Press, 1969.

Nhat Hanh, Thich. *Peace Is Every Step: The Path of Mindfulness in Everyday Life*. New York: Bantam Books, 1991.

Nhat Hanh, Thich. Foreword to *Hell, Healing, and Resistance: Veterans Speak*, by Daniel William Hallock. Farmington, PA: Plough Publishing House, 1998.

Nhat Hanh, Thich. *Creating True Peace: Ending Violence in Yourself, Your Family, Your Community and the World*. New York: Free Press, 2003.

Norbu, Dawa. *China's Tibet Policy*. Richmond, UK: Curzon Press, 2001.

Oommen, T. K. *Charisma, Stability, and Change: An Analysis of Bhoodan-Gramdan Movement in India*. Delhi: Thomson Press, 1972.

Philpott, Daniel. "Reconciliation: An Ethic for Peacebuilding." In *Strategies of Peace: Transforming Conflict in a Violent World*, edited by Daniel Philpott and Gerard F. Powers, 91–118. New York: Oxford University Press, 2010.

Polinska, Wioleta. "Christian-Buddhist Dialogue on Loving the Enemy." *Buddhist-Christian Studies* 27, no. 1 (2007): 89–107.

Poethig, Kathryn. "Movable Peace: Engaging the Transnational in Cambodia's Dhammayietra." *Journal for the Scientific Study of Religion* 41, no. 1 (2002): 19–28.

Schwartz, Ronald D. *Circle of Protest: Political Ritual in the Tibetan Uprising.* London: Hurst and Company, 1994.

Smyer Yu, Dan. *The Spread of Tibetan Buddhism in China: Charisma, Money, Enlightenment.* London: Routledge, 2011.

Stolte, Carolien, and Harald Fischer-Tiné. "Imagining Asia in India: Nationalism and Internationalism (ca. 1905–1940)." *Comparative Studies in Society and History* 54, no. 1 (2012): 65–92.

Thapar, Romilla. *Somanatha, The Many Voices of History.* London: Verso, 2005.

Thurman, Robert. *Why the Dalai Lama Matters: His Act of Truth as the Solution for China, Tibet, and the World.* New York: Atria Books, 2008.

Tian, Lin. *The Diaries of My Tibet Journey.* Beijing: Chinese Tibetology Press, 1997.

Tuttle, Gray. *Tibetan Buddhists in the Making of Modern China.* New York: Columbia University Press, 2005.

van der Veer, Peter. "Playing or Praying: A Sufi Saint's Day in Surat." *Journal of Asian Studies* 51, no. 3 (1992): 545–564.

van der Veer, Peter. *Religious Nationalism: Hindus and Muslims in India.* Berkeley: University of California Press, 1994.

van der Veer, Peter. "Syncretism, Multiculturalism and the Discourse of Tolerance." In: *Syncretism/Anti-Syncretism: The Politics of Religious Synthesis*, edited by Charles Stewart and Rosalind Shaw, 196–212. London: Routledge, 1994.

van der Veer, Peter. 2001. *Imperial Encounters: Religion and Modernity in India and Britain.* Princeton, NJ: Princeton University Press, 2001.

van der Veer, Peter. *The Spirit of Asia. The Spiritual and the Secular in China and India.* Princeton, NJ: Princeton University Press, 2013.

Xu, Chang'an. "Scholars Admonishing the Dalai Lama: Turning the Clock Back Will Meet a Dead End." *Chinese News*, March 27, 2010. www.ln.chinanews.com.

Wang, Zuoan. "The Religious Circle Should Play Its Positive Role in Cultural Building." The United Front Work Department of CPC Central Committee. 2011. http://www.zytzb.org.cn/publicfiles/business/htmlfiles/tzb2010/S1821/201112/719164.html.

Yamazaki, Jane W. *Japanese Apologies for World War II: A Rhetorical Study.* New York: Routledge, 2006.

Zhu, Xiaoming. "Regarding the History and the Current State of the Research on Tibet as a Part of China since the Ancient Time." *Red Flag Journal*, no. 4 (2012): 16–20.

CHAPTER 17

....

PEACEBUILDING IN THE MUSLIM WORLD

....

S. AYSE KADAYIFCI-ORELLANA

DURING his trip to Egypt and Kuwait in February 2011, British Prime Minister David Cameron stated, "Freedom and democracy are the best way to bring peace and prosperity to the Middle East."[1] He further argued that democracy often goes hand in hand with open markets and insisted that "instead of trying to impose democracy or pick sympathetic leaders for Middle Eastern states. . . the West should support the full range of free institutions, including an independent judiciary, a free press, and open markets." While in Cairo, responding to his critics about the potential of the Muslim Brotherhood coming into power, Cameron also suggested that "the Egyptian uprising suggested a desire for Western-style freedoms, not for Islamic extremism" and stated: "What is so refreshing about what's been happening is that this is not an Islamist revolt, this is not extremists on the streets; this is people who want to have the sort of basic freedoms that we take for granted in the UK."[2] The Muslim Brotherhood's Mohammed Morsi was announced to be the new president of Egypt following the June 2012 elections, putting a question mark on Cameron's observations and analysis of the situation.

Prime Minister Cameron's discourse during his trip is an example of what Oliver Richmond calls "the contemporary liberal peacebuilding project."[3] Liberal peacebuilding has been part of many peacebuilding initiatives in various Muslim countries such as Bosnia and Herzegovina, Iraq, Afghanistan, and Libya, to name a few. The liberal peace approach is not limited to Muslim contexts, however. As Richmond notes, "it has been deployed in something like fifty to sixty post-conflict and fragile states"[4] since the 1990s. Although it has made significant contributions to peacebuilding, development, and human rights practices and has set important standards, this chapter argues that the liberal peace approach failed to bring about the promised peace and stability and failed to respond constructively to many conflicts around the world, including ethno-religious conflicts in Muslim communities. In Iraq and Afghanistan, for instance, peacebuilding efforts failed to bring even basic security, while security in Pakistan is decreasing rapidly. The situation in Darfur has not improved. Even in Bosnia and Herzegovina, communities are more divided than ever.

Focusing only on Muslim contexts, this chapter argues that one reason for the failure of the liberal peace framework has been its secular, rational problem-solving approach that either views religion as an instigator of conflict or ignores it altogether because religious issues cannot be addressed from the empirical and positivist perspective they favor.[5] It offers a critical examination of liberal peace approaches that inform peacebuilding efforts and proposes to expand them to include a justpeace perspective, which, recognizing the complex ways in which religio-cultural traditions play both constructive and destructive roles in ethno-religious conflicts, is better suited to respond to conflicts in the Muslim world.

More specifically, this chapter argues that peacebuilding strategies in Muslim contexts should engage Islamic conceptions of peace and justice, and work together with credible agents of peace, including religious leaders. After a brief discussion of the liberal peace approach, this chapter elaborates on Islamic principles of peace and focuses on religious actors as important agents of peace in Islamic contexts. Thanks to the respect they receive as religious leaders who know their religious tradition and history well, Muslim religious actors often have more legitimacy than secular peacebuilders in their communities. Their long-term involvement in the community also often adds to their credibility and bolsters trust.[6] Their familiarity with the needs, hopes, and limitations of the communities they are working with also gives them a better understanding of how to approach conflicts. However, Muslim religious leaders also face significant challenges and obstacles. These include systemic challenges such as the impact of globalization; experiences of colonization, orientalization, modernization, and urbanization; and competing interpretations of Islam, as well as context-specific challenges such as a lack of capacity, training, and resources. It is critically important to understand these challenges and explore ways to enable these agents of peace, and to respond to them constructively within their own unique historical, social, and political contexts.

LIBERAL PEACE IN MUSLIM CONTEXTS

International institutions such as the United Nations (UN), European Union (EU), and the World Bank, as well as various governments including but not limited to the United States, United Kingdom, Germany, Canada, and France are leading the peacebuilding efforts in many Muslim contexts.[7] Rooted in the liberal peace tradition, their peacebuilding approach emphasizes democratization, secularization, advancing women's rights, promoting development, and opening up markets as keys to successful peacebuilding in Muslim countries and elsewhere. As such, they have become important international policy intervention tools in the aftermath of the Cold War.[8] Although the involvement of external actors in war-affected communities and politics is certainly not new, peacebuilding interventions have increased rapidly since the 1990s. Daniel Philpott observes that "since 1988, the United Nations (UN) has undertaken peacebuilding operations in revolutionary number and frequency."[9]

The conceptual definition of peacebuilding was articulated by former UN General-Secretary Boutros Boutros-Ghali in "An Agenda for Peace," published in 1992. In this document, he defined peacebuilding as "actions to identify and support structures which will tend to strengthen and solidify peace in order to avoid relapse into conflict."[10] Boutros-Ghali further identified the UN's role as assisting peacebuilding in differing contexts: rebuilding the institutions and infrastructures of nations torn by civil war and strife; building bonds of mutual benefit between nations formerly at war; and addressing the deepest causes of conflict such as economic despair, social injustice, and political oppression. Paragraph 81 specifically focused on the process of democratization, the promotion of human rights, and the protection of vulnerable minorities.

As Vivienne Jabri notes, the hegemonic liberal peace, which informs modern-day peacebuilding efforts, is a distinctly modern idea, associated with concepts such as progress, emancipation, and civil society.[11] The liberal peace approach puts forth a particular understanding of peace that privileges market economic policies, vibrant civil society, human rights, the rule of law, and democracy as preconditions for a peaceful society. This understanding of peace is rooted in the philosophical, epistemological, and methodological traditions of the Enlightenment and the Western experience and brings a particular set of conflict resolution assumptions and tools that are mainly top-down and elite-led institution-building strategies, as is the case in Iraq, Afghanistan, and Bosnia and Herzegovina.[12] Liberal peacebuilding strategies employ what Robert Cox calls "problem-solving approaches,"[13] which take existing social and political institutions as starting points for analysis and aim to find solutions to the problems arising from these starting points.[14] These approaches offer economic, social, and political "solutions" and support reforms that promote democratization, human rights, and market economies, and other liberal institutions. John Heathershaw also supports this view when he argues that this understanding of peace "reflects a rationalist understanding of human affairs, one which embodies a problem-solving ethos and assumes a universal ethical framework."[15] He adds that liberal peace intervention strategies, such as "structural adjustment," "good governance," and "civil society" are born out of these ethics.[16] Similarly, Eva Bertram defines UN peacebuilding in this way: since it is "designed to address the root causes of conflict, it entails building the political conditions for a sustainable democratic peace, generally in countries long divided by social strife, rather than keeping or enforcing peace between hostile states and armed parties."[17]

Many of the peacebuilding intervention strategies used in the Muslim world reflect these values and principles of the liberal peace. For instance, UNAMI, the United Nations Assistance Mission for Iraq that was established in 2003, states that its mission mandate "includes advancing inclusive, political dialogue and national reconciliation, assisting in the electoral process and in the planning for a national census, facilitating regional dialogue between Iraq and its neighbors, and promoting the protection of human rights and judicial and legal reform."[18] The US Agency for International Development's (USAID) strategy in Iraq for 2010–2012 prioritized the establishment of just, representative, and accountable governance; the integration of Iraq into the global economy; and contributing to regional peace and security.[19] Again, the USAID mission in Afghanistan aims to "ensure economic growth led by the private sector, establish a democratic and capable state governed by the rule of law, and provide basic services for its people."[20] The United Nations Assistance Mission in Afghanistan (UNAMA), on the other hand, is focused on leading and coordinating the international civilian efforts with a particular focus on National Priority Programs, cooperating, with NATO/ISAF for transition, reconciliation, elections, regional cooperation, human rights, and humanitarian assistance.[21]

Although their goals are worthy and important, these peacebuilding efforts have failed to bring the promised peace and prosperity to these countries. For example, peacebuilding efforts have not led to peace and security in Iraq or Afghanistan. Despite national and parliamentary elections, constitutional reform, and the emergence of a multi-party system, ethnic and sectarian violence as well as terrorism are increasing in Iraq.[22] Similarly, in Afghanistan, peacebuilding efforts have failed to provide security or democracy. On the contrary, in both contexts, negative reactions to foreign intervention efforts are growing. Attacks on international staff, including international aid workers, are increasing; more aid workers are being killed or kidnapped.[23] Simon Reid-Henry argues that these attacks have grown primarily because in countries from Sudan to Pakistan, Chad, and Papua New Guinea, aid and humanitarian organizations are seen as ever more complicit with state militaries and the Western liberal agenda.[24]

One reason for the failure of the liberal peace framework has been its universalistic, secular, problem-solving approach, which ignores religio-cultural traditions as a resource for peacebuilding. The liberal peace tradition assumes peace to be universal and "attainable if the correct methods are concertedly and consistently applied by a plethora of different actors working on the basis of an agreed peace building consensus, and focusing on the regimes, structures, and institutions required at multiple levels of analysis and in multiple issue areas by liberal governance."[25] This approach determines what peace means, how peace can and should be attained, and who can be considered agents of peace. Such a perspective reduces the social world into binary oppositions and simplistic patterns of cause and effect: war/peace, good/bad, liberal/illiberal, civilized/uncivilized, or what Mahmood Mamdani calls good Muslim/bad Muslim.[26] As Richmond observes, "culture has often been associated with positions that resist modernity or with resistance more generally: hence 'hearts and minds' strategies against insurgencies and repeated attempts to include cultural sites of influence as common opposite numbers in peace processes, while simultaneously denying the legitimacy of their cultural agency."[27] Local culture is often seen as a generic—distant, exotic, and unknowable—"other," "which, where visible, should be incorporated into problem-solving universal institutional and discursive forms of the liberal peace, often in its most conservative of forms."[28] Such an approach denies legitimacy to the worldviews and practices of the local communities and sees religio-cultural traditions as a source of conflict or at least an obstacle to peace.[29] By failing to understand the religio-cultural context of the conflicts they aim to resolve, liberal peace approaches often fall short of constructively engaging the peacemaking traditions of these communities.

Many of the present-day conflicts in Muslim communities can be referred to as "ethno-religious conflicts,"[30] where Islamic values, principles, and worldviews play an important role in defining parties, legitimizing certain ethnic and national objectives, and/or mobilizing the population. Similar to ethno-religious conflicts in other contexts, Muslim clergy and religious institutions in these contexts represent a significant portion of the community, and religious texts, myths, and images serve as lenses through which history and events are interpreted.[31] Religious traditions, like the Islamic tradition, view nonscientific ways of knowing such as dreams or intuition and revelation recorded in their sacred texts as valid sources of knowledge. Religious leaders, such as imams, are often viewed as legitimate authorities to proclaim what the truth is and how to interpret texts accordingly. Religious truths are conveyed in myths—sacred histories.[32] Robert Luyster notes that the "religious significance of an event is revealed only in its associated symbols and myths, for it is only through these that the mind apprehends what it has seen and attempts to express its meaning,"[33] and "it is by means of myth that the symbolic consciousness expresses most completely its understanding of the cosmos."[34] These truths, recorded in sacred texts such as the Bible, the Torah, or the Qur'an, provide a degree of certainty to religious narratives. These truths are then communicated and realized through religious rituals, which connect the faithful to their spiritual sources and provide models for action.

By denying legitimacy to alternative worldviews, epistemologies, and practices, peace-building interventions often inflict what Polly O. Walker calls "ontological violence."[35] Such an attitude colonizes and silences alternative conceptions of peace and ways through which this peace can be attained, imposing what Gayatri Chakravorty Spivak refers to as the "epistemic violence of imperialism,"[36] where the "colonized disappears from the view or are only brought forth through the actions of the colonizer."[37] Jabri agrees with Edward Said that this "epistemic violence is enabled by the positivist social science that denies complexity a space in its epistemological rule-book."[38] Such denigrating attitudes generate resentment, mistrust, and hostility.

Culture as an exotic and distant other, resisting modernity and posing a threat to peace, has been an important discourse in peacebuilding efforts, especially in Muslim contexts.[39] Since the horrific attacks of September 11, 2001, violence in the so-called "Islamic world" has been a major concern, and Samuel Huntington's thesis of "the clash of civilizations" has been revisited.[40] Certainly representations in the media and elsewhere often reinforce a bleak picture of Muslim societies, that are either victimized or vilified. Islam, today, is associated with violence rather than peace, even though it is rich with values and practices that encourage tolerance, peacemaking, and dialogue. Islam and Muslims are the "ultimate other,"[41] and terrorism is defined and explained as Islamic.[42] As Karen Armstrong has observed, Islam has become a "foil against which we [the West] could measure our achievements,"[43] an existential threat to "civilized us" and to the possibility of creating the conditions of a "perpetual peace."[44] As such, Muslims become "the irrational other: all that we are not" or are pigeon-holed into the categories of radical vs. moderate Muslims, or bad vs. good Muslims.[45] This "Culture Talk" holds that "every culture has a tangible essence that defines it, and it explains politics as a consequence of that essence."[46] For instance, in 2003, Bernard Lewis argued that "the confrontation with a force that defines itself as Islam has given a new relevance—indeed, urgency—to the theme of the 'clash of civilizations.'"[47] Consequently, developing effective intervention approaches to build peace in the Muslim world has become a priority in the so-called West. Shahrbanou Tadjbakhsh notes that peacebuilding efforts in Afghanistan have reinforced the dichotomies of liberal, altruist, and benevolent external actors, mostly Western countries, in the role of liberators on the one hand, and Afghans caricatured as non-liberal, non-Western "others" steeped in a conservative culture in need of engineering, on the other.[48] She adds:

> The more the regime of Taliban was constructed as being dangerous and illiberal, the more, by implication, as in colonial situations, the population was painted as primitive, unknowing of its basic rights, and needy of international interventions to restore conditions for security and rights-based institutions. This type of binary seeped through initial assumptions about whose peace and which peace were being built in Afghanistan.[49]

Soumaya Ghannuchi argues that such attitudes reproduce the orientalist discourse that contrasts the irrational, barbaric, and violent Muslims with Western interveners (such as American mediators), the benign outsiders who are rational, civilized, and peace-loving, without examining the historical, social, and political dimensions of the realities on the ground.[50] Today, global economic structures and international norms and values that reflect clear Western hegemony are seen as modern neocolonial policies, and it is not uncommon to hear those in countries like Afghanistan, Pakistan, and Iraq refer to peacebuilding interventions as neocolonial or neo-imperialist strategies that aim to subjugate Muslim societies by stripping off their religious culture and identity.[51] This perception is intensified when political leaders such as Tony Blair and George Bush emphasize the need to distinguish between "good" and "bad" Muslims.[52] According to Mamdani, such a discourse implies that "whether in Afghanistan, Palestine, or Pakistan, Islam must be quarantined and the devil must be exorcised from it by a civil war between good Muslims and bad Muslims."[53] The representation of Islam as a religion in need of reform and efforts to minimize the role of Islam in Muslim contexts present a threat to Islamic identity. This perceived threat often leads to defensiveness and reification of an idealized and essentialized self that is built upon selective elements of the tradition. When the threat is directed at religious identity, reaction also takes on a radicalized and at times fundamentalist religious discourse.[54]

Civil Society and Peacebuilding

Although the liberal peace tradition often privileges the role of official actors, such as individual governments or intergovernmental organizations, in addressing conflicts through first-track diplomatic efforts including mediation, negotiation, and good offices, the creation of a self-sustaining civil peace through local ownership and participation has become an important concern.[55] Additionally, the international community has come to recognize the important roles nonstate and unofficial organizations (such as charity organizations, faith-based groups, humanitarian agencies, and human rights activists) can play in peacebuilding efforts.[56] The emergence of these non-state and unofficial actors is closely related to Kantian liberal peace theory, which privileges an agency-led, emancipatory politics and focuses on the public sphere, citizen participation, and the individual's capacity to assert difference within a wider set of social relations.[57] Kant states that for parties to possess agency for peace, "they must exist in what [he] refers to as a 'legal civil state,' for only such a state can provide the guarantee against the state of nature, which always constitutes a threat."[58] Within this framework, the possibility of peace is associated with the emergence of legal frameworks that supersede the sovereignty of states, thereby linking humanity in a universal terrain sustained beyond a merely moral set of obligations[59] and a civil society.

From a liberal peace perspective, civil society is a key component of the transformation from a state of nature—which is characterized by violence—to a "legal civil state" characterized by peace, human rights, a liberal economy, and democracy, as it assumes that civil society processes will impact political decision-makers.[60] Since it originated in eighteenth-century Western Europe, the term civil society has often been used to refer to the public sphere that is separate from the state and protected by law. In contrast to the "barbaric" state of nature, where emotions prevail, civil society aims to create a peaceful society based on reason and a social contract.[61] Closely tied to the social, economic, and political evolution of Western Europe and the United States, it is often associated with the rule of law, democratization, human rights, and political and economic liberalism, through which citizens can both uphold and resist the state. As such, it is one of the main spheres where relations of power are worked out, relations between the individual and the state are negotiated, and discourses are constantly articulated. Deriving from this particular historical background, "civil society" today refers to grassroots, democratized politics, and ways in which citizens can influence and participate in the process of governance. The emergence of civil society is often viewed as the first step toward democratization and the protection of human rights. Thus, the existence of civil society in non-Western contexts is linked to their attitudes toward democratization, human rights, and individualism, and linked with the civilizing or democratization mission of the West.[62]

Especially since the end of the Cold War, NGOs have become important actors in addressing international conflicts. Pointing to the important role NGOs played in facilitating a connection between global and civil society in Mozambique,[63] Oliver Richmond observes that "it has often been suggested that NGOs can fulfill vital roles that states and their agencies cannot."[64] These organizations may provide humanitarian relief and assistance after a catastrophic event, or facilitate post-conflict reconstruction through legal, educational, political, and medical assistance to communities. They may attempt to avert conflicts or bring conflicting parties together through mediation, problem-solving workshops, and so on. They may help local communities build their capacity by bringing in resources that may not be available locally (such as funds, technology, etc.). They may offer training and know-how regarding conflict management and resolution skills such as negotiation and consensus-building.

Because civil society is considered the *sine qua non* of a peaceful society, many post-conflict reconstruction and peacebuilding initiatives in non-Western contexts exert significant effort to develop a civil society and look for like-minded, Western-oriented organizations and individuals with whom to cooperate. Without taking note of the spatio-temporal situatedness of the modern notion of civil society, they seem to expect NGOs in non-Western contexts to resemble Western ones in structures, attitudes, work towards human rights, democracy, and liberalism, and familiarity with specific grant-writing strategies or evaluation methods.[65] This expectation contributes to grave misunderstandings between Muslim and non-Muslim actors of peace, as many of the former operate within a religio-cultural context that is significantly different from the ones in which Western actors operate.[66]

Furthermore, because Western organizations often fail to understand local customs and traditions, as well as power relations, their intervention efforts can be perceived to threaten existing power structures and local customs; therefore, they may provoke hostility among local authorities and in the community itself. In some cases, such as in Iraq, Afghanistan, and Pakistan, these Western organizations are perceived to be agents of the West and a threat to traditional ways of life. Especially within the context of military intervention and peacebuilding processes, such as in Iraq, international NGOs are often viewed with grave suspicion.[67]

Pakistan is a case in point. The current madrasa system in Pakistan, which places a strong emphasis on spiritual studies, purification of the belief system, and the rejection of imperialism and its values, was a direct response to the form of Western education that was introduced by the British during the colonial period.[68] Considering the local people uncivilized and "backward," the British initiated a civilizing mission through the transformation of various institutions, including the educational institutions, which were forced to change. During this period, missionary churches were also encouraged to convert as many locals as possible; educational institutions such as missionary schools played an important role in this process. Western-based institutions that aim to introduce modern scientific subjects to reform madrasas in Pakistan are still associated with this period, and thus have been perceived with grave suspicion and hostility.[69]

It is important to recognize that the relationship between state and society in each community evolves as a result of its own unique circumstances. Derived from particular religious and cultural contexts, Muslim communities display unique characteristics that make it difficult for observers unfamiliar with Muslim societies and peacemaking traditions to identify peace efforts and local agents of peace. Many Muslim societies have traditional structures that are different from European or American social structures. Some of these traditional structures may emphasize tribal, religious, or ethnic identities; may be based on hierarchical social divisions rooted in their religio-cultural systems; and may be perceived by outsiders to obstruct effective peacebuilding efforts and contribute in many ways to the continuation of conflicts. Although there are an increasing number of NGOs in Muslim regions similar to the ones in the West, oftentimes agents of peace are individuals—their peacebuilding work is assumed in that identity—that is, as individuals, they are engaged in charity or humanitarian efforts. They are local leaders or imams, working from their mosques or homes, doing the work of intervening in conflicts, not only between local people but also between communities. Such actors are doing extremely constructive and critical work in their communities under very difficult conditions and not without success. Working effectively with these actors would contribute to overcoming many of the misunderstandings between these communities and outsiders and would definitely strengthen their capacity as peacemakers. Unfamiliarity with these situations, on the other hand, may deepen misunderstandings and miscommunication that can be unproductive, even destructive, in the long run.

Justpeace and Peacebuilding in Muslim Contexts

Peacebuilding initiatives in Muslim contexts must take into consideration the religio-cultural context, which provides a set of values, worldviews, rituals, and role models, because for peace to be sustainable, peace initiatives must be broadly supported by the society in general. These initiatives must be sensitive to the particular needs and historical, cultural, and religious backgrounds of these societies. Peacebuilding strategies and approaches must empower local community members and address the social, economic, psychological, and environmental needs of the parties as the parties themselves define them. These initiatives must also cultivate a feeling of ownership rather than an imposition. This requires conflict resolution interventions and peacebuilding initiatives to be perceived as legitimate by the society. Therefore they must take into consideration local sources of legitimacy,[70] indigenous knowledge, and traditions.[71]

The perspective of justpeace realizes that for peacebuilding to be sustainable, it must be considered legitimate, acceptable, and meaningful by the communities. Rooted in the constructivist tradition, justpeace recognizes that knowledge is both socially constructed and intersubjective[72] and that violent conflict is co-constructed through the actions of individuals situated in their own unique religio-cultural contexts.[73] This view holds that conflicts involve the construction of meaning and interpretation of events, which in turn can contribute to either escalation or de-escalation of the conflict.[74] Within its own history, each community develops its own definition of what peace is, how it should be attained, and who should declare it. Finally, justpeace recognizes that even within a single community, based on a common religio-cultural tradition, there are different narratives regarding peace.

The justpeace approach does not dismiss the critical contributions of liberal peace approaches. On the contrary, it builds on its strengths and complements them by emphasizing the reduction of violence and destructive conflict while increasing justice, mutual respect, and understanding. Furthermore, justpeace recognizes that working effectively with communities who have different sources of legitimacy, worldviews, linguistic constructs, forms of social organization, myths, historical narratives, and power relations requires understanding them and developing strategies that incorporate them and empower local agents of peace. The justpeace approach promotes human rights, economic prosperity, good governance, and equality as well as environmental sustainability, but does not offer a particular form or method that can be applied to all contexts. On the contrary, it emphasizes the importance of ownership of the process and promotes a tailored approach to peacebuilding by engaging in a creative, participatory process of articulating an approach that responds to the unique needs and historical, cultural, and political context of each community. Rather than viewing communities as victims who are unable to understand and respond to the conflict they have experienced constructively, it aims to create an opportunity for communities to engage with their own tradition in a reflective manner. Justpeace aims to do that by working towards establishing just social, economic, political, and cultural institutions to address the needs of the members of the community through a creative, bottom-up, and participatory process that involves various local and international actors. This approach is based on the premise that "people are the best resources for building and sustaining peace and [it] aims to strengthen community capacities to resolve disputes peacefully; to develop trust, safety, and social cohesion within and between communities; and to promote inter-ethnic and inter-group dialogue."[75] Consequently, it engages credible actors, members of the grassroots, policymakers, and key decision-makers in order not only to reduce violence but also to build institutions, policies, and relationships locally and globally. As such, it serves as a mirror through which it reflects the best of each tradition to address their conflicts and establish sustainable peacebuilding.

The justpeace perspective recognizes the complex relationship between religio-cultural traditions, violence, and peacemaking. Religious texts, images, symbols, and myths are often used and abused to evoke various emotions such as heroism, chivalry, bravery, vengeance, and violence, perpetuating a culture of violence.[76] It also recognizes that religious traditions can bring moral, social, and spiritual resources to peacebuilding and inspire a sense of engagement and commitment to the process.[77] Religious rituals (e.g., cleansing ceremonies) and values and principles (forgiveness, patience, mercy, accountability, or predestination, etc.), can facilitate healing and trauma management. Religious texts and prophetic stories can provide examples of peacemaking, forgiveness, and compassion that can lead to a change of attitudes and behaviors and encourage interacting or even making peace with the "other." Recognizing their constructive potential, justpeace creates space for religious actors and traditions to play a critical role in peacebuilding and transforming deadly conflict by an ethos of tolerance and nonviolence. David Little and R. Scott Appleby describe this process as religious peacebuilding.[78]

In this process, faith-based actors such as religious leaders, individuals, groups, and organizations that are motivated by their faith engage in activities that aim to find a lasting solution to the conflict, repair and build relationships, and encourage reconciliation. Religious leaders and institutions often have a reputation for integrity and service through constant contact with people.[79] As middle-range leaders, who have access to both high-level leadership and the grassroots, religious actors are typically "long-term players who live and belong to the communities involved in conflict."[80] They often have a long record of charitable work and a privileged status that gives them authority and legitimacy. They can legitimately interpret the tradition's sacred texts from a new perspective to highlight values such as justice, mercy, acceptance of accountability, compassion, and forgiveness. They can also set a moral example as peacemakers through their interactions with, sermons about, or attitudes toward the adversaries.[81]

Agents of Peace in an Islamic Context

Muslim communities are replete with historical and contemporary examples of men and women, inspired by their faith, working to bring peace and justice to their societies. Qamar-ul Huda observes that "real initiatives in Islamic peacebuilding are occurring in all Muslim communities, every day and throughout the world, from Muslim minorities in the West to majority Muslim societies in Africa, the Middle East, and South and Southeast Asia."[82] As he notes, these initiatives include high-ranking scholars, such as muftis and grand ayatollahs; regional and local-level politicians; imams; teachers; qadis; lawyers; women; and others. One such example is the late Dekha Ibrahim Abdi,[83] founder of the Wajir Peace and Development Committee (WPDC). Inspired by her faith, Islam, Dekha Ibrahim played a critical peacebuilding role in her community. She and a group of women, frustrated by constant violence, arms smuggling, refugee migration, kidnappings, and mistrust among clans, founded WPDC in 1993. Soon after, the Wajir Peace Group was established with the main objective of restoring peace by involving all stakeholders. WPDC evolved into a network of twenty-seven governmental and nongovernmental organizations representing a variety of stakeholders including businesswomen, elders, and religious leaders, operating mainly in the Wajir District of Northwestern Kenya.[84]

WPDC employs a variety of approaches, such as interfaith dialogue, forming early warning teams, and engaging all stakeholders in the peace process, and they have been quite successful in reducing and preventing violence. WPDC utilizes traditional Somali conflict resolution tools, such as religious and traditional laws rooted in the Islamic tradition. Local religious leaders and elders, who are well respected in their community and have significant moral and spiritual legitimacy and leverage, play an important role during these conflict resolution processes. Dekha Ibrahim expressed that her religious and spiritual identity as a Muslim formed a strong foundation for her peace work.[85] In particular, Islam informed her vision of how peace is to be achieved, and she often referred to Qur'anic teachings to understand what is necessary for bringing about a sincere and durable peace. "She also encouraged individuals and communities affected by conflict to critically analyze themselves using the verses from the Qur'an, which she stated would enable them to build their conflict transformation on a religious and spiritual base."[86]

Imam Ashafa, a Muslim preacher who, together with Pastor Wuye, founded the Muslim-Christian Dialogue and Interfaith Mediation Center in the Kaduna region of Nigeria, is another example of an effective peacemaker.[87] The center aims to mediate and encourage dialogue among youth, women, religious leaders, and the government as well as to promote diversity, dialogue, and tolerance. Inspired by Islamic principles of peace and tolerance, Imam Ashafa has been propagating values and virtues of religious harmony and peaceful coexistence in his community. In his work, he utilizes Islamic values and principles rooted in the Qur'an and the Prophet's example as positive tools for pursuing the cause of social justice, equality, healing, and peace for humanity.

In yet another example, five of the most influential leaders of Aceh, Indonesia—including the heads of the Provincial Office of National Education, the Provincial Office for Religious Affairs, the Consultative Council of the *Ulema* of Aceh, and the rectors of the Ar-Raniry State Institute for Islamic Studies and Syiah Kuala University—initiated the Peace Education Program to promote Islamic peacemaking and to elevate indigenous mechanisms for solving conflicts.[88] The manuals developed for this program included Qur'anic verses and prophetic tradition as well as Acehnese proverbs. According to Asna Husin, Qur'anic verses or prophetic tradition included in the beginning of every module gave an inspiration for the whole text, a starting point for further discussion, and meaning to issues included in the module, while Acehnese proverbs from the local indigenous culture and language were used to validate the issue under discussion, to increase a sense of ownership, and also to reclaim the Acehnese religious and cultural heritage amidst cultural contestations among local, national, and international spheres.[89]

In addition to these local initiatives of peacemaking by local actors, Muslim states and actors have led various initiatives at international levels. [90] For instance, in 2010, Pakistani Imam Tahir ul-Qadri, the leader of Minhaj-ul-Quran International, a global Muslim group that is said to have hundreds of thousands of followers, issued a six-hundred-page fatwa specifically to enact a firm prohibition against terrorism, which bans suicide bombing without any excuses, pretexts, or exceptions.[91] Also, all heads of state from the Organization of Islamic Cooperation (OIC) issued the *Mecca Al-Mukarramah* Declaration in December 2005, which stated, "the Islamic civilization is an integral part of human civilization, based on the ideals of dialogue, moderation, justice, righteousness, and tolerance as noble human values that counteract bigotry, isolationism, tyranny, and exclusivism."[92] Additionally, the Salam Institute for Peace and Justice, based in Washington, DC, has been providing research, conflict resolution and dialogue training, intra- and inter-faith dialogue, and curriculum development, combining conflict transformation approaches with Islamic values and principles of peacebuilding as well as indigenous traditions in various Muslim countries including Niger, Chad, Sudan, Jordan, Iraq, and Iran.[93]

As these cases indicate, in each Muslim community, the type of mechanism used to resolve conflicts often depends on local factors, the nature of the dispute, and the specific cultural context. It is quite common for a community to have a variety of formal and informal mechanisms and practices to resolve conflicts including arbitration, consultation, mediation, and reconciliation. These mechanisms often incorporate Islamic and local cultural values of peace and coexistence and reflect the requirements of the unique social, historical, and political context and cultural traditions of each community. For example, the most favored mechanism in Afghanistan, particularly in rural areas, is the community or tribal council of elders (known as the *jirga* or *shura*).[94] In the context of the Middle East, *sulha* or *musalaha*, a ritualized process of restorative justice and peacemaking, is often the preferred mechanism to respond to community conflicts.[95] However, as their associated vocabulary indicates, all these different mechanisms are rooted in the Qur'anic notion of *sulh* (reconciliation/peacebuilding). They derive their inspiration from and base their practices on the same Islamic sources, namely the Qur'an, the Hadith (sayings of the Prophet), and the Sunna (the practices of the Prophet).

Islamic Principles of Peace

As Huda stresses, effective and lasting peacebuilding strategies and conflict resolution practices in Muslim communities should be constructed within an Islamic framework[96] because Islam plays an important role in social and political life, and religion is one of the key components of people's identity both as a cultural framework and as a religious creed. In these societies, Islamic discourse becomes an important source of legitimacy upon which notions of truth, justice, and peace are built. Legitimacy in many Muslim societies can be characterized as being based on what Weber calls subjective sources—mostly an ambiguous mixture of religion and custom.[97] In these societies, Islamic tradition derives its legitimacy in virtue of the sanctity of its roughly 1,400-year-old rules and customs derived from the Holy Book, the Qur'an. Holy texts, such as the Qur'an, Hadith, and the Sunna, contain sacred truths that form the basis for Islamic ethics and inform the actions of believers. Islamic rules and customs call for obedience to the persons who occupy a position of authority according to the Islamic tradition. Therefore, peacebuilding strategies must acknowledge Qur'anic evidence, other religious texts and narratives, the fields of jurisprudence, philosophy, and theology, and essential foundational doctrines, creeds, beliefs, and practices of Islam.[98]

However, it is important to note that Islamic culture is not a "'thing' that can be reified into one objective or dimension";[99] nor is it shared uniformly among all Muslims. Culture is always in the making, constantly evolving and changing with the experiences of the society. Cultural difference incorporates self-articulation and representation, both of which are situated in relation to a wider constitutive context of symbolic orders, social norms, and institutional continuities. Thus, it is located within the relations of power. "The symbolic orders and frameworks of meaning that confer identity to an individual or community are continually produced in social interaction, at one and the same time both drawing on established practices recalled through traces of memory and deep-rooted interactions as well as reenacting the situatedness of the individual self."[100] As Homi Bhabha has argued, understanding the political significance of cultural difference does not emerge from the attribution of characteristics deriving from static points of origin, but is rather dependent upon the practices wherein cultural difference comes into force, where such difference is articulated in intersubjective settings.[101]

Moreover, there is more than one culture and various subcultures within each community. "By linking cultures to individuals and emphasizing the number and diversity of social and experiential settings that individuals encounter," Kevin Avruch "expands the scope of reference of culture to encompass not just quasi- or pseudo-kinship groupings (tribes, ethnic group, and nation are the usual ones), but also groupings that derive from profession, occupation, class, religion, or region."[102] This definition recognizes "culture is always psychologically and socially distributed in a group."[103]

Vivienne Jabri goes further to emphasize that it is also important to recognize the individual's capacity for moral choice and action. She argues that "the self situated within the continuities of social life is also recursively implicated in the reproduction of its discursive and institutional norms."[104] Individual reflexivity and interpretive capacity impact the way each person relates to these institutional and discursive norms. As a result, every individual reacts to and interacts differently with his or her culture within specific historical, institutional, and discursive contexts.[105] Thus, although religio-cultural traditions impact the construction of identity, notions of peace, and perspectives on how to resolve conflicts, they do not necessarily determine individual behavior.

As the religion of more than 1.7 billion people around the world, Islam includes many different linguistic, cultural, and ethnic groups. Reflecting this diversity, Islam is not monolithic and static, but includes multiple understandings of what Islam is. What it means to be a Muslim, what Islam is, who is a Muslim, and who has the authority to define who a Muslim is, are highly contested issues among Muslims. Islam as a dynamic theology is shaped by and in turn shapes its historical, social, cultural, and political context. It includes diverse practices and interpretations reflecting the particular historical, social, political, and economic evolution of each group. "Islam, like every other religious tradition, is the product of both its heritage—itself the synthesis of ideas, beliefs and the concrete lived experience of the earlier Muslims and the way that heritage is interpreted by every generation."[106] Islamic discourse contains what Jabri calls "a complex array of memory, myth, symbolic orders and self-imagery [that] come to constitute the life-world of the situated individual."[107] It changes over time due to external and internal factors. Islamic discourse is always situated within a wider societal realm constituted by a religio-cultural context and institutional and discursive structures that both constrain what Islam and Muslim mean and at the same time enable different narratives to emerge. Contextual factors go through meaning systems that are shaped by religio-cultural constructions and institutional and discursive structures that enable the emergence of multiple interpretations that claim to hold the Islamic Truth.[108] Each of these narratives emerges at the nexus of events and texts. Although events are shaped by some set of ideas, beliefs, and rules embodied in ritual, symbols, or speech, they also transform these same cultural objects and social structures.[109] Each narrative de-historicizes various textual elements and takes them as the fixed, identical, and self-sufficient origins of meaning, upon which a particular interpretation of the sacred texts and an "Islamic Truth" are constructed.[110] In this process, creativity and subjectivity also play an important role in individual moral choices and actions. Not recognizing this would be "an unreflexive naming of individuals that denies them their space, their subjectivity, their creativity."[111] Particular relations of power, also rooted within the religio-cultural traditions and the social and historical context, influence which of these narratives becomes hegemonic.[112]

Contemporary peacebuilding activities in the Muslim world reflect this unity and diversity. For example, conflict resolution practices among the Pashtun communities of Afghanistan and Pakistan are often combined with the local tradition called *Pashtunwali*.[113] Among Somali communities, Islamic tradition is often used in combination with traditional Somali cultural values and the *xeer* tradition of conflict resolution.[114] Similarly, *sulha* practices in the Middle East reflect local traditions and history.

Although Muslim peacebuilding actors in different regions respond to the unique needs of their communities and also are influenced by their local cultural traditions and historical experiences, they all operate within an Islamic discourse that both constrains and enables their definitions of peace, how to achieve it, and who can legitimately intervene in conflicts. "Islam as a discourse refers to a body of thought and writing that is united by having a common object of study, a common methodology used by Islamic scholars and a set of common terms and ideas it incorporates which is linguistically and culturally specific."[115] Islamic discourse makes it possible for all Muslims who have been socialized under its authority to speak and act together,[116] as Muslims across the world agree on the sources of Islamic teachings (i.e., the Qur'an and the recorded sayings and deeds of the Prophet Muhammad) and basic tenets of Islam. This discourse constrains Muslim agents of peace by drawing the borders of what they can legitimately say or do in the name of Islam and enables the emergence of various narratives. These sources and tenets create a unified community (umma) and provide Islamic approaches to peace with a common vocabulary, a set of values and principles. Many of these values promote reconciliation and peace among Muslims and between Muslims and non-Muslims. Some of these principles and values shared by Muslims include justice, compassion, and mercy; social responsibility as God's agents on earth; belief in the original constitution of human beings as good, created in the "best of molds" (Qur'an 95:4); the unity of God and all God's creation; diversity and multiplicity as God's blessing and divine plan; forgiveness; and love. They provide religious imagery and sacred myths stories that urge Muslims to establish divine harmony and can inspire people to change and act.[117]

Islamic Principles of Peace

Irrespective of the Islamic tradition they adhere to, Muslims agree that Islam is a religion of peace and that the application of Islamic principles will bring justice, harmony, and order, therefore peace.[118] The Islamic conception of peace begins with God, as As-Salam is one of the most beautiful names of God. Many references to peace (e.g., *salam, silm, sulh*) in the Qur'an suggest that peace together with justice is the central theme in the Islamic discourse.[119]

The Islamic concept of peace is broader than a negative understanding of peace that is defined as the absence of war, oppression, and tyranny. Similar to the justpeace perspective, peace is viewed in Islam as a process in which human beings strive to establish foundations for interacting with each other—and with nature—in harmony and to institute just social, economic, and political structures where they can flourish and fulfill their potential.[120] It also implies a positive state of safety or security, which includes being at peace with oneself, one's fellow human beings, nature, and God.[121] This definition of peace requires a condition of both internal and external order and encompasses both individual and social spheres, as "the individual must be endowed with the necessary qualities to make peace an enduring reality, not only in the public sphere but also in the private domain."[122]

Peace in Islam is not passivity: "it is being fully active against the menaces of evil, destruction, and turmoil, which may come from within or without,"[123] as God constantly calls believers to the "abode of peace" (Qur'an 10:25) and to strive to establish harmony, justice, and peace on earth. As Tawakkol Karman, the Nobel Peace Prize Laureate for 2011, noted in her lecture, the Qur'an urges, "o ye who believe, enter ye into peace, one and all."[124] Therefore, in their struggle to establish conditions for durable peace, Muslims are urged to take into consideration key Islamic values and principles.

The principle of *Tawhid* (unity of God) asks Muslims to actively pursue unity and harmony to maintain the balance established by God, while the principle of *fitrah* (the original constitution of human beings, which is good) reminds Muslims that irrespective of gender, religion, race, and so on, all human beings are created in the image of God, therefore they are all sacred. As such, the idea of *fitrah* becomes a safeguard against dehumanizing "the other." Closely tied to the idea of *fitrah* is *khilafah* (stewardship or vicegerency), which underscores the Islamic understanding of social responsibility and reminds all Muslims that they are responsible for the order on earth as they are God's representatives (Qur'an 2:30 and 33:72). Accordingly, Muslims should contribute to bringing all creatures under the sway of equilibrium and harmony and live in peace with creation.[125] Consequently, while through the principle of *Tawhid* Islam asks Muslims to respect pluralism and diversity and calls for solidarity among humanity, the principles of *fitrah* and *khilafah* invite Muslims to recognize the universality, dignity, and sacredness of humanity and call for social empowerment and doing good.

Islam recognizes that without justice (*Al-Adl*) it is not possible to have durable peace. According to Qur'anic discourse, justice is the key to establishing harmony and sustainable peace among God's creation, because the Qur'anic conception of peace cannot be attained unless a just order is first established, "for peace is predicated upon the availability of equal rights and opportunities for all to realize their goals and potentials."[126] Islamic justice transcends any consideration of gender, religion, race, or creed. It is the responsibility of all Muslims to work toward the establishment of justice for all, including social and economic justice (Qur'an 4:135; 57:25; 5:8; 2:178; 2:30; 16:90). This notion of justice extends to both men and women, Muslim and non-Muslim, and cannot be achieved without an active, socially engaged community. Therefore, this principle asks Muslims to pursue justice, equality, and fairness. This principle was invoked in the preamble of the Women's Islamic Initiative in Spirituality and Equality (WISE), which stated, "justice, fairness, and equality are core values of Islam."[127]

Afu (forgiveness) is another critical principle of Islamic peacebuilding. As an act of goodness (*ihsan*) and the basis for reconciliation, Islam urges believers to forgive those who have wronged them to re-establish harmony. Forgiveness is closely related to the Islamic values of *rahmah* (compassion) and *rahim* (mercy). These twin values remind believers that a true Muslim must be merciful and compassionate to all human beings, irrespective of their ethnicity, religion, or gender, and that they cannot be insensitive to the suffering of other beings. For instance, these values have played an important role in the work of Thai peacemaker Soraya Jamjuree to create harmonious and peaceful relations between Buddhists and Muslims in South Thailand.[128] Thus torture, willfully harming another human being, contradicts Islamic commands. Principles of *afu*, *rahman*, and *rahim* often inspire Muslims to transform their relationships and rehumanize the "other." These principles also call for reconciliation and healing of broken relationships.

Love (*hubb* and *muwadda*) is another key principle of Islamic peacebuilding as it plays a crucial role in transforming violent conflicts. Love comes from God and is often associated with peace, mercy, and forgiveness and is a sign to be reflected upon (Qur'an 30:21). Islam recognizes that transforming enmity into love is a sign of the mercy of God and emphasizes the importance of transforming hostile relations into love and friendship. The Islamic conception of love has often encouraged Muslims in their work for peace and justice. For instance, Sheikha Cemalnur Sargut of Turkey summarized the Islamic perspective of peace rooted in divine love in this way:

> We should be in a state to forgive and love others, then Allah will not be leaving us alone and he will shower his choicest blessings on us. . .

Let us unite and let us be the one committed to spread the message of Allah: of his love, compassion, peace and tranquility to humanity at large which is now reeling under hatred, violence and wickedness.[129]

Finally, *sabr* (patience), which is seen as the antidote to violence, is another central tenet of Islamic peace. The Qur'an often asks believers to be patient when faced with conflict and violence. However, the Islamic principle of patience should not be equated with inaction, as the Qur'an does not ask Muslims to stay idle and accept injustice. On the contrary, it asks Muslims to work hard and strive to ensure justice for all through active, creative nonviolent methods that would restore harmony among God's creation. In this process, justice, compassion, mercy, and forgiveness should be central to the way Muslims deal with our current problems and conflicts. Nonviolent Muslim leaders like Ghaffar Khan of India in the 1940s and Jawdat Said of Syria today have argued that *sabr* is the antithesis of violence from an Islamic view.[130]

Based on these principles, the Islamic understanding of peace, with its strong emphasis on justice, is quite similar to the justpeace perspective and can be defined as a process in which human beings can establish foundations for interacting with each other and with nature in harmony, instituting just socioeconomic structures where human beings can flourish and fulfill their potential. Consequently, tyranny, discrimination, and oppression that perpetuate injustice toward any group in the Muslim society are viewed as being among the greatest threats to peace and harmony.

Features of Muslim Peacebuilding Actors

Muslim peacebuilding actors often employ these Islamic values and principles of peace in combination with other local traditions and practices, and not without success. Although they share some similarities, many Muslim peacebuilding actors differ from Western-based peacebuilding organizations.[131] First, Islam is often inseparable from other aspects of life. With the exception of a few countries like Turkey, in most Muslim societies it is very difficult to separate the religious from the nonreligious. Even in those cases, religious discourse is interwoven into various assumptions about conflict and peace, and it influences the interactions between actors as a cultural/discursive framework. Peacebuilding activities are no exception. Peace work in many Islamic discursive contexts is seen as a duty of re-establishing God's harmony between people; thus, it is a religious duty. As such, peacebuilding activities and initiatives are not viewed as a separate job, but as a social and religious responsibility of the individual, part of one's life and leadership role. Because peacebuilding activities are viewed as part of the social and religious responsibility of religious leaders, and because most of the time, the local imam or sheikh or other religious leaders and elders undertake peacebuilding activities in their personal capacity, quite often they do not feel the need to indicate or emphasize the role of Islam in their work, but take it for granted. Thus, they do not explicitly refer to their organization or work as specifically "Muslim" or "Islamic."[132]

Second, agents of peace in the Muslim world draw on Islamic values, social relations, and rituals, which are critical to legitimize their efforts.[133] The Qur'an often discourages conflict, warns against its detrimental effects on the community, and urges Muslims to resolve their disputes peacefully (49:9 and 8:46). There is a strong sense of community, solidarity of people, and a collaborative understanding of freedom that is embedded in the notion of umma, the community of Muslims. Integration of the umma and creating harmony within the community are called for by the principle of *Tawhid*, as has been discussed. Therefore, in many Muslim communities, conflict is seen as a negative phenomenon destructive of the social fabric and order; to protect the unity of the social group, it must be avoided. Values and rituals focus on repairing and maintaining social relationships; emphasize linkages between people and group identity, collective responsibility for wrongdoing, face-saving, restorative justice, and maintenance of social harmony; and call for reconciliation, public apology, forgiveness, and compensation, among other things.[134] For example, conflict resolution mechanisms such as *sulha* in the Middle East, *xeer* in Somalia and *jirga* in Afghanistan view wrongdoing as an offense both against the individual and the community; therefore, they involve offenders and victims as well as the whole community in a participatory dialogue process to address the needs of the parties, restore a sense of justice, and re-establish order and harmony within the community. These processes stress the importance of restoring broken relationships and compensating victims, but do not go as far as ostracizing the offenders to a point where their integration into society is no longer possible.[135] The process aims to empower the victims of the conflict and the affected communities, while reaffirming collective values, minimizing retribution, and maximizing restoration of community harmony through a collective decision-making process.[136] Acceptance of responsibility, repentance (*tawba*), and offering apology and compensation rather than *qisas* (retribution) are encouraged by invoking unity, harmony, and Islamic principles such as forgiveness and reconciliation.

Furthermore, Muslim peacebuilding actors heavily utilize Islamic rituals, mythology, terminology, and stories stated in the Qur'an and Prophet's examples as well as historical examples to support their peacebuilding efforts and to rehumanize the "others." These Islamic principles have been an inspiration to many Muslim peacebuilding actors. Basing their work on Islamic texts and the Prophet's example enables Muslim peacebuilding actors to work more effectively because Islam provides concepts, language, and terminology that are familiar and meaningful to Muslims. For instance, Soraya Jamjuree—the founder of Friends of Victimized Families and a lecturer at Prince Songklah University in Pattani Province of South Thailand—derives a strong sense of responsibility from the Islamic principles of vicegerency and justice. She invokes Islamic principles of forgiveness, apology, and compassion to prevent militants from creating hate between Muslims and Buddhists.[137] Similarly, Imam Ashafa says that Islam is his compass in life and states:

> You should take care of God's creation. When you destroy the animals or plants, when you pollute the environment, you do the same level of harm as you do to fellow human beings. My religion is about love for all creation.[138]

A group of leading Islamic scholars from Afghanistan also has issued a declaration where they have identified the Islamic principle of peace and condemned violence and terrorist attacks in the name of Islam.[139] Based on Qur'anic verses and the Prophet's example, this document states that the best mode of jihad—struggle for the sake of God—is nonviolent struggle. In order to support their position, these religious scholars refer to Qur'anic verses and values of patience, justice, and compassion, among others, and draw on the Prophet's examples of resolving conflicts peacefully.

Third, peacemaking practices in Muslim contexts are rarely undertaken by stable institutions such as NGOs. Rather, they are often ad hoc and informal, initiated by religious leaders, such as sheikhs or imams, who intervene either upon the request of one of the parties or on their own initiative. Indigenous conflict resolution mechanisms such as *sulha* and *jirga* are based on the formation of an ad-hoc delegation to intervene in conflict, mostly upon the request of one of the parties. Peacemakers in Islamic contexts are often cultural insiders whose efforts are accepted because they have a better understanding of the way the community members make sense of the world and the way they think. Peace work is regarded as a collective responsibility, and those who know Islamic history and tradition—elders and religious leaders, such as *zaumas* in Lebanon, *mohtars* in Turkey, as well as imams and *qadis* in other places—are often perceived as natural peacemakers. They are expected to possess a deep knowledge of the conflict and of local customs. Their wisdom gives them the necessary qualifications and authority to set the procedures and establish ground rules of mediation. Especially in Muslim Arab families, mediators should possess such qualities as high status, kinship ties, previous experience, honor, and authority.[140] In Somalia, as well as in Afghanistan, mediators are often a jury of elders in the community who know the customary law in addition to the Islamic law.[141] In addition to being trustworthy, these elders have knowledge of the parties and the history of the conflict, which is important because they are a first step in understanding and resolving the conflict. Peacemakers are also expected to have the ability to articulate the situation well, to use the right rhetoric, idioms, stories, and references to the past.[142] Because peacemakers are traditionally chosen for these characteristics, it is not common in Muslim communities to establish separate and enduring institutions that are devoted only to peace work. Much of the peacebuilding work, such as education, advocacy, observation, and so on, takes place at mosques through sermons, at religious educational sites such as madrasas, and at informal gatherings or other meetings. Even though with the impact of Western groups and missionary churches, Muslim communities are now more familiar with NGOs, they are still not very common. Recently established Western-inspired peacebuilding organizations often lack regular staff, resources, and infrastructure. They are rarely familiar with budgeting systems or grant-writing practices expected by Western funders or other organizations.

Although building consensus is an important element of decision-making in conflict resolution processes such as *jirgas, xeer,* or *sulha*, and community involvement is encouraged, hierarchical and authoritarian procedures and structures are often accepted to ensure the protection of community interests and relationships. These peacemakers often have a high degree of control over the process of local peacemaking efforts. In many Muslim contexts, the credibility and power of the peacemakers are derived from their social ranking as opposed to education or professional training. As people of faith, religious leaders have an important role as peacemakers because of their religious and spiritual legitimacy and their authority to warn those who have committed crimes and done wrong. This view is supported by Imam Ashafa, who states that, because of his role as a religious leader, his community turns to him for guidance, especially in times of conflict.[143] The leverage of religious leaders stems from their close tribal, family, social, or sectarian linkages as well as their knowledge of the community and religio-cultural traditions. Such close relations and affiliations are not viewed as a weakness but a strength: their close connections allow them to put enormous pressure upon the disputants to settle and abide by the agreement.[144] In Pashtun communities in Afghanistan and Pakistan, third parties may even raise a volunteer group to enforce the decision in some cases, which gives them enormous power in the process. This status helps them persuade parties and reframe conflict in ways that are acceptable to the parties and the communities.

In addition, peace work in Muslim communities is often combined with developmental and humanitarian assistance. Muslim communities have a long tradition of social services, community assistance, and charitable work. Many Muslim organizations, such as Merhamet in Bosnia and Herzegovina,[145] Kimse Yok Mu[146] in Turkey, and Islamic Relief Worldwide operate as relief and humanitarian agencies. Still, in conflict-affected regions, many of these humanitarian organizations extend their efforts to include activities such as peacebuilding and pursuing justice and reconciliation. Peace work is often seen as an integral aspect of their other work. Religious and local leaders who are familiar with the physical, emotional, and spiritual needs of the community are often viewed as more effective and legitimate in providing the necessary assistance. For these reasons, there is less need to establish separate institutions devoted solely to peacebuilding.

Cultural differences between Muslim peacebuilding actors and their Western counterparts often lead to misunderstandings between the two. Building working relationships with Muslim peace actors in these regions requires an understanding of these cultural communication differences. For example, Muslim communities tend to be high-context cultures;[147] less individualistic and more community-oriented. They may be more emotionally expressive, prefer indirect communication styles, and display discomfort at saying no or refusing another person directly. Peacemaking processes in Muslim contexts recognize that conflicts can raise emotions such as anger, an urge to get revenge, or embarrassment. Spontaneous and emotional acts are considered part of conflict resolution, and parties are allowed to express their feelings and vent. Especially in the Middle East, individuals often engage in "heart-to-heart" conversations where interruptions with expressions of empathy and support are quite common.[148] Interrupting others and talking together is not considered rude but an expression of concern. Although negative emotions such as anger, hate, and fear are considered part of the human experience, they are seen as being harmful to group unity and harmony, and for that reason they must be transformed. For instance, Qur'anic verse 3:134[149] associates repression of anger with doing good. Also, the Prophet is recorded to have said: "The strong is not the one who overcomes the people by his strength, but the strong is the one who controls himself while in anger."[150]

Peacemaking traditions in Muslim communities often rely more on body language than words to avoid shame and to save face, which is critical. They tend to concentrate on relationships, make linkages between people and group identity, and emphasize collective responsibility for wrong. Because shame, honor, dignity, and reputation are the driving forces toward ultimate resolution, conflict resolution processes pay special attention to saving face for all those involved, especially the offender. Conflict resolution mechanisms such as *jirga*, *sulha*, and *xeer* pay special attention to protecting the honor and dignity of all parties, take measures to avoid humiliating the parties further, and look for ways to restore dignity, honor, and respect.[151] Managing the emotions of the parties as well as the communication between them is the responsibility of the third parties; nevertheless, expressive emotional reactions are perceived as a normal aspect of the process. In this context they call for reconciliation, public apology, and compensation. These stylistic differences may lead to misunderstanding between the non-regional and Muslim actors.

Strengths and Limitations of Agents of Peace in Islamic Contexts

Although research in this area is lagging, emerging literature suggests that engaging local traditions and values of peacemaking through a participatory process can significantly contribute to peacebuilding in the Muslim world. For example, some local peacebuilding organizations such as Cooperation for Peace and Unity (CPAU) and Sanayee Development Organization (SDO) in Afghanistan have successfully implemented local peacebuilding initiatives rooted in the local traditions.[152] These initiatives were effective in increasing resolution of conflicts; lowering levels of violence, including domestic violence; creating greater community cohesion and resilience to external threats or events; expanding development activity; and successfully reintegrating of returnees.[153]

In this process, Muslim peacebuilding actors often have unique strengths as well as limitations. It is usually the case that Muslim actors—such as Imam Ashafa of Nigeria, Jawdat Said of Syria, Imam Tahir-ul-Qadri of Canada,[154] and Grand-Mufti Mustafa Ceric of Bosnia and Herzegovina—are more effective than secular institutions because as religious leaders who know the Islamic tradition, history of the conflict, and the parties, they have moral and spiritual legitimacy and are perceived to be even-handed and trustworthy. They are highly respected, and their opinions are generally held in high regard within their communities. They know the history and the traditions of the parties, and they also know the needs (both physical and emotional) of their communities. Thus, they are better equipped to reach out to the people, mobilize them, and rehumanize the "other." They employ Islamic values such as justice for all, forgiveness, harmony, and human dignity to motivate the people to work toward peace. As a result, they have been much more effective in mobilizing and motivating their communities to change their behavior and attitudes than secular organizations. For example, Tahir-ul-Qadri was able to gather tens of thousands of people to march nonviolently against corruption in Pakistan in January 2013.[155]

The moral and spiritual authority of religious leaders—their reputation as honest and even-handed people of God—also places them in a better position to mediate between conflicting parties. Islamic practices and rituals of conflict resolution, such as *suluh* or *musalaha* (reconciliation), are important for Muslim communities because they are familiar with these local mechanisms; thus they are considered authentic and legitimate. Employing traditional conflict resolution methods, Muslim actors have contributed significantly to altering negative frames of mind; fighting the negative stereotypes of Muslim leaders through speeches, sermons, and education; reducting violence; promoting disarmament, demilitarization, and reintegration; and encouraging reconciliation and interfaith dialogue in places like Nigeria, Lebanon, and Indonesia. For example, the Wajir Peace and Development Committee has been successful in reducing violence by establishing rapid response teams that have intervened in disputes and prevented them from escalating into violent conflicts. They persuaded the government to provide peace education in schools, and it has become part of the school curriculum in the district.[156] Also the peace *shura* of one peacemaker in Afghanistan, Mohamed Suleman, is based on the Wajir model.[157]

Muslim groups also have a broad community base, which provides them with a wide pool from which to draft committed and unwavering volunteers. These volunteers can devote the necessary time to mediation, reconciliation, or peace education as part of their service to

God. Muslim leaders have access to community members through mosques, community centers, and educational institutions, such as Qur'an schools. They are part of an international Muslim network, which they often connect to for support. Consequently, they have the capacity to mobilize the community as well as national and international support for the peace process. Through their networking potential, they can also help spread peace work to wider communities. This allows them to reach out to larger numbers of individuals than secular groups can, and to increase their effectiveness. Grand-Mufti Mustafa Ceric of Bosnia and Herzegovina, for instance, was able to elicit support from Islamic communities for his work in peace and reconciliation there. His religious identity provided him with access to those communities. Similarly, OIC often aims to provide support to Muslim communities in areas of peace and reconciliation, and it has been increasing allocation of resources to support peacebuilding, development, and education initiatives in various Muslim contexts.[158]

At the same time, peacebuilding actors in the Muslim world face enormous challenges that hinder their work. For instance, many Muslim societies have traditional structures that restrict effective peacebuilding efforts and contribute to the continuation of conflicts in many ways. Deep-rooted traditional customs and structures, which usually serve the interests of certain groups, become strong barriers for these actors, especially in traditional societies such as Pakistan, Afghanistan, and Sudan. Some of these traditional structures include hierarchical social structures and discrimination based on religious affiliation or gender. In some cases, these structures prevent women or youth from taking active roles in peacebuilding efforts.[159] Transforming these structures and challenging these customs are quite difficult and require resilience, perseverance, and courage. Still, operating within an Islamic discursive field by referring to various Qur'anic verses and historical examples, and with their moral authority and knowledge of sacred texts, Muslim peacebuilding actors can reinterpret religious texts and challenge these traditional structures. For example, in the Wajir district, women were often excluded from public decision-making processes, as these were reserved for male elders. The WPDC initiative, which was started by a group of women, initially faced enormous challenges as a result. However, their commitment, their understanding of the cultural and religious context, and their incorporation of religious values and principles have helped them transform these structures, and eventually their role in public decision-making was solidified when a woman was invited to participate in the council of elders for the first time.[160]

Similarly, the Sixth Clan movement founded by Asha Hagi Elmi during the Somali peace talks in Arta in 2000 is another example in which women's peacebuilding efforts have helped them overcome traditional structures. Through empowerment, advocacy, awareness, and mobilization, Sixth Clan aimed to respond to conflict among tribes in Somalia and worked to include women's voices in the peace process.[161] Their efforts enabled women to be invited to the negotiation table as equal partners in decision-making. In addition, their work helped establish the Ministry for Gender and Family Affairs. Sixth Clan was able to secure a 12 percent quota for women representatives in the Transitional Federal Parliament and ensure a 30 percent quota for women in district and regional councils, national commissions, and local committees and conferences. The movement also introduced fair gender formatting (he/she) in the charter language. Finally, Elmi became the first woman to be represented in a peace process in Somalia. Her success represents the achievements of Somalian women during the thirteen years of civil war. Her achievements are particularly impressive considering the challenges women faced during this period.

Locating their work within the Islamic tradition was an important aspect of the Sixth Clan movement. They were able to effectively utilize Islamic texts and history, and they consciously avoided connections to feminist movements. Women involved in the movement also had very high levels of Islamic education and knew the sharia quite well. Thus they were able to vehemently reject any language that contradicted Islam during discussions and meetings. They chose to adhere to the Islamic code of conduct and modes of dress.[162] They gained credibility through their religiosity and alliances with moderate Islamic groups. Along with their allied groups, they supported the perspective that adherence to Islam should not be an obstacle to competent women who want to take leadership roles.[163] Opposition groups were unable to criticize them for a lack of religious piety or for posing a threat to Islamic identity. Additionally, their legal agenda focused on gaining total equality with men beyond Wahhabi conceptions and the Somali contexts used by *Shafii* jurists.[164]

Both men and women Muslim peacebuilding actors have to deal with competing Islamic narratives regarding issues of war, peace, and justice within their communities. Some of these narratives incite violence towards the "others." Peacemakers such as Dekha Ibrahim, Asha Hagi, and Imam Ashafa often face challenges from and attacks by extremist groups or conservative leaders in their communities. Deep-rooted fears and mistrust of Western communities, including peacebuilding organizations, based on the experiences of colonization, globalization, and imperialism, among others, influence the way the intentions of Westerners are perceived and the way religious texts are understood and interpreted. Educational systems of poor quality do not provide the necessary education and training in addressing issues regarding peace, tolerance, and Islam, and frustrated young people are easily seduced by radical and fundamentalist interpretations of sacred texts. Imam Ashafa supports this view when he states that "the fear of the unknown and of another culture" is an important barrier to creating a culture of peace in his context and adds that the second barrier is

> incapable scholars with ignorant followers. They assume they know the best of their traditions, but unfortunately they are half-baked scholars because they have the knowledge of the texts but they don't have the knowledge of the environment. They cannot conceptualize the reality of their traditions in the light of the modern challenges that they find themselves in.[165]

In such a situation, Muslim agents of peace need to compete with these more radical narratives, constantly negotiate what it means to be a Muslim, and negotiate what that means, in turn, to pursue justice and establishing peace. Hostile and suspicious groups attempt to undermine the work of peacebuilding actors by stating that they are aiming to create another religion, serving the interests of Westerners, and so on. They may initiate slandering campaigns against peace-oriented actors and fault them for being collaborators. For example, Imam Ashafa discusses the divisions within his community:

> The divisions within the Muslim community were very sharp at that time and they are to this day. The majority of Muslims are Sufis and they are moderate. They belong mostly to two orders, the Tijaniyya and the Qadiriyya. They represent maybe 70 percent of the population. But the other tendencies (and especially the Salafis), though they are a minority, are very vocal so they have far more influence. They represent new tendencies, with ideas that have come from other places. They also have this Islamicizing mission in a very different way from the more traditional groups and leaders.[166]

In another interview, Imam Ashafa refers to the opposition they faced in their religious communities when he came together with Pastor Wuye to promote interfaith initiatives and local reconciliation. He remembers that there was strong rejection of their work and they were branded as compromising traitors:

> Sceptics mocked us and our idea. But today we have majority support in my country and we are being called upon by other countries, organisations and small communities to sort out conflicts before they get out of hand and sometimes to quench already smouldering conflicts threatening to engulf communities.[167]

For Muslim peacebuilders, locating their efforts in Islamic peacemaking traditions and values becomes especially important to respond to these challenges.

Finally, lack of basic resources is another challenge faced by these peacebuilding actors. Especially in Africa, or in countries like Pakistan or Bangladesh, many communities have no access or only very limited access to basic resources such as electricity, phones, email, and fax. Poverty and unequal access to resources are major issues. This lack of resources negatively affects the local peacebuilding actors who travel to remote parts of their country with very limited resources under extremely difficult conditions. It particularly hinders their ability to communicate with the international community and damages their organizational capacity and effectiveness. Many Muslim peacebuilding actors lack educational resources such as libraries, books, even pens and paper. Especially when combined with high illiteracy rates in these communities, the lack of resources becomes a major challenge.

CONCLUSION

In an age of ethno-religious conflicts, where communities from different religio-cultural frameworks come into conflict, it is important to expand our epistemological and methodological frame to create space for alternative truths about the nature and agents of peace. The liberal peace perspective rests on positivist epistemology and insists that there is only one way to achieve peace. Articulating a universal peace that is a-cultural and a-temporal, this perspective emphasizes the role civil society plays in building peace. The emergence of civil society is considered necessary for establishing a peaceful society; however, the modern understanding of civil society centers on democracy, human rights, and the market economy. As a result, many liberal peacebuilding initiatives focus on building civil society organizations that promote these institutions. Those organizations and actors that do not fit in this framework are either seen as a threat or deemed irrelevant. Hegemonic discourses and practices of peace thus deny the existence of these actors.

It is increasingly becoming evident that for peacebuilding efforts to be effective, they must take into consideration local peacebuilding traditions and actors, as these mechanisms and leaders are considered legitimate, trustworthy, and credible. Especially in the Muslim world, in spite of the grave difficulties they face, many religious leaders and groups have taken up the challenges involved in peacemaking. At a time when religious violence is prevalent, and individuals and groups are committing violence and inciting hatred and intolerance in the name of Islam, it is critical to understand the unique characteristics of these agents of peace and to empower them. Due to their major differences from the West in their sources of legitimacy, worldviews, and ways of knowing, as well as in the organizational structures they use, they are often associated with backwardness or fundamentalism. As a result, Muslim peacebuilders are often ignored or denied a legitimate role. Nevertheless, the most effective response to radical and militant voices is the voice of those religious leaders and groups who have the courage, the knowledge, and the capacity to stand up and present the Islamic values of peace, tolerance, and dialogue based on authentic Islamic sources such as the Qur'an, the Hadith, and the Sunna.

In order to engage with these actors, we need to broaden our perspective to include these local worldviews, practices, and agents within the framework of peace and conflict resolution. Peacebuilding strategies and approaches in the Muslim world, thus, need to take into consideration epistemological foundations rooted in the Islamic discourse as well as the unique needs of these societies. In order to empower these communities, peacebuilding initiatives should adopt an elicitive approach that sees culture as a seedbed—as a resource—that can be built upon through a participatory process that includes all stakeholders and combines top-down and bottom-up approaches. This requires expanding our epistemological and ontological horizons and making space for alternative articulations of what peace is and who can be agents of peace. Conflict resolution approaches that are rooted in the positivist perspective often fail to engage constructively with peacebuilding and conflict resolution traditions that are rooted in different epistemological and ontological perspectives. The just-peace approach, on the other hand, recognizes the constructive role local traditions and religious values can play in peacebuilding, and is therefore better equipped than a liberal peace approach to create conditions for establishing sustainable peace in Muslim communities.

NOTES

1. James Kirkup, "Democracy Is Route to Peace in Middle East, Says David Cameron," *Telegraph*, February 21, 2011, http://www.telegraph.co.uk/news/worldnews/middleeast/8339054/Democracy-is-route-to-peace-in-Middle-East-says-David-Cameron.html.
2. Kirkup, "Democracy Is Route to Peace in Middle East."
3. Oliver P. Richmond and Jason Frank, *Liberal Peace Transitions: Between Statebuilding and Peacebuillding* (Edinburgh: Edinburgh University Press, 2010), 22.
4. Oliver P. Richmond, *A Post-Liberal Peace* (London: Routledge, 2011), 1.
5. Jacob Bercovitch and S. Ayse Kadayifci-Orellana, "Religion and Mediation: The Role of Faith-Based Actors in International Conflict Resolution," *International Negotiation* 14, no. 1 (2009): 177.
6. This dynamic is not limited to Muslim communities. The moral power, credibility, and perceived legitimacy of religious leaders have been discussed by scholars such as R. Scott Appleby, *The Ambivalence of the Sacred: Religion, Violence, and Reconciliation* (Lanham, MD: Rowman and Littlefield, 2000); David Little, ed., with the Tanenbaum Center for Interreligious Understanding, *Peacemakers in Action: Profiles of Religion in Conflict Resolution* (New York: Cambridge University Press, 2007); Bercovitch and Kadayifci-Orellana, "Religion and Mediation."
7. Daniel Philpott and Gerard F. Powers, eds., *Strategies of Peace: Transforming Conflict in a Violent World* (New York: Oxford University Press, 2010), 3.

8. Devon Curtis, "Introduction: The Contested Politics of Peacebuilding in Africa," in *Peacebuilding, Power, and Politics in Africa*, ed. Devon Curtis and Gwinyayi A. Dzinesa (Athens: Ohio University Press, 2012), 1–28.

9. Philpott and Powers, *Strategies of Peace*, 3. Michael Pugh states that the modern version of the liberal peace approach is derived from the 1989 Washington Consensus, which connects economic and developmental dimensions of peacebuilding to political ones, and rests upon an implicit agreement between international actors, such as the UN, international finance institutions, and NGOs, on a "peacebuilding consensus." Pugh, "The Political Economy of Peacebuilding: A Critical Theory Perspective," *International Journal of Peace Studies* 10, no. 2 (2005): 23, 24. Although there has been a discussion on whether the Washington Consensus is "dead," Pugh argues that a revised version continues to link political economy and development to peace. On the "death" of the Washington Consensus, see Simon Maxwell, "The Washington Consensus is Dead! Long Live the Meta-Narrative!" ODI Working Paper 243, January 2005; and Santosh Mehrotra and Enrique Delamonica, "The Private Sector and Privatization in Social Services: Is the Washington Consensus Dead?" *Global Social Policy* 5, no. 2 (2005): 141–174.

10. Boutros Boutros-Ghali, "An Agenda for Peace: Preventive Diplomacy, Peacemaking and Peace-Keeping," UN document A/47/277 (New York: United Nations, 1992), para. 21. http://www.globalpolicy.org/component/content/article/226/32313.html.

11. Vivienne Jabri, *War and the Transformation of Global Politics* (New York: Palgrave Macmillan, 2007), 68.

12. For thorough discussions of liberal peace, see Michael Doyle, "Three Pillars of Liberal Peace," *American Political Science Review* 99, no. 3 (2005): 463–466; Edward Newman, Roland Paris, and Oliver Richmond, eds., *New Perspectives on Liberal Peacebuilding* (Tokyo: United Nations Press, 2009); Oliver Richmond and Jason Frank, *Liberal Peace Transitions: Between Statebuilding and Peacebuilding* (Edinburgh: Edinburgh University Press, 2010); Shahrbanou Tadjbakhsh, ed., *Rethinking the Liberal Peace: External Models and Local Alternatives* (Oxon: Routledge, 2011); Philpott and Powers eds. *Strategies of Peace: Transforming Conflict in a Violent World* (New York: Oxford University Press, 2010). p. 4.

13. Robert Cox, "Social Forces, States and World Orders: Beyond International Relations Theory," *Millennium* 10, no. 2 (1981): 128–129.

14. Steve Smith, "The Contested Concept of Security," in *Critical Security Studies and World Politics*, ed. Ken Booth (Boulder, CO: Lynne Rienner Publishers, 2005), 40–41.

15. John Heathershaw, "Unpacking the Liberal Peace: The Dividing and Merging of Peacebuilding Discourses," *Millennium* 36, no. 3 (2008): 601.

16. Heathershaw, "Unpacking the Liberal Peace," 597.

17. Eva Bertram, "Reinventing Governments: The Promises and Perils of United Nations Peace Building," *Journal of Conflict Resolution* 39, no. 3 (1995): 388.

18. United Nations Assistance Mission for Iraq, http://unami.unmissions.org/Default.aspx?tabid=2832&language=en-US.

19. See USAID Iraq at http://iraq.usaid.gov/node/3.

20. See USAID Afghanistan at http://afghanistan.usaid.gov/en/about/about_usaid_afghanistan.

21. See UNAMA at http://unama.unmissions.org/Default.aspx?tabid=12255&language=en-US. See also Shahrbanou Tadjbakhs, "Liberal Peace and the Dialogue of the Deaf in Afghanistan" in *Rethinking the Liberal Peace: External Models and Local Alternatives*, ed. Shahrbanou Tadjbakhsh (Oxon: Routledge, 2011), 206–220.

22. See A. Slash and P. Tom, "Is Liberal Democracy Possible in Iraq?" in Tadjbakhsh, *Rethinking the Liberal Peace*, 194–205.

23. Simon Reid-Henry writes that lethal attacks on aid workers have grown from around thirty a year in the mid-1990s to more than 150 in 2008. See Reid-Henry, "Why Western Aid Workers Are Coming Under Threat," *Guardian*, May 27, 2011, http://www.guardian.co.uk/global-development/poverty-matters/2011/may/27/western-aid-workers-under-threat.

24. Reid-Henry, "Why Western Aid Workers Are Coming Under Threat."

25. Oliver P. Richmond, *The Transformation of Peace* (New York: Palgrave Macmillan, 2007), 183.

26. See Mahmood Mamdani, *Good Muslim, Bad Muslim: America, the Cold War, and the Roots of Terror* (New York: Pantheon, 2004).

27. Richmond, *A Post-Liberal Peace*, 46

28. Richmond, *A Post-Liberal Peace*, 50.

29. The "clash of civilizations" thesis is an example of this perspective. Religious discourses also present a challenge to the liberal peace thesis as they often involve different epistemologies, such as revelation. It can be argued that certain unique characteristics of religion make it extremely hard to operationalize or rationalize it from a positivist epistemological perspective. One such characteristic is that religious discourses rest on a "claim to Truth" defined in terms of the absolute, the complete, and the changeless and that does not need to be verified by logic or empirical evidence. See S. Ayse Kadayifci-Orellana, "Ethno-Religious Conflicts: Exploring the Role of Religion in Conflict Resolution," in *The Sage Handbook of Conflict Resolution*, ed. Jacob Bercovitch, Victor Kremenyuk, and I. William Zartman (London: Sage Publications, 2008), 264–284.

30. I define ethno-religious conflicts as those conflicts where religion is a key identity marker and an integral aspect of social and cultural life; where religious institutions represent a significant portion of the community; where religious identity becomes an important divider; and where religious myths, symbols, and texts are used to fuel intolerance and hatred, create enemy images, and justify violence toward the "other." These conflicts often take place between communities that live in close proximity, whose history is filled with hostility, resentment, trauma, and violence. Religious and political leaders do not hesitate to use religious texts, images, symbols, and myths to justify their policies and evoke various emotions such as heroism, chivalry, bravery, and vengeance, among others, perpetuating a culture of violence. For more information, see Kadayifci-Orellana, "Ethno-Religious Conflicts," 264–267. Also on ethno-religious conflicts, see Appleby, *Ambivalence of the Sacred*; and Little with the Tanenbaum Center, *Peacemakers in Action*. For a thorough literature review and discussion of religion and peacemaking, see Chapter 1 of this volume.

31. Kadayifci-Orellana, "Ethno-Religious Conflicts."

32. Mircae Eliade, *Myth and Reality*, trans. W. Trask (New York: Harper and Row, 1963).

33. Robert Luyster, "The Study of Myth: Two Approaches," *Journal of Bible and Religion* 34, no. 3 (1966) 235

34. Luyster, "The Study of Myth," 236.

35. Polly O. Walker, "Decolonizing Conflict Resolution: Addressing the Ontological Violence of Westernization," *American Indian Quarterly* 28, no. 3/4 (2004): 527.

36. Gayatri Chakravorty Spivak, *A Critique of Postcolonial Reason: Toward a History of the Vanishing Present* (Cambridge, MA: Harvard University Press, 1999), 277.

37. Jabri, *War and the Transformation of Global Politics*, 149.

38. Jabri, *War and the Transformation of Global Politics*, 149.

39. Richmond, *A Post-Liberal Peace*.

40. Samuel Huntington, "The Clash of Civilizations?" *Foreign Affairs* 72, no. 3 (1993): 22–49.

41. Farid Esack, "The Contemporary Democracy and the Human Rights Project for Muslim Societies," in *Contemporary Islam: Dynamic not Static*, ed. Abdul Aziz Said, Mohammed Abu Nimer, and Meena Sharify-Funk (London: Routledge, 2006), 117–128.

42. Mamdani, *Good Muslim, Bad Muslim*, 17.

43. Karen Armstrong, *Mohammed: A Western Attempt to Understand Islam* (London: Orion, 1991), 39.

44. Jabri, *War and the Transformation of Global Politics*, 139.

45. See, for example, Mamdani, *Good Muslim, Bad Muslim*.

46. Mamdani, *Good Muslim, Bad Muslim*, 17.

47. Bernard Lewis, "I'm Right, You're Wrong, Go To Hell," *The Atlantic* 291, no. 4 (May 2003), http://www.theatlantic.com/doc/200305/lewis. See also Bernard Lewis, *The Crisis of Islam: Holy War and Unholy Terror* (New York: Random House, 2003); and Michael Dunn, "The 'Clash of Civilizations' and the 'War on Terror,'" *49th Parallel*, no. 20 (Winter 2006–2007), xv.

48. Tadjbakhsh, "Liberal Peace," 209.

49. Tadjbakhsh, "Liberal Peace," 209.

50. Soumaya Ghannoushi, "The Propagation of Neo-Orientalism," *Al Jazeera*, January 27, 2011, http://www.aljazeera.com/indepth/opinion/2011/01/201112611591745716.html. Orientalism, which depicted the non-Western Orient as the childlike, irrational, and barbaric other that needs to be redeemed, while depicting the West as rational, evolved, and civilized, has been instrumental in legitimizing colonialism. See Edward Said, *Orientalism* (New York: Vintage, 1979). Orientalist policies in Muslim communities were based on the argument that Islam was the source of backwardness and called for secularization of the Muslim communities in order to modernize them.

51. In fact, during his aforementioned trip, Prime Minister Cameron acknowledged that supporting liberal democracy in the Middle East will benefit the UK's interests when he stated, "Since democracy often goes hand-in-hand with open markets, more freedom in the Middle East could deliver commercial opportunities for Britain." See Kirkup, "Democracy Is Route to Peace in Middle East."

52. Mahmood Mamdani, "Good Muslim, Bad Muslim: A Political Perspective on Culture and Terrorism," *American Anthropologist* 104, no. 3 (2002): 766.

53. Mamdani, "Good Muslim, Bad Muslim: A Political Perspective," 766.

54. This argument is supported by Tadjbakhsh's research in Afghanistan, where she interviewed community members, conducted focus groups, and asked the respondents to describe their view of these value systems: liberalism, Islam, and traditional understandings. She notes that during her interviews, respondents voiced suspicions about the ulterior motives of the international community, which might use liberal peace as an excuse to impose a secular model on the country and launch an assault on local values systems. The suspicions would then increase determination to "preserve" Afghan values and traditions in the name of *namous* (honor), *ezzat* (honor), and Islam. Tadjbakhsh, "Liberal Peace," 216.

55. Richmond, *A Post-Liberal Peace*, 27, 30.

56. Pamela Aall, "What Do NGOs Bring to Peacemaking?" in *Turbulent Peace: The Challenges of Managing Interstate Conflict*, ed. Chester A. Crocker, Fen Osler Hampton, and Pamela Aall (Washington, DC: US Institute of Peace Press, 2001), 365–384.

57. Jabri, *War and the Transformation of Global Politics* 70.

58. Jabri, *War and the Transformation of Global Politics*, 72–73.

59. Jabri, *War and the Transformation of Global Politics*, 68.

60. Oliver Richmond, *Maintaining Order, Making Peace* (Basingstoke, UK: Palgrave, 2002), 96.

61. See D. Pietrzyk, "Civil Society—Conceptual History from Hobbes to Marx," *International Politics*, Marie Curie Working Papers no. 1 (2001); Colas Alejandro *International Civil Society* (Cambridge: Polity, 2002); Benny D. Setianto, "Somewhere in Between: Conceptualizing Civil Society," *International Journal of Not-for-Profit Law* 10, no. 1 (2007): 109–118.

62. For a discussion of the construction of the religious/secular and public/private binaries associated with the liberal peace, and how they are embedded within a particular European historical narrative and Christian conceptions of personhood and autonomy, see Talal Asad, *Formations of the Secular: Christianity, Islam, Modernity* (Stanford, CA: Stanford University Press, 2003).

63. Richmond, *Maintaining Order*, 96.

64. Oliver Richmond, "NGOs, Peace, and Human Security," in *Mitigating Conflict: The Role of NGOs*, ed. Henry F. Carey and Oliver Richmond (London: Frank Cass, 2003), 1–11.

65. See, for example, Ziad Abdel Samad, "Civil Society in the Arab Region: Its Necessary Role and the Obstacles to Fulfillment," *International Journal of Not-for-Profit Law* 9, no. 2 (2007); and Salam Nawaf, "Civil Society in the Arab World: The Historical and Political Dimensions" (Occasional Publications 3, Islamic Legal Studies Program, Harvard Law School, October 2002), 3.

66. For a discussion of Muslim NGOs and peacebuilding actors, see Mohammed Abu-Nimer and S. Ayse Kadayifci-Orellana, "Muslim Peacebuilding Actors in the Balkans, Horn of Africa, and the Great Lakes Regions," Salam Institute for Peace and Justice, May 23, 2005, http://salaminstitute.org/MuslimPeacebuildingActorsReport.pdf. Also, Imam Ashafa of Nigeria states that many Western-based peace organizations operating in that country are viewed with suspicion; they are seen to be there to destroy the communities or monopolize them. See "A Discussion with Pastor James Wuye and Imam Muhammad Ashafa," *Berkeley Center for Religion, Peace, and World Affairs*, October 31, 2011, http://berkleycenter.georgetown.edu/interviews/a-discussion-with-pastor-james-wuye-and-imam-muhammad-ashafa.

67. For a thorough discussion of international NGOs in Iraq, see Cécile Génot, "International NGOs in Iraq: Actors or Witnesses in the Evolution of the Iraqi NGO Sector?" NCCI NGO Coordination Committee for Iraq, Draft Report 2, December 2010, http://south-sudanngoforum.org/wp-content/uploads/2011/05/NCCI-Survey-INGOs-Iraqi-NGOs-Draft-2.pdf.

68. International Crisis Group, "Pakistan: Madrasas, Extremism and the Military,"Asia Report no. 36, July 29, 2002, p. 5. See also Mohammed Abu-Nimer and S. Ayse Kadayifci-Orellana, "Evaluation of International Center for Religion and Diplomacy's Madrasa Reform Project in Pakistan," Salam Institute for Peace and Justice, September 2008, p. 15.

69. See Abu-Nimer and Kadayifci-Orellana, "Evaluation of International Center."

70. For more on legitimacy and conflict resolution, see S. Ayse Kadayifci-Orellana, *Standing on an Isthmus: Islamic Approaches to War and Peace in Palestine* (Lanham MD: Lexington, 2007) and S. Kadayifci-Orellana, *Ethno-Religious Conflicts*.

71. At this point it is important to note that religio-cultural traditions are not unified. They are not shared uniformly among a tradition's members over time and space. Oftentimes they are interpreted to promote direct, structural, or cultural violence. I do not recommend

that only cultural resources can resolve conflicts, but suggest that in order to develop effective mechanisms, cultural traditions must be taken into account. In addition, individual experiences and choices also cause certain actors to become agents of peace. This issue will be addressed later in the section "Islamic Principles of Peace."

72. Oliver Richmond, *Peace in International Relations* (London: Routledge, 2008), 123.

73. John Paul Lederach, *Preparing for Peace: Conflict Transformation Across Cultures* (Syracuse, NY: Syracuse University Press, 1995).

74. Lederach, *Preparing for Peace*, 9.

75. Matt Waldman, "Community Peacebuilding in Afghanistan: The Case for a National Strategy," Oxfam International Research Report, p. 3, http://www.oxfam.de/files/20080228_communitypeacebuildinginafghanistan_359kb.pdf.

76. Defined by Johan Galtung as those religious, ideological, or linguistic symbols that legitimize direct or structural violence, cultural violence contributes to the continuation of conflict by teaching, preaching, or condoning those acts that dehumanize and satanize the opponent, justify discrimination, and incite hatred. In order to transform these violent conflicts into peaceful relations, there is a need to first replace the cultural violence with a cultural peace by tapping into religious, cultural, and national symbols, values, myths, and images that promote reconciliation, coexistence, and peace. Johan Galtung, "Violence, Peace, and Peace Research," *Journal of Peace Research* 6, no. 3 (1996): 167–191.

77. Mohammed Abu-Nimer, "Conflict Resolution, Culture, and Religion: Toward a Training Model of Interreligious Peacebuilding," *Journal of Peace Research* 38, no. 6 (2001): 686.

78. David Little and R. Scott Appleby, "A Moment of Opportunity? The Promise of Religious Peacebuilding in an Era of Religious and Ethnic Conflict," in *Religion and Peacebuilding*, ed. Harold Coward and Gordon S. Smith (Albany: State University of New York Press, 2004), 5. For more on religion and peace, see David Little, "Religion, Nationalism, and Intolerance," in *Between Terror and Tolerance: Religious Leaders, Conflict, and Peacemaking*, ed. Timothy D. Sisk (Washington, DC: Georgetown University Press, 2011), 9–28; Douglas Johnston and Cynthia Sampson, eds., *Religion, the Missing Dimension of Statecraft* (New York: Oxford University Press, 1994); and Appleby, *Ambivalence of the Sacred*.

79. See Little and Appleby, "A Moment of Opportunity," 3; Little with the Tanenbaum Center, *Peacemakers in Action*; Jacob Bercovitch and S. Ayse Kadayifci-Orellana, "Religion and Mediation: The Role of Faith-Based Actors in International Conflict Resolution," *Journal of International Negotiation* 14, no. 1 (2009): 175–204.

80. Little and Appleby, "A Moment of Opportunity," 3. See also Bercovitch and Kadayifci-Orellana, "Religion and Mediation."

81. Not all religious leaders are agents of peace. In fact, in many ethno-religious conflicts, religious leaders use religious texts, myths, and images to incite hatred and escalate conflict. Recognizing the complex and conflicting roles religious actors play, however, this paper focuses on the role of religious actors as agents of peace only.

82. Qamar-ul Huda, ed., *Crescent and Dove: Peace and Conflict Resolution in Islam* (Washington, DC: United States Institute of Peace Press, 2010), xxiii.

83. The peacebuilding community lost Dekha Ibrahim in a tragic accident in July 2011.

84. Abu-Nimer and Kadayifci-Orellana, "Muslim Peacebuilding Actors."

85. See The Right Livelihood Awards, "Dekha Ibrahim Abdi (Kenya)," http://rightlivelihood.org/abdi.html.

86. Right Livelihood Awards, "Dekha Ibrahim Abdi (Kenya)."

87. Abu-Nimer and Kadayifci-Orellana, "Muslim Peacebuilding Actors," 21.

88. See Asna Husin, "Islamic Peace Education: Changing Hearts and Minds," in *Crescent and Dove: Peace and Conflict Resolution in Islam*, ed. Qamar-ul Huda (Washington, DC: United States Institute of Peace Press, 2010), 152.

89. See Husin, "Islamic Peace Education," 159–162.

90. For information on other Muslim peace initiatives, see David Smock and Qamar-ul Huda, "Islamic Peacemaking Since 9/11," US Institute of Peace Special Report 218, January 1, 2009.

91. Dominic Casciani, "Islamic Scholar Tahir ul-Qadri Issues Terrorism Fatwa," BBC, March 2, 2010, http://news.bbc.co.uk/2/hi/uk_news/8544531.stm.

92. Ghazi bin Mohammed bin Talal, *True Islam and the Islamic Consensus on the Amman Message* (Amman: Hashemite Kingdom of Jordan, 2006). For the complete declaration see Huda, *Crescent and Dove*, Appendix 1.

93. For more information on the Salam Institute's work and activities, see www.salaminstitute.org.

94. Waldman, "Community Peacebuilding in Afghanistan," 4.

95. For more information on Sulha, see Mohammed Abu-Nimer, "Conflict Resolution Approaches: Western and Middle Eastern Lessons and Possibilities," *American Journal of Economics and Sociology* 55, no. 1 (1996): 35–55; Abu-Nimer, "Conflict Resolution in an Islamic Context: Some Conceptual Questions," *Peace and Change* 21, no. 1 (1996): 22–40; George Irani, "Reconciliation and Peace: Rituals for the Middle East," *Middle East Insight* (September–October 1998): 24–26; Irani, "Islamic Mediation Techniques for Middle Eastern Conflicts," *MERIA (Middle East Review of International Affairs) Journal* 3, no. 2 (1999), http://www.gloria-center.org/1999/06/irani-1999-06-01/; Irani and Nathan C. Funk, "Rituals of Reconciliation: Arab-Islamic Perspectives," *Arab Studies Quarterly* 20, no. 4 (1998):53–73; and Hussein Tarabeih, Deborah Shmueli, and Rassem Khamaisi, "Sulha as a Cultural Peacemaking Method for Managing and Resolving Environmental Conflicts among Arab Palestinians in Israel," *Journal of Peacebuilding and Development* 5, no. 1 (2009):50–64.

96. Huda, *Crescent and Dove*, xxv.

97. Kadayifci-Orellana, *Standing on an Isthmus*, 46.

98. Huda, *Crescent and Dove*, xxv.

99. Abu-Nimer *Nonviolence and PeaceBuilding in Islamic Theory and Practice* (Gainseville FL: University Press of Florida, 2003). 5.

100. Jabri, *War and the Transformation of Global Politics*, 141.

101. Jabri, *War and the Transformation of Global Politics*, 141.

102. Kevin Avruch, *Culture and Conflict Resolution* (Washington, DC: US Institute of Peace Press, 1998), 5.

103. Avruch, *Culture and Conflict Resolution*. 5,6

104. Jabri, "Explorations of Difference in Normative International Relations," in *Women, Culture, and International Relations*, ed. Vivienne Jabri and Eleanor O'Gorman (Boulder, CO: Lynne Rienner Publishers, 1999), 46.

105. Kadayifci-Orellana, *Standing on an Isthmus*, 46.

106. Esack, "The Contemporary Democracy," 119.

107. Jabri, "Explorations of Difference," 45–46.

108. For a discussion of different Islamic narratives of peace, see Kadayifci-Orellana, *Standing on an Isthmus*.

109. M. Sahlins, "The Return of the Event, Again: With Reflections on the beginnings of the Great Fijian War of 1843 to 1855 between the Kingdoms of Bau and Rewa," in *Clio in Oceania: Toward a Historical Anthropology*, ed. Aletta Biersack (Washington, DC: Smithsonian, 1991), 37–100; W. R. Sewell, "Three Temporalities: Toward an Eventful Sociology," in *The Historic Turn in the Human Sciences*, ed. T. J. McDonald (Ann Arbor: University of Michigan Press, 1996), 245–280; Stephen Ellingson, "Understanding the Dialectic of Discourse and Collective Action: Public Debate and Rioting in Antebellum Cincinnati," in *Social Movements: Readings on Their Emergence, Mobilization, and Dynamics*, ed. Doug McAdam and David A. Snow (Los Angeles: Roxbury Publishing Company, 1997): 268–280.

110. See Kadayifci-Orellana, *Standing on an* Isthmus.

111. Jabri, "Explorations of Difference," 44.

112. Jabri, "Explorations of Difference."

113. See Hassan M. Yousufzai and Ali Gohar, *Towards Understanding Pukhtoon Jirga: An Indigenous Way of Peacebuilding and More. . .* (Peshawar, Pakistan: Just Peace International, 2005), peace.fresno.edu/docs/Pukhtoon_Jirga.pdf.

114. See Abdile Mahdi, "Customary Dispute Resolution in Somalia," *African Conflict and Peacebuilding Review* 2, no. 1 (2012): 87–110; and Abdullahi Mohammed Shirwa, "Making Peace in the Traditional Somali Way," Mennonite Central Committee *Peace Office Newsletter* 33, no. 2 (2003): 6.

115. Kadayifci-Orellana, *Standing on an Isthmus*, 46.

116. Kadayifci-Orellana, *Standing on an Isthmus*, 46.

117. For more on Islamic discourses of peace, see Kadayifci-Orellana, *Standing on an Isthmus*.

118. Kadayifci-Orellana, *Standing on an Isthmus*. 101.

119. Kadayifci-Orellana, "Religion, Violence, and the Islamic Tradition of Nonviolence," *Turkish Yearbook of International Relations* 34 (2003): 43.

120. Kadayifci-Orellana, *Standing on an Isthmus*.

121. Ibrahim Kalin, "Islam and Peace," in *Crescent and Dove: Peace and Conflict Resolution in Islam*, ed. Qamar-ul Huda (Washington, DC: US Institute of Peace Press, 2010), 8.

122. Kalin, "Islam and Peace," 8.

123. Kalin, "Islam and Peace," 8.

124. Tawakkol Karman, "Nobel Lecture" (Oslo, Norway, December 10, 2011), http://www.nobelprize.org/nobel_prizes/peace/laureates/2011/karman-lecture_en.html.

125. William C. Chittick, "The Theological Roots of Peace and War According to Islam," *Islamic Quarterly* 34, no. 3 (1990): 156.

126. Kalin, "Islam and Peace," 8.

127. Women's Islamic Initiative in Spirituality and Equality, "Jihad Against Violence: Muslim Women's Struggle for Peace," July 2009, p. 4. http://www.wisemuslimwomen.org/images/uploads/Jihad_against_Violence_Digest%28color%29.pdf.

128. Aaron Goodman, "Thailand: Women for Peace Offering Solace to Victims of Conflict," *Frontline*, August 9, 2007, http://www.pbs.org/frontlineworld/rough/2007/08/thailand_women.html.

129. Zafar Alam Khan, "There Are Different Paths to the Kaaba: Cemalnur Sargut," interview with Cemalnur Sargut during the International Conference on Sufism, *The Pioneer*, Delhi, India, November 25, 2011, http://www.sufinews.org/paths-to-the-kaabah/.

130. See Kadayifci-Orellana *Standing on an Isthmus*.

131. See Mohammed Abu-Nimer and S. Ayse Kadayifci-Orellana, "Muslim Peacebuilding Actors in Africa and the Balkans," *Peace and Change* 33, no.4 (October 2008): 549–581.

132. For more information, see Abu-Nimer and Kadayifci-Orellana, "Muslim Peacebuilding Actors."

133. For more information, see Irani and Funk, "Rituals of Reconciliation."

134. Abu-Nimer, "Conflict Resolution in an Islamic Context"; S. Ayse Kadayifci-Orellana, *Standing on an Isthmus*.

135. Mahdi, "Customary Dispute Resolution," 98.

136. Unisaro Alice Karakezi, Alphonso Nshimiyimana, and Beth Mutamba "Localizing Justice: Gacaca Courts in Post-Genocide Rwanda" in *My Neighbor, My Enemy: Justice and Community in the Aftermath of Mass Atrocity*, ed. Eric Strover and Harvey M. Weinstein (Cambridge: Cambridge University Press, 2004): 69–84

137. Goodman, "Thailand: Women for Peace."

138. "The Imam and the Pastor: Cooperating for Peace; Interview with Imam Muhammad Ashafa and Pastor James Wuye," *SGI Quarterly* (April 2008), http://www.sgiquarterly.org/feature2008apr-4.html.

139. Khalil Nouri and Matthew Cappiello, "Islam and Conflict Resolution in Afghanistan: Cross-Cultural Leadership and Constructive Engagement," New World Strategies Coalition, Inc., August 19, 2010. http://www.ariaye.com/english/noori2.pdf.

140. Mohammed Faour, "Conflict Management within the Muslim Arab Family," in *Conflict Resolution in the Arab World: Selected Essays*, ed. Paul Salem (Beirut: American University of Beirut, 1997), 175–197. See also Abu-Nimer, "Conflict Resolution in an Islamic Context."

141. Shirwa, "Making Peace in the Traditional Somali Way," 6.

142. Yousufzai and Gohar, *Towards Understanding Pukhtoon Jirga*.

143. "A Discussion with Pastor James Wuye and Imam Muhammad Ashafa."

144. Abu-Nimer, "Conflict Resolution in Islamic Context," 14.

145. See Abu-Nimer and Kadayifci-Orellana, "Muslim Peacebuilding Actors."

146. For more information, see the website of Kimse Yok Mu at http://global.kimseyokmu.org.tr/?lang=en.

147. Edward T. Hall, *Beyond Culture* (New York: Anchor Books, 1981). See also Abu-Nimer and Kadayifci-Orellana, *Muslim Peacebuilding Actors*.

148. Irani, "Islamic Mediation Techniques."

149. The verse reads: "Those who spend [in Allah's Cause—deeds of charity, alms, etc.] in prosperity and in adversity, who repress anger, and who pardon men; verily, Allah loves *Al-Muhsinûn* [the gooddoers]."

150. Hadith: Sahih Al-Bukhari 8:135, narrated by Abu Huraira.

151. S. Ayse Kadayifci-Orellana, Mohammed Abu-Nimer, and Amjad Mohamed-Saleem, "Understanding an Islamic Framework for Peacebuilding," Islamic Relief Working Paper Series No. 2013-02, 2013.

152. According to a report by Oxfam, external evaluators have found these initiatives creative and enabling and supporting what is truly wanted by Afghan partners. Oxfam, "Afghanistan: Development and Humanitarian Priorities," 2008, http://policy-practice.oxfam.org.uk/publications/afghanistan-development-and-humanitarian-priorities-126000. Also, Tadjbakhsh notes that most of the respondents in her research stated that Islam was in fact the best methodology of peace in Afghanistan because Afghans were believers who respected religion. Tadjbakhsh, "Liberal Peace," 215.

153. Oxfam, "Afghanistan: Development and Humanitarian Priorities," 4.

154. Tahir-ul-Qadri is a Canada-based Islamic scholar of Pakistani origin.

155. See M. Ilyas Khan, (12 January 2013) "Tahirul Qadri—Pakistan's Latest Political 'Drone'?" BBC, January 12, 2013, http://www.bbc.co.uk/news/world-asia-20998010.
156. Abu-Nimer and Kadayifci-Orellana, "Muslim Peacebuilding Actors," 16.
157. Right Livelihood Award, "Interview with Dekha Ibrahim," November 6, 2007, http://www.rightlivelihood.org/dekha_ibrahim_abdi_interview.html.
158. See the OIC website at http://www.oic-oci.org/home.asp.
159. See S. Ayse Kadayifci-Orellana and Meena Sharify-Funk, "Women Peacemakers in the Muslim World," in *Crescent and Dove: Peace and Conflict Resolution in Islam*, ed. Qamar ul-Huda (Washington, DC: USIP, 2010).
160. S. Ayse Kadayifci-Orellana, "In Pursuit of Peace: Women's Involvement in Peace-Building," in *Women and Peace in the Islamic World: Gender, Agency and Influence*, ed. Yasmin Saikia and Chad Haines (London: I.B. Tauris, 2014), 191–223.
161. See SSWC information at http://wiserearth.org/organization/view/607d00e8ab5b98a7c8 824a56a622b829. For more information on SSWC, see also Sunni Said Salah, "Somalia Aid Group Assists Women and Children," *Somalia Report*, April 9, 2011, http://www.somali-areport.com/index.php/post/486/Somali_Aid_Group_Assists_Women_and_Children.
162. Interview with Asha Hagi in Abdurrahman M. Abdullahi, "Women and Constitutional Debate in Somalia: Legal Reforms during Reconciliation Conference (2000–03)," http://www.scribd.com/doc/15421298/Women-and-Constitutional-Debate-in-Somalia, 13.
163. Interview with Asha H. Elmi in Abdullahi, "Women and Constitutional Debate in Somalia," 13.
164. Abdullahi, "Women and Constitutional Debate in Somalia," 14.
165. "The Imam and the Pastor."
166. "A Discussion with Pastor James Wuye and Imam Muhammad Ashafa."
167. Bunmi Akpata-Ohohe, "The Imam and the Pastor," *Africa Today*, December 29, 2006, http://www.africatoday.com/cgi-bin/public.cgi?sub=news&action=one&cat=76 &id=878.

BIBLIOGRAPHY

Aall, Pamela. "What Do NGOs Bring to Peacemaking?" In *Turbulent Peace: The Challenges of Managing Interstate Conflict*, edited by Chester A. Crocker, Fen Osler Hampton, and Pamela Aall, 365–384. Washington, DC: US Institute of Peace Press, 2001.

Abdalla, Amr. "Principles of Islamic Interpersonal Conflict Intervention: A Search within Islam and Western Literature." *Journal of Law and Religion* 15, no. 1/2 (2000): 151–184.

Abdel Samad, Ziad. "Civil Society in the Arab Region: Its Necessary Role and the Obstacles to Fulfillment." *International Journal of Not-for-Profit Law* 9, no. 2 (2007). http://www.icnl.org/research/journal/vol9iss2/special_1.htm.

Abu-Nimer, Mohammed. "Conflict Resolution in an Islamic Context: Some Conceptual Questions." *Peace and Change* 21, no. 1 (1996): 22–40.

Abdullahi, Abdurrahman M. "Women and Constitutional Debate in Somalia: Legal Reforms during Reconciliation Conference (2000–03)." http://www.scribd.com/doc/15421298/Women-and-Constitutional-Debate-in-Somalia.

Abu-Nimer, Mohammed. "Conflict Resolution Approaches: Western and Middle Eastern Lessons and Possibilities." *American Journal of Economics and Sociology* 55, no. 1 (1996): 35–52.

Abu-Nimer, Mohammed. "Conflict Resolution, Culture, and Religion: Toward a Training Model of Interreligious Peacebuilding." *Journal of Peace Research* 38, no. 6 (2001): 685–704.

Abu-Nimer, Mohammed. *Nonviolence and Peacebuilding in Islamic Theory and Practice.* Gainseville, FL: University of Florida 2003.

Abu-Nimer, Mohammed, and S. Ayse Kadayifci-Orellana. "Muslim Peacebuilding Actors in the Balkans, Horn of Africa, and the Great Lakes Regions." *Salam Institute for Peace and Justice*, May 23, 2005. http://salaminstitute.org/MuslimPeacebuildingActorsReport.pdf.

Abu-Nimer, Mohammed, and S. Ayse Kadayifci-Orellana, "Muslim Peacebuilding Actors in Africa and the Balkans," *Peace and Change* 33, no.4 (October 2008): 549–581.

Abu Nimer, Mohammed, and S. Ayse Kadayifci-Orellana. "Muslim Peace-Building Actors in Africa and the Balkan Context: Challenges and Needs." *Peace and Change* 33, no. 4 (2008): 549–581.

Abu-Nimer, Mohammed, and S. Ayse Kadayifci Orellana. "Evaluation of International Center for Religion and Diplomacy's Madrasa Reform Project in Pakistan." *Salam Institute for Peace and Justice*, September 2008.

Abu-Nimer, Mohammed, Amal I. Khoury, and Emily Welty. *Unity in Diversity: Interfaith Dialogue in the Middle East.* Washington, DC: US Institute of Peace Press, 2007.

Akpata-Ohohe, Bunmi. "The Imam and the Pastor." *Africa Today*, December 29, 2006. http://www.africatoday.com/cgi-bin/public.cgi?sub=news&action=one&cat=76&id=878.

Appleby, R. Scott, ed. *Spokesmen for the Despised: Fundamentalist Leaders of the Middle East.* Chicago: University of Chicago Press, 1997.

Appleby, R. Scott. *The Ambivalence of the Sacred: Religion, Violence, and Reconciliation.* Lanham, MD: Rowman and Littlefield, 2000.

Armstrong, Karen. *Mohammed: A Western Attempt to Understand Islam.* London: Orion, Armstrong, 1991.

Ausburger, David W. *Conflict Mediation across Cultures: Pathways and Patterns.* Louisville, KY: John Knox Press, 1992.

Avruch, Kevin. *Culture and Conflict Resolution.* Washington, DC: US Institute of Peace Press, 1998.

Bercovitch, Jacob, and S. Ayse Kadayifci Orellana. "Religion and Mediation: The Role of Faith-Based Actors in International Conflict Resolution." *International Negotiation* 14, no. 1 (2009): 175–204.

Bertram, Eva. "Reinventing Governments: The Promises and Perils of United Nations Peace Building." *Journal of Conflict Resolution* 39, no. 3 (1995): 387–418.

Boutros-Ghali, Boutros. *An Agenda for Peace: Preventive Diplomacy, Peacemaking and Peace-Keeping.* UN document A/47/277. New York: United Nations, 1992. http://www.globalpolicy.org/component/content/article/226/32313.html.

Casciani, Dominic. "Islamic Scholar Tahir ul-Qadri Issues Terrorism Fatwa." *BBC*, March 2, 2010. http://news.bbc.co.uk/2/hi/uk_news/8544531.stm.

Chakravorty Spivak, Gayatri. *A Critique of Postcolonial Reason: Toward a History of the Vanishing Present.* Cambridge, MA: Harvard University Press, 1999.

Chittick, William C. "The Theological Roots of Peace and War According to Islam." *Islamic Quarterly* 34, no. 3 (1990): 145–163.

Cohen, Raymond. *Culture and Conflict in Egyptian/Israeli Relations.* Bloomington: Indiana University Press, 1990.

Cohen, Raymond. *Negotiating across Cultures: Communication Obstacles in International Diplomacy.* Washington, DC: US Institute of Peace Press, 1991.

Cohen, Raymond. *International Negotiation*, 2nd ed. Washington, DC: US Institute of Peace Press, 1997.

Colás, Alejandro. *International Civil Society*. Cambridge: Polity Press, 2002.

Comte, August. *System of Positive Polity or Treatise on Sociology*. New York: Burt Franklin, 1973.

Cox, Robert. "Social Forces, States and World Orders: Beyond International Relations Theory." *Millennium* 10, no. 2 (1981): 126–155.

Crow, Karim Douglas. "Divided Discourse: Muslim Discussion on Islam and Peace." Paper presented at Nonviolence International, Washington, DC, July 1997.

Curtis, Devon. "Introduction: The Contested Politics of Peacebuilding in Africa." In *Peacebuilding, Power, and Politics in Africa*, edited by Devon Curtis and Gwinyayi A. Dzinesa, 1–28. Athens: Ohio University Press, 2012.

Curtis, Devon, and Gwinyayi A. Dzinesa, eds. *Peacebuilding, Power, and Politics in Africa*. Athens: Ohio University Press, 2012.

Der Derian, James. "The Boundaries of Knowledge and Power in International Relations." In *International/Intertextual Relations: Postmodern Readings of World Politics*, edited by James Der Derian and Michael J. Shapiro, 3–22. Lexington, MA: Lexington Books, 1998.

Dicenso, James J. *Hermeneutics and the Disclosure of Truth: A Study on the Work of Heidegger, Gadamer, and Ricoeur*. Charlottesville: University Press of Virginia, 1990.

Doyle, Michael. "Three Pillars of Liberal Peace." *American Political Science Review* 99, no. 3 (2005): 463–466.

Dunn, Michael. "The 'Clash of Civilizations' and the 'War on Terror.'" *49th Parallel*, no. 20 (Winter 2006–2007). http://www.49thparallel.bham.ac.uk/back/issue20/Dunn.pdf.

Eliade, Mircae. *Myth and Reality*. Translated by W. Trask. New York: Harper and Row, 1963.

Ellingson, Stephen. "Understanding the Dialectic of Discourse and Collective Action: Public Debate and Rioting in Antebellum Cincinnati." In *Social Movements: Readings on Their Emergence, Mobilization, and Dynamics*, edited by Doug McAdam and David A. Snow, 268–280. Los Angeles: Roxbury Publishing Company, 1997.

Esack, Farid. "The Contemporary Democracy and the Human Rights Project for Muslim Societies." In *Contemporary Islam: Dynamic Not Static*, edited by Abdul Aziz Said, Mohammed Abu Nimer, and Meena Sharify-Funk, 117–128. London: Routledge, 2006.

Faour, Mohammed. "Conflict Management within the Muslim Arab Family." In *Conflict Resolution in the Arab World: Selected Essays*, edited by Paul Salem, 175–197. Beirut: American University of Beirut, 1997.

Foucault, Michel. *History of Sexuality: An Introduction*. New York: Vintage Books, 1978.

Foucault, Michel. "The Subject and Power." *Critical Inquiry* 8, no. 4 (1982): 777–795.

Foucault, Michel. *Power/Knowledge: Selected Interviews and Other Writings, 1972–1977*. Edited by Colin Gordon, translated by Colin Gordon et al. New York: Pantheon Books, 1980.

Gadamer, Hans-Georg. *Truth and Method*. Translated by Joel Weinsheimer and Donald G. Marshall, 2nd ed. New York: Crossroad, 1989.

Gadamer, Hans-George. "Universality of the Hermeneutical Problem." In *Philosophical Hermeneutics*, edited and translated by David E. Linge, 3–17. Los Angeles: University of California Press, 1997.

Ghannoushi, Soumaya. "The Propagation of Neo-Orientalism." *Al Jazeera*, January 27, 2011. http://www.aljazeera.com/indepth/opinion/2011/01/201112611591745716.html.

Goodman, Aaron. "Thailand: Women for Peace Offering Solace to Victims of Conflict." *Frontline*, August 9, 2007. http://www.pbs.org/frontlineworld/rough/2007/08/thailand_women.html.

Gopin, Marc. "Religion, Violence, and Conflict Resolution." *Peace and Change* 22, no. 1 (1991): 1–31.

Gopin, Marc. *Between Eden and Armageddon: The Future of World Religions, Violence, and Peacemaking*. New York: Oxford University Press, 2000.

Gopin, Marc. *Holy War, Holy Peace: How Religion Can Bring Peace to the Middle East*. New York: Oxford University Press, 2002.

Hall, Edward T. *Beyond Culture*. New York: Anchor Books, 1981.

Hansen, Greg. "The Ethos-Practice Gap: Perceptions of Humanitarianism in Iraq." *International Review of the Red Cross* 9, no. 869 (2008): 119–136. http://www.icrc.org/eng/assets/files/other/irrc-869_hansen.pdf.

Heathershaw, John. "Unpacking the Liberal Peace: The Dividing and Merging of Peacebuilding Discourses." *Millennium* 36, no. 3: 597–621.

Huda, Qamar-ul, ed. *Crescent and Dove: Peace and Conflict Resolution in Islam*. Washington, DC: US Institute of Peace Press, 2010.

Huntington, Samuel. "The Clash of Civilizations?" *Foreign Affairs* 72, no. 3 (1993): 22–49.

Husin, Asna. "Islamic Peace Education: Changing Hearts and Minds." In *Crescent and Dove: Peace and Conflict Resolution in Islam*, edited by Qamar-ul Huda, 151–178. Washington, DC: US Institute of Peace Press, 2010.

Irani, George. "Reconciliation and Peace: Rituals for the Middle East." *Middle East Insight* (September–October 1998): 24–26.

Irani, George. "Islamic Mediation Techniques for Middle Eastern Conflicts." *MERIA (Middle East Review of International Affairs) Journal* 3, no. 2 (1999). http://www.gloria-center.org/1999/06/irani-1999-06-01/.

Irani, George E., and Nathan C. Funk. "Rituals of Reconciliation: Arab-Islamic Perspectives." *Arab Studies Quarterly* 20, no. 4 (1998): 53–73.

Jabri, vivienne. *Discourses on Violence: Conflict Analysis Reconsidered*. Manchester: Manchester University Press, 1996.

Jabri, Vivienne. "Explorations of Difference in Normative International Relations." In *Women, Culture, and International Relations*, edited by Vivienne Jabri and Eleanor O'Gorman, 39–60. Boulder, CO: Lynne Rienner Publishers, 1999.

Jabri, Vivienne. *War and the Transformation of Global Politics*. Basingstoke, UK: Palgrave Macmillan, 2007.

Johansen, Robert C. "Radical Islam and Nonviolence: A Case Study of Religious Empowerment and Constraint among Pashtuns." *Journal of Peace Research* 34, no. 1 (1997): 53–71.

Johnston, Douglas M. "Religion and Conflict Resolution." *Fletcher Forum of World Affairs* 20, no. 1 (Winter/Spring 1996): 53–61.

Johnston, Douglas M., and Cynthia Sampson, eds. *Religion, The Missing Dimension of Statecraft*. New York: Oxford University Press, 1994.

Kadayifci-Orellana, "Religion, Violence, and the Islamic Tradition of Nonviolence," *Turkish Yearbook of International Relations* 34 (2003): 23–62.

Kadayifci-Orellana, S. Ayse. "Islamic Nonviolence Paradigm." In *Islamic Peace Paradigms*, edited by Abdul Karim Bangura, Chapter 4. Dubuque, IA: Kendall Hunt, 2005.

Kadayifci-Orellana, S. Ayse. "Interfaith Dialogue and Peace Making." Paper presented at Solidarity and Stewardship: Interfaith Approaches to Global Challenges Conference, Al Akhawayn University, Ifrane, Morocco, June 4–5, 2007.

Kadayifci-Orellana, S. Ayse. "Islamic Tradition of Nonviolence: A Hermeneutical Approach." In *Identity, Morality, and Threat: Studies in Violent Conflict*, edited by Daniel Rothbart and Karina Korostelina, 211–237. Lanham, MD: Lexington Books, 2007.

Kadayifci-Orellana, S. Ayse. "In Pursuit of Peace: Women's Involvement in Peace-Building." In *Women and Peace in the Islamic World: Gender, Agency and Influence*, edited by Yasmin Saikia and Chad Haines, 191–223. London: I.B. Tauris, 2014.

Kadayifci-Orellana, S. Ayse. "Living Walls: Among Muslims, Peace Takes on Its Own Distinct Forms." *Harvard Divinity Bulletin* 35, no. 4 (2007).

Kadayifci-Orellana, S. Ayse. *Standing on an Isthmus: Islamic Approaches to War and Peace in Palestinian Territories*. Lanham, MD: Lexington Books, 2007.

Kadayifci-Orellana, S. Ayse. "Ethno-Religious Conflicts: Exploring the Role of Religion in Conflict Resolution." In *The Sage Handbook of Conflict Resolution*, edited by Jacob Bercovitch, Victor Kremenyuk, and I. William Zartman, 264–284. London: Sage Publications, 2008.

Kadayifci-Orellana, S. Ayse, and Meena Sharify-Funk. "Women Peacemakers in the Muslim World." In *Crescent and Dove: Peace and Conflict Resolution in Islam*, edited by Qamar-ul Huda, 179–204. Washington, DC: US Institute of Peace Press, 2010.

Kalin, Ibrahim. "Islam and Peace." In *Crescent and Dove: Peace and Conflict Resolution in Islam*, edited by Qamar-ul Huda, 3–17. Washington, DC: US Institute of Peace Press, 2010.

Karakezi, Unisaro Alice, Alphonso Nshimiyimana, and Beth Mutamba. "Localizing Justice: Gacaca Courts in Post-Genocide Rwanda." In *My Neighbor, My Enemy: Justice and Community in the Aftermath of Mass Atrocity*, edited by Eric Strover and Harvey M. Weinstein, 68–84. Cambridge: Cambridge University Press, 2004.

Karman, Tawakkol. "Nobel Lecture." Oslo, Norway, December 10, 2011. http://www.nobelprize.org/nobel_prizes/peace/laureates/2011/karman-lecture_en.html.

Khan, Ilyas. "Tahirul Qadri—Pakistan's Latest Political 'dDone'?" *BBC*, January 12, 2013. http://www.bbc.co.uk/news/world-asia-20998010.

Kirkup, James. "Democracy Is Route to Peace in Middle East, Says David Cameron." *Telegraph*, February 21, 2011. http://www.telegraph.co.uk/news/worldnews/middleeast/8339054/Democracy-is-route-to-peace-in-Middle-East-says-David-Cameron.html.

LeBaron, Michelle. *Bridging Cultural Conflicts: A New Approach for a Changing World*. San Francisco: Jossey-Bass, 2003.

Lederach, John Paul. *Preparing for Peace: Conflict Transformation across Cultures*. Syracuse, NY: Syracuse University Press, 1995.

Lederach, John Paul. *Building Peace: Sustainable Reconciliation in Divided Societies*. Washington, DC: US Institute of Peace Press, 1997.

Lewis, Bernard. "I'm Right, You're Wrong, Go to Hell." *The Atlantic* 291, no. 4 (May 2003). http://www.theatlantic.com/doc/200305/lewis.

Lewis, Bernard. *The Crisis of Islam: Holy War and Unholy Terror*. New York: Random House, 2003.

Little, David. ed., with the Tanenbaum Center for Interreligious Understanding. *Peacemakers in Action: Profiles of Religion in Conflict Resolution*. New York: Cambridge University Press, 2007.

Little, David, and R. Scott Appleby. "A Moment of Opportunity? The Promise of Religious Peacebuilding in an Era of Religious and Ethnic Conflict." In *Religion and Peacebuilding*, edited by Harold Coward and Gordon S. Smith, 1–23. Albany: State University of New York Press, 2004.

Luyster, Robert. "The Study of Myth: Two Approaches." *Journal of Bible and Religion* 34, no. 3 (1996): 235–243.

Mahdi, Abdile. "Customary Dispute Resolution in Somalia." *African Conflict and Peacebuilding Review* 2, no. 1 (2012): 87–110

Mamdani, Mahmood. "Good Muslim, Bad Muslim: A Political Perspective on Culture and Terrorism." *American Anthropologist* 104, no. 3 (2002): 766–775.

Mamdani, Mahmood. *Good Muslim, Bad Muslim: America, the Cold War, and the Roots of Terror*. New York: Pantheon, 2004.

Maxwell, Simon. "The Washington Consensus Is Dead! Long Live the Meta-Narrative!" ODI Working Paper 243, January 2005.

Mehrotra, Santosh, and Enrique Delamonica. "The Private Sector and Privatization in Social Services: Is the Washington Consensus Dead?" *Global Social Policy* 5, no. 2 (2005): 141–174.

Newman, Edward, Roland Paris, and Oliver Richmond, eds. *New Perspectives on Liberal Peacebuilding*. Tokyo: United Nations Press, 2009.

Nietzsche, Fredriech. *In the Genealogy of Morals and Ecce Homo*. Translated by Walter Kaufmann. New York: Vintage Books, 1989.

Nouri, Khalil, and Matthew Cappiello. "Islam and Conflict Resolution in Afghanistan: Cross-Cultural Leadership and Constructive Engagement." New World Strategies Coalition, Inc. August 19, 2010. http://www.ariaye.com/english/noori2.pdf.

Omar, Atalia. "Religious Peacebuilding: The Exotic, the Good and the Theatrical." *Practical Matters Journal* no. 5. http://www.practicalmattersjournal.org/issue/5/centerpieces/religious-peacebuilding.

Oxfam. "Afghanistan: Development and Humanitarian Priorities." 2008. http://policy-practice.oxfam.org.uk/publications/afghanistan-development-and-humanitarian-priorities-126000.

Philpott, Daniel, and Gerard F. Powers, eds. *Strategies of Peace: Transforming Conflict in a Violent World*. New York: Oxford University Press, 2010.

Pietrzyk, D. "Civil Society—Conceptual History from Hobbes to Marx." *International Politics*, Marie Curie Working Papers no. 1 (2001).

Pugh, Michael. "The Political Economy of Peacebuilding: A Critical Theory Perspective." *International Journal of Peace Studies* 10, no. 2 (2005): 23–42.

Reid-Heny, Simon. "Why Western Aid Workers Are Coming Under Threat." *Guardian*, May 27, 2011. http://www.guardian.co.uk/global-development/poverty-matters/2011/may/27/western-aid-workers-under-threat.

Richmond, Oliver P. *Maintaining Order, Making Peace*. Basingstoke, UK: Palgrave, 2002.

Richmond, Oliver P. "NGOs, Peace, and Human Security." In *Mitigating Conflict: The Role of NGOs*, edited by Henry F. Carey and Oliver P. Richmond, 1–11. London: Frank Cass, 2003.

Richmond, Oliver P. *The Transformation of Peace*. New York: Palgrave Macmillan, 2007.

Richmond, Oliver P. *Peace in International Relations*. London: Routledge, 2008.

Richmond, Oliver P. *A Post-Liberal Peace*. London: Routledge, 2011.

Richmond, Oliver P., and Jason Frank. *Liberal Peace Transitions: Between Statebuilding and Peacebuilding*. Edinburgh: Edinburgh University Press, 2010.

Sahlins, M. "The Return of the Event, Again: With Reflections on the beginnings of the Great Fijian War of 1843 to 1855 between the Kingdoms of Bau and Rewa." In *Clio in Oceania: Toward a Historical Anthropology*, edited by Aletta Biersack, 37–100. Washington, DC: Smithsonian, 1991.

Said, Abdul Aziz, and Nathan C. Funk. "The Role of Faith in Cross-Cultural Conflict Resolution." *Peace and Conflict Studies* 9, no. 1 (2002): 37–50.

Said, Abdul Aziz, Nathan C. Funk, and S. Ayse Kadayifci, eds. *Peace and Conflict Resolution in Islam: Precept and Practice*. New York: University Press of America, 2001.

Said, Abdul Aziz, Nathan C. Funk, and S. Ayse Kadayifci. "Islamic Approaches to Conflict Resolution and Peace." The Emirates Occasional Papers 48. The Emirates Center for Strategic Studies and Research, Abu Dhabi. 2002.

Salam, Nawaf. "Civil Society in the Arab World: The Historical and Political Dimensions." Occasional Publications 3. Islamic Legal Studies Program, Harvard Law School, Cambridge, MA. October 2002.

Samad, Ziad Abdel, "Civil Society in the Arab Region: Its Necessary Role and the Obstacles to Fulfillment," *International Journal of Not-for-Profit Law* 9, no. 2 (2007). http://www.icnl.org/research/journal/vol9iss2/special_1.htm.

Sampson, Cynthia. "To Make the Real Bond between Us All: Quaker Conciliation During Nigerian Civil War." In *Religion, the Missing Dimension of Statecraft*, edited by Douglas Johnston and Cynthia Sampson, 88–118. New York: Oxford University Press, 1994.

Sampson, Cynthia. "Religion and Peacebuilding." In *Peacemaking in International Conflict: Methods and Techniques*, edited by W. Zartman and L. Rasmussen, 273–316. Washington, DC: US Institute of Peace Press, 1997.

Sampson, Cynthia, and John Paul Lederach, eds. *From the Ground Up: Mennonite Contributions to International Peacebuilding*. New York: Oxford University Press, 2000.

Saunders, Harold. *A Public Peace Process*. London: Macmillan, 1999.

Setianto, Benny D. "Somewhere in Between: Conceptualizing Civil Society." *International Journal of Not-for-Profit Law* 10, no. 1 (2007): 109–118.

Sewell, W. R. "Three Temporalities: Toward an Eventful Sociology." In *The Historic Turn in the Human Sciences*, edited by T. J. McDonald, 245–280. Ann Arbor: University of Michigan Press, 1996.

Shirwa, Abdullahi Mohammed. "Making Peace in the Traditional Somali Way." Mennonite Central Committee *Peace Office Newsletter* 33, no. 2 (2003).

Smith, Steve. "The Contested Concept of Security." In *Critical Security Studies and World Politics*, edited by Ken Booth, 27–62. Boulder, CO: Lynne Rienner Publishers, 2005.

Smock, David. *Religious Perspectives on War*. Washington, DC: US Institute of Peace Press, 1992.

Smock, David. *Interfaith Dialogue and Peacebuilding*. Washington, DC: US Institute of Peace Press, 2002.

Smock, David, and Qamar-ul Huda. "Islamic Peacemaking since 9/11." US Institute of Peace Special Report 218. January 1, 2009.

Tadjbakhsh, Shahrbanou. "International Peacemaking in Tajikistan and Afghanistan Compared: Lessons Learned and Unlearned." Centre d'études et de recherches internationales. Sciences Po. April 2008. http://www.operationspaix.net/DATA/DOCUMENT/5355~v~International_Peacemaking_in_Tajikistan_and_Afghanistan_Compared__Lessons_Learned_and_Unlearned.pdf.

Tadjbakhsh, Shahrbanou, ed. *Rethinking the Liberal Peace: External Models and Local Alternatives*. Oxon: Routledge, 2011.

Tadjbakhsh, Shahrbanou. "Liberal Peace and the Dialogue of the Deaf in Afghanistan." In *Rethinking the Liberal Peace: External Models and Local Alternatives*, edited by Shahrbanou Tadjbakhsh, 206–220. Oxon: Routledge, 2011.

Tarabeih, Hussein, Deborah Shmueli, and Rassem Khamaisi. "Sulha as a Cultural Peacemaking Method for Managing and Resolving Environmental Conflicts among Arab Palestinians in Israel." *Journal of Peacebuilding and Development* 5, no. 1 (2009): 50–64.

Ul-Huda, Qamar, eds. *Crescent and Dove: Peace and Conflict Resolution in Islam*. Washington, DC: United States Institute of Peace Press, 2010.

US Institute of Peace. "Can Faith-Based NGOs Advance Interfaith Reconciliation? The Case of Bosnia and Herzegovina." Special Report 103. March 2003.

US Institute of Peace. "Faith-based NGOs and International Peacebuilding." Special Report 76. October 22, 2001.

Yousufzai, Hassan M., and Ali Gohar. *Towards Understanding Pukhtoon Jirga: An Indigenous Way of Peacebuilding and More. . .* Peshawar, Pakistan: Just Peace International, 2005. peace. fresno.edu/docs/Pukhtoon_Jirga.pdf.

Waldman, Matt. "Community Peacebuilding in Afghanistan: The Case for a National Strategy." Oxfam International Research Report. February 2008. http://www.oxfam.de/files/20080228_communitypeacebuildinginafghanistan_359kb.pdf.

Walker, Polly O. "Decolonizing Conflict Resolution: Addressing the Ontological Violence of Westernization." *American Indian Quarterly* 28, no. 3/4 (2004): 527–550.

Wehr, Paul, and John Paul Lederach. "Mediating Conflict in Central America." In *Resolving International Conflict: The Theory and Practice of Mediation*, edited by Jacob Bercovitch, 55–76. Boulder, CO: Lynne Rienner Publishers, 1996.

Women's Islamic Initiative in Spirituality and Equality. "Jihad Against Violence: Muslim Women's Struggle for Peace." July 2009. http://www.wisemuslimwomen.org/images/uploads/Jihad_against_Violence_Digest%28color%29.pdf.

Zafar Alam Khan. "There Are Different Paths to the Kaaba: Cemalnur Sargut." Interview with Cemalnur Sargut during the International Conference on Sufism. *The Pioneer*, Delhi, India, November 25, 2011. http://www.sufinews.org/paths-to-the-kaabah/.

CHAPTER 18

....

YOUTH AND INTERFAITH
CONFLICT TRANSFORMATION

....

EBOO PATEL AND CASSIE MEYER

MARTIN Luther King Jr. opened his 1959 Palm Sunday sermon at Dexter Avenue Baptist Church in Montgomery with a refrain of the old hymn, "When I Survey the Wondrous Cross," and a reflection on the mystery and darkness of the church's time of waiting for the crucifixion. He ended his sermon with an altar call. "We open the doors of the church now. Is there one who will accept the Christ this morning just as you are? Who will make that decision as we stand and sing together?"[1]

Not atypical bookends, perhaps, to a Palm Sunday sermon in an African American church in the South during the sweltering middle days of the civil rights movement. It is the heart of this sermon, however, that we are primarily interested in. Having just returned from a pilgrimage to India to see the legacy of Gandhi's *Satyagraha* movement of nonviolent resistance, King explained he wanted to spend the bulk of his sermon focusing on Gandhi, for he, "more than anybody else in the modern world, caught the spirit of Jesus Christ and lived it more completely in his life."[2] Elsewhere, King reflected that before coming across Gandhi's work, he had understood Jesus's nonviolent ethic in the Sermon on the Mount to be strictly about interpersonal relationships. Gandhi—who himself was influenced deeply by his understanding of Jesus in the Christian Gospels—suggested to King that it could in fact offer a real strategy for resistance and peacebuilding. King wrote, "Christ furnished the spirit and motivation while Gandhi furnished the method," providing profound inspiration—both spiritual and practical—for King in his leadership.[3] Indeed, King's relationship with those of other faiths and traditions was not limited to his admiration for Gandhi—he marched arm in arm with the Rabbi Abraham Joshua Heschel in Selma, joined the Buddhist monk Thich Nhat Hanh in decrying the Vietnam War, and worked closely with A. Philip Randolph, an organizer of the March on Washington and an atheist who later signed the Humanist Manifesto.

And yet, King's sermon strikes us as radical even fifty years later. Religious diversity, along with contestations of religious belonging, pluralism, and inclusion, has become an increasingly fraught topic in American public discourse and public life, particularly since September 11, 2001. Consider just a few examples circulating during the time of this writing: ongoing illiteracy about President Barack Obama's faith commitments; the unwillingness of many Americans to consider voting for a religious minority or atheist for president; furor across the political spectrum around the connections between religious liberty, access to health care, and reproductive rights.[4] Given how stark religious divides seem today, it is worth recalling the interfaith undercurrents within King's leadership and the American civil rights movement more broadly, and the power of working across lines of difference toward a shared goal.[5] We are struck that King so effortlessly moved from a Christian altar call to hailing Gandhi as "the greatest Christian of the twentieth century [and] not a member of the Christian Church."[6] Without wading into the deep theological waters this claim surely poses, we are interested in how examples of King's work with those of other faiths may offer an additional frame on his legacy, one that complements narratives of him as a civil rights leader, Christian leader, architect of nonviolent resistance, and peacebuilder. What can we take from King's story to imagine what leadership around religious diversity might look like today?

This overlooked frame we call "interfaith leadership," and we define as an interfaith leader someone who is equipped with the relevant knowledge ("interfaith literacy") and skills of mobilization and bridge-building to bring people of diverse religious and nonreligious identities together around issues of shared concern.[7] King offers us a concrete picture of what interfaith leadership might look like and the potential power of such an approach, and examining his accomplishments from this angle prompts the question of how we could foster the development of interfaith leadership today. As religious diversity remains so divisive, in the United States and beyond, we are interested in the role religious and nonreligious actors might play not only in easing tensions, countering bigotry, and diffusing conflict, but also in contributing to a longer-term *justpeace* marked by sustained networks of engagement and social capital between diverse groups.[8] Our purpose in this article is to offer our own constructive framework for the work of interfaith leaders that is attentive to relevant theory as well as clear practical application. We write as practitioners who work for the Chicago-based Interfaith Youth Core (IFYC, www.ifyc.org), but with a keen interest in the theories that inform the strategy, impact, and outcomes of our work. We will begin, then, by acknowledging the context of our work and laying out our understanding of religious pluralism, which is the practical and theoretical goal of our work. From there, we will explore the particular challenges religious diversity poses to peaceful communities within our context; while outright conflict is often not a threat, recent data and research suggest religious diversity poses a real difficulty to social cohesion for diverse communities within the United States. This analysis informs our strategy for building religious pluralism, namely to support interfaith leaders who are equipped to increase appreciative knowledge and positive encounters across lines of difference within their communities. We will then outline our definition of interfaith leadership, and conclude with some reflections on how a movement of leaders committed to building religious pluralism might look.

Before we proceed, it is important to pause and offer a brief description of our work and how it may relate to the broader peacebuilding literature in general, as well as this volume in particular. The organization that we work for, IFYC, focuses on American colleges and universities as a key space for modeling sustainable interfaith cooperation, and college students as key actors in building such cooperation.[9] Therefore our focus will be on religious diversity and peacebuilding in the United States, which will necessarily be concerned primarily with easing tensions and intolerance, and the preventive work of building social capital and routinizing the practices of interfaith cooperation, rather than conflict resolution or post-violence reconciliation work that international interfaith work may entail. Additionally, our work and methodology are shaped by our particular context, one in which religious identity is often framed (explicitly or implicitly) in terms of individual autonomy and choice in a way that may look unfamiliar to many outside of the United States.

However, in focusing primarily on the leadership and agency of young people, and a strategy of movement building, whereby college students are working to catalyze their peers for interfaith action, we find relevant the goal of strategic peacebuilding to "nurture constructive human relationships" so as to lay the groundwork for long-term justice-seeking.[10] In exploring the particular role of religious communities and actors in peacebuilding efforts, Gerard Powers reflects that the important question is not whether religion is a problem in conflict, but the role that religious actors take: "the relevant distinction is. . . between those religious actors who play a negative role in conflict and those who play a positive one—between extremists and non-extremists."[11] In many ways, our organizational mission is to build a growing number of "non-extremists," and to do so in a way that is proactive and catalytic; the more young people equipped with the knowledge, skills, and inspiration of interfaith cooperation, the more likely that interfaith cooperation will become normalized, and religious intolerance, bigotry, and extremism will be marginalized.

Defining Religious Pluralism

Before we explore the particular challenges posed by religious diversity in our context, we must clearly define the good we are moving toward. According to Diana Eck, America is the most religiously diverse country in the world, and the most religiously devout country in the West.[12] In 2008, more than 80 percent of Americans reported that they considered themselves religious, and the diversity of those affiliations only continues to grow.[13] Although diversity is often taken to be a good in and of itself, Eck cautions that diversity is merely descriptive: it may describe the kinds of people in a given society, but tells us nothing certain about how they interact with one another.[14] In light of this, Eck argues we must build what she calls "pluralism," or the active engagement of religious diversity to a constructive end. If diversity is a mere descriptive fact, "pluralism is an achievement" and a normative goal. Building on Eck's definition, in our work we articulate three characteristics of a community characterized by religious pluralism: respect for religious and nonreligious identity, mutually inspiring relationships, and common action around issues of shared social concern.

By *respect for religious and nonreligious identity*, we mean to insist that actors in a community have the freedom to practice and express their distinctive identities—in so far as they are not harmful to others—and a right to an accurate and fair representation of their beliefs, practices, texts, and traditions within the public square. This is first a civic argument: it insists that in a diverse community, individuals and sub-communities should have the opportunity to represent their traditions as they understand them and be allowed the space to nurture appreciation for their distinctiveness and contributions to the wider society. We look to the multiculturalism movement in the United States as an analogy here, which, broadly speaking, maintains that America is a nation made up of—and richer for—the contributions of multiple racial and ethnic communities who contribute positively to the civic fabric. Similarly, we argue for the need to create space for religious and nonreligious communities and actors to offer their own representation of their beliefs and contributions, particularly in light of rancorous public discourse and smear campaigns aimed at many religious and nonreligious minorities. Through the lens of pluralism, America can be seen as a nation stronger for the ways its many religious and nonreligious communities have contributed to institutions that make up our civic fabric, such as hospitals, schools, and social service agencies. It is worth noting that this idea remains in many ways an ideal; the dynamics of power and who in fact has access to the public square matter for whether it becomes a reality. For now, discrimination related to gender, race, age, class, and other characteristics may impinge on the individual's right to such self-expression.

Acknowledging such concerns, respect for others should not lead to a watering down of religious and ethical commitments nor be blindly apologetic about the real differences, disagreements, and shortcomings within diverse traditions. Pluralism must also include space for individuals to believe that they are right and others are wrong, that their beliefs are true and others' are not; this is necessary and pragmatic. If we insist that one has to renounce exclusive truth claims in order to participate in interfaith action or peacebuilding work, we run the risk of bringing into that work only the most liberal of every religious or identity group, which tends to be a minority of religious adherents worldwide. Furthermore, allowing authentic differences ensures that individuals can justify their interfaith work based on the unique and powerful strains within traditions that speak to values like cooperation, reconciliation, and neighbor-love, rather than resorting to a less compelling least-common-denominator approach. As Powers insists, "the solution is not to downplay religious identity but to find those elements within that identity that can contribute to peacebuilding."[15] That said, communities and groups need guidelines for how to navigate these potential inflammatory topics while maintaining a safe space for relationship building; such guidelines should acknowledge that agreement is not necessary. However, an orientation of goodwill should guide participants' interactions when contentious topics arise. Concretely, we ask the college students we work with to generate their own guidelines to maintain the safe space, where something akin to the directive to "acknowledge that others' religious or nonreligious identity and perspectives are as important to them as yours is to you" generally emerges.

Secondly, a community characterized by religious pluralism will be marked by mutually inspiring relationships among people of different backgrounds. As we will explore in more depth in a moment, at least within the United States, it appears diversity can go in multiple ways—toward conflict, toward isolation, or toward cooperation. We mean to be normative about the types of relationships to be sought within a diverse society. In the traditional model for interfaith dialogue, senior religious leaders, often men, from different traditions come together in order to articulate and issue joint statements about how their communities may speak to a given theological tenet or value. As Powers rightly warns, this model often leads to diminishing the distinctiveness of diverse traditions and potentially leading to more division.[16] Instead, in a community marked by pluralism, individuals' relationships are embodied by what Ashutosh Varshney has called "networks of engagement," or the web of connections across lines of difference that may exist in a diverse community.[17] Researching Hindus and Muslims in India, Varshney found these networks to be much stronger when they were "associational"—that is, intentional, institutionalized, and built on deep mutuality, like a Muslim-Hindu phone tree system or neighborhood watch groups—as opposed to "quotidian" (those more casual interactions that happen in a diverse community, such as buying groceries from or having as a doctor someone of a different religious identity). Those communities that had more associational types of relationships were likely to be stronger in the face of tension or conflict at the national level. Positive relationships between people of different religious backgrounds are not simply a hedge against violence or isolation; they are an inspiring good in and of themselves. Broadly speaking, many of the most inspiring images in American public consciousness are cross-racial; when we have in mind the image of King and Heschel marching arm in arm, however, it can both be the image of a black and a white man working together for a common purpose *and* the image of a reverend and a rabbi. Such relationships maintain space for real disagreement but also inspiration, growth, and change. As relationships across lines of difference move beyond a first-time encounter to become authentic friendships, real conversations about differences but also resonances become possible, with a sense that each partner gains from the conversation and relationship.

The third characteristic of pluralism, common action around issues of shared social concern, works to reinforce the space for identity- and relationship-building by activating shared values as a motivation for common action. Robert Putnam and others have argued that religious communities are a huge source of social capital in the United States, fostering ethics of service and volunteerism and building institutions such as schools, hospitals, and social service agencies. Putnam warns, however, that diversity and social capital appear to be *inversely* related, so that the more diverse a given community is, the more likely it is that individuals in that community will withdraw from common life, and in Putnam's words, "hunker down." In his research, not only were the bonds between different groups weakened in a more diverse society (such as across lines of race, ethnicity, or religion, what he calls "bridging social capital"), but "bonding social capital" decreased as well, so that even like groups are less inclined to connect with one another. Generally speaking, the more homogenous a community is, the higher its social capital; the more diverse, the lower its social capital.[18] Left unengaged, a diverse community will be more likely to have weak inter- and intra-communal bonds, and be more susceptible to fracturing in the face of tension or conflict. Acknowledging the need for bridging social capital, Putnam takes Varshney's idea of associational networks a step further, by advocating working together on issues of shared social concern, thereby enacting the shared religious and nonreligious values. With the students we work with, this might mean setting up a sustainable tutoring program with local schools or planting and maintaining a community garden. Not only do such activities reinforce a commitment to the community, but they speak to and create an opportunity to articulate those deeply held religious and ethical values around which students can build deeper relationships. In other words, we imagine the three characteristics of pluralism to be mutually reinforcing.[19]

THE CHALLENGES OF RELIGIOUS DIVERSITY AND THE SCIENCE OF INTERFAITH COOPERATION

The recent public discourse around America's religious diversity—particularly around the role of Muslims in society, but also Mormons, atheists, and countless others—suggests that we cannot simply assume that diversity is a good in and of itself and that there is significant work to be done to build social cohesion and social capital in the face of growing religious diversity. Although America has seen little outright religious conflict, religious diversity poses real challenges to its civic fabric: weaker communities, a decline of social capital, and a tendency toward division or conflict. We are interested, then, in what recent data on American attitudes and behaviors related to religious diversity reveal about how interfaith leaders might overcome these challenges in order to build pluralism. In particular, we will look at a general tendency toward religious illiteracy in America, and attitudes of ambivalence or outright bigotry toward many of the nation's religious groups. From there, we will explore how recent research suggests we may counter these challenges in a way that leads to measurable and reinforcing outcomes.

In a 2010 study conducted by the Pew Forum on Religion and Public Life on Americans' religious knowledge, the average American could correctly answer only half of thirty-two questions meant to test religious literacy.[20] Stephen Prothero famously gives America an "F" on religion and suggests that religious illiteracy is one of the greatest challenges for contemporary civic life.[21] More importantly for our purposes, it appears that religious ignorance is not necessarily benign. Several studies suggest that the amount and type of knowledge one has about a religion correspond to one's attitudes toward that religion. For example, in 2007, 58 percent of Americans said they knew little to nothing about Islam; those who knew less about Islam were significantly more likely to have negative views of Islam or Muslims. Additionally, 48 percent of those who have negative views of Islam say they get their information about Muslims from the media.[22] A recent study out of Ohio State University found that only 28 percent of Americans who believed *false* information about Islam were willing to reject their erroneous beliefs when presented with accurate information, a finding that suggests religious misinformation may be particularly difficult to counter.[23]

Not only do Americans in general suffer from a lack of literacy about diverse religious traditions, but their attitude toward those of other faiths remains ambivalent. On the one hand, Americans at a surface level appear to be relatively tolerant: a 2008 Pew Forum on Religion and Public Life survey finds a majority of Americans to be "non-dogmatic," and nearly 70 percent open to wisdom and truth in other religious traditions. Robert Putnam and David Campbell find 80 percent of Americans to be tolerant of a diversity of religious views.[24] Nevertheless, in a recent Gallup poll, 52 percent of Americans said their view of Islam was unfavorable, and 43 percent admitted to feeling prejudiced toward Muslims.[25] A 2010 Pew report found that favorable opinions of Muslims had decreased between 2005 and 2010 by nearly 10 percentage points, and that unfavorable views had risen.[26] Depending on the survey, evangelical Christians, Mormons, and atheists also do not fare well in the general public perception; it was not that long ago that anti-Semitic and anti-Catholic sentiments would have been clear in American public attitudes. The expression of these attitudes often corresponds to exclusionary actions; we doubt it is a coincidence that American attitudes toward Muslims were on the decline at the same time that outright resistance to Muslim communities increased. Aside from the high-profile resistance to Park51, the proposed Muslim community center in Lower Manhattan, between 2008 and 2010, thirty-five proposed mosques and Islamic centers across America encountered outright resistance from the communities of which they sought to be a part. In many cases, concerns about traffic and noise were cited as the main reason for resistance; fear of Islam, terrorism, and sharia were named outright in others.[27]

The flipside of these concerning trends, however, is that by improving appreciative knowledge, and promoting opportunities for positive, meaningful encounters between people from different religious backgrounds, we may be able to counter the challenges posed by religious diversity and offer a constructive strategy for improving attitudes. Indeed, social science data indicate that there is a strong correlation between attitudes, appreciative knowledge, and meaningful relationships, what we might call the "interfaith triangle." That is, gaining appreciative knowledge of other religions tends to have a measureable, positive effect on one's attitudes toward those religions. Similarly, those who engage in positive relationships with those of diverse backgrounds will as a result likely demonstrate an increase in appreciative knowledge and an improvement in attitudes toward the group as a whole. Thus, attitudes, knowledge, and relationships/behaviors appear to be mutually reinforcing. Further, positive attitudes, appreciative knowledge, and behaviors that build social capital may be the best proxy to measure the strength of pluralism in a community.

As we have noted, the more one knows about a religion, the more likely one is to have a positive view of that religion—but religious misinformation seems to be particularly difficult to counter with correct information. Given this, we are concerned with how to foster knowledge that is amenable to pluralism and relationship building. We call such knowledge "interfaith literacy," an appreciative knowledge of diverse traditions that promotes the values of pluralism. Additionally, we advocate for creating opportunities for the kinds of meaningful encounters that both transform negative or ambivalent attitudes toward religious diversity and build social capital. Just as gaining knowledge about a religious tradition has the power to shift perceptions from negative to positive, actually knowing someone of a particular faith positively impacts one's attitudes towards that tradition as a whole. For example, of the 43 percent of Americans in the 2007 Pew study who reported a favorable view of Muslims, 56 percent had at least one personal relationship with a Muslim. Of the 35 percent with an unfavorable view, only 29 percent had a relationship with a Muslim.[28] Putnam and Campbell refer to this as the "Pal Al" or "Aunt Sue" phenomenon—if one has a friend or family member of a given religious perspective, the more likely one is to have positive attitudes toward that group overall.[29] Personal relationships break down stereotypes and distrust, and help individuals generalize positive attitudes toward the larger group. Further, Putnam and Campbell think these relationships are strongest and have the most influence on broader attitudes when they involve common activities that build social capital. This finding corresponds to more classic theories of inter-group relations suggesting that prejudice and conflict can be overcome by giving individuals on opposing sides opportunities to work together on a common project. Thus, if you not only know but also engage in cooperative work with your "Pal Al," your positive inclination toward others in Pal Al's group will be even stronger.[30]

Given the relationships between attitudes, knowledge, and behaviors, our hypothesis is that we can accelerate the development of pluralism in a community—and in the United States more broadly—by offering programs and projects that seek to leverage appreciative knowledge and positive relationships. At first blush, this might seem intuitive: of course interfaith initiatives with the end goal of building sustained religious pluralism ought to focus on encounters and knowledge. However, such an acknowledgment allows a more data-driven and scientific approach to interfaith cooperation, focusing on those programs and projects that bring communities together around shared values to foster knowledge and relationships. We can begin to ask how interfaith programs can maximize the increase of knowledge and relationships. Furthermore, we can evaluate the kinds of initiatives that will be most effective in building bridged social capital. We may realize, for example, that an interfaith debate about the Middle East is not the most effective tool for building positive relationships and spreading appreciative knowledge. Instead, a program that brings individuals from diverse religious and nonreligious backgrounds together to discuss and enact how their various traditions speak to the shared value of mercy is a more effective approach because it builds appreciative knowledge and positive relationships rather than reinforcing preexisting divisions. Should the interfaith movement, broadly speaking, focus its efforts on these known factors, prioritizing initiatives that increase positive knowledge and foster opportunities for relationships, we think the ideal of interfaith cooperation becoming normative may indeed be a real possibility.

If such efforts were to take place on a large scale, fostered by a grassroots movement of interfaith leaders, precisely what outcomes might we expect? We believe it would be reasonable to see noticeable and measurable changes in Americans' attitudes, knowledge, and behaviors toward religious diversity. For example, more Americans would report that they have a personal relationship with someone from a background different from their own, and they would report engaging in intentional, community-focused activities across lines of religious difference. Americans would fare much better on Pew's religious literacy quiz, and more than that would be able to talk about things they admired about other religious traditions, or articulate values that different traditions share.[31] Further, each of these trends would be mutually reinforcing, so that the more positive encounters one had, the more appreciative knowledge one would gain and the more likely one would be to report positive attitudes toward groups other than their own; the more one knew about diverse religious traditions, the more willing one would be to work with those from different backgrounds, and so on. In other words, by encouraging interfaith leaders to spread appreciative knowledge and to build opportunities for positive encounters in the communities where they work, we believe we may not only see measurable change in attitudes, but communities marked by the characteristics of religious pluralism.

A WORKING DEFINITION OF INTERFAITH LEADERSHIP: SKILLS AND KNOWLEDGE

But in order to make that ideal a reality, we argue there must be a critical mass of actors equipped with the skills and knowledge to work toward religious pluralism in their communities. A central concern of our strategy, then, is to find and support those actors who will create opportunities to foster appreciative knowledge and experience meaningful encounters. As America's religious diversity grows both in scope and divisiveness, an ability to navigate religious diversity in multiple leadership and community settings is becoming a civic imperative. Interfaith leaders, then, are those actors equipped to manage religious diversity and work constructively to build religious pluralism in their communities. We see young people as particularly well equipped to make religious pluralism widely normative, both amongst their peers and as they enter the professional world.[32] First, young people have played significant roles in many other social movements—consider the Student Nonviolent Coordinating Committee's role in the civil rights movement, or how young both King and

Gandhi were when they began organizing. Secondly, young people have a unique lens on the issues surrounding religious diversity. Even as public discourse around religious diversity remains tense, an unprecedented number of American young people have grown up having friendships with people of different faiths. Further, members of the so-called millennial generation (those born in 1981 or later) demonstrate a significant commitment to service and civic engagement, opening up space to connect to the shared values of social action embodied in religious pluralism.[33]

If the task of an interfaith leader, then, is to build appreciative knowledge and create opportunities for positive encounters, what skills and knowledge does she need? We identify three main categories of skills needed for interfaith leadership: (1) the ability to articulate a compelling vision for religious pluralism; (2) the ability to bring people of diverse backgrounds together around common projects, or organizing skills; (3) the ability to bring people of diverse backgrounds together for dialogue, or facilitation skills. Complementary to these, an interfaith leader needs to develop her own "interfaith literacy," a specific framing for knowledge about religious diversity in contrast to mere religious literacy. We categorize such knowledge into four themes for further discussion: (1) a personal theology or ethic of "interfaith cooperation"; (2) appreciative knowledge of diverse religious traditions; (3) knowledge of the shared values between diverse religious traditions; (4) and knowledge of the history or legacy of interfaith cooperation.[34] We will look at each of these pieces in turn.

Given the divisiveness that often surrounds religious diversity, an interfaith leader needs to be able to cast and articulate a constructive vision for religious pluralism, shifting the conversation about the role religion plays in society. Such skills help open up the space for collaboration across lines of religious difference, and essentially tell members of a community that they can build relationships and work together in spite of deep lines of difference or division. When diverse religious leaders took a public stance against the furor surrounding Park51, they were naming the vision of religious pluralism.[35] Sharing a vision for religious pluralism also identifies and claims the powerful and often counter-cultural act of working together across lines of difference. Secondly, an interfaith leader must be able to bring people together in shared activities, the kind of activities that create more "Pal Als," and, in doing so, build social capital. This ability entails concrete skills of community organizing, relationship- and consensus-building, communication, and networking, all while navigating the realities of different religious communities' needs and expectations. The students at the University of Illinois who organized an interfaith action event that brought together thousands of volunteers from diverse backgrounds to package meals for Haiti in the aftermath of the 2010 Haiti earthquake demonstrated these skills.[36] An interfaith leader also must know how to bring a community together in meaningful conversation, creating opportunities for dialogue and relationship-building around common values and diverse identities. It is through such conversations that community members may have the opportunity to learn more about a tradition or identity other than their own, and to build lasting, positive relationships that can then transform their attitudes not just toward individual groups but toward the wider community that each group represents. When coupled with common action—again, the kind of action likely to increase social capital in a community—these conversations can begin with the shared values they have enacted and then open up real discussions about difference even while starting from a place of shared commitment to a community or issue. Many of the skills of interfaith leadership draw from other community-building approaches such as asset-based community development or best practices in community organizing, but with a particular attention to the concerns, practices, and values of the diverse groups that will necessarily be involved in interfaith action.

To understand the imperative of interfaith literacy, that is, the knowledge required of interfaith leadership, we return to the idea of *religious* literacy. While many would agree that religious literacy overall is weak in the United States, there may be some disagreement about the kind of knowledge necessary to remedy that religious illiteracy. For Prothero, religious literacy is a fundamentally civic project: what one knows about religion impacts whether one has the vocabulary to follow presidential races, foreign affairs, domestic politics, and civic issues. Thus, he argues, religious literacy should "stick close to the facts," and explore traditions with an eye to what is most relevant for active engagement in civic life.[37] But if indeed appreciative knowledge plays a part in improving attitudes and behaviors, and we are dealing not just with a lack of knowledge but misinformation, we must work toward the explicitly normative goal of actively cultivating *appreciative* knowledge. Such knowledge should equip an interfaith leader to create spaces where others can build positive attitudes and relationships, and to actively counter stereotypes and misinformation that might hinder interfaith cooperation.

The first facet of interfaith literacy, then, is a theology or ethic of interfaith cooperation, which we understand as a fluency in the resources, stories, texts, and practices in one's own tradition that speak to interfaith cooperation. A theology or ethic of interfaith cooperation makes those pieces salient, interprets and applies them to the contemporary dynamic of religious diversity, and strings them together in a coherent narrative. For some traditions, such an ethic or theology may have a long and weighty history, like the understanding many Muslims have of Christians and Jews as the "people of the Book." For other traditions, as many of the evangelical Christian students we work with insist, the line of thinking is there within a tradition's orthodoxy, but has not always found a clear voice. Many of the young people we work with wonder whether they come to interfaith work simply because they are generally tolerant, progressive young people who grew up amidst relative religious diversity and are therefore simply predisposed to undertake interfaith work due to their context. From this perspective, interfaith work may seem tangential—rather than integral—to their particular religious or nonreligious identity. The question of how to engage with religious diversity in America in the twenty-first century is in many ways a new question, but that does not mean that there are not resources available within traditions that can help develop a coherent and authentic expression of interfaith cooperation. A theology or ethic of interfaith cooperation allows an interfaith leader to articulate answers to questions around religious diversity in ways that make sense of a tradition or community's religious commitments, and offer an imperative for action.

The second facet of interfaith literacy is an appreciative knowledge of diverse religious traditions. In *Toward a True Kinship of Faiths: How the World's Religions Can Come Together*, the Dalai Lama recounts being disturbed by violence he saw committed in the name of Islam.[38] At the same time, he did not feel comfortable dismissing the entirety of a world religion as inherently violent and destructive. Realizing the shallowness of his personal knowledge of Islam, he began to study: reading the Qur'an more closely, looking for themes of compassion in the tradition, and uncovering stories of mercy and justice. Whereas religious literacy may begin with the basic tenets and practices of major religious traditions, interfaith literacy focuses on those texts, practices, leaders, and stories that speak to widely shared values such as compassion and hospitality, or cultural contributions of a given tradition to, for example, art or literature. Such an approach need not be overly apologetic, skimming over the real difficulties or complexities of a given tradition. Rather, recognizing that much of what is "known" about many religious minorities is either negative or incorrect, we see knowledge of what is beautiful in diverse traditions as a powerful tool for those seeking to build religious pluralism to gain for themselves and to cultivate in others.

Thirdly, interfaith literacy involves comparisons, asking what one can learn by looking at the ways that different traditions speak to values important to shared life or the "common good." Such an approach might explore how Christianity, Islam, Hinduism, and atheism, for example, all have something to say about values like compassion, justice, love, or mercy, and articulate such values not only as a counter to the narrative that religious diversity necessitates violence, but also as a call to common action. Many of these are deeply powerful, motivating values for practitioners of these traditions, and may offer a theological or spiritual connection to the work of interfaith cooperation. Focusing on commonalities should not lead to downplaying the differences between traditions, but rather consider how the particular theologies, stories, and practices related to shared values also uncover real difference between traditions. What Christianity has to say about compassion, embodied in God's love for humanity on the cross, is not the same thing as what Islam says in naming God "the most compassionate, the most merciful" in the most commonly recited prayer in the tradition. There are irreconcilable theological differences. That said, both perspectives offer rich motivation to engage in real work to enact compassion in a local community. People from different religious traditions may live out values in common, even while prizing their particularity; an interfaith leader should be able to identify these values, articulate her own tradition's understandings of them, know at least broadly how other traditions understand these values, and prompt reflections in others to this end.

The final component of interfaith literacy seeks to highlight the many moments in history when faith communities and leaders have worked together to enact shared values. From King's first attention to the power of nonviolent resistance in Gandhi to King's collaboration with Rabbi Heschel, interfaith relationships were a powerful instrument for social change in one of the most poignant social change movements in American history. Similarly, the story of peaceful interfaith coexistence in Cordoba, Spain, in medieval Europe is often lost in the contemporary story of conflict between Christians, Muslims, and Jews. Again, such an approach need not be blindly apologetic, but should propose that amid the better-known stories of conflict, there are also rich stories of cooperation that can inspire and prompt interfaith cooperation today.

Though not the primary focus of this chapter, our organizational strategy focuses on colleges and universities as a central institution to building religious pluralism in the United States, and it is worth pausing to explore the unique role higher education can play in developing interfaith leadership among young people. If indeed cultivating appreciative knowledge and positive encounters are the key strategies for building religious pluralism within our context, American colleges and universities offer a unique opportunity for training young people as interfaith leaders and creating opportunities to practice interfaith cooperation. Many campuses serve as microcosms of America's broader religious diversity, where students of different religious and nonreligious backgrounds regularly interact with one another in close quarters, often for the first time. This happens in a place where they are encouraged to question, challenge, and explore their own identities and those of others. If students practice a faith in college, it is often because they have deliberately chosen to, rather than resulting from family expectations or habit. In other words, questions of identity, diversity, and relationships may be raised both organically and provocatively by the simple reality of the campus context. Further, one way of understanding higher education is in terms of its civic role: it educates students for global citizenship, contributes to the common good, and strengthens social cohesion. Such education demands an engagement with the reality of religious diversity as well as creates ample opportunity to advance both the appreciative knowledge and meaningful encounters that religious pluralism requires. For campuses that are concerned not just with the knowledge students obtain in the classroom, but also the kinds of relationships they will have on campus and the ways they will be involved in their communities beyond graduation, engaging religious diversity proactively should be a key priority. Institutions of higher education have already played a leadership role in many of the social change movements of the past; campuses have proactively engaged topics such as multiculturalism, LGBTQ issues, gender equality, and environmental sustainability, leading to culture shifts around each of these issues and giving an imperative and model for campuses to engage religious diversity. If colleges and universities engage religious diversity with the same ambition and resources that they dedicate to other diversity or civic issues, they can make a lasting impact beyond the sphere of higher education to the broader culture.

We have argued that we are in need of a concrete strategy to address the challenges of religious diversity in the United States and that social science research gives us cues into the kinds of strategies that may be effective in that effort: building opportunities for positive encounters and increasing appreciative knowledge. As an organization, our strategy is to cultivate college students as interfaith leaders who have the skills and knowledge to create opportunities for their peers to engage constructively with religious diversity, and to see colleges and universities as the key institution to support this leadership development work. The framework we have laid out names highly specialized skills and knowledge, and considers interfaith literacy in particular as an ongoing project of leadership development. We also recognize there will be a small subset of the young people we work with or who are involved in interfaith work who will have cultivated these skills at a young age. For this reason, much of the work we do with student leaders is spent fostering a long-term commitment to interfaith leadership that can play out across multiple vocations, exploring what it means to be an interfaith leader beyond college, for example as an educator, a doctor, a politician, or a clergy person. Indeed, this is part of why we find the image of King—and the civil rights movement more broadly— to be such a resonant story in our work: it is a movement wherein, at least in certain moments and relationships, religious pluralism does indeed look normative, and interfaith leaders were able to harness the power of religious diversity to contribute to real social change. It is also a story of a movement where young people were authentic agents of change, and where there was a sustained attempt to value diverse leadership styles and actors. Though the work of the civil rights movement surely remains unfinished, we are heartened by the possibility of what a movement of young people today, committed to their own identities, to one another, and to shared social concerns, might do to create real and sustainable change.

CONCLUSION: KING AS INTERFAITH LEADER

We close with a return to the story we opened with: of the Rev. Martin Luther King Jr. as an interfaith leader. To see his ability to articulate a compelling vision for religious pluralism, consider King's image of the "world house" from his Nobel Peace Prize lecture, and note how salient he considers connections between not just diverse racial identities, but also diverse religious identities:

> This is the great new problem of mankind. We have inherited a big house, a great "world house" in which we have to live together—black and white, Easterners and Westerners, Gentiles and Jews, Catholics and Protestants, Moslem [sic] and Hindu, a family unduly separated in ideas, culture, and interest who, because we can never again live without each other, must learn, somehow, in this one big world, to live with each other.[39]

King's skills of bringing those of different backgrounds together are so obvious they need little description, except to mention again the numerous and deliberate ways in which he sought common ground with individuals deeply committed to faith or philosophical traditions that differed vastly from his own Baptist Christianity. King also embodies interfaith literacy—from his appreciative knowledge of Hinduism as embodied in his admiration for Gandhi, to the way he activated shared values between different traditions when he stood with Buddhist Vietnamese monks in opposition to the Vietnam War. As he wrote in "A Time to Break Silence," love was the motivating factor behind his nonviolent work:

> When I speak of love I am not speaking of some sentimental and weak response. I am speaking of that force which all of the great religions have seen as the supreme unifying principle of life.. . . This Hindu-Moslem-Christian-Jewish-Buddhist [sic] belief about the ultimate reality is beautifully summed up in the first epistle of St. John: "Let us love one another; for love is God and everyone that loveth is born of God and knoweth God. . ."[40]

King's articulation of the "beloved community" can be understood as his articulation of a theology of interfaith cooperation, and his reflection on the *Satyagraha* movement and the involvement of those of different faiths in his Palm Sunday Sermon as a knowledge of the legacy of interfaith cooperation.

We end, reflecting that King's journey of interfaith leadership arguably started while he was just a college student at Morehouse College, where he first heard the story of Gandhi from the President of Morehouse, Benjamin Mays, who was a great admirer of the Mahatma. Just a few years later—when he was only thirty—he closed his Palm Sunday Sermon with this prayer: "O God, our gracious heavenly father, we thank thee for the fact that you have defined men and women in all nations, in all cultures. We call you this name. Some call thee Allah, some call you Elohim. Some call you Jehovah, some call you Brahma. Some call you the Unmoved Mover."[41]

Notes

1. King, Martin Luther, Jr., "Palm Sunday Sermon on Mohandas K. Gandhi, Delivered at Dexter Avenue Baptist Church." *The Martin Luther King, Jr. Papers Project*. March 22, 1959. http://mlk-kpp01.stanford.edu/primarydocuments/Vol5/22Mar1959_PalmSundaySermononMohandasK.Gandhi,DeliveredAtDext.pdf.
2. King, "Palm Sunday Sermon."
3. Quoted in Charles Marsh, *The Beloved Community: How Faith Shapes Social Justice, From the Civil Rights Movement to Today* (New York: Basic Books, 2005), 45.
4. See, for example: Frank Newport, "Many Americans Can't Name Obama's Religion," *Gallup Politics*, published June 22, 2012, accessed June 29, 2012, http://www.gallup.com/poll/155315/Many-Americans-Cant-Name-Obamas-Religion.aspx.   Jeffrey M. Jones, "Atheists, Muslims, See Most Bias as Presidential Candidates," *Gallup*, published June 21, 2012, http://www.gallup.com/poll/155285/Atheists-Muslims-Bias-Presidential-Candidates.aspx.
5. "Interfaith" is the term we use to describe work, dialogue, or other community-building interactions between people of different religious and non-religious identities. Though the language is imperfect, we find "interfaith" to be more inclusive than "inter-religious," as many atheists, agnostic, humanists, etc., do not consider themselves religious, but are willing to grant "faith" in, for example, human worth and dignity.
6. King, "Palm Sunday Sermon."
7. Though potentially noninclusive and cumbersome, we use "nonreligious" to refer to those who identify as atheist, agnostic, humanist, or otherwise for whom "religious" would not be a proper descriptor. While our organization's early work focused strictly on young people who claimed strong affiliation with one religious community or another, we soon found many young people who did not identify as religious, or who identified as "spiritual but not religious," interested in doing interfaith work and who found little resonance with the assumed divide between religious and secular people and communities. Additionally, as the so-called Nones are the fastest-growing "religious" identity within the millennial generation, such an approach allows us to be inclusive of a growing swath of our constituency. For the view of a young atheist (and alumnus of IFYC's programming) on why the nonreligious should be involved in interfaith work, see Chris Stedman, *Faithiest: How an Atheist Found Common Ground with the Religious* (Boston: Beacon, 2012). For more on the faith (or non-faith) identity of young people, see Christian Smith, *Souls in Transition: The Religious and Spiritual Lives of Emerging Adults* (Oxford: Oxford University Press, 2009).
8. Drawing from John Paul Lederach and R. Scott Appleby, we understand "justpeace" as a sustainable culture of peace that strategically and actively engages multiple layers of society. John Paul Lederach and R. Scott Appleby, "Strategic Peacebuilding: An Overview," in *Strategies of Peace: Transforming Conflict in a Violent World*, ed. Daniel Philpott and Gerard F. Powers (Oxford: Oxford University Press, 2010), 23–24.
9. For a lengthier discussion of our understanding of the role that colleges and universities can play in making interfaith cooperation normative in this country, see Eboo Patel and Cassie Meyer, "The Civic Relevance of Interfaith Cooperation for Colleges and Universities," *The Journal of College and Character* 12, no. 1 (2011): 1–9. doi:10.2202/1940-1639.1764.
10. Lederach and Appleby, "Strategic Peacebuilding," 22.

11. Gerard F. Powers, "Religion and Peacebuilding," in *Strategies of Peace: Transforming Conflict in a Violent World*, ed. Daniel Philpott and Gerard F. Powers (Oxford: Oxford University Press, 2010).

12. Diana Eck, *A New Religious America* (San Francisco: HarperCollins, 2001), 2.

13. Pew Forum on Religion and Public Life, *U.S. Religious Landscape Survey* (Washington, DC: Pew Research Center, 2008), 12.

14. Diana Eck, "What is Pluralism?" *The Pluralism Project at Harvard University*, n.d., accessed June 29, 2012, http://pluralism.org/pages/pluralism/what_is_pluralism.

15. Powers, "Religion and Peacebuilding," 341.

16. Powers, "Religion and Peacebuilding," 340.

17. Ashutosh Varshney, *Ethnic Conflict and Civic Life: Hindus and Muslims in India* (New Haven: Yale University Press, 2003).

18. Robert Putnam, "*E Pluribus Unum*: Diversity and Community in the 21st Century," *Scandinavian Political Studies* 30, no. 2 (2007): 137–174. doi: 10.1111/j.1467-9477.2007.00176.x.

19. Finding issues of "common concern" is often not without contention. For example, at a recent IFYC Interfaith Leadership Institute (three- to four-day conferences to gather and train student leaders and their campus allies in interfaith leadership and organizing skills), we had students advocating for interfaith work around gay rights out of a conviction that their traditions embody love and inclusion, and other students advocating for interfaith work to oppose the Patient Protection and Affordable Care Act out of concern that it violated core religious freedoms. In such a situation, we push students to consider that if religious pluralism is indeed the end goal, they should work on projects that will be the most inclusive of those of diverse religious (and therefore political) views. This is not to downplay the reality that such divisive and also significant issues are often interlaced with students' religious or nonreligious identities and values, but to ask students to work through conflicting agendas, goals, and values in light of the goal of pluralism. Such an approach also seeks deeper relationship-building that may indeed help students to tackle dividing issues with a renewed commitment to their relationships and stronger social capital. In other words, if two students build a house together and talk about why they care about that project and *then* have a conversation about gay rights, abortion, Israel-Palestine, etc., their relationship may be bolstered to handle the stresses of the conversation.

20. Pew Forum on Religion and Public Life, *U.S. Religious Knowledge Survey* (Washington, DC: Pew Research Center, 2010).

21. Stephen Prothero, *Religious Literacy: What Every American Needs to Know—And Doesn't* (New York: Harper Collins, 2007).

22. "Public Expresses Mixed Views of Islam, Mormonism," Pew Forum on Religion and Public Life, published September 25, 2007, accessed June 29, 2012, http://www.pewforum.org/Public-Expresses-Mixed-Views-of-Islam-Mormonism.aspx.

23. Erik Nisbet and Kelly Garrett. *Belief in Rumors Hard to Dispel: Fact Checking Easily Undermined by Images, Unrelated Facts* (Columbus: Ohio State University, 2010).

24. Pew, *U.S. Religious Landscape Survey*; Robert Putnam and David Campbell, *American Grace: How Religion Divides and Unites Us* (New York: Simon & Schuster, 2010).

25. "In U.S., Religious Prejudice Stronger Against Muslims," Gallup Center for Muslim Studies, published January 21, 2010, accessed June 29, 2012, http://www.gallup.com/poll/125312/religious-prejudice-stronger-against-muslims.aspx.

26. "Public Remains Conflicted Over Islam," Pew Forum on Religion and Public Life, published August 24, 2010, accessed June 29, 2012, http://www.pewforum.org/Muslim/Public-Remains-Conflicted-Over-Islam.aspx.

27. "Controversies Over Mosques and Islamic Centers in the U.S.," Pew Forum on Religion and Public Life, published September 29, 2011, accessed June 29, 2012, http://features.pew-forum.org/muslim/controversies-over-mosque-and-islamic-centers-across-the-us.html.

28. "Mixed Views of Islam, Mormonism," Pew.

29. Putnam and Campbell, *American Grace*.

30. See Putnam, "*E Pluribus Unum*"; Putnam and Campbell, *American Grace*; and Muzafer Sherif et al., *The Robbers Cave Experiment: Intergroup Conflict and Cooperation* (Middletown, CT: Wesleyan University Press, 1988).

31. IFYC is in the second year of administering a survey on religious diversity at colleges and universities, the Campus Religious and Spiritual Climate Survey, that measures students' attitudes, knowledge, and behavior toward religious diversity and allows campuses to measure the effectiveness and impact of their programming. We offer the survey in partnership with two researchers, Dr. Alyssa Rockenbach of North Carolina State University and Dr. Matthew Mayhew at New York University. Our ultimate goal is to do national benchmarking as well as longitudinal research to measure the impact of interfaith programming on young people's attitudes across the country and over time. Information on the survey is available at www.ifyc.org/crscs.

32. Patel and Meyer, "Civic Relevance."

33. Andrea Stone, "'Civic Generation' Rolls Up Sleeves in Record Numbers," USAToday.com, published April 19, 2009, accessed June 29, 2012, http://www.usatoday.com/news/sharing/2009-04-13-millenial_N.htm.

34. Recognizing that what constitutes a tradition is itself contested, and keeping in mind the pragmatic, civic goal of our work, when we talk about "knowledge" of a tradition, we are interested primarily in knowledge shaped by lived religion (how practitioners in a given context interpret and embody their traditions within that context) and those texts, stories, and traditions that may be interpreted as contributing to pluralism. This is particularly important when working with our demographic, American young people, who often lack literacy about their own inherited or adopted traditions, let alone those of others. At the same time, we are making a normative claim that religious traditions have resources that contribute to a theology or ethic of pluralism or cooperation.

35. Laurie Goodstein, "Concern is Voiced Over Religious Intolerance," *New York Times*, published September 17, 2010, accessed June 29, 2012, http://www.nytimes.com/2010/09/08/us/08muslim.html

36. Mohammad Jaber, "First Person: Taking Part in One Million Meals for Haiti," *The Online Gargoyle*, published April 29, 2010, accessed June 29, 2012, http://www.uni.illinois.edu/og/features/2010/04/first-person-taking-part-million-.

37. Prothero, *Religious Literacy*, 173.

38. His Holiness the Dalai Lama, *Toward a True Kinship of Faiths: How the World's Religions Can Come Together* (New York: Random House, 2010).

39. King, Martin Luther, Jr., "The Quest for Peace and Justice" (Nobel Peace Prize Lecture, Oslo, Norway, December 11, 1964), accessed June 29, 2012, http://www.nobelprize.org/nobel_prizes/peace/laureates/1964/king-lecture.html.

40. King, Martin Luther, Jr., "A Time to Break Silence," in *A Testament of Hope: The Essential Writings and Speeches of Martin Luther King Jr.*, ed. James M. Washington (San Francisco: Harper San Francisco, 1986), 243.

41. Taylor Branch, *Parting the Waters: America in the King Years, 1954–62* (New York: Simon & Schuster, 1988), 255.

BIBLIOGRAPHY

Branch, Taylor. *Parting the Waters: America in the King Years, 1954–62.* New York: Simon and Schuster, 1988.

"Controversies Over Mosques and Islamic Centers in the U.S." Pew Forum on Religion and Public Life. Last modified September 29, 2011. http://features.pewforum.org/muslim/controversies-over-mosque-and-islamic-centers-across-the-us.html.

Eck, Diana. *A New Religious America: How a "Christian Country" Has Become the World's Most Religiously Diverse Nation.* San Francisco: HarperCollins, 2001.

Eck, Diana. "What is Pluralism?" The Pluralism Project at Harvard University. N.d. http://pluralism.org/pages/pluralism/what_is_pluralism.

Goodstein, Laurie. "Concern is Voiced Over Religious Intolerance." *New York Times,* September 17, 2010. http://www.nytimes.com/2010/09/08/us/08muslim.html.

His Holiness the Dalai Lama. *Toward a True Kinship of Faiths: How the World's Religions Can Come Together.* New York: Random House, 2010.

"In U.S., Religious Prejudice Stronger Against Muslims." Gallup Center for Muslim Studies. Last modified January 21, 2010. http://www.gallup.com/poll/125312/religious-prejudice-stronger-against-muslims.aspx.

Jaber, Mohammad. "First Person: Taking Part in One Million Meals for Haiti." *The Online Gargoyle,* April 29, 2010. http://www.uni.illinois.edu/og/features/2010/04/first-person-taking-part-million-.

Jones, Jeffrey M. "Atheists, Muslims, See Most Bias as Presidential Candidates." Gallup, June 21, 2012. http://www.gallup.com/poll/155285/Atheists-Muslims-Bias-Presidential-Candidates.aspx.

King, Martin Luther, Jr. "A Time to Break Silence." In *A Testament of Hope: The Essential Writings and Speeches of Martin Luther King Jr.,* edited by James M. Washington, 231–244. San Francisco: Harper, 1986.

King, Martin Luther, Jr. "Palm Sunday Sermon on Mohandas K. Gandhi, Delivered at Dexter Avenue Baptist Church." The Martin Luther King, Jr. Papers Project, March 22, 1959. http://mlk-kpp01.stanford.edu/primarydocuments/Vol5/22Mar1959_PalmSundaySermonon-MohandasK.Gandhi,DeliveredAtDext.pdf.

King, Martin Luther, Jr. "The Quest for Peace and Justice." Nobel Peace Prize Lecture, Oslo, Norway, December 11, 1964. http://www.nobelprize.org/nobel_prizes/peace/laureates/1964/king-lecture.html.

Lederach, John Paul and R. Scott Appleby. "Strategic Peacebuilding: An Overview." In *Strategies of Peace: Transforming Conflict in a Violent World,* edited by Daniel Philpott and Gerard F. Powers, 19–44. Oxford: Oxford University Press, 2010.

Marsh, Charles. *The Beloved Community: How Faith Shapes Social Justice, From the Civil Rights Movement to Today.* New York: Basic Books, 2005.

Newport, Frank. "Many Americans Can't Name Obama's Religion." Gallup Politics, June 22, 2012. http://www.gallup.com/poll/155315/Many-Americans-Cant-Name-Obamas-Religion.aspx.

Nisbet, Erik and Kelly Garrett. *Belief in Rumors Hard to Dispel: Fact Checking Easily Undermined by Images, Unrelated Facts.* Columbus: Ohio State University, 2010.

Patel, Eboo and Cassie Meyer. "The Civic Relevance of Interfaith Cooperation for Colleges and Universities." *The Journal of College and Character* 12, no. 1 (2011): 1–9. doi:10.2202/1940-1639.1764.

Pew Forum on Religion and Public Life. *U.S. Religious Landscape Survey*. Washington, DC: Pew Research Center, 2008.

Pew Forum on Religion and Public Life. *U.S. Religious Knowledge Survey*. Washington, DC: Pew Research Center, 2010.

Powers, Gerard F. "Religion and Peacebuilding." In *Strategies of Peace: Transforming Conflict in a Violent World*, edited by Daniel Philpott and Gerard F. Powers, 317–352. Oxford: Oxford University Press, 2010.

Prothero, Stephen. *Religious Literacy: What Every American Needs to Know—And Doesn't*. New York: Harper Collins, 2007.

"Public Expresses Mixed Views of Islam, Mormonism." Pew Forum on Religion and Public Life. Last modified September 25, 2007. http://www.pewforum.org/Public-Expresses-Mixed-Views-of-Islam-Mormonism.aspx.

"Public Remains Conflicted Over Islam." Pew Forum on Religion and Public Life. Last modified August 24, 2010. http://www.pewforum.org/Muslim/Public-Remains-Conflicted-Over-Islam.aspx.

Putnam, Robert. "*E Pluribus Unum*: Diversity and Community in the 21st Century." *Scandinavian Political Studies* 30, no. 2 (2007): 137–174. doi: 10.1111/j.1467-9477.2007.00176.x.

Putnam, Robert and David Campbell. *American Grace: How Religion Divides and Unites Us*. New York: Simon & Schuster, 2010.

Sherif, Muzafer, O.J. Harvey, B. Jack White, William R. Hood, and Carolyn W. Sherif. *The Robbers Cave Experiment: Intergroup Conflict and Cooperation*. Middletown, CT: Wesleyan University Press, 1988.

Smith, Christian. *Souls in Transition: The Religious and Spiritual Lives of Emerging Adults*. Oxford: Oxford University Press, 2009.

Stone, Andrea. "'Civic Generation' Rolls Up Sleeves in Record Numbers." USAToday.com, April 19, 2009. Accessed June 29, 2012. http://www.usatoday.com/news/sharing/2009-04-13-millenial_N.htm.

Stedman, Chris. *Faithiest: How an Atheist Found Common Ground with the Religious*. Boston: Beacon, 2012.

Varshney, Ashutosh. *Ethnic Conflict and Civic Life: Hindus and Muslims in India*. New Haven: Yale University Press, 2003.

CHAPTER 19

....

THE POSSIBILITIES AND LIMITS OF INTER-RELIGIOUS DIALOGUE

....

PETER OCHS

WHEN we refer to inter-religious or interfaith dialogue, do we mean inter-*cultural* dialogue or inter-*religious* dialogue?[1] And if these refer to different kinds of dialogue, which is most pertinent to inter-religious peacebuilding? This essay explores a single, somewhat narrow line of response to these questions. It is a study of what, with a twinkle of the eye, I will dub "hearth-to-hearth dialogue." This is dialogue that is not only inter-religious but also one that emerges from places of maximal warmth, depth, and fire within each religious community and tradition that is engaged in the dialogue. I shall report on a twenty-year experiment in nurturing this kind of dialogue, what a group of us formally calls "scriptural reasoning" (SR).[2] I shall characterize SR as at once the potentially most dangerous form of inter-religious dialogue *and* the one that, when handled properly, is most likely to contribute to long-term conflict transformation.

First, a note on what this chapter is not addressing. I am not examining forms of religious dialogue that could be characterized as forms of cultural sharing: for example, when two or more groups discuss their beliefs or practices or when such groups gather for the sake of discovering what they share in common. These forms of dialogue are religious in the sense that they address the behaviors of people formed by religious communities. According to the definitions I employ in this chapter, however, they are not religious in the strict sense of pertaining directly to "the human response to a reality perceived as sacred."[3] I will define the sacred as pertaining to that feature of religion that is strictly unassimilable to any other aspect of human experience and inter-religious dialogue as dialogue between places of sacrality within each religion. What "sacrality" means will be articulated only within the terms each religion brings to the dialogue, and that dialogue, alone, will display what it means for one source of sacrality to converse, as it were, with another. I introduce the term "hearth" as part of an analytic or etic vocabulary for commenting *about* the shape of inter-religious dialogue, not as a substitute for any indigenous terms for sacrality. We may find, moreover, that the space of sacrality that is invoked through these dialogues is not named at all by the traditions and that, in practice, our term "hearth-to-hearth" names a manner of interaction that can be recognized only by its consequences.

I am not, furthermore, examining dialogue *about* the beliefs individuals hold within religious communities.[4] I assume that, once beliefs are articulated in language through an individual's voice, it is no longer possible to judge whether or not these beliefs characterize *religiosity* per se. There is no formal way to distinguish statements of religious beliefs from statements of philosophical or cultural or other kinds of belief.[5] What an individual verbalizes *as* religious belief may behave in effect like any other cultural practice, and what an individual verbalizes *as* extra-religious may behave effectively as an expression of religiosity. My interest is in religiosity as a category of effective behavior, judged by its fruits in practice, rather than in what individuals intend when they say something. The goal of this study is to explore the possibility of conducting dialogues between the "hearths" of religious groups. These are sources of dialogue that are irreducible to any category of experience, cognition, or feeling other than that which is unique to religiosity per se. My working hypothesis is that such points of religiosity are specific to social entities ("religious communities") and that each social entity articulates its "religiosity" in a unique way. This means that one mark of religiosity is uniqueness and that one mark of uniqueness is "that which can be articulated in no other way," or that which is "unassimilable" to all other uses of language. If I were about to write a paper demonstrating the character of such an anomaly, the most I could do is depict a possible world or what might conceivably be or not be. But I belong to a society of scholars who have worked for twenty years to articulate and test the postulate that we can observe and measure such a world and that our observations and measurements of it are directly pertinent to any inter-religious dialogue that is conducted for the sake of peacebuilding.[6]

Observers of SR sometimes ask if our scriptural reasoning practices are "natural" to each of the participating scriptural traditions. My response is that if SR were already natural to these traditions, the world would be a much safer place and we would not have had to do this work on SR. Observers may then ask how SR differs from other colonializing efforts to impose models of peace from outside the religions in question. My response is to say: thank you, this question enables me to identify what is most distinctive about SR. SR is accompanied by a universe of discourse that includes relative terms like "inner and outer," "indigenous and outsider," "emic and etic," but it does not define these as contradictory pairs that need always appear in contrast sets. This universe of discourse also allows conjoining these terms so that they may legitimately refer to something (a practice, a relation) that is inner *and* outer, and so on. As for the matter at hand, we say that SR is introduced artificially: facilitators invite participants from all three Abrahamic traditions to share in a practice they have previously never tried, or perhaps even considered. But we have also observed that, over time and contrary to their expectations, participants tend to claim that, while their tradition lacks any term for something like SR, the practice seems to fall within the bounds of authorized or legitimate behavior and appears, in fact, to strengthen traditional faith even while it stimulates collegial bonds across the borders of the traditions. In other words, participants tend to experience SR as something unprecedented but nonetheless acceptable.[7]

Inter-religious dialogue as typically understood is comparable to peace negotiations sponsored by a diplomatic corps or some NGO. There tend to be three parties in such dialogues: participants from two religions in conflict plus those who sponsor the dialogue. Hearth-to-hearth dialogue works the same way; it is constructed artificially by sponsors who seek to introduce something relatively new into the world. The goal of hearth-to-hearth dialogue is, therefore, not to eliminate third-party sponsors but to reduce the degree to which third-party notions of peace, dialogue, or religion influence the terms of the dialogue. To this end, hearth-to-hearth dialogue is informed by a set of procedures and strategies rather than by a predetermined set of ethical, political, or metaphysical postulates about the nature of religion, dialogue, or peace. By way of introduction, here is a skeletal outline of the procedures of hearth-to-hearth dialogue.

- The setting is some form of conflict between members of two or more religious groups.
- Some third party (peopled by individuals from these communities or from another group or society altogether) enters into working relations with some subset of participants from these groups. I will refer to the third party as "the sponsor," and members of groups in conflict as "participants."
- Through various field-specific activities, over a given period of time, the sponsor gains the trust and interest of appropriate subgroups from each of the participants.
- Participants are invited to engage in a series of meetings extended over some period of time. While the goal of these meetings is to effect some inter-religious, political change in real time, each meeting also serves immediate purposes. For participants, meetings should be occasions of dialogue and study, aspects of which should be appealing and interesting beyond their consequences for peace. For sponsors, each meeting should serve as a *laboratory* in the development and testing of the hearth-to-hearth approach to dialogue. In the case of inter-Abrahamic dialogue, for example, participants from the Society for Scriptural Reasoning (SSR) have found it intrinsically enjoyable to share in periods of inter-Abrahamic study. Sponsors of the SSR have, at the same time, instituted sessions of scriptural study as laboratories that test and refine methods of scriptural study as practices of peacebuilding. Here, the term "laboratory" should carry the connotations of something like a chemistry lab: an artificial environment set up by researchers to test certain theories about the consequences of bringing a certain set of chemicals into relation with certain others under certain environmental conditions.[8]
- In the hearth-to-hearth laboratory, sponsors seek to test if and how certain forms of inter-religious study will serve as occasions of encounter between sources of sacrality in two or more religious traditions. Part of the research is to test theories about how to measure the presence of such sources of sacrality as well as how to measure the effects of their interaction.
- Scriptural reasoning names a form of inter-religious peacebuilding that emerges between such points of sacrality. After twenty years of testing, members of the SSR believe that they have ascertained procedures for identifying how to construct peacebuilding dialogues between any given set of religious communities. Even after twenty years, however, this testing is incomplete, since it has been applied to a broad range of contexts *except* for the processes of peacebuilding in the context of heated regional conflict. Engaging with the work of peacebuilding entities such as the University of Notre Dame's Kroc Institute for International Peace Studies is therefore of great significance for participants in SR, since such entities specialize in approaches to conflict transformation in regions of this kind. The goal of this chapter is, in dialogue with members of the Kroc Institute, to offer testable hypotheses about how to extend the work of the SSR into regions of immediate conflict.

HEARTH-TO-HEARTH DIALOGUE
IN INTER-RELIGIOUS DIPLOMACY

In this, the primary section of the chapter, I offer a four-step argument for taking inter-religious dialogue seriously as an agent of inter-religious conflict transformation. I introduce scriptural reasoning (SR) as one effective set of guidelines for conducting this dialogue.

1. It Is Time to Change the Standard Western Paradigm for Resolving Inter-Religious Conflict

Throughout most of the past century, European and American international diplomacy has tended to follow the Enlightenment account of religion and violence. The account goes somewhat like this. *The problem: Religion incites violence.* It does so because religion is a source of deep and irreconcilable differences among different individuals, communities, and peoples. Differences stimulate disagreement. Religion invests disagreement with a maximal degree of passion. Impassioned, irreconcilable disagreement leads to violence. *The solution: Minimize differences among individuals, communities, and peoples in conflict.* Seek, therefore, to minimize the presence and or influence of religion in any process of diplomacy or peace.

In the past three decades, an increasing number and range of scholarly voices have called for a change in this paradigm for diplomacy: philosophers have offered a general critique of the Enlightenment paradigm, and scholars of peacebuilding have completed the critique by demonstrating the efficacy of inter-religious conflict transformation. For example, the philosopher and public intellectual Charles Taylor has written that modernity's wholly negative portrayal of religion emerged not from dispassionate scientific study of the character of religious behavior and the phenomena of violence, but from a worldview that presumed, a priori, that religion is its adversary. One expression of this worldview is what Max Weber called the "secularization hypothesis"—that, as the practices of Enlightenment reasoning spread further and further, Western society will come increasingly to reject religion as an expression of mere superstition that is unmasked and replaced by the clear light of reason.[9] In *A Secular Age*, Taylor argues that the secularization hypothesis has been disconfirmed by the steady persistence of religion since the Enlightenment and, moreover, by the global expansion of religion at the very same time that Western civilization's rational discourses have extended around the globe.[10] In *The Myth of Religious Violence*, the historian of theology William Cavanaugh argues that the term "religion" is itself a construction of post-Enlightenment rationalism. The communities of practice labeled "religion" by Western thinkers tend not to name themselves "religious," since it is not their practice to identify different parts of human life as distinct and separable one from the other: ethics here, agriculture there, and religion somewhere else.[11] These communities have names for different aspects of an integrated human existence, but these are not the same names invented by post-Enlightenment thinkers. For Cavanaugh, as for Taylor and an increasing number of scholars,[12] there is little evidence for the presumption of secularism that there is an isol-able activity we can call "religion," let alone that this activity incites violence. In such loose terms, there is no less evidence for "secular violence."[13] In Appleby's words, "neither religion nor religious militancy per se is a source of deadly conflict: the problem is extremism. Yet the nonviolent 'warrior for peace' could be more influential in the long run than the religious extremist."[14]

Until recent years, Western foreign policy experts and diplomats have tended to follow the secularist paradigm.[15] In *The Might and the Almighty*, for example, Madeleine Albright acknowledges that, as US Ambassador to the United Nations and Secretary of State, she along with other Western international leaders held the conventional view of foreign policy specialists—that religion is not an appropriate or relevant subject for analysis or discussion.[16] But Albright's more recent change of heart anticipates an emergent recognition that the secularist paradigm was inadequate. Like a growing number of specialists in international affairs, Gerard Powers notes, Albright now admits that this secularist paradigm is no longer adequate; understanding international affairs today requires an understanding of religion.[17]

Appleby and other scholars of strategic peacebuilding have been perhaps the most atten-tive to this change:

> [Appleby's] "ambivalence of the sacred" thesis. . . is grounded in recognition of the inter-nal pluralities of religious traditions, consequently articulating a non-essentialist and non-reductionist constructive and contextually sensitive framework. It is this insight that sparked the industry of religious peacebuilding and carved out space for a theological and hermeneutical focus on peace-promoting motifs and resources within religious traditions.[18]

2. Inter-Religious Peacebuilding Must Be Guided by Sources Deep within the Religious Groups that Are in Conflict

How is it that the very religions that are in conflict contain within themselves sources for resolving this conflict? The Society for Scriptural Reasoning set itself this question twenty years ago and then worked, largely through trial-and-error experiments, to identify a means of answering it. An initial group of thirty Christian, Jewish, and Muslim scholars, followed over the years by dozens of additional groups, pursued numerous lines of investigation and on-the-ground experimentation that generated a broad set of theses about how to respond to inter-religious tension and conflict. I have selected the following theses as most pertinent to the themes of this chapter:

1) Our task in scriptural reasoning is not to define "what religion really is." It is instead to characterize how what we call "religion" appears to us in the field, operationally, in everyday social life and in theaters of conflict. And it is important for us to adopt terms and schemes of classification that can evolve through the process of exam-ining and responding to inter-religious conflict. To this end, we adopt the general (etic) terms "religion/religious" as informal labels for our general subjects of study. In dealings with, and descriptions of, religions in conflict in a given locale, we prefer

to use emic terms as introduced by indigenous practitioners.[19] Appleby's definition of religion—"human response to a reality perceived as sacred"—is useful when we are called to explain our subject of study to other scholars or peacebuilders and diplomats. His use of the term "sacred" roughly corresponds to our notion of the "unassimilable" "hearth" of a religion, its "sacrality," which refers functionally, rather than descriptively, to sources of "warmth" around which members of a religious group gather. The central work of SR is to construct practices of engagement that would allow selected members from each of the groups in conflict to meet and speak with each other from out of these places of warmth.

2) Indigenous practitioners tend rarely to identify "religion" with a distinct sphere of conduct, separate from what we observers might call spheres of economics, politics, language, shared feelings, and so on. We therefore expect any conflict among religious groups to involve most of these spheres. It will be difficult to classify a conflict as engaging only "religion" or any other single sphere.

3) For the work of conflict transformation, we need to introduce operational distinctions that are useful only to the extent that they contribute to successful outcomes. The operational goal is to distinguish dimensions of the conflict that can be addressed though religion-specific peacebuilding (in this case, SR) from those that should be addressed through economic, psychosocial, or other modes of conflict transformation. We will assume that every kind of activity we observe (economic, etc.) will also display a religious valence (or character), and that it will display this as a matter of degree: operationally, a particular activity will display a greater or lesser religious valence.[20] It is possible, moreover, to identify a single criterion according to which a behavior can be measured as "more or less religious" and, therefore, more or less amenable to SR work. This criterion is best introduced through an account of the way it is employed operationally. Say a team of SR researchers examines a given behavior, each researcher employing his or her own style of observation. After the researchers have observed a number of behaviors, they gather to compare notes. Say that they list all the behaviors the team as a whole has observed, and alongside each behavior, they describe all the ways it was characterized by the team as a whole. *In this case*, behaviors that are described in very similar ways by all members of the team carry what we, operationally, may call a "lower religious valence." Behaviors that are described in the greatest variety of different ways by the team carry what we may call a "higher religious valence." (This operation is based on our account of the "unassimilable" features of a religion. Behaviors of a higher religious valence will tend to appear differently to different researchers, because they display more unassimilable features. Such features appear differently in relation to different modes of observation.) SR facilitators will want to work with the latter set of behaviors.

4) Reversing the standard Western approach to religious conflict, SR scholars isolate the "most religious" behaviors as those that will contribute most significantly to the work of repairing inter-religious conflict.

5) Researchers will encounter several "most religious" behaviors. From among these, SR peacebuilders should select the ones that appear in a cognate or similar form among all the communities involved in the conflict. If the conflict took place, for example, in traditional Micronesia, these behaviors would most likely concern "religious"

dimensions of navigational lore. Among Abrahamic peoples, they may concern the study of sacred scriptures.

6) The primary work of SR is, through a series of intermediate efforts I will not spell out here, to engage participants from these communities in a new, shared activity that touches on one of these cognate religious behaviors. The participants' mode of engagement will be neither neutral and impersonal (the approach to religious literatures in the academy) nor wholly passionate or intimate (the approach taken in the privacy of one's own "religious home"). The approach will be something between these two poles; one may call it a third approach. For conflicts among Abrahamic peoples, SR has introduced an activity of shared scriptural study that works across religious borders and independently of traditional patterns of religious authority. The issue of authority is a sensitive one. On the one hand, inter-religious peacebuilders rarely succeed in their efforts without negotiating appropriate working relations with the relevant religious authorities. On the other hand, one ground rule for successful hearth-to-hearth dialogue is that inter-religious study must be conducted in ways that do not privilege the authority of any one participant or tradition. SR facilitators must attend both to the politics of religious leadership and to the art of spirit-to-spirit encounter.

7) In the vast majority of cases, participants in SR-sponsored projects report an unexpected shift in their perceptions of both their own religious behavior and that of members of the other religions. They do not report a change in their religious beliefs. Often, in fact, participants report that these sessions leave them with a greater affection for their own religion. There is, however, one significant change. Participants may come to SR study convinced that their religious behavior has only one meaning; but they leave SR study perceiving that, within the frame of their own religion, their behavior displays more than one meaning. Participants will usually affirm the beliefs they came in with. *They will not, however, define their belief as the only legitimate one in their religion.* They may still regard others who do not share their belief as somewhat weak and in need of teaching. But their attitude toward these others will lack the all-or-nothing judgments they may have brought to the SR study: that those who do not share their beliefs represent intolerable threats to their beliefs. We believe this to be the only change that is necessary to transform the conditions for violent disagreement (where A is true, B is false, and there are no other possible options) into conditions for nonviolent disagreement (where A is true and several other options are less true).

3. In Inter-Religious Conflict, Religion Is a Source of Both the Problem and the Solution

For its initial twenty years, the work of SR has focused primarily on conflict among the three Abrahamic traditions. We have found that the study of scripture can be measured as among the "most religious" behaviors of Abrahamic communities prone to inter-religious conflict. These people display other kinds of "very religious behavior," such as prayers and lifecycle rituals. But following the procedures noted above, we identified scriptural study as the behavior around which we could build a best practice of inter-Abrahamic peace.

Scholars of SR have discovered that the insider study of scripture is one place where Abrahamic practitioners share their most heartfelt religious commitments, while also opening these commitments to the gaze of others within the same religious house. We infer that a place of intimate scriptural study is therefore a place of great warmth but also of great danger. Were a stranger to appear suddenly within such an intimate place, those present would most likely interrupt their speech, just as one might cover up an intimate part of the body if exposed to a stranger's gaze. Moreover, if the face that suddenly appeared were of an apparent opponent to the speakers' religion, then the threat would appear all the more dangerous and the reaction to it would be all the more volatile. Would those whose study was interrupted merely stop their study or turn aggressively against the intruder? Asking such questions enables SR scholars to accept one of the Enlightenment's claims: places of great religiosity are also places that open deep and sometimes dangerous passions. SR scholars do not, however, accept the second Enlightenment claim, that religion is part of the problem and never the solution. The claim of SR is that *in cases of inter-religious conflict, religion is both a source of the problem and a major source of the solution. To open the latter source, SR coaxes potential adversaries to share with one another some of the warmth and honesty they typically display only within the intimacy of their religious homes.*

Here is an illustration of that process. For cases of inter-Abrahamic conflict, the SR approach is to invite Muslim, Jewish, and Christian participants to join small "SR fellowships of study." Each fellowship, of five to nine individuals, meets regularly for one or more one-and-a-half-hour sessions of scriptural study. Participants read together and discuss brief selections (three to six verses) from each of the three Abrahamic canons of scripture. The mode of study is not as intimate as study within the various religious homes, nor as dispassionate as study in the university. It is a third kind of study that may currently be unique to SR, but that can be practiced in many environments. Participants usually bring to SR the conviction that the words and verses of scripture deliver a single true meaning to those who believe in those scriptures. Because it is unambiguous, this meaning flatly contradicts any other meaning that may be ascribed to the same words or verses. Should the true meaning concern matters of urgency in contemporary life, then these contradictory meanings will be perceived as intolerable. SR fulfills its goal when such participants leave their SR fellowship with the modified conviction that their own reading of scripture may be the best or truest one, but that the scripture also tolerates a few other readings. As a result, participants may conclude that those who prefer other readings may be weaker in their commitments, but not in an intolerable way.

SR scholars have asked themselves what operational model of inter-religious behavior can best account for these changes in the way participants perceive the meanings of scripture. Over the last several years, these scholars have offered several different but complementary accounts of how the experience of SR tends to change participants' perceptions. They have noted, for example, changes in friendship relations within each study fellowship; changes in what it feels like to study with other kinds of religious people; changes in the quality and quantity of emotions participants attach to religious disagreements; subtle changes in patterns of reasoning, from scripture to the world and back to scripture; and, as introduced above, changes in the range of meanings that scripture appears to tolerate. Within the limits of this report, I offer only a few comments on this last account. Through the process of SR study, participants appear to modify their perceptions of what, more technically, we call the semantic range and domain of the words and verses of scripture. SR participants might, for example, begin with the assumption that scripture speaks directly to all humanity, delivering a single, clear, and distinct message. For participants who feel they know that message, each word and verse of scripture appear to deliver a clearly identifiable part of that larger message. For participants who display what we call "very religious behavior," the singularity of scripture's message implies that any understanding of scripture that appears to contradict this message thereby contradicts the goodness and truth that these participants associate with scripture itself. If such participants are wont to behave aggressively toward those who misrepresent this true message, then we believe the most efficient means of ameliorating their aggression is to introduce them to an environment like that of SR—where, over time, they will most likely come to entertain a somewhat more complicated perception of the range of meanings that scripture itself allows. To recognize that scripture tolerates, say, two meanings of a crucial verse, and not only one, is already to soften the rage that such participants may feel toward those whose readings differ from theirs. In place of rage, such participants may adopt, for example, a superior and patronizing—but nonviolent—attitude toward these others as errant, but guilty only of a weaker reading of scripture rather than a reading that defies the very truth of things.

This change in perception is modest, but it makes all the difference. It marks the decisive change from the perception that other scriptural traditions represent *threats that need to be aggressively resisted* to the perception that one may, indeed, enter into dialogue with members of those other traditions (since, in light of one's own scripture, other scriptures are inadequate but display qualities that may ennoble their devotees and enable them to converse productively with members of one's own tradition). How to account for this change? I am currently working on the hypothesis that the SR setting enables participants, for a brief time, to relax their customary defenses and display some of the attitudes of warmth, intimacy, trust, and honesty they display at "home," in their traditional circles of scriptural study. I do not mean to imply that these are "good" attitudes, as if attitudes of caution and protectiveness were "not good." I mean to suggest, instead, that the traditions wisely recognize that attitudes of trust and warmth are usually appropriate only at home, since the public square may indeed prove to be a dangerous or at least inappropriate place for ingenuous, religious self-expression. "Hearth-to-hearth" dialogue is not universally a good thing, since it may lower appropriately protective walls in the wrong way at the wrong time. Such dialogue is called for, urgently, in times of inter-religious crisis, when the potential benefits outweigh the risks. At such times, SR provides a protective environment, away from the more open public square, in which religious adversaries may risk sharing practices of intimate, "warm" study that are otherwise appropriate only at home. At times of crisis, such shared warmth may, within such environments of study, transform what seem to be opposing bodies of scripture into complementary sources of interpersonal, inter-religious discovery and recognition. Out of those sources, participants may draw reparative forms of speech and reasoning that will serve as instruments of conflict transformation for this particular crisis at this particular time. I repeat the phrase "for this time," because I believe these forms of speech and reasoning will emerge only within the hearth of SR (or comparable) study and will prove to be useful instruments of conflict transformation only for this moment of crisis. When the heat of conflict and the warmth of study have faded, these "instruments of peace" will appear either as semantically dull relics of another time or as ordinary instruments for this or that quotidian use.

4. Scriptural Reasoning Offers One Effective Means of Drawing out Intra-Religious Guidelines for Inter-Religious Peacebuilding

SR retains the Enlightenment's commitment to social justice and human rights and to the pursuit of scientific rationality as society's primary instrument for uncovering the sources of injustice and oppression. But it reverses the Enlightenment's paradigm for addressing issues of religion and conflict. While acknowledging religion's role in inter-religious conflict, SR scholars argue that the religions that participate in such conflict also possess resources for resolving that conflict. They argue that there is no hard evidence that excluding religious actors from the work of inter-religious peacemaking in any way increases the likelihood of successful peacebuilding. Over twenty years, SR has been tested through close to two thousand sessions of inter-Abrahamic study among a great variety of groups (from scholars and congregational leaders to students, children, and prison inmates) in many different geographic areas (universities, schools, and religious institutions throughout North America and the UK, with more modest numbers of groups in Europe, the Middle East, Pakistan, South Africa, Russia, and China), and with individuals displaying varying degrees of religiosity.

SR has drawn from traditional methods of scriptural study new resources for engaging individuals in peaceful dialogue and argument across significant borders of religious difference. In this sense, SR has successfully drawn on the resources of Abrahamic religiosity to ameliorate cases of inter-religious conflict. But these have been cases of only nonviolent conflicts of beliefs and emotions. We hope to test, but have not yet tested, SR practices of inter-religious engagement in environments of serious conflict. Its more immediate applications may come from the broader hypotheses SR scholars have formulated on how to improve the academic and social scientific study of religious behavior, the way teachers teach the subjects of "religion" and "religions," and the way potential peacebuilders examine religious conflicts and propose ways of healing them. In the next, concluding section of this chapter, I suggest ways that SR approaches to peacebuilding might be restated in the terms of recent efforts in "strategic peacebuilding,"[21] as introduced to me by Kroc Institute scholars. I hope this restatement will help expand the resources for testing and refining SR.

SCRIPTURAL REASONING IN THE VOCABULARY OF STRATEGIC PEACEBUILDING

As articulated by Scott Appleby, John Paul Lederach, Daniel Philpott, and others, the peacebuilding model of "strategic peacebuilding" offers an appropriate framework for introducing some of the central features of SR. Here are brief accounts of seven features of strategic peacebuilding (SP), each one followed by a comment on correlative features of SR. In this account, I will adopt the second person plural, "we," to personify, first, the founders of SR and, then, my sense of dominant tendencies among the broader membership of SSR.

1. Moving to Complexity

SP: Lederach and Appleby argue that the increasingly complex character of regional conflicts "exposes the need for strategic. . . peacebuilders [who] must embrace complexity and find within any given situation or issue practical approaches that stitch together key people and initiatives to reduce violence, change destructive patterns, and build healthy relationships and structures.. . . Strategic peacebuilders. . . encourage the deeper and more frequent convergence of mission, resources, expertise, insight, and benevolent self-interest that characterizes this as the most fruitful multilateral collaboration in the cause of peace."[22] Atalia Omer notes in Chapter 1 of this volume that, for Lederach and Appleby, strategic peacebuilding "focuses on transforming inhumane social patterns, flawed structural conditions, and open violent conflict that weakens the conditions necessary for a flourishing human community."

SR: The origins of SR may share some features with those of SP. The project of SR began in 1993–1994 with a fellowship of two Anglican scholars and one Jewish scholar, who studied scriptures together for up to a week at a time, searching for what we considered better ways of teaching and learning scriptural texts and traditions and scriptural-text approaches to religious studies and theology. SR took something like its current form after a Sunni scholar joined the fellowship and the four colleagues generated what we called Abrahamic SR. After its formation in 1996, the Society for Scriptural Reasoning (SSR) nurtured a fellowship of thirty scholars, who met together biannually, once for four days and once for two days, with regional subgroups meeting occasionally at other times. The SSR developed two forms of study. One was small-group "formational SR," which worked well only with small groups of five to nine participants. When the entire group gathered, it would therefore spend most of its time in small group sessions, customarily holding four of these per day (one-and-a-half-hours each), along with one or two plenary sessions. Each small group would maintain its membership for most of the two- to four-day conference. We found that the most profound consequences of SR study emerged only after the same small group of readers worked through the same small sampling of scriptural verses for at least a day and a half and ideally for two or more days. The second form of SSR study was to gather these small teams into larger plenary discussions, where the small teams' discoveries—typically "hot," new, and inchoate—were "cooled" into what, over the years, have become the SSR's descriptive and analytic writings about SR. Members of SSR came gradually to agree that the practices of SR could not be taught by way of these writings, but only through apprenticeship or training in the practices themselves. The "reasoning" dimension of scriptural reasoning—the activity that transformed the participants' sundry disciplines and traditions of text interpretation into integrative processes of inquiry—appeared to display its distinctive characteristics only during the times of small-group study. Over twenty years, the membership of SSR has expanded to several hundred scholars, and SSR members have offered training sessions that, by now, have been attended by more than ten thousand students (including academics, clergy, members of local congregations, and also graduate, undergraduate, and secondary and primary school students). Members of SSR are, typically, academics, teachers, or clergy, each active in both a religious community of some kind and some educational or service profession. Most have been Christian, Jewish, or Muslim. The religious affiliations or interests of SSR members have expanded in the past several years, with emergent efforts at Hindu, Buddhist, Taoist, and Confucian SR, along with emergent attention to Baha'i and other religions and efforts to nurture SR-like approaches to philosophic and comparative literary studies.

The founders of SR were initially moved by concerns about how philosophy, religion, and scripture tend to be taught and researched in the university. We were concerned that faculty tended to examine these complex subjects through narrow lenses: that is, through the analytic tools favored by only one or two academic guilds and in ways that tended to delegitimize the methods of other guilds and, to be sure, approaches that fell outside such guilds. We were not critical of the favored tools—only of the tendency to exclude many other approaches. Our concern, furthermore, was not a matter of principle so much as a response to results: that certain elemental features of scriptural traditions were absent altogether from most academic curricula and that comparable omissions were also evident in the teaching of more general topics in religion, theology, and philosophy. SR began as an experiment in seeing what would happen if more methods of inquiry were admitted into the classroom: if, for example, academic and traditional scriptural commentaries were placed side by side in the classroom, and if academic approaches to scripture and to religion included, for example, performative studies, semiotics, pragmatics, literary studies, and anthropology as well as text-critical histories of scriptural traditions.[23]

In this sense, SR was an effort to attend more to the *complexity* of our subjects of study, employing a greater variety of analytic tools and more highly sensitive modes of inquiry that could attend to subtler expressions of difference and change in the way scriptural texts were read and interpreted in traditions of religion and of thought. The SR founders did not at first think of SR as a method of peacebuilding. The thought came from others who observed SR groups in which orthodox religious Muslims, Christians, and Jews had worked closely together for several years. They asked SR scholars if we realized how unusual it was to observe this kind of intense work among people of very different religious commitments sharing scriptural study and commentary. In response, we turned to the more public, peacebuilding implications of SR work in addition to the ongoing academic project.[24]

2. Expanding the Field

SP: Part of the increasing complexity of strategic peacebuilding is the way it expands the field of play and the players engaged in inter-religious conflict transformation:

> The players have multiplied. In the post–Cold War era a wider range of actors and institutions mattered.... [And] the field of play was enlarged to encompass and link two previously unlikely spheres of action: the local and the global. At the local level, the capacity and need for communities to activate and mobilize resources to face the realities of internal conflicts rose sharply. It was impossible to think about peace without engaging, including, and respecting the local community.[25]

There is also a need to balance a variety of interests and resources:

> striving for social justice, ending violent conflict, and building healthy cooperative relationships in conflict-ridden societies.... These processes of transformation are interrelated most

fundamentally at the local level; even when violence originates and occurs at the national or regional level, its impact is felt most keenly and directly in neighborhoods, towns, villages, cities—in local communities.[26]

There will be a need to move to national and international areas and agents of conflict management, but to move there too quickly will undermine rather than foster conditions for long-lasting peace, and social conditions in the beginning and the end operate locally.

Lederach and Appleby speak, furthermore, of the challenge to

> *specify the roles of religious actors in the building of a sustainable peace.* . . . The practice of strategic peacebuilding develops around the critical question of "who" and "what types of processes" will be needed to initiate, develop, and sustain the desired transformation. Our assumption is simple: in settings of deep-rooted conflict, pursuing transformation requires an alliance of key people and processes that converge in a more precise and coordinated way on the overall desired change. It requires us, no matter our expertise or access within the wider system, to recognize that the quality of the change process we seek depends on bringing together key relationships and influences that would not naturally converge. Strategic peacebuilders therefore think carefully about a range of resources and relationships that go beyond their natural niche, their most immediate circle of influence, access, and exchange. This does not mean that any specific activity, research, or approach is not important on its own; it simply means that "strategic peacebuilding" must build toward a common, coordinated set of goals.[27]

SR: For scriptural reasoning, as for strategic peacebuilding, expanding the complexity of study also meant expanding the field of play and the field of players. As we began, in the later 1990s, to extend SR into the work of peacebuilding, we were surprised to discover how rarely religion was examined in the literature on international diplomacy. Until we came across the early writings of Scott Appleby, Marc Gopin, and comparable authors,[28] we were also surprised to see how, in the peace studies literature, religion tended to be examined only as a source of conflict, very rarely as a contribution to peace. We understood the matter very differently. We were well aware of the role of religions in interethnic conflict, but we also understood religion to be as inseparable from human life as was speech or tool-making. For us, religion referred to a multi-leveled complex of human activities, beliefs, and aspirations, touching and touched by every other aspect of individual and societal life, but also touching and touched by that which remains unassimilable to the human (or to any other form of finite life): what, for the sake of this chapter, I call "religiosity" and place, metaphorically, at the "hearth" of a religion. Our experience, over twenty years, was that a certain type of inter-scriptural dialogue enables some members of different, often conflicting religious communities to converse (according to our account) from religious "hearth to hearth" and, in the process, to uncover and share sources of peace that appeared only by way of such dialogue. Observing that other modes of encounter may uncover sources of conflict or even hate, we concluded that it is unhelpful and inaccurate to categorize religion in either/or terms as necessarily a source of conflict or of peace. We concluded, instead, that in cases of inter-religious conflict, there is reason to look *within* the religions involved in the conflict for possible resources for resolving the conflict. *How* to "look" is one of the primary subjects of this chapter.

3. Moving to the Local and Immediate While Also Addressing the Global and the Long-Term

SP: In the words of Naomi Roht-Arriaza, "to build a lasting peace, national responses are not enough. For teaching, peace builders must look both out—to the international sphere—and down, to the local, to do what needs to be done."[29] "Strategic peacebuilding must work equally on a local and regional and global level, and the local often needs to come first. National and international initiatives should be aware of (and not undermine) local processes."[30] In Lederach and Appleby's words, "The *theory* of peacebuilding is built upon the insight that most deadly conflicts today are: [a] 'local,' involving face to face, 'tribe to tribe,' ethnically and religiously inflected confrontations; [b] unfold over years, decades or even generations; foster enduring resentments and create 'wounds' of various kinds that cannot be healed or transformed merely by a 'getting to yes' process of conflict transformation or negotiation of 'presenting symptoms'; and [c] recur over time, precisely because such wounds are left to fester."[31]

Accordingly, peacebuilding practices across the cycle of conflict must be double-visioned, with one eye on responding to immediate and short-term crises, and another on creating and nurturing relationships, practices, and institutions designed to repair wounds over the long term:

> A sustainable peace, the historical record shows, requires long-term, ongoing activities and operations that may be initiated and supported for a time by outsiders but must eventually become the ordinary practices of the citizens and institutions of the society in question. We believe, furthermore, that peacebuilding occurs in its fully realized mode when it addresses every stage of the conflict cycle and involves all members of a society in the nonviolent transformation of conflict, the pursuit of social justice, and the creation of cultures of sustainable peace. Properly understood, the building and sustaining of a culture of peace and its supporting institutions requires a range of relationship-building activities encompassing the entire cycle, rather than merely the post-accord, coming-out-of-violence period. Accordingly, activities that constitute peacebuilding run the gamut of conflict transformation, including violence prevention and early warning, conflict management, mediation and resolution, social reconstruction and healing in the aftermath of armed conflict, and the long, complex work of reconciliation throughout the process.[32]

SR: As both an academic and a peacebuilding practice, scriptural reasoning also addresses local practices and immediate concerns and crises while serving global and long-term networks of relations and aspirations. The center of SR activity is local: engaging participants from mutually antagonistic groups in circles of inter-religious study and conversation.[33] The primary appeal of SR activity is immediate: engaging in types of inter-religious exchange that members of particular religious groups find intrinsically attractive (joyful, interesting, of value for the sake of learning or skills or to answer curiosities). The somewhat long-range purpose of SR is reparative: healing relations among different groups.[34] The broader context and source of wisdom for SR is global, but through expanding networks of relations rather than through hastier appeals to purportedly universal principles and beliefs.[35] The greatest number of SR scholars resides in North America and the United Kingdom, but an increasing number work out of institutions in Europe, the Middle East, Africa, the Indian sub-continent (Pakistan in particular), and East Asia (China in particular). These scholars tend to describe and promote SR in ways that are shaped by region-specific interests and discourses. They express their SR work in academic writings but also (and, for some, primarily) in practices of study and teaching.

4. Attending to Indigenous Contexts, Practices, and Vocabularies

SP: For strategic peacebuilders, attention to the local contexts of peacebuilding also means attention to the local conditions of speech, action, and belief:

> The setting and the people cannot be seen as the problem and the outsider as the answer. Rather, the long-term goal of transformation demands that external agents of change take as the primary task of accompaniment the validation of the people and the expansion of resources within the setting.. . . Would-be strategic peacebuilders [therefore ask]: how do we build the global movement for justice while at the same time empowering the voice and capacity of local communities? [36]

SR: The primary vocabularies of SR are drawn from the local groups involved in direct conflict and, by way of peacebuilding efforts, in direct dialogue. As noted, these do not yet include cases of hot or armed conflict. There have been several cases of political conflict (such as among Muslim, Jewish, and Christian clerics in Cape Town, South Africa; or among Jews and Palestinians in Israel/Palestine) and of ethnic/religious tension (such as among Muslim and Christian inmates in London prisons, and among students in British secondary schools). Most cases have involved either intra-religious disagreements (among different denominations or factions of Jews, Muslims, or Christians) or inter-religious suspicion and criticism across Abrahamic traditions or, more recently, Abrahamic and Asian traditions.

SR theory and method emerge "bottom up," as ways of characterizing tendencies that have been observed in region-specific practices and in local, group-to-group encounters and dialogue. Any human practice can be generalized to varying degrees; in that sense, SR scholars can learn more general wisdom from each encounter or dialogue they observe. The work of SR scholarship is not to over- or under-generalize, but to collect a broad range of evidence about the various ways that understanding, dialogue, and peace can be nurtured. On the academic side, SR's analytic vocabularies are disciplined by the human sciences, hermeneutic theory, philosophy, and logic, but in ways that should continually be readjusted and reshaped in light of local evidences and in terms of local or indigenous vocabularies and the local or indigenous frames of meaning and action in terms of which, *alone,* those vocabularies are meaningful.[37] For SR, "local" and "general" are not contradictories but, rather, relative vectors. This means that every local activity has some generalizable lesson to teach and every general theory is limited to its own contexts of meaning (whose deictic markers are often veiled).[38]

5. Taking Religion Seriously as a Resource for Peacebuilding

SP: Religion is often a significant factor among the indigenous practices and vocabularies. One of the most evident innovations of strategic peacebuilders is taking religion seriously as a resource for peacemaking. In Powers's words,

> faith-based peacebuilding intervenes in these various stages of conflict through a broad array of roles and activities at the local, national, and international levels. Adapting typologies proposed by Lederach and Sampson, David Steele groups these roles into four types: observation and witness. . ., education and formation. . ., advocacy and empowerment. . ., and conciliation and mediation. Because it involves multiple stages of conflict and multiple roles and activities, peacebuilding also involves multiple time horizons: before ceasefires and regime changes, during the conflict itself, the immediate aftermath, and the often decades-long process of reconstruction and reconciliation after the violence ends.[39]

Philpott's essay in the same volume seeks to restore points of religiosity to their role as a resource for intra- and inter-religious engagement.[40] And Omer adds in Chapter 1 of this volume that

> Philpott's approach. . . diverges significantly from a view of liberal peace (the corollary of an unrevised liberal political theory) with its distinct presuppositions about religion and how it relates to conflict, peace, and public discourse. These premises involve analyzing religious violence as a matter of epistemological dispute, the solution of which necessitated the rise of the modern liberal state and conceptions of toleration. The field of religious peacebuilding. . . has not challenged these premises, but rather has operated within them. Philpott offers a correction that resonates with a rich body of literature and, by now, a perhaps increasingly resolved conversation in religious ethics that challenges and revises presumptions concerning the non-publicity of religion. Tapping into the religion and public life debates, however, proves a valuable maneuver, indicating the need to theoretically enrich religious peacebuilding. Yet unawareness of theoretical and methodological debates that take place in the study of religion can diminish the effectiveness of theorizing about religion in the religious peacebuilding subfield.[41]

SR: Scriptural reasoning scholars do not, first, examine something called "religion," since that term might not correspond to indigenous understandings of what corresponds, in my terms, to sacrality or religiosity per se. SR began as a response to the absence of indigenous discourses as a focus of attention in religious studies and, in particular, in the academic study of the scriptural traditions. Seeking to account for this absence, SR scholars theorized that modern academics tend to rely on an overly narrow set of analytic tools and methods, favoring more familiar Western academic tools even when these tools inhibited rather than promoted discerning studies of non-Western or extra-academic subjects of study. SR scholars sought to pay greater attention to how the scriptural traditions described themselves, continually reshaping the customary academic tools so that they were attentive to these descriptions. Over time, the SR scholars concluded that these tools were most accurately reshaped when the toolmakers first engaged in what we now call SR fellowships of study: long sessions of interactive scriptural study. Following such sessions, SR scholars were better able to perceive indigenous categories of belief, practice, and meaning, and better able to reshape their academic disciplines so that they were attentive to these categories. The English term "religion" rarely corresponds to any of these indigenous categories. Nonetheless, it served initially as a helpful class name for the set of indigenous categories that were often omitted from academic study. As SR scholars entered into conversation with scholars of peacebuilding, the term acquired new uses—as, for example, a helpful class name for categories of experience and practice previously omitted from studies of conflict transformation. For scholars of SP and of SR, the term also seems to help identify dimensions of religious practice and experience that are not well detected through the tools of social, cultural, textual, and psychological sciences. For SR, it remains very important to distinguish between the second-order analytic uses of the term "religion" and first-order or descriptive uses of indigenous terms and categories. SR study fellowships are designed to bring the latter into conversational use among parties to inter-religious conflict, among peacebuilders, and among academic scholars of religion.

6. Examining "the Sacred" Within Religion

SP: Within the context of inter-religious strategic peacebuilding, Lederach and Appleby define religion in a way that anticipates SR's focus on those dimensions of religious practice and experience that are not easily detected through most tools of academic science. They say that religion can be defined simply as the "human response to a reality perceived as sacred."[42] Religious actors, in turn, can be defined as "people who have been formed by a religious community and who are acting with the intent to uphold, extend, or defend its values and precepts."[43]

How, then, can strategic peacebuilders discern whether or not a community and the actors who comprise it are in fact "religious?" By what criteria can one identify a "human response to a reality perceived as sacred"? Appleby's account of "religious traditions" provides one answer. A religious tradition, he writes, is an example of a "living tradition":

> The philosopher Alasdair MacIntyre defines a "living tradition" as "an historically extended, socially embodied argument, and an argument precisely in part about the goods which constitute that tradition." MacIntyre's formulation, coupled with Newman's notion of religious "ideas" awaiting development in each historical period, suggests a working definition of a "religious tradition" as a sustained argument, conducted anew by each generation, about the contemporary significance and meaning of the sources of sacred wisdom and revealed truth (i.e., sacred Scriptures, oral and written commentaries, authoritative teachings, and so on). The argument alternately recapitulates, ignores, and moves beyond previous debates but draws on the same sacred sources as did previous generations of believers. Modernity-negotiating, birth-control-debating Roman Catholics and Shiite Muslims, at least those who engage the great argument that is tradition, are doing what the religious have always done: they are seeking the good in the nexus between inherited wisdom and the possibilities of the present moment.[44]

Following MacIntyre and Newman, Appleby suggests that a "religious community" is one that identifies what it means for its members to respond to the sacred. Such responses are recorded in the community's memory, for example, in its scriptures, scriptural commentaries, and authoritative teachings, and the transmission of this memory from generation to generation constitutes a "living tradition." This is a "tradition," because it authorizes—"argues for"—what it means to be socialized as a member of this community in particular. And it is "living," because authority is not a static good, carried through time like some indestructible yet mobile rock, but an *activity* of argumentation through which each generation restates, reaffirms, and remembers what it means to be a member of this community: in the case of a religious community, what it means to respond to the sacred. Because authority means actively authorizing, tradition is dynamic and ever-changing:

> Religious traditions can adapt to their environments without eroding continuity with the sacred past because the past is capacious. [Traditions retain an] "internal pluralism": . . . an array of laws, doctrines, moral norms, and "practices" (socially embedded beliefs) [that are] sacralized and sanctioned at various times by the community and its religious authorities. This storehouse of religiously approved options is available to religious leaders whenever new circumstances call for change in religious practice.[45]

Strategic peacebuilders can therefore recognize "religion" in the way that a religious community, through all its complexity and pluralism, reauthorizes each generation to articulate what it means to "respond to the sacred." The peacebuilder is not called to be a witness to the *sacred*, per se, but to be skilled in observing a given community's way of authorizing its members to give voice to such a witness. Powers writes, for example of the peacebuilding practices of the Acholi in northern Uganda. The Acholi carry out a ceremony called *matu oput*, or drinking the bitter herbs, which involves a recognition of a wrong and reconciliation with the victim's family. A separate ceremony, involving stepping on a nag, is used to cleanse those who have been away from home and allow them to return.[46] Powers's account of these ceremonies is a peacebuilder's account of how the Acholi community authorizes its members to give personal and public witness to acts of reconciliation or return.

SR: What Appleby calls "the sacred" may correspond closely to what I am calling "the unassimilable" in religious experience or the "hearth" of a religion. "Hearth" refers figuratively to observable places of "warmth," around which members of a given group display signs of ease and at-home-ness and where they gather to share matters of intimate belief. These places are typically closed to outsiders. To intrude on such a place is to elicit defensive reactions, at the very least, and quite possibly aggressive or violent reactions (and thus to feel "heat" rather than "warmth"). The discovery and thesis of SR is that these sources of warmth are, contrary to all our expectations, the best resources for long-lasting conflict transformation. The method of SR is to evaluate, within a given locale, which sets of practices would enable selected members from each group to engage in relatively warm, inter-group conversations over an extended period of time. Over years of testing, SR scholars have concluded that a kind of shared scriptural study is the best resource for conflict transformation among traditionally religious practitioners in the Abrahamic traditions. Here, "scriptural study" represents a religious "hearth" within each group and "inter-scriptural reasoning" the best practice for hearth-to-hearth dialogue. Other forms of engagement are recommended for antagonists from other religious traditions (and from a minority of Abrahamic groups). Places of warmth are also places of potential "fire" within any group in conflict or even mere tension with another group. There is reason, therefore, for the modern West's commonplace assumption that religiosity is a potential source of conflict. The source of potential violence is, however, also the source of potentially enduring peace. If the stakes are high enough, peacebuilders may recognize that it is worth the risk to work closer to the fire. The initial cost is disciplined work: SR, for example, emerges from years of disciplined inquiry into hearth-to-hearth inter-religious dialogue.

One lesson from SR inquiry is that there are few generalizations to be offered about the "hearth." As the philosopher Charles Peirce found in his studies of "material" rather than ideal or "mathematical" infinity, the infinite makes its appearances in this material world in context-specific ways that are weakly captured in wholly general formulae. There are rules of thumb, but the actual thumbprint will include unique and contingent features that can be observed only after the fact, and these features will appear more indefinite the more precisely we seek to measure them. The hearth of religion is thus the "unassimilable." But what disciplined inquiry—or science—could SR scholars pursue if the center of SR practice is, in this sense, unknowable? As Immanuel Kant argued against David Hume, the science we seek is a science of *human behavior in relation to the unknowable*, not of human cognition alone. The science of SR is a science of human behavior in relation to the unassimilable in religion and, in particular, to the unassimilable as a source of both conflict and potential conflict transformation among religious groups. In this sense, like any other contemporary empirical science (from quantum physics to sociology), SR is a probabilistic science, recommending best practices as they have emerged and been refined through trial-and-error observation and testing.

7. Restorative Justice and Justpeace

SP: These six features of strategic peacebuilding are joined to the overall purpose of justpeace:

> Peacebuilding theory articulates the end goal of. . . disparate but interrelated phases of conflict transformation. The end goal is perhaps best expressed by the idea of justpeace, a dynamic state of affairs in which the reduction and management of violence and the achievement of social and economic justice are undertaken as mutual, reinforcing dimensions of constructive change. Sustainable transformation of conflict requires more than the (necessary) problem solving associated with mediation, negotiated settlements, and other elements of conflict transformation; it requires the redress of legitimate grievances and the establishment of new relations characterized by equality and fairness according to the dictates of human dignity and the common good.
>
> To say that a justpeace is the end goal of peacebuilding is not to suggest that peacebuilding ends when the fundamental requirements of a justpeace are established; rather, the practices of peacebuilding that help bring about this desired state of affairs must become routinized in the society.. . . Effective institutions for participatory government, once established, require continual oversight, nurturing, and renewal.[47]

SR: As defined by scholars of strategic peacebuilding, the goals of "justpeace" and restorative justice contribute a more acute direction and terminology to the work of SR. *One shared emphasis is on the local and immediate.* In Omer's words,

> Justpeace and complexity. . . frame the topic as one about religious peacebuilding rather than religion and peace to capture the dynamic, multidisciplinary, multidirectional, and deeply contextual frameworks that need to guide one's exploration of theory and praxis about religion, conflict, and peacebuilding. *The concept of peacebuilding entails an active engagement with particular conflicts. It is not a general and decontextualized reflection on religion and peace. The peace sought is this-worldly* (social, political, economic), although the this-worldliness should not be viewed as necessarily dichotomous with inner-spirituality or with other-worldly and transcendent conceptions of peace.[48]

For SR, religion must itself be defined in emic terms that are specific to the groups engaged in a particular conflict. The methods of SR must also be reshaped in ways that address the religious "hearth" of each of these groups, which means that SR fieldworkers and facilitators must be ever-vigilant, attending at once to their knowledge of previous best practices, to the terms of this particular setting, and to the ever-changing outcomes of their work in the field.

Another shared emphasis between strategic peacebuilding and scriptural reasoning is on repair. In Powers's words,

> Peacebuilding can be defined quite broadly as everything implied by a robust, positive under-standing of a just peace. Alternatively, it can be defined more narrowly as an approach to heal-ing broken societies, or, even more narrowly, as a set of nonviolent methods of dealing with conflict, from mediation and interfaith dialogue to relationship building and reconciliation programs.[49]

SR scholars often cite "healing" and "repair" as the end goal of SR. This goal is consistent with the goal of "pragmatic" inquiry as articulated by Charles Peirce and John Dewey: inquiry that is stimulated by a "problematic situation," or the interruptive observation that something is amiss, and that is quieted or completed once what is wrong has been repaired. SR scholars therefore refer to SR as "reparative reasoning."[50] *One signal difference between SP and SR is that scriptural reasoning is of more limited scope*: a contribution, one might say, to one of the many levels of repair that are included in strategic peacebuilding. SR is a specialized instru-ment for identifying religion in the field, identifying unassimilable religiosity within the practices of religious groups, identifying and facilitating best practices for hearth-to-hearth dialogue, evaluating the outcomes of such dialogue, and refining its methods on the basis of those outcomes.

In conjunction with a discussion between SR scholars and foreign affairs officers, Deputy Assistant Secretary of State Jerry White challenged me to consider the broader implications of "SR wisdom" for addressing conflicts beyond the sphere of religion. In reply, I noted that SR scholars are critical of efforts to generalize approaches to conflict transformation beyond the contexts of any peacebuilder's concrete work. At the same time, I said I was not averse to logical studies of the formal properties of current SR work, provided there is no presumption about whether and how such properties might reappear in efforts to repair other species of conflict. In these terms, I can say that SR inquiry is stimulated by the observation of conflicts that can be mapped formally by sets of contradictories A vs. B, such that A+B defines a per-ceived universe of beliefs or practices in which either A or B is true (as perceived by members of A and B). The method of SR is not to eliminate A or B or to recommend any "mediating" third term, C, so that A+B=C. The method is, instead, to redefine both A and B, separately, as infinite sets, so that each one contains an indefinite number of features, several subsets of which can be put in one-to-one correspondence with several subsets of the other.

This last step represents what one might call the "similarity-seeking" or "liberal" stage of SR peacebuilding: for later use, SR facilitators gather evidence that (a) A and B cannot be contradictories, since neither infinite series can be fully defined, which means it cannot be assigned a finite identity that could contradict some other finite identity; (b) any finite claim a^n or b^n about A or B can be supplemented by another claim a^o or b^o that is contrary to (other than) the first one but not contradictory to it (so that a^n or b^n alone is true). This implies that, however much individual members of A and B may have good reason to *prefer* certain claims (such as a^n rather than a^o; and b^n rather than b^o), they have no evidence that additional claims are impossible; (c) A and B cannot define a complete universe of beliefs or practices, since A and B are contraries (other than one another) but not contradictories; it is possible that A and B are supplemented by C, D, and so on. This means that A could be true and B not false, or vice versa; that they could overlap to varying degrees; and so on.

The information gathered in the first stage of SR peacebuilding could conceivably be used to "educate" members of A and B about their many similarities and about the lack of evidence for their being literal contradictories of one another and, in that sense, enemies. But this information would come from a third party (SR observers) and does not include group-specific sources of motivation for attending to this information in some form or for engaging in any transformational activities either within a group or across group borders. The purpose of the information is therefore to guide further work by SR peacebuilders, rather than to dictate direct dealings with members of either group. SR researchers turn, therefore, to the next, "difference-seeking" or "post-liberal" stage of SR peacebuilding. SR researchers look for evidence that the sets of features gathered in Stage 1 include the feature of "material infinity," or a subset of features every member of which also includes all relations among every member plus the subset itself. This is one way to characterize the feature of "unassimilability": that which, for example, characterizes some aspect of a religion that can be observed (we see evidence of this aspect) but not fully known (always displays more features than we can possibly enumerate). The philosopher Kant attributes this feature to every human being, every one of which, he says, has "infinite worth" and "dignity": that is, its character is unassimilable and, therefore, unique or different from every other. According to our definition, this feature is not at all to be equated with that which is wholly obscure or recondite, or without characteristic marks. *To the contrary, the unassimilable does not lack observable characteristics but displays more characteristics than we can possibly enumerate.* Members of religions tend to attribute this kind of unassimilability to certain features of their religious experience (including those Appleby calls "the sacred"). But in answer to White's challenge, I assume that some readers will identify unassimilability with other realms of behavior and experience.

The third stage of SR peacebuilding is to observe how members of A and B address, or behave in relation to, any unassimilable features of A or B, respectively. Let us use the symbols A_i and B_i to refer to these features and the symbols $a_{i,j,k}$ and $b_{i,j,k}$ to refer to the ways members behave in relation to these features. The defining work of SR is to construct forms of engagement in which selected members of A and B will address, dialogue with, work with, and/or engage one another in ways that include some of these behaviors $a_{i,j,k}$ and $b_{i,j,k}$. The surprising discovery of scriptural reasoning is that, if constructed properly, these forms of engagement may be attractive to members of A and B and may move them, over time, to recognize features of unassimilability in one another and in A and B. This recognition constitutes a transformation of relations of contradiction (A contradicts B) into relations of contrariety (A is different from B) and leads members of A and B toward the observations that concluded Stage 1 above (A and B cannot be contradictories, and so on). SR has tested this process only for relations among Abrahamic religious groups and only by engaging group members in the study of scripture. But some readers may seek to test this with respect to other kinds of contradictories and other kinds of behavior.

A Concluding Note

By way of conclusion, here is an illustration of how scriptural reasoning approaches to peacebuilding might be reframed as policy recommendations for leaders in government and conflict transformation.[51]

- Inter-religious peace cannot be won by suppressing inter-religious difference. Whether attempted through prudent speeches or by force of arms, the suppression of inter-religious difference introduces the seeds of violence rather than peace, because religions live in and through their differences.
- It makes sense that religious freedom is a primary goal of governmental policy, because religions wrap their worldly arms around what they consider sources or symbols of the unassimilable freedom that resides within each religion. Religious people cherish and protect such sources. Whatever appears to threaten these sources is an object of fear and loathing, and potentially a target of violent behavior. Whatever appears to protect, uphold, or cherish these sources, on the other hand, is an object of care, compassion, love, and protection.
- In cases of inter-religious conflict, peacebuilders have reason to search after what each party to the conflict cherishes as such a source. Because there are no universal criteria for identifying such sources, peacebuilders cannot be guided by their a priori assumptions about what a religion will look like in the field. They must come and look for themselves, one case at a time. Peacemaking begins with careful, empirical observation.
- In sum, religions cannot be left out of the work of inter-religious conflict transformation. Religion cannot be comprehended, however, in general, in the classroom or conference room. Each religion appears differently in ways that have to be observed directly in the field to be understood.
- Religious people will be quick to recognize how their government or another government acts in relation to what this people cherishes and to how they cherish it. They will feel threatened and react against any government that appears indifferent to what and how they cherish. This will include any government that appears to predefine the character and content of a people's religion before coming to observe it. It will also include any government that appears to predetermine how inter-religious conflicts should be resolved in general, before observing the specific characteristics of a given conflict.

Notes

1. I am grateful to Scott Appleby and Atalia Omer for encouraging me to participate in this project and to get to know their work at the Kroc Institute, as well as for their crucial editorial guidance. They have also inspired and guided my entry into the literature and practices of "strategic peacebuilding," which are of urgent significance for the future of inter-religious conflict transformation and which give new direction to the public work of scriptural reasoning.

    I am grateful to Jerry White, US Deputy Assistant Secretary of State, for his careful attention to the place of religion in international diplomacy and for his encouragement and counsel in this effort to examine inter-religious diplomacy from the perspectives of scriptural reasoning. The second part of this essay, "Hearth-to-Hearth Dialogue in Inter-religious Diplomacy," emerges from a report I prepared for him; that report emerged, in turn, from extended discussions and research undertaken in 2012 by a team of colleagues and students in the "Scripture, Interpretation, and Practice" graduate area of Religious Studies at the University of Virginia. The members of this team were Ashley Elser, Nauman Faizi, Emily Filler, Kelly Figueroa-Ray, Mark James, Betsy Mesard, Matt Puffer, Reuben Shank, and Professors Ahmed Al-Rahim and Chuck Matthewes.

2. For an introduction to SR, see the following SR websites:

- The Journal of Scriptural Reasoning (University of Virginia): http://jsr.lib.virginia.edu/
- The Scriptural Reasoning Forum (University of Virginia): http://jsrforum.lib.virginia.edu/
- Cambridge University Scriptural Reasoning: http://www.scripturalreasoning.org/
- The Cambridge Inter-faith Programme (Cambridge University): http://www.divinity.cam.ac.uk/cip/
- Three Faiths Forum (London): http://www.3ff.org.uk/index.htm

   For introductory, academic books, see David F. Ford and C. C. Pecknold, eds., *The Promise of Scriptural Reasoning* (Oxford: Blackwell, 2006); and Peter Ochs and Stacy Johnson, eds., *Crisis, Call and Leadership in the Abrahamic Traditions* (New York: Palgrave Macmillan, 2009).

3. See R. Scott Appleby, *The Ambivalence of the Sacred: Religion, Violence, and Reconciliation* (Lanham, MD: Rowman and Littlefield, 2000), 27.

4. I am not therefore interested in dialogue for the sake of agreement. As Gerard Powers writes, "In the face of religious nationalism, effective religious peace building is less about finding common ground on religious issues, per se and more about retrieving theological and moral teaching on the appropriate relationship between religion and politics and between religion and national identity." Powers, "Religion and Peacebuilding," in *Strategies of Peace: Transforming Conflict in a Violent World*, ed. Daniel Philpott and Gerard F. Powers (New York: Oxford University Press, 2010), 325–326.

5. Attention to general statements of belief may be unhelpful, "because, as Appleby points out, 'it is not apparent that even broad concepts such as forgiveness and reconciliation are universal beyond their most generalized usage. . . . Religions, in short, have not arrived at a universal set of values or priorities in pursuing peace." In Powers's words,

> It is not necessary to discover or agree on a global theology and ethics of peace building for religion to be effective in peace building. Efforts to do so usually take an enormous amount of time and resources and usually produce a least common-denominator approach to religious peace building whose impact is minimal, in part because it emasculates the richness and distinctiveness of existing traditions, thereby reducing the ability of religious concepts to motivate and inspire people.
>
> Efforts to find common ground can be especially counterproductive in identity conflicts where a community's religious and communal identity and even survival are threatened. In those cases, efforts to deemphasize what is distinctive in one's own religious tradition can exacerbate the problem of what Gopin calls negative identity, the tendency to define one's religion in opposition to the other. The solution is not to downplay religious identity but to find those elements within the identity that can contribute to peace building.

6. For an overview of the kinds of thinking exhibited in SR, see Peter Ochs, "The Rules of Scriptural Reasoning," *Journal of Scriptural Reasoning* 2, no. 1 (2002): 1–20. http://jsr.lib.virginia.edu/volume-2-no-1-may-2002-the-rules-of-scriptural-reasoning/the-society-of-scriptural-reasoning-the-rules-of-scriptural-reasoning7/.

7. For a sample of SR in Islamic, Jewish, and Christian studies, see Basit Bilal Koshul and Steven Kepnes, eds., *Scripture, Reason and the Contemporary Islam-West Encounter: Studying the "Other," Understanding the "Self"* (New York: Palgrave MacMillan, 2007).

8. For a sampling of firsthand accounts of the experience of participating in public, SR fellowships of study, see Carol Brévart-Demm, "Not Consensus But Friendship," *Swarthmore College Bulletin*, January 2009, http://media.swarthmore.edu/bulletin/?p=131; Rose Aslan, "Scriptural Reasoning: A Creative Approach to Interfaith Engagement," *Huffington Post,* October 10, 2012, http://www.huffingtonpost.com/rose-aslan/creative-approach-to-interfaith-engagement_b_1825953.html; Miriam Lorie, "Scriptural Reasoning: A How-to Guide," Cambridge Inter-faith Programme, www.youtube.com/watch?v=rjNlc9agkUc&feature=relmfu and www.youtube.com/watch?v=Iy9RJ2VAC1k; and Kelly Rankin, "Reading Abrahamic Scriptures Together," *U of T News*, University of Toronto, December 8, 2011, www.news.utoronto.ca/r eading-abrahamic-scriptures-together.

9. See Basit Bilal Koshul, *The Postmodern Significance of Max Weber's Legacy* (New York: Palgrave Macmillan, 2005), 36–38; Steven Smith, *The Disenchantment of Secular Discourse* (Cambridge, MA: Harvard University Press, 2010); and Peter Berger, *The Desecularization of the World: Resurgent Religion and World Politics* (Washington, DC: Ethics and Public Policy Center, 1999).

10. Charles Taylor, *The Secular Age* (Cambridge, MA: Harvard University Press, 2007).

11. William Cavanaugh, *The Myth of Religious Violence: Secular Ideology and the Roots of Modern Conflict* (New York: Oxford University Press, 2009).

12. From philosophers of religion like Alasdair MacIntyre and Stanley Hauerwas to sociologists of religion like Peter Berger, Robert Bellah, and James Hunter. This is of course a focus for all SR scholars. See, for example, Randi Rashkover, "Cultivating Theology: Overcoming America's Skepticism about Religious Rationality," *CrossCurrents* 55, no. 2 (2005): 241–251.

13. See also Cavanaugh, *The Myth of Religious Violence*, 17–20.

14. Appleby, *Ambivalence of the Sacred*, 13.

15. In Powers' words,

On the question of religion, there is a significant gap between the views of the policy elites in Washington, London, Paris, Berlin, Moscow, and Tokyo and the views of ordinary people around the world. In fall 2003, the Zogby polling firm and the University of Rochester released what they called the first ever worldwide poll on religious beliefs, which found that people care about religion far more than politics, that a clear majority associated violence within their own country with politics not religion, and that a majority says that their country would be better if it were more religious. Poll results are summarized at www.zogbyworldwide.com/news/ReadNewsI.cfm. (Powers, "Religion and Peacebuilding," 349–350n25).

16. Powers, "Religion and Peacebuilding," 317n1.

17. Powers, "Religion and Peacebuilding," 318.

18. Atalia Omer, "Religious Peacebuilding: The Exotic, the Good, and the Theatrical," Chapter 1 of this volume.

19. Powers writes,

> The indigenous nature of much religious peacebuilding is strengthened by the fact that many religious institutions are relatively transnational actors. They are deeply rooted in local communities yet also have a global reach that can surpass that of governments, international institutions, or multinational companies. Their global reach enables them to bridge the global divide between zones of conflict and power and zones of peace and prosperity. Their indigenous character enables them to provide early warnings of simmering conflicts and can help outsiders better understand and respond to the dynamics of a particular conflict. (Powers, "Religion and Peacebuilding," 327.)

20. This discovery was as surprising to members of SR research teams as it may be to anyone reading this chapter.

21. By way of illustration, I comment here on John Paul Lederach and R. Scott Appleby, "Strategic Peacebuilding: An Overview," in Philpott and Powers, *Strategies of Peace*, 19–44.

22. Lederach and Appleby, "Strategic Peacebuilding," 22.

23. For a sample of this kind of academic SR, See Basit Bilal Koshul and Muhammad Suheyl Umar, eds., *Muhammad Iqbal*: A Contemporary, Articles from the International Seminar Held at the University of Cambridge, June 19–20 2008 (Lahore: Iqbal Academy Pakistan, 2010).

24. For an example of this public orientation of SR, see Tom Greggs, "Inter-faith Pedagogy for Muslims and Christians: Scriptural Reasoning and Christian and Muslim Youth Work," *Discourse* 9, no. 2 (2010): 201–226. For media coverage, see "Scriptural Reasoning," *Religion and Ethics Weekly*, episode no. 1106, Public Broadcasting Service, October 12, 2007, http://www.pbs.org/wnet/religionandethics/week1106/cover.html.

25. Lederach and Appleby, "Strategic Peacebuilding," 26–27.

26. Lederach and Appleby, "Strategic Peacebuilding," 26–27.

27. Lederach and Appleby, "Strategic Peacebuilding," 36–37.

28. Many of whom are included or cited in this volume.

29. Naomi Roht-Arriaza, "Human Rights and Strategic Peacebuilding: The Roles of Local, National, and International Actors," in Philpott and Powers, *Strategies of Peace*, 232–233.

30. Roht-Arriaza, "Human Rights," 240.

31. From an informal introductory sheet composed by Scott Appleby.

32. Lederach and Appleby, "Strategic Peacebuilding," 23.

33. SR peace workers will need to make strategic decisions about which actors in these groups will best serve and be served by these instruments of small-group study. Some actors will be selected because their antagonisms are judged to be genuinely religious; others because they are motivated to close engagement with their antagonists; others because they may contribute to future negotiations; others because they hold positions of social leadership and cannot be overlooked; others because they have the capacity to teach or influence other members of their society.

34. Note how important it is to distinguish between the immediate and longer-range goal of SR interaction: the interaction needs to have immediate value *in order* for it to succeed as an instrument of healing or repair!

35. Illustrating the global orientation, see David F. Ford, "God and Our Public Life: A Scriptural Wisdom" in *Liberating Texts? Sacred Scriptures in Public Life*, ed. Sebastian Kim and Jonathan Draper (London: SPCK, 2008), 29–56; and Ford, "Knowledge, Meaning, and the World's Great Challenges," *Scottish Journal of Theology* 57, no. 2 (2004): 181–202.

36. Lederach and Appleby, "Strategic Peacebuilding," 28.

37. In this way SR appears to share what Appleby calls SP's ongoing integration of theory and practice, or ways in which theories are continually refined by reference to "local or indigenous frames of meaning" and action, and the ways in which local meanings and practices are generalized and compared across localities and regions.

38. By "deictic marker" I mean some, often subtle, embedded indicator or sign of the finite location or source or reference or optimal usefulness of a speech act or claim or general theory. On SR and the university, see Mike Higton, "Can the University and the Church Save Each Other?" *CrossCurrents* 55, no. 2 (2005): 172–183; and Mike Higton, *A Theology of Higher Education* (New York: Oxford University Press, 2012).

39. Powers, "Religion and Peacebuilding," 323.

40. Daniel Philpott, "Reconciliation: An Ethic for Peacebuilding," in Philpott and Powers, *Strategies of Peace*, 91–118.

41. Omer cites Daniel Philpott, "Reconciliation, Politics, and Peabebuilding," Chapter 13 in this volume.

42. Lederach and Appleby, "Strategic Peacebuilding," 27.

43. Lederach and Appleby, "Strategic Peacebuilding," 28.

44. Appleby, *Ambivalence of the Sacred*, 33.

45. Appleby, *Ambivalence of the Sacred*, 33.

46. Powers, "Religion and Peacebuilding," 332. For background on the Acholi, see, *inter alia*, Kamari Maxine Clarke, *Fictions of Justice: The International Criminal Court and the Challenge of Legal Pluralism in Sub-Saharan Africa* (Cambridge: Cambridge Studies in Law and Society, 2009), 127.

47. Lederach and Appleby, "Strategic Peacebuilding," 24. In Philpott's words ("Reconciliation"):

> Some religious traditions also bring to peace building the foundations of an ethic of reconciliation—especially its core ideas of restorative justice and mercy. . . . In the Jewish scriptures, the Hebrew words that translate to justice in English are the same words that translate into righteousness (*sedeq* and *mishpat*), the condition of the people of Israel living in comprehensive right relationship according to the covenant God made with them. This state of right relationship is also closely related to shalom, the Jewish concept of peace, a thoroughgoing condition of right relationship. Lederach and Appleby's concept of *justpeace* is indeed much like shalom. . . .
>
> In the New Testament, the Greek words translated to reconciliation are found—*katallage and katallosso*—appearing there fifteen times, twelve of these in the letters of Paul. This meaning is either the process of restoration of right relationship or the condition of right relationship that results from this restoration. . . . Although the meanings of justice, peace, reconciliation, and mercy in Islam are not precisely equivalent to those in the Jewish scriptures or the New Testament, they converge closely with their meanings in the present ethics of reconciliation. The Qur'an's words for justice, *'adl* and *qist*, with some interpretive effort, can be understood as comprehensive right relationship. . . . The Arabic word for peace, *salam*, is closely related, both linguistically and in meaning, to the Jewish shalom, and describes a broad state of harmony. ("Reconciliation," 99–100.)

Later, he adds:

> Reconciliation is not true reconciliation if it is not based on justice and should not be mistaken for the irenicism of the peace agreement that fails to ensure fundamental elements of justice like basic human rights, including those of minorities. Dictators must be defeated, *shalom*, *tsedek*, positive peace, *justpeace* must be established. ("Reconciliation," 105.)

48. See Chapter 1 of this volume. Emphases mine.
49. Powers, "Religion and Peacebuilding," 322.
50. See Nicholas Adams, "Reparative Reasoning," *Modern Theology* 24, no. 3 (2008): 447–457.
51. Powers notes that "An extensive report on US government engagement with religion by the Center for Strategic and International Studies concluded that despite a significant increase in attention to religion since 9/11, major obstacles remain to effective US engagement with religion." Among these, in the report's words, are:

  • We government officials are often reluctant to address the issue of religion, whether in response to a secular US legal and political tradition, or the context of America's Judeo-Christian image oversees, or simply because religion is perceived as too complicated or sensitive.

  • Current US government frameworks for approaching religion are narrow, often approaching religions as problematic or monolithic.

(Powers, "Religion and Peacebuilding," 345, citing Liora Danan, "Mixed Blessings: U.S. Government Engagement with Religions in Conflict-Prone Settings; A Report of the Post-Conflict Reconstruction Project," Center for Strategic and International Studies, July 2007, p. 3).

BIBLIOGRAPHY

Adams, Nicholas. "Reparative Reasoning." *Modern Theology* 24, no. 3 (2008): 447–457.
Appleby, Scott. *The Ambivalence of the Sacred: Religion, Violence, and Reconciliation.* Lanham, MD: Rowman and Littlefield, 2000.
Aslan, Rose. "Scriptural Reasoning: A Creative Approach to Interfaith Engagement." *Huffington Post*, October 10, 2012. http://www.huffingtonpost.com/rose-aslan/creative-approach-to-interfaith-engagement_b_1825953.html.
Berger, Peter. *The Desecularization of the World: Resurgent Religion and World Politics.* Washington, DC: Ethics and Public Policy Center, 1999.
Brévart-Demm, Carol. "Not Consensus But Friendship." *Swarthmore College Bulletin*, January 2009. http://media.swarthmore.edu/bulletin/?p=131.
Cavanaugh, William. *The Myth of Religious Violence: Secular Ideology and the Roots of Modern Conflict.* New York: Oxford University Press, 2009.
Danan, Liora. "Mixed Blessings: U.S. Government Engagement with Religion in Conflict-Prone Settings; A Report of the Post-Conflict Reconstruction Project." Center for Strategic and International Studies. July 2007. http://csis.org/files/media/csis/pubs/070820_religion.pdf.
Ford, David F. "Knowledge, Meaning, and the World's Great Challenges." *Scottish Journal of Theology* 57, no. 2 (2004): 181–202.
Ford, David F. "God and Our Public Life: A Scriptural Wisdom." In *Liberating Texts? Sacred Scriptures in Public Life*, edited by Sebastian Kim and Jonathan Draper, 29–56. London: SPCK, 2008.
Ford, David F., and C. C. Pecknold, eds. *The Promise of Scriptural Reasoning.* Oxford: Blackwell, 2006.
Gopin, Marc. *Between Eden and Armageddon: The Future of World Religions, Violence, and Peacemaking.* New York: Oxford University Press, 2000.

Greggs, Tom. "Inter-faith Pedagogy for Muslims and Christians: Scriptural Reasoning and Christian and Muslim Youth Work." *Discourse* 9, no. 2 (2010): 201–226.

Higton, Mike. "Can the University and the Church Save Each Other?" *CrossCurrents* 55, no. 2 (2005): 172–183.

Higton, Mike. *A Theology of Higher Education.* New York: Oxford University Press, 2012.

Koshul, Basit Bilal. *The Postmodern Significance of Max Weber's Legacy.* New York: Palgrave Macmillan, 2005.

Koshul, Basit Bilal, and Steven Kepnes, eds. *Scripture, Reason, and the Contemporary Islam-West Encounter: Studying the "Other," Understanding the "Self."* New York: Palgrave MacMillan, 2007.

Koshul, Basit Bilal, and Muhammad Suheyl Umar, eds. *Muhammad Iqbal*: A Contemporary; Articles from the International Seminar Held at the University of Cambridge, June 19–20, 2008. Lahore: Iqbal Academy Pakistan, 2010.

Lederach, John Paul, and R. Scott Appleby. "Strategic Peacebuilding: An Overview." In Philpott and Powers, *Strategies of Peace*, 19–44.

Lorie, Miriam. "Scriptural Reasoning; A How-to Guide." Cambridge Inter-faith Programme. www.youtube.com/watch?v=Iy9RJ2VAC1k; www.youtube.com/watch?v=rjNlc9agkUc&feature=relmfu.

Ochs, Peter. "The Rules of Scriptural Reasoning." *Journal of Scriptural Reasoning* 2, no. 1 (2002): 1–20.

Ochs, Peter, and Stacy Johnson, eds. *Crisis, Call, and Leadership in the Abrahamic Traditions.* New York: Palgrave Macmillan, 2009.

Philpott, Daniel, ed. *The Politics of Past Evil: Religion, Reconciliation, and the Dilemmas of Transitional Justice.* Notre Dame, IN: University of Notre Dame Press, 2006.

Philpott, Daniel. "Reconciliation: An Ethic for Peacebuilding." In Philpott and Powers, *Strategies of Peace*, 91–118.

Philpott, Daniel. *Just and Unjust Peace.* New York: Oxford University Press, 2012.

Philpott, Daniel, and Gerard F. Powers, eds. *Strategies of Peace: Transforming Conflict in a Violent World.* New York: Oxford University Press, 2010.

Powers, Gerard F. "Religion and Peacebuilding." In Philpott and Powers, *Strategies of Peace*, 317–352.

Rankin, Kelly. "Reading Abrahamic Scriptures Together." *U of T News*, University of Toronto, December 8, 2011. www.news.utoronto.ca/reading-abrahamic-scriptures-together.

Rashkover, Randi. "Cultivating Theology: Overcoming America's Skepticism about Religious Rationality." *CrossCurrents* 55, no. 2 (2005): 241–251.

Roht-Arriaza, Naomi. "Human Rights and Strategic Peacebuilding: The Roles of Local, National, and International Actors." In Philpott and Powers, *Strategies of Peace*, 231–246.

"Scriptural Reasoning." *Religion and Ethics Weekly*, episode no. 1106. Public Broadcasting Service. October 12, 2007. http://www.pbs.org/wnet/religionandethics/week1106/cover.html.

Smith, Steven. *The Disenchantment of Secular Discourse.* Cambridge, MA: Harvard University Press, 2010.

Taylor, Charles. *The Secular Age.* Cambridge, MA: Harvard University Press, 2007.

CHAPTER 20

··

RITUAL, RELIGION, AND PEACEBUILDING

··

LISA SCHIRCH

It takes more than a sharp intellect, searing analysis, comprehensive planning, and quick diplomacy to build peace. These are all important components of peacebuilding, but none can transform deeply held traumas, beliefs, and fears like religious ritual. There is a symbolic element to conflict, one founded on psychosocial wounds and worldviews of identity and religious beliefs. Cold rationality cannot touch these sacred parts of conflict. Peacebuilding requires both ritual and rational approaches.

The 2012 discovery of the Higgs boson or the so-called God particle confirmed the long-held belief that there was a pervasive energy force that shaped the mass of the universe. Religious ritual is like the Higgs boson of conflict. Religion is like the invisible subatomic parts that attract and build mass in the atom, invisibly creating a reality, a mass, or a conflict that can be seen. Researchers cannot easily isolate or track down the specific causal influence or impact of religious beliefs, symbols, or rituals. Rather, acknowledging these often invisible forces within conflict allow us to find symbolic, ritualized pathways out of violence and toward peace.

This chapter describes the role of religious ritual in the process of peacebuilding. It looks at the role of ritual in traditional religions and then shows how specific religious leaders use rituals and even develop new ones in order to foster reconciliation or transformation to support peace. Drawing on a wide set of interdisciplinary research on ritual, the chapter identifies distinct types and characteristics of ritual that support peacebuilding.

TYPES AND FUNCTIONS OF RITUAL

··

Anthropologists,[1] sociologists,[2] religious scholars,[3] and even political scientists[4] and community organizers[5] have written a great deal about ritual's roles and characteristics. In this literature, ritual has two broad meanings. In everyday use, people refer to routine acts such as washing hands or brushing teeth as rituals. In this chapter and in most literature, the term "ritual" refers to a symbolic act that holds significant meaning.

Figure 20.1
Spectrum of Types
Formal------------------Informal Traditional---------------Improvised Socializing---------------Transforming Constructive-------------Destructive Religious-----------------Secular

The literature identifies a variety of types of ritual that fall roughly along a set of spectrums, as Figure 20.1 illustrates.[6] Formal rituals such as inaugurations or graduations have a set of protocols that must be followed in order for them to feel authentic to those participating in them. Informal rituals such as lighting a candle or eating a meal together have some sense of pattern and meaning to them, but can be carried out in a more flexible manner. Traditional rituals refer to symbolic acts that people have carried out for many years, decades, or even centuries. Improvised rituals, on the other hand, refer to symbolic acts that have no history of performance but rather develop out of a specific context that calls for the creation of a new ritual. Socializing rituals aim to reinforce current values, beliefs, and social practices within a community, such as singing hymns or songs with religious content. Transforming rituals are those that aim to bring about change, such as a wedding that transforms single people into a married couple. Constructive rituals affirm and protect life. Destructive rituals aim to destroy life or increase social divisions.

Most important to this chapter is a distinction between religious and secular rituals. Religious rituals are those whose content contains reference to sacred themes relating to a sense of the divine or the purpose of existence. Since conflict calls into question the very meaning and purpose of life, it often takes on religious dimensions. Some people use elaborate religious justifications for the use of violence through religious discourse and may even see waging war or committing acts of terrorism as religious rituals. Secular rituals are those that do not refer to themes related to religious meaning, values, or acts.

Any ritual can fall in more than one category. For example, a Hindu prayer can be formal, traditional, religious, socializing, and constructive. A group of young neo-Nazi men can perform a punk music dance that is informal, improvised, transforming, and destructive.

The religious use of ritual and its application to the field of peacebuilding are the focus of this chapter. All religious traditions use rituals. Religiously motivated people create spaces to perform symbolic acts that communicate significant meaning about the purpose of life, and specific values and rules for how to live and relate to other people and the divine.

SHARED TASKS OF RELIGION AND PEACEBUILDING

The earliest religious rituals developed as humans began to live together in small communities, seeking protection and safety in their unity. Archaeological evidence shows that these early human beings faced great violence from large predator animals and competition with other humans for scarce food sources. Communities began to sacrifice goats and other ani-mals by placing them outside of their community as a way of feeding the predators or com-petitors to prevent them from attacking the community. This ritual of the "scapegoat" that diverted violence away from the community and toward a symbolic object of a substitute sacrifice, often a goat, allowed communities to maintain unity and safety. Scapegoat rituals of symbolic sacrifices grew and developed over generations to include other kinds of early religious rituals on sacred altars.[7]

Today, religions use ritual to embody unity and wholeness among members. Symbolic acts such as drinking wine and eating bread in remembrance of the sacrificial body of Christ, or holding a Seder dinner to remember Jewish ancestors, or observing the Ramadan fast are rituals that bind communities together while reinforcing important stories and values.

The Latin root of the word "religion" is *ligar*—the same root of the word ligament, the con-nective tissue binding muscle and bone. In this sense, the word "religion" means connecting, or reconnecting.[8] From the very beginning of early religious practice, religion was funda-mentally about binding individuals together in a community. Religion built relationships between people, fostering a sense of a collective whole rather than competing parts.[9] This "wholeness" or "holiness" was felt as a sacred, religious experience. Émile Durkheim refers to this as the "collective effervescence" or the inherent social nature of religion in his socio-logical analysis of *The Elementary Forms of the Religious Life* where everyday life is "profane" and people have religious or "sacred" experiences in collective social gatherings.[10]

People experience wholeness, holiness, and a religious high when they perform rituals that emphasize their relationships with others. Rituals bring a sense of unity or relationship that fulfills what psychologists say is a human need for connection and belonging.[11] This includes traditional rituals as diverse as worshipers kneeling in unison, singing in unison, or washing feet together to more secular rituals of warlords and diplomats smoking a ciga-rette in the halls of the United Nations, sports spectators cheering in unison, or audiences at rock concerts lighting candles and waving at musicians. Often these rituals are a process of remembering—re-membering—or putting disparate parts back into relationship.

Religion is a sociological as well as a theological pursuit; it links people together while also explicitly linking people to the divine. Religious rituals can affirm both spiritual and com-munity relationships. Communities and societies have long relied on religion to help form a common set of rituals and rule of law to help people coexist with each other. Religious rituals teach young and old members of a community common values and rules while affirming a shared identity among community members.

Peacebuilding and religions share common traits: they include a set of values, methods, and rituals that create connective tissue between groups of people torn apart by structural or direct violence.[12] Peacebuilding is a relational task, seeking to improve the quantity and quality of relationships between people and their environment.[13] Peacebuilding emphasizes the interdependence of life on a fragile planet where state boundaries and guarded neigh-borhoods separating rich and poor can never truly isolate the haves from the have-nots. Peacebuilding rituals, such as shaking hands after signing a peace agreement, serve as a non-verbal promise to acknowledge the humanity and dignity of another. Religious rituals that support peacebuilding, described in this chapter, hold a special role in both bringing human beings back into relationship after the experience of conflict or violence and in bringing back a sense of spiritual wholeness or holiness where humans have suffered a spiritual crisis of meaning or departed from their religious values in the midst of conflict.

Religion and peacebuilding have a shared task: to overcome the similar concepts of "sin" and "violence," which divide and break relationships between people, their environment, and their creator and sacred values. Sin and violence represent actions done that hurt others, without recognizing the interdependence and connection between parts of creation. Religion and peacebuilding heal while sin and violence wound.[14]

It is important to note here that religious ritual's ability to unite is not all-inclusive. Sometimes members of religious communities unite with each other against what they perceive is a common enemy: people of another religion or identity. Or political leaders hijack religious identities to persuade people to support structural or direct violence against another group, resulting in harms and humiliations to their human rights. Inter-religious conflicts often need peacebuilding processes to enable coexistence between groups. While acknowledging religion's detrimental role in conflict, it is also important to acknowledge that religious rituals have a significant role to play in peacebuilding. Religion is relevant to peacebuilding in several ways,[15] outlined below.

RELIGIONS CREATE RITUALS TO FOSTER RECONCILIATION

Religious actors are often motivated to lead or participate in peacebuilding efforts because of their religious values stressing reconciliation and charity toward others. At their best, religions create a space where people in conflict can express themselves, heal themselves, and reconcile themselves through ritual, symbol, and the arts.

Indigenous religious traditions articulate reconciliation as a primary value, shaping every aspect of their life. An indigenous view of relationships is expansive. A Native prayer remembers every element of creation; it thanks the animals, the plants, and the forces of nature for working the way that they do. The most sacred principle of life in many indigenous communities is the concept of remembering and respecting "all my relations." Indigenous traditions emphasize the relationships and need for reconciliation between all parts of creation: people with their creator, people with each other, and people with creation, animals, plants, and the environment in which they live. All elements of creation have a spiritual nature. Indigenous religious rituals remind people of these relationships.[16]

For example, among North American indigenous nations and communities, the smudging ceremony is a ritual supporting peacebuilding. Performed by elders at the beginnings of meetings and by families and individuals on a daily basis, the smudging ceremony affirms relationships between people, their environment, and their creator. The smudging ceremony begins with lighting powerful-smelling herbs like sage and sweetgrass, and a prayer recognizing "all my relations." People cup the smoke from the herbs in their hands and pull it over their head for clear thinking, toward their eyes and ears to see and hear good intentions in other people, and to their mouths so that they speak respectfully to others. The smoke from the burning herbs then drifts upwards, taking the people's prayers for clarity, good intentions, and respect to the creator. The smudging ceremony purifies the participants in preparation for their interactions. It can also preempt conflict by creating a space that is sacred, where people are reminded of their relationships and have intentionally washed their eyes, ears, mouth, mind, and heart of any bad intentions. The smudging ceremony is a ritualized way of communicating "we want to get along with each other."[17]

In Buddhist traditions, the concept of "mindfulness" and the practice of meditation emphasize ritualized reconciliation.[18] Buddhists practice being mindful by bringing their attention to the present and being mindful of each passing thought and feeling with the goal of recognizing and accepting them. Buddhists meditate through a ritual of sitting or walking quietly. Meditation can include chanting and the ringing of a bell to begin and end the session and remind people throughout of the need to bring back their attention to the present. Recognizing that suffering, separation, and division are common human experiences, Buddhist meditation helps people practice self-regulation to become aware of their relationships with others and their environment.

In a variety of Christian traditions, foot-washing is a ritual of reconciliation between people. Christians who practice this ritual draw inspiration from John 13:1–17, where Jesus performs this act. In verse 14–16, Jesus says, "If I then, your Lord and Teacher, have washed your feet, you also ought to wash one another's feet. For I have given you an example that you should do as I have done to you. Most assuredly, I say to you, a servant is not greater than his master; nor is he who is sent greater than he who sent him." Often after practicing the ritual of Communion where Christians remember Jesus's sacrifice, members of a congregation will engage in the ritual of washing each other's feet. One member will kneel before another, taking their feet into a pan of water and washing them. Christians practice this ritual to illustrate humility and service to others.

These religious rituals illustrate their relevance to peacebuilding. But the practice and potential contribution of religious ritual to peacebuilding go much further.

PEACEBUILDING AS A RELIGIOUS TASK OF CREATION

Religions have a narrative or story about the act of creation. In some religions, God is creator and humans are passive subjects to a divine will or plan. Some religious leaders link a sinful human nature with a brutish violence, where all people have the capacity and propensity to be violent toward others. The story of how the world came to be as it is, and what power humans have in this world to create or recreate the world to support justice and peace—a justpeace—is fundamentally religious in nature.

In peacebuilding, humans are part of the story of creation: they act as "co-creators" with God in designing and forming a world with less division and violence. In the words of Shakespeare, "all life is a stage," and humans can build peace on this stage. All humans are actors in a series of grand and not-so-grand ritual acts that involve symbols, actions, and their senses in the pursuit of justpeace.

The field of peacebuilding rests on the premise that violence is not distributed equally across all individuals or societies. Some individuals make choices that harm others. Some leaders support policies that result in structural and direct violence, which in turn leads to greater levels of violence and crime at intrapersonal, interpersonal, community, and national levels. The political, economic, cultural, and social structure of a community and nation determines in large part the level of violence that it suffers. However, a peacebuilding lens views the violence exhibited by individuals as individuals or within the context of social and political conflicts in a non-essentializing manner as potentially capable of being transformed.

Peacebuilding recognizes human agency in changing a destructive environment. It does not accept that the world simply is "person against person." Rather, it looks at patterns of violence, identifying many areas of relative peace and examining the conditions that breed greed, violence, and division. Peacebuilding requires a belief that humans can create and design societies that are more peaceful.

Peacebuilding includes a wide range of efforts by diverse actors in government and civil society to address both the root causes and immediate impacts of violence before, during, and after particular conflicts. Peacebuilding supports human security; where people have freedom from fear, freedom from want, and freedom from humiliation. Peacebuilding is strategic when multiple efforts address diverse sectors in economics, politics, security, health, education, and other areas related to conflict; when these diverse actors communicate with each other to best complement each other's efforts; and when it spans short-term crisis response to long-term preventive efforts.[19]

Religious ritual is part of this empowering, creative, artistic, and sensual tradition of social transformation. Rituals often seem timeless, as if they have always existed. But all rituals have a history. Humans created them and began passing them down as a way of shaping values, stories, and communities. Religious rituals evolved in response to human crisis, as a way of preventing conflict between individuals and groups.

The Ugandan poet Okot p'Bitek's book *Artist the Ruler* argues that artists are the unacknowledged rulers in any society, for they have the means to spin images in people's minds that shape their lives.[20] Postmodern theorist Theodor Adorno agrees, claiming that there is now a "culture industry" through which the elite class takes over the production of art and culture to repress and pacify any critique of the social structure by producing mind-numbing music, entertainment, and other media.[21] Adorno argues that people have given up their own power that p'Bitek describes as creating culture.

Peacebuilding requires an explicit or implicit theology of creation where people are co-creators with the divine. Like artists, peacebuilders design, create, orchestrate, and direct human energies toward a more ideal world. Like artists, they tap into the inspiration of other artists. They draw inspiration from religious rituals developed by men and women over millennia. They draw on long-standing traditions. But they are also not afraid to invent, to discover, and to improvise new rituals required for bringing divergent groups together.

This act of creation requires empowerment. Peacebuilders are the choreographers, directors, and set designers of a drama centered on the visually engaging process of building peace. Peacebuilding involves people immersed in conflict in a democratic and participatory process of creation or re-creation of their relationship.

RELIGIOUS RITUAL AS TRAUMA HEALING

Ritual is not new to peacebuilding. Traditional societies and some symbol-savvy peacebuilding facilitators are already using ritual to help communities transition toward peace.

Only a scant literature documents these efforts, however. It is no great surprise that societies that value ritual may place less value on written forms of communication. Three case studies illustrate how several regions are using different types of rituals to promote peace.

Walking Meditation: Cambodia

As the supreme patriarch of Cambodian Buddhism, Maha Ghosananda recognized the need to use familiar rituals and religious symbols in helping his country transition to peace and democracy. Ghosananda, who was known as the Cambodian Gandhi, lost his entire family to violence led by Cambodia's Khmer Rouge. Every year Ghosananda led a walking meditation, known as the Walk for Peace and Reconciliation or the Dhammayietra, the pilgrimage of truth, across Cambodia's minefields and deforested land. Walking with Buddhist monks who would immerse flowers into water and then sprinkle this water onto shops and homes as they walked by, Ghosananda created culturally and spiritually informed rituals supporting reconciliation that even some Khmer Rouge welcomed.

In 1993, the Dhammayietra walked through open fighting. Ghosananda announced, "We must remove the land mines in our hearts which prevent us from making peace—greed, hatred, and delusions. We can overcome greed with weapons of generosity, we can overcome hatred with the weapon of loving kindness, we can overcome delusions with the weapon of wisdom."[22] Anthropologist Monique Skidmore writes that

> the Dhammayietra ritual, or "peace walk," may provide a way through the symbolic "washing-away" of Khmer Rouge memories, the creation of new collective memories, and the reclaiming of a physical manifestation (Angkor War) of the Buddhist-centered world view— for some Cambodians to emerge, at least in part, from the sensorially numb space they necessarily created in order to survive the terrors of the Khmer Rouge era.[23]

Drawing on religious values and rituals may have made Cambodia's political forces more accepting of Ghosananda than if his message had been explicitly political. Ghosananda did not shy away from also saying, "Reconciliation does not mean that we surrender rights and conditions, but rather that we use love."[24] As a religious leader, Ghosananda had a powerful charisma and spirituality in his leadership to speak to Cambodia's divided political leadership. But like many religious leaders, Ghosananda was not an administrator or an effective leader delegating tasks that might have made the Dhammayietra a more significant religious and political force within the region.[25]

Healing and Purification Rituals: Mozambique

In many traditional and tribal communities, reconciliation between clashing tribes and the collective healing of trauma may take place over the sacrifice of a cow or goat or through a community ritual. In Kenya, for example, tribes sacrifice a white bull and share a meal together in a ritual of reconciliation to put violent conflict behind them and move forward with peaceful relations.[26]

In Mozambique, communities used ritual in a healing process to welcome home return-ing soldiers, many of them children, and to mark a path toward recovery. Ritual was a natu-ral part of peacebuilding in Mozambique in part because both rebel and government forces had used grotesque and violent rituals to terrorize the country during fifteen years of war. Unlike in Western forms of trauma healing, which focus on helping individuals return to "normal" through verbalizing painful experiences, in many traditional and indigenous com-munities, trauma is viewed as a collective experience requiring symbolic group healing and purification rituals. Mozambican communities used rituals to cleanse and purify returning soldiers or rebels who had been "tainted" by the war, and to capture and put to rest the spirits of people who were not buried properly during the war.[27]

For example, one Mozambican community prepared a purification ceremony for a nine-year-old boy who had been kidnapped by Renamo soldiers. The boy entered a special "house of the spirits." A family member then directed the boy to take off his clothes. The relative then set the hut on fire and helped the boy out. The community then cleansed the boy both internally and externally. The boy inhaled an herbal remedy, took a ritual bath, and drank a medicine. Drawing on traditional religions as well as Catholic rites, these rituals gave the boy and his community a way of symbolically acknowledging the trauma while giv-ing him a rite of passage into his future life, all without requiring the boy to talk about what happened to him during his time with Renamo armed forces.[28]

In other communities, family elders organized a ritual purification process called *tim-hamba* for Renamo and government soldiers after the war. The ritual would begin at dawn as an elder called the names of relatives who died during the war as well as the names of other ancestors. Elders would tell the soldiers about the current family matters and thank them for protection and guidance during the war. Then, elders would sacrifice a goat, ox, or chicken under a *gandzelo* tree as a symbolic bridge between the living and the dead. After eating the sacrificial animal, the family and community drum, dance, and sing together.[29] Some observ-ers argued these traditional rituals had an unquestionably positive effect on Mozambique as a whole in the post-conflict recovery period, facilitating recovery and rebirth, cleansing and forgiveness, and transforming individuals, communities, and the nation.[30]

Public Memorials as Ritualized Spaces for Reconciliation: Argentina and Iraq

Institutional approaches to peacebuilding often overlook or avoid addressing the psy-chological and spiritual dimensions of conflict. Transitional justice processes require both legitimate truth-telling processes and criminal investigations as well as symbolic memorials and rituals that address the messy emotional and existential elements that simply cannot be wrapped up neatly in a judicial process.[31] Ceremonies, rituals, memo-rializing processes, and other arts-based trauma recovery processes help people move from the confusion and trauma of their memories to a place where they can express themselves through written or oral vehicles of communication. This can also include symbolic forms of accountability for offenders (truth-telling) and symbolic repara-tion to victims and restorative justice in national transitional justice processes. As communities find appropriate ways to symbolize their experiences of the past, a non-verbal catharsis and processing of these experiences can help ready people to begin to verbalize their lament over the past.

Public memorials can play similar roles to traditional rituals. Creating a public memorial to foster a ritual of trauma healing is a complex process involving diverse actors. International and local transitional justice experts work with historians, museum designers, public artists, trauma specialists, and human rights activists to create new memorialization processes in diverse countries. While often involving the help of outsiders, memorialization only works when insiders are in the lead, owning the process and involved in making decisions related to the memorial. Insiders must see a memorialization process as legitimate and impartial, so that all sides of the conflict perceive the ritual space as a symbol of their shared grief. Just as institutional justice processes are not sufficient in helping a country move toward reconciliation, memorials themselves are also only helpful if they are one part of a multifaceted approach addressing issues of justice, accountability, human rights, and reconciliation within a country.[32]

Many memorials suffer from top-down processes, often led by outsiders or political interests. Without community support or broad public ownership, even the human rights activists and artists who created a memorial in Sri Lanka to victims on all sides of the conflict abandoned it over the years.[33] In its rundown state, the memorial symbolized an abandonment of efforts to heal trauma in a society that ultimately turned to extreme violence, creating even greater numbers of victims. The most successful memorials see memorialization as a long-term process and build direct, verbal communication to complement nonverbal, ritualized elements.

For example, in Argentina, eight human rights organizations, including religious leadership, developed a memorial called Memoria Abierta or "open memory." They identified hundreds of detention and torture sites. They collected oral histories and photographs, and then made these accessible in public archives to document the past. The memorialization process includes public workshops, trainings, and events aiming to hold together images of the country's violent history. As part of a global network called the International Coalition of Sites of Conscience, Memoria Abierta illustrates the potential of ritualized memorials to help transform a society.[34]

Traditional rituals and memorials of trauma healing are not without problems. Leaders can use them for political gain, to urge people to forget the past, and thus can undermine a sense of justice and human rights. Profit-minded leaders can take them over, commercializing memorials. In Kurdistan, for example, Kurds themselves destroyed the Halabja Monument memorializing five thousand Kurds killed by a chemical warfare attack. Observers noted Kurds were angry that the monument had become an "emblem of tyranny and greed" for local authorities that used the monument to make money for themselves.[35]

Each of these examples illustrates the general relevance of ritual to peacebuilding. Next, this chapter looks at the research detailing why ritual is relevant to peacebuilding, first by explaining the anatomy of the human brain and the way the mind processes information, particularly in the midst of violence and with the help of ritual. The chapter then examines how ritual functions in ways that assist the process of communication about and transformation of conflict.

THE IMPACT OF VIOLENCE AND
TRAUMA ON THE BRAIN

Trauma is an event, a series of events, or a threat of an event that causes lasting physical, emotional, or spiritual injury. Trauma can result from natural disasters, perpetual structural violence, or specific acts of crime, abuse, or war.[36] People in conflict-affected regions often experience psychosocial impacts of trauma.

The diagram below illustrates a trauma-induced cycle of violence.[37] Following a traumatic event, stress hormones flood the body. People may immediately experience shock and pain and then begin to question "Why did this happen to me?" They may experience "survivor guilt" if others around them did not make it through the traumatic event. People often begin to feel shame and humiliation about their victimization. Feelings of depression, desire for revenge, or a combination (hoping that revenge will relieve feelings of depression) may set in. Some people recovering from trauma may commit themselves to getting revenge, which they perceive as justice. A cycle of violence may begin, in which efforts to seek revenge for the original violence lead to more violence in response and groups escalate their harms against each other. The diagram in Figure 20.2 can be a useful map for people to identify for themselves their emotional journey and responses to trauma.

Neurobiologists describe how in normal circumstances, the brain's neurological structures demand a simplification and categorization of complex reality so that people do not drown in the overwhelming information. The brain creates categories that are actual physical structures that guide how the brain processes new information.[38] Non-traumatized

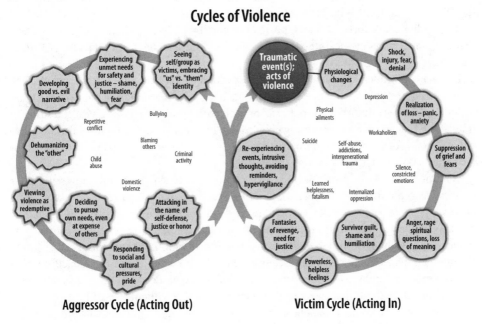

Cycles of Violence

Aggressor Cycle (Acting Out)   **Victim Cycle (Acting In)**

FIGURE 20.2

people are more likely to think through difficult situations with their cerebral cortex, or the front part of the brain that allows for logical and rational thought and problem-solving.

When threatened by or in the midst of a traumatic event, however, people often respond from the two older parts of the brain rather than the cerebral cortex or "rational" brain. People with traumatic experiences may respond more often out of part of the central part of the brain that controls automatic responses and instincts, or the "fight or flight" approach. Adrenalin and chemicals running through the body can trigger a range of physical reactions. These include perspiration, rapid heartbeat, and shaking. The rational brain cannot, in some cases, identify and process the crisis situation. The prefrontal lobe of the brain responsible for language can freeze up, making it difficult for people to articulate what is happening to them. The part of the brain called the amygdala, responsible for emotional regulation, can physically enlarge as it is flooded with stimuli. The part of the brain called the hippocampus, responsible for memory and helping people sort through and make sense of their experiences, can become smaller, making it more difficult for people to remember exact details of what happened. The part of the brain called the prefrontal or cerebral cortex, which develops responses to emotional stimuli, can also freeze up, thus forcing people to respond instinctually rather than thoughtfully to traumatic experiences or memories.[39] Memories of real-world events that sparked trauma or crisis can stay in the brain for years afterwards.

Emotional responses to events or memories of trauma can permeate cognition, impacting how well people can remember, and how well they can think through complex problems.[40] Trauma and conflict can overwhelm the rational brain, making it difficult to develop solutions to problems or work toward a less violent future. Instinctual reactions can override reflection. Each individual develops particular "buttons" or triggers that, when "pushed," lead to reactions that often flow along deeply engraved patterns of response that have biological form in the brain. Media images and sounds can push these buttons. For example, people who more frequently viewed repeated television images of the planes crashing into the World Trade Center on September 11, 2001, experienced more depression.[41] Lack of understanding and efforts to address post-traumatic stress disorder then make it more likely that individual psychological impacts of trauma will have wider social impacts that make peacebuilding more challenging.

Trauma can influence a society's ability to address current problems and conflicts. The brain's structure is relevant to peacebuilding, because peacebuilding requires changes, including transforming thought patterns reinforced by years of conflict. Peacebuilding in traumatized societies requires helping people to identify harms, assert their needs, and move out of the cycle of violence and onto a path toward reconciliation, acceptance, and contributing to human security.[42]

Building peace with traumatized people requires understanding and addressing their trauma. Peacebuilding is a persuasive, not coercive, approach to change. In peacebuilding processes, people come to understand themselves, others, institutions, and relationships in a new way. Peacebuilding is not a transfer of information. Rather, it is a process that must persuade people to change through multiple mediums: facts, emotions, and senses.

Trauma impacts the brain so drastically because it is an experience that impacts people's beliefs, emotions, and senses and obstructs rational thought. Peacebuilding cannot just use rational, direct methods that engage only the cerebral cortex without also addressing the fact that in the midst of conflict, people are more likely to be highly emotionally and sensually engaged, and they may struggle to think through problems in a straightforward approach because of the way the brain works.

Figure 20.3 below illustrates the psychological progress people make when they move out of the victim and aggressor cycles, leave behind the cycle of violence, and begin to take part in peacebuilding and opening the possibility of reconciliation. Rituals can be an important part of this journey.

People are more likely to pay attention to a new idea, attitude, or behavior represented in multiple ways or contexts. Cognitive researchers note the dramatic impact of images on the brain. While the forefront or cerebral cortex part of the brain processes logic and words, images and music cause the two older and larger parts of our brain, the so-called reptilian and the limbic systems, to trigger emotions and instincts like the "fight or flight" reaction. All three parts of the brain are important to the change process. People gather information using all the body's senses and communicate both verbally and nonverbally.

Peacebuilding often requires breaking through the perceptual defense mechanisms all people use in order to bring order and meaning to their experiences. It is challenging to help people see each other and the conflict they experienced in new ways because the process of perception works against change and seeks to reconfirm old ideas. If the old ideas or ways of thinking happen to be the dehumanization of some "other," then there will be great

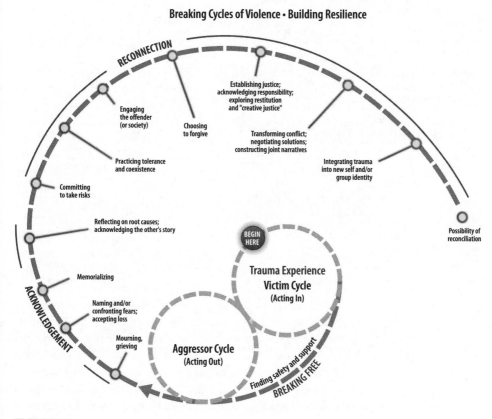

FIGURE 20.3

resistance to seeing that other as human. Most of the time people change their minds gradually, not in one specific moment or with one revelation.

For centuries, religious traditions have used rituals to help in this process of cognitive transformation and trauma healing. Special characteristics of ritual—especially religious ritual—make it particularly useful for peacebuilding. The following sections outline ritual spaces, ritual's means for communication, and ritual's role in transformation.

RITUAL PEACEBUILDING TAKES PLACE
IN SYMBOLIC SPACES

First, ritual takes place in a unique space with symbols that create a sense of meaning for what is happening. Humans make sense of a situation and, at least in part, know how to act according to their physical context. In a ritual, *what* happens relates directly to the physical space *where* it happens. Context is tied to meaning. Ritual space "tells" participants what is going on within its borders of time and space through the interaction of symbols.

Religious rituals usually take place in a special place marked with special symbols. Doors, arches, gates, or other physical markers such as labyrinths, stone circles, or grand temples, cathedrals, and mosques often mark ritual space.[43] Indigenous rituals often take place in special geographic locations such as beside rivers, on mountains, or near geological rock formations. Religious rituals often include symbolic elements such as fire, earth, water, flowers, and foods that give meaning and order to a setting. Humans created some of the earliest buildings to be sacred spaces. These early structures relied on candles or lamps to provide light. Candles were originally used in sacred shrines to give light. Today, lighting a candle almost automatically creates a sacred place because of this historic connotation and the contrast to electrical forms of lighting used in many places. Candles are thus symbols that help separate ritual space from non-ritual space.[44] Religious leaders also mark off sacred, ritual space with specific smells, sounds, or tastes. Some religions burn incense to provide a powerful, physical cloud of pungent air to set ritual space apart from normal life. The smudging ceremony begins with the sweet pungent smell of sweetgrass, sage, tobacco, and cedar. Specific sounds may also mark ritual space. Buddhist rituals often begin with the ringing of a bell. And some religions mark ritual space with a specific food or drink. In the South Pacific, for example, Fijian indigenous leaders drink a mildly sedating herbal drink called kava to begin a ceremony.

Ritual spaces, marked by specific times, locations, symbols, tastes, smells, and sounds can create a special "oasis for peace" where people in conflict can find respite from conflict's destruction. Anthropologist Victor Turner describes ritual contexts as "liminal spaces." Liminal spaces are in-between, set-aside, or separate contexts where the rules for acting and interpreting meaning are different from the rest of life.[45] Ritual spaces are "thresholds" or "places in limbo" that are symbolically separated from other social settings. Mythologist Joseph Campbell describes ritual space as

> a room or a certain hour or so a day, where you don't know what was in the newspapers that morning, you don't know who your friends are, you don't know what you owe anybody, you

don't know what anybody owes you. This is a place where you can simply experience and bring forth what you are and what you might be. This is the place of creative incubation.[46]

These liminal places and times create an opening or give permission to try out new or different ways of interacting.

For these reasons, ritual space is relevant to peacebuilding. Peacebuilding efforts can create a separate, ritualized space that allows people to temporarily step out of the places where they are experiencing conflict, threats, or violence. The typical negotiation room is set up with people sitting across a table from each other. The table itself becomes a symbol of the divisive issues between the people. Peacebuilding planners can be more intentional about the symbols they include in a peacebuilding effort. Other contexts, such as sharing a meal at a round table with candles and flowers, hold more cooperative images and connotations. Creating a ritual space may help people feel more comfortable and open in a peacebuilding process.

Peacebuilding planners should design physical and temporal spaces for peacebuilding that are liminal, safe spaces that symbolically support the desired transformation of perceptions and relationships. Efforts to foster conflict transformation work best when they are not just rational and verbal, but when the places where peacebuilding takes place include symbols, and invite people to include their emotions, senses, and bodies in the learning process. Ideally, peacebuilding rituals provide opportunities for people to interact physically and emotionally with each other and to act out new ways of being with each other, which may better enable them to catalyze change and experience their shared humanity.

A variety of peacebuilding efforts already indicate an awareness of the need for rituals. Some mediators and facilitators choose to bring adversaries together in a symbolic space that invites emotion and sensual interaction. For example, Norwegian mediation efforts frequently take place in mountain chalets where gourmet food and gorgeous views inspire conversations of family and create a safe space to imagine alternative futures.[47] In Latin America, the Catholic Church uses its religious spaces as human rights monuments to those tortured and disappeared, allowing an emotional catharsis and a form of advocacy that comes from religious values more than political posturing. The Outward Bound Center for Peacebuilding brings together diverse groups to meet in recreational outdoor parks or wilderness areas where nature creates a context that highlights shared human appreciation for the beauty of wilderness and the shared fragility of being human in the wild.[48]

A carefully designed, symbolically supportive environment can mean sitting at round tables with a facilitator who can help constructively frame conversations and paraphrase areas of convergence and divergence, followed by evenings that invite participants to sing, dance, joke, drink, and laugh with each other. While hard logical negotiations are the typical primary elements of peacebuilding dialogue, symbolic support enables people to build trust, reduce fear, and form relationships in which tough issues can be discussed.

These separate spaces can remove some of the pressures facing people in conflict-affected regions, allowing them to try out new ways of thinking and behaving. It may be impossible in the midst of conflict to create a safe place where people can think with their cerebral cortex rather than respond instinctively with the limbic portion of their brain. Moreover, what happens in these separate spaces may not automatically induce or support sustainable transformation in systems, institutions, and relationships that are addicted to conflict.[49] Ritual certainly does not appear to be a solution on its own. It can, however, be an important component to complement a broader set of peacebuilding strategies.

Ritual Peacebuilding Engages People's Bodies, Senses, and Emotions

Second, ritual communicates through symbols, emotions, and using all the senses (taste, touch, hearing, seeing, and smelling). In ritual, people communicate and learn by doing. There is a preference for nonverbal communication using bodies, senses, and emotions rather than words. Communication researchers estimate that between 60 and 90 percent of communicated meaning comes from nonverbal cues.[50] Education theorists argue there are "multiple forms of intelligence" and "multiple ways of knowing."[51]

Peacebuilding requires an ability to find mutually acceptable solutions to complex challenges. The cerebral cortex involved in complex thought is essential to this sophisticated reasoning. But relying only on direct, rational forms of communication to arrive at negotiated solutions or manage tensions in conflict is a mistake. Solving complex problems requires the full capacity of the human brain, including the parts responsible for emotions and senses. Ritual's way of communicating through symbols may be more effective in the midst of conflict.

Peacebuilding requires impacting people's beliefs, emotions, and senses. Humans make sense of the world by seeing, hearing, touching, feeling, and tasting it. Centuries of religious practice recognize the power of symbols and rituals to impact the human mind. Gregory Bateson was the first to emphasize the impact of the connection between the body and the mind, noting that this contradicted both "the biologists [who had] worked hard to un-mind the body; and the philosophers [who had] disembodied the mind."[52] Any process of cognitive transformation attempting to impact the way people think has to take into consideration this mind-body connection.[53]

People change their minds as a result of a combination of forces that together foster or inhibit change.[54] Advertising researchers and media professionals recognize that a convincing effort to persuade an audience to buy a product or to watch a television show must in some way touch people emotionally or sensually. Humans have bodies, senses, emotions, and minds. Peacebuilding that only engages the mind without the other elements is unlikely to be effective.

Ritual and rationality are not opposites. Ritual is not the opposite of thought and reason. Rather, ritual communicates through symbols, which humans use to create meaning systems.[55] Words themselves constitute symbols that communicate about the world. Early theorists such as Charles Peirce and Kenneth Burke described symbols as significant elements in the meaning-making process.[56] Individuals perceive and understand their environment through symbols that attach meaning to experiences. Symbols are basic to thought: humans transform all of their experiences in the physical world into symbols. Susanne Langer defines the "symbolic transformation of experience" as a process in which the mind takes information from the environment and creates symbolic forms to capture experiential information that is stored for later "re-cognition" of another environment.[57]

Theologian Theodore Jennings describes what he calls "ritual knowledge" to explain what humans learn and communicate through ritual. In ritual, people learn through symbols; senses such as seeing, hearing, smelling, and tasting; and the bodily expression of emotions, such as crying, anger, and joy. Jennings notes that "ritual knowledge is gained by and through the body... not by detached observation or contemplation but through action."[58] In his article "On Ritual Knowledge," he claims the body undergoes changes during ritual:

> It is not so much that the mind 'embodies' itself in ritual action, but rather that the body 'minds' itself or attends through itself in ritual action.... It is in and through the action that ritual knowledge is gained, not in advance of it, nor after it.... Ritual knowledge is gained not through detachment but through engagement—an engagement that does not leave things as they are but which alters and transforms them.[59]

Symbols are particularly effective means of communicating on issues related to conflict. Political scientist David Kertzer argues that symbolic forms act in three ways: through condensation, multivocality, and ambiguity.[60] Symbols condense information about the world into a single unified form. Symbols communicate multiple messages. And symbols are flexible, so that different people can interpret them in different ways.

For example, the Dhammayietra peace walk is a symbol of a condensed message communicating Buddhist religious practice, or compassion for Cambodian victims, or a plea for a new, more peaceful future for the country. The Dhammayietra is multivocal, allowing the Khmer Rouge to interpret it as an acceptable religious expression, while, at the same time, human rights activists interpret it as an act of political defiance. The Dhammayietra is ambiguous and flexible because the symbols leave the Khmer Rouge, for example, uncertain of whether the walk is in fact an act of political defiance. The walk is ambiguous enough to make it acceptable to all.

Ritual communication lends itself to cross-cultural communication, where people with different languages can still communicate through symbols they can each interpret. Theater scholar Richard Schechner claims ritual and theater are particularly effective means of communicating across cultures.

> When one group wants to communicate to another across various boundaries (linguistic, political, cultural, and geographical) the main initial signal is an exchange of performances, a mutual display of rituals. There is something about dance, music, theatre and ritual that needs no translating—even as there is very much that is so culturally specific that it takes a lifetime of study to understand the performances of a culture not one's own.[61]

Schechner asserts that humans seem to develop or use rituals precisely when humans are in conflict with each other and require these delicate "conflict dances" that remain ambiguous enough to not pose a direct threat.

> In both animals and humans, rituals arise or are devised around disruptive, turbulent, and ambivalent interactions where faulty communication can lead to violent or even fatal encounters.... 'You get the message, don't you!?!' says that what a ritual communicates is very important yet problematic. The interactions that rituals surround, contain, and mediate almost always concern hierarchy, territory, and sexuality/mating.... If these interactions are the 'real events' rituals enfold, then what are the rituals themselves? They are ambivalent symbolic actions pointing at the real transactions even as they help people avoid too direct a confrontation with these events.[62]

Ritual provides an opportunity to people in conflict to communicate with each other through symbols that are less confrontational or threatening than ordinary conversation.

Media such as movies, television, and radio shows and commercials use background music, images, and special lighting to evoke particular emotions and convey important messages. Words are often kept to a minimum—allowing people to use the sights and sounds to make sense of the message. Journalists choose photos or videos to accompany their stories knowing that the images may have a more lasting impact than their words. Social marketers use bright colors and flashy advertisements to capture an audience's attention. For example, a series of stunning ads seeking international condemnation of armed conflict and action to support child soldiers uses gripping video along with catchy and uplifting music to draw an audience into supporting the cause.[63]

Rituals often include words as well. Ritual phrases or "performatives" are spoken with the intent that saying something *as if* it were true within a ritual context will actually convince people that it is true.[64] Leaders *declare* a peace agreement in a performative statement when by their authority and official context, they suggest that the declaration of peace is perhaps more "true" than the reality suggests, since almost half of all peace agreements end up failing. So when a religious leader such as Cambodia's Ghosananda says "we must remove the landmines in our hearts" during the Dhammayietra walk, the ritual context of the walk gives his words an added power to reach and impact those listening.

The formal and sometimes spiritual context that ritual creates makes it an effective means for communicating messages where there is doubt. As Sally Moore and Barbara Myerhoff assert,

> Since ritual is a good form for conveying a message as if it were unquestionable, it often is used to communicate those very things that are most in doubt. Thus where there is conflict, or danger, or political opposition, where there is made-upness and cultural invention, ritual may carry the opposite message in form as well as in content.[65]

Likewise, in their book *Brain, Symbol and Experience* authors Eugene d'Aquili, Charles Laughlin, and John McManus describe how some cultures use ritual as a healing agent since the words used in a ritual can be so potent and rich in symbolism that the words themselves can "penetrate disorder and affect a cure."[66]

When elders in Mozambique perform a religious purification to help individuals and their communities reconcile after a war, the performance of the cleansing becomes real. The use of symbols to "penetrate" the human mind and its worldview seems essential to the "magic" of performatives. These rituals of performance can also help people believe that real change is happening in a peacebuilding process.

South Africa's Truth and Reconciliation Commissions were largely symbolic, ritual exercises. The courts accepted the truth of public confession to crimes in exchange for amnesty given to perpetrators of violence. The ritualized exercise of truth-telling and accountability—without criminal punishment or even symbolic reparations in the form of financial payments in most cases—was a performance of reconciliation. Without the TRC process, it is hard to know what might have happened in South Africa. Yet critics note the lack of accountability and the use of pure symbolism may have undercut respect for human rights in the long term.

Rituals—especially those in South Africa's anti-apartheid movement—often include art and music. Researchers claim that the repetition, rhythm, juxtaposition, and pattern found in ritual, music, and art can have a physical impact on the brain, helping people to think and see differently. Symbols and symbolic forms of communication seem to be able to penetrate, integrate, and communicate between different parts of the body and brain. Ritual triggers altered states of consciousness, or simply a shiver up one's back. These are signs of a neurological reorganizing and transforming of the brain's cognitive system, allowing people to make new connections and to change the way they view the world and understand problems.[67]

Like rituals, emotional stories of courageous people undertaking dramatic actions for peace, told through the arts and media, can sometimes make a profound impact on people. In a media project titled "Jerusalem Stories," artists pair images and narratives of the trauma and loss of Palestinians and Jews living in Jerusalem together in a photo-journalism display and also in a theatrical performance. Theater itself can be a ritual space where people may be more open to seeing and hearing new ideas. The project enables people to make an emotional connection with individual Palestinians and Israelis who have suffered through the conflict. In building this empathy, the project aims to build greater awareness of the commonality of suffering and the possibility of coexistence.[68]

Ritual's method of learning or pedagogy stands in contrast to most reconciliation efforts that emphasize rational negotiation and direct communication. But ritual is not a replacement of these peacebuilding methods. Rather, rituals and the symbols they include can be an effective complement to more direct approaches to peacebuilding, particularly when more direct methods of communication are not possible.

RITUAL PEACEBUILDING'S ROLE IN SOCIALIZATION AND TRANSFORMATION

Third, rituals can advance violence or peace as they socialize and transform people and their relationships. Ritual holds the destructive potential to turn civilians into warriors and drive a wedge of enmity between ethnic groups. It also has the power to transform inter-group hostility by re-establishing relationships, rules, and values of harmony. Ritual's "liminal" space offers the possibility of intrapersonal, interpersonal, cultural, and structural change. Ritual marks and assists the process of forming or transforming people's worldviews, identities, and relationships, as well as the process of personal and relational transformation. It gives people a "prism," or a new way of looking at themselves, their identity, their experiences, and their relationships with others. Ritual can "heal" wounded identities, or create new identities. Ritual can create a constructive pathway for expressing conflict between groups.

Ritual's power to transform is not always used constructively. Ideally, rituals foster community relations and affirm interdependence and the value of common good between people. At times, however, leaders use ritual to mobilize one group against another by heightening cultural anxiety around particular traumas or glories from the generational memory of a community that may serve to escalate conflict.[69] Destructive rituals that mobilize people toward war, highlight divisive points in history, or dehumanize other groups must be countered by equally potent symbolic rituals of redemption and healing. The logic of ritual, steeped in symbol and metaphor, is sometimes more powerful than direct, logical, or rational forms of discourse in these cases. So when tribes kill or capture symbols of power and pride in opposing groups, reconciliation should restore not only the economic value, but the symbolic value, the dignity, and the spirituality of the offended group. Adversaries can begin to see the humanity of others not through the logic of their arguments but rather by sharing a meal together, sharing family photos, visiting each other's homes, or taking other actions that signify trust, relationship, and humanity.

Ritual actions can symbolize transformation in a variety of ways. In South Africa, activists pinned photos of those disappeared and tortured to a wooden cross, indicating that these people had not died in vain but that their lives were a sacrifice recognized by the community in the pursuit of a more just future. Other peacebuilding workshops invited people from different sides of a conflict to add a section to a quilt of patches representing peacebuilding efforts. A group of women used salt water in a ritual to mark each other as survivors of sexual violence, with the water representing their shared tears and sadness but also the transformation they are making from seeing themselves as victims to announcing themselves as survivors who are agents in their own recovery. Participants in a peacebuilding training workshop with mixed identity walked through an arbor to recognize their transformation toward constructive relationships with each other. Rituals can assist the process of peacebuilding by enabling groups to meet together in a safe, liminal space; engage with emotions, senses, and symbols as well as direct communication; and to act out and make real the process of transformation.[70]

THE PRACTICE OF RELIGIOUS RITUAL IN PEACEBUILDING

Ritual offers a paradox to peacebuilders facing an increasingly technological world. It is not a simple method for sorting out and analyzing conflict. Rather, ritual acknowledges that conflict is messy, confusing, and oftentimes not rational. Its symbolism and reliance on nonverbal methods of communication make it useful to peacebuilding precisely because there are so many elements of conflict that cannot be neatly addressed in a negotiation. Wounds from trauma cannot be negotiated away. A healing ritual, a memorial, or a public symbol recognizing trauma cannot wipe away trauma, either. However, they may offer a balm to begin the long path to healing.

Ritual images, objects, and actions can have the effect of opening up traumas by penetrating and opening worldviews that may lead to a recovery process. Of course, there are dangers in opening up traumas as well. Re-traumatizing people is a real risk. Leaders should always inform participants in a ritual of what will happen so they can make an informed choice about whether to participate.

The empowerment of participants in a peacebuilding process is always essential. Participants themselves are the best authors of rituals that draw on symbols of trauma but that offer a possibility to transform or recover from past events through new ritualized experiences. Facilitators can ask participants, "What rituals could help people heal their identity or change their understanding of themselves from victims to survivors of trauma? What rituals could help groups change the way they perceive traumatic events?"

Ritual can become a prism that offers a new way to look at past events that can allow people to see multiple points of view and attain a deeper understanding of the causes and factors that led to a traumatizing event. Rituals can help groups come to see each other as fully human and find mutually satisfying ways of meeting their needs. It can create a safe space, set aside from normal life, for groups of people who normally do not meet. Familiar and appealing sights, sounds, tastes, and symbols can help people feel safe and comfortable enough to engage with each other. Planners can choose the geographic location and the size and shape of the room and meeting space to maximize participants' ability to hear and see each other in ways that are less adversarial and more focused on identifying and addressing common problems. Facilitators can listen for symbolic "keys" in the victims' stories to help identify specific symbols that trigger memories of trauma or open the possibility of recovery. Facilitators can engage people's senses and emotions as much as possible and make "channels" or ritual spaces where emotions are both allowed and valued. Finally, they can plan activities that encourage people to interact physically and emotionally with each other and to act out new ways of being with each other—a first step toward building a just and lasting peace.

Notes

1. For example, see Arnold van Gennep, *The Rites of Passage* (Chicago: University of Chicago Press, 1960); Victor Turner, *The Ritual Process: Structure and Anti-Structure* (Chicago: Aldine Pub. Co., 1969).

2. For example, see Robert Bocock, *Ritual in Industrial Society: A Sociological Analysis of Ritualism in Modern England* (London: Allen and Unwin, 1974). Also, Kenneth Burke, "Symbolic Action," in *Kenneth Burke: On Symbols and Society*, ed. Joseph R. Gusfield (Chicago: University of Chicago Press, 1989), 77–85.

3. For example, see Roy Rappaport, *Ritual and Religion in the Making of Humanity* (Cambridge: Cambridge University Press, 1999).

4. For example, see David I. Kertzer, *Ritual, Politics, and Power* (New Haven, CT: Yale University Press, 1988).

5. For example, see Tom Faw Driver, *The Magic of Ritual: Our Need for Liberating Rites That Transform Our Lives and Our Communities* (San Francisco: HarperSanFrancisco, 1991).

6. Lisa Schirch, *Ritual and Symbol in Peacebuilding* (Bloomfield, MA: Kumarian Press, 2005).

7. Barbara Ehrenreich, *Blood Rites: Origins and History of the Passions of War* (New York: Henry Holt and Company, 1997); René Girard, "Violence and the Sacred: Sacrifice," in *Readings in Ritual Studies*, ed. Ronald L. Grimes (New Jersey: Prentice Hall, 1996), 239–256.

8. There is some debate about which Latin root forms the basis of the word "religion." Some say *religare*, meaning similarly "to fasten or bind," is the root. Other interpretations purport that *relegere* is the root, meaning "to re-read or go over a text." A third option, *re-eligere*, means "to choose again." See "Roots of 'Religion,'" *Jewish Daily Forward*, May 25, 2007, http://www.forward.com/articles/10776/roots-of-religion.

9. Ehrenreich, *Blood Rites*.

10. Émile Durkheim, *The Elementary Forms of the Religious Life*, trans. Joseph Swain (New York: The Free Press, 1965).

11. John Burton, *Conflict: Human Needs Theory* (New York: St. Martin's Press, 1990).

12. Schirch, *Ritual and Symbol.*

13. Lisa Schirch, *The Little Book of Strategic Peacebuilding* (Intercourse, PA: Good Books, 2004).

14. Ted Grimsrud, *God's Healing Strategy* (Telford, PA: Pandora Press, 2000).

15. See also R. Scott Appleby, *The Ambivalence of the Sacred: Religion, Violence, and Reconciliation* (Lanham, MD: Rowman and Littlefield, 2000); Marc Gopin, *Holy War, Holy Peace: How Religion Can Bring Peace to the Middle East* (New York: Oxford University Press, 2002); Douglas Johnston, ed., *Faith-Based Diplomacy: Trumping Realpolitik* (New York: Oxford University Press, 2003).

16. Winona LaDuke, *All My Relations: Native Struggles for Land and Rights* (Cambridge, MA: South End Press, 1999).

17. For more information on the smudging ceremony, see Schirch, *Ritual and Symbol.*

18. Thich Nhat Hahn, *Being Peace* (Berkeley, CA: Parallax Press, 1987).

19. Lisa Schirch, *Conflict Assessment and Peacebuilding Planning* (Bloomfield, MA: Kumarian Press, 2013).

20. Okot p'Bitek, *Artist the Ruler* (Nairobi, Kenya: East African Educational Publishers, 1992).

21. Theodor Adorno with Max Horkheimer, *Dialectic of Enlightenment*, trans. Edmund Jephcott (Stanford, CA: Stanford University Press, 2002).

22. Quoted in Marc Gopin, *Between Eden and Armageddon: The Future of World Religions, Violence and Peacemaking* (New York: Oxford University Press, 2000), 45.

23. Monique Skidmore, "In the Shade of the Bodhi Tree: Dhammayietra and the Re-awakening of Community in Cambodia," *Crossroads* 10, no. 1 (1996): 1–32.

24. See "Dhammayietra: Pilgrimages of Truth in Cambodia," Buddhist Travel, http://www.buddhistravel.com/index.php?id=30,597,0,0,1,0.

25. Appleby, *The Ambivalence of the Sacred*, 129–131.

26. Kana Roba Duba et al., *Honey and Heifer: Grasses, Milk and Water; A Heritage of Diversity in Reconciliation* (Nairobi, Kenya: Mennonite Central Committee, 1997).

27. Alcinda Honanda, "Sealing the Past, Facing the Future: Trauma Healing in Rural Mozambique," *Accord*, no. 3 (1998): 75–80.

28. Honanda, "Sealing the Past," 78–79.

29. Honanda, "Sealing the Past," 79.

30. Honanda, "Sealing the Past," 80.

31. Judy Barsalou, "Trauma and Transitional Justice in Divided Societies," Special Report, US Institute of Peace, April 2005.

32. Judy Barsalou and Victoria Baxter, "The Urge to Remember: The Role of Memorials in Social Reconstruction and Transitional Justice," Stabilization and Reconstruction Series, no. 5, US Institute of Peace, January 2007, p. 13.

33. Barsalou and Baxter, "Urge to Remember," 15.

34. See the Memoria Abierta website at http://www.memoriaabierta.org.ar.

35. Robert F. Worth, "Kurds Destroy Monument in Rage at Leadership," *New York Times*, March 17, 2006.

36. Carolyn Yoder, *The Little Book of Trauma Healing* (Intercourse, PA: Good Books, 2005).

37. These diagrams were developed by the STAR program at Eastern Mennonite University's Center for Justice and Peacebuilding. STAR stands for Strategies for Trauma Awareness

and Resilience, a program that began for caregivers of victims and family members of the September 11, 2001, attacks.

38. Charles D. Laughlin, John McManus, and Eugene G. d'Aquili, *Brain, Symbol and Experience: Toward a Neurophenomenology of Human Consciousness* (Boston, MA: Shambhala Publications, 1990).

39. For further research, see Rachel Yehuda and Joseph LeDoux, "Response Variation Following Trauma: A Translational Neuroscience Approach to Understanding PTSD," *Neuron* 56, no. 1 (2007): 19–32; and Michelle Rosenthal, "Trauma and the Brain: Understanding What Happens and Why You Feel Changed," The Survivors Club, http://www.thesurvivorsclub.org/health/neurological/trauma-and-the-brain-understan.

40. Richard J. Davidson with Sharon Begley, *The Emotional Life of Your Brain* (New York: Hudson Street Press, 2012).

41. J. Ahern, S. Galea, H. Resnick, D. Kilpatrick, M. Bucuvalas, J. Gold, and D. Vlahov, "Television Images and Psychological Symptoms After the September 11 Terrorist Attacks," *Psychiatry* 65, no. 4 (2002): 289–300.

42. Barry Hart, ed., *Peacebuilding in Traumatized Societies* (Lanham, MD: University Press of America, 2008).

43. van Gennep, *Rites of Passage*.

44. Mary Catherine Bateson, "Ordinary Creativity," in *Social Creativity*, edited by Alfonso Montuori and Ronald E. Purser (New Jersey: Hampton Press, 1999).

45. Victor Turner, *The Anthropology of Performance* (New York: PAJ Publishers, 1988), 34.

46. Joseph Campbell with Bill Moyers, *The Power of Myth*, ed. Betty Sue Flowers (New York: Doubleday, 1988), 92.

47. Jane Corbin, *The Norway Channel: The Secret Talks That Led to the Middle East Peace Accord* (New York: Atlantic Monthly Press, 1994), 139.

48. See the website of the Outward Bound Center for Peacebuilding at http://www.outward-boundpeace.org/.

49. See for example Mohammed Abu-Nimer, *Dialogue, Conflict Resolution, and Change: Arab-Jewish Encounters in Israel* (New York: State University of New York Press, 1999).

50. Julia Wood, *Spinning the Symbolic Web: Human Communication as Symbolic Interaction* (Norwood, NJ: Ablex Publishing Corporation, 1992).

51. For example, see Mary Belenky, *Women's Ways of Knowing: The Development of Self, Voice, and Mind* (New York: Basic Books, 1997).

52. Gregory Bateson, *A Sacred Unity: Further Steps to an Ecology of Mind* (San Francisco: HarperSanFrancisco, 1991), xvii. See also Bateson, *Mind and Nature: A Necessary Unity* (New York: Dutton, 1979).

53. Humberto Maturana and Francisco J. Varela, *Autopoiesis and Cognition: The Realization of the Living* (Dordrecht, Netherlands: D. Reidel, 1980).

54. Howard Gardner, *Changing Minds: The Art and Science of Changing Our Own and Other People's Minds* (Cambridge, MA: Harvard Business School Press, 2004).

55. Roy A. Rappaport, *Ritual and Religion in the Making of Humanity* (Cambridge: Cambridge University Press, 1999).

56. Charles Peirce, *The Philosophy of Peirce: Selected Writings*, ed. J. Buchler (New York: Dover, 1940); Kenneth Burke, "The Symbol as Formative," in *Kenneth Burke: On Symbols and Society*, ed. Joseph R. Gusfield (Chicago: University of Chicago Press, 1989), 107–113.

57. Susanne Langer, *Philosophy in a New Key: A Study in the Symbolism of Reason, Rite, and Art* (New York: Penguin Books, 1948).
58. Theodore W. Jennings Jr., "On Ritual Knowledge," in *Readings in Ritual Studies*, ed. Ronald L. Grimes (New Jersey: Prentice Hall, 1996), 324–334.
59. Jennings, "On Ritual Knowledge."
60. David I. Kertzer, *Ritual, Politics, and Power* (New Haven, CT: Yale University Press, 1988).
61. Richard Schechner, *The Future of Ritual: Writings on Culture and Performance* (New York: Routledge, 1993).
62. Schechner, *The Future of Ritual*.
63. See the videos at WarChild.org.
64. J. L. Austin, *How To Do Things With Words* (Cambridge, MA: Harvard University Press, 1962).
65. Sally F. Moore and Barbara Myerhoff, "Introduction: Secular Ritual: Forms and Meanings," in *Secular Ritual*, ed. Sally F. Moore and Barbara Myerhoff (Amsterdam: Van Gorcum, 1977), 3–24.
66. Laughlin, McManus, and d'Aquili, *Brain, Symbol and Experience*.
67. Eugene G. d'Aquili, Charles D. Laughlin, and John McManus, introduction to *The Spectrum of Ritual: A Biogenetic Structural Analysis*, ed. Eugene G. d'Aquili, Charles D. Laughlin, and John McManus (New York: Columbia University Press, 1979), 1–50.
68. See "Jerusalem Stories" at www.jerusalemstories.org.
69. Vamik D. Volkan, Joseph Montville, and Demetrios Julius, *The Psychodynamics of International Relationships* (Lexington, MA: Lexington Books, 1990).
70. These stories are told in Schirch, *Ritual and Symbol*.

BIBLIOGRAPHY

Abu-Nimer, Mohammed. *Dialogue, Conflict Resolution, and Change: Arab-Jewish Encounters in Israel*. New York: State University of New York Press, 1999.

Adorno, Theodor, with Max Horkheimer. *Dialectic of Enlightenment*. Translated by Edmund Jephcott. Stanford, CA: Stanford University Press, 2002.

Ahern, J., S. Galea, H. Resnick, D. Kilpatrick, M. Bucuvalas, J. Gold, and D. Vlahov. "Television Images and Psychological Symptoms After the September 11 Terrorist Attacks." *Psychiatry* 65, no. 4 (2002): 289–300.

Appleby, R. Scott. *The Ambivalence of the Sacred: Religion, Violence, and Reconciliation*. Lanham, MD: Rowman and Littlefield, 2000.

Austin, J. L. *How To Do Things With Words*. Cambridge, MA: Harvard University Press, 1962.

d'Aquili, Eugene G., Charles D. Laughlin, and John McManus. *The Spectrum of Ritual: A Biogenetic Structural Analysis*. New York: Columbia University Press, 1979.

Barsalou, Judy. "Trauma and Transitional Justice in Divided Societies." Special Report. US Institute of Peace. April 2005.

Barsalou, Judy, and Victoria Baxter. "The Urge to Remember: The Role of Memorials in Social Reconstruction and Transitional Justice." Stabilization and Reconstruction Series, no. 5. US Institute of Peace. January 2007.

Bateson, Gregory. *Mind and Nature: A Necessary Unity*. New York: Dutton, 1979.

Bateson, Gregory. *A Sacred Unity: Further Steps to an Ecology of Mind*. San Francisco: HarperSanFrancisco, 1991.

Bateson, Mary Catherine. "Ordinary Creativity." In *Social Creativity*, edited by Alfonso Montuori and Ronald E. Purser. New Jersey: Hampton Press, 1999.

Belenky, Mary. *Women's Ways of Knowing: The Development of Self, Voice, and Mind*. New York: Basic Books, 1997.

Bocock, Robert. *Ritual in Industrial Society: A Sociological Analysis of Ritualism in Modern England*. London: Allen and Unwin, 1974.

Burke, Kenneth. "Symbolic Action." In *Kenneth Burke: On Symbols and Society*, edited by Joseph R. Gusfield, 77–85. Chicago: University of Chicago Press, 1989.

Burke, Kenneth. "The Symbol as Formative." In *Kenneth Burke: On Symbols and Society*, edited by Joseph R. Gusfield, 107–113. Chicago: University of Chicago Press, 1989.

Burton, John. *Conflict: Human Needs Theory*. New York: St. Martin's Press, 1990.

Campbell, Joseph, with Bill Moyers. *The Power of Myth*. Edited by Betty Sue Flowers. New York: Doubleday, 1988.

Corbin, Jane. *The Norway Channel: The Secret Talks That Led to the Middle East Peace Accord*. New York: Atlantic Monthly Press, 1994.

Davidson, Richard J., with Sharon Begley. *The Emotional Life of Your Brain*. New York: Hudson Street Press, 2012.

Driver, Tom Faw. *The Magic of Ritual: Our Need for Liberating Rites That Transform Our Lives and Our Communities*. San Francisco: HarperSanFrancisco, 1991.

Duba, Kana Roba, et al. *Honey and Heifer: Grasses, Milk and Water; A Heritage of Diversity in Reconciliation*. Nairobi, Kenya: Mennonite Central Committee, 1997.

Durkheim, Émile. *The Elementary Forms of the Religious Life*. Translated by Joseph Swain. 1915. Reprint, New York: The Free Press, 1965.

Ehrenreich, Barbara. *Blood Rites: Origins and History of the Passions of War*. New York: Henry Holt and Company, 1997.

Gardner, Howard. *Changing Minds: The Art and Science of Changing Our Own and Other People's Minds*. Cambridge, MA: Harvard Business School Press, 2004.

van Gennep, Arnold. *The Rites of Passage*. Chicago: University of Chicago Press, 1960.

Girard, René. "Violence and the Sacred: Sacrifice." In *Readings in Ritual Studies*, edited by Ronald L. Grimes, 239–256. New Jersey: Prentice Hall, 1996.

Gopin, Marc. *Between Eden and Armageddon: The Future of World Religions, Violence, and Peacemaking*. New York: Oxford University Press, 2000.

Gopin, Marc. *Holy War, Holy Peace: How Religion Can Bring Peace to the Middle East*. New York: Oxford University Press, 2002.

Grimsrud, Ted. *God's Healing Strategy*. Telford, PA: Pandora Press, 2000.

Hart, Barry, ed. *Peacebuilding in Traumatized Societies*. Lanham, MD: University Press of America, 2008.

Jennings, Theodore W., Jr. "On Ritual Knowledge." In *Readings in Ritual Studies*, edited by Ronald L. Grimes, 324–334. New Jersey: Prentice Hall, 1996.

Johnston, Douglas, ed. *Faith-Based Diplomacy: Trumping Realpolitik*. New York: Oxford University Press, 2003.

Honwana, Alcinda. "Sealing the Past, Facing the Future: Trauma Healing in Rural Mozambique." *Accord*, no. 3 (1998): 75–80.

Kertzer, David I. *Ritual, Politics, and Power*. New Haven, CT: Yale University Press, 1988.

LaDuke, Winona. *All My Relations: Native Struggles for Land and Rights*. Cambridge, MA: South End Press, 1999.

Langer, Susanne. *Philosophy in a New Key: A Study in the Symbolism of Reason, Rite, and Art*. New York: Penguin Books, 1948.

Laughlin, Charles D., John McManus, and Eugene G. d'Aquili. *Brain, Symbol and Experience: Toward a Neurophenomenology of Human Consciousness.* Boston, MA: Shambhala Publications, 1990.

Maturana, Humberto, and Francisco J. Varela. *Autopoiesis and Cognition: The Realization of the Living.* Dordrecht, Netherlands: D. Reidel, 1980.

Moore, Sally F., and Barbara Myerhoff, eds. *Secular Ritual.* Amsterdam: Van Gorcum, 1977.

Nhat Hahn, Thich. *Being Peace.* Berkeley, CA: Parallax Press, 1987.

p'Bitek, Okot. *Artist the Ruler.* Nairobi, Kenya: East African Educational Publishers. 1992.

Peirce, Charles. *The Philosophy of Peirce: Selected Writings.* Edited by J. Buchler. New York: Dover, 1940.

Rappaport, Roy A. *Ritual and Religion in the Making of Humanity.* Cambridge: Cambridge University Press, 1999.

Rosenthal, Michelle. "Trauma and the Brain: Understanding What Happens and Why You Feel Changed." The Survivors Club. http://www.thesurvivorsclub.org/health/neurological/trauma-and-the-brain-understan.

Schechner, Richard. *The Future of Ritual: Writings on Culture and Performance.* New York: Routledge, 1993.

Schirch, Lisa. *The Little Book of Strategic Peacebuilding.* Intercourse, PA: Good Books, 2004.

Schirch, Lisa. *Ritual and Symbol in Peacebuilding.* Bloomfield, MA: Kumarian Press, 2005.

Schirch, Lisa. *Conflict Assessment and Peacebuilding Planning.* Boulder, CO: Lynne Rienner Publishers, 2013.

Skidmore, Monique. "In the Shade of the Bodhi Tree: Dhammayietra and the Re-awakening of Community in Cambodia." *Crossroads* 10, no. 1 (1996): 1–32.

Turner, Victor. *The Ritual Process: Structure and Anti-Structure.* Chicago: Aldine, 1969.

Turner, Victor. *The Anthropology of Performance.* (New York: PAJ Publishers, 1988).

van Gennep, Arnold. *The Rites of Passage.* Chicago: University of Chicago Press, 1960.

Volkan, Vamik D., Joseph Montville, and Demetrios Julius. *The Psychodynamics of International Relationships.* Lexington, MA: Lexington Books, 1990.

Wood, Julia. *Spinning the Symbolic Web: Human Communication as Symbolic Interaction.* Norwood, NJ: Ablex Publishing Corporation, 1992.

Yehuda, Rachel, and Joseph LeDoux. "Response Variation Following Trauma: A Translational Neuroscience Approach to Understanding PTSD." *Neuron* 56, no. 1 (2007): 19–32.

Yoder, Carolyn. *The Little Book of Trauma Healing.* Intercourse, PA: Good Books, 2005.

CHAPTER 21

....

SPIRITUALITY AND RELIGIOUS PEACEBUILDING

....

JOHN PAUL LEDERACH

INTRODUCTION

....

THIS chapter explores the spiritual resources emergent in and sustaining the practice of religious peacebuilding. While this constitutes a significant subfield within the wider area of religion and peacebuilding,[1] our focus will narrow even further. My particular interest is how people with religious identity and commitment engage the dilemmas inherent in developing relationships across lines of enmity. Faith-inspired peacebuilders in deeply divided societies find themselves enmeshed in and facing both direct violence and the pressures of protracted conflict. At the same time, they choose to reach out and create and hold a space for being in relationship and conversation with those who represent the face of threat and harm in the midst of conflict. To attain this creativity and sustenance, they tap a range of potential spiritual and inner resources rarely explored in the formal literature.[2]

The convergence of spirituality and creativity entails a number of personal and social dilemmas and real dangers. Less visible but equally important, the act of reaching out emanates from and must return to the deep inner world. Here I refer to the less accessible or empirically observable interior world of the individual where competing voices, anxieties, and debates arise *within* the potential peacebuilder as she or he encounters perceived and real enemies. A probe into the spiritual and ultimately creative worlds, the inner and outer, invites us to explore the nexus and confluence of tributaries that provide insight into and nurture the *quality of presence* required to sustain constructive encounter with the enemy-other.

To develop an inquiry into quality of presence, we must first explore several key concepts with reference to but venturing beyond the existing literature. These include a review of the dynamics and characteristics of protracted conflict, clarification of the proposed *nexus* that touches on both inner and outer expressions, the concept of the enemy-other, and the paradoxical nature of the dilemmas faced by religious peacebuilding. With these foundations more clearly developed, we can then turn attention toward the tributaries, capacities, and practices of spirituality and creativity that flow together toward a quality of presence that seems to underpin or in some instances may be projected as the aspirational horizon of the religious peacebuilder. We begin with a review of protracted violent conflict, the context within which these tributaries must flow. Realistic engagement of this context facilitates our understanding of the deep dilemmas faced by religious peacebuilding.

THREE WINDOWS: FAITH-INSPIRED DISPATCHES FROM THE GROUND

This chapter faces two significant challenges. How do we distinguish between the empirical and the aspirational when approaching faith-inspired action? How do we ground an exploration of the inner world of peacebuilding? I prefer the phrase "faith-inspired" precisely because it opens up this difficult yet significant doorway into the world of religious peacebuilding. "Faith-based" suggests a root that would seem mostly permanent within a particular tradition or belief.[3] Sometimes people come from and are identified with a particular tradition yet may or may not consider themselves particularly religious or faithful, even while engaging in the most extraordinary acts of spiritual imagination in the midst of conflict. Sometimes people dig deep within their tradition to find the resources necessary to reach beyond what may seem to be humanly possible. By my view, "faith-inspired" has an inclusive quality. It suggests an unfolding, a blossoming that may tap not fully recognized resources yet displays an emergent quality of creativity. To a large degree it is this emergent quality, responsive and relevant to the patterned yet everyday dynamic nature of lived conflict, that we wish to explore. As much of this chapter will necessarily explore a series of potentially abstract (and easily perceived as aspirational) constructs, I wish to begin with a series of short but grounded stories. I face the particular challenge in writing this chapter that I come from the vocation of a faith-inspired peacebuilder.[4] Some of what emerges in this chapter comes not only from my observations of others with whom I have worked but also from a practice of reflective spirituality, that is, intentional and regular observation of my own experiences, both inner and outer, in reference to this material.[5] So I start with an early experience, the first really that I had, where the quality of presence finds expression, followed by two shorter examples from other religious traditions and contexts.

Walking to the Stadium: A Personal story and Question

In the mid- to late 1980s I worked in support of an interdenominational conciliation team in Nicaragua mediating between Yatama, the indigenous armed insurgents of the east coast of Nicaragua, and the Sandinista government. The case has been well documented and studied.[6] While I could elaborate on numerous aspects of this early experience I will focus on one particular event near the conclusion of our activity in order to highlight a less explored component of the engagement.

Following numerous years and with considerable frustration, our team led by a Baptist pastor and medical doctor, Gustavo Parajón, and the then-superintendent of the Moravian Church, the Rev. Andy Shogreen, we successfully facilitated a negotiation between Yatama and the Sandinista government. Near the conclusion of a full week of negotiations, a last request was made just prior to the formal signing. The indigenous leaders proposed a trip to the east coast of Nicaragua. The government agreed and proposed a joint trip through a series of visits to villages along the coast and rivers, the heartland of the uprising.

Our conciliation team was tasked with facilitating the trip and meetings. Over the course of several weeks we traveled, mostly by outboard motor wood canoes from Bluefields near the Costa Rican border to Puerto Cabezas, the stronghold of the Miskito Indians, and then along the Rio Coco, the dividing frontier with Honduras. Among our many challenges in those days was a lack of basic infrastructure. We had no way to announce our arrival times, formulate agendas, or deal with potential local issues. The latter came in fits and starts as these unexpected and unusual meetings began. Villagers gathered after the ringing of a church bell and stared, surprised at the presence of the highest-level representatives of two warring sides in their hometown. Each village had its internal conflicts, divisions, and deep pain rising from years of violence, displacement, and betrayals. Peace processes do not emerge in safe and peaceful conditions. They are born in the cauldron of violence, still present and pending in all its imaginative forms. In the early portion of the trip we experienced the full breadth of division and animosity. While we could facilitate, prepare, and accompany, we had no capacity to control events, emotions, and in some cases the outpouring of bitterness. Following one of our meetings, several government cadres stationed nearby were attacked and died. The risk and demands on subsequent meetings rose incrementally. The government became more wary of the process, and the escalated potential for renewed conflict slowly put pressure on our team to call off the agreed-upon trip. The indigenous leaders, in spite of the risk to their own lives, believed fervently that the agreement to meet with their people must not be rescinded and pushed ahead.

The culminating point of the trip came around the largest public event in Puerto Cabezas. Government leaders became increasingly determined that the event should not happen, perhaps in part driven by the assessment that this was the symbolic return of leaders from years of exile to the heartland of their movement, perhaps legitimately concerned that events could not be fully controlled. What became apparent to us was rather simple. The threats of violence if the public event took place were rising, stoked in large part by pro-government allies, troops, and party cadres who became increasingly active on the radio and the streets. At the same time, the majority who sympathized with the return of the Indian leaders became equally adamant that the meeting must take place.

The night before the meeting, our conciliation team received separate visits from the two sides. The Indian leaders indicated their intention to hold the meeting no matter what came. The government leaders in a last plea told us they had "lost control" of their own people. They could not guarantee anyone's safety, including ours. They asked us to call off the event or not attend. Our response, decided ahead of time, was that both sides had agreed to this trip and to this meeting. We agreed that the potential for violence was high, but we also indicated that our presence to accompany the process and the leaders was required to help mitigate the violence. We encouraged the government leaders to do what they could to call off the squads that were well prepared and headed for the streets in the morning. Our view, to be honest, was that the government had not lost control but was in fact using the conditions to strike back against and decrease the potential impact of the returning indigenous leaders.

The next morning, our team rose early, had breakfast, and then prayed together for about thirty minutes. Those thirty minutes I have never forgotten. The prayers came from the various religious leaders. They were not vague or abstract pleas. Dr. Parajón and Rev. Shogreen prayed for each leader of significance on both sides by name. They prayed for each as a person with a simple recognition that these individual leaders from different sides of a conflict each faced a difficult day. Rev. Shogreen was praying for people who in earlier days had him arrested, and from whom he had received death threats on more than one occasion. They prayed for the leaders' well-being knowing full well that some of these people were putting in motion violent actions that we would face later that morning. It was the first time I had been part of a prayer for the well-being of people, by name, who were about to do us and me harm.

We left the house and walked with the indigenous leaders to the baseball stadium. It was early morning, but the streets were already filled with gangs of young people preparing for a fight. We stopped several times to talk with them. Walking to the stadium, those prayers seemed to reverberate internally. The public utterance of those words represented something much deeper, a flow of preparation these religious leaders had nurtured across years of navigating the division, violence, and personal animosity they had each experienced. Now we knew we were about to live through the very thing we professed to believe. You could see it in the streets. You could feel it in the eyes.

The morning unfolded about as we expected. Crowds gathered from both sides. Gangs of youth provoking conflict emerged carrying chains, clubs, and machetes. The public talk was held amidst a cacophony of abusive chants and gunfire at the edges of the stadium. Riots broke out as we accompanied the key Indian leaders to safety. A few of us, myself included, ended up in makeshift emergency care locations from the blows and beating we took.

How does one prepare for loving one's enemy? Thirty-five years later I am still searching for the answer.

The Long Rough Road

In 1965, Thich Nhat Hanh wrote a poem to young students engaged in Buddhist response to the war in Vietnam. He found himself in exile, having been forced from his homeland, yet attempted through this poetry to carve the difficult space of refusing to accept violence and refusing to take sides. The poem titled "Recommendation" had a single purpose, according to this beloved teacher who went more often by the name Thay: "Prepare to die without hatred."[7]

> Promise me,
> Promise me this day,
> Promise me now,
> While the sun is overhead
> Exactly at the zenith
> Promise me:
>
> Even as they
> Strike you down
> With a mountain of hatred and violence;
> Even as they step on you and crush you
> Like a worm,
> Even as they dismember and disembowel you,

Remember, brother,
Remember:

Man is not our enemy.
The only thing worthy of you is compassion—
Invincible, limitless, unconditional.
Hatred will never let you face
The beast in man.
One day when you face this beast alone,
With your courage intact, your eyes kind,
Untroubled
(even as no one sees them),
out of your smile
will bloom a flower.

And those who love you
Will behold you
Across ten thousand worlds of birth and dying.

Alone again,
I will go on with bent head,
Knowing that love has become eternal.
On the long, rough road,
The sun and the moon
Will continue to shine.[8]

In the midst of warfare and violence of the kind Thay knew in flesh and life, the hard realist schools of political engagement may well ask, of what significance is a life of walking meditation, blooming smiles, and compassion? Yet over a lifetime Thay inspired generations of rising leaders, as he says in the poem on the long, rough road, aimed at finding the humanity in the other, not taking sides to unify a fragmented community both within and across his religious tradition, within his country, and internationally. By all accounts the journey had much pain and suffering. When one of his earliest novitiates immolated herself in protest against the war in Vietnam, Thay spent months in isolated meditation. Yet he persisted in engaging the other, in cultivating compassion for those who saw and pursued him as an enemy.

To Revenge in a Different Way

The Parents Circle–Families Forum bills itself as a "grassroots organization of bereaved Palestinians and Israelis" who promote "reconciliation as an alternative to hatred and revenge."[9] One might expect this represents the view of those seeking an end to the armed conflict by way of a liberal peace, but that is not the case. Members of this movement are individuals and families who have, in the words of one of founders, "lost relatives from the first degree, sons or fathers or sisters or brothers. And they follow a strange way, to sit and dialogue, to revenge in a different way, to sit and make dialogue."[10]

It may be useful to look more carefully at how revenge in a different way takes place. Their practices involve a number of approaches, the primary one being the act of sitting with other parents and listening to the story of their life, their loss, and their bereavement. This sitting together happens at the level of people to people across the lines of deep and historical enmity.

They believe that being human with each other, with the "simple" people who have experienced great loss, opens the way toward healing and dignity. In the aftermath of a death, the families gather and sit together. Sometimes in the early days of tragedy, their mutual presence takes the form of only tears. "We start to cry. That's it. Because when you've lost something from your family it means a lot. It means no Fridays with the son. No social occasions with the son. Everything gone away."

When violence erupts, like in the case of a bombing or shelling, and dozens of people are rushed to hospitals, the families act together. In pairs or groups they find their way, Palestinians and Israelis, Muslims, Christians, and Jews, to emergency rooms and hospitals to give blood together. They call the initiative "Blood Relations." It does not fit any existing category of government or NGO funding; in fact it requires no funding. It literally comes from the heart and spilled blood. They call this a different kind of revenge, one that displays a spontaneous determination to uphold the basic dignity of the human person and family.

How do historical enemies who themselves have lost their most precious gift, members of their own families, make a journey that permits them to share and act together with those who come from the other side of the conflict divide that produced the greatest source of their suffering? From what inner processes and resources does such engagement and interaction emerge?

THE NATURE OF PROTRACTED CONFLICT

Since the 1980s the terminology of protracted or intractable conflict has emerged to describe settings that combine cyclical violence, often in the form of fighting conducted by armed groups, with long-standing identity-based animosities and social division. In the majority of these cases, internal conflicts unfold between groups living within the borders of the same nation-state. At the same time, these "internal" conflicts exhibit significant international elements and influences. For example, weapons flow in from outside the country, armed groups operate in fluid border areas, and civilians, displaced from their homes by violence within their own countries, move toward neighboring countries and far beyond. Such conflicts with significant internal and internationalized characteristics and dynamics are typically protracted.

The descriptors of protracted or intractable conflict highlight distinguishing temporal traits that the groups in conflict have experienced, notably generational and trans-generational division and animosities. Historically, the patterns will include periods of intense, sometimes sustained levels of open violence and periods of latent social division simmering below the surface. In essence the groups in conflict have a long history of grievance and division that merges with direct personal experience of violence and significant shared personal, family, and community trauma. The protracted nature underscores both the longevity and the depth of the division which, when expressed in narratives of the conflict, includes generational transference of trauma and the assessment of blame, the pain of exclusion and oppression, and demands for rights and protection. More often than not, people perceive themselves to be in a fight not just around the demands for land, political recognition, or economic inclusion but for their very survival.[11]

By their very nature, these internal armed conflicts carry a geographic proximity that differentiates them from "international" wars fought in distant battlefields. The "enemy" rarely lives on the other side of the globe but rather next door, in the back yard, in the adjoining neighborhood or village. Literally, as in the case of Northern Ireland, they share and co-inhabit spaces divided only by a street. This proximity, coupled with the experience of historical and immediate violence, creates sharp social divisions with nearly impermeable social identity groups. In many locations the construction of identity relates closely to finding oneself born into and living daily with the defining boundaries of "in" and "out" groups, the "us" and "them" prevalent in the everyday language. These defining boundaries of identity can materialize around ethnicity, language, geographic location, shades of pigmentation, and of course religion. For the religious actor, the lines of division have deep connection to the ways in which their fundamental belief system provides for ethics, the gathering and parameters of their shared faith community, and the intriguing ways in which those same ethics also portray the "other," the "stranger," and the "outsider." At times, within the warrants of religious affiliation are requirements of sharing if not proselytizing the other toward the in-group truth, a significant source for conflict. Less explored is the liminal experience itself, that is, how the religious actor in a context of division assumes, defines, and engages the where, how, and how deep the separation between in- and out-group must attain. The very act of defining the line, and doing so often amid competing internal mandates within a tradition, to protect truth yet engage the other create a special location for the religious actor within the landscape of deep social division.

The dynamics of this social polarization hold particular salience for the purpose of this chapter and merit a brief description, with emphasis on the research emergent in sociology and social psychology.[12]Certain shifts or transformations affect individuals, collectives, and social structures. For example, as conflict escalates, and in particular if violence emerges in significant ways, people seek safety, often through the formation of "in" groups of shared identity and affiliation, which are differentiated from the source of perceived threat, the "out" group. As conflict escalates, the frequency and intensity of interaction between people within an identity group increase, while contact between groups who disagree decreases. In essence, people spend more time with those who agree with them and have less and less contact with those who may express different or oppositional views, or are perceived to be on the "other" side.[13]

These crisis-driven alignments trigger a significant change in communication patterns. In the midst of conflict, people seek the safety of others who agree with them. Decreasing levels of interaction with those of different views translates into reliance on indirect sources of information regarding what the other side may say or seek. Accuracy of information suffers as the very source and structure of communication no longer has direct exchange or input. In protracted settings, those defined as having a trans-generational history of division (Northern Ireland, Israel/Palestine, Sudan and South Sudan, to mention a few that have significant religious overlay), this pattern becomes more rigid over years, decades, and generations. A person is born into a divided social context that will mark his or her life and identity. In a setting of protracted conflict, contact and movement to engage with the "other" perceived as coming from the "enemy" side become in themselves questioned, as they can easily be portrayed as signs of disloyalty to the in-group. People experience a strong social pressure to interact only with the in-group and minimize contact with the out-group. Those who find themselves in relationship with both sides feel a sharp and demanding pressure to choose a side or suffer the consequences of suspicion and distance, a dynamic that diminishes relational space over time and can eliminate a middle or more moderate ground of connections between people.

Increased in-group interaction over time creates shared narratives of perception and interpretation of complex realities. Formative historical explanation and even "truth" about lived and inherited situations—in other words, how the conflict is viewed and explained, including the portrayal of both "our" plight and the justification of our demands, how the other side should be seen, and what motivates them—is conveyed in a single, shared, and unquestioned narrative. The shared narrative, what some call the chosen traumas and chosen glories, imparts strong predisposed perceptions and interpretations of immediate social realities and information.[14]People see what they look for, and pressure exists within the group to accept and not dissent from the shared understandings of the narrative. Alternative views will be assessed and interpreted to match the existing narrative. The outsider, who does not have the filter of generationally based perceptions and narrative combined with the experience of trauma and the immediacy of violence, may see the insider narratives as carrying significant elements of irrationality. Nothing is seen as irrational from within the conflict, however, given that survival has often required an interpretation leaning toward and driven by worst-case expectations of the purpose and motivations of the enemy group.

Individuals and leaders who may have been perceived as extreme in their view of the threat during periods of less polarization rise into more significant and prominent leadership within their group as conflict escalates.[15]Their exclusivist and extreme portrayal of the other often plays on the immediate and historical experiences of exploitation and mistreatment, and solidifies an environment of imminent threat, fear, and survival. Those who hold moderate views lose ground and prominence during periods of escalation. There is little appreciation in particular for those who may advocate contact with the other and a more complex, nuanced understanding of the conflict.

Lewis Coser observed that conflict has a number of social functions.[16] He noted, for example, that outside threat increases internal cohesion and agreement. To sustain that cohesion, ambiguity must be minimized if not eliminated. Thus, in periods of sharp polarization, little room exists for internal disagreement within an identity group, and very little interaction with alternative views of complex histories and events is sought or socially sanctioned.

Sustained over time, and reinforced by periods of violence, this social polarization can create a shift in goals. Rather than focus on addressing originating issues in order to arrive at an understanding with an adversary, people in settings of protracted conflicts often conclude they must separate completely from the other community or eliminate them in order to survive and find safety. In armed conflicts this decision carries significant impact. Deep suspicion bordering on paranoia is not the outcome of twisted perceptions produced by irrational emotions. Rather, sustained and deeply held suspicion functions as a method of survival in a context with a great deal of unpredictability.

To this we add the religious dimension. Religious faith and beliefs about the sacred amplify the search for and portrayal of truth. Religious truth emerges from and interacts with frames of reference that describe (or lend themselves to description of) right and wrong, evil and threat. As well noted by Scott Appleby, religion carries an embedded "ambivalence" of interpretation that has the capacity to mobilize people in ways that inflame and justify violence to defend their ultimate truth and faith tradition, or that can incite constructive engagement with the other, even one perceived and known to be an enemy.[17]

In settings of deep-rooted, protracted conflict where religious identity plays a significant role, then, we observe complex dynamics and characteristics that dominate social interaction. Highly escalated conflict, particularly when violence has come through iterative and generational experiences, creates sharply defined in- and out-group affiliations that provide few spaces for constructive interaction with the other side. "Truth" about history, about "us" and "them," when mixed with religious identity divisions, is similarly exclusive and defensive. Sustained experiences of violence and trauma, and generational patterns of suspicion and mistreatment, deepen the incommensurable nature of the rival self-understandings and narratives.[18]

We wish to explore spiritual practices in such contexts that flow into a quality of being and presence that opens toward and engages the enemy-other against the gravitational forces of polarization, escalated conflict, and historical but exclusive narratives. In many regards this can be conceived as an exploration into positive social deviance: in a context that pushes people toward mistrust, separation, and demonization of the other, how do some people, in this case religiously motivated peacebuilders, reach out and engage perceived enemies against the socially sanctioned norms that justify violence?

PRESENCE: SPIRITUALITY AND ENGAGED RESPONSE

The challenge protracted conflict poses for religious peacebuilders has layers not always apparent on the surface. Prominently, the embedded peacebuilder must locate strategies for day-to-day survival when violence carries both historical patterns and repeated direct expression. Violence engenders significant personal and social loss. In protracted conflict it leaves a social genealogy and shared legacy. Inherited, lived, and re-enacted violence is not an abstract concept. In these contexts a focus on spiritual resources of religiously inspired peacebuilding tends to gravitate toward exploring coping mechanisms for survival, interpretive schemes that attempt to account for the inexplicable, and the personal sources of resilience that respond to the emergent threat and trauma. Referring back to our opening examples, how does a Moravian pastor who was jailed and threatened come to pray for the well-being of individuals who later that same day would wreak physical harm on him and his family? How did a Buddhist monk encourage the front line of his devotees to dedicate themselves to offer their lives nonviolently without hate or bitterness? How did Palestinian and Israeli parents who had lost children at the hands of their respective enemy communities *go together* to give blood in hospitals as a response to violence, no matter the source or victim? When the response to lived violence, rooted in a religious understanding, contributes to peacebuilding (as opposed to revenge or the justification of counter-violence) and seeks to understand and engage the "enemy-other," outsiders may perceive this "reaching out" as "otherworldly."

Academic attempts to identify the source and nature of such responses often start with categorizing *spiritual* motivations and practices from across different traditions by comparing the warrants found within sacred texts or theological interpretation of the same.[19] However, comparative typologies scratch only the surface of a richly textured and complex set of human responses and creativity. Even the combination of the two terms, "spiritual" and "practice," carries a paradoxical quality. *Spirituality* points toward mystery if not mysticism.

Practice evokes the image of habit or daily activities of the devotee. Thus the phrase *spiritual practices* may draw our attention toward quasi-technical explorations of behavior and action, a kind of religiously based classification useful for cross comparison responsive to questions like these: How do religiously motivated persons explain their action? What rituals do they follow? What preparation do they practice? These questions reflect a pragmatic orientation to "spiritual practices," but they rarely dig deeper, toward the more profound ways of being and attitudes that may help explain creative forms of positive deviance in response to enmity.

My colleague Scott Appleby and I recently completed an initial annotated bibliography based on five bodies of literature to explore the nexus of creativity, spirituality, and compassion in fields as diverse as neuroscience, contemplative traditions, helping professions, peacebuilding, and the arts.[20] The points of convergence are relatively few and thus striking. The core practices most commonly found within and across these disciplinary fields were forms of meditation and prayer, yoga and exercise, the ritual use of symbol, and engagement of the arts, not least music. Spiritual habits reflected the search for "centering" and "balancing" the practitioner, for forging the connection with a "sacred space apart" from the daily demands of work, and a reconnection with a sense of purpose. Empirical research suggests some of these practices do in fact impact the physical functioning of the brain in a way that ripples into attitude and behavior changes.[21] Their regular practice, particularly that focused on mindfulness, produces greater curiosity and openness, a calmer and less reactive demeanor in the face of threat or challenge, and the ability to engage constructively with the other.

The present chapter proposes a perhaps more nuanced approach to the notion of spiritual resources for religious peacebuilding than provided by an exercise in comparative typologies of rituals or sacred texts. The approach requires that we explore the understanding and perspectives that undergird the practices, the terrain, and meaning at a deeper level than the description of a particular technique. At the same time, such an inquiry will not rely exclusively on a theological framing of spirituality. Both theology and particular practices provide insight, but they deliver limited understanding into *the dynamism of being and response* that emerges in peacebuilding and evinces a creative and transcendent character in its constructive engagement of violence and the "enemy-other." Our interest here requires an exploration into the *nexus, the confluence* of personal grounded experience, lived faith with its roots in a robust theological imagination, and the formation of self. The nurturing of a resilient soul capable of sustaining a healthy self and creative engagement of the other unveils the mystery of the pathways that connect the inner world with the ever present threat of the outer world.

This nexus represents one way to explore the concept of *quality of presence* identified by a range of authors as key to transformative processes in the midst of conflict and in peacebuilding.[22] The nuances and layered meanings behind the idea of a "quality of presence" cannot be comprehended merely by listing particular spiritual practices or by ascribing to the practices a specific set of resulting actions and responses. The very nature of *presence* has elements inclusive of worldview and attitude, spirituality and theological grounding, as well as practices and creativity. As such, "presence" encompasses multiple tributaries of focus and resources that appear paradoxical. Each particular tributary contains differentiated qualities and character, connected and interdependent with others; thus a particular tributary cannot be taken as separate from or exclusive of other distinctive elements. These spiritual tributaries mix and converge across a range of potential combinations, which in turn emerge creatively as patterns of response and engagement. A brief review of the layers and levels of paradox we will encounter is necessary to clarify my meaning. Three levels of paradox seem particularly salient. They are identified here as a core set of dilemmas faced by religious peacebuilders, particularly those from and responding to settings of protracted conflict.

NEXUS: THE CONFLUENCE OF PARADOXES

By its very nature the notion of "nexus" highlights a spatial quality primarily expressed in the encounter, or visible interaction between people. In his seminal work reflecting on his homeland, his personal experience, and the challenge of enmity, Miroslav Volf understood this primarily as *encounter* with the other.[23] Other layers, perhaps less visible, also have significance for exploring this confluence. Nexus suggests an encounter that must account for how the *inner world* of each person comes alongside the *outer world*, the shared space of encounter with another. In this space the inner world shapes and responds to the interaction with the other and returns inward as a tributary to the deep processes involving perception, interpretation, and meaning. Phenomenologists early tagged this as the extraordinary and instantaneous process by which subjectivity and intersubjectivity meet, interact, and mutually affect the construction of social meaning.[24] At a third level, nexus has a quality that explores how people from different sides of the polarized setting inhabit a common space wherein their very lives are affected and shaped by the continuing impact of violence. We seek here to explore this nexus of encounter, the space where people are aware and present with and to the enemy-other while also attentive to and engaged with the inner world of conflict and mystery they live and experience.

The hyphenated phrase "enemy-other" merits further detail. The challenge of enmity for the religious peacebuilder has been well documented in the wider literature.[25] Our primary focus requires us to look at religious leaders who find themselves in the presence of and in encounter with others whom they (or their communities) perceive as enemies and who pose a threat to their safety. Perception should not be minimized: what is perceived to be real is real in its consequences.[26] In protracted violent conflict, perception plays the core function of noticing and locating a person and events within a frame of reference. Meaning rises from an act of association. How a person is viewed and located, or how particular statements, events, or activities have association provides the basic process of interpretation and construction of social meaning. In reference to our inquiry, we wish to explore the instances when, by way of previous and more immediate experience in the long history of collective and inter-group conflict, a person finds him- or herself in the presence of another who represents the face of that which has caused harm to their primary community, immediate family, or self. Our focus will be oriented toward sustained encounters and relationships across the lines of enmity in which each perceives the "other" as representative and defender of those things that have caused damage, and as one who may well seek the very elimination of "me," "us," or "our" community.[27] This I refer to as an encounter with the *enemy-other*.

Such an encounter holds several key dilemmas with paradoxical qualities. First, conflict has dynamics that both divide and bind groups. Coser noted that conflict has functions that serve to separate and push individuals and groups apart yet also contains elements that hold them together.

In settings of armed conflict, people have commonalities that bind them together. For example, they inhabit a landscape of immediate conflict. They learn to navigate and read the signs of this conflict, which streets are safe to travel and when, what buses to take or not, what neighborhoods are safe or not for their group. They share a social geography of identity, which whether chosen or not places them as with or from one side or another. More often than not, in-group identity is shaped more by having a clearly defined enemy than a well-articulated self or group identity. They share a world of suspended trust and pressures to have narrowly defined sets of relationships corresponding to the divisions of historical animosities.

We typically understand enmity as creating *centrifugal* energies that drive people apart, the polarizing effect sharply delineated in the creation and sustenance of in- and out-groups described earlier. Within this framework, the image and concept of the *other*, by whatever form it takes, collective or very personalized, has prominence. By virtue of the boundary demarcating the in- and out- group, the "other" creates the countenance of threat and enmity. At the same time, enemies in protracted conflict experience, though rarely externalize, a *centripetal* quality in conflict. They share in common the inherited legacy of trans-generational trauma, the pain of experienced loss, survival through cycles of violence, and the all too familiar pressures of guilt, blame, and demands felt within their community. Herein we find the first paradox in protracted conflicts: Though framed as mutually exclusive and differentiated in the competing narratives, the enemies are held together by the wars they fight. Yet for the religious peacebuilder, this paradox creates a bridge for engagement with the other! By harnessing the powers of the centripetal capacity, that is, by noticing the commonality of their human experience rather than reinforcing the justification of distance and exclusion—the powers of the centrifugal force—the religious peacebuilder bridges the divide by seeking connection. This we could call the *bridging dilemma*, the step required to reach out toward the other rather than pull back and distance oneself from the perceived enemy.

The second level of paradox has roots in the movement between the *lived internal world* that seeks meaning and purpose and the *external life* that seeks safety, understanding, and respect. The inner world, hidden except in rare moments, holds a series of running debates about the nature of one's life journey, the greater purpose in life, the competing sense of loyalty to a just cause and to bloodline—all compounded by the nagging questions of meaningless that endless bloodshed bequeaths to those who must live on, into, and through the next encounter, the ever proximate battle. The religious peacebuilder is potentially embedded within this inner narrative, precisely where the questions of faith and vocation reside. The warrants and moral lenses rising from belief and sacred texts, when cross-referenced with the lived experience of violence, pose paradoxical dilemmas that ultimately lead to a deep uncertainty about the very nature of the sacred and the human. Inevitably one confronts the paradox of the nexus, the point of intersection and encounter between the "I and Thou" (or between the "us and them"): How do I protect my/our dignity and yet recognize and acknowledge the dignity of the other? At essence, the paradox of the nexus compels one to understand how, in a space defined by enmity, the face of the divine or sacred is noticed in the other. How is it that humanity was noticed and recovered in spite of imminent threat and fear? This we could call the *dilemma of human dignity*, the natural openness and capacity of even the combatant to notice something of the common spark of life, vulnerability, and the sacred in the other.[28]

The third paradox relates most directly to the lived experience of violence. Violence has a numbing effect. In its aftermath people find ways to survive, often by closing down and controlling certain emotional features of their internal landscape. This is more pronounced if the pattern of violence remains active and present, affording little or no space for distance from the events or people that have caused it, a situation most face in protracted conflict. Narrowing the explanations toward less complexity or suspending the deeper search for meaning may facilitate internal control. Some will search the endless labyrinth for (nonexistent) logical answers. No rational explanation sufficiently explains what has transpired or been lost in the exclusive and ultimate conclusion that violence represents, leading many to describe the experience as "unspeakable."[29]

In the wider field of peacebuilding, resilience and response to surviving violence come under the exploration of trauma and the processes of healing. In its narrow application, healing may focus on phenomena such as post-traumatic stress syndrome, which is prevalent among returning combatants and among individuals living through periods of escalated violence. Beyond post-traumatic stress disorder, we find the challenge of understanding how collective violence and the wider social impact of sustained armed conflict or structural injustice affect whole populations. In the study of these all-too-prevalent experiences the notions of trans-generational trauma and approaches to social healing have emerged.[30] The religious peacebuilder carries within him- or herself the legacy of this trauma. The paradox is this: the religious peacebuilder hosts her own, unique internal journey of healing. At the same time, by way of the warrants and values present in every religious tradition, she also carries a sense of responsibility that concerns itself with the well-being and healing of those around her.

Let me briefly describe the example of Sister Mary Tarcisia from northern Uganda. As a young novice she found herself fleeing the convent, displaced and on the run following Idi Amin's incursion to the north of Uganda. In subsequent decades, she lost sisters from her convent and from her family to the Lord's Resistance Army incursions. Sister Mary then became the only woman member of the Acholi Religious Leaders Peace Initiative (ARLPI), the first group to seek out and engage the morally sworn enemy Joseph Kony, head of the Lord's Resistance Army, attempting to bring him into negotiations with the government. As the war in the north diminished, she opened the convent to receive abducted child-soldier-mothers who themselves had experienced and participated in violence.[31] In these few short sentences we find a lifetime of facing situations of violence, directly experiencing violence and loss, engaging the enemy, and caring for victims on all sides—a journey filled with inner trauma and response to trauma.

If defined by the impact of polarization, the centrifugal energy, the concern for healing attends only to those within one's own group, and creates a focus exclusively on the well-being of *my* immediate community, our family, our side. This internal caretaking impulse can often be held as separate from the healing of the other, the historic enemy, or those who have done us harm. The engagement of the other thus presents a rather extraordinary paradox at the heart of the nexus: How to recognize the roots, symptoms, and legacy of trauma within one's own life while acknowledging the same in the life of the other, particularly a person or group perceived to have caused one's loss and experience of violence? This we could call the *compassion dilemma*, the challenge to tap the capacity to create a bridge between one's own suffering and that of the enemy-other.

THE MORAL IMAGINATION

Exploring the challenge of these dilemmas in an earlier volume, I described a series of community-level responses to violence that required people creatively to engage their perceived enemy.[32] The focus was on how local leaders and individuals, including religiously motivated peacebuilders, who faced repeated patterns of armed conflict found ways to transcend the cycle of violence while still living in and through its daily expression. Four types of imagination or commitments appeared rather consistently that we would find equally present in the examples starting this chapter and the short description of Sister Mary.

First, in the face of violence, these leaders approach the conflict with a capacity to envision a web of relationships that included their enemies. This suggests relationship-building creates the very tissue in which the response to conflict, the contested issues and the emotional process, emerges. For those facing cycles of violence, this imagination requires the capacity to recognize that ultimately the quality of their community's life, the "in-group," has direct correlation with the quality of life enjoyed by the other community. In essence, to break from the legacy of violence, people have to recognize that the promise to ensure the well-being of their grandchildren has a direct link to the well-being of their enemy's grandchildren.

Second, in these contexts, constructive response to conflict requires a commitment to remain open and inquisitive about understandings and perceptions—including those held by others. I refer to this as a stance of paradoxical curiosity. While each person and side holds to and affirms the lived reality of their experience, the capacity to transcend violence means not rigidly holding to one's own view or experience as exclusive. Rather, these leaders hold open the possibility that a more complex, ever unfolding set of understandings was possible. In conflict settings, the more common view frames issues, history, and reality within a framework of dualism and contradiction that relies on and must accept a mutually exclusive understanding of right and wrong. Such a framing has little or no room for ambiguity and falls prey to the centrifugal dynamics of polarization. Curiosity requires an engagement of social realities with an abiding respect for complexity, a refusal to simply accept the pressures of forced exclusive choice. Curiosity approaches the conflict and the enemy-other with an inquisitiveness about what may hold together seemingly contradictory perceptions and social energies in a greater whole. A commitment to this quality of curiosity—of staying open to new understanding while remaining honest about one's own convictions—does not aim to find quick remedies or compromises based on narrowly shared common denominators. Rather, paradoxical curiosity seeks something beyond what may be immediately visible. It must learn to suspend immediate judgment of others in order to learn more about their perception, history, and understanding. In the process, it also affords the opportunity to deepen one's own understanding.

Third, in every instance, something new and unexpected emerges in the course of response to conflict. In other words, consistent with the very essence of imagination, creativity breaks out, beyond what existed in the cycles of destructive conflict. The creative act captures the dynamic and potential of the human being as artist. And the unexpected also may account for why imagination and artists are sometimes not fully appreciated but misunderstood and portrayed as living "unrealistically" at the edge of society. In a parallel vein, the religious peacebuilder will find she lives at the very edge, as a dweller on the outskirts of both communities she inhabits, the one with which she is identified and the one that poses a threat to her home.

Fourth, in order to overcome violence and destructive patterns of conflict, peacebuilding requires risk. In the midst of violence, risk means taking a step into the unknown *without* any guarantee of success or even safety. By its very nature, risk is mystery lived. People in settings of deep-rooted armed conflict face an extraordinary irony. Violence is known and peace is the unknown. Peace embodies mystery. By its very nature, therefore, religious leadership engaged in constructively transforming conflict must prepare for a journey guided by the imagination of risk, to offer vulnerability without the guarantee of reciprocation.

These four guideposts converge in what I call the moral imagination. While they provide a first window into our inquiry about the quality of presence, we must identify more fully the spiritual resources and the underflow of tributaries that constitute this way of being. This takes us to the heart of the nexus and more fully into practices.

By practices I mean personal disciplines and capacities, but not in the narrow sense of skills. Rather, I refer to how a person mixes attitude, empowerment, and mystery. These may seem an odd combination of concepts but they precisely identify the quality of presence we seek to understand. Attitude lifts up the tributary of predisposition, the discipline of how a person observes and notices the world around them. Empowerment enters the tributary of choice, the discipline of how a person envisions and takes up responsibility and engagement. Mystery offers the tributary flowing into the unknown, the discipline of facing and staying with the unfolding of understanding even when it appears to call into question deeply held and fundamental beliefs. As such this notion of practice has a preparatory quality that combines *reminder* with *response*, and complements the cues to *recall* a vocation—the deepest commitment to voice and yearning that stays close and true to what has been learned and known as true and authentic—with the commitment to a value-oriented *imagination* engaged with the not-yet-known. Three practices illustrate the nexus underpinning this quality of presence.

CREATIVITY: THE PRACTICES OF RISK AND HOPE

Earlier we identified the challenge of facing the bridging dilemma as the decision to take steps toward, rather than away from, the enemy-other. This step requires movement against gravity, counter to the centrifugal pressures that grip and drive people toward exclusively defined in-group contact and interaction. The movement to reach beyond the defined, accepted parameters of social relationships in contexts of deep and protracted division carries consequences in the form of increased social pressure against engagement with the other and the potential for isolation from one's own primary group of identity and affiliation. In essence the act gives birth to something that does not exist on its own—the opening of a new relational space. For the religious peacebuilder, what tributaries of attitude and practice—the spirituality of reaching out—facilitate such a birth? The exploration begins with a closer look at the creative act.

Creativity in violent conflict requires a combination of imaginations. Among those identified we find two that establish an intriguing baseline. At a first level, we find an imagination about the web of relationships that lifts up the interdependencies within conflict, that includes engagement with rather than isolation of the enemy-other. At a second level, we encounter the imagination for holding and appreciating complexity rather than reducing history and options to dualistic either/or choices. As I described in *The Moral Imagination*, and as are visible in the stories recounted at the beginning of this chapter, these two—inclusion and complexity—create a way of envisioning the social geography of conflict. Framed in this way, these forms of imagination approach and visualize the outer world. Less explored is a different lens: the discipline that attends to inclusion and complexity within the person—the inner landscape of conflict. Herein resides a key component in the spirituality of creativity: the capacity to hold risk and hope together.

The experience of violence and the lived social geography of conflict replay themselves constantly in the deepest trenches of the inner world. Among the gifts encountered in the long years of seemingly fruitless work of conciliation, moving between people who fear for their very survival and lock down into demanding counter-positions of mutually exclusive justification and blame, we find this: appreciation for the profound and real unfolding of inner debates about engagement with the enemy-other.[33]

Everything learned from years of survival coupled with disappointment and profound distrust of the other community justifies suspicion, skepticism, and extreme caution. Violence teaches you this: nothing can be trusted. Survival requires minimizing and controlling risks, pulling back and away from the other.

At the same time, repeated cycles of violence evoke the nagging voice that sits between reason and despair, and whispers that something at some point must be found to shift the dynamic of so much repeated violence. For the faith-based peacebuilder, this voice appeals to hope and points toward the horizon of the future. I recall an initiative of a colleague who in the midst of a rising exchange of violence in the Basque Country conducted a quiet survey of key hard-line decision-makers on both sides. Only one question in the survey uncovered common ground: a majority agreed they did not want to "pass the legacy of the violence" to future generations. Hope holds open possibility. Risk remains skeptical it can be trusted. The tense nexus where risk and hope meet provides the cauldron of creative engagement. The paradoxical tension remains key. Risk, on its own, shuts down any form of new input, moves with the gravitas of social division, and chooses to stay home and avoid any opening toward the enemy-other, even in the form of engagement. Hope without grounding in the hard geography of violence becomes inauthentic and unconnected wishful thinking. True hope requires acknowledgment and recognition, holding present the experience of loss. Authentic hope remembers. It does not live in the land of forgetfulness.

In more practical terms the tension provides an insight into the creative process. Creativity lies in anchoring risk in a hope shaped by remembering the past but also by offering a first sign of hope, the recognition of dignity in the other as part and parcel of one's own dignity. This risk-taking grounded in hope and recognition opens the possibility of new and surprising connections with the other.

In short, the internal landscape of debate requires the co-habitation of risk and hope. The practice of risk and hope becomes a choice knowingly to move against the history of disappointment and distrust. The step to reach out, however, requires a stance of vulnerability, to which we now turn our attention.

VULNERABILITY: THE PRACTICES OF SINCERITY AND HUMILITY

When religious orientations are expressed in declarations of unyielding identity, exclusive of any and all others, the results often reflect the animosity and social division that accompany exclusive claims to ultimate truth. Such claims come to dominate both social and religious discourse. These contending truths pose exclusive choices. The truths become ultimate when they are linked to perceived, portrayed, and lived experiences of sacrifice, and in the context of violence can express themselves in life-and-death outcomes. Claims become exclusive when one understanding of truth requires the elimination of other understandings. We must remember that the experience of violence and living under threat often solidifies a deep conviction that survival requires ultimate and exclusive demands about and from a faith tradition. In such a context the religious *peacebuilder* stands apart from the exclusivist and absolutist strain and instead embodies a deep vulnerability.

Vulnerability suggests a level of defenselessness. One is exposed. Naked. The etymology of vulnerable, *vulneris* in Latin, traces to the word "wound." When vulnerable, wounds are exposed and open. The poet Mark Nepo has suggested that to live vulnerably requires carrying one's wounds gracefully.[34] For the religious peacebuilder, the embrace of vulnerability, the openness to significant forms of exposure, carries the risk of someone pouring "salt" in the wound, virtually on a daily basis.

The most obvious exposure comes from the threat experienced in encounter with the enemy-other. In settings where the perception and lived experience lead to the conclusion that the enemy-other operates by way of ultimate and exclusive demand, and that one truth must triumph over the other, "our" very survival is at stake in the encounter and struggle with the other. Defending our right, our story, our view becomes central to our survival. Vulnerability appears as a choice of surrender and sacrifice.

A second exposure comes from within the community of shared belief and faith. The general nature of escalating and deeply polarized conflict, as described in the section "The Nature of Protracted Conflict," suggests that outside threat increases internal cohesion, a dynamic that intensifies extreme views of the other and reduces the space for ambiguity in in-group debates and discussions. Within "our" group, truth is known and must be defended. Engagement and relationship with the enemy-other carry the risk of portraying weakness, may dilute the clarity of belief binding the faithful, and only serve to confuse the truth. For the religious peacebuilder, the very act of reaching out exposes her or him to serious condemnation if not denigration from within their own faith community. As suggested by the prophet Zechariah (13:6), few losses create greater pain than the wounds suffered in the house of a friend, the most prominent of which takes the form of betrayal.

A third exposure resides deep within the peacebuilder. This vulnerability unfolds around the very concept of truth. On the one hand, conviction of belief translates toward truth as core principles and tenets of faith that have a defining quality of permanence requiring adherence and observance. On the other, truth also suggests ever-deepening understanding and revelation, a defining quality of impermanence and largesse requiring continued search. Here lies the internal vulnerability of religious peacebuilding: How to hold together truth as a destination reached with truth as an unfolding mystery? Relationship with the enemy-other rises from and returns to this internal debate.

Engagement of the enemy-other is justified in numerous ways. Many rise from pragmatic arguments. This seems particularly true of frameworks that argue for religious dialogue based on tolerance and coexistence. Both concepts and approaches establish laudable goals, particularly in the midst of violence. Their fundamental impulse focuses on the need to accept a regime of rights applicable to all. At times this may be seen as a mechanism to ensure the protection of one's own rights, as seems to be the case with the emphasis on religious liberty. These approaches appear to replicate the secular rationale of the universal declaration of human rights and liberal democracy. They are oriented toward the fundamental notion that religious extremism must be drawn toward a common denominator of rights and acceptance, a convergence that in essence neutralizes the public expression of the spiritual imagination.

Tolerance and coexistence in their more common practice suggest that relationship with the enemy-other will require forms of self-imposed restraint from each side. Logically, this has its most significant utility when applied to ending or limiting the use of violence, particularly in settings where it systemically functions by way of what sociologists call reciprocal causation—unleashing wicked cycles of justified counter-violence.[35] Less visible within the liberal framework is the value placed on forms of compromise, or at a minimum the requirement that the religious practitioner hold back deeply held convictionsthat may be experienced as offensive for the other in order to open and sustain a relationship. This often has a secularist justification that envisions religion as irrational and provocative of conflict.[36]The religious encounter revolves around the protection of common ground between faith views or historic perspectives, often for the purpose of achieving more immediate goals of reducing open conflict or assuring the safety of encounter.

A secular-liberal understanding of religious peacebuilding, however, lands far short of what I here refer to as the spiritual discipline of vulnerability. In a sustained relationship, vulnerability will require two fundamental commitments, quite paradoxical in nature, that also constitute significant tributaries in the quality of presence we seek to understand.

First, vulnerability requires a profound and open honesty, perhaps best described and experienced as sincerity. This honesty has a self-revelatory quality by which the core, fundamental aspects of faith and belief, held as precious and cherished, find their way from the inner world out into the unprotected environment and presence of the other in spite of resistance, dismissal, or expression of offense.

Second, vulnerability requires the practice of humility—a combination of attitude and relational stance that remains permanently open to learning and insight, and regards the other as holding the potential for sharing wisdom.

Associated with authenticity, the word "sincerity" has a rich etymology. Hailing from the Roman Empire, the Latin root of sincerity combines two terms, *sin* and *cera*, or literally in English, "without wax." In this time period builders and sculptors sought high-quality marble for their projects, and a robust business emerged. Vendors wanting to present their wares in the best possible light at times used mixes of wax to cover blemishes and fissures in the stones. At a later stage those working with the quarried marble would sooner or later come across the cover-up. Over time the vendors who sold their stones without wax, that is, who showed the stone as it was, blemishes and all, came to be known as people without wax, *sin cera*, or sincere in their life and livelihood. The story perhaps illustrates the quality of honesty that underscores this tributary we must understand. Vulnerability, a quality of living exposed, requires the honest sharing of how one views the world, the tenets of faith and belief held as truth, even when those may shock or offend. The alternative, refraining from full honesty about deeply held conviction, may have a place in finding diplomatic wording or politically correct engagement, but will fall short of authenticity if it hides, compromises, or refrains from openly sharing belief which at the deepest level is held to be central. At essence, this tributary of vulnerability suggests that the practice of honesty, the sincere sharing of truth as best understood, carries greater worth for the relationship than diplomatic expression, tolerant compromise, or ensuring a shared environment of political and religious correctness.

At the same time vulnerability requires the tributary of humility. Humility may well appear contradictory to honest revelation, in that honesty, when attached to ultimate spiritual values and truth, can easily appear as superiority, even arrogance. Humility with its etymological image of organic, earthy soil creates a firm repudiation of arrogance, a posture that sits above and beyond the inferiors wallowing below. Paradoxically, the practice of humility does lie with a self-effacing stance at times associated negatively with humbleness, particularly in relations defined by social hierarchies, but with the vigorous, full embodiment of curiosity. The tributary we approach with the word humility flows from the wells that feed the seeker, the practices of remaining open and wishing in each moment that something deeper, something more transcendent, something unexpected will emerge that expands and informs his or her understanding of truth. Curiosity does not suggest ignorance or the need for conversion, that is, that a person must drop his or her existing understanding to accept the other's view. Rather, in humility we find curiosity as the practices of open inquisitiveness and awareness in pursuit of truth. Such a practice requires that one align his or her life with commitment to continued growth and learning. In this sense humility provides the foundational practice that permits a person to live comfortably in the presence of ambiguity and reduces the need for quick judgment of others. Ultimately, humility carries an appreciation of the gift of complexity (and, it may be added, the grandeur and expansiveness) that accompany and infuse the spheres where the divine and the human meet. As such, humility leads to a deep appreciation of human impermanence, minuteness, and insignificance. Translated into the relational space, the practice of humility creates the disposition toward learning and the appreciation of the other, even the enemy-other, as teacher, even mentor.

Where sincere honesty and humility meet, the practice of lived vulnerability emerges as a spiritual discipline. We could engage this more carefully with the early stories in this chapter,which expressed the quality of honesty and humility embedded in the religious peacebuilder, but it must be noted that these qualities have limited application in one-time encounters and high-profile religious events. Within committed relationships, over time, they encourage and build the quality of presence. The practices of vulnerability, honest sincerity, and humility provide the conditions whereby faith finds expression as an artistic unfolding of engagement. The spirituality of risk and hope is not the absence of grounded realism but the offer of honest openness.

COMPASSION: THE PRACTICE OF NOTICING
YOURSELF IN THE OTHER

At an everyday level, many people associate compassion with an act of empathy for the suffering experienced by a fellow human being. These more commonly are experienced as spontaneous, nearly fleeting moments of connection. We feel for the other. We feel something of our own vulnerability when we see the pain of another. In my and my colleague's recent review of literatures about compassion, a striking observation emerged around how seldom the formal field of peacebuilding directly engaged the topic of compassion. It perhaps speaks to the domination of Western authors, as opposed to Asian or Buddhist authors who place compassion—the search to recognize, understand, and ultimately alleviate suffering—at the very center of peace. Yet one could argue, as numerous authors have recently done, that compassion represents the shared heart across religious traditions.[37]

While not denying the centrality of compassion in religious belief systems, our interest here is not primarily on compassion as a common denominator. Rather, the inquiry wishes to explore the spiritual practices flowing from and back into compassion—that is, the tributaries that link it primarily to the unexpected response apparent in a quality of presence engaged with the enemy-other. Key to this search we find a rather simple affirmation that merits exploration. The primary tributary of compassion emerges in the act of noticing oneself in the other and at the same time noticing something sacred, even divine, in the other. Hidden in this affirmation we find the *locus* of compassion. In essence, compassion bridges two vibrant inner worlds.

In the late 1990s, neurologists began to study topics like meditation and compassion.[38] Their interest focused on the brain and shifts in patterns within the brain, particularly among lifelong practitioners of meditative practices. Tibetan monks participating in one of the early studies found their heads strapped with probes and sensors to track the internal processes of interest to the neurologists. Assuming the purpose centered on understanding compassion, the monks found this funny and misguided. Compassion, they suggested, was not located in the head. Not much will be found there. Its source sits in the stomach and abdomen.

Comparatively this also matches the language for compassion of other traditions. Nouwen, McNeill, and Morrison (2005), theologians from the Christian tradition, highlighted the particular language used by New Testament authors when they described Jesus and acts of compassion. Consistently it emerges as a phrase: Jesus was "moved by compassion" in responding to human suffering and need. They note the Greek word for locating compassion—*splangchnizomai*—refers to the entrails. Compassion, so to say, moved Jesus in his guts. The parallel choice of word in Hebrew—*rachamim*—refers to the womb of God. The location of compassion is located deep in the core of our creation experience. In essence, *feeling* of this kind touches an aspect of embodied emotion that penetrates and shakes the lived experience to the very center where life itself emerges. If we accept both the emic-based experience of the Tibetan monks and the etymology of various languages, our search suggests the *locus* of compassion crosses between two inner worlds *gut-to-gut*. Here, too, we find the location of authenticity, the nexus of honest sincerity and humility. Compassion and authenticity feel connection in the gut before they find rational explanation in the head.

The tributaries flowing under compassion require a robust form of intuition, though this term does not fully capture the quality of "being" present to the inner world that stays intimately in touch with the deepest gut feeling. At the same time, compassion requires a vigilance of presence attuned to the inner, gut-world of another. Curiously, the more accurate term for "feeling it in the guts" may be found in an understanding that this has a womb-like character.[39] Womb lifts forward a crucible-like image for birthing, the inner location that holds and nurtures the smallest seed of life, an image that highlights at once the quality of vulnerability with the act of creativity.

I note in my own experience how often people who engage their enemy vacillate in their explanation of motivation between a *pragmatism* driven by their lived experience and the *hope* of shifting the relationship toward something qualitatively more life-giving. The first emerges as rational explanation, traversing the long review of hard facts and realities that make engagement unlikely to succeed but necessary to end undesired violence. The second expresses a generational legacy and concern. It dips toward the womb metaphor, emphasizing at once children and parentage. A priest in Colombia noted his engagement of the enemy-other in moments of direct threat with this simple phrase, "I remind myself that behind the gun is someone's son."[40] Or one is reminded of the often-heard explanation that God or the sacred has a primary reference as a parent with a phrase such as "we are all children of the same creator."

Here we find a primary tributary of compassion. People pay attention to a gut feeling that notices the shared humanity, the divine spark of life intrinsic in each person. The capacity to notice has significance, as discipline and practice. It requires awareness of one's own fragility and need for protection, even as it simultaneously recalls that fragility of life in the other. In essence, this form of noticing requires the capacity to first feel and then see *oneself in the other*. This bridge, the act of feeling and seeing, has an intimate connection with the transcendent, the sense that within each person the place of meeting at the womb has a sacred quality that returns to the very gift of one's own life for which no human being had control or responsibility.

Here the various tributaries converge in a compassionate quality of presence. The act of noticing oneself in another, and at the same time recognizing the sacred nature of the bridge that connects two inner worlds, emerges when risk and hope meet, when honest sincerity and humility embrace. In such a space the gut sensation of the experience appears as something simple yet profound: the recovery and restoration of humanity. In conflict and violence, the sustained processes of dehumanization create a vacuum of unspoken numbness not easily explained with words. The quality of presence that regenerates authentic human engagement with the enemy-other suggests that the loss of humanity is not inherent to the person but lies with our incapacity to find and engage the divine spark, our incapacity to notice ourselves in each other.

CONCLUSION

In this chapter we examined the spiritual resources, the inner world as it links to the lived outer world of protracted conflict, violence, and engagement of the enemy-other. Our purpose required an exploration into the significance of how a quality of presence that permits such an engagement emerges. We noted that three significant dilemmas or tensions must be faced and addressed by the religiously inspired peacebuilder that arise from the very nature of deep-rooted social conflict and the experience of escalated violence.

First, the religious peacebuilder moves to reach out toward the other instead of following the pressures of conflict dynamics within and across groups to pull back and have little or no contact with the other side. This reaching out, we noted, also had to address the internal tensions unfolding within the religious peacebuilder, the debates of right and wrong, risk and protection of self. Second, beyond reaching out, the religious peacebuilder faces the challenge of noticing both the humanity and divine nature of the enemy-other rather than dismissing their story or demonizing their character and purpose. Here perhaps we find in the examples provided the particular resource of how the faith tradition inspires and mobilizes the sense of fundamental connectedness among human beings. Third, the religious peacebuilder faces the challenge of how to link his or her personal and ongoing experience of suffering with the suffering of the enemy-other. This link forms the bridge of compassion that requires a form of coming alongside the other in a more sustained relationship. When these three dilemmas are faced, entered, and held—for one does not resolve a dilemma but rather chooses to live with its inherit tension—what takes shape, in situ and in specific relationships, can be characterized as a felt quality of presence.

Our exploration suggests that this quality of presence builds from and mobilizes several key forms of imagination that distinguish the nature of the *religious* in peacebuilding in part because it rises from the mysterious depth seeking the unfolding of faith, understanding, and ultimately truth in the cauldron of facing violence and suffering in the human condition. The first imagination we find in the act of creativity embedded in the process of reaching out across lines of enmity that defies the push and pull of violence and division. This involves mobilizing the religious imagination that hope and risk translate toward the belief that change and healing of self, other, and society are possible.

The second imagination requires commitment to honesty and humility. Rarely held together, the two give rise to the presence of being vulnerable in settings where history and experience demand self-protection and isolation. This vulnerability, carrying a wound gracefully and offering to be present with the wounds of another, requires a religious imagination built on awe and the expansive belief that truth unfolds endlessly through daily experience and encounter. Vulnerability built on honesty and humility provides for a continuous openness, the offer to shed the callused outer skin and be open to learning about self and the other. As noted by Gopin,[41] honesty and humility in relationship require the practice of deep self-reflection.

Finally, we find the imagination that gives rise to and nurtures compassion, the capacity to notice oneself in another and build a bridge of care for suffering experienced as mutual, parallel, and fundamentally human. This imagination with deep eschatological roots in the very nature of creation and ultimate purpose of shared humanity suggests that healing has an inclusive character that must address the deep inner wounds of self and the other.

Quality of presence in the end does not approach the context or relationships with an emphasis on finding quick solutions. It opens toward a way of being with oneself and with the enemy-other. While on the outside this appears as building relationships across lines of enmity, less visible are the ways in which the inner worlds open spaces toward forms of mutual accompaniment of healing. With commitment toward longer-term relationships, being with and engaging the other seek a wholeness of internal and external brokenness. As such, this quality of presence chooses to live with rather than resolve the experienced ambiguities without retreat or reaction, creating the conditions for personal and social healing.

Notes

1. The body of literature is widely cited in this volume. For purposes of this chapter, see Douglas Johnston and Cynthia Sampson, eds., *Religion, the Missing Dimension of Statecraft* (New York: Oxford University Press, 1994); Daniel Buttry, *Christian Peacemaking: From Heritage to Hope* (Valley Forge, PA: Judson Press, 1994); R. Scott Appleby, *The Ambivalence of the Sacred: Religion, Violence, and Reconciliation* (Lanham, MD: Rowman and Littlefield, 2000); Gopin (2002); Abu-Nimer (2003); Douglas Johnston, *Faith-Based Diplomacy: Trumping Realpolitik* (New York: Oxford University Press, 2003); Harold Coward, and Gordan S. Smith, eds., *Religion and Peacebuilding* (Albany: State University of New York Press, 2004); Mohammed Abu-Nimer, Amal I. Khoury, and Emily Welty, *Unity in Diversity: Interfaith Dialogue in the Middle East* (Washington, DC: US Institute of Peace Press, 2007); David Little, ed., with the Tanenbaum Center for Interreligious Understanding, *Peacemakers in Action: Profiles of Religion in Conflict Resolution* (New York: Cambridge University Press, 2007); Susan Thistlethwaite and Glen Stassen, "Abrahamic Alternatives to War: Jewish, Christian, and Muslim Perspectives on Just Peacemaking," US Institute of Peace Special Report 214, October 2008; Robert J. Schreiter, R. Scott Appleby, and Gerard F. Powers, eds, *Peacebuilding: Catholic Theology, Ethics, and Praxis* (Maryknoll, NY: Orbis Books, 2010); Timothy D. Sisk, ed., *Between Terror and Tolerance: Religious Leaders, Conflict, and Peacemaking* (Washington, DC: Georgetown University Press, 2011); and John Witte Jr. and M. Christian Green, eds., *Religion and Human Rights: An Introduction* (New York: Oxford University Press, 2011).
2. Gopin's recent volume, *Bridges Across an Impossible Divide: The Inner Lives of Arab and Jewish Peacemakers* (New York: Oxford University Press, 2012), opens the specific issue of the inner lives of Arab and Jewish peacemakers.
3. See Johnston, *Faith-Based Diplomacy*.
4. I come from the Mennonite tradition, have been significantly influenced in my conciliation work by Quaker mentors, and have worked closely with Catholic colleagues in many parts of the world, including my academic home at the University of Notre Dame. I have had significant inter-religious engagement in settings of protracted conflict, where I have worked with teams of colleagues from Jewish, Muslim, Buddhist, Hindu, and indigenous traditions. For a better understanding of the formative traditions, see John Howard Yoder, *The Politics of Jesus* (Grand Rapids, MI: Eerdmans, 1972); Adam Curle, *Making Peace* (London: Tavistock Books, 1972); Thomas Merton, *The Seven Storey Mountain* (New York: Harcourt Brace and Co., 1948).
5. See as examples *The Journey Toward Reconciliation* (Scottdale, PA: Herald Press, 1999) and *The Moral Imagination: The Art and Soul of Building Peace* (New York: Oxford University Press, 2005).
6. See Paul Wehr and John Paul Lederach, "Mediating Conflict in Central America," *Journal of Peace Research* 28, no. 1 (1991): 85–98; Bruce Nichols, "Religious Conciliation Between the Sandinistas and the East Coast Indians of Nicaragua," in *Religion, the Missing Dimension of Statecraft*, ed. Douglas Johnston and Cynthia Sampson (New York: Oxford University Press, 1994), 64–87; Buttry, *Christian Peacemaking*; and Lederach, *Journey Toward Reconciliation*.

7. Thich Nhat Hanh, *Call Me by My True Names* (Berkeley, CA: Parallax Press, 1996).

8. Reprinted with permission from *Call Me by My True Names: The Collected Poems of Thich Nhat Hanh* (Berkeley, CA: Parallax Press, 1996). www.parallax.org.

9. See website at http://www.theparentscircle.com.

10. Gopin, *Bridges Across an Impossible Divide*, 10–11.

11. See Vamik D. Volkan, *Bloodlines: From Ethnic Pride to Ethnic Terrorism*. New York: Farrar, Straus and Giroux, 1997; Volkan, 1999; and Montville, 1999 for clear description of the nature of chosen trauma and chosen glory, where the generational narrative capture the deep sense that the conflict represents a threat to survival and can in fact justify preemptive forms of violence.

12. From classic sociological conflict studies, see in particular Simmel (1950); James Coleman, *Community Conflict* (Glencoe, IL: The Free Press, 1957); and Lewis Coser, *The Functions of Social Conflict* (New York: The Free Press, 1956).

13. As example, Coser (*The Functions of Social Conflict*) in his seminal work on the functions of social conflict identifies this very dynamic, arguing that outside threat increases internal cohesion during times of conflict escalation. Coleman (*Community Conflict*), studying community conflicts, found the dynamic repeatedly emerging that as conflict escalates, the community divides into groups where contact increases between people who agree on a particular issue but significantly decreases among those who do not share their viewpoint. This creates two common phenomena, the formation of "in" and "out" groups and the rise of indirect systems of communication between adversaries.

14. See Volkan, *Bloodlines*, and 1999 and Montville, 1999.

15. This was one of the functions of conflict identified by Coser and has held rather consistently through internal conflicts. See more recent studies focused on the role of religious leaders in locations like Northern Ireland (John Brewer, Gareth Higgins, and Francis Teeney, *Religion, Civil Society and Peace in Northern Ireland* [New York: Oxford University Press, 2011]) or the Balkans (Montville, 1999). Miroslav Volf (*Exclusion and Embrace: A Theological Exploration of Identity, Otherness and Reconciliation* [Nashville: Abingdon Press, 1996]) provides a personal account of his own need to engage, or in his words "embrace," the other when escalation pushed toward more extreme leadership in his home country.

16. Coser, *The Functions of Social Conflict*.

17. Appleby, *Ambivalence of the Sacred*.

18. In *The Moral Imagination* I trace the ways in which the past is alive and active in the present tracing to the narratives of how a group or people explain their sense of identify and belonging as part of the landscape of making sense of contemporary expressions of conflict. This has parallel with Judy Atkinson *Trauma Trails* (North Melbourne, Australia: Spinifex Press, 2002); Volkan, *Bloodlines*; Volkan, Gabriele Ast, and William F. Greer Jr., eds, *The Third Reich in the Unconscious: Transgenerational Transmission and Its Consequences* (New York: Brunner-Routledge, 2002); and theological works like Walter Brueggemann, *The Prophetic Imagination*, 2nd ed. (Minneapolis: Fortress Press, 2001).

19. See, as examples, Karen Armstrong's body of work on world religions with the cross-comparison on compassion (*Twelve Steps to a Compassionate Life* [New York: First Anchor Books, 2011]); David Smock, *Interfaith Dialogue and Peacebuilding* (Washington, DC: US Institute of Peace Press, 2002); and Paul Hedges, *Controversies in Interreligious Dialogues and The Theology of Religions* (New York: SCM Press,).

20. See Appleby, Lederach and Rojas (2013) posted at www.kroc.nd.edu. It includes more than one hundred entries from the five different disciplines on the topics of compassion, creativity, and spirituality.

21. See, as examples, Daniel Siegel, *The Mindful Brain* (New York: W. W. Norton, 2007); Siegel, *Mindsight* (New York: Bantam Books, 2010); and Harald Walach, Stefan Schmidt, and Wayne B. Jonas, eds., *Neuroscience, Consciousness and Spirituality* (New York: Springer, 2011), all of which document recent studies on the physical and overall well-being emergent from practices of mindfulness, including the recent neuroscience focus on meditation and music.

22. Edwin Friedman, *Generation to Generation* (New York: The Guilford Press, 1985); Friedman, *A Failure of Nerve* (New York: Church Publishing Inc., 2007); Parker Palmer, *Let Your Life Speak* (San Francisco: Jossey Bass, 1999); Lederach, *The Moral Imagination*.

23. Miroslav Volf, *Exclusion and Embrace*, includes a personal rendering of how difficult and complex engaging the enemy-other becomes in settings of lived violence.

24. See the work of Alfred Schutz (*Phenomenology of the Social World* [Chicago: Northwestern University Press, 1967]); Herbert Blumer (*Symbolic Interactionism* [Los Angeles: University of California Press, 1986]); and Peter Berger and Thomas Luckman (*The Social Construction of Reality* [New York: First Anchor Books, 1967]).

25. See for example Volkan, *The Need to Have Enemies and Allies: From Clinical Practice to International Relationships* (Northvale, NJ: J. Aronson, 1988); Donald Shriver, *An Ethic for Enemies* (New York: Oxford University Press, 1995); and Volf, *Exclusion and Embrace*.

26. Sociologist W. I. Thomas described this in his work on definition of a situation (*The Unadjusted Girl* [Boston: Little, Brown, and Co., 1923]).

27. See also Emmanuel Levinas, *Humanity of the Other* (Chicago: University of Illinois Press, 2005) and the parallel with Martin Buber's notion of the I and Thou (*I and Thou* [New York: Charles Scribner and Sons, 1970]), though the context we explore here is not a generalized other, but an "other" perceived as enemy.

28. Donna Hicks's essay on dignity (*Dignity: The Essential Role It Plays In Resolving Conflict* [New Haven, CT: Yale University Press, 2011]) provides an extraordinary exploration into the centrality of acknowledging and respecting dignity as the key to the constructive transformation of conflict.

29. This was more extensively explored in John Paul Lederach and Angela Jill Lederach, *When Blood and Bones Cry Out: Journeys Through the Soundscape of Healing And Reconciliation* (New York: Oxford University Press, 2010), and has been well documented in recent explorations in the field of trauma and healing by Carolyn Yoder (*The Little Book of Trauma Healing* [Intercourse, PA: Good Books, 2005]), Judith Herman (*Trauma and Recovery: The Aftermath of Violence from Domestic Abuse to Political Terror* [New York: Basic Books, 1997]), and Barry Hart (ed., *Peacebuilding in Traumatized Societies* [Lanhan, MD: University Press of America, 2008]).

30. See in particular Volkan et. al., *The Third Reich in the Unconscious*; Atkinson, *Trauma Trails*; and Lederach and Lederach, *When Blood and Bones Cry Out*.

31. See John Paul Lederach, "The Long Road Back to Humanity: Catholic Peacebuilding With Armed Actors," in *Peacebuilding: Catholic Theology, Ethics, and Praxis*, ed. Robert Schreiter, R. Scott Appleby, and Gerard Powers (New York: Orbis Books, 2010) for a more extensive discussion of Sister Mary's life, views, and peacebuilding work.

32. See Lederach, *The Moral Imagination*, and for a more recent description of religious leadership, see Janna Hunter-Bowman and John Paul Lederach, "Building Peace: Religious Leadership in Divided Communities," in *Religious Leadership: A Reference Handbook*, vol. 2, ed. Sharon Henderson Callahan (London: SAGE, 2013), 464–474.

33. Gopin (*Bridges Across an Impossible Divide*) provides one of very few "inner" ethnographies of this landscape. His careful and detailed interviews with Palestinian and Israeli peacebuilders in particular open a window into the difficult unfolding of the inner

struggle that simultaneously takes place within the peacebuilder yet is replicated and provoked by external conversations and events. See, for example, pages 22–23 on one family's discussion about whether to invite or permit people from the other side to grieve the loss of a son in the intimacy of their home.

34. See Mark Nepo, *Finding Inner Courage* (San Francisco, CA: Conari Press, 2011).

35. A term coined by James Coleman (*Community Conflict*), "reciprocal causation" suggests that at a highly escalated point of conflictive behavior between groups, the cause of the conflict corresponds more to the cycle of responses to the latest perceived provocation of the other side than to the originating issues creating the conflict, thus creating a "reciprocal" causation in the dynamics of the conflict.

36. See Appleby (2005); Anna Lännström, *Promise and Peril: The Paradox of Religion as Resource and Threat* (Notre Dame, IN: University of Notre Dame Press, 2003); or the extended conversation by Charles Taylor (2007).

37. See Armstrong, *Twelve Steps*; Marc Barasch, *The Compassionate Life* (San Francisco: Barrett-Koehler, 2009).

38. See, for example, Richard Davidson and Anne Harrington, *Visions of Compassion* (New York: Oxford University Press, 2002).

39. See, for example, the work of theologian Marcus Borg (*Meeting Jesus Again for the First Time* [New York: HarperCollins, 1994]).

40. See Lederach, "The Long Road Back to Humanity."

41. Gopin, *Bridges Across an Impossible Divide*.

Bibliography

Abu-Nimer, Mohammed, Amal I. Khoury, and Emily Welty. *Unity in Diversity: Interfaith Dialogue in the Middle East*. Washington, DC: US Institute of Peace Press, 2007.

Appleby, R. Scott. *The Ambivalence of the Sacred: Religion, Violence, and Reconciliation*. Lanham, MD: Rowman and Littlefield, 2000.

Armstrong, Karen. *Twelve Steps to a Compassionate Life*. New York: First Anchor Books, 2011.

Atkinson, Judy. *Trauma Trails*. North Melbourne, Australia: Spinifex Press, 2002.

Barasch, Marc. *The Compassionate Life*. San Francisco: Barrett-Koehler, 2009.

Berger, Peter, and Thomas Luckman. *The Social Construction of Reality*. New York: First Anchor Books, 1967.

Blumer, Herbert. *Symbolic Interactionism*. Los Angeles: University of California Press, 1986.

Borg, Marcus. *Meeting Jesus Again for the First Time*. New York: HarperCollins, 1994.

Brewer, John, Gareth Higgins, and Francis Teeney. *Religion, Civil Society and Peace in Northern Ireland*. New York: Oxford University Press, 2011.

Brueggemann, Walter. *The Prophetic Imagination*. 2nd ed. Minneapolis: Fortress Press, 2001.

Buber, Martin. *I and Thou*. New York: Charles Scribner and Sons, 1970.

Buttry, Daniel. *Christian Peacemaking: From Heritage to Hope*. Valley Forge, PA: Judson Press, 1994.

Coleman, James. *Community Conflict*. Glencoe, IL: The Free Press, 1957.

Coser, Lewis. *The Functions of Social Conflict*. New York: The Free Press, 1956.

Coward, Harold, and Gordan S. Smith, eds. *Religion and Peacebuilding*. Albany: State University of New York Press, 2004.

Curle, Adam. *Making Peace*. London: Tavistock Books, 1972.

Davidson, Richard, and Anne Harrington. *Visions of Compassion*. New York: Oxford University Press, 2002.

Friedman, Edwin. *Generation to Generation*. New York: The Guilford Press, 1985.

Friedman, Edwin. *A Failure of Nerve*. New York: Church Publishing Inc., 2007.

Gopin, Marc. *Between Eden and Armageddon: The Future of Religion, Violence, and Peacemaking*. New York: Oxford University Press, 2000.

Gopin, Marc. *Holy War, Holy Peace: How Religion Can Bring Peace to the Middle East*. New York: Oxford University Press, 2002.

Gopin, Marc. *Bridges Across an Impossible Divide: The Inner Lives of Arab and Jewish Peacemakers*. New York: Oxford University Press, 2012.

Hart, Barry, ed. *Peacebuilding in Traumatized Societies*. Lanhan, MD: University Press of America, 2008.

Hedges, Paul. *Controversies in Interreligious Dialogues and The Theology of Religions*. New York: SCM Press, 2010.

Herman, Judith. *Trauma and Recovery: The Aftermath of Violence from Domestic Abuse to Political Terror*. New York: Basic Books, 1997.

Hicks, Donna. *Dignity: The Essential Role It Plays In Resolving Conflict*. New Haven, CT: Yale University Press, 2011.

Hunter-Bowman, Janna, and John Paul Lederach. "Building Peace: Religious Leadership in Divided Communities." In *Religious Leadership: A Reference Handbook*, vol. 2, edited by Sharon Henderson Callahan, 464–474. London: SAGE, 2013.

Johnston, Douglas. *Faith-based Diplomacy: Trumping Realpolitik*. New York: Oxford University Press, 2003.

Johnston, Douglas, and Cynthia Sampson, eds. *Religion, the Missing Dimension of Statecraft*. New York: Oxford University Press, 1994.

Lännström, Anna. *Promise and Peril: The Paradox of Religion as Resource and Threat*. Notre Dame, IN: University of Notre Dame Press, 2003.

Lederach, John Paul. *Preparing for Peace: Conflict Transformation Across Cultures*. Syracuse, NY: Syracuse University Press, 1995.

Lederach, John Paul. *Building Peace: Sustainable Reconciliation in Divided Societies*. Washington, DC: US Institute of Peace Press, 1997.

Lederach, John Paul. *The Journey Toward Reconciliation*. Scottdale, PA: Herald Press, 1999.

Lederach, John Paul. *The Little Book of Conflict Transformation*. Intercourse, PA: Good Books, 2003.

Lederach, John Paul. *The Moral Imagination: The Art and Soul of Building Peace*. New York: Oxford University Press, 2005.

Lederach, John Paul. "The Long Road Back to Humanity: Catholic Peacebuilding With Armed Actors." In *Peacebuilding: Catholic Theology, Ethics, and Praxis*, edited by Robert Schreiter, R. Scott Appleby, and Gerard Powers. New York: Orbis Books, 2010.

Lederach, John Paul, and Angela Jill Lederach. *When Blood and Bones Cry Out: Journeys Through the Soundscape of Healing And Reconciliation*. New York: Oxford University Press, 2010.

Levinas, Emmanuel. *Humanity of the Other*. Chicago: University of Illinois Press, 2005.

Little, David, ed., with the Tanenbaum Center for Interreligious Understanding. *Peacemakers in Action: Profiles of Religion in Conflict Resolution*. New York: Cambridge University Press, 2007.

Merton, Thomas. *The Seven Storey Mountain*. New York: Harcourt Brace and Co., 1948.

Montville, Joseph. *Conflict and Peacemaking in Multiethnic Societies.* Lexington, MA: Lexington Press, 1990.

Nepo, Mark. *Finding Inner Courage.* San Francisco, CA: Conari Press, 2011.

Nhat Hanh, Thich. *Call Me by My True Names.* Berkeley, CA: Parallax Press, 1996.

Nichols, Bruce. "Religious Conciliation Between the Sandinistas and the East Coast Indians of Nicaragua." In *Religion, the Missing Dimension of Statecraft,* edited by Douglas Johnston and Cynthia Sampson, 64–87. New York: Oxford University Press, 1994.

Palmer, Parker. *Let Your Life Speak.* San Francisco: Jossey Bass, 1999.

Philpott, Daniel, and Gerard F. Powers, eds. *Strategies of Peace: Transforming Conflict in a Violent World.* New York: Oxford University Press, 2010.

Shriver, Donald. *An Ethic for Enemies.* New York: Oxford University Press, 1995.

Schreiter, Robert J., R. Scott Appleby, and Gerard F. Powers, eds. *Peacebuilding: Catholic Theology, Ethics, and Praxis.* Maryknoll, NY: Orbis Books, 2010.

Schutz, Alfred. *Phenomenology of the Social World.* Chicago: Northwestern University Press, 1967.

Siegel, Daniel. *The Mindful Brain.* New York: W. W. Norton, 2007.

Siegel, Daniel. *Mindsight.* New York: Bantam Books, 2010.

Sisk, Timothy D., ed. *Between Terror and Tolerance: Religious Leaders, Conflict, and Peacemaking.* Washington, DC: Georgetown University Press, 2011.

Smock, David. *Interfaith Dialogue and Peacebuilding.* Washington, DC: US Institute of Peace Press, 2002.

Thistlethwaite, Susan, and Glen Stassen "Abrahamic Alternatives to War: Jewish, Christian, and Muslim Perspectives on Just Peacemaking." US Institute of Peace Special Report 214. October 2008.

Thomas, W. I. *The Unadjusted Girl.* Boston: Little, Brown, and Co., 1923.

Volf, Miroslav. *Exclusion and Embrace: A Theological Exploration of Identity, Otherness and Reconciliation.* Nashville: Abingdon Press, 1996.

Volkan, Vamik D. *The Need to Have Enemies and Allies: From Clinical Practice to International Relationships.* Northvale, NJ: J. Aronson, 1988.

Volkan, Vamik D. *Bloodlines: From Ethnic Pride to Ethnic Terrorism.* New York: Farrar, Straus and Giroux, 1997.

Volkan, Vamik D., Gabriele Ast, and William F. Greer Jr., eds. *The Third Reich in the Unconscious: Transgenerational Transmission and Its Consequences.* New York: Brunner-Routledge, 2002.

Walach, Harald, Stefan Schmidt, and Wayne B. Jonas, eds. *Neuroscience, Consciousness and Spirituality.* New York: Springer, 2011.

Wehr, Paul, and John Paul Lederach. "Mediating Conflict in Central America." *Journal of Peace Research* 28, no. 1 (1991): 85–98.

Witte, John, Jr., and M. Christian Green, eds. *Religion and Human Rights: An Introduction.* New York: Oxford University Press, 2011.

Yoder, Carolyn. *The Little Book of Trauma Healing.* Intercourse, PA: Good Books, 2005.

Yoder, John Howard. *The Politics of Jesus.* Grand Rapids, MI: Eerdmans, 1972.

CHAPTER 22

....

THE INTERSECTION
OF CHRISTIAN THEOLOGY
AND PEACEBUILDING

....

HEATHER M. DUBOIS AND
JANNA HUNTER-BOWMAN[*]

BOTH of us were working in peacebuilding, one in direct practice in Colombia, one in program management in New York, when pressed by our experiences to do graduate study in theology.[1] We found, from our different vantage points, that a lack of deep appreciation for theologies—embodied as well as verbal—limits understanding of social change processes, skews interpretations of religious actors, and undermines positive outcomes of peacebuilding. Now situated at the intersection of peacebuilding and theology,[2] we see that this gap in the practice of peacebuilding exists also in the academy. Therefore, we argue for explicit, theoretically robust, and practically grounded theological reflection. In doing so, we join those who are already critically stretching the subfield of religious peacebuilding. Further, we seek an expansion of peacebuilding generally, because without theological capacity, scholarship and practice tend to neglect significant dimensions of existing—and potential—peacebuilding. First, we consider how theological methods may fill gaps in theory addressing experiences of violence and peace. Then, in a second mode of analysis, we begin with an existing set of peacebuilding theories and excavate its operative theological roots. In effect, both sections of the chapter provide resources for countering detrimental effects of the "liberal peace."

Theology's fluency in first-order religious sources and discourse can contribute to religious peacebuilding's methodological expansion. In some ways, the subfield has become confined by its own success as a descriptor and proponent of an otherwise excluded demographic, namely religious actors. Additional theoretical and critical lenses will enable a more reflective and a more substantial participation in peacebuilding by religious communities and their interpreters. In turn, this will enable stronger interdisciplinary, inter-religious and religious-secular research and praxis. Theology can also break new ground in peacebuilding—especially in contextual, strategic peacebuilding[3]—even when such work is not religious. Fulfilling this potential entails engaging subjective as well as objective dimensions of violence, peace, rupture, and healing. Listening more closely to theologies may challenge peacebuilders' working assumptions about what is happening and what is possible. It can help in identifying the presence and persistence of secularist and positivist assumptions embedded in the liberal peace that would ignore, reduce, or erase religious and spiritual ways of knowing and being.[4] These same processes of attention to theology can recognize existential, psychic, and emotional dimensions of the human person that are relevant to peacebuilding, yet often neglected by its researchers.[5]

As the most visible and resourced paradigm in the field, the liberal peace overdetermines peacebuilding activity such that practitioners and scholars can be inattentive to alternative forms of perceiving, reasoning, and acting. This sometimes occurs even amidst constructive efforts to include religious voices.[6]Inattentiveness to these voices, when chronic, can be an obstacle to transformations of conflict. Expansions of religious peacebuilding and strategic peacebuilding alike would confront precisely this type of diminishment of opportunity.

Developing alternatives to the liberal peace requires theoretical frames that are broad and flexible enough to include multiple sociolinguistic communities and academic disciplines and thereby draw upon a range of epistemologies and imaginaries. To illustrate the possibilities inherent in opening up the range of methods and frameworks for peacebuilding, we focus on a practitioner-scholar whose work challenges the prevailing logic of the liberal peace, John Paul Lederach. Looking closely at the processes of Lederach's theory-making, we find interdisciplinary exploration that emerges from the posture of responsiveness to context. We also identify a logic, or form of reasoning, emergent from Lederach's particular religious tradition, which he employs while living and working with people who claim a variety of other identities and interpretive frameworks. We conclude from this case that an imagination in part *theologically* formed has played a substantive role in creating theories that contribute to the strategic peacebuilding paradigm.

Our theological analysis centers on Lederach's theories related to time, especially his notions of "expansive time" and the "beckoning horizon." Throughout his career, Lederach has been prompted by his experiences in conflict settings and by his Mennonite tradition to challenge the singular, linear view of history presumed in much of conflict resolution and in some peacebuilding and peace studies. Specifically, Lederach cites the Christian eschatology and apocalyptic ethics of Mennonite theologian John Howard Yoder as a significant influence on his thinking and action.[7] Broadly defined, eschatology—the study of the eschaton—points to "the edge or horizon spatially or temporally."[8] As the last or ultimate things, the eschaton may function as a telos. Apocalyptic is a type of eschatology in which this telos is understood to have interruptive qualities, identified or forecast as God's activity in history. While not wholly responsible for Lederach's various approaches to temporal aspects of peacebuilding, the elements of eschatology that he embraces[9] undergird his work. As we will explain, this theological background helped him to articulate the scaffolding of justpeace in theory and envision unforeseen and unpredictable possibilities in the pursuit of justpeace in practice.[10]

We seek to make this operative theology accessible to a general peacebuilding audience, while honoring Lederach's decision to write without explicit Christian categories for much of his professional life.[11] Drawing Lederach into conversation with other scholars who critique "linear time" and "instrumental reason," we highlight the employment of "hybrid reasoning" derived from multiple sociolinguistic communities and disciplines. In this way, we explicate an example of theologically rich social change theory that can be nonviolently and coherently deployed in inter-religious and religious-secular contexts.

DOING NEW THEOLOGICAL WORK

Only now is theology—as an explicit disciplinary partner—entering the field of peacebuilding, though it has long been substantively present in the related fields of war and peace, peace and justice, and reconciliation. Within the paradigm of strategic peacebuilding, theology is a part of a multidisciplinary agenda, in addition to being a relevant factor in the work or biography of individual scholars and practitioners. Prior to this development, theology was carried implicitly into the conversation through the practices, texts, and biographies of religious persons. The span of actors includes grassroots peacebuilders, combatants, government officials, heads of international nongovernmental organizations, "track two" diplomats, leaders of religious communities, and academics. Religious peacebuilding has made sufficiently clear that religion still matters in history and that religious persons should be encouraged to articulate themselves on their own terms. Notwithstanding the now obvious necessity and benefits of this approach, it directs religious studies and theological work to the task of interpreting the presence and agency of religious actors. This direction has negative as well as positive consequences.

An identification of theology with religious actors makes the religion and peacebuilding conversation identity-based, for example, with one result being a focus on inclusion and another being (an apparent) reluctance to offer critique. Framed in terms of "including" a neglected demographic, compensatory efforts tend to rely on persuasion or apologetics: to persuade peacebuilders to take religion (or a particular religion) more seriously, and to persuade religious people to be peacebuilders.[12] These are important goals, and yet they must be supplemented for a full development of the field, and for their own integrity. Broader theoretical engagement can create a "wider community of inquiry" in which it is possible to "test further our best insights and all our claims that we have indeed recognized some manifestation of truth."[13] An expansion of methods can help peacebuilders to engage particular instantiations of religion and culture without reducing them to functional tools or deeming them too sacred or inaccessible to be evaluated or fully included in conversation.

Writing in 2010, religious peacebuilding scholar Katrien Hertog notes that leaders in the subfield have been calling for more robust analysis and theory for a decade. She finds that the largest category of literature is case studies, "which often remain on the descriptive level." There is still "no general theory on religious peacebuilding as such. Rather, different authors are contributing from their own background and in their own way."[14] The importance of persons acting on their own terms, speaking out of their perspectives and experiences, is core to the contextual model of peacebuilding. Yet, as Atalia Omer has incisively mapped in Chapter 1 of this volume, "local," identity-based, or community-based approaches require self-reflexivity and critique, as do all peacebuilding approaches. This is one of the benefits of intentional interdisciplinary conversation: it allows for the fact that all perspectives are limited, and it aspires to transform this reality into a productive change process.

Without explicit theological reflection in peacebuilding, there is likewise a missed opportunity for the discipline of theology. Omer also points to this lacuna in Chapter 1 when she critiques the tendency to frame religious peacebuilding as a "unidirectional process." Again, filling this gap will require an expansion of goals and methods beyond inclusion and apologetics, but theological methods exist to respond to this need. Religious peacebuilding can engage and in some ways resemble the internal debates of religious traditions, which include contestation about everything from ethical norms to the meaning of foundational symbols and doctrines. While some communities of practice may resemble "closed systems," it is more common for borders of influence to be relatively porous, such that even communities that present themselves as, or appear to be, homogeneous *de facto* include "other" or "outside" perspectives filtered through the diversified or hybrid identities of their members.[15]

Filling a Gap with Theological Methods

Without attempting to present a survey of theological methods, we suggest a broad typology of how theologians typically deal with "tradition" or "religious experience" or "God-talk." On the one hand, there are narrative or hermeneutical approaches, and on the other, there are experiential or epistemological approaches.[16] Sometimes these are parsed as two starting points: linguistic expression and pre-linguistic experience.[17] The first emphasizes the role that sociolinguistic community plays in shaping human capacity to perceive and experience (or not). The second emphasizes contingency and the possibility of experience that alters or eludes existing languages and paradigms. We use this delineation only as a useful analytical construct; in reality, both facets of knowing and expressing are always already operating in dialogical tension with one another. Making space in practice and scholarship for articulating new or dissonant experiences enables better assessment and understanding of the power and reach of "living traditions." Learning the histories of narratives' interpretations sheds light on the range of possible modes of experience that are readily available within a tradition.

Keeping in mind the need for further theoretical and interdisciplinary rigor, the subfield of religion and peacebuilding has begun to focus due attention on narratives (including cosmologies, sacred texts, stories of exemplars) that animate peacebuilding.[18] We will expand this conversation in the next section by examining the role apocalyptic eschatology plays in theories and concrete processes of peacebuilding. In this section we explore the lacuna surrounding expression and analysis of psycho-spiritual experiences related to conditions of violence and peace. In short, peacebuilding would benefit from reflection on the processes by which people discern and ascribe language to events and ways of being that a community or tradition has not previously encountered or may still not understand. Theology is especially equipped to stimulate this conversation because a great portion of its language revolves around attempts to speak well about that which cannot be fully grasped intellectually—whether the prevailing concern is divinity, the transcendent, the sacred, the numinous, the liminal, unconditional love, justice, alienation, suffering, comfort, bliss, violence, or peace.

Situations of violence intensify and multiply obstacles to articulating new or acute experiences. It is evident that trauma, displacement, physical wounds, and political turmoil disrupt physical, emotional, psychological, and spiritual patterns of living. They also disrupt patterns of thought, language, and interpretation. To think strategically about peacebuilding in such spaces includes discerning which forms of expression are most likely to circumvent these obstacles. It includes enabling people for whom nonlinear communication is preferable (or necessary because of a response to trauma) to "tell" their stories. It is important to have multiple ways to address needs for expression—and corresponding modes of reflecting upon that expression—because of inevitable ranges in personal and communal capacities and preferences.

This is true not least because healing is a multifaceted process, one that is subjective as well as objective. Consider the fact that hospitals with advanced technologies have found that illness requires more than a physical-biological response and now advocate multidimensional approaches to healing, often intentionally creating spaces for lamentation, meaning-making, and reconciliation.[19] In peacebuilding, also, healing is facilitated by holistic engagement with multilayered persons and communities. Or consider the fact that many forms of expression are indirect: parable, symbol, poetry, visual art, music, kinesthetic arts.[20] Such modes of understanding are in part subjective, but that need not imply that they are completely relative, inaccessible to another, or even abstract in the sense of being detached from the physical world. Healing and peacebuilding involve concrete participation in some things that can only be grasped and communicated indirectly, but when they are accessed, it is nonetheless in and through the material, sensate world.

Sometimes the very acts of naming violence and peace begin with inchoate, subjective perceptions. This means that it is incumbent upon peacebuilders to invest in understanding and expanding the available means through which people express them.[21] Identifying and categorizing violence and peace can give the experiences standing, without which they can remain at the margins of consciousness and of political awareness.[22] This can be especially vital in relation to cultural and structural violence, cognizance of which may be suppressed by causal agents and sometimes by victims as well. When significant experiences remain inchoate in expression, people lose the opportunity to name injustices, discern opportunities for change, and advance processes of healing.[23]

That naming can be a struggle, indeed may happen only in fragmentary ways, is to be expected and embraced. One way to get a handle, so to speak, on such experiences is with the language of encounter[24]—less a description of something that has happened and more a description of meeting or finding someone or something. Encounter denotes a meeting that is unexpected, perhaps even *in the* meeting of something or someone *familiar*. The language of encounter might be a way to approach positive or negative liminal experiences. For instance, it can be used to articulate what theologian Edward Schillebeeckx, drawing from Theodor Adorno, called "negative contrast experiences"—encounters with the absence of "what ought to be."[25] Whether language through which one expresses an encounter has already been learned or is in the process of development, the capacity to name positive and negative encounters can open up a static situation. Reflection on how we do this can help us to facilitate the positive. In some sense, people must learn how to experience the possibility of peace as a genuine alternative to violence. A belief in long-term change may develop only through continual, mutual sharing of occasional and fragmentary glimpses of this reality.

In terms of religious peacebuilding, some people use the language of encounter to trace and pay attention to the presence of spirits, angels, ancestors, gods, or God in their lives. This type of description is often explicit in prayer and in pastoral care, for instance, including the evocation and invocation of that presence. When sustained and given language or other expressive form, encounter can become accompaniment and solidarity, the experience of a trustworthy and supportive presence. To understand how this may happen in the lives of individuals and communities, consider again the broad typology of narrative and experience. People who are spiritually or psychically accompanied may be unreflectively presuming and/or intentionally participating in religious narrative(s). For example, internally displaced persons may interpret their experience as living the Exodus. These same accompanied persons may be instead *or also* regularly engaging prelinguistic experience through memory, meditation, ritual, and worship. Recognizing the impact of such phenomena involves appreciating the enriching effects of silence and nonverbal communication. In other words, an absence of language is not necessarily a deficit.

Paying attention to ways in which people find language for experiences that are difficult to articulate or perhaps ineffable can help us to understand when and why expression is *not* possible. While honoring positive experiences of silence, it is equally important to seek to recognize and deal appropriately with negatively experienced distortion and blockage of personal and communal expression. A preliminary step for an individual or community might be locating disruptions and perversions in existing religious and cultural narratives, perhaps elements of practice and belief that can no longer be taken for granted.[26] Prolonged conflict and violence can create their own unique cultures within broader geographical and historical complexities. In these situations even the very word "peace" may have suffered desertification and distortion. Careful listening, including but not limited to theological diagnosis, can help track change that would otherwise be overlooked. This should be part and parcel of contextual approaches to peacebuilding.

The importance of such reflection is attested in a seminal work on strategic peacebuilding. Years of working with communities around the world have convinced John Paul Lederach and R. Scott Appleby that the "spiritual dimension of humanity" plays pivotal roles in dynamics of conflict and peace. In their "Overview" chapter to *Strategies of Peace,* they go so far as to state that "reconciliation and healing" are the "*sine qua non*" of peacebuilding, and these require restoration of "the soul, the psyche, and the moral imagination." They note that these "personal and social spheres. . . directly and indirectly shape the national and political spheres."[27] Yet the multidisciplinary volume that follows these framing remarks does not fulfill the promise of this direction; only one of the authors even touches upon these themes.[28]

Without theological (or artistic or literary or other) contextualization and analysis, terms like "spiritual," "soul," and even "healing" are amorphous. If left unpacked, they can be read as idiosyncratic to the authors themselves. The average peace scholar trained in the social sciences might ask Lederach and Appleby: "What exactly do you mean by soul, psyche, and moral imagination?[29] Moreover, what can be done about them?"[30] Theologians and religious studies scholars themselves struggle with how to address the spiritual.[31] (And some would argue that the very word "spiritual" invokes an interiority that is individualistic and alien to their way of being religious.) Nevertheless, indispensable facets of peacebuilding exist or take place specifically within such contested, messy terrains at the borders of our capacity to express and conceptualize. Describing them carefully, consistently, and as wholly as possible seems essential to peacebuilding that would be strategic, that would begin to comprehend the full range of human experience of violence, pain, reconciliation, and healing.

Thus far, in inviting peacebuilding to more explicit engagement with the discipline of theology, we have noted a particular site for enhancement, the articulation of psycho-spiritual and other subjective experiences. Thoroughly developed in a contextual manner, specific theological interventions of this type would challenge secularist and positivist assumptions of the liberal peace and its influences on religious and strategic peacebuilding. The remainder of this chapter is an extended exposition of one theoretical framework that stands in radical, intentional contrast to the liberal peace. Namely, we examine theologically John

Paul Lederach's understandings of time, acknowledging their foundational role in strategic peacebuilding theory and the work of many practitioners.

ELUCIDATING AN ALTERNATIVE
THEORETICAL FRAMEWORK

To alter the liberal peace at its foundation and provide viable alternatives requires theoretical frameworks able to bear more fully and respond to diverse ways of engaging complex and contingent historical realities—and to do so without abandoning coherence, meaning, and pragmatic action. Lederach's work offers such frames. Theological analysis can help to explain his theories by elucidating their internal logic so they can be more thoroughly compared with other theoretical options in peacebuilding. Though Lederach is not a theologian, he has made his work ripe for theological reflection by self-consciously exploring the links between his social theory and his religious heritage and commitments.[32] Moreover, resistance to prevailing notions, including those related to secularist and positivist frameworks, marks his work.

Lederach is one of the pioneers of the contextual approach that we take as our starting point. In *Building Peace: Sustainable Reconciliation in Divided Societies*, he breaks theoretical ground by changing the subject of politics from institutions and laws of the state to local communities and processes.[33] A relational focus permeates most of his work, and he often explicitly reflects on his own immersion with communities in situations of protracted conflict to articulate his theoretical innovations. For Lederach, historical change happens through relationship, and the possibility for strategic change lies in the quality of "improbable relationships."[34] Also in *Building Peace,* he insists that peacebuilding must engage context at multiple levels, illustrated with the now ubiquitous "conflict pyramid" composed of elite, middle-range, and grassroots actors. This holistic commitment to context enables his work to be responsive, even to the point of overturning the premises of his formal training.

Lederach was trained as a sociologist and as a specialist in conflict resolution with the tools germane to that profession and social science. The vast array of sources from which he now draws, from physics to anthropology to poetry and music, has gradually expanded as he has sought to respond to the concrete situations and contexts before him.[35] Illustrating one facet of the aforementioned conceptual dichotomy of experience versus narrative, he utilizes an experience-based approach to theory-making and praxis, allowing new things to alter his existing languages and frameworks. In his corpus, for instance, he repeatedly refers to observations from his conflict mediation fieldwork with Mennonite church agencies in the 1980s and 1990s to explain the monumental shift from conflict resolution to conflict transformation. On the other hand, we might also say that Lederach's work illustrates a narrative-based approach. At least implicitly, he deploys the frames of the sociolinguistic communities to which he belongs as he perceives and digests the conflicts in which he works. For our purposes, it is noteworthy that these are multiple: the conflict resolution/transformation/peacebuilding fields, the sociological academy, the variety of religious and secular communities with which he has worked, and the sacred stories and cosmology of his Mennonite Christianity.

Diversifying the Interpretation of Time

Lederach's body of work offers theories related to culture, relationship, imagination, healing, and other dynamics of social change. We choose to focus on time because it is a pivotal category underpinning the conceptualization and analysis of historical processes.[36] Moreover, time and space are considered fundamental categories of contrast among interpretive frameworks that impact daily life. Without fully entering critical debates about the construction and deployment of such frameworks, we underscore the fact that there is not one self-evident conception of time. As such, we appreciate cultural anthropologist Talad Asad's articulation of

> heterogeneous time: of embodied practices rooted in multiple traditions, of the differences between horizons of expectation and spaces of experience—differences that continually dislocate the present from the past, the world experienced from the world anticipated, and call for their revision and reconnection. These simultaneous temporalities embrace both individuals and groups in complexities that imply more than a simple process of secular time.[37]

In his seminal work *A Secular Age*, Charles Taylor also points to the existence of "more than one kind of time," contrasting "ordinary time" and "higher time."[38] Such scholarship recognizes that depictions of time matter, and that a singular, flat depiction is inadequate for fully understanding the world. For Lederach, this claim is directly related to peacebuilding.

Lederach's innovative understanding of how conflicts change through time and how time functions in conflicts emerged in part through creative dissonance among the practitioner-scholar's sociolinguistic communities. A linear model of time is often assumed in conflict resolution, peacebuilding, and peace studies. Many scholars and practitioners envision necessary sequences in social change and politics, particularly as they are striving to grasp why or how events unfold. In contrast, Lederach's field experience taught him that constructing peacebuilding plans and projects in exclusively linear fashion distorts and fails to account for much that is crucial to actual peacebuilding processes. In Lederach's first writings the reader can feel the struggle beneath the text as he searches for language in various academic disciplines to express the multi-directionality and simultaneity that he saw and experienced "in the field."

For example, early on, Lederach borrows anthropologist Edward Hall's notions of monochronic and polychronic time to critique a causal sequenced linear model. As a cross-cultural scholar, Hall found that monochronic cultures tend to handle events sequentially, while those with a polychronic vision have the ability to attend to multiple events simultaneously. Lederach suggests a polychronic departure point to attain the ability to envision simultaneity and social interaction as key elements in a process linking reconciliation and time.[39] This stands in contrast to the linearity he describes, in the language of chemistry, as issuing causal formulas based on categories of past, present, and future suggestive of a "chemical reaction."[40] Building on the same theme, he writes decades later in *The Moral Imagination* that the crux of the problem is that conflict envisioned as a single line poses a way of looking at change processes that predisposes short-term thinking and solutions; emphasizes the "more visible and often destructive expression of the conflict"; and may occlude from view the "relational epicenter of conflict" that "generates the fighting."[41] Drawing on his work in Central and South America, the Philippines, Nepal, and the Horn of Africa, Lederach insists that "in the real world, the element that historically assures extinction [of a constructive process] is uni-directionality and tunnel vision, a single-mindedness of process and response in pursuit of a purpose."[42]

Such tunnel vision prevents observation of incipient and small-scale peacebuilding efforts. It occludes cultivation of "peace-time conditions" that may exist even during the most intense violence of an armed conflict. As put by Fr. Roberto Layson, a parish priest in Pikit, Philippines, "My experience told me that it was not possible to do [rehabilitation] during the war. You had to wait until it was over."[43] This was Layson's reasoning before he began to do just what he had thought was impossible. In retrospect, he says, "I became aware that we had to try to give the people hope again, to show them that life goes on even in the midst of war." Layson began working with others to create "spaces for peace communities" into which displaced persons could return. "In the beginning it was difficult to convince the people, but after the agreement of [the military and the other armed group] the people began to move back. We started to implement several social projects. Even the NGOs started to believe. It was something unique: rehabilitation with a war going on! This contradicted many theories on peacebuilding. Then we expanded it. . . ."[44]

Among other examples of unlikely peace-amidst-war are those less connected to conflicts' official parties and the NGOs and other actors tasked with addressing them. For instance, Lederach highlights the story of the women of Wajir, Kenya, who "did not set out to stop a war." In his telling, "They just wanted to make sure they could get food for their families. The initial idea was simple enough: Make sure that the market is safe for anyone to buy and sell." Yet stop the war they did, through a series of small successes and relationship-building. Their efforts eventually led to the Wajir Peace and Development Committee, which operates early warning mechanisms, conflict resolution training, and more, still now over twenty years later.[45] Lederach also tells the story of the 1987 birth of the Association of Peasant Workers of Carare in Colombia: with the community facing expulsion or immediate death at the hands of a "notoriously violent captain of the Colombian army" if they did not join the fight against the guerillas, a peasant named Josué spoke out. "Captain, with all due respect, we do not plan to join your side, their side, or any side. And we are not leaving this place. We are going to find our own solution." Thus began a "living laboratory" of unarmed civilian resistance that would be awarded the Alternative Nobel Peace Prize in 1990.[46] Movements such as these, born of necessity and creativity, defy the totalizing logic of war—and the linear logic of most peace processes.

And yet, despite such evidence to the contrary, exclusively linear models of time persist and have broad impact. According to critical theorists Max Horkheimer and Theodor W. Adorno, this dominant view—that history unfolds in a necessary sequence of phases—emerges through the use of instrumental reason, enabled by what Max Weber described as the rationalization and segmentation of time. Within this interpretive framework, it is a logical conclusion that human problems are akin to engineering problems, and solutions can be attained through principles, technology, and deductive knowledge. As one scholar observes, "Instrumental reason is a way of exercising reason that determines the means to a given end by objectifying and quantifying the components of natural and social systems—including human beings—and deploying and manipulating those components in the most efficient way possible to achieve that end."[47]

Lederach questions the application of an engineering mentality to social change in his analysis of the state of the peacebuilding field. He observes:

Practitioners and academics seem to have a need for the analytical project, the breaking of complex reality into pieces, the creation of categories, and the pursuit of knowledge by taxonomy. Thus it was that at some point conflict came to be seen as a linear progression of phases. In the case of sustained, organized violence, otherwise known as war, the rise and descent of violent conflict became a single wave-like timeline. On this wave categories were located, indicating what should be done when by whom in response to escalating conflict and the building of peace.[48]

One peace researcher, for instance, issues recommendations on how to take action "In the Nick of Time,"[49] a prescription that is only comprehensible from within sequence-dependent time. This timeline view of the way the world works is germane to conflict and peace well outside journal articles. The "curve of conflict" is a heuristic device used widely in conflict analysis to depict the "evolution of conflict." In this model, time runs along the horizontal axis and depth of peace or intensity of violence runs along the vertical axis. Represented in these two dimensions, the conflict appears to move in a smooth line—which ends with "post-conflict" peacebuilding, despite compelling arguments that this phrase is usually a misnomer at best. Without dismissing the contributions of such models, Lederach seeks to diversify the way peacebuilders view time and, in effect, the types of reason they deploy. As we explain below, one source for his insights into the need and possibility for such plurality is participation in a religious tradition that entails alternatives to instrumental reason and linear time.

Hybrid Reasoning and Logics of Time

Though Lederach does not explicitly reflect upon the origins of linear time, his actions and writings presume that it is not natural or "true." We argue that he is able to counter what many accept as given because he has consciously embraced a normative paradigmatic alternative and listened closely to his experiences in the field. Through his simultaneous commitments to his own religious perspective and to the contexts where he works, he has come to some of the same conclusions as other critics of instrumental reason. The peacebuilder's perspective can be likened to that of Johann Baptist Metz, who integrated the insights of Horkheimer and Adorno into his political theology. Metz underscored that within instrumental rationality, questions about what constitutes life worth seeking are not asked, or the answers are presumed. This, in turn, offers little resistance to the teleological narratives of those with power.

A German writing after World War II, Metz engaged—in the words of his translator and friend Matthew Ashley—"the sudden eruption of cruelty and suffering in history, even and precisely the history of a Europe that optimistically understood itself to be governed by Enlightenment ideals of rationality, freedom, and the equality of all persons."[50] Wrestling with this contradiction, he concluded that instrumental reason cannot be accepted as a "universal, abstract faculty."[51] For Metz and Lederach, reason is *mediated* by experience and thus can be understood as practical without being reductionistic and as contextual without being solipsistic. This understanding has led the theologian to emphasize the "primacy of practice" just as the peacebuilder has emphasized reflective praxis. Thereby, both have developed hybrid conceptualizations of reason that include the logics of multiple sociolinguistic communities. Moreover, both thinkers have promoted the importance of memory as a relational category that includes the dead and makes demands upon the living. For Metz, this takes the form of "dangerous memory,"[52] and for Lederach, memory enables us to acknowledge a "long past with emergent present."[53] Lederach's temporal horizon reflects such a hybrid form of reasoning insofar as he does not completely reject linearity, but insists that it not stand alone. As we shall see, this means that the linear quality of *social* change is not one of "cause and effect."

His perspective is represented in the framing chapter of *Strategies of Peace*, as Lederach and Appleby underscore the significance of how social actors and social theory represent and experience time. Encapsulating the contrast between Lederach's alternative temporal horizon and the dominant view, the authors ask "under what [temporal] conditions would the word *strategic* not apply?" and then respond "when the time horizon is too narrow or constricted." Among other suggestions, they advise practitioners to "develop a capacity to think simultaneously rather than sequentially." All research and practice, they claim, should be "time expansive" (i.e., take account of historical patterns, dynamics of exclusion and oppression, historical experiences of trauma, and so on). Like Lederach in his independent writing, the coauthors do not ignore the importance of emergency responses or other works that "engage particular timeframes of action." They advocate that these be a part of "encompassing analysis" that is "wider and deeper" than the majority of peacebuilding has been to date and located within an expansive "time horizon" that people and processes collaborate to "realize."[54]

Through the perspective of theology, and with some knowledge of these authors' religious education and other works, it is not difficult to see that the "wider and deeper" of strategic peacebuilding signals a vision of reality beyond what can be explained by a positivist reading of the evidence alone. We argue that theological literacy partially accounts for Lederach and Appleby's capacity to perceive and articulate a "bigger picture" of peacebuilding. Going forward, we will dwell particularly on the theological resources that have influenced Lederach's multidimensional understanding of time and history.[55] While these have been largely embedded in his imagination and have functioned implicitly, some of his lesser-known writings (and conversations with him) explicitly identify the eschatological thinking of theologian John Howard Yoder as one influence. In Lederach's own words: "How did this impact my thought and work? [. . .] from early on I carried from Yoder an insatiable optimism based on the notion that the whole of human history is moving toward this reconciliation."[56] Elsewhere he reflects: "The foundation on which I built a vocational pathway outside of theology per se came directly from [*The Politics of Jesus*]. I refer to this influence as providing me a sense of the 'big picture.'"[57] It is to the substance of Yoder's influence that we now turn.

Eschatological Influences

Lederach's social theory can be meaningfully understood as, in part, a second-order description of the realization of God's reign in history. Though eschatology is sometimes read and constructed in a purely linear, sequential, or millennial key, these are not the types of eschatologies that animate Lederach's view of time and history. Lederach's reading of Yoder enables him to perceive and describe social processes that are *multidirectional* and *multidimensional* and not exclusively causal, rational, and logical in the dominant sense we have outlined. Describing the broad flow of history in which *multidirectional* change processes unfold, Lederach writes:

> Yoder operated with a very expansive view of history.. . . It seemed to emerge from a defining, paradigmatic question: 'From what source and toward what horizon is human history flowing?' Yoder's answer, as I understood it, was simple. History bubbles forward from the compassionate love of God and flows back toward God whose historic purpose is reconciliation with all of creation.[58]

For Yoder, the shape of the cosmos in which this history flows is disclosed by Jesus the Lord: to see history "doxologically"—through a life of confessional claim and praise—is to "grasp which end is up and which way is forward."[59] It involves discerning "which historical developments can be welcomed as progress. . . and which are setbacks. Not all historical movement is forward."[60] In other words, in contrast with a sense of progress in which history necessarily advances in a forward motion and in a positive direction and, consequently, is inevitably linear, "progress" is a contextual and contingent designation. Thus, this perspective has cognitive and emotional capacity to thoroughly recognize adversity and failure while simultaneously enabling constructive responses of resistance and resilience.

In this eschatology, there is a historical process of realizing, making actual, God's will in time. Yet this movement toward humanity's ultimate destiny of reconciliation occurs through transhistorical or multidimensional processes, involving—to use typical theological temporal metaphors—that which is "inside" and "outside" mundane time. While God's reconciliation is *not yet* complete in history, through God's grace it is *already* accessible and even partially realized on earth. This means that the Kingdom of God is within reach in the "here and now"; God's love, reconciliation, and justice "break" into human history as its sign[61] and foretaste. In some ways, the anticipation of complete reconciliation—a future with God and fulfillment of God's promises—allows humans to trigger and actualize in the present what is nevertheless beyond their full grasp. In Yoder's words, "the ethic supports the promise and vice versa."[62]

In terms of peacebuilding, it is vital to note that humans may participate in this divine in-breaking and interruption of reality. One of the basic presumptions of eschatological perspectives is that the totality of reality is not self-evident. There exist possibilities that we may see in fragments, or not at all. (Recall this is how we earlier described the elusive quality of peace.) To bring about or realize this potentiality requires that we "live into" it—partaking and creating at once. In some Christian eschatologies, *that which* persons live into *and how* to do it is modeled by the life of Jesus, who shows humans how to "operationalize" the Kingdom of God he inaugurated. Lederach articulates these points in describing Yoder's way of understanding and enabling positive change:

> Through our shenanigans we humans create a series of messes, structures and misadventures that we euphemistically refer to as 'reality' and we take these constructions as the actual flow of history. But time and again Yoder would argue a different view. The key to wisdom, understanding, and faithfulness is to align oneself with the flow of God's purpose in history best known through the actual way that Jesus lived.[63]

Aligning with "the reconciling and nonviolent love of God that sustains all of creation" enables people to carry on with a vision of purpose despite it being "at times made invisible" by human action.[64] In conflict, this may mean transcending and breaking destructive patterns and cycles by imagining and generating constructive, perhaps unpredictable, responses that do not yet tangibly exist.

That Lederach the Mennonite sympathizes with a particular eschatological view is perhaps not surprising. That Lederach the peacebuilder has developed social change theory rooted in this particular theological matrix may be surprise, and perhaps even trouble, for some readers, especially those who have used his work and are not Christian. As should now be clear, the extended theological analysis of Lederach's work in this chapter is not an attempt to reveal the "real Lederach" but rather to illustrate what many have guessed, that theological imaginations are *already* operative—in the work of scholars and pioneering practitioners, as well as religious actors on the ground. This fact in itself should be no cause for alarm. However, it does reinforce our argument that explicit theological work, including theoretically rigorous analysis, can play an important role in peacebuilding. Such work can enable theories like Lederach's to be evaluated more completely and thus deployed more conscientiously and effectively. Now that we have introduced Lederach's implicit apocalyptic eschatology, we move on to explore how it is operative in his theorization of time, before assessing the significance of its presence.

Telos in Lederach's Time Images

In the pithy book *The Little Book of Conflict Transformation*, Lederach describes a "horizon that provides direction and purpose," which corresponds with what Yoder calls "an overarching divine purposefulness active in history."[65] By Lederach's account, conflict transformation "requires" this horizon, which "represents a social energy that informs and creates orientation."[66] He cites colleagues in Latin America who communicate the same theme when they say "We have to seek 'Our North.'"[67] Lederach explains that this active vision of the future shapes practitioners' perception and attitude, bringing to the fore meta questions about where they are going or what is the destiny of their hope. One can hear an echo of Metz's critique that instrumental reason has an unreflexive telos when Lederach writes: "If we do not know where we are going it is difficult to get there."[68]

Lederach describes the horizon of purpose as twofold, both object and subject. He advocates nurturing one's sight of it (as an object) as a cognitive exercise.[69] "The horizon of the future," he writes, "harnesses an impulse that points toward possibilities of what could be constructed or built."[70] Concurrently, he describes the horizon as a quasi-personal subject beckoning toward a daily "journey."[71] Lederach traces the latter conceptual move to New Testament scholarship that highlights Jesus's pedagogical mode of teaching "on the way."[72] Viewed through an eschatological lens, the beckoning horizon functions broadly like the message of Jesus does for Christians. In first-order language, it can set people in a new direction, disclosing that humans are not self-enclosed but are called to participate in God's action for the reconciliation of the world. In a world "not yet redeemed," Lederach writes, "God moves people and history towards a redeemed, transformed humanity and creation."[73] In Lederach's second-order language, the beckoning horizon invites people to work in collaboration with a horizon of purpose headed toward justpeace. Whichever language is foregrounded—and one need not assume a one-to-one correspondence between the two—this vision opens new possibilities for actions (such as "improbable relationships") and closes others (such as violence). A new kind of multidimensional agency is made possible and intelligible through recognition of a chosen telos.

Conceptually dependent on this telos, Lederach's "nested paradigm" of the temporal dimension of peacebuilding is another foundational model that arguably rises from his eschatological big picture. Lederach projects this theory in a visual image that features four concentric circles: immediate action, short-range planning, "decades thinking" and "generational vision."[74] As a frame of interpretation, it gives us a lens to see a "long past" interacting with the "emergent present."[75] The nested or embedded nature of time (and action in time) reveals a necessary correspondence between the tactics of the moment and the envisioned destiny. Lederach writes, "taken as a whole the nested paradigm demonstrates that we must respond to immediate crises in a manner that is informed by a longer-term vision."[76] Here we see that, for Lederach, a presumed eschatological time horizon governs or inspires strategic peacebuilding's leitmotif: "crisis responsive, not crisis driven."[77] Rather than consider short-term possibilities governed by historical precedent, the emphasis is as follows: Why, right now, in this very place does the extant political order deny justice and reconciliation? How shall we be instruments of God's action to perform and reveal these truths in this place? The nested paradigm provides focus on immediate needs within view of a broader horizon for the journey as peoples on the way.

The horizon of purpose and the nested paradigm are two core elements of Lederach's peacebuilding. They are intriguing and useful on their own, but powerful and transformative in combination with one another and a rich understanding of the contextually based telos of justpeace. That these theories have functioned well in a variety of settings around the globe indicates that their integrity is not dependent on their theological valences. Nonetheless, we claim that considering them in the light of their origins within the author's imagination illuminates further potential parallels, resonances, and applications. Moreover, we hope that this demonstration of theological influences invites other practitioners and scholars (and hybrids thereof) to self-reflexively and creatively include their own multiplicity of sociolinguistic communities in their work.

Drawing from Yoder in Heterogeneous Contexts

The eschatological influences that we have brought to the fore exemplify how social theory and praxis can draw upon developed theological categories to challenge and break with dominant paradigms. One aspect of the theological perspective undergirding Lederach's temporal horizon—and peacebuilders' participation in and with it—empowers radical critique. Evoking the prophet Jeremiah (23:29), Yoder writes that the "behavior God calls for" interrupts "like a fire, like a hammer that breaks rocks into pieces,"[78] and it "does not let present empirical readings of possibility have the last word."[79] Such imagery portrays the rupture that happens to history when people live counter to the dominant paradigms, social patterns, and structures. (In Lederach's case, this includes living counter to the logic of coercion, as in Metz's case it was countering the Weberian "iron cage" of instrumental reason.) Because this eschatology confronts strong, seemingly impenetrable or self-evident ways of living and organizing our world with "interruption" and "in-breaking," it can be categorized as apocalyptic.[80] Yoder uses apocalyptic perspectives to contest the "frame of normalcy" and as a way of interrupting history "from below."[81] Likewise, Metz helped to bring this category into political theology, convinced that it alone had the strength to counter the "bourgeois apathy" of Christians in postwar Europe, who were beginning to forget the suffering of the dead.

Of course an eschatological matrix, whether apocalyptic or not, does not necessarily lead to critical interpretation of reality or creative, nonviolent, transformative social engagement; it may also result in support for the status quo, violence, and escapism.[82] As we have already noted, Yoder's eschatology is shaped substantively by his interpretation of the political work of Christ, which for him activates a critical interpretation of particular situations of violence and a robust vision of creative nonviolent peacemaking. Jesus is normative for how Christians are to "look at the moving of history,"[83] see the world and live in it. "In Jesus," Yoder writes, "we have a clue to which kinds of causation, which kinds of community-building, which kinds of conflict management, go with the grain of the cosmos."[84]

Yoder nevertheless recognizes the "cosmological conversions" that have led others who are not operating within the same Christological matrix to see this same directionality.[85] For example, Yoder writes that Gandhi—though speaking in a Hindu and inter-religious key—formulates in his teaching of the "unity of means and ends" the same truth that immediate or short-term responses should be governed by an ultimate reality. Yoder noted that Martin Luther King Jr. also affirmed the unity of means and ends. For King, this means following the "moral arc of the universe" with the knowledge that "there is something in the universe that unfolds for justice." For Yoder, it demands seeing more than present empirical facts to disrupt the friend-foe logic and to move toward "new and higher forms of creativity."[86] Though his own understanding of the universe is thoroughly Christological, Yoder claims that he is also simply describing the way social processes work.[87]

Yoder's eschatological big picture is totalizing—it uses a particular category to interpret reality writ large—yet also vulnerable. The latter facet is drawn out in a "radical democratic" reading of Yoder, which gives primacy to discursive nonviolence, susceptibility to rejection, and open dialogue with other traditions.[88] Oriented by an interpretation of Christ's work as nonviolent and deeply political, and grounded in non-coercive, relationally oriented, transformative practices, this reading is explicitly and intentionally subversive of Christian theologies that underwrite domination and hegemony and that view political power "from above" as natural. Normatively speaking, it refuses to be tamed by the logic, presuppositions, and structures they espouse. In this vision, a Christ-centered orientation does not only mean refusing to kill or participate in other coercive actions; it means methodological nonviolence as well. It commends patience and receptivity, not only in social processes but also in conversation with other communities and methods. It views itself as an invitation that is accessible to other social groups and that they all are free to reject.

Lederach has developed a unity of theological grounding and broadly accessible social theory, like that which Yoder invited, through his multidisciplinary and contextual approach and careful use of second-order language. In brief, Lederach has sought to overcome the embedded, "unintended residue of imperialism" that he identifies in traditional conflict mediation theories. In his view, this residue takes the form of tendencies of control and imposition entangled in these theoretical legacies of colonialism. In terms related to the broader concerns of this chapter, his emphasis on reflexive practice has included sensitivity to his own Christian identity particularly in light of the Christian tradition's participation in imperialism and colonialism.[89] Yet the continuity between his theology and social theory raises questions: do Lederach's approaches to conflict transformation operate as a counter-force to violent legacies tied to colonization and missionizing? Do they succeed in transcending the problems he critiques and providing a theoretical and practical corrective? Or does his even implicit use of Christian theological categories undermine his otherwise nonviolent approach? Does our analysis prove it inappropriate for use in diverse cultural, religious, and secular settings?

What King and Yoder call the "arc" and "grain" of the universe, Lederach names a "horizon of purpose" operating in "nested time," aiming at justpeace. This strategic peacebuilder gives a broad audience access to the insights of an eschatological imagination in a way that does not explicitly rely upon nor necessitate confessional or religious commitment. That he has succeeded in doing so to some extent is attested by the widespread use of the theories. To what degree further work should be done to broaden and enrich his theoretical frames, particularly with a view to further actualize this inclusive posture, is beyond the scope of this chapter. Yet in the spirit of a bidirectional process of inquiry, we invite peacebuilders who have used Lederach's theory to reflect upon how these theological insights enrich or diminish the theory from their perspectives; and we invite theologians to trouble the admittedly partial correlations we have drawn between apocalyptic eschatology and a peacebuilder's perspective of time and history.

CONCLUSION

In this chapter, we identify theology as a relatively new, relevant, and distinct disciplinary partner in strategic peacebuilding. As theologians, we suggest that explicit theological study—including first-order discourse and sources—enriches theoretical analysis. As peacebuilding practitioners, we encourage a multidirectional conversation among theology, peacebuilding, and particular, contingent, historical, and present realities. We demonstrate that theology offers peacebuilding ways to consider a larger spectrum of human experience, in addition to further critical and appreciative investigation of operative narratives. Moreover, through a theological examination of John Paul Lederach's peacebuilding theory, we illustrate how theological resources—however embedded in a peacebuilder's interpretive framework and imagination—can address crucial, otherwise neglected dimensions of peacebuilding.

A core insight of interdisciplinary research is that each perspective has contributions and limitations; each discloses one or more dimensions of existence and each is inattentive to others. Theology has unique offerings, as do each of the disciplines at the peacebuilding table, due to their historical development and particularity. The intersection of theology and peacebuilding is large, rich, and fraught. While we have foregrounded the positive and the constructive, we perceive the need for scholars and practitioners together to also articulate and analyze the negative and indeed the violent theologies among us. Of course, contestation about which is which will be central to such endeavors.

Gesturing toward the full scope of inquiry that lies ahead, we offer a few parting questions: How might theological analysis of the formation of conscience introduce new questions to peacebuilding? What could a theologian help a practitioner articulate about the "meaning" of suffering or the "benefits" of prayer? What might an interdisciplinary study of the genre as well as the content of sacred texts bring to peacebuilding conversations about imagination and memory? How do definitions of sin operate within a particular culture of violence, and how does gender analysis affect these? What could peacebuilders do with theological investigation of different kinds of power and the interrelationship of divine and human agency? How does a scholar-practitioner deal with the varieties of intra- and inter-personal alienation experienced in conflict? How does increased understanding of trauma affect speech about healing, reconciliation, redemption, and other (ultimate) goals? Finally, but not least, what other questions emerging from the experiences and narratives of our colleagues in other traditions will enable stronger contextual, interdisciplinary peacebuilding?

Notes

* In alphabetical order
1. Janna Hunter-Bowman worked with Justapaz: the Christian Center of Nonviolence and Direct Action in Colombia, South America, for more than eight years between 2001 and 2010. She focused on political violence, U.S. foreign policy and peacebuilding initiatives. Heather M. DuBois worked for three years with the Tanenbaum Center for Interreligious Understanding's Religion and Conflict Resolution program, which honors, supports, and shares the stories of local religious peacemakers in armed conflict zones around the globe. Coincidentally, Ricardo Esquivia Ballestas, founder of Justapaz, is a "Tanenbaum Peacemaker."
2. We write as Christian theologians, moreover as a Mennonite and a Catholic. Cognizant that persons and narratives are historically embedded and that context matters, we take as axiomatic that our vantage points are broadened in some ways, limited in others, by the fact that we live and work from within these particular traditions. We further locate ourselves as disquieted and mindful inheritors of the interlaced legacies—and current manifestations—of Christian proselytizing, colonialism, orientalism, and patriarchy. We are aware that the field of peacebuilding is not free from these challenges. We note, for example, that Christian theology implicitly dominates some discussions of reconciliation and forgiveness through uncritical use of these terms, which have deep resonances with Christianity. It is within this fraught yet fecund matrix that we embrace the monikers "theologian" and "peacebuilder."
3. The Kroc Institute for International Peace Studies adopted the phrase "strategic peacebuilding" as a conceptual hub for its work. Several scholars from the Kroc Institute worked together on the 2010 volume *Strategies of Peace: Transforming Conflict in a Violent World* (ed. Daniel Philpott and Gerard F. Powers [New York: Oxford University Press, 2010]), which begins to flesh out this paradigm. While theological reflection has certainly not been completely absent in peacebuilding—see, for example, Kroc's neighbor, Anabaptist Mennonite Biblical Seminary—this movement in the field calls for reflection that is qualitatively new by virtue of its intentional and wide-ranging engagement with other disciplines. For an earlier discussion of what makes peacebuilding strategic, see Lisa Schirch, *The Little Book of Strategic Peacebuilding* (Intercourse, PA: Good Books, 2005).
4. In terms of religious-secular debates, we have in mind particularly the works of Elizabeth Shakman Hurd and Talal Asad, which name the secular as a constructed and pluriform reality shaped by national and global power dynamics. See Elizabeth Shakman Hurd, *The Politics of Secularism in International Relations* (Princeton, NJ: Princeton University Press, 2008); and Talal Asad, *Formations of the Secular: Christianity, Islam, Modernity* (Stanford,

CA: Stanford University Press, 2003). The larger conversation from which we draw includes the works of Peter Berger, Charles Taylor, and Saba Mahmood. See also Michael Warner, Jonathan VanAntwerpen, and Craig Calhoun, eds., *Varieties of Secularism in a Secular Age* (Cambridge, MA: Harvard University Press, 2010).

5. For an exposition of secularist assumptions limiting the range of experiences and expressions even of secular persons, see William Connolly, *Why I Am Not a Secularist* (Minneapolis: University of Minnesota Press, 2000).

6. This is evident in many consensus-based approaches to ethics. See, for example, Daniel Philpott's recent work, *Just and Unjust Peace: An Ethic of Political Reconciliation* (New York: Oxford University Press, 2012). Philpott gives religion a privileged place in making the biblical concept "right relationship" core to his ethic. Yet he specifically rejects "distributive justice" (193–198), arguably the current term of reference that most resembles the economic dimensions of right relationship. Thereby, his ethic leaves untouched presumptions of the liberal peace related to neoclassical market orthodoxy, presumptions that weaken the very concept through which he seeks to include religious perspectives.

    Or consider Jacques Maritain's theoretical rationalization for the 1948 Universal Declaration of Human Rights. Working out of a background in Christian natural law, Maritain believed that consensus on human rights was possible by virtue of a shared "secular faith," through which peoples of diverse "belief systems" could come together through a set of "practical points of convergence." See Jacques Maritain, *Man and the State* (Washington, DC: Catholic University Press, 1951). Pragmatic, consensus-based approaches have produced powerfully positive results, yet the model is vulnerable to critiques that it is substantively illusory and reductionistic. There is not really consensus if the agreement is largely or merely semantic and dissolves into irreconcilable contestations when particular situations of rights are at issue.

7. John Howard Yoder has a complicated legacy. In contradiction with his powerful writing on ethics and peace, he engaged in sexually abusive acts towards women. Amidst this repugnant history of harm, his writings continue to influence widely and inspire new readers. The Mennonite Church USA (MCUSA) and Anabaptist Mennonite Biblical Seminary announced in the summer of 2013 a denominational process to discern a response to Yoder's legacy. See Ervin Stutzman, "Denominational Response to John Howard Yoder's Legacy," *Menno Snapshots*, Mennonite Church USA, August 9, 2013, http://www.mennoniteusa.org/2013/08/19/denominational-response-to-john-howard-yoder-legacy/; and Sara Wenger Shenk, "Revisiting the Legacy of John Howard Yoder," *Practicing Reconciliation*, Anabaptist Mennonite Biblical Seminary, July 25, 2013 http://www.ambs.edu/publishing/2013/07/Revisiting-the-Legacy-of-John-Howard-Yoder.cfm. The Discernment Group convened by MCUSA releases updates on the process and iniciatives. See "A Way Forward: Sexual Abuse and the Church," Mennonite Church USA, June 19, 2014, http://www.mennoniteusa.org/an-update-from-the-discernment-group-on-sexual-abuse/.

8. Catherine Keller, *Apocalypse Now and Then: A Feminist Guide to the End of the World* (Minneapolis: Fortress Press, 2005), 20.

9. Lederach does not perform a uniform or comprehensive appropriation of Yoderian eschatology. Moreover, to do so would require rigorous theological analysis, if it were even possible, because interwoven in Yoder's corpus are several types or forms of eschatology.

10. This neologism, signaling the simultaneous reduction of violence and fostering of justice, was born through Lederach's engagement with Colombian Mennonite church leaders.

Founded in 1990, the Colombian Mennonite peacebuilding center of the same name, Justapaz in Spanish, is suggestive of the shared roots.

11. Explicit Christological terms were salient in the early years of his work, when the practitioner was working mostly with church communities. In the years since, in the course of his engagement with communities of different religious traditions, Hindu and Buddhist among others, most Christological formulations of his theories have fallen away. See also footnote 32.

12. Roland Czada, Thomas Held, and Markus Weingardt, eds., *Religions and World Peace: Religious Capacities for Conflict Resolution and Peacebuilding* (Osnabrück, Germany: Nomos Publishers, 2012) echoes many of the themes in foundational works such as: R. Scott Appleby, *The Ambivalence of the Sacred: Religion, Violence, and Reconciliation* (Lanham, MD: Rowman and Littlefield, 2000); Marc Gopin, *Between Eden and Armageddon: The Future of World Religions, Violence, and Peacemaking* (New York: Oxford University Press, 2000); Raymond G. Helmick, SJ, and Rodney L. Petersen, eds., *Forgiveness and Reconciliation: Religion, Public Policy, and Conflict Transformation* (Philadelphia: Templeton Foundation Press, 2001); Douglas Johnston, ed., *Faith-Based Diplomacy: Trumping Realpolitik* (New York: Oxford University Press, 2003); Gordon S. Smith and Harold Coward, eds., *Religion and Peacebuilding* (Albany: State University of New York Press, 2004); James J. Busuttil and Gerrie ter Haar, eds., *Bridge or Barrier: Religions, Violence and Visions for Peace* (Boston: Brill, 2004).

13. David Tracy wrote these words in 1987 while observing the end of the "reign of method," which entailed a carryover of natural science methods into other disciplines. It is instructive for our purposes to note that he argued for a basic appreciation of method (not "methodologism") over against a potential return to "one more round of romanticism" that would valorize "symbol, metaphor, and narrative" without realizing they too are open to hermeneutical study, in other words, method, explanation, and theory. Tracy, *Plurality and Ambiguity: Hermeneutics, Religion, Hope* (San Francisco: Harper and Row, 1987), 30–34.

14. Katrien Hertog, *The Complex Reality of Religious Peacebuilding: Conceptual Contributions and Critical Analysis* (New York: Lexington Books, 2010), 38–39.

15. Hybridity as an analytical lens has been developed in postcolonial studies, and other fields have begun to adopt it as well. For example, theologian Jeanine Hill-Fletcher draws on feminist scholarship to argue that all Christians have hybrid identities: *Monopoly on Salvation? A Feminist Approach to Religious Pluralism* (New York: Continuum, 2005). A special issue of the *Journal of Peacebuilding and Development* argues for the use of the concept to understand peacebuilding and development contexts; the opening essay is by Roger Mac Ginty and Sanghera Gurchathen, "Hybridity in Peacebuilding and Development: An Introduction," *Journal of Peacebuilding and Development* 7, no. 2 (2012): 3–8.

16. These are multiply attested categories. For one scholar's exposition of them, among other methodological strands, see Francis S. Fiorenza, "Systematic Theology: Task and Methods," in *Systematic Theology: Roman Catholic Perspectives*, vol. 1, ed. Fiorenza and John P. Galvin (Minneapolis: Augsburg Fortress Press, 1991), 1–89.

17. To take a prominent example, in *The Nature of Doctrine* (Philadelphia: Fortress Press, 1984), theologian George Lindbeck gives one account of these two modes, naming them "cultural linguistic" and "experiential expressivist." Whereas Lindbeck argued for the former against the latter, we see them as complementary. Other Christian exemplars of theology emphasizing narrative include Hans Frei and Stanley Hauerwas. Philosopher Alasdair

MacIntyre's work on tradition is foundational for many authors using this approach. In the experiential group, again looking at Christian theologians, Karl Rahner is one who draws on transcendental philosophy. Using different types of sources, F. D. E. Schleiermacher, Edward Schillebeeckx, and various liberation theologians also "start with" experience.

18. See, for example, Mohammed Abu-Nimer, *Nonviolence and Peace Building in Islam: Theory and Practice* (Gainesville: University Press of Florida, 2003); Marc Gopin, *Holy War, Holy Peace: How Religion Can Bring Peace to the Middle East* (New York: Oxford University Press, 2002); David Little, ed., with the Tanenbaum Center for Interreligious Understanding, *Peacemakers in Action: Profiles of Religion in Conflict Resolution* (New York: Cambridge University Press, 2005); and Robert J. Schreiter, R. Scott Appleby, and Gerard F. Powers, eds., *Peacebuilding: Catholic Theology, Ethics, and Praxis* (Maryknoll, NY: Orbis Books, 2010). These works self-identify as part of conflict resolution or peacebuilding literatures. A broader scope would include related subfields such as reconciliation studies, spiritualities of peace, and pastoral theology. See, for instance, Emmanuel Katongole and Chris Rice, *Reconciling All Things: A Christian Vision for Justice, Peace and Healing* (Downers Grove, IL: InterVarsity Press, 2008).

   Relevant to the conceptual binary we have sketched, a growing number of religious and theological works emphasize narrative and/or what has been called a turn to tradition or a turn to culture. Stanley Hauerwas stands out among these because he has led a broadly popular and visible movement in Christian theology, and, moreover, one of his signature concerns is peace. For recent analysis of the benefits and dangers of his approach, see Ted A. Smith, "Redeeming Critique: Resignations to the Cultural Turn in Christian Theology and Ethics," *Journal of the Society of Christian Ethics* 24, no. 2 (2004): 89–113; and Jennifer A. Herdt, "Hauerwas Among the Virtues," *Journal of Religious Ethics* 40, no. 2 (2012): 202–227. Both authors point to the need for greater theoretical and critical reflection and acknowledgment of hybridity. Smith advocates "resignation to a culture that is neither entirely other, nor whole, nor ideal" (97). Herdt explains that though Hauerwas is "ambivalent" about the degrees and forms of his particularism, he often deploys the rhetoric of "exclusive particularism," the dangers of which she outlines. For pointing us in Smith's direction and for countless conversations at the foundational stages of this writing process, we thank Kyle Lambelet.

19. For information on these and various related topics, see Mark R. Cobb, Christina M. Puchalski, and Bruce Rumbold, eds., *Oxford Textbook of Spirituality in Healthcare* (New York: Oxford University Press, 2012). For a reflection on the cultural shift, see Robbie E. Davis-Floyd and Gloria St. John, *From Doctor to Healer: The Transformative Journey* (New Brunswick, NJ: Rutgers University Press, 1998). For an emerging approach that accounts for these needs, see Rita Charon, *Narrative Medicine: Honoring the Stories of Illness* (New York: Oxford University Press, 2008).

20. There is a growing interest in the intersection of peacebuilding and the arts. The European Graduate School in Switzerland now offers a three-year master's degree in the Expressive Arts in Conflict Transformation and Peacebuilding. Brandeis University's International Center for Ethics, Justice, and Public Life runs a program called Peacebuilding and the Arts. See also Michael Shank and Lisa Schirch, "Strategic Arts-Based Peacebuilding," *Peace and Change* 33, no. 2 (April 2008): 217–242.

21. We focus here on processes of expression, yet a more complete account would focus equally on the vital presence of willing and capable listeners. Trauma survivor and philosopher Susan J. Brison explains that survivors often have to "remake a self" and argues

that this type of healing is inherently relational. Facing others' refusal or inability to hear their stories "makes it difficult for survivors to tell them even to themselves." Brison writes, "In order to construct self-narratives, then, we need not only the words with which to tell our stories but also an audience able and willing to hear us and to understand our words as we intend them." Brison, "Outliving Oneself: Trauma, Memory, and Personal Identity," in *Feminists Rethink the Self*, ed. Diana Tietjens Meyers (Boulder, CO: Westview Press, 1997), 21–22.

22. For an account of discursive versus non-discursive experiences of oppression, see Iris Marion Young, "Abjection and Oppression: Dynamics of Unconscious Racism, Sexism, and Homophobia," in *Crises in Continental Philosophy*, ed. A. B. Dallery and C. B. Scott (Albany: State University of New York Press, 1990), 201–213.

23. See, for instance, Atalia Omer's work on the impact of silencing in Chapter 24 of this volume. Also, the work of "naming" has been foundational to various liberation theologies (including but not limited to Mujerista, Hispanic, Black, Womanist, African, Minjung, Native American, Asian, Queer, and Feminist). For example, Latin American liberation theology was groundbreaking in part because it named poverty as structural violence. See Gustavo Gutiérrez, *A Theology of Liberation: History, Politics, and Salvation* (Maryknoll, NY: Orbis Books, 1988). For a recent interdisciplinary and inter-contextual analysis of liberation theologies, see Thia Cooper, ed., *The Reemergence of Liberation Theologies: Models for the Twenty-First Century* (New York: Palgrave Macmillan, 2013).

24. Our use of the term has connecting points but does not overlap with its use in psychology and existential philosophy.

25. As Schillebeeckx explained, "All our negative experiences cannot brush aside the 'nonetheless' of trust which is revealed in human resistance and which prevents us from simply surrendering human beings, human society, and the world to total meaninglessness. This trust in the ultimate meaning of human life seems to me to be the basic presupposition of human action in history." *The Understanding of Faith*, trans. N. D. Smith (London: Sheed and Ward, 1974), 96–97.

26. In her classic psychological text *Trauma and Recovery*, Judith Herman articulates how severe and totalizing such disruptions can be: "The traumatic event challenges an ordinary person to become a theologian, a philosopher, and a jurist. The survivor is called upon to articulate the values and beliefs that she once held and that the trauma destroyed. She stands mute before the emptiness of evil, feeling the insufficiency of any known system of explanation. Survivors of atrocity of every age and every culture come to a point in their testimony where all questions are reduced to one, spoken more in bewilderment than in outrage: Why? The answer is beyond human understanding." Judith Herman, *Trauma and Recovery: The Aftermath of Violence—from Domestic Abuse to Political Terror* (New York: Basic Books, 1992), 178.

27. John Paul Lederach and R. Scott Appleby, "Strategic Peacebuilding: An Overview," in *Strategies of Peace: Transforming Conflict in a Violent World*, ed. Daniel Philpott and Gerard F. Powers (New York: Oxford University Press, 2010), 28.

28. See Daniel Philpott's chapter, "Reconciliation: An Ethic for Peacebuilding," in Philpott and Powers, *Strategies of Peace*, 91–118.

29. John Paul Lederach brought the term "moral imagination" into peacebuilding literature through *The Moral Imagination: The Art and Soul of Building Peace* (New York: Oxford University Press, 2005). Lederach defines the moral imagination functionally: "The kind of imagination to which I refer is mobilized when four disciplines and capacities are held

together and practiced by those who find their way to rise above violence. Stated simply, the moral imagination requires the capacity to imagine ourselves in a web of relationships that includes our enemies; the ability to sustain a paradoxical curiosity that embraces complexity without reliance on dualistic polarity; the fundamental belief in and pursuit of the creative act; and the acceptance of the inherent risk of stepping into the mystery of the unknown that lies beyond the far too familiar landscape of violence" (5).

30. In *When Blood and Bones Cry Out*, another work published in the same year and by the same publishing house as *Strategies of Peace,* Lederach and Lederach delve deeply into the defining (often nonlinear) dynamics of healing. Comparing the two books and their bibliographies illustrates some of the subdivisions within peacebuilding and some of the lack of cross-fertilization among disciplinary interests that we describe. John Paul Lederach and Angela Jill Lederach, *When Blood and Bones Cry Out: Journeys through the Soundscape of Healing and Reconciliation* (New York: Oxford University Press, 2010).

31. For one Christian perspective, see Bernard McGinn, "The Letter and the Spirit: Spirituality as an Academic Discipline," *Christian Spirituality Bulletin* 1, no. 2 (1993): 13–22. For the perspective of a cultural historian and Buddhist-Christian religious practitioner, see Ann Taves, "Detachment and Engagement in the Study of 'Lived Experience,'" *Spiritus: A Journal of Christian Spirituality* 3, no. 2 (2003): 186–208.

32. See especially Lederach, *The Journey Toward Reconciliation* (Scottdale, PA: Herald Press, 1998) reprinted as *Reconcile: Conflict Transformation for Ordinary Christians* (Scottdale, PA: Herald Press, 2014), and Lederach and Cynthia Sampson, eds., *From the Ground Up: Mennonite Contributions to International Peacebuilding* (New York: Oxford University Press, 2000).

33. *Building Peace: Sustainable Reconciliation in Divided Societies* (Washington, DC: US Institute of Peace Press, 1997). See graph on p. 78.

34. In the interest of deeper illustration, we note that "meeting places," an early metaphor depicting Lederach's signature contribution of relational spaces, arose from reflection on Psalm 85 alongside war-weary Central American communities in the 1980s. Later publishing this insight, Lederach describes reconciliation as the "dynamic social space" where Psalm 85 "characters" Truth, Mercy, Justice, and Peace stand together. *Journey Toward Reconciliation*, 60.

35. "I adopt elements from across the disciples to help me articulate what I see to be true," he said in an April 2013 conversation with one of the authors.

36. For an elaboration of this point, see Paul S. Minear, "Time and the Kingdom," *Journal of Religion* 26, no. 2 (1944): 7.

37. Talad Asad, *Formations of the Secular*, 179.

38. Charles Taylor, *A Secular Age* (Cambridge, MA: Harvard University Press, 2007), 54–61.

39. *Journey Toward Reconciliation*, 78.

40. *Journey Toward Reconciliation*, 78.

41. Lederach, *The Moral Imagination*, 46–47.

42. Lederach, *The Moral Imagination*, 119.

43. Layson is referring to what is known as Filipino President Joseph Estrada's 2000 "all-out war" against the Moro Islamic Liberation Front (MILF), which led to the displacement of nearly one million people in Mindanao.

44. Interview with Roberto Layson, OMI, *Oblate Communications*, http://www.omi-world.org/content.asp?catID=4&artID=268&N=. For more on the "spaces of peace" in Mindanao, see Hannah Neumann and Martin Emmer, "Peace Communication: Building a Local Culture of Peace Through Communication," in *Forming a Culture of Peace: Reframing Narratives of Intergroup Relations, Equity, and Justice*, ed. Karina V. Korostelina (New York: Palgrave Macmillan, 2012), 227–255.

45. Lederach, *The Moral Imagination*, 10–13. For more information, see *The Wajir Story*, a documentary commissioned by Responding to Conflict (Birmingham, UK) and produced by Trojan Horse Productions Ltd (http://www.respond.org/data/files/LPP_video_notes/lpp_wajir_story_video_notes.pdf), as well as Dekha Ibrahim and Janice Jenner, "Breaking the Cycle of Violence in Wajir," in *Transforming Violence: Linking Local and Global Peacemaking*, ed. Robert Herr and Judy Zimmerman Herr (Scottdale, PA: Herald Press, 1998), 133–148.

46. Lederach notes that the movement's success was not without "its price": several leaders, including Josué, were assassinated. Lederach, *The Moral Imagination*, 13–16.

47. J. Matthew Ashley, introduction to Johann Baptist Metz, *Faith in History and Society: Toward a Practical Fundamental Theology*, trans. J. Matthew Ashley, (Mainz, Germany: Grünewald, 1977; New York: Crossroad Publishing Company, 2011), 11. Citations refer to the Crossroad edition.

48. Lederach, *The Moral Imagination*, 43.

49. Patrick M. Regan and Allan C. Stam, "In the Nick of Time: Conflict Management, Mediation Timing, and the Duration of Mediation Disputes," *International Studies Quarterly* 44, no. 2 (2000): 239–260.

50. Ashley, "Introduction," 4.

51. Ashley, "Introduction," 12.

52. See Parts II and II of *Faith in History and Society*.

53. Lederach, *The Moral Imagination*, 131.

54. Lederach and Appleby, "Strategic Peacebuilding," 36–37.

55. Others also arrive at the same conclusion about a broader, more comprehensive notion of time, though with a different texture. As we have noted, Lederach's understanding of time is sourced from non-theological as well as theological sources. For example, he draws upon physicists who employ empirical methods yet operate with a time horizon that is broader than linear time.

56. "Recollections and the Construction of a Legacy: The Influence of John Howard Yoder on My Life and Work" (paper presented at the Believers Church Conference, University of Notre Dame, Notre Dame, IN, March 7–9, 2002), 9.

57. "Recollections," 8.

58. "Recollections," 8.

59. John Howard Yoder, "To Serve God and to Rule the World," in *The Royal Priesthood: Essays Ecclesiological and Ecumenical*, ed. Michael G. Cartwright (Scottdale, PA: Herald Press, 1998), 129.

60. Yoder, "To Serve God," 132.

61. In Christian eschatology, the word "sign" has a venerable lineage going back to Augustine, who emphasized that humans can find analogs of the heavenly city on earth.

62. John Howard Yoder, "North Park Symposium" (1990) as published in Thomas Schaffer, *Moral Memoranda From John Howard Yoder: Conversation on Law, Ethics and the Church from a Mennonite Theologian and a Hoosier Lawyer* (Eugene: Wipf & Stock Pub., 2002), 54.

63. Lederach, "Recollections," 8.

64. Lederach, "Recollections," 8.

65. John Howard Yoder, *For the Nations: Essays Public and Evangelical* (Grand Rapids, MI: Eerdmans, 1997), 240.

66. John Paul Lederach, *The Little Book of Conflict Transformation* (Intercourse, PA: Good Books, 2003), 36–37.

67. Lederach, *Conflict Transformation*, 45.

68. Lederach, *Building Peace*, 77.
69. Lederach, *Conflict Transformation*, 14–15.
70. Lederach, *Conflict Transformation*, 37.
71. Lederach, *Building Peace*, 77.
72. Personal correspondence with Lederach, May 2013. See, e.g., Willard M. Swartley, *Covenant of Peace: The Missing Peace in New Testament Theology and Ethics* (Grand Rapids, MI: Eerdmans, 2006).
73. John Paul Lederach, "The Mystery of Transformative Times and Spaces," in *Artisans of Peace: Grassroots Peacemaking*, ed. Mary Ann Cejka and Thomas Bamat (Maryknoll, NY: Orbis Books, 2003), 258.
74. *Building Peace*. See graph on p. 78.
75. *The Moral Imagination*, 142.
76. *The Moral Imagination*, 78.
77. For one formulation of this, see *Journey Toward Reconciliation*, 38.
78. Yoder, *For the Nations*, 212.
79. Yoder, *For the Nations*, 216.
80. It is noteworthy that Lederach's appropriations of Yoder's apocalyptic ethics do not seamlessly integrate with his use—explained above—of the concept of telos. His writings demonstrate exploratory analysis of what is happening (and what could happen) rather than systematic development of overarching notions of time, history, divine and human agency, etc.
81. Yoder, *For the Nations*, 136ff.
82. See for instance, Keller, *Apocalypse Now and Then*, for an extensive treatment of the ambiguities of apocalypse as a genre, with particular attention to the dangers of the logic of dualism.
83. Yoder, *The Politics of Jesus*, 2nd ed. (Grand Rapids, MI: Eerdmans, 1994), 233.
84. Yoder, *The Politics of Jesus*, 165.
85. John Howard Yoder, *Nonviolence: A Brief History; The Warsaw Lectures*, ed. Paul Martens (Waco, TX: Baylor University Press), 4, 22–26.
86. Yoder, *For the Nations*, 106.
87. For Yoder, the claim that Christ is Lord provides a "Lordship axiom." This is a theological (and political) claim that Christ is Lord (ruler) over the cosmos—including "real-world" history. It means that destruction and violence do not, as he says, "have the last word." Instead, "existing order" is distinct from the "order of redemption," and the latter is the ultimate truth. See, e.g., "Why Ecclesiology Is Social Ethics: Gospel Ethics Versus the Wider Wisdom," in *The Royal Priesthood*, 103.
88. See, for example, Joseph R. Wiebe, "Fracturing Evangelical Recognitions of Christ: Inheriting the Radical Democracy of John Howard Yoder with the Penumbral Vision of Rowan Williams," and Romand Coles, "The Wild Patience of John Howard Yoder: 'Outsiders' and the 'Otherness of the Church,'" both in *The New Yoder*, ed. Peter Dula and Chris K. Huebner (Eugene, OR: Cascade, 2010), 294–316 and 216–252, respectively.
89. In his early pioneering texts outlining the theoretical contours of conflict transformation, Lederach critiqued conflict resolution as grounded in imperialist presuppositions. The ways he problematizes conflict resolution, statist diplomacy, and the liberal peace have conceptual links with theories contributing to structural violence, including cultural violence (Felipe MacGregor and Marcial Rubio, "Rejoinder to the Theory of Structural Violence," in *Culture of Violence*, ed. Marcial Rubio Correa and

Kumar Rupesinghe (New York: UN Press, 1994), 42–58) and symbolic violence (Pierre Bourdieu, *The Logic of Practice* (Stanford: Standford University Press, 1990). Efforts to correct for condescending by local and foreign elites (Jean-Philippe Colin and Bruno Losch, "'Touche pas à mon planteur': Réflexions sur les 'encadrements' paysans à travers quelques exemples ivoiriens," *Politique Africaine* 40 (1990): 83–99.) and the systematic denial of local knowledge and culture (Xavier Albó, "Ethnic Violence: The Case of Bolivia," in *Culture of Violence*, ed. Marcial Rubio Correa and Kumar Rupesinghe (New York: UN Press, 1994), 119–143) are deeply present in practical ways in his method and framework from early on.

Bibliography

Works Cited

Abu-Nimer, Mohammed. *Nonviolence and Peace Building in Islam: Theory and Practice.* Gainesville: University Press of Florida, 2003.Albó, Xavier. "Ethnic Violence: The Case of Bolivia." In *Culture of Violence*, edited by Marcial Rubio Correa and Kumar Rupesinghe, 119–143. New York: UN Press, 1994.

Appleby, R. Scott. *The Ambivalence of the Sacred: Religion, Violence, and Reconciliation.* Lanham, MD: Rowman and Littlefield, 2000.

Asad, Talal. *Formations of the Secular: Christianity, Islam, Modernity.* Stanford, CA: Stanford University Press, 2003.

Baker, David L. *Tight Fists or Open Hands? Wealth and Poverty in Old Testament Law.* Grand Rapids, MI: Eerdmans, 2009.

Benjamin, Walter. *Illuminations: Essays and Reflections.* Edited and with an introduction by Hannah Arendt, translated by Harry Zohn. New York: Schocken, 1968.

Bock, Darrell L. "The Parable of the Rich Man and Lazarus and the Ethics of Jesus." *Southwestern Journal of Theology* 40, no. 1 (1997): 63–72.

Bourdieu, Pierre. *The Logic of Practice.* Stanford: Standford University Press, 1990.

Brison, Susan J. "Outliving Oneself: Trauma, Memory, and Personal Identity." In *Feminists Rethink the Self*, edited by Diana Tietjens Meyers, 12–39. Boulder, CO: Westview Press, 1997.

Busuttil, James J., and Gerrie ter Haar, eds. *Bridge or Barrier: Religions, Violence and Visions for Peace.* Boston: Brill, 2004.

Charon, Rita. *Narrative Medicine: Honoring the Stories of Illness.* New York: Oxford University Press, 2008.

Cobb, Mark R., Christina M. Puchalski, and Bruce Rumbold, eds. *Oxford Textbook of Spirituality in Healthcare.* New York: Oxford University Press, 2012.

Colin, Jean-Philippe and Bruno Losch. "'Touche pas à mon planteur': Réflexions sur les 'encadrements' paysans à travers quelques exemples ivoiriens." *Politique Africaine*, 40 (1990): 83–99.

Connolly, William. *Why I Am Not a Secularist.* Minneapolis: University of Minnesota Press, 2000.

Cooper, Thia, ed. *The Reemergence of Liberation Theologies: Models for the Twenty-First Century.* New York: Palgrave Macmillan, 2013.

Czada, Roland, Thomas Held, and Markus Weingardt, eds. *Religions and World Peace: Religious Capacities for Conflict Resolution and Peacebuilding.* Osnabrück, Germany: Nomos Publishers, 2012.

Davis-Floyd, Robbie E., and Gloria St. John. *From Doctor to Healer: The Transformative Journey*. New Brunswick, NJ: Rutgers University Press, 1998.

Donahue, John R. *The Gospel in Parable*. Philadelphia: Fortress Press, 1988.

Dula, Peter, and Chris K. Huebner, eds. *The New Yoder*. Eugene, OR: Cascade, 2010.

Fiorenza, Francis S. "Systematic Theology: Task and Methods." In *Systematic Theology: Roman Catholic Perspectives*, vol. 1, edited by Francis S. Fiorenza and John P. Galvin, 1–89. Minneapolis: Augsburg Fortress Press, 1991.

Gopin, Marc. *Between Eden and Armageddon: The Future of World Religions, Violence, and Peacemaking*. New York: Oxford University Press, 2000.

Gopin, Marc. *Holy War, Holy Peace: How Religion Can Bring Peace to the Middle East*. New York: Oxford University Press, 2002.

Gutiérrez, Gustavo. *A Theology of Liberation: History, Politics, and Salvation*. New York: Orbis Books, 1988.

Helmick, Raymond G., SJ, and Rodney L. Petersen, eds. *Forgiveness and Reconciliation: Religion, Public Policy, and Conflict Transformation*. Philadelphia: Templeton Foundation Press, 2001.

Herdt, Jennifer A. "Hauerwas Among the Virtues." *Journal of Religious Ethics* 40, no. 2 (2012): 202–227.

Hertog, Katrien. *The Complex Reality of Religious Peacebuilding: Conceptual Contributions and Critical Analysis*. New York: Lexington Books, 2010.

Hill-Fletcher, Jeanine. *Monopoly on Salvation? A Feminist Approach to Religious Pluralism*. New York: Continuum, 2005.

Ignatieff, Michael. *The Warrior's Honor: Ethnic War and the Modern Conscience*. New York: Henry Holt and Co., 1998.

Johnston, Douglas, ed. *Faith-Based Diplomacy: Trumping Realpolitik*. New York: Oxford University Press, 2003.

Katongole, Emmanuel, and Chris Rice. *Reconciling All Things: A Christian Vision for Justice, Peace and Healing*. Downers Grove, IL: InterVarsity Press, 2008.

Keller, Catherine. *Apocalypse Now and Then: A Feminist Guide to the End of the World*. Minneapolis: Fortress Press, 2005.

Lederach, John Paul. *Building Peace: Sustainable Reconciliation in Divided Societies*. Washington, DC: US Institute of Peace Press, 1997.

Lederach, John Paul. *Journey Toward Reconciliation*. Scottdale, PA: Herald Press, 1998.

Lederach, John Paul. *The Little Book of Conflict Transformation*. Intercourse, PA: Good Books, 2003.

Lederach, John Paul. "The Mystery of Transformative Times and Spaces." In *Artisans of Peace: Grassroots Peacemaking*, edited by Mary Ann Cejka and Thomas Bamat, 256–268. Maryknoll, NY: Orbis Books, 2003.

Lederach John Paul. *Moral Imagination: The Art and Soul of Building Peace*. New York: Oxford University Press, 2005.

Lederach, John Paul, and R. Scott Appleby. "Strategic Peacebuilding: An Overview." In Philpott and Powers, *Strategies of Peace*, 19–44.

Lederach, John Paul, and Angela Jill Lederach. *When Blood and Bones Cry Out: Journeys through the Soundscape of Healing and Reconciliation*. New York: Oxford University Press, 2010.

Lindbeck, George. *The Nature of Doctrine*. Philadelphia: Fortress Press, 1984.

Little, David, ed., with the Tanenbaum Center for Interreligious Understanding. *Peacemakers in Action: Profiles of Religion in Conflict Resolution*. New York: Cambridge University Press, 2005.

Longenecker, Bruce W. *Remember the Poor: Paul, Poverty, and the Greco-Roman World*. Grand Rapids, MI: Eerdmans, 2010.

Mac Ginty, Roger, and Sanghera Gurchathen. "Hybridity in Peacebuilding and Development: an Introduction." *Journal of Peacebuilding and Development* 7, no. 2 (2012): 3–8.

MacGregor, Felipe and Marcial Rubio. "Rejoinder to the Theory of Structural Violence." In *Culture of Violence*, edited by Marcial Rubio Correa and Kumar Rupesinghe, 42–58. New York: UN Press, 1994.

Maritain, Jacques. *Man and the State*. Washington, DC: Catholic University Press, 1951.

McGinn, Bernard. "The Letter and the Spirit: Spirituality as an Academic Discipline." *Christian Spirituality Bulletin* 1, no. 2 (1993): 13–22.

Metz, Johann Baptist. *Faith in History and Society: Toward a Practical Fundamental Theology*. Translated by J. Matthew Ashley. New York: Crossroad Publishing Company, 2011. First published 1977 by Grünewald.

Minear, Paul S. "Time and the Kingdom." *Journal of Religion* 26, no. 2 (1944): 77–88.

Neumann, Hannah, and Martin Emmer. "Peace Communication: Building a Local Culture of Peace Through Communication." In *Forming a Culture of Peace: Reframing Narratives of Intergroup Relations, Equity, and Justice*, edited by Karina V. Korostelina, 227–255. New York: Palgrave Macmillan, 2012.

Philpott, Daniel. "Reconciliation: An Ethic for Peacebuilding." In Philpott and Powers, *Strategies of Peace*, 91–118.

Philpott, Daniel. *Just and Unjust Peace: An Ethic of Political Reconciliation*. New York: Oxford University Press, 2012.

Philpott, Daniel, and Gerard F. Powers, eds. *Strategies of Peace: Transforming Conflict in a Violent World*. New York: Oxford University Press, 2010.

Regan, Patrick M., and Allan C. Stam. "In the Nick of Time: Conflict Management, Mediation Timing, and the Duration of Mediation Disputes." *International Studies Quarterly* 44, no. 2 (2000): 239–260.

Sampson, Cynthia, and John Paul Lederach, eds. *From the Ground Up: Mennonite Contributions to International Peacebuilding*. New York: Oxford University Press, 2000.

Schillebeeckx, Edward. *The Understanding of Faith*, translated by N. D. Smith. London: Sheed and Ward, 1974.

Schirch, Lisa. *The Little Book of Strategic Peacebuilding*. Intercourse, PA: Good Books, 2005.

Schreiter, Robert J., R. Scott Appleby, and Gerard F. Powers, eds. *Peacebuilding: Catholic Theology, Ethics, and Praxis*. Maryknoll, NY: Orbis Books, 2010.

Shakman Hurd, Elizabeth. *The Politics of Secularism in International Relations*. Princeton, NJ: Princeton University Press, 2008.

Shank, Michael, and Lisa Schirch. "Strategic Arts-Based Peacebuilding." *Peace and Change* 33, no. 2 (2008): 217–242.

Smith, Gordon S., and Harold Coward, eds. *Religion and Peacebuilding*. Albany: State University of New York, 2004.

Smith, Ted A. "Redeeming Critique: Resignations to the Cultural Turn in Christian Theology and Ethics." *Journal of the Society of Christian Ethics* 24, no. 2 (2004): 89–113.

Spohn, William C. "Jesus and Christian Ethics." *Theological Studies* 56, no. 1 (1995): 92–107.

Swartley, Willard M. *Covenant of Peace: The Missing Peace in New Testament Theology and Ethics*. Grand Rapids, MI: Eerdmans, 2006.

Taves, Ann. "Detachment and Engagement in the Study of 'Lived Experience.'" *Spiritus: A Journal of Christian Spirituality* 3, no. 2 (2003): 186–208.

Taylor, Charles. *A Secular Age*. Cambridge: Harvard University Press, 2007.

Tracy, David. *Plurality and Ambiguity: Hermeneutics, Religion, Hope*. San Francisco: Harper and Row, 1987.

Warner, Michael, Jonathan VanAntwerpen, and Craig Calhoun, eds. *Varieties of Secularism in a Secular Age*. Cambridge, MA: Harvard University Press, 2010.

Witte, John, Jr., and Johan David van der Vyver, eds. *Religious Human Rights in Global Perspective: Religious Perspectives*. Boston: Nijhoff Publishers, 1996.

Yoder, John Howard. *The Politics of Jesus*. 2nd ed. Grand Rapids, MI: Eerdmans, 1994.

Yoder, John Howard. *For the Nations: Essays Public and Evangelical*. Grand Rapids, MI: Eerdmans, 1997.

Yoder, John Howard. *The Royal Priesthood: Essays Ecclesiological and Ecumenical*. Edited by Michael G. Cartwright. Scottdale, PA: Herald Press, 1998.

Yoder, John Howard. *Nonviolence: A Brief History; The Warsaw Lectures*. Edited by Paul Martens. Waco, TX: Baylor University Press, 2010.

Young, Iris Marion. "Abjection and Oppression: Dynamics of Unconscious Racism, Sexism, and Homophobia." In *Crises in Continental Philosophy*, edited by A. B. Dallery and C. B. Scott, 201–213. Albany: State University of New York Press, 1990.

Further Reading

Bellinger, Charles K. "Religion and Violence: A Bibliography." Wabash Center for Teaching and Learning in Theology and Religion. http://www.wabashcenter.wabash.edu/resources/article2.aspx?id=10516.

McCarty James W., III, and Joseph Wiinikka-Lydon. "Resources in Religion, Violence, and Peacebuilding: An Annotated Bibliography." *Practical Matters*, no. 5 (Spring 2012). http://practicalmattersjournal.org/issue/5/teaching-matters/resources-in-religion-violence-and-peacebuilding.

CHAPTER 23

....

RELIGIOUS COMMUNITIES
AND POSSIBILITIES
FOR JUSTPEACE

....

CECELIA LYNCH

THIS volume details the critical importance of peacebuilding with and through religious communities. In this chapter I take up several of the major principles of strategic peacebuilding to probe important issues that arise when we consider religious communities' involvement in global processes as well as local issues, historically and in the present. In particular, I am concerned with the degree to which contemporary religious humanitarianism, peacebuilding, and development work are shaped by dominant powers' security and economic discourses, versus the degree to which religious ethics can or do transcend these discourses in order to work toward what the literature refers to as *justpeace*.[1] This concern is motivated by the conviction that the conditions of justpeace require awareness and reflexivity vis-à-vis "dominant discourses" (a term that appeals to Foucault, which I explain below), and that in order to cultivate this sensibility, we must examine more fully several of strategic peacebuilding's principle tenets for problem spots and potential contradictions. Given my concerns, I welcome the openness with which the authors solicit substantive and theoretical questioning, deepening, and broadening of the concept of justpeace in this book.

The concept of justpeace is an extremely helpful one, and indeed, it is critical for peacebuilding to succeed. It denotes the "end goal" of strategic peacebuilding, according to its proponents. Justpeace describes "a dynamic state of affairs in which the reduction and management of violence and the achievement of social and economic justice are undertaken as mutual, reinforcing dimensions of constructive change."[2] Justpeace, therefore, implies the reduction if not elimination of (primarily physical forms of) violence, along with the realization of human dignity and movement toward equality for all regardless of their racial, gender, ethnic, religious, or class identity. By "dominant discourses," I refer not only to the language used to explain and justify particular modes of action, but also the material forms that are constitutive of that language. The linguistic/ideational and the material are mutually constituted, as Michel Foucault demonstrated in his detailed studies of the workings of power.[3] Power relationships form an integral part of any political, economic, or social relationship, and so, I argue, we need to investigate the discursive power at issue in situations of conflict and in attempts to bring about justpeace.

When we focus on the intersection of the conditions for justpeace, given the nature of dominant discourses, and the role of the increasing number of religious actors in peacebuilding, important, intersecting questions arise that require further investigation before we can understand the potential for justpeace. The first question concerns the requirements of justpeace given dominant discourses in the past and present. What are these dominant discourses and how do they shape strategic peacebuilding? Is it important to understand the colonial history of religious communities and their involvement in postcolonial societies (where peacebuilding efforts frequently occur)? I argue that it is indeed important to uncover and analyze the complex layers of the religious community's involvement in colonial and postcolonial strategic projects, and that we need to probe any areas in which the peacebuilding literature has not yet fully bridged the analytical as well as on-the-ground contradictions involved in actualizing justpeace.

The power of dominant discourses to shape religious actors' engagement in peacebuilding is not new; it was also part and parcel of the successive waves of missionary activity that accompanied and frequently justified conquest and colonization. Perhaps, then, we should examine the mistakes of external religious communities' involvement in colonialism, especially the certainties they carried with them and with which they intervened in the lives of others, and the extraordinary conviction that this intervention was both beneficial and necessary for colonial societies.

Today, peacebuilding efforts are worked out in contexts dominated by liberal economic pressures for free markets, foreign investment, and self-help development policies, as well as contemporary security discourses that prioritize actions against what is called a global war on terror. They are also worked out in contexts of ever-increasing numbers of professional development, humanitarian, and peacebuilding experts, many of them external to the societies in conflict they hope to assist. We should investigate, therefore, whether re-examining the legacies of colonialism can assist the development of a more reflexive peacebuilding stance that might enable stronger challenges to the dominant discourses of today. This, of course, raises the question of to what degree peacebuilding activities and concepts accord with some of these discourses, or at least insufficiently challenge them, and how they might be strengthened to accord with the goals of justpeace.

After examining the vast field of religious actors engaged in peacebuilding efforts, I focus on the globalized security and economic discourses that confront the complex of actors, especially faith-based organizations, in their work, bringing together past and present. Global discourses of security, political economy, and culture sometimes work in conjunction with each other but often are contradictory. Nevertheless, these global logics and the interactions that flow from them shape actors' goals and, hence, accepted peacebuilding norms and guidelines. Peacebuilding work unfolds in sites marked by particular power relations that are shaped by historical as well as contemporary events. As a result, the ethics and actions of state and international organization (IO) actors as well as nonstate and religious actors each constitute the contemporary ethos of "peacebuilding," shaping it in particular ways. We should examine these disparate motivations critically in order to assess both the contributions and contradictions of peacebuilding processes in the twenty-first century.

The questions I investigate in this chapter arise from several aspects of my current research, including interviews with dozens of humanitarian, development, and peacebuilding NGO representatives in West, Central, and East Africa, along with interviews of NGO representatives in Europe and the United States who work in Africa. They also arise from my reading of scholarship on postcolonial histories, practices, and theology,[4] and from observations, news accounts, and more informal discussions on issues of aid, humanitarianism, and peace I encountered while in various research sites.

THE SCOPE AND ROLE OF RELIGIOUS COMMUNITIES IN PEACEBUILDING

As John Paul Lederach and Scott Appleby point out, there exists a "dizzying array of international and transnational, governmental and non-governmental actors" involved in peacebuilding efforts today.[5] This array includes religious communities, which themselves include churches, mosques, temples, other sacred communities and sites, religiously supported nongovernmental organizations, mission organizations, intra- and interfaith organizations (local, national, and transnational); states and their donor agencies, such as the US State Department and the US Agency for International Development, or USAID, the British Foreign Office and the UK Department for International Development, or DFID; militaries; private companies tasked with feeding, supplying, or providing expertise to militaries; international organizations (IOs) and their agencies (the UN Security Council as well as the UN High Commissioner for Refugees, or UNHCR, the World Health Organization, and others); and a vast array of local, national, and transnational nongovernmental organizations (NGOs) and other nonstate, civil society actors.

If we focus on the already wide range of actors in this array who define themselves as religious, we can distill several types and functions. First are the communities that have long existed in particular areas, largely due to migration, trade, the importation of labor for railways and mines, and missionaries' long-standing efforts to convert local populations. Thus Sufi Muslim communities in parts of Sub-Saharan Africa are frequently quite old and well established, dating from the ninth century,[6] and Christian communities on both the West and East African coasts originated with the Portugese and continued to be settled with successive waves of missionary activity and colonization. Today, these Muslim and "mainline" Christian communities (Catholic, Anglican, Methodist, Baptist, Presbyterian) have developed strong local roots and become "indigenized," meaning that they tend to be run by clergy from the societies in which they are situated, instead of clergy from outside. In addition to Sufi communities, especially in places like Senegal where the Mouride brotherhood is integral to the economy and norms of Senegalese society, Sunni Muslim communities are found across the continent and Shi'ite groups are also present in many places.

There are also numerous religious communities that settled due to labor migration patterns, sometimes forced. For example, Indians were brought by the British to South and East Africa as indentured laborers to work on railroads, plantations, and coal mines, establishing Hindu (as well as Muslim) communities in these regions. Still other religious communities are much more recent, including Pentecostal and evangelical Christian groups that have spread quickly across the continent over the past two decades and represent growing numbers of Christians on the continent. Conversely, the African Initiated or African Indigenous

Churches, which split from mainline denominations in the early twentieth century to incorporate and preserve traditional religious beliefs, represent significant religious populations in many places, particularly East African countries such as Kenya. Still other religious actors include transnational NGOs and mission groups. NGOs operating in Africa include large numbers of Christian and Muslim groups, and some Hindu, Buddhist, and Jewish groups. Christian and Muslim groups, which form the vast majority, include Caritas and Catholic Relief Services, Episcopal Relief and Development, United Methodist Committee on Relief, Lutheran World Relief, the Mennonite Central Committee, the American Friends Service Committee, Adventist Development and Relief Agency, Christian Children's Fund, Baptist World Aid, Brethren Disaster Ministries, Southern Baptist Disaster Relief, Samaritan's Purse, Presbyterian Relief and Development Agency, Action by Churches Together, World Vision, Christian Aid, Islamic Relief, Muslim Aid, the Aga Khan Foundation, the Ahmadiyya Mission, the Cordoba Foundation, and numerous others. Traditionalists are also beginning to organize across regions, particularly in organizations that promote non-Western forms of healing, such as Prometra International, or non-Western forms of adjudication and cultural and religious mores (Leebon Ci Leer in Senegal and the Noyam Institute in Ghana). On the national level, both Christian and Muslim groups are strong in many countries, and are grouped into National Christian and Supreme Muslim councils in many countries. Finally, interfaith groups, taking off from the movement begun by the World Conference of Religions for Peace in 1970, are increasingly active in numerous countries. In addition to national and transnational interfaith groups such as Interfaith Action for Peace in Africa and the Programme for Christian-Muslim Relations in Africa, local groups have arisen such as that in the coastal region of Kenya to promote understanding and joint action for Muslim human rights in the post–9/11 era.[7]

The landscape of religious actors potentially, if not actually, involved in peacebuilding is, therefore, vast. Many of the most significant peacebuilding actors are "faith-based"—in churches, mosques, monasteries, synagogues, temples, and religious educational and social service organizations. There are two primary reasons why faith-based actors are believed to provide unique advantages to peacebuilding efforts. First, some religious communities are seen as major assets to peacebuilding because they have established long-term roots in given societies. With these roots come trust on the part of local populations, decision-making authority (many form part of formal or informal decision-making councils on the local as well as regional or national levels), and, much more often than not, histories of working side by side with people of different faith traditions. Second, religious communities and faith-based organizations frequently provide services not provided by governments, including health clinics, schools, and basic needs such as food, shelter, and clothing. Their role in providing these services has continued to increase with successive economic and political crises since the 1980s, with governments being unable, unwilling, too corrupt, or a combination of these factors to provide adequate levels of services themselves.

These features of religious communities support the argument of religious peacebuilding advocates that the positive functions of religious actors are often overlooked in contemporary analyses of peace and conflict. Religion, these advocates argue, is still too often equated with conflict and violence instead of peace despite more than a decade of new academic work on the subject. Gerard Powers, for example, acknowledges that religious actors can abet the dynamics of conflict, especially when conflict originates in or incorporates religiously articulated reasons for violence, but he also argues that the resources of religious actors—both ethical and material—that are or can be put in the service of peacebuilding are too often overlooked.[8] Moreover, Powers argues that the role of external religious actors, including interfaith groups, in promoting peace and finding mechanisms for conflict resolution, especially where "religion" is not a central motivation in the conflict or in promoting violence—is often underappreciated by those who charge religion with exclusivism and violence promotion. Here the emphasis is on the resources and networks that religious actors possess and that can be mobilized to work out mechanisms for conflict resolution.

Yet we also need to appreciate that religious communities that engage in peacebuilding do so in conjunction with the ideas, discourses, and activities of state, international institutional, and nonstate actors. They do not operate independently of these other actors, or of the discourses that these actors produce and perpetuate. Indeed, they never have. In many societies, what is not frequently acknowledged is the fact that these long-term religious connections have colonial roots. The intersection of missionizing with colonizing and conquest has left extremely complicated legacies that should be taken into account in assessing the role of religious communities in peacebuilding engagements both past and present.

We need to acknowledge, therefore, that the areas of the world where strategic peacebuilding is most at issue are almost always areas that were colonized by the United States and/or by European or Middle Eastern powers over the past several centuries. This is certainly true of almost all states in Africa. Independence from European powers is only a twentieth-century phenomenon (as it was a century before for Latin American countries), and postcolonial economic, strategic, and political vises have remained extremely strong, creating elite coalitions of colonists and postcolonists who have established economic, political, and legal systems that favor themselves over local populations. Mainline Christian and Muslim leaders may or may not align with elites or former colonial interests. In many cases they have been the strongest advocates for restructuring wealth, educating the marginalized, and providing health care to all. Yet it is also necessary to go beyond mainline religions and incorporate traditional practices and systems of authority when analyzing religious contributions to peacebuilding in Africa. This is because there are at least two facets of religious experience that bear further investigation for strategic peacebuilders. First, while Christian and Muslim religious traditions have long been essential components of African societies, what are known as traditional African religions (or simply African religion[9]) also remain integral. This is despite numerous historical and contemporary attempts by both Christians and Muslims to eradicate, condemn, or dismiss traditional beliefs and practices. In the past, traditional practices from female circumcision to ancestor worship to the use of herbs and pouring of libations were condemned by mainline Christian denominations. Second, however, many forms of syncretism resulted, ranging from those that incorporated traditional practices into essentially mainstream varieties of Christianity or Islam, to those that borrowed bits and pieces from Christianity and/or Islam to graft onto traditional beliefs. In the post–World War II period, both the Vatican and many Protestants opened the door to a somewhat broader range of "cultural" practices, but the Catholic Church made new efforts to rein in its followers under Popes John Paul II and Benedict XVI.[10] Today, however, it is primarily the Pentecostal and evangelical mega-churches that condemn traditional religions as engaging in satanic rituals, even as traditional religions and Pentecostalism share an affinity for practices that combine rather than separate spirit, mind, and body.[11]

Tradition is used here to refer to a dynamic, not static, state of affairs, that includes practices, commitments, and beliefs that both have long histories and evolve with changing circumstances. This is akin to Alasdair MacIntyre's notion of tradition as lived rather than tradition as artifact,[12] although in my interviews and informal discussions in Senegal, Cameroon, and Ghana, interlocutors articulated tradition as dynamic and possessing multiple layers, without reference to MacIntyre or other philosophers and theologians. Traditional commitments and religions involve practices and rituals of healing, birth, entry into adulthood, marriage, death and burial, and appeals to and worship of ancestors. Traditional religions and the hybrid practices that combine them with Christianity, Islam, or other transnational religions have been debated, acknowledged, and condemned to different degrees by Catholic, Protestant, Muslim, and other religious leaders, in the past as well as the present.

Past and Present Relationships Between Dominant Discourses and Religious Communities

Christian missionaries came to Africa as part of discourses of colonization and "civilization." As Siba Grovogui argues, Western colonizers viewed African societies as repositories of culture but not of civilization,[13] implying that they were exotic but not able to govern themselves properly. Moreover, the "*mission civilisatrice*" that European states believed was their right as well as duty was frequently accompanied by Christian missionary efforts. Dominant discourses of European superiority characterized political, economic, and religious motivations for influence in Africa. Today, there exists much debate about the definition, purpose, and impact of "mission," a term which some theologians argue must become much broader to incorporate understanding of multifaceted and religiously plural conceptions of God's movement in the world rather than remaining ensconced in efforts to spread adherence to more exclusivist versions of religious commitment.[14] Yet the activities of today's faith-based NGOs, given their critical relationship with states and international organizations, are also embedded in broader political and economic discourses that should be examined if just-peace is to be achieved in situations of conflict.

Military and economic logics shaped missionaries' efforts to convert local populations in the Americas, Asia, and Africa from the fifteenth through the twentieth centuries. These logics promoted conquest and colonization for prestige, territory, and mercantilist economic policies, which, under the guise of civilizing local populations and improving their livelihoods, created highly unequal economic relationships that extracted wealth from colonies and sent it to the metropoles, or colonial powers. Moreover, the slave trade flourished simultaneously with attempts to convert local populations to Christianity. Some missionaries were strong advocates of colonialist discourses and practices, while others tried to moderate or even challenge them, and still others became inculturated into local religious practices, producing various forms of religious hybridity on the part of missionaries as well as of local populations.[15]

Religious communities that participate in development and humanitarian efforts today also must negotiate contemporary dominant political and economic discourses.

Contemporary discourses that shape the peacebuilding context for religious communities include the ongoing global war on terror, which under the George W. Bush administration promoted military interventionism, and under the Obama administration has promoted multilateral interventions. They also include the discourses of market liberalization and individual rights, which are sometimes contradictory and sometimes complementary, and are tied to liberal economic and social traditions that are more constitutive of donor societies than recipient ones.

Regarding the war on terror, religious communities need to decide whether to challenge (openly or covertly) military interventionism and whether to accept military escorts for humanitarian and development assistance. Discourses related to the war on terror have also increased suspicion of Muslim groups in some areas, making interfaith collaboration more difficult, for example in Nigeria, Somalia, and Mali. Muslim groups, in turn, frequently feel a need to play down their own religious motivations to be acceptable partners for Western donors as well as both secular and Christian NGOs.[16]

Discourses of market liberalization and human rights also produce numerous NGO discursive trends in which faith-based NGOs can be willing participants. These include programs that emphasize concepts such as "sustainability," "capacity-building," and "self-help." Sustainability, however, often refers to a local population's ability to take over the financing of an externally driven program, rather than ecological or cultural sustainability. Capacity-building can refer to providing beneficial educational or training opportunities, but can also refer to training for programs that meet needs designed by donors rather than recipients. Finally, self-help signals a form of assistance that differs from the charity models of the past. More importantly, the use of each of these terms tends to accord with the push for technical solutions for peacebuilding as well as reflecting the market values of donors, rather than allowing for sustained investigations into the requirements of social and economic justice. This is why, I argue elsewhere, microfinance took off in the 2000s with such ubiquity, such that almost all NGOs, including both Christian and Muslim faith-based groups, developed their own microfinance programs.[17]

Challenging or transcending these discourses is difficult for religious communities in the midst of active engagement in conflict resolution and peacebuilding. Time is at a premium, activities and programs to assist local populations depend on meeting donor requirements (and constantly asking for additional resources), and socialization pressures into these discourses are strong. Resistance to the power of these discourses, however, exists. Christian groups on the coast of Kenya, for example, have for some time supported Muslim groups in their demands for increased rights against government deportations.[18] Groups in the DRC, among others, recognize the necessity of attacking structural forms of injustice.[19] More groups are asking what happened to religious communities' strong denunciations of injustices during seminal moments such as the struggle against apartheid in South Africa, or the inter-religious work that promoted an end to violence in Liberia (both of these questions were posed at a June 2013 conference in Cape Town on peacebuilding in Africa sponsored by the Institute for Justice and Reconciliation and the Program on Religion and Reconciliation at Notre Dame's Kroc Institute for International Peace Studies). Religious voices such as the Circle of Concerned African Women Theologians, which was founded in 1989, have long articulated powerful critiques of the intertwined discourses of militarism, neoliberal postcolonialism, and patriarchy.[20]

What does this comparison of past and present tell us? First, in both past and present, dominant political and economic discourses entangle and incorporate religious communities' involvement in development, humanitarianism, and hence peacebuilding. Religious communities both stand within these discourses and at times challenge them and complicate their legacies. It is difficult but critically necessary, therefore, for peacebuilders to practice reflexivity about their own assumptions, connections, and relationships with all actors and processes in the peacebuilding environment—those that are obvious and those that are less obvious. Second, strategic peacebuilders must ask whether and how the experiences of the past continue to shape strategies in the present, and whether any of the mistakes of the past are being renewed in the present.[21] Third, religious peacebuilders, in particular, must reclaim the "prophetic voice" present in all religious traditions that challenges how discourses of power breed specific injustices in given temporal contexts. In the next section, I dissect several assumptions and terms used in the strategic peacebuilding literature to examine these questions.

ISSUES FOR STRATEGIC PEACEBUILDING: ASSUMPTIONS, TERMS, AND GOALS

The peacebuilding literature excels in its call to understand the complexity of post-conflict situations, as well as its attempts to be inclusive. Within and despite this complexity, peacebuilding is guided by core principles: "At its core, peacebuilding nurtures constructive human relationships." The "strategic" element comes from doing this purposefully, "at every level of society and across the potentially polarizing lines of ethnicity, class, religion, and race." Strategic peacebuilding, therefore, is both a strategy and a cultivated ability, resulting in "the capacity to develop strategies to maximize the impact of initiatives for constructive change within this complexity." Moreover, it is extremely comprehensive, focusing "on transforming inhumane social patterns, flawed structural conditions, and open violent conflict that weaken the conditions necessary for a flourishing human community."[22] The concept of justpeace, used as one word to highlight the symbiotic nature of peace and justice, is highly significant. Strategic peacebuilders recognize that peace without justice is likely to be fleeting, only skimming the surface of the conditions that produce violence and conflict in the first place.

As a result, "strategic peacebuilders take advantage of emerging and established patterns of collaboration and interdependence for the purposes of reducing violence and alleviating the root causes of deadly conflict," according to Lederach and Appleby. In order to do so, a broad temporal range of activity is also required: peacebuilding must include strategies of conflict prevention mediation and negotiation of peace during the conflict itself, and post-conflict implementation of political reforms, and it must combine both "the reduction and management of violence and the achievement of social and economic justice" as mutually-reinforcing components"[23]

Yet the role of strategic peacebuilders and the end goal of justpeace also prompt questions about who in religious communities are the peacebuilders and how we know whether they have attacked "root causes" of conflict, given the dominance of liberal, neoliberal, and war-on-terror discourses discussed above, and the difficulties inherent in challenging and transcending them.

Given the high level of skill, awareness, knowledge, experience, and training required to understand and adapt to complexity as well as keep "the big picture," or end goal, always in the forefront, it is unlikely that anyone, any given person, can become a strategic peacebuilder. Strategic peacebuilders must be able to recognize and build upon any movement toward dialogue and cooperation among adversaries, and therefore be able to discern the difference between false starts and promising developments. How much of these skills are innate or capable of development within any given person remains in question.

Nevertheless, the description of the qualities that strategic peacebuilders must possess suggests that external actors are important to the process. For example, Lederach and Appleby discuss the problems of allowing enough time for peacebuilding practices to take root and of ensuring there is agreement on end goals, noting:

> Such sobering considerations might give pause to politicians and policymakers, potential donors, intergovernmental organizations, and other critical contributors to any peacebuilding operation that would be planned according to the requirements of our comprehensive definition. Presumably, no one wants to sink (much less dive) into what looks like a quagmire—which is how long-term interventions within "bloody borders" far from home can readily be depicted.[24]

Certainly external actors have been extremely important in brokering dialogue, negotiations, and agreements, as the experience of the Community of Sant'Egidio in Mozambique shows. Moreover, external actors can bring a fresh perspective that is less attached to the interests of those who initiate violence, practices of corruption, or patterns of exploitation than actors in the midst of conflict who might be allies of these groups. External actors can therefore be viewed as "honest brokers" in a conflict. Finally, external actors motivated by religiously articulated ethics of relief of suffering, nonviolence, and promotion of dignity can appeal to key groups in local communities to strengthen these values, thereby enhancing processes of dialogue and conflict resolution (note that these ethics can also be articulated in secular ways by actors who define themselves in secular terms).

Yet we should also be careful to think through the assumptions about and limitations of external actors in peacebuilding processes. Strategic peacebuilding assumes that sustainable peacebuilding tasks must be taken over by local leaders and populations to be successful. But we also need to ask whether external actors are necessarily better at seeing "the bigger picture," or whether they can also be more compromised by dominant discourses emanating largely from their own societies and norms. As a re-examination of the role of missionaries vis-à-vis colonialism indicates, a reflexive stance on the part of both external and internal actors vis-à-vis the dominant discourses of their times is critical. Many of the contemporary challenges to dominant discourses, as discussed in the section "Past and Present Relationships Between Dominant Discourses and Religious Communities," emanate from voices "internal" to the societies at issue, bringing together an analysis of past and present to articulate powerful religious foundations for peacebuilding that do not ignore either the colonial past or the postcolonial present, and that integrate African with missionary religious insights. A more direct challenge on the part of the strategic peacebuilding literature to the assumptions of broader literatures on development and conflict resolution, which tend to assume that external actors (NGOs, IOs, etc.) must play major roles in the different phases of peacebuilding, is therefore warranted.

Inevitably, external actors have *already* been implicated to greater or lesser degrees in the conditions that led to violence and conflict, as committed peacebuilders such as Lederach are all too aware. Conflicts are rarely if ever produced by processes that are completely internal to a given society. Particularly in postcolonial contexts, the ongoing role of external powers, multinational firms, and sometimes religious leaders is considerable. While religious actors involved in peacebuilding may not be directly implicated, questions for them include a) what their relationship to actors involved in the conflict has been, b) to what degree they are resistant to or complicit in the conditions (economic, political, cultural) that result in conflict situations, and c) whether and how they use their faith-based ethics to challenge problematic or unjust conditions and work across multiple identity categories (religious, ethnic, gender) to do so.

Thus, for example, some would-be peacebuilders from the Western powers have found it difficult to act in areas of the world in which US foreign, military, or economic policy is heavily criticized. Christian groups working in Somalia are one example, and it is unclear that many of them should try to participate in peacebuilding efforts in that context, even though some groups I have interviewed would like to have more of a presence in the country. Similar issues are present in Chad and Mali. And despite the enormous problems magnified by the Mugabe regime in Zimbabwe, external actors must tread carefully due to the continued power of anticolonial discourses that continue to be wielded more or less successfully by the regime.[25]

Moreover, understanding historical legacies of colonialism, racial oppression, and also liberation are important, complicating external versus internal categories. Gerard Powers makes the point that indigenous religious actors bring both pros and cons to peacebuilding processes. They have deep connections in local societies and possess considerable authority. Yet they can also favor their own religious community over others, resulting in a loss of legitimacy with other faith populations.[26] But there are also degrees of what it means to be "indigenous." For example, it made an important difference, when parts of Kenya erupted in violence after the 2007 presidential election, that high-level mediation was conducted by an eminent group of *African* elders, including former UN Secretary-General Kofi Annan and Archbishop Desmond Tutu, rather than external actors from outside the continent. "The Elders," as they became known, did not operate alone; indeed, Kenyan civil society, sometimes supported by transnational NGOs, rapidly organized to press for peace.[27] Yet the primary roles could only be played by activists and leaders from the continent. Similarly, the "Arab Spring" uprisings across North Africa and the Middle East demonstrate the relative impotence of external actors to create the conditions for comprehensive peacebuilding. Even as some of the Egyptian protesters looked to the examples of Gandhi and Martin Luther King Jr., their ideas and strategies could not be articulated by outsiders, at least in part because of historical legacies of intervention and oppression.

Finally, Christian and Muslim participation in past colonial enterprises continues to color the cultural practices that must be understood and investigated to engage in successful peacebuilding. To what degree are "traditional" practices opposed by local Christian and Muslim communities and to what degree are they integrated into them? The implications of the enormous range of religious syncretisms present in Africa as well as Asia and even Latin America means that there is an equally broad diversity of responses to traditional practices of herbal healing; divining; respecting, appealing to, and worshipping ancestors; and decisions about keeping social order and punishing violators. Some Muslims and Christians purport to reject all traditional practices and beliefs, although according to my interviews such a rigid stance has little active support in many parts of the African continent. Others engage openly and easily in a range of hybrid religious practices, while still others participate in local religious practices along with Islam or Christianity but attempt to keep each separate from the other because of condemnation from either or both sides. And some on the extreme end of traditionalism have created their own allegedly pan-African practices that reject the "colonial" religions of both Christianity and Islam.[28] While in numerous places, traditional and "colonial" religious actors support and reinforce peacebuilding efforts, this layering of traditional and transnational religions can have consequences for peacebuilding when Christian and Muslim communities attempt to label and eradicate traditional practices. Some of these practices, for example, female circumcision, can be harmful, but problems for peacebuilding can arise if they are isolated and prioritized above other social and economic concerns. Here again, "internal" actors can lead efforts to connect such practices to broader issues, as indicated by Jackie Ogega's programs in her own Kisii community of Kenya.[29]

A second problem that the strategic peacebuilding literature should address is the potential contradiction between inclusiveness in listening to all parties as equals at the peacebuilding table and attacking the root causes of conflict in order to achieve a sustainable justpeace. The inclusiveness of dialogue and participation in peacebuilding processes recalls liberal criteria for democratic participation, such as Jürgen Habermas's well-known conditions for dialogue, in which adversaries debate from positions of equality. The strategic peacebuilding literature should take extra care to address the critique of Habermas—that he takes insufficient account of asymmetrical power relations that prevent a dialogue among equals[30]—in order to clarify the difficulties of its own positionality in addressing the "root causes" of conflict. At the core is a difficult conundrum: many of the most powerful actors at any negotiating table are those who have reaped the benefits of oppressing others and who thus want to cut a deal to end the violence that leaves their power essentially intact. Conversely, those who have been oppressed (frequently by a combination of external and internal collaborators) stand to gain a reduction in bloodshed but not the economic or political restructuring necessary to eliminate gross inequalities and social suffering. As the base communities and liberation theologians in much of Central America discovered after the civil wars of the 1970s and 1980s, the advent of peace came about while keeping the same oligarchies in charge of state and regional economies, while the violence that engulfed the poor moved from paramilitaries into criminal activity. Similar results obtained in South Africa, where processes of reconciliation, while enormously cathartic for many, did little to change conditions that resulted most recently in the 2012 miners' strike and its violent repression. The strategic peacebuilding literature should acknowledge more forcefully the reasons for the partial nature of these and other peace processes, and emphasize the importance of the prophetic role of local religious actors in insisting on structural changes in favor of social and economic justice.

A major example of such structural issues, which also ties together past and present, is the problem of land—its use, tenure, and ownership by individuals, communities, and external actors such as multinational corporations—a problem that is critical in creating the conditions for conflict or peace. The legacies of colonialism, which disrupted communal systems of authority and control over land, added numerous problems for local communities that are still being felt today. One of the most comprehensive cases of land-grabbing, or "mass scale corporate land occupations" that are "expanding throughout Africa," occurred in Madagascar between 2008 and 2011.[31] In this case, the Daewoo Corporation of South Korea attempted to sign a long-term lease to use 1.3 million hectares of national land for biofuel production, a lease whose provisions would force local people off the land and also send the biofuel to South Korea. In Madagascar, systems of traditional authority and local people's use of the land for economic and religious reasons were upended by coalitions of foreign companies and the state elites, and the grassroots mobilization that opposed the deal caused a major political crisis. This type of land expropriation is not an isolated phenomenon: a similar instance of land-grabbing for biofuel production by a Norwegian company was resisted by a grassroots coalition in the Tamale area of northern Ghana,[32] and other cases are occurring all over the continent. In both the cases of both Madagascar and Ghana, grassroots mobilizations developed locally, although eventually they developed coalitions with transnational NGOs. Land-grabs are frequently justified by liberal discourses of legal and economic development, using arguments that assert that biofuel or agricultural production will be increased and jobs generated by corporate control, and/or that contractual obligations that specify and codify land leases can clarify ownership of land and therefore move forward the rule of law. But these arguments deny the social dislocations and legal confusion resulting from the takeover of land by elite and corporate interests; such takeovers are certain to be a major cause of conflict in the future. As a result, land-grabs raise broader questions for faith-based strategic peacebuilders regarding when and how preventive peacebuilding can occur, and whether both local and transnational religious communities can be at the forefront of resisting them in the name of justpeace. And if such land-grabs are to be resisted, what place do pro-development elites and foreign interests have at the negotiating table?

This is one example, albeit an important one, of the types of specific issues that justpeace theorists and practitioners must confront in their work. The issue of who articulates, decides upon, and enacts the content and parameters of justpeace poses significant problems given existing social and economic structures. The discussion above is not intended to diminish the importance of the concept of justpeace in the strategic peacebuilding literature, but rather to point to specific reasons why reflexivity is warranted and specific issues that justpeace must take into account.

Conclusion

In assessing these substantive and theoretical issues that the strategic peacebuilding framework should address, I do not mean to deny the progress made, either in scholars' vision of peacebuilding or in the carrying out of peacebuilding by practitioners. But, as Lederach and Appleby argue, peacebuilding must be "comprehensive and sustainable."[33] Moreover, the practices of peacebuilding need to become part of the fabric of social life, and become "routinized in society." My goal is to point out that the component parts of the vision for achieving comprehensive justpeace in the peacebuilding literature, such as inclusion of all segments of society, rule of law, democracy, and particular conceptions of human rights, accord to a significant degree with liberal discourses that are both dominant and salient in contemporary global or cosmopolitan thought and that are understood and promoted, albeit selectively, by major powers and donors. These discourses, while containing many promising components, also reflect an era in which substantive, structural mechanisms for redistribution of wealth and power are often pushed aside by major powers and external actors in the resolution of conflicts. Religious communities map onto these discourses while also carrying their own historical baggage. Yet religious communities also possess enormous ethical resources and commitments that can challenge inequality and oppression. Advocates of justpeace, to their credit, have restored social and economic justice to their central place in the theory and practice of sustainable peace. The question is whether they, along with local religious communities, can specify how strategic peacebuilding practices can challenge and transcend systemic oppression, economic inequality, and the links between foreign and local elites that maintain them.

While the strategic peacebuilding literature has thus far addressed numerous critical issues, it has not yet incorporated a full reckoning with the implications of today's dominant discourses and the implications of religious actors' histories into its conceptual and theoretical apparatus. It should also rely more centrally on local actors, scholars, and religious leaders' articulations of the bases for social and economic justice in the postcolonial present. This chapter is an attempt to engage with these issues and resources, although they require and, I would argue, strongly merit, further discussion, debate, and conceptual clarification. It may not be viable, for example, to resolve many of these tensions in the strategic peacebuilding apparatus. If it is, however, it will need at a minimum ongoing reflection as well as conceptual and contextual flexibility to implement.

Notes

1. John Paul Lederach and R. Scott Appleby, "Strategic Peacebuilding: An Overview," in *Strategies of Peace: Transforming Conflict in a Violent World*, ed. Daniel Philpott and Gerard F. Powers (New York: Oxford University Press, 2010), 19–44.

2. Lederach and Appleby, "Strategic Peacebuilding," 23. See also John Paul Lederach, *Preparing for Peace* (Syracuse, NY: Syracuse University Press, 1995); Lisa Schirch, *The Little Book of Strategic Peacebuilding* (Intercourse, PA: Good Books, 2004); and Pierre Allan and Alexis Keller, *What Is a Just Peace?* (New York: Oxford University Press, 2006).

3. Michel Foucault, *The History of Sexuality*, vol. 1, *An Introduction* (New York: Vintage, 1990); Foucault, *Discipline and Punish: The Birth of the Prison*, 2nd ed. (New York: Vintage, 1995).

4. See, for example, Franz Fanon, *The Wretched of the Earth*, trans. Richard Philcox (Paris: François Maspero, 1961; New York: Grove Atlantic, 2005); Ngugi wa Thiong'o, *Decolonizing the Mind: The Politics of Language in African Literature* (London: James Currey, 1986); Achille Mbembe, *On the Postcolony* (Berkeley: University of California Press, 2011); Mercy Amba Oduyoye, *Daughters of Anowa: African Women and Patriarchy* (Maryknoll, NY: Orbis Books, 1995); and Stacey M. Floyd-Thomas and Miguel A. De La Torre, eds., *Beyond the Pale: Reading Ethics from the Margins* (Louisville: Westminster/John Knox Press, 2011).

5. Lederach and Appleby, "Strategic Peacebuilding," 26.

6. Ousmane Oumar Kane, *Non-Europhone Intellectuals*, trans. Victoria Bawtree (Dakar: Council for the Development of Social Science Research in Africa [CODESRIA], 2012).

7. See Cecelia Lynch, "Local and Global Influences on Islamic NGOs in Kenya," *Journal of Peacebuilding and Development* 6, no. 1 (2011): 21–34.

8. Gerard F. Powers, "Religion and Peacebuilding," in *Strategies of Peace: Transforming Conflict in a Violent World*, edited by Daniel Philpott and Gerard F. Powers (New York: Oxford University Press, 2010), 317–352.

9. See Laurenti Magesa, "On Speaking Terms: African Religion and Christianity in Dialogue," in *Reconciliation, Justice and Peace: The Second African Synod*, ed. Agbonkhianmeghe E. Orobator, SJ (Maryknoll, NY: Orbis Books, 2011), 25–36.

10. S. Wesley Ariarajah, *Gospel and Culture: An Ongoing Discussion within the Ecumenical Movement* (Geneva: World Council of Churches, 1998); Musa W. Dube, ed., *Other Ways of Reading: African Women and the Bible* (Geneva: World Council of Churches Publications, 2001); Magesa, "On Speaking Terms."

11. Birgit Meyer, *Translating the Devil: Religion and Modernity Among the Ewe in Ghana* (Edinburgh: Edinburgh University Press, 1999); Rosalind I. J. Hackett, "Discourses of Demonization in Africa and Beyond," *Diogenes* 50, no. 3 (2003): 61–65.

12. Alasdair MacIntyre, *Three Rival Versions of Moral Enquiry: Encyclopedia, Genealogy, and Tradition* (Notre Dame, IN: University of Notre Dame Press, 1997). See also R. Scott Appleby, *The Ambivalence of the Sacred: Religion, Violence, and Reconciliation* (Lanham, MD: Rowman and Littlefield, 2000).

13. Siba N'Zatioula Grovogui, *Sovereigns, Quasi Sovereigns, and Africans* (Minneapolis: University of Minnesota Press, 1996).

14. Christopher Duraisingh, "From Church-Shaped Mission to Mission-Shaped Church," *Anglican Theological Review* 92, no. 1 (2010): 7–28.

15. Ariarajah, Gospel and Culture Dube, Other Ways of Reading; Max Assimeng, Religion and Social Change inWest Africa, 2nd ed. (Accra, Ghana: Woeli, 2010).

16. Cecelia Lynch, "Religion, Identity, and the War on Terror: Insights from Religious Humanitarianism," in *Religion, Identity, and Global Governance*, ed. Patrick James, 108–127 (Toronto: University of Toronto Press, 2010); Lynch, "Local and Global Influences."

17. Cecelia Lynch, "Neoliberal Ethics, the Humanitarian International, and Practices of Peacebuilding," in *Globalization, Social Movements, and Peacebuilding*, ed. Jackie Smith and Ernesto Verdeja, 47–68 (Syracuse, NY: Syracuse University Press, 2013).

18. Lynch, "Local and Global Influences."

19. Pyana Symphorien, "Grassroots Peacebuilding in (Eastern) DR Congo: Role of Religion and Local Culture," *Critical Investigations into Humanitarianism in Africa (CIHA) Blog*, July 30, 2013, www.cihablog.com.

20. See the website of the Circle of Concerned African Women Theologians at www.thecircle-cawt.org.

21. Johan Galtung, "A Structural Theory of Imperialism," *Journal of Peace Research* 8, no. 2 (1971): 81–117.

22. Lederach and Appleby, "Strategic Peacebuilding," 22.

23. Lederach and Appleby, "Strategic Peacebuilding," 22, 23.

24. Lederach and Appleby, "Strategic Peacebuilding, "25.

25. Ian Phimister and Brian Raftopoulos, "Mugabe, Mbeki, and the Politics of Anti-Imperialism," *Review of African Political Economy* 31, no. 101 (2004): 385–400.

26. Powers, "Religion and Peacebuilding."

27. Lych, "Local and Global Influences."

28. Marlene DeWitte, "Spirit Media: Charismatics, Traditionalists, and Mediation Practices in Ghana" (PhD diss., University of Amsterdam, 2008), http://dare.uva.nl/record/273202.

29. Jackie Ogega, *Pervasive Violence* (Create Space Independent Publishing Platform, 2012).

30. See Craig Calhoun, *Critical Social Theory* (Cambridge, MA: Basil Blackwell, 1995), 51–53.

31. Stefan Christoff, "Madagascar: Community Resistance to Corporate Land Theft," *Food Crisis and the Global Land Grab*, April 6, 2011, http://farmlandgrab.org/post/view/18406.

32. Author interview with activist on land issues in Tamale, Ghana, September 2, 2012.

33. Lederach and Appleby, "Strategic Peacebuilding," 23.

BIBLIOGRAPHY

Allan, Pierre, and Alexis Keller. *What Is a Just Peace?* New York: Oxford University Press, 2006.

Appleby, R. Scott. *The Ambivalence of the Sacred: Religion, Violence, and Reconciliation.* Lanham, MD: Rowman and Littlefield, 2000.

Ariarajah, S. Wesley. *Gospel and Culture: An Ongoing Discussion within the Ecumenical Movement.* Geneva: World Council of Churches, 1998.

Assimeng, Max. *Religion and Social Change in West Africa.* 2nd ed. Accra, Ghana: Woeli, 2010.

Calhoun, Craig. *Critical Social Theory.* Cambridge, MA: Basil Blackwell, 1995.

Christoff, Stefan. "Madagascar: Community Resistance to Corporate Land Theft." *Food Crisis and the Global Land Grab*, April 6, 2011. http://farmlandgrab.org/post/view/18406.

Confortini, Catia. "A Feminist Humanism? Outlining a Future for Gender-Responsive Strategic Peacebuilding." In *Global Governance and the Future of Strategic Peacebuilding*, edited by R. Scott Appleby. New York: Oxford University Press, forthcoming.

DeWitte, Marlene. "Spirit Media: Charismatics, Traditionalists, and Mediation Practices in Ghana." PhD diss., University of Amsterdam, 2008. http://dare.uva.nl/record/273202.

Dube, Musa W., ed. *Other Ways of Reading: African Women and the Bible.* Geneva: World Council of Churches Publications, 2001.

Duraisingh, Christopher. "From Church-Shaped Mission to Mission-Shaped Church." *Anglican Theological Review* 92, no. 1 (2010): 7–28.

Fanon, Franz. *The Wretched of the Earth.* Translated by Richard Philcox. New York: Grove Atlantic, 2005. First published 1961 by François Maspero.

Floyd-Thomas, Stacey M., and Miguel A. De La Torre, eds. *Beyond the Pale: Reading Ethics from the Margins.* Louisville: Westminster/John Knox Press, 2011.

Foucault, Michel. *Discipline and Punish: The Birth of the Prison.* 2nd ed. New York: Vintage, 1995.

Foucault, Michel. *The History of Sexuality.* Vol. 1, *An Introduction.* New York: Vintage, 1990.

Galtung, Johan. "A Structural Theory of Imperialism." *Journal of Peace Research* 8, no. 2 (1971): 81–117.

Grovogui, Siba N'Zatioula. *Sovereigns, Quasi Sovereigns, and Africans.* Minneapolis: University of Minnesota Press, 1996.

Hackett, Rosalind I. J. "Discourses of Demonization in Africa and Beyond." *Diogenes* 50, no. 3 (2003): 61–65.

Kane, Ousmane Oumar. *Non-Europhone Intellectuals.* Translated by Victoria Bawtree. Dakar: Council for the Development of Social Science Research in Africa (CODESRIA), 2012.

Lederach, John Paul. *Preparing for Peace.* Syracuse, NY: Syracuse University Press, 1995.

Lederach, John Paul, and R. Scott Appleby. "Strategic Peacebuilding: An Overview." In *Strategies of Peace: Transforming Conflict in a Violent World*, edited by Daniel Philpott and Gerard F. Powers, 19–44. New York: Oxford University Press, 2010.

Lynch, Cecelia. "Local and Global Influences on Islamic NGOs in Kenya." *Journal of Peacebuilding and Development* 6, no. 1 (2011): 21–34.

Lynch, Cecelia. "Neoliberal Ethics, the Humanitarian International, and Practices of Peacebuilding." In *Globalization, Social Movements, and Peacebuilding*, edited by Jackie Smith and Ernesto Verdeja. Syracuse, 47–68. New York: Syracuse University Press, 2013.

Lynch, Cecelia. "Religion, Identity, and the War on Terror: Insights from Religious Humanitarianism," in *Religion, Identity, and Global Governance*, edited by Patrick James, 108–127. Toronto: University of Toronto Press, 2011.

MacIntyre, Alasdair. *Three Rival Versions of Moral Enquiry: Encyclopedia, Genealogy, and Tradition*. Notre Dame, IN: University of Notre Dame Press, 1997.

Magesa, Laurenti. "On Speaking Terms: African Religion and Christianity in Dialogue." In *Reconciliation, Justice and Peace: The Second African Synod*, edited by Agbonkhianmeghe E. Orobator, SJ, 25–36. Maryknoll, NY: Orbis Books, 2011.

Mbembe, Achille. *On the Postcolony*. Berkeley: University of California Press, 2011.

Meyer, Birgit. *Translating the Devil: Religion and Modernity Among the Ewe in Ghana*. Edinburgh: Edinburgh University Press, 1999.

Oduyoye, Mercy Amba. *Daughters of Anowa: African Women and Patriarchy*. Maryknoll, NY: Orbis Books, 1995.

Ogega, Jackie. *Pervasive Violence*. Create Space Independent Publishing Platform, 2012.

Philpott, Daniel. "Reconciliation: An Ethic for Peacebuilding." In *Strategies of Peace: Transforming Conflict in a Violent World*, edited by Daniel Philpott and Gerard F. Powers, 91–118. New York: Oxford University Press, 2010.

Phimister, Ian, and Brian Raftopoulos. "Mugabe, Mbeki, and the Politics of Anti-Imperialism." *Review of African Political Economy* 31, no. 101 (2004): 385–400.

Powers, Gerard F. "Religion and Peacebuilding." In *Strategies of Peace: Transforming Conflict in a Violent World*, edited by Daniel Philpott and Gerard F. Powers, 317–352. New York: Oxford University Press, 2010.

Richmond, Oliver. "A Pedagogy of Peacebuilding: Infrapolitics, Resistance, and Liberation." *International Political Sociology* 6, no. 2 (2012): 115–131.

Schirch, Lisa. *The Little Book of Strategic Peacebuilding*. Intercourse, PA: Good Books, 2004.

Smith, Jackie, and Ernesto Verdeja, eds. *Globalization, Social Movements, and Peacebuilding*. Syracuse, NY: Syracuse University Press, 2013.

Symphorien, Pyana. "Grassroots Peacebuilding in (Eastern) DR Congo: Role of Religion and Local Culture." *Critical Investigations into Humanitarianism in Africa (CIHA) Blog*, July 30, 2013. www.cihablog.com.

wa Thiong'o, Ngugi. *Decolonizing the Mind: The Politics of Language in African Literature*. London: James Currey, 1986.

CHAPTER 24

RELIGION, NATIONALISM, AND SOLIDARITY ACTIVISM

ATALIA OMER

INTRODUCTION

"TELL them to get the hell out of Palestine" is what the late Helen Thomas (1920–2013)—the former esteemed dean of the White House press corps—said in response to Rabbi David Nessenoff's question as to whether she had something to say about Israel.[1] Nessenoff, who hosts the right-wing-leaning website www.rabbilive.com, captured Thomas's response on camera during his 2010 visit to the White House to celebrate Jewish Heritage Month. Explaining her blunt comment, Thomas continued her interview with Nessenoff: "Remember these people are occupied, and it's their land. It's not Germany, and it's not Poland." In response to Nessenoff's further question as to where "they" should go, Thomas replied: "They could go home." "Where is their home?" Nessenoff asks. "Poland, Germany... and America and everywhere else. Why push people out of there who have lived there for centuries?" was her reply. After a clip of the interview circulated, Thomas resigned from her iconic position at the White House and terminated her long and distinguished career as a journalist for the Hearst newspapers.

After showing the infamous clip to his audience, Jon Stewart, the host of the satirical *The Daily Show*, asked, "Yes. *Why* did the Jews ever leave Germany and Poland?" Stewart is of course pointing to the complex history that surely Thomas was aware of.[2] The comment seemed to have erased the memories of the Holocaust and oversimplified a very complicated historical situation. Thomas knew the "Jews" could not "just go home." To begin with, Germany and Poland are not home for the millions of Jews born in Palestine/Israel. Nor are they home for the millions of Mizrahi or Arab Jews (Jews who trace their ancestry to Arab and Islamic lands). They may be a home for some Jews who chose to move or stay there, but they are certainly no longer the "home" in a Jewish narrative and ethos so centrally shaped by the experiences of anti-Semitism and near extinction in Germany, Poland, and Europe more broadly. Thomas's remark is analogous to telling every American citizen of European descent who has benefited from the occupation, expulsion, and exploitation of Native Americans (and arguably they all did, directly or indirectly) to go back to Europe.

Indeed, despite her presumed intention to voice silenced Palestinian grievances, Thomas's comments may be interpreted as a "reactionary" counter-silencing. She departed from the usual expunging of anti-Semitic connotations exhibited by other proponents of the Palestine cause whom I associate with a global Palestine solidarity movement. Many Palestine solidarity activists in the "West" explicitly state that their anti-Israel position does not by any means imply any personal hatred of Jews. In other words, "it's nothing personal," but rather it is the self-evident and universally wrong reality of a colonial occupation. This is how many pro-Palestine groups frame their passionate struggle for justice to the Palestinians.[3] Hence, Thomas's obvious dismissal of the Holocaust legacy, an experience very personal indeed, appears out of step with the attitude of a global Palestine activism. Yet, as I argue in this chapter, her critique is more an exemplar than an aberration of the movement's counter-hegemonic stances and its complicity with a pattern of mutual silencing.

What I call "the global Palestine solidarity movement" comprises diverse groups and individuals, from trade unions and churches to politicians and celebrities, Palestinian and non-Palestinian alike.[4] Palestine solidarity is also pivotal to Islamist and Arab rhetorical construal of Palestine as a signifier of colonial subjugation and of Israel as the embodiment, the taskmaster, and/or the instrument of Western domination. This rhetoric reacts to dominant and enduring orientalist discursive formations that undergird the effectiveness of the pro-Israel lobby.

Peacebuilding, I contend, must move beyond advertent or inadvertent complicity with the pattern of mutual silencing that has informed both pro-Palestine and pro-Israel activism. This process requires both a discursive critique of religio-cultural and social attitudes and formations as well as a constructive engagement with how religion might relate to the transformation of attitudes and patterns of solidarity. My intention, therefore, is to scrutinize the rhetorically inflammatory mimesis of mutual silencing in an effort to think constructively about the concept of solidarity beyond the totalizing and homogenizing deployments of Palestinian and Jewish narratives as well as their symbolic appropriations—their deployment, for instance, as a symbol of colonial oppression, Western domination, as a step in an end-time drama, or as a paradigm of suffering, humiliation, and nonnegotiable claims. While not unique, the Israeli-Palestinian case highlights the explosive dynamics of abstractions born out of the interfaces among various foci of solidarities. The chapter, therefore, calls attention to why solidarities that I view as a type of diaspora activism may exacerbate, often despite their best intentions, the concrete realities of national conflicts.

Interrogating the specific case of Israel-Palestine will expose why it has generated such emotions, activism, and polarities. Hence, my research questions are not only *how* and *why* the Palestine trope is invoked, but also *why* it works so effectively as such a trope. How does Palestine as a utopia construed in Islamist and Arab rhetoric echo the rhetorical representation of Israel? What are the implications of turning Palestine and Israel into symbols for issues of peace and justice? What are the roles of the religious imagination in diasporic imaginings? Is the symbolization of Israel-Palestine unique or indicative of broader patterns of diaspora and solidarity activism? This method does not amount to a privileging of the case of Israel/Palestine but rather to scrutiny of the discursive topographies that inform its perceived uniqueness and centrality to perceptions concerning "world peace." The question of why a 2003 poll commissioned by the European Union indicates that a large number of Europeans rank Israel as the greatest threat to world peace (above Iran and North Korea) is a relevant question and one that demands considering historical, cultural, and religious underpinnings.[5]

I explore these questions through a comparative consideration of the case of Tibet, its symbolization, and its rhetorical functionalism. I begin by introducing the central analytic utility of orientalism as a discursive formation. I then apply the insights of discursive critique in scrutinizing the limitations of realist and value-essentialist approaches to the analysis of cultural affinities as a factor in conflict cycles.

In the second part of the chapter, I develop a typology of diaspora nationalism that explores the roles of "home" and "diasporas"—real or perceived—in transforming geography into a utopia and/or a symbolic landscape of devotion. This approach is consistent with the metaphorical study of diasporas, which defies a simple dichotomy of homeland versus host-land and perceives the "diasporic" as a potential subversive space.[6] I interpret the concept of "diaspora" not only as denoting a physical dislocation from a "homeland," but also as encompassing solidarity networks as well as symbolic experiences of displacement. Likewise, it entails normative (in addition to geopolitical) destinations. Here I build on theorist of nationalism Rogers Brubaker's critique of the overuse of the category of diaspora so that it loses all analytic distinctiveness. The embrace of de-territoriality—marking the supposed cosmopolitan merging of the study of migration, transnationalism, and diasporas—has not entailed relinquishing metaphysical and essentialist conceptions of identity. Brubaker, instead, offers a non-essentialist lens for thinking of diaspora as a "category of practice." Instead of diaspora as a bounded entity, that is, he views diaspora as "an idiom, a stance, a claim." In other words, "'diaspora' is used to make claims, to articulate projects, to formulate expectations, to mobilize energies, to appeal to loyalties. It is often a category with a strong normative change. It does not so much *describe* the world as seek to *remake* it."[7] Hence, it is a distinct normative orientation that marks diaspora nationalism and not mere ethnic links. On this account, my typology of direct, indirect, symbolic, and pluralizing "diasporas" foregrounds the notion of solidarity. Outlining this typology engages the fluid overlaps among various discursive fields through an exposition of the cases of Tibet and Palestine. The third part of this chapter further situates the question of solidarity activism within the broader discussion of peacebuilding, a comprehensive process intent on transforming the patterns of mutual silencing. Religion relates centrally to this analysis in that it interlaces with the construction, reconstruction, and contestations of questions of national membership (whether within or without the geopolitical boundaries of a nation-state). Diasporas, in this context, can play many roles, from reifying exclusionary interpretations of intersecting cultural, religious, and national boundaries, which often contribute to support of belligerent agendas, to challenging such reification and exclusionary interpretations. This inquiry is further pertinent to broader questions of religion, conflict, and peacebuilding because deep sociocultural attitudes that underlie the formations of solidarities and perceptions of various "others" are not unrelated to authorizing various interventions, favoring certain parties, and policy-making more broadly. Illuminating the enduring relevance of the orientalist discourse in informing the theory and practice of international relations points to why transforming perceptions and attitudes is a critical step in substantive processes of conflict transformation. Orientalism has particular cultural, historical, and religious dimensions that invite a methodical analysis pertaining to how it informs attitudes, solidarities, intercultural affinities, and policy-making.

I. Mutual Silencing

Orientalism

The notion of discourse is central to my discussion. Helen Thomas's silencing of Jewish histories constitutes an example of reactionary counter-discourse to the prevailing orientalist discourse in which her words were sounded and consequently interpreted as threatening the bounds of convention.

Famously, the orientalist discourse was observed and critiqued by the Christian Palestinian and American scholar Edward Said in his seminal book *Orientalism* (1978), in which he applies and develops French historian and philosopher Michel Foucault's notion of discourse as an epistemic construction or a "regime of knowledge." He does so in order to decipher and deconstruct how and why "the Orient" has been represented as morally and culturally inferior to "the West."[8] Based on Foucault's engagement primarily with Friedrich Nietzsche's non-essentialist conceptualization of the relation between appearance and the *thing in itself*, truth and morality for Foucault are ineradicably yet non-reductively constituted by power.[9] "Truth," he writes, "is a thing of this world: it is produced only by virtue of multiple forms of constraint. And it induces regular effects of power. Each society has its regime of truth, its 'general politics' of truth: that is, the types of discourse which it accepts and makes function as true."[10] A discursive formation is the formalized manner in which we perceive our world, interpret social and normative boundaries, and discern the normal versus the abnormal or the perverse. Social norms are so embedded and embodied that they prompt self-regulation without external coercion. Discourse also entails the comprehensive participation of intellectual and cultural productions in maintaining and authorizing systemic power configurations, without reducing such productions to power. Indeed, though critics of Foucault frame his theory of power as too diffused for agency or change, there is always a possibility that novel epistemic regimes of knowledge will emerge. Because power is constituted through accepted ways of knowing, change and resistance would depend on exposing discourse and its accompanying epistemic fields.[11]

Said's critique of orientalism also draws on Italian political theorist and linguist Antonio Gramsci's notion of cultural hegemony as exercised by political and socioeconomic elites and as supported by intellectual productions and the coercive infrastructures of state apparatuses.[12] Said illuminates the interconnections between the imperial project (including its later postcolonial, neo-imperial cultural variations) and the development of the orientalist discourse. Critically, the "West" and the "Orient" are constitutive of one another, and this relation is interwoven with the project of empire. The sense of modernity, rationality, and progress associated with the West is constructed in a binary relation to the construct of traditionalism, despotism, and backwardness attributed to the Orient. This perception of the Orient was reproduced and reinforced by (pseudo-) scientific observations, respectable forms of knowledge and knowing that emboldened the "regime of truth" underlying colonial, imperial (and later neoliberal) structures of domination.

Said later situates his discussion of Palestine in this broader colonial and postcolonial discourse, deconstructing the silencing of Palestinian histories and voices from mainstream representation and official production of attitudes toward the Israeli-Palestinian conflict.[13]

Orientalism in Reverse

Said's thesis generated diverse responses. His many critics primarily challenged the lack of historical precision in his broad observations.[14] But as one interpreter of *Orientalism*, Alexander Lyon Macfie, explains, this does not detract from Said's task of identifying and deconstructing orientalism as a discourse in the Foucauldian sense. While many of his critics remained beholden to a conventional realist approach to history, Said's study of the orientalist discourse was intended primarily to expose orientalism as a regime of knowledge deployed in the service of empire.[15] Imagining essentialist constructs such as the "Arab mind" or "Arab society" underwrote empire, revealing the intricacies of power and knowledge production.[16] Contrary to critics' dismissal of orientalism as depriving the "object" of agency, the object-subject reciprocity, and consequently the possibility of change[17] (a critique also levelled against Foucault's notion of power), for Said, deconstructing orientalism optimally would have meant an analysis of "the dialectic between Orientalist and the Oriental." It would also have invited a focus on "the restorative dialectic by which the Oriental asserts his actuality."[18]

Indeed, as Said asserts in "Orientalism Reconsidered," the deconstructive turn would ideally lead to "nothing less than the creation of new objects for a new kind of knowledge."[19] In the same way in which early waves of feminism reimagine women (resisting and deconstructing gender essentialism), this creation would empower the formerly silenced and subjugated oriental other.[20] While critics wish to rescue the *thing in itself* (the actual existing human beings located within the "Orient") from Said's *Orientalism* by showing "empirical facts," Said deploys Foucault's notion of truth as a function of multiple forms of constraint, inextricably but non-reductively beholden to power. Rather than being ahistorical, Said's rereading of Middle Eastern history through the prism of orientalism reveals profound dissonances between myths and concrete realities. Those dissonances potentially constitute constructive tools not only in challenging the dominant discourse, but also in offering possible resources for rethinking (or even subverting) it.[21] Certainly, if categories such as "the West" and "the Orient" constitute interpretive constructs, they could also be reinterpreted, but this reinterpretation must entail a discursive analysis. Yet the notion of agency that emerges out of Said's critique, as I show below, lends itself to a transvaluation that, in its radical mirroring of the "norms," ironically remains beholden to the orientalist logic, thereby perpetuating the patterns of mutual silencing.

My reference to "mutual silencing" draws on the deconstructive insight that animates the work of cultural theorists working within the Saidian-Foucauldian tradition. It is not only the case that pro-Palestine and pro-Israel actors offer contradictory claims and arguments within a normatively and socioculturally neutral public space where the relative validity of their claims is then reasonably debated. "The public space," as cultural anthropologist Talal Asad aptly observed, "is not an empty space for carrying out debates. It is constituted by the sensibilities—memories and aspirations, fears and hopes—of speakers and listeners."[22] Sometimes, the quality of "being heard" (which is ultimately the objective of speaking) requires "the disruption of established assumptions structuring debates in the public sphere. More strongly: they may *have* to disrupt existing assumptions to be heard."[23] This is precisely what Thomas's provocative words intended to accomplish in introducing a counter-discourse about Israel/Palestine. However, her counter-discourse, as I show below, intersected with another form of discursive violence, namely anti-Semitism, and thus silenced Israeli and non-Israeli Jewish histories, memories, and narratives. The key to peace-building, therefore, is to move, through a process of reinterpretation, away from such patterns of mutual silencing.

Notably, Said himself was accused by Sadik Jalal al-'Azm, a specialist in the study of Arab cultures, of essentializing the Occident in a way akin to his critique of the reification of the Orient.[24] In similar fashion other critics, perhaps misreading Said's aforementioned intent to recognize the dialectical relations between colonizer and colonized, illuminated the hetero-geneity of the orientalist discourse and the multi-directionality and interfaces between colo-nizers and colonized. The relationships between colonizer and colonized, East versus West are, therefore, much more complex than the conceptualization of this relation in binaries that only replicate the orientalist logic.[25] "Orientalism in reverse," al-'Azm explains, informs conceptions of Arab superiority and instrumentality in guiding "humanity out of the state of decadence to which Western leadership has brought it."[26] This line of argumentation indeed reverses the discursive logic of orientalism. An Islamic variation of this reversed discourse emerged in full force in the aftermath of the Iranian Revolution. Accordingly, "the national salvation so eagerly sought by the Arabs since the Napoleonic occupation of Egypt" will not arise by operationalizing secular nationalism in its various forms, but rather through a return to an authentic, popular Islam.[27] This counter-hegemonic discourse—one that mir-rors the logic of political scientist Samuel Huntington's thesis of the "clash of civilizations"— is typified in speeches given by personalities such as former Iranian president Mahmoud Ahmadinejad and Osama bin Laden.[28] It is also characterized by conflating Israel with the West and the interrelated metaphorical invocation of Palestine as a symbol of the broader redemptive scheme outlined above.

In the case of Islamist rhetoric, therefore, "home" is transformed into a moral and utopian destination. It is indeed a "stance" rather than a place or ethnic identity. Muslims throughout the world become, in a sense, a Palestinian diaspora. Within this frame, along with rectify-ing the humiliation born out of the experiences of colonialism and imperialism, a liberated Palestine signifies redemption and return, mirroring the traditional Jewish conceptualiza-tion of return to the land of Zion as a redemptive moment of auto-emancipation and/or a divine restoration of a golden age. It represents an aspirational utopia (literally a "no-place") outside ordinary historical time and place. Indeed, as Brubaker argues, diaspora as a cat-egory of practice is not about describing the world, but rather about a longing to transform it. Yet deploying Palestine as a trope overlooks the complexities of place and history, akin to Thomas's request that Jews go "back home." It also loudly echoes Zionist blindness to the indigenous and concrete presence of Palestinians in the land. This blindness, I illustrate below, is deeply rooted in the orientalist and colonial discourses and their interrelations with Christo-centrism (which morphed into Judeo-Christian-centrism after World War II).

The relation of mimesis between the metaphorical invocation of the causes of Palestine and Israel is further amplified by the theo-political imagination of Christian Zionists, whose support of Israeli policies is grounded in an instrumentalist view of the Zionist project as a necessary chapter in their end-time saga.[29] This theo-political position is contested by Palestinian liberation theology as well as a host of other Christian denominations. For exam-ple, the Presbyterian Church USA laments Christian Zionism's pervasive influences on geo-political agendas and underscores its hermeneutical flaws as a Christian theology.[30] Other critics challenge the reigning discourses through contestating homogenizing and reified narratives. Such efforts that draw upon internal pluralities may facilitate the reimagining of discursive fields as a process of conflict transformation. But this reimagining would have to interrogate the elastic boundaries of place and belonging. I will attempt this interrogation by introducing an overlapping typology of diaspora nationalism, focusing especially on the symbolization of "home" and/or a national cause. Before proceeding with the typology, however, I will briefly review existing realist and cultural essentialist accounts of solidarities as they relate to the dynamics of conflicts in the global arena.

Between the Prisms of Realism and Cultural Essentialism

The typology I will develop below goes beyond existing works on diasporas in that it includes solidarity movements. De-essentializing diaspora as a category of practice and a normative stance, rather than positing it as a self-evident (and countable) demographic category, challenges the teleologies inherent in classical nation-state-centric as well as in post-national accounts of diasporas.[31] Critically, a non-essentialist conception of the "nation," a contested construct, is pivotal. Developing this conception remains necessary despite the teleological cosmopolitan valorizing of heterogeneity and hybridity as the upshot of the cosmopolitan condition and as an antidote to ethnic chauvinism (by which diaspora or the diasporic serves as destination rather than mono-cultural, national self-determination). Such a conception contests the conservative fixity entailed in the task of "boundary maintenance," conventionally articulated as an essential criterion of diaspora.[32] But this non-essentialist stance nonetheless retains the "nation" as the conceptual "other," albeit as a highly hermeneutical and embodied construct. In this framing, the possibility of overcoming chauvinistic and homogenizing national historiographies, ostensibly integral for peacebuilding, is not achieved through dissolving collective passions (boundary erosion), but through reimagining them by way of a discursive analysis that denaturalizes what appears and/or is projected as the "same," regardless of time and space differentials.[33] In other words, the constructive peacebuilding potential for a diaspora is not reliant necessarily on cosmopolitan post-nationalist presumptions about overcoming ethnocentric and chauvinistic passions but rather on reinterpreting exclusionary claims through engagement with internal diversities. The non-essentialist lens views diasporic communities as related to "nation" in complex and varied ways. Religion is intricately related to this process not the least because within the topographies of Western multicultural societies, religious spaces such as mosques, churches, synagogues, and Hindu temples are highly ethnicized and nationalized.

Highlighting, as I do shortly, the type of "pluralizing diaspora" as pivotal for reimagining solidarities and normative commitments to national projects counters the grim essentialist and deeply orientalist prediction (projection) contained in Huntington's notion of the "kin country syndrome." Accordingly, what Huntington dubbed "civilization commonality" would, in the post–Cold War era, replace political ideology as the principal basis for cooperation and coalitions.[34] Yet solidarities and cultural affinities are infinitely more complex than the fixity entailed in his "clash of civilizations" thesis, which is but a contemporary manifestation of the orientalist discourse.[35] Solidarities and affinities are likewise more complex than political realism's reluctant recognition of "culture" and "solidarities" as restraints on acting on a state's geopolitical interests. Geopolitical agendas, in other words, can never simply be a function of mere "realist" or "idealist" interests. Such interests are always embedded within discursive constraints that outline what may appear as a self-evidently realist or value agenda.

Ironically, the curious case of the United States' supposedly unconditional love of Israel prompted even devout political realists to consider broad cultural and political solidarities as relevant variables in the analysis of US involvement in the Middle East and the Israeli-Palestinian conflict. In their controversial *The Israel Lobby and U.S. Foreign Policy*, John Mearsheimer and Stephen M. Walt contend that an amalgam of loosely connected pressure groups, ranging from politically active American Jews to Christian Zionists, influences the course of US policy concerning Israel and involvement in the Middle East, contra to actual American regional interests.[36] The authors, as many of their critics decried, overstated the influence of the Israel lobby, thereby, in even inadvertently suggesting likeness to classical tropes of Jewish conspiracies, becoming susceptible to the charge of anti-Semitism so often directed to critics of the Israeli status quo vis-à-vis the Palestinians.[37]

While as "realists," Mearsheimer and Walt are motivated by perceived American interests rather than by a particular concern with the plight of the Palestinians or by any hatred of the Jews, their thesis does echo (despite itself) a disproportional attribution of power and influence to the Israel lobby.[38] Such an attribution does sound like a conspiratorial cabal, a hallmark of an antecedent and enduring anti-Jewish discursive formation. It overlooks an analysis of the broader American lobbying culture that is also marked by other exceedingly powerful lobbies. The narrative makes no mention of failures of the Israel lobby to sway American foreign policies, or of the relevance of the American imperialist agenda and oil interests.

While a simple categorization of Mearsheimer and Walt's thesis as anti-Semitic is misguided, it is likewise wrong to dismiss the suggestion that the seeming plausibility of this thesis plays into deep-seated receptivity for anti-Semitic explanatory paradigms such as the one outlined in the *Protocols of the Elders of Zion*.[39] In the same way that, in the aftermath of September 11, 2001, the clash of civilizations thesis resonated as "true" in the minds of those already conditioned within the discourses of orientalism, *The Israel Lobby* resonates with those culturally (even if inadvertently) receptive to anti-Semitism. The point of this analogy is to bring to the fore the need to engage in discursive analyses that historicize and scrutinize cultural affinities or lack thereof. Discursively, a reliance on orientalist and essentializing renderings of Islam as especially prone to the so-called phenomenon of "religious violence"[40] lent an ahistoric prism through which to comprehend the violence of September 11th. Indeed, the discursive formations associated with this orientalist positionality are at the heart of the "war on terror," rising Islamophobia, and popular perceptions of and attitudes toward Israel/Palestine.[41]

Of course, the tragic events of 2001 marked more broadly the discovery of religion by theorists and other commentators of international relations (IR). With few exceptions,[42] however, IR thinking retains the dominant paradigms of liberalism, realism, and constructivism for analyzing international and global politics. Religion need not receive special analytic attention, beyond its function as another form of (ideological or spiritual) legitimization and/or transnational activism. This is how political scientists Jack Snyder and Emily Cochran Bech synthesize a volume devoted to the topic of whether religion deserves a new kind of theorizing in IR.[43] Yet these authors do acknowledge the indebtedness of the reigning paradigms of IR to a particularistic European history and equally particularistic (despite its universalist outlook) philosophical, cultural, and religious traditions. It is not clear how integrating this kind of discursive critique—one that illuminates the kind of violence inflicted by classifying as "religious" everything that seems to be consistent with a Christian-centric conception of faith—leaves those lenses of IR only slightly adjusted. For the purposes of this chapter, however, it is important to note that retaining the presuppositions of IR is precisely what cripples the analysis of the supposedly unique case of the Israel lobby recounted above. Without scrutiny of how the cultural and religious imaginations relate to the construction and reproduction of underlying discourses about the Middle East, in this case, the analysis of intercultural and transnational solidarities presumes the tale of the *Protocols of the Elders of Zion* contains a kernel of truth in the same way that the "clash of civilizations" confirmed orientalist underpinnings.

Because of its emphasis on cultural and social interests and loose collaboration, the thesis of *The Israel Lobby* indeed departs from the materialist reductionism otherwise associated with the realist approach. It exposes some of the ways in which broad solidarities with a national project contribute to the course of a conflict; that is, the levels of regional imperial involvement and support influence direct forms of violence and/or peace initiatives. However, this realist discovery of culture and religion, specifically how the Israel lobby constitutes a "strategic liability" to U.S. interests in the Middle East, provides a narrow explanatory account of the cultural affinities between the United States and Israel. It exemplifies how the lack of discursive sensibility constrains the scope of intellectual inquiry. What presents itself as an empirical truth (the cabal-like relations between the loose Israel lobby) is deeply embedded in various intersecting discourses. A discursively critical account will have to address American civil religion and national ethos as well as the discourse of orientalism and its cognate construct of Judeo-Christianity informing America's national self-perception.[44] This discursive topography is aided structurally and culturally by the framework of multicultural identity politics. While encouraging religious plurality, the multicultural landscape also encourages the practice of fossilizing, essentializing, domesticating, and ethnicizing religious groups.[45] Instead, defaulting on what appears as an anti-Jewish explanatory framework, the thesis of *The Israel Lobby* overlooks the complex religio-cultural interlacing and discursive formations informing US solidarity with Israel. Likewise, the supposed descriptive power of the "clash of civilizations" is limited by its normative orientalist presuppositions.

II. TELL ME WHO YOUR FRIENDS ARE: A TYPOLOGY OF DIASPORA NATIONALISM

Real Homes

By "direct diaspora" I refer to communities that experience firsthand physical displacement from a homeland. Certainly, the "directness" of this displacement could extend inter-generationally, potentially reclassifying this diaspora nationalism as "indirect" and/or "symbolic." The symbolization of home transforms "homeland" from geopolitical place to the object of collective devotion and/or messianic aspiration.

Indeed, symbolic and indirect diaspora nationalisms could easily blend into one another. In the paradigmatic Jewish case, its indirectness (ostensibly, all Jews can "recall" the experience of dispersion from the biblical homeland) is also symbolic, in that a return to the land signifies, in the Jewish theological imagination, the coming of messianic redemption. A return "home," in other words, entails the fulfillment of Jewish destiny and redemption from the constraints of historical space and time. Within the secular Zionist teleological narratives, Israel likewise epitomizes Jewish self-reliance, resistance, and redemption from persecutions that are always imminent. It is in reaction to the homogenizing scope of such teleological construal that some Jewish critics in the diasporas (as well as within the geo-political space called Israel) react by revalorizing "dispersal" over and against a supposed "return" to utopia. These are the voices that I classify as "pluralizing diasporas," highlighting their contestations of homogenizing narratives pertaining to the relations between Jewish history and identity and the Israeli political project. Such pluralizing diasporas reject the conflation and essentialist fixity of the Jewish people and the presumption that Israel is their self-appointed spokesperson.

"Indirect diaspora," therefore, refers precisely to the perceptions of homeland articulated by those communities that have not necessarily experienced direct displacement, but for whom a distant homeland has become a defining feature of their identity as well as a focus of devotion (financial, spiritual, political). Indirect as well as direct diasporants, for whom return to an imagined homeland is denied, embrace "home" as a symbolic and at times utopian destination and focus of veneration which, within the diasporic context, is often conflated with one's religio-cultural identity. As noted, various Palestine solidarity groups imagine or project Palestine as a utopia. Tibet stands as a comparative utopia that shares many discursive similarities with and notable differences from the symbolic appropriations of Palestine/Israel. For Tibetans in Dharamsala, for instance, this devotion results in the construal of their space-in-exile as the "Little Lhasa of India" and in considerable artistic representations of places from Tibet.[46] These processes of identity construction illuminate the interfaces among direct, indirect, and symbolic diasporas. As political scientist Dibyesh Anand reflects: "For the older generation of refugees, the homeland is the place where they once lived. For later generations of refugees, the homeland is, in a certain sense, not a real place; it is a utopia. For them, the longing is for a home they never inhabited."[47] Anand terms this nostalgia for a pre-1959 Tibet "the space-time projection": "like the Palestinians, the Tibetans conceive a common homeland as a moral as well as geographical location."[48] Illuminating these similarities with and divergences from Palestine, as I do below, further exposes the interfaces between various discursive fields and demonstrates how such synergies affect national agendas and solidarities with such causes.

Metaphorical Homes

The first discursive similarity returns us to the discussion of orientalism. Within the so-called "Western imagination," both Palestine and Tibet have been demonized at times and idealized at others. Certainly the colonial trajectories in the Middle East were distinctly different from those in the Far East and Asia. But both modes of imagining Tibet and Palestine are deeply orientalist and embedded in colonial and missionary discourses. The case of Tibet especially exemplifies why the discursive context can transform home from geography to utopia and/or self-referential metaphor for various forms of solidarities, from direct to indirect and symbolic diasporas. I explain this below.

The colonial context of the nineteenth century enabled missionary work in the Tibetan region that usually produced knowledge about Tibet with a characteristic air of European superiority, framing local culture as backward and primitive.[49] This colonial juncture also signaled the launch of the study of Buddhism by Orientalists (scholars of the Orient) who, by and large, considered Tibetan Buddhism as an aberration of "pure" or "original" Buddhism. The term "Lamaism" came to denote this dismissive attitude toward Tibetan Buddhism, a degenerate religion (or not a religion at all), mired in magic, superstition, excessive sexuality, blind obedience to religious figures, and other familiar attributes of "despotic orientalism."[50]

Countering this dominant Western construal of Tibet, the theosophical movement in the nineteenth century appropriated the Tibetan eschatological myth of Sambhala (based on the texts of Kalacakra Tantra) concerning a hidden land behind impassable mountains, the site of perfect harmony and wisdom that stands in total contrast to the worldly chaos beyond this destination. The theosophists accordingly imagined Tibet as a spiritual center, untouched by the claws of modernity, a repository of secret and sublime knowledge, and undamaged by the signs of the time. Sambhala therefore began to be synonymized with Tibet, even if the Tibetans themselves did not think of their land as a place of perfect harmony.[51] The fantasies of Tibet as Sambhala illustrate the complex multi-directionality of orientalist projection. The notion of Tibet as a spiritual destination as well as the negative dismissal of Tibetan practices as degenerate are indicative of Western and European agendas and longings, and to this degree they are self-referential. At the same time, Tibet, with its cultural and ethnic diversity, cannot be reduced to Western fantasies and colonial policies. The Tibetan eschatological myth of Sambhala is Tibetan, after all. Yet its realness is not a *thing in itself*, an unchanged ahistorical essence outside the constraints of discursive formations.

To be sure, the influence of the theosophist movement on Western imaginings of Tibet is culturally far-ranging.[52] Despite decades of encounters with Tibetans in exile (after the Chinese occupation) and of Tibetan Buddhism as a lived religion, Tibet in the popular Western imagination has remained a positive yet overly uncritical construct. The charismatic person of the Fourteenth Dalai Lama, the projection of his image and philosophy upon Tibetans, homogenizing what is heterogeneous, once again produced Tibet as "a metaphor of good, as the last refuge of spirituality amidst a materialistic and radically demythologized world."[53] In his related discussion of the role of Tibet in the New Age movement, Frank J. Korom outlines how dabbling in Tibetan Buddhism by New Age practitioners concurrently popularizes and trivializes Tibet and Tibetan knowledge. The myth of Sambhala and its supposed universalist millenarianism is construed as consistent with the notion of millenarianism that defines New Age thinking.[54] This conflation of the particular with the universal functions, simultaneously, to market Tibet as a New Age cause while also emptying it of its concrete and historical complexities. Once again, transforming a cause into a symbol of greater and vaguer liberation (spiritual longings, in this case), deconcretizes the actual historicity of Tibetans and Tibet.

Along those lines, the scholar of religious studies Donald Lopez famously lamented in a groundbreaking book that Tibetans are, in effect, "prisoners of Shangri-La."[55] This provocative statement encapsulates the point that the orientalist romanticization of Tibet and Tibetan appropriations of Western projections work against the real and concrete interests of the Tibetan struggle against Chinese occupation, repression, and cultural genocide.[56] Lopez argues that, in their strategic efforts to garner support for their cause and to resist their virtual imprisonment under China, Tibetans have become prisoners of idealizing Western fantasies of them. Shangri-La is, of course, the fictional location described by British author James Hilton in his text *Lost Horizon*. It is a mystical hidden valley that strongly resonates with the myth of Sambhala. The orientalism at the core of the struggle for the liberation of Tibet, Lopez argues, glosses over internal historical complexities and cultural nuances of Tibetans.[57] It traps the political struggle for independence in the idealized and exoticized image of Sambhala.

Both the exoticization of Tibet as the destination of secret knowledge, sublime wisdom, and spiritual harmony as well as its demonization as a realm of magic, superstition, and darkness are characterized by an overemphasis on religion, bracketing out and selectively neglecting other cultural aspects of Tibetan lived experiences. Clearly, the construal of Tibet as utterly spiritual, disembodied, and a metaphorical contrast to the materialism of modern secular life betrays a deeply Christocentric conception of religion qua faith, a conception central to the classificatory system undergirding colonial domination. The ambivalent representation of Tibet either as Shangri-La or the embodiment of feudal servitude, both equally orientalist, produced either Tibetophiles or Tibetophobes.[58] Yet neither of these positions has any necessary connection to the predicaments of real Tibetans.

The growing solidarity with Tibet and the indebtedness of this solidarity to Western fantasies of Tibet qua Shangri La notwithstanding, the question remains whether generating an idealized image of Tibet works to the benefit of actual Tibetans. Are Tibetans, in other words, prisoners and/or manipulators of the intrinsically apolitical image of Shangri La, as Lopez exclaims?

In responding to the exoticization of Tibet thesis, some scholars challenge the perception of Tibetans as mere victims of projected Western images. These scholars point out that Tibetans are prisoners of China and Chinese imperial policies that frame the takeover of Tibet as a "liberation."[59] This rhetorical maneuver is all too familiar in reframing occupation as the benevolent liberation from one's own civilizational backwardness. Incidentally, this is also why the "Left" in the West initially (while still intoxicated with the Communist leader Mao Zedong) welcomed the Chinese "liberation" of Tibet. In countering what they deem Lopez's conservative approach to Tibetan culture, Tsering Shakya and David Germano stress the agency exercised by Tibetans themselves while not denying the constructive intercultural exchanges with exogenous discursive currencies such as environmentalism, world peace, indigenous sovereignty, and nonviolent resistance.[60] These critics contend that Tibetans in exile appropriate and deploy selective imaginings of Tibetan-ness merely as political tactics to mobilize necessary support.[61] This does not mean, however, that Tibet and Tibetan-ness do not exist outside Western fantasizing of them.

Important parallels can be observed between the symbolization of the Tibetan and Palestinian causes. The imaginings of Tibet and Palestine have also appropriated the currencies of the universalizing discourses of human rights and nationalism without which any claims for national self-determination or violation of this right as well as others would have been nonsensical. Yet, like the imagining of Palestinian-ness, Tibetan-ness was dialectically shaped by the experiences of missionizing, colonialism, displacement, exile and repression, modernity, and the dominance of the discourse of nation-states. To be sure, the "space-time projection" of Tibet as a utopia, regardless of its concrete realities, is accompanied by processes of objectification and essentialization of Tibetan culture and religion, as well as the commodification of Tibetan-ness for Western consumption, which is then also internalized and appropriated within Tibetan discourse of national identity.[62]

Indeed, in imagining Tibet as a cohesive national identity, the experience of exile enabled an unprecedented homogenizing. For instance, the political control of the Dalai Lama transcended its traditional jurisdiction in the U-Tsang region to also encompass the Kham and Amdo regions and their constituencies (diasporic or not).[63] This act of imagining a nation through dispersal is a common motif in other nationalisms.[64] A complex network of local city-centered affiliations in Palestine has likewise been transformed into a more encompassing and cohesive national and cross-regional identity. The shared experience of displacement and occupation has forced such cohesion. But merely to attribute the imagining of nationhood to physical displacement and repression would overlook the complex interfacing among antecedent cultural, political, and religious resources and the modernist nationalist impulse toward cultural standardization.

As in the case of Israeli and Palestinian nationalisms, the influence of the discourse of nationalism with its homogenizing impulse is pervasive and multidimensional in the broader Tibetan context. Tibetans, like Palestinians, are subject to multiple levels of stereotyping and thus to sets of cultural licenses authorizing socioeconomic and political domination. While Zionism is a much more complex phenomenon than mere colonialism, this movement (upon its varieties) cannot be analyzed without accounting for orientalism and Western colonialism. Euro-Zionists internalized those discourses, as is evident in their presumption that the land of Palestine was a "land without people for a People without a land," as the Zionist slogan proclaimed. Likewise, the Eurocentricity of the Zionist movement (later enshrined in the Israeli self-conception as constituting a part of the "West") authorized discrimination against non-European Jews as well as non-Jews. In a similar way, the case of imagining a distinct Tibetan culture (the subject of protection under a universal discourse of nation-statehood qua human right) needs to be analyzed within the complexity of Sino-centrism as well as the theosophist gaze. The modes of imagining Tibet and Tibetan-ness by Tibetans take place within and in counter-distinction from the (Han) Chinese imagining and representation of Tibet and the cultural stereotyping that have authorized Chinese policies. Despite the wide-ranging ethnic diversity within China, the ruling Communist Party projects Han as constituting the parameters of authentic and normative Chinese-ness. The criteria by which various populations are classified as "Han" are flexible, allowing for standardization of language and customs and the construal of "a fictional homogenous unity," as noted by one scholar of East Asian politics.[65] Tibetans constitute only one of the (approximately fifty-five) non-Han minorities in China, a normatively stratified landscape where ethnic diversity is allowed if subsumed within the logic of cultural hegemony: not unlike the civilizational mission legitimizing French colonialism, Chinese domination accommodates the possibility of cultural evolution and assimilation through overcoming "backward" cultural practices and norms and embracing the "superior" practices and norms characteristic of Han Chinese society. Imperial China's traditional perception of its cultural superiority and universal scope and mission regarded other inhabitants of China as "barbarians."[66] Han Chinese perception of superiority and stereotyping of non-Han groups as animalistic are deeply embedded within Confucian notions concerning social hierarchy,[67] once again demonstrating the relevance of analyzing how religion interlaces with cultural, political, and structural forms of violence in order to think constructively about the role of religion in transforming such sociocultural and political formations. In the same way in which the discursive investigation of Euro-American perceptions and attitudes about Palestine/Israel requires analysis of the co-imbrication of orientalist, colonial, and Judeo-Christian discourses, so does the study of Chinese imperialism and patterns of interactions with various non-Han communities entail an analysis of Confucian underpinnings and their enduring influences in authorizing violent destructive practices against the non-Han others. In this context of cultural and political domination, rescuing Tibetan-ness entailed a form of strategic essentialism, turning an internally diverse group into a "cause," comparable to other national causes and thus consistent with a discourse of universal rights.

The homogenization and cultural codification enabled the transformation of Tibet from geography to utopian topography as a corollary of the nation-making process, a process of self-creation (self-determination). But this imagining of Tibetan-ness is embedded in broader symbolic fields saturated with orientalist projections and appropriations. The upshot of this symbolization, as the critics claim, might amount to the diminishment of the concrete experiences of Tibetans. In a similar way, the symbolization of Palestine as a utopia in Islamist rhetoric may resonate with the moral topography of direct and indirect Palestinian diasporas, but it also altogether functions to reify Palestinian-ness while emptying this signifier of its embedded concreteness. Yet Palestinian national identity is, in effect, an elastic construct, contested on multiple fronts, in Palestine and its multivalent diasporas.[68] The patterns of symbolization and de-concretization, therefore, illuminate the interconnectedness between national and transnational discourses. Hence, pointing out the pertinence of discursive formations does not deny the agency or actuality of Tibetans or Palestinians; rather, it illuminates the impossibility of distilling subjectivity. It is implausible, that is, to assume that recovering selfhood is unencumbered by the intricacies of intersubjectivity and the intersection of discursive fields.

Certainly, the kind of internalization and appropriation of Tibetan-ness in the image of Western fantasies is instructive, in that Tibet as a utopia may deflate the effectiveness of Tibet as a movement for national self-determination and cultural survival. While the utopianization of Palestine within various Palestine solidarity groups is not the same as the utopianization of Tibet by the Free Tibet movement (with its theosophist motifs[69]) and by Tibetan exiles themselves, both cases illuminate the importance of further scrutinizing the role of solidarity by situating solidarities within their discursive formations, probing into the connections between their religio-cultural underpinnings and their fantasies, their agendas, their frustrations, and their all-too-local concerns. It is also critical to locate the dynamic synergies between direct, indirect, and symbolic diaspora nationalisms. In other words, without framing them as mere reactionary outcomes of colonial realities, both Palestinian and Tibetan identities are deeply shaped by hegemonic and ahistoricizing orientalist representations and fantasies as well as by the homogenizing logic of the discourse of modern nationalism. This second discursive similarity between the cases of Palestine and Tibet, with its typical homogenizing impulse, is intricately related to the transformation of home from geopolitical destination to a utopia and/or a moral imperative.

Yet, as I anticipated in my critique of realist and essentialist analytic lenses, any comparative analysis of the utopianization of Palestine and Tibet has to account for the comparative imagining and representation of Zion/Israel and China and how their respective nationalist agendas might fit into the sociocultural, religious, and national positionality of those who stand in solidarity with or in opposition to them. In the case of Palestine, the national discourse is amplified by Zionist colonial practices authorized in part by a particular narration of Jewish history and religious claims as well as by the Jewish experience of the Shoah (the Holocaust) and anti-Semitism more broadly. In the case of Tibet, its struggle emerges in a context of Sino-centrism, which shares affinities with traditional Confucian notions of social hierarchy that presume the cultural inferiority of Tibetans and thus their subordinate and yet integral position within the Han-dominated ethnic mosaic that constitutes Greater China. This cultural datum informs the Chinese commitment to a territorial maximalist vision of China, of which Tibet is an integral part. An independent Tibet, in this context, amounts to a violation of the territorial integrity of a multinational China. In defending this position, the Chinese leadership relies on a particular Sino/Han-centric reading of history that delegitimizes Tibetan claims and aspirations for cultural, socioeconomic, and geopolitical autonomy. Going back to the Tang dynasty in the seventh century, the marriage of the Chinese princess Wen Chang and Songzain Gambo, the ruler of Tibet at the time, is marked as a crucial chapter in the story of integrating Tibet into the Middle Kingdom. The official Chinese chronicles attribute to Wen Chang the introduction of Buddhism to Tibet. This as well as the China-Tibet treaty of 821 represent examples of an ethnocentric and selective reading of history deeply challenged and countered by Tibetan perceptions of the same historical events. Tibetans read the treaty as designed to secure territorial integrity rather than to validate their incorporation into Greater China. It was only under the Mongolian Khans (thirteenth and fourteenth centuries) that Tibet became a military protectorate of China in return for spiritual autonomy under the newly minted institution of the Dalai Lama. While within the Tibetan self-perception, Tibet continuously remained distinct from China, official Chinese narratives deny this perception and incorporate Tibet and Tibetans into a broader Chinese landscape. The argument from history is then compounded with a perception that Chinese rule has "enlightened" a backward Tibet—here one can identify the elective affinities between Maoist-Leninist socio-historical evolutionary outlooks and traditional prejudices against Tibetans as they have been enabled by Confucian motifs and practices. The Communist occupation of Tibet in the 1950s thus supposedly amounted to the liberation of Tibetans from their captivity in feudalism and an otherwise barbaric existence. In addition to drawing on these historical and cultural justifications of the Chinese occupation of Tibet, Chinese officials have worked systematically to discredit the Dalai Lama and portray any support of Tibetan activism as interference in internal Chinese affairs.[70] What this brief overview suggests is that nationalism understood as a right to cultural and ethnic protection contradicts the traditional logic of Han ethnocentrism with its embrace of a deeply stratified multinational society that rejects, by definition, secessionist ethno-national causes. While Tibet is the sacred home of Tibetans, the object of their aspiration for self-determination, for official China, what is sacred is the territorial integrity of Greater China, a commitment profoundly rooted in and authorized by Han-centrism. China's control of Tibet is naturalized through historical arguments and normatively justified by way of asserting cultural superiority. On one level, the occupation of Palestinian territories by Jewish Israelis reflects, as already alluded to, a comparable interrelation between (Jewish) ethnocentricity and the broader legitimating discourses of orientalism and colonialism. On the other hand, the meanings of Zion within the Jewish theological and cultural imaginations represent a significant difference in terms of the four-way comparison between Tibet/Palestine and China/Israel. Since the time of diasporic dispersal associated with the biblical narratives, Zion has been "home" and "destination" regardless of whether "home" means geopolitical hegemony. In fact, for most of Jewish history, such an interpretation of return was considered blasphemous, and Zion represented a utopia a no-place outside historical time and requiring divine initiation. Tibet, in contrast, is "destination" only insofar as Chinese control over it reaffirms the territorial maximalist view of China authorized by Han-centrism, Confucian underpinnings, and affinities with communists' evolutionary outlooks of human progress. I highlight these broad distinctions in order to illuminate both the relevance of religio-cultural imaginations in authorizing various political projects (including the Chinese one) and the relevance of such imaginings to the formation of solidarities with various national causes.

Palestine and Israel readily became moral destinations and normative symbolic topographies for diverse groups, such as non-Israeli Jews; non-Palestinian Islamists; Christian Zionists; college-educated, urban professionals; non-Muslims; non-Palestinian Boycott, Divestment, Sanctions (BDS) activists; and, of course, Palestinians and Israelis, too. Which of the causes of Israel or Palestine qua utopia do these groups take on as their moral destinations? A response to this question is not necessarily defined by ethnic or religious links. In fact, Jews whose commitment to human rights discourses overwhelms their devotion to Zionism may end up participating, as I show below, in the kind of symbolic or discursive silencing associated with various Palestine solidarities—this is the case despite their critiques of the discourses informing injustice toward the Palestinians. As noted, Islamist and non-Islamist Palestine solidarity constitute a reactionary counter-discourse about Israel. While the predominant rhetoric of Western Palestine solidarity consciously anticipates the accusation of anti-Semitism,[71] its simultaneous diminishment of the Jewish meanings of Israel functions in a fashion similar to Islamist rhetoric.

The multivalent symbolic force of the Israeli-Palestinian conflict, however, extends beyond explicit solidarities. The various sides and causes of the conflict are appropriated in numerous fronts—from Northern Ireland, where Protestants hang "shalom" signs at the thresholds of their homes, to India, where Hindu nationalists fight against "*their* Muslims," to the framing of Kosovo as "*our* Jerusalem" by Serb nationalists.[72] Why is the case of Israel/Palestine unique in generating such diverse and polarizing symbolic significances?

While Tibet's statelessness strongly resonates in the popular imagination, its symbolic scope and applicability are significantly less expansive. The discursive interfacing of Tibetan activism with the kind of "good" orientalism that informs the Free Tibet activism of Hollywood celebrities and other sympathizers has not resulted in significant policy shifts or transformation of the Tibetan predicament. The weak transformative effectiveness of this movement, despite its occasional shiny spokesperson and its embodiment in the Dalai Lama, may be a testament to the pragmatic decision to assume a nonconfrontational attitude toward the increasingly formidable Chinese super-power. The liberation of Tibet is desirable, but not at any cost. Clearly, China is not Israel.

First, China is not Israel in that its own fixation with Tibet is so deeply culture-specific and does not necessarily intersect with other cultural or religious currents that could then generate patterns of solidarity comparable to the kinds the Zionist project has spawned. Second, China's history in relation to Tibet has not included episodes of near annihilation and existential threats. To this extent, the struggle of Tibetans resembles historical Jewish uprootedness. After all, as noted, the Jewish diasporic narrative offers a historical as well as theoretical paradigm or ideal type for explaining the diasporic experience in relation to home qua territory and utopia. This point about the parallels between Tibetan and Jewish longings for their respective homes exposes the added complexity of the Israel/Palestine case. There is no "Chinese Holocaust" to add to the equation. Indeed, the Japanese war crimes during World War II are often referred to as the "forgotten Holocaust," and the Chinese populations endured unspeakable atrocities. However, this experience is not centrally relevant to the

Chinese occupation of Tibet. Nor was the brutal systematic killing during the era of Japanese imperialism related to scientific racism aided by some parallel to the centuries of classical anti-Semitism intricately woven into the very fabric of cultural formations in Christian contexts. And yet conflicts in both arenas—the Middle East and Asia—are deeply related to the legacies of Western colonialism. The emergence of Japanese imperialism is often explained as a reaction to and emulation of Western colonialism and one authorized by a conception of national chosen-ness and cultural prestige. As one Japanese leader wrote in 1882, "We shall someday raise the national power of Japan so that not only shall we control the natives of China and India as the English do today, but we shall also possess in our hands the power to rebuke the English and to rule Asia ourselves."[73] This legacy and the forgotten Holocaust surely influence Chinese resistance to Western impositions concerning the Tibetan case. But while various cultural undercurrents affirm the sanctity of Greater China, Tibet is not definitional to (Han) Chinese identity in the same way that Zion is for Jews. Third, China is not Israel in that inter-religio-cultural affinities do not cloud geopolitical global considerations and political judgments. The U.S. does not like human rights violations in China, but it is more than willing to overlook those. Of course, it also overlooks and/or is complicit with Israel's persistent construction of settlements in the Palestinian territories occupied in 1967. This oversight along with the broader support of Israeli agendas, however, realist political analysts claim, work against the United States' best geopolitical interests.

Of course, there are always the considerations of *realpolitik*. To return to my critique of the thesis of *The Israel Lobby*, the reason behind the relatively weak effectiveness of Palestine solidarity is not merely pragmatic geopolitical factors (a complication that puzzles realists such as Walt and Mearsheimer), but also a comparably strong normative and deeply engrained commitment to Israel and its Jewishness on the part of Jewish Americans and their well-placed Gentile supporters. While the charges of colonialism and apartheid are applicable to Israeli policies, Israeli "colonialism" is distinct, in that it also represents the fulfillment of a Jewish return "home." Likewise, it constitutes the normative antidote to the horrors of Nazism. For Jews in Israel, unlike the Chinese colonialists in Tibet, simply going "back home," as Thomas suggested, is a violent proposition. While the violent implications of Islamist rhetoric may be explicit in their conflation of anti-Jewish and anti-Zionist antagonisms and their appropriation of anti-Semitic motifs, the violence of self-proclaimed activists for peace and Palestine solidarity may be much more subtle.[74] Enumerating above the distinctions between Chinese and Jewish-Israeli occupations of Tibet and Palestine, respectively, already suggests that simply rendering Zionism as a "colonial" or "apartheid" project offers a partial explanatory frame that overlooks or silences critical cultural, historical, and religious dimensions pertaining to the analysis and transformation of the Israeli-Palestinian conflict.

Obviously, the fact that various interested colonial players, like Lord Arthur Balfour, were in the habit of handing out land for settlement is indebted to orientalist and colonialist discourses.[75] That Palestine, within the colonial imagination, was perceived as being out there, seemingly frozen in biblical time (as British travelers often portrayed it), served to exoticize and idealize its inhabitants.[76] And those images were also further projected by the Euro-Zionists who came "home" to recover a lost self-sufficiency epitomized in the natives. This leitmotif was later trans-valued, in that, within Zionist mythology, Palestinians turned into strangers to the land—morally questionable, primitive, and fitting other pejorative orientalist attributes[77] that are not unlike the Sino-centric stereotyping and representations of

Tibetans. On the other hand, it was the orientalist framework that also enabled the Zionist colonization of this land, a process not unrelated to the emergence of the aforementioned Christian Zionist lobbying within the colonial landscapes. The ahistorical projection of Zion/Palestine facilitated the reframing of religious longings as "historical" claims for return to the landscape of the Tanach. The land was supposedly left untouched by millennia of indigenous life. This fed the infamous Zionist slogan that Palestine was "a land without people, for a people without a land." Clearly, the rhetorical (and reactionary) symbolization of Palestine as a utopia (as in the Islamist and occasional Arab framing of solidarity with Palestine) or even the supposedly normatively neutral pursuit of Palestine as a moral destination (Thomas, for example) depends on a careful analysis of Israel qua utopia. As in the cases of Tibet and Palestine, imagining utopia is also intricately interwoven with the homogenizing impulse of nationalism.

Problems in Utopia and the Trans-Locality of Pluralizing Diasporas

The Zionist project—a Eurocentric, Ashkenazi one—has imagined Jewish national identity as secular, Western, enlightened, and cultured. This was set in contrast to the situation of Arab Jews (and indigenous Palestinian Arabs), while nonetheless co-opting Mizrahi histories into a grand narrative of expulsion, persecution, and "negation of exile." Millennia of Jewish learning and existence in the diasporas were rendered irrelevant by this homogenizing narrative.[78] Still, the ethos of the negation of exile proved inherently and increasingly contradictory to the desire to cultivate Israel as a Jewish majoritarian democratic nation-state. Nonetheless, Zionism has entailed a universalizing and homogenizing historiography. Accordingly, the Jewish people has been imagined as one body with various tentacles, suspended in empty diasporic time and awaiting a return to and ingathering in the land. This narrative of return betrays a contestable political theology, even if Jewish identity has been dominantly framed as secular, historical, ethnic, and cultural rather than religious. The fact that Zionism qua secular nationalism relied on traditional Jewish conceptions of the messianic era points to what Max Weber correctly observed as the "elective affinity" among signifiers such as ethnicity, nationality, religion, and culture. The affinity among these signifiers is elastic, selective, and multidirectional.[79]

Therefore, the conceptual basis of the fourth type of pluralizing diaspora as a potential site for contesting national teleologies and their violent implications is the view of identity as continuously constructed and contested, despite efforts to project it as a natural unchanged essence.[80] Such nationalist framing that imagines homogeneity in the face of plurality commits violence, internally as well as externally. Sometimes this violence is direct, as in the case of the repression of the Palestinians, but it is also cultural and symbolic in that Zionist historiography has homogenized and universalized thoroughly plural Jewish communities and experiences. But while internal pluralities were glossed over for the sake of unification projects, they could not be imagined away. Additionally, the homogenizing logic and infrastructures of nationalism generate novel hybrid identities that can offer further embodied critique and reframing of national belonging.[81] But this kind of pluralizing is more likely to occur in contexts where the quest for national self-determination is already settled.

"Home" as utopia is indeed a central feature of traditional Jewish conceptions of return to the land of Zion. The secular Zionist movement transformed meta-historical and messianic longings into a historical and human-initiated project. Of course, there were "problems in utopia." To begin with, there were other people there. There was also the aforementioned marginalization of groups that did not fit the projected homogenizing national historiography. It is from within those marginalized spaces that the critique and reimagining of national belonging can emerge by first exposing and denaturalizing cultural and symbolic forms of violence. Notably, cultural counter-currents within the mosaic of Israeli society reclaim their lost and negated homes in Iraq, Iran, North Africa, and other locations in the "Orient" through the embrace of music, languages, folkloristic practices, and even pilgrimages (within the possibilities afforded by tense geopolitics). This process of cultural reclaiming denaturalizes a Zionist teleology with its characteristic Eurocentricity and with its definitional (even if ambiguous) ethos of the negation of exile. In the process of critique, Israeli society itself turns into the diasporic context within which Mizrahi Jews reside. Mizrahi voices, in other words, constitute a form of pluralizing diaspora in that they denaturalize what may appear axiomatic within the homogenizing and nationalist discourses of home.[82]

The America-based Jewish Voice for Peace provides another prominent example of a pluralizing diaspora. Particularly pertinent is the articulation of its platform by political and cultural theorist Judith Butler, who challenges the supposed union of the Jewish people and the universalizing scope of Zionist historiography and teleology. She does so through a rereading of non-nationalist Jewish thinkers such as Hannah Arendt and Walter Benjamin and their non-teleological conceptualization of Jewish history and identity, and through echoing some postcolonial Israeli critics of Zionist historiography (some of whom are closely associated with the Mizrahi critique mentioned earlier).

Butler and other Jewish activists and thinkers challenge the framing of Israel as the focus of Jewish devotion and the telos of Jewish history. They argue that the overwhelming logic of Zionism marginalized other Jewish responses to modernity. They resist the emptying of their own embedded realities in the name of a cause that is not their own.[83] Butler consequently argues that "a diasporic frame may be crucial for the theorization of cohabitation and binationalism" and that such geopolitical rearrangements cannot come to fruition on the back of continuous "colonial subjugation."[84] Butler's view of ethics as relationality, therefore, leads her to conclude that political Zionism needs to be dismantled as a precondition for ethical cohabitation. In other words, the resources for ethical reframing cannot be found exclusively within Judaism because an exclusive reliance on Jewish resources will reinforce the kind of chauvinistic privileging that needs to be overcome. Hence, she illuminates how her own valorization of the diasporic and alterity resonates with Edward Said's late-in-life illumination of the experience of uprootedness and dispersal as a moral foundation for a potential reframing of the Israeli-Palestinian conflict.[85] "Relationality," Butler explains, "displaces ontology," and this displacement constitutes the condition for justice.[86] It is only through relationality, a form of "ethical self-departure," that ontological claims to identity can be contested.[87] But contesting or "interrupting" identity, Butler underscores, "is not the same as self-annihilation."[88]

In a different vein, the teleological and hegemonic Zionization of Jewishness led American public intellectual Peter Beinart to declare that the forceful drive of the Jewish establishment to ensure that American Jews "check their liberalism at Zionism's door" gave way to a situation in which "many young Jews have checked their Zionism instead."[89] Beinart illuminates, on the basis of sociological studies, that young Jews increasingly feel a profound sense of dissonance between their liberalism and Israeli policies and wish to dissociate themselves from a seemingly simplistic victim mentality that often has undergirded the all-powerful trump card of the "security argument." This supposed attempt to find consistency between liberalism and Zionism is not novel. In fact, it often amounts to normalizing the 1948 boundaries of a Jewish-Israeli nation-state, through an exclusive focus on the 1967 Occupation as an aberration of the original intent of the Jewish home and social experiment. Despite the supposedly high moral ground of Jewish-Zionist critics of Israel and of an American Jewish community's traditional blindness to Israeli illiberal practices, such critics' commitment to liberal Zionism avoids challenging the universalizing scope of Zionist teleology and the enduring commitment to Jewish majoritarianism (within a two-state constellation, usually).[90]

On the other hand, the aforementioned critique that draws on non-nationalistic Jewish ethical traditions challenges the conflation of Judaism, Israeliness, and Zionism. This kind of contesting typifies what I mean by "pluralizing diaspora." In my analysis, therefore, I move beyond a Weberian focus on the institution of the "modern state" as the geopolitical locus for the contestations of national identities and claims of entitlement. In providing the typology of diaspora nationalisms, I show that the interpretive elasticity of the perceived boundaries of the nation is multi- and trans-local. The diaspora does not constitute the exclusive place where critique can happen. Nor does diaspora necessarily denote de-territoriality, since a sense of estrangement from "home" is as much cultural, religious, and socioeconomic as it is geographical. Therefore, diaspora may be especially but not exclusively inclined to the tasks of reframing ethno-religious national ideological formations with their homogenizing tendencies.[91]

But to be effective, reframing national claims through a hermeneutical process requires overcoming both internal and external essentializing and symbolizing of national causes and identities. This kind of reframing means different things in different cases. In the case of the Jewish diaspora, it would amount to pluralizing and contesting homogenizing and hegemonic national narratives in order to dissociate supposedly unified Jewish imperatives and interests from specific Israeli policies.

The quest for an elusive consistency between liberalism and Zionism may denote a limited range in the kind of solidarities non-Israeli Jews harbor toward Israel. This range is limited owing to the elusiveness of liberal Zionism and the unproblematized framing of Israel as a "Jewish home" or "home for the Jews." What similarly remains unproblematized are the calls for cohabitation within Palestine/Israel as a unitary space. The retrieval of non-nationalistic Jewish ethical traditions brackets out a philosophical and theo-political engagement with land and communal passions. An inherent distaste for collective passions or "love" (to allude to Arendt's famous rejection of the "love of Israel")[92] theorizes those attachments out of existence. Such theorizing, despite its pluralizing effectiveness, may also participate in the dynamics of mutual silencing. While challenging the homogenization of Zionist teleology, non-nationalist imagining of ethical cohabitation in Palestine/Israel counter it by revalorizing the diasporic, being without a land and estranged, as the most authentic Jewish condition. This maneuver ahistoricizes Jewish-Israeliness as a focus of authentic, even if contested and elastic, collective commitment. In theorizing nationalism out of existence in a way that recognizes no significant difference between Jewish cohabitation within political spaces in Israel or Switzerland, this type of pluralizing diaspora offers no specific currency for conflict transformation beyond its deconstructive challenge to the Zionization of Jewish identity.[93] Certainly, like Helen Thomas's call for Jews to "get the hell out of Palestine," this deconstructive lens would, from the perspective of Jewish Israelis, amount to an erasure of their authenticity. Interrupting ontology, despite protestations to the contrary, does translate into "self-annihilation." As such, Butler's call to "dismantle political Zionism" loses its ethical and transformative force. It merely partakes in patterns of mutual silencing.

In explicating the theological and philosophical aspects of the tension between Judaism and Zionism, historians of religion Daniel and Jonathan Boyarin re-situate the discussion within the classical dialectic between Paul and the rabbis. On the one hand is Paul's dualism of body and spirit, with its devaluation of flesh and universalizing impulses. On the other, the rabbinic emphasis on the centrality of peoplehood is "a necessary critique of Paul, for if the Pauline move had within it the possibility of breaking out of the tribal allegiances and commitments to one's own family, as it were, it also contains the seeds of an imperialist and colonizing missionary practice."[94]

The Boyarins offer a penetrating comparative critique of how Christianity plus power produced empire and Judaism plus power produced fascism. The latter embodied in the ideology of modern Zionism subverted the rabbinic reinterpreting of space as a meta-historical destination and the rabbinic invention of the "diaspora" as fundamental for and constitutive of Jewish identity. In doing so, the Boyarins not only become, like so many other critics of Zionism, complicit with the enduring Pauline logic. They also reintroduce the rabbinic-Pauline tension to problematize the forceful inclination of conventional critics of Israeli policies to dissolve peoplehood and land through a reliance on universalizing discourses. They write that, where Christianity is the hegemonic power in Europe and the United States, "the resistance of Jews to being universalized can be a critical force and model for the resistance of all peoples to being Europeanized out of a particular bodily existence." Yet when Judaism constitutes the hegemonic force, as in Israel, "it becomes absolutely, vitally necessary to accept Paul's critical challenge—although not his universalizing, disembodying solution—and to develop an equally passionate concern for all human beings."[95] Critically, accepting the Pauline challenge does not amount to dissolving genealogy to fulfill universality; this universality is, of course, deeply ethnocentric itself.

The Boyarins, then, return to the rabbinic valorization of diaspora as the key space for a synthesis "that will allow for stubborn hanging on to ethnic, cultural specificity but in the context of deeply felt and enacted human solidarity." Hence, while retaining the notion of peoplehood that other Jewish critics of Zionism eschew, the Boyarins' framing of diaspora qua utopia (where Jews could take care of their own without it being interpreted as hegemony) still does not provide hermeneutical tools for rethinking Jewish-Israeliness within its historical specificity.

Indeed, for the Boyarins, the culprit in Zionism as a perversion of Judaism is not the supposedly inherent "racism" of Judaism, but rather the myth of autochthony inherent in the nationalist discourse. But as critics of the discourse of multiculturalism have noted, even the valorization of the diasporic condition within a context of multi-nationality will always be constrained by cultural, social, political, and linguistic boundaries. In other words, the political proposal implicit in the Boyarins' thesis is a veiled multicultural liberalism that domesticates and depoliticizes religion, a discourse deeply steeped in a Christocentric conceptualization of religion and secularity. When one reflects on the comparative case of Tibet/China, one acknowledges, as I have, that nationalism in its narrower sense as the protection of a particular culture within the infrastructure of a political state, or as the exercise of "self-determination"—one that presumes a particular "self"—is highly pivotal in the struggle of Tibetans against Chinese domination. This narrow and culture-specific discourse of nationalism stands in contrast to the multinational stratified Han-centric conception of Chinese society, where Tibetans have been assimilated in a subordinated position into the broader stratified cultural and ethnic landscape. When viewed this way, the discourse of modern nationalism constitutes an empowering currency (even while engaging in strategic essentializing) rather than a form of sociopolitical perversion. The path for transforming exclusionary and chauvinistic perceptions of the nation does not traverse through an intellectualist overcoming of collective passions and attachments, embodied in the conception of the diasporic as "post-national," but rather through denaturalizing and reinterpreting such passions. This process necessitates an analysis of how religion relates to cultural, social, and political practices and beliefs, assessing those from a multi-perspectival lens attentive to inter- and intra-cultural discursive topographies.

Symbolization

The symbolization of national causes takes place in multiple arenas. One is the level of nationalization, a process that often involves the standardization, ethnicization, and essentialization of religion and culture. This move is strategic for the purpose of marketing a cause but also reflects an authentic desire for a homogenizing formation and cultural preservation. This is the purview of nationals inside and outside the contested geopolitical frame. When integrating the notion of pluralizing diaspora, the imagining of the meanings and boundaries of national identity becomes not only a territorially based process of introspection, but also one that is substantially trans-local, from subaltern contestations to macro-rethinking of homogenizing narratives. Butler, for one, rejects her automatic inclusion in Jewish-Israeli peoplehood. Mizrahim in Israel potentially reject the Eurocentric normativity of Israeli society. The second level of symbolization occurs in the various interfaces among multi- and trans-local contestations of the discourse of national authenticity, the utopianization of home, and the broader normative landscapes that enable further symbolic abstractions of contested geographies and victims of territorial and ethnocultural displacements.

"Symbolic diaspora nationalism" therefore denotes not only the transformation of "home" into a devotional destination and a totemic expression of one's identity while "abroad" or "dispersed." It also refers to the metaphorical deployment of a national cause (Palestine, Israel, Tibet) as a proxy or symbol for a broader and vaguer kind of liberation: the hope to rectify the humiliation associated with Western colonialism and the dissolution of the Muslim empires, to fulfill an end-time drama, to adopt a counter-hegemonic stance against the forces of neoliberalism, to pursue a New Age spiritual quest, and so forth. It also might denote a diasporic consciousness and a sense of displacement that is not grounded in a direct or indirect physical experience of dislocation or marginalization. The sense of displacement could instead result from an experience of religious alienation in a secular age and the kind of internal de-centering of "religion" that secularist ideologies have entailed.[96] It might also suggest a more "secular" and "humanistic" reaction to neoliberal imperialism. This type of abstraction and symbolization is distinct from, yet interconnected with, the symbolization associated with the multi-local level of nationalization. It is this type of symbolic diaspora nationalism that encompasses solidarity movements whose normative commitment needs to be explicated through cultural, religious, socioeconomic, and national contextualization.

Right Is Not Always Just

The foregrounding of solidarity as the analytic category for explaining diaspora nationalism facilitates a scrutiny of how various national causes fit into broader cultural discourses and why discursive analyses could function as a pivotal dimension of peacebuilding. Solidarity movements and other global networks supporting a "cause" associated with civil or other wars fight on behalf of a group's rights without necessarily claiming any "common origins and cultural attributes." Yet such solidarity movements tend to reify their "cause" and represent a bifurcated account of "rights" and "wrongs," one that may indeed function as "strategic essentialism" but is not necessarily contributing to constructive processes of conflict transformation. The case of the global Palestine solidarity movement exemplifies this problem. In its participation in the cycle of mutual silencing, the human rights talk it deploys to preempt the charge of anti-Judaism is perceived by Israeli and non-Israeli Jews often as a false moral neutrality.[97] This perception invalidates the normative force of self-proclaimed humanitarian interventions by those who stand in solidarity.

As I mentioned earlier, to merely accept Jews qua individuals and Judaism qua faith/religion as Palestine solidarity groups frequently do (i.e., there is nothing personal against Jews in their critique of Israeli policies) is an act of cultural violence.[98] It is violent because it dissolves the centrality of peoplehood and land through the imposition of modern categories, such as reducing religion to interiorized faith, conscience, or culture. However, to recognize the centrality of land within the Jewish imagination, to allude to the Boyarins, does not mean that what that land constitutes is not a hermeneutically contested, elastic construct: one that moves from literal geography to messianic topography. Nor does acknowledging complexities over and against simplistic renderings of Israel as apartheid or colonialist detract from the urgency of resisting the evils associated with Israeli settlement and occupation of Palestine. Hence, in anticipating the argument that conflict transformation would entail breaking the patterns of mutual silencing, I now problematize the role of solidarities as self-appointed agents of peacebuilding. The Helen Thomas episode exemplifies this explosiveness, but it is by no means unique.

In fact, just a few days before the Thomas controversy, Israeli commandoes attacked the flotilla that sailed from Turkey to the shores of Gaza in violation of the Israeli naval blockade—a blockade that had by all accounts exacerbated an already devastating humanitarian crisis in the densely populated strip. This crisis is attributed to Israeli policies and the imposition of collective punishment on Gazans under Hamas leadership. The flotilla mission was engineered by the Free Gaza Movement but involved a wide coalition of interested parties. In reference to the violence that erupted on the *Mavi Marmara*—the main ship of the flotilla and the one that carried a Turkish flag—Chairperson of the Free Gaza Movement Huwaida Arraf admitted the difficulties of maintaining a uniform commitment to nonviolent action while cultivating an intricately complex coalition for advancing the cause of Palestinian liberation.[99] Reports of activists onboard the ships point to a violent Israeli raid that left nine civilians dead. The activists involved with the flotilla framed their undertaking as merely "humanitarian," but radical changes in Turkey's geopolitical involvement point to other possible agendas that may have attracted the heavy Turkish sponsorship of this tragic humanitarian mission.

To point to other agendas does not dismiss the deep moral outrage that the humanitarian crisis in Gaza evokes; rather, it highlights why rallying behind the cause of Palestine may also indicate internal transformations and signal a turn away from Turkey's catering to US geopolitical interests and its desire to integrate into the EU. Still, Turkey's choice to support the Gaza flotilla and vocally react to the Israeli raid against it does not explain why it was the cause of Palestine that signifies Turkey's change of course toward the United States. The bodies of the victims of the Israeli raid were buried in Turkey with great honor and anti-Israeli proclamations; Israeli and American flags were burned in a variety of locations around the world; and more aid ships were dispatched en route to Gaza, with the intention of again broadcasting to the world Israel's moral bankruptcy in the face of a humanitarian initiative to alleviate obvious Palestinian suffering.

But the Gaza flotilla and its aftermath show that this loose coalition of activist groups, which can be classified as a global social movement because of the global critique it puts forward (connecting Israeli policies and oppression of the Palestinians to neoliberal imperialism and enduring political, military, and cultural Western hegemony), needs to interrogate not only global and local structures of injustice enabling the occupation of Palestinian territories, but also its own biases, cultural and political constraints, and motivations, as well as its long-term plans for involvement in peacebuilding processes in the region. Does the campaign for the social, political, cultural, and economic emancipation of the Palestinians also entail the delegitimization and silencing of Jewish and Israeli narratives? If not, why is it so easily framed this way by the flag-burning practices around the world and by someone so liberal and enlightened as Helen Thomas?

On the level of theory, the limits of the movement reside in what is often framed as a "bottom-up approach to global integration." While proponents of this approach are aware of global systemic structural injustices and how they may relate to local identity conflicts, they overlook the relevance of discursive formations and their complex implications for power and culture. One upshot is the tendency to locate the cause of the conflict primarily in neoliberal, globalizing ideologies and institutional instruments, thereby explaining "religion" and "culture" merely as epiphenomenal manifestations of deeper "real" and "material" causes. This oversight is not incidental, but rather indicative of a reductive interpretation of identity within systemic analyses of global structures of injustices.[100] In attempting to move away from neoliberal conventions, the bottom-up orientation privileges other forms of transmission mechanisms, such as a thin conception of human rights as a model for restructuring both locally and globally. As in the case of Thomas's comment, a sense of moral outrage and the deployment of a universal and de-contextualized platform for evaluating "rights" and "wrongs" very quickly become a "conversation stopper."[101] They stop conversation precisely because a rights-centered prism enables the counter-discursive silencing of Jewish narratives, memories, and histories. To recall, my analysis of the pattern of mutual silencing recognizes that various opinions and arguments are not articulated in a neutral public arena. Instead, this "publicity" is imbued by power and is constitutive of sets of cultural sensibilities and assumptions. Helen Thomas's words sought to subvert those assumptions, but in the process of subverting and challenging the enduring orientalist discourse that structures debates about the Middle East, she participated not in a counter-argumentation—a necessary dimension of a healthy contestation—but rather in a counter-silencing discourse and one that inadvertently intersects with anti-Semitism.

Hence, while obviously different from Islamist invocations of Palestine as a utopia, the solidarity movement's rallying behind Palestine as a moral destination is equally violent in the cultural sense, for it dismisses or overlooks historical complexities such as the Holocaust and the enduring yet hermeneutically flexible meanings of land within the Jewish theo-political and messianic imaginations. Critically, global Palestine solidarity movements are intricately interwoven with the discourses of orientalism, colonialism, nationalism, and neoliberalism, as well as the counter-discourses confronting these hegemonic formations. I therefore categorize both Islamist and Western Palestine solidarity as a form of symbolic diaspora nationalism in that Palestine functions as a multivalent symbol, interconnected to broader symbolic and discursive fields. Both forms of symbolization deconcretize Palestine and the geopolitical Palestinian cause in a way akin to the deconcretizing of the Tibetan cause, and both resonate, albeit to varying degrees, with a new appropriation of classical anti-Jewish tropes.

To overcome the cycle of mutual silencing, Palestine solidarity movements would have to recognize how their imagining of Palestine as a normative category substantially relates to Palestine/Israel in its multidimensional cultural and historical intricacies. A failure to do so, as I illustrate in my exposition of Thomas's comments, will prove the movement ineffective in terms of peacebuilding. Symbolizing and rhetorically transforming a national cause from geopolitics to utopianism violently dismisses those whose embodied experiences do not fit a homogenizing construal of authentic identity (Tibetans from Tibet, Mizrahim in Israel). This constitutes a moralistic one-sidedness or unidirectional and mono-perspectival perception of destiny (e.g., national or supra-national historiographies, in the cases of Zionist teleology and Islamist rhetoric, respectively). It also dismisses those whose physical presence and historical experiences do not accord with ideological commitments and presumed historical necessities (Christian Palestinians, for instance).

It is in these discursive contexts that solidarity movements could become culprits in the cycles of mutual silencing, even while carrying badges of courage (sometimes martyrdom) for their pursuit of justice under fire. To think constructively about transforming the unproductive mutual silencing that marks the Israeli-Palestinian conflict, it is therefore important to expose the discursive topography in which it is located. Assigning significance to Western fantasies, orientalism, and the theo-political imagination does not entail reducing Tibetan-ness, Palestinian-ness, or Jewish-Israeliness to those discursive forces. Instead, what is at stake is a much more complex exploration of the interfaces among moral topographies and geopolitical projects and agendas in order to constructively interrupt ontological claims by recognizing relationality or a multi-perspectival theorizing of justice. While not unique in its dynamics of symbolization, the case of Israel-Palestine offers an especially apt illustration of this point, primarily because it consistently evokes disparate normative orientations that, in their patterns of mutual silencing, fail to build peace and transform conflict. The comparative discussion of China vis-à-vis Tibet brings to the fore not the inherent uniqueness of the Israel/Palestine case but the limits of the comparison between China and Israel, the two oppressors in the respective stories of Palestinians and Tibetans' victimization and nation-statelessness. Those limits relate to the comparability between the Tibetan and Jewish longing for their respective "homes" in addition to the absence of a narrative of Chinese victimization akin to centuries of anti-Semitism. Furthermore, the limits of comparability between the cases relate to the cultural affinities among Western "Judeo-Christian" sensibilities and Zionism as well as to the projection of Israel as an outpost of the "West" in the "East," a self-perception very much embedded within the orientalism inherent in Euro-Zionism. These are the kind of cultural "stuff" that delimits the scope of public debate about Israel/Palestine. In the Chinese case, the non-negotiability of Tibet and the integrity of Greater China more broadly relates to a reaffirmation of Sino-centrism, and thus Chinese officials view any form of activism to free Tibet as meddling in its internal affairs and as instances of Western imperialism, which resonates strongly also with the experience of the Chinese Holocaust in the era of Japanese imperialism. The broad point behind the complex comparative undertaking here is to show the complex intersections between local and global discursive formations and geopolitical projects. More specifically, the comparative effort demonstrates that simply framing Israel as a colonial villain and calling upon Jews to return home constitute a reactionary counter-discourse whose cultural underpinnings deserve scrutiny. Recognizing the dynamic of discourse and counter-discourse not only stresses the centrality of cultural formations, but also suggests potential constructive interventions in efforts to transform the unproductive interlocking associated with mutual silencing.

III. Breaking the Silences

Diasporas, Conflicts, and Peacebuilding

Diasporas in Conflict: Peace-Makers or Peace-Wreckers?, edited by Hazel Smith and Paul Stares, constitutes a nascent attempt to connect the study of diasporas, a field that emerged in full force in the 1990s, to the study of conflict and peace.[102] The conceptual orientation of this edited volume privileges the conventional focus of political science on power and how, in the words of one of the editors, "the nature of diaspora interventions in conflict is a result of the respective power relations within diasporas and between diaspora, home and host country." A reluctance or inability to intervene in the dynamics of conflict and peacebuilding, therefore, simply indicates a seemingly obvious insight in political science: "Diasporas without access to power of some sort, whether direct or surrogate, do not intervene in conflicts."[103] This general point echoes other authors' attempts to deploy the explanatory paradigm of historical materialism as a frame for the analysis of diaspora activism.[104]

On the basis of the book's diverse empirical studies of diasporas' interventions in conflicts and peacebuilding efforts, one editor concludes that the question of whether diasporas would be inclined to play positive or negative roles or neither in the so-called "conflict cycle paradigm" would depend on their ability to exercise agency as well as on structural conditions that shape transnational opportunities.[105]

What this form of analysis does is contextualize the agency of individual diasporas within broader historical and structural conditions. Moving beyond and supplementing this political scientific focus, my study of diasporas as they relate to homeland conflicts further embeds this structural analysis in its sociocultural and discursive underpinnings. This broader analysis seeks to explain why certain solidarities emerge and contribute to escalating or transforming national agendas and conflicts, and what kind of resources may be available for reframing belligerent and chauvinistic agendas.

The specialized scholarship on diaspora activism certainly recognizes the influences of diasporas, as nonstate actors, upon the dynamics of "homeland" conflicts. It further acknowledges the heterogeneity of these diasporas and their fluctuating divergences from the objectives and agendas of communities in the homeland.[106] But the mere recognition of a hybrid subjectivity does not preclude the need to explore how and why cultural and national conceptions of membership change. It is, therefore, crucial to connect the study of diasporas to discussions of migration, multiculturalism, and nationalism as well as to broad analyses of the discourses and legacies informing international politics, including orientalism, colonialism, and neoliberalism. Engaging in such a multidimensional and contextually embedded analysis could offer descriptive observations of when, how, and whether diasporas effectively influence the course of a conflict in their homelands. It also provides constructive angles to think of why and when diasporas could positively influence the dynamics of conflict by constructively challenging homogenizing interpretations of national claims and narratives as well as broader discursive formations. The scrutiny of discursive formation integrates into the discussion of diasporas and conflict consideration not only direct forms of violence and how they might be enabled by broader and transnational geopolitical considerations and forces, but also how local conflicts relate to broader symbolic and cultural forms of violence and how might they inform cycles of mutual silencing.

Hence, while the focus on the role of de-territorialized national and ethnic groups in the dynamics of conflict and peace is valuable, this focus is too confining to be an explanatory framework. It contributes to a conceptual separation of the solidarity activism of direct and indirect diasporas from other forms of solidarities that likewise contribute to escalation and de-escalation. Instead, I connect the study of direct and indirect diasporas to the study of symbolic diasporas (that rhetorically deploy a national cause as a symbol of redemption from broader ills such as colonialism, neoliberalism, and cultural imperialism) by showing how the elusive concept of "home" is normative as much as it is geopolitical and that this normativity underpins complex and interrelated ideological landscapes of activists and interested parties. This line of analysis calls attention to how the industry of peacebuilding, including humanitarian and nongovernmental aid organizations, might be implicated in the counterproductive dynamics of mutual silencing.[107]

Conclusion: Breaking Silences as a Peacebuilding Process

My intention in this exposition was to foreground discourse analysis in order to scrutinize, and potentially overcome, the dynamics of mutual silencing. The challenge to the rigidity of Westphalian lines cannot be limited to the presumption of synonymy between nation and state; it must also recognize that the contestation of the subjective boundaries of nationhood constitutes a multi-local engagement, involving diasporas in their expansive and overlapping meanings as direct, indirect, symbolic, and pluralizing.

As my analysis of China/Tibet and Israel/Palestine and the various patterns of solidarity and stereotyping they provoke or instrumentalize illustrates, religion enters this discussion as it interrelates with other facets of identity. Simplistically compartmentalizing religion as faith precludes the complex relations of religion to national identities and transnational cultural affinities. It also delimits the scope of religion's potential positive engagement with conflict transformation to "faith diplomacy" and "interfaith dialogue." While religious peacebuilding in these mediums can be constructive, it risks evading a scrutiny of how the selective retrieval of religio-cultural attitudes, symbols, motifs, and conceptions of person-hood and agency is interlaced with the dominant discourses in international relations and how they still lurk even behind secular political projects.[108] Such scrutiny would then be supplemented by a constructive reimagining of cultural, national, and transnational affini-ties, a broad process that will include religious and nonreligious actors. The point is that the kind of scrutiny afforded by a discourse analysis pushes beyond the homogenizing and essentializing tendencies of national rhetoric, enabling a process of rethinking I associate with a pluralizing diaspora.

The focus on discursive analysis in order to decipher how and why cultural and religious affinities influence geopolitical decisions coheres with and complements recent attempts to theorize peacebuilding as a "strategic," comprehensive, and multidimensional process. The aim of scrutinizing and transforming mutual silencing through the interrogation of interconnected discursive fields is oriented by and expands upon the composite concept of *justpeace*,[109] which entails the transformation of conflicts as a process that moves beyond the confines of "liberal peace" toward the approximation of justice and just relations.[110] This transformative aim needs to take into account not only local cultural forces, inter-ests, and grievances influencing the course of the conflict, but also those interested global and trans-local agendas and cultural affinities that likewise participate in the dynamics of conflict. While the meaning of justpeace is always contextually contested in conflict zones defined by ethno-religious national claims, it also conveys a strong normative stance that could radically challenge the ethos and narratives of identity groups, locked in seemingly intractable conflicts. However, interrupting ontological claims is merely silencing if its pre-condition is a total dismantling of such claims. This approach seems to confuse an aspira-tional ethical destination with the processes needed to approximate it.

In other words, deploying a normative orientation that is thoroughly relational and multi-perspectival does not mean dismissing the lived authenticity of collective identities. Nor does it translate into a paternalistic dictation of what "ought" to be. Instead, the con-cept of justpeace provides a prism through which the analyst may be able to connect the trans-local, national, and sub-national symbolic fields with broader discursive formations and imaginings of places such as Palestine, Zion, Tibet, and Greater China. This connection helps to illuminate why the analysis of ethno-religious national conflicts needs to interrogate the roles of various solidarities and alliances, even if the latter are framed as merely realist or altruistic, in perpetuating the unproductive cycles of mutual silencing.

NOTES

1. May 27, 2010.
2. For a clip of this episode, see "Thank You, South Carolina: The Race to Replace Disgrace," *The Daily Show with John Stewart*, June 7, 2010, http://www.thedailyshow.com/watch/mon-june-7-2010/thank-you--south-carolina---the-race-to-replace-disgrace.
3. I address this issue also in Atalia Omer, "'It's Nothing Personal': The Globalization of Justice, the Transferability of Protest, and the Case of the Palestine Solidarity Movement," *Studies in Ethnicity and Nationalism* 9, no. 3 (2009): 497–518.

4. For a partial list of the individuals and groups who make up this movement, see the endorsements of the Palestinian Call for Boycott, Divestment, and Sanctions (BDS), reproduced in Omar Barghouti, *Boycott, Divestment, Sanctions: The Global Struggle for Palestinian Rights* (Chicago: Haymarket Books, 2011), 239–247.

5. See Arjan El Fassed, "EU Poll: 'Israel Poses Biggest Threat to World Peace,'" *The Electronic Intifada*, November 3, 2003, http://electronicintifada.net/content/eu-poll-israel-poses-biggest-threat-world-peace/4860.

6. For examples of this broad approach, see James Clifford, "Diasporas," in *Routes: Travel and Translation in the Late Twentieth Century* (Cambridge, MA: Harvard University Press, 1997), 244–277; Arjun Appadurai, *Modernity at Large: Cultural Dimensions of Globalization* (Minneapolis: University of Minnesota Press, 1996); Homi Bhabha, *The Location of Culture* (London: Routledge, 1994); Homi Bhabha, *Nation and Narration* (London: Routledge, 1990); Stuart Hall, "Cultural Identity and Diaspora," in *Identity: Community, Culture, Difference*, ed. J. Rutherford (London: Lawrence and Wishard, 1990), 222–237; Paul Gilroy, *"There Ain't No Black in the Union Jack": The Cultural Politics of Race and Nation* (Chicago: University of Chicago Press, 1991); Andre Levi and Alex Weingrod, eds., *Homelands and Diasporas: Holy Lands and Other Places* (Stanford, CA: Stanford University Press, 2005); Karen Olwig Fog, "Place, Movement and Identity: Processes of Inclusion and Exclusion in a 'Caribbean Family,'" Susanne Schwalgin, "Why Locality Matters: Diaspora Consciousness and Sedentariness in the Armenian Diaspora in Greece," and Martin Sökefeld, "Religion or Culture? Concepts of Identity in the Alevi Diaspora," in *Diaspora, Identity and Religion: New Directions in Theory and Research*, ed. Waltraud Kokot, Khachig Tölölyan, and Carolin Alfonso (London: Routledge, 2004), 53–71, 72–92, and 143–165; and Liisa Malkki, "Citizens of Humanity: Internationalism and the Imagined Community of Nations," *Diaspora* 3, no. 1 (1992): 41–68.

7. Rogers Brubaker, "The 'Diaspora' Diaspora," *Ethnic and Racial Studies* 28, no. 1 (2005): 12.

8. Edward W. Said, *Orientalism* (New York: Pantheon Books, 1978); Said produced many other relevant and interrelated works.

9. Michel Foucault, *Power/Knowledge* (New York: Pantheon Books, 1980).

10. Foucault, *Power/Knowledge*, 131.

11. See, for instance, Michel Foucault, *The History of Sexuality*, vol. 1, *The Will to Knowledge* (London: Penguin, 1998), 100–101. For another work that illuminates the possibility of resistance and change in Foucault, see Jason A. Springs, "'Dismantling the Master's House': Freedom as Ethical Practice in Brandom and Foucault," *Journal of Religious Ethics* 37, no. 3 (2009): 419–448. For other attempts to "rescue" the notion of agency by also problematizing unreconstructed feminist assumptions concerning agency-qua-resistance, see Saba Mahmood, *Politics of Piety: The Islamic Revival and the Feminist Subject* (Princeton, NJ: Princeton University Press, 2005); and Elizabeth Bucar, *Creative Conformity: The Feminist Politics of U.S. Catholic and Iranian Shi'i Women* (Washington, DC: Georgetown University Press, 2011).

12. See Antonio Gramsci, *The Modern Prince* (New York: International Publishers, 1957), 124.

13. Edward Said, *The Question of Palestine* (New York: Times Books, 1979); Said, *Peace and Its Discontents: Essays on Palestine in the Middle East Peace Process* (New York: Vintage Books, 1996); Said, *Out of Place: A Memoir* (New York: Knopf, 1999); Said, *The Politics of Dispossession: The Struggle for Palestinian Self-Determination, 1969–1994*

(New York: Pantheon Books, 1994); and Said, *The End of the Peace Process: Oslo and After* (New York: Pantheon Books, 2000).

14. For prominent examples, see David Kopf, "Hermeneutics versus History," *Journal of Asian Studies* 39, no. 3 (1980): 495–506; Bernard Lewis, *Islam and the West* (New York: Oxford University Press, 1993), especially chap. 6; and John MacKenzie, "Edward Said and the Historians," *Nineteenth-Century Contexts* 18, no. 1 (1994): 9–25.

15. For a critique of Said's use of Foucault, see Aijaz Ahmad, "Between Orientalism and Historicism," reproduced in *Orientalism: A Reader*, ed. Alexander Lyon Macfie (New York: New York University Press, 2000), 285–297. For a further exposition of the critiques of Orientalism, see Zachary Lockman, *Contending Visions of the Middle East: The History and Politics of Orientalism* (Cambridge: Cambridge University Press, 2010).

16. See, for instance, Edward Said, "Shattered Myths," reproduced in Macfie, *Orientalism*, 89–103.

17. For an example of such a critique from the disciplinary vantage point of anthropology, see Michael Richardson, "Enough Said," *Anthropology Today* 6, no. 4 (1990): 16–19.

18. Said, "Shattered Myths," 101.

19. Edward Said, "Orientalism Reconsidered," reproduced in Macfie, *Orientalism*, 347.

20. Said, "Orientalism Reconsidered," especially 348–349.

21. See also Edward Said, *Culture and Imperialism* (New York: Knopf, 1993).

22. Talal Asad, *Formations of the Secular: Christianity, Islam, Modernity* (Stanford, CA: Stanford University Press: 2003), 185.

23. Asad, *Formations of the Secular*, 185.

24. Sadik Jalal al-'Azm, "Orientalism and Orientalism in Reverse," reproduced in Macfie, *Orientalism*, 217–238.

25. For a similar argument, see the editors' introduction to Carol Appadurai Breckenridge and Peter van der Veer, eds., *Orientalism and the Postcolonial Predicament: Perspectives of South Asia* (Philadelphia: University of Pennsylvania Press, 1993); and John MacKenzie, *Orientalism: History, Theory and the Arts* (Manchester: Manchester University Press, 1995).

26. al-'Azm, "Orientalism and Orientalism in Reverse," 233.

27. al-'Azm, "Orientalism and Orientalism in Reverse," 234.

28. For characteristic examples, see "Bin Laden Tape Urges War on Israel, Taunts U.S.," NBC News, January 14, 2009, http://www.msnbc.msn.com/id/28652698/#.UABNApFSSgQ. See also bin Laden's post–9/11 speech. He ends it as follows: "As to America, I say to it and its people a few words: I swear to God that America will not live in peace before peace reigns in Palestine, and before all the army of infidels depart the land of Muhammad peace be upon him." See "Osama bin Laden, Videotaped Address, October 7, 2011," http://www.press.uchicago.edu/Misc/Chicago/481921texts.html, and a characteristic speech by Mahmoud Ahmadinejad, "Address by H.E. Dr. Mahmoud Ahmadinejad, President of the Islamic Republic of Iran, Before the 66th Session of the United Nations General Assembly," *General Assembly of the United Nations*, September 22, 2011, http://gadebate. un.org/sites/default/files/gastatements/66/IR_en.pdf.

29. For instructive accounts of Christian Zionism, see Donald M. Lewis, *The Origins of Christian Zionism: Lord Shaftesbury and Evangelical Support for a Jewish Homeland* (Cambridge: Cambridge University Press, 2010); Stephen Spector, *Evangelicals and Israel: The Story of American Christian Zionism* (New York: Oxford University Press, 2009); and Paul Charles Merkley, *Christian Attitudes Towards the State of Israel* (Montreal: McGill-Queen's University Press, 2001).

30. For an example of a critique from the vantage point of a Christian Palestinian liberation theology, see Naim Stifan Ateek, *Challenging Christian Zionism: Theology, Politics and the Israel-Palestine Conflict* (London: Melisende, 2005).

31. For a notable example of a classical articulation of diaspora (deeply rooted in the paradigmatic case of the Jewish diaspora), see William Safran, "Diasporas in Modern Societies: Myths of Homeland and Return," *Diaspora* 1, no. 1 (1991): 83–99. For Safran's model, the orientation to the homeland as a source of authority, authenticity, and values is pivotal. This model came under criticism in the 1990s with the proliferation of diaspora studies, especially in the journal *Diaspora*. For critiques of Safran's classical approach, see James Clifford, "Diasporas," *Cultural Anthropology* 9, no. 3 (1994): 302–338; Floya Anthias, "Evaluating 'Diaspora': Beyond Ethnicity," *Sociology* 32, no. 3 (1998): 557–580; and Mark Anthony Falzon, "'Bombay, Our Cultural Heart': Rethinking the Relation between Homeland and Diaspora," *Ethnic and Racial Studies* 26, no. 4 (2003): 662–683. These authors attempt to de-center the teleologies of origin and return by stressing the aspiration for multi-local cultural recreation. For post-national articulations of "diasporas" with their emphasis on hybridity, creolization, and boundary erosion, see the examples listed in footnote 6 above.

32. See, for example, Khachig Tölölyan, "Rethinking Diasporas(s): Stateless Power in the Transnational Moment," *Diaspora* 5, no. 1 (1996): 3–36. For a helpful exposition of the tension between boundary maintenance and boundary erosion as it plays out in diaspora studies, see Brubaker, "The 'Diaspora' Diaspora," 6–7.

33. This resonates with theoretical headways in the subfield of the cultural sociology of religion, where increased attention is devoted to the relation between symbolic boundaries and sociopolitical practice. For a state-of-the-art review, see Penny Edgell, "A Cultural Sociology of Religion: New Directions," *Annual Review of Sociology* 38 (2012): 247–265.

34. Samuel Huntington, *The Clash of Civilizations and the Remaking of World Order* (New York: Simon and Schuster, 1997), 272.

35. Notably, Huntington's theory came under intense scrutiny, especially from theorists and other commentators who integrated into their analyses Edward Said's critique of orientalism. In fact, Said himself challenged the Huntington frame, positioning it within his broader critique of the discourse. For an insightful collection of critiques of the premises inherent in Huntington's thesis, see Emran Qureshi and Michael Anthony Sells, eds., *The New Crusades: Constructing the Muslim Enemy* (New York: Columbia University Press, 2003).

36. John J. Mearsheimer and Stephen M. Walt, *The Israel Lobby and U.S. Foreign Policy* (New York: Farrar, Straus and Giroux, 2008).

37. For an example of such critiques, see Stephen Zunes, "The Israel Lobby: How Powerful Is It Really?" *Mother Jones*, May 18, 2006, http://www.motherjones.com/politics/2006/05/israel-lobby-how-powerful-it-really.

38. For a clear articulation of this point, refer to David Remnick, "The Lobby," *New Yorker*, September 3, 2007, http://www.newyorker.com/talk/comment/2007/09/03/070903taco_talk_remnick.

39. *The Protocols of the Elders of Zion* is an anti-Semitic document published in Russia in 1903. It describes the supposed minutes of meeting of a Jewish cabal planning a global takeover. While discredited, the text has continued to circulate and be translated into various languages, including Arabic and Persian.

40. For a critique of this argument, see William T. Cavanaugh, *The Myth of Religious Violence: Secular Ideology and the Roots of Modern Conflict* (New York: Oxford University Press, 2009) and Talal Asad, *On Suicide Bombing* (New York: Columbia University Press,

2007). For an important work that explores the interrelations between the history of colonialism, orientalism, and rising Islamophobia in France as indicated in the "veil controversy," see Joan Wallach Scott, *The Politics of the Veil* (Princeton, NJ: Princeton University Press, 2007).

41. For an insightful exposition of the unique species of American orientalism, see Melani McAlister, *Epic Encounters: Culture, Media, and U.S. Interests in the Middle East, 1945–2000* (Berkeley: University of California Press, 2005).

42. For a critique that takes up the discursive constraints and blind spots of international relations theories, see Elizabeth Shakman Hurd, *The Politics of Secularism in International Relations* (Princeton, NJ: Princeton University Press, 2008). For an account of the role of religion in structuring the Westphalian system of nation-states, see Daniel Philpott, *Revolutions in Sovereignty: How Ideas Shaped Modern International Relations* (Princeton, NJ: Princeton University Press, 2001). Philpott is also notable in his non-reductionist approach to religion in global politics, as religion relates to both conflict and peacebuilding. For representative works, see Philpott, *Just and Unjust Peace: An Ethic of Political Reconciliation* (New York: Oxford University Press, 2012); and Monica Duffy Toft, Daniel Philpott, and Timothy Samuel Shah, *God's Century: Resurgent Religion and Global Politics* (New York: W. W. Norton, 2011). For a multidisciplinary report on how integrating religion into the analysis of global politics might translate into policy recommendations, see R. Scott Appleby and Richard Cizik, "Engaging Religious Communities Abroad: A New Imperative for U.S. Foreign Policy," Chicago Council on Global Affairs, 2010, http://www.thechicagocouncil.org/UserFiles/File/Task%20Force%20Reports/2010%20Religion%20Task%20Force_Full%20Report.pdf.

43. See Emily Cochran Bech and Jack L Snyder, "Conclusion: Religion's Contribution to International Relations Theory," in *Religion and International Relations Theory*, ed. Jack L. Snyder (New York: Columbia University Press: 2011), 204.

44. For relevant accounts of American civil religion and national ethos (the motifs of a "City upon a Hill," American exceptionalism, the New Israel, and so forth), see Atalia Omer and Jason Springs, *Religious Nationalism: A Reference Handbook* (Santa Barbara: ABC-CLIO, 2012), especially chaps. 2 and 3. See also Scott Hibbard, *Religious Politics and Secular States: Egypt, India, and the United States* (Baltimore,: Johns Hopkins University Press, 2010).

45. For an account that helpfully illuminates how the politics of identity within the multicultural context influences the consolidation, homogenization, and ethnicization of religious identities (especially as it pertains to the case of Indian/Hindu diasporas), see Prema Kurien, "Who Speaks for Indian Americans? Religion, Ethnicity, and Political Formation," *American Quarterly* 59, no. 3 (2007): 759–783.

46. Dibyesh Anand, "(Re)imagining Nationalism: Identity and Representation in the Tibetan Diaspora of South Asia," *Contemporary South Asia* 9, no. 3 (2000): 277.

47. Anand, "(Re)imagining Nationalism," 277.

48. Anand, "(Re)imagining Nationalism," 277.

49. Thierry Dodin and Heinz Räther, "Imagining Tibet: Between Shangri-La and Feudal Oppression: Attempting a Synthesis," in *Imagining Tibet: Perceptions, Projections, and Fantasies*, ed. Thierry Dodin and Heinz Räther (Somerville, MA: Wisdom Publications, 2001), 392–393. These authors do highlight the exception to this trend represented in the case of Moravian missionaries who exhibited greater constructive tolerance that, nonetheless, constituted a calculated missionizing strategy. For an account of earlier missionary reports, which were inclined to reflect Catholic-Protestant contestations at home in

their articulation of images of Tibet, see Rudolf Kaschewsky, "The Image of Tibet in the West before the Nineteenth Century," in Dodin and Räther, *Imagining Tibet*, 3–20.

50. Dodin and Räther, "Between Shangri-La and Feudal Oppression," 394; see also L. Austine Waddell, *The Buddhism of Tibet or Lamaism* (Cambridge: Heffer, 1971 [1895]).

51 Dodin and Räther, "Between Shangri-La and Feudal Oppression," 395–396.

52. For a detailed account, see Poul Pedersen, "Tibet, Theosophy, and the Psychologization of Buddhism," in Dodin and Räther, *Imagining Tibet*, 151–166.

53. Dodin and Räther, "Between Shangri-La and Feudal Oppression," 409.

54. Frank J. Korom, "The Role of Tibet in the New Age Movement," in Dodin and Räther, *Imagining Tibet*, 180.

55. Donald Lopez, *Prisoners of Shangri-La: Tibetan Buddhism and the West* (Chicago: University of Chicago Press, 1998).

56. This argument is echoed in various ethnographic and theoretical works in cultural and political geography. See Emily T. Yeh, "Exile Meets Homeland: Politics, Performance, and Authenticity in the Tibetan Diaspora," *Environmental and Planning D: Society and Space* 25, no. 4 (2007): 648–667; and Serin Houston and Richard Wright, "Making and Remaking Tibetan Diasporic Identities," *Social and Cultural Geography* 4, no. 2 (2003): 217–232.

57. For nuanced accounts of Tibet's diverse cultural, political, and religious institutions as well as social attitudes, see P. Jeffrey Hopkins, "Tibetan Monastic Colleges: Rationality versus the Demands of Allegiance," in Dodin and Räther, *Imagining Tibet*, 257–268.

58. Dodin and Räther, "Between Shangri-La and Feudal Oppression," 403. For additional important accounts of the representations and projections of Tibet, see Peter Bishop, *The Myth of Shangri-La: Tibet, Travel Writing, and the Western Creation of Sacred Landscape* (Berkeley: University of California Press, 1989) and Bishop, *Dreams of Power: Tibetan Buddhism and the Western Imagination* (London: Athlone, 1993).

59. Robert A. F. Thurman, "Critical Reflections on Donald S. Lopez Jr.'s *Prisoners of Shangri-La: Tibetan Buddhism and the West*," *Journal of the American Academy of Religion* 69, no. 1 (2001): 195.

60. Tsering Shakya, "Who Are the Prisoners?" *Journal of the American Academy of Religion* 69, no. 1 (2001): 183–189; and David Germano, "Encountering Tibet: The Ethics, Soteriology, and Creativity of Cross-Cultural Interpretation," *Journal of the American Academy of Religion* 69, no. 1 (2001): 165–182.

61. Christian P. Klieger, "Shangri-La and Hyperreality: A Collision in Tibetan Refugee Expression," in *Tibetan Culture in the Diaspora: Papers Presented at a Panel of the 7th Seminar of the International Association for Tibetan Studiesed*. Frank Korom (Wien: Österreichische Akademie der Wissenschaften Philosophisch-Historische Klasse, 1997), 59–68.

62. Anand, "(Re)imagining Nationalism," 277–279. See also Robert E. Wood, "Touristic Ethnicity: A Brief Itinerary," *Ethnic and Racial Studies* 21, no. 2 (1998): 218–241. The point concerning the homogenizing and metaphorical construal of Tibet, within a context of diasporic contestation over an authentic Tibetan history, is also echoed in Carole McGranahan's notion of "arrested history." McGranahan argues that the history of armed Tibetan resistance is denied in the process of producing, reproducing, and projecting the Tibetan struggle as inherently political and nonviolent. The homogenization of a Tibetan identity in the diaspora glosses over regional complexities in the geographic space of Tibet itself. See McGranahan, "Truth, Fear, and Lies: Exile Politics and Arrested Histories of the Tibetan Resistance," *Cultural Anthropology* 20, no. 4 (2005): 570–600.

63. Anand, "(Re)imagining Nationalism," 274.

64. As scholar of religion Jonathan Z. Smith clearly encapsulates in *To Take Place: Toward Theory in Ritual* (Chicago: University of Chicago Press, 1987), the experience of dispersal was foundational for Judaism as a collective identity reflective of one fraction of an antecedent diverse society.

65. Thomas Heberer, "Old Tibet a Hell on Earth? The Myth of Tibet and Tibetans in Chinese Art and Propaganda," in Dodin and Räther, *Imagining Tibet*, 112.

66. Heberer, "Old Tibet," 113.

67. Heberer, "Old Tibet," 114–115.

68. To get a glimpse at the complexities and contestations of Palestinian identities, see Loren D. Lybarger, *Identity and Religion in Palestine: The Struggle between Islamism and Secularism in the Occupied Territories* (Princeton, NJ: Princeton University Press, 2007).

69. For an example of the endurance of theosophist motifs, see the opening quote from Richard Gere, Chair of the Board of the International Campaign for Tibet, as it is reproduced on the official website of the International Campaign for Tibet (http://www.savetibet.org/resource-center/all-about-tibet): "Tibet is a human rights issue as well as a civil and political rights issue. But there's something else too—Tibet has a precious culture based on principles of wisdom and compassion. This culture addresses what we lack in the world today; a very real sense of inter-connectedness. We need to protect it for the Tibetan people, but also for ourselves and our children."

70. Anne F. Thurston, "The Chinese View of Tibet—Is Dialogue Possible?" February 22, 2010 *Cultural Survival Quarterly* 12, no. 1 (1988): 70–73.

71. For an example of such conscious and preemptive distancing from the potential attribution as "anti-Jewish," see the stated aim of the Palestine Solidarity Campaign: "The Palestine Solidarity Campaign (PSC) campaigns for justice for the Palestinians. . . PSC is established to campaign. . . in opposition to racism, including anti-Jewish prejudice and Islamophobia, and the apartheid and Zionist nature of the Israeli state." http://www.palestinecampaign.org/Index5b.asp?m_id=1&l1_id=2&l2_id=10.

72. For a relevant discussion of the parallels between the Hindu and Zionist struggles and their interlacing with broader orientalist frameworks in terms of their lobbying efforts, see Atalia Omer, "Rethinking 'Home' Abroad: Religion and the Reinterpretation of National Boundaries in the Indian and Jewish Diasporas in the U.S.," *International Journal of Peace Studies* 16, no. 1 (2001): 23–51. For an example of the use of the phrase "Kosovo is our Jerusalem," see a May 31, 2010, interview with Serbian Foreign Minister Vuk Jeremic at *Spiegel Online International*, http://www.spiegel.de/international/europe/serbian-foreign-minister-vuk-jeremic-kosovo-is-our-jerusalem-a-697725.html.

73. Quoted in William R. Nester, *Power Across the Pacific: A Diplomatic History of American Relations with Japan* (New York: New York University Press, 63). For a succinct analysis of Japanese imperialism, see Bill Gordon, "Explanations of Japan's Imperialistic Expansion, 1894–1910," http://wgordon.web.wesleyan.edu/papers/imperialism.htm.

74. Atalia Omer and Jason Springs, "The Cultural Violence of Peace Research" (in progress).

75. The so-called Balfour Declaration (issued on November 2, 1917) promised the support of the United Kingdom for the establishment of a Jewish home in Palestine. The British, however, also issued competing promises to various representatives of the Palestinians (see the recommendations of the Peel Commission of 1937; White Paper issued in 1939; and the McMahon-Hussein Correspondence of 1915).

76. For an interesting overview of the interfaces among the colonial project and projections of the "Holy Land," see Laura Robson, *Colonialism and Christianity in Mandate Palestine*

(Austin: University of Texas Press, 2011). For an account of the projection of Palestine within the framework of American orientalism, see Hilton Obenzinger, *American Palestine: Melville, Twain, and the Holy Land Mania* (Princeton, NJ: Princeton University Press, 1999).

77. For examples of postcolonial rereadings of Zionist mythology, see Ella Shohat, *Israeli Cinema: East/West and the Politics of Representation* (Austin: University of Texas Press, 1989); Idith Zertal, *Israel's Holocaust and the Politics of Nationhood* (Cambridge: Cambridge University Press, 2005); and Yehouda Shenhav, *The Arab Jews: A Postcolonial Reading of Nationalism, Religion, and Ethnicity* (Stanford, CA: Stanford University Press, 2006).

78. For important works addressing the motif of the "negation of exile" and other dimensions of the early Jewish Zionist ethos, see Yael Zerubavel, *Recovered Roots: Collective Memory and the Making of Israeli National Tradition* (Chicago: University of Chicago Press, 1995); Zertal, *Israel's Holocaust*; and Baruch Kimmerling, *The Invention and Decline of Israeliness: State, Society, and the Military* (Berkley: University of California Press, 2001).

79. This Weberian insight is carried through in different ways in scholarship on religion and nationalism by David Little, Scott Hibbard, and Atalia Omer. See, for instance, Hibbard, *Religious Politics and Secular States*; David Little, "Religion, Nationalism, and Intolerance," in *Between Terror and Tolerance: Religious Leaders, Conflict, and Peacemaking*, ed. Timothy D. Sisk (Washington, DC: Georgetown University Press, 2011), 9–28; and Atalia Omer, *When Peace Is Not Enough: How the Israeli Peace Camp Thinks about Religion, Nationalism, and Justice* (Chicago: University of Chicago Press, 2013).

80. Liisa Malkki, "Citizens of Humanity: Internationalism and the Imagined Community of Nations," *Diaspora* 3, no. 1 (1994): 41–68.

81. In an earlier work, I focus on subaltern hybridities as spaces for critique and reframing of national historiography and practices. See Omer, *When Peace Is Not Enough*.

82. For related examples of diasporic contestations within the nation-state framework, see Hanna Herzog, "Shifting Boundaries: Palestinian Women Citizens of Israel in Peace Organizations" and Lisa Anteby-Yemini, "From Ethiopian Villager to Global Villager: Ethiopian Jews in Israel," in *Homelands and Diasporas: Holy Lands and Other Places*, ed. André Levi and Alex Weingrod (Stanford, CA: Stanford University Press, 2005), 200–219 and 220–246. For an influential ethnographic study of diaspora as a liminal and transformative space for rethinking nationalism and links to land/territory, see Liisa H. Malkki, *Purity and Exile: Violence, Memory, and National Cosmology Among Hutu Refugees in Tanzania* (Chicago: University of Chicago Press, 1995).

83. For a selection of accounts that point to the internal plurality and heterogeneity of Jewish communities and their conflicted and contested conceptions of home, see Danny Ben-Moshe and Zohar Segev, eds., *Israel, The Diaspora and Jewish Identity* (Portland: Sussex Academic Press, 2010).

84. Judith Butler, *Parting Ways: Jewishness and the Critique of Zionism* (New York: Columbia University Press, 2012), 7.

85. For Butler's engagement with Said's work in constructing her argument about cohabitation in Palestine/Israel, see Butler, *Parting Ways*, especially 205–224.

86. Butler, *Parting Ways*, 5.

87. Butler, *Parting Ways*, 6–7, for example. Butler applies Said's own conception of justice to the complex Israel-Palestine case, recognizing the intricate interconnectedness of Israeli/ Jewish and Palestinian histories (they cannot be told apart from one another). He suggests that justice will only entail a process of demystifying chauvinism through secularism; see Edward Said, "A Method for Thinking about Just Peace," in *What Is a Just Peace?*, ed. Pierre Allan and Alexis Keller (New York: Oxford University Press, 2006).

88. Butler, *Parting Ways*, 6.

89. Peter Beinart, "The Failure of the American Jewish Establishment," *New York Review of Books* 57, no. 10 (2010): 16–20, http://www.nybooks.com/articles/archives/2010/jun/10/failure-american-jewish-establishment/.

90. Omer, *When Peace Is Not Enough*.

91. For an analysis of the potentially positive role of diasporas in reframing the discourse of belligerence in the case of Sri Lankan diasporas, see Camilla Orjuela, "Distant Warriors, Distant Peace Workers? Multiple Diaspora Roles in Sri Lanka's Violent Conflict," *Global Networks* 8, no. 4 (2008): 436–452.

92. Arendt's critique of the "love of Israel" (*ahavat Yisrael*) unfolds across the pages of her correspondence with Gershom Scholem in 1963. She writes: "How right you are that I have no such love [*ahavat Yisrael*] and for two reasons: first, I have never in my life 'loved' some nation or collective—not the German, French, or American nation, or the working class, or whatever else might exist. The fact is that I love only my friends and am quite incapable of any other sort of love." See *Gershom Scolem: A Life in Letters, 1914–1982*, ed. and trans. Anthony David Skinner (Cambridge, MA: Harvard University Press, 2002), 398–399.

93. For a further elaboration of this critique of the model of cohabitation as articulated by Butler, see Omer, *When Peace Is Not Enough*, especially chap. 5.

94. Daniel Boyarin and Jonathan Boyarin, "Diaspora: Generation and the Ground of Jewish Diaspora," in *Theorizing Diaspora*, ed. Jana Evans Braziel and Anita Mannur (Oxford: Blackwell Publishing, 2003), 98.

95. Boyarin and Boyarin, "Diaspora," 107.

96. The concept of *jahiliyya* as articulated by Sayyid Qutb, the ideologue of the Egyptian Muslim Brotherhood, captures this sense of estrangement (literally the pre–Qur'anic revelation sense of ignorance) within Egyptian society itself in his *Milestones*.

97. This perception played out tragically in the case of the young American activist Rachel Corrie, who was crushed to death by a bulldozer in her attempt to protest and prevent house demolition in the Occupied Territories. That the event was defined as an "accident" in the Israeli court illustrates the kind of resistance and resentment of such activism. For coverage of this point, see, for instance, Harriet Sherwood, "Rachel Corrie Lawsuit Result 'Dangerous Precedent' Say Human Rights Group," *Guardian*, August 28, 2012, http://www.guardian.co.uk/world/2012/aug/28/rachel-corrie-dismissal-dangerous-precedent. The Israeli government increasingly constrained the ability of humanitarian and human rights organizations to operate freely in Israel and Palestine.

98. I treat this issue with greater detail in Omer, "'It's Nothing Personal.'"

99. Amy Goodman and Juan González, "Flotilla Passengers Huwaida Arraf of free Gaza Movement and Retired Army Col. Ann Wright Respond to Israeli Claims on Deadly Assault," *Democracy Now*, June 3, 2010, http://www.democracynow.org/2010/6/3/huwaida.

100. See, for examples, Peter Uvin, "Global Dreams and Local Anger: From Structural to Acute Violence in a Globalizing World," in *Rethinking Global Political Economy: Emerging Issues, Unfolding Odysseys*, ed. Mary Ann Tétreault, Robert A. Denemark, Kenneth P. Thomas, and Kurt Burch (London: Routledge, 2003), 147–162; Paul Collier, "Economic Causes of Civil Conflict and Their Implications for Policy," in *Leashing the Dogs of War: Managing Global Chaos*, ed. Chester A. Crocker and Fen Osler Hampson, with Pamela Aall (Washington, DC: US Institute of Peace Press, 2000), 197–218; and David

Laitin, "Ethnicity, Insurgency, and Civil War," *American Political Science Review* 97, no. 1 (2003): 75–90.

101. Michael Ignatieff, *Human Rights as Politics and Idolatry* (Princeton, NJ: Princeton University Press, 2001).

102. Hazel Smith and Paul Stares, eds., *Diasporas in Conflict: Peace-Makers of Peace-Wreckers?* (Tokyo: United Nations University Press, 2007). Analysts have grappled with the role of diasporas as political, social, and cultural actors in international and national politics. The discussion became especially acute in light of cosmopolitan post-nationalist idealism and global neoliberal restructuring, bringing about the supposed diminishment of state sovereignty and territorial nationalism. For an example of such a focus on neoliberal restructuring, see Yossi Shain and Aharon Barth, "Diasporas in International Relations Theory," *International Organization* 57, no. 2 (2003): 449–479. For a prominent example of the cosmopolitan framework, see Arjun Appadurai, *Modernity at Large: Cultural Dimensions of Globalization* (Minneapolis: University of Minnesota Press, 1996).

103. Hazel Smith, "Diasporas in International Conflict," in Smith and Stares, *Diasporas in Conflict*, 5; for a schematic articulation of the findings, see 9–12.

104. Latha Varadarajan, "Back to the Future: Historical Materialism, Diaspora Politics, and the Limits of Novelty," *International Political Sociology* 6, no. 1 (2012): 95–99.

105. Smith, "Diasporas in International Conflict," 9.

106. See, for example, Orjuela, "Distant Warriors, Distant Peace Workers"; and Bahar Baser and Ashok Swain, "Diasporas as Peacemakers: Third-Party Mediation in Homeland Conflicts," *International Journal of World Peace* 25, no. 3 (2008): 7–28.

107. Resonating with this argument is Peter Uvin's critique of development work in Africa as a contributing factor in perpetuating forms of structural violence that undergird the eruptions of genocidal practices. See, for example, Uvin, *Aiding Violence: The Development Enterprise in Rwanda* (West Hartford, CT: Kumarian Press, 1998).

108. For an explication of this argument and for a conceptual mapping of the subfield of religious peacebuilding, see Chapter 1 of this volume.

109. See Daniel Philpott and Gerard Powers, eds., *Strategies of Peace* (New York: Oxford University Press, 2010), especially the chapter by R. Scott Appleby and John Paul Lederach, "Strategic Peacebuilding: An Overview," 19–44.

110. See also Philpott, *Just and Unjust Peace*, and Philpott, "Beyond Politics as Usual: Is Reconciliation Compatible with Liberalism?," in *The Politics of Past Evil: Religion, Reconciliation, and the Dilemmas of Transitional Justice*, ed. Philpott (Notre Dame, IN: University of Notre Dame Press, 2006), 11–44.

Bibliography

Ahmad, Aijaz. "Between Orientalism and Historicism." In *Orientalism: A Reader*, edited by Alexander Lyon Macfie, 285–297. New York: New York University Press, 2000.

Anand, Dibyesh. "(Re)imagining Nationalism: Identity and Representation in the Tibetan Diaspora of South Asia." *Contemporary South Asia* 9, no. 3 (2000): 271–287.

Anteby-Yemini, Lisa. "From Ethiopian Villager to Global Villager: Ethiopian Jews in Israel." In *Homelands and Diasporas: Holy Lands and Other Places*, edited by André Levi and Alex Weingrod, 220–246. Stanford, CA: Stanford University Press, 2005.

Anthias, Floya. "Evaluating 'Diaspora': Beyond Ethnicity." *Sociology* 32, no. 3 (1998): 557–580.

Appadurai Breckenridge, Carol, and Peter van der Veer, eds. *Orientalism and the Postcolonial Predicament: Perspectives of South Asia.* Philadelphia: University of Pennsylvania Press, 1993.

Appadurai, Arjun. *Modernity at Large: Cultural Dimensions of Globalization.* Minneapolis: University of Minnesota Press, 1996.

Appleby, R. Scott, and Richard Cizik. "Engaging Religious Communities Abroad: A New Imperative for U.S. Foreign Policy." Chicago Council on Global Affairs, 2010. http://www.thechicagocouncil.org/UserFiles/File/Task%20Force%20Reports/2010%20Religion%20Task%20Force_Full%20Report.pdf.

Appleby, Scott, and John Paul Lederach. "Strategic Peacebuilding: An Overview." In Philpott and Powers, *Strategies of Peace*, 19–44. New York: Oxford University Press, 2010.

Arendt, Johanna. *Gershom Scolem: A Life in Letters, 1914–1982.* Edited and translated by Anthony David Skinner. Cambridge, MA: Harvard University Press, 2002.

Asad, Talal. *Formations of the Secular: Christianity, Islam, Modernity.* Stanford, CA: Stanford University Press, 2003.

Asad, Talal. *On Suicide Bombing.* New York: Columbia University Press, 2007.

Ateek, Naim Stifan. *Challenging Christian Zionism: Theology, Politics, and the Israel-Palestine Conflict.* London: Melisende, 2005.

Barghouti, Omar. *Boycott, Divestment, Sanctions: The Global Struggle for Palestinian Rights.* Chicago: Haymarket Books, 2011.

Baser, Bahar, and Ashok Swain. "Diasporas as Peacemakers: Third Party Mediation in Homeland Conflicts." *International Journal of World Peace* 25, no. 3 (2008): 7–28.

Bech, Cochran Emily and Jack L Snyder. "Conclusion: Religion's Contribution to International Relations Theory." In *Religion and International Relations Theory*, edited by Jack L. Snyder, 200–209. New York: Columbia University Press: 2011.

Beinart, Peter. "The Failure of the American Jewish Establishment." *New York Review of Books* 57, no. 10 (2010): 16–20. http://www.nybooks.com/articles/archives/2010/jun/10/failure-american-jewish-establishment/?pagination=false.

Ben-Moshe, Danny, and Zohar Segev, eds. *Israel, the Diasora and Jewish Identity.* Portland: Sussex Academic Press, 2010.

Bhabha, Homi. *Nation and Narration.* London: Routledge, 1990.

Bhabha, Homi. *The Location of Culture.* London: Routledge, 1994.

"Bin Laden Tape Urges War on Israel, Taunts U.S." NBC News. January 14, 2009, http://www.msnbc.msn.com/id/28652698/#.UABNApFSSgQ.

Bishop, Peter. *The Myth of Shangri-La: Tibet, Travel Writing, and the Western Creation of Sacred Landscape.* Berkeley: University of California Press, 1989.

Bishop, Peter. *Dreams of Power: Tibetan Buddhism and the Western Imagination.* London: Athlone, 1993.

Boyarin, Daniel, and Jonathan Boyarin. "Diaspora: Generation and the Ground of Jewish Diaspora." In *Theorizing Diaspora*, edited by Jana Evans Traziel and Anita Mannur, 85–118. Oxford: Blackwell Publishing, 2003.

Brubaker, Rogers. "The 'Diaspora' Diaspora." *Ethnic and Racial Studies* 28, no. 1 (2005): 1–19.

Bucar, Elizabeth. *Creative Conformity: The Feminist Politics of U.S. Catholic and Iranian Shi'i Women.* Washington, DC: Georgetown University Press, 2011.

Butler, Judith. *Parting Ways: Jewishness and the Critique of Zionism.* New York: Columbia University Press, 2012.

Cavanaugh, William T. *The Myth of Religious Violence: Secular Ideology and the Roots of Modern Conflict.* New York: Oxford University Press, 2009.

Clifford, James. "'Diasporas.'" *Cultural Anthropology* 9, no. 3 (1994): 302–338.

Clifford, James. "Diasporas." In *Routes: Travel and Translation in the Late Twentieth Century*, 244–277. Cambridge, MA: Harvard University Press, 1997.

Collier, Paul. "Economic Causes of Civil Conflict and Their Implications for Policy." In *Leashing tThe Dogs of War: Managing Global Chaos*, edited by Chester A. Crocker and Fen Osler Hampson, with Pamela Aall, 197–218. Washington, DC: US Institute of Peace Press, 2000.

Dodin, Thierry, and Heinz Räther. "Imagining Tibet: Between Shangri-La and Feudal Oppression: Attempting a Synthesis." In *Imagining Tibet: Perceptions, Projections, and Fantasies*, edited by Thierry Dodin and Heinz Räther. Somerville, MA: Wisdom Publiations, 2001. 339–356.

Duffy Toft, Monica, Daniel Philpott, and Timothy Samuel Shah. *God's Century: Resurgent Religion and Global Politics*. New York: W. W. Norton, 2011.

Edgell, P. "A Cultural Sociology of Religion: New Directions." *Annual Review of Sociology* 38 (2012): 247–265.

El Fassed, Arjan. "EU Poll: 'Israel Poses Biggest Threat to World Peace.'" *The Electronic Intifada*, November 3, 2003. http://electronicintifada.net/content/eu-poll-israel-poses-biggest-threat-world-peace/4860.

Falzon, Mark Anthony. "'Bombay, Our Cultural Heart': Rethinking the Relation between Homeland and Diaspora." *Ethnic and Racial Studies* 26, no. 4 (2003): 662–683.

Foucault, Michel. *Power/Knowledge*. New York: Pantheon Books, 1980.

Foucault, Michel. *The History of Sexuality*. Vol. 1, *The Will to Knowledge*. London: Penguin, 1998.

Germano, David. "Encountering Tibet: The Ethics, Soteriology, and Creativity of Cross-Cultural Interpretation." *Journal of the American Academy of Religion* 69, no. 1 (2001): 165–182.

Goodman, Amy, and Juan González. "Flotilla Passengers Huwaida Arraf of free Gaza Movement and Retired Army Col. Ann Wright Respond to Israeli Claims on Deadly Assault." *Democracy Now*, June 3, 2010. http://www.democracynow.org/2010/6/3/huwaida.

Gilroy, Paul. *"There Ain't No Black in the Union Jack": The Cultural Politics of Race and Nation*. Chicago: University of Chicago Press, 1991.

Gordon Bill. "Explanations of Japan's Imperialistic Expansion, 1894–1910." http://wgordon.web.wesleyan.edu/papers/imperialism.htm.

Gramsci, Antonio. *The Modern Prince*. New York: International Publishers, 1957.

Hall, Stuart. "Cultural Identity and Diaspora." In *Identity: Community, Culture, Difference*, edited by J. Rutherford, 222–237. London: Lawrence and Wishard, 1990.

Heberer, Thomas. "Old Tibet a Hell on Earth? The Myth of Tibet and Tibetans in Chinese Art and Propaganda." In *Imagining Tibet: Perceptions, Projections, and Fantasies*, edited by Thierry Dodin and Heinz Räther. Somerville, MA: Wisdom Publications, 2001.

Herzog, Hanna. "Shifting Boundaries: Palestinian Women Citizens of Israel in Peace Organizations." In *Homelands and Diasporas: Holy Lands and Other Places*, edited by André Levi and Alex Weingrod, 200–219. Stanford, CA: Stanford University Press, 2005.

Hibbard, Scott W. *Religious Politics and Secular States: Egypt, India, and the United States*. Baltimore: Johns Hopkins University Press, 2010.

Hopkins, P. Jeffrey. "Tibetan Monastic Colleges: Rationality versus the Demands of Allegiance." In *Imagining Tibet: Perceptions, Projections, and Fantasies*, edited by Thierry Dodin and Heinz Räther, 257–268. Somerville, MA: Wisdom Publications, 2001.

Houstin, Serin, and Richard Wright. "Making and Remaking Tibetan Diasporic Identities." *Social and Cultural Geography* 4, no. 2 (2003): 217–232.

Huntington, Samuel. *The Clash of Civilizations and the Remaking of World Order.* New York: Simon and Schuster, 1997.

Ignatieff, Michael. *Human Rights as Politics and Idolatry.* Princeton, NJ: Princeton University Press, 2001.

Jalal al-'Azm, Sadik. "Orientalism and Orientalism in Reverse." In *Orientalism: A Reader,* edited by Alexander Lyon Macfie, 217–238. New York: New York University Press, 2000.

Kaschewsky, Rudolf. "The Image of Tibet in the West Before the Nineteenth Century." In *Imagining Tibet: Perceptions, Projections, and Fantasies,* edited by Thierry Dodin and Heinz Räther, 3–20. Somerville, MA: Wisdom Publications, 2001.

Kimmerling, Baruch. *The Invention and Decline of Israeliness: State, Society, and the Military.* Berkeley: University of California Press, 2001.

Klieger, Christian P. "Shangri-La and Hyperreality: A Collision in Tibetan Refugee Expression." In *Tibetan Culture in the Diaspora: Papers Presented at a Panel of the 7th Seminar of the International Association for Tibetan Studies,* edited by Frank Korom, 59–68 Wien: Österreichische Akademie der Wissenschaften Philosophisch-Historische Klasse, 1997.

Kopf, David. "Hermeneutics versus History." *Journal of Asian Studies* 39, no. 3 (1980): 495–506.

Korom, Frank J. "The Role of Tibet in the New Age Movement." In *Imagining Tibet: Perceptions, Projections, and Fantasies,* edited by Thierry Dodin and Heinz Räther. Somerville, MA: Wisdom Publications, 2001.

Kurien, Prema. "Who Speaks for Indian Americans? Religion, Ethnicity, and Political Formation." *American Quarterly* 59, no. 3 (2007): 759–783.

Laitlin, David. "Ethnicity, Insurgency, and Civil War." *American Political Science Review* 97, no. 1 (2003): 75–90.

Levi, Andre, and Alex Weingrod, eds. *Homelands and Diasporas: Holy Lands and Other Places.* Stanford, CA: Stanford University Press, 2005.

Lewis, Bernard. *Islam and the West.* New York: Oxford University Press, 1993.

Lewis, Donald M. *The Origins of Christian Zionism: Lord Shaftesbury and Evangelical Support for a Jewish Homeland.* Cambridge: Cambridge University Press, 2010.

Little, David. "Religion, Nationalism, and Intolerance." In *Between Terror and Tolerance: Religious Leaders, Conflict, and Peacemaking,* edited by Timothy D. Sisk, 9–28. Washington, DC: Georgetown University Press, 2011.

Lockman, Zachary. *Contending Visions of the Middle East: The History and Politics of Orientalism.* Cambridge: Cambridge University Press, 2010.

Lopez, Donald. *Prisoners of Shangri-La: Tibetan Buddhism and the West.* Chicago: University of Chicago Press, 1998.

Lybarger, Loren D. *Identity and Religion in Palestine: The Struggle between Islamism and Secularism in the Occupied Territories.* Princeton, NJ: Princeton University Press, 2007.

MacKenzie, John. "Edward Said and the Historians." *Nineteenth Century Contexts* 18, no. 1 (1994): 9–25.

MacKenzie, John. *Orientalism: History, Theory and the Arts.* Manchester: Manchester University Press, 1995.

Mahmood, Saba. *Politics of Piety: The Islamic Revival and the Feminist Subject.* Princeton, NJ: Princeton University Press, 2005.

Malkki, Liisa. "Citizens of Humanity: Internationalism and the Imagined Community of Nations." *Diaspora* 3, no. 1 (1994): 41–68.

Malkki, Liisa. *Purity and Exile: Violence, Memory, and National Cosmology Among Hutu Refugees in Tanzania.* Chicago: University of Chicago Press, 1995.

McAlister, Melani. *Epic Encounters: Culture, Media, and U.S. Interest in the Middle East, 1945–2000.* Berkeley: University of California Press, 2005.

McGranahan, Carole. "Truth, Fear, and Lies: Exile Politics and Arrested Histories of the Tibetan Resistance." *Cultural Anthropology* 20, no. 4 (2005): 570–600.

Mearsheimer, John J., and Stephen M. Walt. *The Israel Lobby and U.S. Foreign Policy.* New York: Farrar, Straus, and Giroux, 2008.

Merkley, Paul Charles. *Christian Attitudes Towards the State of Israel.* Montreal: McGill-Queen's University Press, 2001.

Nester, William R. *Power Across the Pacific: A Diplomatic History of American Relations with Japan.* New York: New York University Press, 1996.

Obenzinger, Hilton. *American Palestine: Melville, Twain, and the Holy Land Mania.* Princeton, NJ: Princeton University Press, 1999.

Olwig Fog, Karen. "Place, Movement, and Identity: Processes of Inclusion and Exclusion in a 'Caribbean Family.'" In *Diaspora, Identity and Religion: New Directions in Theory and Research*, edited by Waltraud Kokot, Khachig Tölölyan, and Carolin Alfonso, 53–71. London: Routledge, 2004.

Omer, Atalia. "Rethinking 'Home' Abroad: Religion and the Reinterpretation of National Boundaries in the Indian and Jewish Diasporas in the U.S." *International Journal of Peace Studies* 16, no. 1 (2001): 23–51.

Omer, Atalia. "'It's Nothing Personal': The Globalization of Justice, the Transferability of Protest, and the Case of the Palestine Solidarity Movement." *Studies in Ethnicity and Nationalism* 9, no. 3 (2009): 497–518.

Omer, Atalia. *When Peace Is Not Enough: How the Israeli Peace Camp Thinks About Religion, Nationalism, and Justice.* Chicago: University of Chicago Press, 2013.

Omer, Atalia, and Jason Springs. *Religious Nationalism: A Reference Handbook.* Santa Barbara, CA: ABC-CLIO, 2012.

Omer, Atalia, and Jason Springs. "The Cultural Violence of Peace Research." In progress.

Orjuela, Camilla. "Distant Warriors, Distant Peace Workers? Multiple Diaspora Roles in Sri Lanka's Violent Conflict." *Global Networks* 8, no. 4 (2008): 436–452.

Pedersen, Poul. "Tibet, Theosophy, and the Psychologization of Buddhism." In *Imagining Tibet: Perceptions, Projections, and Fantasies*, edited by Thierry Dodin and Heinz Räther, 151–166. Somerville, MA: Wisdom Publications, 2001.

Philpott, Daniel. *Revolutions in Sovereignty: How Ideas Shaped Modern International Relations.* Princeton: Princeton University Press, 2001.

Philpott, Daniel. "Beyond Politics as Usual: Is Reconciliation Compatible with Liberalism?" In *The Politics of Past Evil: Religion, Reconciliation, and the Dilemmas of Transitional Justice*, edited by Daniel Philpott, 11–44. Notre Dame, IN: University of Notre Dame Press, 2006.

Philpott, Daniel. *Just and Unjust Peace: An Ethic of Political Reconciliation.* New York: Oxford University Press, 2012.

Philpott, Daniel, and Gerard F. Powers, eds. *Strategies of Peace: Transforming Conflict in a Violent World.* New York: Oxford University Press, 2010.

Qureshi, Emran, and Michael Anthony Sells, eds. *The New Crusades: Constructing the Muslim Enemy.* New York: Columbia University Press, 2003.

Remnick, David. "The Lobby." *New Yorker*, September 3, 2007. http://www.newyorker.com/talk/comment/2007/09/03/070903taco_talk_remnick.

Richardson, Michael. "Enough Said." *Anthropology Today* 6, no. 4 (1990): 16–19.

Robson, Laura. *Colonialism and Christianity in Mandate Palestine.* Austin: University of Texas Press, 2011.

Safran, William. "Diasporas in Modern Societies: Myths of Homeland and Return." *Diaspora* 1, no. 1 (1991): 83–99.

Said, E. *Orientalism*. New York: Pantheon Books, 1978.

Said, Edward. *The Question of Palestine*. New York: Times Books, 1979.

Said, Edward. *Culture and Imperialism*. New York: Knopf, 1993.

Said, Edward. *The Politics of Dispossession: The Struggle for Palestinian Self-Determination, 1969–1994*. New York: Pantheon Books, 1994.

Said, Edward. *Peace and Its Discontents: Essays on Palestine in the Middle East Peace Process*. New York: Vintage Books, 1996.

Said, Edward. *Out of Place: A Memoir*. New York: Knopf, 1999.

Said, Edward. *The End of the Peace Process: Oslo and After*. New York: Pantheon Books, 2000.

Said, Edward. "Orientalism Reconsidered." In *Orientalism: A Reader*, edited by Alexander Lyon Macfie, 345–361. New York: New York University Press, 2000.

Said, Edward. "A Method for Thinking about Just Peace." In *What Is a Just Peace?*, edited by Pierre Allan and Alexis Keller, 176–194. New York: Oxford University Press, 2006.

Said, Edward. "Shattered Myths." In *Orientalism: A Reader*, 89–103. Edited by Alexander Lyon Macfie. New York: New York University Press, 2000.

Schwalgin, Susanne. "Why Locality Matters: Diaspora Consciousness and Sedentariness in the Armenian Diaspora in Greece." In *Diaspora, Identity and Religion: New Directions in Theory and Research*, edited by Waltraud Kokot, Khachig Tölölyan, and Carolin Alfonso, 72–92. London: Routledge, 2004.

"Serbian Foreign Minister Juk Veremic: Kosovo 'Is Our Jerusalem.'" *Spiegel Online International*, May 31, 2010. http://www.spiegel.de/international/europe/serbian-foreign-minister-vuk-jeremic-kosovo-is-our-jerusalem-a-697725.html.

Shain, Yossi, and Aharon Barth. "Diasporas in International Relations Theory." *International Organization* 57, no. 2 (2003): 449–479.

Shakman Hurd, Elizabeth. *The Politics of Secularism in International Relations*. Princeton, NJ: Princeton University Press, 2008.

Shakya, Tsering. "Who Are the Prisoners?" *Journal of the American Academy of Religion* 69, no. 1 (2001): 183–189.

Shenhav, Yehouda. *The Arab Jews: A Postcolonial Reading of Nationalism, Religion, and Ethnicity*. Stanford, CA: Stanford University Press, 2006.

Sherwood, Harriet. "Rachel Corrie Lawsuit Result 'Dangerous Precedent' Say Human Rights Groups." *Guardian*. August 28, 2012. http://www.guardian.co.uk/world/2012/aug/28/rachel-corrie-dismissal-dangerous-precedent.

Shohat, Ella. *Israeli Cinema: East/West and the Politics of Representation*. Austin: University of Texas Press, 1989.

Smith, Hazel. "Diasporas in International Conflict." In *Diasporas in Conflict: Peace-Makers or Peace-Wreckers?*, edited by Hazel Smith and Paul Stares. Tokyo: United Nations University Press, 2007.

Smith, Jonathan Z. *To Take Place: Toward Theory in Ritual*. Chicago: University Press, 1987.

Sökefeld, Martin. "Religion or Culture? Concepts of Identity in the Alevi Diaspora." In *Diaspora, Identity and Religion: New Directions in Theory and Research*, edited by Waltraud Kokot, Khachig Tölölyan, and Carolin Alfonso, 143–165. London: Routledge, 2004.

Spector, Stephen. *Evangelicals and Israel: The Story of American Christian Zionism*. New York: Oxford University Press, 2009.

Springs, Jason A. "Dismantling the Master's House: Freedom as Ethical Practice in Brandom and Foucault." *Journal of Religious Ethics* 37, no. 3 (2009): 419–448.

"Thank You, South Carolina: The Race to Replace Disgrace." *The Daily Show with John Stewart*, June 7, 2010. http://www.thedailyshow.com/watch/mon-june-7-2010/thank-you--south-carolina---the-race-to-replace-disgrace.

Thurman, Robert A. F. "Critical Reflections on Donald S. Lopez Jr.'s *Prisoners of Shangri-La: Tibetan Buddhism and the West.*" *Journal of the American Academy of Religion* 69, no. 1 (2001): 191–201.

Thurston, Anne F. "The Chinese View of Tibet—Is Dialogue Possible?" *Cultural Survival Quarterly* 12, no. 1 (1988): 70–73. http://www.culturalsurvival.org/ourpublications/csq/article/the-chinese-view-tibet-is-dialogue-possible.

Tölölyan, Khachig. "Rethinking Diaspora(s): Stateless Power in the Transnational Moment." *Diaspora* 5, no. 1 (1996): 3–36.

Uvin, Peter. *Aiding Violence: The Development Enterprise in Rwanda.* West Hartford, CT: Kumarian Press, 1998.

Uvin, Peter. "Global Dreams and Local Anger: From Structural to Acute Violence in a Globalizing World." In *Rethinking Global Political Economy: Emerging Issues, Unfolding Odysseys*, edited by Mary Ann Tétreault, Robert A. Denemark, Kenneth P. Thomas, and Kurt Burch, 147–162. London: Routledge, 2003.

Varadarajan, Latha. "Back to the Future: Historical Materialism, Diaspora Politics, and the Limits of Novelty." *International Political Sociology* 6, no. 1 (2012): 95–99.

Waddell, L. Austine. *The Buddhism of Tibet or Lamaism.* Cambridge: Heffer, 1971.

Wallach Scott, Joan. *The Politics of the Veil.* Princeton, NJ: Princeton University Press, 2007.

Wood, Robert E. "Touristic Ethnicity: A Brief Itinerary." *Ethnic and Racial Studies* 21, no. 2 (1998): 218–241.

Yeh, Emily T. "Exile Meets Homeland: Politics, Performance, and Authenticity in the Tibetan Diaspora." *Environmental and Planning D: Society and Space* 25, no. 4 (2007): 648–667.

Zertal, Idith. *Israel's Holocaust and the Politics of Nationhood.* Cambridge: Cambridge University Press, 2005.

Zerubavel, Yael. *Recovered Roots: Collective Memory and the Making of Israeli National Tradition.* Chicago: University of Chicago Press, 1995.

Zunes, Stephen. "The Israel Lobby: How Powerful Is It Really?" *Mother Jones*, May 17, 2006. http://www.motherjones.com/politics/2006/05/israel-lobby-how-powerful-it-really.

PART FIVE

THE GROWING EDGE OF THE CONVERSATION

CHAPTER 25

···

RELIGION, CONFLICT, AND PEACEBUILDING: SYNTHETIC REMARKS

···

ATALIA OMER

JUSTPEACE: A NORMATIVE ORIENTATION

···

A pivotal aspect of our conversation during the framing workshop for this volume was to illuminate the tension between the complex concept of *justpeace* elucidated in an essay coauthored by R. Scott Appleby and John Paul Lederach, and the more familiar tradition of the "liberal peace." The neologism of justpeace entails, in the words of the coauthors, "a dynamic state of affairs in which the reduction and management of violence and the achievement of social and economic justice are undertaken as mutual, reinforcing dimensions of constructive change."[1] Justpeace is a normative orientation that informs the development of the notion of peacebuilding as a strategic, multidisciplinary, multi-perspectival, and multidimensional engagement that is comprehensive, interdependent, architectonic, sustainable, and integrative.[2] The strategic angle, grounded in a justpeace orientation, allows for thinking about conflict transformation as a long-term process aimed at analyzing the root causes of deadly violence and its relation to cultural and structural forms of violence, histories, memories, global structures, and local and global power dynamics. Likewise, this lens provides a framework for thinking and acting pragmatically and proactively to articulate and link immediate and long-term views of desired change. According to this view, justpeace critiques, complements, and supplements the liberal peace. Most of the contributors to this volume took up the challenge to wrestle with the justpeace orientation in developing their respective chapters.

In his contribution, comparative ethicist David Little, for instance, critically connects the discussion of the liberal peace to a typology of nationalism, fluctuating between the ideal types of civic/liberal and ethnic/illiberal. He argues on the basis of empirical evidence that illiberal forms of nationalism positively correlate with an increased probability of deadly violence. Little recognizes the validity of some critiques of this typology—including the unavoidable ethnocentricity of every nationalism and the tension between a supposed commitment to universal rights and the parochial, chauvinistic, nationalist impulse to cater to "members only." Yet he insists that his robust view of liberal forms of nationalism and the attendant understanding of the liberal peace offer sufficient conceptual parameters for thinking about peacebuilding and change. For Little, in short, a justpeace agenda does not constitute a radical paradigm shift.

To illustrate why the search for a radically different paradigm for conflict analysis and peacebuilding is not only unnecessary but conceptually misguided, Little examines "afresh the historical origins of nationalism as background to the idea of liberal peace." This effort takes him back to the Protestant Reformation as well as to antecedent influences of Renaissance humanism and Catholic conciliarism. Resisting the oversimplified way in which critics of the liberal peace dismiss liberal political theory and practice as a hegemonic and monochromatic discourse, Little insists on recovering the complexity, contextuality, and resources for self-correction inherent in the liberal tradition itself. These resources (especially found in liberal Calvinism), Little argues, are well equipped to respond to valid critiques from the perspective of a justpeace orientation, the most pertinent of which are the need for an emphasis on social and economic justice to counter the marriage of the free-market agenda with liberalism and the need to address the modes of local and global structural violence associated with this agenda.

Similarly, in his chapter on "Religion, Nationalism, and the Politics of Secularism," political scientist Scott Hibbard follows Little's conceptual foundations in arguing that "ecumenical secularism," which he views as foundational to a robust interpretation of liberalism, is highly consistent with a justpeace orientation with its focus on economic, cultural, social, and political forms of justice, including a commitment to deep plurality. For Hibbard, "the important question is not whether states are religious or secular per se, but, rather, how do different interpretations of religion (and secularism) inform competing visions of the nation?" This question informs his comparative study of the "resurgence" of religious politics in the latter part of the twentieth century, in contexts as diverse as the United States, Egypt, and India, and his engagement with two sets of interlocutors: the deconstructive critics of secularism associated with the work of anthropologist Talal Asad, and the scholars associated with the justpeace orientation who criticize the "liberal peace," which they see as a tradition and a set of political practices unaware of their own modes of injustice. Hibbard critiques what he calls "irreligious secularism" as an untenable position. "Religion," he writes, "provides a normative language for political action, informs nationalist mythologies, and helps to define collective identities." "Ecumenical secularism" is capable, Hibbard affirms, of cultivating deep plurality within what Little refers to as the paradoxical constraints of bounded political entities.

Little and Hibbard's reclaiming of the liberal peace tradition, especially as it relates to the discussion of religion and politics in particular national arenas, recognizes the validity of some of the critiques of the restrictive view of violence associated with the liberal lens—that is, a view of violence as (merely) physical, direct, and deadly. Indeed, both Little's historical investigation and Hibbard's reimagining of secularism intend to address the conventional lack of attention to cultural, religious, and systemic violence. Rather than dismiss secularism and liberalism altogether, however, they argue that there is much in these traditions that is worth salvaging and that is highly consistent with the justpeace conceptualization. To this extent, these two "defenders" of the liberal peace tradition are critical caretakers[3]: they recognize its limitations, its historicity, its flaws—and also its multiple resources for self-correction.

DIFFERENT CONCEPTIONS OF VIOLENCE

This mode of critical caretaking is consistent with justpeace, broadly construed. Thus the editors devoted attention to how different conceptions of violence could expand the scope of analysis as well as bring greater nuance to the fields of practice. Indeed, pondering how religion might relate to those expanded discussions of violence offers many new and productive avenues for future research. In his contribution to the volume, ethicist and religious studies scholar Jason A. Springs provides a genealogy of the concepts of structural and cultural violence as they have emerged in debates within the precincts of peace studies, and of the affinities such debates share with critical theory and discourse analysis. Springs demonstrates how cross-fertilization with such debates requires expanding the scope of the discussion concerning the relation between religion, conflict, and peacebuilding from a preoccupation with deadly violence to a more complex multidimensional engagement with how religious leaders, resources, vocabularies, and infrastructures relate to structural and cultural forms of violence. Springs examines the relevance of this analysis to potentially transforming direct and deadly as well as cultural and structural violence. Indeed, he argues that structural and cultural forms of violence demand the attention of peacebuilders even if—perhaps *especially* when—those forms of violence do not erupt in, or trigger, explicit, direct, deadly violence. Certainly, the aforementioned defenders of the liberal peace—a tradition now re-positioned by Little and Hibbard as revisable and self-correcting—accept the lessons of such a multifocal account of violence, recognizing the cultural and structural forms of violence with which secular liberalism itself became complicit.

However, if Little and Hibbard insist on retaining a robust and self-correcting liberalism as both an analytic lens as well as a roadmap for peacebuilding, political scientist and peace studies scholar Daniel Philpott critiques the liberal peace paradigm as too narrow a ground for imagining and accomplishing processes of political reconciliation. In his chapter, Philpott articulates "an ethic of peacebuilding" which, he argues, is grounded in religious traditions rather than in the secular tradition informing liberal political theory. By religious traditions, he refers to the three Abrahamic so-called "world religions." The selectively retrieved "ethic of peacebuilding," Philpott then suggests, could become instrumental in contexts of "transitional justice," a construct he adopts with caution. On his account, the liberal peace paradigm dominates the discourse of the international community on the question of justice in the wake of mass atrocities. The concept of justice inherent in the liberal peace, which focuses on individual rights and liberties and the rule of law, emerged from the Enlightenment, according to the standard narrative. Being a dominant discourse, the liberal peace, Philpott writes, is also "a set of contemporary actors and institutions" and the "set of activities that these actors carry out: establishing the rule of law, human rights, and free markets, carrying out elections, and the range of measures that promote relief and settlement at the end of armed conflict."

A focus on the concept and practice of reconciliation from South Africa and Sierra Leone to El Salvador and Guatemala suggests the deep rootedness of the notion of reconciliation in religious traditions and the creative hermeneutical work of theologians, religious actors, and scholars who extend reconciliation to political spheres of interactions. The concept of reconciliation, contra the liberal peace, cannot be reduced to a discussion of "rights, entitlements, and deserved punishment." Instead, Philpott underscores reconciliation as entailing a different conception of justice as "the comprehensive set of obligations that define right relationship in all spheres of life." Reconciliation, therefore, means the restoration of right relationship through redressing the wounds of injustices.

Redressing of wounds then translates into several practices, some overlapping with the liberal peace frame and others departing not only from its current scope but also from its premises. These practices include building socially just institutions, acknowledgment of wrongdoing, reparations, punishment, apology, and forgiveness. Forgiveness, with its highly religious and Christian-centric connotations, is singled out as the most at odds with the liberal peace frame but also as the most promising area for further research and peacebuilding practice. Philpott, in other words, presents reconciliation with an emphasis on forgiveness as a radically different paradigm of peacebuilding, one in tension with the hegemonic liberal peace and its enduring domination among the various actors and institutions involved in transitional justice processes.

While not referring explicitly in his chapter to the concept of justpeace, Philpott's explication of reconciliation resonates with a focus on root causes and holistic transformation of conflict. His underscoring of the religious and primarily Christian model of forgiveness for his new paradigm or ethic of peacebuilding could, however, be resisted on various grounds. As mentioned, the critical caretaking approach adopted by the defenders of the liberal peace paradigm retrieves resources from within the liberal tradition for corrective and economic justice. Is the contrast between justpeace and liberal peace therefore overstated? Philpott's construal of these two paradigms as occasionally overlapping but as essentially grounded in radically different worldviews suggests that it is accurate to perceive a sharp contrast between the two. The "debate" between Little and Hibbard, on the one hand, and Philpott, on the other, underscores another dimension of our workshop's deliberations: the importance of historicist and genealogical critique of the very terms of the conversation.

In charting the failures of secular humanitarian and relief and development agencies to lift people out of poverty, and their reluctant recognition, over the last two decades, of the inadequacy of their engagement (or lack thereof) with local and regional religious and cultural actors, R. Scott Appleby's discussion of the nexus between religion, peacebuilding, and development also turns on an explicit critique of the liberal peace model. Precisely in its previous tendency virtually to ignore "local wisdom" regarding what constitutes "authentic" human development in specific geographic and cultural settings, and its accompanying blindness to the various ways in which top-down development projects trigger violent conflict among ethnic, religious, and political actors on the ground, the so-called World Bank approach has proved counterproductive. Yet Appleby also indicates, à la Little and Hibbard, that the liberal secularist paradigm is giving evidence of its capacity to incorporate appropriate reforms, in that some sectors of the World Bank and other traditional "mainstream" development agencies are gradually opening themselves up to religious expertise and partnerships with local religious actors. The progress in this regard is halting, indeed, and it is too early to say whether it represents accommodation of or definitive resistance to the introduction of justpeace imperatives into a model of development that remains staunchly rooted in liberal peace assumptions.

Appleby prefers to see the glass as half full: his chapter traces a growing awareness among the three sets of actors—development experts, peacebuilders, and religious actors—regarding the affinities and opportunities for collaboration among them. He argues that their previously separate and self-contained understandings and practices are converging in three areas, creating a nexus for collaboration, a common ground, that should be cultivated by religious leaders, development experts, and peacebuilders alike. These areas of convergence respond to and address key requirements and methods of building a justpeace: 1) the priority of the local community, as engaged in its full creative potential by local and external actors alike through an elicitive method of discernment and practice; 2) an emerging set of "rules of engagement," rooted in reflexive practice, with trans-local and transnational partners; and 3) perhaps most challenging, a growing recognition of the fluid and shifting criteria for "authentic" human development. The challenges of transforming these commonalities into actual sites of convergence and collaboration, however, are significant.

CRITIQUE

Appleby's chapter illuminates the point that navigating the tensions between the positive and negative conceptions of peace associated with the lenses of justpeace and the liberal peace, respectively, necessitates attentiveness to the theoretical tools of critique. The concepts we use have histories, contested meanings, ethical presuppositions, and political applications. For example, scholars must be attentive to how one term in a dichotomous pair defines its opposite and vice versa: universal versus particular, global versus local, theory versus practice, negative versus positive, religious versus secular. Some of the contributors engaged those complexities explicitly.

Hibbard, as indicated above, problematizes the tendency of some critics of the secular tradition to delegitimize secularism as an authorizing discourse of modernity, colonialism, neo-imperialism, and neoliberalism. He specifically highlights Talal Asad's understanding of secularism as inherently exclusivist and repressive of certain worldviews and voices of dissent. Acknowledging Asad's assertion that the public space is a space articulated by power and that only those voices that conform to the norms of liberal modernity can be tolerated and possibly heard, Hibbard asks rhetorically: "Does it mean that the elimination of constitutional restraint would be preferable?" Committed to rehabilitating rather than discarding secularism, Hibbard deploys the notion of "ecumenical secularism" in order to respond to the critiques of liberalism and secularism, without falling into the potential traps of relativism, on the one hand, or utopianism, on the other. Given that the public space will always be articulated by power, the only recourse is to devise mechanisms to push back against hegemonic power agendas. The task is to negotiate and enhance the meanings of plurality in the aftermath of the critique of the liberal discourse of tolerance and in the face of illiberal religious and other challenges to democratic institutions and practices. Thus, according to Hibbard, it is not necessary to abandon the liberal tradition in its entirety, including the principle and practice of secularity that inhabits the heart of the aspiration for multi-ethnic and multi-religious plurality as a desirable normative good—and one highly compatible with the justpeace orientation and nonviolent modes of conflict transformation and management.

Like Hibbard, sociologist of religion Slavica Jakelić stresses the limits of the critics of secularism in overcoming what she calls "secularist parochialism." The conceptual premises of the critique of secularism put the critics in "great danger of falling into another extreme—that of marginalizing and neglecting the positive role of secularism for establishing and sustaining peace." Focusing on the case of the Polish Solidarity movement in the 1980s and on patterns of collaboration between secular (atheist) and religious Polish activists, Jakelić challenges the deconstructive critiques of secular agency articulated by Asad and those working within the Asadian premises, such as anthropologist Saba Mahmood. Drawing on Rajeev Bhargava's intervention into the growing industry of secularism studies, Jakelić underscores that the problem is not that secularism entails a normative orientation but rather the pretense that it is normatively neutral. Hence, she suggests, by way of introducing her case study, that an embrace of secularism as a normative orientation "guided by a drive to enable the human flourishing of all" is paramount to a justpeace agenda with its definitional appreciation of relational interpretations of justice and injustice. Historicizing and critiquing the discourses of secularism, Jakelić argues, is indispensable for discerning the role of religion in peacebuilding. However, to think constructively about conflict transformation would require moving beyond the critique of secularism. It would necessitate deciphering the ethical and institutional, not merely the instrumental, roles of religion underlying potential secular-religious engagements in peacebuilding.

Atalia Omer's "Religious Peacebuilding: The Exotic, the Good, and the Theatrical" likewise ascertains, by way of mapping the field, the indispensability yet insufficiency of critique in theorizing and imagining the role of religion and religious people and institutions in processes of conflict transformation. Most of what takes place in the field of religious peacebuilding, Omer argues, has been grounded, implicitly or explicitly, in historian and peace studies scholar Scott Appleby's *The Ambivalence of the Sacred* (2000)[4] and his phenomenological approach to religion. Appleby's thesis ignited the industry of religious peacebuilding owing to its emphasis on internal pluralities of religious traditions, an emphasis that made room for theological and hermeneutical investigations or acts of retrieval as well as recognition of the instrumentality of religious leaders and institutions in various arenas of peacebuilding. However, the study of religion and peace, Omer argues, is itself beholden to a secularist paradigm, which explains its preoccupation with direct and obvious forms of violence. Taking up a justpeace orientation instead would lead to a consideration of the relevance of religion to structural and cultural forms of violence, including those varieties of violence that transpire in religious traditions and the communities that embody them. In other words, the thesis of the "ambivalence of the sacred" is misapplied if it represents only the inverse of essentializing and ahistoricizing interpretive frames that render "religion" or "civilizational identities" as the causes of violent conflicts.

This reductive approach to the analysis of religion and conflict was most recently popularized by the late Harvard political scientist Samuel Huntington in his influential thesis on the "clash of civilizations."[5] He argued that conflict in the post–Cold War era will erupt along "civilizational" rather than ideological fault lines and will, most likely, involve Islam (infamously exclaiming that "Islam has bloody borders"). While Huntington's thesis gained traction as a supposedly new paradigm for explicating conflict, his view of "Islamic civilization" as incompatible with Judeo-Christian "Western civilization" clearly locates the framework within a long history of orientalism and thus opens this approach to the study of religion and conflict to the same kind of critique that exposed the orientalist discourse.[6]

Omer, to reiterate, argues that interpreting Appleby's "ambivalence of the sacred" merely as the inverse of Huntington's essentialism by focusing on retrieving internal pluralities within religious traditions offers only a limited conceptual scope for the study of religion, conflict, and peacebuilding.

In a complementary chapter reprinted here, Appleby maps the state of scholarship on the question of religion and violence as falling into three orientations. The first, which he terms "strong religion," refers to theoretical works that presume religion either as a cause of and motivation behind deadly violence or an independent variable animating movements that are also oriented by more "secular" projects such as a struggle for national self-determination. This mode of "strong religion" lends itself to Girardian functionalism and to an analysis of religious violence as categorically different from normal, routine, and rational secular violence. The second mode in which religion figures into interpretive frames is "weak" or epiphenomenal: religion is interpreted as a dependent variable in deadly violence. Through this analytic prism, the *real* cause of violence is always "secular" and supposedly more basic than religious. One thread that Appleby associates with the "weak religion" camp is theoretical engagement with the formation of nationalisms as an outcome of some process of manipulation by political elites of antecedent religious and cultural narratives, symbols, sentiments, and practices. A related thread of the literature is preoccupied with the relevance of colonial encounters and discourses in weakening religious traditions in such a way that they become resources for power manipulations. The third mode of analysis is "pathological religion." This interpretive frame explores the "fundamentalist mindset," secular or religious, and locates mass violence as perversion and pathology writ large. Proponents of this approach, Appleby argues, do not only "choose the extreme point on the spectrum as the representative of the whole," but also, and perhaps most importantly from a peace studies perspective, "fail to explain why the majority of the world's fundamentalists *do not* take up the sword."

In his own discussion of religious militancy, historian Patrick Q. Mason employs case studies from the struggle for and against civil rights in the United States in order to underscore the crucial significance of religious literacy as a shield against "facile manipulation" by violent religious and secular militants. And yet he cautions against the "textual cherry-picking" associated with the field of religious peacebuilding and its associated tendency to declare certain aspects of a tradition "inauthentic." While detouring to explore some of the historicist critiques of the modernist, orientalist, and Christian-centric assumptions embedded within the very categories of the "religious" and "secular" and their supposed binary location that informs the discourse about religious militancy, Mason affirms the Protestant theologian and scholar of religion Paul Tillich's notion of religion as "ultimate concern." Appealing to Tillich at this point may strike some readers as odd in that it attempts a theological response to the secular/religious dichotomy by absorbing the "secular" into a more basic category of "religion" as ultimate concern. This move has been widely critiqued within religious studies as reductionist in that it derives a fundamental, all-encompassing (and arguably anthropological) category of religion from a theological and tradition-specific one.[7] If this is a question intriguingly raised by Mason's chapter, it is a question to which one finds equally compelling responses in philosopher Peter Ochs's chapter on scriptural reasoning (SR) as a range of practices and skills capable of facilitating interfaith engagements that avoid the tendency to reduce tradition-specific categories to more fundamental categories of religion.

Offering a reflection on his twenty-year experiment with SR, Ochs clarifies his move away from the cognitive and individualist biases animating modernist and secularist views of religion. Instead, he understands "religiosity as a category of effective behavior, judged by its fruits in practice, rather than in what individuals intend when they say something." Accordingly, SR's potential contributions to peacebuilding and conflict transformation revolve around a focus on a dialogue occurring, in Ochs's metaphor, from "hearth to hearth." "Hearth" is an etic term that by no means is intended to replace or override emic notions of the sacred. Critically, Ochs illuminates how the practice of SR does not constitute another instance of hegemonic imposition of foreign or colonial models of peace, for it resists defining relative terms like "inner and outer," "indigenous and outsider," "emic and etic" as sets of contradictions. In response to the question whether the practice of SR itself amounts to an imposition, Ochs replies that even when it is not "indigenous" to the traditions, participants' experiences eventually suggest that SR "seems to fall within the bounds of authorized or legitimate behavior and appears, in fact, to strengthen traditional faith even while it stimulates collegial bonds across the borders of the traditions."

Ochs's discussion illuminates the effectiveness of SR as a practice of inter-religious conflict transformation, but he remains tentative with respect to the potential application of SR in conflict zones dominated by direct forms of violence. Importantly, however, SR as a set of practices does increase the level of religious literacy, which strengthens religious actors' ability to resist manipulation by religious and other political entrepreneurs.

This exploratory avenue naturally engages the various critiques of "religion" as a post-Enlightenment construct deeply embedded within Western colonialism. One such critique challenges the myth of origins of the Western concepts of liberal tolerance and secularity, which holds them to be the evolutionary outcome of taming and domesticating irrational and inherently divisive religious passions. The myth presents religious violence as categorically different from secular and rational violence, a thesis debunked by the theologian William Cavanaugh.[8] Both Mason's emphasis on "pedagogical peacebuilding" and Ochs's imagining of SR as a form of inter-religious conflict transformation build on Cavanaugh's challenge to "the myth of religious violence."

Cavanaugh's thesis also animates scholar of Islamic and religious studies A. Rashied Omar's chapter on religious and state violence. With particular attention devoted to the case of South Africa, Omar demonstrates that the hegemonic hold of the secularist discourse that differentiates categorically between religious and secular forms of violence explains the paucity of scholarship addressing state violence and terrorism. While highlighting a few exceptions in the works of Michael Sells and David Chidester, he argues forcefully that a lacuna in the literature has prevented scholars from recognizing the role and complicity of the state in producing violence by religious actors. Clearly, this critique of state violence invites a contextual discussion of religion and nationalism. It also echoes Jakelić's engagement with the various critiques of secularism as political and normative projects, which lead to a pivotal consideration of cultural and systemic violence as they may relate to the need to decipher how and why state violence is authorized. What cultural and religious memories, symbols, and authorities legitimize acts of state violence? This is where a careful discussion of nationalism as a theory of political legitimacy allows for broadening the analytic scope of the discussion of religion, conflict, and peacebuilding.

However, a good deal of theorizing about religion and peacebuilding builds upon Cavanaugh's critique in articulating an argument about religious agency outside the surveillance logic of the secular state and its claim to a monopoly over the legitimate use of force. Accordingly, the state is posited as a Leviathan whose tentacles are ever expanding into the interiority and consciences of individual members of the society. In Cavanaugh's *Myth of Religious Violence,* his radical orthodoxy (while muted in this particular book) intersects with Asad's reading of Foucault's notion of governmentality. The modern state and the modern political liberal secular project are interpreted only as a violent and insidious disruption of tradition and as an instrument of empire, without substantive engagements with the multifaceted tradition of liberalism and its potential to correct itself through geneaological and historicist scrutiny of its sometimes tainted legacy and to develop more fully in the direction of ecumenical secularism as discussed by the aforementioned defenders of this tradition. Pursuing Cavanaugh's line of critique, therefore, entails positing the state as an abstraction or aberration born out of an intra-Christian theological mistake while expressing no interest in questions of liberalism's relation to the realities and demands of religious pluralisms and other demands of ethno-cultural justice not easily accommodated by traditional theological and political imaginations and frameworks. Such a state-centric approach and the homogenizing narration of modernity as "fall" re-inscribe (despite purporting to deconstruct) the rigid binary logic of anti-religious secularism. As a result, the analysis of the "state" overlooks how the "nation" (with its own "elective affinities" with religious and cultural symbols, motifs, narratives, memories) authorizes the political infrastructure of the state.

Cavanaugh's deconstructing of the narrative of the secular state as the "peacemaker" responsible for resolving religiously based conflicts also makes an appearance in the contribution of legal scholars W. Cole Durham Jr. and Elizabeth A. Clark. Their argument that the protection of religious freedom is "fundamental to the structure of peacebuilding" draws on Cavanaugh's historicizing of the so-called wars of religion. Durham and Clark underscore that protecting the freedom of religion can function as a preventive measure with a long-term, flexible, and context-specific outlook cognizant of the peace dividend and the social goods and virtues of religious traditions that can function to reinforce the sociopolitical order rather than threaten its stability. Durham and Clark agree with Cavanaugh's critique of liberal political theory's exaggerated concern with religious difference and with his equally sharp critique of the creation, out of the irrational and divisive bloody passions of the so-called European wars of religion, of both a myth of religious violence and a corresponding myth of the peaceable secular state. Most critically, they build on Cavanaugh's rereading of the mythology of the modern West to suggest that the cause of religious violence was not religious passions or doctrinal differences but rather "state-imposed restrictions on religion." The abstract, generic state is the source of violence in this story and the role of religion as a causal factor of violence is significantly downplayed. Indeed, for Cavanaugh (drawing on Asad and scholars working in his intellectual tradition), "religion" was invented by the state for the purposes of advancing geopolitical agendas abroad and displacing, marginalizing, taming, and dominating potential opposition domestically. Durham and Clark's conclusion is simple and elegant: the protection of the freedom of religion and belief is a long-term guarantee of stability; accordingly, a focus on the legal structures and practices of these freedoms is a crucial contribution to peacebuilding, conflict transformation, and the cultivation of justpeace.

Intersecting with Little and Hibbard's conceptualization of liberal political theory as a tradition with clear potential for self-correction, as well as with Jakelić's notion of parochial secularism, Durham and Clark defend a robust Lockean account attentive to the relationship between law and conscience. They do so in order to underscore the instrumentality and relevance of the maintenance and protection of social pluralism for peacebuilding and the prevention of violent conflict. The claim to equality, they argue, constitutes a mere façade if it "confuses a right to sameness with an equal right to be different." Beyond expanding Locke's theorizing of the relation between legal theory and the protection of conscience, Durham and Clark underscore that Locke's limits to toleration can be extended to permit various forms of radical dissent and exclusivist worldviews as long as those do not subvert the very institutions allowing for pluralism. Their potential for subversion is then countered by the cultivation of mutual respect, commitment to human dignity, and legal mechanisms designed for "filtering" out destructive and subversive religious agendas through the language of limitations.

This is yet another recognition in this volume of the critique of liberalism with its conventional arguments about the logic underlying the liberal peace. As is the case for Little and Hibbard, however, the challenges to liberalism from the justpeace perspective do not require throwing out the baby with the proverbial bathwater. For Durham and Clark, the strategy for revising and expanding liberal political theory is not just the practice of ecumenical secularism as a counter to parochial secularism. Nor is it an aspiration to respond to the post-structuralist critics of political liberalism. Rather, Durham and Clark voice a concern that the silencing of religious voices and institutions is detrimental for peace and the prevention of deadly violence. Religion's constructive engagements with the legal framework informing the discourse concerning the basic freedom of religion are also put in jeopardy by this occlusion, they worry. The management of pluralism through a non-doctrinaire vocabulary of legal equality is a product of modernity not to be dispensed with. Rather, it is a legacy that ought to be at the heart of a comprehensive and strategic peacebuilding lens, which focuses on long-term, integrative, context-sensitive processes of change and nonviolent conflict transformation. Durham and Clark's expansive reading of Locke also involves a critical challenge to the conceptualization of religion as private and interiorized, a conceptualization born out of the Lockean distinction between the temporal and spiritual spheres. Instead, the public and communal dimensions of religion need to be incorporated into nation-specific as well as international legal arguments about the protection of religion and belief as they span diverse constitutional and sociopolitical contexts.

By now it is clear that Durham and Clark's focus on the protection of religious freedom as a crucial dimension of peacebuilding aspires to reform the liberal tradition and its conceptualization of peace as it relates to challenges from a justpeace perspective. Their approach also relies on a de-privatized interpretation of religion and therefore contains the capacity to respond, at least in part, to potential critics who would otherwise classify these legal scholars as beholden to a narrow and highly specific theorizing of religion qua belief. Participants in this mode of critique[9] are highly suspicious of who gets to define what religion is, what agendas that defining serves, and how the contemporary focus on the protection of religious freedoms relates to the tainted colonial legacy of religious taxonomies. Also called into question are the instrumental nature of the language of protection in the so-called war on terror(ism) and the legal structures through which the supposedly ever-expanding scope of government unfolds, among other discursive and genealogical foci.

When read alongside the contributions by Little, Hibbard, Jakelić, and others, Durham and Clark's chapter offers a strong constructive response to such critics. First, their nuanced rereading of the liberal tradition and secularity complicates the inclination of the critics to

see the discourse of religious freedoms as an instrument of geopolitical domination to nar-
rate a homogenized story of modernity. This narrative tells a story about the emergence of
the liberal state as a Leviathan, manifesting itself with the same surveillance logic and legal
mechanisms, regardless of contexts, and thereby disrupting traditional modalities of agency
and personhood.[10] Second, Durham and Clark offer empirical data and the tools of legal
theory to suggest the productive correlation between the protection of religious freedom
and the conditions necessary for nourishing other virtues and social goods associated with
peacebuilding. Regardless of its potential limitations, this approach recognizes the empowering dimensions of the legal vocabulary of protection. The critics, on the other hand, remain
beholden to a deconstructive lens and thus contribute little to thinking about sociopolitical
transformations, including affirmation of basic universal standards for human flourishing.

Indeed, Durham and Clark's framing constructively intervenes in mediating the tension
between the justpeace and liberal peace orientations through the affirmation of pluralism.
Similarly, they offer resources to illuminate the importance of protecting the freedom of
religion and belief for operationalizing the archeology and strategy of peacebuilding. And
yet their analysis still needs to grapple with Jakelić's critique that the problem is not that
secularism offers a normative prism but rather that it presents itself as normatively neutral. The presumption that the secular can be neutral vis-à-vis religion underlies Durham
and Clark's retrieval of Locke in the service of their legal theorizing. Once again there is
an assumption here that the "state" is authorized through a set of abstract principles and
not through an affirmation of a collective identity, culture, and passions, the protection of
which is worth dying for. If this is indeed the case, how can one distinguish between the
United States, Canada, and Sweden? Beyond the presumption of the possibility of state neutrality, the public aspect of religion that Durham and Clark underscore contra the modernist
assumption of religion qua interiorized faith is not accompanied by a related challenge to the
framing of religion qua choice nor the related cognitive bias that underpins the early decades
of the comparative study of religion and that Asad and many others have critiqued and historicized. In the modernist view, an individual's religiosity is a function of choice (affirming
the "right to exit" religious communities and institutions) and thus cognitive consent. Such
assumptions—when re-inscribed without attention to their problematic pretense to universality nor their historical legacy and complicity with empire—are vulnerable to the mode of
critique described above.

One may ask whether it is relevant to discuss the complicity of the Anglo-Saxon thinker's ideas with colonial domination and displacement. Similarly, when shifting away from
a narrow focus on deadly violence, can the robust Lockean rereading of liberalism address
more expansive accounts of structural and cultural violence within religious communities
and institutions, especially as they pertain to gender equality? How might the negotiability
between liberal peace and justpeace perspectives play out in resolving the tension between
equality and the wiring of patriarchy into the very structures of religious traditions? How
might the analysis in Durham and Clark's chapter account for power dynamics internal to
religious communities and their protected practices? What of the protection of internal pluralities within religious communities? And what of the related perennial question of the critics of the discourse of religious freedoms: who gets to talk on behalf of such communities
and why?[11]

In sum, Durham and Clark's engagement with the legal theories governing the protection
of the freedom of religion could be pushed even further to confront the broader question of

how the mechanism of protection, while contributing to stability and peacebuilding through the guarded affirmation of pluralism, also entrenches internal, typically patriarchal, traditional systems and institutions that by virtue of their protection from the state, may not benefit from pluralizing forces they would otherwise embrace for the sake of their preservation and protection. As in Cavanaugh's narrow focus on the (ir)relevance of religion to deadly violence—a focus that enables his debunking of the myth of religious violence—Durham and Clark's underscoring of the freedom of religion is not concerned with various modes of silent and structural violence associated with the institutions and practices of religious communities themselves. The right to exit currently is an anemic right and, frequently, not a choice at all.

Cavanaugh's critique of the myth of religious violence also lurks in the background of Timothy Shah's chapter, titled "Secular Militancy as an Obstacle for Peacebuilding." Shah's chapter echoes more closely a lament about the loss (as well as the violence) associated with secularism, a development he narrates as disruptive of the fabric of the antecedent worldview and related institutions. He provides a genealogy of secularism that brackets consideration of the colonial and persistently Christian-centric contexts of secularization processes. Likewise, it posits secularism as a normative worldview (a "religion" in fact involving a "leap of faith") that is inherently militant, both as intellectual and political project. Gesturing toward internal pluralities and divergent shapes of secularism, Shah nonetheless laments the secular as a misguided and highly ideological, false construct that detracts from the ability to analyze violence and conflict.

Shah's critique of secularism stands in fundamental tension with Little's discussion of the influences of the Reformation on the emergence of modern liberal and illiberal conceptions of nationalism, Hibbard's discussion of ecumenical secularism, and Jakelić's affirmation of secularism as a normative orientation, pivotal for a justpeace orientation with respect to conflict transformation and peacebuilding. Shah's critique reflects a teleological conception of modernity that affirms an interpretation of the Enlightenment that has come under scrutiny in various and interrelated disciplinary conversations.[12] While Shah laments the secularism paradigm, however, the rabbi and scholar-practitioner Marc Gopin celebrates this legacy as instrumental for his work in religious or faith-based diplomacy. The mention of Gopin leads us explicitly to another thematic thread that animates this volume, namely the tension and complex relations between theory and practice.

THEORY AND PRACTICE

Like Jakelić, Gopin discusses the possibility of negotiating and collaborating across religious and secular lines, albeit from a different point of departure that does not attend to the critiques and internal pluralities of secularism. The myth of religious violence that Cavanaugh debunks remains an operative framing of Gopin's work as a religious peacebuilder who is all too aware of the bloody legacy of religious people and institutions. "Organized religion," Gopin stresses, "has been one of the most important handmaidens and apologists for the worst empires and states of history, not only failing to analyze structural injustice but actively constructing the most long-standing forms of structural injustice, against nonbelievers, against women, against homosexuals, even against children sometimes, and always available to bless the destruction of enemies beyond the borders of the empire or state." In contrast to this "priestly" type of religiosity, however, religious traditions also carry histories including many instances of *prophetic* critiques of injustice and resources for reform. It is this insight that animates Appleby's thesis of the "ambivalence of the sacred," which also informs Gopin's actual justpeace-building work in Palestine/Israel, Syria, and other arenas of conflict, where he strives to strike a balance between the liberal peace and the "elicitive, religious-cultural peace" models. Gopin underscores the need for conflict resolution efforts, international relations, and diplomacy to overcome the secular myopia that has dominated these spheres and skewed capacities for peacebuilding. While he does not wish to overstate the uniqueness of religion and religious people in offering counter-hegemonic critiques, the empirical record suggests the effectiveness of so-called faith-based diplomacy, a growing practice of which Gopin has been an integral part.

Religious peacebuilding also involves hermeneutical engagement with texts, narratives, and memories, a process which he understands as one that would elicit themes consistent with "tolerance (even love) of the other." Such a process could complement and embolden the framework of the liberal peace, especially in efforts to promote reconcilitation.

Endorsing Philpott's work on the role of religion in efforts for political reconciliation, Gopin nonetheless affirms the liberal tradition and its premises. He upholds a conception of "a shared public space in which no one group or religion has a monopoly" as a building block of his view of the role of religion and religious voices in justpeace-building. This overarching commitment to such a notion of the public and the pluralism it may facilitate—an innovation which, Gopin exclaims, "we owe. . . to the Enlightenment"—informs his view of religious peacebuilding as an occasion to return and imagine the "best ethical moorings" of religious traditions. Hence, in contrast to Shah's critique of secularism as an error, Gopin joins some of the other contributors to this volume in affirming the secular as a space inherently ripe for religious peacebuilding oriented by the kind of relationality entailed in a justpeace perspective, one that is deeply embedded within a commitment to and recognition of a plurality of voices, experiences, and narratives of injustice.

Whereas Gopin's peacebuilding efforts reflect a focus on the instrumentality of religious people in conflict transformation, theological retrieval, and hermeneutical innovation, his work reflects attentiveness to the particular contextual complexities of the zones of conflict he engages as well as to self-reflexivity in terms of the engrained complicity of religious institutions, leaders, and definitional texts and narratives with structural forms of violence internal to the religious communities themselves. This orientation, in turn, informs a broad view of religious peacebuilding that underscores the instrumentality of religious leaders as well as laypeople.

In a similar manner to Gopin's guarded endorsement of Philpott's focus on the comparative religious ethics of reconciliation, John Kelsay's chapter takes the reader back to the traditional preoccupation of comparative religious ethics with the regulation of force. This time, however, the comparative religious ethicist does so with a particular attention to the relevance of his scholarly tradition to enlarging the scope of peace research and practice. Kelsay worries that the overemphasis of some contributors to this volume on the positive roles of religious actors and sources in peacebuilding undermines the urgency of attending to traditional and historical conversations concerning religion's participation in authorizing the use of force. He underscores the importance of scrutinizing the ways in which the "historical frameworks intended to regulate armed force are changing in the here and now."

In particular, he focuses on the emergence and consolidation of war conventions during the Abbasid caliphate, tracing the development of this conversation concerning the legitimate use of force in the pursuit of peace and justice through various historical epochs in Islamic histories.

A sketch of the sustained tradition of the ethics of the use of force in Islam also illuminates a distinct vocabulary authorizing the use of violence in extraordinary situations or emergencies "when the ordinary structures of command and control might break down." Suggesting a crisis of legitimacy of traditional structures of authority, Kelsay writes, this emergency mode informs much of the contemporary discourse about jihad as a duty incumbent on every Muslim. Hence, analysis of the role of religion in transforming violent conflict needs substantively to engage the historical frames as well as the contemporary dynamics and colonial and geopolitical legacies underpinning the sense of emergency and with it the breakdown or suspension of ordinary conventions, including those concerning inflicting collateral damage.

Beyond the potential contribution to a deeper analysis of the role of religion in authorizing violence, the sub-field of comparative religious ethics, Kelsay suggests, can participate also in constructively imagining the virtues of peacebuilding as they connect with long-standing ethical thinking about the cultivation of patience, hope, the ability to combine a sense of justice and practical wisdom, and self-discipline. Here Kelsay illustrates for the reader the resonances between accounts of virtues found in Thomas Aquinas and Nasir al-Din Tusi (as representative examples from the contexts of Christianity and Islam, respectively) with the more political accounts of the virtues necessary for peacebuilding articulated by the late Swedish statesman and philosopher Dag Hammarskjöld.

In their study of various Asian contexts, Tam Ngo, Dan Smyer Yu, and Dutch anthropologist Peter van der Veer articulate a different view of religion and peacebuilding. They underscore the social effectiveness of what they refer to as charismatic "moral exemplars," specifically Gandhi, the Dalai Lama, and Thich Nhat Hanh. They suggest that the Asian context presents an altogether different instance for exploring the connections between religion and peace because (Judeo-)Christianity and Islam, which allegedly inform much of the discussion of that topic, constitute only minority traditions in Asia. Thus, an exploration of case studies in Asia offers an opportunity to reflect on the intersection of religion and peacebuilding in non-Abrahamic resources, drawn primarily from Hinduism and Buddhism. While accounting for the conceptual as well as geopolitical implications of colonial encounters and how they play out in informing social, cultural, and political engagements as well as ideas about the meanings of peace in Asia, these authors underscore the context-specific distinctiveness of the personalist and charismatic models of peacebuilding.

The focus on moral exemplars such as the three men mentioned above is a common tendency in the study of religion and peacebuilding, and the uniqueness of the Asian cases may therefore be overdrawn. There are religious exemplars in every context. Many Christian religious peacebuilders who are laypeople assume this vocation, for instance, owing to their internalized view of Jesus's vocation. While this is clearly a non-elitist view, it nonetheless attests to the pertinence of the moral exemplar to Christian peacebuilding. More to the point, celebrating the greatness of Gandhi, the Dalai Lama, and Thich Nhat Hanh, as Ngo et al. do, without references to critiques of these exemplars could significantly delimit the horizons of religion and peacebuilding to religious elites. Critiques that need to be taken into account include those concerning Gandhi's sexual practices, or fractures in the presumption that the

Dalai Lama embodies and personifies all Tibetans, or a critique from a gender or class perspective of heralding male and elite players as virtually the only exemplars for peacebuilding.

In fact, such tensions and challenges are raised and illuminated upon a careful reading of S. Ayse Kadayifci-Orellena's chapter on "Peacebuilding in the Muslim World." Providing a detailed overview of Islamic principles of peace, Kadayifci-Orellana profiles a variety of Muslim peace initiatives and concrete efforts in conflict transformation engaged from a variety of perspectives and by diverse actors: from official religious leaders and Islamic states to nongovernmental transnational initiatives oriented toward the promotion of Islamic peacebuilding. However, she especially underscores the potential role of middle-range religious leadership and Muslim women in various processes of social critique and peacebuilding. For instance, she profiles the case of the late Dekha Ibrahim Abdi, a Somali founder of the Kenyan Wajir Peace and Development Committee (WPDC). Inspired by their Islamic identity, Abdi and other women founded this organization in 1993 to combat various violent practices and conflictual relations in Kenya. The organization grew into an extensive network of governmental and nongovernmental organizations, drawing on the support and activism of a wide spectrum of "stakeholders," as Kadayifci-Orellana puts it. The WPDC, like many other comparable organizations that resonate with the "elicitive" approach to peacebuilding in contexts as diverse as Nigeria, Afghanistan, Pakistan, and Indonesia, reflects a creative synthesis between a hermeneutical reflection on Islamic resources and local peacebuilding practices and structures of leadership and ethnic/tribal networks and affiliations.

In her analysis of peacebuilding practices within Muslim contexts, as well as in her theological excavation of "peace" motifs along the lines of Philpott's comparative study of Abrahamic sources for forgiveness and reconciliation, Kadayifci-Orellana depicts the liberal peace frame as essentially alien to the Muslim and other indigenous practices and resources of justpeace-building. Pivotal for this critique is her emphasis on the historical legacies of colonialism, Christian missionary activities, orientalism, and neoliberalism as persistently alive in the memories and experiences of Muslims across diverse contexts. She also stresses the need to overcome the epistemological presuppositions inherent in the liberal peace approach in order to expand the meanings of and scope of potential actors engaged in religious and specifically Muslim peacebuilding.

The indispensability of a rehabilitated conception of and commitment to the secular as a normative orientation facilitating deep pluralism may be more obvious in discussions of religion and conflict in the United States than in the Middle East or Africa. Indeed, an implicit affirmation of the concept of ecumenical secularism animates Eboo Patel and Cassie Meyer's reflection on their Chicago-based Interfaith Youth Core (IFYC). IFYC intends to promote and deepen pluralism specifically, but not exclusively, within the culturally textured context of American universities.

In their reflection on what they call "interfaith leadership," Patel and Meyer add one name to the same list of "exemplars" enumerated by Ngo et al. This is Martin Luther King Jr., who "marched arm in arm with Rabbi Abraham Joshua Heschel in Selma, joined the Buddhist monk Thich Nhat Hahn in decrying the Vietnam War, and worked closely with A. Philip Randolph, an organizer of the March on Washington and an atheist who later signed the Humanist Manifesto." King, according to these two authors, offers a model of interfaith leadership and the qualities that they seek to cultivate through the programs and conversations they facilitate on college campuses with the young adults affiliated with IFYC. Theoretically, the IFYC's approach is oriented by scholar of religion Diana Eck's work on pluralism, political scientist Ashutosh Varshney's study of inter-group "networks of engagement," and Robert Putnam's focus on the cultivation of social capital. Put simply, the more one knows about the other and the more relationships one has developed with people across cultural and religious divides, the less likely one is to engage in violent confrontation with that other. Not only does one need to develop intra-tradition literacy, however; one also needs to engage in promoting "interfaith literacy," which cultivates the value of tolerance of pluralism and a commitment to the democratic practices associated with nonviolent negotiations of differences within public arenas.

This attentiveness to deepening the pluralistic landscape is certainly consistent with the notion of ecumenical and rehabilitated secularism. And yet, the IFYC's approach may face challenges if expanded beyond the United States. On one level, Patel and Meyer overlook the relevance of the discussion of nationalism and how the interrelations between religion and nationalism then shape questions concerning religious pluralism. On another level, they uphold and celebrate ecumenical secularism without fully attending to the kind of critique Jakelić articulates of secular agency, its historicity, and especially its cognitive and individualistic biases. The focus, however, on young adults as the engine of interfaith literacy and subsequently religious peacebuilding stands in constructive tension with Ngo and his coauthors' preoccupation with moral exemplars in abstraction from the complex mosaics of social and cultural contexts in which such models resonate as exemplary and virtuoso. Varshney's work, which has exerted a profound influence on establishing social capital and inter-group cooperation on various issues as a preventive shield against the eruption of communal violence, was conducted within the specific, complex context of India, the context within which Gandhi emerged as a moral exemplar. The Gandhian legacy notwithstanding, peacebuilding across communal divides is empirically reliant on mundane familiarity and collaboration with the "other" and could become even stronger with increased inter-religious and inter-communal literacy.

In "Women, Religion, and Peacebuilding," Susan Hayward continues with this effort to pluralize the agency of peacebuilders: her subjects are not male moral exemplars or just male diplomats and leaders but also the regular college student, women, and other laypeople. Hayward describes how these ordinary actors promote processes of conflict transformation through deep and interpretive engagements with the cultural, social, political, and religious fabrics they embody and are embedded within. She opens her reflection with the observation that despite an increased (albeit still marginal) focus on the role of gender in international relations, diplomacy, and conflict and peace more broadly, scholarly accounts of the intersections between religion, peacebuilding, and gender are rather limited in scope. As someone who, as part of her work for the US Institute of Peace, is actually in the field, Hayward underscores that the scarcity of such scholarly conversations "is not a reflection of the state of the field *in* the field." It is simply self-evident to any observer in conflict zones that women are highly instrumental in spearheading and implementing peacebuilding projects and grassroots initiatives. The 2011 Nobel Peace Prize winners, Leymah Gbowee and Tawakkol Karman, are but two female role models who emerged onto the scene seemingly recently but who have been, in effect, in the scene all along.

Hayward's chapter provides a stimulating intersection of theory and practice. It combines a practitioner's observations of actual cases and "women of faith" on the ground with attentiveness to feminist theorizing. Consequently, Hayward recognizes both the validity and the limitations of conventional feminist romanticization of agency primarily as resistance to the mode of structural violence most definitional of women's roles, namely patriarchy, which is often interwoven with religion and religious authority structures. This tension is particularly evident where women strategically operationalize their invisibility and disempowered positionality. Providing a rich list of examples of women's concentrated efforts to reach beyond religious, ethnic, and other divides, Hayward concludes that "women's marginalization from the top tier of institutional religious and political leadership situates them for this sort of cross-boundary work. Less visible and less constrained by institutional commitments, they are freer to make moves that would otherwise be considered politically or socially risky."

This recognition of the instrumentality of marginality notwithstanding, a feminist prism invites profound challenges to the marginality of women and invites, in practice, intentional efforts to transform such marginality on the levels of peacebuilding initiatives, diplomacy, and so forth. Framing female agency as essentially "secular" and anti-patriarchal does not cohere with the empirical realities of women, including the already mentioned Dekha Ibrahim of Kenya, Venerable Mae Chee Sansanee of Thailand, and Sister Marie-Bernard Alima of the Democratic Republic of Congo. Their activism and peacebuilding work are deeply embedded in and draw sustenance from their religiosity, often through mining their traditions for empowering resources, including the biblical characters Esther and Vashti. This hermeneutical process illuminates the potential to overcome the hegemony of male hermeneutics, which, as feminist critics have argued, has consolidated and hallowed male privileges and gender norms that constitute forms of structural and cultural violence and are otherwise open to interpretation and deconstruction. Women's hermeneutical mediation of their traditions does not necessarily result, however, in the emergence of a Western feminist modality of agency, as discussed in anthropologist Saba Mahmood's study of the piety movement in Egypt. But it does afford a degree of empowering religious literacy, a concept articulated differently in Ochs's discussion of "hearth-to-hearth" inter-religious dialogue, Mason's chapter on religious militancy, Gopin's focus on hermeneutical retrieval, and Kadayifci-Orellena's account of peacebuilding in Muslim contexts, to recall only a few of the previously discussed contributions.

Hayward's application of the justpeace angle, her "on-the-ground" engagement with women actors, and a generally expansive view of peacebuilding gesture toward creative ways for intervening in the theoretical discussion of agency as articulated by Mahmood and other critics of the kind of feminism associated with the "West" and "secularity." Mahmood's effort to deconstruct Western agency and pluralize modalities of female agency in such a way that a female agent is not only one who engages in overthrowing patriarchal norms and structures is deeply grounded in a refusal to articulate explicitly any kind of a telos or a theory of justice. This refusal, some critics underscore, can amount to endorsing a form of relativism, which is not the same as the relational conception of justice interwoven into the justpeace prism (once that prism is expanded to incorporate the tools of critique). In other words, the value of illuminating, as Mahmood does, the self-perception of pious women who embrace what they interpret as the feminine Muslim norms of submissiveness remains merely ethnographic if the author does not also engage in scrutiny of these very norms. This may be the prerogative of an abstract academic theorizing. But when one is accompanying or observing women who must resist the threat of systematic rape in their daily lives, for instance, suspending normative judgments would seem at best absurd and at worst complicit with this violent reality. Hence, the intersection of theory and practice, as Hayward's chapter demonstrates, complicates the operating presumptions of both. It also suggests a fundamental tension with the kind of hermeneutics Philpott deploys and the male normativity that Ngo and her coauthors re-inscribe in their analysis.

While Hayward challenges the gendered dimensions of conventional peacebuilding, illuminating how unreconstructed secularist assumptions about agency relate to an enduring male domination in the upper echelons of peace work, she also shows how a justpeace approach can be expanded to incorporate feminist critique and, in so doing, remain in creative tension with what Little, Hibbard, and Jakelić, among other contributors, may refer to as a robust conception of the liberal and secular.

Lisa Schirch, the peace studies scholar and director of a policy program of the Alliance for Peacebuilding, has expanded the scope of peacebuilding through her work on rituals. In her contribution to this volume, she focuses on the symbolic elements of conflict and specifically on the transformative potential of rituals defined as "symbolic act[s] that hold significant meaning." Drawing on social functionalist theories of religion and ritual practice, Schirch presents religion and peacebuilding as sharing several traits. "They include a set of values, methods, and rituals that create connective tissue between groups of people torn apart by structural or direct violence," she writes. Recognizing that religion has been complicit with much divisiveness and violence, Schirch emphasizes that religion and peacebuilding also share a task, namely "to overcome the similar concepts of 'sin' and 'violence' which divide and break relationships between people, their environment, and their creator and sacred values." Religious actors and rituals are indispensable for peacebuilding processes aimed at transforming root causes of conflict and healing traumas as well as at the level of negotiation of agreements and other diplomatic encounters on the "track one" level of engagement. Religion, Schirch stresses, is especially equipped to provide reconciliatory spaces through art, symbols, and rituals and the sense of vocation and spiritual nurturing of religious people (such as the women Hayward introduces) involved in peacebuilding processes. Substantiating her argument with many examples from diverse contexts, including Maha Ghosananda's peace marches in Cambodia, cleansing rituals in Mozambique, public memorials as ritualized spaces for reconciliation in Argentina and Iraq, a smudging ceremony among Northern American indigenous populations, and the practice of feet-washing in Christianity, Schirch intriguingly draws on neuroscientific research to illuminate the elasticity of the brain in responding to, remembering, and possibly recovering from trauma. Rituals and art could provide often nonverbal transformative contexts, with liminality being an operative concept which deeply challenges the conventional focus of peacebuilding on the cerebral cortex or the "rational" brain. Importantly, in her analysis of rituals as embedded within symbols which are non-cognitive, Schirch strives to avoid and overcome a dualistic framing of mind versus body. "Ritual's liminal space," she writes, "offers the possibility of intrapersonal, interpersonal, cultural, and structural change."

Drawing on insights from the Ugandan poet Okot p'Bitek and the cultural theorist Theodor Adorno, Schirch alludes to the empowering practice of art. p'Bitek celebrates the artist as a powerful agent because s/he constructs images that populate people's imaginations. Adorno mourns the relinquishment of this power to the "culture industry," to elites' dominating agenda. For Schirch, peacebuilding constitutes an artistic act of creation that shares crucial affinities with the religious imagination, especially as it pertains to the view of human agency in creation and re-creation of the world in pursuit of justice and meaning. Hence, peacebuilding is necessarily embedded within "an explicit or implicit religious theology of creation where people are co-creators with the divine." Peacebuilders are like artists because, she writes, "they tap into the inspiration of other artists. They draw inspiration from religious rituals developed by men and women over millennia. They draw on long-standing traditions." And yet, their indebtedness to traditions does not prevent them from innovating, improvising, and imagining new horizons and practices. This view of the peacebuilder qua artist animates Mennonite peace scholar and practitioner John Paul Lederach's reflection on "spiritual practices" in his own contribution to this volume.

In his exploration of spiritual resources and creativity in the face of deadly conflict, Lederach focuses on a context radically different from Ochs's laboratory-like conditions of the practice of SR or "hearth-to-hearth" dialogue. Yet he offers a similarly nuanced exploration of potentially bridging practices that enable people to retain a strong and deeply rooted sense of "self" while, at the same time, allowing for vulnerability and humility in relation to the "other." Presenting the practitioner equivalent to Kelsay's retrieval of virtue ethics as a relevant interlocutor with peacebuilding, Lederach ponders the processes of accessing the most vulnerable spaces of one's own position (the "hearth" in Ochs's terminology) as a necessary step or a form of spiritual practice inevitable for peacebuilders involved in processes of conflict transformation. The question is how to access and cultivate a quality of *being* and *presence* that allows for engaging the "enemy other" substantively and with compassion while recognizing that in the midst of fire, the possibility of accessing internal pluralities, alternative narratives of the group, and reconciliatory resources is significantly constrained, and that doing so would involve standing against the tide, a position Schirch recognizes as entailing at least an implicit theology.

What Lederach calls a "quality of presence" constitutes, therefore, a key to transformative processes involving a creative moral imagination and a set of spiritual practices that are capable of sustaining a robust sense of self. To reach an aspired capacity to imagine better possibilities in the midst of fire, a moral imagination that enables the "quality of presence" would require spiritual formation, intuition, and practices that include *creativity* or practices of risk and hope, a pulling against "centrifugal pressures that grip and drive people toward exclusively defined in-group contact and interaction." To be "present" also requires *vulnerability,* a spiritual discipline that suggests the practices of honest sincerity and humility, which inform the "curiosity paradox," as well as *compassion*, which requires the practice of seeing oneself in the other. These practices, however, also enable, through the confluence of a robust theological imagination, personal experiences, and spiritual intelligence, building bridges to the "enemy other" as a matter of basic recognition of the other's humanity, dignity, and suffering.

Lederach illuminates this quality of presence as emerging out of contexts filled with paradoxes and dilemmas. Protracted conflicts exert mostly "centrifugal energies," but years of entanglements also produce an interlocking "centripetal quality" that bind groups together in their shared experiences of trauma. A religious peacebuilder, Lederach argues, is able constructively to cultivate the centripetal aspects by overcoming what he calls a "bridging dilemma." Resonating with Schirch's discussion of peacebuilding as a religious act of participating in (re)creation, Lederach's second paradox revolves around the tension between the inner and personal life, involving the search for meaning and dignity in the midst of suffering and loss, and the recognition of dignity in the "other." This tension or paradox relates to the "dilemma of human dignity," which is inextricably related to the third "compassion dilemma." The ability of local leaders creatively to engage the "other" across lines of enmity necessitates a "moral imagination"—the ability to imagine one's location within "a web of relationships" and to cultivate a "paradoxical curiosity" concerning the other's perspectives and experiences. This mode enables relinquishing a totalizing hold on the truth, retaining space for dynamic artistic creativity along the lines described by Schirch, and taking risks on the road to "peace," which, in contexts of protracted violent conflict, constitutes an unknown, often with no guarantees of tangible success or reciprocation.

While peacebuilding for Schirch and Lederach are not necessarily the exclusive purview of religious peacebuilders per se, in both their accounts, the practices of peacebuilding are described as deeply religious or as sharing overlapping qualities with the (Christian) religious and theological imaginations. Two PhD students in the joint program in theology and peace studies at the Kroc Institute for International Peace Studies at the University of Notre Dame, Janna Hunter-Bowman and Heather M. DuBois, endorse this approach and offer an attempt to explicate the deep theological dimensions of both Lederach's work and Roman Catholic approaches to peacebuilding, in order to demonstrate the relevance of the theological imagination to peacebuilding and the kind of commitments such a vocation requires. More broadly, the coauthors gesture toward the potential nexus of Christian theologies with peace studies as a field of inquiry and peacebuilding as a practice. In their chapter, DuBois and Hunter-Bowman likewise draw on Christian theological resources, but they do so to show the need for the interpretive and expressive capacities of the discipline of theology within the interdisciplinary work of justpeace-building. They demonstrate that theological theory and methods can enrich work like Schirch's and Lederach's by enabling contestation over the meanings of rituals and symbols, by offering language to further describe what is happening in the "liminal space," and by contextualizing terms like "spiritual." While affirming the need for additional practices that engage theological and spiritual dimensions of thought and action, the theologian-practitioners emphasize a corresponding need for theoretical analysis attuned to the range of narratives and experiences that such practices invoke and engage. Moreover, they argue that theological methods can serve as vehicles to address the oft-neglected existential, psychic, and emotional dimensions of peacebuilding as well. Whereas Lederach focuses on personal and collective resources for choosing alternatives in the midst of violence, DuBois and Hunter-Bowman explicate the worldviews and forms of reason that shape or undergird what is possible in those moments of decision. Thereby, they offer means to contest whether an explicit or implicit theology is indeed operative, as Schirch suggests, and, moreover, whether secularist and positivist assumptions are limiting the scope of inquiry and practice in particular contexts.

To demonstrate the salience of their categorical claim, in the second half of their chapter, DuBois and Hunter-Bowman use theological analysis to explore how Lederach's temporal images and concepts constitute an alternative to the linear temporal frameworks currently dominant in peacebuilding. In this specific case, they explain that elements of Christian eschatology have helped Lederach to articulate his signature understandings of "expansive time" and the "beckoning horizon." The authors illustrate that he has also drawn upon the apocalyptic ethics of Mennonite theologian John Howard Yoder to make sense of experiences in which the logic of a violent conflict is "interrupted" by peacebuilding practice. Through their analysis of the work of this one practitioner-scholar, who draws upon his Christian tradition in conjunction with concrete contexts and (Christian and non-Christian) communities, they demonstrate the value of scholarship and practice sourced from multiple sociolinguistic communities, traditions, and disciplines, including theology.

From a different vantage, political scientist and peace studies scholar Cecelia Lynch reminds us that what is meant by "religious peacebuilding" needs to be continuously interrogated with attention to global structures of cultural and structural violence. This scrutiny requires historicizing religious activism "abroad," bringing into full focus the colonial and missionary underpinnings and pasts of peacebuilding agendas. Hence, the assumptions, theological imaginations, and motivations of self-proclaimed peacebuilders are not beyond the scope of critique, even if they are presented as altruistic and heroic. To suggest a constructive expansion of the justpeace lens, Lynch, therefore, deploys Foucauldian modes of critique in reflecting on how contemporary religious humanitarianism and development work are shaped by dominant economic and security discourses. Describing the vast landscape of actual or potential religious peacebuilding in various contexts and acknowledging the importance of a growing attention to the relevance of religious communities in peacebuilding processes, Lynch underscores the need to acknowledge the embeddedness of such actors within local and international discourses and institutional arrangements, as well as the enduring legacies of the religious dimensions of colonialism, usually in contexts where peace efforts appear urgent. It is through such a process of self-reflexivity on the part of peacebuilders that justpeace and strategic peacebuilding can become more fully realized, interrogating their own legacies and confronting enduring assumptions.

This focus on illuminating the discursive patterns of peace and justice activism is also the thrust of Atalia Omer's "Religion, Nationalism, and Solidarity Activism." In this contribution, Omer situates solidarity and diaspora activism for the two national causes of Palestine and Tibet within their broader discursive topographies, including the persistence of various types of orientalisms and anti-Semitism but also the conflation of such discursive formations with critiques of neoliberalism and globalism and, in the case of Islamism, imperial "Western" secularism. The study of the two cases of Tibet and Palestine activism in the diasporas foregrounds counterproductive patterns of mutual silencing in which, to take one example, a well-meaning actor such as the late esteemed Helen Thomas, the former dean of the White House press corps, can so easily "solve" the Israeli-Palestinian conflict by "tell[ing] them [Israeli-Jews] to get the hell out of Palestine" and suggesting that "they could go home to Poland, Germany. . . and America and everywhere else." Thomas was reacting to the systematic silencing of Palestinian voices and experiences, a silencing much indebted to the persistence of orientalism and compounded by the United States and Israel's parallel and mutually reinforcing so-called wars on [Islamic] terrorism and by the complex religio-cultural affinities they share. However, Thomas's own dismissal of Jewish narratives, most immediately the fact that "Germany, Poland, and everywhere else" is *not* home to Israeli Jews (even if some Jews do choose to reside in those countries) and for rather obvious historical reasons, illuminates how one's peace activism can intersect with discourses (in this case anti-Semitism) that themselves participate in deeply rooted forms of cultural, structural, and deadly violence. To reiterate a recurrent conclusion in this volume, critiquing the discursivity that informs normative positions in the discussion of religion and conflict is a necessary stage, but the practice is insufficient in thinking constructively about conflict transformation and peacebuilding. Therefore, Omer's chapter aspires to expose the dynamics of mutual silencing in order to suggest a broader view of the analysis of religion's role in trans-local dimensions of conflict and peacebuilding. It is conventional in political science to relate the influences of international structures, powers, and institutions to the dynamics of conflict and peacebuilding. Less conventional is recognizing how cultural and religious vocabularies, experiences, and narratives selectively authorize geopolitical discourses and transnational affinities. Within an expanded view of justpeace, by contrast, normativity pivots around a multi-perspectival approach to justice and a deconstructive critique that avoids its counterproductive excesses. Accordingly, Omer shows how trans-local, international, and transnational intersecting discursive formations unfold in local zones of conflict as well as in the formation and potential reframing of solidarity activism of various sorts. Such activism must pass through a hermeneutical engagement that not only denaturalizes but also contributes to the reimagining of conventional frames.

Like many of the other contributions to this volume, Omer's chapter engages the tension between justpeace and the assumptions inherent in the liberal peace tradition. This involves, as we have seen, scrutinizing the connection between theory and practice, and gauging the effectiveness but also the limits of the theoretical tools of critique as they pertain to the analysis of conflict and to processes of peacebuilding. Grounding their analyses on cases from diverse contexts including Sri Lanka, Somalia, Cambodia, Morocco, Mozambique, Honduras, Argentina, Congo, Kenya, Nigeria, Indonesia, Afghanistan, Pakistan, Thailand, Liberia, Northern Uganda, Palestine, Israel, the Philippines, the U.S., Syria, Tibet, and Colombia, the various authors attend to these issues with varying degrees of intensity, highlighting one or two of the interlaced tensions that inform the broader framing of this volume. Viewed synthetically, the contributions illuminate how the broadening scope of both research and practice profoundly relate to the broadening analytic interpretations of the scopes and meanings of violence. Analyzing how religion relates to structural and cultural forms of violence (locally and trans-locally) is where we locate the growing edges of the field of religion, conflict, and peacebuilding.

NOTES

1. John Paul Lederach and R. Scott Appleby, "Strategic Peacebuilding: An Overview," in Daniel Philpott and Gerard Powers, eds., *Strategies of Peace: Transforming Conflict in a Violent World* (New York: Oxford University Press, 2010), 23.
2. Lederach and Appleby, "Strategic Peacebuilding," especially 33–41.
3. For further reflections on the notion of "critical caretaking," see Atalia Omer, "Can a Critic Be a Caretaker Too? Religion, Conflict, and Conflict Transformation," *Journal of the American Academy of Religion* 79, no. 2 (2011): 459–496.
4. R. Scott Appleby, *The Ambivalence of the Sacred: Religion, Violence, and Reconciliation* (Lanham, MD: Rowman and Littlefield, 2000).
5. Samuel P. Huntington, "The Clash of Civilizations?," *Foreign Affairs* vol. 72, no. 3 (1993): 22–49.
6. See, for example, Emran Qureshi and Michael Sells, eds., *The New Crusades: Constructing the Muslim Enemy* (New York: Columbia University Press, 2003).
7. Jonathan Z. Smith, "Tillich['s] Remains. . .," *Journal of the American Academy of Religion* 78, no. 4 (2010): 1139–1170.
8. William T. Cavanaugh, *The Myth of Religious Violence: Secular Ideology and the Roots of Modern Conflict* (New York: Oxford University Press, 2009).
9. See, for instance, contributions to Saba Mahmood and Peter G. Danchin, eds., "Politics of Religious Freedom: Contested Genealogies," special issue, *South Atlantic Quarterly* (Duke University Press), 113, no. 1 (2014).

10. For a further account of this line of analysis, see Atalia Omer, "Modernist Despite Themselves? The Limits of Critique as an Instrument of Change," *Journal of the American Academy of Religion* (forthcoming).

11. See, for example, Winnifred Fallers Sullivan and Lori G. Beaman, eds., *Varieties of Religious Establishment* (Burlington, VT: Ashgate, 2013).

12. See, for example, William E. Connolly, "Europe: A Minor Tradition," in *Powers of the Secular Modern: Talal Asad and His Interlocutors*, ed. David Scott and Charles Hirschkind (Stanford, CA: Stanford University Press, 2006), 75–92.

BIBLIOGRAPHY

Appleby, R. Scott. *The Ambivalence of the Sacred: Religion, Violence, and Reconciliation.* Lanham, MD: Rowman and Littlefield, 2000.

Cavanaugh, William T. *The Myth of Religious Violence: Secular Ideology and the Roots of Modern Conflict.* New York: Oxford University Press, 2009.

Connolly, William E. "Europe: A Minor Tradition." In *Powers of the Secular Modern: Talal Asad and His Interlocutors*, edited by David Scott and Charles Hirschkind, 75–92. Stanford, CA: Stanford University Press, 2006.

Huntington, Samuel P. "The Clash of Civilizations?" *Foreign Affairs* 72, no. 3 (1993): 22–49.

Lederach, John Paul, and R. Scott Appleby. "Strategic Peacebuilding: An Overview." In *Strategies of Peace: Transforming Conflict in a Violent World*, edited by Daniel Philpott and Gerard Powers, 19–44. New York: Oxford University Press, 2010.

Mahmood, Saba, and Peter G. Danchin, eds. "Politics of Religious Freedom: Contested Genealogies." Special issue, *South Atlantic Quarterly* (Duke University Press) 113, no. 1 (2014).

Omer, Atalia. "Can a Critic Be a Caretaker Too? Religion, Conflict, and Conflict Transformation." *Journal of the American Academy of Religion* 79, no. 2 (2011): 459–496.

Omer, Atalia. "Modernist Despite Themselves? The Limits of Critique as an Instrument of Change." *Journal of the American Academy of Religion* (forthcoming).

Qureshi, Emran, and Michael Sells, eds. *The New Crusades: Constructing the Muslim Enemy.* New York: Columbia University Press, 2003.

Smith, Jonathan Z. "Tillich['s] Remains. . ." *Journal of the American Academy of Religion* 78, no. 4 (2010): 1139–1170.

Sullivan, Winnifred Fallers, and Lori G. Beaman, eds. *Varieties of Religious Establishment.* Burlington, VT: Ashgate, 2013.

Index

Figures and tables are indicated by "f" and "t" following page numbers. Surnames starting with "al-" are alphabetized by the subsequent part of the name (e.g., al-Banna is found in the B's.)